Aboriginal Legal Issues
Cases, Materials & Commentary
Fourth Edition

John J. Borrows
B.A., M.A., J.D., LL.M., Ph.D., F.R.S.C.
of the Chippewas of the Nawash, Anishinaabe Nation
Robina Professor of Law, Public Policy and Society
University of Minnesota Law School

Leonard I. Rotman
B.A., LL.B., LL.M., S.J.D.
Purdy Crawford Chair in Business Law and Professor
Schulich School of Law, Dalhousie University

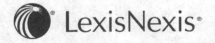

Aboriginal Legal Issues: Cases, Materials & Commentary, 4th edition
© LexisNexis Canada Inc. 2012
August 2012

Library and Archives Canada Cataloguing in Publication

Borrows, John, 1963-
     Aboriginal legal issues : cases, materials & commentary / John J. Borrows, Leonard I. Rotman. — 4th ed.

Includes index.
ISBN 978-0-433-47101-1

     1. Native peoples—Legal status, laws, etc.—Canada—Cases. I. Rotman, Leonard Ian II. Title.

KE7709.B67 2012	342.7108'72	C2007-903706-2
KF8205.B67 2012		

Published by LexisNexis Canada, a member of the LexisNexis Group
LexisNexis Canada Inc.
123 Commerce Valley Dr. E., Suite 700
Markham, Ontario
L3T 7W8

Customer Service
Telephone: (905) 479-2665 • Fax: (905) 479-2826
Toll-Free Phone: 1-800-668-6481 • Toll-Free Fax: 1-800-461-3275
Email: customerservice@lexisnexis.ca
Web Site: www.lexisnexis.ca

Printed and bound in Canada.

To our partners, Kim and Tammy,

thanks for your patience and support

PREFACE TO THE FOURTH EDITION

Boozhoo Nindinawemaaganidog

It has been 30 years since Aboriginal and treaty rights were formally added to Canada's constitution through section 35(1) of the *Constitution Act, 1982*. Aboriginal peoples were suspicious of this initiative because most declared that they were in a nation-to-nation relationship with the Crown, as demonstrated by treaties with the Queen and the protection of Aboriginal rights through Royal Proclamation and other instruments. As a result, many Aboriginal people did not regard the domestication of their rights with much enthusiasm. With three decades of experience we may now ask whether this apprehension was misplaced, or whether Aboriginal peoples were right to express grave misgivings about the domestic constitutionalization of Aboriginal and treaty rights.

There are likely varied assessments about section 35(1)'s usefulness in building a nation-to-nation relationship between Aboriginal peoples and the Crown. We encourage readers to make their own evaluation in this regard by reference to the cases and materials which follow. The cases and materials included in this book represent the current state of the field as expressed by courts, legislatures and academic commentaries as of April 1, 2012. These materials should enable students, professors, practitioners and judges to form their own opinions about section 35(1)'s effectiveness in building Aboriginal nations and the Canadian state. While our casebook demonstrates that the volume of Aboriginal cases is vast, our own view is that much work remains to be done to meet this broader goal. As a result, this casebook poses questions throughout which delve deeper into the courts' own reasons for judgment while simultaneously considering the broader policy questions raised by their opinions.

We continue to see this casebook as a teaching tool, first and foremost. Thus, we have organized the materials to allow students and teachers to understand how the cases developed chronologically and see how they relate to the wider field. At the same time this book could also function as a general reference book for those interested in getting a snapshot of various legal issues affecting Aboriginal peoples. Given the growing number of cases, we expect that teachers will make choices to highlight selected aspects of this field for their students. While a class which meets 4 hours a week, for 13 weeks, will be able to study most of this book, we recognize that shorter courses will require more focus. Thus we have designed these materials to allow teachers to make their own editorial selections. Each chapter has sufficient information to stand alone as a teaching unit. This is also the case with many sections within each chapter. Even with this in mind, we have often had to make editorial choices which drastically pared down the number of pages devoted to each topic, in order to streamline the book. While there is always more that might be included in a book of this nature, we are confident that our choices will allow teachers and students to gain an excellent understanding of the field.

There are many people and institutions that support a work of this breadth. We are especially thankful to Fran Cudlipp at LexisNexis Canada for her encouragement and patience as we completed this edition. We also express appreciation for the Faculties of Law at the University of Minnesota and the University of Windsor. We are grateful for their continued financial assistance and general support of this project.

Ahow. Maajitaadaa.

John Borrows
Victoria, BC

Len Rotman
Windsor, ON

April 2012

ABOUT THE AUTHORS

John J. Borrows, B.A., M.A., J.D., LL.M. (Toronto), Ph.D. (Osgoode Hall Law School), F.R.S.C., is Professor and Robina Chair in Law and Society at the University of Minnesota Law School and a member of the British Columbia Bar. Formerly: Law Foundation Chair of Aboriginal Law and Justice at the University of Victoria Law School; Professor in the Faculty of Law at the University of Toronto; Associate Professor and First Nations Legal Studies Director, Faculty of Law at the University of British Columbia; Associate Professor and Director of the Intensive Programme in Lands, Resources and First Nations Governments at Osgoode Hall Law School. Professor Borrows has served as a Visiting Professor and Acting Executive Director of the Indian Legal Program at Arizona State University College of Law in Phoenix, Arizona; Visiting Professor at the Faculty of Law of the University of New South Wales, Australia; New Zealand Law Foundation Distinguished Visitor at Waikato University in New Zealand; Visiting Professor at J. Rueben Clark Law School at BYU; Vine Deloria Distinguished Visitor at the University of Arizona James E. Rogers School of Law; and L.G. Pathy Professor in Canadian Studies at Princeton University. He teaches in the areas of Constitutional Law, Indigenous Law and Environmental Law. His publications include *Recovering Canada: The Resurgence of Indigenous Law* (Donald Smiley Award for the best book in Canadian Political Science, 2002), *Canada's Indigenous Constitution* (Canadian Law and Society Best Book Award 2011), and *Drawing Out Law: A Spirit's Guide*, all from the University of Toronto Press. Professor Borrows is a recipient of an Aboriginal Achievement Award in Law and Justice, a Fellow of the Trudeau Foundation, and a Fellow of the Academy of Arts, Humanities and Sciences of Canada (RSC), Canada's highest academic honour. He is Anishinaabe/Ojibway and a member of the Chippewa of the Nawash First Nation in Ontario, Canada.

Leonard I. Rotman, B.A. (Toronto), LL.B. (Queen's), LL.M. (Osgoode Hall), S.J.D. (Toronto), is Professor and Purdy Crawford Chair in Business Law at the Schulich School of Law, Dalhousie University. He was previously on faculty at the Faculty of Law, University of Windsor and the Faculty of Law, University of Alberta, and a member of the Ontario Bar. Professor Rotman has been invited to serve as Visiting Professor at the Washington and Lee University School of Law, Lexington, VA and University of Denver Sturm College of Law, Denver, CO, was named the inaugural Visiting Scholar at the Hennick Centre for Business and Law at Osgoode Hall Law School, York University, a Visiting Scholar at the Center for the Study of Law and Society at the University of California Berkeley, Boalt Hall School of Law, and awarded a T.C. Beirne Distinguished Visiting Fellowship at the T.C. Beirne School of Law, University of Queensland in Brisbane, Australia. In addition to his work in Aboriginal Law, Professor Rotman teaches and writes predominantly in the areas of Constitutional Law, Corporate Law and Governance, and Fiduciary Law. His book

Fiduciary Law (2005) was shortlisted for the 2007 Walter Owen book prize as the best new book in Canadian law. He is also the author of *Parallel Paths: Fiduciary Doctrine and the Crown-Native Relationship in Canada* (1996), Contributing Editor (with Bruce Welling and Lionel Smith) of *Canadian Corporate Law: Cases, Notes & Materials*, 4th ed. (2010), and Contributing Editor-in-Chief of *Constitutional Law: Cases, Commentary and Principles* (2008) (with Bruce Elman and Gerald Gall, eds.). Professor Rotman is the author of numerous essays, chapters and law review articles addressing substantive issues in Aboriginal Law, Constitutional Law, Corporate Law and Governance, Equity, Fiduciary Law, Legal History, Remedies, Trusts, Unincorporated Associations, and Unjust Enrichment/Restitution. He is also formerly Editor-in-Chief of the peer-reviewed journal *Windsor Yearbook of Access to Justice*. He has presented papers at conferences and law schools in Canada, the United States, England, France, Israel and New Zealand, and his work has been cited by domestic and international commissions and courts.

ACKNOWLEDGEMENTS

A casebook on such a wide subject necessarily contains a great deal of references to the work of others. The authors and publishers of these articles and textbooks have been most generous in giving permission for the reproduction in this text of works already in print. References, of course, appear where necessary and possible in the text. It is convenient for us to list below, for the assistance of the reader, the publishers and authors for whose courtesy we are most grateful. The following is organized by author in alphabetical order.

Amnesty International, *No More Stolen Sisters: The Need for a Comprehensive Response to Discrimination and Violence against Indigenous Women in Canada* (London: Amnesty International Publications International, 2009), <http://www.amnesty.ca/amnestynews/upload/AMR200122009.pdf>. Reproduced with permission of Amnesty International.

Jim Anglin, "Risk, Well-being, and Paramountcy in Child Protection: The Need for Transformation" (2002) 31 Child and Youth Care Forum 233 at 248-49. Reprinted with permission of Springer Science & Business Media.

Michael Asch and Patrick Macklem, "Aboriginal Rights and Canadian Sovereignty: An Essay on *R. v. Sparrow*" (1991) 29 Alta. L. Rev. 498 at 501-503, 505, 507-508, 510, 515-16. Reproduced with permission of the Alberta Law Review.

Catherine Bell, "Métis Constitutional Rights in Section 35(1)" (1997) 36 Alta. L. Rev. 180 at 184, 189-90. Reproduced with permission of the Alberta Law Review.

Thomas Berger, *Conciliator's Final Report: Nunavut Land Claims Agreement Implementation Planning Contract Negotiations for the Second Planning Period* – Letter to Minister Prentice, March 1, 2006 at <http://www.ainc-inac.gc.ca/pr/agr/nu/lca/lca1_e.html>. Reproduced with the permission of the Minister of Public Works and Government Services, 2007, and courtesy of the Department of Indian and Northern Affairs.

John Borrows, *Canada's Indigenous Constitution* (Toronto: University of Toronto Press, 2010) at 10-11, 59-60, 155-65.

John Borrows, "Domesticating Doctrines: Aboriginal Peoples after The Royal Commission" (2001) 46 McGill L.J. 615 at 655-57. Reproduced under a licence given by Copibec.

John Borrows, "Ground Rules: Indigenous Treaties and Legal Foundations" (2006) 36 N.Z.U. L. Rev. 188 at 195, 197-98. Reprinted with permission of the author.

John J. Borrows, *Indigenous Legal Traditions* (Ottawa: Law Commission of Canada, 2006). Reproduced with the permission of the Minister of Public Works and Government Services, 2007.

John Borrows, "Let Obligations Be Done". Reprinted with permission of the author.

John Borrows, *Living Law on a Living Earth* (unpublished manuscript, 2007). Reprinted with permission of the author.

John J. Borrows, "Wampum at Niagara: The Royal Proclamation, Canadian Legal History and Self-Government". This excerpt is reprinted with permission of the publisher from *Aboriginal and Treaty Rights in Canada: Essays on Law, Equality and Respect for Difference* (Vancouver: University of British Columbia Press, 1997) by Michael Asch, ed. © University of British Columbia Press 1997. All rights reserved by the Publisher.

British Columbia Civil Liberties Association, Principles, <http://www.bbcla.org/positions/political/00nonaboriginal.html>. Reproduced with permission of the British Columbia Civil Liberties Association.

Canada, Office of the Auditor General, "Programs for First Nations on Reserve: Status Report of the Auditor General of Canada to the House of Commons" (Ottawa: Office of the Auditor General, 2011), Chapter 4 at 2-6, <http://www.oag-bvg.gc.ca/internet/docs/parl_oag_201106_04_e.pdf>.

Canada, Office of the Auditor General, "2011 June Status Report of the Auditor General of Canada" (Ottawa: Office of the Auditor General, 2011), Chapter 4 at 23-25, <http://www.oag-bvg.gc.ca/internet/docs/parl_oag_201106_04_e.pdf>.

Canada, Presentation to the Commission of First Nations and Metis People and Justice Reform (Correctional Service) of Canada, May 2003, in Commission on First Nations and Metis Peoples and Justice Reform, *Final Report*, Vol. II: Submissions to the Commission (Saskatchewan Justice, December 2003) at 3-9 to 3-10, 7-7 to 7-8. © Correctional Service Canada 2003. Reproduced with the permission of the Minister of Public Works and Government Services Canada, 2007.

Canada, Royal Commission on Aboriginal Peoples, *Report of the Royal Commission on Aboriginal Peoples*, Vol. I, Looking Forward, Looking Back at 78-79, 82, 85, 128-30, 173-76, 317; Vol. II, Restructuring the Relationship at

105-06, 108-14, 186-90, 290-93, 535-39, 543, 544-49; Vol. III, Gathering Strength at 23, 29-33, 52-53, 87; Vol. IV, Perspectives and Realities at 24-33, 33-36, 36-37, 39-42, 68-71, 199-203, 278-81, 285, 288, 290-92. The Commission © 1996. Reproduced with the permission of the Minister of Public Works and Government Services, 2007, and courtesy of the Privy Council Office; *Bridging the Cultural Divide: A Report on Aboriginal People and Criminal Justice in Canada* at xi, 7, 28-33, 109, 110, 116. Royal Commission on Aboriginal Peoples © 1996 (Ottawa: Privy Council Office, 1996). Reproduced with the permission of the Minister of Public Works and Government Services Canada, 2007, and courtesy of the Privy Council Office.

Canadian Association of Elizabeth Fry Societies, "Aboriginal Women", <http://elizabethfry.ca/wwdcms/uploads/Aboriginal%20Women.pdf>.

Canadian Judicial Council, letter dated July 24, 2002.

Larry Chartrand, "Metis Identity and Citizenship" (2001) 12 Windsor Rev. Legal Soc. Issues 5 at 6-10, 19-23, 25-26, 37-41, 47-52. Reproduced with permission of the Windsor Review of Legal and Social Issues.

Chiefs of Ontario Magazine (1998) Winter, <http://www.chiefs-of-ontario.org/magazine/4-02.html#1>.

Pamela Gough, *Manitoba's Child Welfare System* (Toronto: University of Toronto, Faculty of Social Work, 2006), <http://www.cecw-cepb.ca/DocsEng/ManitobaChildWelfareSystem34E.pdf>. Reprinted with permission of the author.

A.C. Hamilton and C.M. Sinclair, *The Justice System and Aboriginal People: Report of the Aboriginal Justice Inquiry of Manitoba, Vol. 1* (Winnipeg: Queen's Printer, 1991), at 115-16, 127, 130-35, 137, 256-64, 475-87, 509-20. Reproduced with permission of the Province of Manitoba.

Sonia Harris-Short, "The Road Back from Hell? Self-Government and the Decolonisation of Aboriginal Child Welfare in Canada" (2003, unpublished). Reprinted with permission of the author.

Inuit Land Claims – A Chronology <http://www.itk.ca/5000-year-heritage/land-claims.php>. Reproduced with permission of Inuit Tapiriit Kanatami.

Dean Jacobs, "Consulting and Accommodating First Nations in Canada: A Duty that Reaps Benefits", July 25, 2006 at <http://www.bkejwanong.com>. Reprinted with permission of Bkejwanong.

Andre Le Dressay, "A Brief Tax (on a me) of First Nations Taxation and Economic Development" in *Sharing the Harvest: The Road to Self-Reliance*,

Report of the National Round Table on Aboriginal Economic Development and Resources at 218-20. Royal Commission on Aboriginal Peoples © 1993. Reproduced with the permission of the Minister of Public Works and Government Services, 2007, and courtesy of the Privy Council Office.

Kent McNeil, "Aboriginal Title and Section 88 of the *Indian Act*" (2000) 34:1 U.B.C. L. Rev. 159 at 165-69.

Kent McNeil, "The Onus of Proof of Aboriginal Title" (1999) 37 Osgoode Hall L.J. 775 at 776-82, 800-803. Reprinted with permission of the Osgoode Hall Law Journal and the author.

Patricia Monture, "A Vicious Circle: Child Welfare and the First Nations" (1989) 3 C.J.W.L. 1 at 11, 12, 14. Reprinted with permission from University of Toronto Press (www.utpjournals.ca).

Zebedee Nungak, *Exiles in the High Arctic*. Nunavut Department of Education. High Arctic Relocation: Grade 10 English Language Arts [Draft] (Iqaluit: Nunavut Department of Education, 2002). Used with permission of the Department of Education, Government of Nunavut.

Jarich Oosten, Frédéric Laugrand and Wim Rasing, eds., *Interviewing Inuit Elders: The Oral Traditions Project, Volume 2: Perspectives on Inuit Law* (Iqaluit: Nunavut Arctic College, 1999) at 1-3, 33, 35-38, 190.

Pine Tree Legal Assistance, *Wabanaki Legal News*, Summer 1999. Reproduced with permission of Pine Tree Legal Assistance.

Leonard I. Rotman, *Fiduciary Law* (Toronto: Thomson/Carswell, 2005) at 244, 247, 253, 278-79, 280, 283-84, 286, 290, 294-96, 532-35, 543-46, 547-49, 586-91. Reprinted by permission of Thomson Carswell, a division of Thomson Canada Limited. Footnotes have been omitted.

Leonard I. Rotman, "Taking Aim at the Canons of Treaty Interpretation in Canadian Aboriginal Rights Jurisprudence" (1997) 46 U.N.B.L.J. 1 at 13-18. Reproduced with permission of the University of New Brunswick Law Journal.

Leonard I. Rotman, *Parallel Paths: Fiduciary Doctrine and the Crown-Native Relationship in Canada* (Toronto: University of Toronto Press, 1996) at 3-4, 11-18, 192-93, 221, 238-39, 251-53, 279-80. Reprinted by permission of University of Toronto Press Incorporated © 1996.

Leonard I. Rotman, "Provincial Fiduciary Obligations to First Nations: The Nexus Between Governmental Power and Responsibility" (1994) 32 Osgoode Hall L.J. 735 at 743-45, 754-58, 760-63. Reproduced with permission of the Osgoode Hall Law Journal and the author.

Douglas Sanders, "We Intend to Live Here Forever: A Primer on the Nisga'a Treaty" (1999) U.B.C. L. Rev. 103-128. Reprinted with permission of University of British Columbia Law Review © 1996.

Saskatchewan Child Welfare Review Panel Report, *For the Good of Our Children and Youth: A New Vision, A New Direction*, November 2010, <http://saskchildwelfarereview.ca/CWR-panel-report.pdf>.

Chief John Snow, *These Mountains Are Our Sacred Places: The Story of the Stoney Indians* (Toronto: Samuel Stevens, 1977) at 2-3, 12-13.

D.N. Sprague, "Canada's Treaties with Aboriginal Peoples" (1996) 23 Man. L.J. 341 at 341-44. Reproduced with permission of Manitoba Law Journal.

The Women's Press, "Retrospective", *Enough is Enough: Aboriginal Women Speak Out* (Toronto: The Women's Press, 1987) at 243-45. Reprinted with permission of Women's Press.

Janice Tibetts, "Adoptive Family Wins Custody of Native Boy Supreme Court will not Deliver Written Reasons for Ruling" *National Post* (18 February 1999). Reprinted with permission of Southam News.

Mary Ellen Turpel, "Home/land" (1991) 10 Can. J. Fam. L. 17 at 30. Reproduced with permission of Canadian Journal of Family Law.

Wen'de: We Are Coming to the Light of Day (Ottawa, 2005), at 14-15, 38-40. Reproduced with permission of First Nations Child and Family Caring Society of Canada.

William Wicken, "The Mi'kmaq and Wuastukwiuk Treaties" (1994) 44 U.N.B.L.J. 241 at 241-42, 249-53. Reproduced with permission of the University of New Brunswick Law Journal.

Kerry Wilkins, "Still Crazy After All These Years: Section 88 of the Indian Act at Fifty" (2000) 38 Alta. L. Rev. 458 at 465-80, 482-83, 485-87, 497-99, 501-03. Reprinted with permission of Alberta Law Review.

Daniel Wilson, "Checking the right wing's math on First Nations tax exemptons", *This Magazine*, June 15, 2011, <http://this.org/magazine/2011/06/15/first-nations-tax-exemption/>.

TABLE OF CONTENTS

TABLE OF CASES

[A page number in boldface type indicates that a case
has been excerpted in the text.]

CHAPTER 1

GOVERNANCE

A. INTRODUCTION

Aboriginal peoples exercised powers of governance for millennia prior to the arrival of Europeans and others in North America. These powers of governance varied according to clan and nation, and were suited to the varieties of languages and cultures represented on the continent. There were alliances, confederacies, powerful families, democracies and empires. Traditions of governance were often closely connected to land and family, and many emphasized the connection of the spiritual, familial, economic and political spheres.

The arrival of others challenged the governing structures of Aboriginal nations and tested their ability to perpetuate their institutions. These challenges were both internal and external. Internally, the appearance of alternative values and options for governance provided a greater range of choice to individuals and communities. Some chose to depart from or alter their traditions in response to these influences and, in the process, severely weakened the fabric of their governing structures. Others had little choice in the matter and were forced to surrender their traditional ways. Externally, the coercive implementation of the *Indian Act* (now R.S.C. 1985, c. I-5) and the associated onslaught of "civilizing" programs such as residential schools and child welfare policies tested the ability of Aboriginal people to perpetuate their traditional governance. Today, despite these difficulties, many Aboriginal people continue to be guided by their ancient practices and traditions in their approaches to governance.

The materials that follow explore the legal principles relevant to Aboriginal governance in Canada today.

B. ABORIGINAL VIEWS ON GOVERNANCE

REPORT OF THE ROYAL COMMISSION ON ABORIGINAL PEOPLES: RESTRUCTURING THE RELATIONSHIP, VOL. 2

(Ottawa: Ministry of Supply and Services, 1996) at 105-6, 108-14
(references omitted)

CONCEPTS AND TRADITIONS OF GOVERNANCE

IN THE TIME BEFORE there were human beings on Earth, the Creator called a great meeting of the Animal People.

During that period of the world's history, the Animal People lived harmoniously with one another and could speak to the Creator with one mind. They were very curious about the reason for the gathering. When they had all assembled together, the Creator spoke.

"I am sending a strange new creature to live among you," he told the Animal People. "He is to be called Man and he is to be your brother.

"But unlike you he will have no fur on his body, will walk on two legs and will not be able to speak with you. Because of this he will need your help in order to survive and become who I am creating him to be. You will need to be more than brothers and sisters, you will need to be his teachers.

"Man will not be like you. He will not come into the world like you. He will not be born knowing and understanding who and what he is. He will have to search for that. And it is in the search that he will find himself.

"He will also have a tremendous gift that you do not have. He will have the ability to dream. With this ability he will be able to invent great things and because of this he will move further and further away from you and will need your help even more when this happens.

"But to help him I am going to send him out into the world with one very special gift. I am going to give him the gift of the knowledge of Truth and Justice. But like his identity it must be a search, because if he finds this knowledge too easily he will take it for granted. So I am going to hide it and I need your help to find a good hiding-place. That is why I have called you here."

A great murmur ran through the crowd of Animal People. They were excited at the prospect of welcoming a new creature into the world and they were honoured by the Creator's request for their help. This was truly an important day.

One by one the Animal People came forward with suggestions of where the Creator should hide the gift of knowledge of Truth and Justice.

"Give it to me, my Creator," said the Buffalo, "and I will carry it on my hump to the very centre of the plains and bury it there."

"A good idea, my brother," the Creator said, "but it is destined that Man should cover most of the world and he would find it there too easily and take it for granted."

"Then give it to me," said the Salmon, "and I will carry it in my mouth to the deepest part of the ocean and I will hide it there."

"Another excellent idea," said the Creator, "but it is destined that with his power to dream, Man will invent a device that will carry him there and he would find it too easily and take it for granted."

"Then I will take it," said the Eagle, "and carry it in my talons and fly to the very face of the Moon and hide it there."

"No, my brother," said the Creator, "even there he would find it too easily because Man will one day travel there as well."

Animal after animal came forward with marvellous suggestions on where to hide this precious gift, and one by one the Creator turned down their ideas. Finally, just when discouragement was about to invade their circle, a tiny voice spoke from the back of the gathering. The Animal People were all surprised to find that the voice belonged to the Mole.

The Mole was a small creature who spent his life tunnelling through the earth and because of this had lost most of the use of his eyes. Yet because he was always in touch with Mother Earth, the Mole had developed true spiritual insight.

The Animal People listened respectfully when Mole began to speak.

"I know where to hide it, my Creator," he said. "I know where to hi[de] gift of the knowledge of Truth and Justice."

"Where then, my brother?" asked the Creator. "Where should I hid[e] gift?"

"Put it inside them," said the Mole. "Put it inside them because then on- ly the wisest and purest of heart will have the courage to look there."

And that is where the Creator placed the gift of the knowledge of Truth and Justice.

. . . . .

1. Aboriginal Perspectives

1.1 Basic Concepts

... [H]uman beings are born with the inherent freedom to discover who and what they are. For many Aboriginal people, this is perhaps the most basic definition of sovereignty — the right to know who and what you are. Sovereignty is the natural right of all human beings to define, sustain and perpetuate their identities as individuals, communities and nations.

Many Aboriginal people see sovereignty as much as a human right as a political and legal one. Seen in this way, sovereignty is an inherent human attribute that cannot be surrendered or taken away.

> What is sovereignty? Sovereignty is difficult to define because it is intangi- ble, it cannot be seen or touched. It is very much inherent, an awesome power, a strong feeling or the belief of a people. What can be seen, however, is the exercise of Aboriginal powers. For our purposes, a working definition of sovereignty is the ultimate power from which all specific political powers are derived.

> Roger Jones, Councillor and Elder
> Shawanaga First Nation
> Sudbury, Ontario, 1 June 1993*

As an inherent human quality, sovereignty finds its natural expression in the principle of self-determination. Self-determining peoples have the freedom to choose the pathways that best express their identity, their sense of themselves and the character of their relations with others. Self- determination is the power of choice in action.

> Self-determination is looking at our desires and our aspirations of where we want to go and being given the chance to attain that ... for life itself, for ex- istence itself, for nationhood itself ... .

> René Tenasco, Councillor
> Kitigan Zibi Anishinabeg Council
> Maniwaki, Quebec, 2 December 1992

Self-government is one path Aboriginal people may take in putting the principle of self-determination into effect. Self-government flows from the principle of self-determination. In its most basic sense, it is the ability to assess and satisfy needs without outside influence, permission or restriction. In a study prepared for the Commission, the Metis Family and Community Justice Services of Saskatchewan asserts the following:

The political movement towards Métis self-government may be understood as a viable alternative to a mainstream political and administrative system that has consistently failed to address our goals and needs. Our desire to control our own affairs should be viewed as a positive step, as an expression of nationhood, built upon a history in which the right to self-determination was never relinquished, in which the governing apparatus will have legitimacy in the eyes of its citizens.

Of course, self-government may take a variety of forms. For some peoples, it may mean establishing distinct governmental institutions on an 'exclusive' territory. For others, it may mean setting up a public government generally connected with modern treaties or land claims agreements. Alternatively, self-government may involve sharing power in joint governmental institutions, with guaranteed representation for the nations and peoples involved. In other instances, it may involve setting up culturally specific institutions and services within a broader framework of public government. ...

While the terms sovereignty, self-determination and self-government have distinct meanings, they are versatile concepts, with meanings that overlap one another. They are used by different peoples in different ways.

. . . . .

Sovereignty, in the words of one brief, is "the original freedom conferred to our people by the Creator rather than a temporal power." As a gift from the Creator, sovereignty can neither be given nor taken away, nor can its basic terms be negotiated. This view is shared by many Aboriginal people, whose political traditions are infused with a deep sense of spirituality and a sense of the inter-connectedness of all things. Such concepts as sovereignty, self-government and the land, which for some Canadians have largely secular definitions, all retain a spiritual dimension in contemporary Aboriginal thinking. Dave Courchene, Jr. alluded to this point in his testimony to the Commission:

> The underlying premise upon which all else was based was to recognize and fulfil the spirit of life within oneself and with all others in the circle of individuals, relationship or community and the land. This was achieved through concerted effort on developing the spirit through prayer, meditation, vision quests, fasting, ceremony, and in other ways of communicating with the Creator.
>
> Dave Courchene, Jr.
> Fort Alexander, Manitoba
> 30 October 1992

From this perspective, sovereignty is seen as an inherent attribute, flowing from sources within a people or nation rather than from external sources such as international law, common law or the Constitution. Herb George of the Gitksan and Wet'suwet'en stated:

> What is required here is not an inquiry of the current law or international law to determine the source of our rights. What is required here is the recognition that our rights exist in spite of what international law says, in spite of what the common law says, and in spite of what have been the policies of this government to the present day.

If this issue is to be dealt with in a fair way, then what is required is a strong recommendation from this Commission to government that the source of our rights, the source of our lives and the source of our government is from us. That the source of our lives comes from Gitksan-Wet'suwet'en law.

Herb George
Gitksan-Wet'suwet'en Government
Commission on Social Development
Kispiox, British Columbia, 16 June 1992

While Aboriginal sovereignty is inherent, it also has an historical basis in the extensive diplomatic relations between Aboriginal peoples and European powers from the early period of contact onward. In the eyes of many treaty peoples, the fact that the French and British Crowns concluded alliances and treaties with First Nations demonstrates that these nations were sovereign peoples capable of conducting international relations. The president of the Union of Nova Scotia Indians said to the Commission:

We see our right of self-government as an inherent right which does not come from other governments. It does not originate in our treaties. The right of self-government and self-determination comes from the Mi'kmaq people themselves. It is through their authority that we govern. The treaties reflect the Crown's recognition that we were, and would remain, self-governing, but they did not create our nationhood. ... In this light, the treaties should be effective vehicles for the implementation of our constitutionally protected right to exercise jurisdiction and authority as governments. Self-government can start with the process of interpreting and fully implementing the 1752 Treaty, to build onto it an understanding of the political relationship between the Mi'kmaq people and the Crown.

Alex Christmas
Eskasoni, Nova Scotia
6 May 1992

Some interveners spoke of the need for caution in using the term sovereignty. They noted that the word has roots in European languages and political thought and draws on attitudes associated with the rise of the unitary state, attitudes that do not harmonize well with Aboriginal ideas of governance. For example, in some strands of European thought, sovereignty is coloured by theories suggesting that absolute political authority is vested in a single political office or body, which has no legal limits on its power. The classic notion of the sovereignty of Parliament as developed in British constitutional thought reflects such an approach.

This understanding of sovereignty is very different from that held by most Aboriginal people.

I don't even like the word sovereignty because ... it denotes the idea that there's a sovereign, a king, or a head honcho, whatever. I don't think that native people govern themselves that way ... .I think native peoples' government was more of a consultative process where everyone was involved — women, men and children.

Greg Johnson
Eskasoni, Nova Scotia
6 May 1992

Gerald Alfred makes similar observations in a study dealing with the meaning of self-government among the Mohawk people of Kahnawake:

> The use of the term 'sovereignty' is itself problematic, as it skews the terms of the debate in favour of a European conception of a proper relationship. In adopting the English language as a means of communication, Aboriginal peoples have been compromised to a certain degree in that accepting the language means accepting basic premises developed in European thought and reflected in the debate surrounding the issues of sovereignty in general and Aboriginal or Native sovereignty in particular.

A better term for political authority, Alfred suggests, is the Mohawk word tewatatowie, which means 'we help ourselves'. Tewatatowie is linked to philosophical concepts embodied in the Iroquois Kaianerekowa, or Great Law of Peace. It is understood not only in terms of interests and boundaries, but also in terms of land, relationships and spirituality. The essence of Mohawk sovereignty is harmony, achieved through balanced relationships. This requires respect for the common interests of individuals and communities, as well as for the differences that require them to maintain a measure of autonomy from one another. For the Mohawk, as for many other Aboriginal peoples, sovereignty does not mean establishing an all-powerful government over a nation or people. It means that the people take care of themselves and the lands for which they are responsible. It means using political power to express the people's will.

Commissioners heard differing views about what Aboriginal sovereignty means for the relationship between Aboriginal peoples and Canada. Some Aboriginal people spoke about degrees of sovereignty and joint jurisdiction. A number of treaty nations used the term 'shared sovereignty' and maintained that their treaties created a confederal relationship with the Crown, or a form of treaty federalism. For example, the Federation of Saskatchewan Indian Nations outlined a vision of shared but equal sovereignties, affirmed by treaties between First Nations and the Crown. This view envisages relations among First Nations governments, provincial governments and the federal government that are based on principles of coexistence and equality.

Others adopt a more autonomous stance. For example, the Mohawk people draw a clear distinction between co-operating with Canada at an administrative level and surrendering sovereignty. They hold that the first does not necessarily involve the second. They consider the freedom to make associations an essential element of self-determination and self-government. The point is elaborated in a joint statement by the Mohawk Council of Akwesasne, Kahnawake and Kanesatake:

> We see self-determination and governance as discrete concepts. But by believing that our Nation constitutes a sovereign power, we are not precluding political or economic cooperation with Canada. Self-determination is a right we have and which must be respected, but we recognize that it is a right which operates within the context of a political and economic reality. From our perspective, our right to self-determination is not detrimentally affected by the arrangements and agreements we reach with Canada for the mutual benefit of our peoples. Our position with respect to any agreement must be

based upon our assessment of our current capabilities to govern and administer, it in no way derogates from the unlimited right to change those arrangements in the future upon reflection.

The right of self-determination is also a basic concept for Inuit. This right is grounded in their identity as a distinct people, the strong bonds they have with their homelands, and the fact that they have governed themselves on those lands for thousands of years. They call for their rights to be viewed within a human rights framework as opposed to an ethnic rights framework:

> If more emphasis was placed on examining the self-government question from a human rights perspective, the dominating principles would be the universality of human rights and the equality of all peoples. This would lead to a recognition of the right of aboriginal peoples, like other peoples, to self-determination. Self-determination is not defined as an ethnic right internationally. It is a fundamental human right of peoples, not of ethnic groups.

In the eyes of Inuit, self-determination has both international and domestic aspects. Nevertheless, they have clearly indicated that they wish to exercise their right of self-determination mainly through constitutional reform and the negotiation of self-government agreements. Rosemarie Kuptana, former president of Inuit Tapirisat of Canada, has expressed this position as follows:

> The implementation of our right to self-determination will be pursued in a co-operative and practical manner with all Arctic States including Canada, but the Inuit agenda is first and foremost premised upon our recognition as a people. We are a people who have been subjected to the sovereignty of Canada without our consent, without recognition of our collective identity as a people and in violation of our right to self-determination under international law. This must be rectified by several initiatives: the negotiation of regional self-government agreements, constitutional entrenchment of the inherent right of self-government, and the full recognition of the right of indigenous peoples to self-determination, under international human rights standards.

Métis people also maintain that they have a right of self-determination as a distinct people. This right forms the background to their assertion of the right to govern themselves and, more generally, to control their own social, cultural and economic development. The Métis right of self-determination arises from their distinctive political history, which has taken different forms in different parts of Canada. For example, the political consciousness of Métis people in western Canada is rooted in the unique character and status of the Métis Nation, which emerged in the prairies during the eighteenth and nineteenth centuries in the course of activities centred on the fur trade and buffalo hunting. The historical dimensions of self-determination are emphasized in a study by the Metis Society of Saskatchewan:

> At the outset, it is important to note that our self-determination objectives, through self-government, are not new. Metis history bears witness to a lengthy legacy of struggles aimed at asserting our fundamental right to control our own destiny. In what is now the province of Saskatchewan, for example, ever escalating political, economic, social and cultural disputes

between the Metis and the European settlers culminated in the well known Metis resistance to Ottawa in 1885. Other sites in nineteenth century Western Canada were also scenes of conflict over many of the same issues. As might be expected, while the military conflicts that sometimes erupted were relatively short-lived, the political struggle to protect Metis economic, social and cultural values and goals has persisted.

This enduring theme in our Metis history — that we as a people have struggled against often overwhelming odds to reclaim our traditional Homeland and assert our sense of nationhood — lies behind much of the current drive towards self-government.

Métis people in eastern and central Canada also point to their long-standing and unique history, their position as mediators between First Nations and incoming Europeans and their involvement in the earliest treaties of peace and friendship. They also emphasize the continuity between their own traditions and those of other Aboriginal people.

While they ground their right of self-determination in international law, Métis people see Canada as the main venue for exercising that right.

The Métis Nation, while believing that it possesses the right of self-determination in the context of international law, has consistently pursued the recognition of its autonomy within the confines of the Canadian state and has vigorously advocated the need to negotiate self-government arrangements.

Métis organizations have urged Canadian governments to ratify a Métis Nation accord, similar to the Charlottetown Accord of 1992. They have also called for the explicit entrenchment of the inherent right of Métis self-government in the Canadian constitution. Such measures would allow Métis people to negotiate self-government agreements as a "nation within a nation".

In summary, while Aboriginal people use a variety of terms to describe their fundamental rights, they are unanimous in asserting that they have an inherent right of self-determination arising from their status as distinct or sovereign peoples. This right entitles them to determine their own governmental arrangements and the character of their relations with other people in Canada. As Elder Moses Smith of the Nuu-chah-nulth Nation told Commissioners:

> What we have — the big thing within our system ... Ha Houlthee. That is the very basic of our political setup, is Ha Houlthee, which is, we might say, putting it in English, that is true sovereignty ... .That is absolutely the key, the key of why we are today now, is that we have always been. That was never taken away from us.

C. THE COURTS' VIEW ON ABORIGINAL GOVERNANCE

Historically, Aboriginal peoples often expressed their powers of governance through relations with others. These agreements were originally carried on with attention to Aboriginal protocol and were respected by non-Aboriginal nations because of the power Aboriginal nations exercised. The Supreme Court of Canada has recognized the autonomy and independence of Aboriginal peoples in early North American relations and has provided contemporary protection for treaties formed in this period. The case of *R. v. Sioui*, below, illustrates the inherent nature of Aboriginal governance powers that provided Aboriginal peoples with authority to enter into nation-to-nation agreements with France and Great Britain.

R. v. SIOUI

[1990] S.C.J. No. 48, [1990] 1 S.C.R. 1025, 70 D.L.R. (4th) 427 (S.C.C.)

[Four members of the Huron nation were charged with cutting trees, camping and making fires in a provincial park, contrary to provincial regulations in Quebec. The Huron admitted performing the acts for which they were charged, but claimed they were practising ancestral customs and religious rites guaranteed by a treaty with the British in 1760. In resolving this appeal in favour of the Huron, the Supreme Court considered the unique relationship of First Nations to European powers at the time the treaty was signed, and commented on the independence of the Huron at this date.]

Lamer J. (Dickson C.J.C., Wilson, La Forest, L'Heureux-Dubé, Sopinka, Gonthier, Cory and **McLachlin JJ.** concurring): —
... On September 5, 1760, France and England were engaged in a war begun four years earlier, which ended with the Treaty of Paris signed on February 10, 1763. About a year earlier, the battle of the Plains of Abraham had allowed the British to take control of Quebec City and the surrounding area. During the year following this victory, British troops had worked to consolidate their military position in Canada and to solve the supply and other practical problems engendered by the very harsh winter of 1759.
... General Murray at that time invited French soldiers to surrender and Canadians to lay down their arms. He had made it widely known that he would pardon those who surrendered and allow them to keep their land. He had also promised them that he would make larger grants of land and protect them. He gave those who responded to his appeal and took the oath of allegiance to the British Crown safe conducts to return to their parishes. Steps were also taken to inform the Indians who were allies of the British of these changes of allegiance so as to ensure that they would not be attacked on the way back.
As the advantageous position and strength of the British troops became more and more apparent, several groups did surrender and it appears that this movement accelerated in the days preceding that on which the document at issue was signed. In his Historical Journal, at the entries for September 1, 2 and 3, 1760, Knox indicates that:

> The whole parish of Varenne have surrendered, delivered up their arms, and taken the oaths; their fighting-men consisted of five companies of militia: two

other parishes, equally numerous, have signified their intentions of submitting to-morrow.

. . . . .

The Canadians are surrendering every-where; they are terrified at the thoughts of Sir William Johnson's Indians coming among them, by which we conjecture they are near at hand.

. . . . .

In fact, the total defeat of France in Canada was very near: the Act of Capitulation of Montreal, by which the French troops stationed in Canada laid down their arms, was signed on September 8, 1760 and signaled the end of France's de facto control in Canada.

Great Britain's *de jure* control of Canada took the form of the Treaty of Paris of February 10, 1763. ... Some months later, the *Royal Proclamation* of October 7, 1763 organized the territories recently acquired by Great Britain and reserved two types of land for the Indians: that located outside the colony's territorial limits and the establishments authorized by the Crown inside the colony...

I consider that ... we can conclude from the historical documents that both Great Britain and France felt that the Indian nations had sufficient independence and played a large enough role in North America for it to be good policy to maintain relations with them very close to those maintained between sovereign nations.

The mother countries did everything in their power to secure the alliance of each Indian nation and to encourage nations allied with the enemy to change sides. When these efforts met with success, they were incorporated in treaties of alliance or neutrality. This clearly indicates that the Indian nations were regarded in their relations with the European nations which occupied North America as independent nations. The papers of Sir William Johnson (The Papers of Sir William Johnson, 14 vol.), who was in charge of Indian affairs in British North America, demonstrate the recognition by Great Britain that nation-to-nation relations had to be conducted with the North American Indians. As an example, I cite an extract from a speech by Sir Johnson at the Onondaga Conference held in April 1748, attended by the Five Nations:

> Brethren of the five Nations I will begin upon a thing of a long standing, our first *Brothership*. My Reason for it is, I think there are several among you who seem to forget it; It may seem strange to you how I a *Foreigner* should know this, But I tell you I found out some of the old Writings of our Forefathers which was thought to have been lost and in this old valuable Record I find, that our first *Friendship* Commenced at the Arrival of the first great Canoe or Vessel at Albany . . . (Emphasis added.) (The Papers of Sir William Johnson, vol. I, 1921, at pp. 157-58.)

As the Chief Justice of the United States Supreme Court said in 1832 in *Worcester v. State of Georgia*, 31 U.S. (6 Pet.) 515 (1832), at pp. 548-49, about British policy towards the Indians in the mid-eighteenth century:

Such was the policy of Great Britain towards the Indian nations inhabiting the territory from which she excluded all other Europeans; such her claims, and such her practical exposition of the charters she had granted: *she considered them as nations capable of maintaining the relations of peace and war; of governing themselves, under her protection; and she made treaties with them, the obligation of which she acknowledged.* (Emphasis added.)

Further, both the French and the English recognized the critical importance of alliances with the Indians, or at least their neutrality, in determining the outcome of the war between them and the security of the North American colonies.

Following the crushing defeats of the English by the French in 1755, the English realized that control of North America could not be acquired without the co-operation of the Indians. Accordingly, from then on they made efforts to ally themselves with as many Indian nations as possible. The French, who had long realized the strategic role of the Indians in the success of any war effort, also did everything they could to secure their alliance or maintain alliances already established. ...

England also wished to secure the friendship of the Indian nations by treating them with generosity and respect for fear that the safety and development of the colonies and their inhabitants would be compromised by Indians with feelings of hostility. One of the extracts from Knox's work which I cited above reports that the Canadians and the French soldiers who surrendered asked to be protected from Indians on the way back to their parishes. Another passage from Knox, also cited above, relates that the Canadians were terrified at the idea of seeing Sir William Johnson's Indians coming among them. This proves that in the minds of the local population the Indians represented a real and disturbing threat. The fact that England was also aware of the danger the colonies and their inhabitants might run if the Indians withdrew their co-operation is echoed in the ... documents ... and by analogy Governor Murray's *Journal of the Siege of Quebec*, entry of December 31, 1759, at pp. 15-16.

This "generous" policy which the British chose to adopt also found expression in other areas. The British Crown recognized that the Indians had certain ownership rights over their land, it sought to establish trade with them which would rise above the level of exploitation and give them a fair return. It also allowed them autonomy in their internal affairs, intervening in this area as little as possible.

[Drawing on this historical context and noting the need to reconcile the independence of the Huron with the colonial aspirations of the British, the Court found that the Hurons exercised their autonomy in the period in question by entering into a treaty to protect their religious liberties and customs. They further found that this treaty was still valid, that the acts protected by its terms were not incompatible with Crown suzerainty and that, therefore, the treaty provided an effective defence against the acts for which the Huron were charged.]

D. THE HISTORICAL RECOGNITION OF ABORIGINAL GOVERNANCE

As recognized in the *Sioui* case, the early history of Aboriginal-Crown relations in eastern North America demonstrates that the Crown often recognized the autonomy of Aboriginal Nations. Practices and principles were developed to affirm this fact and to facilitate productive relations between the parties. One of the most important was the creation of treaties between the parties. While Crown-Aboriginal treaties are the focus of Chapter 4, as Rotman indicates in the following excerpt, the treaties played an important role in the reciprocal recognition of British and Aboriginal governance and made use of diplomatic practices previously used by the parties in their interactions with other independent nations.

LEONARD I. ROTMAN, FIDUCIARY LAW

(Toronto: Thomson/Carswell, 2005) at 532-35 (references omitted)

Britain's relations with the Aboriginal peoples were both cumulative and evolutionary. The initial grassroots interaction between the parties was not superseded by the broader, more formal relations that developed, but was incorporated into the continually evolving relationship between the parties. These more substantial alliances were often solemnized in written treaties. Under these treaties, trade relations and military alliances were solidified. Britain's alliances with the Aboriginals enabled it to engage in profitable trade while furthering its ambitions of empire through the establishment and maintenance of colonies in North America. These alliances also proved beneficial to the Aboriginal peoples, providing them with recognition of their rights, protection from their enemies, and the ability to acquire British goods.

The process of relationship building through the increased and intensified scope of the parties' interaction was consistent with prior Aboriginal practices. Aboriginal diplomacy was based upon the continuous reaffirmation and renewal of alliances. Once a relationship was established, Aboriginal peoples regarded the regularized affirmation of its existence and purpose as an imperative. This was accomplished through the presentation of gifts, the oral reaffirmation of existing alliances or, in some situations, the expansion of existing alliances. As Borrows explains:

> [r]enewal and re-interpretation were practised to bring past agreements into harmony with changing circumstances. First Nations preferred this articulation of treaty-making to exercise their powers of self-government because it was consistent with their oral tradition. The idea of the principles of a treaty being "frozen" through terms written on paper was an alien concept [to the Odawa].

> Therefore, to convey the meaning of the treaties, First Nations sovereignty was exercised through the spoken word and Wampum belts, and not through written statements. The reception of presents was also a part of the traditional ceremonial and oral nature of treaties. The gathering for presents provided an opportunity to meet in council and exchange words and material goods to reaffirm or modify previous agreements according to changing

conditions. This explains why First Nation leaders would travel such long distances to receive a few trinkets that were monetarily of trivial value.

In contrast, traditional British diplomacy was premised upon the drafting of formal treaties. These treaties established the entire terms of the relations between the parties as of the date the treaty was signed. The functional life of a treaty was dependent upon the continued existence of harmonious relations between the treating parties. Rather than regularly tending to or affirming its alliances, Britain simply relied upon the reasonable expectations created by a treaty. Another point of distinction is that, under British practice, subsequent treaties automatically superseded the terms and conditions of any previous treaties between the same parties absent any express indication to the contrary.

The nature of Britain's relations with the Aboriginal peoples in North America necessitated a change in its traditional approach to making and maintaining alliances. Indeed, Britain's historical engagements with Aboriginal peoples in North America demonstrates that it adopted Aboriginal methods of diplomacy in its relations with the Aboriginal peoples. In addition to giving gifts and reaffirming existing alliances, British diplomats invoked Aboriginal rhetoric and made extensive use of wampum, all of which had previously been foreign to them. A speech made in 1764 by Sir William Johnson, Northern Superintendent-General of Indian Affairs, represents how Britain used these practices in its diplomatic relations with the Aboriginal peoples:

> [b]rothers of the Western Nations, Sachems, Chiefs and Warriors: You have now been here for several days, during which time we have frequently met to renew and Strengthen our Engagements and you have made so many Promises of your Friendship and Attachment to the English that there now remains for us only to exchange the great Belt of the Covenant Chain that we may not forget our mutual Engagements.

> I now therefore present you the great Belt by which I bind all your Western Nations together with the English, and I desire that you will take fast hold of the same, and never let it slip, to which end I desire that after you have shewn this Belt to all Nations you will fix one end of it with the Chipeweighs at St. Marys [Michilimackinac] whilst the other end remains at my house, and moreover I desire that you will never listen to any news which comes to any other Quarter. If you do it, it may shake the Belt.

Thus, it may be seen that these Aboriginal practices were merged with existing British customs to create a unique method of diplomacy that was shaped by Aboriginal demands and Britain's need for Aboriginal alliances.

... Both the use of formal treaties as well as the rhetoric implemented by British diplomats are consistent with nation-to-nation relations. British representations to the Aboriginal peoples further affirm that Britain dealt with the Aboriginal peoples as autonomous nations. Moreover, these representations remained unvaried from the earliest formal alliance between the groups, the *Treaty of Albany, 1664*, through to the largest gathering of Aboriginal peoples for the purposes of treating with Britain, the *Treaty of Niagara, 1764*.

1.   The *Treaty of Albany*

The *Treaty of Albany, 1664* was the first formal alliance between Aboriginal peoples in North America and the British Crown. At the time of the treaty, the Iroquois were more numerous and powerful than the British in North America. Equally important, they had become catalysts in the struggle between Britain and France for economic and military pre-eminence in North America. The Iroquois had been allies of the Dutch prior to Britain's acquisition of New Netherland, renamed New York by Britain in 1664. Through the treaty, Britain sought to ally itself with a powerful ally. Meanwhile, the Iroquois sought to continue the relationship they had previously enjoyed with the Dutch.

ARTICLES BETWEEN COL. CARTWRIGHT AND THE NEW YORK INDIANS, 24 SEPTEMBER 1664

in E.B. O'Callaghan, ed., *Documents Relative to the Colonial History of the State of New York*, 11 vols. (Albany: Weed, Parsons, 1853-61), Vol. 3, at 67-68

ARTICLES made and agreed upon the 24th day of September 1664 in Fort Albany between Ohgehando, Shanarage, Soachoenighta, Sachamackas of y[e] Maques; Anaweed Conkeeherat Tweasserany, Aschanoondah, Sachamakas of the Synicks, on the one part; and Colonell George Cartwright, in the behalf of Colonell Nicolls Governour under his Royall Highnesse the Duke of Yorke of all his territoryes in America, on the other part, as followeth, vizt–

1.   Imprimis. It is agreed that the Indian Princes above named and their subjects, shall have all such wares and commodities from the English for the future, as heretofore they had from the Dutch.

2.   That if any English Dutch or Indian (under the proteccôn of the English) do any wrong injury or violence to any of ye said Princes or their Subjects in any sort whatever, if they complaine to the Governor at New Yorke, or to the Officer in Chiefe at Albany, if the person so offending can be discovered, that person shall receive condigne punishm[t] and all due satisfaccôn shall be given; and the like shall be done for all other English Plantations.

3.   That if any Indian belonging to any of the Sachims aforesaid do any wrong injury or damage to the English, Dutch or Indians under the proteccôn of the English, if complaint be made to ye Sachims and the person be discovered who did the injury, then the person so offending shall be punished and all just satisfaccôn shall be given to any of His Maties subjects in any Colony or other English Plantacôn in America.

4.   The Indians at Wamping and Espachomy and all below the Manhatans, as also all those that have submitted themselves under the

proteccôn of His Matie are included in these Articles of Agreement and Peace;

In confirmacôn whereof the partyes above mencôned have hereunto sett their hands the day and yeare above written.

GEORGE CARTWRIGHT

THESE ARTICLES following were likewise proposed by the same Indian Princes & consented to by Colonell Cartwright in behalfe of Colonell Nicolls the 25th day of September 1664.

1. That the English do not assist the three Nations of the Ondiakes Pinnekooks and Pacamtekookes, who murdered one of the Princes of the Maques, when he brought ransomes & presents to them upon a treaty of peace.

2. That the English do make peace for the Indian Princes, with the Nations down the River.

3. That they may have free trade, as formerly.

4. That they may be lodged in houses, as formerly.

5. That if they be beaten by the three Nations above mencôned, they may receive accommodacôn from ye English.

The written version of the *Treaty of Albany* provided for separate British and Iroquois jurisdiction in criminal matters involving their own citizens. The written treaty provided Britain's understanding of the nature of the agreement between the parties and reflected the separate governing rights of the parties over their own citizens. This understanding of the compact between the nations was affirmed by the Iroquois' own understanding of what transpired between them at Albany. In addition to the parchment treaty, a wampum belt was presented by the Iroquois to the British to mark the former's understanding of the compact between them. Wampum belts were created by making beads from shells, such as those from clams, that were then pierced and sewn into patterns on animal hides. The belt presented to the British at Albany became known as the Two-Row Wampum because of the pattern depicted on it.

The pattern of the Two-Row Wampum, and its significance, is described below:

> The belt showed two parallel rows of purple wampum on a background of white wampum. The white wampum symbolized the purity of the agreement. The two purple rows denoted the spirit of the nations' ancestors and the separate, but parallel paths which they would each take in their respective vessels. One vessel, a birch-bark canoe, was for the Iroquois people, their laws, customs, and way of life; the other, a ship, was for the British, their laws, customs, and way of life. Three beads of wampum — symbolizing peace, friendship, and respect — separated the two rows. The three beads were the link between the nations, but just as their paths never cross on the wampum belt, neither was to attempt to steer the other's vessel.

As the first formal alliance between Britain and the Aboriginal peoples, the *Treaty of Albany* made use of forms existing within each culture that were duly representative of the solemnity with which the parties pledged their peace, friendship and respect. The use of formally-written treaties on parchment was a practice that Britain had reserved for its relations with independent, sovereign powers. Meanwhile, the Iroquois' representation of the compact on a wampum belt, which was highly valuable and required great skill to fashion, demonstrated the sanctity with which they viewed their alliance with Britain. The use of formal agreements by Aboriginal peoples was also a practice that had been used prior to contact with European nations.

Future agreements between the Aboriginal peoples and Britain built upon the foundation provided by the *Treaty of Albany* and the Two-Row Wampum. Aboriginal peoples did not view treaties as disconnected agreements as the British tended to. Rather, they regarded individual treaties as continuations of earlier alliances. Thus, the *Treaty of Albany*, from the Aboriginal point of view, was not an isolated agreement. Rather, it provided the basis for the Covenant Chain alliance that was forged between them and that extended beyond the signing of the *Treaty of Niagara* in 1764.

2. The Covenant Chain

The Covenant Chain alliance was a military, political, social, and economic alliance that existed initially between the Dutch and River Indians of the Hudson River region, but was later forged between the British and the Iroquois Confederacy and then extended to include other Aboriginal nations. The status of the *Treaty of Albany* as the foundation for the Covenant Chain alliance is supported by a statement made by the Onondaga Chief Canasatego in 1744:

> About two Years after the Arrival of the English, an English Governor came to Albany, and finding what great Friendship subsisted between us and the Dutch, he approved it mightily, and desired to make as strong a League, and to be upon as good Terms with us as the Dutch were, with whom he was united, and to become one People with us: and by his further Care in looking into what had passed between us, he found that the Rope which tied the Ship to the great Mountain was only fastened with Wampum, which was liable to break and rot, and to perish in a Course of Years; he thereafter told us, he would give us a Silver Chain which would be much stronger, and would last for ever. This we accepted, and fastened the Ship with it, and it has lasted ever since.

As described by Chief Canasatego, the treaty relationship between Britain and the Iroquois was symbolized as a ship (Britain) that was tied to an immoveable object, such as a great tree (the Tree of Peace) or mountain (usually at Onondaga, the council fire of the Iroquois Confederacy). Each of the participants in the alliance was a link in the chain and their compact was symbolized by the notion of each party placing its arms through the chain's links.

The Covenant Chain was perhaps the primary example of the use of treaties building upon each other and serving as reminders of the alliance forged between the groups. While the Covenant Chain was designed as a permanent alliance, it was expected that the nations would regularly renew their respective undertakings. This process of renewal — which was often described as "polishing the chain" — was designed to remind the parties of the solemn compact that they had entered into. When the chain was neglected through a lack of renewed commitment, it was described as "tarnished" or "rusted."

Renewing the Covenant Chain was accomplished in different ways. It took the form of the exchange of presents or wampum belts, restating the nations' solidarity, by agreements of further undertakings of union, or the extension of the alliance to include other Aboriginal groups. The periodical renewal of historic alliances was a practice familiar to the Aboriginal peoples. In addition to giving the parties an opportunity to reaffirm the nature of their alliance, the renewal process enabled them to make any necessary alterations arising from changing circumstances or needs. As John Borrows explains in "Negotiating Treaties and Land Claims: The Impact of Diversity Within First Nations Property Interests":

> Traditionally, First Nations did not allocate property in the exercise of their treaty decision-making powers by conducting their relations with other people in a static way. Relationships were continually renewed and reaffirmed through ceremonial customs. Renewal and re-interpretation were practised to bring past agreements into harmony with changing circumstances. First Nations preferred this articulation of treaty-making to exercise their powers of self-government because it was consistent with their oral tradition. The idea of the principles of a treaty being "frozen" through terms written on paper was an alien concept.
>
> . . . . .
>
> Therefore, to convey the meaning of the treaties, First Nations sovereignty was exercised through the spoken word and Wampum belts, and not through written statements. The reception of presents was also a part of the traditional ceremonial and oral nature of treaties. The gathering for presents provided an opportunity to meet in council and exchange words and material goods to reaffirm or modify previous agreements according to changing conditions. This explains why First Nation leaders would travel such long distances to receive a few trinkets that were monetarily of trivial value.[1]

The process of initiating and renewing treaty relations that had commenced with the *Treaty of Albany* and was continued through the Covenant Chain alliance established the parameters of British-Aboriginal relations in North America. These treaties were compacts between independent nations, as the following excerpt indicates.

LEONARD I. ROTMAN, "TAKING AIM AT THE CANONS OF TREATY INTERPRETATION IN CANADIAN ABORIGINAL RIGHTS JURISPRUDENCE"

(1997) 46 U.N.B.L.J. 1 at 13-18 (references omitted)

... Although there is no firm definition of what constitutes a treaty in Canadian law, the parties' intentions, not their adherence to a certain protocol, is most relevant in ascertaining whether a valid treaty exists. Justice Lamer, as he then was, stated in the *Sioui* case that a treaty exists where there is an agreement between Aboriginal peoples and the Crown that demonstrates "the intention to create obligations, the presence of mutually binding obligations and a certain measure of solemnity."

. . . . .

Treaties were mutual compacts which recognized the independence of the European and Aboriginal nations that were parties to them. The very nature of the treaty-making process indicated the autonomy of the parties, since a nation did not need to treat with its own subjects.

. . . . .

That the Aboriginal peoples considered themselves independent actors, notwithstanding their alliances with particular European nations is also indicated in the statement of the Ojibway Chief Minavavana to English trader Alexander Henry at Michilimackinac in 1764, "Englishman, although you have conquered the French, you have not yet conquered us. We are not your slaves. These lakes, these woods and mountains, were left to us by our ancestors. They are our inheritance; and we will part with them to none."

In addition to recognizing the autonomy of the parties involved, the treaties also solidified the relationship between the Crown and the Aboriginal people. ... As the basis of the origins and continuation of Crown-Native relations, the treaties were the building blocks of the modern Canadian state.

---

3. The *Royal Proclamation of 1763*

The *Royal Proclamation of 1763* figured prominently in the *Sioui* decision as evidence of a policy of peaceful alliance the Crown pursued with Indians. The *Royal Proclamation* and its associated history have significant implications for the recognition of Aboriginal self-government in contemporary affairs.

The relevant portions of the *Proclamation* are reproduced below:

ROYAL PROCLAMATION OF 7 OCTOBER, 1763
R.S.C. 1985, App. II, No. 1

Whereas We have taken into Our Royal Consideration the extensive and valuable Acquisitions in America, secured to our Crown by the late Definitive Treaty of Peace, concluded at Paris, the 10th Day of February last; and being desirous that all Our loving Subjects, as well of our Kingdom as of our Colonies in America, may avail themselves with all convenient Speed, of the great Benefits and Advantages which must accrue therefrom to their Commerce, Manufactures, and Navigation, We have thought fit, with the Advice of our Privy Council, to issue this our Royal Proclamation, hereby to publish and declare to all our loving Subjects, that we have, with the Advice of our

Said Privy Council, granted our Letters Patent, under our Great Seal of Great Britain, to erect, within the Countries and Islands ceded and confirmed to Us by the said Treaty, Four distinct and separate Governments, styled and called by the names of Quebec, East Florida, West Florida and Grenada. ...

And whereas it is just and reasonable, and essential to our Interest, and the Security of our Colonies, that the several Nations or Tribes of Indians with whom We are connected, and who live under our Protection, should not be molested or disturbed in the Possession of such Parts of Our Dominions and Territories as, not having been ceded to or purchased by Us, are reserved to them, or any of them, as their Hunting Grounds. — We do therefore, with the Advice of our Privy Council, declare it to be our Royal Will and Pleasure, that no Governor or Commander in Chief in any of our Colonies of Quebec, East Florida, or West Florida, do presume, upon any Pretence whatever, to grant Warrants of Survey, or pass any Patents for Lands beyond the Bounds of their respective Governments, as described in their Commissions; as also that no Governor or Commander in Chief in any of our other Colonies or Plantations in America do presume for the present, and until our further Pleasure be known, to grant Warrants of Survey, or pass Patents for any Lands beyond the Heads or Sources of any of the Rivers which fall into the Atlantic Ocean from the West and North West, or upon any Lands whatever, which, not having been ceded to or purchased by Us as aforesaid, are reserved to the said Indians, or any of them.

And We do further declare it to be Our Royal Will and Pleasure, for the present as aforesaid, to reserve under our Sovereignty, Protection, and Dominion, for the use of the said Indians, all the Lands and Territories not included within the Limits of Our said Three new Governments, or within the Limits of the Territory granted to the Hudson's Bay Company, as also all the Lands and Territories lying to the Westward of the Sources of the Rivers which fall into the Sea from the West and North West as aforesaid.

And We do strictly forbid, on Pain of our Displeasure, all our loving Subjects from making any Purchases or Settlements whatever, or taking Possession of any of the Lands above reserved, without our especial leave and Licence for that Purpose first obtained.

And, We do further strictly enjoin and require all Persons whatever who have either wilfully or inadvertently seated themselves upon any Lands within the Countries above described, or upon any other Lands which, not having been ceded to or purchased by Us, are still reserved to the said Indians as aforesaid, forthwith to remove themselves from such Settlements.

And whereas great Frauds and Abuses have been committed in purchasing Lands of the Indians, to the great Prejudice of our Interests, and to the great Dissatisfaction of the said Indians, In order, therefore, to prevent such Irregularities for the future, and to the end that the Indians may be convinced of our Justice and determined Resolution to remove all reasonable Cause of Discontent, We do, with the Advice of our Privy Council strictly enjoin and require, that no private Person do presume to make any purchase from the said Indians of any Lands reserved to the said Indians, within those parts of our Colonies where, We have thought proper to allow Settlement; but that, if at any Time any of the Said Indians should be inclined to dispose of the said Lands, the same shall be Purchased only for Us, in our Name, at some public Meeting or Assembly of the said Indians, to be held for that Purpose by the Governor or Commander in Chief of our Colony respectively within which they shall lie; and in case they shall lie within the limits of any Proprietary Government, they shall be purchased only for the Use and in the name of such Proprietaries, conformable to such Directions and Instructions as We or they shall think proper to give for that Purpose.

. . . . .

Given at our Court at St. James's the 7th Day of October 1763, in the Third Year of our Reign.

———————

The *Royal Proclamation* was declared to delineate boundaries and define jurisdiction between Aboriginal people and the Crown. The *Proclamation* attempted to convince Indians that the British would respect existing political and territorial jurisdiction by incorporating Aboriginal under-standings of this relationship in the document. The *Proclamation* does this by implying that no lands would be taken from Indians without their con-sent. However, in order to consolidate the Crown's position in North America, words were also placed in the document that did not accord with Aboriginal viewpoints. For example, the British inserted statements in the *Proclamation* that claimed "Dominion" and "Sovereignty" over the territo-ries that First Nations occupied. In placing these divergent notions within the *Proclamation* the British were trying to convince Native people that they had nothing to fear from the colonists, while at the same time trying to in-crease their own political and economic power. The British perceptively realized that alleviating Indian discontent required Native people to be-lieve that their jurisdiction and territory were protected. However, the British also realized that the colonial enterprise required an expansion of the Crown's sovereignty and dominion over Indian lands. Thus, while the *Proclamation* seemingly reinforced Indian preferences that their territories remain free from European settlement, it also opened the door for the ero-sion of these same preferences. The *Royal Proclamation* uncomfortably straddles contradictory aspirations. This is documented in the following two excerpts.

LEONARD I. ROTMAN, FIDUCIARY LAW

(Toronto: Thomson/Carswell, 2005) at 543-46, 547-49 (references omitted)

The principles of peace, friendship, and respect that connected the parallel paths of Britain and the Iroquois in the Two-Row Wampum in the 17th century ... continued to provide the basis for the parties' interaction throughout the Covenant Chain alliance that remained vibrant well into the second half of the 18th century. During this period, Britain's practice of entering into alliances with the Aboriginal peoples on a nation-to-nation basis had become a firmly-entrenched element of Britain's New World policy. ...

Prior to the conquest of New France in 1760-61, Aboriginal groups had occupied strategic roles on both sides of British-French battles for North American supremacy. This was a fact not lost on either Britain or France. Because of their superior strength as well as military and trade positioning, the Aboriginal peoples were potentially dangerous enemies to the Europeans as well as much sought-after allies. With Britain and France competing to achieve predominance in North America in the 18th century, the Aboriginals for their own benefit were able to play off the two European powers against each other.

. . . . .

The Aboriginal peoples were shrewd negotiators who were well aware of the strategic value of their positions in the European struggle in North America. They also realized that their own interests were best served by maintaining the balance of power between the two European nations. Maintaining this balance ensured the Aboriginals' autonomy. It also enhanced their bargaining position and necessitated that they be treated with respect by the Europeans. This situation changed drastically, however, in the second half of the 18th century.

Once France ceased to be a major power in North America, the pre-existing relationship between Britain and the Aboriginal peoples was placed in jeopardy. France's defeat marked a significant change to the middle ground that had served Aboriginal interests from the second half of the 17th century. The conquest of New France had other equally significant effects upon the Aboriginals. While Britain had strengthened its position in North America by virtue of its wars with France, those same wars had drastically reduced the Aboriginals' military strength. Further, the combined effects of disease, lengthy wars, colonial expansion, and Aboriginal dependence on European goods rendered the Aboriginal peoples more heavily dependent upon Britain than they had ever been. The result was that British-Aboriginal relations that had long been dominated by the Aboriginals were now tilted in favour of Britain. The practical implications of this occurrence was expressed by General Thomas Gage, who stated that "[a]ll North America in the hands of a single power robs [the Aboriginals] of their Consequence, presents, & pay."

After the conquest of New France, there was a rift in British attitudes towards the Aboriginal peoples. On the one hand, military leaders such as Gage and General Jeffrey Amherst thought that Britain could now unilaterally dictate the future course of British-Aboriginal relations. As White explains, "General Amherst's new vision of the *pays d'en haut* was a simple one: the British were conquerors; the Indians were subjects." However, Sir William Johnson and his right-hand man, George Croghan, believed that British relations with the Aboriginal peoples should continue as they had prior to the conquest. They contended that any change in the *status quo* would lead to Aboriginal revolt that would be costly to Britain's colonial desires. This split between Britain's diplomatic and military representatives in North America was responsible for an ensuing inconsistency in British attitudes towards the Aboriginal peoples. This inconsistency was most apparent in the years between the conquest of New France and the release of the *Royal Proclamation of 1763* ...

Despite the split in British diplomatic and military *attitudes* towards the Aboriginal peoples from the conquest of New France until the American Revolution, Britain's *representations* to the Aboriginal peoples during this period were consistent. Britain continued to indicate to the Aboriginal peoples that its relations with them were on a nation-to-nation basis. Effectively, this created a new "middle ground" that emerged in the aftermath of the conquest, which may be seen in a variety of sources, including the representations of British officials, colonial instruments, and instructions given to military leaders.

It may be seen, therefore, that in spite of the change in power relations between Britain and the Aboriginal peoples and the change in some British attitudes towards its relations with the latter, the foundational principles of peace, friendship, and respect proved to be the basis upon which Britain continued to represent its dealings to the Aboriginal peoples. Even in the context of offering its protection to the Aboriginal peoples and their lands in the *Royal Proclamation of 1763*, Britain indicated its continued respect for Aboriginal autonomy.

The *Royal Proclamation of 1763* affirms the special relationship between the Crown and Aboriginal peoples through its recognition of pre-existing Aboriginal rights and its protection of Aboriginal peoples and their lands. The *Proclamation* also bridges the gap between pre- and post-conquest British-Aboriginal relations through its entrenchment of the principles of peace, friendship, and respect solidified through the Covenant Chain alliance. ...

The *Proclamation* characterizes the Crown-Aboriginal relationship as existing between autonomous entities coexisting in a peaceful and mutually beneficial manner. Its description of "the several Nations or Tribes with whom We are connected, and who live under our Protection" indicates that the Aboriginal peoples were not conceived of as subjects of the Crown, but allied nations in receipt of British military support. British correspondence contemporaneous with the issuing of the *Proclamation* supports the proposition that the *Proclamation* recognizes the Aboriginal peoples as allies rather than subjects. ... As the Royal Commission on Aboriginal Peoples explains in its report entitled *Treaty Making in the Spirit of Co-existence*:

> ... while the Royal Proclamation asserted suzerainty over Aboriginal peoples living "under Our Protection", it also recognized that these people were "Nations" connected with the Crown by way of treaty and alliance. ... [T]he Proclamation acknowledged the retained sovereignty of Aboriginal peoples under the Crown's protection, and adopted measures to secure and protect their Territorial rights. This arrangement is the historical basis of the enduring constitutional relationship between Aboriginal nations and the Crown and provides the source of the Crown's fiduciary duties to those nations.

By simultaneously asserting British suzerainty *vis-à-vis* European nations while affirming the independence of the Aboriginal peoples, the *Proclamation* is consistent with the symbiotic nature of Crown-Aboriginal relations established in the *Treaty of Albany* and solidified through the Covenant Chain alliance.

The terms of the *Proclamation* denote the Crown's recognition of its historical commitments to protect the Aboriginal peoples. The *Proclamation*'s prohibition of the exploitation of Aboriginal peoples and their lands is designed to maintain the integrity of Crown-Aboriginal relations. ... That is not to suggest that the document did not sow the seeds for the onslaught of colonialism that ultimately become the dominant characteristic of Crown-Aboriginal relations. However, while the *Proclamation* may have provided a framework for the realization of Britain's colonialist desires in North America, it did not ignore Britain's historical undertakings and responsibilities towards the Aboriginal peoples. The *Treaty of Niagara, 1764* demonstrates the validity of this assertion.

JOHN BORROWS, "WAMPUM AT NIAGARA: THE ROYAL PROCLAMATION, CANADIAN LEGAL HISTORY AND SELF-GOVERNMENT"

In Michael Asch, ed., *Aboriginal and Treaty Rights in Canada: Essays on Law, Equality and Respect for Difference*
(Vancouver: U.B.C. Press, 1997) 155 at 161-65, 168-69

The Treaty of Niagara

Since the wording of the [Royal] Proclamation is contradictory in describing the autonomy and jurisdiction of First Nations, and since the Proclamation was drafted under the control and preference of the colonial power, the spirit and intent of the Royal Proclamation can best be discerned by reference to a treaty with First Nations representatives at Niagara in 1764. At this gathering a nation-to-nation relationship between settler and First Nation peoples was renewed and extended, and the Covenant Chain of Friendship, a multination alliance in which no member gave up their sovereignty, was affirmed. The Royal Proclamation became a treaty at Niagara because it was presented by the colonialists for affirmation, and was accepted by the First Nations. However, when presenting the Proclamation, both parties made representations and promises through methods other than the written word, such as oral statements and belts of wampum. It is significant to note that Sir William Johnson, superintendent of Indian affairs, had earlier agreed to meet with the First Nations and reassert their mutual relationship through requirements prescribed by the Aboriginal peoples, which involved the giving and receiving of wampum belts. Some principles that were implicit in the written version of the Proclamation were made explicit to First Nations in these other communications. For example, First Nation peoples approved terms of the

Proclamation that encompassed more than a system of land allotment, including express guarantees of First Nations sovereignty.

In the winter after the Royal Proclamation was issued, First Nation leaders throughout the northeast, mid-east, and mid-west of North America were invited to attend a conference to be held the following summer to discuss the formation of principles that would govern their relationship with the Crown. The people of the Algonquin and Nipissing nations met with the British superintendent of Indian affairs at Oswegatchie and were persuaded to be messengers in inviting other First Nations to attend a peace council at Niagara in the summer of 1764. Representatives of these two nations travelled throughout the winter of 1763-4 with a printed copy of the Royal Proclamation, and with various strings of wampum, in order to summons the various First Nations to a council with the British.

William Johnson described the purpose of the intended meeting at Niagara as a "Treaty of Offensive and Defensive Alliance" that would include British promises to assure them of a Free Fair & Open trade, at the principal Posts, & a free intercourse, & passage into our Country, That we will make no Settlements or Encroachments contrary to Treaty, or without their permission. That we will bring to justice any persons who commit Robberys or Murders on them & that we will protect & aid them against their & our Enemys, & duly observe our Engagements with them." It is clear that, in conjunction with their issuance of the Proclamation, the British proposed that a treaty be entered into to negotiate and formalize the principles upon which their relationship would be based. The invitation to treaty, with the accompanying promises that were to govern the parties' relationship, demonstrates the intent of the British to enter into momentous negotiations with the First Nations of North America. Johnson further proposed, on behalf of the British, that: at this treaty ... we should tie them down (in the Peace) according to their own forms of which they take the most notice, for example by exchanging a very large belt with some remarkable & intelligible figures thereon. Expressive of the occasion which should always be shown to remind them of their promises." Thus, the treaty at Niagara was to be recorded in the manner that the First Nations were familiar with. Wampum belts were to be exchanged which would communicate the promises exchanged, and which would form the record of the agreement.

The treaty at Niagara was entered into in July and August 1764, and was regarded as "the most widely representative gathering of American Indians ever assembled," as approximately two thousand chiefs attended the negotiations. There were over twenty-four Nations gathered with "representative nations as far east as Nova Scotia, and as far west as Mississippi, and as far north as Hudson Bay." It is also possible that representatives from even further afield participated in the treaty as some records indicate that the Cree and Lakota (Sioux) nations were also present at this event. It is obvious that a substantial number of First Nations people attended the gathering at Niagara. Aboriginal people throughout the Great Lakes and northern, eastern, and western colonial regions had travelled for weeks and months to attend this meeting.

When everyone was assembled, William Johnson presented the terms of what he hoped would prove a Pax Britannica for North America. Johnson read the terms of the Royal Proclamation to representatives of the nations and a promise of peace was given by Aboriginal representatives and a state of mutual non-interference established. Presents were exchanged to certify the binding nature of the promises being exchanged. Johnson then presented the Covenant Chain and wampum belts and stated:

> Brothers of the Western Nations, Sachems, Chiefs and Warriors; You have now been here for several days, during which time we have frequently met to renew and Strengthen our Engagements and you have made so many Promises of your Friendship and Attachment to the English that there now remains for us only to exchange the great Belt of the Covenant Chain that we may not forget out mutual Engagements.
>
> I now therefore present you the great Belt by which I bind all your Western Nations together with the English, and I desire that you will take fast hold of the same, and never let it slip, to which end I desire that after you have shewn this Belt to all Nations you will fix one end of it with the Chipeweighs at St. Marys [Michilimackinac] whilst the other end remains at my house, and moreover I desire that you will never listen to any news which comes to any other Quarter. If you do it, it may shake the Belt.

By this speech, and an exchange of presents and wampum, a treaty of alliance and peace was established between the parties. When Johnson had finished speaking, a two-row wampum belt was used by First Nation peoples to reflect their understanding of the treaty of Niagara and the words of the Royal Proclamation.

The two-row wampum belt reflects a diplomatic convention that recognizes interaction and separation of settler and First Nation societies. This agreement was first struck by the Haudonosaunee (Iroquois) upon contact with the Europeans, and the principles it represents were renewed in 1764. The symbolism of the two-row wampum belt has been commented on by a leading Native legal academic, Robert A. Williams, Jr.:

> When the Haudenosaunee first came into contact with the European nations, treaties of peace and friendship were made. Each was symbolized by the Gus-Wen-Tah, or Two Row Wampum. There is a bed of white wampum which symbolizes the purity of the agreement. There are two rows of purple, and those two rows have the spirit of your ancestors and mine. There are three beads of wampum separating the two rows and they symbolize peace, friendship and respect. These two rows will symbolize two paths or two vessels, travelling down the same river together. One, a birch bark canoe, will be for the Indian people, their laws, their customs and their ways. The other, a ship, will be for the white people and their laws, their customs, and their ways. We shall each travel the river together, side by side, but in our own boat. Neither of us will try to steer the other's vessel.

The two-row wampum belt illustrates a First Nation/Crown relationship that is founded on peace, friendship, and respect, where each nation will not interfere with the internal affairs of the other. An interpretation of the Proclamation using the Treaty of Niagara discredits the claims of the Crown to exercise sovereignty over First Nations. In fact, Sir William Johnson indicated as much when he commented on a questionable treaty in 1865:

> These people had subscribed to a Treaty with me at Niagara in August last, but by the present Treaty I find, they make expressions of subjection, which must either have arisen from the ignorance of the Interpreter, or from some mistake; for I am well convinced, they never mean or intend anything like it, and that they can not be brought under our laws, for some Centuries, neither have they any word which can convey the most distant idea of subjection, and should it be fully explained to them, and the nature of subordination punishment ettc [sic], defined, it might produce infinite harm ... and I dread its consequences, as I recollect that some attempts towards Sovereignty not long ago, was one of the principal causes of all our troubles.

One can see that Sir William Johnson did not regard the extension of the Royal Proclamation and the Treaty at Niagara as an assertion of sovereignty over the First Nations. Records such as the two-row wampum belt, and statements such as Johnson's, further allow First Nations to assert that their jurisdiction cannot be molested or disturbed without Aboriginal consent.

The evidence surrounding the Treaty of Niagara demonstrates that the written text of the Proclamation, while it contains a partial understanding of the agreement at Niagara, does not fully reflect the consensus of the parties. The concepts found in the Proclamation have different meanings when interpreted in accord with the wampum belt. For example, the belt's denotation of each nation pursuing its own path while living beside one another in peace and friendship casts new light on the Proclamation's wording "The several Nations ... with whom we are connected ... should not be molested or disturbed." These words, read in conjunction with the two-row wampum, demonstrate that the connection between the nations spoken of in the Proclamation is one that mandates colonial noninterference in the land use and governments of First Nations. Therefore, First Nations regarded the agreement, represented by the Proclamation and the two-row wampum, as one that affirmed their powers of self-determination in, among other things, allocating land. This agreement, at the start of the formal relationship between the British and the First Nations of Canada, demonstrates the foundation-building principles of peace, friendship, and respect agreed to between the parties.

Conclusion

The promises made at Niagara and echoed in the Royal Proclamation have never been abridged, repealed, or rendered nugatory. Since Aboriginal rights are presumed to continue until the contrary is proven, the supposed "increasing weight" of colonial history and its disregard of the Treaty of Niagara does not render void the Aboriginal rights under its protection. Furthermore, since the Proclamation is not a unilateral declaration of the Crown but part of a treaty into which First Nations had considerable input, it therefore must be interpreted as it would be "naturally understood" by them. A "natural understanding" of the Proclamation by First Nations prompts an interpretation that includes the promises made at Niagara. These promises are: a respect for the sovereignty of First Nations, the creation of an alliance ("The several Nations ... with whom we are connected"), free and open trade and passage between the Crown and First Nations ("Shall not be molested or disturbed"), permission or consent needed for settlement of First Nations territory ("Same shall be purchased for use ... at some public meeting or assembly of Indians"), the English provision of presents to First Nations, mutual peace, friendship, and respect ("That the Indians may be convinced of our Justice and determined resolution to remove all reasonable cause of discontent"). The promises made at Niagara, and their solemnization in proclamation and treaty, demonstrate that there was from the outset considerable doubt about the Crown's assertion of sovereignty and legislative power over Aboriginal rights. The securing of these significant promises demonstrates that First Nations treated with the Crown as active and powerful partners in making provisions for the future relationship between the parties.

The relationship between the *Royal Proclamation of 1763* and the *Treaty of Niagara* and their implications was taken up in the *Chippewas of the Sarnia* case below.

CHIPPEWAS OF SARNIA BAND v. CANADA (ATTORNEY GENERAL)

[2000] O.J. No. 4804, 195 D.L.R. (4th) 135;
[2001] 1 C.N.L.R. 56 (Ont. C.A.)

BY THE COURT (**Osborne A.C.J.O., Finlayson, Doherty, Charron** and **Sharpe JJ.A.**): —

[48] In the first half of the 18th century the English Crown showed little interest in the First Nations of North America. Unlike its Catholic counterparts in France and Spain, the English Crown did not pursue active efforts to "civilize" the First Nations peoples and convert them to Christianity. Relationships between the First Nations and English colonies in North America were left primarily to the individual colonies and developed on an *ad hoc* basis. By the 1750s, however, French imperialist ambitions, aided and abetted by First Nations allies, threatened the security of English interests in North America. Those who shaped imperial policy came to see the military need to develop better relations with First Nations peoples in North America.

[49] An Indian Department under the control of English Ministers of the Crown was established in the 1750s. Sir William Johnson was appointed Superintendent of the Northern District [of British North America]. ... Johnson and members of his family played a key role in the administration of English-First Nations relations in the latter part of the 18th and the early part of the 19th century. All were familiar with First Nation customs and appear to have been well regarded by the First Nations.

[50]   At first, the Crown's policy was aimed at gaining the military support, or at least the neutrality of First Nations in England's ongoing war with the French. When that war ended with an English victory in 1763, English control over the territories it had won from France depended in part on maintaining good relations with the First Nations. The English Crown continued its wartime Indian policy in the hope of forging new military alliances with First Nations who had supported the French ... and avoiding ... uprisings like that led by Chief Pontiac of the Odawa in 1763.

[51]   The Indian Department underwent many changes between 1750 and 1860. The lines of responsibility and the titles of various officials changed repeatedly. As the bureaucracy grew, responsibility for different aspects of the policy fell to various Crown agencies. Despite these many bureaucratic changes, two fundamental tenets of the Crown's policy towards First Nations remained constant until 1860. First and foremost, dealings between the English Crown and First Nations were viewed as involving relations between sovereign nations to be governed by agreements or treaties made by the English Crown and the First Nations. Relations with the First Nations were an imperial concern to be administered primarily through the exercise of the royal prerogative. Like all imperial policies, Indian policy was formulated in England and those responsible for the implementation of it in North America reported to Crown officials. Indian affairs were no concern of the colonial legislatures.

[52]   Second, the English Crown, primarily for military reasons, actively pursued the support of the First Nations. In doing so, it sought to address First Nations' grievances. Those grievances had arisen out of incursions by white settlers onto Indian lands and the dishonest actions of some of those who traded with the First Nations. In an effort to gain First Nations support, the Crown sought to assure the First Nations that they would not be deprived of their lands or cheated in their (trade) dealings with the white man. The Crown pursued these goals by recognizing First Nations' land rights, taking steps to protect those rights against white settlers, and regulating trade between the white man and First Nations.

[53]   The *Royal Proclamation* [*of 1763*, R.S.C. 1985, App. II, No. 1] was an important, albeit not the first, manifestation of Crown imperial policy as it applied to Indian lands. The Royal Proclamation:

- recognized that First Nations had rights in their lands;
- established imperial control over settlement on Indian lands whether those lands were within or beyond the boundaries of the established British colonies in North America;
- prohibited private purchase of Indian lands and required that alienation of Indian rights in their lands be by way of surrender to the Crown; and
- established a process by which surrenders of Indian land would be made to the Crown. The surrender process accepted that Indian rights in their lands were collective and not individual.

[54] After setting out its policy in the Royal Proclamation, the Crown took extraordinary steps to make the First Nations aware of that policy and to gain their support on the basis that the policy as set down in the Royal Proclamation would govern Crown-First Nations relations. In the summer of 1764, at the request of the Crown, more than 2,000 First Nations chiefs representing some twenty-two First Nations ... attended a Grand Council at Niagara. Sir William Johnson, the Crown representative, who was well known to many of the chiefs present, read the provisions of the Royal Proclamation respecting Indian lands and committed the Crown to the enforcement of those provisions. The chiefs, in turn, promised to keep the peace and deliver up prisoners taken in recent hostilities. The singular significance of the Royal Proclamation to the First Nations can be traced to this extraordinary assembly and the treaty it produced.

[55] The First Nations chiefs prepared an elaborate wampum belt to reflect their understanding of the Treaty of Niagara. That belt described the relationship between the Crown and the First Nations as being based on peace, friendship and mutual respect. The belt symbolized the Crown's promise to all of the First Nations who were parties to the Treaty that they would not be molested or disturbed in the possession of their lands unless they first agreed to surrender those lands to the Crown.

[56] The meeting at Niagara and the Treaty of Niagara were watershed events in Crown-First Nations relations. The Treaty established friendly relations with many First Nations who had supported the French in the previous war. It also gave treaty recognition to the nation-to-nation relationship between the First Nations and the British Crown, Indian rights in their lands and the process to be followed when Indian lands were surrendered.

[57] Between 1764 and 1774, the commanders of the British forces in North America who were responsible for Indian relations emphasized the applicability and the importance, not only of the specific terms of the Royal Proclamation, but also of the policies underlying it.

[58] In 1774, the English Parliament passed the *Quebec Act*. That Act radically changed the government of the province of Quebec and extended the boundaries of that province to include what is now southwestern Ontario. ... It is safe to say, however, that those responsible for First Nations relations after 1776 continued to follow the central policies underlying the Royal Proclamation. The historical record is replete with references to the Royal Proclamation and its policies. ...

[59] ... the Crown continued to recognize Indian rights in their lands, continued to require that those rights be surrendered only to the Crown on consent, and continued to regard those rights as communal and capable of surrender only by a public manifestation of the First Nations' consent to the surrender.

[60] The Crown policy towards the First Nations was reflected not only in official documents like the Royal Proclamation, but also in the day-to-day conduct of those relations. People like Sir William Johnson had long-standing connections with First Nations peoples and long-standing associations with them. They were aware of and respected the manner in which

First Nations peoples conducted business. Formal meetings between Crown officials and First Nations were held at public Council meetings attended by the chiefs and other members of the First Nations. Certain formalities became an accepted part of these meetings and served to emphasize the nation-to-nation nature of the dealings. Many of those formalities reflected aboriginal customs and usages. The First Nations peoples attached considerable importance to compliance with these formalities and the Crown representatives were aware of the importance of these formalities to the First Nations.

By examining historical events and Aboriginal perspectives on the meaning of the right to governance, there is evidence that many Aboriginal people did not intend to surrender their power. They intended to continue living according to ancient customs, practices and laws. In short, they desired to live by and continue to develop the systems and values that had organized their conduct for generations. While they encountered great resistance in following these ways, the sovereignty and autonomy of Aboriginal governance found some limited recognition in early Canadian case law.

The practice of recognizing and participating in Aboriginal customs and practices and incorporating them into legal relationships with non-Aboriginal people occurred on a personal level as well. These events also had important implications for the development of constitutional principles relative to Aboriginal peoples. This development was perhaps first foreshadowed by the courts in Canada in the case of *Connolly v. Woolrich* (1867), 17 R.J.R.Q. 75 (Que. Ct. Q.B.), discussed below in an extract from a report by the *Royal Commission on Aboriginal Peoples*.

REPORT OF THE ROYAL COMMISSION ON ABORIGINAL PEOPLES: RESTRUCTURING THE RELATIONSHIP, VOL. 2

(Ottawa: Ministry of Supply and Services, 1996) at 186-190
(references omitted)

In about 1802, a young Quebec lad by the name of William Connolly left his home near Montreal and went west to seek his fortune in the fur trade with the North-West Company. A year or so later, William married a young woman of the Cree Nation, Suzanne by name. Suzanne had an interesting background. She was born of a Cree mother and a French-Canadian father and was the stepdaughter of a Cree chief at Cumberland House, located west of Lake Winnipeg. The union between William and Suzanne was formed under Cree law by mutual consent, with a gift probably given to Suzanne's stepfather. It was never solemnized by a priest or minister. Marriages of this kind were common in the fur trade during that era.

William and Suzanne lived happily together for nearly 30 years and had six children, one of whom later became Lady Amelia Douglas, the wife of the first governor of British Columbia. William Connolly prospered in the fur trade. He was described by a contemporary as "a veritable *bon garçon*, and an Emeralder of the first order." When the North-West Company merged with the Hudson's Bay Company, he continued on as a chief trader and was later promoted to the position of chief factor.

In 1831, William left the western fur trade and returned to the Montreal area with Suzanne and several of their children. Not long after, however, William decided to treat his first marriage as invalid and he married his well-to-do second cousin, Julia Woolrich, in a Catholic ceremony. Suzanne eventually returned west with her younger children and spent her final years living in the Grey Nuns convent at St. Boniface, Manitoba, where she was supported by William and later by Julia. When William died in the late 1840s, he willed all his property to Julia and their two children, cutting Suzanne and her children out of the estate.

Several years after Suzanne's death in 1862, her eldest son, John Connolly, sued Julia Woolrich for a share of his father's estate. This famous case, *Connolly v. Woolrich*, was fought through the courts of Quebec and was eventually appealed to the privy council in Britain before being settled out of court. The judgement delivered in the case sheds a remarkable light on the constitutional status of Aboriginal nations and their relations with incoming French and English settlers.

In support of his claim, John Connolly argued that the marriage between his mother and William Connolly was valid under Cree law and that the couple had been in 'community of property', so that each partner to the marriage was entitled to one-half of their jointly owned property. When William died, only his half-share of the property could be left to Julia, with the other half passing automatically to Suzanne as his lawful wife. On Suzanne's death, her children would be entitled to inherit her share of the estate, now in the hands of Julia.

The initial question for the Quebec courts was whether the Cree marriage between Suzanne and William was valid. The lawyer for Julia Woolrich argued that it was not valid. He maintained that English common law was in force in the northwest in 1803 and that the union between Suzanne and William did not meet its requirements. Moreover, he said, in an argument that catered to the worst prejudices of the times, the marriage customs of so-called uncivilized and pagan nations could not be recognized by the court as validating a marriage even between two Aboriginal people, much less between an Aboriginal and a non-Aboriginal person.

The Quebec Superior Court rejected Julia Woolrich's arguments. It held that the Cree marriage between Suzanne and William was valid and that their eldest son was entitled to his rightful share of the estate. This decision was maintained on appeal to the Quebec Court of Queen's Bench.

In his judgement, Justice Monk of the Superior Court stated that he was prepared to assume, for the sake of argument, that the first European traders to inhabit the northwest brought with them their own laws as their birthright. Nevertheless, the region was already occupied by "numerous and powerful tribes of Indians; by aboriginal nations, who had been in possession of these countries for ages". Assuming that French or English law had been introduced in the area at some point, "will it be contended that the territorial rights, political organization, such as it was, or the laws and usages of the Indian tribes, were abrogated; that they ceased to exist, when these two European nations began to trade with the aboriginal occupants?" Answering his own question in the negative, Justice Monk wrote: "In my opinion, it is beyond controversy that they did not, that so far from being abolished, they were left in full force, and were not even modified in the slightest degree, in regard to the civil rights of the natives."

Justice Monk supported this conclusion by quoting at length from *Worcester v. Georgia*, a landmark case decided in 1832 by the United States Supreme Court under Chief Justice Marshall. Justice Marshall, describing the policy of the British Crown in America before the American Revolution, states:

> Certain it is, that our history furnishes no example, from the first settlement of our country, *of any attempt on the part of the Crown to interfere with the internal affairs of the Indians*, farther than to keep out the agents of foreign powers, who, as traders or otherwise, might seduce them into foreign alliances. The king purchased their lands when they were willing to sell, at a price they were willing to take; but never coerced a surrender of them. *He also purchased their alliance and dependence by subsidies; but never intruded into the interior of their affairs, or interfered with their self-government, so far as respected themselves only*. [emphasis supplied by Justice Monk]

According to this passage, the British Crown did not interfere with the domestic affairs of its Indian allies and dependencies, so that they remained self-governing in internal matters. Adopting this outlook, Justice Monk concluded that he had no hesitation in holding that "the Indian political and territorial right, laws, and usages remained in full force" in the northwest at the relevant time. This decision portrays Aboriginal peoples as autonomous nations living within the protection of the Crown but retaining their territorial rights, political organizations and common laws.

A number of lessons can be drawn from *Connolly v. Woolrich*. First, the sources of law and authority in Canada are more diverse than is sometimes assumed. They include the common laws and political systems of Aboriginal nations in addition to the standard range of Euro-Canadian sources.

Second, in earlier times, the history of Canada often featured close and relatively harmonious relations between Aboriginal peoples and newcomers. The fur trade, which played an important role in the economy of early Canada, was based on long-standing alliances between European fur traders and Aboriginal hunters and traders. At the personal level, these alliances resulted in people of mixed origins, who sometimes were assimilated into existing groups but in other cases coalesced into distinct nations and communities, as with the Métis of Red River.

Connolly v. Woolrich demonstrates that newcomers have sometimes found it convenient to forget their early alliances and pacts with Aboriginal peoples and to construct communities that excluded them and suppressed any local roots. Despite these efforts, however, the courts have periodically upheld the original relationship between newcomers and Aboriginal peoples and enforced the rights it embraced. Among these was the right of Aboriginal peoples to conduct their affairs under their own laws, within a larger constitutional framework linking them with the Crown.

The decision in *Connolly v. Woolrich* stands in contrast, then, to the common impression that Aboriginal peoples do not have any general right to govern themselves. It is often thought that all governmental authority in Canada flows from the Crown to Parliament and the provincial legislatures, as provided in the constitution acts — the basic enactments that form the core of our written constitution. According to this view, since the constitution acts do not explicitly recognize the existence of Aboriginal governments, the only governmental powers held by Aboriginal peoples are those delegated to them by Parliament or the provincial legislatures, under such statutes as the *Indian Act* and the Alberta *Metis Settlements Act*.

This outlook assumes that all law is found in statutes or other written legal instruments. Under this view, if a right has not been enshrined in such a document, it is not a legal right. At best, it is regarded as only a moral or political right, which does not have legal status and so cannot be enforced in the ordinary courts. Since the constitution acts do not explicitly acknowledge an Aboriginal right of self-government, such a right does not exist as a matter of Canadian law.

However, this view overlooks important features of our legal system. The laws of Canada spring from a great variety of sources, both written and unwritten, statutory and customary. It has long been recognized, for example, that the written constitution is based on fundamental unwritten principles, which govern its status and interpretation. In Quebec, the general laws governing the private affairs of citizens trace their origins in large part to a body of French customary law, the *Coûtume de Paris*, which was imported to Canada in the 1600s and embodied in the *Civil Code of Lower Canada* in 1866. In the other provinces, the foundation of the general private law system is English common law, a body of unwritten law administered by the courts, with its roots in the Middle Ages. English common law has never been reduced to statutory form, except in partial and fragmentary ways. Over the years, it has become a supple legal instrument, capable of being adapted by the courts to suit changing circumstances and social conditions.

Given the multiple sources of law and rights in Canada, it is no surprise that Canadian courts have recognized the existence of a special body of 'Aboriginal rights'. These are not based on written instruments such as statutes, but on unwritten sources such as long-standing custom and practice. In the *Sparrow* case, for example, the Supreme Court of Canada recognized the Aboriginal fishing rights of the Musqueam people on the basis of evidence "that the Musqueam have lived in the area as an organized society long before the coming of European settlers, and that the taking of salmon was an integral part of their lives and remains so to this day." The court went on to hold that government regulations governing the Aboriginal fishing right were incapable of delineating the content and scope of the right.

Aboriginal rights include rights to land, rights to hunt and fish, special linguistic, cultural and religious rights, and rights held under customary systems of Aboriginal law. Also included is the right of self-government. This broad viewpoint is reflected in the words of John Amagoalik, speaking for the Inuit Committee on National Issues in 1983:

> Our position is that aboriginal rights, aboriginal title to land, water and sea ice flow from aboriginal rights; and all rights to practise our customs and traditions, to retain and develop our languages and cultures, and the rights to self-government, all these things flow from the fact that we have aboriginal rights ... .In our view, aboriginal rights can also be seen as human rights, because these are the things that we need to continue to survive as distinct peoples in Canada.

This point was echoed by Clem Chartier, speaking on behalf of the Métis National Council:

> What we feel is that aboriginal title or aboriginal right is the right to collective ownership of land, water, resources, both renewable and non-renewable. It is a right to self-government, a right to govern yourselves with your own institutions ... .

A similar view underlies a resolution passed by the Quebec National Assembly in 1985. This recognizes the existing Aboriginal rights of the indigenous nations of Quebec. It also urges the government of Quebec to conclude agreements with indigenous nations guaranteeing them

   (a) the right to self-government within Quebec;

   (b) the right to their own language, culture and traditions;

   (c) the right to own and control land;

   (d) the right to hunt, fish, trap, harvest and participate in wildlife management; and

   (e) the right to participate in, and benefit from, the economic development of Quebec ... [translation]

The doctrine of Aboriginal rights is not a modern innovation, invented by courts to remedy injustices perpetrated in the past. The doctrine was reflected in the numerous treaties of peace and friendship concluded in the seventeenth and eighteenth centuries between Aboriginal peoples and the French and British Crowns. Aboriginal rights are also apparent in the *Royal Proclamation of 1763* and other instruments of the same period, and in the treaties signed in Ontario, the west, and the northwest during the late nineteenth and early twentieth century. These rights are also considered in the many statutes dealing with Aboriginal matters from earliest times and in a series of judicial decisions extending over nearly two centuries. As such, the doctrine of Aboriginal rights is one of the most ancient and enduring doctrines of Canadian law.

The principles behind the decision in *Connolly v. Woolrich* form the core of the modern Canadian law of Aboriginal rights. This body of law provides the basic constitutional context for relations between Aboriginal peoples and the Crown and oversees the interaction between general Canadian systems of law and government and Aboriginal laws, government institutions and territories.

E. THE INDIAN ACT'S CHALLENGE TO ABORIGINAL GOVERNANCE

The vision of Aboriginal sovereignty and governance reflected in the early agreements and case law has not received the high level of judicial recognition foreshadowed by these earlier events. In fact, encroachments on Aboriginal governments have occurred time and again throughout Canadian history. On the west coast the Potlatch, a central governing institution of the Indians, was outlawed under the provisions of the *Indian Act*. The Sun Dance on the Prairies suffered a similar fate. In Ontario, the case of the Haudenosaunee Confederacy (Iroquois) is a particularly striking example of the disregard for Aboriginal governance. Before we explore the Canadian government's interference with the Confederacy's governance, its historic formation and structure will be examined.

1. Haudenosaunee Governance and the Great Law: Before the *Indian Act*

Haudenosaunee people, known more widely as the Iroquois Confederacy, historically lived in fortified villages in lands now called Southern Ontario, Southern Quebec, New York and Wisconsin. The confederacy was first made up of five nations: the Mohawk, Oneida, Onondaga, Cayuga and Seneca. They were joined by the Tuscaroras in 1722 when they migrated from Carolina. The confederacy is still organized in this manner and resides within its historic territories.

Haudenosaunee governmental and legal traditions are complex and sophisticated. Their Great Law of Peace, *Kaianerekowa*, bound Iroquois Nations together into a confederacy of considerable strength. Its narrative and principles brought peace, power and righteousness to generations of Iroquois people. The *Kaianerekowa* stands among the world's great legal codes as a testament to the power of human creativity and accomplishment. The Great Law of Peace is one of North America's most recognizable Indigenous Constitutions.

There are numerous written descriptions of the Great Law but its primary authority continues to reside in its spoken version. The Great Law begins with the Peacemaker, who was born into the Wendat Nation of a virgin mother.[2] His early life is filled with trials until his grandmother is told in a dream that the Creator has a great work for him to perform. When he is old enough the Peacemaker travels in a white stone canoe away from his people, who reject his message. He lands in the Mohawk Nation, where war, chaos, destruction and cannibalism abound, and he delivers the Creator's message that war must cease. The Peacemaker is rejected by the Mohawks and taken in by Jikonsahseh, a strong woman who changes her life when she accepts his message. As a result of her willingness to hear the Peacemaker's words Jikonsahseh becomes the Mother of Nations and women are given the role of Clan Mothers in the National

Confederacy that the Peacemaker proposes. The Peacemaker explains to her the principles of Peace, Power and Righteousness and the concept of the longhouse as a metaphor for the Great Law.

The Great Law narration continues with the Peacemaker journeying onward where he meets Hiawatha, after spying on him from the roof of his house, observing his cannibalism. Hiawatha spots the Peacemaker's reflection in the pot of soup he is about to eat and is transformed by the experience. The Peacemaker teaches him the evils of cannibalism and counsels him to eat deer meat, whose antlers will become symbols of authority in the Confederacy.

With Hiawatha, the Peacemaker journeys back to the Mohawks where he once again proclaims his message. He gives a great demonstration of his power by emerging unscathed from a fall into a deep ravine (from a tall tree that was chopped down from underneath him). The Mohawk chiefs accept his message of peace and he seeks out the Onondaga. The Peacemaker is prevented from meeting them by an evil [trickster] Tododaho. Hiawatha also faces trials with the Onondaga as Osinoh, a witch who transformed into an owl, murders his daughters. These challenges cause Hiawatha to battle with depression that he only partially overcomes with wampum strings. Hiawatha then takes these strings to the Mohawks, who receive him as an honoured chief. From this meeting Hiawatha teaches the Mohawks proper protocols for creating peaceful relations, such as announcing the arrival of a peaceful visitor by building a signal fire at the village edge, and making and using wampum strings to deliver messages. The Peacemaker next teaches Hiawatha even deeper principles about wampum as he removes his depression by using eight of 13 wampum strings made by Hiawatha. These actions free Hiawatha's mind from pain and the Peacemaker determines that wampum will be used to carry this idea as the Creator's message.

At this point the Peacemaker searches for Tododaho, a twisted, evil man, to receive his message with the Onondaga. The Peacemaker sends transformed animals and messages to convey his words but each time he is rebuffed. While the Peacemaker is seeking Tododaho he continues to proclaim his message and the Cayuga, Oneida and Seneca join the Confederacy. With these four nations having joined the Confederacy the Peacemaker leads them to Tododaho and the Onondoga to sing about the Confederacy, the *Kaianerekowa* and their ancestors. The Peacemaker leads this procession in an attempt to soothe Tododaho's wrath. Tododaho finally accepts the message of peace when he receives a promise that his position in the Confederacy would be central and that Onondaga would be the capital of the League.

The Peacemaker and Hiawatha then create chieftainships to protect the peace. They are given instructions on how to live their lives and run their councils, through roll calls, and protocols. The Clan's central role in the Confederacy's structure is described and future warnings are given. The Chiefs are endowed with deer antlers to note their authority. The path to communication is then cleared. Wing fans and poles are used to sweep dirt and keep unwanted beings away from the council fire. Metaphors are then spoken of in greater detail to teach the law in greater depth. These details speak of the five fireplaces of the longhouse, wampum, the Tree of Peace, the circle of chiefs, the eagle, the white roots of peace, the burying of weapons under the tree, a feast of beaver tail, the binding of five arrows and the council fire's smoke which pierces the sky. Each of these symbols communicates detailed aspects of the law. The Great Law's narration continues as laws are proclaimed relating to adoption, emigration, individual rights and international relations. A Condolence Ceremony is outlined for use when a chief dies to help maintain the stability and mental health of the Confederacy's Chiefs. Once these principles are taught the Peacemaker departs, leaving a promise of his return and a warning not to use his name except in special cases.

The Great Law is built on the consensus and agreement of the people. Future generations were considered as a formal part of their deliberations. Unanimity was necessary for the adoption of council decisions. Each of the nations joined to the League kept its independence and individuality in the midst of a centralized decision-making structure. The council of 50 chiefs administered Confederacy business as they repeatedly passed ideas across a fire to explore and analyze ideas before actions were taken. Any Iroquois nation of the Haudenosaunee could request a meeting of the council by sending runners with wampum belts to indicate the time, place and agenda of the meeting. The Onondaga nation, as the firekeepers of the council, could decide whether the issue would come for full debate before the Confederacy.

2. Challenges to Haudenosaunee Governance: Introducing the *Indian Act*

The Haudenosaunee Confederacy has consistently insisted on its independent governmental status. It draws this independence from the agreements it entered into throughout its history. Treaties such as the Covenant Chain of friendship and the two-row wampum are examples of this status. There are numerous expressions of Haudenosaunee sovereignty. For example, in 1876, the year the first consolidated *Indian Act* was passed, 33 Onondaga Chiefs wrote, from the Oshweken Council House of the Six Nations Indians on August 17, 1876:

> To the Honourable Mr. D. Laird Superintendent of Indian Affairs:

> We the undersigned Chiefs & Members of the Six United Nation Indian Allies to the British Government residing on the Grand River, Township of Tuscarora, Onondaga and Oneida, in the counties of Brant and Haldimand Ont., to your Honourable our Brother by the treaty of Peace we thought it is fit and proper to bring a certain thing under your Notice which is a very great hindrance and grievance in our council for we believe in this part it is your duty to take it into consideration with your government to have this great hindrance and grievance to be removed in our council and it is this, one says we are subjects to the British Government and ought to be controled under those Laws which was past in the Dominion Parliament by your Government you personally and the others (That is us) says we are not subjects but we are Allies to the British Government; and to your Honourable our Brother we will now inform you and your Government, personally, that we will not deny to be Allies but we will be Allies to the British Gov-

ernment as our forefathers were; we will further inform your Honourable
our Brother and to your Government that we do now seprate from them
henceforth we will have nothing to do with them anymore as they like to be
controled under your Laws we now let them go to become as your own
people, but us we will follow our Ancient Laws and Rules, and we will not
depart from it.[3]

Despite these repeated agreements, and their strong assertions of
independence, the Confederacy's government has been disregarded by
Canadian law. In the 1920s the Chiefs prepared a case and sent their leaders to London, England and Geneva, Switzerland to secure recognition of
their sovereignty before the international community.[4] They were unsuccessful in their attempts, but their efforts created considerable anxiety
within the Canadian government. As a result, the deputy superintendent
general of Indian Affairs, Duncan Campbell Scott, secured approval from
the federal Cabinet to displace the confederacy council and replace it with
an elected one under the *Indian Act*. Without prior notice to the chiefs, they
were removed from office by an order-in-council on the morning of October 7, 1924. The Royal Canadian Mounted Police seized the wampum used
to sanction council proceedings, and posted a proclamation on the doors of
the council house announcing the date and procedures for an elected government on the Six Nations reserve. The following case represents Canadian
law's treatment of the Confederacy.

LOGAN v. STYRES

(sub nom. Logan v. Canada (Attorney General))

(1959), 20 D.L.R. (2d) 416, [1959] O.W.N. 361 (Ont. H.C.J.)

King J.: — In the statement of claim the plaintiff is described as a member of the Six Nations Indian Band residing upon the Six Nations Indian
Reserve near Brantford, Ontario, and the wife of Joseph Logan, Jr., a Mohawk Chief of the Six Nations Indians. The constituent members of the
said Six Nations Indians are the Mohawk, the Oneida, the Onondaga, the
Cayuga, the Seneca and the Tuscarora.

In the course of her evidence the plaintiff stated that she was nominated
to bring the action on behalf of the hereditary Chiefs of the Six Nations
Indian Band and although the defendants submitted that the plaintiff, as
an individual member of the Six Nations Indian Band, had no status to
maintain the action for the relief claimed, I have nevertheless allowed the
action to proceed.

The defendant, Clifford E. Styres, is chief councillor of the elected council of the said Six Nations Indian Band and the defendant R.J. Stallwood is
superintendent of the Six Nations Indian Agency at Brantford, Ontario.

The Six Nations Indian Reserve at Brantford consists of slightly more
than 45,000 acres of land set aside for the use and benefit of the Six Nations
Band.

The present action is for an injunction to restrain the defendants from
taking any steps to facilitate the surrender of 3.05 acres of land being a part

of the said Reserve and for a declaration that Order in Council P.C. 1629 dated September 17, 1924 and Order in Council P.C. 6015 [[1951] S.O.R. 528] dated November 12, 1951 are *ultra vires* the powers of His Excellency the Governor-General of Canada acting for and with the advice and consent of the Queen's Privy Council for Canada.

Briefly, the position taken by the plaintiff is that the Six Nations Indians in the latter part of the eighteenth century and subsequently were the faithful allies of the British Crown and that they continue to the present day to be such faithful allies and that they never were and are not today subjects of the Crown. The plaintiff then takes the further position that the Six Nations Indians, not being subjects of the Crown, it was *ultra vires* the powers of the Parliament of the United Kingdom to enact section 91(24) of the *B.N.A. Act*, whereby the legislative authority of the Parliament of Canada is made to extend to all matters coming within the classification "Indians, and Lands reserved for the Indians" insofar as the said Six Nations Indians are concerned. If this be so the plaintiff then states that it is *ultra vires* the powers of the Parliament of Canada to enact the *Indian Act*, R.S.C. 1952, c. 149, insofar as the said Six Nations Indians are concerned and that likewise the Orders in Council already referred to and made pursuant to the *Indian Act* are likewise *ultra vires* insofar as the Six Nations Indians are concerned.

If the plaintiff is able to establish the above then I am of the opinion that judgment should be given for the relief asked but of course it is a formidable task that the plaintiff has undertaken.

The difficulties would appear to have arisen with the Orders in Council already referred to. Almost from time immemorial the Indian Bands which formed, first the Five Nations Confederacy, and later the Six Nations Confederacy were governed by their hereditary Chiefs. I have used the term "Hereditary Chiefs" to describe the system whereby the Clan Mothers designated a Chief from among the male members of certain families within the Clan. The Orders in Council to which objection is taken set up a system whereby elected Councillors would supplant the [hereditary] Chiefs among other matters in dealing with the surrender of Reserve lands. It would appear that many of the Six Nations Indians, a great majority in fact, do not recognize the authority of the Parliament of Canada to provide for elected Councillors or to provide for the surrender of Reserve lands by means of a vote. Such members of the Six Nations Indians, it would appear, simply refrain from voting at all and in the proposed surrender of the lands in question when a vote was held on July 27, 1957, only 53 votes were cast out of which 30 voted for surrender and 23 against surrender and this out of about, 3,600 eligible voters. It is the elected Councillors who negotiate the terms of surrender. ...

It should be remembered that the *Indian Act* provides in ss. 39 and 40 that the Governor in Council may accept or refuse a surrender of land so that it is still quite possible for the Governor in Council to take the position that the surrender of the land in question in this action should be refused. From the evidence given at the trial it is difficult to see what advantage would accrue to the Six Nations Indians by surrendering the land in question.

Before turning to the evidence in this action I should say that in my opinion all of the witnesses were honest witnesses who were endeavoring to tell the truth. Indeed, there is no dispute about any facts of any consequence. I should say, however, that the plaintiff was given some leeway in presenting the historical background of the plaintiff's claim and in putting forward the merits of the hereditary system of Chiefs as opposed to the elective system of Councillors. The defendants did not consider it necessary to present any evidence with respect to the merits of the hereditary system as opposed to the elective system so that only one side of this matter was before the Court.

A start has to be made at some stage and I believe a satisfactory point at which to begin is with the Haldimand Deed dated October 25, 1784, which followed the conclusion of the American Revolution and which in its recitals sets out a sufficient background. It is as follows:

> *Frederick Haldimand Captain General* and *Governor in chief* of the province of *Quebec* and *Territories* depending thereon *etc etc etc General* and *Commander in Chief* of His Majesty's Forces in said province and the Frontiers thereof — etc — etc — etc —
>
> *Whereas His Majesty* having been pleased to direct that in consideration of the early attachment to his cause manifested by the *Mohawk Indians* and of the loss of their settlement which they thereby sustained — that a convenient tract of land under his protection should be chosen as a safe and comfortable retreat for them and others of the *Six Nations*, who have either lost their settlements within the *Territory* of the *American States*, or wish to retire from them to the British — I have at the earnest desire of many of these *His Majesty's Faithful allies* purchased a tract of land from the *Indians* situated between the *Lakes Ontario, Erie* and *Huron*, and I do hereby in His Majesty's name authorize and permit the said *Mohawk Nation* and such others of the *Six Nation Indians* as wish to settle in that quarter to take possession of and settle upon the Banks of the *River* commonly called *Ouse* or *Grand River*, running into *Lake Erie*, allotting to them for that purpose *six miles deep* from *each side* of the river beginning at Lake Erie and extending *in that proportion to the head of the said river* which them and their posterity are to enjoy for ever.
>
> *Given* under my hand and seal at arms at the *Castle of St. Lewis* at *Quebec* this *twenty-fifth* day of *October* one thousand seven hundred and *eighty-four* and in the *twenty-fifth* year of the reign of our Sovereign *Lord George The Third* by the Grace of *God* of Great Britain, France and Ireland *King* Defender of the *Faith* and *so forth*. ...
> (Emphasis in original)

However, there is another document upon which the Six Nations Indians rely and it is known as the "Simcoe Deed" dated January 14, 1793, and it is as follows:

John Graves Simcoe
(Great Seal of Canada)
George the Third, by the Grace of God, King of Great Britain, France and Ireland, Defender of the Faith, and so forth. To all to whom these presents shall come, Greeting!
Know ye, that whereas the attachment and fidelity of the Chiefs, Warriors, and people of the Six Nations, to Us and Our Government has been made manifest on divers Occasions by their spirited and zealous Exertions,

and by the Bravery of their Conduct, and We being desirous of showing Our Approbation of the same and in recompense of the Losses they may have sustained of providing a convenient Tract of Land under Our protection for a safe and suitable Retreat for them and their Posterity, Have of Our Special Grace, certain Knowledge and mere motion, given and granted and by these Presents Do Give and Grant to the Chiefs, Warriors, Women and People of the said Six Nations and their Heirs forever, All that District or Territory of Land, being Parcel of a certain District ... To have and to Hold the said District or Territory of Land so bounded as aforesaid of Us, Our Heirs and Successors, to them the Chiefs, Warriors, Women and People of the Six Nations, and to and for the sole use and Behoof of them and their Heirs for ever, Freely and Clearly of and from, all, and all manner of rents, fines, and services whatever to be rendered by them or any of them to Us or Our Successors for the same, and of and from all conditions, stipulations and agreements whatever, except as hereinafter by Us expressed and declared. Giving and granting, and by these Presents confirming to the said Chiefs, Warriors, Women, and People of the said Six Nations and their Heirs, the full and entire possession, use, benefit and advantage of the said district or territory, to be held and enjoyed by them in the most free and ample manner, and according to the several customs and usages of them the said Chiefs, Warriors, Women, and People of the said Six Nations; Provided always, and be it understood to be the true intent and meaning of these Presents, that, for the purpose of assuring the said lands, as aforesaid to the said Chiefs, Warriors, Women, and People of the Six Nations, and their Heirs, and of securing to them the free and undisturbed possession and enjoyment of the same, it is Our Royal will and pleasure that no transfer, alienation, conveyance, sale, gift, exchange, lease, property or possession, shall at any time be had, made, or given of the said district or territory, or any part or parcel thereof, by any of the said Chiefs, Warriors, Women or People, to any other nation or body of people, person, or persons whatever, other than among themselves the said Chiefs, Warriors, Women and People, but that any such transfer, alienation, conveyance, sale, gift, exchange, lease or possession shall be null and void, and of no effect whatever, and that no person or persons shall possess or occupy the said district or territory or any part or parcel thereof, by or under pretence of any such alienation, title or conveyance as aforesaid, or by or under any pretence whatever, upon pain of Our severe displeasure.

And that in case any person or persons other than them, the said Chiefs, Warriors, Women and People of the said Six Nations, shall under pretence of any such title as aforesaid presume to possess or occupy the said district or territory or any part or parcel thereof, that it shall and may be lawful for Us, Our heirs and successors, at any time hereafter, to enter upon the lands so occupied and possessed by any person or persons other than the people of the said Six Nations, and them the said intruders thereof and therefrom, wholly to dispossess and evict, and to resume the part or parcel so occupied to Ourselves, Our heirs and successors; Provided, always, that if at any time the said Chiefs, Warriors, Women and People of the said Six Nations should be inclined to dispose of and surrender their use and interest in the said district or territory or any part thereof, the same shall be purchased for Us, Our heirs and successors, at some public meeting or assembly of the Chiefs, Warriors, and People of the said Six Nations, to be holden for that purpose by the Governor, Lieutenant-Governor, or person administering Our Government in Our Province of Upper Canada. ...

(Signed) Wm. Jarvis, Secretary. Recorded February 20th, 1837...

The purpose of the Simcoe Deed would seem to be to confirm the grant already made by the Haldimand Deed. In each of these deeds it is made clear that those of the Six Nations Indians settling on the lands therein described do so under the protection of the Crown. In my opinion, those of the Six Nations Indians so settling on such lands, together with their posterity, by accepting the protection of the Crown then owed allegiance to the Crown and thus became subjects of the Crown. Thus, the said Six Nations Indians from having been the faithful allies of the Crown became, instead, loyal subjects of the Crown.

The position which the Six Nations Indians have taken throughout the years is perhaps best stated in their own words in the submission made by them to the representatives of the United Nations at San Francisco, California, U.S.A., on April 13, 1945 and which was as follows:

> On behalf of the people of the Six Nations Indians settled upon part of the territory granted to them pursuant to the pledge given by the British Crown and granted under the terms of the Haldimand Treaty of March 1784, we, the representatives of the above named people of the Six Nations Indians, appeal to the conscience of the democratic nations for action to correct the deep injustice under which we are suffering.
>
> In accord with the terms of the proposal made to us by representatives of the English Crown, we as a sovereign people accepted the terms of the Haldimand Treaty and settled upon the territory thereby granted to us. A few years after our occupation of the territory and before it was fully settled a large part of the territory was alienated from us by methods and on terms which did a deep injustice to our people and all their descendents. One, Joseph Brant, using an alleged power of attorney from the Six Nations Indians dated November 2, 1796, leased large sections of our territory to white people. No revenue whatsoever accrued to the people of the Six Nations Indians for such leases and until now we have been unable to secure either restoration of the property which was granted to us and our descendents and friends in perpetuity, nor to secure compensation for its alienation.
>
> Our claim for abrogation of the so-called leases under which this property was alienated from us or, failings such abrogation, compensation for such alienation or revenues from all such lands, is based upon the fact that, according to the terms of the India Act (which deny to Indians the legal status of a person) and the terms under which the land was granted to us, the methods by which the above named Brant disposed of said lands were illegal and cannot be justified either in the eyes of the law or by the conscience of governments.
>
> We appeal to the representatives of the governments and peoples of the United Nations gathered here in this historic conference at San Francisco to aid the people of the Six Nations Indians in securing these fundamental rights. Our appeal for restoration of the property rights guaranteed to us in 1784 is based first of all upon our duty, as parents, to protect the rights and the futures of our children, but it is based also upon our solemn obligation to protect the rights of our people as a whole. We, the people of the Six Nations Indians, who fought as allies of the British Crown during the American revolutionary war, accepted the grant of lands described in the Haldimand Treaty and came to Canada from the United States to settle on those lands in the spirit and in the understanding that we were doing so as a sovereign people. As a nation we now appeal to the conscience of the nations of the world. We appeal for the restoration of those lands which the terms of the

Haldimand Treaty guaranteed the people of the Six Nations and their posterity are to enjoy forever.
Verification of all the above statements is to be found in the copy of Session-
al Paper No. 151 tabled in the House of Commons Canada on April 5th,
1945, which is attached.
ON BEHALF Of the people of the Six Nations Indians on the Grand River at
Brantford, Ontario ...

From the evidence before me however it would appear the strongest
case for the Six Nations Indians should be based upon the submission that
Parliament should not make the Order in Council to which objection is
taken applicable to the Six Nations Indians rather than that Parliament
cannot make such Orders in Council applicable. It seems to me much
might be said on that score.

I am of the opinion that the Six Nations Indians are entitled to the protection of the laws of the land duly made by competent authority and at
the same time are subject to such laws. While it might be unjust or unfair
under the circumstances for the Parliament of Canada to interfere with
their system of internal Government by hereditary Chiefs, I am of the opinion that Parliament has the authority to provide for the surrender of
Reserve land, as has been done herein, and that Privy Council Order P.C.
6015 is not *ultra vires*. It should be noted that P.C. 1629 has been revoked
by P.C. 6015, so it is not necessary to consider P.C. 1629 further.

In my opinion, therefore, the plaintiff is not entitled to an injunction and
is not entitled to the declaration asked for.

The plaintiff's action is therefore dismissed but, under the circumstances, without costs.

Action dismissed.

How does the discussion in *Logan v. Styres* compare with the understanding
of Haudenosaunee governance expressed by the Cayuga chief Deskaheh in
the following excerpt?

"THE LAST SPEECH OF DES-KA-HEH"

March 10, 1925

[Deskaheh (1873-1925), or Hi-wyi-iss, Levi General, was a Cayuga chief of
the Younger Bear Clan of the Six Nations Indians. In 1923, as the government was taking steps to replace the traditional Six Nations government at
the Grand River with an *"Indian Act"* elective system; Deskaheh, who opposed the change, travelled to London and Geneva to make his case before
the British government and the League of Nations. Returning to Canada he
felt his freedom was threatened, and he therefore spent the rest of his days
in exile south of the border. His last speech, part of which follows, was
made over the radio in Rochester, New York, on March 10, 1925.]

My home is on the Grand River. Until we sold off a large part, our
country extended down to Lake Erie, where, 140 winters ago, we had a

little sea-shore of our own and a birch-bark navy. You would call it Canada. We do not. We call the little ten-miles square we have left the "Grand River Country." We have the right to do that. It is ours. We have the written pledge of George III that we should have it forever as against him or his successors and he promised to protect us in it. We didn't think we would ever live long enough to find that a British promise was not good. An enemy's foot is on our country and George V knows it for I told him so but he will not lift his finger to protect us nor will any of his ministers ...

In some respects we are just like you. We like to tell our troubles. You do that. You told us you were in great trouble a few winters ago because a great big giant with a big stick was after you. We helped you whip him. Many of our young men volunteered and many gave their lives for you. You were willing to let them fight in the front ranks in France. Now we want to tell our troubles to you — I do not mean that we are calling on your governments. We are tired of calling on the governments of pale-faced peoples in America and Europe. We have tried that and found it was no use. They deal only in fine words ... We have a little territory left — just enough to live and die on. Don't you think your governments ought to be ashamed to take that away from us by pretending it is part of theirs? You ought to be ashamed if you let them. Before it is all gone we mean to let you know what your governments are doing. If you are a free people you can have your own way. The governments at Washington and Ottawa have a silent partnership of policy — It is aimed to break up every tribe of Red-men so as to dominate every acre of their territory. Your high officials are the nomads today — not the Red People. Your officials won't stay at home. Over in Ottawa they call that policy "Indian Advancement". Over in Washington they call it "Assimilation." We, who would be the helpless victims, say it is tyranny ...

We want none of your laws or customs that we have not willingly adopted for ourselves. We have adopted many. You have adopted some of ours — votes for women for instance — We are as well behaved as you and you would think so if you knew us better. We would be happier to-day, left alone, than you who call yourselves Canadians and Americans. We have no jails and do not need them. You have many jails, but do they hold all the criminals you convict? And do you convict or prosecute all your violators of the thousands of laws you have?

Your governments have lately resorted to new practices in their Indian policies. In the old days they often bribed our chiefs to sign treaties to get our lands. Now they know that our remaining territory can easily be gotten away from us by first taking our political rights away in forcing us into your citizenship, so they give jobs in their Indian offices to the bright young people among us who will take them and who, to earn their pay, say that our people wish to become citizens with you and that we are ready to have our tribal life destroyed and want your governments to do it. But that is not true. Your governments of today learned that method from the British. The British have long practiced it on weaker peoples in carrying out their policy of subjugating the world, if they can, to British Imperialism. Under cover of it, your law-makers now assume to govern other peoples too weak to resist your courts. There are no three-mile limits or twelve-mile limits to strong governments who wish to do that. About three winters ago the Canadian government set out to take mortgages on farms of our returned soldiers to secure loans made to them intending to use Canadian courts to enforce those mortgages in the name of Canadian authority within our country. When Ottawa tried that our people resented it. We knew that would mean the end of our own government. Because we did so the Canadian government began to enforce all sorts of Dominion and Provincial laws over us and quartered armed men among us to enforce Canadian laws and customs upon us. We appealed to Ottawa in the name of our right as a separate people and by right of our treaties and the door was closed in our faces. We then went to London with our treaty and asked for the protection it promised and got no attention. Then we went to the League of Nations at Geneva with its covenant to protect little peoples and to enforce respect for treaties by its members and we spent a whole year patiently waiting but got no hearing.

To punish us for trying to preserve our rights, the Canadian government has now pretended to abolish our government by Royal Proclamation and has pretended to set up a Canadian-made government over us, composed of the few traitors among us who are willing to accept pay from Ottawa and do its bidding. Finally Ottawa officials, under pretence of a friendly visit, asked to inspect our precious wampum belts, made by our Fathers centuries ago as records of our history, and when shown to them those false-faced officials seized and carried away those belts as bandits take your precious belongings ... The Ottawa government thought that with no wampum belts to read in the opening of our Six Nations Councils, we would give up our home rule and self-government, the victims of superstition. Any superstition of which the Grand River People have been victims are not in reverence for wampum belts but in their trust in the honor of governments who boast of a higher civilization ...

We are not as dependent in some ways as we were in the early days. We do not need interpreters now. We know your language and can understand your words for ourselves and we have learned to decide for ourselves what is good for us. It is bad for any people to take the advice of an alien people as to that.

You Mothers, I hear, have a good deal to say about your government. Our Mothers have always had a hand in ours. Maybe you can do something to help us now. If you white mothers are hard-hearted and will not, perhaps you boys and girls who are listening and who have loved to read stories about our people — the true ones, I mean — will help us when you grow up if there are any of us left then to be helped. If you are bound to treat us as though we were citizens under your government then those of your people who are land hungry will get our farms away from us by hooks and crooks under your property laws and in your courts that we do not understand and do not wish to learn. We would then be homeless and have to drift into your big cities to work for wages, to buy bread and have to pay rent, as you call it, to live on this earth and to live in little rooms in which we would suffocate. We would then be scattered and lost to each other and lost among so many of you. Our boys and girls would then have to intermarry with you or not at all. If consumption took us off or if we brought no children into the world or our children mixed with the ocean of your blood then there would be no Iroquois left ...

Boys — think this over. Do it before your minds lose the power to grasp the idea that there are other peoples in this world beside your own and with an equal right to be here. You see that a people as strong as yours is a great danger to other peoples near you. Already your will comes pretty near being law in this world where no one can whip you, think then what it will mean if you grow up with a will to be unjust to other peoples; to believe that whatever your government does to other peoples is no crime however wicked. I hope the Irish-Americans hear that and will think about it — they used to when that shoe pinched their foot.

This is the story of the Mohawks, the story of the Oneidas, of the Cayugas — I am a Cayuga — of the Onondagas, the Senecas and the Tuscaroras. They are the Iroquois. Tell it to those who have not been listening. Maybe I will be stopped from telling it. But if I am prevented from telling it over, as I hope to do, the story will not be lost. I have already told it to thousands of listeners in Europe — it has gone into the records where your children can find it when I may be dead or be in jail for daring to tell the truth — I have told this story in Switzerland. They have free speech in little Switzerland. One can tell the truth over there in public even if it is uncomfortable for some great people.

This story comes straight from Des-ka-heh, one of the Chiefs of the Cayugas. I am the speaker of the Council of the Six Nations, the oldest League of Nations now existing. It was founded by Hiawatha. It is a League which is still alive and intends, as best it can, to defend the rights of the Iroquois to live under their own laws in their own little countries.

The dispute between the Canadian government and the Haudenosaunee Confederacy continues. The issues lying at the root of *Logan v. Styres* and Deskaheh's speech remain unresolved. In 1995, the Six Nations band at Oshweken initiated litigation against the federal and provincial government for breaches of their duty to respect First Nations' land and to account for assets managed or held by the Crown for the benefit of the Six Nations. In the meantime, development continued on lands which the Haudenosaunee regarded as rightfully their own. On February 26, 2006, a group of Haudenosaunee people occupied a portion of a 40-hectare site in Caledonia, near Hamilton, Ontario on which residential property development had commenced. They sought to reclaim their land and exercise their governance rights over it. Many of the Haudenosaunee people at Caledonia do not regard themselves as Canadians and see their political citizenship and allegiance as aligned with the Confederacy.

The developers sought and obtained an injunction to remove the Haudenosaunee occupiers, who had constructed a barricade to control access to the impugned site. The Ontario Provincial Police were called in and arrests were made, but the barricade and the protest remained. The Ontario government later purchased the land in question from the developers and the injunction against the occupiers was vacated, but the land was held in trust pending the negotiated outcome of the dispute. Both the federal and Ontario governments appointed prominent former politicians as their negotiators; the elected Six Nations representatives have worked with the Haudenosaunee hereditary chiefs in the negotiations. The Caledonia dispute remains unresolved.

3. The *Indian Act* and the General Challenge to Aboriginal Governance

The Haudenosaunee are not the only First Nation to have their governance challenged by the federal government. One can see from the implications underlying the case of *Logan v. Styres* that the *Indian Act* potentially threatens all traditional governance structures. Many First Nations feel this pressure today and live with the resulting tensions. Fortunately, very few Indian bands in Canada had their traditional governments forcibly ejected from power as was the case with the Haudenosaunee at Six Nations. Many First Nations blended traditional forms of governance with the elected requirements of the *Indian Act*. Other First Nations attempted to keep the two systems apart. Still others have tried to subjugate the *Indian Act* governance structure to traditional forms or values and principles. A variety of governance forms exist in relation to the *Indian Act* as a result.

The problem in maintaining Aboriginal governmental diversity is that the *Indian Act*'s provisions narrowly define and heavily regulate their citizenship, land rights, succession rules, political organization, economic opportunities, fiscal management, educational patterns and attainment. Despite these challenges First Nations have responded creatively to the *Act*'s restrictions. A few examples of the *Indian Act*'s reach and application demonstrate how it potentially complicates the issue of Aboriginal governance.

Section 2(1) of the *Indian Act* defines an Indian "band" as a "body of Indians." *Indian Act* regulations setting out procedures for conducting Band Council meetings are found in the *Indian Band Council Procedures Regulations*, C.R.C. 1978, c. 950. Section 2(1) of the *Indian Act* also states that an Indian band council can be "chosen according to the custom of the band." One in three Indian bands have chosen to organize their political affairs in accordance with their own customs. The fact that Indian bands continue to function under a degree of their own inherent authority demonstrates that, rather than extinguishing Indian governance, the *Indian Act* could be interpreted as explicitly recognizing and affirming pre-existing governance powers.

Land is often a primary issue over which governance is exercised. Section 20 of the *Indian Act* outlines procedures for allocation and possession of reserve lands by individual Indians. There is no individual fee simple ownership of reserve land because the land is owned by the Crown. Section 20 states that "no Indian is lawfully in possession of land in a reserve, unless, with the approval of the Minister, possession of land has been allotted to him by the council of the band." Most Indian bands have acted as if the *Indian Act* permitted a choice about how lands were to be used: collectively or individually. The bands that chose to use land in an individual fashion often adopted certificates of possession. In these cases bands often allotted lands to individuals who were historically in possession of what later became land parcels under the *Indian Act*. Other bands have acted in accordance with the idea that a "band means a body of Indians for whose use and benefit in common, lands, the legal title to which is vested in Her Majesty, have been set apart" (section 2(1)(*a*)). For those bands who took this interpretation "common" use and benefit was interpreted as allowing their collective land use allocation. Finally, it is estimated that over half the individually allotted lands on reserves are not held by certificate procedures but in accordance with the band's customs. It would be difficult to classify those holding such lands as trespassers on their own lands, when land is held in accordance with their own customs and with the implied consent of their governments. While some judicial decisions hold that custom or band action, without more, cannot grant a legal interest to an individual enforceable under the *Indian Act* (*Lower Nicola Indian Band v. Trans-Canada Displays Ltd.*, [2000] B.C.J. No. 1672, [2000] 4 C.N.L.R. 185 (B.C.S.C.); *Joe v. Findlay*, [1987] B.C.J. No. 20, [1987] 2 C.N.L.R. 75 (B.C.S.C.)) this interpretation has not been universally followed by the courts (*George v. George*, [1996] B.C.J. No. 1929, [1997] 2 C.N.L.R. 62 (B.C.C.A.); *Stoney Band v. Poucette*, [1999] 3 C.N.L.R. 321 (Alta. Q.B.), affd [1998] A.J. No. 842 (Alta. C.A.)). These examples potentially suggest that while the *Indian Act* heavily regulated Aboriginal governance, it did not extinguish those powers.

Under section 81 of the *Indian Act*, the band can exercise governance through by-laws. The Act states that the Band Council may not make by-laws inconsistent with the *Indian Act* or with any regulation made by the federal Cabinet or Minister. A band can pass by-laws related to the following limited range of subjects:

(*a*)   to provide for the health of residents on the reserve and to prevent the spreading of contagious and infectious diseases;

(*b*)   the regulation of traffic;

(*c*)   the observance of law and order;

(*d*)   the prevention of disorderly conduct and nuisances;

(*e*)   the protection against and prevention of trespass by cattle and other domestic animals, the establishment of pounds, the appointment of pound-keepers, the regulation of their duties and the provision for fees and charges for their services;

(*f*)   the construction and maintenance of watercourses, roads, bridges, ditches, fences and other local works;

(*g*)   the dividing of the reserve or a portion thereof into zones and the prohibition of the construction or maintenance of any class of buildings or the carrying on of any class of business, trade or calling in any zone;

(*h*)   the regulation of the construction, repair and use of buildings, whether owned by the band or by individual members of the band;

(*i*)   the survey and allotment of reserve lands among the members of the band and the establishment of a register of Certificates of Possession and Certificates of Occupation relating to allotments and the setting apart of reserve lands for common use, if authority therefor has been granted under section 60;

(*j*) the destruction and control of noxious weeds;

(*k*) the regulation of bee-keeping and poultry raising;

(*l*) the construction and regulation of the use of public wells, cisterns, reservoirs and other water supplies;

(*m*) the control or prohibition of public games, sports, races, athletic contests and other amusements;

(*n*) the regulation of the conduct and activities of hawkers, peddlers or others who enter the reserve to buy, sell or otherwise deal in wares or merchandise;

(*o*) the preservation, protection and management of fur-bearing animals, fish and other game on the reserve;

(*p*) the removal and punishment of persons trespassing on the reserve or frequenting the reserve for prohibited purposes;

(*p*.1) the residence of band members and other persons on the reserve;

(*p*.2) to provide for the rights of spouses or common-law partners and children who reside with members of the band on the reserve with respect to any matter in relation to which the council may make by-laws in respect of members of the band;

(*p*.3) to authorize the Minister to make payments out of capital or revenue moneys to persons whose names were deleted from the Band List of the band;

(*p*.4) to bring subsection 10(3) or 64.1(2) into effect in respect of the band;

(*q*) with respect to any matter arising out of or ancillary to the exercise of powers under this section; and

(*r*) the imposition on summary conviction of a fine not exceeding one thousand dollars or imprisonment for a term not exceeding thirty days, or both, for violation of a by-law made under this section.

From the above list one can see the extremely limited nature of governance powers under the *Indian Act*. For most First Nations, the *Indian Act* is an unacceptable base upon which to build their governance. Its assimilative premises are racist and outmoded. Its presumption of delegated authority is offensive because it ignores or undermines inherent, pre-existing sources of power. This has led to proposals for its repeal. The Royal Commission on Aboriginal Peoples outlined one proposal that was particularly attractive to the Assembly of First Nations in the early 1980s:

[T]he 1983 Special Committee on Indian Self-Government, chaired by Keith Penner, MP ... recommended ... the immediate recognition of Indian First Nations as a distinct, constitutionally protected order of government within Canada and with a full range of government powers. In short, their vision was a return to that of the imperial tripartite system: a status equal to that of the colonies (now provinces), with the federal Crown in the role of protector originally assumed by imperial authorities.

Thus, the Penner report proposed an active and protective federal role to recreate the original partnership that Indians have never ceased to call for. As the protector and guarantor of Indian self-government, the federal Crown would pass legislation that under normal constitutional paramountcy rules would oust the provinces from regulating anything to do with "Indians, and Lands reserved for the Indians" under section 91(24) of the *Constitution Act, 1867*. Having secured a space in which to legislate exclusively for Indians, Parliament would withdraw its laws to allow the laws of federally recognized self-governing Indian First Nations to regulate matters occurring on Indian reserves.

Ultimately, the Penner committee saw Indian First Nations as equivalent to provinces. Thus, in the same way that provinces are immune from each other's law-making powers, Indian First Nations laws and provincial laws would have had no effect on each other. In the event of conflict, federal laws in the same areas would be paramount over Indian First Nations laws, as is the case with provincial laws. The federal government would support Indian First Nations programs, services and operations through a system of grants like those available to the provinces under the rules of fiscal federalism. Eventually, the whole arrangement would be entrenched in the constitution. Neither the federal government nor the provincial governments endorsed the approach of the Penner report.[5]

The Royal Commission on Aboriginal Peoples subsequently crafted a proposal somewhat similar to that of the Penner Commission. It suggested the passage of an *Aboriginal Nations Recognition and Government Act* (see *Report of the Royal Commission on Aboriginal Peoples: Restructuring the Relationship*, Vol. 2 (Ottawa: Supply and Services, 1996) at Chapter 3). Under this proposal the federal government would extend its policies through legislation to recognize and support Indigenous governments. The Commission suggested that, if implemented, the Act could "enable the federal government to vacate its legislative authority under section 91(24) of the *Constitution Act, 1867* with respect to core powers deemed needed by Aboriginal nations and to specify which additional areas of federal jurisdiction the Parliament of Canada is prepared to acknowledge as being core powers to be exercised by Aboriginal governments."

4. Supplementing the *Indian Act*?

As demonstrated by the Penner Commission and other historical events, First Nations want to govern themselves. They want to get rid of the *Indian Act*. However, they do not want to abolish the Act if it is a step towards assimilation. When the Trudeau government proposed the *Indian Act*'s elimination in a 1969 White Paper, First Nations opposed that initiative because it was part of a package designed to eliminate their rights. The White Paper's main points were to: eliminate the legislative recognition of Indian status, abolish Indian reserves and impose taxation, dismantle treaty obligations, and off-load federal Indian programs and services to provinces, municipalities and First Nations. At the time, Harold Cardinal spoke for many First Nations people when he wrote:

We do not want the Indian Act retained because it is a good piece of legislation. It isn't. It is discriminatory from start to finish. ... but we would rather continue to live in bondage under the inequitable Indian Act than surrender our sacred rights. Any time the government wants to honour its obligations to us we are more than ready to devise new Indian legislation.[6]

Shawn Atleo, the Grand Chief of the Assembly of First Nations ("AFN"), has recently called upon the federal government to work with the AFN to eliminate the *Indian Act*. In the past decade there has been heated debate about whether the *Indian Act* should be reformed or supplemented by other federal legislation. First Nations have resisted such proposals out of a concern that such legislation could be regarded as a delegation of authority from the federal government to the First Nations. While there are individual exceptions, First Nations have not generally been supportive of this approach because they want to build their governance on a base of inherent rights, which are not subject to the whims of other governments. Legislation passed by the Canadian government can always be amended or repealed. This is why First Nations have sought to protect their rights to governance under section 35(1).

The following report from Canada's Auditor General outlines four issues that should be addressed if reform to the *Indian Act* comes through Parliament, rather than through litigation or negotiation.

"PROGRAMS FOR FIRST NATIONS ON RESERVES" STATUS REPORT OF THE AUDITOR GENERAL OF CANADA TO THE HOUSE OF COMMONS

(Ottawa: Office of the Auditor General, 2011), Chapter 4 at 2-6
<http://www.oag-bvg.gc.ca/internet/docs/parl_oag_201106_04_e.pdf>

Structural impediments explain the lack of progress on reserves

In our view, many of the problems facing First Nations go deeper than the existing programs' lack of efficiency and effectiveness. We believe that structural impediments severely limit the delivery of public services to First Nations communities and hinder improvements in living conditions on reserves. We have identified four such impediments:

- lack of clarity about service levels,
- lack of a legislative base,
- lack of an appropriate funding mechanism, and
- lack of organizations to support local service delivery.

Lack of clarity about service levels. Most of the services provided to communities throughout Canada are the responsibility of provincial and municipal governments, but this is not the case on reserves. Under the *Constitution Act, 1867*, the federal government has exclusive authority to legislate on matters pertaining to "Indians, and Lands reserved for Indians." INAC has been the main federal organization exercising this authority. While the federal government has funded the delivery of many programs and services, it has not clearly defined the type and level of services it supports.

Mainly through INAC, the federal government supports many services on reserves that are normally provided by provincial and municipal governments off reserves. It is not always evident whether the federal government is committed to providing services on reserves of the same range and quality as those provided to other communities across Canada. In some cases, the Department's documents refer to services that are reasonably comparable to those of the provinces. But comparability is often poorly defined and may not include, for instance, the level and range of services to be provided.

To provide true comparability, it would be important to include a clear statement of comparability in program objectives and define comparability on a program-by-program basis. Roles and responsibilities would also need to be specified, as would the level of services required for comparability. In addition, the costs of achieving comparability would have to be determined and programs would have to be adequately funded. It would be necessary to establish measures for evaluating performance and determining whether the program was achieving the desired outcomes.

Lack of a legislative base. Provincial legislation provides a basis of clarity for services delivered by provinces. A legislative base for programs specifies respective roles and responsibilities, eligibility, and other program elements. It constitutes an unambiguous commitment by government to deliver those services. The result is that accountability and funding are better defined.

The federal government has often developed programs to support First Nations communities without establishing a legislative or regulatory framework for them. Therefore, for First Nations members living on reserves, there is no legislation supporting programs in important areas such as education, health, and drinking water. Instead, the federal government has developed programs and services for First Nations on the basis of policy. As a result, the services delivered under these programs are not always well defined and there is confusion about federal responsibility for funding them adequately.

Lack of an appropriate funding mechanism. The federal government uses contribution agreements to fund the delivery of services on First Nations reserves. Through these agreements, First Nations receive a certain level of funding to provide various programs and services in their communities. We see several problems with the use of this funding mechanism for the provision of core government services. One problem is that, while the agreements state the services or actions to be provided, they do not always focus on service standards or results to be achieved.

The timing for provision of funds under contribution agreements is also problematic. Most contribution agreements must be renewed yearly. In previous audits, we found that the funds may not be available until several months into the period to be funded; one reason is that new agreements cannot be finalized until departments have reviewed documentation and confirmed that funds from the previous period were used appropriately. Consequently, First Nations must often reallocate funds from elsewhere to continue meeting community service requirements. However, INAC recognizes the importance of providing certain services on an ongoing basis, such as health care and education. The Department therefore continues to fund these and other essential services even before it has confirmed appropriate spending of funds for the previous period.

The use of contribution agreements between the federal government and First Nations may also inhibit appropriate accountability to First Nations members. It is often unclear who is accountable to First Nations members for achieving improved outcomes or specific levels of services. First Nations often cite a lack of federal funding as the main reason for inadequate services. For its part, INAC maintains that the federal government funds services to First Nations but is not responsible for the delivery or provision of these services.

Contribution agreements involve a significant reporting burden, especially for small First Nations with limited administrative capacity. Communities often have to use scarce administrative resources to respond to numerous reporting requirements stipulated in their agreements. We followed up on INAC's efforts to reduce the reporting requirements of First Nations and found progress to date to be unsatisfactory even though the Department had taken various actions …

The use of contribution agreements to fund services for First Nations communities has also led to uncertainty about funding levels. Statutory programs such as land claim agreements must be fully funded, but this is not the case for services provided through contribution agreements. Accordingly, it is not certain whether funding levels provided to First Nations in one year will be available the following year. This situation creates a level of uncertainty for First Nations and makes long-term planning difficult. In contrast, legislation may commit the federal government to provide statutory funding to meet defined levels of service. A legislative base including statutory funding could remove the uncertainty that results when funding for services depends on the availability of resources.

Lack of organizations to support local service delivery. Over the decades, provinces have established many organizations and structures to support local delivery of programs and services to communities. For example, provinces have developed school boards, health services boards, and social service organizations. These organizations can supply vital expertise, facilitate career advancement, and develop a means of efficient and effective delivery of services.

There are few similar organizations to support service delivery within First Nations communities. The federal government established each First Nation band as an autonomous entity and provides separate program funding to each. Many of these First Nations are small, consisting of communities that often have fewer than 500 residents. There are more than 600 First Nations across Canada. Many of them are hampered by the lack of expertise to meet the administrative requirements for delivering key programs within their reserves. They often do not have the benefit of school boards, health boards, or other regional bodies to support the First Nations as they provide services to community members.

In an attempt to address the lack of organizations supporting the delivery of services, INAC has developed new approaches and worked with groups representing various First Nations. For example, the Department has worked with First Nations organizations and provincial governments to develop improved child and family service programs in several provinces. It has also recently launched the Reforming First Nation Education Initiative, which includes support for establishing partnerships with First Nations regional organizations and provinces; for example, it has provided funding to organizations such as the First Nations Education Steering Committee in British Columbia and the First Nations Education Council in Quebec. This is a start, but much remains to be done.

Change is needed if meaningful progress is to be realized

Despite the federal government's many efforts to implement our recommendations and improve its First Nations programs, we have seen a lack of progress in improving the lives and well-being of people living on reserves. Services available on reserves are often not comparable to those provided off reserves by provinces and municipalities. Conditions on reserves have remained poor. Change is needed if First Nations are to experience more meaningful outcomes from the services they receive. We recognize that the issues are complex and that solutions will require concerted efforts of the federal government and First Nations, in collaboration with provincial governments and other parties.

. . . . .

We recognize that the federal government cannot put all of these structural changes in place by itself since they would fundamentally alter its relationship with First Nations. For this reason, First Nations themselves would have to play an important role in bringing about the changes. They would have to become actively engaged in developing service standards and determining how the standards will be monitored and enforced. They would have to fully participate in the development of legislative reforms. First Nations would also have to co-lead discussions on identifying credible funding mechanisms that are administratively workable and that ensure accountable governance within their communities. First Nations would have to play an active role in the development and administration of new organizations to support the local delivery of services to their communities.

Addressing these structural impediments will be a challenge. The federal government and First Nations will have to work together and decide how they will deal with numerous obstacles that surely lie ahead. Unless they rise to this challenge, however, living conditions may continue to be poorer on First Nations reserves than elsewhere in Canada for generations to come.

One change the federal government has recently made which may affect First Nations' governance is to make the *Canadian Human Rights Act*, R.S.C. 1985, c. H-6 applicable to Indian Bands. Prior to this change, section 67 of the *Canadian Human Rights Act* read: "Nothing in this Act affects any provision of the *Indian Act* or any provision made under or pursuant to that Act." Now, after *An Act to amend the Canadian Human Rights Act*, S.C. 2008, c. 30, section 67 of the Act reads:

1. Section 67 of the *Canadian Human Rights Act* is repealed.

1.1 For greater certainty, the repeal of section 67 of the *Canadian Human Rights Act* shall not be construed so as to abrogate or derogate from the protection provided for existing aboriginal or treaty rights of the aboriginal peoples of Canada by the recognition and affirmation of those rights in section 35 of the *Constitution Act, 1982*.

1.2 In relation to a complaint made under the *Canadian Human Rights Act* against a First Nation government, including a band council, tribal council or governing authority operating or administering programs and services under the *Indian Act*, this Act shall be interpreted and applied in a manner that gives due regard to First Nations legal traditions and customary laws, particularly the balancing of individual rights and interests against collective rights and interests, to the extent that they are consistent with the principle of gender equality.

2(1) Within five years after the day on which this Act receives royal assent, a comprehensive review of the effects of the repeal of section 67 of the *Canadian Human Rights Act* shall be jointly undertaken by the Government of Canada and any organizations identified by the Minister of Indian Affairs and Northern Development as being, in the aggregate, representative of the interests of First Nations peoples throughout Canada.

(2) A report on the review referred to in subsection (1) shall be submitted to both Houses of Parliament within one year after the day on which the review is undertaken under that subsection.

3. Despite section 1, an act or omission by any First Nation government, including a band council, tribal council or governing authority operating or administering programs or services under the *Indian Act*, that was made in the exercise of powers or the performance of duties and functions conferred or imposed by or under that Act shall not constitute the basis for a complaint under Part III of the *Canadian Human Rights Act* if it occurs within 36 months after the day on which this Act receives royal assent.

4. The Government of Canada, together with the appropriate organizations representing the First Nations peoples of Canada, shall, within the period referred to in section 3, undertake a study to identify the extent of the preparation, capacity and fiscal and human resources that will be required in order for First Nations communities and organizations to comply with the *Canadian Human Rights Act*. The Government of Canada shall report to both Houses of Parliament on the findings of that study before the expiration of the period referred to in section 3.

As a result of this legislation, First Nations will be challenged by their own members to comply with human rights law in the coming years. In the United States, any such challenges would be litigated in tribal courts under the *Indian Civil Rights Act*: see *Santa Clara Pueblo v. Martinez*, 436 U.S. 49 at 72 n.32 (USSC 1978). Though there are challenges associated with this approach as well (largely due to lack of financial resources to support such courts), in many places this has led to a vibrant Indigenous jurisprudence within Native American communities: see Justin B. Richland and Sarah Deer, eds., *Introduction to Tribal Legal Studies*, 2nd ed. (Lanham, MD: Altamira Press, 2010); Carrie E. Garrow and Sarah Deer, eds., *Tribal Criminal*

Law and Procedure (Walnut Creek, MD: Altamira Press, 2004). The question remains: can or should Indians seek governance reform through the legislative process? What are the risks and opportunities present in such an approach? What is the place of First Nations courts and dispute resolution bodies in Indigenous governance? In answering these questions, consider the words of Lumbee Nation Professor David Wilkins of the University of Minnesota:

> "The vaccination will come from the same society as the disease." — Leonardo Vitteri

> "The Master's tools will never dismantle the Master's house." — Audre Lord

> These two powerful and contradictory epigraphs reflect the two dominant sentiments held by a majority of Native nations when they are asked to assess their historic and contemporary political and legal status vis-à-vis the United States.

> Some adhere to the idea that the federal government, as a democratic state founded on the rule of law, contains within its legal and political institutions and ideologies a framework that provides the necessary vaccines that will eventually cure the various and sundry indigenous ailments generated throughout American society by its social, economic, political and legal institutions.

> By contrast, there are others who vigorously argue that the prevailing institutions of governance and law of the United States are incapable of providing justice to First Nations because they entail systems, ideologies, and values that represent non-Indians and thus they cannot possibly adequately address the distinctive aboriginal, treaty, and trust based rights of indigenous nations.[7]

F.   CONTEMPORARY CASES: LITIGATING GOVERNANCE

Contemporary Canadian jurisprudence has only recently addressed the issue of Aboriginal rights to self-government. The current case law has defined Aboriginal powers of governance in a narrower manner than historic practice may warrant, or Aboriginal people may desire. This reduction in Aboriginal rights to governance simultaneously vests ever-widening powers of governance in non-Aboriginal institutions. The courts closely and carefully scrutinize Aboriginal expressions of governance, while allowing broad assertions of Crown sovereignty to go unchallenged. The unequal application of Aboriginal and non-Aboriginal sovereignty has not yet been adequately explained. The cases of *R. v. Pamajewon*, and *Delgamuukw v. British Columbia*, provide an indication of the court's current interpretation of Aboriginal governance rights.

R. v. PAMAJEWON

[1996] S.C.J. No. 20, [1996] 2 S.C.R. 821, 138 D.L.R. (4th) 204 (S.C.C.)

[Pamajewon and his co-accused, each a member of either the Shawanaga First Nation or Eagle Lake Band, were convicted of keeping a common gaming house contrary to section 201 of the *Criminal Code*. The gaming activities were conducted on reserves, though many of the participants were non-natives. On appeal the Band members argued, *inter alia*, that the activities in question were protected as an Aboriginal right under section 35(1) or as an incident of the inherent right of self-government claimed by the two First Nations. The Ontario Court of Appeal and the Supreme Court of Canada dismissed the appeals.]

Lamer C.J.C. (La Forest, Sopinka, Gonthier, Cory, McLachlin, Iacobucci and Major JJ. concurring): —

[1]   This appeal raises the question of whether the conduct of high stakes gambling by the Shawanaga and Eagle Lake First Nations falls within the scope of the aboriginal rights recognized and affirmed by s. 35(1) of the *Constitution Act, 1982*.

. . . . .

[21]   The appellants appealed on the basis that the Court of Appeal erred in restricting aboriginal title to rights that are activity and site specific and in concluding that self-government only extends to those matters which were governed by ancient laws or customs. The appellant argued further that the Court of Appeal erred in concluding that the *Code* extinguished self-government regarding gaming and in not addressing whether the *Code*'s gaming provisions unjustifiably interfered with the rights recognized and affirmed by s. 35(1) of the *Constitution Act, 1982*.

. . . . .

[23]   The resolution of the appellants' claim in this case rests on the application of the test, laid out by this Court in *R. v. Van der Peet*, [1996] 2 S.C.R. 507, for determining the aboriginal rights recognized and affirmed by s. 35(1) of the *Constitution Act, 1982*. The appellants in this case are claiming that the gambling activities in which they took part, and their respective bands' regulation of those gambling activities, fell within the scope of the aboriginal rights recognized and affirmed by s. 35(1). *Van der Peet, supra,* lays out the test for determining the practices, customs and traditions which fall within s. 35(1) and, as such, provides the legal standard against which the appellants' claim must be measured.

[24]   The appellants' claim involves the assertion that s. 35(1) encompasses the right of self-government, and that this right includes the right to regulate gambling activities on the reservation. Assuming without deciding that s. 35(1) includes self-government claims, the applicable legal standard is nonetheless that laid out in *Van der Peet, supra*. Assuming s.

35(1) encompasses claims to aboriginal self-government, such claims must be considered in light of the purposes underlying that provision and must, therefore, be considered against the test derived from consideration of those purposes. This is the test laid out in *Van der Peet, supra*. In so far as they can be made under s. 35(1), claims to self-government are no different from other claims to the enjoyment of aboriginal rights and must, as such, be measured against the same standard.

[25] In *Van der Peet, supra*, the test for identifying aboriginal rights was said to be as follows, at para. 46:

> . . . In order to be an aboriginal right an activity must be an element of a practice, custom or tradition integral to the distinctive culture of the aboriginal group claiming the right.

In applying this test the Court must first identify the exact nature of the activity claimed to be a right and must then go on to determine whether, on the evidence presented to the trial judge, and on the facts as found by the trial judge, that activity could be said to be (*Van der Peet*, at para. 59) "a defining feature of the culture in question" prior to contact with Europeans.

[26] I now turn to the first part of the *Van der Peet* test, the characterization of the appellants' claim. In *Van der Peet, supra*, the Court held at para. 53 that:

> To characterize an applicant's claim correctly, a court should consider such factors as the nature of the action which the applicant is claiming was done pursuant to an aboriginal right, the nature of the governmental regulation, statute or action being impugned, and the practice, custom or tradition being relied upon to establish the right.

When these factors are considered in this case it can be seen that the correct characterization of the appellants' claim is that they are claiming the right to participate in, and to regulate, high stakes gambling activities on the reservation. The activity which the appellants organized, and which their bands regulated, was high stakes gambling. The statute which they argue violates those rights prohibits gambling subject only to a few very limited exceptions (laid out in s. 207 of the *Code*). Finally, the applicants rely in support of their claim on the fact that the "Ojibwa people ... had a long tradition of public games and sporting events, which pre-dated the arrival of Europeans". Thus, the activity in which the appellants were engaged and which their bands regulated, the statute they are impugning, and the historical evidence on which they rely, all relate to the conduct and regulation of gambling. As such, the most accurate characterization of the appellants' claim is that they are asserting that s. 35(1) recognizes and affirms the rights of the Shawanaga and Eagle Lake First Nations to participate in, and to regulate, gambling activities on their respective reserve lands.

[27] The appellants themselves would have this Court characterize their claim as to "a broad right to manage the use of their reserve lands". To so characterize the appellants' claim would be to cast the Court's inquiry at a level of excessive generality. Aboriginal rights, including any asserted right to self-government, must be looked at in light of the specific

circumstances of each case and, in particular, in light of the specific history and culture of the aboriginal group claiming the right. The factors laid out in *Van der Peet*, and applied, *supra*, allow the Court to consider the appellants' claim at the appropriate level of specificity; the characterization put forward by the appellants would not allow the Court to do so.

[28] I now turn to the second branch of the *Van der Peet* test, the consideration of whether the participation in, and regulation of, gambling on the reserve lands was an integral part of the distinctive cultures of the Shawanaga or Eagle Lake First Nations. The evidence presented at both the Pamajewon and Gardner trials does not demonstrate that gambling, or that the regulation of gambling, was an integral part of the distinctive cultures of the Shawanaga or Eagle Lake First Nations. In fact, the only evidence presented at either trial dealing with the question of the importance of gambling was that of James Morrison, who testified at the Pamajewon trial with regards to the importance and prevalence of gaming in Ojibwa culture. While Mr. Morrison's evidence does demonstrate that the Ojibwa gambled, it does not demonstrate that gambling was of central significance to the Ojibwa people. Moreover, his evidence in no way addresses the extent to which this gambling was the subject of regulation by the Ojibwa community. His account is of informal gambling activities taking place on a small-scale; he does not describe large-scale activities, subject to community regulation, of the sort at issue in this appeal.

[29] I would note that neither of the trial judges in these cases relied upon findings of fact regarding the importance of gambling to the Ojibwa; however, upon review of the evidence I find myself in agreement with the conclusion arrived at by Osborne J.A. when he said first, at p. 400, that there "is no evidence to support a conclusion that gambling generally or high stakes gambling of the sort in issue here, were part of the First Nations' historic cultures and traditions, or an aspect of their use of their land" and, second, at p. 400, that "there is no evidence that gambling on the reserve lands generally was ever the subject matter of aboriginal regulation". I also agree with the observation made by Flaherty Prov. Ct. J. in the Gardner trial when he said that

> commercial lotteries such as bingo are a twentieth century phenomena and nothing of the kind existed amongst aboriginal peoples and was never part of the means by which those societies were traditionally sustained or socialized.

[30] Given this evidentiary record, it is clear that the appellants have failed to demonstrate that the gambling activities in which they were engaged, and their respective bands' regulation of those activities, took place pursuant to an aboriginal right recognized and affirmed by s. 35(1) of the *Constitution Act, 1982*.

[**L'Heureux-Dubé J.** concurred in separate reasons.]

Appeal dismissed.

One of the difficulties emanating from the *Pamajewon* judgment is the manner in which the Supreme Court essentially recharacterized the appellants' claim from one of self-government, namely, their right to determine how to financially support their communities (such as by high-stakes gambling), to whether the appellants possessed a right to engage in high-stakes gambling on their reserves. In so doing, the court removed the all-important context for the appropriate resolution of the appellants' claim and trivialized the importance of the dispute in question.

The Supreme Court held, at para. 27, that the appellants "would have this Court characterize their claim as to 'a broad right to manage the use of their reserve lands'". In describing the appellants' desired characterization as "cast[ing] the Court's inquiry at a level of excessive generality" (para. 27) the court explicitly states, *ibid.*, that:

> Aboriginal rights, including any asserted right to self-government, must be looked at in light of the specific circumstances of each case and, in particular, in light of the specific history and cluture of the aboriginal group claiming the right. The factors laid out in *Van der Peet*, and applied, *supra*, allow the Court to consider the appellant's claim at the appropriate level of specificity; the characterization put forward by the appellants would not allow the Court to do so.

Do you agree with the Supreme Court's characterization of the scenario posed by the appellants' claim in *Pamajewon*? Consider the following account of what transpired in the Supreme Court's judgment, given by the lead plaintiff "Delgam uukw" at the opening of the *Delgamuukw* case at trial.

GISDAY WA AND DELGAM UUKW, THE SPIRIT IN THE LAND: THE OPENING STATEMENT OF THE GITKSAN AND WET'SUWET'EN HEREDITARY CHIEFS IN THE SUPREME COURT OF BRITISH COLUMBIA MAY 11, 1987

(Gabriola, B.C.: Reflections, 1989) at 7-9

DELGAM UUKW SPEAKS Smithers, Gitksan and Wet'suwet'en Territories, May 11, 1987.

My name is Delgam Uukw. I am a Gitksan Chief and a plaintiff in this case. My House owns territories in the Upper Kispiox Valley and the Upper Nass Valley. Each Gitksan plaintiffs House owns similar territories. Together, the Gitksan and Wet'suwet'en Chiefs own and govern the 22,000 square miles of Gitksan and Wet'suwet'en territory.

For us, the ownership of territory is a marriage of the Chief and the land. Each Chief has an ancestor who encountered and acknowledged the life of the land. From such encounters come power. The land, the plants, the animals and the people all have spirit — they all must be shown respect. That is the basis of our law.

The Chief is responsible for ensuring that all the people in his House respect the spirit in the land and in all living things. When a Chief directs his House properly and the laws are followed, then that original power can be recreated. That is the source of the Chief's authority. That authority is what gives the 54 plaintiff Chiefs the right to bring this action on behalf of their House members — all Gitksan and Wet'suwet'en people. That authority is what makes the Chiefs the real experts in this case.

My power is carried in my House's histories, songs, dances and crests. It is recreated at the Feast when the histories are told, the songs and dances performed, and the crests displayed. With the wealth that comes from respectful use of the territory, the House feeds the name of the Chief in the Feast Hall. In this way, the law, the Chief, the territory, and the Feast become one. The unity of the Chief's authority and his House's ownership of its territory are witnessed and thus affirmed by the other Chiefs at the Feast.

By following the law, the power flows from the land to the people through the Chief; by using the wealth of the territory, the House feasts its Chief so he can properly fulfill the law. This cycle has been repeated on my land for thousands of years. The histories of my House are always being added to. My presence in this courtroom today will add to my House's power, as it adds to the power of the other Gitksan and Wet'suwet'en Chiefs who will appear here or who will witness the proceedings. All of our roles, including yours, will be remembered in the histories that will be told by my grandchildren. Through the witnessing of all the histories, century after century, we have exercised our jurisdiction.

The Europeans did not want to know our histories; they did not respect our laws or our ownership of our territories. This ignorance and this disrespect continues. The former Delgam Uukw, Albert Tait, advised the Chiefs not to come into this Court with their regalia and their crest-blankets. Here, he said, the Chiefs will not receive the proper respect from the government. If they are wearing their regalia then, the shame of the disrespect will be costly to erase.

Officials who are not accountable to this land, its laws or its owners have attempted to displace our laws with legislation and regulations. The politicians have consciously blocked each path within their system that we take to assert our title. The courts, until perhaps now, have similarly denied our existence. In your legal system, how will you deal with the idea that the Chiefs own the land? The attempts to quash our laws and extinguish our system have been unsuccessful. Gisday Wa has not been extinguished.

If the Canadian legal system has not recognized our ownership and jurisdiction but at the same time not extinguished it, what has been done with it? Judges and legislators have taken the reality of aboriginal title as we know it and tried to wrap it in something called "aboriginal rights". An aboriginal rights package can be put on the shelf to be forgotten or to be endlessly debated at constitutional conferences. We are not interested in asserting aboriginal rights — we are here to discuss territory and authority. When this case ends and the package has been unwrapped, it will have to be our ownership and our jurisdiction under our law that is on the table.

Our histories show that whenever new people came to this land, they had to follow its laws if they wished to stay. The Chiefs who were already here had the responsibility to teach the law to the newcomers. They then waited to see if the land was respected. If it was not, the newcomers had to pay compensation and leave. The Gitksan and Wet'suwet'en have waited and observed the Europeans for a hundred years. The Chiefs have suggested that the newcomers may want to stay on their farms in their towns and villages, but beyond the farm fences the land belongs to the Chiefs. Once this has been recognized, the Court can get on with its main task which is to establish a process for the Chiefs' and the newcomers' interests to be settled. The purpose of this case then, is to find a process to Gitksan and Wet'suwet'en ownership and jurisdiction within the context of Canada. We do not seek a decision as to whether our system might continue or not. It will continue.

DELGAMUUKW v. BRITISH COLUMBIA

[1997] S.C.J. No. 108, [1997] 3 S.C.R. 1010 (S.C.C.)

. . . . .

D. Has a claim to self-government been made out by the appellants?

[170] In the courts below, considerable attention was given to the question of whether s. 35(1) can protect a right to self-government, and if so, what the contours of that right are. The errors of fact made by the trial judge, and the resultant need for a new trial, make it impossible for this Court to determine whether the claim to self-government has been made out. Moreover, this is not the right case for the Court to lay down the legal principles to guide future litigation. The parties seem to have acknowledged this point, perhaps implicitly, by giving the arguments on self-government much less weight on appeal. One source of the decreased emphasis on the right to self-government on appeal is this Court's judgment in *Pamajewon*. There, I held that rights to self-government, if they existed, cannot be framed in excessively general terms. The appellants did not have the benefit of my judgment at trial. Unsurprisingly, as counsel for the Wet'suwet'en specifically concedes, the appellants advanced the right to self-government in very broad terms, and therefore in a manner not cognizable under s. 35(1).

[171] The broad nature of the claim at trial also led to a failure by the parties to address many of the difficult conceptual issues which surround the recognition of aboriginal self-government. The degree of complexity involved can be gleaned from the *Report of the Royal Commission on Aboriginal Peoples*, which devotes 277 pages to the issue. That report describes different models of self-government, each differing with respect to their conception of territory, citizenship, jurisdiction, internal government organization, etc. We received little in the way of submission that would help us grapple with these difficult and central issues. Without assistance from the

parties, it would be imprudent for the Court to step into the breach. In these issues, the issue of self-government will fall to be determined at trial.

In its brief two-paragraph examination of self-government, the Supreme Court of Canada revealed the effects of its unreflective acceptance of Crown sovereignty on its comprehension of the issues before it. After relying on assertions of Crown sovereignty to ground Crown rights throughout the judgment (see the further discussion of *Delgamuukw* in Chapter 3), the Court did not extend to Aboriginal peoples equivalent generous treatment concerning the effects of Aboriginal sovereignty. Relying on its earlier judgment in *R. v. Pamajewon*, above, the Court reasserted that Aboriginal rights to self-government, if they existed, cannot be framed in excessively general terms. This contrast in the Court's treatment of Crown and Aboriginal sovereignty could not be more profound. The Court was quite willing to frame Crown rights to self-government in the most excessive and general of terms — simple utterances were sufficient to grant the Crown the widest possible range of entitlements to other's ancient rights. On the other hand, detailed evidence concerning Gitksan and Wet'suwet'en sovereignty (houses, clans, chiefs, feasts, crests, poles, laws, *etc.*) over specific people and territory was too broad to "lay down the legal principles to guide future litigation". As a result the Court held that the advancement of the Aboriginal right to self-government in the supposedly very broad terms in the case before it was not cognizable under section 35(1) of the *Constitution Act, 1982*. Is the Crown's assertion of broad rights of Crown sovereignty any more cognizable given its unexamined extension and unquestioned acceptance by the Court in this case?

It would be interesting to subject the Court's treatment of Crown sovereignty to the same standards it expects for evidence of Aboriginal self-government. If this approach was followed could it not also be said of Crown sovereignty, as the Court wrote of Aboriginal sovereignty:

> The broad nature of the claim at trial also led to a failure by the parties to address many of the difficult conceptual issues which surround the recognition of [Crown] self-government. … We received little in the way of submissions that would help us to grapple with these difficult and central issues. Without assistance from the parties it would be imprudent for the Court to step into the breach. In these circumstances the issue of [Crown] self-government will fall to be determined at trial.

The implications of the assertion of Crown sovereignty need to be more carefully scrutinized to assess the justice of colonialism in British Columbia. Without such an examination, the unequal treatment of Aboriginal and Crown sovereignty perpetuates historical injustices and therefore fails to respect the distinctive cultures of pre-existing Aboriginal societies in contemporary Canadian society.

When British Columbia entered Confederation in 1871, Indians composed a majority of people within the province, yet did not participate in its creation. Most continued to live within their own governments on their lands as they had done for centuries, with little or no thought for British assertions of sovereignty. As stated by former United States Supreme Court Justice John Marshall in *Worcester v. Georgia*, 31 U.S. (6 Pet.) 515, 8 L.Ed. 483 (1832):

> It is difficult to comprehend the proposition that the inhabitants of the globe could have rightful original claims of dominion over the inhabitants of the other, or over the lands they occupied; or that the discovery of either by the other should give the discoverer rights in the country discovered which annulled the pre-existing rights of its ancient possessions.

It should be asked how, then, under such circumstances did the Indians become subject to the legislative authority of Canada? Is it because they "became a conquered people, not by force of arms, for that was not necessary, but by an invading culture and a relentless energy with which they would not, or could not compete", as the trial judge, McEachern C.J., suggested in his judgment in *Delgamuukw v. British Columbia*, [1991] B.C.J. No. 525, [1991] 3 W.W.R. 97 at 269 (B.C.S.C.). Or did this subjection come about by the assertion of British sovereignty through unjust and discriminatory laws? In 1881, 10 years after union, Indians were still the majority population in British Columbia: there were 28,704 Indians, 4,195 Chinese and 19,069 settlers of European origin. Yet in 1872, a year after union, when the Indian population was closer to 40,000 and the settler population was smaller still, one of the new province's first legislative acts was to remove voting rights from the Indians. This same government continued to uphold laws that denied Indians fee simple title to pre-empted lands taken up through settlement, a right freely granted to non-Aboriginal people in British Columbia. Furthermore, this government only allowed for the surveying of extremely small reserves for Indians, and would not recognize any Aboriginal title to land. When Aboriginal peoples in British Columbia tried to dispute this mistreatment the province responded by further diminishing their land and political rights, and the federal government eventually followed suit by amending the *Indian Act* and making it virtually illegal to raise these matters before the courts.

"Taking the perspective of the aboriginal people themselves, on the meaning of the rights at stake" it should be asked whether the authority of an imposed, obstructionist and unrepresentative government, should be recognized as legally infringing or extinguishing any "Aboriginal legislative or other jurisdiction" which Aboriginal people possess. In these circumstances, is the assertion of British sovereignty over Aboriginal peoples in British Columbia a "morally and politically defensible conception of aboriginal rights"? Does it "perpetuate historical injustice suffered by aboriginal peoples at the hands of the colonizers"? Is it consistent with the "noble and prospective purpose of the Constitutional entrenchment of aboriginal and treaty rights in the Constitution"? If assertions of sovereignty operate as they have done throughout Western European legal thought, should we ask whether "an unjust and discriminatory doctrine of that kind can any longer be accepted"?

G. NEGOTIATING GOVERNANCE AGREEMENTS

Thus far, litigation has been very ineffective in addressing the issue of Aboriginal governance. One productive way in which new legal under-standings of Aboriginal governance have emerged is through negotiated self-government agreements, such as the Cree-Naskapi (see *Cree-Naskapi (of Quebec) Act*, S.C. 1984, c. 18), the Sechelt Indians on the Sunshine Coast of British Columbia (see *Sechelt Indian Band Self-Government Act*, S.C. 1986, c. 27), the *Champagne and Aishihik Self-Government Agreement* (Yukon), and the *Westbank First Nation Self-Government Act* (S.C. 2004, c. 17). None of these agreements protects self-government under section 35(1) of the *Constitution Act, 1982*. Self-government agreements outside of section 35(1) have also been signed pursuant to the 1992 *Gwich'in Comprehensive Land Claim Agreement* and the 1994 *Sahtu Dene and Metis Comprehensive Land Claim Agreement*. Nunavut has a public model of governance rather than an Inuit-exclusive government structure that does not benefit from protection under section 35. The Inuit of the East-ern Arctic negotiated this arrangement outside of the *Nunavut Land Claims Agreement Act*, S.C. 1993, c. 29. Other Aboriginal peoples have negotiated governance within section 35(1), including the 1999 Nisga'a Final Agreement, the *TliCho Land Claims and Self Government Agreement Act* (S.C. 2005, c. 1) and the *Labrador Inuit Land Claims Agreement Act* (S.C. 2005, c. 27). Other nations have proceeded with self-government initia-tives through sectoral agreements in education, health, resources man-agement, *etc.* These smaller agreements allow communities to gain expe-rience in areas of strategic importance to a First Nation.

The *Report of the Royal Commission on Aboriginal Peoples: Restructuring the Relationship*, Vol. 2 (Ottawa: Ministry of Supply and Services, 1996), at 215 suggested that Aboriginal people are free to implement their inherent right to self-government through self-starting initiatives, without the need for agreements with federal or provincial governments. These initiatives can occur in what the commission called "core" areas of Aboriginal jurisdiction. While they considered it preferable for governance to be negotiated, to min-imize the potential for misunderstanding by creating mechanisms for recip-rocal recognition, the commission defined the core to include all matters that:

- are of vital concern to the life and welfare of a particular Aboriginal people, its culture and identity;
- do not have a major impact on adjacent jurisdictions; and
- are not otherwise the object of transcendent federal or provincial concern.

The commission then defined a "periphery" of Aboriginal jurisdiction which "takes up the remainder of inherent Aboriginal jurisdiction."

In 1995 the federal government issued a policy guide, entitled *Aboriginal Self-Government*, often referred to as the inherent rights policy. This policy lists the areas of governance the federal government thinks Aboriginal peoples have within the scope of their jurisdiction. It views Aboriginal jurisdiction as extending to "matters that are internal to the group, integral to its distinct Aboriginal culture, and essential to its operation as a government." These areas include: internal constitutions, elections, membership, marriage, adoption and child welfare, language, culture, education, health, social services, administration and enforcement of Aboriginal laws, policing, internal land management, agriculture, taxation of members, housing, transportation and licensing of local businesses.

In January 1998, the federal government released *Gathering Strength — Canada's Aboriginal Action Plan* to deal with the issue of Aboriginal governance. In the document the government said it:

- was "open to further discussions on the departmental and institutional arrangements that could improve existing systems";
- would "consult with Aboriginal organizations and the provinces and territories on appropriate instruments to recognize Aboriginal governments";
- would focus on improving the capacity of First Nations to negotiate and implement self-government;
- would work with Treaty First Nations to achieve self-government within the context of the treaty relationship.

The 1995 inherent right policy was directly implemented for the first time with the 1999 *Nisga'a Final Agreement*. This Agreement came into effect on 11 May 2000 after being ratified by the Nisga'a, the British Columbia Legislative Assembly and the federal Parliament. The context within which Nisga'a governance was negotiated and recognized within section 35(1) of the *Constitution Act, 1982* will be addressed in greater detail below. It provides an interesting case study regarding the interaction of First Nation traditional laws and structures with the broader Canadian constitutional framework.

1. Nisga'a Law and the Nisga'a Agreement

JOHN BORROWS, INDIGENOUS LEGAL TRADITIONS

(Ottawa: Law Commission of Canada, 2006) (Footnotes omitted)

The Nisga'a people divide themselves into four clans or *pdeek*: *Gisk'ahaast* (Killer Whale), *Laxgibuu* (Wolf), *Ganada* (Raven) and *Laxsgiik* (Eagle). Nisga'a people also historically organized themselves into *wilps* or house groups. Each *wilp* had its own chiefs, territories, rights, history, stories, songs, dances and traditions. These possessions are handed down through matrilineal succession.

Wilps are matrilineal and matrilocal. The highest ranking woman in a *wilp* is called the *sigidimnak'* and she makes the ultimate decisions concerning names and inheritance. Upon her death her position would be assumed by her oldest sister or daughter. The highest ranking man within a *wilp* is called the *sim'oogit*. When he dies his entitlements are usually passed on to his eldest living brother or the oldest son of his eldest sister.

Wilp Chiefs are responsible for transmitting *adaawks* and associated prerogatives from one generation to the next. This is usually done through a series of feasts to make public these prerogatives and have them validated by other Chiefs.

Each *wilp* has an *adaawk* which describes how their ancient territories were acquired and they can take the listener's mind back to the beginning of time. The *adaawk* will also describe the *wilp's* ancient migrations, territorial defense, and "major events in the life of the house, such as natural disasters, epidemics, war, the arrival of new peoples, the establishment of trade alliances, and major shifts in power." The *adaawk* records property rights such as fishing sites, hunting territories, gathering grounds. It also details family law rights and responsibilities. For example, *adaawks* convey information about how their ancestors were given animals to be used as crests by each *wilp* to show them how to live, eat and prepare food. They also relate details about how these entitlements and obligations should be passed on to the next generation.

The Nisga'a people are assisted in remembering their *adaawks* by reference to their *ayuukhl*. The *ayuukhl* is an ancient legal code that has guided Nisga'a social, economic and political relationships from "time of memory." Centuries before Canada proclaimed itself a nation "founded upon the principles that recognize the supremacy of God and the rule of law," the people of the Nass River were living according to *Ayuukhl Nisga'a*, an ancient code of laws that will stand comparison to any modern constitution or declaration of statehood and nationality." The *ayuukhl*, in conjunction with the *adaawk*, historically governed land ownership, succession, citizenship, the institutions of the chieftain and matriarch, education, marriage and divorce, war, peace, trading relationships, and restitution, though these have been modified in some degree by a recent treaty. For example, on matters of succession, property is passed on when a *wilp* Chief dies and his next older brother or his oldest sister's son assumes the role of custodian for all the property of the House. This process occurs through a sophisticated ceremony known as a Settlement Feast. Like a deed in a land registry office, the Settlement Feast is a formal registration of title and ownership. Some *ayuukhl* are related to the Nisga'a narrative regarding their origins, being placed in *Ginsk'eexkw* by *K'amligihahlhaahl* who is regarded as the Supreme God. Other *ayuukhl* are founded upon *K'amligihahlhaahl* teachings to *Txeemsim*, the trickster, who identified central legal tenets for Nisga'a peace and order. His deeds and misdeeds illustrate consequences that can flow from certain behaviors.

Some *ayuukhl* seem to come from the direct experience and observation of the people. There are many cases of people being rewarded or punished because of the respect or disrespect they showed in following the *ayuukhl*. For example, Chief Joe Gosnell has spoken about an *ayuukhl* that warns against disrespect for animals. In this *ayuukhl* young boys were playing with salmon and setting tiny pitch lamps in their backs to watch the lights swim away upriver. Chief Gosnell reported that: "For this crime, the animals took their vengeance upon the valley, causing the eruption of a dormant volcano known as *Wilksi Baxhl Mihl*. More than 2,000 of our people were entombed in the lava that flowed from the volcano, and the lava beds remain the dominant feature of much of the Nass Valley to this day." This account demonstrates that Nisga'a legal principles can also be embedded in the very landscape of their nation.

As one reads Nisga'a law it is apparent that sanctions and restitution are an important part of their legal regime. Nisga'a Elder Bert McKay has recounted the shaming and cleansing nature of Nisga'a law. He related:

> And the last of our laws were, I guess you would call them, penalties. One is called restitution, or *Ksiiskw*. It's a very, very difficult and important law. When a life is lost over carelessness or over greed the law states very plainly, that before the sun sets if the offending family does not settle the issue with the grieved family, then those people have a right to take double the lives that they lost. So the only way that was resolved was by restitution payment. And then the other part, where certain of the ten laws were broken, not restitution but to make amends, to make a complete break from the shame that you imposed on your family, and that was called public cleansing.

Nisga'a legal traditions cover many significant aspects of human behavior. The Nisga'a *ayuukhl* and *adaawks* are an important part of their legal traditions because they connect them to their territories, families and past. They teach them how to live in relationship with the earth around them.

Recently the Nisga'a nation has modified their legal traditions to a degree by entering into the Nisga'a final agreement with the Canadian and British Columbian governments. After initiating the *Calder* case before the Supreme Court and gaining recognition of the justiciability of their legal position in Canadian law, the Nisga'a entered into a two-decade long negotiation that culminated in a comprehensive treaty in 1999. The Agreement is an ambitious one, providing for collective Nisga'a ownership of approximately 2,000 square kilometres of land in the Nass Valley watershed in northwestern British Columbia. The treaty covers such diverse issues as land titles, minerals, water, forests, fisheries, wildlife, governance, the administration of justice, fiscal relations (including taxation), cultural property, and dispute resolution. Many of these provisions provide significant benefits for Nisga'a people that are far greater than anything contemplated under the current *Indian Act*. Of particular importance is the Agreement's reference to the *Ayuukhl* as a source of Nisga'a law, and the creation of Nisga'a courts to determine its meaning in the context of the new treaty. This institution will help Nisga'a stories to rise to the surface and perforate the cover of Canadian legal fictions that had denied them rights in their traditional territories.

Nisga'a laws such as the *ayuukhl* will now operate in a contemporary Canadian context through the Nisga'a Lisims Government because of the *Nisga'a Final Agreement Act* (R.S.C. 2000, c. 7; S.B.C. 1999 c. 2). They will be adapted and find articulation in Nisga'a parliamentary procedure. They will be evident in statutory laws governing marriage, divorce, commerce, resource use, education, dispute resolution, will and estates, citizenship, governance and land. They will be the background "common law" principles in Nisga'a courts. The Nisga'a final agreement recognizes the continued importance of Nisga'a legal traditions in its preamble:

> WHEREAS the Parties acknowledge the ongoing importance to the Nisga'a Nation of the Simgigat and Sigidimhaanak (hereditary chiefs and matriarchs) continuing to tell their Adaawk (oral histories) relating to their Ango'oskw (family hunting, fishing, and gathering territories) in accordance with the Ayuuk (Nisga'a traditional laws and practices).

The "Ayuukhl Nisga'a" and "Ayuukl" is defined within the Final Agreement to mean "the traditional laws and practices of the Nisga'a Nation." Through such agreement Nisga'a legal traditions continue to exist today. Their authority and use is evidence of the potential for tolerance and respect of Indigenous legal traditions in contemporary Canada.

Since the Nisga'a Final Agreement came into effect the *Wilp Si'ayuukhl Nisga'a* has enacted over 30 Acts and other pieces of legislation. During Wilp Si'ayuukhl Nisga'a meetings, all members are able to make statements, participate in question periods, introduce petitions, raise urgent matters, and debate Nisga'a bills introduced. Legislation is enacted by Wilp Si'ayuukhl' Nisga'a when there is: Introduction of the Bill; Consideration of the Bill; Final Vote of the Bill; and Signing of the Bill by the President. Some of the acts passed are: *Nisga'a Effective Day Procedures Act*, *Nisga'a Lisims Government Act*, *Nisga'a Interpretation Act*, *Nisga'a Citizenship Act*, *Nisga'a Elections Act*, *Nisga'a Financial Administration Act*, *Nisga'a Capital Finance Commission Act*, *Nisga'a Administrative Decisions Review Act*, *Nisga'a Personnel Administration Act*, *Nisga'a Land Act*, *Nisga'a Land Designation Act*, *Nisga'a Village Entitlement Act*, *Nisga'a Nation Entitlement Act*, *Nisga'a Land Title Act*, *Nisga'a Fisheries and Wildlife Act*, *Nisga'a Forest Act*, *Nisga'a Programs and Services Delivery Act*, and the *Nisga'a Offence Act*. The *Nisga'a* Constitution describes how law making power is to be exercised by the *Wilp Si'ayuukhl Nisga'a* and has rules describing the process for enacting laws. Furthermore a Nisga'a Executive has the power to enact regulations under laws enacted by the *Wilp Si'ayuukhl Nisga'a* and Village Governments also have jurisdiction in their areas of law making authority.

Under the *Nisga'a Final Agreement*, *Nisga'a* Government has no exclusive jurisdiction. It is always concurrent with federal or provincial jurisdiction which made it necessary to provide for rules that determine which law prevails in the event of inconsistency or conflict. "Generally, Nisga'a laws prevail in relation to matters that are internal to the Nisga'a Nation, integral to their distinct culture or essential to the operation of their government or the exercise of their other treaty rights. In some cases, Nisga'a laws must comply with provincial standards in order to be valid. If those standards are met or exceeded, then Nisga'a laws prevail. In other cases, Canada, British Columbia and the Nisga'a Nation agreed that, while Nisga'a Government should have the authority to make laws, if there is a conflict, federal or provincial laws should prevail. Finally, there are many subject matters over which Nisga'a Government has no jurisdiction."

Under the *Nisga'a Final Agreement* Edmond Wright has argued that Nisga'a laws prevails in the following matters: Administration, management and operation of Nisga'a Government; Creation, continuation, amalgamation, dissolution, naming or renaming of Nisga'a Villages on Nisga'a Lands, and Nisga'a Urban Locals; Nisga'a citizenship; Preservation, promotion and development of Nisga'a language and Nisga'a culture; Use, management, possession, disposition of Nisga'a Lands owned by the Nisga'a Nation, a Nisga'a Village or a Nisga'a Corporation and similar matters relating to the property interests of the Nisga'a Nation, Nisga'a Villages and Nisga'a Corporations; Nisga'a Lands Use, management, planning, zoning, development and similar matters related to the regulation and administration of Nisga'a Lands, including establishment of a land title or land registry system, designation of Nisga'a Lands; Use, possession, management and similar matters relating to the property interests of the Nisga'a Nation, Nisga'a Villages and Nisga'a Corporations in their assets other than real property on Nisga'a Lands; Organization and structure for the delivery of health services on Nisga'a Lands; Authorization or licensing of Aboriginal healers on Nisga'a Lands, including measures in respect of competence, ethics and quality of practice that are reasonably required to protect the public; Child and family services on Nisga'a Lands, if Nisga'a laws include standards comparable to provincial standards intended to ensure the safety and well-being of children and families; Adoption of Nisga'a children, if Nisga'a laws expressly provide that the best interests of the child is the paramount consideration and that British Columbia and Canada are provided with records of all adoptions occurring under Nisga'a laws; Pre-school to grade 12 education on Nisga'a Lands of Nisga'a children, if Nisga'a laws include provisions for curriculum, examination and other standards that permit transfers between school systems, and for appropriate certification of teachers; Post-secondary education within Nisga'a Lands, if Nisga'a laws include standards comparable to provincial standards in respect of matters such as institutional structure and accountability, admission and curriculum standards; Devolution of cultural property (ceremonial regalia and similar property associated with a Nisga'a clan and other personal property having cultural significance to the Nisga'a Nation) of a Nisga'a citizen who dies intestate.

The Nisga'a Treaty is the first modern-day treaty in British Columbia. and was the 14th modern treaty in Canada to be negotiated since 1976. Chief Gosnell expressed his community's struggle for the agreement in the following speech before the agreement was ratified in the B.C. legislature.

CHIEF GOSNELL'S HISTORIC SPEECH TO THE BRITISH COLUMBIA LEGISLATURE

Official Report of the Legislative Assembly (B.C. *Hansard*), Wednesday December 2, 1998, Vol. 12, No. 17

Madame Speaker, Honourable Members, ladies and gentlemen.

Today marks a turning point in the history of British Columbia. Today, aboriginal and non-aboriginal people are coming together to decide the future of this province.

I am talking about the Nisga'a Treaty — a triumph for all British Columbians — and a beacon of hope for aboriginal people around the world.

A triumph, I believe, which proves to the world that reasonable people can sit down and settle historical wrongs. It proves that a modern society can correct the mistakes of the past. As British Columbians, as Canadians, we should all be very proud.

A triumph because, under the Treaty, the Nisga'a people will join Canada and British Columbia as free citizens — full and equal participants in the social, economic and political life of this province, of this country.

A triumph because, under the Treaty, we will no longer be wards of the state, no longer beggars in our own lands.

A triumph because, under the Treaty, we will collectively own about 2,000 square kilometres of land, far exceeding the postage-stamp reserves set aside for us by colonial governments. We will once again govern ourselves by our own institutions, but within the context of Canadian law.

It is a triumph because, under the Treaty, we will be allowed to make our own mistakes, to savor our own victories, to stand on our own feet once again.

A triumph because, clause by clause, the Nisga'a Treaty emphasizes self-reliance, personal responsibility and modern education. It also encourages, for the first time, investment in Nisga'a lands and resources, and allows us to pursue meaningful employment from the resources of our own territory, for our own people.

To investors, it provides economic certainty and gives us a fighting chance to establish legitimate economic independence — to prosper in common with our non-aboriginal neighbors in a new and proud Canada.

A triumph, Madame Speaker and Honorable Members, because the Treaty proves, beyond all doubt, that negotiations — not lawsuits, not blockades, not violence — are the most effective, most honorable way to resolve aboriginal issues in this country.

A triumph that signals the end of the *Indian Act* — the end of more than a century of humiliation, degradation and despair.

In 1887, my ancestors made an epic journey from the Nass River here to Victoria's inner harbor.

Determined to settle the Land Question, they were met by a Premier who barred them from the Legislature.

He was blunt. Premier Smithe rejected all our aspirations to settle the Land Question. Then he made this pronouncement, and I quote: "When the white man first came among you, you were little better than wild beasts of the field."

Wild beasts of the field! Little wonder then, that this brutal racism was soon translated into narrow policies which plunged British Columbia into a century of darkness for the Nisga'a and other aboriginal people.

Like many colonists of the day, Premier Smithe did not know, or care to know, that the Nisga'a is an old nation, as old as any in Europe.

From time immemorial, our oral literature, passed down from generation to generation, records the story of the way the Nisga'a people were placed on earth, entrusted with the care and protection of our land.

Through the ages, we lived a settled life in villages along the Nass River. We lived in large, cedar-planked houses, fronted with totem poles depicting the great heraldry and the family crests of our nobility. We thrived from the bounty of the sea, the river, the forest and the mountains.

We governed ourselves according to Ayuukhl Nisga'a, the code of our own strict and ancient laws of property ownership, succession, and civil order.

Our first encounters with Europeans were friendly. We welcomed these strange visitors, visitors who never left.

The Europeans also valued their encounters with us. They thought we were fair and tough entrepreneurs, and no doubt today, negotiators. In 1832, traders from the Hudson Bay Company found us living, in their words, in "two story wooden houses the equal of any in Europe." For a time, we continued to prosper.

But there were dark days to come.

Between the late 1700s and the mid-1800s, the Nisga'a people, like so many other coastal nations of the time, were devastated by European diseases, such as smallpox, measles and fevers. Our population, once 30,000, dwindled to about 800 people. Today, I am pleased to report, our population is growing again. Today, we number 5,500 people.

We took to heart the promises of King George III, set out in the Royal Proclamation of 1763, that our lands would not be taken without our permission, and that treaty-making was the way the Nisga'a would become part of this new nation.

We continued to follow our ayuukhl, our code of laws. We vowed to obey the white man's laws, too, and we expected him to obey his own law — and to respect ours.

But the Europeans would not obey their own laws, and continued to trespass on our lands. The King's governments continued to take our lands from us, until we were told that all of our lands had come to belong to the Crown, and even the tiny bits of land that enclosed our villages were not ours, but belonged to the government.

Still, we kept faith that the rule of law would prevail one day, that justice would be done. That one day, the Land Question would be settled fairly and honorably.

In 1913, the Nisga'a Land Committee drafted a Petition to London. The Petition contained a declaration of our traditional land ownership and governance and it contained the critical affirmation that, in the new British colony, our land ownership would be respected. In part the Petition said quote:

> We are not opposed to the coming of the white people into our territory, provided this be carried out justly and in accordance with the British principles embodied in the Royal Proclamation. If therefore as we expect the aboriginal rights which we claim should be established by the decision of His Majesty's Privy Council, we would be prepared to take a moderate and rea-

sonable position. In that event, while claiming the right to decide for ourselves, the terms upon which we would deal with our territory, we would be willing that all matters outstanding between the province and ourselves should be finally adjusted by some equitable method to be agreed upon which should include representation of the Indian Tribes upon any Commission which might then be appointed.

The above statement was unanimously adopted at a meeting of the Nisga'a Nation or Tribe of Indians held at the village of Kincolith on the 22nd day of January, 1913.

Sadly, this was not to be the case.

Also in 1913, Duncan Campbell Scott became deputy superintendent of Indian Affairs. His narrow vision of assimilation dominated federal aboriginal policy for years and years to come and was later codified as the *Indian Act*.

Mr. Scott said, I want to get rid of the Indian problem. "Our objective is to continue until there is not a single Indian in Canada that has not been absorbed into the body politic and there is no Indian question."

One of this man's earliest efforts was to undermine the influence of the Nisga'a Petition to London and to deflect attention away from political action.

But these men, Smithe and Scott failed; and are now deservedly only dusty footnotes in history.

Still, the situation of the Nisga'a worsened. In 1927, Canada passed a law to prevent us from pursuing our land claims, from hiring lawyers to plead our case.

At the same time, our central institution of tribal government, the potlatch system (yuukw), was outlawed by an Act of Parliament. It was against the law for us to give presents to one another during our ceremonies, which our laws instructed us to do. It was even made illegal for us to sing, to dance.

But still, we never gave up. And then finally, under the leadership of President Emeritus Frank Calder, the Nisga'a Land Committee was reborn as the Nisga'a Tribal Council in 1955. In 1968, we took our Land Question to the B.C. Supreme Court. We lost but appealed to the Supreme Court of Canada, where in 1973 — in what is now known as the *Calder Case* — the judges ruled that aboriginal title existed prior to Confederation. This initiated the modern day process of land claims negotiations.

The government of Canada agreed it was best to negotiate modern-day treaties. Canada agreed it was time to build a new relationship, based on trust, respect, and the rule of law.

In time, as you well know Madame Speaker, the Province of British Columbia came to the negotiating table as well. For the past twenty-five years, in good faith, the Nisga'a struggled to negotiate this Treaty and finally, it was initialed in August in our village of New Aiyansh.

How the world has changed. Two days ago and one hundred and eleven years after Smithe's rejection, I walked up the steps of this Legislature as the sound of Nisga'a drumming and singing filled the rotunda. To the Nisga'a people, it was a joyous sound, the sound of freedom.

What does "Freedom" mean? I looked it up in the dictionary. It means "The state or condition of being free, the condition of not being under another's control; the power to do, say, or think as one pleases."

Our people have enjoyed the hospitality and warmth of this Legislature, this capital city, its sights and its people — in churches, schools, malls, streets and public places. Our people have been embraced, welcomed and congratulated by the people of British Columbia, Madame Speaker. ...

To us, a Treaty is a sacred instrument. It represents an understanding between distinct cultures and shows respect for each other's way of life. We know we are here for a long time together. A Treaty stands as a symbol of high idealism in a divided world. That is why we have fought so long, and so hard.

I have been asked, has it been worth it? Yes, a resounding yes. But, believe me, it has been a long and hard-fought battle. Some may have heard us say that a generation of Nisga'a men and women has grown old at the negotiating table. Sadly, it is very, very true. ...

We are not naive. We know that some people do not want this Treaty. We know there are naysayers, some sitting here today. We know there are some who say Canada and B.C. are "giving" us too much. And a few who want to re-open negotiations in order to "give" us less.

Others — still upholding the values of Smithe and Scott — are practising a willful ignorance. This colonial attitude is fanning the flames of fear and ignorance in this province and re-igniting a poisonous attitude so familiar to aboriginal people.

But these are desperate tactics — doomed to fail. By playing politics with the aspirations of aboriginal people these naysayers are blighting the promise of the Nisga'a Treaty — not only for us, but for non-aboriginal people as well.

Because, Madame Speaker, this is about people. We are not numbers. In this Legislative debate, you will be dealing with the lives of our people; with the futures of our individual people. This is about the legitimate aspirations of people no longer willing to step aside or be marginalized.

We intend to be free and equal citizens, Madame Speaker. Witness the flags that have been waved in this Chamber over the past two days — by the Nisga'a people of British Columbia, the Nisga'a people of Canada.

Now, on the eve of the 50th anniversary of the Declaration of Human Rights, this Legislature embarks on a great debate about aboriginal rights. The Nisga'a people welcome that debate — one of the most important in the modern history of British Columbia.

And we have every confidence that elected members of this Legislature will look beyond narrow politics to correct a shameful and historic wrong. I ask every honorable member to search their hearts deeply and to allow the light of our message to guide their decision.

We have worked for justice for more than a century. Now, it is time to ratify the Nisga'a Treaty, for aboriginal and non-aboriginal people to come together and write a new chapter in the history of our Nation, our province, our country and indeed, the world.

The world is our witness.

Be strong. Be steadfast. Be true.

The Preamble to the Nisga'a Final Agreement reads as follows:

WHEREAS the Nisga'a Nation has lived in the Nass Area since time immemorial;

WHEREAS the Nisga'a Nation is an aboriginal people of Canada;

WHEREAS section 35 of the *Constitution Act, 1982* recognizes and affirms the existing aboriginal and treaty rights of the aboriginal peoples of Canada, which the Courts have stated include aboriginal title;

WHEREAS the Nisga'a Nation has never entered into a treaty with Canada or British Columbia;

WHEREAS the Nisga'a Nation has sought a just and equitable settlement of the land question since the arrival of the British Crown, including the preparation of the Nisga'a Petition to His Majesty's Privy Council, dated 21 May, 1913, and the conduct of the litigation that led to the decision of the Supreme Court of Canada in *Calder v. the Attorney-General of British Columbia* in 1973, and this Agreement is intended to be the just and equitable settlement of the land question;

WHEREAS Canadian courts have stated that the reconciliation between the prior presence of aboriginal peoples and the assertion of sovereignty by the Crown is best achieved through negotiation and agreement, rather than through litigation or conflict;

WHEREAS the Parties intend that this Agreement will result in this reconciliation and establish a new relationship among them;

WHEREAS this Agreement sets out Nisga'a section 35 rights inside and outside of the area that is identified in this Agreement as Nisga'a Lands;

WHEREAS the Parties acknowledge the ongoing importance to the Nisga'a Nation of the *Simgigat* and *Sigidimhaanak* (hereditary chiefs and matriarchs) continuing to tell their *Adaawak* (oral histories) relating to their *Ango'oskw* (family hunting, fishing, and gathering territories) in accordance with the *Ayuuk* (Nisga'a traditional laws and practices);

WHEREAS the Parties intend their relationship to be based on a new approach to mutual recognition and sharing, and to achieve this mutual recognition and sharing by agreeing on rights, rather than by the extinguishment of rights; and

WHEREAS the Parties intend that this Agreement will provide certainty with respect to Nisga'a ownership and use of lands and resources, and the relationship of federal, provincial and Nisga'a laws, within the Nass Area.

Chapter 2 of the Agreement, outlining its General Provisions begins:

This Agreement is a treaty and a land claims agreement within the meaning of sections 25 and 35 of the *Constitution Act, 1982.*

DOUGLAS SANDERS, "WE INTEND TO LIVE HERE FOREVER: A PRIMER ON THE NISGA'A TREATY"

(1999) 33 U.B.C. Law Rev. 103-128

... [T]he Nisga'a Treaty has generated a level of controversy in British Columbia that is reminiscent of the debates over the Meech Lake and Charlottetown Accord packages of constitutional amendments. What are the elements of this public debate?

Supporters of the Treaty argue that it will move us away from the old, paternalistic system under the *Indian Act*, toward Nisga'a self-government based on constitutionally protected treaty rights. The government of Canada was determined to extricate itself from the burdens and obligations of paternalism. To this end, Nisga'a lands will no longer fall under federal jurisdiction nor will they be governed under the *Indian Act*. Secondly, the Treaty settles land claims in the Nass River Valley by a compromise that gives a portion to the Nisga'a, while leaving most of the land and resources under the dominant legal system. The government of British Columbia wanted a treaty in order to bring investment certainty to the province's resource-based economy and to stop recurring confrontations and court challenges. Thirdly, the Nisga'a government will be both recognized and integrated into the constitutional system of Canada, with most parts of federal and provincial laws applying to the Nisga'a and their lands.

Public criticism of the Treaty has been dominated by non-Indian voices. These critics argue that the Treaty establishes a system of rights and self-government that are "race-based" and, therefore, comparable to apartheid. Secondly, they argue that a constitutionally protected self-government system is a permanent and dramatic shift in Canadian constitutional architecture and, as such, either requires or deserves a public referendum. Thirdly, it has been said, that non-Nisga'a living on Nisga'a lands will become second-class citizens, denied the right to vote or hold public office in the local government that affects parts of their lives.

Phil Fontaine, National Chief of the Assembly of First Nations, supports the Treaty on the basis that it represents what the Nisga'a people want. Support, on those terms, has also come from various tribal councils in British Columbia and from the First Nations Summit. But in general, First Nations people are critical of the Treaty. The sharpest Indian critics call it a "custodial agreement" or the "B.C. *Indian Act*." Some Indian critics say that the Treaty gives the Provincial government a much stronger constitutional role than in the past, in spite of historic treaties that have directly affected the relationship between Canada and its First Nations. The Treaty is also criticized for creating only a limited self-government. Accordingly, the powers involved are said to be modest and said to be "municipal" in character. The Treaty does not address, much less settle, issues surrounding Indian sovereignty. It is also said to represent a settlement but not a new relationship; that is, it is not a commitment to Indian survival, development, or achievement within the Canadian system, because it gives Indians too little and involves too much outside control. Others among the critics say that they will never agree to such provisions as the ending of tax exemptions under the *Indian Act*.

Four court challenges to the Treaty and its the process have been filed. In 1997, some of the Nisga'a community went to court with the claim that their leaders did not have the authority to sign the Treaty. They failed, however, because they could not demonstrate significant support for their position and were refused a pre-trial injunction. One court challenge is based on a border dispute between the Gitanyow and the Nisga'a. Another, by Reform MP John Cummins and the Fisheries Survival Coalition (a group that has actively protested Indian fishing rights for a number of years), has been brought. However, the leading challenge is that of the provincial Liberal party — the official opposition party in British Columbia. The Liberal party's case focuses primarily on the self-government provisions of the Treaty.

The decision dismissing the Liberal party of British Columbia's challenge to the Nisga'a treaty is found in *Campbell v. British Columbia (Attorney General)*, [2000] B.C.J. No. 1524, 189 D.L.R. (4th) 333 (B.C.S.C.). The main issue in the *Campbell* case was whether the Nisga'a Treaty was inconsistent with the division of powers granted to Parliament and the Legislative Assemblies of the Provinces by sections 91 and 92 of the *Constitution Act, 1867*. The Liberal party argued the Agreement was of no force or effect, *to the extent* that it purports to provide the Nisga'a government with legislative jurisdiction, or provides that the Nisga'a government may make laws that prevail over federal and provincial laws. Justice Williamson, of the British Columbia Supreme Court, ruled against the challenge, finding that self-government was a constitutionally protected right within the Nisga'a Agreement. His reasons for decision are as follows:

CAMPBELL v. BRITISH COLUMBIA (ATTORNEY GENERAL)

[2000] B.C.J. No. 1524, 189 D.L.R. (4th) 333 (B.C.S.C.)

Williamson J.: —

. . . . .

THE NISGA'A TREATY

[34] The Nisga'a Final Agreement, now a "treaty", is a complex tripartite agreement which purports to define in an exhaustive way the treaty rights of the Nisga'a Nation. Counsel for the plaintiffs have characterized the Treaty as having four basic components. The first is the substitution for aboriginal title with a grant of a fee simple to the Nisga'a Nation of just under 2,000 square kilometres of land in the Nass Valley. This would, to use the word in the Treaty, "modify" the existing aboriginal title. It is an area much smaller than that originally claimed by the Nisga'a.

[35] Second, the Treaty defines existing hunting, fishing and trapping rights in the Nisga'a lands, but also permits participation in wildlife and fisheries management over a much larger area known as the Nass Wildlife Area. Thus, it is important to note that there are two areas of land involved. The first is the smaller fee simple area owned by the Nisga'a Nation and over which it has defined legislative power. The second is the larger area in which the Nisga'a have certain specified hunting, fishing and trapping rights.

[36] The third basic component is the payment of money over a period of years which can be seen as compensation for what the Nisga'a have given up or possibly for the negative impact upon the Nisga'a which followed upon the arrival of Europeans.

[37] The fourth component is described by the plaintiffs as "a new order of government", a government with certain legislative jurisdiction specified in Chapter 11 of the Treaty. I have put the words "a new order of government" in quotation marks as there is some dispute about whether this government can be called new, except as to its structure.

[38] The Nisga'a government is divided into two groups: the Nisga'a Lisims Government and the Nisga'a Village Governments, intended to govern the Nisga'a Nation and the Nisga'a villages respectively. The Nisga'a Lisims Government is responsible for intergovernmental relations between the Nisga'a Nation and Canada or British Columbia. Each of these governments is a separate legal entity which can enter into contracts and agreements, acquire and hold property, raise and spend money, sue and be sued, and do those things ancillary to the exercise of its powers. The Agreement provides for the creation, continuation, amalgamation, or dissolution of Nisga'a villages.

[39] The Treaty provides for a Nisga'a Constitution which must, however, be consistent with the Treaty.

[40] The Treaty also provides for the creation of Nisga'a Urban Locals, a provision designed to ensure that the Nisga'a who live away from the Nass Valley in three specified areas (Greater Vancouver, Terrace and Prince Rupert/Port Edward) will be able to participate in the Nisga'a Lisims Government.

[41] The *Canadian Charter of Rights and Freedoms* is stated expressly to apply to Nisga'a government "in respect of all matters within its authority, bearing in mind the free and democratic nature of Nisga'a Government" as set out in the Treaty.

[42] Nisga'a citizenship, or enrolment under the agreement, is the subject of detailed provisions. Individuals are eligible to be enrolled if they are of Nisga'a ancestry and if their mother was born into one of the Nisga'a tribes, as are descendants and adopted children of such individuals. An "enrolment committee" is established to consider applications for enrolment under the Treaty.

[43] Another provision in the Treaty allows other Aboriginal Canadians who marry a Nisga'a citizen, and are adopted into one of the four Nisga'a tribes in accordance with the *Ayuuk̲hl Nisga'a* (that is, traditional Nisga'a law), to apply for enrolment. In regards to non-Nisga'a citizens

resident on Nisga'a lands, the Agreement requires the Nisga'a government to consult with them concerning decisions which "directly and significantly affect them".

[44] ... [t]he plaintiffs do not challenge the transfer to the Nisga'a Nation of fee simple title to the Nisga'a lands, the confirmation of hunting, fishing and trapping rights, or the payment of compensation. They limit their constitutional challenge to what they submit is the establishment of a new order of government. I will therefore survey briefly the legislative powers of the Nisga'a nation as set out in the Treaty.

LEGISLATIVE POWERS OF THE NISGA'A GOVERNMENT

[45] The Nisga'a Government has power to make laws in a number of different areas which can be divided generally into two groupings. In the first category, when Nisga'a law conflicts with federal or provincial law, the Nisga'a law will prevail, although in many cases only if it is consistent with comparable standards established by Parliament, the Legislative Assembly, or relevant administrative tribunals.

[46] Generally speaking, the subjects in this category are matters which concern the identity of the Nisga'a people, their education, the preservation of their culture, the use of their land and resources, and the means by which they will make decisions in these areas. As noted, however, some of these areas remain subject to comparable provincial standards. For example, adoption laws must provide for the best interests of the child, just as does the *Adoption Act*, R.S.B.C. 1996, c. 5. The provision for Nisga'a control of education is subject to various comparable provincial educational standards.

[47] Other jurisdictions of the Nisga'a government in this category have specific matters carved out and reserved to the Crown, or to laws generally applicable in the subject area. For example, the right to regulate the use and development of Nisga'a Lands rests with the Nisga'a, but rights of way held or required by the Crown are subject to special provisions. The right to regulate businesses, professions and trades on Nisga'a lands rests with the Nisga'a, but it is subject to provincial laws concerning accreditation, certification and regulation of the conduct of professions and trades.

[48] In the second classification of jurisdiction, when a Nisga'a law conflicts with federal or provincial law, the federal or provincial law will prevail.

[49] The Treaty permits the Nisga'a to establish police services and a police board. Any regimes established pursuant to these provisions require the approval of the provincial cabinet. If the Attorney General of the province is of the opinion that "effective policing in accordance with standards prevailing elsewhere in British Columbia" is not in place, she or he may provide or reorganize policing on the Nisga'a lands, appointing constables or using the provincial police (the R.C.M.P.) as a police force.

[50] The Treaty also provides that the Nisga'a Lisims Government may decide to establish a Nisga'a Court. But again, if that course is followed, its

structure and procedures, and the method of selecting judges, must be approved by the provincial cabinet. Further, an appeal from a final decision of the Nisga'a Court lies to the Supreme Court of British Columbia. The Court section of the Treaty includes a number of references to the requirement that any Nisga'a court system must operate in accordance with generally accepted principles. For example, a Nisga'a Court and its judges must comply with "generally recognized principles in respect of judicial fairness, independence and impartiality".

[51] The Nisga'a Government has no authority to make criminal law (that power remains with Parliament). Importantly, a person accused of any offence for which he or she may be imprisoned under Nisga'a law has the right to elect to be tried in the Provincial Court of British Columbia rather than a Nisga'a Court. Any provincial court proceedings would be subject to rights of appeal to the Supreme Court of British Columbia or the Court of Appeal.

[52] Labour relations law, or what in the Agreement is called industrial relations, is governed by federal and provincial laws. However, the Nisga'a Lisims Government has a right in some instances to make representations concerning the effect of a particular aspect of labour relations law upon Nisga'a culture.

[53] While the Treaty defines the right of the Nisga'a to harvest fish and aquatic plants in Nisga'a fisheries areas, all the fisheries rights of the Nisga'a are expressly subject to measures that are necessary for conservation and to legislation enacted for the purposes of public health or safety. Nisga'a peoples' harvest of fish is subject to limits set by the federal Minister of Fisheries. Any laws made by the Nisga'a government concerning fish or aquatic plants harvested by the Nisga'a are subject to relevant federal or provincial laws.

[54] The Nisga'a government may make laws concerning assets the Nisga'a Nation, a Nisga'a village or Nisga'a corporation may hold off Nisga'a lands, but in the event of a conflict between such laws and federal or provincial laws of general application, the latter prevail.

[55] Similarly, while the Nisga'a may make laws concerning the sale and consumption of alcohol (intoxicants) on Nisga'a lands, they are subject to federal and provincial laws in the area in the event of conflict.

[56] British Columbia retains the right to licence or approve gambling or gaming facilities on Nisga'a lands, but the Agreement provides that the province will not do so except in accordance with terms established by the Nisga'a government. Such terms, however, must not be inconsistent with federal and provincial laws.

[57] The above paragraphs do not list every jurisdiction and every rule set out in this lengthy and complex agreement about which law will prevail. This review, however, is enough to show that the legislative powers of the Nisga'a Government are significantly limited by the Treaty itself, without considering the effect of s. 35 of the *Constitution Act, 1982*.

[58] Recognizing these restrictions, the plaintiffs submit that it is only those portions of the Treaty which allocate legislative power in the Nisga'a Government, and which provide that in the event of a conflict with federal or provincial law Nisga'a law will prevail, which are unconstitutional.

[59] The heart of this argument is that any right to such self-government or legislative power was extinguished at the time of Confederation. Thus, the plaintiffs distinguish aboriginal title and other aboriginal rights, such as the right to hunt or to fish, from the right to govern one's own affairs. They say that in 1867, when the then *British North America Act* (now called the *Constitution Act, 1867*) was enacted, although other aboriginal rights including aboriginal title survived, any right to self-government did not. All legislative power was divided between Parliament and the legislative assemblies. While they concede that Parliament, or the Legislative Assembly, may delegate authority, they say legislative bodies may not give up or abdicate that authority. To do so, they argue, is unconstitutional.

[60] For this reason, they ask this court to strike down those provisions of the Nisga'a Treaty which so provide.

. . . . .

SECTIONS 91 AND 92: THE DIVISION OF POWERS

[62] I turn first to the significance of the division of powers between the federal and provincial governments originally set out in 1867 by the Parliament of the United Kingdom in ss. 91 and 92 of the *British North America Act*. It is necessary to ask whether the passage of the *British North America Act* effectively concentrated all law making power in Parliament and the Legislative Assemblies. ...

[64] These sections, in view of the submissions of the plaintiffs, lead to at least two related questions. First, when the Parliament of the United Kingdom enacted the *British North America Act* in 1867 was all legislative power distributed through Sections 91 and 92? Second, is the legislative power granted to the Nisga'a Nation a new order of government? I have concluded the answer to both of these questions is "no".

THE PREAMBLE TO THE CONSTITUTION ACT, 1867

[65] The argument that Sections 91 and 92 exhaustively distribute all legislative power does not sufficiently consider the preamble to the *Act*. That opening statement provides that the intention of the statute is to endow Canada "with a Constitution similar in Principle to that of the United Kingdom". In considering this Preamble, the Supreme Court of Canada has recognized that there are a number of constitutional principles and powers not set out in writing in the *Constitution Act, 1867* which nevertheless are fundamental to the Constitution.

[66] In *Reference re Remuneration of Judges of the Provincial Court of Prince Edward Island (the Provincial Court Judges Reference)*, [1997] 3 S.C.R. 3 at 75, the Chief Justice, speaking for the court...wrote:

> ... the preamble is not only a key to construing the express provisions of the *Constitution Act, 1867* but also invites the use of those organizing principles to fill out gaps in the express terms of the constitutional scheme. It is the means by which the underlying logic of the Act can be given the force of law.

[67] Some two years later in *Reference Re Secession of Quebec*, [1998] 2 S.C.R. 217, the Court referred to the *Provincial Court Judges Reference* and again affirmed, at page 239, that the Constitution "embraces unwritten as well as written" rules.

[68] British imperial policy, reflected in the instructions given to colonial authorities in North America prior to Confederation, recognized a continued form, albeit diminished, of aboriginal self-government after the assertion of sovereignty by the Crown. This imperial policy, through the preamble to the *Constitution Act, 1867*, assists in filling out "gaps in the express terms of the constitutional scheme".

[69] The history of the negotiation of treaties by the executive branch after Confederation indicates that the distribution of power in Sections 91 and 92, and in particular the designation of "Indians, and Lands reserved for the Indians" as a parliamentary responsibility in Section 91(24), did not interfere with the royal or executive prerogative to negotiate treaties with aboriginal nations.

[70] Nor did the distribution of power in Sections 91 and 92 terminate the development of the common law, law binding upon citizens and enforceable by the courts. And until the *Statute of Westminster* was passed in 1931, 64 years after Confederation, all legislation enacted in Canada was subject to the overriding powers of the Parliament of the United Kingdom. In short, long before the 1982 enactment of s. 35, aboriginal rights formed part of the unwritten principles underlying our constitution.

DO SECTIONS 91 AND 92 EXHAUST LEGISLATIVE POWER?

[71] The plaintiffs argue that all legislative power in Canada is "exhaustively" distributed between Parliament and the legislative assemblies by virtue of the *Constitution Act, 1867*. Consequently, they submit, an amendment to the constitution would be required to allow aboriginal governments, such as the Lisims Government of the Nisga'a Nation established by the Treaty, the power to make laws which prevail over federal or provincial laws. ... For example, in *A.G. Ont. v. A.G. Canada*, [1912] A.C. 571, a case which did not concern aboriginal rights but which was considered in detail by the Court of Appeal in *Delgamuukw*, the Privy Council, while discussing the *British North America Act*, said at p. 581:

> Now, there can be no doubt that under this organic instrument the powers distributed between the Dominion on the one hand and the provinces on the other hand cover the whole area of self-government within the whole area of Canada.

[72] This is the heart of the plaintiffs' argument. If the powers granted to Parliament and the legislatures combined "cover the whole area of self-government" within Canada, there can be no legislative power left to aboriginal peoples.

[73] The flaw in this submission, however, becomes evident when one considers what the Privy Council said in the same judgment three pages on at p. 584:

For whatever belongs to self-government in Canada belongs either to the Dominion or to the provinces, *within the limits* of the British North America Act. (emphasis added)

[74] What are "the limits of the British North America Act"?

[75] In *R. v. Secretary of State for Foreign and Commonwealth Affairs, ex parte Indian Association of Alberta and others,* [1982] 2 All E.R. 118, the English Court of Appeal dealt with the question of whether after Canada obtained independence obligations owed by the Crown to aboriginal peoples remained with the Crown in right of the United Kingdom or became the responsibility of the Crown in right of Canada. The court found that such obligations had become the responsibility of the Crown in right of Canada. In his reasons, May L.J. quoted with approval the following passage from the decision of Watson J. in *Liquidators of the Maritime Bank of Canada v. Receiver-General of New Brunswick,* [1892] A.C. 437 at 441-2:

> The object of the [*British North America Act*] ... was accomplished by distributing between the Dominion and the provinces, all powers executive and legislative, and all public property and revenues *which had previously belonged to the provinces*; so that the Dominion government should be vested with such of these powers, property, and revenues as were necessary for the due performance of its constitutional functions, and that the remainder should be retained by the provinces for the purposes of provincial government. (emphasis added)

[76] Thus, what was distributed in ss. 91 and 92 of the *British North America Act* was all of (but no more than) the powers which until June 30, 1867 had belonged to the colonies. Anything outside of the powers enjoyed by the colonies was not encompassed by ss. 91 and 92 and remained outside of the power of Parliament and the legislative assemblies just as it had been beyond the powers of the colonies.

[77] In the *Quebec Secession Reference,* the Supreme Court of Canada reviewed the historical context of the events leading to Confederation. The Court observed, at pp. 244-5, that:

> Federalism was a legal response to the underlying political and cultural realities that existed at Confederation and continue to exist today. At Confederation, political leaders told their respective communities that the Canadian union would be able to reconcile diversity with unity.

> . . . . .

> The federal-provincial division of powers was a legal recognition of the diversity that existed among the initial members of Confederation, and manifested a concern to accommodate that diversity within a single nation ...

> Federalism was the political mechanism by which diversity could be reconciled with unity.

[78] This demonstrates that the object of the division of powers in ss. 91 and 92 between the federal government and the provinces was not to extinguish diversity (or aboriginal rights), but to ensure that the local and distinct needs of Upper and Lower Canada (Ontario and Quebec) and the maritime provinces were protected in a federal system.

[79] Several pages on in the same judgment, at para. 82, the Court spoke of the explicit protection for aboriginal and treaty rights in ss. 25 and 35 of the *Constitution Act, 1982*, as being consistent with a tradition of respect for minority rights reflecting "an important underlying constitutional value".

[80] The unique relationship between the Crown and aboriginal peoples, then, is a underlying constitutional value. In *Mitchell v. Peguis Indian Band* [1990] 2 S.C.R. 85 both Dickson C.J.C. and La Forest J. discussed this "unique historical relationship". After discussing *Guerin v. The Queen*, [1984] 2 S.C.R. 335; 13 D.L.R. (4th) 321 (S.C.C.), the Chief Justice wrote at pp. 108-9 that since 1867:

> ... the Crown's role has been played, as a matter of the federal division of powers, by Her Majesty in right of Canada, with the *Indian Act* representing a confirmation of the Crown's historic responsibility for the welfare and interests of these peoples. However, the Indians' relationship with the Crown or sovereign has never depended on the particular representatives of the Crown involved. From the aboriginal perspective, any federal-provincial divisions that the Crown has imposed on itself are internal to itself and do not alter the basic structure of Sovereign-Indian relations.

[81] A consideration of these various observations by the Supreme Court of Canada supports the submission that aboriginal rights, and in particular a right to self-government akin to a legislative power to make laws, survived as one of the unwritten "underlying values" of the Constitution outside of the powers distributed to Parliament and the legislatures in 1867. The federal-provincial division of powers in 1867 was aimed at a different issue and was a division "internal" to the Crown.

· · · · ·

RECOGNITION OF ABORIGINAL LAW AFTER CONFEDERATION

[84] ... The common law has long recognized "customs" or rules that have obtained the force of law in a particular locality. Agreements such as treaties negotiated and entered into by exercise of executive prerogative will be enforced by the courts.

[85] History, and a review of the authorities, persuades me that the aboriginal peoples of Canada, including the Nisga'a, had legal systems prior to the arrival of Europeans on this continent and that these legal systems, although diminished, continued after contact. Aboriginal laws did not emanate from a central print oriented law-making authority similar to a legislative assembly, but took unwritten form. Lord Denning, in *R. v. Secretary of State For Foreign and Commonwealth Affairs* at p. 123 likened aboriginal laws to "custom":

> These customary laws are not written down. They are handed down by tradition from one generation to another. Yet beyond doubt they are well established and have the force of law within the community.

[86] The continued existence of indigenous legal systems in North America after the arrival of Europeans was articulated as early as the 1820s by the Supreme Court of the United States. But the most salient fact,

for the purposes of the question of whether a power to make and rely upon aboriginal law survived Canadian Confederation, is that since 1867
courts in Canada have enforced laws made by aboriginal societies. This
demonstrates not only that at least a limited right to self-government, or a
limited degree of legislative power, remained with aboriginal peoples after
the assertion of sovereignty and after Confederation, but also that such
rules, whether they result from custom, tradition, agreement, or some other decision making process, are "laws" in the Dicey constitutional sense.

[A review of historic and contemporary cases recognizing Aboriginal governance and law-making power is omitted.]

THE FRAMEWORK

[167] The Supreme Court of Canada has referred to s. 35 as a "framework" for reconciling the prior existence of aboriginal peoples with the
sovereignty of the Crown. In *Van der Peet*, Lamer C.J.C. wrote at pp. 533-9:

> In my view, the doctrine of aboriginal rights exists, and is recognized and af-
> firmed by s. 35 (1), because of one simple fact: when Europeans arrived in
> North America, aboriginal peoples, <u>were already here</u>, living in communi-
> ties on the land, and participating in distinctive cultures, as they had done
> for centuries. It is this fact, and this fact above all others, which separates
> aboriginal peoples from all other minority groups in Canadian society and
> which mandates their special legal, and now constitutional, status.

> More specifically, what s. 35(1) does is provide the constitutional framework
> through which the fact that aboriginals lived on the land in distinctive socie-
> ties, with their own practices, traditions and cultures, is acknowledged and
> reconciled with the sovereignty of the Crown. The substantive rights which
> fall within the provision must be defined in light of this purpose; ... [under-
> lining in original]

[168] That the purpose of s. 35(1) is to provide a framework within
which the prior existence of aboriginal peoples may be reconciled with the
sovereignty of the Crown can mean nothing other than that there are existing aboriginal rights which have not yet been so reconciled. In much of
Canada, these rights were reconciled through the negotiation of treaties. In
most of British Columbia they were not.

[169] There are two ways to achieve the definition of "the substantive
rights" which fall within s. 35(1): by resort to the courts, or by the negotiation of treaties. The Supreme Court of Canada, as have other courts, has
stated a number of times that negotiation is the preferred method.

. . . . .

[171] Section 35(1), then, provides the solid constitutional framework
within which aboriginal rights in British Columbia may be defined by the
negotiation of treaties in a manner compatible with the sovereignty of
the Canadian state. I conclude that what Canada, British Columbia and the
Nisga'a have achieved in the Nisga'a Final Agreement is consistent both

with what the Supreme Court of Canada has encouraged, and consistent with the purpose of s. 35 of the *Constitution Act, 1982.*

[172] The idea that treaties could be the vehicle to define rights to be given constitutional protection by s. 35 is supported by a consideration of the records of meetings of the framers of s. 35, and a consideration of a temporary provision in the *Constitution Act, 1982,* s. 37, the provision which mandated a first ministers' conference within one year of the passage of that *Act.*

[173] The meeting required by this section took place in March of 1983. It was at this conference that the First Ministers agreed to add s. 35(3) to the Constitution. They also agreed to add s. 37(2) which stated that a future conference would include in the agenda

> ... an item respecting constitutional matters that directly affect the aboriginal peoples of Canada, including the identification and definition of the rights of those peoples to be included in the Constitution of Canada ...

[174] At the 1983 conference, transcripts of which are in evidence, the then Prime Minister said that one matter for the meeting was the "the identification of rights" to be included in s. 35. He went on to say that:

> ... the heart of the matter, the crux of our efforts to improve the condition of our aboriginal peoples and strengthen their relationships with other Canadians, is found within the set of issues concerning aboriginal government.

[175] Twelve years later in December of 1995, in another document in evidence, the federal government published a policy statement entitled *Aboriginal Self-Government: the Government of Canada's Approach to Implementation of the Inherent Right and the Negotiation of Aboriginal Self-Government.* That policy statement said, at p. 3, that:

> The Government of Canada recognizes the inherent right of self-government as an existing aboriginal right under section 35 of the *Constitution Act, 1982.* It recognizes, as well, that the inherent right may find expression in treaties...

[176] These extrinsic documents are evidence that the framers of s. 35(3) considered that a form of self-government yet to be defined was to be included in the bundle of rights protected by that section, and that the Crown in right of Canada accepted treaties as a method of defining such rights as part of its policy.

[177] The Supreme Court of Canada recognized in 1990 that the rights guaranteed by s. 35 required definition. In *Sparrow* at p. 1108, the Court wrote of s. 35 as a "solemn commitment that must be *given meaningful content*" (emphasis added). The Nisga'a Final Agreement provides, with respect to the Nisga'a, that content.

SUMMARY

[179] For the reasons set out above, I have concluded that after the assertion of sovereignty by the British Crown, and continuing to and after the time of Confederation, although the right of aboriginal people to govern themselves was diminished, it was not extinguished. Any aboriginal right to self-government could be extinguished after Confederation and before 1982 by federal legislation which plainly expressed that intention, or it could be replaced or modified by the negotiation of a treaty. Post-1982, such rights cannot be extinguished, but they may be defined (given content) in a treaty. The Nisga'a Final Agreement does the latter expressly.

[180] I have also concluded that the *Constitution Act, 1867* did not distribute all legislative power to the Parliament and the legislatures. Those bodies have exclusive powers in the areas listed in Sections 91 and 92 (subject until 1931 to the Imperial Parliament). But the *Constitution Act, 1867*, did not purport to, and does not end, what remains of the royal prerogative or aboriginal and treaty rights, including the diminished but not extinguished power of self-government which remained with the Nisga'a people in 1982.

[181] Section 35 of the *Constitution Act, 1982*, then, constitutionally guarantees, among other things, the limited form of self-government which remained with the Nisga'a after the assertion of sovereignty. The Nisga'a Final Agreement and the settlement legislation give that limited right definition and content. Any decision or action which results from the exercise of this now-entrenched treaty right is subject to being infringed upon by Parliament and the legislative assembly. This is because the Supreme Court of Canada has determined that both aboriginal and treaty rights guaranteed by s. 35 may be impaired if such interference can be justified and is consistent with the honour of the Crown.

[182] The Nisga'a Final Agreement, negotiated in full knowledge of the limited effect (a fact accepted by the Nisga'a Nation in these proceedings) of the constitutional promise of s. 35, itself limits the new Nisga'a governments' rights to legislate. In addition, it specifies that in a number of areas, should there be any conflict between Nisga'a laws and federal or provincial laws, federal or provincial laws will prevail.

[183] Thus, the Nisga'a government, subject as it is to both the limitations set out in the treaty itself and to the limited guarantee of s. 35 of the *Constitution Act, 1982*, does not have absolute or sovereign powers.

[184] As set out above, the submission that the Nisga'a Treaty impinges improperly upon the offices of the Governor General and the Lieutenant Governor is answered by a plain reading of s. 55 of the *Constitution Act, 1867*. The challenges based upon the *Canadian Charter of Rights and Freedoms* are answered by s. 25 of the *Charter*.

RESULT

[185] In the result, I find the Nisga'a Final Agreement, and the settlement legislation passed by Parliament and the Legislative Assembly of the

Province of British Columbia, establish a treaty as contemplated by Section 35 of the *Constitution Act, 1982*. The legislation and the Treaty are constitutionally valid. The application for a declaration that the settlement legislation and the Treaty are in part void and of no effect is dismissed.

H. CONCLUSION

The facilitation and implementation of more ample forms of Aboriginal governance have been very slow in coming. Respect for and acceptance of Aboriginal governance has not been easy to accomplish, even though historic precedent would allow it and contemporary instruments in domestic and international law can accommodate it. For many who struggle from day to day under intolerable conditions the pace of change is painstakingly slow. Decades have passed since Prime Minister Pierre Trudeau attempted to eliminate Indian rights in Canada via the 1969 White Paper. As excerpted above, Harold Cardinal's book *The Unjust Society* was a response to the White Paper intended to refute this drive. He described the denial of Indian citizenship and governance rights that faced Aboriginal people at that time. His message captured the feelings of Aboriginal people across Canada. He chronicled a disturbing tale of how Indians were marginalized through bureaucratic neglect, political indifference and societal ignorance. He labelled Canada's treatment of Indians as "cultural genocide", and, in the process, gave widespread literary presence to the absence of Indian rights. In convincing tones he outlined thoughtful solutions to overcome threats to Aboriginal governance, organized around the central theme of Indian control of Indian affairs. His work in proposing the contours for Aboriginal governance was ground-breaking. He advocated the strengthening of Indian organizations, the abolition of the Department of Indian Affairs, educational reform, restructured social institutions, broad-based economic development and the "immediate recognition of all Indian rights for the re-establishment, review and renewal of all existing Indian treaties". Cardinal's ideas resonated within Indian country and parallel proposals became the mainstay of Indian political discourse for the next three decades.

Three decades later the massive five-volume *Report of the Royal Commission on Aboriginal Peoples* ("RCAP report") was released. It contained many of the same ideas Cardinal had put forward a generation earlier. The Commission provided an account of the violation of Aboriginal rights and called for their immediate recognition and renewal. The Report recorded the continued diminishment of Aboriginal control over their affairs of life and governance. It also indicated that the problems Cardinal profiled so many years previously stubbornly remained in existence. Despite some notable achievements in the intervening years, such as the recognition and affirmation of Aboriginal rights in the Constitution, the RCAP report illustrated how Indigenous citizenship is increasingly tenuous.

In their broad outlines, Cardinal and the RCAP report's messages are remarkably similar. Aboriginal people are suffering, their rights are being abrogated, and the answer to this challenge is Aboriginal control of Aboriginal affairs. Like Cardinal, though more elaborately and expansively, the RCAP report recommended a series of legislative and policy goals, including: the strengthening of Aboriginal nations; the abolition of the Department of Indian Affairs; educational reform; restructured social institutions; broad-based economic development; and the immediate recognition of all Aboriginal rights for the re-establishment, review, renewal and creation of treaties.

It has now been more than 15 years since the RCAP report was released. Little progress in the field of Aboriginal governance has been made in this period. In fact, it is arguable that valuable momentum has been lost. The *Indian Act* still grinds its assimilative ways and threatens the entire fabric of First Nations' life. Only a few communities have escaped its racist grasp through negotiated self-government agreements. For most of Canada's 634 bands, though, the *Indian Act* retains its disturbing and twisted hold. Furthermore, Métis people and their governance have been virtually ignored by governments throughout this entire period.

The contemporary dynamics of legal, political, economic and social power place non-Aboriginal governments in a domineering position relative to Aboriginal governments. Unburdening Aboriginal governance from the constrictions and obstacles they encounter will continue to be a great challenge. The traditional laws, values and principles that guided Aboriginal people in their past, and which still have a great presence in many communities today, are stifled by alien institutions and ideologies. Acceptance of these laws by non-Aboriginal governments is also restrained by bias and prejudice that discounts the authenticity and utility of these ancient legal genealogies. Yet Indigenous legal traditions are strong, dynamic and can be interpreted flexibly to deal with the pressing issues Aboriginal communities encounter. Their principles can be drawn from ancient stories, customs and codes, historic agreements with the Crown, Canadian common law, constitutional law and contemporary international instruments. They can be implemented through proclamation, direct action, litigation and negotiation. The existing framework of the *Indian Act* does not provide a sound base on which to build healthy and productive communities. Aboriginal law and philosophies can — and should — be given a more central place within First Nations communities. Historic agreements could be recognized and affirmed as a base upon which contemporary relations with Canadian levels of government can be forged. Section 35(1) of the *Constitution Act* should be interpreted in a broad and generous way to recognize and affirm an inherent jurisdictional base for First Nations governance. This chapter has introduced these significant issues in the hope that further critical and constructive inquiry can illuminate the path for the achievement of effective Aboriginal governance.

ENDNOTES

1.   (1992) 12 Windsor Y.B. Access. Just. 179 at 191-92 (references omitted).
2.   The structure of this overview follows the outline of the Great Law of Peace found at <http://www.sixnations.org/Great_Law_of_Peace/> (date accessed: May 7, 2007).
3.   NAC RGIO, Red Series, volume 1995, file 6897, MR C11130, 17 August 1876 [original spelling and punctuation preserved]; cited in The *Report of the Royal Commission on Aboriginal Peoples, Looking Forward, Looking Back, Vol. 1* (Ottawa: Supply and Services, 1996), at 182.
4.   Appeal of the Six Nations to the League, *League of Nations Official Journal*, June 24, 1924, 829-837.
5.   *Report of the Royal Commission on Aboriginal Peoples: Looking Forward, Looking Back,* Vol. 1, Chapter 9 — The Indian Act (Ottawa: Ministry of Supply and Services, 1996) at 317 (references omitted).
6.   Harold Cardinal, *The Unjust Society: The Tragedy of Canada's Indians* (Edmonton: Hurtig, 1969) at 140.
7.   Indian Nations as Reserve Sovereigns, *Indian Country Today* (June 13, 2003).

ABORIGINAL RIGHTS

A. INTRODUCTION

The earliest practitioners of law in North America were its original Indigenous inhabitants. These peoples are known as the Aboriginal peoples of the continent. There are over one million people of Aboriginal ancestry in Canada today. They are members of ancient nations that pre-existed the arrival of the French, British and other early settlers that initiated the Dominion of Canada. The term Aboriginal conceals the great diversity among peoples and includes, among others, the ancient and contemporary nations of the Mi'kmaq, Maliseet, Abenaki, Innu, Cree, Anishinabek, Haudenosaunee, Wendat, Dakota, Lakota, Nakota, Assinaboine, Saulteaux, Blackfoot, Kootenay Secwepemec, Nlha7kapmx, Salish, Nuu-Chah-Nulth, Kwakwaka'wakw, Haida, Heiltsuk, Carrier, Tsimshian, Nisga'a, Gitksan, Tahltan, Tlingit, Gwichin, Dene, Inuit and Métis. Indigenous peoples' traditions could be as historically different from one another as other nations and cultures in the world. For example, Canadian Indigenous peoples speak over 50 different Aboriginal languages from 11 distinct language families, which have as wide a variation as do the language families of Europe and Asia. These nations' linguistic, genealogical, political and legal descent can be traced back through millennia to different regions or territories in northern North America. This explains the wide variety of laws between Indigenous groups.

Aboriginal rights exist because they are derived from Aboriginal laws, governance, practices, customs and traditions. They exist in Canadian law not as a result of governmental recognition, but because they were not extinguished upon British or French assertions of sovereignty or establishment of governmental authority in what is now Canada. Aboriginal rights are therefore unlike other forms of rights that exist in Canadian society. Aboriginal rights are a part of Canadian common law and Canadian constitutional law, even though they did not arise under these regimes. Thus, Aboriginal rights also continue to be protected and reflected in Aboriginal legal systems.

Canada is a multi-juridical country. The interaction of common law, civil law and Indigenous legal systems demonstrate Canada's deep legal pluralism. Aboriginal rights have sometimes been described as "rights plus", insofar as they exist in addition to Aboriginal people's other common law, civil law or Indigenous legal system's rights. This chapter attempts to provide context for the appreciation of the unique nature of Aboriginal rights and their place within the Canadian constitutional order.

B. ABORIGINAL PEOPLES, CANADA AND THE CONSTITUTION

Despite the prior and continued existence of Aboriginal rights, Canada's Constitution has not generally protected Aboriginal peoples as individuals or groups. For most of the country's history Aboriginal government has been suppressed, land denied, treaty rights ignored, children forcibly taken, and traditional economic pursuits criminalized. There has been a negation of rights of religious freedom, association, due process and equality. The failure of Canada's Constitution to limit federal and provincial interference with Aboriginal rights has often greatly harmed Aboriginal communities.

1. Canadian Constitutional Sources

The "Dominion" of Canada was initially formed by the union of three British colonies in 1867: Canada (consisting of Ontario and Quebec), Nova Scotia and New Brunswick. Its architects chose not to itemize all constitutional powers in one document. Canada's Constitution comprises various written texts, an assortment of established practices and a diverse array of oral traditions. The open nature of Canada's Constitution is mandated by the preamble to the *British North America Act, 1867* (now the *Constitution Act, 1867*) which established it as "a Constitution similar in Principle to that of the United Kingdom". The United Kingdom's Constitution is largely unwritten and draws upon customs, conventions and deeply embedded principles to structure government. Since Canada's Constitution is similar in principle to that of the United Kingdom it is obvious that Canada's Constitution also contains many unwritten terms.

Aboriginal rights could be considered one organizing feature of Canada's unwritten constitution. A recent British Columbia judgment found that the unique relationship between Aboriginal peoples and the Crown is an "underlying constitutional value" that can be given the force of law (*Campbell v. British Columbia (Attorney General)*, [2000] B.C.J. No. 1524, 189 D.L.R. (4th) 333 (B.C.S.C.) at para. 81, as reproduced in Chapter 1). Despite Canada's unwritten constitutional traditions, the conventional view of early constitution-making in Canada has concentrated on formal British Imperial instruments. This focus has not served Aboriginal peoples well. Section 91(24) of the *Constitution Act, 1867* is the only provision to deal with Aboriginal peoples and has provided only minimal protection for their rights.

2. Constitutional Suspicions

As a result of the minimal protection of Aboriginal rights in the *Constitution Act, 1867*, Aboriginal groups have regarded Canada's Constitution with great suspicion. A deep distrust of the Canadian state has made it very challenging for Aboriginal leaders to present Canadian constitutional reform to their people in a positive light. Most Aboriginal people have been very wary of constitutional reform because of the government's repeated attempts to forcibly eliminate Aboriginal languages, laws, land, government and culture. They wonder why they should desire greater incorporation within a state that has almost shattered Aboriginal ways of life and community structures. Thus, many have concerns that the constitutionalization of Aboriginal rights could lead to a further erosion of Indigenous languages, cultures and governments. In fact, many Aboriginal peoples regard constitutional entrenchment as an attack on their inherent rights as peoples and feel that their distinct legal personality is potentially undermined through such provisions. This is particularly so for those First Nations who signed historic treaties with the British Crown, a nation separate from Canada. They regard their incorporation within Canada's Constitution as a breach of these international obligations, particularly since they were not consulted about this constitutional framework change. At the same time, Aboriginal people who have not signed treaties sometimes regard themselves as being outside of the Canadian legal framework. They resent being forcibly included within its structures without their consent. Thus, constitutional reform has not always been regarded as a universal good by Aboriginal peoples, even if the goal of formalized entrenchment of Aboriginal rights in Canada's highest written laws seems positive.

3.   Constitutional Discussions

There have been numerous attempts to reform Canada's Constitution since 1867. Until 1982 Canada's written Constitution could not be amended without legislative action by the British Parliament (where Canada's constitutional statutes resided). These statutes included the *Constitution Act, 1867*, numerous amendments, various statutes admitting different colonies into Confederation, and the *Statute of Westminister, 1931*, which gave Canada equality and a broader degree of legislative independence from Great Britain. While the *Statute of Westminister* gave Canada some independence, it still did not allow for the amendment of Canada's written Constitution without British Parliamentary agreement. For most Canadians, the lack of a domestic amending formula led them to seek constitutional reform in 1935-1936, 1950, 1960-61, and 1964. Aboriginal peoples did not take part in any of these initiatives.

In 1968, the Liberal government of the day (under Prime Minister Pierre Trudeau) sought to introduce issues broader than patriation into the constitutional debate, such as changes to governmental institutions, distribution of powers, and the entrenchment of a Bill of Rights. There was no discussion of constitutional protection for Aboriginal rights during this period. In fact, the federal government seemed to have planned the exact opposite for Aboriginal peoples. The infamous White Paper of 1969 explicitly proposed the assimilation of Aboriginal peoples and the elimination of treaty rights and any other special or separate status. This initiative was regarded by most Aboriginal peoples in the worst possible light. It was deemed a great offence and has been described as "the single most powerful catalyst of the Indian nationalist movement".[1] Although the White Paper was never implemented, it played an important role by mobilizing Aboriginal peoples and facilitating the development of many Aboriginal political organizations to resist Canadian initiatives aimed at assimilation.

Despite Aboriginal opposition to the White Paper, wider constitutional debate continued. In 1971, the provinces and federal government obtained a tentative agreement on broader constitutional principles in a document called the Victoria Charter. Once again, there was no mention of Aboriginal issues. Ultimately, however, consensus over the Victoria Charter broke down because of changes in political leadership and concerns about Quebec's reaction to specific income security provisions. Other attempts to patriate the Constitution in the mid 1970s also ended in failure. Aboriginal peoples were largely shut out of these constitutional discussions and were not very supportive of the entire enterprise.

4. Constitutional Amendment: Strategies and Debates

In 1978, constitutional reform once again came to the forefront of Canadian political life. Since Aboriginal people did not feel included in constitutional processes and distrusted the Canadian government they presented a considerable threat to reform. They held parallel meetings and resisted the domestication of their rights through advocacy in the United Kingdom. The Union of British Columbia Indians resolved to organize a "Constitutional Express" which travelled from Vancouver to Ottawa to raise awareness of their position. This event eventually attracted 500 participants. When the Express arrived in Ottawa it generated a great deal of press coverage. The arrival also corresponded with a meeting of 2,000 other Indians, hosted by the Assembly of First Nations, which generated further media attention. The group drafted a *Declaration of the First Nations* and presented it to the Governor General as a statement of their inherent rights, independent from Canada's control. It was also decided that some members of the Express would continue on to New York, London and Rotterdam to create international pressure against constitutionalization without their consent. Finally, the Assembly of First Nations resolved it would not participate in a Special Joint Committee meeting on the Constitution because governmental recognition of its position was lacking.

In the summer of 1981, the Indian Association of Alberta commenced litigation before the English Courts disputing the erosion of their nation-to-nation relationship with the United Kingdom. Their core arguments were that while treaties were domestic agreements, the British Crown had never explicitly transferred responsibility for Indians to Canada, making treaty implementation Britain's continuing responsibility. First Nations organizations from Saskatchewan and British Columbia did not participate in this case because of differences in opinion on legal strategy. The Federation of Saskatchewan Indian Nations did not agree that their treaties were domestic agreements, and the Union of British Columbia Indians argued that the treaties were a part of Canada's constitutional order, but that their consent was needed to patriate the Constitution.

Despite a strong campaign in England, Lord Denning M.R. of the English Court of Appeal rejected the Alberta Indians' arguments. In *R. v. Secretary of State for Foreign and Commonwealth Affairs, ex parte Indian Association of Alberta and Others*, [1982] 2 All E.R. 118 at 128 (C.A.), he found that:

> ... the Crown was no longer single and indivisible. It was separate and divisible for each self-governing dominion or province or territory.

> ... Thus, the obligations to which the Crown bound itself in the Royal Proclamation of 1763 are now to be confined to the territories to which they related and binding on the Crown only in respect of those territories. None of them is any longer binding on the Crown in respect of the United Kingdom.

Meanwhile back in Canada the provinces also failed to persuade the courts that their consent to constitutional patriation was needed. On September 28, 1981, the Supreme Court of Canada wrote, in *Reference re Amendment of the Constitution Act of Canada*, [1981] S.C.J. No. 58, [1981] 1 S.C.R. 753 (S.C.C.), that a "unilateral" patriation of the Constitution by the federal government was legal. However, it also noted that a "substantial degree" of provincial consent was required by constitutional convention before the federal-provincial relationship could be fundamentally altered by a request to Britain for constitutional amendment. The Court's politically astute judgment, coupled with the pressure created by Aboriginal peoples in Britain, sent the federal government back to the bargaining table with the provinces, with an additional promise to include Aboriginal and treaty rights in the final document.

Unfortunately, when the provinces and federal government sat down to negotiate on November 5, 1981, Aboriginal rights were dropped from the tabled accord. Aboriginal groups were shocked by this development. Provincial pressure and federal timidity were the cause of this troubling set-back. This turn of events placed the National Indian Brotherhood ("NIB"), the forerunner of the Assembly of First Nations, in a tenuous position with its membership. Since the NIB was uncertain about whether it could support the reinstatement of Aboriginal provisions in the Constitution without full First Nations backing, the political initiative was taken by other Aboriginal groups with much smaller memberships. It was led by such organizations as the Native Council of Canada, the Inuit Committee on National Issues, the Native Woman's Association of Canada, the Dene Nation and the Council of Yukon Indians under the banner of the Aboriginal Rights Coalition ("ARC"). The federal government responded positively to ARC's submissions, but insisted it could not act without provincial consent. This response resulted in a series of large Indian demonstrations in nine cities across Canada to protest the provincial position. The provinces reacted to this pressure and reconsidered their position on Aboriginal rights, eventually agreeing to their reintroduction in the accord. Thus, while most Indigenous peoples (particularly Indian Bands) did not want their rights domesticated in a

Canadian constitutional document, strategic protests by other Indigenous groups somewhat ironically facilitated constitutional inclusion.

5. Constitutional Entrenchment

On April 17, 1982, Aboriginal and treaty rights officially became a part of Canada's written Constitution. Section 35 in Part II of the *Constitution Act, 1982*, being Schedule B to the *Canada Act 1982* (U.K.), 1982, c. 11, came into force and originally read as follows:

> (1) The existing Aboriginal and Treaty Rights of the Aboriginal Peoples of Canada are hereby recognized and affirmed.
>
> (2) In this Act, "aboriginal peoples of Canada" includes the Indian, Inuit and Metis peoples of Canada.

In addition to section 35, which was intended to provide a substantive guarantee of rights, section 25 was included in Part I of the *Constitution Act, 1982* to provide, *inter alia*, important context for the interpretation of section 35 and its place in the Canadian constitutional order:

> The guarantee in this Charter of certain rights and freedoms shall not be construed so as to abrogate or derogate from any aboriginal, treaty or other rights or freedoms that pertain to the aboriginal peoples of Canada including
>
> > (a) any rights or freedoms that have been recognized by the Royal Proclamation of October 7, 1763;

As well, section 37 was added, which provided that:

> (1) A constitutional conference composed of the Prime Minister of Canada and the first ministers of the provinces shall be convened by the Prime Minister of Canada within one year after this Part comes into force.
>
> (2) The conference convened under subsection (1) shall have included in its agenda an item respecting constitutional matters that directly affect the aboriginal peoples of Canada, including the identification and definition of the rights of those peoples to be included in the Constitution of Canada, and the Prime Minister of Canada shall invite representatives of those peoples to participate in the discussions on that item. (3) The Prime Minister of Canada shall invite elected representatives of the governments of the Yukon Territory and the Northwest Territories to participate in the discussions on any item on the agenda of the conference convened under subsection (1) that, in the opinion of the Prime Minister, directly affects the Yukon Territory and the Northwest Territories.

The first constitutional conference in 1983 mandated under section 37, produced amendments to sections 35 and 25 of the *Constitution Act, 1982*. As a result of negotiations and agreement during this conference, subsections 35(3) and (4), 25(*b*) and 37.1(1) were added to the *Constitution Act, 1982* by the *Constitution Amendment Proclamation, 1983*. Thereafter Section 35 contained additional amendments which more accurately reflected the breadth of its application in the present and into the future:

> (3) For greater certainty, in subsection (1) "treaty rights" includes rights that now exist by way of land claims agreements or may be so acquired.

(4) Notwithstanding any other provision of this Act, the aboriginal and treaty rights referred to in subsection (1) are guaranteed equally to male and female persons.

Section 25 was amended by inserting an additional qualification that *Charter* rights were not to be construed as abrogating or derogating from:

any rights or freedoms that may be acquired by the aboriginal peoples of Canada by way of land claims settlement.

Finally, section 37 was amended to provide for an additional two First Ministers conferences with Aboriginal organizations. These provisions, sections 25, 35 and 37 of the *Constitution Act, 1982*, became the primary sections identifying Aboriginal and treaty rights in Canada's written Constitution, along with section 91(24) of the *Constitution Act, 1867*.

6. The Future

The effects of formally constitutionalizing Aboriginal and treaty rights are still being analyzed more than a generation after their entrenchment. It is still too early to tell whether, on balance, the entrenchment of Aboriginal rights was a positive development that will benefit Aboriginal peoples. On the positive side, as we will see, section 35(1) appears to prevent Canada from unilaterally *extinguishing* Aboriginal and treaty rights. On the negative side, the Crown's broad power to *infringe* Aboriginal and treaty rights seems to undermine much of the autonomy and powers of governance many were seeking prior to section 35's entrenchment. Furthermore, constitutionalization seems to have led some Canadians to believe that Aboriginal peoples' rights are best protected through Canadian constitutional instruments. Since a large number of Aboriginal people do not share this opinion, the future will likely be clouded by continuing disputes over this issue.

C. THE CHARACTERIZATION OF ABORIGINAL RIGHTS BY THE COURTS

In many instances pre-existing Aboriginal rights were not abrogated by Canada's Constitution; rather, they were affirmed through treaties and historical practices. Aboriginal rights remained in place and were, in fact, received into British law by a process known as the Doctrine of Continuity.[2] For example, in *Connolly v. Woolrich* (1867), 17 R.J.R.Q. 75 (Que. S.C.), discussed in Chapter 1 and reported during the first year of Canada's confederation, the Quebec Superior Court affirmed the existence of Cree law on the Prairies and recognized it as part of the common law. Justice Monk wrote, at 79:

Will it be contended that the territorial rights, political organization such as it was, or the laws and usages of Indian tribes were abrogated — that they ceased to exist when these two European nations began to trade with [A]boriginal occupants? In my opinion it is beyond controversy that they did not — that so far from being abolished, they were left in full force, and were not even modified in the slightest degree. ....

The courts have held there was no widespread extinguishment of Aboriginal rights through military conquest, occupation or legislative enactment. As the Supreme Court has observed, "European settlement did not terminate the interests of Aboriginal peoples arising from their historical occupation and use of the land. To the contrary, Aboriginal interests and customary laws were presumed to survive the assertion of sovereignty…" (*R. v. Mitchell*, [2001] S.C.J. No. 33, [2001] 1 S.C.R. 911 (S.C.C.) at para. 8). The Court has also held that: "Aboriginal peoples were here when Europeans came, and were never conquered" (*Haida Nation v. British Columbia (Minister of Forests)*, [2004] S.C.J. No. 70, [2004] 3 S.C.R. 511 (S.C.C.) at para. 25). Thus, Aboriginal rights and Indigenous laws continue to exist in Canada unless, as McLachlin C.J.C. wrote in *Mitchell*: "(1) they were incompatible with the Crown's assertion of sovereignty, (2) they were surrendered voluntarily via the treaty process, or (3) the government extinguished them". Barring one of these exceptions, the practices, customs and traditions that defined the various Aboriginal societies as distinctive cultures continue as part of the law of Canada today.

Whether received into the common law through treaties or under the Doctrine of Continuity, Aboriginal rights are enforceable under the common law. The extent to which the common law recognized and enforced these rights, however, was rather limited in practice until after 1982, as noted above.

Since Aboriginal rights exist because of circumstances that arose independently of Europeans' arrival in North America, it would appear logical that the existence of Aboriginal rights would not be dependent upon their recognition by European governments or laws. Yet, Canadian courts have only recently recognized that the existence of those rights is not dependent upon such positive, external recognition.

One of the first cases to recognize that Aboriginal rights had an independent existence and did not have to be recognized by the common law or governmental authority was *Calder v. British Columbia (Attorney General)*, [1973] S.C.J. No. 56, [1973] S.C.R. 313, [1973] 4 W.W.R. 1, 34 D.L.R. (3d) 145 (S.C.C.), which is reproduced in Chapter 3. The same assertion was made more recently in Lamer C.J.C.'s majority judgment in the Supreme Court of Canada's decision in *R. v. Adams*, [1996] 3 S.C.R. 101, [1996] 4 C.N.L.R. 1 (S.C.C.) at para. 33:

> … [T]he fact that a particular practice, custom or tradition continued following the arrival of Europeans, but in the absence of the formal gloss of legal recognition from the European colonizers, should not undermine the protection accorded to aboriginal peoples. Section 35(1) would fail to achieve its noble purpose of preserving the integral and defining features of distinctive aboriginal societies if it only protected those defining features which were fortunate enough to have received the legal approval of British and French colonizers.[3]

The *Adams* decision and its companion case *R. v. Côté*, [1996] S.C.J. No. 93, [1996] 3 S.C.R. 139, 202 N.R. 161, 138 D.L.R. (4th) 385, 110 C.C.C. (3d) 122, [1996] 4 C.N.L.R. 26 (S.C.C.) are excerpted later in this chapter.

One of the leading cases on the understanding of Aboriginal rights in Canadian law is *R. v. Sparrow*. The *Sparrow* case focused on the ability of fishing regulations enacted pursuant to the federal *Fisheries Act*, R.S.C. 1970, c. F-14 (now R.S.C. 1985, c. F-14) to restrict the ability of an Aboriginal person to exercise Aboriginal fishing rights. Through its discussion of section 35 of the *Constitution Act, 1982*, the *Sparrow* case initiated an entirely new context for the appreciation and protection of Aboriginal rights in Canada.

R. v. SPARROW

[1990] S.C.J. No. 49, [1990] 1 S.C.R. 1075, 70 D.L.R. (4th) 385,
[1990] 4 W.W.R. 410, 46 B.C.L.R. (2d) 1, 56 C.C.C. (3d) 263,
11 N.R. 241, [1990] 3 C.N.L.R. 160 (S.C.C.)

The judgment of the court was delivered by

Dickson C.J.C. and **La Forest J.**: —

. . . . .

The context of this appeal is the alleged violation of the terms of the Musqueam food fishing licence which are dictated by the *Fisheries Act*, R.S.C. 1970, c. F-14, and the regulations under that Act. The issue is whether Parliament's power to regulate fishing is now limited by s. 35(1) of the *Constitution Act, 1982*, and, more specifically, whether the net length restriction in the licence is inconsistent with that provision.

Facts

The appellant, a member of the Musqueam Indian Band, was charged under s. 61(1) of the *Fisheries Act* of the offence of fishing with a drift-net longer than that permitted by the terms of the band's Indian food fishing licence. The fishing which gave rise to the charge took place on May 25, 1984 in Canoe Passage which is part of the area subject to the band's licence. The licence, which had been issued for a one-year period beginning March 31, 1984, set out a number of restrictions including one that drift-nets were to be limited to 25 fathoms in length. The appellant was caught with a net which was 45 fathoms in length. He has throughout admitted the facts alleged to constitute the offence, but has defended the charge on the basis that he was exercising an existing aboriginal right to fish and that the net length restriction contained in the band's licence is inconsistent with s. 35(1) of the *Constitution Act, 1982* and therefore invalid.

. . . . .

The Appeal

... On November 24, 1987, the following constitutional question was stated:

Is the net length restriction contained in the Musqueam Indian Band Indian Food Fishing Licence dated March 30, 1984, issued pursuant to the *British Columbia Fishery (General) Regulations* and the *Fisheries Act*, R.S.C. 1970, c. F-14, inconsistent with s. 35(1) of the *Constitution Act, 1982*?

. . . . .

Analysis

We will address first the meaning of "existing" aboriginal rights and the content and scope of the Musqueam right to fish. We will then turn to the meaning of "recognized and affirmed", and the impact of s. 35(1) on the regulatory power of Parliament.

"Existing"

The word "existing" makes it clear that the rights to which s. 35(1) applies are those that were in existence when the *Constitution Act, 1982* came into effect. This means that extinguished rights are not revived by the *Constitution Act, 1982*. A number of courts have taken the position that "existing" means being in actuality in 1982.

. . . . .

Further, an existing aboriginal right cannot be read so as to incorporate the specific manner in which it was regulated before 1982. The notion of freezing existing rights would incorporate into the Constitution a crazy patchwork of regulations. Blair J.A. in *Agawa, supra* [(1988), 53 D.L.R. (4th) 101 (S.C.C.)] had this to say about the matter:

> Some academic commentators have raised a further problem which cannot be ignored. The *Ontario Fishery Regulations* contain detailed rules which vary for different regions in the province. Among other things, the *Regulations* specify seasons and methods of fishing, species of fish which can be caught and catch limits. Similar detailed provisions apply under the comparable fisheries *Regulations* in force in other provinces. These detailed provisions might be constitutionalized if it were decided that the existing treaty rights referred to in s. 35(1) were those remaining after regulation at the time of the proclamation of the *Constitution Act, 1982*.

As noted by Blair J.A., academic commentary lends support to the conclusion that "existing" means "unextinguished" rather than exercisable at a certain time in history. Professor Slattery, "Understanding Aboriginal Rights" (1987), 66 Can. Bar Rev. 727, at pp. 781-82, has observed the following about reading regulations into the rights:

> This approach reads into the Constitution the myriad of regulations affecting the exercise of aboriginal rights, regulations that differed considerably from place to place across the country. It does not permit differentiation between regulations of long-term significance and those enacted to deal with temporary conditions, or between reasonable and unreasonable restrictions. Moreover, it might require that a constitutional

amendment be enacted to implement regulations more stringent than those in existence on 17 April 1982. This solution seems unsatisfactory.

. . . . .

The unsuitability of the approach can also be seen from another perspective. Ninety-one other tribes of Indians, comprising over 20,000 people (compared with 540 Musqueam on the reserve and 100 others off the reserve) obtain their food fish from the Fraser River. Some or all of these bands may have an aboriginal right to fish there. A constitutional patchwork quilt would be created if the constitutional right of these bands were to be determined by the specific regime available to each of those bands in 1982.

Far from being defined according to the regulatory scheme in place in 1982, the phrase "existing aboriginal rights" must be interpreted flexibly so as to permit their evolution over time. To use Professor Slattery's expression, in "Understanding Aboriginal Rights," *ibid.*, at p. 782, the word "existing" suggests that those rights are "affirmed in a contemporary form rather than in their primeval simplicity and vigour". Clearly, then, an approach to the constitutional guarantee embodied in s. 35(1) which would incorporate "frozen rights" must be rejected.

The Aboriginal Right

We turn now to the aboriginal right at stake in this appeal. The Musqueam Indian Reserve is located on the north shore of the Fraser River close to the mouth of that river and within the limits of the City of Vancouver. There has been a Musqueam village there for hundreds of years. This appeal does not directly concern the reserve or the adjacent waters, but arises out of the band's right to fish in another area of the Fraser River estuary known as Canoe Passage in the South Arm of the river, some 16 kilometres (about 10 miles) from the reserve. The reserve and those waters are separated by the Vancouver International Airport and the Municipality of Richmond.

The evidence reveals that the Musqueam have lived in the area as an organized society long before the coming of European settlers, and that the taking of salmon was an integral part of their lives and remains so to this day. Much of the evidence of an aboriginal right to fish was given by Dr. Suttles, an anthropologist, supported by that of Mr. Grant, the Band administrator. The Court of Appeal thus summarized Dr. Suttles' evidence:

> Dr. Suttles was qualified as having particular qualifications in respect of the ethnography of the Coast Salish Indian people of which the Musqueams were one of several tribes. He thought that the Musqueam had lived in their historic territory, which includes the Fraser River estuary, for at least 1,500 years. That historic territory extended from the north shore of Burrard Inlet to the south shore of the main channel of the Fraser River including the waters of the three channels by which that river reaches the ocean. As part of the Salish people, the Musqueam were part of a regional social network

covering a much larger area but, as a tribe, were themselves an organized social group with their own name, territory and resources. Between the tribes there was a flow of people, wealth and food. No tribe was wholly self-sufficient or occupied its territory to the complete exclusion of others.

Dr. Suttles described the special position occupied by the salmon fishery in that society. The salmon was not only an important source of food but played an important part in the system of beliefs of the Salish people, and in their ceremonies. The salmon were held to be a race of beings that had, in "myth times", established a bond with human beings requiring the salmon to come each year to give their bodies to the humans who, in turn, treated them with respect shown by performance of the proper ritual. Toward the salmon, as toward other creatures, there was an attitude of caution and respect which resulted in effective conservation of the various species.

While the trial for a violation of a penal prohibition may not be the most appropriate setting in which to determine the existence of an aboriginal right, and the evidence was not extensive, the correctness of the finding of fact of the trial judge "that Mr. Sparrow was fishing in ancient tribal territory where his ancestors had fished from time immemorial in that part of the mouth of the Fraser River for salmon" is supported by the evidence and was not contested. The existence of the right, the Court of Appeal tells us, was "not the subject of serious dispute". It is not surprising, then, that, taken with other circumstances, that court should find that "the judgment appealed from was wrong in . . . failing to hold that Sparrow at the relevant time was exercising an existing aboriginal right".

In this Court, however, the respondent contested the Court of Appeal's finding, contending that the evidence was insufficient to discharge the appellant's burden of proof upon the issue. It is true that for the period from 1867 to 1961 the evidence is scanty. But the evidence was not disputed or contradicted in the courts below and there is evidence of sufficient continuity of the right to support the Court of Appeal's finding, and we would not disturb it.

What the Crown really insisted on, both in this Court and the courts below, was that the Musqueam Band's aboriginal right to fish had been extinguished by regulations under the *Fisheries Act*.

[The Court then summarized the progressive restriction and regulation of the fisheries.]

It is this progressive restriction and detailed regulation of the fisheries which, respondent's counsel maintained, have had the effect of extinguishing any aboriginal right to fish. The extinguishment need not be express, he argued, but may take place where the sovereign authority is exercised in a manner "necessarily inconsistent" with the continued enjoyment of aboriginal rights. ... The consent to its extinguishment before the *Constitution Act, 1982* was not required; the intent of the sovereign could be effected not only by statute but by valid regulations. Here, in his view, the regulations had entirely displaced any aboriginal right. There is, he submitted, a fundamental inconsistency between the communal right to fish embodied in the aboriginal right, and fishing under a special licence or permit issued to individual Indians (as was the case until 1977) in the discretion of the Minister and subject to terms and conditions which, if breached, may result in cancellation of the licence. The *Fisheries Act* and its regulations were, he argued, intended to constitute a complete code inconsistent with the continued existence of an aboriginal right.

At bottom, the respondent's argument confuses regulation with extinguishment. That the right is controlled in great detail by the regulations does not mean that the right is thereby extinguished.

. . . . .

The test of extinguishment to be adopted, in our opinion, is that the sovereign's intention must be clear and plain if it is to extinguish an aboriginal right.

There is nothing in the *Fisheries Act* or its detailed regulations that demonstrates a clear and plain intention to extinguish the Indian aboriginal right to fish. The fact that express provision permitting the Indians to fish for food may have applied to all Indians and that for an extended period permits were discretionary and issued on an individual rather than a communal basis in no way shows a clear intention to extinguish. These permits were simply a manner of controlling the fisheries, not defining underlying rights.

We would conclude then that the Crown has failed to discharge its burden of proving extinguishment. In our opinion, the Court of Appeal made no mistake in holding that the Indians have an existing aboriginal right to fish in the area where Mr. Sparrow was fishing at the time of the charge. This approach is consistent with ensuring that an aboriginal right should not be defined by incorporating the ways in which it has been regulated in the past.

The scope of the existing Musqueam right to fish must now be delineated. The anthropological evidence relied on to establish the existence of the right suggests that, for the Musqueam, the salmon fishery has always constituted an integral part of their distinctive culture. Its significant role involved not only consumption for subsistence purposes, but also consumption of salmon on ceremonial and social occasions. The Musqueam have always fished for reasons connected to their cultural and physical survival. As we stated earlier, the right to do so may be exercised in a contemporary manner.

The British Columbia Court of Appeal in this case held that the aboriginal right was to fish for food purposes, but that purpose was not to be confined to mere subsistence. Rather, the right was found to extend to fish consumed for social and ceremonial activities. The Court of Appeal thereby defined the right as protecting the same interest as is reflected in the government's food fish policy.

. . . . .

[I]t was contended before this Court that the aboriginal right extends to commercial fishing. While no commercial fishery existed prior to the arrival of European settlers, it is contended that the Musqueam practice of bartering in early society may be revived as a modern right to fish for commercial purposes. The presence of numerous interveners representing commercial fishing interests, and the suggestion on the facts that the net length restriction is at least in part related to the probable commercial use of fish caught under the Musqueam food fishing licence, indicate the possibility of conflict between aboriginal fishing and the competitive commercial fishery with respect to economically valuable fish such as salmon. We recognize the existence of this conflict and the probability of its intensification as fish availability drops, demand rises and tensions increase.

Government regulations governing the exercise of the Musqueam right to fish, as described above, have only recognized the right to fish *for food* for over a hundred years. This may have reflected the existing position. However, historical policy on the part of the Crown is not only incapable of extinguishing the existing aboriginal right without clear intention, but is also incapable of, in itself, delineating that right. The nature of government regulations cannot be determinative of the content and scope of an existing aboriginal right. Government policy *can* however regulate the exercise of that right, but such regulation must be in keeping with s. 35(1).

In the courts below, the case at bar was not presented on the footing of an aboriginal right to fish for commercial or livelihood purposes. Rather, the focus was and continues to be on the validity of a net length restriction affecting the appellant's *food fishing licence*. We therefore adopt the Court of Appeal's characterization of the right for the purpose of this appeal, and confine our reasons to the meaning of the constitutional recognition and affirmation of the existing aboriginal right to fish for food and social and ceremonial purposes.

"Recognized and Affirmed"

We now turn to the impact of s. 35(1) of the *Constitution Act, 1982* on the regulatory power of Parliament and on the outcome of this appeal specifically.

. . . . .

[I]n finding the appropriate interpretive framework for s. 35(1), we start by looking at the background of s. 35(1).

It is worth recalling that while British policy towards the native population was based on respect for their right to occupy their traditional lands, a proposition to which the Royal Proclamation of 1763 bears witness, there was from the outset never any doubt that sovereignty and legislative power, and indeed the underlying title, to such lands vested in the Crown.... And there can be no doubt that over the years the rights of the Indians were often honoured in the breach.

. . . . .

For many years, the rights of the Indians to their aboriginal lands —
certainly as *legal* rights — were virtually ignored. The leading cases
defining Indian rights in the early part of the century were directed at
claims supported by the Royal Proclamation or other legal instruments,
and even these cases were essentially concerned with settling legislative
jurisdiction or the rights of commercial enterprises. For fifty years after the
publication of Clement's *The Law of the Canadian Constitution*, 3rd ed.
(1916), there was a virtual absence of discussion of any kind of Indian
rights to land even in academic literature. By the late 1960s, aboriginal
claims were not even recognized by the federal government as having any
legal status. Thus the *Statement of the Government of Canada on Indian Policy*
(1969), although well meaning, contained the assertion (at p. 11) that
"aboriginal claims to land . . . are so general and undefined that it is not
realistic to think of them as specific claims capable of remedy except
through a policy and program that will end injustice to the Indians as
members of the Canadian community". In the same general period, the
James Bay development by Quebec Hydro was originally initiated without
regard to the rights of the Indians who lived there, even though these were
expressly protected by a constitutional instrument: see *The Quebec
Boundary Extension Act, 1912*, S.C. 1912, c. 45. It took a number of judicial
decisions and notably the *Calder* case in this court (1973) to prompt a
reassessment of the position being taken by government.

In the light of its reassessment of Indian claims following *Calder*, the
federal Government on August 8, 1973 issued "a statement of policy"
regarding Indian lands. By it, it sought to "signify the Government's
recognition and acceptance of its continuing responsibility under the British
North America Act for Indians and lands reserved for Indians", which it
regarded "as an historic evolution dating back to the Royal Proclamation
of 1763, which, whatever differences there may be about its judicial
interpretation, stands as a basic declaration of the Indian people's interests
in land in this country". (Emphasis added.) See *Statement made by the
Honourable Jean Chrétien, Minister of Indian Affairs and Northern Development
on Claims of Indian and Inuit People*, August 8, 1973. The remarks about
these lands were intended "as an expression of acknowledged
responsibility". But the statement went on to express, for the first time, the
government's willingness to negotiate regarding claims of aboriginal title,
specifically in British Columbia, Northern Quebec, and the Territories, and
this without regard to formal supporting documents. "The Government",
it stated, "is now ready to negotiate with authorized representatives of
these native peoples on the basis that where their traditional interest in the
lands concerned can be established, an agreed form of compensation or
benefit will be provided to native peoples in return for their interest."

It is obvious from its terms that the approach taken towards aboriginal
claims in the 1973 statement constituted an expression of a policy, rather
than a legal position.

. . . . .

It is clear, then, that s. 35(1) of the *Constitution Act, 1982*, represents the culmination of a long and difficult struggle in both the political forum and the courts for the constitutional recognition of aboriginal rights. The strong representations of native associations and other groups concerned with the welfare of Canada's aboriginal peoples made the adoption of s. 35(1) possible and it is important to note that the provision applies to the Indians, the Inuit and the Métis. Section 35(1), at the least, provides a solid constitutional base upon which subsequent negotiations can take place. It also affords aboriginal peoples constitutional protection against provincial legislative power. We are, of course, aware that this would, in any event, flow from the *Guerin* case ... but for a proper understanding of the situation, it is essential to remember that the *Guerin* case was decided after the commencement of the *Constitution Act, 1982*. In addition to its effect on aboriginal rights, s. 35(1) clarified other issues regarding the enforcement of treaty rights.

. . . . .

In our opinion, the significance of s. 35(1) extends beyond these fundamental effects. Professor Lyon in "An Essay on Constitutional Interpretation" (1988), 26 Osgoode Hall L.J. 95, says the following about s. 35(1), at p. 100:

> . . . the context of 1982 is surely enough to tell us that this is not just a codification of the case law on aboriginal rights that had accumulated by 1982. Section 35 calls for a just settlement for aboriginal peoples. It renounces the old rules of the game under which the Crown established courts of law and denied those courts the authority to question sovereign claims made by the Crown.

The approach to be taken with respect to interpreting the meaning of s. 35(1) is derived from general principles of constitutional interpretation, principles relating to aboriginal rights, and the purposes behind the constitutional provision itself. Here, we will sketch the framework for an interpretation of "recognized and affirmed" that, in our opinion, gives appropriate weight to the constitutional nature of these words.

. . . . .

... The nature of s. 35(1) itself suggests that it be construed in a purposive way. When the purposes of the affirmation of aboriginal rights are considered, it is clear that a generous, liberal interpretation of the words in the constitutional provision is demanded....

In *Nowegijick v. The Queen*, [1983] 1 S.C.R. 29 [at p. 36], the following principle that should govern the interpretation of Indian treaties and statutes was set out:

> . . . treaties and statutes relating to Indians should be liberally construed and doubtful expressions resolved in favour of the Indians.

In *R. v. Agawa, supra,* Blair J.A. stated that the above principle should apply to the interpretation of s. 35(1). He added the following principle to be equally applied:

> The second principle was enunciated by the late Associate Chief Justice MacKinnon in *R. v. Taylor and Williams* (1981), 34 O.R. (2d) 360. He emphasized the importance of Indian history and traditions as well as the perceived effect of a treaty at the time of its execution. He also cautioned against determining Indian rights 'in a vacuum'. The honour of the Crown is involved in the interpretation of Indian treaties and, as a consequence, fairness to the Indians is a governing consideration.

> ... In our opinion, *Guerin*, together with *R. v. Taylor and Williams* (1981), 34 O.R. (2d) 360, ground a general guiding principle for s. 35(1). That is, the Government has the responsibility to act in a fiduciary capacity with respect to aboriginal peoples. The relationship between the Government and aboriginals is trust-like, rather than adversarial, and contemporary recognition and affirmation of aboriginal rights must be defined in light of this historic relationship.

We agree with both the British Columbia Court of Appeal below and the Ontario Court of Appeal that the principles outlined above, derived from *Nowegijick, Taylor and Williams* and *Guerin*, should guide the interpretation of s. 35(1). As commentators have noted, s. 35(1) is a solemn commitment that must be given meaningful content.

. . . . .

In response to the appellant's submission that s. 35(1) rights are more securely protected than the rights guaranteed by the *Charter*, it is true that s. 35(1) is not subject to s. 1 of the *Charter*. In our opinion, this does not mean that any law or regulation affecting aboriginal rights will automatically be of no force or effect by the operation of s. 52 of the *Constitution Act, 1982*. Legislation that affects the exercise of aboriginal rights will none-the-less be valid, if it meets the test for justifying an interference with a right recognized and affirmed under s. 35(1).

There is no explicit language in the provision that authorizes this court or any court to assess the legitimacy of any government legislation that restricts aboriginal rights. Yet, we find that the words "recognition and affirmation" incorporate the fiduciary relationship referred to earlier and so import some restraint on the exercise of sovereign power. Rights that are recognized and affirmed are not absolute. Federal legislative powers continue, including, of course, the right to legislate with respect to Indians pursuant to s. 91(24) of the *Constitution Act, 1867*. These powers must, however, now be read together with s. 35(1). In other words, federal power must be reconciled with federal duty and the best way to achieve that reconciliation is to demand the justification of any government regulation that infringes upon or denies aboriginal rights. Such scrutiny is in keeping with the liberal interpretive principle enunciated in *Nowegijick, supra,* and the concept of holding the Crown to a high standard of honourable dealing with respect to the aboriginal peoples of Canada as suggested by *Guerin v. The Queen, supra.*

We refer to Professor Slattery's "Understanding Aboriginal Rights", *ibid.*, with respect to the task of envisioning a s. 35(1) justificatory process. Professor Slattery, at p. 782, points out that a justificatory process is required as a compromise between a "patchwork" characterization of aboriginal rights whereby past regulations would be read into a definition of the rights, and a characterization that would guarantee aboriginal rights in their original form unrestricted by subsequent regulation. We agree with him that these two extreme positions must be rejected in favour of a justificatory scheme.

Section 35(1) suggests that while regulation affecting aboriginal rights is not precluded, such regulation must be enacted according to a valid objective. Our history has shown, unfortunately all too well, that Canada's aboriginal peoples are justified in worrying about government objectives that may be superficially neutral but which constitute *de facto* threats to the existence of aboriginal rights and interests. By giving aboriginal rights constitutional status and priority, Parliament and the provinces have sanctioned challenges to social and economic policy objectives embodied in legislation to the extent that aboriginal rights are affected. Implicit in this constitutional scheme is the obligation of the legislature to satisfy the test of justification. The way in which a legislative objective is to be attained must uphold the honour of the Crown and must be in keeping with the unique contemporary relationship, grounded in history and policy, between the Crown and Canada's aboriginal peoples. The extent of legislative or regulatory impact on an existing aboriginal right may be scrutinized so as to ensure recognition and affirmation.

The constitutional recognition afforded by the provision, therefore, gives a measure of control over government conduct and a strong check on legislative power. While it does not promise immunity from government regulation in a society that, in the twentieth century, is increasingly more complex, interdependent and sophisticated, and where exhaustible resources need protection and management, it does hold the Crown to a substantive promise. The government is required to bear the burden of justifying any legislation that has some negative effect on any aboriginal right protected under s. 35(1).

In these reasons, we will outline the appropriate analysis under s. 35(1) in the context of a regulation made pursuant to the *Fisheries Act.* We wish to emphasize the importance of context and a case-by-case approach to s. 35(1). Given the generality of the text of the constitutional provision, and especially in light of the complexities of aboriginal history, society and rights, the contours of a justificatory standard must be defined in the specific factual context of each case.

Section 35(1) and the Regulation of the Fisheries

Taking the above framework as guidance, we propose to set out the test for *prima facie* interference with an existing aboriginal right and for the justification of such an interference.

. . . . .

The first question to be asked is whether the legislation in question has the effect of interfering with an existing aboriginal right. If it does have such an effect, it represents a *prima facie* infringement of s. 35(1). Parliament is not expected to act in a manner contrary to the rights and interests of aboriginals, and, indeed, may be barred from doing so by the second stage of s. 35(1) analysis. The inquiry with respect to interference begins with a reference to the characteristics or incidents of the right at stake. Our earlier observations regarding the scope of the aboriginal right to fish are relevant here. Fishing rights are not traditional property rights. They are rights held by a collective and are in keeping with the culture and existence of that group. Courts must be careful, then, to avoid the application of traditional common law concepts of property as they develop their understanding of what the reasons for judgment in *Guerin* ... referred to as the *"sui generis"* nature of aboriginal rights: See also Little Bear, "A Concept of Native Title," [1982] 5 Can. Legal Aid Bul. 99.

While it is impossible to give an easy definition of fishing rights, it is possible, and, indeed, crucial, to be sensitive to the aboriginal perspective itself on the meaning of the rights at stake. For example, it would be artificial to try to create a hard distinction between the right to fish and the particular manner in which that right is exercised.

To determine whether the fishing rights have been interfered with such as to constitute a *prima facie* infringement of s. 35(1), certain questions must be asked. First, is the limitation unreasonable? Secondly, does the regulation impose undue hardship? Thirdly, does the regulation deny to the holders of the right their preferred means of exercising that right? The onus of proving a *prima facie* infringement lies on the individual or group challenging the legislation. In relation to the facts of this appeal, the regulation would be found to be a *prima facie* interference if it were found to be an adverse restriction on the Musqueam exercise of their right to fish for food. We wish to note here that the issue does not merely require looking at whether the fish catch has been reduced below that needed for the reasonable food and ceremonial needs of the Musqueam Indians. Rather the test involves asking whether either the purpose or the effect of the restriction on net length unnecessarily infringes the interests protected by the fishing right. If, for example, the Musqueam were forced to spend undue time and money per fish caught or if the net length reduction resulted in a hardship to the Musqueam in catching fish, then the first branch of the s. 35(1) analysis would be met.

If a *prima facie* interference is found, the analysis moves to the issue of justification. This is the test that addresses the question of what constitutes legitimate regulation of a constitutional aboriginal right. The justification analysis would proceed as follows. First, is there a valid legislative objective? Here the court would inquire into whether the objective of Parliament in authorizing the department to enact regulations regarding fisheries is valid. The objective of the department in setting out the particular regulations would also be scrutinized. An objective aimed at preserving s. 35(1) rights by conserving and managing a natural resource, for example, would be valid. Also valid would be objectives purporting to prevent the exercise of s. 35(1) rights that would cause harm to the general populace or to aboriginal peoples themselves, or other objectives found to be compelling and substantial.

The Court of Appeal below held ... that regulations could be valid if reasonably justified as "necessary for the proper management and conservation of the resource *or in the public interest*". (Emphasis added.) We find the "public interest" justification to be so vague as to provide no meaningful guidance and so broad as to be unworkable as a test for the justification of a limitation on constitutional rights.

The justification of conservation and resource management, on the other hand, is surely uncontroversial.

. . . . .

[T]he value of conservation purposes for government legislation and action has long been recognized. Further, the conservation and management of our resources is consistent with aboriginal beliefs and practices, and, indeed, with the enhancement of aboriginal rights.

If a valid legislative objective is found, the analysis proceeds to the second part of the justification issue. Here, we refer back to the guiding interpretive principle derived from *Taylor and Williams* and *Guerin, supra*. That is, the honour of the Crown is at stake in dealings with aboriginal peoples. The special trust relationship and the responsibility of the government *vis-à-vis* aboriginals must be the first consideration in determining whether the legislation or action in question can be justified.

The problem that arises in assessing the legislation in light of its objective and the responsibility of the Crown is that the pursuit of conservation in a heavily used modern fishery inevitably blurs with the efficient allocation and management of this scarce and valued resource. The nature of the constitutional protection afforded by s. 35(1) in this context demands that there be a link between the question of justification and the allocation of priorities in the fishery. The constitutional recognition and affirmation of aboriginal rights may give rise to conflict with the interests of others given the limited nature of the resource. There is a clear need for guidelines that will resolve the allocational problems that arise regarding the fisheries. We refer to the reasons of Dickson J., [as he then was], in *Jack v. The Queen*, [1980] [1 S.C.R. 294] for such guidelines.

In *Jack*, the appellants' defence to a charge of fishing for salmon in certain rivers during a prohibited period was based on the alleged constitutional incapacity of Parliament to legislate such as to deny the

Indians their right to fish for food. They argued that art. 13 of the *British Columbia Terms of Union* imposed a constitutional limitation on the federal power to regulate. While we recognize that the finding that such a limitation had been imposed was not adopted by the majority of this Court, we point out that this case concerns a different constitutional promise that asks this Court to give a meaningful interpretation to recognition and affirmation. That task requires equally meaningful guidelines responsive to the constitutional priority accorded aboriginal rights. We therefore repeat the following passage from *Jack*, at p. 313:

> Conservation is a valid legislative concern. The appellants concede as much. Their concern is in the allocation of the resource after reasonable and necessary conservation measures have been recognized and given effect to. They do not claim the right to pursue the last living salmon until it is caught. Their position, as I understand it, is one which would give effect to an order of priorities of this nature: (i) conservation; (ii) Indian fishing; (iii) non-Indian commercial fishing; or (iv) non-Indian sports fishing; the burden of conservation measures should not fall primarily upon the Indian fishery.

> I agree with the general tenor of this argument. ... With respect to whatever salmon are to be caught, then priority ought to be given to the Indian fishermen, subject to the practical difficulties occasioned by international waters and the movement of the fish themselves. But any limitation upon Indian fishing that is established for a valid conservation purpose overrides the protection afforded the Indian fishery by art. 13, just as such conservation measures override other taking of fish.

The constitutional nature of the Musqueam food fishing rights means that any allocation of priorities after valid conservation measures have been implemented must give top priority to Indian food fishing. If the objective pertained to conservation, the conservation plan would be scrutinized to assess priorities. While the detailed allocation of maritime resources is a task that must be left to those having expertise in the area, the Indians' food requirements must be met first when that allocation is established. The significance of giving the aboriginal right to fish for food top priority can be described as follows. If, in a given year, conservation needs required a reduction in the number of fish to be caught such that the number equalled the number required for food by the Indians, then all the fish available after conservation would go to the Indians according to the constitutional nature of their fishing right. If, more realistically, there were still fish after the Indian food requirements were met, then the brunt of conservation measures would be borne by the practices of sport fishing and commercial fishing.

. . . . .

We acknowledge the fact that the justificatory standard to be met may place a heavy burden on the Crown. However, government policy with respect to the British Columbia fishery, regardless of s. 35(1), already dictates that, in allocating the right to take fish, Indian food fishing is to be given priority over the interests of other user groups. The constitutional entitlement embodied in s. 35(1) requires the Crown to ensure that its regulations are in keeping with that allocation of priority. The objective of this requirement is not to undermine Parliament's ability and responsibility with respect to creating and administering over-all conservation and management plans regarding the salmon fishery. The objective is rather to guarantee that those plans treat aboriginal peoples in a way ensuring that their rights are taken seriously.

Within the analysis of justification, there are further questions to be addressed, depending on the circumstances of the inquiry. These include the questions of whether there has been as little infringement as possible in order to effect the desired result; whether, in a situation of expropriation, fair compensation is available; and, whether the aboriginal group in question has been consulted with respect to the conservation measures being implemented. The aboriginal peoples, with their history of conservation-consciousness and interdependence with natural resources, would surely be expected, at the least, to be informed regarding the determination of an appropriate scheme for the regulation of the fisheries.

We would not wish to set out an exhaustive list of the factors to be considered in the assessment of justification. Suffice it to say that recognition and affirmation requires sensitivity to and respect for the rights of aboriginal peoples on behalf of the government, courts and indeed all Canadians.

Application to this Case — Is the Net Length Restriction Valid?

The Court of Appeal below found that there was not sufficient evidence in this case to proceed with an analysis of s. 35(1) with respect to the right to fish for food. In reviewing the competing expert evidence, and recognizing that fish stock management is an uncertain science, it decided that the issues at stake in this appeal were not well adapted to being resolved at the appellate court level.

· · · · ·

According to the Court of Appeal, the findings of fact were insufficient to lead to an acquittal. There was no more evidence before this Court. We also would order a re-trial which would allow findings of fact according to the tests set out in these reasons.

The appellant would bear the burden of showing that the net length restriction constituted a *prima facie* infringement of the collective aboriginal right to fish for food. If an infringement were found, the onus would shift to the Crown which would have to demonstrate that the regulation is justifiable. To that end, the Crown would have to show that there is no underlying unconstitutional objective such as shifting more of the resource to a user group that ranks below the Musqueam. Further, it would have to show that the regulation sought to be imposed is required to accomplish the needed limitation. In trying to show that the restriction is necessary in the circumstances of the Fraser River fishery, the Crown could use facts pertaining to fishing by other Fraser River Indians.

In conclusion, we would dismiss the appeal and the cross-appeal and affirm the Court of Appeal's setting aside of the conviction. We would accordingly affirm the order for a new trial on the questions of infringement and whether any infringement is nonetheless consistent with s. 35(1), in accordance with the interpretation set out here.

. . . . .

Appeal and cross-appeal dismissed. The constitutional question should be sent back to trial to be answered according to the analysis set out in these reasons.

In *Sparrow*, the Supreme Court affirmed that section 35(1) of the *Constitution Act, 1982* prevented the extinguishment of Aboriginal rights found to exist on or after April 17, 1982. It also affirmed that section 35(1) was not subject to the limitation on rights provided by section 1 of the *Canadian Charter of Rights and Freedoms*. Nevertheless, it did allow for the infringement of Aboriginal rights on or after April 17, 1982 through the justificatory test it created.

From the *Sparrow* decision, the Court held that Aboriginal rights were those practices that were "integral to the distinctive cultures" of Aboriginal peoples. The Court also explained that Aboriginal rights could not be frozen at a particular point in time (as discussed in relation to treaty rights in Chapter 4). On these points, the *Sparrow* decision marked a significant departure from previous judicial decisions on Aboriginal rights and their status in law.

D. ABORIGINAL RIGHTS: INHERENT RIGHTS OR CONTINGENT RIGHTS?

While the *Sparrow* decision illustrated a variety of judicial interpretations of Aboriginal rights, a key element of the decision was predicated upon pre-*Calder* characterizations about the nature of Aboriginal rights. In fact, the underlying basis of the *Sparrow* decision raises questions about the Court's understanding of Aboriginal rights and whether they exist independently of the common law or governmental recognition. In the following excerpt from their article "Aboriginal Rights and Canadian Sovereignty: An Essay on *R. v. Sparrow*," Michael Asch and Patrick Macklem address this through the characterizations of Aboriginal rights as "inherent" or "contingent".

MICHAEL ASCH & PATRICK MACKLEM, "ABORIGINAL RIGHTS AND CANADIAN SOVEREIGNTY: AN ESSAY ON R. v. SPARROW"

(1991) 29 Alta. L. Rev. 498 at 501-3, 505, 507-8, 510, 515-16
(references omitted)

. . . . .

II. TWO THEORIES OF ABORIGINAL RIGHT

. . . . .

A contingent rights approach views the existence or non-existence of aboriginal rights to be contingent upon the exercise of state authority. It therefore assumes the legitimacy of executive and legislative authority over First Nations and imagines rights as emanating from state recognition of a valid aboriginal claim to freedom from state interference. An aboriginal right to fish, for example, is dependent upon the state conferring such a right on the relevant aboriginal population by legislative or executive action.

. . . . .

A contingent theory of aboriginal right gives rise to a particular conception of the meaning of First Nations sovereignty and self-government. Under a contingent rights approach, First Nations sovereignty would not exist as a constitutional right until expressed by way of constitutional amendment. Until such a time, aboriginal self-government exists only to the extent it is given force by legislation or executive action. ... Thus, under a contingent theory of aboriginal rights, self-government is a label for a bundle of rights that attach to Native people as a result of legislative or executive action or constitutional amendment, and is not dependent upon a prior acceptance of First Nations sovereignty. In fact, a contingent theory of aboriginal right implicitly denies any assertion of First Nations sovereignty by viewing the existence or non-existence of aboriginal rights, including rights of self-government, as dependent upon the exercise of Canadian sovereign authority.

. . . . .

An inherent theory of aboriginal right generates an approach to First Nations sovereignty and self-government that stands in stark contrast to that envisioned by a contingent rights perspective. According to an inherent rights approach, First Nations sovereignty is a term used to describe the totality of powers and responsibilities necessary or integral to the maintenance and reproduction of aboriginal identity and social organization. Under an inherent rights theory, First Nations sovereignty and aboriginal forms of government, as the means by which aboriginal identity and social organization are reproduced, pre-existed the settlement of Canada and continue to exist notwithstanding the interposition of the Canadian state. The Canadian state may choose to recognize aspects of

First Nations sovereignty and aboriginal forms of self-government through executive, legislative or judicial action. Unlike a contingent theory of aboriginal right, however, such action is not necessary for the existence of First Nations sovereignty and native forms of self-government, only their recognition in Canadian law.

The debate … as to the legal nature of aboriginal rights was initially put to rest in 1984 by Dickson J. (as he then was) in *Guerin v. The Queen*. Describing the nature of the Musqueam Indian Band's interest in their land as "a pre-existing legal right not created by Royal Proclamation, by s. 128(1) of the *Indian Act*, or by any other executive order or legislative provision," Dickson J. in *Guerin* firmly opted for an inherent theory of aboriginal right. Yet, prior to the passage of the *Constitution Act, 1982*, the legal embrace of an inherent theory of aboriginal right was restricted to the common law. Although aboriginal rights in *Guerin* were conceived as not contingent upon the exercise of legislative or executive authority, they nonetheless existed only at common law. Common law aboriginal rights were therefore always subject to regulation or extinguishment by the appropriate legislative authority. The judicial recognition of the inherent nature of aboriginal rights thus occurred in the context of a tacit acceptance of the sovereign authority of the Canadian state over its indigenous population. As a result, the vision of First Nations sovereignty and native forms of self-government generated by an inherent theory of aboriginal right remained outside the purview of Canadian law.

III. THE *SPARROW* DECISION

. . . . .

In *R. v. Sparrow* … the Supreme Court of Canada was provided with the occasion to give meaning to s. 35(1). As stated previously, the Court accepted that Canada enjoys sovereignty and is therefore entitled to exercise legislative authority over First Nations. The court held, however, that aboriginal rights that exist at common law are now "recognized and affirmed" by s. 35(1), and that, as a result, laws that interfere with the exercise of such rights must conform to constitutional standards of justification.

. . . . .

In so holding, the Court re-affirmed Dickson J.'s holding in *Guerin* that aboriginal rights are not contingent upon the exercise of legislative or executive authority, and to this extent the Court in *Sparrow* embraced an inherent theory of aboriginal right. In the Court's view, the reason for concluding that the Musqueam Nation enjoys a right to fish lies not in the presence of state action conferring such a right, but instead arises from the fact that fishing is integral to Musqueam self-identify and self-preservation. …

. . . . .

The Court also implicitly relies on a contingent theory of aboriginal right in the definition it gives s. 35(1)'s requirement that aboriginal rights be "existing" before they receive constitutional recognition and affirmation. An inherent theory of aboriginal right would suggest that the existence of aboriginal rights is not to be determined by reference to actions of the Canadian state. The Court, however, held that prior to 1982 aboriginal rights could be extinguished by the Canadian state. If extinguished prior to 1982, aboriginal rights no longer "exist" within the meaning of s. 35(1) and their exercise is not protected against state action. ... State action, in other words, defines the parameters of s. 35(1) rights, which is a central tenet of a contingent theory of aboriginal right.

. . . . .

In sum, although the Court in *Sparrow* pays attention to an inherent theory of aboriginal right, its reasons ultimately betray a reliance on a contingent rights perspective, which serves to rein in the scope of s. 35(1) rights. The assertion of Canadian sovereignty is sufficient to nullify and render non-existent any pre-existing claims of aboriginal sovereignty, which would otherwise constitute an "existing aboriginal right" within the meaning of s. 35(1). ...

. . . . .

In our view, the assertion of Canadian sovereignty over aboriginal peoples, as well as the contingent theory of aboriginal right that it generates, ultimately rest on unacceptable notions about the inherent superiority of European nations. ...

. . . . .

... [W]e are drawn to the following statement by Justice Hall in the *Calder* case written more than twenty years ago:

> [t]he assessment and interpretation of the historical documents and enactments tendered in evidence must be approached in the light of present-day research and knowledge disregarding ancient concepts formulated when understanding of the customs and culture of our original people was rudimentary and incomplete and when they were thought to be wholly without cohesion, laws or culture, in effect a subhuman species.

... In our view, it is equally applicable to the invocation of a contingent theory of aboriginal right in the context of s. 35(1) of the *Constitution Act, 1982*. The stability of a contingent rights approach to s. 35(1) ultimately depends on a belief in the superiority of European nations. In our view, Canada ought not to be constituted by a reliance on such a belief, and constitutional interpretation surrounding Canada's relation with First Nations should heed Justice Hall's sage advice. An inherent theory of aboriginal right remains true to the belief of equality of peoples and as such should form an integral part of Canada's constitutional identity.

How do Asch and Macklem's views sit with those expressed by Binnie J. in *Mitchell v. M.N.R.*, [2001] S.C.J. No. 33, [2001] 1 S.C.R. 911 (S.C.C.), where he said:

> The common law concept of aboriginal rights is built around the doctrine of sovereign succession in British colonial law. The framers of the *Constitution Act, 1982* undoubtedly expected the courts to have regard in their interpretation of s. 35(1) to the common law concept. This point was made by McLachlin J. (as she then was) (dissenting in the result) in *Van der Peet, supra*, at paras. 227 and 262:
>
> > The issue of what constitutes an aboriginal right must, in my view, be answered by looking at what the law has historically accepted as fundamental aboriginal rights. ...
> >
> > ... The *Constitution Act, 1982* ushered in a new chapter but it did not start a new book. Within the framework of s. 35(1) regard is to be had to the common law ("what the law has historically accepted") to enable a court to determine what constitutes an aboriginal right.

How do Justice Binnie's comments mesh with those of Noel Lyon, which were expressly adopted by the Supreme Court of Canada in *Sparrow*? Did section 35(1) usher in a new chapter in the approach to Aboriginal rights or did it begin a new book? What do you think? Does your answer differ if you consider only the approach to be taken with respect to those rights as opposed to the content of those rights?

E. POST-*SPARROW* CONSIDERATIONS OF ABORIGINAL RIGHTS

Until the Supreme Court of Canada's decisions in the *Van der Peet* trilogy — *R. v. Van der Peet* and *R. v. Gladstone*, which are reproduced below, and *R. v. N.T.C. Smokehouse Ltd.*, [1996] S.C.J. No. 78, [1996] 2 S.C.R. 672, [1996] 4 C.N.L.R. 130, [1996] 9 W.W.R. 114, 23 B.C.L.R. (3d) 114, 137 D.L.R. (4th) 528, 50 C.R. (4th) 181, 109 C.C.C. (3d) 129, 200 N.R. 321 (S.C.C.) — the Supreme Court of Canada had not undertaken a substantive discussion of the effects of section 35(1) of the *Constitution Act, 1982* since its decision in *Sparrow* some six years previously. Through these decisions, in particular *Van der Peet* and *Gladstone*, the Supreme Court may be seen to have made some fundamental changes to its characterization of Aboriginal rights in *Sparrow*.

R. v. VAN DER PEET

[1996] S.C.J. No. 77, [1996] 2 S.C.R. 507, [1996] 4 C.N.L.R. 177,
[1996] 9 W.W.R. 1, 23 B.C.L.R. (3d) 1, 50 C.R. (4th) 1, 137 D.L.R. (4th) 289,
109 C.C.C. (3d) 1, 200 N.R. 1 (S.C.C.)

La Forest, Sopinka, Gonthier, Cory, Iacobucci and **Major JJ.** concur with **Lamer C.J.C.**: —

I. *Introduction*

[1] This appeal ... raises the issue left unresolved by this Court in its judgment in *R. v. Sparrow*, [1990] 1 S.C.R. 1075: How are the Aboriginal rights recognized and affirmed by s. 35(1) of the *Constitution Act, 1982* to be defined?

[2] In *Sparrow*, Dickson C.J. and La Forest J., writing for a unanimous Court, outlined the framework for analyzing s. 35(1) claims. First, a court must determine whether an applicant has demonstrated that he or she was acting pursuant to an Aboriginal right. Second, a court must determine whether that right has been extinguished. Third, a court must determine whether that right has been infringed. Finally, a court must determine whether the infringement is justified. In *Sparrow*, however, it was not seriously disputed that the Musqueam had an Aboriginal right to fish for food, with the result that it was unnecessary for the Court to answer the question of how the rights recognized and affirmed by s. 35(1) are to be defined. It is this question and, in particular, the question of whether s. 35(1) recognizes and affirms the right of the Sto:lo to sell fish, which must now be answered by this Court.

[3] In order to define the scope of Aboriginal rights, it will be necessary first to articulate the purposes which underpin s. 35(1), specifically the reasons underlying its recognition and affirmation of the unique constitutional status of Aboriginal peoples in Canada. Until it is understood why Aboriginal rights exist, and are constitutionally protected, no definition of those rights is possible. ...

[4] This judgment will thus, after outlining the context and background of the appeal, articulate a test for identifying Aboriginal rights which reflects the purposes underlying s. 35(1), and the interests which that constitutional provision is intended to protect.

II. *Statement of Facts*

[5] The appellant Dorothy Van der Peet was charged under s. 61(1) of the *Fisheries Act*, R.S.C. 1970, c. F-14, with the offence of selling fish caught under the authority of an Indian food fish licence, contrary to s. 27(5) of the *British Columbia Fishery (General) Regulations*, SOR/84-248. At the time at which the appellant was charged s. 27(5) read:

> 27. . . . (5) No person shall sell, barter or offer to sell or barter any fish caught under the authority of an Indian food fish licence.

[6] The charges arose out of the sale by the appellant of 10 salmon on September 11, 1987. ... The appellant, a member of the Sto:lo, has not contested these facts at any time, instead defending the charges against her on the basis that in selling the fish she was exercising an existing aboriginal right to sell fish. The appellant has based her defence on the position that the restrictions imposed by s. 27(5) of the Regulations infringe her existing aboriginal right to sell fish and are therefore invalid on the basis that they violate s. 35(1) of the *Constitution Act, 1982*.

. . . . .

V. *Analysis*

Introduction

[15] I now turn to the question which ... lies at the heart of this appeal: How should the aboriginal rights recognized and affirmed by s. 35(1) of the *Constitution Act, 1982* be defined?

[16] In her factum the appellant argued that the majority of the Court of Appeal erred because it defined the rights in s. 35(1) in a fashion which "converted a Right into a Relic"; such an approach, the appellant argued, is inconsistent with the fact that the aboriginal rights recognized and affirmed by s. 35(1) are *rights* and not simply aboriginal practices. The appellant acknowledged that aboriginal rights are based in aboriginal societies and cultures, but argued that the majority of the Court of Appeal erred because it defined aboriginal rights through the identification of pre-contact activities instead of as pre-existing legal rights.

[17] While the appellant is correct to suggest that the mere existence of an activity in a particular aboriginal community prior to contact with Europeans is not, in itself, sufficient foundation for the definition of aboriginal rights, the position she would have this Court adopt takes s. 35(1) too far from that which the provision is intended to protect. Section 35(1), it is true, recognizes and affirms existing aboriginal *rights*, but it must not be forgotten that the rights it recognizes and affirms are *aboriginal*.

[18] In the liberal enlightenment view, reflected in the American Bill of Rights and, more indirectly, in the *Charter*, rights are held by all people in society because each person is entitled to dignity and respect. Rights are general and universal; they are the way in which the "inherent dignity" of each individual in society is respected: *R. v. Oakes*, [1986] 1 S.C.R. 103 at p. 136; *R. v. Big M Drug Mart Ltd.*, [[1985] 1 S.C.R. 295] at p. 336.

[19] *Aboriginal* rights cannot, however, be defined on the basis of the philosophical precepts of the liberal enlightenment. Although equal in importance and significance to the rights enshrined in the *Charter*, aboriginal rights must be viewed differently from *Charter* rights because they are rights held only by aboriginal members of Canadian society. They arise from the fact that aboriginal people are *aboriginal*. As academic commentators have noted, aboriginal rights "inhere in the very meaning of aboriginality" ...

[20] The task of this Court is to define aboriginal rights in a manner which recognizes that aboriginal rights are *rights* but which does so without losing sight of the fact that they are rights held by aboriginal people because they are *aboriginal*. The Court must neither lose sight of the generalized constitutional status of what s. 35(1) protects, nor can it ignore the necessary specificity which comes from granting special constitutional protection to one part of Canadian society. The Court must define the

scope of s. 35(1) in a way which captures *both* the aboriginal and the rights in aboriginal rights.

[21] The way to accomplish this task is, as was noted at the outset, through a purposive approach to s. 35(1). It is through identifying the interests that s. 35(1) was intended to protect that the dual nature of aboriginal rights will be comprehended. ... A purposive approach to s. 35(1), because ensuring that the provision is not viewed as static and only relevant to current circumstances, will ensure that the recognition and affirmation it offers are consistent with the fact that what it is recognizing and affirming are "rights". Further, because it requires the court to analyze a given constitutional provision" in the light of the interests it was meant to protect" (*Big M Drug Mart Ltd.*, *supra*, at p. 344), a purposive approach to s. 35(1) will ensure that that which is found to fall within the provision is related to the provision's intended focus: aboriginal people and their rights in relation to Canadian society as a whole.

. . . . .

General Principles Applicable to Legal Disputes Between Aboriginal Peoples and the Crown

[23] Before turning to a purposive analysis of s. 35(1), however, it should be noted that such analysis must take place in light of the general principles which apply to the legal relationship between the Crown and aboriginal peoples. In *Sparrow* [*R. v. Sparrow*, [1990] 1 S.C.R. 1075], this Court held at p. 1106 that s. 35(1) should be given a generous and liberal interpretation in favour of aboriginal peoples. ...

[24] This interpretive principle, articulated first in the context of treaty rights ... arises from the nature of the relationship between the Crown and aboriginal peoples. The Crown has a fiduciary obligation to aboriginal peoples with the result that in dealings between the government and aboriginals the honour of the Crown is at stake. Because of this fiduciary relationship, and its implication of the honour of the Crown, treaties, s. 35(1), and other statutory and constitutional provisions protecting the interests of aboriginal peoples, must be given a generous and liberal interpretation. ... This general principle must inform the Court's analysis of the purposes underlying s. 35(1), and of that provision's definition and scope.

[25] The fiduciary relationship of the Crown and aboriginal peoples also means that where there is any doubt or ambiguity with regards to what falls within the scope and definition of s. 35(1), such doubt or ambiguity must be resolved in favour of aboriginal peoples. In *R. v. Sutherland*, [1980] 2 S.C.R. 451, at p. 464, Dickson J. held that paragraph 13 of the Memorandum of Agreement between Manitoba and Canada, a constitutional document, "should be interpreted so as to resolve any doubts in favour of the Indians, the beneficiaries of the rights assured by the paragraph". This interpretive principle applies equally to s. 35(1) of the

Constitution Act, 1982 and should, again, inform the Court's purposive analysis of that provision.

Purposive Analysis of Section 35(1)

. . . . .

[27] When the court identifies a constitutional provision's purposes, or the interests the provision is intended to protect, what it is doing in essence is explaining the rationale of the provision; it is articulating the reasons underlying the protection that the provision gives. With regards to s. 35(1), then, what the court must do is explain the rationale and foundation of the recognition and affirmation of the special rights of aboriginal peoples; it must identify the basis for the special status that aboriginal peoples have within Canadian society as a whole....

[28] In identifying the basis for the recognition and affirmation of aboriginal rights it must be remembered that s. 35(1) did not create the legal doctrine of aboriginal rights; aboriginal rights existed and were recognized under the common law. ... The pre-existence of aboriginal rights is relevant to the analysis of s. 35(1) because it indicates that aboriginal rights have a stature and existence prior to the constitutionalization of those rights and sheds light on the reasons for protecting those rights.

. . . . .

[30] In my view, the doctrine of aboriginal rights exists, and is recognized and affirmed by s. 35(1), because of one simple fact: when Europeans arrived in North America, aboriginal peoples *were already here*, living in communities on the land, and participating in distinctive cultures, as they had done for centuries. It is this fact, and this fact above all others, which separates aboriginal peoples from all other minority groups in Canadian society and which mandates their special legal, and now constitutional, status.

[31] More specifically, what s. 35(1) does is provide the constitutional framework through which the fact that aboriginals lived on the land in distinctive societies, with their own practices, traditions and cultures, is acknowledged and reconciled with the sovereignty of the Crown. The substantive rights which fall within the provision must be defined in light of this purpose; the aboriginal rights recognized and affirmed by s. 35(1) must be directed towards the reconciliation of the pre-existence of aboriginal societies with the sovereignty of the Crown.

. . . . .

[35] The view of aboriginal rights as based in the prior occupation of North America by distinctive aboriginal societies, finds support in the early American decisions of Marshall C.J. Although the constitutional structure of the United States is different from that of Canada, and its aboriginal law has developed in unique directions, I agree with Professor

Slattery both when he describes the Marshall decisions as providing "structure and coherence to an untidy and diffuse body of customary law based on official practice" and when he asserts that these decisions are "as relevant to Canada as they are to the United States" ...

. . . . .

[38] The High Court of Australia has also considered the question of the basis and nature of aboriginal rights. Like that of the United States, Australia's aboriginal law differs in significant respects from that of Canada. ...Despite these relevant differences, the analysis of the basis of aboriginal title in the landmark decision of the High Court in *Mabo v. Queensland [No. 2]* (1992), 175 C.L.R. 1, is persuasive in the Canadian context.

[39] The *Mabo* judgment resolved the dispute between the Meriam people and the Crown regarding who had title to the Murray Islands. The islands had been annexed to Queensland in 1879 but were reserved for the native inhabitants (the Meriam) in 1882. The Crown argued that this annexation was sufficient to vest absolute ownership of the lands in the Crown. The High Court disagreed, holding that while the annexation did vest radical title in the Crown, it was insufficient to eliminate a claim for native title.

[40] ... Brennan J., writing for a majority of the Court ... consider[ed] the nature and basis of aboriginal title:

> Native title has its origin in and is given its content by the traditional laws acknowledged by and the traditional customs observed by the indigenous inhabitants of a territory. The nature and incidents of native title must be ascertained as a matter of fact by reference to those laws and customs. ...

This position is the same as that being adopted here. "Traditional laws" and "traditional customs" are those things passed down, and arising, from the pre-existing culture and customs of aboriginal peoples. ... To base aboriginal title in traditional laws and customs, as was done in *Mabo*, is, therefore, to base that title in the pre-existing societies of aboriginal peoples. This is the same basis as that asserted here for aboriginal rights.

[41] Academic commentators have also been consistent in identifying the basis and foundation of the s. 35(1) claims of aboriginal peoples in aboriginal occupation of North America prior to the arrival of Europeans. ....

[42] ... In his comment on *Delgamuukw v. British Columbia* ("British Imperial Constitutional Law and Aboriginal Rights: A Comment on *Delgamuukw v. British Columbia*" (1992), 17 *Queen's L.J.* 350), Mark Walters suggests at pp. 412-13 that the essence of aboriginal rights is their bridging of aboriginal and non-aboriginal cultures:

> The challenge of defining aboriginal rights stems from the fact that they are rights peculiar to the meeting of two vastly dissimilar legal cultures; consequently there will always be a question about which legal culture is to provide the vantage point from which rights are to be defined. ... a morally

and politically defensible conception of aboriginal rights will incorporate both legal perspectives. [Emphasis added.]

Similarly, Professor Slattery has suggested that the law of aboriginal rights is "neither English nor aboriginal in origin: it is a form of intersocietal law that evolved from long-standing practices linking the various communities" …

. . . . .

The Test for Identifying Aboriginal Rights in Section 35(1)

[44] In order to fulfil the purpose underlying s. 35(1) — *i.e.*, the protection and reconciliation of the interests which arise from the fact that prior to the arrival of Europeans in North America aboriginal peoples lived on the land in distinctive societies, with their own practices, customs and traditions — the test for identifying the aboriginal rights recognized and affirmed by s. 35(1) must be directed at identifying the crucial elements of those pre-existing distinctive societies. It must, in other words, aim at identifying the practices, traditions and customs central to the aboriginal societies that existed in North America prior to contact with the Europeans.

[45] In *Sparrow, supra*, this Court did not have to address the scope of the aboriginal rights protected by s. 35(1); however, in their judgment at p. 1099 Dickson C.J. and La Forest J. identified the Musqueam right to fish for food in the fact that…participation in the salmon fishery is an aboriginal right because it is an "integral part" of the "distinctive culture" of the Musqueam. This suggestion is consistent with the position just adopted; identifying those practices, customs and traditions that are integral to distinctive aboriginal cultures will serve to identify the crucial elements of the distinctive aboriginal societies that occupied North America prior to the arrival of Europeans.

[46] In light of the suggestion of *Sparrow, supra*, and the purposes underlying s. 35(1), the following test should be used to identify whether an applicant has established an aboriginal right protected by s. 35(1): in order to be an aboriginal right an activity must be an element of a practice, custom or tradition integral to the distinctive culture of the aboriginal group claiming the right.

. . . . .

Factors to be Considered in Application of the Integral to a Distinctive Culture Test

[48] The test just laid out — that aboriginal rights lie in the practices, customs and traditions integral to the distinctive cultures of aboriginal peoples — requires further elaboration with regards to the nature of the inquiry a court faced with an aboriginal rights claim must undertake. I will now undertake such an elaboration. …

Courts must take into account the perspective of aboriginal peoples themselves

[49] In assessing a claim for the existence of an aboriginal right, a court must take into account the perspective of the aboriginal people claiming the right. In *Sparrow, supra*, Dickson C.J. and La Forest J. held, at p. 1112, that it is "crucial to be sensitive to the aboriginal perspective itself on the meaning of the rights at stake". It must also be recognized, however, that that perspective must be framed in terms cognizable to the Canadian legal and constitutional structure. As has already been noted, one of the fundamental purposes of s. 35(1) is the reconciliation of the pre-existence of distinctive aboriginal societies with the assertion of Crown sovereignty. Courts adjudicating aboriginal rights claims must, therefore, be sensitive to the aboriginal perspective, but they must also be aware that aboriginal rights exist within the general legal system of Canada. To quote again Walters, at p. 413: "a morally and politically defensible conception of aboriginal rights will incorporate both [aboriginal and non-aboriginal] legal perspectives". The definition of an aboriginal right must, if it is truly to reconcile the prior occupation of Canadian territory by aboriginal peoples with the assertion of Crown sovereignty over that territory, take into account the aboriginal perspective, yet do so in terms which are cognizable to the non-aboriginal legal system.

[50] ... [T]he only fair and just reconciliation is, as Walters suggests, one which takes into account the aboriginal perspective while at the same time taking into account the perspective of the common law. True reconciliation will, equally, place weight on each.

Courts must identify precisely the nature of the claim being made in determining whether an aboriginal claimant has demonstrated the existence of an aboriginal right

[51] Related to this is the fact that in assessing a claim to an aboriginal right a court must first identify the nature of the right being claimed; in order to determine whether a claim meets the test of being integral to the distinctive culture of the aboriginal group claiming the right, the court must first correctly determine what it is that is being claimed.

[52] ... The nature of an applicant's claim must be delineated in terms of the particular practice, custom or tradition under which it is claimed; the significance of the practice, custom or tradition to the aboriginal community is a factor to be considered in determining whether the practice, custom or tradition is integral to the distinctive culture, but the significance of a practice, custom or tradition cannot, itself, constitute an aboriginal right.

[53] To characterize an applicant's claim correctly, a court should consider such factors as the nature of the action which the applicant is claiming was done pursuant to an aboriginal right, the nature of the governmental regulation, statute or action being impugned, and the practice, custom or tradition being relied upon to establish the right. In this case, therefore, the Court will consider the actions which led to the

appellant's being charged, the fishery regulation under which she was charged and the practices, customs and traditions she invokes in support of her claim.

[54] It should be acknowledged that a characterization of the nature of the appellant's claim from the actions which led to her being charged must be undertaken with some caution. In order to inform the court's analysis the activities must be considered at a general rather than at a specific level. Moreover, the court must bear in mind that the activities may be the exercise in a modern form of a practice, custom or tradition that existed prior to contact, and should vary its characterization of the claim accordingly.

In order to be integral a practice, custom or tradition must be of central significance to the aboriginal society in question

[55] To satisfy the integral to a distinctive culture test the aboriginal claimant must do more than demonstrate that a practice, custom or tradition was an aspect of, or took place in, the aboriginal society of which he or she is a part. The claimant must demonstrate that the practice, custom or tradition was a central and significant part of the society's distinctive culture. He or she must demonstrate, in other words, that the practice, custom or tradition was one of the things which made the culture of the society distinctive — that it was one of the things that truly *made the society what it was.*

[56] This aspect of the integral to a distinctive culture test arises from fact that aboriginal rights have their basis in the prior occupation of Canada by distinctive aboriginal societies. To recognize and affirm the prior occupation of Canada by distinctive aboriginal societies it is *to what makes those societies distinctive* that the court must look in identifying aboriginal rights. The court cannot look at those aspects of the aboriginal society that are true of every human society (e.g., eating to survive), nor can it look at those aspects of the aboriginal society that are only incidental or occasional to that society; the court must look instead to the defining and central attributes of the aboriginal society in question. It is only by focusing on the aspects of the aboriginal society that make that society distinctive that the definition of aboriginal rights will accomplish the purpose underlying s. 35(1).

[57] Moreover, the aboriginal rights protected by s. 35(1) have been said to have the purpose of reconciling pre-existing aboriginal societies with the assertion of Crown sovereignty over Canada. To reconcile aboriginal societies with Crown sovereignty it is necessary to identify the distinctive features of those societies; it is precisely those distinctive features which need to be acknowledged and reconciled with the sovereignty of the Crown.

[58] As was noted earlier, Lambert J.A. erred when he used the significance of a practice, custom or tradition as a means of identifying what the practice, custom or tradition is; however, he was correct to recognize that the significance of the practice, custom or tradition is

important. The significance of the practice, custom or tradition does not serve to identify the nature of a claim of acting pursuant to an aboriginal right; however, it is a key aspect of the court's inquiry into whether a practice, custom or tradition has been shown to be an integral part of the distinctive culture of an aboriginal community. The significance of the practice, custom or tradition will inform a court as to whether or not that practice, custom or tradition can be said to be truly integral to the distinctive culture in question.

[59] A practical way of thinking about this problem is to ask whether, without this practice, custom or tradition, the culture in question would be fundamentally altered or other than what it is. One must ask, to put the question affirmatively, whether or not a practice, custom or tradition is a defining feature of the culture in question.

The practices, customs and traditions which constitute aboriginal rights are those which have continuity with the practices, customs and traditions that existed prior to contact

[60] The time period that a court should consider in identifying whether the right claimed meets the standard of being integral to the aboriginal community claiming the right is the period prior to contact between aboriginal and European societies. Because it is the fact that distinctive aboriginal societies lived on the land prior to the arrival of Europeans that underlies the aboriginal rights protected by s. 35(1), it is to that pre-contact period that the courts must look in identifying aboriginal rights.

[61] The fact that the doctrine of aboriginal rights functions to reconcile the existence of pre-existing aboriginal societies with the sovereignty of the Crown does not alter this position. Although it is the sovereignty of the Crown that the pre-existing aboriginal societies are being reconciled with, it is to those pre-existing societies that the court must look in defining aboriginal rights. It is not the fact that aboriginal societies existed prior to Crown sovereignty that is relevant; it is the fact that they existed *prior to the arrival of Europeans in North America*. As such, the relevant time period is the period prior to the arrival of Europeans, not the period prior to the assertion of sovereignty by the Crown.

[62] That this is the relevant time should not suggest, however, that the aboriginal group claiming the right must accomplish the next to impossible task of producing conclusive evidence from pre-contact times about the practices, customs and traditions of their community. It would be entirely contrary to the spirit and intent of s. 35(1) to define aboriginal rights in such a fashion so as to preclude in practice any successful claim for the existence of such a right. The evidence relied upon by the applicant and the courts may relate to aboriginal practices, customs and traditions post-contact; it simply needs to be directed at demonstrating which aspects of the aboriginal community and society have their origins pre-contact. It is those practices, customs and traditions that can be rooted in the pre-contact societies of the aboriginal community in question that will constitute aboriginal rights.

[63] … Where an aboriginal community can demonstrate that a particular practice, custom or tradition is integral to its distinctive culture today, and that this practice, custom or tradition has continuity with the practices, customs and traditions of pre-contact times, that community will have demonstrated that the practice, custom or tradition is an aboriginal right for the purposes of s. 35(1).

[64] The concept of continuity is also the primary means through which the definition and identification of aboriginal rights will be consistent with the admonition in *Sparrow, supra*, at p. 1093, that "the phrase 'existing aboriginal rights' must be interpreted flexibly so as to permit their evolution over time". The concept of continuity is, in other words, the means by which a "frozen rights" approach to s. 35(1) will be avoided. Because the practices, customs and traditions protected by s. 35(1) are ones that exist today, subject only to the requirement that they be demonstrated to have continuity with the practices, customs and traditions which existed pre-contact, the definition of aboriginal rights will be one that, on its own terms, prevents those rights from being frozen in pre-contact times. The evolution of practices, customs and traditions into modern forms will not, provided that continuity with pre-contact practices, customs and traditions is demonstrated, prevent their protection as aboriginal rights.

[65] I would note that the concept of continuity does not require aboriginal groups to provide evidence of an unbroken chain of continuity between their current practices, customs and traditions, and those which existed prior to contact. It may be that for a period of time an aboriginal group, for some reason, ceased to engage in a practice, custom or tradition which existed prior to contact, but then resumed the practice, custom or tradition at a later date. Such an interruption will not preclude the establishment of an aboriginal right. Trial judges should adopt the same flexibility regarding the establishment of continuity that, as is discussed, *infra*, they are to adopt with regards to the evidence presented to establish the prior-to-contact practices, customs and traditions of the aboriginal group making the claim to an aboriginal right.

[66] Further, I would note that basing the identification of aboriginal rights in the period prior to contact is not inconsistent with the fact that s. 35(2) of the *Constitution Act, 1982* includes within the definition of "aboriginal peoples of Canada" the Métis people of Canada.

[67] Although s. 35 includes the Métis within its definition of "aboriginal peoples of Canada", and thus seems to link their claims to those of other aboriginal peoples under the general heading of "aboriginal rights", the history of the Métis, and the reasons underlying their inclusion in the protection given by s. 35, are quite distinct from those of other aboriginal peoples in Canada. As such, the manner in which the aboriginal rights of other aboriginal peoples are defined is not necessarily determinative of the manner in which the aboriginal rights of the Métis are defined. At the time when this Court is presented with a Métis claim under s. 35 it will then, with the benefit of the arguments of counsel, a factual context and a specific Métis claim, be able to explore the question of the purposes underlying s. 35's protection of the aboriginal rights of Métis

people, and answer the question of the kinds of claims which fall within s. 35(1)'s scope when the claimants are Métis. The fact that, for other aboriginal peoples, the protection granted by s. 35 goes to the practices, customs and traditions of aboriginal peoples prior to contact, is not necessarily relevant to the answer which will be given to that question. It may, or it may not, be the case that the claims of the Métis are determined on the basis of the pre-contact practices, customs and traditions of their aboriginal ancestors; whether that is so must await determination in a case in which the issue arises.

Courts must approach the rules of evidence in light of the evidentiary difficulties inherent in adjudicating aboriginal claims

[68] In determining whether an aboriginal claimant has produced evidence sufficient to demonstrate that her activity is an aspect of a practice, custom or tradition integral to a distinctive aboriginal culture, a court should approach the rules of evidence, and interpret the evidence that exists, with a consciousness of the special nature of aboriginal claims, and of the evidentiary difficulties in proving a right which originates in times where there were no written records of the practices, customs and traditions engaged in. The courts must not undervalue the evidence presented by aboriginal claimants simply because that evidence does not conform precisely with the evidentiary standards that would be applied in, for example, a private law torts case.

Claims to aboriginal rights must be adjudicated on a specific rather than general basis

[69] Courts considering a claim to the existence of an aboriginal right must focus specifically on the practices, customs and traditions of the particular aboriginal group claiming the right. In the case of *Kruger* [*Kruger v. The Queen*, [1978] 1 S.C.R. 104] this Court rejected the notion that claims to aboriginal rights could be determined on a general basis. This position is correct; the existence of an aboriginal right will depend entirely on the practices, customs and traditions of the *particular aboriginal community claiming the right*. As has already been suggested, aboriginal rights are constitutional rights, but that does not negate the central fact that the interests aboriginal rights are intended to protect relate to the specific history of the group claiming the right. Aboriginal rights are not general and universal; their scope and content must be determined on a case-by-case basis. The fact that one group of aboriginal people has an aboriginal right to do a particular thing will not be, without something more, sufficient to demonstrate that another aboriginal community has the same aboriginal right. The existence of the right will be specific to each aboriginal community.

For a practice, custom or tradition to constitute an aboriginal right it must be of independent significance to the aboriginal culture in which it exists

[70] In identifying those practices, customs and traditions that constitute the aboriginal rights recognized and affirmed by s. 35(1), a court must ensure that the practice, custom or tradition relied upon in a particular case is independently significant to the aboriginal community claiming the right. The practice, custom or tradition cannot exist simply as an incident to another practice, custom or tradition but must rather be itself of integral significance to the aboriginal society. Where two customs exist, but one is merely incidental to the other, the custom which is integral to the aboriginal community in question will qualify as an aboriginal right, but the custom that is merely incidental will not. Incidental practices, customs and traditions cannot qualify as aboriginal rights through a process of piggybacking on integral practices, customs and traditions.

The integral to a distinctive culture test requires that a practice, custom or tradition be distinctive; it does not require that that practice, custom or tradition be distinct

[71] The standard which a practice, custom or tradition must meet in order to be recognized as an aboriginal right is *not* that it be *distinct* to the aboriginal culture in question; the aboriginal claimants must simply demonstrate that the practice, custom or tradition is *distinctive*. A tradition or custom that is *distinct* is one that is unique — "different in kind or quality; unlike" (*Concise Oxford Dictionary*, *supra*). A culture with a distinct tradition must claim that in having such a tradition it is different from other cultures; a claim of distinctness is, by its very nature, a claim relative to other cultures or traditions. By contrast, a culture that claims that a practice, custom or tradition is *distinctive* — "distinguishing, characteristic" — makes a claim that is not relative; the claim is rather one about the culture's own practices, customs or traditions considered apart from the practices, customs or traditions of any other culture. It is a claim that this tradition or custom makes the culture *what it is*, not that the practice, custom or tradition is different from the practices, customs or traditions of another culture. The person or community claiming the existence of an aboriginal right protected by s. 35(1) need only show that the particular practice, custom or tradition which it is claiming to be an aboriginal right is distinctive, not that it is distinct.

· · · · ·

The influence of European culture will only be relevant to the inquiry if it is demonstrated that the practice, custom or tradition is only integral because of that influence

[73] The fact that Europeans in North America engaged in the same practices, customs or traditions as those under which an aboriginal right is claimed will only be relevant to the aboriginal claim if the practice, custom or tradition in question can only be said to exist because of the influence of

European culture. If the practice, custom or tradition was an integral part of the aboriginal community's culture prior to contact with Europeans, the fact that that practice, custom or tradition continued after the arrival of Europeans, and adapted in response to their arrival, is not relevant to determination of the claim; European arrival and influence cannot be used to deprive an aboriginal group of an otherwise valid claim to an aboriginal right. On the other hand, where the practice, custom or tradition arose solely as a response to European influences then that practice, custom or tradition will not meet the standard for recognition of an aboriginal right.

Courts must take into account both the relationship of aboriginal peoples to the land and the distinctive societies and cultures of aboriginal peoples

[74] As was noted in the discussion of the purposes of s. 35(1), aboriginal rights and aboriginal title are related concepts; aboriginal title is a sub-category of aboriginal rights which deals solely with claims of rights to land. The relationship between aboriginal title and aboriginal rights must not, however, confuse the analysis of what constitutes an aboriginal right. Aboriginal rights arise from the prior occupation of land, but they also arise from the prior social organization and distinctive cultures of aboriginal peoples on that land. In considering whether a claim to an aboriginal right has been made out, courts must look at both the relationship of an aboriginal claimant to the land *and* at the practices, customs and traditions arising from the claimant's distinctive culture and society. Courts must not focus so entirely on the relationship of aboriginal peoples with the land that they lose sight of the other factors relevant to the identification and definition of aboriginal rights.

. . . . .

Application of the Integral to a Distinctive Culture Test to the Appellant's Claim

[76] The first step in the application of the integral to a distinctive culture test requires the court to identify the precise nature of the appellant's claim to have been exercising an aboriginal right. In this case the most accurate characterization of the appellant's position is that she is claiming *an aboriginal right to exchange fish for money or for other goods*. She is claiming, in other words, that the practices, customs and traditions of the Sto:lo include as an integral part the exchange of fish for money or other goods.

[77] That this is the nature of the appellant's claim can be seen through both the specific acts which led to her being charged and through the regulation under which she was charged. Mrs. Van der Peet sold 10 salmon for $50. Such a sale, especially given the absence of evidence that the appellant had sold salmon on other occasions or on a regular basis, cannot be said to constitute a sale on a "commercial" or market basis. These actions are instead best characterized in the simple terms of an exchange of fish for money. It follows from this that the aboriginal right pursuant to which the appellant is arguing that her actions were taken is,

like the actions themselves, best characterized as an aboriginal right to exchange fish for money or other goods.

[Lamer C.J.C. then held that the trial judge made no error justifying an appellate court's substituting its finding of fact. These findings included: (1) prior to contact, exchanges of fish were only "incidental" to fishing for food purposes; (2) there was no "regularized trading system" among the Sto:lo prior to contact; (3) the trade engaged in between the Sto:lo and the Hudson's Bay Company, while certainly of significance to the Sto:lo society of the time, was found by the trial judge to be qualitatively different from that which was typical of the Sto:lo culture prior to contact; and (4) the Sto:lo exploitation of the fishery was not specialized and that suggested that the exchange of fish was not a central part of Sto:lo culture. As a result Lamer C.J.C. held that the appellant failed to demonstrate that the exchange of fish for money or other goods was an integral part of the distinctive Sto:lo culture that existed prior to contact, and he dismissed the appeal.]

. . . . .

[Justice L'Heureux-Dubé and McLachin J. wrote separate dissenting opinions in the *Van der Peet* case. Justice L'Heureux-Dubé would have characterized Aboriginal rights at a fairly high level of abstraction. She wrote:]

[157] Accordingly, s. 35(1) should be viewed as protecting, not a catalogue of individualized practices, traditions or customs, as the Chief Justice does, but the "distinctive culture" of which aboriginal activities are manifestations. Simply put, the emphasis would be on the significance of these activities to natives rather than on the activities themselves.

. . . . .

[162] … The criterion of "distinctive aboriginal culture" should not be limited to those activities that only aboriginal people have undertaken or that non-aboriginal people have not. Rather, all practices, traditions and customs which are connected enough to the self-identity and self-preservation of organized aboriginal societies should be viewed as deserving the protection of s. 35(1). Further, a generous, large and liberal construction should be given to these activities in order to give full effect to the constitutional recognition of the distinctiveness of aboriginal culture. Finally, it is almost trite to say that what constitutes a practice, tradition or custom distinctive to native culture and society must be examined through the eyes of aboriginal people, not through those of the non-native majority or the distorting lens of existing regulations.

[Justice L'Heureux-Dubé also critiqued Lamer C.J.C.'s reliance on non-Aboriginal arrival and activity in setting dates for reconciling Aboriginal rights. She wrote:]

[166] First, relying on the proclamation of sovereignty by the British imperial power as the "cut-off" for the development of aboriginal

practices, traditions and customs overstates the impact of European influence on aboriginal communities ...

[167] ... Second, crystallizing aboriginal practices, traditions and customs at the time of British sovereignty creates an arbitrary date for assessing existing aboriginal rights. ...

[168] ... As a third point, in terms of proof, the "frozen right" approach imposes a heavy and unfair burden on the natives: the claimant of an aboriginal right must prove that the aboriginal practice, tradition or custom is not only sufficiently significant and fundamental to the culture and social organization of the aboriginal group. ... This test embodies inappropriate and unprovable assumptions about aboriginal culture and society. ...

[As an alternative, L'Heureux-Dubé J. adopted what she termed a "dynamic rights" approach to Aboriginal rights. She wrote:]

[172] ... [A]boriginal rights must be permitted to maintain contemporary relevance in relation to the needs of the natives as their practices, traditions and customs change and evolve with the overall society in which they live. This generous, large and liberal interpretation of aboriginal rights protected under s. 35(1) would ensure their continued vitality.

[173] Distinctive aboriginal culture would not be frozen as of any particular time but would evolve so that aboriginal practices, traditions and customs maintain a continuing relevance to the aboriginal societies as these societies exist in the contemporary world. Instead of considering it as the turning point in aboriginal culture, British sovereignty would be regarded as having recognized and affirmed practices, traditions and customs which are sufficiently significant and fundamental to the culture and social organization of aboriginal people. ...

. . . . .

[175] ... Consequently, in order for an aboriginal right to be recognized and affirmed under s. 35(1) ... the determining factor should only be that the aboriginal activity has formed an integral part of a distinctive aboriginal culture — *i.e.*, to have been sufficiently significant and fundamental to the culture and social organization of the aboriginal group — for a substantial continuous period of time as defined above.

. . . . .

[178] In short, the substantial continuous period of time necessary to the recognition of aboriginal rights should be assessed based on (1) the type of aboriginal practices, traditions and customs, (2) the particular aboriginal culture and society, and (3) the reference period of 20 to 50 years. Such a time frame does not minimize the fact that in order to benefit from s. 35(1) protection, aboriginal activities must still form the core of the lives of native people ...

[Applying this test, L'Heureux-Dubé J.'s dissent concluded that the Sto:lo Band possessed a constitutionally protected Aboriginal right to sell, trade and barter fish for livelihood, support and sustenance purposes.]

. . . . .

[Justice McLachlin's dissent in *Van der Peet* also took issue with Lamer C.J.C.'s opinion and disposition of the case. She was critical of the Chief Justice's reliance on non-Aboriginal activity in defining Aboriginal rights. She regarded Aboriginal laws as underlying aboriginal rights. She wrote:]

[247] ... I cannot agree with the Chief Justice ... that it is essential that a practice be traceable to pre-contact times for it to qualify as a constitutional right. Aboriginal rights find their source not in a magic moment of European contact, but in the traditional laws and customs of the aboriginal people in question. ... One finds no mention in the text of s. 35(1) or in the jurisprudence of the moment of European contact as the definitive all-or-nothing time for establishing an aboriginal right. The governing concept is simply the traditional customs and laws of people prior to imposition of European law and customs. What must be established is continuity between the modern practice at issue and a traditional law or custom of the native people. Most often, that law or tradition will be traceable to time immemorial; otherwise it would not be an ancestral aboriginal law or custom. But date of contact is not the only moment to consider. What went before and after can be relevant too.

[248] My concern is that we not substitute an inquiry into the precise moment of first European contact — an inquiry which may prove difficult — for what is really at issue, namely the ancestral customs and laws observed by the indigenous peoples of the territory. ... I see no reason why evidence as to the laws and customs and territories of the aboriginals in this interval should not be considered in determining the nature and scope of their aboriginal rights. ...

[Justice McLachlin also criticized the breadth of Lamer C.J.C.'s "integral to a distinctive culture test" as being too broad and too indeterminate (at paras. 255-257). She argued that Aboriginal rights should be defined with reference to common law analogies. She wrote:]

[261] In my view, the better approach to defining aboriginal rights is an empirical approach. Rather than attempting to describe *a priori* what an aboriginal right is, we should look to history to see what sort of practices have been identified as aboriginal rights in the past. From this we may draw inferences as to the sort of things which may qualify as aboriginal rights under s. 35(1). Confronted by a particular claim, we should ask, "Is this like the sort of thing which the law has recognized in the past?". This is the time-honoured methodology of the common law. Faced with a new legal problem, the court looks to the past to see how the law has dealt with similar situations in the past. The court evaluates the new situation by reference to what has been held in the past and decides how it should be characterized. In this way, legal principles evolve on an incremental, pragmatic basis.

[Applying this framework, McLachlin J. held that the Sto:lo possessed Aboriginal rights to exchange fish for commercial purposes. Her dissent concluded:]

[282] The evidence establishes that by custom of the aboriginal people of British Columbia, the Sto:lo have lived since time immemorial at the place of their present settlement on the banks of the Fraser River. It also establishes that as a fishing people, they have for centuries used the fish from that river to sustain themselves. One may assume that the forest and vegetation on the land provided some of their shelter and clothing. However, their history indicates that even in days prior to European contact, the Sto:lo relied on fish, not only for food and ceremonial purposes, but also for the purposes of obtaining other goods through trade. Prior to contact with Europeans, this trade took place with other tribes; after contact, sales on a larger scale were made to the Hudson's Bay Company, a practice which continued for almost a century. In summary, the evidence conclusively establishes that over many centuries, the Sto:lo have used the fishery not only for food and ceremonial purposes, but also to satisfy a variety of other needs. Unless that right has been extinguished, and subject always to conservation requirements, they are entitled to continue to use the river for these purposes. To the extent that trade is required to achieve this end, it falls within that right.

Appeal dismissed.

———————

The Supreme Court's characterization of Aboriginal rights in *Van der Peet* as arising only where an activity was an element of a practice, tradition, or custom integral to the distinctive culture of the Aboriginal group claiming the right and traceable to pre-contact practices may be seen to have marked a significant departure from the previous standard, as set out in *Sparrow*. It also gives rise to a variety of questions:

1. Is Lamer C.J.C.'s restriction of Aboriginal rights to pre-contact practices evidence of an adherence to frozen rights theory?
2. Are temporal considerations key determinants in establishing Aboriginal rights?
3. When is "contact" for the purposes of establishing the existence of Aboriginal rights? What ought this be based upon?
4. Can post-contact practices created to replace pre-contact practices rendered ineffective by European settlement be protected under Lamer C.J.C.'s analysis in *Van der Peet*?

While the *Van der Peet* decision made significant changes to *Sparrow's* characterization of Aboriginal rights, the Supreme Court of Canada's decision in *R. v. Gladstone*, [1996] S.C.J. No. 79, [1996] 2 S.C.R. 723 (S.C.C.) also altered the precedent that had been established in *Sparrow*. In *Gladstone*, the Supreme Court of Canada also addressed the application of the justification test outlined in *Sparrow* to laws that unduly interfered with the exercise of Aboriginal commercial fishing rights. Gladstone was a member of the Heiltsuk Band, charged with attempting to sell herring spawn on kelp without a proper licence. His defence to the charge was that he was exercising a pre-existing right to fish for commercial purposes. After his conviction was upheld by both the Supreme Court of British Columbia and the Court of Appeal, the accused appealed to the Supreme Court of Canada. A majority of the Court (La Forest J. dissenting) found that there was an Aboriginal right that had not been extinguished, and that there was a *prima facie* infringement. The Chief Justice held the commercial sale or barter of herring spawn on kelp to be an Aboriginal right, since it was found to constitute a central, significant and defining feature of the culture of the Heiltsuk prior to contact. The majority also found that there was no clean and plain intention to extinguish the right, and therefore that the regulation of the right was *prima facie* an infringement. The key elements of *Gladstone*, as reproduced below, are those aspects of the decision relating to the justificatory standard that had been established in *Sparrow*.

R. v. GLADSTONE

[1996] S.C.J. No. 79, [1996] 2 S.C.R. 723, [1996] 4 C.N.L.R. 65,
[1996] 2 S.C.R. 723, [1996] 9 W.W.R. 149, 23 B.C.L.R. (3d) 155,
50 C.R. (4th) 111, 200 N.R. 189, 137 D.L.R. (4th) 648, 109 C.C.C. (3d) 193,
79 B.C.A.C. 161 (S.C.C.) 129 W.A.C. 161 (S.C.C.) (references omitted)

Sopinka, Gonthier, Cory, Iacobucci and **Major JJ.** concur with

Lamer C.J.C.: —

I. *Facts*

[1] Donald and William Gladstone, the appellants, are members of the Heiltsuk Band. The appellants were charged under s. 61(1) of the *Fisheries Act*, R.S.C. 1970, c. F-14, with the offences of offering to sell herring spawn on kelp caught under the authority of an Indian food fish licence, contrary to s. 27(5) of the *British Columbia Fishery (General) Regulations*, SOR/84-248 and of attempting to sell herring spawn on kelp not caught under the authority of a Category J herring spawn on kelp licence, contrary to s. 20(3) of the *Pacific Herring Fishery Regulations*, SOR/84-324. Only the charges arising under s. 20(3) of the *Pacific Herring Fishery Regulations* are still at issue in this appeal.

[2] The charges arose out of events taking place in April of 1988. On approximately April 27, 1988 the appellants shipped 4,200 pounds of herring spawn on kelp from Bella Bella to Richmond, a suburb of Vancouver. On April 28, 1988 the appellants took a pail containing approximately 35 pounds of herring spawn on kelp to Seaborn Enterprises Limited, a fish store in Vancouver. At Seaborn Enterprises the appellants had a conversation with Mr. Katsu Hirose, the owner of the store, in which they asked Mr. Hirose if he was "interested" in herring spawn on kelp. Mr.

Hirose informed the appellants that he did not purchase herring spawn on kelp from Native Indians. Upon leaving Seaborn Enterprises the appellants, who had been under surveillance by fisheries officers throughout these events, were arrested and the entire 4,200 pounds of herring spawn on kelp was seized. Upon arrest the appellant William Gladstone produced an Indian food fish licence permitting him to harvest 500 pounds of herring spawn on kelp.

. . . . .

Justification

[54] In *Sparrow* [*R. v. Sparrow*, [1990] S.C.J. No. 49, [1990] 1 S.C.R. 1075], Dickson C.J. and La Forest J. articulated a two-part test for determining whether government actions infringing aboriginal rights can be justified. ...

. . . . .

[56] In this case, where, particularly at the stage of justification, the context varies significantly from that in *Sparrow*, it will be necessary to revisit the *Sparrow* test and to adapt the justification test it lays out in order to apply that test to the circumstances of this appeal.

[57] Two points of variation are of particular significance. First, the right recognized and affirmed in this case — to sell herring spawn on kelp commercially — differs significantly from the right recognized and affirmed in *Sparrow* — the right to fish for food, social and ceremonial purposes. That difference lies in the fact that the right at issue in *Sparrow* has an inherent limitation which the right recognized and affirmed in this appeal lacks. The food, social and ceremonial needs for fish of any given band of aboriginal people are internally limited — at a certain point the band will have sufficient fish to meet these needs. The commercial sale of the herring spawn on kelp, on the other hand, has no such internal limitation; the only limits on the Heiltsuk's need for herring spawn on kelp for commercial sale are the external constraints of the demand of the market and the availability of the resource. This is particularly so in this case where the evidence supports a right to exchange fish on a genuinely commercial basis; the evidence in this case does not justify limiting the right to harvest herring spawn on kelp on a commercial basis to, for example, the sale of herring spawn on kelp for the purposes of obtaining a "moderate livelihood". ...

[58] The significance of this difference for the *Sparrow* test relates to the position taken in that case that, subject to the limits of conservation, aboriginal rights holders must be given priority in the fishery. In a situation where the aboriginal right is internally limited, so that it is clear when that right has been satisfied and other users can be allowed to participate in the fishery, the notion of priority, as articulated in *Sparrow*, makes sense. In that situation it is understandable that in an *exceptional*

year, when conservation concerns are severe, it will be possible for aboriginal rights holders to be alone allowed to participate in the fishery, while in more ordinary years other users will be allowed to participate in the fishery after the aboriginal rights to fish for food, social and ceremonial purposes have been met.

[59] Where the aboriginal right has no internal limitation, however, what is described in *Sparrow* as an exceptional situation becomes the ordinary: in the circumstance where the aboriginal right has no internal limitation, the notion of priority, as articulated in *Sparrow*, would mean that where an aboriginal right is recognized and affirmed that right would become an exclusive one. Because the right to sell herring spawn on kelp to the commercial market can never be said to be satisfied while the resource is still available and the market is not sated, to give priority to that right in the manner suggested in *Sparrow* would be to give the right-holder exclusivity over any person not having an aboriginal right to participate in the herring spawn on kelp fishery.

. . . . .

[61] The basic insight of *Sparrow* — that aboriginal rights holders have priority in the fishery — is a valid and important one; however, the articulation in that case of what priority means, and its suggestion that it can mean exclusivity under certain limited circumstances, must be refined to take into account the varying circumstances which arise when the aboriginal right in question has no internal limitations.

[62] Where the aboriginal right is one that has no internal limitation then the doctrine of priority does not require that, after conservation goals have been met, the government allocate the fishery so that those holding an aboriginal right to exploit that fishery on a commercial basis are given an exclusive right to do so. Instead, the doctrine of priority requires that the government demonstrate that, in allocating the resource, it has taken account of the existence of aboriginal rights and allocated the resource in a manner respectful of the fact that those rights have priority over the exploitation of the fishery by other users. This right is at once both procedural and substantive; at the stage of justification the government must demonstrate both that the process by which it allocated the resource and the actual allocation of the resource which results from that process reflect the prior interest of aboriginal rights holders in the fishery.

[63] The content of this priority — something less than exclusivity but which nonetheless gives priority to the aboriginal right — must remain somewhat vague pending consideration of the government's actions in specific cases. ... [U]nder *Sparrow*'s priority doctrine, where the aboriginal right to be given priority is one without internal limitation, courts should assess the government's actions not to see whether the government has given exclusivity to that right (the least drastic means) but rather to determine whether the government has taken into account the existence and importance of such rights.

[64] That no blanket requirement is imposed under the priority doctrine should not suggest, however, that no guidance is possible in this area, or that the government's actions will not be subject to scrutiny. Questions relevant to the determination of whether the government has granted priority to aboriginal rights holders are those enumerated in *Sparrow* relating to consultation and compensation, as well as questions such as whether the government has accommodated the exercise of the aboriginal right to participate in the fishery (through reduced licence fees, for example), whether the government's objectives in enacting a particular regulatory scheme reflect the need to take into account the priority of aboriginal rights holders, the extent of the participation in the fishery of aboriginal rights holders relative to their percentage of the population, how the government has accommodated different aboriginal rights in a particular fishery (food *versus* commercial rights, for example), how important the fishery is to the economic and material well-being of the band in question, and the criteria taken into account by the government in, for example, allocating commercial licences amongst different users. These questions, like those in *Sparrow*, do not represent an exhaustive list of the factors that may be taken into account in determining whether the government can be said to have given priority to aboriginal rights holders; they give some indication, however, of what such an inquiry should look like.

. . . . .

[69] I now turn to the second significant difference between this case and *Sparrow*. In *Sparrow*, while the Court recognized at p. 1113 that, beyond conservation, there could be other "compelling and substantial" objectives pursuant to which the government could act in accordance with the first branch of the justification test, the Court was not required to delineate what those objectives might be. Further, in delineating the priority requirement, and the relationship between aboriginal rights-holders and other users of the fishery, the only objective considered by the Court was conservation. ...

[70] Considering this question is made more difficult in this case because, as will be discussed below, almost no evidence has been provided to this Court about the objectives the government was pursuing in allocating the herring resource as it did. Absent some concrete objectives to assess, it is difficult to identify the objectives other than conservation that will meet the "compelling and substantial" standard laid out in *Sparrow*. That being said, however, it is possible to make some general observations about the nature of the objectives that the government can pursue under the first branch of the *Sparrow* justification test.

. . . . .

[73] Aboriginal rights are recognized and affirmed by s. 35(1) in order to reconcile the existence of distinctive aboriginal societies prior to the arrival of Europeans in North America with the assertion of Crown sovereignty over that territory; they are the means by which the critical

and integral aspects of those societies are maintained. Because, however, distinctive aboriginal societies exist within, and are a part of, a broader social, political and economic community, over which the Crown is sovereign, there are circumstances in which, in order to pursue objectives of compelling and substantial importance to that community as a whole (taking into account the fact that aboriginal societies are a part of that community), some limitation of those rights will be justifiable. Aboriginal rights are a necessary part of the reconciliation of aboriginal societies with the broader political community of which they are part; limits placed on those rights are, where the objectives furthered by those limits are of sufficient importance to the broader community as a whole, *equally* a necessary part of that reconciliation.

[74] The recognition of conservation as a compelling and substantial goal demonstrates this point. Given the integral role the fishery has played in the distinctive cultures of many aboriginal peoples, conservation can be said to be something the pursuit of which can be linked to the recognition of the existence of such distinctive cultures. Moreover, because conservation is of such overwhelming importance to Canadian society as a whole, including aboriginal members of that society, it is a goal the pursuit of which is consistent with the reconciliation of aboriginal societies with the larger Canadian society of which they are a part. In this way, conservation can be said to be a compelling and substantial objective which, provided the rest of the *Sparrow* justification standard is met, will justify governmental infringement of aboriginal rights.

[75] Although by no means making a definitive statement on this issue, I would suggest that with regards to the distribution of the fisheries resource after conservation goals have been met, objectives such as the pursuit of economic and regional fairness, and the recognition of the historical reliance upon, and participation in, the fishery by non-aboriginal groups, are the type of objectives which can (at least in the right circumstances) satisfy this standard. *In the right circumstances, such objectives are in the interest of all Canadians and, more importantly, the reconciliation of aboriginal societies with the rest of Canadian society may well depend on their successful attainment.*

. . . . .

[77] Other than with regards to the first aspect of the government's regulatory scheme, the evidence and testimony presented in this case is insufficient for this Court to make a determination as to whether the government's regulatory scheme is justified. ...

. . . . .

[82] ... A new trial on the question of justification will remedy this deficiency.

[83] A new trial is not, however, necessary with regards to the first aspect of the government's scheme; the evidentiary record clearly demonstrates that this aspect of the government's scheme was justified.

Witnesses testified as to the conservation objectives of setting the stock at 20 per cent and as to the difficulties encountered by the herring fishery when the catch was set at much higher levels, as was the case in the 1960s. Moreover, the defence witness Dr. Gary Vigers testified that "fisheries management is full of uncertainty"; in the context of such uncertainty this Court must grant a certain level of deference to the government's approach to fisheries management.

. . . . .

[85] In the result, the appeal is allowed and a new trial directed on the issue of guilt or innocence and, with regards to the constitutionality of s. 20(3), on the issue of the justifiability of the government's allocation of herring.

[L'Heureux-Dubé J., in separate reasons, concurred with the Chief Justice. McLachlin J., in separate reasons, would have allowed the appeal to the extent of confirming the existence of an Aboriginal right of the Heiltsuk to sell herring spawn on kelp for sustenance purposes, and would have ordered a new trial to decide whether that right had been infringed, and if so, whether such an infringement had been justified. La Forest J. dissented and would have dismissed the appeal, holding that the right of the Heiltsuk band to sell herring spawn on kelp, assuming that it was an Aboriginal right, had been extinguished by the Crown.]

─────────────

The extension of the *Sparrow* justificatory standard in *Gladstone* has garnered significant criticism. In particular, Lamer C.J.C.'s majority judgment has been criticized for allowing infringements of Aboriginal rights based on public interest standards, something that the unanimous decision in *Sparrow* had rejected as being "so vague as to provide no meaningful guidance and so broad as to be unworkable as a test for the justification of a limitation on constitutional rights".[4] As McLachlin J. explained in her judgment in *Van der Peet*:

> The extension of the concept of compelling objective to matters like economic and regional fairness and the interests of non-Aboriginal fishers, by contrast, would negate the very Aboriginal right to fish itself, on the ground that this is required for the reconciliation of Aboriginal rights and other interests and the consequent good of the community as a whole. This is not limitation required for the responsible exercise of the right, but rather limitation on the basis of the economic demands of non-Aboriginals. It is limitation of a different order than the conservation, harm prevention type of limitation sanctioned in *Sparrow*.

Kent McNeil has also commented that the former Chief Justice's approach to justification allows Aboriginal rights to be overridden "on broad policy grounds relating to economic and regional fairness, and even to support the economic interests of particular groups such as commercial fishers whose historic use of the fishery may well have been a violation of aboriginal rights all along".[5]

While *Gladstone* altered *Sparrow*'s justificatory standard for legislative infringements of Aboriginal rights, the Supreme Court in *Delgamuukw v. British Columbia, infra,* further altered that test to render it applicable to infringements of Aboriginal title. Aboriginal title is one important category of Aboriginal rights which will be discussed in greater detail in Chapter 3. The discussion of the justificatory standard for Aboriginal title in *Delgamuukw* is also important for its summary of the standard for infringements of Aboriginal rights from *Sparrow* through *Gladstone.*

DELGAMUUKW v. BRITISH COLUMBIA

[1997] S.C.J. No. 108, [1977] 3 S.C.R. 1010 (S.C.C.)

Cory, McLachlin, and **Major JJ.** concur with

Lamer C.J.C.: —

(f) *Infringements of Aboriginal Title: the Test of Justification*

(i)   *Introduction*

The aboriginal rights recognized and affirmed by s. 35(1), including aboriginal title, are not absolute. Those rights may be infringed, both by the federal (e.g., *Sparrow*) and provincial (e.g., *Côté*) governments. However, s. 35(1) requires that those infringements satisfy the test of justification. In this section, I will review the Court's nascent jurisprudence on justification and explain how that test will apply in the context of infringements of aboriginal title.

(ii)   *General Principles*

The test of justification has two parts, which I shall consider in turn. First, the infringement of the aboriginal right must be in furtherance of a legislative objective that is compelling and substantial. I explained in *Gladstone* that compelling and substantial objectives were those which were directed at either one of the purposes underlying the recognition and affirmation of aboriginal rights by s. 35(1), which are (at para. 72):

> ... the recognition of the prior occupation of North America by aboriginal peoples or ... the reconciliation of aboriginal prior occupation with the assertion of the sovereignty of the Crown.

I noted that the latter purpose will often "be most relevant" (at para. 72) at the stage of justification. I think it important to repeat why (at para. 73) that is so:

> Because ... distinctive aboriginal societies exist within, and are part of, a broader social, political and economic community, over which the Crown is

sovereign, there are circumstances in which, in order to pursue objectives of compelling and substantial importance to that community as a whole (taking into account the fact that aboriginal societies are part of that community), some limitation of those rights will be justifiable. *Aboriginal rights are a necessary part of the reconciliation of aboriginal societies with the broader political community of which they are part; limits placed on those rights are, where the objectives furthered by those limits are of sufficient importance to the broader community as a whole, equally a necessary part of that reconciliation.* [Emphasis added; "equally" emphasized in original.]

The conservation of fisheries, which was accepted as a compelling and substantial objective in *Sparrow*, furthers both of these purposes, because it simultaneously recognizes that fishing is integral to many aboriginal cultures, and also seeks to reconcile aboriginal societies with the broader community by ensuring that there are fish enough for all. But legitimate government objectives also include "the pursuit of economic and regional fairness" and "the recognition of the historical reliance upon, and participation in, the fishery by non-aboriginal groups" (para. 75). By contrast, measures enacted for relatively unimportant reasons, such as sports fishing without a significant economic component (*Adams, supra*) would fail this aspect of the test of justification.

The second part of the test of justification requires an assessment of whether the infringement is consistent with the special fiduciary relationship between the Crown and aboriginal peoples. What has become clear is that the requirements of the fiduciary duty are a function of the "legal and factual context" of each appeal (*Gladstone, supra*, at para. 56). *Sparrow* and *Gladstone*, for example, interpreted and applied the fiduciary duty in terms of the idea of *priority*. The theory underlying that principle is that the fiduciary relationship between the Crown and aboriginal peoples demands that aboriginal interests be placed first. However, the fiduciary duty does not demand that aboriginal rights always be given priority. As was said in *Sparrow, supra*, at pp. 1114-15:

> The nature of the constitutional protection afforded by s. 35(1) *in this context* demands that there be a link between the question of justification and the allocation of priorities in the fishery. [Emphasis added.]

Other contexts permit, and may even require, that the fiduciary duty be articulated in other ways (at p. 1119):

> Within the analysis of justification, there are further questions to be addressed, depending on the circumstances of the inquiry. These include the questions of whether there has been as little infringement as possible in order to effect the desired result; whether, in a situation of expropriation, fair compensation is available; and, whether the aboriginal group in question has been consulted with respect to the conservation measures being implemented.

Sparrow did not explain when the different articulations of the fiduciary duty should be used. Below, I suggest that the choice between them will in large part be a function of the nature of the aboriginal right at issue.

In addition to variation in the *form* which the fiduciary duty takes, there will also be variation in degree of scrutiny required by the fiduciary duty of the infringing measure or action. The degree of scrutiny is a function of the nature of the aboriginal right at issue. The distinction between *Sparrow* and *Gladstone*, for example, turned on whether the right amounted to the exclusive use of a resource, which in turn was a function of whether the right had an internal limit. In *Sparrow*, the right was internally limited, because it was a right to fish for food, ceremonial and social purposes, and as a result would only amount to an exclusive right to use the fishery in exceptional circumstances. Accordingly, the requirement of priority was applied strictly to mean that (at p. 1116) "any allocation of priorities after valid conservation measures have been implemented must give top priority to Indian food fishing".

In *Gladstone*, by contrast, the right to sell fish commercially was only limited by supply and demand. Had the test for justification been applied in a strict form in *Gladstone*, the aboriginal right would have amounted to an exclusive right to exploit the fishery on a commercial basis. This was not the intention of *Sparrow*, and I accordingly modified the test for justification, by altering the idea of priority. ... After *Gladstone*, in the context of commercial activity, the priority of aboriginal rights is constitutionally satisfied if the government had taken those rights into account and has allocated a resource "in a manner respectful" (at para. 62) of that priority. A court must be satisfied that "the government has taken into account the existence and importance of [aboriginal] rights" (at para. 63) which it determines by asking the following questions (at para. 64):

> Questions relevant to the determination of whether the government has granted priority to aboriginal rights holders are ... questions such as whether the government has accommodated the exercise of the aboriginal right to participate in the fishery (through reduced licence fees, for example), whether the government's objectives in enacting a particular regulatory scheme reflect the need to take into account the priority of aboriginal rights holders, the extent of the participation in the fishery of aboriginal rights holders relative to their percentage of the population, how the government has accommodated different aboriginal rights in a particular fishery (food *versus* commercial rights, for example), how important the fishery is to the economic and material well-being of the band in question, and the criteria taken into account by the government in, for example, allocating commercial licences amongst different users.

(iii) *Justification and Aboriginal Title*

... In the wake of *Gladstone*, the range of legislative objectives that can justify the infringement of aboriginal title is fairly broad. Most of these objectives can be traced to the *reconciliation* of the prior occupation of North America by aboriginal peoples with the assertion of Crown sovereignty, which entails the recognition that "distinctive aboriginal societies exist within, and are a part of, a broader social, political and economic community" (at para. 73). In my opinion, the development of agriculture, forestry, mining, and hydroelectric power, the general economic development of the interior of British Columbia, protection of the environment or endangered species, the building of infrastructure and the settlement of foreign populations to support those aims, are the kinds of objectives that are consistent with this purpose and, in principle, can justify the infringement of aboriginal title. Whether a particular measure or government act can be explained by reference to one of those objectives, however, is ultimately a question of fact that will have to be examined on a case-by-case basis.

The manner in which the fiduciary duty operates with respect to the second stage of the justification test — both with respect to the standard of scrutiny and the particular form that the fiduciary duty will take — will be a function of the nature of aboriginal title. Three aspects of aboriginal title are relevant here. First, aboriginal title encompasses the right to *exclusive* use and occupation of land; second, aboriginal title encompasses *the right to choose* to what uses land can be put, subject to the ultimate limit that those uses cannot destroy the ability of the land to sustain future generations of aboriginal peoples; and third, that lands held pursuant to aboriginal title have an inescapable *economic component*.

The exclusive nature of aboriginal title is relevant to the degree of scrutiny of the infringing measure or action. For example, if the Crown's fiduciary duty requires that aboriginal title be given priority, then it is the altered approach to priority that I laid down in *Gladstone* which should apply. What is required is that the government demonstrate ... "both that the process by which it allocated the resource and the actual allocation of the resource which results from that process reflect the prior interest" of the holders of aboriginal title in the land. By analogy with *Gladstone*, this might entail, for example, that governments accommodate the participation of aboriginal peoples in the development of the resources of British Columbia, that the conferral of fee simples for agriculture, and of leases and licences for forestry and mining reflect the prior occupation of aboriginal title lands, that economic barriers to aboriginal uses of their lands (e.g., licensing fees) be somewhat reduced. This list is illustrative and not exhaustive. This is an issue that may involve an assessment of the various interests at stake in the resources in question. No doubt, there will be difficulties in determining the precise value of the aboriginal interest in the land and any grants, leases or licences given for its exploitation. These difficult economic considerations obviously cannot be solved here.

Moreover, the other aspects of aboriginal title suggest that the fiduciary duty may be articulated in a manner different than the idea of priority. This point becomes clear from a comparison between aboriginal title and the aboriginal right to fish for food in *Sparrow*. First, aboriginal title encompasses within it a right to choose to what ends a piece of land can be put. The aboriginal right to fish for food, by contrast, does not contain within it the same discretionary component. This aspect of aboriginal title suggests that the fiduciary relationship between the Crown and aboriginal peoples may be satisfied by the involvement of aboriginal peoples in decisions taken with respect to their lands. There is always a duty of consultation. Whether the aboriginal group has been consulted is relevant to determining whether the infringement of aboriginal title is justified, in the same way that the Crown's failure to consult an aboriginal group with respect to the terms by which reserve land is leased may breach its fiduciary duty at common law: *Guerin*. The nature and scope of the duty of consultation will vary with the circumstances. In occasional cases, when the breach is less serious or relatively minor, it will be no more than a duty to discuss important decisions that will be taken with respect to lands held pursuant to aboriginal title. Of course, even in these rare cases when the minimum acceptable standard is consultation, this consultation must be in good faith, and with the intention of substantially addressing the concerns of the aboriginal peoples whose lands are at issue. In most cases, it will be significantly deeper than mere consultation. Some cases may even require the full consent of an aboriginal nation, particularly when provinces enact hunting and fishing regulations in relation to aboriginal lands.

Second, aboriginal title, unlike the aboriginal right to fish for food, has an inescapably economic aspect, particularly when one takes into account the modern uses to which lands held pursuant to aboriginal title can be put. The economic aspect of aboriginal title suggests that compensation is relevant to the question of justification as well, a possibility suggested in *Sparrow* and which I repeated in *Gladstone*. Indeed, compensation for breaches of fiduciary duty are a well-established part of the landscape of aboriginal rights: *Guerin*. In keeping with the duty of honour and good faith on the Crown, fair compensation will ordinarily be required when aboriginal title is infringed. The amount of compensation payable will vary with the nature of the particular aboriginal title affected and with the nature and severity of the infringement and the extent to which aboriginal interests were accommodated. Since the issue of damages was severed from the principal action, we received no submissions on the appropriate legal principles that would be relevant to determining the appropriate level of compensation of infringements of aboriginal title. In the circumstances, it is best that we leave those difficult questions to another day.

One may also query whether the distinction between the requirement for proof of Aboriginal rights — that they must be integral to the distinctive culture of the group claiming the right and identifiable prior to European contact under the *Van der Peet* standard — versus that for proof of Aboriginal title — that the group claiming title must have been in exclusive occupancy of the land in question at the time the Crown asserted sovereignty over the land, as established in *Delgamuukw v. British Columbia*, [1997] S.C.J. No. 108, [1997] 3 S.C.R. 1010 (S.C.C.) — under section 35(1) is an appropriate one. Are there valid reasons for looking to contact to determine Aboriginal rights, but looking to the time of the Crown's assertion of sovereignty to determine Aboriginal title? In *Delgamuukw*, *supra*, Lamer C.J.C. provided the following explanation at 1098:

> [I]n the context of Aboriginal title, sovereignty is the appropriate time period to consider for several reasons. ... Aboriginal title is a burden on the Crown's underlying title. However, the Crown did not gain this title until it asserted sovereignty over the land in question. Because it does not make

sense to speak of a burden on the underlying title before that title existed, aboriginal title crystallized at the time sovereignty was asserted. Secondly, aboriginal title does not raise the problem of distinguishing between distinctive, integral aboriginal practices, customs and traditions and those influenced or introduced by European contact. Under common law, the act of occupation or possession is sufficient to ground aboriginal title and it is not necessary to prove that the land was a distinctive or integral part of the aboriginal society before the arrival of Europeans. Finally, from a practical standpoint, it appears that the date of sovereignty is more certain than the date of first contact. It is often very difficult to determine the precise moment that each Aboriginal group had first contact with European culture. ... For these reasons, I conclude that Aboriginals must establish occupation of the land from the date of the assertion of sovereignty in order to sustain a claim for Aboriginal title.

In Lamer C.J.C.'s explanation of why the time period for establishing Aboriginal title differs from that in which to establish Aboriginal rights, his final point is one of expediency — that the date of sovereignty is more certain than the date of first contact and the former is easier to demonstrate. If expediency is a legitimate rationale for establishing a particular temporal period as a basis for the existence of a right, is there any reason why it ought to apply only to Aboriginal title and not to Aboriginal rights?

Although the *Delgamuukw* decision is significant for its differentiation of the test for demonstrating Aboriginal title versus that for Aboriginal rights, the Supreme Court of Canada previously considered the relationship between Aboriginal rights and Aboriginal title in its decisions in *R. v. Adams* and *R. v. Côté* (both of which are excerpted below). These cases are important for the distinctions they create between Aboriginal rights as a general category, and Aboriginal title as a specific right within the general categorization of Aboriginal rights. As you read *Adams* and *Côté*, ask yourself whether these distinctions and categorizations are supportable. Also ask yourself about the implications of these distinctions for Aboriginal peoples continuing to exercise Indigenous law-making power over their lands and people.

R. v. ADAMS

[1996] S.C.J. No. 87, [1996] 4 C.N.L.R. 1, [1996] 3 S.C.R. 101, 202 N.R. 89, 138 D.L.R. (4th) 657, 110 C.C.C. (3d) 97 (S.C.C.) (references omitted)

The judgment of **Lamer C.J.C.** and **La Forest, Sopinka, Gonthier, Cory, McLachlin, Iacobucci** and **Major JJ.** was delivered by

The Chief Justice: —

I. *Introduction*

[1] This appeal and the appeal of *R. v. Côté*, [1996] [3 S.C.R. 139] have been released simultaneously and should be read together in light of the closely related issues raised by both cases.

[2] The appellant, a Mohawk, was charged with the regulatory offence of fishing without a licence in Lake St. Francis in the St. Régis region of Quebec. He challenges his conviction on the basis that he was exercising an Aboriginal right to fish as recognized and affirmed by s. 35(1) of the *Constitution Act, 1982*.

[3] In resolving this appeal and the appeal in *Côté*, this Court must answer the question of whether Aboriginal rights are necessarily based in Aboriginal title to land, so that the fundamental claim that must be made in any Aboriginal rights case is to Aboriginal title, or whether Aboriginal title is instead one sub-set of the larger category of Aboriginal rights, so that fishing and other Aboriginal rights can exist independently of a claim to Aboriginal title.

[4] In the trilogy of *R. v. Van der Peet*, [1996] 2 S.C.R. 507, *R. v. N.T.C. Smokehouse Ltd.*, [1996] 2 S.C.R. 672, and *R. v. Gladstone*, [1996] 2 S.C.R. 723, this Court had opportunity to consider the question of the scope of the Aboriginal rights recognized and affirmed by s. 35(1). This case and *Côté* will require the application of the principles articulated in those cases to the question of the relationship between Aboriginal title and the other Aboriginal rights, particularly fishing rights, recognized and affirmed by s. 35(1). Furthermore, these two related appeals involve the claim of an Aboriginal right to fish within the historical boundaries of New France. As such, this Court must answer the question of whether, under the principles of the *Van der Peet* trilogy, the constitutional protection of s. 35(1) extends to Aboriginal customs, practices, and traditions which may not have achieved legal recognition under the colonial regime of New France prior to the transition to British sovereignty in 1763.

. . . . .

V. *Analysis*

Aboriginal Title and Aboriginal Rights

. . . . .

[26] In *Van der Peet* ... Aboriginal rights were said to be best understood as,

> ... first, the means by which the Constitution recognizes the fact that prior to the arrival of Europeans in North America the land was already occupied by distinctive Aboriginal societies, and as, second, the means by which that prior occupation is reconciled with the assertion of Crown sovereignty over Canadian territory.

From this basis the Court went on to hold ... that Aboriginal rights are identified through the following test:

> ... in order to be an Aboriginal right an activity must be an element of a practice, custom or tradition integral to the distinctive culture of the Aboriginal group claiming the right.

What this test, along with the conceptual basis which underlies it, indicates, is that while claims to Aboriginal title fall within the conceptual framework of Aboriginal rights, Aboriginal rights do not exist solely where a claim to Aboriginal title has been made out. Where an Aboriginal group has shown that a particular activity, custom or tradition taking place on the land was integral to the distinctive culture of that group then, *even if they have not shown that their occupation and use of the land was sufficient to support a claim of title to the land*, they will have demonstrated that they have an Aboriginal right to engage in that practice, custom or tradition. ... *Van der Peet* establishes that s. 35 recognizes and affirms the rights of those peoples who occupied North America prior to the arrival of the Europeans; that recognition and affirmation is not limited to those circumstances where an Aboriginal group's relationship with the land is of a kind sufficient to establish title to the land.

[27] To understand why Aboriginal rights cannot be inexorably linked to Aboriginal title it is only necessary to recall that some Aboriginal peoples were nomadic, varying the location of their settlements with the season and changing circumstances. ...

[28] Moreover, some Aboriginal peoples varied the location of their settlements both before and after contact. The Mohawks are one such people ... That this is the case may (although I take no position on this point) preclude the establishment of Aboriginal title to the lands on which they settled; however, it in no way subtracts from the fact that, wherever they were settled before or after contact, *prior to contact the Mohawks engaged in practices, traditions or customs on the land which were integral to their distinctive culture.*

. . . . .

[30] The recognition that Aboriginal title is simply one manifestation of the doctrine of Aboriginal rights should not, however, create the impression that the fact that some Aboriginal rights are linked to land use or occupation is unimportant. Even where an Aboriginal right exists on a tract of land to which the Aboriginal people in question do not have title, that right may well be site specific, with the result that it can be exercised only upon that specific tract of land. For example, if an Aboriginal people demonstrates that hunting on a specific tract of land was an integral part of their distinctive culture then, even if the right exists apart from title to that tract of land, the Aboriginal right to hunt is nonetheless defined as, and limited to, the right to hunt on the specific tract of land. A site-specific hunting or fishing right does not, simply because it is independent of Aboriginal title to the land on which it took place, become an abstract

fishing or hunting right exercisable anywhere; it continues to be a right to hunt or fish *on the tract of land in question.*

Aboriginal Rights and The Colony of New France

[31] The respondent raises another important question concerning the doctrine of Aboriginal rights under s. 35(1). The Aboriginal right to fish claimed in this instance relates to a tract of territory, specifically Lake St. Francis, which falls within the boundaries of New France prior to 1763. The respondent argues that this claimed right should be rejected as the French colonial regime never legally recognized the existence of Aboriginal title or any incident Aboriginal right to fish prior to the commencement of British sovereignty.

[32] Under the British law governing colonization, the Crown assumed ownership of newly discovered territories subject to an underlying interest of indigenous peoples in the occupation and use of such territories. By contrast, it is argued that under the French regime of colonization, the French monarch assumed full and complete ownership of all newly discovered territories upon discovery and symbolic possession. In the absence of a specific concession, colonists and Aboriginal peoples were only entitled to enjoy the use of the land through the grace and charity of the French monarch, but not by any recognized legal right. ... In brief, the respondent submits that regardless of the actual fishing practices of the Mohawks both prior to and during the French regime, the French Crown never formally recognized any legal right of the Mohawks to fish in Lake St. Francis, and thus no such right was received into the common law with the transition to British sovereignty in 1763.

[33] For the reasons developed in *Côté, supra*, this argument must be rejected. The respondent's characterization of the status of Aboriginal rights under French colonial law is open to question, although, as in *Côté*, I need not decide the point here. What is important is that, as explained in *Van der Peet, supra*, the purpose of the entrenchment of s. 35(1) was to extend constitutional protection to the practices, customs and traditions central to the distinctive culture of Aboriginal societies prior to contact with Europeans. If the exercise of such practices, customs and traditions effectively continued following contact in the absence of specific extinguishment, such practices, customs and traditions are entitled to constitutional recognition subject to the infringement and justification test outlined in *Sparrow, supra*, and more recently, in *Gladstone, supra*. The fact that a particular practice, custom or tradition continued following the arrival of Europeans, but in the absence of the formal gloss of legal recognition from the European colonizers, should not undermine the protection accorded to Aboriginal peoples. Section 35(1) would fail to achieve its noble purpose of preserving the integral and defining features of distinctive Aboriginal societies if it only protected those defining features which were fortunate enough to have received the legal approval of British and French colonizers.

. . . . .

VI. *Disposition*

[60] In the result the appeal is allowed and the appellant's conviction is set aside.

[61] For the reasons given above, the constitutional question must be answered as follows:

Question :   Is s. 4(1) of the *Quebec Fishery Regulations*, as they read on May 7, 1982, of no force or effect with respect to appellant in the circumstances of these proceedings in virtue of s. 52 of the *Constitution Act, 1982* by reason of the Aboriginal rights within the meaning of s. 35 of the *Constitution Act, 1982* invoked by appellant.

Answer :   Yes.

Appeal allowed.

As the *Adams* decision indicates, it was considered jointly with the appeal of the decision in *Côté*, below. Thus, it is necessary to consider both decisions together in order to acquire a true appreciation of the entirety of the issues considered by the Supreme Court of Canada therein.

R. v. CÔTÉ

[1996] S.C.J. No. 93, [1996] 4 C.N.L.R. 26, [1996] 3 S.C.R. 139, 202 N.R. 161, 138 D.L.R. (4th) 185, 110 C.C.C. (3d) 122 (S.C.C.) (references omitted)

The judgment of **Lamer C.J.C.** and **Sopinka, Gonthier, Cory, McLachlin, Iacobucci** and **Major JJ.** was delivered by

The Chief Justice: —

I. Introduction

[1] This appeal and the appeal of *R. v. Adams*, [1996] 3 S.C.R. 101, have been released simultaneously and should be read together in light of the closely related issues raised by both cases.

[2] The appellants, members of the Algonquin people, were convicted of the offence of entering a controlled harvest zone in the Outaouais region of Quebec without paying the required fee for motor vehicle access. The appellant Côté was additionally convicted of the offence of fishing within the zone in the absence of a valid licence. The appellants jointly challenge their convictions on the basis that they were exercising an aboriginal right and a concurrent treaty right to fish on their ancestral lands as recognized and protected by s. 35(1) of the *Constitution Act, 1982*.

[3] The appellant Côté was convicted under the same federal fishing regulation as the accused in *Adams*. In resolving both this appeal and *Adams*, this Court must answer the question of whether an aboriginal

fishing or other right must be necessarily incident to a claim of aboriginal title in land, or whether an aboriginal right may exist independently of a claim of aboriginal title. ...

[4] Additionally, these two related appeals involve the claim of an aboriginal right within the historic boundaries of New France. As such, this Court must answer the question of whether, under the principles of the *Van der Peet* trilogy, the constitutional protection of s. 35(1) extends to aboriginal practices, customs and traditions which did not achieve legal recognition under the colonial regime of New France prior to the transition to British sovereignty in 1763.

. . . . .

A. *Aboriginal Rights*

Aboriginal Rights and Aboriginal Title

[35] Throughout the proceedings below, the appellants framed their ancestral right to fish on the Z.E.C. territory as an aboriginal right incidental to a claim of aboriginal title.

. . . .

[38] For the reasons I have given in the related appeal in *Adams*, *supra*, I find that aboriginal rights may indeed exist independently of aboriginal title. As I explained in *Adams* ... aboriginal title is simply one manifestation of the doctrine of aboriginal rights. ...

[39] However, as I stressed in *Adams* ... a protected aboriginal right falling short of aboriginal title may nonetheless have an important link to the land. An aboriginal practice, custom or tradition entitled to protection as an aboriginal right will frequently be limited to a specific territory or location, depending on the actual pattern of exercise of such an activity prior to contact. As such, an aboriginal right will often be defined in site-specific terms, with the result that it can only be exercised upon a specific tract of land.

. . . . .

Aboriginal Rights within New France

[42] In the proceedings below, the respondent adopted the position that the Algonquins could not assert the existence of aboriginal title within the former boundaries of New France in light of the process of French colonization and the legal transition to British sovereignty following capitulation. ...

[43] The argument of the respondent is fairly straightforward. Under the British law of discovery, the British Crown assumed ownership of newly discovered territories subject to an underlying interest of indigenous peoples in the occupation and use of such territories. Accordingly, the Crown was only able to acquire full ownership of the

lands in the New World through the slow process of negotiations with aboriginal groups leading to purchase or surrender.

[44] Unlike the British process of colonization, however, it is suggested that the French Crown did not legally recognize any subsisting aboriginal interest in land upon discovery. Rather, the French Crown assumed full ownership of all discovered lands upon symbolic possession and conquest. Accordingly, French colonizers never engaged in the consistent practice of negotiating formal territorial surrenders with the aboriginal peoples. G. F. G. Stanley, summarized this process in "The First Indian 'Reserves' in Canada", *Revue d'histoire de l'Amérique française*, 4, 2 (1950): 178-210:

> One point of interest emerges with respect to the Indian reserves of the Ancien Régime. At no time was there any recognition on the part of the French crown of any aboriginal proprietary rights in the soil. The French settler occupied his lands in Canada without any thought of compensating the native. There were no formal surrenders from the Indians, no negotiations, and no treaties such as marked the Indian policy of the British period. The lands which were set aside for the Indians were granted not of right but of grace, not to the Indians themselves but to the religious orders who cared for them. The nearest approach to any grant to the Indians themselves was the Sillery grant of 1651. Whatever rights the Indians acquired flowed not from a theoretical aboriginal title but from the clemency of the crown or the charity of individuals.

... The French monarch did cede important specific lands to missions for the purpose of organizing and evangelizing the indigenous residents of New France. As well, colonial authorities did indeed tolerate the fact that aboriginal peoples occupied and engaged in traditional practices and activities (such as fishing and hunting) on Crown lands. However, it is contended that the toleration of such activities represented a general liberty accorded to all of the King's subjects, rather than the recognition of a special right enjoyed by aboriginal peoples.

[45] The respondent further argues that following capitulation, pre-existing French colonial law was fully received under the terms of *The Quebec Act, 1774* and under the general principles of the British law of conquest.... In the absence of a formal renunciation of the French colonial system, it is submitted that the common law thus incorporated the non-existence of aboriginal rights within New France in its doctrine of aboriginal title.

[46] ... I am not persuaded that the status of French colonial law was as clear as the respondent suggests. As H. Brun admitted in "Les droits des Indiens" ... while French law never explicitly recognized the existence of a *sui generis* aboriginal interest in land, [TRANSLATION] "nor did it [explicitly] state that such an interest did not exist". Indeed, some legal historians have suggested that the French Crown never assumed full title and ownership to the lands occupied by aboriginal peoples in light of the nature and pattern of French settlement in New France.

[47] According to this historical interpretation, from the time of Champlain to 1763, French settlements within New France fell almost exclusively within the St. Lawrence Valley. At the date of Champlain's

arrival in the Montreal area in 1603, the surrounding region was largely devoid of indigenous inhabitants. In one of the mysteries of the history of New France, the Iroquois people who occupied the region at the date of Jacques Cartier's visit in 1534 had simply disappeared by 1603. The French colonists thus claimed and occupied this particular area as *terra nullius*. But these historians argue that the French chose not to further encroach on the traditional lands of the aboriginal peoples surrounding the valley. In the west of New France, for instance, French seigneuries did not extend further than the Long-Sault, stopping well before the vague eastern boundary of the ancestral lands of the Algonquins. The French, of course, had good reason for not encroaching upon these lands, as they were both outnumbered and surrounded by potentially hostile forces in the Valley. Content with occupation of the *terra nullius* of the Valley, the French thus never engaged in a pattern of surrender and purchase similar to British colonial policy. In this interpretation, it is argued that the French Crown only assumed ownership of the lands lining the St. Lawrence River which it actually occupied and organized under the Seigneurial system. ...

[48] This argument is supported by the fact that, in its diplomatic relations, the French Crown maintained that aboriginal peoples were sovereign nations rather than mere subjects of the monarch. As Cumming and Mickenberg chronicle in *Native Rights in Canada* ... in the diplomatic period following the Treaty of Utrecht, 1713, the French officially maintained that they could not cede title to lands occupied by aboriginal peoples in the Maritimes and Upper New York State as such peoples were independent nations allied with the French Crown, rather than mere royal subjects. The French similarly disavowed responsibility for Indian attacks on the British, on the grounds that aboriginal nations were independent allies of the French monarch rather than his royal subjects. ... While such assertions were raised in the context of subtle diplomatic manoeuvring between the two European powers, they do not appear to have been received as entirely hollow.

[49] Furthermore, even under the assumption that the respondent's characterization of French colonial system is accurate, it is not at all clear that French colonial law governing relations with aboriginal peoples was mechanically received by the common law upon the commencement of British sovereignty. It is true that under *The Quebec Act, 1774*, and under the legal principles of British conquest, the pre-existing laws governing the acquired territory of New France were received and continued in the absence of subsequent legislative modification. It is by these legal means that the distinct civilian system of private law continues to operate and thrive within the modern boundaries of the province of Quebec. But while the new British regime received and continued the former system of colonial law governing the proprietary relations between private individuals, it is less clear that the advent of British sovereignty continued the French system of law governing the relations between the British Crown and indigenous societies. In short, the common law recognizing aboriginal title was arguably a necessary incident of British sovereignty

which displaced the pre-existing colonial law governing New France. As Professor Slattery argues in "Understanding Aboriginal Rights"...:

> The doctrine of aboriginal rights, like other doctrines of colonial law, applied automatically to a new colony when the colony was acquired. In the same way that colonial law determined whether a colony was deemed to be 'settled' or 'conquered', and whether English law was automatically introduced or local laws retained, it also supplied the presumptive legal structure governing the position of native peoples. The doctrine of aboriginal rights applied, then, to every British colony that now forms part of Canada, from Newfoundland to British Columbia. Although the doctrine was a species of unwritten British law, it was not part of English common law in the narrow sense, and its application to a colony did not depend on whether or not English common law was introduced there. Rather the doctrine was part of a body of fundamental constitutional law that was logically prior to the introduction of English common law and governed its application in the colony.

Indeed, this Court has held that the law of aboriginal title represents a distinct species of federal common law rather than a simple subset of the common or civil law or property law operating within the province. ...

[50] However, I do not rely on such reasoning to reject the position of the respondent on the reception of French colonial law. Rather, I believe that the respondent's submission is best addressed under the terms and purpose of the constitutional enactment of s. 35(1) of the *Constitution Act, 1982.*

[51] I do not believe that the intervention of French sovereignty negated the potential existence of aboriginal rights within the former boundaries of New France under s. 35(1). The entrenchment of aboriginal ancestral and treaty rights in s. 35(1) has changed the landscape of aboriginal rights in Canada. As explained in the *Van der Peet* trilogy, the purpose of s. 35(1) was to extend constitutional protection to the practices, customs and traditions central to the distinctive culture of aboriginal societies prior to contact with Europeans. If such practices, customs and traditions continued following contact in the absence of specific extinguishment, such practices, customs and traditions are entitled to constitutional recognition subject to the infringement and justification tests outlined in *Sparrow, supra*, and *Gladstone, supra.*

[52] As such, the fact that a particular practice, custom or tradition continued, in an unextinguished manner, following the arrival of Europeans *but* in the absence of the formal gloss of legal recognition from French colonial law should not undermine the constitutional protection accorded to aboriginal peoples. Section 35(1) would fail to achieve its noble purpose of preserving the integral and defining features of distinctive aboriginal societies if it only protected those defining features which were fortunate enough to have received the legal recognition and approval of European colonizers. I should stress that the French Regime's failure to recognize legally a specific aboriginal practice, custom or tradition (and indeed the French Regime's tacit toleration of a specific practice, custom or tradition) clearly cannot be equated with a "clear and

plain" intention to extinguish such practices under the extinguishment test of s. 35(1). ...

[53] The respondent's view, if adopted, would create an awkward patchwork of constitutional protection for aboriginal rights across the nation, depending upon the historical idiosyncrasies of colonization over particular regions of the country. In my respectful view, such a static and retrospective interpretation of s. 35(1) cannot be reconciled with the noble and prospective purpose of the constitutional entrenchment of aboriginal and treaty rights in the *Constitution Act, 1982*. Indeed, the respondent's proposed interpretation risks undermining the very purpose of s. 35(1) by perpetuating the historical injustice suffered by aboriginal peoples at the hands of colonizers who failed to respect the distinctive cultures of pre-existing aboriginal societies. ...

[54] Therefore, even on the assumption that the French Crown did not legally recognize the right of the Algonquins to fish within the Z.E.C. prior to the commencement of British sovereignty, it remains open to the appellants to establish that they enjoyed an aboriginal right to fish within the Z.E.C. under the principles of *Van der Peet*, *Gladstone*, and *N.T.C. Smokehouse Ltd*.

. . . . .

Appeal allowed in part.

─────────

As *Adams*, *supra*, and *Côté*, *supra*, indicate, Aboriginal title is a species of Aboriginal right. Thus, the "clear and plain" test for extinguishing Aboriginal title that is discussed further in Chapter 3 pertains equally to Aboriginal rights. Therefore, as the Supreme Court explained in *Côté*, "... the French Regime's failure to recognize legally a specific Aboriginal practice, custom or tradition (and indeed the French Regime's tacit toleration of a specific practice, custom or tradition) clearly cannot be equated with a clear and plain intention to extinguish such practices. ..."[6]

The *Adams* and *Côté* decisions also indicate, however, that Aboriginal rights exist independently of Aboriginal title. Thus, an Aboriginal group claiming the existence of Aboriginal rights such as hunting or fishing rights does not need to first demonstrate the existence of Aboriginal title to the land upon which those rights are exercised. Yet, because Aboriginal rights do not need to be tied to Aboriginal title does not necessarily mean that those rights are entirely unconnected to land, as the Court explained in *Adams*.

Another issue raised by the *Côté* decision was the extent of the application of the *Sparrow* justificatory test. In *Côté*, Chief Justice Lamer held that the *Sparrow* test applied equally to Aboriginal and treaty rights. He relied upon the Supreme Court of Canada's earlier decision in *R. v. Badger*, [1996] S.C.J. No. 39, [1996] 1 S.C.R. 771, [1996] 4 W.W.R. 457, 37 Alta. L.R. (3d) 153, 195 N.R. 1, 105 C.C.C. (3d) 289, 133 D.L.R. (4th) 324 (S.C.C.) to support this proposition. This was subsequently affirmed in the

Marshall cases — *R. v. Marshall*, [1999] S.C.J. No. 55, [1999] 3 S.C.R. 456, 177 D.L.R. (4th) 513 (S.C.C.) and *R. v. Marshall*, [1999] S.C.J. No. 66, [1999] 3 S.C.R. 533, 179 D.L.R. (4th) 193 (S.C.C.) ("*Marshall No. 2*") — where the applicable test was referred to as the "*Badger* test". This issue is examined in greater detail in Chapter 4.

Returning more generally to the issue of Aboriginal rights and their definition rather than their limitation, a useful synopsis of the Supreme Court of Canada's understanding of the status of Aboriginal rights may be seen in the majority's judgment in *Mitchell v. M.N.R.*, at paras. 9 to 13, as excerpted below.

MITCHELL v. M.N.R.

[2001] S.C.J. No. 33, [2001] 1 S.C.R. 911 (S.C.C.) (references omitted)

McLachlin C.J.C.: —

. . . . .

[9] Long before Europeans explored and settled North America, aboriginal peoples were occupying and using most of this vast expanse of land in organized, distinctive societies with their own social and political structures. The part of North America we now call Canada was first settled by the French and the British who, from the first days of exploration, claimed sovereignty over the land on behalf of their nations. English law, which ultimately came to govern aboriginal rights, accepted that the aboriginal peoples possessed pre-existing laws and interests, and recognized their continuance in the absence of extinguishment by cession, conquest, or legislation ... At the same time, however, the Crown asserted that sovereignty over the land, and ownership of its underlying title, vested in the Crown: *Sparrow, supra*. With this assertion arose an obligation to treat aboriginal peoples fairly and honourably, and to protect them from exploitation, a duty characterized as "fiduciary" in *Guerin* ...

[10] Accordingly, European settlement did not terminate the interests of aboriginal peoples arising from their historical occupation and use of the land. To the contrary, aboriginal interests and customary laws were presumed to survive the assertion of sovereignty, and were absorbed into the common law as rights, unless (1) they were incompatible with the Crown's assertion of sovereignty, (2) they were surrendered voluntarily via the treaty process, or (3) the government extinguished them ... Barring one of these exceptions, the practices, customs and traditions that defined the various aboriginal societies as distinctive cultures continued as part of the law of Canada ...

[11] The common law status of aboriginal rights rendered them vulnerable to unilateral extinguishment, and thus they were "dependent upon the good will of the Sovereign": see *St. Catherine's Milling and Lumber Co. v. The Queen* ... This situation changed in 1982 when Canada's Constitution was amended to entrench existing aboriginal and treaty rights ... The enactment of s. 35(1) elevated existing common law aboriginal rights to constitutional status (although, it is important to note,

the protection offered by s. 35(1) also extends beyond the aboriginal rights recognized at common law: *Delgamuukw v. British Columbia ...*). Henceforward, aboriginal rights falling within the constitutional protection of s. 35(1) could not be unilaterally abrogated by the government. However, the government retained the jurisdiction to limit aboriginal rights for justifiable reasons, in the pursuit of substantial and compelling public objectives: see *R. v. Gladstone* ...

[12] In the seminal cases of *R. v. Van der Peet* ... and *Delgamuukw* ... this Court affirmed the foregoing principles and set out the test for establishing an aboriginal right. Since s. 35(1) is aimed at reconciling the prior occupation of North America by aboriginal societies with the Crown's assertion of sovereignty, the test for establishing an aboriginal right focuses on identifying the integral, defining features of those societies. Stripped to essentials, an aboriginal claimant must prove a modern practice, tradition or custom that has a reasonable degree of continuity with the practices, traditions or customs that existed prior to contact. The practice, custom or tradition must have been "integral to the distinctive culture" of the aboriginal peoples, in the sense that it distinguished or characterized their traditional culture and lay at the core of the peoples' identity. It must be a "defining feature" of the aboriginal society, such that the culture would be "fundamentally altered" without it. It must be a feature of "central significance" to the peoples' culture, on [sic] that "truly *made the society what it was*" ... This excludes practices, traditions and customs that are only marginal or incidental to the aboriginal society's cultural identity, and emphasizes practices, traditions and customs that are vital to the life, culture and identity of the aboriginal society in question.

[13] Once an aboriginal right is established, the issue is whether [an] act ... is an expression of that right. Aboriginal rights are not frozen in their pre-contact form: ancestral rights may find modern expression. The question is whether the impugned act represents the modern exercise of an ancestral practice, custom or tradition. ...

Does this synopsis in *Mitchell* add to or detract from anything that had been said in cases such as *Sparrow* and *Van der Peet*?

In the next case, the Supreme Court of Canada considered whether Mi'kmaq and Maliseet people in Nova Scotia and New Brunswick possessed Aboriginal rights to harvest wood for "personal use". In examining this issue the Court re-characterized the right as one of "domestic use". As you read *Sappier and Gray*, consider the implications of the Court's characterization of the right for issues like Aboriginal governance, title and commercial access. Ask yourself whether the court's interpretation of the right is beneficial to the Crown, Aboriginal peoples, both, or neither. *Sappier and Gray* was regarded as a test case and attracted 18 legal intervenors, including the federal government, most provinces, Aboriginal organizations and forestry industry representatives. Does the Court narrow or broaden Aboriginal rights through this decision?

R. v. SAPPIER; R. v. GRAY

[2006] S.C.J. No. 54, [2006] 2 S.C.R. 686 (S.C.C.)

Bastarache J. (McLachlin C.J.C. and LeBel, Deschamps, Fish, Abella, Charron and Rothstein JJ. concurring): —

1. *Introduction*

[1] The three respondents were charged with unlawful possession or cutting of Crown timber. Messrs. Sappier and Polchies are Maliseet, and Mr. Gray is Mi'kmaq. All three respondents argued in defence that they possess an aboriginal and treaty right to harvest timber for personal use. Mr. Gray has since abandoned his treaty right claim.

[2] The respondents submit that the practice of harvesting timber for personal use was an integral part of the distinctive culture of the Maliseet and Mi'kmaq peoples prior to contact with Europeans. The claimed right refers to the practice of harvesting trees to fulfill the domestic needs of the pre-contact communities for such things as shelter, transportation, fuel and tools. The Maliseet and Mi'kmaq were migratory living from hunting and fishing, and using the rivers and lakes of Eastern Canada for transportation. The central question on appeal is how to define the distinctive culture of such peoples, and how to determine which pre-contact practices were integral to that culture. The Crown submits that the evidence of wood usage in pre-contact Maliseet and Mi'kmaq societies was primarily a reference to the need for harvesting wood on a daily basis in order to survive. In the Crown's submission, this is not sufficient to establish a defining practice, custom or tradition that truly made the society what it was.

[3] For the reasons that follow, I find that all three respondents have established an aboriginal right to harvest wood for domestic uses. Given this Court's decision on the aboriginal right issue, I need not decide whether Messrs. Sappier and Polchies also benefit from a treaty right to harvest wood.

. . . . .

4.   *The Aboriginal Right Claim*

4.1   *Characterization of the Respondents' Claim*

[20] In order to be an aboriginal right, an activity must be an element of a practice, custom or tradition integral to the distinctive culture of the aboriginal group claiming the right: *R. v. Van der Peet*, [1996] 2 S.C.R. 507, at para. 46. ... In this case, the respondents were charged with the unlawful cutting and possession of Crown timber. They claimed an aboriginal right to harvest timber for personal use so as a defence to those charges. The statute at issue prohibits the unauthorized cutting, damaging, removing and possession of timber from Crown lands. The respondents rely on the pre-contact practice of harvesting timber in order to establish their aboriginal right.

[21] The difficulty in the present cases is that the practice relied upon to found the claims as characterized by the respondents was the object of very little evidence at trial. Instead, the respondents led most of their evidence about the importance of wood in Maliseet and Mi'kmaq cultures and the many uses to which it was put. This is unusual because the jurisprudence of this Court establishes the central importance of the actual practice in founding a claim for an aboriginal right. Aboriginal rights are founded upon practices, customs, or traditions which were integral to the distinctive pre-contact culture of an aboriginal people. They are not generally founded upon the importance of a particular resource. In fact, an aboriginal right cannot be characterized as a right to a particular resource because to do so would be to treat it as akin to a common law property right. In characterizing aboriginal rights as *sui generis*, this Court has rejected the application of traditional common law property concepts to such rights: *Sparrow*, at pp. 1111-12. In my view, the pre-contact practice is central to the *Van der Peet* test for two reasons.

[22] First, in order to grasp the importance of a resource to a particular aboriginal people, the Court seeks to understand how that resource was harvested, extracted and utilized. These practices are the necessary "aboriginal" component in aboriginal rights. ... The goal for courts is, therefore, to determine how the claimed right relates to the pre-contact culture or way of life of an aboriginal society. This has been achieved by requiring aboriginal rights claimants to found their claim on a pre-contact practice which was integral to the distinctive culture of the particular aboriginal community. It is critically important that the Court be able to identify a *practice* that helps to define the distinctive way of life of the community as an aboriginal community. The importance of leading evidence about the pre-contact practice upon which the claimed right is based should not be understated. In the absence of such evidence, courts will find it difficult to relate the claimed right to the pre-contact way of life of the specific aboriginal people, so as to trigger s. 35 protection.

[23] Second, it is also necessary to identify the pre-contact practice upon which the claim is founded in order to consider how it might have evolved to its present-day form. This Court has long recognized that aboriginal rights are not frozen in their pre-contact form, and that ancestral rights may find modern expression: *Mitchell v. M.N.R.*, [2001] 1 S.C.R. 911, 2001 SCC 33, at para. 13; *Van der Peet*, at para. 64.

[24] In the present cases, the relevant practice for the purposes of the *Van der Peet* test is harvesting wood. It is this practice upon which the respondents opted to found their claims. However, the respondents do not claim a right to harvest wood for any and all purposes — such a right would not provide sufficient specificity to apply the reasoning I have just described. The respondents instead claim the right to harvest timber for personal uses; I find this characterization to be too general as well. ... The way of life of the Maliseet and of the Mi'kmaq during the pre-contact period is that of a migratory people who lived from fishing and hunting and who used the rivers and lakes of Eastern Canada for transportation. Thus, the practice should be characterized as the harvesting of wood for

certain uses that are directly associated with that particular way of life. The record shows that wood was used to fulfill the communities' domestic needs for such things as shelter, transportation, tools and fuel. I would therefore characterize the respondents' claim as a right to harvest wood for domestic uses as a member of the aboriginal community.

[25] The word "domestic" qualifies the uses to which the harvested timber can be put. The right so characterized has no commercial dimension. The harvested wood cannot be sold, traded or bartered to produce assets or raise money. This is so even if the object of such trade or barter is to finance the building of a dwelling. In other words, although the right would permit the harvesting of timber to be used in the construction of a dwelling, it is not the case that a rightholder can sell the wood in order to raise money to finance the purchase or construction of a dwelling, or any of its components.

[26] The right to harvest wood for domestic uses is a communal one. Section 35 recognizes and affirms existing aboriginal and treaty rights in order to assist in ensuring the continued existence of these particular aboriginal societies. The exercise of the aboriginal right to harvest wood for domestic uses must be tied to this purpose. The right to harvest (which is distinct from the right to make personal use of the harvested product even though they are related) is not one to be exercised by any member of the aboriginal community independently of the aboriginal society it is meant to preserve. It is a right that assists the society in maintaining its distinctive character.

4.2   *The Integral to a Distinctive Culture Test*

4.2.1   *The Evidentiary Problem*

[27] The question before the Court at this stage is whether the practice of harvesting wood for domestic uses was integral to the distinctive culture of the Maliseet and Mi'kmaq, pre-contact. As previously explained, very little evidence was led with respect to the actual harvesting practice. Nevertheless, this Court has previously recognized an aboriginal right based on evidence showing the importance of a resource to the pre-contact culture of an aboriginal people. In *R. v. Adams*, [1996] 3 S.C.R. 101, this Court recognized an aboriginal right to fish for food in Lake St. Francis despite the fact that "[t]he fish were not significant to the Mohawks for social or ceremonial reasons" (para. 45). The Court based its holding on the fact that "[the fish] were an important and significant source of subsistence for the Mohawks" (para. 45). In other words, the Court recognized a right to fish for food based on the importance of the resource. Fishing was such a significant practice as to constitute a way of life. In this sense, it was part of what made the pre-contact Mohawk community distinctive.

[28] In the present cases, the evidence established that wood was critically important to the Maliseet and the Mi'kmaq, pre-contact. The learned trial judge in the *Sappier* and *Polchies* prosecutions found that the Maliseet people used wood or wood products from the forest in which

they lived to construct shelters, implements of husbandry and perhaps in the construction of what might be called rude furnishings (para. 12). Cain Prov. Ct. J. also referred to evidence that was led to the effect that the pre-European Maliseet society revered wood and considered it sacred (para. 13). Referring to the *Gray* prosecution, Cain Prov. Ct. J. stated that, "[t]here is no question that the evidence of Mr. Sewell in Gray (*supra*) clearly established an historical pattern and tradition of the use of wood from Crown lands for the construction of furniture and housing" (para. 27). He went on to comment that, "[s]imilar evidence was led in the case at bar" (para. 27).

[29] In the *Gray* prosecution, the trial judge declared the defence witness, Mr. Sewell, an expert "regarding oral traditions and customs which have been passed down through the generations and more particularly in the field of describing practices and customs relating to the use of and gathering of wood by aboriginals in the geographical area encompassed by the terms of the charge" (Arsenault Prov. Ct. J., at p. 3). As previously mentioned, Mr. Sewell is Mi'kmaq and a status Indian who is recognized as an elder and historian within his community. ...

[30] Mr. Sewell testified about the many uses to which wood was and continues to be put. He spoke of using the inner bark of a cedar tree for rope, and of cutting strips of it to be used in the construction of the old birch bark canoes. Birch bark and ash were used to make baskets. Birch, poplar and black spruce were fashioned into paddles. Any leftover birch or maple was used for firewood. He spoke of using cedar to make drums, and of how the aboriginal peoples were also carvers. He testified that some of the figure-heads on the first ships to arrive in Canada were done by aboriginals. Mr. Sewell spoke of building camps and making pots out of wood. He testified that the pots were made out of large logs, using fire first to burn out the centre and then chiselling it out. He spoke of using bird's eye maple and curly maple in the construction of axe handles and boat paddles, either for sale or for gifts. He confirmed that the extraction of sap from maple and birch trees had been known to the Mi'kmaq for centuries (testimony of Gilbert Sewell, presented during examination-in-chief, October 4, 2000, pp. 16-19 (A.R., at pp. 80-83). Finally, he spoke of the practice of fashioning spears for fishing out of ash (A.R., at p. 94).

[31] Mr. Sewell concluded that, "[s]o, as far back as I can read in history or the oral tradition that has been passed down to me, it's been — we've been always gathering and we've been always using wood as, as, as a way of life" (A.R., at p. 81). This evidence detailing the many uses to which wood was put by the Mi'kmaq as a whole is important given the communal nature of aboriginal rights. The trial judge accepted this evidence as proof that the practice of harvesting wood for domestic uses was integral to the pre-contact Mi'kmaq way of life.

[32] Before this Court, the Crown conceded in the *Sappier* and *Polchies* appeal that wood was important to the Maliseet for survival purposes in the pre-contact period (appellant's factum, at para. 46). The Crown also acknowledged that "wood was undeniably used in many facets of aboriginal life" (*ibid.*, at para. 46). In the *Gray* appeal, the Crown similarly

conceded that "wood was used in Mi'kmaq society to ensure survival" (*ibid.*, at para. 44).

[33] As in *Adams*, I infer from this evidence that the practice of harvesting wood for domestic uses was also significant, though undertaken primarily for survival purposes. Flexibility is important when engaging in the *Van der Peet* analysis because the object is to provide cultural security and continuity for the particular aboriginal society. This object gives context to the analysis. For this reason, courts must be prepared to draw necessary inferences about the existence and integrality of a practice when direct evidence is not available.

[34] Flexibility is also important in the present cases with regard to the relevant time frame during which the practice must be found to have been integral to the distinctive culture of the aboriginal society in question. ... Before this Court, the Attorney General of Nova Scotia, intervener, objected to some of Mr. Sewell's evidence insofar as he did not specify to which time period he was referring when describing the uses to which harvested wood was put by the Mi'kmaq. In other words, it was respectfully submitted that it was unclear whether he was always describing pre-contact practices. In dismissing this concern, I need only repeat what was said in *Van der Peet*, and reiterated more recently in *Mitchell* at para. 29, about the adapted rules of evidence applicable in aboriginal rights litigation and the use of post-contact evidence to prove the existence and integrality of pre-contact practices ...

4.2.2 *Whether a Practice Undertaken for Survival Purposes Can be Considered Integral to an Aboriginal Community's Distinctive Culture*

[35] The principal issue on appeal is whether a practice undertaken for survival purposes can meet the integral to a distinctive culture test. The learned trial judge in the *Sappier* and *Polchies* trial concluded that it could not. Cain Prov. Ct. J. was of the view that:

> The practice of using wood to construct shelters, irrespective of whether they were wigwams or wooden building or of using wood to make furniture, was not in any way integral to the distinctive culture of the ancestors of the Woodstock First Nation in pre European times. From the evidence adduced it is clear that they used wood or wood products from the forest in which they lived to construct shelters, implements of husbandry and perhaps in the construction of what might be called rude furnishings. Any humane society who would have been living on the same lands in New Brunswick at the same time would have used wood and wood products for the same purpose [pp. 12-13]

[36] In making these comments, Cain Prov. Ct. J. relied on a statement made by Lamer C.J. in *Van der Peet*, at para. 56:

> To recognize and affirm the prior occupation of Canada by distinctive aboriginal societies it is to what makes those societies distinctive that the court must look in identifying aboriginal rights. <u>The court cannot look at those aspects of the aboriginal society that are true of every human society (e.g., eating to survive)</u>, nor can it look at those aspects of the aboriginal

society that are only incidental or occasional to that society; the court must look instead to the defining and central attributes of the aboriginal society in question. It is only by focussing on the aspects of the aboriginal society that make that society distinctive that the definition of aboriginal rights will accomplish the purpose underlying s. 35(1). [Emphasis added.]

Relying on this passage, Cain Prov. Ct. J. concluded that harvesting timber to construct a shelter was akin to eating to survive. This statement by Lamer C.J. appears to have resulted in considerable confusion as to whether a practice undertaken strictly for survival purposes can found an aboriginal right claim. However, further in his decision, Lamer C.J. clarifies that the pre-contact practice, custom or tradition relied need not be distinct; it need only be distinctive. In so doing, he confirms that fishing for food can, in certain contexts, meet the integral to a distinctive culture test:

> That the standard an aboriginal community must meet is distinctiveness, not distinctness, arises from the recognition in *Sparrow, supra*, of an aboriginal right to fish for food. Certainly no aboriginal group in Canada could claim that its culture is "distinct" or unique in fishing for food; fishing for food is something done by many different cultures and societies around the world. What the Musqueam claimed in *Sparrow, supra*, was rather that it was fishing for food which, in part, made Musqueam culture what it is; fishing for food was characteristic of Musqueam culture and, therefore, a distinctive part of that culture. Since it was so it constituted an aboriginal right under s. 35(1). [Emphasis in original deleted; para. 72.]

[37] More recently, this Court has recognized a right to fish for food in *Adams* and in *R. v. Côté*, [1996] 3 S.C.R. 139. In *Adams*, the Court specifically noted that fish were only important as a source of subsistence. In *Côté*, Lamer C.J. emphasized that "[f]ishing was significant to the Algonquins, as it represented the predominant source of subsistence during the season leading up to winter" (para. 68). Moreover, this Court has previously suggested that the scope of s. 35 should extend to protect the means by which an aboriginal society traditionally sustained itself, and that the *Van der Peet* test emphasizes practices that are vital to the life of the aboriginal society in question: see *R. v. Pamajewon*, [1996] 2 S.C.R. 812, at para. 28; and *Mitchell*, at para. 12, respectively. I wish to clarify, however, that there is no such thing as an aboriginal right to sustenance. Rather, these cases stand for the proposition that the traditional *means* of sustenance, meaning the pre-contact practices relied upon for survival, can in some cases be considered integral to the distinctive culture of the particular aboriginal people.

[38] I can therefore find no jurisprudential authority to support the proposition that a practice undertaken merely for survival purposes cannot be considered integral to the distinctive culture of an aboriginal people. Rather, I find that the jurisprudence weighs in favour of protecting the traditional means of survival of an aboriginal community.

[39] McLachlin C.J. explained in *Mitchell* that in order to satisfy the *Van der Peet* test, the practice, custom or tradition must have been integral to the distinctive culture of the aboriginal peoples, in the sense that

it distinguished or characterized their traditional culture and lay at the core of the peoples' identity. It must be a "defining feature" of the aboriginal society, such that the culture would be "fundamentally altered" without it. It must be a feature of "central significance" to the peoples' culture, one that "truly made the society what it was" (*Van der Peet, supra,* at paras. 54-59 ...). [Emphasis in original; para. 12.]

[40] As I have already explained, the purpose of this exercise is to understand the way of life of the particular aboriginal society, pre-contact, and to determine how the claimed right relates to it. This is achieved by founding the claim on a pre-contact practice, and determining whether that practice was integral to the distinctive culture of the aboriginal people in question, pre-contact. Section 35 seeks to protect integral elements of the way of life of these aboriginal societies, including their traditional means of survival. Although this was affirmed in *Sparrow, Adams* and *Côté,* the courts below queried whether a practice undertaken strictly for survival purposes really went to the core of a people's identity. Although intended as a helpful description of the *Van der Peet* test, the reference in *Mitchell* to a "core identity" may have unintentionally resulted in a heightened threshold for establishing an aboriginal right. For this reason, I think it necessary to discard the notion that the pre-contact practice upon which the right is based must go to the core of the society's identity, i.e. its single most important defining character. This has never been the test for establishing an aboriginal right. This Court has clearly held that a claimant need only show that the practice was integral to the aboriginal society's pre-contact distinctive culture.

[41] The notion that the pre-contact practice must be a "defining feature" of the aboriginal society, such that the culture would be "fundamentally altered" without it, has also served in some cases to create artificial barriers to the recognition and affirmation of aboriginal rights. The trial judge in the *Sappier* and *Polchies* prosecution concluded that Maliseet culture would not have been fundamentally altered had wood not been available to it. In his opinion, "[t]he society would in all probability have used some other available material" (p. 13). In response, I would adopt the following comments made by Robertson J.A., on behalf of the Court of Appeal:

> ... I am at a loss to speculate on what other natural resource might have been used had wood not been available. Snow houses would have provided New Brunswick's aboriginal societies with adequate shelter during the winter months only. Whether fish and wildlife by-products would have served as an alternative source of fuel, and an adequate one, is a question on which I need not speculate. There is also the question as to how the aboriginal societies of New Brunswick would have traversed the lakes and rivers of this Province, in pursuit of fish and wildlife, without the traditional means of transportation: canoes. [para. 91]

I further agree with Robertson J.A. that courts should be cautious in considering whether the particular aboriginal culture would have been fundamentally altered had the gathering activity in question not been pursued. The learned judge correctly notes that "[a] society that fishes for sustenance will survive even if it does not consume meat and the converse is equally true" (para. 92).

4.2.3 *Applying the Van der Peet Test: the Meaning of "Distinctive Culture"*

[42] This brings us to the question of what is meant by "distinctive culture"? As previously explained, this Court in *Van der Peet* set out to interpret s. 35 of the Constitution in a way which captures both the aboriginal and the rights in aboriginal rights. Lamer C.J. spoke of the "necessary specificity which comes from granting special constitutional protection to one part of Canadian society" (para. 20). It is that aboriginal specificity which the notion of a "distinctive culture" seeks to capture. However, it is clear that "Aboriginality means more than interesting cultural practices and anthropological curiosities worthy only of a museum" (C. C. Cheng, "Touring the Museum: A Comment on *R. v. Van der Peet*" (1997), 55 *U.T. Fac. L. Rev.* 419, at para. 34). R. L. Barsh and J. Youngblood Henderson argue that as a result of the *Van der Peet* decision, "'culture' has implicitly been taken to mean a fixed inventory of traits or characteristics" ("The Supreme Court's *Van der Peet* Trilogy: Naive Imperialism and Ropes of Sand" (1997), 42 *McGill L.J.* 993, at p. 1002).

[43] Many of these concerns echo those expressed by McLachlin J. (as she then was) and by L'Heureux-Dubé J. in dissenting opinions in *Van der Peet*. L'Heureux-Dubé J. was of the view that "the approach based on aboriginal practices, traditions and customs considers only discrete parts of aboriginal culture, separating them from the general culture in which they are rooted" (para. 150). McLachlin J. opined that "different people may entertain different ideas of what is distinctive", thereby creating problems of indeterminacy in the *Van der Peet* test (para. 257).

[44] Culture, let alone "distinctive culture", has proven to be a difficult concept to grasp for Canadian courts. Moreover, the term "culture" as it is used in the English language may not find a perfect parallel in certain aboriginal languages. Barsh and Henderson note that "[w]e can find no precise equivalent of European concepts of "culture" in Mi'kmaq, for example. How we maintain contact with our traditions is *tan'telo'tlieki-p*. How we perpetuate our consciousness is described as *tlilnuo'lti'k*. How we maintain our language is *tlinuita'sim*. Each of these terms connotes a process rather than a thing" (p. 1002, note 30). Ultimately, the concept of culture is itself inherently cultural.

[45] The aboriginal rights doctrine, which has been constitutionalized by s. 35, arises from the simple fact of prior occupation of the lands now forming Canada. The "integral to a distinctive culture" test must necessarily be understood in this context. As L'Heureux-Dubé J. explained in dissent in *Van der Peet*, "[t]he 'distinctive aboriginal culture' must be taken to refer to the reality that, despite British sovereignty, aboriginal people were the original organized society occupying and using Canadian lands: *Calder v. Attorney-General of British Columbia*, *supra*, at p. 328, *per* Judson J., and *Guerin*, *supra*, at p. 379, *per* Dickson J. (as he then was)" (para. 159). The focus of the Court should therefore be on the *nature* of this

prior occupation. What is meant by "culture" is really an inquiry into the pre-contact way of life of a particular aboriginal community, including their means of survival, their socialization methods, their legal systems, and, potentially, their trading habits. The use of the word "distinctive" as a qualifier is meant to incorporate an element of aboriginal specificity. However, "distinctive" does not mean "distinct", and the notion of aboriginality must not be reduced to "racialized stereotypes of Aboriginal peoples" (J. Borrows and L. I. Rotman, "The *Sui Generis* Nature of Aboriginal Rights: Does it Make a Difference?" (1997), 36 *Alta. L. Rev. 9*, at p. 36).

[46] In post-hearing submissions to the Court of Appeal in the *Sappier* and *Polchies* case, the Crown admitted that gathering birch bark for the construction of canoes or hemlock for basket-making were practices likely integral to the distinctive Maliseet culture (para. 94). But it would be a mistake to reduce the entire pre-contact distinctive Maliseet culture to canoe-building and basket-making. To hold otherwise would be to fall in the trap of reducing an entire people's culture to specific anthropological curiosities and, potentially, racialized aboriginal stereotypes. Instead, the Court must first inquire into the way of life of the Maliseet and Mi'kmaq, pre-contact. As previously explained, these were migratory communities using the rivers and lakes of Eastern Canada for transportation and living essentially from hunting and fishing. The Court must therefore seek to understand how the particular pre-contact practice relied upon relates to that way of life. In the present cases, the practice of harvesting wood for domestic uses including shelter, transportation, fuel and tools is directly related to the way of life I have just described. I have already explained that we must discard the idea that the practice must go to the core of a people's culture. The fact that harvesting wood for domestic uses was undertaken for survival purposes is sufficient, given the evidence adduced at trial, to meet the integral to a distinctive culture threshold.

[47] I therefore conclude that the practice of harvesting wood for domestic uses was integral to the pre-contact distinctive culture of both the Maliseet and Mi'kmaq peoples.

4.3 *Continuity of the Claimed Right with the Pre-Contact Practice*

[48] Although the nature of the *practice* which founds the aboriginal right claim must be considered in the context of the pre-contact distinctive culture of the particular aboriginal community, the nature of the *right* must be determined in light of present day circumstances. As McLachlin C.J. explained in *R. v. Marshall*, [2005] 2 S.C.R. 220, 2005 SCC 43, at para. 25, "[l]ogical evolution means the same sort of activity, carried on in the modern economy by modern means". It is the practice, along with its associated uses, which must be allowed to evolve. The right to harvest wood for the construction of temporary shelters must be allowed to evolve into a right to harvest wood by modern means to be used in the construction of a modern dwelling. Any other conclusion would freeze the right in its pre-contact form.

[49] Before this Court, the Crown submitted that "[l]arge permanent dwellings, constructed from multi-dimensional wood, obtained by modern methods of forest extraction and milling of lumber, cannot resonate as a Maliseet aboriginal right, or as a proper application of the logical evolution principle", because they are not grounded in traditional Maliseet culture (appellant's factum in *Sappier* and *Polchies* appeal at para. 76; appellant's factum in *Gray* appeal at para. 80). I find this submission to be contrary to the established jurisprudence of this Court, which has consistently held that ancestral rights may find modern form: *Mitchell*, at para. 13. In *Sparrow*, Dickson C.J. explained that "the phrase 'existing aboriginal rights' must be interpreted flexibly so as to permit their evolution over time" (p. 1093). Citing Professor Slattery, he stated that "the word 'existing' suggests that those rights are 'affirmed in a contemporary form rather than in their primeval simplicity and vigour'" (p. 1093, citing B. Slattery, "Understanding Aboriginal Rights" (1987), 66 *Can. Bar Rev.* 727, at p. 782). In *Mitchell*, McLachlin C.J. drew a distinction between the particular aboriginal right, which is established at the moment of contact, and its expression, which evolves over time (para. 13). L'Heureux-Dubé J. in dissent in *Van der Peet* emphasized that "aboriginal rights must be permitted to maintain contemporary relevance in relation to the needs of the natives as their practices, traditions and customs change and evolve with the overall society in which they live" (para. 172). If aboriginal rights are not permitted to evolve and take modern forms, then they will become utterly useless. Surely the Crown cannot be suggesting that the respondents, all of whom live on a reserve, would be limited to building wigwams. If such were the case, the doctrine of aboriginal rights would truly be limited to recognizing and affirming a narrow subset of "anthropological curiosities", and our notion of aboriginality would be reduced to a small number of outdated stereotypes. The cultures of the aboriginal peoples who occupied the lands now forming Canada prior to the arrival of the Europeans, and who did so while living in organized societies with their own distinctive ways of life, cannot be reduced to wigwams, baskets and canoes.

4.4 *The Site-Specific Requirement*

[50] This Court has imposed a site-specific requirement on the aboriginal hunting and fishing rights it recognized in *Adams*, *Côté*, *Mitchell*, and *Powley*. ...

[51] The characterization of the claimed right in the present cases, as in *Adams*, *Côté* and *Mitchell*, imports a necessary geographical element, and its integrality to the Maliseet and Mi'kmaq cultures should be assessed on this basis: *Mitchell*, at para. 59. ...

[52] At the trial of Messrs. Sappier and Polchies, the Crown conceded that "the issue of territoriality does not arise in the trial of the defendants on the charges set out herein" (agreed statement of facts at para. 12, reproduced in the trial decision at p. 296). ... Territoriality is therefore not at issue in the *Sappier* and *Polchies* prosecution.

[53] In the *Gray* trial, the trial judge accepted Mr. Sewell's evidence that the Mi'kmaq had traditionally used the Crown lands in question for the purpose of tree harvesting. The Court of Appeal noted that the Crown did not dispute this finding (para. 15). I would conclude on this basis that Mr. Gray has established an aboriginal right to harvest wood for domestic uses on Crown lands traditionally used for this purpose by members of the Pabineau First Nation.

4.5   *Infringement and Justification*

[54] In the *Sappier* and *Polchies* litigation, the Crown accepted that the relevant provisions of the *Crown Lands and Forests Act* infringed the alleged right and that the infringement could not be justified under the test set out in *Sparrow* and in *Badger* (Court of Appeal reasons at para. 3). The Crown did not argue otherwise before this Court. Before the Court of Appeal in the *Gray* case, the Crown did not challenge the trial judge's conclusions that the impugned legislation infringed the right and that the Crown had failed to justify the infringement (para. 26).

[55] The aboriginal right to harvest wood for domestic uses is subject to regulation pursuant to the ordinary rules applicable in that regard. However, given that the Crown did not attempt to justify the infringement in the present cases, this is a question that need not be addressed in the circumstances of these appeals.

4.6   *Extinguishment*

[56] The Crown did not allege before the Court of Appeal in the *Sappier* and *Polchies* litigation that the aboriginal right was extinguished by either pre- or post-Confederation legislation (see Court of Appeal reasons at para. 3). ... The argument was advanced on appeal in the *Gray* case, where Robertson J.A. explicitly held that:

> My concurring opinion and that of Justice Daigle in *Bernard* is a sufficient basis for purposes of disposing of any argument that an existing aboriginal right was extinguished by either pre- or post-Confederation provincial legislation: see *Bernard* at paras. 176-179 and 523-541. [para. 25]

[57] The Crown bears the burden of proving extinguishment. Before this Court, it relied on four pre-Confederation statutes enacted by the New Brunswick legislature between 1840 and 1862 as evidence of the Crown's intent to extinguish any aboriginal right to harvest wood. A clear intent is necessary in order to extinguish aboriginal rights. However, that intent need not be express and therefore aboriginal rights may also be extinguished implicitly: *Sparrow*, at p. 1099; *R. v. Gladstone*, [1996] 2 S.C.R. 723, at paras. 31 and 34.

[58] First, it must be emphasized that during the colonial period, the power to extinguish aboriginal rights rested with the Imperial Crown: *Delgamuukw v. British Columbia*, [1997] 3 S.C.R. 1010, at para. 15. Given the submissions advanced on behalf of the respondents and the Assembly of

First Nations, intervener, it is not at all clear that the colonial legislature of New Brunswick was ever granted the legal authority by the Imperial Crown to extinguish aboriginal rights. I do not deal with this argument in any detail as I conclude that the pre-Confederation legislation does not indicate a clear intention to extinguish aboriginal rights.

[59] The legislation relied upon by the Crown as proof of extinguishment is primarily regulatory in nature, although it does introduce prohibitions and create misdemeanour offences. ...

[60] Following this Court's decision in *Sparrow*, the regulation of Crown timber through a licensing scheme does not meet the high standard of demonstrating a clear intent to extinguish the aboriginal right to harvest wood for domestic uses. ...

[61] For this reason, I find that the Crown has not discharged its onus of proving that the aboriginal right to harvest wood for domestic uses has been extinguished.

5. *The Treaty Right Claim*

[The treaty right aspect of this case is covered in Chapter 4. The court concluded: "Given the Court's decision on the aboriginal rights issue, there is no need to consider the treaty right claim in further detail."]

6. *Incorporation of Extrinsic Evidence by the Court of Appeal*

[The court held that that extrinsic evidence was not improperly incorporated into the learned judge's reasons by Robertson J.A. of the Court of Appeal].

7. *Conclusion*

[72] For the above reasons, I conclude that the respondents have made out the defence of aboriginal right. The respondent Mr. Gray possesses an aboriginal right to harvest wood for domestic uses on Crown lands traditionally used for that purpose by members of the Pabineau First Nation. The respondents Messrs. Sappier and Polchies possess an aboriginal right to harvest wood for domestic uses. That right is also site-specific, such that its exercise is necessarily limited to Crown lands traditionally harvested by members of the Woodstock First Nation.

[73] Accordingly, I would dismiss the appeals.

Binnie J. (concurring): —

[74] I agree with my colleague, Bastarache J., about the disposition of this appeal for the reasons he gives except, with respect, for his ruling that

[t]he harvested wood cannot be sold, traded or bartered to produce assets or raise money. This is so even if the object of such trade or barter is to finance the building of a shelter. In other words, although the right would permit the harvesting of timber to be used in the construction of a shelter, it is not

the case that a rightholder can sell the wood in order to raise money to finance the purchase or construction of a home, or any of its components. [para. 25]

In aboriginal communities pre-contact, as in most societies, there existed a division of labour. This should be reflected in a more flexible concept of the exercise of aboriginal rights *within* modern aboriginal communities, especially considering that the aboriginal right itself is communal in nature. Barter (and, its modern equivalent, sale) within the reserve or other local aboriginal community would reflect a more efficient use of human resources than requiring all members of the reserve or other local aboriginal community to which the right pertains to do everything for themselves. They did not do so historically and they should not have to do so now. On the one hand, it seems to me a Mi'kmaq or Maliseet should be able to sell firewood to his or her aboriginal neighbour or barter it for, say, a side of venison or roofing a house. On the other hand, I agree that trade, barter or sale <u>outside</u> the reserve or other local aboriginal community would represent a commercial activity outside the scope of the aboriginal right established in this case. In other respects I agree with my colleague.

1. Under what legal doctrine or theory can the Crown remove wood from Crown lands for commercial purposes? Is the Crown treated differently than Aboriginal peoples when it comes to utilizing resources like wood on those lands? If not, then why does the Crown (and those individuals and corporations whose rights flow from the Crown) not have to show that its right to take wood from the forest is rooted in practices prior to the Crown's arrival in North America, as Aboriginal claims must? If the Crown's claims are not treated differently than Aboriginal claims, how do you explain the Crown's seeming advantage over prior Aboriginal populations when it comes to harvesting wood?

2. The Court characterized the right in this case as a "right to harvest wood for domestic uses as a member of the aboriginal community" (para. 24). The Court further held that "The right so characterized has no commercial dimension" (para. 25). Can this conclusion be true, even if the "harvested wood cannot be sold, traded or bartered to produce assets or raise money"? Doesn't any use of resources have an economic dimension? For example, if individuals harvest wood for themselves, doesn't that produce an economic benefit in that they don't have to purchase wood on the market?

3. Does the judgment in *Sappier and Gray* attempt to quantify how much wood can be harvested for an individual's use? Does it set any rules on how individuals may dispose of goods they have made out of wood harvested on Crown land?

4. How will conflicts over wood be resolved between forestry companies and Aboriginal peoples? For example, who will have priority over trees located on Crown land which have been leased to forestry

companies? Is there a logical inference within the decision that Aboriginal peoples can harvest these logs, and that any commercial loss to the companies may be a matter of negotiation or litigation between the companies and the provincial government involved?

5. Why did Bastarache J. discard the idea that the practice of harvesting wood for domestic use "must go to the core of a people's culture" (para. 48)?

6. Justice Bastarache wrote that "A clear intent is necessary in order to extinguish aboriginal rights. However, that intent need not be express and therefore aboriginal rights may also be extinguished implicitly: *R. v. Sparrow*, [1990] S.C.J. No. 49, [1990] 1 S.C.R. 1075 at 1099 (S.C.C.); *R. v. Gladstone*, [1996] S.C.J. No. 79, [1996] 2 S.C.R. 723, at paras. 31 and 34" (para. 57). Can or should Aboriginal rights be capable of implicit extinguishment? The paragraphs cited from *Gladstone* contain the following statement: "While to extinguish an aboriginal right the Crown does not, *perhaps*, have to use language which refers expressly to its extinguishment of aboriginal rights, it must demonstrate more than that, in the past, the exercise of an aboriginal right has been subject to a regulatory scheme" (*R. v. Gladstone*, [1996] S.C.J. No. 79, [1996] 2 S.C.R. 723 (S.C.C.) at para. 34).

The Supreme Court's most recent Aboriginal rights decision revisits and re-inscribes the "integral to a distinctive culture test" in Canadian law. The Court once again addressed the scope of Aboriginal rights in relation to pre-contact Aboriginal practices. As you read the *Lax Kw'alaams* case, below, identify the benefits the Crown receives from the "integral to a distinctive culture" test.

LAX KW'ALAAMS INDIAN BAND v. CANADA (ATTORNEY GENERAL)

[2011] S.C.J. No. 56, [2011] 3 S.C.R. 535 (S.C.C.)

The judgment of the Court was delivered by

Binnie J.: —

[1] This appeal involves the claim of the Lax Kw'alaams First Nation and other First Nations ... whose ancestral lands stretch along the northwest coast of British Columbia between the estuaries of the Nass and lower Skeena Rivers, to the commercial harvesting and sale of "all species of fish" within their traditional waters. ...

. . . . .

IV. Issues

[37] The Lax Kw'alaams raise the following issues:

1. Did the courts below err by characterizing the appellants' Aboriginal rights claim based on the pleadings rather than an enquiry into pre-contact practices?
2. Did the courts below err in isolating the ancestral practice of trading in eulachon grease "as a practice of its own" rather than focusing more comprehensively on the Coast Tsimshian "fishing way of life"?
3. Did the courts below err by refusing to consider whether the appellants had established a "lesser" right to fish on a "moderate" scale "to sell to others in order to acquire money, goods or services to sustain [their] communities" or to an Aboriginal right to fish for food, social and ceremonial purposes? ...

V. Analysis

[38] The Lax Kw'alaams First Nation and its ancestors have inhabited the northwest coast of British Columbia for thousands of years. In the pre-contact period prior to 1793, the basis of their culture and sustenance was the fishery. The principal issue in the present action is whether its ancestral practices, customs and traditions provide a proper legal springboard to the right to harvest and sell all varieties of fish in a modern *commercial* fishery — a right that would be protected and privileged by s. 35(1) of the *Constitution Act, 1982*.

[39] In a series of decisions over the last 15 years the Court has worked out the test to establish such a right in the context of a defence to prosecutions for regulatory offences: see in particular *Van der Peet*; *R. v. Gladstone*, [1996] 2 S.C.R. 723; *N.T.C. Smokehouse*; *R. v. Marshall*, 2005 SCC 43, [2005] 2 S.C.R. 220 ("*Marshall (2005)*"); and *R. v. Sappier*, 2006 SCC 54, [2006] 2 S.C.R. 686. In such cases, it is the prosecution that establishes the boundaries of the controversy by the framing of the charge. Here, however, the Lax Kw'alaams First Nation is the moving party, and it lay in its hands to frame the action, within the *Supreme Court Civil Rules*, B.C. Reg. 168/2009, as it saw fit.

A. *Did the Trial Judge Err in her Approach to Characterizing the Lax Kw'alaams' Claim?*

[40] The heart of the Lax Kw'alaams' argument on this point is that "before a court can characterize a claimed aboriginal right, it must first inquire and make findings about the pre-contact practices and way of life of the claimant group" (A.F., at para. 57 (emphasis in original)). I would characterize this approach as a "commission of inquiry" model in which a commissioner embarks on a voyage of discovery armed only with very general terms of reference. Quite apart from being inconsistent with the jurisprudence that calls for "characterization of the claim" as a first step, the "commission of inquiry" approach is not suitable in civil litigation, even in civil litigation conducted under rules generously interpreted in Aboriginal cases to facilitate the resolution in the public interest of the underlying controversies.

[41] I would reject the appellants' approach for three reasons. Firstly, it is illogical. The relevance of evidence is tested by reference to what is in issue. The statement of claim (which here did undergo significant amendment) defines what is in issue. The trial of an action should not resemble a voyage on the *Flying Dutchman* with a crew condemned to roam the seas interminably with no set destination and no end in sight.

[42] Secondly, it is contrary to authority. In *Van der Peet*, Lamer C.J. emphasized that the *first* task of the court, even in the context of a defence to a regulatory charge, is to characterize the claim:

> … in assessing a claim to an aboriginal right … [t]he correct characterization of the appellant's claim is of importance because whether or not the evidence supports the appellant's claim will depend, in significant part, on what, exactly, that evidence is being called to support. [Emphasis added; para. 51.]

[43] Thirdly, it defies the relevant rules of civil procedure. Pleadings not only serve to define the issues but give the opposing parties fair notice of the case to meet, provide the boundaries and context for effective pre-trial case management, define the extent of disclosure required, and set the parameters of expert opinion. Clear pleadings minimize wasted time and may enhance prospects for settlement.

. . . . .

[46] With these considerations in mind, and acknowledging that the public interest in the resolution of Aboriginal claims calls for a measure of flexibility not always present in ordinary commercial litigation, a court dealing with a s. 35(1) claim would appropriately proceed as follows:

1. First, at the characterization stage, identify the precise nature of the First Nation's claim to an Aboriginal right based on the pleadings. If necessary, in light of the evidence, refine the characterization of the right claimed on terms that are fair to all parties.
2. Second, determine whether the First Nation has proved, based on the evidence adduced at trial:
   a. the existence of the pre-contact practice, tradition or custom advanced in the pleadings as supporting the claimed right; and
   b. that this practice was integral to the distinctive pre-contact Aboriginal society.
3. Third, determine whether the claimed modern right has a reasonable degree of continuity with the "integral" pre-contact practice. In other words, is the claimed modern right demonstrably connected to, and reasonably regarded as a continuation of, the pre-contact practice? At this step, the court should take a generous though realistic approach to matching pre-contact practices to the claimed modern right. As will be discussed, the pre-contact practices must engage the essential elements of the modern right, though of course the two need not be exactly the same.

4. Fourth, and finally, in the event that an Aboriginal right to trade *commercially* is found to exist, the court, when delineating such a right should have regard to what was said by Chief Justice Lamer in *Gladstone* (albeit in the context of a *Sparrow* justification), as follows:

> Although by no means making a definitive statement on this issue, I would suggest that with regards to the distribution of the fisheries resource after conservation goals have been met, objectives such as the pursuit of economic and regional fairness, and the recognition of the historical reliance upon, and participation in, the fishery by non-aboriginal groups, are the type of objectives which can (at least in the right circumstances) satisfy this standard. _In the right circumstances, such objectives are in the interest of all Canadians and, more importantly, the reconciliation of aboriginal societies with the rest of Canadian society may well depend on their successful attainment._ [Emphasis in the original; para. 75.] ...

[47] In my view the trial judge proceeded correctly in her approach to characterization of the claim based on the pleadings and this ground of appeal should be rejected.

B. *Did the Trial Judge Err in Refusing to Consider a Modern Commercial Fishery to be the Logical Evolution of a Pre-Contact Trade in Eulachon Grease?*

[48] The trial judge interpreted the pleadings as a single claim to an existing Aboriginal right within the meaning of s. 35(1) of the *Constitution Act, 1982*, "to harvest and sell on a commercial scale all species of Fisheries Resources in the Claimed Territories" (para. 97). Although the Lax Kw'alaams sought two distinct and separate declarations, the fusion into a single claim for declaratory relief made by the trial judge was quite appropriate. There can be no sale without a prior harvesting of the fish and the whole point of harvesting the fish, according to the Second Amended Statement of Claim, was for commercial sale. The two elements of the claim are inextricably tied together.

[49] If established, an Aboriginal right is not frozen at contact, but is subject to evolution both in terms of the subject matter and the method of its exercise, depending on the facts.

[50] In terms of the mode of exercise, the courts have repeatedly recognized that fishing methods continue to evolve. The Aboriginal source of fishing rights does not require rights holders in the Pacific Northwest to fish from dugout canoes. Pre-contact trade in Pacific smoked salmon (if established) should not exclude preparation and sale of the frozen product when the technology became available. (All of this, of course, is subject to the interest of conservation and other substantial and compelling interests: *Sparrow*, at pp. 1108-1110; and *N.T.C. Smokehouse*, at para. 96.)

[51] However, when it comes to "evolving" the *subject matter* of the Aboriginal right, the situation is more complex. A "gathering right" to berries based on pre-contact times would not, for example, "evolve" into a right to "gather" natural gas within the traditional territory. The surface

gathering of copper from the Coppermine River in the Northwest Territories in pre-contact times would not, I think, support an "Aboriginal right" to exploit deep shaft diamond mining in the same territory. While courts have recognized that Aboriginal rights must be allowed to evolve within limits, such limits are both quantitative and qualitative. "[A] pre-sovereignty Aboriginal practice cannot be transformed into a different modern right": *Marshall (2005)*, at para. 50.

[52] The trial judge was satisfied that the ancestors of the Lax Kw'alaams "harvested a wide variety of Fish Resources and Products through an array of fishing techniques. They have proved that the harvesting and consumption of Fish Resources and Products, including the creation of a surplus supply for winter consumption, was an integral part of their distinctive culture" (para. 494 (emphasis added)). She further found

> that the pre-contact Coast Tsimshian existed primarily within a subsistence economy until the arrival of the fur traders who influenced the creation of trade monopolies and chiefdoms [although they were also] involved in some form of loosely termed trade before the date of contact. This trade involved primarily gift exchange between kin at feasts and potlatches, or exchange of luxury goods such as slaves, coppers, dentalium and eulachon grease. [para. 495]

However, and this is the crucial point, the trial judge held that "trade in any other Fish Resource or Product beside eulachon grease" (*ibid.* (emphasis added)) could *not* be described as integral to their distinctive culture. Such sporadic trade as took place in other fish products was peripheral to the pre-contact society and did not define what made Coast Tsimshian society what it was.

[53] The Lax Kw'alaams argue that such sporadic trade in other fish products was nonetheless part of their ancestral "way of life" and, on that account, they should be allowed to continue to engage in trade in fish generally under the protection of s. 35(1) of the *Constitution Act, 1982*. In other words, the Lax Kw'alaams' argument is that proof of even sporadic trade as part of pre-contact society is sufficient to support a modern trading right in "all species of fish" and that the test applied by the trial judge is too strict. It should be enough to show that trade was part of their ancestors' pre-contact "way of life" whether or not "distinctive" or "integral" as required by *Van der Peet*.

[54] The Lax Kw'alaams place reliance on references to "way of life" in *Sappier*, at paras. 24 and 40. However, the reference in *Sappier* to a pre-contact "way of life" should not be read as departing from the "distinctive culture" test set out in *Van der Peet*, where Chief Justice Lamer stated:

> To satisfy the integral to a distinctive culture test the aboriginal claimant must do more than demonstrate that a practice, custom or tradition was an aspect of, or took place in, the aboriginal society of which he or she is a part. The claimant must demonstrate that the practice, custom or tradition was a central and significant part of the society's distinctive culture. He or she must demonstrate, in other words, that the practice, custom or tradition was one of the things which made the culture of the society distinctive — that it

was one of the things that truly <u>made the society what it was</u>. [First emphasis added; second emphasis in original; para. 55.] ...

[55] Counsel for the Lax Kw'alaams argues that, even if pre-contact trade had been limited to eulachon grease (which they deny), the modern right should not be "frozen" but should be generalized and "evolved" to include all other fish species and fish products.

[56] However, such an "evolution" would run counter to the trial judge's clear finding that the ancestors of the Lax Kw'alaams fished all species but did not *trade* in any significant way in species of fish or fish products other than eulachon. Extension of a modern right to all species would directly contradict her view that only the "species specific" trade in eulachon grease was integral to the distinctive culture of the pre-contact society. A general commercial fishery would represent an outcome qualitatively different from the pre-contact activity on which it would ostensibly be based, and out of all proportion to its original importance to the pre-contact Tsimshian economy.

[57] The "species specific" debate will generally turn on the facts of a particular case. Had it been established, for example, that a defining feature of the distinctive Coast Tsimshian culture was to catch whatever fish they could and trade whatever fish they caught, a court ought not to "freeze" today's permissible catch to species present in 1793 in the northwest coastal waters of British Columbia. As the oceans have warmed, new species have come north from southern waters and the migratory pattern of some of the old species may have shifted towards Alaska. To ignore the evolution of the fisheries resources of the Pacific Northwest would be uncalled for in the absence of some compelling reason to the contrary on the particular facts of a particular case ...

[58] The trial judge made no findings regarding the quantity of eulachon grease traded in those ancient times (and presumably had no means of doing so given the lack of evidence), but it may be assumed that, given the very short eulachon fishing season and the laborious method of extraction of the grease previously described, the quantities were small relative to the overall pre-contact fishing activity of the industrious and productive Coast Tsimshian peoples. Accordingly, to extrapolate a modern commercial fishery from the pre-contact trade in eulachon grease would lack proportionality in *quantitative* terms relative to the overall pre-contact fishing activity as well.

......

C. *Did the Trial Judge Err in Refusing to Make a Declaration in Relation to "Lesser and Included Rights"?*

[60] The Lax Kw'alaams seek a declaration of "lesser included" Aboriginal rights to harvest fish of all species for consumption and sale "to sustain their communities and generate wealth and maintain and develop their economy" ... The Lax Kw'alaams also seek a declaration of entitlement to a s. 35(1) right to a food, social and ceremonial ... .

[61] The categories of fishery are thus portrayed as falling along a spectrum with a subsistence food fishery at the bottom end and a full commercial fishery at the top end. Where this "lesser" commercial-type fishery falls on the spectrum is not altogether clear. In their final written argument at trial the Lax Kw'alaams characterized the *lesser* right as "a right to harvest all species of Fisheries Resources in the Lax Kw'alaams Territory, for the purpose of selling those Fisheries Resources and their products, <u>on a commercial scale,</u> to sustain the Lax Kw'alaams communities accumulate and generate wealth" ... It is therefore a "lesser" right but nevertheless a *commercial* right, albeit on a more modest scale. How much more modest is not clear. The Lax Kw'alaams particularized the "amount of Fisheries Resources that the Plaintiffs need to sustain their communities" as "depending on a number of factors including availability of stocks and availability of markets for their Fisheries Resources. The Plaintiffs require enough Fisheries Resources which, when converted to money, will enable the communities to develop and maintain a prosperous economy" ... .

[62] It seems to me that by rejecting the claim to the "greater" commercial fishery on the basis that *trade* in fish other than eulachon was not integral to pre-contact society, the trial judge was equally required to reject a "lesser" commercial right to fish "all species". Her problem on this branch of the argument was not only the scale of the commercial fishery but whether and to what extent "trade" in the pre-contact period could support *any* sort of modern commercial fishery — whether full scale or "lesser" in scope. Her conclusion that *trade* in fish apart from eulachon grease was *not* integral to Coastal Tsimshian pre-contact society was as fatal to the lesser commercial claim as it was to the greater commercial claim.

. . . . .

[67] This is not like a treaty case where the court may be obliged to interpret its terms — however vague — because that is what the parties agreed to. Here nothing in this respect has been agreed to. The economic implications of even a "lesser" commercial fishery could be significant, and the Crown is entitled to proper notice of what "declaration" it was supposed to argue about and to test the evidence directed to that issue.

[68] In summary, the Lax Kw'alaams' claim to a declaration of an aboriginal right to a "lesser" commercial fishery was properly rejected, in my opinion.

. . . . .

VI. <u>Disposition</u>

[73] Large amounts of time and resources were dedicated to a year-long trial to determine the commercial fisheries issue. Notwithstanding the facts that the people of the Coast Tsimshian have deep roots in the coastal fishery of what is now British Columbia, the evidence satisfied the trial judge that they were not a *trading* people, except in the limited area of

species specific eulachon grease. This is not to say the Lax Kw'alaams are without s. 35(1) rights. Their claim to Aboriginal title remains outstanding. ...

[74] The appeal must be dismissed ... .

---

1. Identify the benefits the Crown receives from the "integral to a distinctive culture" test as applied in the *Lax Kw'alaams* case.
2. The "integral to a distinctive culture" test significantly narrows activities that might qualify as Aboriginal rights because Aboriginal peoples can only claim rights to specific practices that lie in the distant past. As the *Lax Kw'alaams* case demonstrates, Aboriginal peoples cannot generalize from these practices to broader possible rights. Furthermore, they cannot claim rights for activities that are generated as a result of European influence. One might question whether this is a "large, liberal and generous" conception of Aboriginal rights, as *Sparrow* counselled. Compare the Supreme Court of Canada's approach to the one which underlies much of "Federal Indian Law" in the United States. Felix Cohen expressed the U.S. Supreme Court's view as follows: "An Indian tribe possesses, in the first instance, all the powers of any sovereign state."[7] When First Nations possess sovereign powers, they have the ability to engage in trade, resource use, and other activities without proving they historically exercised these powers. Do you think the *Lax Kw'alaams* and other cases dealing with Aboriginal rights would be better resolved using an approach which first recognizes the sovereignty of First Nations and other Aboriginal peoples?

F. CONCLUSION

The judiciary's focus on Aboriginal rights in cases such as *Sparrow* and *Van der Peet* has often appeared to be more on the limitation of those rights than on facilitating their understanding or protection. Moreover, the restrictive understandings of Aboriginal rights in the majority judgments in the *Van der Peet* trilogy, as well as in *Adams* and *Côté*, appear to have eliminated the sensitivity to Aboriginal perspectives that had been recognized in *Sparrow*.[8] Even in a case that appears to be a victory, like *Sappier and Gray*, Aboriginal rights appear to be narrowed when one considers the Crown's entitlements and the context in which they are upheld. These approaches seem inconsistent with the purposive approach to interpreting section 35(1) of the *Constitution Act, 1982* indicated in both *Sparrow* and *Van der Peet*. If Aboriginal rights are to have substantive protection from section 35(1), Canadian courts must infuse their understandings of Aboriginal rights with more meaningful content that pays heed to Aboriginal perspectives and understandings. They must also interpret them in light of who they are meant to apply to and protect: "peoples". The courts have spent so much time and energy focusing on the Aboriginal within Aboriginal rights, it has seemingly overlooked that what is protected are the rights of Aboriginal *peoples* in Canada. As constitutional protection of Aboriginal rights continues to develop, section 35(1) clearly provides a constitutional imperative for the judiciary to interpret them with these considerations in mind.

ENDNOTES

1. Sally Weaver, *Making Canadian Indian Policy: The Hidden Agenda* (University of Toronto Press, 1981) at 171.

2. See *Campbell v. Hall* (1774), 1 Cowp. 204, 98 E.R. 1045, [1558-1774] All E.R. Rep. 252 (K.B.); *Re Southern Rhodesia*, [1919] A.C. 211 at 233 (P.C.); *Amodu Tijani v. Southern Nigeria (Secretary)*, [1921] 2 A.C. 399 at 407 (P.C.); *Oyekan v. Adele*, [1957] 2 All E.R. 785 at 788, [1957] 1 W.L.R. 876 (P.C.); B. Slattery, ed., "The Doctrine of Continuity," in *Ancestral Lands, Alien Laws: Judicial Perspectives on Aboriginal Title* (Saskatoon: University of Saskatchewan Native Law Centre, 1983) at 10-11.

3. *R. v. Adams*, [1996] S.C.J. No. 87, [1996] 3 S.C.R. 101, [1996] 4 C.N.L.R. 1 at 14 (S.C.C.). See also *R. v. Côté*, [1996] S.C.J. No. 93, [1996] 3 S.C.R. 139, [1996] 4 C.N.L.R. 26 at 48 (S.C.C.), in which this quotation is repeated almost verbatim; also *Delgamuukw v. British Columbia*, [1997] S.C.J. No. 108, [1997] 3 S.C.R. 1010, at 1093 (S.C.C.): "the existence of a particular aboriginal right at common law is not a *sine qua non* for the proof of an aboriginal right that is recognized and affirmed by s. 35(1)." The *Adams* and *Côté* decisions are notable for their findings that Aboriginal rights still exist in the former French colony of New France, notwithstanding long-standing arguments to the contrary by historians and jurists.

4. *R. v. Sparrow*, [1990] S.C.J. No. 49, [1990] 1 S.C.R. 1075, [1990] 4 W.W.R. 410, 46 B.C.L.R. (2d) 1, 56 C.C.C. (3d) 263, 82 N.R. 206, 65 Sask. R. 176, 70 D.L.R. (4th) 385 at 412 (S.C.C.).

5. K. McNeil, "How Can Infringements of the Constitutional Rights of Aboriginal Peoples be Justified?" (1997) 8 Constitutional Forum 33 at 39.

6. *Côté, supra*, note 3 at 48.

7. Felix Cohen, *Handbook of Federal Indian Law* (Washington, DC: Department of Interior, 1941) at 123.

8. Interestingly, the Supreme Court's judgment in *Delgamuukw, supra*, note 3 was arguably more sensitive to Aboriginal perspectives, even in the establishment of a justificatory standard for legislative infringements on Aboriginal title, than those in either the *Van der Peet* trilogy, *Adams* or *Côté*.

CHAPTER 3

ABORIGINAL TITLE

A. INTRODUCTION

Land is a central element of Aboriginal societies. The sacredness of land to Aboriginal peoples is illustrated in the following statement made by the Shawnee leader Tecumseh:

> No tribe has the right to sell, even to each other, much less to strangers. ... Sell a country! Why not sell the great sea, as well as the earth? Did not the Great Spirit make them all for the use of his children?[1]

While not all Aboriginal issues revolve around land, Aboriginal rights, and some treaty rights, are strongly tied to Aboriginal relationships to land.

The link between Aboriginal rights and land exists because many of those rights stem from Aboriginal traditions, customs, or practices associated with land. Common examples are hunting, fishing, or trapping rights. These rights may exist either as Aboriginal rights or they may have been incorporated into a treaty as treaty rights. While these rights are derived from an association with land, their existence is not dependent upon a finding of Aboriginal title. As the Supreme Court of Canada decisions in *R. v. Adams*, [1996] S.C.J. No. 87, [1996] 3 S.C.R. 101, 202 N.R. 89, 138 D.L.R. (4th) 657, 110 C.C.C. (3d) 97, 4 C.N.L.R. 1 (S.C.J.) and *R. v. Côté*, [1996] S.C.J. No. 93, [1996] 3 S.C.R. 139, 202 N.R. 161, 138 D.L.R. (4th) 385, 110 C.C.C. (3d) 122, [1996] 4 C.N.L.R. 26 (S.C.C.) illustrate (see the excerpts of these cases in Chapter 2), Aboriginal rights exist independently of title and may be exercised without the need to demonstrate title to a particular area. This same premise also holds true of treaty rights that affirm pre-existing Aboriginal rights.

B. THE IMPORTANCE OF LAND TO ABORIGINAL CULTURES

Aboriginal peoples traditionally viewed land in a different manner than Europeans. They did not generally regard land as something to be owned, as Europeans did. Rather, they viewed land as something to be used and cared for. While the notion of stewardship was not necessarily a foreign concept to the Europeans of the 15th and 16th centuries, they did not give it much weight. Because of their different emphasis and understandings, Aboriginal and European peoples each viewed the others' actions regarding land according to their own conceptions. Thus, when the Aboriginal peoples shared their lands with the Europeans, they did not generally imagine that what they regarded as sharing would be conceived of by the Europeans as a surrender of their interests.

THE JUSTICE SYSTEM AND ABORIGINAL PEOPLE: REPORT OF THE ABORIGINAL JUSTICE INQUIRY OF MANITOBA, VOL. 1

(Winnipeg: Queen's Printer, 1991)
(A.C. Hamilton and C.M. Sinclair, Commissioners) c. 5 at 115-16

When Europeans came to the Americas they were considered outsiders but, in accordance with the Aboriginal view, were permitted to share in the land and its resources. Elders have told us that, in the eyes of the Creator, the Europeans as outsiders could not enjoy the same rights as the original inhabitants. Whatever rights the Europeans wanted had to be sought from those who were placed upon the land first by the Creator. It is a belief common to many Aboriginal societies that the Creator placed Aboriginal people upon this land first for a reason, and that, as the first one on the land, they were placed in a special relationship to it. In the worldview of Aboriginal people, the Europeans were visitors and, as such, were bound to respect the obligations of that status.

For Aboriginal peoples, the land was part of their identity as a people. The earth was their Mother, the animals were their spiritual kin and all were part of the greater whole, which was life. Their culture was grounded in nature. Time was marked by the changing seasons and the rising and setting of the sun, rather than by numbers, and their existence was marked by an acceptance of and respect for their natural surroundings and their place in the scheme of things. The thinking of Aboriginal peoples was cyclical, rather than linear like that of the Europeans. Everything was thought of in terms of its relation to the whole, not as individual bits of information to be compared to one another. Aboriginal philosophy was holistic, and did not lend itself readily to dichotomies or categories as did European philosophy. So, for Aboriginal people, their rights were — and still are — seen in broad, conceptual terms.

The most fundamental of those rights is the right to their identity as Aboriginal people. Since that identity was derived largely from the land they used and occupied before the arrival of the Europeans, they believe they had — and still have — certain rights in regard to the land, including continuing habitation and use of the land, whether it be for hunting, fishing, trapping, gathering food and medicines, or for any other traditional pursuits.

This excerpt from the Manitoba Aboriginal Justice Inquiry report affirms the central role that land plays in the identity of Aboriginal peoples. Consequently, to be able to properly understand the basis of an Aboriginal claim to land, it is necessary to have an appreciation of the meaning of land to Aboriginal cultures. Of course, individual Aboriginal cultures will view land in their own way. In the following excerpts, Chief John Snow and Professor John Borrows describe the centrality of land for their people. Note that in describing the land's importance they focus not only on relationships to land but also on their way of life and their place within the natural order.

CHIEF JOHN SNOW, THESE MOUNTAINS ARE OUR SACRED PLACES: THE STORY OF THE STONEY INDIANS

(Toronto: Samuel Stevens, 1977) at 2-3, 12-13

Indian traditions and oral history say that my people were always present in this part of the Great Island (the native name for the North American continent), roaming along the foothills out onto the prairies to the east and deep into the Rocky Mountain country to the west. Our traditional hunting territory seems to have extended north to the Brazeau River-Jasper area, south a little past what is now the international border, east beyond the present-day city of Calgary, and west into the Rockies beyond what would become the British Columbia border.

In order to understand the vital importance the mountains had — and still have — to my people, it is necessary to know something of our way of life before the coming of the whiteman. It is not enough to say the mountains were the Stoneys' traditional place of prayer because our life was not a fragmented one with a compartment for religion. Rather, our life was one in which religion (and reverance for nature, which revealed religious truth) was woven throughout all parts of the social structure and observed in conjunction with every activity. Our forefathers were a proud people because they knew they had been selected by the Creator to receive a precious gift of special understanding and they have handed that gift down to us as a sacred trust.

In the days prior to the coming of the whiteman, we lived a nomadic way of life, hunting, fishing, and gathering from the abundance of this good land. There were literally millions of buffalo roaming on the western prairies, along the foothills, and even into the Rocky Mountains themselves. There were game animals of all kinds — moose, elk, deer, wild sheep, and goats — readily available for us to hunt and enjoy. The land was vast, beautiful, and rich in abundant resources. Our Mother Earth called us from the forests, the prairies, the valleys, the mountainous areas, the lakes, rivers, and springs: "Come, my children, anyone who is hungry, come and eat from the fruits and gather from the abundance of this land. Come, everyone who thirsts, come and drink pure spring waters that are especially provided for you." Everywhere the spirits of all living things were alive.

We talked to the rocks, the streams, the trees, the plants, the herbs, and all nature's creations. We called the animals our brothers. They understood our language; we, too, understood theirs. Sometimes they talked to us in dreams and visions. At times they revealed important events or visited us on our vision quests to the mountain tops. Truly, we were part of and related to the universe, and these animals were a very special part of the Great Spirit's creation.

. . . . .

In our migrations, as in our vision quests, my people continued to observe the animals, plants, rocks, trees, streams, winds, sun, moon, stars, and all things. Our teaching has always been that everything was created for a purpose by the Great Spirit. We must, therefore, respect all things of creation and learn as much as we can. There are lessons hidden in creation that we must learn in order to live a good life and walk the straight path. Behind these lessons and teachings is the Creator. These things can only be understood through the Great Spirit.

Century after century, the rugged Rocky Mountains sat there in majesty, and nature seemed to say: "Your thoughts must be as firm as these mountains, if you are to walk the straight path. Your patience and kindness must be as solid as these mountains, if you are to acquire understanding and wisdom."

. . . . .

Upon these lofty heights, the Great Spirit revealed many things to us. Some of my people received powers to heal. They could heal the physical body with herbs, roots, leaves, plants, and mineral spring waters. They could also heal the broken and weary soul with unseen spiritual powers. Others received powers over the weather. These gifted religious men and women could call for a great storm or calm the weather; they could call on the winds, rain, hail, snow, or sleet, and they would come. From these mountain-top experiences my fellow tribesmen and women were given unique tasks to perform to help the tribe prepare for things to come.

Therefore the Rocky Mountains are precious and sacred to us. We knew every trail and mountain pass in the area. We had special ceremonial and religious areas in the mountains. In the olden days some of the neighbouring tribes called us the "People of the Shining Mountains." These mountains are our temples, our sanctuaries, and our resting places. They are a place of hope, a place of vision, a place of refuge, a very special and holy place where the Great Spirit speaks with us. *Therefore, these mountains are our sacred places.*

JOHN BORROWS, LIVING LAW ON A LIVING EARTH

[Unpublished manuscript, 2007] (references omitted)

The Anishinabek Nation surrounds the North American Great Lakes. They are an Algonquian and (more recently) English speaking people who historically organized themselves in a loose confederacy of clans throughout the region. Anishinabek people possess laws pertaining to the earth. These laws have ancient roots but they are not stunted by time. They continue to grow and develop through observation, experience and interaction with other people's more recent presence within their territories. Anishinabek law is a living system of social order, developed through comparing, contrasting, accepting and rejecting legal standards from many sources. Anishinabek legal traditions do not lose their Indigenous status if they adopt viewpoints that address matters not encountered before European contact. Law is not solely a matter of history because it is reinterpreted and reapplied in every generation to remain relevant amidst changing circumstances.

The Anishinabek regard Michee-Makinakong on the narrows between Lake Huron and Michigan near Lake Superior as the world's centre; the place where the land above the water was formed. Michee-Makinakong was where Michabous (Nanabush) recreated the upper earth through breathing life into soil which was brought up from the ocean's depths by a muskrat. The earth grew as the soil was scattered around Michabous' raft and tread upon by this Great Being. The earth's ability to respond to Michabous' actions provided enough space for plants and animals to find a home. When these first animals died the first Anishinabe arose from their corpses. The Anishinabek take their identity and dodem or clan names from these ancestors. Professor Heidi Bohaker has observed that: "This sacred story is part of what Anishinaabe peoples call aadizookaanag, or the grandfathers. Stories of this genre are set in time immemorial; they explain how the world came to have its present form and furnish embedded observations on how the beings who currently inhabit it should relate to one another." These stories contain law.

For the Anishinabek the earth's creation did not end with Michabous' experience on the raft. The earth grows and develops or dies and decays because it is a living being subject to many of the same forces as all other living creatures. Many Anishinabek people characterize the earth as a living entity that has thoughts and feelings, can exercise agency by making choices, and is related to humans at the deepest generative levels of existence.

The subject of the earth's personality is a profound legal issue. Law is implicated in the earth's sentience because its life is considered sacred within most Anishinabek thought. Anishinabek people do not generally worship the earth as one would the Creator but she is regarded with great awe, respect and wonder because of her ability to live a good life and reproduce it in numerous forms. Anishinabek people believe in a Creator, Kitchee Manitou, who gave form and meaning to the earth following a vision. The first elements of Anishinabek creation stories explain how life came into being from a constellation of forces marshaled by the Creator. Later stories convey important spiritual insights by providing instruction about how the earth must be honoured and respected. Within these teachings there is a general recognition that the earth has a soul (chejauk) which animates her many moods and activities. Many believe the Creator, as the Great Master of Life, created a universal bond between all living things which placed the earth at the centre of a vast web of kinship relations. Great power can be attached to these relationships because of the spiritual energy that flows between, from and through them.

The land's sentience is a fundamental principle of Anishinabek law, one upon which many Anishinabek people attempt to build their societies and relationships. Of course, they have not always been successful in this regard; like most peoples, they often fall short of their highest ideals. That is why they developed law, to direct behavior towards more peaceful, orderly, and respectful future.

The relationship between humans and rocks creates mutual obligations and entitlements that must be respected for this community to reproduce in a healthy manner. This legal structure requires humans to consult with both the earth's Creator and to seek the earth's receptiveness before important decisions are undertaken. The Anishinabek will listen to the Creator and/or the earth through ceremonies or they will elect to understand the earth's requirements by observing its interactions with wind, water, fire and other beings to which she relates.

These obligations between Anishinabek and the earth have territorial aspects. At one level the political boundaries of Anishinabek relationships to the earth coincide with the totality of the planet's surface. An Anishinabemowin word that describes this relationship is aen-danee-yauk-kummikuak which means the nature of the land's character from which all derive sustenance. At this broadest level, we are all citizens with and of one land because we depend upon its total existence to survive.

At the same time this wider political ordering does not preclude Anishinabek or the land from being citizens of smaller polities: watersheds, islands, valleys, countries, tribes, cities, reserves, etc. Anishinabek political community contemplates allegiances across global and smaller geographical units. The Anishinabemowin word for boundary is ani-ishkawaek-kummikauk meaning the place along the way of the land's end according to her character. Within Anishinabek thought there is an encouragement to determine the earth's character to make decisions about how to best divide ourselves in ways that are most respectful of her. The ability to relate to the earth on different scales feeds a multiplicity of citizenship rights and responsibilities for Anishinabek people and the earth. A person could be simultaneously a Clan (dodem) member, Anishinabek, Canadian, American, and a world citizen. Likewise, the earth can concurrently be a planet, geological plate, continent or small rock.

Rocks are animate or living in verb-oriented Algonkian languages, of which Anishnabemowin is one. The very way in which Anishinabek people conceive of the land as alive is hardwired through language. You cannot even describe the world without acknowledging this fact. Their active nature means rocks have an agency of their own which must be respected when Anishinabek people use them. As such it would be inappropriate to use rocks without their acquiescence and participation because such action could oppress their liberty in some circumstances. Using rocks without their consent could be considered akin to using another person against their will. Their enslavement could lead to great calamities for the earth and its people. Therefore, to ensure that rocks and land are appropriately used there are particular ceremonies, or legal permissions, needed to engage in such action.

Since Anishinabek law regards some rocks (or places on earth) as living they could not be owned or allocated if such ownership implied control of the earth without its involvement. However, a kind of ownership can occur if undertaken in accordance with appropriate Anishinabek principles. As such, the pipe ceremony is a particularly important certification-like process preceding the appropriate use or ownership of land. When one smokes the sacred pipe under the guidance of proper leaders, the earth's legal personality is acknowledged during this process. While the smoke is said to ascend to the Creator and demonstrate thankfulness for existence; prayers of thanksgiving are expressed for the rocks, plants, animals and other humans as the smoke rises from the pipe. The pipe itself represents earth's different orders: "the earth, whose elemental substance was rock, made up the pipe; the plant, tobacco was the sacrificial victim; the animal, symbolized by feathers and fur, was appended to the sacred pipe of rock; man was the celebrant." (Basil Johnston, Ojibway Heritage, Toronto: McClelland and Stewart, 1976 at 24-25)

The pipe's use is a token of peace between people and the land, and between peoples settling on the land. The earth was best used by celebrating her contributions and consulting with her Creator in this way. This is why, when treaties were signed, Anishinabek people often included non-Indigenous people in this relationship, and both would use the pipe to register their mutual agreement concerning her use. Anishinabek Elder Basil Johnston has observed that rocks are the elemental substance of life and must be continually acknowledged for their role in sustaining other orders of life. While plants, animals and humans all come to an end, the earth lives on. It is contrary to certain interpretations of Anishinabek law to claim to absolute ownership of the earth, which is called a mother because of her role in bringing forth life. In this vein Dr. Johnston has written:

> No man can own his mother. This principle extends even into the future. The unborn are entitled to the largess of the earth, no less than the living. During his life a man is but a trustee of his portion of the land and must pass on to his children what he inherited from his mother. At death, the dying leave behind the mantle that they occupied, taking nothing with them but a memory and a place for others still to come.

Thus, for many Anishinabek "ownership" is differently construed when compared with other Canadian legal traditions. The analogy of a trustee when explaining limitations concerning Anishinabek land use is somewhat helpful in understanding Anishinabek law. A trust in equity, as merged through the common law, is a right held by one person (the trustee) for the benefit of another person (the beneficiary). Under Anishinabek law, land is held by the present generation for future generations. Land does not ultimately belong to a person or people in the sense that they have absolute discretion and control; land is provisionally held for contemporary sustenance and for those unborn.

However, analogies to trust law can also create confusion in understanding Anishinabek legal traditions if carried too far. Under

Anishinabek law, while the earth is somewhat dependent on other orders of life for its health and vitality — plants, animals and humans are much more reliant on the earth for their survival. In this sense, the earth could be considered the trustee for its beneficiaries (plants, animals and humans). This analogy may be a stretch for the common law legal imagination because of the legal personality the earth possesses under Anishinabek law as a living being. The common law does not generally regard the earth in this light. Nevertheless Anishinabek legal traditions recognize interdependence between rocks and humans because of their mutual agency. The concept of reciprocal obligations between rocks and humans is an important part of Anishinabek law. People are the beneficiaries of the earth's care, and under Anishinabek law this creates duties for the beneficiaries as well as for the earth (as the so-called trustee).

A contemporary applied example of these principles is demonstrated by the Anishinabek people of the Bruce Peninsula, who live between the waters of Lake Huron and Georgian Bay. Ten years ago the people of Neyashiingmiing, the Chippewas of the Nawash on the Cape Croker Indian Reserve, had to make a decision about moving the site of an annual summer festival on their reserve. Each August a powwow is held in their park, drawing thousands of people in a celebration of Anishinabek resilience and culture. A move was contemplated to accommodate the increasing number of park users during this annual event. One suggestion was to move the powwow to "the prairie", a broad, flat and largely treeless stretch of land lying below Jones Bluff just beyond the shores of Sydney Bay. The prairie had the advantage of being able to accommodate large crowds with easy access to the main road. The area affords beautiful views of the surrounding escarpments, lake and ever-changing skies. It is also easy to see from the park and other vantage points around the community. The idea to move the powwow to the prairie seemed to make sense by most principles of efficiency. To any casual observer the land looked empty in terms of human use, and did not seem to be productively used by most economic measures.

However, when it became apparent that a road would be built to facilitate access to the prairie a widespread community movement developed that drew upon Anishinabek legal principles. The land is host to a significant alvar, which is a rock-barren or natural pavement-like feature with little or no brush or tree cover. The alvar is a limestone plain composed of dolostone bedrock with a surface that is almost completely exposed to the air. The alvar is among the oldest exposed stone in Ontario, having an age in excess of four hundred and forty million years. For many Anishinabek the alvar is a story-teller that recounts the time when the land was younger and covered by shallow tropical seas. It is related to the surrounding limestone escarpments and fossil strewn beaches formed when the area once likely resembled the Great Barrier Reef of Australia's north-eastern coast. Furthermore, in those areas where a very thin layer of organic matter covers the alvar it accommodates a unique community of resilient mosses, lichens and plants which are very well adapted to extreme conditions of intense cold, heat, drought and flooding.

The alvar is also home to spiritually significant 'spirit trails' which wend their way through the area. Family stories amongst the Anishinabek speak of the place as having significant sacred power with accounts of bear-walkers, deceased relatives and supernatural transformers traversing over the area. Armed with this knowledge, there was consultation, debate, discussion, direct experience on the land, prayer and persuasion when making a decision about the alvar's use. Scientists and Anishinabek lawyers, band councillors, grandmothers, Elders, artists, medicine people, community employees and others participated in a process that drew most strongly on Anishinabek law respecting Anishinabek spiritual beliefs. Ceremonies were conducted and traditional teachings reviewed. This led to a decision to stop the prairie's development to respect and reverence the life force of what others might regard as barren rock.

This brief review of Anishinabek law demonstrates that Anishinabek beliefs concerning the earth as a living being can be legally recognized and affirmed, within that legal system. It also shows how Anishinabek law can lead to land being accorded political citizenship with its other close relations. The attentiveness to land's character and the desire to respect significant sites where it manifests sacred power give the earth a place within this jurisprudential system.

C. THE DOCTRINE OF ABORIGINAL TITLE

Aboriginal peoples used and occupied lands in what is now known as Canada long before the first arrival of Europeans to North America. During that time, they put the land to various uses in order to provide for the sustenance and continuation of their societies. When European traders and settlers arrived in North America, they required the assistance of the Aboriginal peoples in order to survive in a strange and distant land. The Aboriginals shared their land, resources, and knowledge with the Europeans. The groups also engaged in mutually-beneficial trade of fish, furs, and other resources.

As the number of Europeans grew significantly, disputes between the European and Aboriginal peoples arose over rights to land. The doctrine of Aboriginal title in English common law originated from the historical circumstances arising from these competing European and Aboriginal land interests. The Europeans, who sought ownership and control of North American lands, laid claim to those lands through a variety of means. In actual fact, European claims to lands in the New World had been initiated prior to the Europeans' arrival on North American shores. In 1455, King Alfonso V of Portugal had been granted the exclusive "right" to conquer and enslave all "pagan" nations — and to seize their lands — by Pope Nicholas V in his bull *Romanus Pontifex*. When Spain ignored the exclusivity of this grant by sending Columbus to the New World in the latter stages of the 15th century, Pope Alexander VI divided the rights that had been granted to Portugal between it and Spain in his 1493 bull *Inter*

Caetera. Being snubbed by the papacy once again, England and France sent explorers to claim lands in the New World on their own authorization. King Henry VII granted Letters Patent to John Cabot in 1496 which authorized him to "subdue, occupy and possess all such townes, cities, castles and isles of them found, which [he] can subdue, occupy and possess".[2] France, meanwhile, issued its own commission to Jean François de La Rocque, Sieur de Roberval, in 1541, which granted him "full power and authority over those *lands that he shall have been able to acquire for us in this voyage*".[3] Soon, Russia, the Netherlands, and Sweden also joined in the race to claim lands in the New World.

1.   Aboriginal Title and the Law of Nations

Aside from papal bulls and royal charters, European nations attempted to reinforce their claims to lands in the New World through the doctrines of discovery, occupation/settlement, adverse possession, conquest, and cession. These concepts were creatures of the *jus gentium*, or Law of Nations, which governed controversies between its member states, including those surrounding their attempts to acquire new territories. The question remains, however, what the effects of these concepts were *vis-à-vis* the Aboriginal peoples of North America.

THE JUSTICE SYSTEM AND ABORIGINAL PEOPLE: REPORT OF THE ABORIGINAL JUSTICE INQUIRY OF MANITOBA, VOL. 1

(Winnipeg: Queen's Printer, 1991) (A.C. Hamilton and C.M. Sinclair, Commissioners) c. 5 at 127, 130-5, 137 (references omitted)

One of the primary issues with which Canadian society has to come to grips is the historical legacy of its acquisition of Aboriginal lands. ... The issue involves how Canadian and American legal systems have addressed the nature and form of the Aboriginal legal interest in the land now within Canada and the United States, and of the legal techniques used to assert dominion over lands which enjoyed some degree of legal protection in international law.

The Use of Doctrines of International Law

Since the beginning of the Age of Discovery, European states have engaged relentlessly in the process of divesting indigenous peoples of their lands, and have sought to justify and legitimate this practice through the use of the doctrines of discovery, occupation, adverse possession, conquest and cession. On the whole, domestic courts have either ignored or generally misapplied and misinterpreted these doctrines in their discussions of "Aboriginal title," thereby upholding the status quo of Aboriginal dispossession.

The starting point in determining what rights Aboriginal people had at international law when they first were in contact with Europeans requires an examination of the legal provisions applicable to those nations which asserted authority over North America after contact. We will examine in turn each of the rationales for European claims to sovereignty and underlying title to the discovered territories.

The Doctrine of Discovery

The doctrine of discovery has been — and still is — rigorously advanced by various authors, jurists, legal scholars, nation states and domestic courts as the foundation upon which English, Canadian or American sovereignty in North America is based. The basic premise is that the first state to "discover" an uninhabited region with no other claims to it automatically acquires territorial sovereignty. Originally, the doctrine was limited to *terra nullius* — literally, a barren and deserted area — as reflected by the noted English scholar of the common law, Blackstone, writing in his *Commentaries*. The concept of *terra nullius* was expanded later, without justification, to include any area devoid of "civilized" society. In order to reflect colonial desires, the New World was said by some courts to fall within this expanded definition.

The traditional doctrine of discovery has never been recognized as vesting a valid claim or title to a "discovered" territory. Since [16th-century Spanish scholar Francisco de] Vitoria's vehement rejection of the doctrine in the 16th century, such a claim has been seen only as establishing an initial and incomplete title to the territory in question. This traditional interpretation has been ratified and affirmed in decisions from international courts in this century. While there is some debate among academics about this claim's validity, the dominant view clearly is in favour of the traditional elaboration of this doctrine.

Although the doctrine of discovery has been advanced occasionally by European powers since the "discovery" of the New World, such a claim was based more upon expediency than international law. The validity of the claim is dependent upon the status of the territory as *terra nullius* — an uninhabited land. Because Indians already occupied the land at the arrival of the Europeans, Vitoria unequivocally rejected such a title when it was asserted in the New World. Although there were many attempts to found claims based on discovery, the doctrine, by itself, was not considered sufficient to establish a valid claim, and does not appear to have been accepted officially by the competing states themselves, unless the discoverer was able to demonstrate an actual and effective governmental presence.

In *Johnson v. M'Intosh*, 21 U.S. (8 Wheat.) 543 (1823), however, the United States Supreme Court applied the doctrine of discovery in order to justify American sovereignty over the land included in what is now the United States of America. The court held that:

- The principle of discovery was acknowledged by all Europeans because it was in their interests to do so.
- The nation making the "discovery" had "the sole right of acquiring the soil and establishing settlements on it."

- The rule regulated the relations among the competing interests of European powers.
- The original inhabitants had the right to retain possession of their land, but were without any powers of alienation other than to the "discoverers" who had obtained exclusive title by virtue of making the "discovery."

When one considers both the international legal reality of the time and state practice, this decision appears to be more an effort to justify the taking of Indian territory that had already occurred than a serious analysis and application of the principles demanded by international law. Quite simply, the concept that Aboriginal inhabitants could only alienate their interest in the land to the "discoverer" was a legal fiction, because that concept did not originally exist in international law. In the *Island of Palmas* case (1928), 2 R.I.A.A. 829, the doctrine of discovery, as a means to justify the taking of Aboriginal lands, was considered and rejected definitively in just such a situation by the Permanent Court of Arbitration.

The Doctrine of Occupation

It has been argued by some that if discovery was seen to vest only an imperfect title, then discovery plus occupation completed the claim. There was, however, a traditional requirement that the land so discovered and occupied had to be *terra nullius.* At one time, an area devoid of "civilized" society was alleged by some scholars to fall within the scope of such a requirement. The more accurate historical interpretation, which is reflected by the modern jurisprudence in international law, precludes the requirement's application to any region with an indigenous population that is organized socially and politically.

According to the *Island of Palmas* case, a claim based on discovery was incomplete until accompanied by "the effective occupation of the region claimed to be discovered." The term "effective occupation" incorporates the notion of "uninterrupted and permanent possession." Based on such a rule and interpretation, it would appear that the only ones capable of successfully advancing a claim based on discovery and occupation may be the Aboriginal peoples themselves, because they are the ones who could argue best that they first discovered and occupied the vacant territory many thousands of years ago.

There was much debate about the definition of *terra nullius* for some time. Although the term was commonly accepted as meaning "uninhabited," some decisions have held that certain tribal lands could be said to fall within the scope of "uninhabited" if the peoples of the area exhibited an unwillingness to exploit the land in a "civilized" fashion. Such decisions, like many of the European policies of dealing with indigenous peoples, were largely the result of expediency and ethnocentrism. The present state of international law, as expressed by the International Court of Justice in the *Western Sahara Case*, precludes a region from being termed "uninhabited" if nomadic or resident tribes with a degree of social and political organization are present in the area. The issue then becomes, in individual cases, whether a specific indigenous group meets the test by exhibiting a sufficient degree of internal organization to be recognized as a distinct society, so as to effectively occupy the land and administer it as its own.

It appears from the Canadian case law that probably every Aboriginal group would meet this test. The standard is not similarity to European civilization, and no particular level of "sophistication" is required. International law merely requires that the society was organized sufficiently to meet the needs of its members and was recognizable by others as a legal entity that inhabited the territory with a settled system of government.

. . . . .

It should be noted that the colonizing nations themselves applied this test in the 18th and 19th centuries, with the Indian treaties demonstrating its practical application. The *Western Sahara Case*'s adoption of it in 1975 indicates that it reflects current international law. This test, however, should not be confused with international law requirements established for recognition as a nation state, which include additional criteria.

The Doctrine of Adverse Possession

The doctrine of adverse possession has frequently been linked to the above two doctrines to consolidate a valid claim to territory. Adverse possession basically posits that you can acquire title to part of another state's land if you openly occupy it for an extended period of time and the original owner acquiesces to your presence. In order for such a claim to be valid, there must be a *de facto* exercise of sovereignty which is peaceful and unchallenged. This doctrine is similar to one that exists within the Canadian domestic law by virtue of provincial and territorial legislation (the relevant *Limitations Act*, which establishes a 10- or 20-year rule among private parties and 60 years versus the Crown) or through reception of English law (regarding federal Crown land).

It would take little effort to discover in Canadian or Manitoban history sufficient examples of Aboriginal resistance to European occupation of the land to refute the application of this doctrine. Significant European occupation of lands in Manitoba did not occur until the Selkirk Settlement of 1811. That settlement came about as a direct result of Aboriginal consent being negotiated with Indian Chief Peguis by Lord Selkirk prior to the arrival and occupation of the land by the European settlers. The Hudson's Bay Company, which constituted the only significant European presence prior to that era, acknowledged in its practices the Indian sovereignty in the territory, and deliberately did not interfere with Indian control over their territory. In fact, various instructions sent to the trading post managers in North America by the senior officials of the company always emphasized the importance of not interfering in the internal affairs of the Indians, and in ensuring that wherever trading posts were established, the

"Indian title" was purchased. When the company transferred its interest in the territory to Canada, it specifically required that the new Dominion negotiate land surrenders with the Indians, and in 1872 the Canadian government began to do so. Those earlier negotiations between the company and the Indians, as well as the later treaties between the Dominion and the First Nations, enabled the land to be settled by Europeans with Indian consent, as the latter agreed to share their territory.

To the extent that they reflect only a surrender of exclusive Indian title to much of the land, the treaties also amount to a confirmation of the Indian right to retain all other aspects of their Aboriginal title (*i.e.*, their "other" Aboriginal rights), since only the land rights were surrendered.

What is clear, however, is that Canadian sovereignty in western Canada is dependent to a large degree upon the validity of the treaties in those areas covered by them.

The Doctrine of Conquest

With respect to its traditional interpretation, the doctrine of conquest allowed using force or waging war only if a nation's security or rights were threatened. Under traditional international law, a country was no more justified in exploiting another through force than was a private individual. Conquest gave the victorious nation the full right to colonize the vanquished nation and change its legal regime. These rights usually were described in the peace treaty that ended the war. The doctrine of conquest only operated, however, if the conquered territory actually was annexed and possessed by the conqueror. In terms of the indigenous lands in North America, these criteria normally were not met, as no state of war was declared, although hostilities were not infrequent.

The present interpretation of the doctrine of conquest was outlined by the Permanent Court of International Justice in the *Status of Eastern Greenland Case* (1933), 3 W.C.R. 148 at 171. According to this decision:

> [The doctrine of conquest] only operates as a cause of lack of sovereignty when there is a war between two states and by reason of the defeat of one of them sovereignty over territory passes from the loser to the victorious state.

The doctrine of conquest frequently has been confused with the doctrine of discovery. Both are also the cause of further confusion, as they have international and domestic law purposes. At international law, conquest can cause the vanquished to lose sovereignty when the conqueror chooses to annex part or all of the territory of the loser. As has been indicated already, discovery *per se* can justify only the acquisition of sovereignty over uninhabited territories, and even then mere discovery without actual occupation is insufficient.

These two doctrines are also used for an entirely different purpose: determining what law comes to be applied within the newly acquired territory, as opposed to the international law standards governing the legitimacy of the process of acquisition itself. The common law distinguishes among settled, ceded and conquered colonies for the purposes of defining precisely when and on what terms the common law becomes the basic foundational law of the colony. This function is embraced within the English doctrine of reception of laws. It is quite possible, therefore, for a territory to be treated as being acquired at international law by conquest or cession (treaty), and then for the common law to be applied on the basis that the land is treated as a settled colony.

Canada, in fact, is treated largely as a settled colony under the reception of laws doctrine, with the common law being "received" by each colony as it stood on the date the first local colonial statute was passed. The sole example of using the conquest theory for domestic purposes relates to the colony of New France, in which King George III imposed the common law through the *Royal Proclamation of 1763*. French civil law was restored in non-criminal matters through the *Quebec Act of 1774*.

It is clear from our history that conquest was rarely, if ever, relevant in the acquisition of sovereignty over Aboriginal peoples and title to their lands. While this was argued forcefully by the Province of Nova Scotia and a variety of other governments in the *Simon* case, the Supreme Court of Canada decisively rejected its application in relation to the Micmac treaties of 1725 and 1752. The court further stated in *R. v. Simon*, [1985] 2 S.C.R. 387 that the conquest doctrine could apply in Canada only if a declaration of war had been proclaimed previously by the Crown, and there was no evidence of this ever occurring in Aboriginal-Crown relations.

The Doctrine of Cession

From the discussion thus far, it would appear that the consent of indigenous peoples is a necessary precondition to the legitimate acquisition of their territory, except where war has been officially declared and the conquest doctrine applies. The signing of valid treaties would fulfil the requirement for consent but ... the exact legal nature and effect of the Indian treaties are plagued by uncertainty. In some instances, Aboriginal groups voluntarily surrendered their aboriginal title, but in other instances fraud, undue influence and misunderstanding would seem to invalidate the arrangement.

The history of Indian treaties is filled with injustice and dishonesty, if not in the negotiations themselves, then certainly in the implementation and interpretation of the treaties. ... Indian people generally believed that they were only signing an arrangement to share the land with the newcomers, not, as some government officials later asserted, that they were agreeing to an abject surrender of their land and sovereignty. If they had been told that that [the latter] was to be the case, there is much doubt that they ever would have agreed. In fact, there is considerable evidence that many of the assurances given during the treaty negotiations were deliberately ignored by governments.

The Application of International Law to Aboriginal Peoples in Canada

Proper respect for the principles of international law by Canadian governments would have protected Aboriginal people from the treatment they received during the treaty-making era and subsequently. The colonization of the "New World" essentially involved the assertion of territorial and jurisdictional sovereignty by the European governments. In order for each one to legitimate its claims in the eyes of its European competitors, it was necessary for the colonizer to demonstrate a valid legal claim or title to the territory in question. In order to do so, however, reliance had to be placed on international law, yet that law contained principles concerning Aboriginal people which made it clear that the Aboriginal interest in the land could not be ignored. The manner in which legal title was asserted as against the Aboriginal people in subsequent domestic court decisions is clouded by the obvious lack of attention to those principles.

Thus, the traditional international law doctrines of discovery, occupation, adverse possession, conquest and cession bore little resemblance to the way in which they came to be applied in American, English and Canadian case law.

---

2. The Use of Symbolic Acts

In addition to these international law doctrines, the European nations also used symbolic acts, such as the planting of crosses and/or the recitation of words of conquest, to legitimize their claims to sovereignty over such lands. One such act was Jacques Cartier's erection of a cross on the point of the entrance to Gaspé Bay in July of 1534:

> Upon the 25 of the moneth, wee caused a faire high Crosse to be made of the height of thirty foote, which was made in the presence of many of them, upon the point of the entrance of the sayd haven [Gaspé Bay], in the middest whereof we hanged up a Shield with three Floure de Luces in it, and in the top was carved in the wood with Anticke letters this posie, Vive le Roy de France. Then before them all we set it upon sayd point .... So soone as it was up, we altogether kneeled downe before them, with our hands towards Heaven, yeelding God thankes: and we made signes unto them, shewing them the Heavens, and that all our salvation dependeth onely on him which in them dwelleth ... And after wee were returned to our ships, their Captaine clad with an old Beares skin, with three of his sonnes, and a brother of his with him, came unto us in one of their boates ... there he made a long Oration unto us, shewing us the crosse we had set up, and making a crosse with two fingers, then did he shew us all the Countrey about us, as if he would say that all was his, and that wee should not set up any crosse without his leave .... Then did we shew them with signes, that the crosse was but onely set up to be as a light and leader which wayes to enter into the port, and that wee would shortly come againe.[4]

It should be noted that when the Aboriginals inquired about the reasons for Cartier's erection of the cross, the true purpose of the act — to claim the land for France — was denied.

Another surreptitious use of symbolic acts was the Spanish *requerimiento*, or "requirement". The *requerimiento* was to be read aloud to peoples over whom Spain sought to exercise control. The text of the document reads as follows:

On the part of the King, don Fernando, and of doña Juana, his daughter, Queen of Castille and Leon, subduers of the barbarous nations, we their servants notify and make known to you, as the best we can, that the Lord our God, Living and Eternal, created the heaven and the Earth, and one man and one woman, of whom you and I, and all the men of the world, were and are descendants, and all those who come after us. But, on account of the multitude which has sprung from this man and woman in the five thousand years since the world was created, it was necessary that some men should go one way and some another, and that they should be divided into many kingdoms and provinces, for in one alone they could not be sustained.

Of all the nations God our Lord gave charge to one man, called St. Peter, that he should be Lord and Superior of all the men in the world, that all should obey him, and that he should be head of the whole human race, wherever men should live, and under whatever law, sect, or belief they should be; and he gave him the world for his kingdom and jurisdiction.

And he commanded him to place his seat in Rome, as the spot most fitting to rule the world from; but also he permitted him to have his seat in any other part of the world, and to judge and govern all Christians, Moors, Jews, Gentiles, and all other sects. This man was called Pope, as if to say, Admirable Great Father and Governor of men. The men who lived in that time obeyed that St. Peter, and took him for Lord, King, and Superior of the universe; so also have they regarded the others who after him have been elected to the Pontificate, and so it has been continued even until now, and will continue until the end of the world.

One of these Pontiffs ... made donation of these isles and Terra-firme to the aforesaid King and Queen and to their successors, our lords, with all that there are in these territories, as is contained in certain writings which passed upon the subject as aforesaid, which you can see if you wish.

So their Highnesses are kings and lords of these islands and land of Terra-firme by virtue of this donation; and some islands, and indeed almost all those to whom this land has been notified, have received and served their Highnesses ... with good will, without any resistance, immediately, without delay, when they were informed of the aforesaid facts. And also they received and obeyed the priests whom their Highnesses sent to preach to them and to teach them our Holy Faith; and all these, of their own free will, without any reward or condition, have become Christians, and are so, and their Highnesses have joyfully and benignantly received them, and also have commanded them to be treated as their subjects and vassals; and you too are held and obliged to do the same. Wherefore as best we can, we ask and require you that you consider what we have said to you, and that you take the time that shall be necessary to understand and deliberate upon it, and that you acknowledge the Church as the Ruler and Superior of the whole world and the high priest called Pope, and in his name the King and Queen doña Juana our lords, in his place, as superiors and lords and kings of these islands and this Terra-firme by virtue of the said donation, and that you consent and give place that these religious fathers should declare and preach to you the aforesaid.

If you do so, you will do well, and that which you are obliged to do to their Highnesses, and we in their name shall receive you in all love and charity, and shall leave you your wives, and your children, and your lands, free without servitude, that you may do with them and yourselves freely that which you like and think best, and they shall not compel you to turn

Christians, unless you yourselves, when informed of the truth, should wish to be converted to our Holy Catholic Faith, as almost all the inhabitants of the rest of the islands have done. And besides this, their Highnesses award you many privileges and exceptions and will grant you many benefits.

But if you do not do this, and wickedly and intentionally delay to do so, I certify to you that, with the help of God, we shall forcibly enter into your country and shall make war against you in all ways and manners that we can, and shall subject you to the yoke and obedience of the Church and of their Highnesses; we shall take you and your wives and children, and shall make slaves of them, and as such shall sell and dispose of them as their Highnesses may command; and we shall take away your goods, and shall do all the harm and damage that we can, as to vassals who do not obey, and refuse to receive their lord, and resist and contradict him; and we protest that the deaths and losses which shall accrue from this are you fault, and not that of their Highnesses, or our, or of these cavaliers who come with us. And that we have said this to you and made this Requirement, we request the notary here present to give us his testimony in writing, and we ask the rest who are present that they should be witnesses of this Requirement.[5]

While the *requerimiento* was meant to be read aloud by the Spanish to the inhabitants of invaded territories, in practice this did not occur in the intended manner. As indicated by scholar Lewis Hanke:

... the Requirement was read to trees and empty huts when no Indians were to be found. Captains muttered its theological phrases into their beards on the edge of sleeping Indian settlements, or even a league away before starting the formal attack, and at times some leather-lunged Spanish notary hurled its sonorous phrases after the Indians as they fled into the mountains.[6]

Hanke's account of the practical implementation of the *requerimiento* demonstrates that, much like Cartier's erection of a cross illustrated above, there was a marked difference between the purported implications of the symbolic acts engaged in and the subsequent explanations of those actions provided to the Aboriginal peoples concerned.

It is reasonable to question how symbolic acts such as these could form a basis for legitimate claims to territory, superseding those of the Aboriginal peoples, if their very purposes were concealed from those same peoples.

3.   The Doctrine of Discovery and Early Aboriginal Rights Jurisprudence

Of these various international law doctrines and symbolic acts, the primary vehicle used by the Europeans to justify their claims to land was discovery. In *Johnson v. M'Intosh*, 8 Wheat. 543 (U.S. 1823), a case involving a dispute over the ownership of former Indian lands, Chief Justice John Marshall explained the function of discovery as a basis for acquiring title to Aboriginal lands at 572-3:

On the discovery of this immense continent, the great nations of Europe were eager to appropriate to themselves so much of it as they could respectively acquire. ... But, as they were all in pursuit of nearly the same object, it was necessary, *in order to avoid conflicting settlements, and consequent war with each other*, to establish a principle, which all should acknowledge as the law by which the right of *acquisition*, which they all asserted, should be regulated *as between themselves*. This principle was, that discovery gave title to the government by whose subjects or by whose authority it was made, *against all other European governments*, which title might be consummated by possession. [Emphasis added]

The issues raised in *Johnson v. M'Intosh* were soon considered again in *Worcester v. State of Georgia*, 6 Pet. 515 (U.S. 1832), excerpted below. That case dealt with the authority of the state of Georgia to pass laws pertaining to territory that was occupied by the Cherokee Nation but situated within Georgia's state boundaries. Samuel Worcester had entered Cherokee territory, with authority of the United States government, to preach. He was arrested under Georgia law for being on Cherokee territory without state authority and sentenced to four years' hard labour. He appealed his sentence to the United States Supreme Court.

In declaring that Georgia had no authority for passing such laws in Cherokee territory, Chief Justice Marshall and Justice M'Lean rendered classic judgments on the nature of Aboriginal title and the interaction between European and Aboriginal peoples.

WORCESTER v. STATE OF GEORGIA

6 Pet. 515 (U.S. 1832) (references omitted)

Marshall C.J.: — America, separated from Europe by a wide ocean, was inhabited by a distinct people, divided into separate nations, independent of each other and of the rest of the world, having institutions of their own, and governing themselves by their own laws. It is difficult to comprehend the proposition, that the inhabitants of either quarter of the globe could have rightful original claims of dominion over the inhabitants of the other, or over the lands they occupied; or that the discovery of either by the other should give the discoverer rights in the country discovered, which annulled the pre-existing rights of its ancient possessors.

After lying concealed for a series of ages, the enterprise of Europe, guided by nautical science, conducted some of her adventurous sons into this western world. They found it in possession of a people who had made small progress in agriculture or manufactures, and whose general employment was war, hunting, and fishing.

Did these adventurers, by sailing along the coast and occasionally landing on it, acquire for the several governments to whom they belonged, or by whom they were commissioned, a rightful property in the soil, from the Atlantic to the Pacific; or rightful dominion over the numerous people who occupied it? Or has nature, or the great Creator of all things, conferred these rights over hunters and fishermen, on agriculturists and manufacturers?

But power, war, conquest, give rights, which, after possession, are conceded by the world; and which can never be controverted by those on whom they descend. We proceed, then, to the actual state of things, having glanced at their origin; because holding it in our recollection might shed some light on existing pretensions.

The great maritime powers of Europe discovered and visited different parts of this continent at nearly the same time. The object was too immense for any one of them to grasp the whole; and the claimants were too powerful to submit to the exclusive or unreasonable pretensions of any single potentate. To avoid bloody conflicts, which might terminate disastrously to all, it was necessary for the nations of Europe to establish some principle which all would acknowledge, and which should decide their respective rights as between themselves. This principle, suggested by the actual state of things, was, "that discovery gave title to the government by whose subjects or by whose authority it was made, against all other European governments, which title might be consummated by possession."

This principle, acknowledged by all Europeans, because it was the interest of all to acknowledge it, gave to the nation making the discovery, as its inevitable consequence, the sole right of acquiring the soil and making settlements on it. It was an exclusive principle which shut out the right of competition among those who had agreed to it. It regulated the right given by discovery among the European discoverers; but could not affect the rights of those already in possession, either as aboriginal occupants, or as occupants by virtue of a discovery made before the memory of man. It gave exclusive right to purchase, but did not found that right on a denial of the right of the possessor to sell.

. . . . .

Soon after Great Britain determined on planting colonies in America, the king granted charters to companies of his subjects who associated for the purpose of carrying the views of the crown into effect, and of enriching themselves. The first of these charters was made before possession was taken of any part of the country. They purport, generally, to convey the soil, from the Atlantic to the South Seas. This soil was occupied by numerous and warlike nations, equally willing and able to defend their possessions. The extravagant and absurd idea, that the feeble settlements made on the sea coast, or the companies under whom they were made, acquired legitimate power by them to govern the people, or occupy the lands from sea to sea, did not enter the mind of any man. They were well understood to convey the title, which, according to the common law of European sovereigns respecting America, they might rightfully convey, and no more. This was the exclusive right of purchasing such lands as the natives were willing to sell. The crown could not be understood to grant what the crown did not affect to claim; nor was it so understood.

. . . . .

[T]hese grants asserted title against Europeans only, and were considered as blank paper so far as the rights of the natives were concerned.

. . . . .

Fierce and warlike in their character, they [the Indians] might be formidable enemies, or effective friends. Instead of rousing their resentments, by asserting claims to their lands, or to dominion over their persons, their alliance was sought by flattering professions, and purchased by rich presents. The English, the French, and the Spaniards were equally competitors for their friendship and their aid. Not well acquainted with the exact meaning of words, nor supposing it to be material whether they were called the subjects, or the children of their father in Europe; lavish in professions of duty and affection, in return for the rich presents they received; so long as their actual independence was untouched, and their right to self government acknowledged, they were willing to profess dependence on the power which furnished supplies of which they were in absolute need, and restrained dangerous intruders from entering their country: and this was probably the sense in which the term was understood by them.

Certain it is, that our history furnishes no example, from the first settlement of our country, of any attempt on the part of the crown to interfere with the internal affairs of the Indians, farther than to keep out the agents of foreign powers, who, as traders or otherwise, might seduce them into foreign alliances. The king purchased their lands when they were willing to sell, at a price they were willing to take; but never coerced a surrender of them. He also purchased their alliance and dependence by subsidies; but never intruded into the interior of their affairs, or interfered with their self government, so far as respected themselves only.

. . . . .

Such was the policy of Great Britain towards the Indian nations inhabiting the territory from which she excluded all other Europeans; such her claims, and such her practical exposition of the charters she had granted: she considered them as nations capable of maintaining the relations of peace and war; of governing themselves, under her protection; and she made treaties with them, the obligation of which she acknowledged.

This was the settled state of things when the war of our revolution commenced. The influence of our enemy was established; her resources enabled her to keep up that influence; and the colonists had much cause for the apprehension that the Indian nations would, as the allies of Great Britain, add their arms to hers. This, as was to be expected, became an object of great solicitude to congress. Far from advancing a claim to their lands, or asserting any right of dominion over them, congress resolved "that the securing and preserving the friendship of the Indian nations appears to be a subject of the utmost moment to these colonies."

The early journals of congress exhibit the most anxious desire to conciliate the Indian nations. Three Indian departments were established; and commissioners appointed in each, "to treat with the Indians in their respective departments, in the name and on behalf of the United Colonies, in order to preserve peace and friendship with the said Indians, and to prevent their taking any part in the present commotions."

The most strenuous exertions were made to procure those supplies on which Indian friendships were supposed to depend; and every thing which might excite hostility was avoided.

. . . . .

The general law of European sovereigns, respecting their claims in America, limited the intercourse of Indians, in a great degree, to the particular potentate whose ultimate right of domain was acknowledged by the others. This was the general state of things in time of peace. It was sometimes changed in war. The consequence was, that their supplies were derived chiefly from that nation, and their trade confined to it. Goods, indispensable to their comfort, in the shape of presents, were received from the same hand. What was of still more importance, the strong hand of government was interposed to restrain the disorderly and licentious from intrusions into their country, from encroachments on their lands, and from those acts of violence which were often attended by reciprocal murder. The Indians perceived in this protection only what was beneficial to themselves — an engagement to punish aggressions on them. It involved, practically, no claim to their lands, no dominion over their persons. It merely bound the nation to the British crown, as a dependent ally, claiming the protection of a powerful friend and neighbour, and receiving the advantages of that protection, without involving a surrender of their national character.

. . . . .

The Indian nations were, from their situation, necessarily dependent on some foreign potentate for the supply of their essential wants, and for their protection from lawless and injurious intrusions into their country. That power was naturally termed their protector. They had been arranged under the protection of Great Britain: but the extinguishment of the British power in their neighbourhood, and the establishment of that of the United States in its place, led naturally to the declaration, on the part of the Cherokees, that they were under the protection of the United States, and of no other power. They assumed the relation with the United States, which had before subsisted with Great Britain.

This relation was that of a nation claiming and receiving the protection of one more powerful: not that of individuals abandoning their national character, and submitting as subjects to the laws of a master.

. . . . .

The Indian nations had always been considered as distinct, independent political communities, retaining their original natural rights, as the undisputed possessors of the soil, from time immemorial, with the single exception of that imposed by irresistible power, which excluded them from intercourse with any other European potentate than the first discoverer of the coast of the particular region claimed: and this was a restriction which those European potentates imposed on themselves, as well as on the Indians. The very term "nation," so generally applied to them, means "a people distinct from others." The constitution, by declaring treaties already made, as well as those to be made, to be the supreme law of the land, has adopted and sanctioned the ... treaties with the Indian nations, and consequently admits their rank among those powers who are capable of making treaties. The words "treaty" and "nation" are words of our own language, selected in our diplomatic and legislative proceedings, by ourselves, having each a definite and well understood meaning. We have applied them to Indians, as we have applied them to the other nations of the earth. They are applied to all in the same sense.

. . . . .

The actual state of things at the time, and all history since, explain these charters; and the king of Great Britain, at the treaty of peace, could cede only what belonged to his crown. These newly asserted titles can derive no aid from the articles so often repeated in Indian treaties; extending to them, first, the protection of Great Britain, and afterwards that of the United States. These articles are associated with others, recognizing their title to self government. The very fact of repeated treaties with them recognizes it; and the settled doctrine of the law of nations is, that a weaker power does not surrender its independence — its right to self government, by associating with a stronger, and taking its protection. A weak state, in order to provide for its safety, may place itself under the protection of one more powerful, without stripping itself of the right of government, and ceasing to be a state.

. . . . .

The Cherokee nation, then, is a distinct community occupying its own territory, with boundaries accurately described, in which the laws of Georgia can have no force, and which the citizens of Georgia have no right to enter, but with the assent of the Cherokees themselves, or in conformity with treaties, and with the acts of congress.

. . . . .

It is the opinion of this court that the judgment of the superior court for the country of Gwinnett, in the state of Georgia, condemning Samuel A. Worcester to hard labour, in the penitentiary of the state of Georgia, for four years, was pronounced by that court under colour of a law which is void, as being repugnant to the constitution, treaties, and laws of the United States, and ought, therefore, to be reversed and annulled.

M'lean J.: — With the decision, just given, I concur.

. . . . .

By the treaties and laws of the United States, rights are guarantied to the Cherokees, both as it respects their territory and internal polity. By the laws of Georgia these rights are abolished; and not only abolished, but an ignominious punishment is inflicted on the Indians and others; for the exercise of them. The important question then arises, which shall stand, the laws of the United States, or the laws of Georgia? No rule of construction, or subtlety of argument, can evade an answer to this question. The response must be, so far as the punishment of the plaintiff in error is concerned, in favour of the one or the other.

. . . . .

A reference has been made to the policy of the United States on the subject of Indian affairs, before the adoption of the constitution, with the view of ascertaining in what light the Indians have been considered by the first official acts, in relation to them, by the United States. For this object, it might not be improper to notice how they were considered by the European inhabitants, who first formed settlement in this part of the continent of America.

The abstract right of every section of the human race to a reasonable portion of the soil, by which to acquire the means of subsistence, cannot be controverted. And it is equally clear, that the range of nations or tribes, who exist in the hunter state, may be restricted within reasonable limits. They shall not be permitted to roam, in the pursuit of game, over an extensive and rich country, whilst in other parts, human beings are being crowded so closely together, as to render the means of subsistence precarious. The law of nature, which is paramount to all other laws, gives the right to every nation, to the enjoyment of a reasonable extent of country, so as to derive the means of subsistence from the soil.

In this view perhaps, our ancestors, when they first migrated to this country, might have taken possession of a limited extent of the domain, had they been sufficiently powerful, without negotiation or purchase from the native Indians. But this course is believed to have been nowhere taken. A more conciliatory mode was preferred, and one which was better calculated to impress the Indians, who were then powerful, with a sense of the justice of their white neighbours. The occupancy of their lands was never assumed, except upon the basis of contract, and on the payment of a valuable consideration.

This policy has obtained from the earliest white settlements in this country, down to the present time. Some cessions of territory may have been made by the Indians, in compliance with the terms on which peace was offered by the whites; but the soil, thus taken, was taken by the laws of conquest, and always as an indemnity for the expenses of the war, commenced by the Indians.

At no time has the sovereignty of the country been recognized as existing in the Indians, but they have been always admitted to possess many of the attributes of sovereignty. All the rights which belong to self government have been recognized as vested in them. Their right of occupancy has never been questioned, but the fee in the soil has been considered in the government. This may be called the right to the ultimate domain, but the Indians have a present right in possession.

From this discussion of early Crown-Aboriginal interaction and the use of international law doctrines to justify the dispossession of Aboriginal peoples, a number of questions arise. For one, how could the doctrine of discovery be used in relation to Aboriginal lands in North America if the doctrine required land to be *terra nullius*? Second, if discovery only granted to the "discovering" nation the right to *purchase* title from the Aboriginal inhabitants, does that entail that the latter "owned" the lands in their possession? If they did not "own" the lands, who did? Finally, if the Law of Nations was designed to govern controversies between its member states, was it binding on Aboriginal peoples who were not members?

D. THE BRITISH CROWN'S RESPONSE

The pre-emptive right to purchase land from the Aboriginal peoples was highly sought-after by Europeans seeking to establish colonies in North America. By acquiring this right, not only could a European nation obtain title, but it could exclude its European colonial competitors. The wars between Britain and France in North America resulted, in part, from those nations' attempts to acquire or maintain this pre-emptive right.

Following the conquest of New France in 1760-61, Britain endeavoured to consolidate its hold on its North American colonies and reinforce its right to purchase the Aboriginal peoples' interest in land that it laid claim to. The conquest had created concern for the Aboriginal allies of France, who were anxious about its effects on them politically and economically. Britain sought to smooth over these concerns by issuing a policy statement detailing the status of its relations with the Aboriginal peoples.

Britain's initial response, the *Royal Proclamation of 1761*, was an order of the King in Council on a report of the Lords of Trade dated December 2, 1761. At the request of the Lords of Trade, King George III issued his proclamation, which spoke about the importance of existing treaties and treaty relations between Britain and the Aboriginal peoples. This is recognized explicitly in the preamble to the document, which states:

> WHEREAS the peace and security of Our Colonies and Plantations upon the Continent of North America does greatly depend upon the Amity and Alliance of the several Nations or Tribes of Indians bordering upon the said Colonies and upon a just and faithful Observance of those Treaties and Compacts which have been heretofore solemnly entered into with the said Indians by Our Royal Predecessors Kings & Queens of this Realm ...

The *Royal Proclamation of 1761*'s recognition of the importance of existing treaties and other agreements is further reflected in the following portion of the document, under which King George III undertakes to "protect the said Indians in their just Rights and Possessions and to keep inviolable the Treaties and Compacts which have been entered into with them". To ensure this protection, the Proclamation forbids the granting of lands possessed or occupied by Aboriginal peoples or adjacent to those possessed or occupied by them, requires persons wishing to purchase Aboriginal lands to first obtain a Crown licence and mandates that colonial officials immediately remove those non-Aboriginal persons who had "willfully or inadvertently ... seated themselves on any Lands so reserved to or claimed by the said Indians without any lawfull Authority for so doing ..."

Finally, the *Royal Proclamation of 1761* ordered the governors of British colonies in North America to issue their own proclamations designed to appease Aboriginal concerns about their title and treaty rights. One such proclamation, issued by Governor Jonathan Belcher of Nova Scotia on May 4, 1762, has received judicial attention by the Supreme Court of Canada in *R. v. Marshall; R. v. Bernard*, [2005] S.C.J. No. 44, [2005] 2 S.C.R. 220 (S.C.C.). However, the *Royal Proclamation of 1761* was superseded by the *Royal Proclamation of 1763*, R.S.C. 1985, App. II, No. 1 (excerpted in Chapter 1), which made no mention of Crown-Aboriginal treaties or pre-existing Crown promises to the Aboriginal peoples. Nonetheless, the *Royal Proclamation of 1763* did include much the same sentiments regarding the British Crown's expression of its relationship with the Aboriginal peoples and the nature of Britain's claim to title to North American lands.

The *Royal Proclamation of 1763* established British policy for its North American colonies in the wake of many years of warfare with France. Following the defeat of New France, Britain had acquired new territories from France under the *Treaty of Paris, 1763*, February 10, 1763. Yet, Britain still faced a number of threats to its North American ambitions of empire. In addition to the potential threat stemming from the French population of the new colony of Quebec, other issues to contend with included deteriorating British-Indian relations that had led to Pontiac's Rebellion in 1763 and the American colonies' growing expansionist desires. The Proclamation was designed to curb American territorial expansion, establish control over Quebec, and prevent the outbreak of politically and economically costly Indian wars. This was to be accomplished by the creation of an immense Indian hunting ground in the Proclamation which was intended to placate Aboriginal concerns while functioning as a buffer between the French loyalists in Quebec and the agitated American colonists.

In many respects, the *Royal Proclamation of 1763* may be viewed as similar in intention and effect to the version of discovery formulated by Chief Justice Marshall in *Johnson v. M'Intosh*, 21 U.S. (8 Wheat.) 543 (1823), and *Worcester v. State of Georgia*, 6 Pet. 515 (U.S. 1832). The Proclamation provided Britain with the exclusive right to treat with the Aboriginal peoples in those territories claimed by it; it did not provide a right of sovereignty over them and their lands. As the Royal Commission on Aboriginal Peoples has explained:

> [T]he Proclamation portrays Aboriginal nations as autonomous political units living under the Crown's protection and on lands that are already part of the Crown's dominions. Aboriginal nations hold inherent authority over

their internal affairs and the power to deal with the Crown by way of treaty and agreement. In a word, it portrays the link between Aboriginal peoples and the Crown as broadly "confederal".[7]

The protection of Aboriginal interests in the Proclamation may be viewed as qualifications imposed by the Crown upon its own rights. These qualifications stem from the Crown's recognition and affirmation of the Aboriginal peoples' pre-existing right to land. Thus, the Proclamation did not grant new rights to the Aboriginal peoples, it simply affirmed existing rights. As explained in *R. v. Koonungnak* (1963), 42 C.R. 143, [1963-64] 45 W.W.R. 282 at 302 (N.W.T. Terr. Ct.):

> This proclamation has been spoken of as the "Charter of Indian Rights". Like so many great charters in English history, it does not create rights but rather affirms old rights. The Indians and the Eskimos had their aboriginal rights and English law has always recognized these rights.

See also A.C. Hamilton, *A New Partnership*: "The Royal Proclamation of October 7, 1763 recited the legal principles of that day. It did not make new law."[8] Indeed, the Proclamation also carried on the British tradition of requiring Aboriginal peoples interested in alienating their lands to first surrender them to the Crown that had existed previously in the 13 American colonies, as seen, for example, in legislation from Maryland in 1638 and 1649 and from Virginia in 1655.[9] The legal requirements of surrender remain restrictions on the alienability of Aboriginal title to the present day and are discussed in the *Opetchesaht* case, below.

OPETCHESAHT INDIAN BAND v. CANADA
[1997] S.C.J. No. 50, [1997] 2 S.C.R. 119 (S.C.C.)

Major J.: —

. . . . . .

[39] Any sale or lease of land to a third party can only be carried out after a surrender has taken place, with the Crown then acting on the band's behalf to effectuate the transfer to third parties. The Crown prior to the surrender holds the fee simple to the land subject to the Indians' *sui generis* interest. When a band surrenders land, or more correctly, its *sui generis* interest in land, to the Crown, the band's interest is said to merge in the fee held by the Crown. The Crown then holds the land free of the Indian interest. The Crown has a broad discretion in dealing with surrendered land but it is subject to an equitable obligation to deal with the land for the benefit of the Indians and subject to the terms of the surrender from the band. ...

[40] Surrenders may be absolute or qualified, conditional or unconditional. *Smith, supra*, at p. 568, makes clear that upon unconditional and absolute surrender the Indians' rights in the land disappear. However, surrenders may also release only partially or temporarily the interest of the Indians. The point here is that surrenders are required as a general rule not

only when the Indian band is releasing all its interest in the reserve forever, but whenever any interest is given up for any duration of time. Indeed, this has been recognized by the jurisprudence of this Court:

> That there can be a partial surrender of the "personal and usufructuary rights" which the Indians enjoy is confirmed by the *St. Catherine's Milling Company Limited v. The Queen* [(1888), 14 App. Cas. 46], in which there was retained the privilege of hunting and fishing; and I see no distinction in principle, certainly in view of the nature of the interest held by the Indians and the object of the legislation, between a surrender of a portion of rights for all time and a surrender of all rights for a limited time. ...

[41] That this is so is apparent from the face of s. 37. Section 37 is not restricted to sales or complete alienation of lands in a reserve from the Crown to third parties. Leases or other dispositions of "lands in a reserve" also require a surrender by the Indians of their interest to the Crown. Section 38 elaborates what exactly may be surrendered to the Crown:

> 38. (1) A band may surrender to Her Majesty any right or interest of the band and its members in a reserve.
> (2) A surrender may be absolute or qualified, conditional or unconditional.

[42] Section 38 provides that "any right or interest of the band and its members" in a reserve may be surrendered, obviously in reference to s. 37. The bundle of rights which may be surrendered is "any right or interest" in a reserve. Section 35, the expropriation power, specifies that the right to expropriate may similarly be exercised "in relation to lands in a reserve or any interest therein".

[43] Also apparent on the face of s. 37 from the qualification at the beginning of s. 37 is the legislative intention that it operate in conjunction with and subject to other provisions of the *Indian Act*. There is in this qualification an express recognition that other provisions of the *Indian Act* also deal with sales, alienations, leases or other dispositions of lands in a reserve. ...

McLachlin J. (dissenting): —

. . . . .

[65] ... Surrender is a formal process, accompanied by a formal vote by band members and other safeguards to ensure that the people understand and consent to the proposed alienation.

. . . . .

[82] The starting point in an assessment of the relationship between aboriginals and the Crown on the question of land is the *Royal Proclamation, 1763*, R.S.C., 1985, App. II, No. 1. That document, affirmed by Hall J. in *Calder v. Attorney-General of British Columbia*, [1973] S.C.R. 313, at p. 395, as an "Indian Bill of Rights", established as governing principles in Canada (1) the reservation of certain lands to Indians for their exclusive

use and possession, and (2) the creation of a strict process for the purchase of Indian land:

> And whereas it is just and reasonable, and essential to our Interest, and the Security of our Colonies, that the several Nations or Tribes of Indians with whom We are connected, and who live under our Protection, should not be molested or disturbed in the Possession of such Parts of Our Dominions and Territories as, not having been ceded to or purchased by Us, are reserved to them, or any of them, as their Hunting Grounds. . . .

> . . . . .

> And whereas great Frauds and Abuses have been committed in the purchasing Lands of the Indians, to the great Prejudice of our Interests, and to the great Dissatisfaction of the said Indians; In order, therefore, to prevent such Irregularities for the future, and to the end that the Indians may be convinced of our Justice and determined Resolution to remove all reasonable Cause of Discontent, We do, with the Advice of our Privy Council strictly enjoin and require, that no private Person do presume to make any purchase from the said Indians of any Lands reserved to the said Indians, within those parts of our Colonies where, We have thought proper to allow Settlement; but that, if at any Time any of the Said Indians should be inclined to dispose of the said Lands, the same shall be Purchased only for Us, in our Name, at some public Meeting or Assembly of the said Indians, to be held for that Purpose. . . .

[83] As a result of the *Royal Proclamation, 1763*, "lands could be surrendered only on a nation-to-nation basis, from the Indian nation to the British Crown, in a public process in which the assembled Indian population would be required to consent to the transaction" (*Report of the Royal Commission on Aboriginal Peoples* (1996), vol. 1, at p. 261). The Report also notes that the "present *Indian Act* continues to reflect the land surrender procedure first set out in the Royal Proclamation" (p. 261).

[84] The 1952 *Indian Act*, as amended by S.C. 1956, c. 40, reflects the surrender requirements established by the Royal Proclamation. Section 37 of the Act affirms the presence of the Crown as a go-between in transactions involving reserve land, stating that "lands in a reserve shall not be sold, alienated, leased or otherwise disposed of until they have been surrendered to Her Majesty by the band for whose use and benefit in common the reserve was set apart". Section 39(1) mandates that surrenders of reserve land must be made to the Crown, must be assented to by a majority of the electors of the band, and must be accepted by the Governor in Council. This requirement of <u>band</u> approval stands in contrast to the more limited requirements of ss. 28(2) and 58(1) for consent of the <u>band council</u> and Minister to the granting of a permit, or a lease for agricultural or grazing purposes.

[85] The *Indian Act* provisions governing the surrender of reserve lands were created to strike "a balance between the two extremes of autonomy and protection. The band's consent was required to surrender its reserve. Without that consent the reserve could not be sold. But the Crown, through the Governor in Council, was also required to consent to the surrender." . . . The protection of reserve lands for future generations may

be seen as one of the fundamental purposes of the Act. Alienation was viewed as a grave matter, to be effected only in accordance with a highly scrutinized and strictly regulated procedure. The *Indian Act* confirms the general inalienability of Indian lands (s. 37) and safeguards the sanctity of reserve lands, by prohibiting their alienation except to the Crown, with the consent of the band membership as a whole.

———————

The *Royal Proclamation of 1763*'s recognition of Aboriginal land rights has been incorporated into section 25 of the *Constitution Act, 1982*, being Schedule B to the *Canada Act 1982* (U.K.), 1982, c. 11, which reads:

> The guarantee in this Charter of certain rights and freedoms shall not be construed so as to abrogate or derogate from any aboriginal, treaty, or other rights or freedoms that pertain to the aboriginal peoples of Canada including
>
> (a)　any rights or freedoms that have been recognized by the Royal Proclamation of October 7, 1763.

The effect of this recognition has yet to be judicially determined. However, there have been numerous disputes over the effect of the Proclamation's recognition of Aboriginal lands rights. The first of these came in the landmark case of *St. Catherine's Milling & Lumber Co. v. R.*, reproduced below.

E.　EARLY CANADIAN ABORIGINAL TITLE JURISPRUDENCE

The *St. Catherine's* case was the first important consideration of Aboriginal title in Canada. It involved a dispute between the Province of Ontario and the Dominion of Canada over the ownership of former Indian lands and the rights to timber thereon.

ST. CATHERINE'S MILLING & LUMBER CO. v. R.

(1888), 14 App. Cas. 46 (J.C.P.C.)

The judgment of their Lordships was delivered by

Lord Watson: — On the 3rd of October, 1873, a formal treaty or contract was concluded between commissioners appointed by the Government of the Dominion of Canada, on behalf of Her Majesty the Queen, of the one part, and a number of chiefs and headmen duly chosen to represent the Salteaux tribe of Ojibbeway Indians, of the other part, by which the latter, for certain considerations, released and surrendered to the Government of the Dominion, for Her Majesty and her successors, the whole right and title of the Indian inhabitants whom they represented, to a tract of country upwards of 50,000 square miles in extent. By an article of the treaty it is stipulated that, subject to such regulations as may be made by the Dominion Government, the Indians are to have right to pursue their avocations of hunting and fishing throughout the surrendered territory, with the exception of those portions of it which may, from time to time, be required or taken up for settlement, mining, lumbering, or other purposes.

Of the territory thus ceded to the Crown, an area of not less than 32,000 square miles is situated within the boundaries of the Province of Ontario; and, with respect to that area, a controversy has arisen between the Dominion and Ontario, each of them maintaining that the legal effect of extinguishing the Indian title has been to transmit to itself the entire beneficial interest of the lands, as now vested in the Crown, freed from incumbrance of any kind, save the qualified privilege of hunting and fishing mentioned in the treaty.

Acting on the assumption that the beneficial interest in these lands had passed to the Dominion Government, their Crown Timber Agent, on the 1st of May, 1883, issued to the appellants, the St. Catherine's Milling and Lumber Company, a permit to cut and carry away one million feet of lumber from a specified portion of the disputed area. The appellants having availed themselves of that licence, a writ was filed against them in the Chancery Division of the High Court of Ontario, at the instance of the Queen on the information of the Attorney-General of the Province, praying — (1) a declaration that the appellants have no rights in respect of the timber cut by them upon the lands specified in their permit; (2) an injunction restraining them from trespassing on the premises and from cutting any timber thereon; (3) an injunction against the removal of timber already cut; and (4) decree for the damage occasioned by their wrongful acts. The Chancellor of Ontario, on the 10th of June, 1885, decerned with costs against the appellants, in terms of the first three of these conclusions, and referred the amount of damage to the Master in Ordinary. The judgment of the learned Chancellor was unanimously affirmed on the 20th of April, 1886, by the Court of Appeal for Ontario, and an appeal taken from their decision to the Supreme Court of Canada was dismissed on the 20th of June, 1887, by a majority of four of the six judges constituting the court.

Although the present case relates exclusively to the right of the Government of Canada to dispose of the timber in question to the appellant company, yet its decision necessarily involves the determination of the larger question between that government and the province of Ontario with respect to the legal consequences of the treaty of 1873.

. . . . .

The capture of Quebec in 1759, and the capitulation of Montreal in 1760, were followed in 1763 by the cession to Great Britain of Canada and all its dependencies, with the sovereignty, property, and possession, and all other rights which had at any previous time been held or acquired by the Crown of France. A royal proclamation was issued on the 7th of October, 1763, shortly after the date of the Treaty of Paris, by which His Majesty King George erected four distinct and separate Governments, styled respectively, Quebec, East Florida, West Florida, and Grenada, specific boundaries being assigned to each of them. Upon the narrative that it was just and reasonable that the several nations and tribes of Indians who lived under British protection should not be molested or disturbed in the "possession of such parts of Our dominions and territories as, not having been ceded to or purchased by us, are reserved to them or any of them as their hunting grounds," it is declared that no governor or commander-in-chief in any of the new colonies of Quebec, East Florida, or West Florida, do presume on any pretence to grant warrants of survey or pass any patents for lands beyond the bounds of their respective governments, or "until Our further pleasure be known," upon any lands whatever which, not having been ceded or purchased as aforesaid, are reserved to the said Indians or any of them. It was further declared "to be Our Royal will, for the present, as aforesaid, to reserve under Our sovereignty, protection, and dominion, for the use of the said Indians, all the land and territories not included within the limits of Our said three new Governments, or within the limits of the territory granted to the Hudson's Bay Company." The proclamation also enacts that no private person shall make any purchase from the Indians of lands reserved to them within those colonies where settlement was permitted, and that all purchases must be on behalf of the Crown, in a public assembly of the Indians, by the governor or commander-in-chief of the colony in which the lands lie.

The territory in dispute has been in Indian occupation from the date of the proclamation until 1873. During that interval of time Indian affairs have been administered successively by the Crown, by the Provincial Governments, and (since the passing of the British North America Act, 1867), by the Government of the Dominion. The policy of these administrations has been all along the same in this respect, that the Indian inhabitants have been precluded from entering into any transaction with a subject for the sale or transfer of their interest in the land, and have only been permitted to surrender their rights to the Crown by a formal contract, duly ratified in a meeting of their chiefs or head men convened for the purpose. Whilst there have been changes in the administrative authority, there has been no change since the year 1763 in the character of the interest which its Indian inhabitants had in the lands surrendered by the treaty. Their possession, such as it was, can only be ascribed to the general provisions made by the royal proclamation in favour of all Indian tribes then living under the sovereignty and protection of the British Crown. It was suggested in the course of the argument for the Dominion, that inasmuch as the proclamation recites that the territories thereby reserved for Indians had never "been ceded to or purchased by" the Crown, the entire property of the land remained with them. That inference is, however, at variance with the terms of the instrument, which shew that the tenure of the Indians was a personal and usufructuary right, dependent upon the good will of the Sovereign. The lands reserved are expressly stated to be "parts of Our dominions and territories;" and it is declared to be the will and pleasure of the sovereign that, "for the present," they shall be reserved for the use of the Indians, as their hunting grounds, under his protection and dominion. There was a great deal of learned discussion at the Bar with respect to the precise quality of the Indian right, but their Lordships do not consider it necessary to express any opinion upon the point. It appears to them to be sufficient for the purposes of this case that there has been all along vested in the Crown a substantial and paramount estate, underlying the Indian title, which became a plenum dominium whenever that title was surrendered or otherwise extinguished.

By an Imperial statute passed in the year 1840 (3 & 4 Vict. c. 35), the provinces of Ontario and Quebec, then known as Upper and Lower Canada, were united under the name of the Province of Canada, and it was, *inter alia*, enacted that, in consideration of certain annual payments which Her Majesty had agreed to accept by way of civil list, the produce of all territorial and other revenues at the disposal of the Crown arising in either of the united Provinces should be paid into the consolidated fund of the new Province. There was no transfer to the Province of any legal estate in the Crown lands, which continued to be vested in the Sovereign; but all moneys realized by sales or in any other manner became the property of the Province. In other words, all beneficial interest in such lands within the provincial boundaries belonging to the Queen, and either producing or capable of producing revenue, passed to the Province, the title still remaining in the Crown. That continued to be the right of the Province until the passing of the British North America Act, 1867. Had the Indian inhabitants of the area in question released their interest in it to the Crown at any time between 1840 and the date of that Act, it does not seem to admit of doubt, and it was not disputed by the learned counsel for the Dominion, that all revenues derived from its being taken up for settlement, mining, lumbering, and other purposes would have been the property of the Province of Canada. The case maintained for the appellants is that the Act of 1867 transferred to the Dominion all interest in Indian lands which previously belonged to the Province.

The Act of 1867, which created the Federal Government, repealed the Act of 1840, and restored the Upper and Lower Canadas to the condition of separate Provinces, under the titles of Ontario and Quebec, due provision being made (sect. 142) for the division between them of the property and assets of the United Province, with the exception of certain items specified in the fourth schedule, which are still held by them jointly. The Act also contains careful provisions for the distribution of legislative powers and of revenues and assets between the respective Provinces included in the Union, on the one hand, and the Dominion, on the other. The conflicting claims to the ceded territory maintained by the Dominion and the Province of Ontario are wholly dependent upon these statutory provisions. In construing these enactments, it must always be kept in view that, wherever public land with its incidents is described as "the property of" or as "belonging to" the Dominion or a Province, these expressions merely import that the right to its beneficial use, or to its proceeds, has been appropriated to the Dominion or the Province, as the case may be, and is subject to the control of its legislature, the land itself being vested in the Crown.

Sect. 108 enacts that the public works and undertakings enumerated in Schedule 3 shall be the property of Canada. As specified in the schedule, these consist of public undertakings which might be fairly considered to exist for the benefit of all the Provinces federally united, of lands and buildings necessary for carrying on the customs or postal service of the Dominion, or required for the purpose of national defence, and of "lands set apart for general public purposes." It is obvious that the enumeration cannot be reasonably held to include Crown lands which are reserved for Indian use. The only other clause in the Act by which a share of what previously constituted provincial revenues and assets is directly assigned to the Dominion is sect. 102. It enacts that all "duties and revenues" over which the respective legislatures of the United Provinces had and have power of appropriation, "except such portions thereof as are by this Act reserved to the respective legislatures of the Provinces, or are raised by them in accordance with the special powers conferred upon them by this Act," shall form one consolidated fund, to be appropriated for the public service of Canada. The extent to which duties and revenues arising within the limits of Ontario, and over which the legislature of the old Province of Canada possessed the power of appropriation before the passing of the Act, have been transferred to the Dominion by this clause, can only be ascertained by reference to the two exceptions which it makes in favour of the new provincial legislatures.

The second of these exceptions has really no bearing on the present case, because it comprises nothing beyond the revenues which provincial legislatures are empowered to raise by means of direct taxation for Provincial purposes, in terms of sect. 92 (2). The first of them, which appears to comprehend the whole sources of revenue reserved to the provinces by sect. 109, is of material consequence. Sect. 109 provides that "all lands, mines, minerals, and royalties belonging to the several Provinces of Canada, Nova Scotia, and New Brunswick, at the union, and all sums then due or payable for such lands, mines, minerals, or royalties, shall belong to the several Provinces of Ontario, Quebec, Nova Scotia, and New Brunswick, in which the same are situate or arise, subject to any trusts existing in respect thereof, and to any interest other than that of the Province in the same." In connection with this clause it may be observed that, by sect. 117, it is declared that the Provinces shall retain their respective public property not otherwise disposed of in the Act, subject to the right of Canada to assume any lands or public property required for fortifications or for the defence of the country. A different form of expression is used to define the subject-matter of the first exception, and the property which is directly appropriated to the Provinces; but it hardly admits of doubt that the interests in land, mines, minerals, and royalties, which by sect. 109 are declared to belong to the Provinces, include, if they are not identical with, the "duties and revenues" first excepted in sect. 102.

The enactments of sect. 109 are, in the opinion of their Lordships, sufficient to give to each Province, subject to the administration and control of its own Legislature, the entire beneficial interest of the Crown in all lands within its boundaries, which at the time of the union were vested in the Crown, with the exception of such lands as the Dominion acquired right to under sect. 108, or might assume for the purposes specified in sect. 117. Its legal effect is to exclude from the "duties and revenues" appropriated to the Dominion, all the ordinary territorial revenues of the Crown arising within the Provinces. That construction of the statute was accepted by this Board in deciding *Attorney General of Ontario v. Mercer*, where the controversy related to land granted in fee simple to a subject before 1867, which became escheat to the Crown in the year 1871. The Lord Chancellor (Earl Selborne) in delivering judgment in that case, said: "It was not disputed, in the argument for the Dominion at the bar, that all territorial revenues arising within each Province from 'lands' (in which term must be comprehended all estates in land), which at the time of the union belonged to the Crown, were reserved to the respective Provinces by sect. 109; and it was admitted that no distinction could, in that respect, be made between lands then ungranted, and lands which had previously reverted to the Crown by escheat. But it was insisted that a line was drawn at the date of the union, and that the words were not sufficient to reserve any lands afterwards escheated which at the time of the union were in private hands, and did not then belong to the Crown. Their Lordships indicated an opinion to the effect that the escheat would not, in the special circumstances of that case, have passed to the Province as "lands;" but they held that it fell within the class of rights reserved to the Provinces as "royalties" by sect. 109.

Had its Indian inhabitants been the owners in fee simple of the territory which they surrendered by the treaty of 1873, *Attorney-General of Ontario v. Mercer* might have been an authority for holding that the Province of Ontario could derive no benefit from the cession, in respect that the land was not vested in the Crown at the time of the union. But that was not the character of the Indian interest. The Crown has all along had a present proprietary estate in the land, upon which the Indian title was a mere burden. The ceded territory was at the time of the union, land vested in the Crown, subject to "an interest other than that of the Province in the same," within the meaning of sect. 109; and must now belong to Ontario in terms of that clause, unless its rights have been taken away by some provision of the Act of 1867 other than those already noticed.

In the course of the argument the claim of the Dominion to the ceded territory was rested upon the provisions of sect. 91 (24), which in express terms confer upon the Parliament of Canada power to make laws for "Indians, and lands reserved for the Indians." It was urged that the exclusive power of legislation and administration carried with it, by necessary implication, any patrimonial interest which the Crown might have had in the reserved lands. In reply to that reasoning, counsel for Ontario referred us to a series of provincial statutes prior in date to the Act of 1867, for the purpose of shewing that the expression "Indian reserves" was used in legislative language to designate certain lands in which the Indians had, after the royal proclamation of 1763, acquired a special interest, by treaty or otherwise, and did not apply to land occupied by them in virtue of the proclamation. The argument might have deserved consideration if the expression had been adopted by the British Parliament in 1867, but it does not occur in sect. 91 (24), and the words actually used are, according to their natural meaning, sufficient to include all lands reserved, upon any terms or conditions, for Indian occupation. It appears to be the plain policy of the Act that, in order to ensure uniformity of administration, all such lands, and Indian affairs generally, shall be under the legislative control of one central authority.

Their Lordships are, however, unable to assent to the argument for the Dominion founded on sect. 92 (24) [*sic*]. There can be no a priori probability that the British Legislature, in a branch of the statute which professes to deal only with the distribution of legislative power, intended to deprive the Provinces of rights which are expressly given them in that branch of it which relates to the distribution of revenues and assets. The fact that the power of legislating for Indians, and for lands which are reserved to their use, has been entrusted to the Parliament of the Dominion is not in the least degree inconsistent with the right of the Provinces to a beneficial interest in these lands, available to them as a source of revenue whenever the estate of the Crown is disencumbered of the Indian title.

By the treaty of 1873 the Indian inhabitants ceded and released the territory in dispute, in order that it might be opened up for settlement, immigration, and such other purpose as to Her Majesty might seem fit, "to the Government of the Dominion of Canada," for the Queen and Her successors for ever. It was argued that a cession in these terms was in effect a conveyance to the Dominion Government of the whole rights of the Indians, with consent of the Crown. That is not the natural import of the language of the treaty, which purports to be from beginning to end a transaction between the Indians and the Crown; and the surrender is in substance made to the Crown. Even if its language had been more favourable to the argument of the Dominion upon this point, it is abundantly clear that the commissioners who represented Her Majesty, whilst they had full authority to accept a surrender to the Crown, had neither authority nor power to take away from Ontario the interest which had been assigned to that province by the Imperial Statute of 1867.

These considerations appear to their Lordships to be sufficient for the disposal of this appeal. The treaty leaves the Indians no right whatever to the timber growing upon the lands which they gave up, which is now fully vested in the Crown, all revenues derivable from the sale of such portions of it as are situate within the boundaries of Ontario being the property of that Province. The fact, that it still possesses exclusive power to regulate the Indians' privilege of hunting and fishing, cannot confer upon the Dominion power to dispose, by issuing permits or otherwise, of that beneficial interest in the timber which has now passed to Ontario. Seeing that the benefit of the surrender accrues to her, Ontario must, of course, relieve the Crown, and the Dominion, of all obligations involving the payment of money which were undertaken by Her Majesty, and which are said to have been in part fulfilled by the Dominion Government. There may be other questions behind, with respect to the right to determine to what extent, and at what periods, the disputed territory, over which the

Indians still exercise their avocations of hunting and fishing, is to be taken up for settlement or other purposes, but none of these questions are raised for decision in the present suit.

Their Lordships will therefore humbly advise Her Majesty that the judgment of the Supreme Court of Canada ought to be affirmed, and the appeal dismissed.

The question of Aboriginal title was raised in *St. Catherine's Milling* simply because governmental and private interests hinged upon its resolution. The same principle held true for the majority of early Canadian Aboriginal rights jurisprudence. Consequently, while Aboriginal title was a primary element of early Aboriginal rights jurisprudence, the Aboriginal peoples whose title was the subject of litigation were rarely, if ever, represented in such litigation. They were neither afforded the direct opportunity to explain the significance of land to their cultures, nor the uses they made of the land. It was not until the decision in *Calder v. British Columbia (Attorney General)*, reproduced below, that Aboriginal conceptions of land and its use were given primary attention by the judiciary. Perhaps not coincidentally, this change in approach to the determination of Aboriginal title resulted in pronouncements that were more consistent with the nature of that title than previous judicial analyses had been.

CALDER v. BRITISH COLUMBIA (ATTORNEY GENERAL)

[1973] S.C.J. No. 56, [1973] S.C.R. 313, 34 D.L.R. (3d) 145,
[1973] 4 W.W.R. 1 (S.C.C.)

[**Martland** and **Ritchie JJ.** concur with **Judson J.**]

Judson J.: — The appellants sue, as representatives of the Nishga Indian Tribe, for a declaration "that the aboriginal title, otherwise known as the Indian title, of the Plaintiffs . . . has never been lawfully extinguished". The action was dismissed at trial. The Court of Appeal rejected the appeal. The appellants appeal from both decisions.

The appellants are member of the Nishga Nation, which is made up of four bands: Gitlakdami, Canyon City, Greenville and Kincolith. They are officers of the Nishga Tribal Council and councillors of each of the four Indian bands. They are descendants of the Indians who have inhabited since time immemorial the territory in question, where they have hunted, fished and roamed. It was agreed for purposes of this litigation that this territory consisted of 1,000 square miles in and around the Nass River Valley, Observatory Inlet, Portland Inlet and the Portland Canal, all located in north-western British Columbia. No other interest has intervened in this litigation to question the accuracy of this agreed statement of facts.

The Crown in right of the Province has made certain grants in this territory, some in fee simple; in other cases rights of pre-emption, mineral and mining rights, petroleum permits, forestry rights and titles, and tree farm licences. However, the vast bulk of the area remains still unalienated.

No treaty or contract with the Crown or the Hudson's Bay Company has ever been entered into with respect to the area by anyone on behalf of the Nishga Nation. Within the area there are a number of reserves but they comprise only a small part of the total land. The Nishga Nation did not agree to or accept the creation of these reserves. The Nishgas claim that their title arises out of aboriginal occupation; that recognition of such a title is a concept well embedded in English law; that it is not dependent on treaty, executive order or legislative enactment. In the alternative they say that if executive or legislative recognition ever was needed, it is to be found in the Royal Proclamation of 1763, in Imperial statutes acknowledging that what is now British Columbia was "Indian Territory", and in Royal instructions to the Governor of British Columbia. Finally, they say that their title has never been extinguished.

. . . . .

In the agreed statement of facts, the mode of life of the Indians is set out in rather bald terms. This description is amplified in the material filed at the hearing. I refer to the *Indian History of British Columbia*, chapter 8, by Wilson Duff, published in 1964:

> It is not correct to say that the Indians did not 'own' the land but only roamed over the face of it and 'used' it. The patterns of ownership and utilization which they imposed upon the lands and waters were different from those recognized by our system of law, but were nonetheless clearly defined and mutually respected. Even if they didn't subdivide and cultivate the land, they did recognize ownership of plots used for village sites, fishing places, berry and root patches, and similar purposes. Even if they didn't subject the forests to wholesale logging, they did establish ownership of tracts used for hunting, trapping, and food-gathering. Even if they didn't sink mine shafts into the mountains, they did own peaks and valleys for mountain goat hunting and as sources of raw materials. Except for barren and inaccessible areas which are not utilized even today, every part of the Province was formerly within the owned and recognized territory of one or other of the Indian tribes.

The Nishga answer to Government assertions of absolute ownership of the land within their boundaries was made as early as 1888 before the first Royal Commission to visit the Nass Valley. Their spokesman said:

> David Mackay — What we don't like about the Government is their saying this: "We will give you this much land." How can they give it when it is our own? We cannot understand it. They have never bought it from us or our forefathers. They have never fought and conquered our people and taken the land in that way, and yet they say now that they will give us so much land — our own land. These chiefs do not talk foolishly, they know the land is their own; our forefathers for generations past had their land here all around us; chiefs have had their own hunting grounds, their salmon streams, and places where they got their berries; it has always been so. It is

not only during the last four or five years that we have seen the land; we have always seen and owned it; it is no new thing, it has been ours for generations. If we had only seen it for twenty years and claimed it as our own, it would have been foolish, but it has been ours for thousands of years. If any strange person came here and saw the land for twenty years and claimed it, he would be foolish. We have always got our living from the land; we are not like white people who live in towns and have their stores and other business, getting their living in that way, but we have always depended on the land for our food and clothes; we get our salmon, berries, and furs from the land.

Any Canadian inquiry into the nature of the Indian title must begin with *R. v. St. Catherines Milling & Lumber Co. v. The Queen.*

. . . . .

There can be no doubt that [in *St. Catherine's Milling*] the Privy Council found that the Proclamation of 1763 was the origin of the Indian title — "Their possession, such as it was, can only be ascribed to the . . . royal proclamation in favour of all Indian tribes then living under the sovereignty and protection of the British Crown."

I do not take these reasons to mean that the Proclamation was the exclusive source of Indian title. The territory under consideration in the *St. Catherines* appeal was clearly within the geographical limits set out in the Proclamation. It is part of the appellants' case that the Proclamation does apply to the Nishga territory and that they are entitled to its protection. They also say that if it does not apply to the Nishga territory, their Indian title is still entitled to recognition by the Courts. These are two distinct questions.

I say at once that I am in complete agreement with judgments of the British Columbia Courts in this case that the Proclamation has no bearing upon the problem of Indian title in British Columbia. I base my opinion upon the very terms of the Proclamation and its definition of its geographical limits and upon the history of the discovery, settlement and establishment of what is now British Columbia.

. . . . .

When the Colony of British Columbia was established in 1858, there can be no doubt that the Nishga territory became part of it. The fee was in the Crown in right of the Colony until July 20, 1871, when the Colony entered Confederation, and thereafter in the Crown in right of the Province of British Columbia, except only in respect of those lands transferred to the Dominion under the Terms of Union.

. . . . .

Although I think it is clear that Indian title in British Columbia cannot owe its origin to the Proclamation of 1763, the fact is that when the settlers came, the Indians were there, organized in societies and occupying the land as their forefathers had done for centuries. This is what Indian title means and it does not help one in the solution of this problem to call it a "personal or usufructuary right". What they are asserting in this action is that they had a right to continue to live on their lands as their forefathers had lived and that this right has never been lawfully extinguished. There can be no question that this right was "dependent on the goodwill of the Sovereign".

It was the opinion of the British Columbia Courts that this right, if it ever existed, had been lawfully extinguished, that with two societies in competition for land — the white settlers demanding orderly settlement and the Indians demanding to be let alone — the proper authorities deliberately chose to set apart reserves for Indians in various parts of the territory and open up the rest for settlements. They held that this had been done when British Columbia entered Confederation in 1871 and that the Terms of Union recognized this fact.

As to Vancouver Island, we have before us a collection of dispatches between the Colonial Office and Governor Douglas in connection with the Indian problem that was confronting him. The first, dated July 31, 1851, contains an admonition that it should be an invariable condition in all bargains or treaties with the natives for the cession of lands possessed by them that subsistence should be supplied in some other shape.

. . . . .

These dispatches are detailed and informative on both sides. They set out the difficulties and problems as they arose and suggestions for their solution. I quote from the last dispatch of the Governor, which conveniently summarizes his efforts:

Victoria, 25th March, 1861.

    My Lord Duke, — I have the honour of transmitting a petition from the House of Assembly of Vancouver Island to your Grace, praying for the aid of Her Majesty's Government in extinguishing the Indian title to the public lands in this Colony; and setting forth, with much force and truth, the evils that may arise from the neglect of that very necessary precaution.

    2. As the native Indian population of Vancouver Island have distinct ideas of property in land, and mutually recognize their several exclusive possessory rights in certain districts, they would not fail to regard the occupation of such portions of the Colony by white settlers, unless the full consent of the proprietary tribes, as national wrongs, and the sense of injury might produce a feeling of irritation against the settlers, and perhaps disaffection to the Government that would endanger the peace of the country.

    3. Knowing their feelings on that subject, I made it a practice up to the year 1859, to purchase the native rights in the land, in every case prior to the settlement of any district; but since that time in consequence of the termination of the Hudson's Bay Company's Charter, and the want of funds, it has not been in my power to continue it. Your Grace must, indeed, be well aware that I have, since then, had the utmost difficulty in raising money enough to defray the most indispensable wants of Government.

. . . . .

The reasons for judgment next deal with a series of Proclamations by James Douglas as Governor of the Colony of British Columbia. The first is dated December 2, 1858, and it is stated to be a Proclamation having the force of law to enable the Governor of British Columbia to have Crown lands sold within the said Colony. It authorized the Governor to grant any land belonging to the Crown in the Colony.

The second Proclamation is dated February 14, 1859. It declared that all lands in British Columbia and all mines and minerals thereunder belonged to the Crown in fee. It provided for the sale of these lands after surveys had been made and the lands were ready for sale, and that due notice should be given of such sales.

The third Proclamation is dated January 4, 1860. It provided for British subjects and aliens who take the oath of allegiance acquiring unoccupied and unreserved and unsurveyed Crown land, and for the subsequent recognition of the claim after the completion of the survey.

The fourth Proclamation is dated January 20, 1860. It provided for the sale of certain lands by private contract and authorized the Commissioner of Land and all Magistrates and Gold Commissioners to make these sales at certain prices.

The fifth Proclamation of January 19, 1861, dealt with further details of land sales.

The sixth Proclamation, dated January 19, 1861, reduced the price of land.

The seventh Proclamation, dated May 28, 1861, dealt with conditions of pre-emption and limited the right to 160 acres per person.

The eighth Proclamation, dated August 27, 1861, was a consolidation of the laws affecting the settlement of unsurveyed Crown lands in British Columbia.

The ninth Proclamation, dated May 27, 1863, dealt with the establishment of mining districts.

Then follow four Ordinances enacted by the Governor by and with the consent of the Legislative Council of British Columbia. The first is dated April 11, 1865. It repeats what the Proclamation had previously said, namely, that all lands in British Columbia and all mines and minerals therein, not otherwise lawfully appropriated, belong [to] the Crown in fee. It goes on to provide for the public sale of lands and the price; that unless otherwise specially announced at the time of the sale, the conveyance of the lands shall include all trees and all mines and minerals within and under the same (except mines of gold and silver). It also deals with rights of pre-emption of unoccupied, unsurveyed and unreserved Crown lands "not being the site of an existent or proposed town, or auriferous land or an Indian reserve or settlement under certain conditions."

The next Ordinance, dated March 31, 1866, restricts those who may acquire lands by pre-emption under the Ordinance of April 11, 1865. British subjects or aliens who take the oath of allegiance have this right but it does not extend without special permission of the Governor to companies or "to any of the Aborigines of this Colony of the Territories neighbouring thereto".

The third Ordinance is dated March 10, 1869. It deals with the payment of purchase money for pre-emption claims.

The last Ordinance is dated June 1, 1870, and is one to amend and consolidate the laws affecting Crown lands in British Columbia.

The result of these Proclamations and Ordinances was stated by Gould, J., at the trial in the following terms [8 D.L.R. (3d) at pp. 81-2]. I accept his statement, as did the Court of Appeal:

> The various pieces of legislation referred to above are connected, and in many instances contain references *inter se*, especially XIII. They extend back well prior to November 19, 1866, the date by which, as a certainty, the delineated lands were all within the boundaries of the Colony of British Columbia, and thus embraced in the land legislation of the Colony, where the words were appropriate. All thirteen reveal a unit of intention to exercise, and the legislative exercising, of absolute sovereignty over all the lands of British Columbia, a sovereignty inconsistent with any conflicting interest, including one as to "aboriginal title, otherwise known as the Indian title", to quote the statement of claim. The legislation prior to November 19, 1866, is included to show the intention of the successor and connected legislation after that date, which latter legislation certainly included the delineated lands.

. . . . .

The Terms of Union under which British Columbia entered into Confederation with the Dominion of Canada are also of great significance in this problem. These terms were approved by Imperial Order in Council dated May 16, 1871, which has, under s. 146 of the *B.N.A. Act*, the force of an Imperial statute. Term 13 reads:

> 13. The charge of the Indians, and the trusteeship and management of the lands reserved for their use and benefit, shall be assumed by the Dominion Government, and a policy as liberal as that hitherto pursued by the British Columbia Government shall be continued by the Dominion Government after the Union.
>
> To carry out such policy, tracts of land of such extent as it has hitherto been the practice of the British Columbia Government to appropriate for that purpose, shall from time to time be conveyed by the Local Government to the Dominion Government in trust for the use and benefit of the Indians on application of the Dominion Government; and in case of disagreement between the two Governments respecting the quantity of such tracts of land to be so granted, the matter shall be referred for the decision of the Secretary of State of the Colonies.

On the question of reserves, it is convenient to mention at this point, though it is out of chronological order, the McKenna-McBride Commission, its Report and the Dominion legislation which followed on its recommendations.

The Commission was established in 1913 to settle all differences between the Dominion and the Province of British Columbia respecting Indian lands and Indian affairs generally in the Province. Seven years later, the recommendations of this Commission were followed by Dominion legislation, 1920 (Can. 2nd Sess.), c. 51.

. . . . .

The recommendations of the Commission resulted in the establishment of new or confirmation of old Indian reserves in the Nass area. They are over thirty in number. Frank Calder, one of the appellants, says that this was done over Indian objections. Nevertheless, the federal authority did act under its powers under s. 91(24) of the *B.N.A. Act, 1867*. It agreed, on behalf of the Indians, with the policy of establishing these reserves.

In the Department of Indian Affairs and Northern Development there exists a Nass River Agency that administers the area in question. The reserves generally correspond with the fishing places that Indians had traditionally used. The Government of the original Crown colony and, since 1871, the Government of British Columbia have made alienations in the Nass Valley that are inconsistent with the existence of an aboriginal title. These have already been referred to and show alienations in fee simple and by way of petroleum and natural gas leases, mineral claims and tree farm licences.

Further, the establishment of the railway belt under the Terms of Union is inconsistent with the recognition and continued existence of Indian title.

. . . . .

There was no reservation of Indian rights in respect of the railway belt to be conveyed to the Dominion Government.

From what I have already said, it is apparent that before 1871 there were no treaties between the Indian tribes and the Colony relating to lands on the mainland. From the material filed, it appears that on Vancouver Island there were, in all, fourteen purchases of Indian lands in the area surrounding Fort Victoria. These are the ones referred to in the correspondence between James Douglas and the Colonial Office. In 1899, Treaty 8 was negotiated and certain tribes of north-eastern British Columbia were grouped with the Cree, Beaver, Chipewyan, Alberta and Northwest Territories' tribes, and included in the treaty. The area covered by this treaty is vast — both in the Northwest Territories and north-eastern British Columbia. There can be no doubt that by this treaty the Indians surrendered their rights in both areas.

. . . . .

In my opinion, in the present case, the sovereign authority elected to exercise complete dominion over the lands in question, adverse to any right of occupancy which the Nishga Tribe might have had, when, by legislation, it opened up such lands for settlement, subject to the reserves of land set aside for Indian occupation.

. . . . .

I would dismiss the appeal and would make no order as to costs.

[**Laskin** and **Spence JJ.** concur with **Hall J.**]

Hall J. (dissenting): — This appeal raises issues of vital importance to the Indians of northern British Columbia and, in particular, to those of the Nishga tribe. The Nishga tribe has persevered for almost a century in asserting an interest in the lands which their ancestors occupied since time immemorial. The Nishgas were never conquered nor did they at any time enter into a treaty or deed of surrender as many other Indian tribes did throughout Canada and in southern British Columbia. The Crown has never granted the lands in issue in this action other than a few small parcels later referred to prior to the commencement of the action. The claim as set out in the statement of claim reads as follows:

> WHEREFORE, the Plaintiffs claim a declaration that the aboriginal title, otherwise known as the Indian title, of the Plaintiffs to their ancient tribal territory hereinbefore described, has never been lawfully extinguished.

. . . . .

It was stated and agreed to by counsel at the hearing in this Court that Parliament had not taken any steps or procedures to extinguish the Indian right of title after British Columbia entered Confederation. The appeal was argued on this basis and on the representation of counsel that no constitutional question was involved.

Consideration of the issues involves the study of many historical documents and enactments received in evidence. ... The Court may take judicial notice of the facts of history whether past or contemporaneous ... and the Court is entitled to rely on its own historical knowledge and researches ...

The assessment and interpretation of the historical documents and enactments tendered in evidence must be approached in the light of present-day research and knowledge disregarding ancient concepts formulated when understanding of the customs and culture of our original people was rudimentary and incomplete and when they were thought to be wholly without cohesion, laws or culture, in effect a subhuman species. This concept of the original inhabitants of America led Chief Justice Marshall in his otherwise enlightened judgment in *Johnson and Grahams' Lessee v. M'Intosh* (1823), 8 Wheaton 543, 21 U.S. 240, which is the outstanding judicial pronouncement on the subject of Indian rights to say [p. 590], "But the tribes of Indians inhabiting this country were fierce savages, whose occupation was war ..." We now know that that assessment is ill-founded. The Indians did in fact at times engage in some tribal wars but war was not their vocation and it can be said that their preoccupation with war pales into insignificance when compared to the religious and dynastic wars of "civilized" Europe of the 16th and 17th centuries. Chief Justice Marshall was, of course, speaking with the knowledge available to him in 1823. Chief Justice Davey in the judgment under appeal [13 D.L.R. (3d) 64, 74 W.W.R. 481], with all the historical research and material available since 1823 and notwithstanding the evidence in the record which Gould, J. [8 D.L.R. (3d) 59, 71 W.W.R. 81], found was given "with total integrity", said of the Indians of the mainland of British Columbia [p. 66]:

> ... they were undoubtedly at the time of settlement a very primitive people with few of the institutions of civilized society, and none at all of our notions of private property.

In so saying this in 1970, he was assessing the Indian culture of 1858 by the same standards that the Europeans applied to the Indians of North America two or more centuries before.

. . . . .

The nature of the title of the interest being asserted on behalf of the Nishgas was stated in evidence by Calder in cross-examination as follows:

> From time immemorial the Naas River Nishga Indians possessed, occupied and used the Naas Valley, Observatory Inlet, and Portland Inlet and Canal, and within this territory the Nishgas hunted in its woods, fished in its waters, streams and rivers. Roamed, hunted and pitched their tents in the valleys, shores and hillsides. Buried their dead in their homeland territory. Exercised all privileges of free men in the tribal territory. The Nishgas have never ceded or extinguished their aboriginal title within this territory.

. . . . .

When asked to state the nature of the right being asserted and for which a declaration was being sought, counsel for the appellants described it as "an interest which is a burden on the title of the Crown; an interest which is usufructuary in nature; a tribal interest inalienable except to the Crown and extinguishable only by legislative enactment of the Parliament of Canada". The exact nature and extent of the Indian right or title does not need to be precisely stated in this litigation. The issue here is whether any right or title the Indians possess as occupants of the land from time immemorial has been extinguished. ... Their position is that they possess a right of occupation against the world except the Crown and that the Crown has not to date lawfully extinguished that right. The essence of the action is that such rights as the Nishgas possessed in 1858 continue to this date. Accordingly, the declaratory judgment asked for implies that the *status quo* continues and this means that if the right is to be extinguished it must be done by specific legislation in accordance with the law.

The right to possession claimed is not prescriptive in origin because a prescriptive right presupposes a prior right in some other person or authority. Since it is admitted that the Nishgas have been in possession since time immemorial, that fact negatives that anyone ever had or claimed prior possession.

The Nishgas do not claim to be able to sell or alienate their right to possession except to the Crown. They claim the right to remain in possession themselves and to enjoy the fruits of that possession. They do not deny the right of the Crown to dispossess them but say the Crown has not done so. There is no claim for compensation in this action. The action is for declaration without a claim for consequential relief. ... However, it must be recognized that if the Nishgas succeed in establishing a right to possession, the question of compensation would remain for future determination as and when proceedings to dispossess them should be taken. British Columbia's position has been that there never was any right or title to extinguish, and alternatively, that if any such right or title did exist it was extinguished in the period between 1858 and Confederation in 1871. The respondent admits that nothing has been done since Confederation to extinguish the right or title.

The appellants do challenge the authority of British Columbia to make grants in derogation of their rights, but because the grants made so far in respect of Nishga lands are so relatively insignificant the appellants have elected to ignore them while maintaining that they were *ultra vires*.

Unlike the method used to make out title in other contexts, proof of the Indian title or interest is to be made out as a matter of fact. In *Amodu Tijani v. Secretary, Southern Nigeria*, [1921] 2 A.C. 399, Lord Haldane said at pp. 402-4:

> Their Lordships make the preliminary observation that in interpreting the native title to land, not only in Southern Nigeria, but other parts of the British Empire, much caution is essential. *There is a tendency, operating at times unconsciously, to render that title conceptually in terms which are appropriate only to systems which have grown up under English law. But this tendency has to be held in check closely.* As a rule, in the various systems of native jurisprudence throughout the Empire, there is no such full division between property and possession as English lawyers are familiar with. *A very usual form of native title is that of a usufructuary right, which is a mere qualification of or burden on the radical or final title of the Sovereign where that exists. In such cases the title of the Sovereign is a pure legal estate, to which beneficial rights may or may not be attached.* But this estate is qualified by a right of beneficial users which may not assume definite forms analogous to estates. (Emphasis added.)

The appellant Calder who is a member of the Legislature of British Columbia testified as follows:

. . . . .

Q. Are you acquainted with the territory outlined in the map, exhibit 2?
A. Yes.
Q. Have the Nishga people every signed any document or treaty surrendering their aboriginal title to the territory outlined in the map, exhibit 2 ?
A. The Nishgas have not signed any treaty or any document that would indicate extinguishment of the title.

Gosnell, Chief Councillor of the Gitlakdamix band, said:

Q. Mr. Gosnell, have the Nishga people ever signed any treaty or document giving up their Indian title to the lands and the waters comprised in the area delineated on the map Exhibit 2 which I am showing you?
A. No.
MR. BROWN: I think I can save my friend some trouble, I think the Attorney-General is prepared to say while denying there is such a thing as an Indian

title in the area, that the inhabitants never did give up or purport to give up that right.

The witnesses McKay, Nyce and Robinson confirmed the evidence of Calder and Gosnell.

. . . . .

At the second Royal Commission hearing in 1915 (the McKenna-McBride Commission), Gideon Minesque for the Nishgas said:

> We haven't got any ill feelings in our hearts but we are just waiting for this thing to be settled and we have been waiting for the last five years — we have been living here from time immemorial — it has been handed down in legends from the old people and that is what hurts us very much because the white people have come along and taken this land away from us. I myself am an old man and as long as I have lived, my people have been telling me stories about the flood and they did not tell me that I was only to live here on this land for a short time. We have heard that some white men, it must have been in Ottawa; this white man said that they must be dreaming when they say they own the land upon which they live. It is not a dream — we are certain that this land belongs to us. Right up to this day the government never made any treaty, not even to our grandfathers or our great-grandfathers.

Wilson Duff, associate professor of anthropology at the University of British Columbia, testified as to the nature of the Nishga civilization and culture in great detail.

. . . . .

Dr. Duff is the author of vol. I of the *Indian History of British Columbia* published by the Government of British Columbia and admitted in evidence as ex. 25. Dr. Duff testified as follows, quoting from ex. 25 and related quotations applicable to the Nishgas:

Q. Now, are you able to tell the Court whether the Nishga Tribe made use of the land and the waters delineated on the map beyond the limits of the reserve that appear on this map in the MacKenna-McBride report?

A. Yes.

. . . . .

Q. Now, prior to the establishment of these reserves what use would the Indian people have made of the areas which flow into the mouths of the streams and rivers?

A. The general pattern in these cases would be that the ownership of the mouth of the stream and the seasonal villages, or habitations that were built there, signify the ownership and use of the entire valley. It would be used as a fishing site itself and a fishing site on the river, but in addition to that the people who made use of this area would have the right to go up the valley for berry picking up on the slopes, for hunting and trapping in the valley and up to forest slopes, usually for the hunting of mountain goats. In other words they made use, more or less intensive use of the entire valley rather than just the point at the mouth of the stream.

. . . . .

Q. To what extent would the use and exploitation of the resources of the Nishga territory have extended in terms of that territory? Would it have extended only through a limited part of the territory or through the whole territory?

A. To a greater or lesser degree of intensity it would extend through a whole territory except for the most barren and inaccessible parts, which were not used or wanted by anyone. But the ownership of an entire drainage basin marked out by the mountain peaks would be recognized as resting within one or other groups of Nishga Indians and these boundaries, this ownership would be respected by others.

. . . . .

On cross-examination he said:

. . . . .

Q. Well, now, I was asking you as to what documentary or other evidence there was that justifies you in using the word 'ownership'. I suggest that that was a concept that was foreign to the Indians of the Nass Agency?

A. I am an anthropologist, sir, and the kind of evidence with which I work is largely not documentary evidence. It is verbal evidence given by people who didn't produce documents and it is turned into documentary form in anthropological and historical reports and in the reports of various Commissions.

Q. All right. Well, that is what I want now.

A. Yes, okay.

Q. I want you to state, so I can go and look them up, the documents you rely upon to support your statement, your use of the word 'ownership', as 'belonging' in the Indian concept.

A. Anthropological reports which I understand Mr. Berger is going to enter into the record, one of them by Philip Drucker, is a general book on the Indians of the Northwest Coast and it would use the term. Another is a book by Viola Garfield as to the Tsimshian Indians in general and in this sense it includes the Nishga which would use a concept of ownership.

Q. Now, are you suggesting that this is anything other than a tribal concept?

A. It includes the tribal concept and it is more besides, yes.

. . . . .

Q. Well, in other words the Indians would speak of the fact that when they attended before a Commission, that they owned the land?

A. Yes.

Q. They would speak in those terms as "We" as a group.

A. Yes.

Q. "Own the land".

A. I think they would go beyond that and say, "And the chief owned that certain territory up Portland Inlet where we used to get this and that," and the whole list of things that I referred to before.

Q. Would one family defend its right like that against other families?

A. It could, yes.

Q. Well, is there evidence of that?

A. There are narratives to that effect, yes.

Q. In the Nishga Valley, in the territory you have marked off there?

A. Yes.

Q. Where? Can you point to that?
A. They are in the unpublished material that I have been referring to.

Possession is of itself at common law proof of ownership ... Unchallenged possession is admitted here.

Dr. Duff also went into details of the Nishga system of succession to property based on a matrilineal line, showing that the Nishgas had a well-developed and sophisticated concept of property.

· · · · ·

An interesting and apt line of questions by Gould, J., in which he endeavoured to relate Duff's evidence as to Nishga concepts of ownership of real property to the conventional common law elements of ownership must be quoted here as they disclose that the trial Judge's consideration of the real issue was inhibited by a preoccupation with the traditional *indicia* of ownership. In so doing, he failed to appreciate what Lord Haldane said in *Amodu Tijani*, [[1991] 2 A.C. at p. 402]:

> Their lordships make the preliminary observation that in interpreting the native title to land, not only in Southern Nigeria, but other parts of the British Empire, much caution is essential. There is a tendency, operating at times unconsciously, to render that title conceptually in terms which are appropriate only to systems which have grown up under English law. But this tendency has to be held in check closely.

The trial Judge's questions and Duff's answers were as follows:

THE COURT:
Q. I want to discuss with you the short descriptive concept of your modern ownership of land in British Columbia, and I am going to suggest to you three characteristics (1) specific delineation of the land, we understand is the lot.
A. Yes.
Q. Specifically delineated down to the lot, and the concept of the survey; (2) exclusive possession against the whole world, including your own family. Your own family, you know that, you want to keep them off or kick them off and one can do so; (3) to keep the fruits of the barter or to leave it or to have your heirs inherit it, which is the concept of wills. Now, those three characteristics — are you with me?
A. Yes.
Q. Specific delineation, exclusive possession, the right of alienation, have you found in your anthropological studies any evidence of that concept being in the consciousness of the Nishgas and having them executing such a concept?
A. My lord, there are three concepts.
Q. Yes, or a combination of them.
A. Could we deal with them one at a time?
Q. Yes, you can do it any way you like. You deal with it.
A. Specific delineation, I think, was phrased by Dr. —
Q. Touched upon by landmarks.
A. Physical landmarks, physical characteristics. The exclusive occupation did not reside in an individual. It rested in a group of people who were a sub-group of the tribe.
Q. The third one was alienation.

A. The owners in this sense had certain rights of alienation. They could give up the tract of land, lose it in warfare, but in practice it would not go to anybody outside of the tribe, that is, a tract of Nishga land might change hands but it wouldn't go to other than a Nishga family.

Q. So am I correct in assuming that there are similarities in the Nishga civilization in the first two characteristics, but not the third? All that alienation means, of course, is that you can sell it to anybody you like?

A. Yes.

Q. Generally speaking, I mean, that is what it does, Two of the three the Nishga Tribe — I don't want to put words in your mouth, now, I want you to tell me. I don't want to tell you anything.

A. Delineation but not by modern surveying methods.

Q. Of course, I understand, yes.

A. Exclusive ownership resting not in an individual.

Q. Possession or occupancy, not ownership?

A. Oh, I see. Possession or occupancy resting in a specific group rather than an individual. The right of alienation, which in practice would leave the land within the same tribe. It was limited.

Q. Could the group having exclusive occupancy select within the tribe, if they chose, another group to whom they wanted to either, to use the modern word, convey it, or would that go by general communal habit, customs or even law?

A. The group could do the thing you suggest. For example, in some cases the chief of a group might convey a property to his son, which would not be the normal way; it would be to his nephew in the normal way.

Q. Yes.

A. And that would , on rare occasions, be accepted.

Q. Always subject to the acceptance of what, the tribe?

A. The tribe, yes.

RE-EXAMINED BY MR. BERGER:

Q. His lordship put to you three characteristics of modern day real property concepts. Having regard to the territory of the Nishga Tribe outlined on the map, Exhibit 2, can you say whether or not there would have been specific delineation of that area in the sense in which it was put to you by his lordship?

A. Of the boundaries of that area?

Q. Yes.

A. Yes.

Q. What would the means of delineation have been?

A. As Dr. Drucker has described them here, landmarks.

Q. By landmarks. Do you mean the mountain tops?

A. Yes, geographical locations.

Q. Now, his lordship put to you the notion of exclusive possession. As regards the territory delineated on the map, Exhibit 2, the Nishga territory, what would have been the application of that concept if it had any in the time before the coming of the white man?

A. It would be recognized by all as Nishga territory. They would exercise exclusive possession of it.

MR. BERGER: I have no further questions.

THE COURT: I have some more now.

Q. I will give you two more characteristics of ownership, the right to destroy it at your own whim, if you like, and the other, that the exclusive possession should be of indeterminable time, that is, cannot be terminated by a person's life; that is, can be passed on to one's heirs. That makes five. Now, you have dealt with three. Now, the right to destroy at whim, set fire to your own house; these matters you have been dealing with, would a group within the Nishga have the right, if the buildings at the mouth of a certain river had been in their exclusive use some time and they will say, "Let's set fire to it," would the tribe prohibit that?

A. I would think that they would have that right.

Q. You would think they would have that right?

A. Yes.

Q. Now, what about the duration of the right, not to destroy, but the right of exclusive ownership, would it go to their heirs?

A. Yes.

Q. Or go back to the tribe for distribution?

A. In theory it belongs within that kinship group through time, with no duration in theory. It always remains with that same kinship group.

Q. There is a matrilineal line?

A. Yes.

THE COURT: Thank you.

In enumerating the *indicia* of ownership, the trial Judge overlooked that possession is of itself proof of ownership. *Prima facie*, therefore, the Nishgas are the owners of the lands that have been in their possession from time immemorial and, therefore the burden of establishing that their right has been extinguished rests squarely on the respondent.

What emerges from the evidence is the following: the Nishgas in fact are and were from time immemorial a distinctive cultural entity with concepts of ownership indigenous to their culture and capable of articulation under the common law.

. . . . .

While the Nishga claim has not heretofore been litigated, there is a wealth of jurisprudence affirming common law recognition of aboriginal rights to possession and enjoyment of lands of aborigines precisely analogous to the Nishga situation here.

. . . . .

The case most frequently quoted with approval dealing with the nature of aboriginal rights is *Johnson and Graham's Lessee v. M'Intosh* (1823), 8 Wheaton 543, 21 U.S. 240. It is the *locus classicus* of the principles governing aboriginal title.

. . . . .

The dominant and recurring proposition stated by Chief Justice Marshall in *Johnson v. M'Intosh* is that on discovery or on conquest the aborigines of newly-found lands were conceded to be the rightful occupants of the soil with a legal as well as a just claim to retain possession of it and to use it according to their own discretion, but their rights to complete sovereignty as independent nations were necessarily diminished and their power to dispose of the soil on their own will to whomsoever they pleased was denied by the original fundamental principle that discovery or conquest gave exclusive title to those who made it.

. . . . .

The view that the Indians had a legal as well as a just claim to the territory they occupied was confirmed as recently as 1946 by the Supreme Court of the United States in the case of *United States v. Alcea Band of Tillamooks et al.* (1946), 329 U.S. 40. In that case it was held that the Indian claims legislation of 1935 did not confer any substantive rights on the Indians, that is, it did not convert a moral claim for taking their land without their consent and without compensation into a legal claim, because they had already had a valid legal claim and there was no necessity to create one.... The judgment is based squarely on the recognition by the Court of "aboriginal Indian title" founded on their previous possession of the land.

. . . . .

The aboriginal Indian title does not depend on treaty, executive order or legislative enactment. ...

. . . . .

Surely the Canadian treaties, made with much solemnity on behalf of the Crown, were intended to extinguish the Indian title. What other purpose did they serve? If they were not intended to extinguish the Indian right, they were a gross fraud and that is not to be assumed. Treaty 8 made in 1899 was entered into on behalf of Queen Victoria and the representatives of Indians in a section of British Columbia and the Northwest Territories. The treaty was ratified by the Queen's Privy Council in Canada. Certain statements in the treaty are entirely inconsistent with any argument or suggestion that such rights as the Indians may have had were extinguished prior to Confederation in 1871.

. . . . .

If there was no Indian title extant in British Columbia in 1899, why was the treaty negotiated and ratified?

Parallelling and supporting the claim of the Nishgas that they have a certain right or title to the lands in question is the guarantee of Indian rights contained in the Proclamation of 1763. This Proclamation was an Executive Order having the force and effect of an Act of Parliament and was described by Gwynne, J., in *St. Catherines Milling* case at p. 652 as the "Indian Bill of Rights". ... Its force as a statute is analogous to the status of Magna Carta which has always been considered to be the law throughout the Empire. It was a law which followed the flag as England assumed jurisdiction over newly-discovered or acquired lands or territories. It follows, therefore, that the *Colonial Laws Validity Act*, 1865 (U.K.), c. 63, applied to make the Proclamation the law of British Columbia.

. . . . .

[It] cannot be challenged that while the west coast lands were mostly unexplored as of 1763 they were certainly known to exist and that fact is borne out by the wording of the ... Proclamation.

. . . . .

This important question remains: were the rights either at common law or under Proclamation extinguished? Tysoe, J.A., said in this regard at p. 95 [13 D.L.R. (3d)] of his reasons: "It is true, as the appellants have submitted, *that nowhere can one find express words extinguishing Indian title* ..." (emphasis added).

The parties here agree that if extinguishment was accomplished, it must have occurred between 1858 and when British Columbia joined Confederation in 1871. ...

Once aboriginal title is established, it is presumed to continue until the contrary is proven. This was stated to be the law by Viscount Haldane in *Amodu Tijani v. Secretary, Southern Nigeria*, [1921] 2 A.C. 399 at pp. 409-10.

. . . . .

The appellants rely on the presumption that the British Crown intended to respect native rights; therefore, when the Nishga people came under British sovereignty ... they were entitled to assert, as a legal right, their Indian title. It being a legal right, it could not thereafter be extinguished except by surrender to the Crown or by competent legislative authority, and then only by specific legislation. There was no surrender by the Nishgas and neither the Colony of British Columbia nor the Province, after Confederation, enacted legislation specifically purporting to extinguish the Indian title nor did Parliament at Ottawa.

. . . . .

[T]he onus of proving that the Sovereign intended to extinguish the Indian title lies on the respondent and that intention must be "clear and plain". There is no such proof in the case at bar; no legislation to that effect.

The Court of Appeal also erred in holding that there "is no Indian Title capable of judicial interpretation ... unless it has previously been recognized either by the Legislature or the Executive Branch of Government" [see p. 70]. Relying on *Cook et al. v. Sprigg*, [1899] A.C. 572 and other cases, the Court of Appeal erroneously applied what is called the Act of State Doctrine. This doctrine denies a remedy to the citizens of an acquired territory for invasion of their rights which may occur during the change of sovereignty. English Courts have held that a municipal Court has no jurisdiction to review the manner in which the Sovereign acquires new territory. The Act of State is the activity of the Sovereign by which he acquires the property. Professor D.P. O'Connell in his work *International Law*, 2nd ed. (1970), at p. 378 says:

> [T]he Act of State doctrine is no more than a procedural bar to municipal law action, and as such is irrelevant to the question whether in international law change of sovereignty affects acquired rights.

The Act of State doctrine has no application in the present appeal for the following reasons: (a) It has never been invoked in claims dependent on aboriginal title. An examination of its rationale indicates that it would be quite inappropriate for the Courts to extend the doctrine to such cases; (b) It is based on the premise that an Act of State is an exercise of the Sovereign power which a municipal Court has no power to review.

. . . . .

In the present case the appellants are not claiming that the origin of their title was a grant from any previous Sovereign, nor are they asking this Court to enforce a treaty of cession between any previous Sovereign and the British Crown. The appellants are *not* challenging an Act of State — they are asking this Court to recognize that settlement of the north Pacific coast did not extinguish the aboriginal title of the Nishga people.

. . . . .

Once it is apparent that the Act of State doctrine has no application, the whole argument of the respondent that there must be some form of "recognition" of aboriginal rights falls to the ground.

On the question of extinguishment, the respondent relies on what was done by Governors Douglas and Seymour and the Council of British Columbia. The appellants, as I have previously mentioned, say that if either Douglas or Seymour or the Council of the Colony of British Columbia did purport to extinguish the Nishga title that any such attempt was beyond the powers of either the Governors or of the Council and that what, if anything, was attempted in this respect was *ultra vires*.

. . . . .

[O]n October 19, 1861 [the Colonial Secretary wrote to Governor Douglas] as follows:

Sir, — I have had under my consideration your despatch No. 24, of the 25th of March last, transmitting an Address from the House of Assembly of Vancouver Island, in which they pray for the assistance of Her Majesty's Government in extinguishing the Indian title to the public lands in the Colony, and set forth the evils that may result from a neglect of this precaution.

I am fully sensible of the great importance of purchasing without loss of time the native title to the soil of Vancouver Island; but the acquisition of the title is a purely colonial interest, and the Legislature must not entertain any expectation that the British taxpayer will be burthened to supply the funds or British credit pledged for the purpose. I would earnestly recommend therefore to the House of Assembly, that they should enable you to procure the requisite means, but if they should not think proper to do so, Her Majesty's Government cannot undertake to supply the money requisite for an object which, whilst it is essential to the interests of the people of Vancouver Island, is at the same time purely Colonial in its character, and trifling in the charge that it would entail.

This reply, while refusing funds to acquire the native rights in land, did not authorize Douglas to take or extinguish those rights without compensation. If the lands were to be taken they had to be paid for by the Colony and not by the British taxpayer. If the Colony had intended extinguishing the Indian title to public lands as referred to in the foregoing letter, it could easily have said, "Indian title to public lands in the Colony is hereby extinguished". No such enactment or one with language to like effect was ever passed.

A number of other Acts, Ordinances and Proclamations were passed or issued between February 14, 1859, and June 1, 1870. All of these were repealed and consolidated by an Ordinance passed July 1, 1870. That Consolidation contained in part the following:

PRE-EMPTION

3. From and after the date of the proclamation in this Colony of Her Majesty's assent to this Ordinance, any male person being a British Subject, of the age of eighteen years or over, may acquire the right to pre-empt any tract of unoccupied, unsurveyed, and unreserved Crown Lands (not being an Indian settlement) not exceeding three hundred and twenty acres in extent in that portion of the Colony situate to the northward and eastward of the Cascade or Coast Range of Mountains, and one hundred and sixty acres in extent in the rest of the Colony. Provided that such right of pre-emption shall not be held to extend to any of the Aborigines of this Continent, except to such as shall have obtained the Governors' special permission in writing to that effect.

This is the provision chiefly relied on by Gould, J., and by the Court of Appeal in making the finding that the Indian title in British Columbia had been extinguished. It is obvious that this enactment did not apply to the Nishga lands on the Naas River. The north-west boundary of the Colony in that area was still in dispute. In any event, this provision is expansive and permissive in so far as it enables aborigines to get title in fee with the Governor's written permission.

If in any of the Proclamations or actions of Douglas, Seymour or of the Council of the Colony of British Columbia there are elements which the respondent says extinguish by implication the Indian title, then it is obvious from the Commission of the Governor and from the Instructions under which the Governor was required to observe and neither the Commission nor the Instructions contain any power or authorization to extinguish the Indian title, then it follows logically that if any attempt was made to extinguish the title it was beyond the power of the Governor or of the Council to do so and, therefore, *ultra vires*.

A further observation in respect of the Letter of Instructions of July 31, 1858, must be made of the phrase, "Let me not omit to observe, that it should be an invariable condition, in all bargains or treaties with the Natives for the *cession* of land possessed by them . . .". Having in mind the use of the word "cession" in this context, how can it logically be said that the Imperial Government was not at the time recognizing that the natives had something to cede? What they had to cede was their aboriginal right and title to possession of the lands, subject to the Crown's paramount title.

. . . . .

I would, therefore, allow the appeal with costs throughout and declare that the appellants' right to possession of the lands delineated in ex. 2 with the exceptions before mentioned and their right to enjoy the fruits of the soil of the forest, and of the rivers and streams within the boundaries of said lands have not been extinguished by the Province of British Columbia or by its predecessor, the Colony of British Columbia, or by the Governors of that Colony.

Pigeon J.: — ... I have to hold that the preliminary objection that the declaration prayed for, being a claim of title against the Crown in the right of the Province of British Columbia, the court has no jurisdiction to make it in the absence of a fiat of the Lieutenant-Governor of that Province. I am deeply conscious of the hardship involved in holding that the access to the Court for the determination of the plaintiff's claim is barred by sovereign immunity from suit without a fiat. However, I would point out that in the United States, claims in respect of the taking of lands outside of reserves and not covered by any treaty were not held justiciable until legislative provisions had removed the obstacle created by the doctrine of immunity. In Canada, immunity from suit has been removed by legislation at the federal level and in most provinces. However, this has not yet been done in British Columbia.

I would therefore dismiss the appeal and make no order as to costs.

Appeal dismissed.

F. THE BEGINNINGS OF MODERN CANADIAN ABORIGINAL TITLE JURISPRUDENCE

The *St. Catherine's* case was the first important consideration of Aboriginal title. After the *Calder* decision, a significant number of claims to Aboriginal title were placed before the Canadian judiciary. One of the most prominent of these post-*Calder* decisions on Aboriginal title came in *Baker Lake (Hamlet) v. Canada (Minister of Indian Affairs and Northern Development)*, reproduced below. The case concerned an action brought by a number of Inuit organizations and individuals who sought (1) a declaration that lands comprising the Baker Lake area in the Northwest Territories belonged to the Inuit residing in or near the area on the basis of Aboriginal title, as well as (2) a declaration of their Aboriginal rights to hunt and fish on those lands. In the end, a declaration was granted with respect to part of the lands included in the Baker Lake area. However, the primary legacy of the case remains its formulation of the requirements to prove the existence of Aboriginal title at common law.

The test devised by Justice Mahoney, and some commentary on it, are excerpted below. Although since superseded by the test established in *Delgamuukw v. British Columbia*, [1997] S.C.J. No. 108, [1997] 3 S.C.R. 1010 (S.C.C.), the *Baker Lake* test remains noteworthy as the prime example of post-*Calder*, pre-*Delgamuukw* considerations of the necessary requirements for proving Aboriginal title.

BAKER LAKE (HAMLET) v. CANADA (MINISTER OF INDIAN AFFAIRS AND NORTHERN DEVELOPMENT)

(1979), 107 D.L.R. (3d) 513 at 542, [1980] 1 F.C. 518, [1980] 5 W.W.R. 193, [1979] 3 C.N.L.R. 17 (T.D.); additional reasons at [1981] 1 F.C. 266 (F.C.T.D.)

Mahoney J.: —

. . . . .

The elements which the plaintiffs must prove to establish an aboriginal title cognizable at common law are:

1. That they and their ancestors were members of an organized society.
2. That the organized society occupied the specific territory over which they assert the aboriginal title.
3. That the occupation was to the exclusion of other organized societies.
4. That the occupation was an established fact at the time sovereignty was asserted by England.

. . . . .

Proof that the plaintiffs and their ancestors were members of an organized society is required by the authorities. In quoting Mr. Justice Judson's *Calder* judgment, I emphasized the phrase "organized in societies" and I repeated the emphasis Mr. Justice Hall had included in quoting the passage from *Worcester v. Georgia*: "having institutions of their own, and governing themselves by their own laws". The *rationale* of the requirement is to be found in the following *dicta* of the Privy Council in *Re Southern Rhodesia*, [1919] A.C. 211 at pp. 233-4:

The estimation of the rights of aboriginal tribes is always inherently difficult. Some tribes are so low in the scale of social organization that their usages and conceptions of rights and duties are not to be reconciled with the institutions or the legal ideas of civilized society. Such a gulf cannot be bridged. It would be idle to impute to such people some shadow of the rights known to our law and then to transmute it into the substance of transferable rights of property as we know them. In the present case it would make each and every person by a fictional inheritance a landed proprietor "richer than all his tribe". On the other hand, there are indigenous peoples whose legal conceptions, though differently developed, are hardly less precise than our own. When once they have been studied and understood they are no less enforcable [*sic*] than rights arising under English law. Between the two there is a wide tract of much ethnological interest, but the position of the natives of Southern Rhodesia within it is very uncertain; clearly they approximate rather to the lower than to the higher limit.

. . . . .

It is apparent that the relative sophistication of the organization of any society will be a function of the needs of its members, the demands they make of it. While the existence of an organized society is a prerequisite to the existence of an aboriginal title, there appears no valid reason to demand proof of the existence of a society more elaborately structured than is necessary to demonstrate that there existed among the aborigines a recognition of the claimed rights, sufficiently defined to permit their recognition by the common law upon its advent in the territory.

. . . . .

The nature, extent or degree of the aborigines' physical presence on the land they occupied, required by the law as an essential element of their aboriginal title is to be determined in each case by a subjective test.

. . . . .

The occupation of the territory must have been to the exclusion of other organized societies. In the *Santa Fe* case [*U.S. v. Santa Fe Pacific Rwy. Co.*, 314 U.S. 339 (1941)], at p. 345, Mr. Justice Douglas, giving the opinion of the court, held:

> Occupancy necessary to establish an aboriginal possession is a question of fact to be determined as any other question of fact. If it were established as a fact that the lands in question were, or were included in, the ancestral home of the Walapais in the sense that they constituted definable territory occupied exclusively by the Walapais (as distinguished from lands wandered over by many tribes), then the Walapais had "Indian title" which, unless extinguished, survived the railroad grant of 1866.

. . . . .

[I]n this context, "time immemorial" runs back from the date of assertion of English sovereignty over the territory which was probably no earlier than 1610 and certainly no later than May 2, 1670 [the date of the granting of the royal charter to the Hudson's Bay Company, giving it control over Rupert's Land].

. . . . .

In the result, I find, on the balance of probabilities on the evidence before me, that at the time England asserted sovereignty over the barren lands west of Hudson Bay, the Inuit were the exclusive occupants of the portion of the barren lands extending from the vicinity of Baker Lake north and east toward the Arctic and Hudson Bay to the boundaries of the Baker Lake R.C.M.P. detachment area as they were in 1954 .... An aboriginal title to that territory, carrying with it the right to freely move about and hunt and fish over it, vested at common law in the Inuit.

Shortly after the *Baker Lake* decision was rendered, and slightly more than a decade after *Calder*, the Supreme Court of Canada again took the opportunity to discuss the nature of Aboriginal title and the effects of the *Royal Proclamation of 1763* in *Guerin v. R.* That case, which dealt primarily with the fiduciary obligations of the federal Crown towards the Musqueam band upon the latter's surrender of reserve lands for leasing purposes, is discussed in greater detail in Chapter 5, but is excerpted here for its discussion of Aboriginal title.

GUERIN v. R.

[1984] S.C.J. No. 45, 13 D.L.R. (4th) 321 at 335, [1984] 2 S.C.R. 335, [1984] 6 W.W.R. 481, 59 B.C.L.R. 301, [1985] 1 C.N.L.R. 120, 20 E.T.R. 6, 36 R.P.R. 1 (*sub nom. Guerin v. Canada*), 55 N.R. 161 (S.C.C.)

Dickson J.: —

. . . . .

In *Calder et al. v. A.-G. B.C.* (1973), 34 D.L.R. (3d) 145, [1973] S.C.R. 313, [1973] W.W.R. 1, this court recognized aboriginal title as a legal right derived from the Indians' historic occupation and possession of their tribal lands. With Judson and Hall JJ. writing the principal judgments, the court split three-three on the major issue of whether the Nishga Indians' aboriginal title to their ancient tribal territory had been extinguished by general land enactments in British Columbia. The Court also split on the issue of whether the Royal Proclamation of 1763 was applicable to Indian lands in that province. Judson and Hall JJ. were in agreement, however, that aboriginal title existed in Canada (at least where it has not been extinguished by appropriate legislative action) independently of the Royal Proclamation of 1763. Judson J. stated expressly that the Proclamation was not the "exclusive" source of Indian title (at pp. 152-3, 156 D.L.R., pp. 322-23, 328 S.C.R.). Hall J. said (at p. 200 D.L.R., p. 390 S.C.R.) that "aboriginal Indian title does not depend on treaty, executive order or legislative enactment".

. . . . .

In recognizing that the Proclamation is not the sole source of Indian title the *Calder* decision went beyond the judgment of the Privy Council in *St. Catherine's Milling & Lumber Co. v. The Queen* (1888), 14 App. Cas. 46. In that case Lord Watson acknowledged the existence of aboriginal title but said it had its origin in the Royal Proclamation. In this respect *Calder* is consistent with the position of Chief Justice Marshall in the leading American cases of *Johnson and Graham's Lessee v. M'Intosh* (1823), 8 Wheaton 543, 21 U.S. 240, and *Worcester v. State of Georgia* (1832), 6 Peters 515, 31 U.S. 530, cited by Judson and Hall JJ. in their respective judgments.

In *Johnson v. M'Intosh*, Marshall C.J., although he acknowledged the Royal Proclamation of 1763 as one basis for recognition of Indian title, was none the less of the opinion that the rights of Indians in the lands they traditionally occupied prior to European colonization both predated and survived the claims to sovereignty made by various European nations in the territories of the North American continent. The principle of discovery which justified these claims gave the ultimate title in the land in a particular area to the nation which had discovered and claimed it. In that respect at least the Indians' rights in the land were obviously diminished; but their rights of occupancy and possession remained unaffected.

. . . . .

The principle that a change in sovereignty over a particular territory does not in general affect the presumptive title of the inhabitants was approved by the Privy Council in *Amodu Tijani v. Secretary, Southern Nigeria*, [1921] 2 A.C. 399. That principle supports the assumption implicit in *Calder* that Indian title is an independent legal right which, although recognized by the Royal Proclamation of 1763, none the less predates it. ... [The Indians'] interest in their lands is a pre-existing legal right not created by Royal Proclamation, by s. 18(1) of the *Indian Act*, or by any other executive order or legislative provision.

It does not matter, in my opinion, that the present case is concerned with the interest of an Indian band in a reserve rather than with unrecognized aboriginal title in traditional tribal lands. The Indian interest in the land is the same in both cases: see *A.-G. Que. v. A.-G. Can.* (1920), 56 D.L.R. 373 at pp. 378-9, [1921] 1 A.C. 401 at pp. 410-11 (the *Star Chrome* case).

. . . . . .

In the *St. Catherine's Milling* case, *supra*, the Privy Council held that the Indians had a "personal and usufructuary right" [p. 54] in the lands which they had traditionally occupied. Lord Watson said that "there has been all along vested in the Crown a substantial and paramount estate, underlying the Indian title, which became a *plenum dominium* whenever the title was surrendered or otherwise extinguished" (at p. 55). He reiterated this idea, stating that the Crown "has all along had a present proprietary estate in the land, upon which the Indian title was a mere burden" (at p. 58). This view of aboriginal title was affirmed by the Privy Council in the *Star Chrome* case. In *Amodu Tijani, supra*, Viscount Haldane, adverting to the *St. Catherine's Milling* and *Star Chrome* decisions, explained the concept of a usufructuary right as "a mere qualification of or burden on the radical or final title of the Sovereign" (p. 403). He described the title of the Sovereign as a pure legal estate, but one which could be qualified by a right of "beneficial user" that did not necessarily take the form of an estate in land. Indian title in Canada was said to be one illustration "of the necessity for getting rid of the assumption that the ownership of land naturally breaks itself up into estates, conceived as creatures of inherent legal principle" [p. 403]. Chief Justice Marshall took a similar view in *Johnson v. M'Intosh, supra,* saying, "All our institutions recognize the absolute title of the Crown, subject only to the Indian right of occupancy" (p. 588).

It should be noted that the Privy Council's emphasis on the personal nature of aboriginal title stemmed in part from constitutional arrangements peculiar to Canada. The Indian territory at issue in *St. Catherine's Milling* was land which in 1867 had been vested in the Crown subject to the interest of the Indians. The Indians' interest was "an interest other than that of the Province", within the meaning of s. 109 of the *Constitution Act, 1867*. Section 109 provides:

> 109. All Lands, Mines, Minerals, and Royalties belonging to the several Provinces of Canada, Nova Scotia, and New Brunswick at the Union, and all Sums then due or payable for such Lands, Mines, Minerals, or Royalties, shall belong to the several Provinces of Ontario, Quebec, Nova Scotia, and New Brunswick in which the same are situate or arise subject to any Trusts existing in respect thereof, and to any Interest other than that of the Province in the same.

When the land in question in *St. Catherine's Milling* was subsequently disencumbered of the native title upon its surrender to the federal government by the Indian occupants in 1873, the entire beneficial interest in the land was held to have passed, because of the personal and usufructuary nature of the Indians' right, to the Province of Ontario under s. 109 rather than to Canada. The same constitutional issue arose recently in this court in *Smith et al. v. The Queen* (1983), 147 D.L.R. (3d) 237, [1983] 1 S.C.R. 554, 47 N.R. 132 *sub nom. Government of Canada v. Smith*, in which the court held that the Indian right in a reserve, being personal, could not be transferred to a grantee, whether an individual or the Crown. Upon surrender the right disappeared "in the process of release".

No such constitutional problem arises in the present case, since in 1938 the title to all Indian reserves in British Columbia was transferred by the provincial government to the Crown in right of Canada.

It is true that in contexts other than the constitutional the characterization of Indian title as "a personal and usufructuary right" has sometimes been questioned. In *Calder, supra*, for example, Judson J. intimated at p. 156 D.L.R., p. 328 S.C.R., that this characterization was not helpful in determining the nature of Indian title. In *A.-G. Can. v. Giroux* (1916), 30 D.L.R. 123, 53 S.C.R. 172, Duff J., speaking for himself and Anglin J., distinguished *St. Catherine's Milling* on the ground that the statutory provisions in accordance with which the reserve in question in *Giroux* had been created conferred beneficial ownership on the Indian band which occupied the reserve. In *Cardinal v. A.-G. Alta.* (1973), 40 D.L.R. (3d) 553, [1974] S.C.R. 695, 13 C.C.C. (2d) 1, Laskin J., dissenting on another point, accepted the possibility that Indians may have a beneficial interest in a reserve. The Alberta Court of Appeal in *Western Industrial Contractors Ltd. v. Sarcee Developments Ltd.* (1979), 98 D.L.R. (3d) 424, [1979] 3 W.W.R. 631 *sub nom. Western Int'l Contractors Ltd. v. Sarcee Developments Ltd.*, 15 A.R. 309, accepted the proposition that an Indian band does indeed have a beneficial interest in its reserve. In the present case this was the view as well of Le Dain J. in the Federal Court of Appeal. See also the judgment of Kellock J. in *Miller v. The King,* [1950] 1 D.L.R. 513, [1950] S.C.R. 168, in which he seems implicitly to adopt a similar position. None of these judgments mentioned the *Star Chrome* case, however, in which the Indian interest in land specifically set aside as a reserve was held to be the same as the "personal and usufructuary right" which was discussed in *St. Catherine's Milling*.

It appears to me that there is no real conflict between the cases which characterize Indian title as a beneficial interest of some sort, and those which characterize it a personal, usufructuary right. Any apparent inconsistency derives from the fact that in describing what constitutes a unique interest in land the courts have almost inevitably found themselves applying a somewhat inappropriate terminology drawn from general property law. There is a core of truth in the way that each of the two lines of authority has described native title, but an appearance of conflict has none the less arisen because in neither case is the categorization quite accurate.

Indians have a legal right to occupy and possess certain lands, the ultimate title to which is in the Crown. While their interest does not, strictly speaking, amount to beneficial ownership, neither is its nature completely exhausted by the concept of a personal right. It is true that the *sui generis* interest which the Indians have in the land is personal in the sense that it cannot be transferred to a grantee, but it is also true, as will presently appear, that the interest gives rise upon surrender to a distinctive fiduciary obligation of the Crown to deal with the land for the benefit of the surrendering Indians. These two aspects of Indian title go together, since the Crown's original purpose in declaring the Indians' interest to be inalienable otherwise than to the Crown was to facilitate the Crown's ability to represent the Indians in dealings with third parties. The nature of the Indians' interest is therefore best characterized by its general inalienability, coupled with the fact that the Crown is under an obligation to deal with the land on the Indians' behalf when the interest is surrendered. Any description of Indian title which goes beyond these two features is both unnecessary and potentially misleading.

The unique, or *sui generis*, nature of Aboriginal land rights indicated in *Guerin* was subsequently referenced in *St. Mary's Indian Band v. Cranbrook (City)*, [1997] S.C.J. No. 19, [1997] 2 S.C.R. 657 (S.C.C.). In that case, Lamer C.J.C., for the Court, held, at para. 14, that the *sui generis* nature of Aboriginal land rights entailed that disputes concerning Aboriginal lands were not to be approached "by strict reference to intractable real property rules". As he further explained, *ibid*. at para. 16:

> The reason the Court has said that common law real property concepts do not apply to native lands is to prevent native intentions from being frustrated by an application of formalistic and arguably alien common law rules. Even in a case such as this where the Indian band received full legal representation ... we must ensure that form not trump substance. It would

be fundamentally unjust to impose inflexible and technical land transfer requirements upon these "autonomous actors"...

While Justice Dickson in *Guerin* attempted to simplify Aboriginal title to facilitate its understanding, it should be emphasized that the *Guerin* judgment was limited by the effects of the Supreme Court of Canada's decision in *Smith v. R.*, [1983] S.C.J. No. 39, [1983] 1 S.C.R. 554, 47 N.R. 132, 147 D.L.R. (3d) 237 (S.C.C.). In *Smith*, the Aboriginal interest in land was characterized as an ephemeral right that disappeared upon surrender (*i.e.* relinquishment of Aboriginal title) and could not be transferred to a grantee, whether the Crown or a private individual: *Smith, ibid.*, at 250. Thus, upon surrender, pre-existing Aboriginal title simply vanished and could never be resurrected. There are problems with this characterization of Aboriginal title, however. If, as in *Guerin*, a band surrenders title for leasing purposes with the intention of having the land revert back to it at the conclusion of the lease, how is it possible for the band to regain the land if its legal interest vanished upon surrender? Furthermore, if the *Smith* characterization of Aboriginal title is accurate, does that not render the treaty-making process between the Crown and Aboriginal peoples redundant, at least with regard to the characterization of treaties as agreements that transfer land (as opposed to conceptions of treaties that regard the document as extinguishing the Aboriginal interest in that land)?

While the *Opetchesaht* case, above, raised the issue of the effect of land surrenders on Aboriginal title, it simply affirmed the *Smith* decision without truly considering its effects on surrenders for lease versus surrenders for sale. *Opetchesaht's* finding that surrenders may partially or temporarily release the Indian interest in land, while consistent with sections 37-38 of the *Indian Act*, creates problems in light of *Smith's* statement that Indian land interests may not be transferred, but simply vanish upon surrender and cannot be resurrected. If *Smith's* characterization is correct, then a band that has temporarily surrendered its land interests (as in a leasing situation) will still be understood to have had those interests eliminated, leaving in doubt the basis upon which the band may reclaim the land upon the termination of the lease. As a result of the incomplete analysis of this issue in *Opetchesaht*, the *Smith* precedent and the problems it created remain.

G. MORE RECENT JUDICIAL CONSIDERATIONS OF ABORIGINAL TITLE

Originally, the doctrine of Aboriginal title, as formulated by British colonial law, was a means of reconciling Aboriginal and European claims to land designed to maintain peaceful relations between the parties. The modern law of Aboriginal title is derived from the nature of the interaction between Aboriginal and European people in North America, their competing claims to land, and the creation of a significant bod y of case law dealing with Aboriginal rights to land.

In spite of important pronouncements such as *Calder* and *Guerin*, Canadian courts have not always provided a consistent basis upon which to appraise questions of Aboriginal title. For a variety of reasons, the courts have evaded many of the primary issues surrounding Aboriginal title. These issues, which include the legitimacy of the British Crown's claims to title and/or sovereignty over Canada, are of primary importance to all Canadians, whether Aboriginal or non-Aboriginal. Questions of title and sovereignty were central to the issues at bar in the case of *Delgamuukw v. British Columbia*, below.

DELGAMUUKW v. BRITISH COLUMBIA

[1997] S.C.J. No. 108, [1997] 3 S.C.R. 1010 (S.C.C.)

Lamer C.J.C. (Cory, Major and **McLachlin JJ.,** concurring)

[1] This appeal is the latest in a series of cases in which it has fallen to this Court to interpret and apply the guarantee of existing aboriginal rights found in s. 35(1) of the *Constitution Act, 1982*. Although that line of decisions, commencing with *R. v. Sparrow*, [1990] 1 S.C.R. 1075, proceeding through the *Van der Peet* trilogy (*R. v. Van der Peet*, [1996] 2 S.C.R. 507; *R. v. N.T.C. Smokehouse Ltd.*, [1996] 2 S.C.R. 672, and *R. v. Gladstone*, [1996] 2 S.C.R. 723) and ending in *R. v. Pamajewon*, [1996] 2 S.C.R. 821; *R. v. Adams*, [1996] 3 S.C.R. 101, and *R. v. Côté*, [1996] 3 S.C.R. 139, have laid down the jurisprudential framework for s. 35(1), this appeal raises a set of interrelated and novel questions which revolve around a single issue — the nature and scope of the constitutional protection afforded by s. 35(1) to common law aboriginal title.

. . . . .

II. *Facts*

. . . . . .

[7] This action was commenced by the appellants, who are all Gitksan or Wet'suwet'en hereditary chiefs, who, both individually and on behalf of their "Houses" claimed separate portions of 58,000 square kilometres in British Columbia. For the purpose of the claim, this area was divided into 133 individual territories, claimed by the 71 Houses. This represents all of the Wet'suwet'en people, and all but 12 of the Gitksan Houses. Their claim was originally for "ownership" of the territory and "jurisdiction" over it. (At this Court, this was transformed into, primarily, a claim for aboriginal title over the land in question.) The province of British Columbia counterclaimed for a declaration that the appellants have no right or interest in and to the territory or alternatively, that the appellants' cause of action ought to be for compensation from the Government of Canada. ...

[At the time of trial the Gitksan consisted of approximately 4,000 to 5,000 persons in the watersheds of the north and central Skeena, Nass and

Babine Rivers. The Wet'suwet'en consisted of approximately 1,500 to 2,000 persons mainly in the watersheds of the Bulkley and parts of the Fraser-Nechako River systems. There were also approximately 30,000 non-aboriginals living in the territory at the time of the trial. There was archeological evidence, which was accepted at trial, that there was some form of human habitation in the territory and its surrounding areas from 3,500 to 6,000 years ago. The trial judge held that the time of direct contact between the Aboriginal peoples in the claimed territory was approximately 1820. The appellants, 51 Chiefs representing most of the Houses of the Gitksan and Wet'suwet'en nations, originally advanced 51 individual claims on their own behalf and on behalf of their houses for "ownership" and "jurisdiction" over 133 distinct territories which together comprise 58,000 square kilometres of northwestern British Columbia. On appeal, that original claim was altered in two ways: (1) replacing the claims for ownership and jurisdiction with claims for aboriginal title and self-government; and (2) amalgamating the 51 individual claims into two communal claims, one for each nation. Lamer C.J.C. held that there was no formal amendment to the first pleading, but a *de facto* amendment to permit "a claim for aboriginal rights other than ownership and jurisdiction" permitted by the trial judge. As a result, he held that there was no prejudice to the respondents by virtue of the first alteration. However, Lamer C.J.C. held that no such amendment was made with respect to the amalgamation of the individual claims brought by the 51 Gitksan and Wet'suwet'en Houses into two collective claims. Given the absence of an amendment to the pleadings, he concluded that the respondents suffered some prejudice that prevented the Court from considering the merits of this appeal. The Chief Justice ordered a new trial as the correct remedy for this defect in the pleadings. The remainder of the judgment was dedicated to other reasons why a new trial should be ordered.]

B. *What is the ability of this Court to interfere with the factual findings made by the trial judge?*

(1) General Principles

[78] ... As a general rule, this Court has been extremely reluctant to interfere with the findings of fact made at trial, especially when those findings of fact are based on an assessment of the testimony and credibility of witnesses. Unless there is a "palpable and overriding error", appellate courts should not substitute their own findings of fact for those of the trial judge. ...

. . . . .

[80] ... [W]hile accepting the general principle of non-interference, this Court has also identified specific situations in which an appeal court can interfere with a finding of fact made at trial. ... In cases involving the

determination of aboriginal rights, appellate intervention is also warranted by the failure of a trial court to appreciate the evidentiary difficulties inherent in adjudicating aboriginal claims when, first, applying the rules of evidence and, second, interpreting the evidence before it. ...

[81] The justification for this special approach can be found in the nature of aboriginal rights themselves. I explained in *Van der Peet* that those rights are aimed at the reconciliation of the prior occupation of North America by distinctive aboriginal societies with the assertion of Crown sovereignty over Canadian territory. They attempt to achieve that reconciliation by "their bridging of aboriginal and non-aboriginal cultures" (at para. 42). Accordingly, "a court must take into account the perspective of the aboriginal people claiming the right. ... while at the same time taking into account the perspective of the common law" such that "[t]rue reconciliation will, equally, place weight on each" (at paras. 49 and 50).

[82] In other words, although the doctrine of aboriginal rights is a common law doctrine, aboriginal rights are truly *sui generis*, and demand a unique approach to the treatment of evidence which accords due weight to the perspective of aboriginal peoples. However, that accommodation must be done in a manner which does not strain "the Canadian legal and constitutional structure" (at para. 49). ...

. . . . .

[84] In practical terms, this requires the courts to come to terms with the oral histories of aboriginal societies, which, for many aboriginal nations, are the only record of their past. ...

. . . . .

[86] Many features of oral histories would count against both their admissibility and their weight as evidence of prior events in a court that took a traditional approach to the rules of evidence. The most fundamental of these is their broad social role not only "as a repository of historical knowledge for a culture" but also as an expression of "the values and mores of [that] culture". ... Dickson J. (as he then was) recognized as much when he stated in *Kruger v. The Queen*, [1978] 1 S.C.R. 104, at p. 109, that "[c]laims to aboriginal title are woven with history, legend, politics and moral obligations." The difficulty with these features of oral histories is that they are tangential to the ultimate purpose of the fact-finding process at trial — the determination of the historical truth. Another feature of oral histories which creates difficulty is that they largely consist of out-of-court statements, passed on through an unbroken chain across the generations of a particular aboriginal nation to the present-day. These out-of-court statements are admitted for their truth and therefore conflict with the general rule against the admissibility of hearsay.

[87] Notwithstanding the challenges created by the use of oral histories as proof of historical facts, the laws of evidence must be adapted in order that this type of evidence can be accommodated and placed on an equal

footing with the types of historical evidence that courts are familiar with. ...

. . . . .

[107] The trial judge's treatment of the various kinds of oral histories did not satisfy the principles I laid down in *Van der Peet*. These errors are particularly worrisome because oral histories were of critical importance to the appellants' case. They used those histories in an attempt to establish their occupation and use of the disputed territory, an essential requirement for aboriginal title. The trial judge, after refusing to admit, or giving no independent weight to these oral histories, reached the conclusion that the appellants had not demonstrated the requisite degree of occupation for "ownership". Had the trial judge assessed the oral histories correctly, his conclusions on these issues of fact might have been very different.

[108] In the circumstances, the factual findings cannot stand. However, given the enormous complexity of the factual issues at hand, it would be impossible for the Court to do justice to the parties by sifting through the record itself and making new factual findings. A new trial is warranted, at which the evidence may be considered in light of the principles laid down in *Van der Peet* and elaborated upon here. In applying these principles, the new trial judge might well share some or all of the findings of fact of McEachern C.J.

C.   *What is the content of aboriginal title, how is it protected by s. 35(1) of the Constitution Act, 1982, and what is required for its proof?*

(1) Introduction

[109] The parties ... have ... a fundamental disagreement over the content of aboriginal title itself, and its reception into the Constitution by s. 35(1). In order to give guidance to the judge at the new trial, it is to this issue that I will now turn.

[110] ... I believe that all of the parties have characterized the content of aboriginal title incorrectly. ... The content of aboriginal title ... is a right in land and, as such, is more than the right to engage in specific activities which may be themselves aboriginal rights. ...

[111] [I]t confers the right to use land for a variety of activities, not all of which need be aspects of practices, customs and traditions which are integral to the distinctive cultures of aboriginal societies. Those activities do not constitute the right *per se*; rather, they are parasitic on the underlying title. However, that range of uses is subject to the limitation that they must not be irreconcilable with the nature of the attachment to the land which forms the basis of the particular group's aboriginal title. This inherent limit ... flows from the definition of aboriginal title as a *sui generis* interest in land, and is one way in which aboriginal title is distinct from a fee simple.

(2) Aboriginal Title at Common Law

(a) *General Features*

[112] The starting point of the Canadian jurisprudence on aboriginal title is the Privy Council's decision in *St. Catherine's Milling and Lumber Co. v. The Queen* (1888), 14 A.C. 46, which described aboriginal title as a "personal and usufructuary right". ... What the Privy Council sought to capture is that aboriginal title is a *sui generis* interest in land. Aboriginal title has been described as *sui generis* in order to distinguish it from "normal" proprietary interests, such as fee simple. However, as I will now develop, it is also *sui generis* in the sense that its characteristics cannot be completely explained by reference either to the common law rules of real property or to the rules of property found in aboriginal legal systems. As with other aboriginal rights, it must be understood by reference to both common law and aboriginal perspectives.

[113] The idea that aboriginal title is *sui generis* is the unifying principle underlying the various dimensions of that title. One dimension is its *inalienability*. Lands held pursuant to aboriginal title cannot be transferred, sold or surrendered to anyone other than the Crown and, as a result, is inalienable to third parties. This Court has taken pains to clarify that aboriginal title is only "personal" in this sense, and does not mean that aboriginal title is a non-proprietary interest which amounts to no more than a licence to use and occupy the land and cannot compete on an equal footing with other proprietary interests: see *Canadian Pacific Ltd. v. Paul*, [1988] 2 S.C.R. 654, at p. 677.

[114] Another dimension of aboriginal title is its *source*. It had originally been thought that the source of aboriginal title in Canada was the *Royal Proclamation, 1763*. ... However, it is now clear that although aboriginal title was recognized by the *Proclamation*, it arises from the prior occupation of Canada by aboriginal peoples. That prior occupation, however, is relevant in two different ways, both of which illustrate the *sui generis* nature of aboriginal title. The first is the physical fact of occupation, which derives from the common law principle that occupation is proof of possession in law. ... Thus, in *Guerin* [*Guerin v. The Queen*, [1984] 2 S.C.R. 335] Dickson J. described aboriginal title, at p. 376, as a "legal right derived from the Indians' historic occupation and possession of their tribal lands". What makes aboriginal title *sui generis* is that it arises from possession *before* the assertion of British sovereignty, whereas normal estates, like fee simple, arise afterward. This idea has been further developed in *Roberts v. Canada*, [1989] 1 S.C.R. 322, where this Court unanimously held at p. 340 that "aboriginal title pre-dated colonization by the British and survived British claims of sovereignty". ... What this suggests is a second source for aboriginal title — the relationship between common law and pre-existing systems of aboriginal law.

[115] A further dimension of aboriginal title is the fact that it is held *communally*. Aboriginal title cannot be held by individual aboriginal persons; it is a collective right to land held by all members of an aboriginal

nation. Decisions with respect to that land are also made by that community. This is another feature of aboriginal title which is *sui generis* and distinguishes it from normal property interests.

(b) *The Content of Aboriginal Title*

[116] Although cases involving aboriginal title have come before this Court and Privy Council before, there has never been a definitive statement from either court on the *content* of aboriginal title. ...

[117] Although the courts have been less than forthcoming, I have arrived at the conclusion that the content of aboriginal title can be summarized by two propositions: first, that aboriginal title encompasses the right to exclusive use and occupation of the land held pursuant to that title for a variety of purposes, which need not be aspects of those aboriginal practices, customs and traditions which are integral to distinctive aboriginal cultures; and second, that those protected uses must not be irreconcilable with the nature of the group's attachment to that land. ...

Aboriginal title encompasses the right to use the land held pursuant to that title for a variety of purposes, which need not be aspects of those aboriginal practices, cultures and traditions which are integral to distinctive aboriginal cultures

[118] The respondents argue that aboriginal title merely encompasses the right to engage in activities which are aspects of aboriginal practices, customs and traditions which are integral to distinctive aboriginal cultures of the aboriginal group claiming the right and, at most, adds the notion of exclusivity; i.e., the exclusive right to use the land for those purposes. However, the uses to which lands held pursuant to aboriginal title can be put are not restricted in this way. This conclusion emerges from three sources: (i) the Canadian jurisprudence on aboriginal title, (ii) the relationship between reserve lands and lands held pursuant to aboriginal title, and (iii) the *Indian Oil and Gas Act.*, R.S.C., 1985, c. I-7. ...

(i) *Canadian Jurisprudence on Aboriginal Title*

[119] Despite the fact that the jurisprudence on aboriginal title is somewhat underdeveloped, it is clear that the uses to which lands held pursuant to aboriginal title can be put is not restricted to the practices, customs and traditions of aboriginal peoples integral to distinctive aboriginal cultures. In *Guerin*, for example, Dickson J. described aboriginal title as an "interest in land" which encompassed "a legal right to occupy and possess certain lands" (at p. 382). The "right to occupy and possess" is framed in broad terms and, significantly, is not qualified by reference to traditional and customary uses of those lands. Any doubt that the right to occupancy and possession encompasses a broad variety of uses of land was put to rest in *Paul* [*Canadian Pacific Ltd. v. Paul*, [1988] 2 S.C.R. 654], where the Court went even further and stated that aboriginal title was "more than the right to enjoyment and occupancy" (at p. 678). Once again,

there is no reference to aboriginal practices, customs and traditions as a qualifier on that right. Moreover, I take the reference to "more" as emphasis of the broad notion of use and possession.

(ii) Reserve Land

[120] Another source of support for the conclusion that the uses to which lands held under aboriginal title can be put are not restricted to those grounded in practices, customs and traditions integral to distinctive aboriginal cultures can be found in *Guerin*, where Dickson J. stated at p. 379 that the same legal principles governed the aboriginal interest in reserve lands and lands held pursuant to aboriginal title. ...

[121] The nature of the Indian interest in reserve land is very broad, and can be found in s. 18 of the *Indian Act*, which I reproduce in full:

> **18.**(1) Subject to this Act, reserves are held by Her Majesty for the *use and benefit* of the respective bands for which they were set apart ...
>
> (2) The Minister may authorize the use of lands in a reserve for the purpose of Indian schools, the administration of Indian affairs, Indian burial grounds, Indian health projects or, with the consent of the council of the band, *for any other purpose for the general welfare of the band,* and may take any lands in a reserve required for those purposes. ... [Emphasis added.]

The principal provision is s. 18(1), which states that reserve lands are held "for the use and benefit" of the bands which occupy them; those uses and benefits, on the face of the *Indian Act*, do not appear to be restricted to practices, customs and traditions integral to distinctive aboriginal cultures. The breadth of those uses is reinforced by s. 18(2), which states that reserve lands may be used "for any other purpose for the general welfare of the band". The general welfare of the band has not been defined in terms of aboriginal practices, customs and traditions, nor in terms of those activities which have their origin pre-contact; it is a concept, by definition, which incorporates a reference to the present-day needs of aboriginal communities. On the basis of *Guerin*, lands held pursuant to aboriginal title, like reserve lands, are also capable of being used for a broad variety of purposes.

(iii) Indian Oil and Gas Act

[122] ...The overall purpose of the statute is to provide for the exploration of oil and gas on reserve lands through their surrender to the Crown. The statute presumes that the aboriginal interest in reserve land includes mineral rights, a point which this Court unanimously accepted with respect to the *Indian Act* in *Blueberry River Indian Band v. Canada,* [1995] 4 S.C.R. 344. On the basis of *Guerin*, aboriginal title also encompass mineral rights, and lands held pursuant to aboriginal title should be capable of exploitation in the same way, which is certainly not a traditional use for those lands. This conclusion is reinforced by s. 6(2) of the Act, which provides:

(2) Nothing in this Act shall be deemed to abrogate the rights of Indian people or preclude them from negotiating for oil and gas benefits in those areas in which land claims have not been settled.

The areas referred to in s. 6(2), at the very least, must encompass lands held pursuant to aboriginal title, since those lands by definition have not been surrendered under land claims agreements. The presumption underlying s. 6(2) is that aboriginal title permits the development of oil and gas reserves.

. . . . .

[124] In conclusion, the content of aboriginal title is not restricted to those uses which are elements of a practice, custom or tradition integral to the distinctive culture of the aboriginal group claiming the right. However, nor does aboriginal title amount to a form of inalienable fee simple, as I will now explain.

(c) *Inherent Limit: Lands Held Pursuant to Aboriginal Title Cannot Be Used in a Manner that Is Irreconcilable with the Nature of the Attachment to the Land Which Forms the Basis of the Group's Claim to Aboriginal Title*

[125] The content of aboriginal title contains an inherent limit that lands held pursuant to title cannot be used in a manner that is irreconcilable with the nature of the claimants' attachment to those lands. This limit on the content of aboriginal title is a manifestation of the principle that underlies the various dimensions of that special interest in land — it is a *sui generis* interest that is distinct from "normal" proprietary interests, most notably fee simple.

[126] I arrive at this conclusion by reference to the other dimensions of aboriginal title which are *sui generis* as well. I first consider the source of aboriginal title. As I discussed earlier, aboriginal title arises from the prior occupation of Canada by aboriginal peoples. That prior occupation is relevant in two different ways: first, because of the physical fact of occupation, and second, because aboriginal title originates in part from pre-existing systems of aboriginal law. However, the law of aboriginal title does not only seek to determine the historic rights of aboriginal peoples to land; it also seeks to afford legal protection to prior occupation in the present-day. Implicit in the protection of historic patterns of occupation is a recognition of the importance of the continuity of the relationship of an aboriginal community to its land over time.

[127] ... The relevance of the continuity of the relationship of an aboriginal community with its land here is that it applies not only to the past, but to the future as well. That relationship should not be prevented from continuing into the future. As a result, uses of the lands that would threaten that future relationship are, by their very nature, excluded from the content of aboriginal title.

[128] Accordingly, in my view, lands subject to aboriginal title cannot be put to such uses as may be irreconcilable with the nature of the occupation of that land and the relationship that the particular group has had with the

land which together have given rise to aboriginal title in the first place. As discussed below, one of the critical elements in the determination of whether a particular aboriginal group has aboriginal title to certain lands is the matter of the occupancy of those lands. Occupancy is determined by reference to the activities that have taken place on the land and the uses to which the land has been put by the particular group. If lands are so occupied, there will exist a special bond between the group and the land in question such that the land will be part of the definition of the group's distinctive culture. It seems to me that these elements of aboriginal title create an inherent limitation on the uses to which the land, over which such title exists, may be put. For example, if occupation is established with reference to the use of the land as a hunting ground, then the group that successfully claims aboriginal title to that land may not use it in such a fashion as to destroy its value for such a use (e.g., by strip mining it). Similarly, if a group claims a special bond with the land because of its ceremonial or cultural significance, it may not use the land in such a way as to destroy that relationship (e.g., by developing it in such a way that the bond is destroyed, perhaps by turning it into a parking lot).

[129] It is for this reason also that lands held by virtue of aboriginal title may not be alienated. Alienation would bring to an end the entitlement of the aboriginal people to occupy the land and would terminate their relationship with it. I have suggested above that the inalienability of aboriginal lands is, at least in part, a function of the common law principle that settlers in colonies must derive their title from Crown grant and, therefore, cannot acquire title through purchase from aboriginal inhabitants. It is also, again only in part, a function of a general policy "to ensure that Indians are not dispossessed of their entitlements". … What the inalienability of lands held pursuant to aboriginal title suggests is that those lands are more than just a fungible commodity. The relationship between an aboriginal community and the lands over which it has aboriginal title has an important non-economic component. The land has an inherent and unique value in itself, which is enjoyed by the community with aboriginal title to it. The community cannot put the land to uses which would destroy that value.

. . . . .

[131] [T]he continuity of the relationship between an aboriginal community and its land, and the non-economic or inherent value of that land, should not be taken to detract from the possibility of surrender to the Crown in exchange for valuable consideration. On the contrary, the idea of surrender reinforces the conclusion that aboriginal title is limited in the way I have described. If aboriginal peoples wish to use their lands in a way that aboriginal title does not permit, then they must surrender those lands and convert them into non-title lands to do so.

[132] … This is not, I must emphasize, a limitation that restricts the use of the land to those activities that have traditionally been carried out on it. That would amount to a legal straitjacket on aboriginal peoples who have

a legitimate legal claim to the land. The approach I have outlined above allows for a full range of uses of the land, subject only to an overarching limit, defined by the special nature of the aboriginal title in that land.

(d) *Aboriginal Title under s. 35(1) of the Constitution Act, 1982*

[133] ... On a plain reading of the provision, s. 35(1) did not create aboriginal rights; rather, it accorded constitutional status to those rights which were "existing" in 1982. The provision, at the very least, constitutionalized those rights which aboriginal peoples possessed at common law, since those rights existed at the time s. 35(1) came into force. Since aboriginal title was a common law right whose existence was recognized well before 1982 (e.g., *Calder, supra*), s. 35(1) has constitutionalized it in its full form.

. . . . .

[136] I hasten to add that the constitutionalization of common law aboriginal rights by s. 35(1) does not mean that those rights exhaust the content of s. 35(1). ... [T]he existence of a particular aboriginal right at common law is not a *sine qua non* for the proof of an aboriginal right that is recognized and affirmed by s. 35(1). Indeed, none of the decisions of this Court handed down under s. 35(1) in which the existence of an aboriginal right has been demonstrated has relied on the existence of that right at common law. The existence of an aboriginal right at common law is therefore sufficient, but not necessary, for the recognition and affirmation of that right by s. 35(1).

. . . . .

(e) *Proof of Aboriginal Title*

(i) *Introduction*

[140] ... To date, the Court has defined aboriginal rights in terms of *activities*. As I said in *Van der Peet* (at para. 46):

> [I]n order to be an aboriginal right an *activity* must be an element of a practice, custom or tradition integral to the distinctive culture of the aboriginal group claiming the right. [Emphasis added.]

Aboriginal title, however, is a *right to the land* itself. ...

[141] This difference between aboriginal rights to engage in particular activities and aboriginal title requires that the test I laid down in *Van der Peet* be adapted accordingly. ... Since the purpose of s. 35(1) is to reconcile the prior presence of aboriginal peoples in North America with the assertion of Crown sovereignty, it is clear from this statement that s. 35(1) must recognize and affirm both aspects of that prior presence — first, the occupation of land, and second, the prior social organization and distinctive cultures of aboriginal peoples on that land. To date the

jurisprudence under s. 35(1) has given more emphasis to the second aspect. ...

[142] The adaptation of the test laid down in *Van der Peet* to suit claims to title must be understood as the recognition of the first aspect of that prior presence. ... [The distinction between the *Van der Peet* test for Aboriginal rights and the test for Aboriginal title, discussed immediately below, is also addressed in Chapter 2, Aboriginal Rights.]

(ii) *The Test for the Proof of Aboriginal Title*

[143] In order to make out a claim for aboriginal title, the aboriginal group asserting title must satisfy the following criteria: (i) the land must have been occupied prior to sovereignty, (ii) if present occupation is relied on as proof of occupation pre-sovereignty, there must be a continuity between present and pre-sovereignty occupation, and (iii) at sovereignty, that occupation must have been exclusive.

The land must have been occupied prior to sovereignty

[144] In order to establish a claim to aboriginal title, the aboriginal group asserting the claim must establish that it occupied the lands in question at the *time at which the Crown asserted sovereignty over the land subject to the title*. ...

[145] [I]n the context of aboriginal title, sovereignty is the appropriate time period to consider for several reasons. First, from a theoretical standpoint, aboriginal title arises out of prior occupation of the land by aboriginal peoples and out of the relationship between the common law and pre-existing systems of aboriginal law. Aboriginal title is a burden on the Crown's underlying title. However, the Crown did not gain this title until it asserted sovereignty over the land in question. Because it does not make sense to speak of a burden on the underlying title before that title existed, aboriginal title crystallized at the time sovereignty was asserted. Second, aboriginal title does not raise the problem of distinguishing between distinctive, integral aboriginal practices, customs and traditions and those influenced or introduced by European contact. Under common law, the act of occupation or possession is sufficient to ground aboriginal title and it is not necessary to prove that the land was a distinctive or integral part of the aboriginal society before the arrival of Europeans. Finally, from a practical standpoint, it appears that the date of sovereignty is more certain than the date of first contact. It is often very difficult to determine the precise moment that each aboriginal group had first contact with European culture. ... For these reasons, I conclude that aboriginals must establish occupation of the land from the date of the assertion of sovereignty in order to sustain a claim for aboriginal title. McEachern C.J. found, at pp. 233-34, and the parties did not dispute on appeal, that British sovereignty over British Columbia was conclusively established by the Oregon Boundary Treaty of 1846. This is not to say that circumstances subsequent to sovereignty may never be relevant to title or compensation;

this might be the case, for example, where native bands have been dispossessed of traditional lands after sovereignty.

[146] There was a consensus among the parties on appeal that proof of historic occupation was required to make out a claim to aboriginal title. However, the parties disagreed on how that occupancy could be proved. ...

[147] This debate over the proof of occupancy reflects two divergent views of the source of aboriginal title. The respondents argue, in essence, that aboriginal title arises from the physical reality at the time of sovereignty, whereas the Gitksan effectively take the position that aboriginal title arises from and should reflect the pattern of land holdings under aboriginal law. However, as I have explained above, the source of aboriginal title appears to be grounded both in the common law and in the aboriginal perspective on land; the latter includes, but is not limited to, their systems of law. It follows that both should be taken into account in establishing the proof of occupancy. ...

[148] This approach to the proof of occupancy at common law is also mandated in the context of s. 35(1) by *Van der Peet*. In that decision, as I stated above, I held at para. 50 that the reconciliation of the prior occupation of North America by aboriginal peoples with the assertion of Crown sovereignty required that account be taken of the "aboriginal perspective while at the same time taking into account the perspective of the common law" and that "[t]rue reconciliation will, equally, place weight on each". I also held that the aboriginal perspective on the occupation of their lands can be gleaned, in part, but not exclusively, from their traditional laws, because those laws were elements of the practices, customs and traditions of aboriginal peoples: at para. 41. As a result, if, at the time of sovereignty, an aboriginal society had laws in relation to land, those laws would be relevant to establishing the occupation of lands which are the subject of a claim for aboriginal title. Relevant laws might include, but are not limited to, a land tenure system or laws governing land use.

[149] However, the aboriginal perspective must be taken into account alongside the perspective of the common law. Professor McNeil has convincingly argued that at common law, the fact of physical occupation is proof of possession at law, which in turn will ground title to the land. ... Physical occupation may be established in a variety of ways, ranging from the construction of dwellings through cultivation and enclosure of fields to regular use of definite tracts of land for hunting, fishing or otherwise exploiting its resources. ... In considering whether occupation sufficient to ground title is established, "one must take into account the group's size, manner of life, material resources, and technological abilities, and the character of the lands claimed". ...

[150] In *Van der Peet*, I drew a distinction between those practices, customs and traditions of aboriginal peoples which were "an aspect of, or took place in" the society of the aboriginal group asserting the claim and those which were "a central and significant part of the society's distinctive culture" (at para. 55). The latter stood apart because they "made the culture of the society distinctive . . . it was one of the things that truly *made the society what it was*" (at para. 55, emphasis in original). The same

requirement operates in the determination of the proof of aboriginal title. As I said in *Adams*, a claim to title is made out when a group can demonstrate "that their connection with the piece of land . . . was of a central significance to their distinctive culture" (at para. 26).

[151] [I]n the case of title, it would seem clear that any land that was occupied pre-sovereignty, and which the parties have maintained a substantial connection with since then, is sufficiently important to be of central significance to the culture of the claimants. As a result, I do not think it is necessary to include explicitly this element as part of the test for aboriginal title.

If present occupation is relied on as proof of occupation pre-sovereignty, there must be a continuity between present and pre-sovereignty occupation

[152] ... Conclusive evidence of pre-sovereignty occupation may be difficult to come by. Instead, an aboriginal community may provide evidence of present occupation as proof of pre-sovereignty occupation in support of a claim to aboriginal title. What is required, in addition, is a *continuity* between present and pre-sovereignty occupation, because the relevant time for the determination of aboriginal title is at the time before sovereignty.

[153] Needless to say, there is no need to establish "an unbroken chain of continuity" (*Van der Peet*, at para. 65) between present and prior occupation. The occupation and use of lands may have been disrupted for a time, perhaps as a result of the unwillingness of European colonizers to recognize aboriginal title. To impose the requirement of continuity too strictly would risk "undermining the very purpose of s. 35(1) by perpetuating the historical injustice suffered by aboriginal peoples at the hands of colonizers who failed to respect" aboriginal rights to land (*Côté*, *supra*, at para. 53). In *Mabo*, [*Mabo v. Queensland* (1992), 107 A.L.R. 1] the High Court of Australia set down the requirement that there must be "substantial maintenance of the connection" between the people and the land. In my view, this test should be equally applicable to proof of title in Canada. ...

[154] I should also note that there is a strong possibility that the precise nature of occupation will have changed between the time of sovereignty and the present. I would like to make it clear that the fact that the nature of occupation has changed would not ordinarily preclude a claim for aboriginal title, as long as a substantial connection between the people and the land is maintained. ...

At sovereignty, occupation must have been exclusive

[155] Finally, at sovereignty, occupation must have been exclusive. The requirement for exclusivity flows from the definition of aboriginal title itself, because I have defined aboriginal title in terms of the right to *exclusive* use and occupation of land. Exclusivity, as an aspect of aboriginal title, vests in the aboriginal community which holds the ability to exclude

others from the lands held pursuant to that title. The proof of title must, in this respect, mirror the content of the right. Were it possible to prove title without demonstrating exclusive occupation, the result would be absurd, because it would be possible for more than one aboriginal nation to have aboriginal title over the same piece of land, and then for all of them to attempt to assert the right to exclusive use and occupation over it.

[156] As with the proof of occupation, proof of exclusivity must rely on both the perspective of the common law and the aboriginal perspective, placing equal weight on each. ... Exclusivity is a common law principle derived from the notion of fee simple ownership and should be imported into the concept of aboriginal title with caution. As such, the test required to establish exclusive occupation must take into account the context of the aboriginal society at the time of sovereignty. For example, it is important to note that exclusive occupation can be demonstrated even if other aboriginal groups were present, or frequented the claimed lands. Under those circumstances, exclusivity would be demonstrated by "the intention and capacity to retain exclusive control" ... Thus, an act of trespass, if isolated, would not undermine a general finding of exclusivity, if aboriginal groups intended to and attempted to enforce their exclusive occupation. Moreover ... the presence of other aboriginal groups might actually reinforce a finding of exclusivity. For example, "[w]here others were allowed access upon request, the very fact that permission was asked for and given would be further evidence of the group's exclusive control" (at p. 204).

[157] A consideration of the aboriginal perspective may also lead to the conclusion that trespass by other aboriginal groups does not undermine, and that presence of those groups by permission may reinforce, the exclusive occupation of the aboriginal group asserting title. For example, the aboriginal group asserting the claim to aboriginal title may have trespass laws which are proof of exclusive occupation, such that the presence of trespassers does not count as evidence against exclusivity. As well, aboriginal laws under which permission may be granted to other aboriginal groups to use or reside even temporarily on land would reinforce the finding of exclusive occupation. Indeed, if that permission were the subject of treaties between the aboriginal nations in question, those treaties would also form part of the aboriginal perspective. ...

[158] In their submissions, the appellants pressed the point that requiring proof of exclusive occupation might preclude a finding of joint title, which is shared between two or more aboriginal nations. ... I would suggest that the requirement of exclusive occupancy and the possibility of joint title could be reconciled by recognizing that joint title could arise from shared exclusivity. ... There clearly may be cases in which two aboriginal nations lived on a particular piece of land and recognized each other's entitlement to that land but nobody else's. However, since no claim to joint title has been asserted here, I leave it to another day to work out all the complexities and implications of joint title, as well as any limits that another band's title may have on the way in which one band uses its title lands. ... In my opinion, this accords with the general principle that the

common law should develop to recognize aboriginal rights (and title, when necessary) as they were recognized by either *de facto* practice or by the aboriginal system of governance. It also allows sufficient flexibility to deal with this highly complex and rapidly evolving area of the law.

[The Chief Justice then considered the test of justification for governmental infringements of Aboriginal title. He concluded that the general principles governing justification, as set out in the *Sparrow* and *Gladstone* decisions, applied to infringements of Aboriginal title with some modifications because of the unique nature of Aboriginal title. The matter of justification was not addressed, as the question of whether the appellants possessed title to the lands in question was sent back to trial for adjudication. The justificatory test for governmental infringement of Aboriginal rights, including title, may be found in Chapter 2.

The appellants' claim to self-government rights was also sent back to trial. The Chief Justice declined to lay down legal principles to guide future self-government litigation, other than to state that "rights to self-government, if they existed, cannot be framed in excessively general terms".

Finally, Lamer C.J.C. held that the province did not have the power to extinguish Aboriginal rights, including title, after its admission into Confederation in 1871, whether under its own jurisdiction or through the operation of section 88 of the federal *Indian Act*. See the discussion of these issues in Chapter 8.]

VI. *Conclusion and Disposition*

For the reasons I have given above, I would allow the appeal in part, and dismiss the cross-appeal. Reluctantly, I would also order a new trial.

. . . . .

[La Forest J., L'Heureux-Dubé J. concurring, agreed with Lamer C.J.C.'s conclusion, but disagreed with the methodology the Chief Justice used to demonstrate whether Aboriginal peoples possess Aboriginal title to land. In particular, La Forest J. disagreed with Lamer C.J.C.'s finding that statutory provisions governing reserve lands — such as section 18 of the *Indian Act* and the *Indian Oil and Gas Act* — should automatically apply to tribal lands. Sopinka J. took no part in the judgment.]

Appeal allowed in part; cross-appeal dismissed.

Canada's Royal Commission on Aboriginal Peoples recommended governmental recognition that the doctrine of discovery is "legally, morally and factually wrong".[10] Did the Supreme Court of Canada adopt a position on the doctrine of discovery in *Delgamuukw*?

In *Delgamuukw*, the onus of proving Aboriginal title was placed squarely upon the Aboriginal claimants. This is nothing new, as evidenced both by *Calder* and the test established in *Baker Lake*. What was new, however, was the test set out by the Supreme Court for proof of Aboriginal title, as well as the Court's articulation of the key temporal frame of reference for such claims.

Kent McNeil questions why Aboriginal peoples bear the onus of proving that they possess title to land, given the fact that Aboriginal peoples "were here first".

KENT McNEIL, "THE ONUS OF PROOF OF ABORIGINAL TITLE"

(1999) 37 Osgoode Hall L.J. 775 at 776-82, 800-3 (footnotes omitted)

Given [the *Delgamuukw* case] criteria for occupation, the Aboriginal peoples probably occupied much, if not all, of what is now Canada at the time of Crown assertion of sovereignty. If so, is it appropriate to apply the presumption of Crown title in this context? Is not reliance on the feudal doctrine of tenures, which had already lost much of its importance in Britain by the time Canada was colonized, counter-intuitive and prejudicial where Aboriginal title is concerned? Why does the known fact of the Aboriginal presence not take precedence over a presumption based on this largely out-dated doctrine? And what of the Aboriginal perspective on this matter? In *Van der Peet*, Lamer C.J.C. said that, "[i]n assessing a claim for the existence of an aboriginal right, a court must take into account the perspective of the aboriginal people claiming the right . ... while at the same time taking into account the perspective of the common law." In placing the onus of proof of Aboriginal title on Aboriginal claimants in *Delgamuukw*, the chief justice does not appear to have taken account of the Aboriginal perspective at all.

One reason why the Supreme Court probably has not relied on the Aboriginal perspective and the historical record to presume that the Aboriginal peoples were in occupation of all of Canada, and so cast the burden on the Crown of rebutting that presumption by proving the opposite where particular lands are concerned, is that the Aboriginal peoples would then be presumed to have held all lands in Canada by Aboriginal title, and that might pose too great a threat to the economic, social, and political stability of the country. ...

A second legal justification for placing the onus of proof on the Aboriginal peoples arises from the fact that they are typically the plaintiffs in actions for a declaration of Aboriginal title. As a general rule, in legal actions the plaintiffs bear the onus of proving the facts on which their claims depend. As the validity of an Aboriginal title claim depends on occupation of the claimed land at the time the Crown asserted sovereignty over the territory where the land is located, and occupation is a question of fact, it is not surprising that the courts have placed the onus of proving occupation of that specific land on the Aboriginal nation making the claim. But if the tables were turned and Aboriginal nations were the defendants rather than the plaintiffs, the onus should be the other way around. Moreover, if an Aboriginal nation brought an action, not for a declaration of Aboriginal title, but for trespass on their Aboriginal title lands, the evidentiary requirements would be different as well, because in that situation they would only have to prove their present possession, not their title. So the identity of the party initiating the legal proceedings, and the form of action, affect both the onus of proof and what has to be proven.

. . . . .

V. CONCLUSIONS

Despite the apparent unfairness of placing the onus of proving their title on the Aboriginal nations, it is unlikely that the Supreme Court will re-examine this issue and require the Crown to initially prove its own title when an Aboriginal title claim is brought to court. Nonetheless, Aboriginal nations should be able to rely on two fundamental common law rules to meet the onus the Court has placed on them: (1) title is presumed from possession; and (2) possession is title as against anyone who cannot prove that he or she has a better title. So in situations where they can establish either present or past possession of lands at any time *after* Crown assertion of sovereignty, Aboriginal nations should be presumed to have a valid Aboriginal title to those lands, and the burden of proving a better title should be cast on the Crown or its grantees.

Where past possession and the presumption of title arising from it are relied on, an action for recovery of land might be more appropriate and more likely to succeed than an action for declaration of Aboriginal title, as judgment in an action for recovery of land would not prejudice possible claims of persons not party to the action. For the same reason, where an Aboriginal nation seeks to protect *present* possession from interference, the preferable action would probably be an action for trespass rather than an action for declaration of title. If it resulted in a positive judgment, an action for recovery of land or for trespass would restore or secure the possession of the Aboriginal nation against the defendant who had wrongfully taken possession of or trespassed on the nation's lands. Such a judgment would presumably act as a deterrent to discourage others from wrongfully interfering with the nation's possession.

. . . . .

An Aboriginal nation that is in a position to rely on present possession of some or all of their lands could also support that possession with continuing uses and activities on and in relation to the land that would make their possession apparent to the world. Using the land in accordance with their traditional lifestyles, which might include fishing, hunting, gathering, horticulture, cutting trees for building houses, maintaining trails, visiting and conducting ceremonies at sacred sites, and so on, would all be means of supporting their possession. But any other uses of the land, whether "traditional" or not, would serve the same purpose. Examples might be constructing roads, controlling water flow, utilizing natural resources, erecting buildings and other structures, pasturing livestock, and putting up fences. Given that Lamer C.J.C. said in *Delgamuukw* that Aboriginal laws are also relevant to proving Aboriginal occupation, affirming or establishing laws in relation to the land would be another way for the nation to support their possession, while exercising their right of self-government. It would also be advisable to mark boundaries and put up signs or other indicators that the land belongs to the Aboriginal nation. Informing outsiders who intrude on the land that they are trespassing, and either asking them to leave or giving them limited permission to stay, would be another important way to make the nation's possession known to the world. In short, the Aboriginal nation could engage in as many uses and peaceful activities on and in relation to the land as practicable, and sustain those activities over time so that their possession would be maintained. This would require community organization and coordination, fostering a common enterprise that virtually every member of the nation could participate in. By means of this direct participation on the ground, they would be contributing to their community by helping to establish the factual basis for their nation's possession, on which the nation's right to the land may well depend.

The issues that were raised in *Delgamuukw* are not peculiar to the situation in Canada. Many of the same claims have been made in other countries. Australia, for instance, saw a rash of Aboriginal land claims following the Australian High Court's decision in *Mabo v. Queensland [No. 2]* (1992), 107 A.L.R. 1 (H.C. Aust.). The *Mabo* case repudiated principles that had all but eliminated Aboriginal land claims in Australia following the decision in *Milirrpum v. Nabalco Pty. Ltd.*, [1971] 17 F.L.R. 141 (Northern Terr. S.C.). However, as a result of subsequent events — including the judgments in *Wik Peoples v. Queensland* (1996), 187 C.L.R. 1 (H.C. Aust.) and *Fejo v. Northern Territory* (1998), 195 C.L.R. 96 (H.C. Aust.) and the promulgation of the *Native Title Act, 1993* (Cth.) and the *Native Title Amendment Act, 1998* (Cth.) which recognize the ability of the Australian government to extinguish Aboriginal title (including by unilateral action) — Aboriginal title claims in Australia have waned, leaving empty the initial promise set out in *Mabo*.

Following *Delgamuukw*, there had been little substantive discussion of Aboriginal title at the Supreme Court of Canada. That changed with the decision in the combined *Marshall* and *Bernard* cases, discussed below. When reading this judgment, consider whether it assists Aboriginal peoples in their attempts to have Aboriginal title recognized under Canadian law.

R. v. MARSHALL; R. v. BERNARD

[2005] S.C.J. No. 44, [2005] 2 S.C.R. 220 (S.C.C.)

McLachlin C.J.C. (Major, Bastarache, Abella and **Charron JJ.** concurring): —

I. *Introduction*

[1] Can members of the Mi'kmaq people in Nova Scotia and New Brunswick engage in commercial logging on Crown lands without authorization, contrary to statutory regulation? More precisely, do they have treaty rights or aboriginal title entitling them to do so? These are the central issues on this appeal.

[2] In the *Marshall* case, Stephen Frederick Marshall and 34 other Mi'kmaq Indians were charged with cutting timber on Crown lands without authorization, contrary to s. 29 of the *Crown Lands Act*, between November 1998 and March 1999. The logging took place in five counties on mainland Nova Scotia and three counties on Cape Breton Island, in the Province of Nova Scotia. The accused admitted all the elements of the offence, except lack of authorization.

[3] In the *Bernard* case, Joshua Bernard, a Mi'kmaq Indian, was charged with unlawful possession of 23 spruce logs he was hauling from the cutting site to the local saw mill in contravention of s. 67(1)(*c*) of the *Crown Lands and Forests Act*, S.N.B. 1980, c. C-38.1, as amended. Another member of the Miramichi Mi'kmaq community had cut the logs from Crown lands in the Sevogle area of the watershed region of the Northwest Miramichi River, in the Province of New Brunswick. Like the accused in *Marshall*, Bernard argued that as a Mi'kmaq, he was not required to obtain authorization to log.

[4] In both cases the trial courts entered convictions. In both cases, these convictions were upheld by the summary appeal court. And in both cases, these decisions were reversed by the Court of Appeal. In *Marshall*, the convictions were set aside and a new trial ordered. In *Bernard*, the conviction was set aside and an acquittal entered.

[5] The significance of these cases transcends the charges at stake. They were used as vehicles for determining whether Mi'kmaq peoples in Nova Scotia and New Brunswick have the right to log on Crown lands for commercial purposes pursuant to treaty or aboriginal title. ...

[6] I conclude that the trial judges in each case correctly held that the respondents' treaty rights did not extend to commercial logging and correctly rejected the claim for aboriginal title in the relevant areas. I would thus allow the appeals, dismiss the cross-appeal in *Marshall* and restore the convictions.

. . . . .

III. *Aboriginal Title*

[37] The respondents claim that they hold aboriginal title to the lands they logged and that therefore they do not need provincial authorization to log. They advance three different grounds for title: common law; the *Royal Proclamation* of 1763 (reproduced in R.S.C. 1985, App. II, No. 1); and *Belcher's Proclamation*. I will consider each in turn.

A. *Aboriginal Title at Common Law*

[38] Where title to lands formerly occupied by an aboriginal people has not been surrendered, a claim for aboriginal title to the land may be made under the common law. Aboriginal peoples used the land in many ways at the time of sovereignty. Some uses, like hunting and fishing, give rights to continue those practices in today's world. ... Aboriginal title, based on occupancy at the time of sovereignty, is one of these various aboriginal rights. The respondents do not assert an aboriginal right to harvest forest resources. They assert aboriginal title *simpliciter*.

[39] The common law theory underlying recognition of aboriginal title holds that an aboriginal group which occupied land at the time of European sovereignty and never ceded or otherwise lost its right to that land, continues to enjoy title to it. Prior to constitutionalization of aboriginal rights in 1982, aboriginal title could be extinguished by clear legislative act (see *Van der Peet*, at para. 125). Now that is not possible. The Crown can impinge on aboriginal title only if it can establish that this is justified in pursuance of a compelling and substantial legislative objective for the good of larger society ... . This process can be seen as a way of reconciling aboriginal interests with the interests of the broader community.

[40] These principles were canvassed at length in *Delgamuukw v. British Columbia*, [1997] 3 S.C.R. 1010, which enunciated a test for aboriginal title based on exclusive occupation at the time of British sovereignty. Many of the details of how this principle applies to particular circumstances remain to be fully developed. In the cases now before us, issues arise as to the standard of occupation required to prove title, including the related issues of exclusivity of occupation, application of this requirement to nomadic peoples, and continuity. If title is found, issues also arise as to extinguishment, infringement and justification. Underlying all these questions are issues as to the type of evidence required, notably when and how orally transmitted evidence can be used.

B. *Standard of Occupation for Title: The Law*

[41] The trial judges in each of *Bernard* and *Marshall* required proof of regular and exclusive use of the cutting sites to establish aboriginal title. The Courts of Appeal held that this test was too strict and applied a less onerous standard of incidental or proximate occupancy.

[42] Cromwell J.A. in *Marshall* ((2003), 218 N.S.R. (2d) 78, 2003 NSCA 105) adopted in general terms Professor McNeil's "third category" of occupation (*Common Law Aboriginal Title* (1989)), "actual entry, and some act or acts from which an intention to occupy the land could be inferred" (para. 136). Acts of "cutting trees or grass, fishing in tracts of water, and even perambulation, may be relied upon" (para. 136).

[43] Daigle J.A. in *Bernard*, ((2003), 262 N.B.R. (2d) 1, 2003 NBCA 55) similarly concluded that it was not necessary to prove specific acts of occupation and regular use of the logged area in order to ground aboriginal title. It was enough to show that the Mi'kmaq had used and occupied an area near the cutting site at the confluence of the Northwest Miramichi and the Little Southwest Miramichi. This proximity permitted the inference that the cutting site would have been within the range of seasonal use and occupation by the Mi'kmaq (para. 119).

[44] The question before us is which of these standards of occupation is appropriate to determine aboriginal title: the strict standard applied by the trial judges; the looser standard applied by the Courts of Appeal; or some other standard? Interwoven is the question of what standard of evidence suffices; Daigle J.A. criticized the trial judge for failing to give enough weight to evidence of the pattern of land use and for discounting the evidence of oral traditions.

[45] Two concepts central to determining aboriginal rights must be considered before embarking on the analysis of whether the right claimed has been established. The first is the requirement that both aboriginal and European common law perspectives must be considered. The second relates to the variety of aboriginal rights that may be affirmed. Both concepts are critical to analyzing a claim for an aboriginal right, and merit preliminary consideration.

[46] *Delgamuukw* requires that in analyzing a claim for aboriginal title, the Court must consider both the aboriginal perspective and the common law perspective. Only in this way can the honour of the Crown be upheld.

[47] The difference between the common law and aboriginal perspectives on issues of aboriginal title is real. But it is important to understand what we mean when we say that in determining aboriginal title we must consider both the common law and the aboriginal perspective.

[48] The Court's task in evaluating a claim for an aboriginal right is to examine the pre-sovereignty aboriginal practice and translate that practice, as faithfully and objectively as it can, into a modern legal right. The question is whether the aboriginal practice at the time of assertion of European sovereignty ... translates into a modern legal right, and if so, what right? This exercise involves both aboriginal and European perspectives. The Court must consider the pre-sovereignty practice from the perspective of the aboriginal people. But in translating it to a common law right, the Court must also consider the European perspective; the nature of the right at common law must be examined to determine whether a particular aboriginal practice fits it. This exercise in translating aboriginal practices to modern rights must not be conducted in a

formalistic or narrow way. The Court should take a generous view of the aboriginal practice and should not insist on exact conformity to the precise legal parameters of the common law right. The question is whether the practice corresponds to the core concepts of the legal right claimed.

[49] To determine aboriginal entitlement, one looks to aboriginal practices rather than imposing a European template: "In considering whether occupation sufficient to ground title is established, 'one must take into account the group's size, manner of life, material resources, and technological abilities, and the character of the lands claimed'" ... . The application of "manner of life" was elaborated by La Forest J. who stated that:

> ... when dealing with a claim of "aboriginal title", the court will focus on the occupation and use of the land as part of the aboriginal society's *traditional way of life*. In pragmatic terms, this means looking at the manner in which the society used the land *to live*, namely to establish villages, to work, to get to work, to hunt, to travel to hunting grounds, to fish, to get to fishing pools, to conduct religious rites, etc. [Emphasis in original; para. 194.]

[50] Thus, to insist that the pre-sovereignty practices correspond in some broad sense to the modern right claimed, is not to ignore the aboriginal perspective. The aboriginal perspective grounds the analysis and imbues its every step. It must be considered in evaluating the practice at issue, and a generous approach must be taken in matching it to the appropriate modern right. Absolute congruity is not required, so long as the practices engage the core idea of the modern right. But as this Court stated in *Marshall 2*, a pre-sovereignty aboriginal practice cannot be transformed into a different modern right.

[51] In summary, the court must examine the pre-sovereignty aboriginal practice and translate that practice into a modern right. The process begins by examining the nature and extent of the pre-sovereignty aboriginal practice in question. It goes on to seek a corresponding common law right. In this way, the process determines the nature and extent of the modern right and reconciles the aboriginal and European perspectives.

[52] The second underlying concept — the range of aboriginal rights — flows from the process of reconciliation just described. Taking the aboriginal perspective into account does not mean that a particular right, like title to the land, is established. The question is what modern right best corresponds to the pre-sovereignty aboriginal practice, examined from the aboriginal perspective.

[53] Different aboriginal practices correspond to different modern rights. This Court has rejected the view of a dominant right to title to the land, from which other rights, like the right to hunt or fish, flow ... . It is more accurate to speak of a variety of independent aboriginal rights.

[54] One of these rights is aboriginal title to land. It is established by aboriginal practices that indicate possession similar to that associated with title at common law. In matching common law property rules to aboriginal practice we must be sensitive to the context-specific nature of common law title, as well as the aboriginal perspective. The common law recognizes that possession sufficient to ground title is a matter of fact, depending on

all the circumstances, in particular the nature of the land and the manner in which the land is commonly enjoyed ... . For example, where marshy land is virtually useless except for shooting, shooting over it may amount to adverse possession ... . The common law also recognizes that a person with adequate possession for title may choose to use it intermittently or sporadically ... . Finally, the common law recognizes that exclusivity does not preclude consensual arrangements that recognize shared title to the same parcel of land ... .

[55] This review of the general principles underlying the issue of aboriginal title to land brings us to the specific requirements for title set out in *Delgamuukw*. To establish title, claimants must prove "exclusive" pre-sovereignty "occupation" of the land by their forebears: *per* Lamer C.J., at para. 143.

[56] "Occupation" means "physical occupation". This "may be established in a variety of ways, ranging from the construction of dwellings through cultivation and enclosure of fields to regular use of definite tracts of land for hunting, fishing or otherwise exploiting its resources ... .

[57] "Exclusive" occupation flows from the definition of aboriginal title as "the right to *exclusive* use and occupation of land ... . It is consistent with the concept of title to land at common law. Exclusive occupation means "the intention and capacity to retain exclusive control", and is not negated by occasional acts of trespass or the presence of other aboriginal groups with consent ... . Shared exclusivity may result in joint title ... . Non-exclusive occupation may establish aboriginal rights "short of title" ... .

[58] It follows from the requirement of exclusive occupation that exploiting the land, rivers or seaside for hunting, fishing or other resources may translate into aboriginal title to the land if the activity was sufficiently regular and exclusive to comport with title at common law. However, more typically, seasonal hunting and fishing rights exercised in a particular area will translate to a hunting or fishing right. This is plain from this Court's decisions in *Van der Peet, Nikal, Adams* and *Côté*. In those cases, aboriginal peoples asserted and proved ancestral utilization of particular sites for fishing and harvesting the products of the sea. Their forebears had come back to the same place to fish or harvest each year since time immemorial. However, the season over, they left, and the land could be traversed and used by anyone. These facts gave rise not to aboriginal title, but to aboriginal hunting and fishing rights.

[59] The distinction between the requirements for a finding of aboriginal title and the requirements for more restricted rights was affirmed in *Côté*, where the Court held the right to fish was an independent right ... . Similarly in *Adams*, the Court held that rights short of title could exist in the absence of occupation and use of the land sufficient to support a claim of title to the land ... . To say that title flows from occasional entry and use is inconsistent with these cases and the approach to aboriginal title which this Court has consistently maintained.

[60] In this case, the only claim is to title in the land. The issue therefore is whether the pre-sovereignty practices established on the evidence correspond to the right of title to land. These practices must be assessed from the aboriginal perspective. But, as discussed above, the right claimed also invokes the common law perspective. The question is whether the practices established by the evidence, viewed from the aboriginal perspective, correspond to the core of the common law right claimed.

[61] The common law, over the centuries, has formalized title through a complicated matrix of legal edicts and conventions. The search for aboriginal title, by contrast, takes us back to the beginnings of the notion of title. Unaided by formal legal documents and written edicts, we are required to consider whether the practices of aboriginal peoples at the time of sovereignty compare with the core notions of common law title to land. It would be wrong to look for indicia of aboriginal title in deeds or Euro-centric assertions of ownership. Rather, we must look for the equivalent in the aboriginal culture at issue.

[62] Aboriginal societies were not strangers to the notions of exclusive physical possession equivalent to common law notions of title: *Delgamuukw*, at para. 156. They often exercised such control over their village sites and larger areas of land which they exploited for agriculture, hunting, fishing or gathering. The question is whether the evidence here establishes this sort of possession.

[63] Having laid out the broad picture, it may be useful to examine more closely three issues that evoked particular discussion here — what is meant by exclusion, or what I have referred to as exclusive control; whether nomadic and semi-nomadic peoples can ever claim title to land, as opposed to more restricted rights; and the requirement of continuity.

[64] The first of these sub-issues is the concept of exclusion. The right to control the land and, if necessary, to exclude others from using it is basic to the notion of title at common law. In European-based systems, this right is assumed by dint of law. Determining whether it was present in a pre-sovereignty aboriginal society, however, can pose difficulties. Often, no right to exclude arises by convention or law. So one must look to evidence. But evidence may be hard to find. The area may have been sparsely populated, with the result that clashes and the need to exclude strangers seldom if ever occurred. Or the people may have been peaceful and have chosen to exercise their control by sharing rather than exclusion. It is therefore critical to view the question of exclusion from the aboriginal perspective. To insist on evidence of overt acts of exclusion in such circumstances may, depending on the circumstances, be unfair. The problem is compounded by the difficulty of producing evidence of what happened hundreds of years ago where no tradition of written history exists.

[65] It follows that evidence of acts of exclusion is not required to establish aboriginal title. All that is required is demonstration of effective control of the land by the group, from which a reasonable inference can be drawn that it could have excluded others had it chosen to do so. The fact that history, insofar as it can be ascertained, discloses no adverse claimants

may support this inference. This is what is meant by the requirement of aboriginal title that the lands have been occupied in an exclusive manner.

[66] The second sub-issue is whether nomadic and semi-nomadic peoples can ever claim title to aboriginal land, as distinguished from rights to use the land in traditional ways. The answer is that it depends on the evidence. As noted above, possession at common law is a contextual, nuanced concept. Whether a nomadic people enjoyed sufficient "physical possession" to give them title to the land, is a question of fact, depending on all the circumstances, in particular the nature of the land and the manner in which it is commonly used. Not every nomadic passage or use will ground title to land; thus this Court in *Adams* asserts that one of the reasons that aboriginal rights cannot be dependent on aboriginal title is that this would deny any aboriginal rights to nomadic peoples ... . On the other hand, *Delgamuukw* contemplates that "physical occupation" sufficient to ground title to land may be established by "regular use of definite tracts of land for hunting, fishing or otherwise exploiting its resources" ... . In each case, the question is whether a degree of physical occupation or use equivalent to common law title has been made out.

[67] The third sub-issue is continuity. The requirement of continuity in its most basic sense simply means that claimants must establish they are right holders. Modern-day claimants must establish a connection with the pre-sovereignty group upon whose practices they rely to assert title or claim to a more restricted aboriginal right. The right is based on pre-sovereignty aboriginal practices. To claim it, a modern people must show that the right is the descendant of those practices. Continuity may also be raised in this sense. To claim title, the group's connection with the land must be shown to have been "of a central significance to their distinctive culture" ... . If the group has "maintained a substantial connection" with the land since sovereignty, this establishes the required "central significance" ... .

[68] Underlying all these issues is the need for a sensitive and generous approach to the evidence tendered to establish aboriginal rights, be they the right to title or lesser rights to fish, hunt or gather. Aboriginal peoples did not write down events in their pre-sovereignty histories. Therefore, orally transmitted history must be accepted, provided the conditions of usefulness and reasonable reliability set out in *Mitchell v. M.N.R.*, [2001] 1 S.C.R. 911, 2001 SCC 33, are respected. Usefulness asks whether the oral history provides evidence that would not otherwise be available or evidence of the aboriginal perspective on the right claimed. Reasonable reliability ensures that the witness represents a credible source of the particular people's history. In determining the usefulness and reliability of oral histories, judges must resist facile assumptions based on Eurocentric traditions of gathering and passing on historical facts.

[69] The evidence, oral and documentary, must be evaluated from the aboriginal perspective. What would a certain practice or event have signified in their world and value system? Having evaluated the evidence, the final step is to translate the facts found and thus interpreted into a modern common law right. The right must be accurately delineated in a

way that reflects common law traditions, while respecting the aboriginal perspective.

[70] In summary, exclusive possession in the sense of intention and capacity to control is required to establish aboriginal title. Typically, this is established by showing regular occupancy or use of definite tracts of land for hunting, fishing or exploiting resources … . Less intensive uses may give rise to different rights. The requirement of physical occupation must be generously interpreted taking into account both the aboriginal perspective and the perspective of the common law … . These principles apply to nomadic and semi-nomadic aboriginal groups; the right in each case depends on what the evidence establishes. Continuity is required, in the sense of showing the group's descent from the pre-sovereignty group whose practices are relied on for the right. On all these matters, evidence of oral history is admissible, provided it meets the requisite standards of usefulness and reasonable reliability. The ultimate goal is to translate the pre-sovereignty aboriginal right to a modern common law right. This must be approached with sensitivity to the aboriginal perspective as well as fidelity to the common law concepts involved.

C. *Application of the Legal Test*

[71] The cases proceeded on the basis that the British had established sovereignty in the middle of the 18th century: in *Bernard* 1759 and in *Marshall* 1713 for Mainland Nova Scotia and 1763 for Cape Breton. The British took sovereignty over lands populated by the French, Acadian settlers and the Mi'kmaq.

[72] The trial judge in each case applied the correct test to determine whether the respondents' claim to aboriginal title was established. In each case they required proof of sufficiently regular and exclusive use of the cutting sites by Mi'kmaq people at the time of assertion of sovereignty.

[73] In *Marshall*, Curran Prov. Ct. J. reviewed the authorities and concluded that the line separating sufficient and insufficient occupancy for title is between irregular use of undefined lands on the one hand and regular use of defined lands on the other. "Settlements constitute regular use of defined lands, but they are only one instance of it" (para. 141).

[74] In *Bernard*, Lordon Prov. Ct. J. likewise found that occasional visits to an area did not establish title; there must be "evidence of capacity to retain exclusive control" (para. 110) over the land claimed.

[75] These tests correctly reflect the jurisprudence as discussed above.

[76] Holding otherwise, Cromwell J.A. in *Marshall* held that this test was too strict and that it was sufficient to prove occasional entry and acts from which an intention to occupy the land could be inferred. Similarly, in *Bernard*, Daigle J.A. held that the trial judge erred in requiring proof of specific acts of occupation and regular use in order to ground aboriginal title. It was not in error to state, as Cromwell J.A. did, that acts from which intention to occupy the land could be inferred may ground a claim to common law title. However, as discussed above, this must be coupled with

sufficiently regular and exclusive use in order to establish title in the common law sense.

[77] Cromwell J.A. found that this additional requirement is not consistent with the semi-nomadic culture or lifestyle of the Mi'kmaq. With respect, this argument is circular. It starts with the premise that it would be unfair to deny the Mi'kmaq title. In order to avoid this result, it posits that the usual indicia of title at common law — possession of the land in the sense of exclusive right to control — should be diminished because the pre-sovereignty practices proved do not establish title on that test. As discussed, the task of the court is to sensitively assess the evidence and then find the equivalent modern common law right. The common law right to title is commensurate with exclusionary rights of control. That is what it means and has always meant. If the ancient aboriginal practices do not indicate that type of control, then title is not the appropriate right. To confer title in the absence of evidence of sufficiently regular and exclusive pre-sovereignty occupation, would transform the ancient right into a new and different right. It would also obliterate the distinction that this Court has consistently made between lesser aboriginal rights like the right to fish and the highest aboriginal right, the right to title to the land: *Adams* and *Côté*.

D. *Assessment of the Evidence*

[78] The question remains whether the trial judges, having applied essentially the right test, erred in their assessment of the evidence or application of the law to the evidence. Absent this, there is no ground for appellate intervention. As discussed, the evidence of aboriginal practices must be assessed from the aboriginal perspective. The question is whether the practices on a broad sense correspond to the right claimed.

[79] Curran Prov. Ct. J. in *Marshall* reviewed the facts extensively and summarized his conclusions as follows:

a) The Mi'kmaq of 18th century Nova Scotia could be described as "moderately nomadic" as were the Algonquins in *Côté*, *supra*. The Mi'kmaq, too, moved with the seasons and circumstances to follow their resources. They did not necessarily return to the same campsites each year. Nevertheless, for decades before and after 1713 local communities on mainland Nova Scotia stayed generally in the areas where they had been.

b) On the mainland the Mi'kmaq made intensive use of bays and rivers and at least nearby hunting grounds. The evidence is just not clear about exactly where those lands were or how extensive they were. It is most unlikely all the mainland was included in those lands. There just weren't enough people for that.

c) As for Cape Breton, there simply is not enough evidence of where the Mi'kmaq were and how long they were there to conclude that they occupied any land to the extent required for aboriginal title.

d) In particular, there is no clear evidence that the Mi'kmaq of the time made any use, let alone regular use, of the cutting sites where these charges arose, either on the mainland or in Cape Breton. The [Respondents] have not satisfied me on the balance of probability that their ancestors had aboriginal title to those sites. [para. 142]

[80] Applying the law to these facts, Curran Prov. Ct. J. "concluded that the Mi'kmaq of the 18th century on mainland Nova Scotia probably had aboriginal title to lands around their local communities, but not to the cutting sites" (para. 143).

[81] In *Bernard*, Lordon Prov. Ct. J. also made a thorough review of the evidence of Mi'kmaq occupation of lands at the time of sovereignty, and concluded that it did not establish title:

> Given the evidence before me, I cannot conclude that the land at the *locus in quo* was used on a regular basis for hunting and fishing. Such trips made there in 1759 would have been occasional at best. Occasional forays for hunting, fishing and gathering are not sufficient to establish Aboriginal title in the land.

> Furthermore, the evidence does not convince me that the Mi'kmaq were the only occasional visitors to the area. From the time of contact onward the Indians welcomed Europeans. ...

> ...

> There was no evidence of capacity to retain exclusive control and, given the vast area of land and the small population they did not have the capacity to exercise exclusive control. In addition, according to the evidence of Chief Augustine, the Mi'kmaq had neither the intent nor the desire to exercise exclusive control, which, in my opinion, is fatal to the claim for Aboriginal title. [paras. 107-8 and 110]

[82] The Nova Scotia Court of Appeal did not criticize the findings of fact in *Marshall*, basing its reversal on the legal test. However, in *Bernard*, the New Brunswick Court of Appeal criticized aspects of Lordon Prov. Ct. J.'s approach to the facts. Daigle J.A. found that the trial judge failed to give appropriate weight to the evidence of the pattern of land use and discounted the evidence of oral traditions. Daigle J.A. emphasized that during the winter, the Mi'kmaq would break into smaller hunting groups and disperse inland, fishing and hunting in the interior. He also emphasized the proximity of the cutting sites to traditional settlement sites. However, these facts, even if overlooked by the trial judge, do not support a finding of aboriginal title on the principles discussed above. They amount only, as Daigle J.A. put it, to "compelling evidence ... that the cutting site area ... would have been within the range of seasonal use and occupation by the Miramichi Mi'kmaq" (para. 127). Assuming the trial judge overlooked or undervalued this evidence, the evidence would have made no difference and the error was inconsequential.

[83] I conclude that there is no ground to interfere with the trial judges' conclusions on the absence of common law aboriginal title.

E. *Extinguishment, Infringement, Justification and Membership*

[84] The Crown argued that even if common law aboriginal title is established, it was extinguished by statutes passed between 1774 and 1862

relating to forestry on Crown lands. Since aboriginal title is not established, it is unnecessary to consider this issue. Nor is it necessary to consider whether the statutes under which the respondents were charged infringe aboriginal title, or if so, whether that infringement is justified. Finally, it is unnecessary to consider continuity issues relating to the sites claimed.

F. *Aboriginal Title Under the Royal Proclamation*

[85] The respondents argue that the *Royal Proclamation* of 1763 ... reserved to the Mi'kmaq title in all unceded, unpurchased land in the former Nova Scotia, which later was divided into Nova Scotia and New Brunswick. I agree with the courts below that this argument must be rejected.

[86] The *Royal Proclamation* must be interpreted liberally, and any matters of doubt resolved in favour of aboriginal peoples ... . Further, the *Royal Proclamation* must be interpreted in light of its status as the "Magna Carta" of Indian rights in North America and Indian "Bill of Rights" ... .

[87] The first issue is whether the *Royal Proclamation* applies to the former colony of Nova Scotia. The *Royal Proclamation* states that it applies to "our other Colonies or Plantations in America" and at the beginning annexes Cape Breton and Prince Edward Island to Nova Scotia. Other evidence, including correspondence between London and Nova Scotia, suggests that contemporaries viewed the *Royal Proclamation* as applying to Nova Scotia (*Marshall*, trial decision, at para. 112). Interpreting the *Royal Proclamation* liberally and resolving doubts in favour of the aboriginals, I proceed on the basis that it applied to the former colony of Nova Scotia.

[88] This brings us to the text of the *Royal Proclamation*. The text supports the Crown's argument that it did not grant the Mi'kmaq title to all the territories of the former colony of Nova Scotia. The respondents rely principally on three provisions of the *Royal Proclamation*.

[89] The first provision is the preamble to the part addressing aboriginal peoples which reads:

> And whereas it is just and reasonable, and essential to our Interest, and the Security of our Colonies, that the several Nations or Tribes of Indians with whom We are connected, and who live under our Protection, should not be molested or disturbed <u>in the Possession of such Parts of Our Dominions and Territories as, not having been ceded to or purchased by Us, are reserved to them, or any of them, as their Hunting Grounds</u>.

[90] As part of the preamble, this does not accord new rights. When the *Royal Proclamation* directed the reservation or annexation of land it used terms of grant ("We do therefore ... declare it to be our Royal Will and Pleasure, that" or "We have thought fit, with the Advice of our Privy Council" or "We do hereby command") and referred to the specific tracts of land ("all the Lands and Territories not included within the Limits of Our said Three new Governments, or within the Limits of the Territory granted to the Hudson's Bay Company").

[91] The second provision of the *Royal Proclamation* relied on by the respondents is the following:

> We do therefore ... declare it to be our Royal Will and Pleasure, that no Governor or Commander in Chief ... in any of our other Colonies or Plantations in America do presume ... to grant Warrants of Survey, or pass Patents for any Lands beyond the Heads or Sources of any of the Rivers which fall into the Atlantic Ocean from the West and North West, <u>or upon any Lands whatever, which, not having been ceded to or purchased by Us as aforesaid, are reserved to the said Indians, or any of them.</u>

[92] The respondents argue that the underlined phrase reserved to the Mi'kmaq all unceded or unpurchased land within the colony of Nova Scotia. However, this phrase merely repeats the wording from the preamble. It does not create new rights in land. This is confirmed by the fact that it does not use the direct and clear language used elsewhere to reserve lands to the Indians, and is reinforced by its relation to subsequent provisions. If the *Royal Proclamation* had reserved virtually the entire province of Nova Scotia to the Mi'kmaq, the subsequent requirement, that settlers leave lands "still reserved to the . . . Indians", would have had the effect of ejecting all the settlers from the colony. Yet the historical evidence suggests extensive settlement of Nova Scotia shortly after the *Royal Proclamation*.

[93] The third provision of the *Royal Proclamation* upon which the respondents rely requires that "no private Person do presume to make any purchase from the said Indians of any Lands reserved to the said Indians, within those parts of our Colonies where, We have thought proper to allow Settlement". The respondents argue that this reinforces reservation of Nova Scotia to the Indians. This language, however, is equally consistent with referring to newly reserved lands as it is to previously reserved lands and does not definitively argue in either direction.

[94] The jurisprudence also supports the Crown's interpretation of the text of the *Royal Proclamation*. In *R. v. Sioui*, [1990] 1 S.C.R. 1025, this Court held that "the Royal Proclamation of October 7, 1763 organized the territories recently acquired by Great Britain and reserved two types of land for the Indians: that located <u>outside the colony's territorial limits</u> and the establishments authorized by the Crown <u>inside the colony</u>" (p. 1052 (emphasis added), *per* Lamer J.).

[95] Finally, the historical context and purpose of the *Royal Proclamation* do not support the claim that the *Royal Proclamation* granted the colony of Nova Scotia to the Indians. The *Royal Proclamation* was concluded in the context of discussions about how to administer and secure the territories acquired by Britain in the first Treaty of Paris in 1763. In the discussions between the Board of Trade and the Privy Council about what would eventually become the *Royal Proclamation*, the imperial territories were from the beginning divided into two categories: lands to be settled and those whose settlement would be deferred. Nova Scotia was clearly land marked for settlement by the Imperial policy promoting its settlement by the "Planters", "Ulster Protestants", Scots, Loyalists and others. The Lords of Trade had urged "the compleat Settlement of Your Majesty's Colony of

Nova Scotia": Lords of Trade to Lord Egremont, June 8, 1763 ... . The settlement aspirations of the British were recognized by Binnie J. for the majority in *Marshall 1* when he stated that the recently concluded treaties with the Mi'kmaq of 1760-61 were designed to facilitate a "wave of European settlement" (para. 21). The *Royal Proclamation* sought to ensure the future security of the colonies by minimizing potential conflict between settlers and Indians by protecting existing Indian territories, treaty rights and enjoining abusive land transactions. Reserving Nova Scotia to the Indians would completely counter the planned settlement of Nova Scotia.

[96] In summary, the text, the jurisprudence and historic policy, all support the conclusion that the *Royal Proclamation* did not reserve the former colony of Nova Scotia to the Mi'kmaq.

G.   *Aboriginal Title Through Belcher's Proclamation*

[97] Colonial governors, including those of the former colony of Nova Scotia, were issued a Royal Instruction on December 9, 1761 forbidding them from granting lands adjacent to or occupied by the Indians, including "any Lands so reserved to or claimed by the said Indians". Pursuant to the instruction, in 1762 the then governor of Nova Scotia, Jonathan Belcher, issued a Proclamation directing settlers to remove themselves from lands "reserved to or claimed by" the Indians. It further directed that "for the more special purpose of <u>hunting, fowling and fishing</u>, I do hereby strictly injoin and caution all persons to avoid all molestation of the said Indians in their said Claims, <u>till His Majesty's pleasure in this behalf shall be signified</u>" (emphasis added).

[98] Three issues arise in determining the applicability of *Belcher's Proclamation*: first the geographical area it covers, second, the activities it covers and third, whether it was concluded with the relevant authority.

[99] First, *Belcher's Proclamation* defines areas from Musquodobiot to Canso, from Canso along the Northumberland Strait to Miramichi, Bay of Chaleur, Gulf of St. Lawrence and along the Gaspé "and so along the coast". Lordon Prov. Ct. J. in *Bernard* found that it granted only a "common right to the Sea Coast" (para. 116). I see no reason to disturb this finding.

[100] Second, Lordon Prov. Ct. J. found that *Belcher's Proclamation* was, on its terms, limited to "hunting, fowling and fishing" and did not cover logging (para. 116). Again, I see no reason to reject this conclusion. These two conclusions alone suffice to resolve this issue.

[101] The third issue is whether *Belcher's Proclamation* was issued with the relevant authority. *Belcher's Proclamation* provoked immediate adverse reaction and dissatisfaction from the Lords of Trade. On July 2, 1762, Belcher wrote to them to explain what he had done. He explained that he had made a return to the Indians "for a Common right to the Sea Coast from Cape Fronsac onwards for Fishing without disturbance or Opposition by any of His Majesty's Subjects". He went on to assure the Lords of Trade that it was only temporary "till His Majesty's pleasure should be signified". In fact, His Majesty never approved *Belcher's Proclamation*. The

text of the Proclamation and the evidence of Drs. Patterson and Wicken accepted by Lordon Prov. Ct. J. confirms its intended temporary nature (para. 116).

[102] On December 3, 1762, the Lords of Trade responded in a strongly worded letter condemning *Belcher's Proclamation* and instructing that the Royal Instruction referred only to "Claims of the Indians, as heretofore of long usage admitted and allowed on the part of the Government and Confirmed to them by solemn Compacts". Interestingly, the Lords of Trade state that if it were necessary to reserve lands for the Indians it should not have been the lands along the coast, "but rather the Lands amongst the woods and lakes where the wild beasts resort and are to be found in plenty", supporting the view that *Belcher's Proclamation* did not grant rights over cutting sites further inland.

[103] By letter of March 20, 1764 the Lords of Trade signified His Majesty's disallowance of *Belcher's Proclamation* to Belcher's successor, Governor Wilmot. The Lords of Trade noted that this claim was "inconsistent with his Majesty's Right, and so injurious to the Commercial Interest of His Subjects". They further stated that the grant of the coastal lands to the Indians was contrary to the true spirit and meaning of the Royal Instructions upon which *Belcher's Proclamation* was based. They referred to "His Majesty's disallowance" of such claim, though nowhere did they state that *Belcher's Proclamation* was void *ab initio*. The Lords of Trade instructed Governor Wilmot to "induce the Indians to recede from so extraordinary and inadmissible a claim, if he had not already done so"; however this was to be done in the "mildest manner". This was apparently done, although no formal action was taken to revoke *Belcher's Proclamation*.

[104] Against this it is argued that what matters is what the Indians thought *Belcher's Proclamation* meant, as opposed to whether Belcher in fact had the power to make the Proclamation. The Proclamation was never formally revoked. The Mi'kmaq were apparently told their claims to the colony's lands were invalid, although in the "mildest manner". However, there is no evidence that the British misled the Mi'kmaq or acted dishonourably toward them in explaining that *Belcher's Proclamation* was disallowed. I see no reason to interfere with the conclusion of Robertson J.A. in *Bernard* that "[t]his is one case where the Crown's silence cannot validate that which is otherwise invalid" (para. 409).

[105] In summary, the defence based on *Belcher's Proclamation* faces formidable hurdles. Did Belcher have the authority to make it, or was it void *ab initio*, as claimed at the time? If it was valid, was it temporary and conditional on further order of His Majesty? If invalid, where is the evidence of Mi'kmaq reliance or dishonorable Crown conduct? Finally, whatever the legal effect of *Belcher's Proclamation*, it seems that it was intended to apply only to certain coastal areas and to "hunting, fowling and fishing". On the evidence before us, it is impossible to conclude that *Belcher's Proclamation* could provide a defence to the charges against the respondents.

IV. *Conclusion*

[106] The trial judge in each case applied the correct legal tests and drew conclusions of fact that are fully supported by the evidence. Their conclusions that the respondents possessed neither a treaty right [this issue is examined in Chapter 4] to trade in logs nor aboriginal title to the cutting sites must therefore stand. Nor is there any basis for finding title in the *Royal Proclamation* or *Belcher's Proclamation*.

. . . . .

LeBel J. (Fish J. Concurring): —

I. *Introduction*

[110] I have read the reasons of the Chief Justice. While I am in agreement with the ultimate disposition, I have concerns about various parts of them. ... On the issue of aboriginal title, I take the view that given the nature of land use by aboriginal peoples — and in particular the nomadic nature of that use by many First Nations — in the course of their history, the approach adopted by the majority is too narrowly focused on common law concepts relating to property interests. ...

. . . . .

III. *Aboriginal Title*

[126] Although the test for aboriginal title set out in the Chief Justice's reasons does not foreclose the possibility that semi-nomadic peoples would be able to establish aboriginal title, it may prove to be fundamentally incompatible with a nomadic or semi-nomadic lifestyle. This test might well amount to a denial that any aboriginal title could have been created by such patterns of nomadic or semi-nomadic occupation or use ...

[127] In my view, aboriginal conceptions of territoriality, land-use and property should be used to modify and adapt the traditional common law concepts of property in order to develop an occupancy standard that incorporates both the aboriginal and common law approaches. Otherwise, we might be implicitly accepting the position that aboriginal peoples had no rights in land prior to the assertion of Crown sovereignty because their views of property or land use do not fit within Euro-centric conceptions of property rights. ...

[128] It is very difficult to introduce aboriginal conceptions of property and ownership into the modern property law concepts of the civil law and common law systems, according to which land is considered to be a stock in trade of the economy. Aboriginal title has been recognized by the common law and is in part defined by the common law, but it is grounded in aboriginal customary laws relating to land. The interest is proprietary in nature and is derived from inter-traditional notions of ownership: "The

idea is to reconcile indigenous and non-indigenous legal traditions by paying attention to the Aboriginal perspective on the meaning of the right at stake" (J. Borrows, "Creating an Indigenous Legal Community" (2005), 50 *McGill L.J.* 153, at p. 173).

[129] This Court has on many occasions explained that aboriginal title is a *sui generis* interest in land. A dimension of the *sui generis* aspect of aboriginal title that is of particular relevance to the issues on appeal is the source of such title. ... The Court must give equal consideration to the aboriginal and common law perspectives. An analysis which seeks to reconcile aboriginal and European perspectives may not draw a distinction between nomadic and sedentary modes of use or of occupation. Both modes would suffice to create the connection between the land and the First Nations which forms the core of aboriginal title.

[130] The role of the aboriginal perspective cannot be simply to help in the interpretation of aboriginal practices in order to assess whether they conform to common law concepts of title. The aboriginal perspective shapes the very concept of aboriginal title. "Aboriginal law should not just be received as evidence that Aboriginal peoples did something in the past on a piece of land. It is more than evidence: it is actually law. And so, there should be some way to bring to the decision-making process those laws that arise from the standards of the indigenous people before the court" (Borrows, at p. 173). ...

[131] At common law, the physical fact of occupation is proof of possession. This explains the common law theory underlying the recognition of aboriginal title that is set out by the Chief Justice at para. 39: "an aboriginal group which occupied land at the time of European sovereignty and never ceded or otherwise lost its right to that land, continues to enjoy title to it". If aboriginal title is a right derived from the historical occupation and possession of land by aboriginal peoples, then notions and principles of ownership cannot be framed exclusively by reference to common law concepts. The patterns and nature of aboriginal occupation of land should inform the standard necessary to prove aboriginal title. The common law notion that "physical occupation is proof of possession" remains, but the nature of the occupation is shaped by the aboriginal perspective, which includes a history of nomadic or semi-nomadic modes of occupation.

[132] At the time of the assertion of British sovereignty, North America was not treated by the Crown as *res nullius*. The jurisprudence of this Court has recognized the factual and legal existence of aboriginal occupation prior to that time. In *Calder v. Attorney-General of British Columbia*, [1973] S.C.R. 313, Judson J. wrote that "when the settlers came, the Indians were there, organized in societies and occupying the land as their forefathers had done for centuries" (p. 328). Hall J., dissenting, also found that indigenous legal traditions pre-existed the Crown's assertion of sovereignty, and he recognized the existence of concepts of ownership that were "indigenous to their culture and capable of articulation under the common law" (p. 375).

[133] The *Royal Proclamation* of 1763 is evidence of British recognition of aboriginal modes of possession of the land. As La Forest J. noted in *Delgamuukw*, the huge tracts of lands that were reserved for aboriginal groups were not limited to villages or permanent settlements (para. 200). In a similar vein, the Robinson Treaties, the Numbered Treaties, and the entire treaty system did not formally acknowledge the existence of aboriginal title, but nonetheless evince the Crown's recognition that aboriginal peoples possessed certain rights in the land even if many of them were nomadic at the time. The Crown's claim to sovereignty did not affect aboriginal rights of occupancy and possession. In *Mitchell v. M.N.R.*, [2001] 1 S.C.R. 911, 2001 SCC 33, McLachlin C.J., writing for the majority, wrote:

> Accordingly, European settlement did not terminate the interests of aboriginal peoples arising from their historical occupation and use of the land. To the contrary, aboriginal interests and customary laws were presumed to survive the assertion of sovereignty, and were absorbed into the common law as rights, unless (1) they were incompatible with the Crown's assertion of sovereignty, (2) they were surrendered voluntarily via the treaty process, or (3) the government extinguished them: see B. Slattery, "Understanding Aboriginal Rights" (1987), 66 *Can. Bar Rev.* 727. [para. 10]

[134] Nomadic peoples and their modes of occupancy of land cannot be ignored when defining the concept of aboriginal title to land in Canada. "The natural and inevitable consequence of rejecting enlarged *terra nullius* was not just recognition of indigenous occupants, but also acceptance of the validity of their prior possession and title" (Hepburn, at p. 79). To ignore their particular relationship to the land is to adopt the view that prior to the assertion of Crown sovereignty Canada was not occupied. Such an approach is clearly unacceptable and incongruent with the Crown's recognition that aboriginal peoples were in possession of the land when the Crown asserted sovereignty. Aboriginal title reflects this fact of prior use and occupation of the land together with the relationship of aboriginal peoples to the land and the customary laws of ownership. This aboriginal interest in the land is a burden on the Crown's underlying title.

[135] This qualification or burden on the Crown's title has been characterized as a usufructuary right. The concept of a community usufruct over land was first discussed by this Court in *St. Catharines Milling and Lumber Co. v. The Queen* (1887), 13 S.C.R. 577. Ritchie C.J. used this concept as an analogy to explain the relationship between Crown and aboriginal interests in the land. The usufruct concept is useful because it is premised on a right of property that is divided between an owner and a usufructuary. A usufructuary title to all unsurrendered lands is understood to protect aboriginal peoples in the absolute use and enjoyment of their lands.

[136] If this form of *dominium utile* is recognized as belonging to aboriginal peoples and the *dominium directum* is considered to be in the Crown, then it seems to follow that the test for proof of aboriginal title cannot simply reflect common law concepts of property and ownership. The nature and patterns of land use that are capable of giving rise to a

claim for title are not uniform and are potentially as diverse as the aboriginal peoples that possessed the land prior to the assertion of Crown sovereignty. The fact that a tract of land was used for hunting instead of agriculture does not mean that the group did not possess the land in such a way as to acquire aboriginal title. Taking into account the aboriginal perspective on the occupation of land means that physical occupation as understood by the modern common law is not the governing criterion. The group's relationship with the land is paramount. To impose rigid concepts and criteria is to ignore aboriginal social and cultural practices that may reflect the significance of the land to the group seeking title. The mere fact that the group travelled within its territory and did not cultivate the land should not take away from its title claim.

[137] The standard of proof required to ground a claim must therefore reflect the patterns of occupation of the land prior to the assertion of British sovereignty. If the presence of an aboriginal group on the land at the time of the assertion of sovereignty is the source of aboriginal title and the explanation for the burden on the Crown's underlying title, then pre-sovereignty patterns of use are highly relevant to the issue of occupation.

[138] As explained above, the common law principle that "occupation is proof of possession in law" supports the proposition that the claimant must demonstrate physical occupation of the land claimed. In the context of aboriginal title claims, the physical fact of sedentary and continuous occupation is only one of the sources of title. According to Lamer C.J. in *Delgamuukw*, aboriginal title affords legal protection to historical patterns of occupation in recognition of the importance of the relationship of an aboriginal community to its land (para. 126). At paragraph 128 he explained that

> one of the critical elements in the determination of whether a particular aboriginal group has aboriginal title to certain lands is the matter of the occupancy of those lands. Occupancy is determined by reference to the activities that have taken place on the land and the uses to which the land has been put by the particular group. If lands are so occupied, there will exist a special bond between the group and the land in question such that the land will be part of the definition of the group's distinctive culture. ...

[139] The aboriginal perspective on the occupation of their land can also be gleaned in part, but not exclusively, from pre-sovereignty systems of aboriginal law. The relevant laws consisted of elements of the practices, customs and traditions of aboriginal peoples and might include a land tenure system or laws governing land use.

[140] In *Delgamuukw*, Lamer C.J. acknowledged having stated in *R. v. Adams*, [1996] 3 S.C.R. 101, that a claim to title is made out when a group can demonstrate "that their connection with the piece of land ... was of a central significance to their distinctive culture" (*Adams*, at para. 26). He concluded that this requirement, while remaining a crucial part of the test for aboriginal rights generally, is subsumed by the requirement of occupancy in the test for aboriginal title. This demonstrates that anyone considering the degree of occupation sufficient to establish title must be mindful that aboriginal title is ultimately premised upon the notion that

the specific land or territory at issue was of central significance to the aboriginal group's culture. Occupation should therefore be proved by evidence not of regular and intensive use of the land but of the traditions and culture of the group that connect it with the land. Thus, intensity of use is related not only to common law notions of possession but also to the aboriginal perspective.

[141] The record in the courts below lacks the evidentiary foundation necessary to make legal findings on the issue of aboriginal title in respect of the cutting sites in Nova Scotia and New Brunswick and, as a result, the respondents in these cases have failed to sufficiently establish their title claim. In the circumstances, I do not wish to suggest that this decision represents a final determination of the issue of aboriginal title rights in Nova Scotia or New Brunswick. A final determination should be made only where there is an adequate evidentiary foundation that fully examines the relevant legal and historical record. The evidentiary problems may reflect the particular way in which these constitutional issues were brought before the courts.

IV. *Summary Conviction Proceedings*

[142] Although many of the aboriginal rights cases that have made their way to this Court began by way of summary conviction proceedings, it is clear to me that we should re-think the appropriateness of litigating aboriginal treaty, rights and title issues in the context of criminal trials. The issues that are determined in the context of these cases have little to do with the criminality of the accused's conduct; rather, the claims would properly be the subject of civil actions for declarations. Procedural and evidentiary difficulties inherent in adjudicating aboriginal claims arise not only out of the rules of evidence, the interpretation of evidence and the impact of the relevant evidentiary burdens, but also out of the scope of appellate review of the trial judge's findings of fact. These claims may also impact on the competing rights and interests of a number of parties who may have a right to be heard at all stages of the process. In addition, special difficulties come up when dealing with broad title and treaty rights claims that involve geographic areas extending beyond the specific sites relating to the criminal charges.

[143] There is little doubt that the legal issues to be determined in the context of aboriginal rights claims are much larger than the criminal charge itself and that the criminal process is inadequate and inappropriate for dealing with such claims. ...

[144] ... Accordingly, when issues of aboriginal title or other aboriginal rights claims arise in the context of summary conviction proceedings, it may be most beneficial to all concerned to seek a temporary stay of the charges so that the aboriginal claim can be properly litigated in the civil courts. Once the aboriginal rights claim to the area in question is settled, the Crown could decide whether or not to proceed with the criminal charges.

V. *Disposition*

[145] For these reasons, I would concur with my colleague, allow the appeals, dismiss the cross-appeal in *Marshall* and restore the convictions.

---

1. Under what legal doctrine or theory did the Crown acquire title to the land at issue in Nova Scotia and New Brunswick?
2. Does Chief Justice McLachlin's judgment imply that portions of Nova Scotia and New Brunswick were terra nullius prior to European sovereignty?
3. Chief Justice McLachlin wrote (at para. 48): "The Court's task in evaluating a claim for an aboriginal right is to examine the pre-sovereignty aboriginal practice and translate that practice, as faithfully and objectively as it can, into a modern legal right." What are the implications for Aboriginal peoples and the Crown in using the doctrine of "translation" as a concept for the interpretation of Aboriginal title?
4. Nigel Bankes has written: "The language use by Chief Justice McLachlin to describe the 'perspective' of indigenous societies seems deliberately designed to deny the normative significance of that perspective. By contrast the perspective of settler society is consistently and exclusively framed in terms of law and legal system. ... The implication is clear that, while [indigenous] practices may be 'facts', they have no normative significance save what the common law chooses to accord to them." (Nigel Bankes, "Marshall and Bernard: Ignoring the Relevance of Customary Property Laws" (2006) 55 U.N.B.L.J. 120 at 125.) Do you agree with this observation?
5. Why did the Court not directly apply Mi'kmaq law as the standard of proof for occupation of land? What would be the potential risks and rewards of applying Mi'kmaq law to determine Mi'kmaq title?
6. Chief Justice McLachlin wrote that she was "[i]nterpreting the *Royal Proclamation* liberally and resolving doubts in favour of the aboriginals" (para. 87). Do you agree with her assessment regarding her treatment of this document? Did she interpret the *Royal Proclamation* liberally and resolve doubts in the Indians' favour? Did Chief Justice McLachlin approach *Belcher's Proclamation* in the same manner?
7. Chief Justice McLachlin found: "... there is no ground to interfere with the trial judges' conclusions on the absence of common law aboriginal title" (para. 83). The *Royal Proclamation* was also not a source of Aboriginal title (paras. 88, 94, 95). If Aboriginal title does not exist on certain lands in Canada prior to European arrival through either common law or the *Proclamation*, what is the significance of this holding, given the Court's interpretation of Aboriginal title in *Guerin*, *supra*, where Justice Dickson wrote:

Judson and Hall JJ. were in agreement, however, that aboriginal title existed in Canada (at least where it has not been extinguished by appropriate legislative action) independently of the *Royal Proclamation of 1763*. Justice Judson stated expressly that the *Proclamation* was not the "exclusive" source of Indian title (at pp. 152-53, 156 D.L.R., pp. 322-23, 328 S.C.R.). Justice Hall said (at p. 200 D.L.R., p. 390 S.C.R.) that "aboriginal Indian title does not depend on treaty, executive order or legislative enactment.

H. ALTERNATIVES TO ABORIGINAL TITLE LITIGATION

From the discussion in this chapter, it is evident that case law on Aboriginal title has not resulted in many favourable decisions for Aboriginal peoples. Nevertheless, Aboriginal title claims are still being pursued by Aboriginal groups in the courts. There are, however, alternatives to pursuing Aboriginal title claims through the litigation process. These alternatives were created by the federal government through its Comprehensive and Specific Claims processes. As the following excerpt from the Royal Commission on Aboriginal Peoples' Report illustrates, these processes suffer from their own deficiencies that reduce their usefulness as viable alternatives to Aboriginal title litigation.

REPORT OF THE ROYAL COMMISSION ON ABORIGINAL PEOPLES: RESTRUCTURING THE RELATIONSHIP, VOL. 2

(Ottawa: Ministry of Supply and Services Canada, 1996)
at 535-39, 543, 544-49 (references omitted)

The comprehensive claims process

As originally defined by government and set out in the 1982 publication, *In All Fairness*, a comprehensive claim is one based on unextinguished Aboriginal title and is, in effect, a request for the negotiation of a treaty. This is reinforced by subsection 35(3) of the *Constitution Act, 1982*, which recognizes and affirms existing Aboriginal and treaty rights: "'treaty rights' includes rights that now exist by way of land claims agreements or may be so acquired".

The comprehensive claims policy has three elements:

1. the criteria for acceptance under the policy;
2. the rights the Aboriginal group in question is asked to relinquish; and
3. the type and quantity of benefits the federal government will consider providing the Aboriginal group in exchange for the relinquishment of the group's rights.

Criteria for acceptance of claims

Under the comprehensive claims policy (as amended in 1986), the minister of Indian affairs will determine whether to accept a claim on advice from the minister of justice about its acceptability according to legal criteria. An Aboriginal group is therefore expected to submit a statement of claim that complies with the following requirements:

- the claimant has not previously adhered to treaty;
- the claimant group has traditionally used and occupied the territory in question, and this use and occupation continue;
- a description of the extent and location of such land use and occupancy together with a map outlining approximate boundaries; and
- identification of the claimant group, including the names of the bands, tribes or communities on whose behalf the claim is being made, as well as linguistic and cultural affiliation and approximate population figures.

This list might suggest relatively liberal criteria for accepting claims, but in practice the criteria used by the department of justice to assess validity are more rigorous, set out in the 1979 Federal Court decision in *Baker Lake*. Under this decision, as elaborated by the federal government, an Aboriginal group must demonstrate all of the following:

- It is, and was, an organized society.
- It has occupied the specific territory over which it asserts Aboriginal title from time immemorial. The traditional use and occupancy of the territory must have been sufficient to be an established fact at the time of the assertion of sovereignty by European nations.
- The occupation of the territory is largely to the exclusion of other organized societies.
- There is continuing use and occupancy of the land for traditional purposes.
- Aboriginal title and rights to use of resources has not been dealt with by treaty.
- Aboriginal title has not been extinguished by other lawful means.

The last part of this test appears to have been somewhat altered by the 1990 *Sparrow* decision, which held that if the federal government's position is that Aboriginal title has been eliminated by "other lawful means", then its intention to extinguish Aboriginal title must have been "clear and plain". Federal policy continues to reflect other parts of the *Baker Lake* decision, however, despite Supreme Court decisions like *Simon* and *Bear Island* that implicitly reject evidentiary tests for Aboriginal claims that are impossible to meet in the absence of written evidence.

·····

What Aboriginal people must relinquish

... [T]he Crown's interpretation of the treaty relationship was, historically, that Aboriginal nations had received specified benefits in exchange for a blanket extinguishment of their title or rights. In keeping with this practice, the original comprehensive claims policy specified that an Aboriginal group must surrender all Aboriginal rights in return for a grant of rights specified in a settlement agreement. The government has moved very little from this position. ... [T]he amended federal policy allows for an "alternative" to the surrender of all Aboriginal rights — "the cession and surrender of Aboriginal title in non-reserved areas", while "allowing any Aboriginal title that exists to continue in specified reserve areas, granting to the beneficiaries defined rights applicable to the entire settlement area". This policy also notes that the only Aboriginal rights to be relinquished are those related to the use of and title to lands and resources. In practice, however, only one of the recent settlements, the Yukon Umbrella Final Agreement, comes under this "alternative". In that agreement the only Aboriginal rights that are not surrendered are surface interests in the lands that are retained as Indian lands. Thus, it would appear that the current policy allows for only minimal divergence from the basic position of requiring a total surrender of all Aboriginal rights.

Scope of the benefits Aboriginal groups can negotiate

Federal policy sets out a number of areas where benefits can be negotiated, including lands (including offshore lands), wildlife harvesting rights, subsurface rights, natural resources revenue sharing, environmental management, local self-government and financial compensation. Certain limitations on each of these areas are especially noteworthy.

First, until the recent federal announcement on self-government, these issues were based on delegated authority, not the inherent right, and were the subject of separate negotiations governed by the federal policy on community self-government negotiations. Under the comprehensive claims policy, issues of self-government will be contained in separate agreements and separate enacting legislation. They will not receive constitutional protection unless there is a general constitutional amendment to this effect.

Second, natural resources revenue-sharing provisions will be subject to limitations, which might include an absolute dollar amount, the duration of the revenue-sharing provisions or a reduction of the percentage of royalties generated. Thus, natural resources revenue-sharing arrangements are seen more correctly as a way of spreading cash compensation over a longer period of time, rather than securing a significant continuing source of revenue for Aboriginal claimants.

Third, on the issue of Aboriginal participation in managing lands and resources, the policy requires that any arrangements recognize the overriding powers of non-Aboriginal governments. While numerous management boards and committees have been set up under the various comprehensive land claims agreements, these bodies remain advisory, although some have found innovative ways to prevent their recommendations from being ignored. Nonetheless, non-Aboriginal governments retain full jurisdiction and final decision-making authority.

The lack of interim measures

One of the most significant weaknesses of comprehensive land claims policy is the lack of any provision for interim measures before submission of a comprehensive claim and during negotiations. Governments are free to create new third-party interests on the traditional lands of Aboriginal claimants right up until the moment a claims agreement is signed.

... It should not be necessary for Aboriginal people to mount blockades to obtain interim measures while their assertions of title are being dealt with.

· · · · ·

The Commission cannot support the extinguishment of Aboriginal rights, either blanket or partial. It seems to us completely incompatible with the relationship between Aboriginal peoples and the land. This relationship is fundamental to the Aboriginal world view and sense of identity; to abdicate the responsibilities associated with it would have deep spiritual and cultural implications. However, we recognize that there will be circumstances where the Aboriginal party to a treaty may agree to a partial extinguishment of rights in return for other advantages offered in treaty negotiations. We would urge, however, that this course of action be taken only after all other options have been considered carefully.

· · · · ·

The specific claims process

As defined by government and set out in the 1982 publication, *Outstanding Business*, a specific claim is one based upon a "lawful obligation" of Canada to Indians. Claims based on unextinguished Aboriginal title are expressly excluded, as were pre-Confederation claims until 1991. A specific claim, from the government's point of view, is little more than a claim for compensation.

... [T]he concept of lawful obligation remains at the centre of specific claims policy, although there is no agreement upon what facts or relationships might constitute such an obligation. In a paper prepared for the department of Indian affairs before publication of the policy, G.V. La Forest suggested that "we are not so much concerned with a *legal obligation* in the sense of enforceable in the courts as with a *government obligation of fair treatment* if a lawful obligation is established to its satisfaction". ... The department of justice, however, assesses the validity of claims in terms of their chances of success in court and applies technical rules of evidence. Thus, legal validity informs the government's assessment of whether a claim properly falls within the scope of federal policy. This assessment is further informed, if not defined, by the examples of lawful obligations set out in the policy itself:

A lawful obligation may arise in any one of the following circumstances:

1. The non-fulfilment of a treaty or agreement between Indians and the Crown.
2. A breach of an obligation arising out of the *Indian Act* or other statutes pertaining to Indians and the regulations thereunder.
3. A breach of an obligation arising out of government administration of Indian funds or other assets.
4. An illegal disposition of Indian land.

The more restrictive view of lawful obligation is that a claim must fall within one of these examples in order to come within the policy. The most restrictive view is that a claim must fall within one of the examples and also within the compensation guidelines; that is, compensation in the form of money or land must be possible.

A narrow and restrictive reading of the policy leads to the exclusion of many claims based on non-fulfilment of treaty obligations. Assertions of the right to exercise hunting and fishing rights, for example, or of rights to education, health and other benefits, are not seen by government as coming within the policy even though they are justiciable rights. Even seemingly uncontroversial obligations, such as the provision of land under the terms of treaties, have been subject to the same narrow reading. ... It is the great irony of the policy, and the most common complaint against it, that it was intended to broaden the concept of negotiable claims beyond those that might be proven strictly in court. In fact, it does precisely the opposite. Nowhere is this more evident than in the failure to incorporate, as a basis of claim, breach of fiduciary obligation, which was established as actionable in 1984 by the Supreme Court of Canada.

In addition, the government's determination of validity involves a clear conflict of interest. The department of justice faces a conundrum, because the policy directs it to ignore technical rules of evidence and the issue of justiciability. Yet how can it advise government that a treaty includes one set of terms, with one meaning for purposes of claims policy, but another set of terms, with a different meaning, for purposes of litigation?

. . . . .

As a result, the department of justice advises on treaties in the same way that it litigates them.

. . . . .

The policy interpretations and practices noted here create the perception, if not the reality, of a policy that is arbitrary, self-serving and operating without due regard to established law. If negotiated settlements are meant to be achieved according to a broad range of rights and obligations than those otherwise enforceable in a court of law, then federal policy must set a clear standard by which their validity can be determined. ... At a minimum, Canada cannot continue to articulate standards that exclude justiciable claims from its policy for negotiated settlements.

The specific claims policy also contains restrictions on compensation, in the form of guidelines, which ensure much delay and confrontation in negotiations. The policy's first rule is that compensation will be based on "legal principles", but nine other guidelines qualify it. Of particular concern is guideline number 10:

> The criteria set out above are general in nature and the actual amount which the claimant is offered will depend on the extent to which the claimant has established a valid claim, the burden of which rests with the claimant. As an example, where there is doubt that the lands in question were ever reserve land, the degree of doubt will be reflected in the compensation offered.

In practice, guideline number 10 means that the federal government may, at any stage, reduce the amount of compensation being offered by 25 per cent, 50 per cent or 75 per cent. The perception is widespread that such determinations are made arbitrarily, or with a view to the budget rather than the facts.

. . . . .

While it is possible to reach a negotiated claims settlement within the policies, it is far from clear that these settlements will deal ultimately with the underlying cause of grievance or implement any significant change over the long term. The Commission believes the number of settlements does not vindicate the specific claims policy or rebut the criticisms levelled against it. Our review of the specific claims policy and process shows that major change is needed.

Claims of a third kind

Claims of a third kind, acknowledged since 1993, are really a subset of specific claims. Such claims are intended to attract "administrative solutions or remedies to grievances that are not suitable for resolution, or cannot be resolved, through the Specific Claims process". The policy provides no definition of what kinds of claims might fall into this category.

... [N]o indication is given of the purpose of negotiation or the potential results. Quite simply, the problem with claims of a third kind is that there is no purpose, no definition, no process, no conclusion and no review.

An appropriate claims process would not require an unarticulated catch-all category like claims of a third kind. Such a policy would include these claims as part of an overall objective of achieving reconciliation and coexistence.

———————

In the Royal Commission on Aboriginal Peoples' opinion — one that is shared by many Aboriginal groups — the federal government's claims processes are plagued by restrictive interpretations of claims, overly rigid applications of claims process criteria, and exclusive reliance on common law conceptions of land. In this sense, these processes replicate many of the problems that exist in Aboriginal title litigation. If the claims processes are to continue as meaningful alternatives to litigation, they need to be modified to account for both common law and Aboriginal understandings of land rights.

I.   CONCLUSION

It may be seen that the law relating to Aboriginal title has undergone a number of changes since the decisions of the United States Supreme Court in the first half of the 19th century. Some of these changes may be observed by comparing the Privy Council's judgment in *St. Catherine's Milling* with that of Justice Hall in *Calder* or, to some extent, Chief Justice Lamer's judgment in *Delgamuukw*. It remains to be seen, though, how the disagreement among the judges in *Marshall/Bernard* will affect the understanding of Aboriginal title. In spite of these changes, can one truly say that there is much of a difference in judicial attitudes generally in dealing with Aboriginal title claims?

In *Mabo*, Justice Brennan held that reliance on ancient doctrines of discovery and settlement as the basis for the Crown's claim to sovereignty may be challenged by contemporary courts. In many more decisions, however, the historic and legal basis of the Crown's claim to sovereignty is simply not questioned. The Supreme Court of Canada's decision in *R. v. Sparrow*, [1990] S.C.J. No. 49, [1990] 1 S.C.R. 1075, [1990] 4 W.W.R. 410, 46 B.C.L.R. (2d) 1, 56 C.C.C. (3d) 263, 70 D.L.R. (4th) 385, 111 N.R. 241, [1990] 3 C.N.L.R. 160 (S.C.C.) is a prime example of this judicial practice. There, the unanimous judgment of the Court stated, at 404 D.L.R., that:

> It is worth recalling that while British policy toward the native population was based on respect for their right to occupy their traditional lands, a proposition to which the Royal Proclamation of 1763 bears witness, there was from the outset never any doubt that sovereignty and legislative power, and indeed the underlying title, to such lands vested in the Crown ...

None of the judgments rendered in the Supreme Court's consideration of *Delgamuukw*, altered this understanding, nor has any subsequent discussion of Aboriginal title by the Court. Consequently, while the law relating to Aboriginal title may have (at least rhetorically) discarded some of the obstacles that have impeded more contextual analyses of the legal nature of the Crown's claim to title and sovereignty over Canada, significant barriers remain.

ENDNOTES

1.   In F.W. Turner III, ed., *The Portable North American Indian Reader* (Harmondsworth, England: Penguin, 1977) at 246.
2.   Letters Patent to John Cabot, 4 March 1496, as reproduced in H.S. Commager, ed., *Documents of American History*, 8th ed. (New York: Appleton-Crofts, 1968) at 5.
3.   See B. Slattery, "Did France Claim Canada Upon 'Discovery'?" in J.M. Bumsted, ed., *Interpreting Canada's Past*, Vol. I (Toronto: Oxford University Press, 1986) at 15.

4. From H.S. Burrage, ed., *Early English and French Voyages, Chiefly from Hakluyt, 1534-1608* (New York: Scribner's, 1906), as quoted in W.E. Washburn, *The Indian and the White Man* (Garden City, N.J.: Anchor Books, 1964) at 10-11.

5. As translated by L. Hanke, *History of Latin American Civilization: Sources and Interpretations*, Vol. I (Boston: Little, Brown, and Company, 1967) at 123-25.

6. L. Hanke, *The Spanish Struggle for Justice in the Conquest of America* (Philadelphia: University of Pennsylvania Press, 1949) at 34.

7. Royal Commission on Aboriginal Peoples, *Report of the Royal Commission on Aboriginal Peoples, Looking Forward, Looking Back*, Vol. 1 (Ottawa: Ministry of Supply and Services, 1996) at 117.

8. (Ottawa: Ministry of Public Works and Government Services Canada, 1995) at 7.

9. L.I. Rotman, *Parallel Paths: Fiduciary Doctrine and the Crown-Native Relationship in Canada* (Toronto: University of Toronto Press, 1996) at 108-9.

10. *Report of the Royal Commission on Aboriginal Peoples: Looking Forward, Looking Back*, Vol. 1 (Ottawa: Supply and Services Canada, 1996) at 696.

CHAPTER 4

TREATIES

The language used in treaties with the Indians should never be construed to their prejudice. If words be made use of which are susceptible of a more extended meaning than their plain import, as connected with the tenor of the treaty, they should be considered as used only in the latter sense. To contend that the word "allotted," in reference to the land guarantied to the Indians in certain treaties, indicates a favour conferred, rather than a right acknowledged, would, it would seem to me, do injustice to the understanding of the parties. How the words of the treaty were understood by this unlettered people, rather than their critical meaning, should form the rule of construction.

Worcester v. State of Georgia, 6 Pet. 515 at 582 (U.S. 1832), *per* M' Lean J.

A. INTRODUCTION

Treaty relations between Britain and the Aboriginal peoples in North America have been a fundamental aspect of the interaction between the groups from earliest times. Treaties are foundational documents in the history of Crown-Native relations. Initially, they established parameters for peaceful intercourse. Later, they served as the basis for the parties' renewal of their historical commitments to each other.

Treaties were the primary means by which diplomatic relations were conducted between Britain and the Aboriginal peoples. Treaties signed between the groups took a variety of forms. Not all of them involved the cession of land, as conventional wisdom might suggest. Some were treaties of alliance, others of peace and friendship. What the treaties did share in common, at least in theory, was their creation or maintenance of mutually beneficial relationships between the Crown and the Aboriginal peoples.

REPORT OF THE ROYAL COMMISSION ON ABORIGINAL PEOPLES: LOOKING FORWARD, LOOKING BACK, VOL. 1

(Ottawa: Ministry of Supply and Services, 1996) at 173-76
(references omitted)

When Europeans landed on the shores of the Americas, they first sought shelter and sustenance, then pursued a lucrative trade with Aboriginal nations, and later made arrangements through treaties to live permanently in Aboriginal territories. These treaties varied in purpose and scope, depending on the circumstances and objectives of the parties making them. Early treaties were made for peace, trade, alliance, neutrality and military support. When settlement grew, treaties were made to establish relationships, as a way of living together in peaceful co-existence, and to acquire Aboriginal lands and resources.

. . . . .

Over time, treaties became more complex and difficult to negotiate. In the early period of contact, when Europeans were a minority and understanding one another was essential to survival, treaty relationships were cultivated and maintained carefully. As time went on and Europeans became a majority, negotiations became complex, difficult and vague in some areas, as the Crown pursued its goal of securing Aboriginal lands to build its new country. The different cultural views, values and assumptions of both parties conflicted in substantial ways. These contradictions were often not evident, or remained unspoken, in the negotiation and conclusion of solemn treaty agreements. In many cases, it is questionable whether the Indian parties understood the legal and political implications of the land conveyance documents they were asked to sign. Many of these transactions are the subject of land claims today.

It is also doubtful in many cases that the First Nations participating in the [post-Confederation] numbered treaties knew that the written texts they signed differed from the oral agreements they concluded. In fact, it was not evident to them until some years after treaties were made that the Crown was not honouring its treaty commitments or was acting in a way that violated treaty agreements. Their reaction to the imposition of government laws and restrictions upon them was seen as a violation of the Queen's promise to protect their way of life and not subject them to the Queen's laws (the *Indian Act*) or the Queen's servants (the Indian agent). The possibility that the party recording the oral agreements and preparing the written text took advantage of the other party's lack of understanding of the legal implications of written texts, or that those interpretations were not communicated to the party that did not read or write, is disturbing. If First Nations depended on the oral version of their treaties, it follows that the oral agreements reached must be compared to the written version to verify the nature and scope of these agreements today. The fact that in most cases the Indian parties were unable to verify the implications of the written text against the oral agreement, because of language and cultural barriers, must be given consideration when interpreting their meaning.

... [F]rom the perspective of the First Nations there were several basic elements or principles involved in the treaty-making process. In making treaties both parties recognized and affirmed one another's authority to enter into and make binding commitments in treaties. In addition, First Nations would not consider making a treaty unless their way of life was protected and preserved. This meant the continuing use of their lands and natural resources. In most, if not all the treaties, the Crown promised not to interfere with their way of life, including their hunting, fishing, trapping and gathering practices.

The Crown asked First Nations to share their lands with settlers, and First Nations did so on the condition that they would retain adequate land

and resources to ensure the well-being of their nations. The Indian parties understood they would continue to maintain their traditional governments, their laws and their customs and to co-operate as necessary with the Crown. There was substantive agreement that the treaties established an economic partnership from which both parties would benefit. Compensation was offered in exchange for the agreement of First Nations to share. The principle of fair exchange and mutual benefit was an integral part of treaty making.

. . . . .

These principles, which were part and parcel of the treaty negotiations, were agreed upon throughout the oral negotiations for Treaties 1 through 11 [the post-Confederation numbered treaties]. They were not always discussed at length, and in many cases the written versions of the treaties are silent on them. In these circumstances, the parties based their negotiations and consent on their own understandings, assumptions and values, as well as on the oral discussions. First Nations were assured orally that their way of life would not change unless they wished it to. They understood that their governing structures and authorities would continue undisturbed by the treaty relationship. They also assumed, and were assured, that the Crown would respect and honour the treaty agreements in perpetuity and that they would not suffer — but only benefit — from making treaties with the Crown. They were not asked, and they did not agree, to adopt non-Aboriginal ways and laws for themselves. They believed and were assured that their freedom and independence would not be interfered with as a result of the treaty. They expected to meet periodically with their treaty partner to make the necessary adjustments and accommodations to maintain the treaty relationship.

Treaty negotiations were usually conducted over a three- to four-day period, with tremendous barriers created by two different cultures with very different world views and experiences attempting to understand and come to terms with one another. Negotiation and dialogue did not, and could not, venture into the meaning of specific terminology, legal or otherwise, and remained at a broad general level, owing to time and language barriers. Issues such as co-existence, non-interference with the Indian way of life, non-interference with hunting and fishing and retention of adequate lands would therefore have been understood at the broadest level. These were matters that would, presumably, be sorted out as time went on.

... [T]he parties had to rely on the trustworthiness, good intentions, and good faith of the other treaty partner and the ability to understand one another better through time. At the time of treaty making, First Nations would not have been sufficiently cognizant of British laws and perspectives, since their previous interaction and exchanges had been primarily through trading relationships. When treaty commissioners proposed a formula (usually called a land quantum formula) to determine how much land would be reserved for Indian nations, for example, it is doubtful that they would have understood the amount of land entailed in one square mile. Similarly, terms such as cede, surrender, extinguish, yield and forever give up all rights and titles appear in the written text of the treaties, but discussion of the meaning of these concepts is not found anywhere in the records of treaty negotiations.

Even as treaty commissioners were promising non-interference with the Indian way of life, treaty documents referred to the Indian nations as "subjects of the Crown". Since First Nations patterned their relationships along kinship lines, they would have understood the relationship they were entering as being more akin to "brothers" or "partners" of the Crown. The First Nations also assumed, since they were being asked for land, that they were the ones giving land to the Crown and that they were the owners of the land. Indeed, the notion that the Crown was in any position to "give" their land to them — for the establishment of reserves, for example — would have been ludicrous, since in many cases it had been their land since time immemorial.

Written texts also placed limits on the agreements and promises being made, unbeknownst to the Indian parties. For example, written texts limiting hunting and fishing to Crown lands stand in contradiction to the oral promise not to interfere, in any way, with their use of wildlife and fisheries resources. These inherent conflicts and contradictions do not appear to have been explained to the Indian parties.

However, it is also clear that both parties wanted to make treaties to secure their respective political and economic objectives. Both sides saw tangible rewards flowing from the treaties and each side worked to secure the terms and conditions they wanted in the treaty. Both parties pledged to honour and uphold their sacred and binding pacts. Each side brought something of value to bargain with — the First Nations brought capital in the form of their land and resources, and the Crown brought the promise of compensation and the promise not to interfere with their way of life and the use of their natural resources as they had in the past. Each believed they had secured their respective objectives — the Crown gained access to Indian lands and resources, and First Nations secured the guarantee of the survival and protection of their nationhood.

B. THE PROCESS OF TREATY-MAKING

Indigenous laws and protocols facilitated treaties between First Nations in early North American legal relationships. Subsequently, Indigenous laws were also instrumental in constructing treaties with people from other continents. For example, various European powers transacted treaties with the Iroquois in accordance with Haudenosaunee legal traditions. The French entered into treaties with Aboriginal peoples of the northern Great Lakes using Anishinabek ideas and ceremonies. The British Crown secured Peace and Friendship agreements with the Mi'kmaq, Maliseet and Passamaquody Nations in what is now Atlantic Canada by following

Indigenous protocols, procedures and practices. As noted in Chapter 1, in 1764 when the British secured a stronger place in the heart of North America after the Seven Years War, they used Indigenous legal traditions to create solemn commitments with First Nations. There have been over 500 treaties in Canada. Many draw on some form of Indigenous legal tradition, even in later eras when Aboriginal peoples enjoyed less political influence. Indigenous laws, legal perspectives and other frameworks have been present throughout much of the treaty-making process in Canada.

The process of initiating and renewing treaty relations that had commenced before Europeans arrived in North America was continued through the Covenant Chain alliance, which established the parameters of British-Aboriginal relations in North America. These treaties were compacts between independent nations. As compacts between independent nations, the treaties provided the guidelines for the parties' interaction and governed disputes between them. In addition, they provided the basis for the reciprocal rights and obligations of the parties through the process.

C. THE CHANGING FACE OF TREATIES

The nature of treaties — and, indeed, the entire treaty-making process — was fundamentally altered by the change in the political situation in North America following Britain's conquest of New France in 1760-61. The strategic importance of the Aboriginal peoples as allies or enemies during the battles between Britain and France for colonial supremacy in North America ended upon the conquest. As Leonard Rotman has explained:

> With Britain and France competing to achieve predominance in North America, the Indians were able to play the two European powers off against each other for their own benefit. They were shrewd negotiators who knew full well that they were the catalysts in the European struggle in North America. They also knew that their precarious interests were best served by maintaining the delicate balance of power between the two European nations.
>
> . . . . . .
>
> The removal of France as a major power in North America forever changed the relationship between the Crown and Native peoples. The Indians could no longer occupy the enviable position of holding the balance of power between Britain and France.[1]

This change in the Aboriginals' position was described by General Thomas Gage, who stated that "All North America in the hands of a single power robs [the Aboriginals] of their Consequence, presents, & pay."[2]

Just as the relationship between Britain and the Aboriginal peoples did not remain static, the nature of their treaty relations also changed over time. As the following excerpt indicates, treaties have taken a variety of forms since their first use in North America.

D.N. SPRAGUE, "CANADA'S TREATIES WITH ABORIGINAL PEOPLES"

(1996) 23 Man. L.J. 341 at 341-44 (references omitted)

VII. The First Treaties, 1763-1850

... The first [treaties] in the eighteenth century were of "peace and friendship"negotiated by representatives of the crown and Native peoples, either for military alliance or neutrality towards competing colonial powers. The French entered such alliances earlier than the British, but more informally. Britain solemnised its simple arrangements with a written text: in return for Aboriginal peace and friendship, British negotiators promised not to disturb the other side in its essential hunting and fishing territories. At the end of the era of inter-imperial rivalry, from the time of Britain's occupation of the St. Lawrence valley in 1760, British generals made their peace with Native peoples formerly allied with the French.

Several "peace and friendship" treaties followed elsewhere in the Atlantic region after 1760. Supremacy of Great Britain in North America, formalised by the Peace of Paris in 1763, set the stage for a new kind of treaty-making announced by a royal proclamation on 7 October 1763. ... [T]he significance of the Royal Proclamation of 7 October 1763 for Canadian Aboriginal treaty matters was and continues to have primary importance.

. . . . . .

What followed after 1763 was a new kind of negotiation with Native people: face to face meetings between specially commissioned agents and representatives of "the several Nations or Tribes" to negotiate lump-sum payments for lands needed by an expanding settler population. ... The first large-scale application of the treaty-making requirement enunciated in 1763 was ... to make land available for Loyalist refugees after the American Revolution. Over the next thirty years almost twenty other "land surrenders" negotiated purchases from Native people, prior to the crown opening such areas to settlers.

By the 1810s, imperial authorities complained that existing means of fulfilling the purpose of the Proclamation placed excessive demands on the colonial treasury. In 1818 a third kind of treaty replaced lump-sum payment for each surrender of Aboriginal land for settlement. J.R. Miller describes the new approach as one that shifted the cost of extinguishing Aboriginal title from the crown to the Natives themselves. What followed was a scheme of district by district promises of annual payments, "annuities," at first amply funded by revenue flowing to the crown from sales of Aboriginal lands to settlers. In Miller's characterisation, "the Indians indirectly funded most of the purchase price of their land through instalment payments made from revenues derived from the land." Almost twenty such arrangements, all in present-day southern Ontario, were made over the next several decades as the new norm for meeting the terms of the Proclamation of 1763.

II. The Robinson Treaties, 1850s

A final step in the evolution of Canadian treaty-making occurred in 1850. The newly autonomous Province of Canada, an experimental union of present-day Ontario and Quebec created in 1840, began to anticipate exploitation of mineral resources and pockets of agricultural land in the geographically enormous, thinly populated territory north of Lakes Huron and Superior (i.e., north of modern-day Sudbury and west beyond Thunder Bay). William Benjamin Robinson, the commissioner for the task, negotiated a surrender of Aboriginal title to the whole vast region in two brief meetings with representatives of Aboriginal occupants on 7 and 9 September 1850. Since the "Robinson treaties" affected twice as much territory as all previous treaties combined, in that aspect alone they signalled a bold departure from earlier practice. They represented an equally important step in the evolution of the Canadian form of treaty-making with Native people in another respect. In addition to the standard commitments to pay annuities, and ceremonial assurances that Native people could continue to hunt and fish on ancestral lands as before, the second innovation was a promise of a reserve of territory for each band signatory to the treaty. Robinson explained to his superiors that while the reserve-promise was a novelty, it was necessary as a cost-saving measure:

> In allowing the Indians to retain reservations of land for their own use I was governed by the fact that they in most cases asked for such tracts as they had heretofore been in the habit of using for purposes of residence and cultivation ... By securing these to them and the right of hunting and fishing over the ceded territory, they cannot say that the Government takes from their usual means of subsistence and therefore have no claims for support.

... The promise of reserves emerged, then, as the cost-effective means for securing extinguishment of Aboriginal title over much larger tracts than had been the case in any negotiations before 1850. The two Robinson treaties ... became normal legal form for the new Dominion of Canada ... In fact, every Canadian treaty after Confederation fit the basic Robinson recipe: negotiated by specially commissioned officers of the crown to extinguish title to relatively large expanses of territory, offering vague assurances for existing hunting and fishing rights, and promising reserves as well as annuities.

As Sprague highlights, treaties underwent a number of changes following the early days of Crown-Native relations. While the Aboriginal peoples continued to view treaties on the same basis as they had since the earliest treaties they had entered into with Britain, Canada's use of treaties after Confederation was economically focused. As Sprague notes, each of the post-Confederation numbered treaties from 1871 to 1921 paralleled some governmental economic interest:

> The one valid generalisation concerning the making of treaties was that extinguishment negotiations occurred sporadically, and only where Canada hoped for large returns from areas of expected boom: Treaties 1 to 7 (1871-1877) extinguished Aboriginal title to the Prairies and Northwestern Ontario to clear the way for the Canadian Pacific Railway and agricultural settlement; Treaty 8 (1899-1900) covered access to the Yukon Territory, established as an administrative district separate from the North West Territory in 1898 after the gold rush that began in 1897; Treaty 9 (1904) followed silver discoveries and expected hydroelectric, pulp and paper development along the routes of newly projected rail lines in northern Ontario; Treaty 10 (1909) served a similar purpose in northern Saskatchewan; and Treaty 11 (1921) followed Imperial Oil's first gusher at Norman Wells in 1920.[3]

D. CONCEPTUALIZING CROWN-NATIVE TREATIES

Once the Crown no longer relied upon the Aboriginal peoples as military or political allies, it tended to view the treaties it concluded with them much more like contractual agreements than compacts between nations.

Unlike this change in the Crown's attitude towards the treaties, the Aboriginal view remained consistent with the understanding emanating from the Covenant Chain, discussed in Chapter 1, which regarded treaties as a series of agreements and renewals that were relationship-based rather than individual agreements that were document-based. Thus, the Aboriginal understanding of treaties included oral promises or collateral representations made during treaty negotiations, not simply the final, written parchment copy. This more inclusive view is often referred to as the "spirit and intent" of the agreement.

REPORT OF THE ROYAL COMMISSION ON ABORIGINAL PEOPLES: LOOKING FORWARD, LOOKING BACK, VOL. 1

(Ottawa: Ministry of Supply and Services, 1996)
at 128-30 (references omitted)

To the Aboriginal nations, treaties are vital, living instruments of relationship. They forged dynamic and powerful relationships that remain in effect to this day. Indeed the spirit of the treaties has remained more or less consistent across this continent, even as the terms of the treaties have changed over time.

Canadians and their governments, however, are more likely to look on the treaties as ancient history. The treaties, to Canada, are often regarded as inconvenient and obsolete relics of the early days of this country. With respect to the early treaties in particular, which were made with the British or French Crown, Canadian governments dismiss them as having no relevance in the post-Confederation period. The fact remains, however, that Canada has inherited the treaties that were made and is the beneficiary of the lands and resources secured by those treaties and still enjoyed today by Canada's citizens.

A final source of misunderstanding about the treaties lies in the fact that the relationship created by treaty has meaning and precedent in the laws and way of life of the Indian nations for which there are no equivalents in British or Canadian traditions.

One aspect of treaty making that is little understood today is the spiritual aspect of treaties. Traditional Aboriginal governments do not distinguish between the political and spiritual role of the chiefs, any more than they draw a sharp demarcation line between the physical and spirit worlds. Unlike European-based governments, they do not see the need to achieve a separation between the spiritual and political aspects of governing:

> Everything is together — spiritual, and political — because when the Creator ... made this world, he touched the world all together, and it automatically became spiritual and everything come from the world is spiritual and so that is what leaders are, they are both the spiritual mentors and political mentors of the people.

This integration of spiritual and political matters extends to treaty making, where sacred wampum, sacred songs and ceremonies, and the sacred pipe are integral parts of making the commitment to uphold the treaty. In affirming these sacred pacts, the treaty partners assured one another that they would keep the treaty for as long as the sun shines, the grass grows and the waters flow.

What sacred pacts, symbols and things of concrete value did the Crown bring to treaty making? The Crown's representatives gave their word and pledged to uphold the honour of the Crown. The symbols of their honour and trustworthiness were the reigning king or queen in whose name the treaty was being negotiated and with whose authority the treaty was vested. Missionaries were a testament to the integrity of the vows that were made and witnesses to the promises that were to be kept. Outward symbols, like flags, the red coats, treaty medals, gifts and feasts were also part of the rituals.

While European treaties borrowed the form of business contracts, Aboriginal treaties were modelled on the forms of marriage, adoption and kinship. They were aimed at creating living relationships and, like a marriage, they required periodic celebration, renewal, and reconciliation. Also like a marriage, they evolved over time; the agreed interpretation of the relationship developed and changed with each renewal and generation of children, as people grew to know each other better, traded, and helped defend each other. This natural historical process did not render old treaties obsolete, since treaties were not a series of specific promises in contracts; rather they were intended to grow and flourish as broad, dynamic relationships, changing and growing with the parties in a context of mutual respect and shared responsibility.

Despite these differences, Europeans found no difficulty adapting to Aboriginal protocols in North America. They learned to make condolence before a conference with the Six Nations, to give and receive wampum, to smoke the pipe of peace on the prairies, to speak in terms of "brothers" (kinship relations), not "terms and conditions" (contract relations). Whatever may have come later, diplomacy in the first centuries of European contact in North America was conducted largely on a common ground of symbols and ceremony. The treaty parties shared a sense of solemnity and the intention to fulfil their promises.

The apparent common ground was real, but under the surface the old differences in world view still existed, largely unarticulated.

Early judicial interpretation of Crown-Native treaties tended to side with the Crown's more focused emphasis on the quid pro quo element of the treaties rather than their relationship basis emanating from the Covenant Chain. Consequently, to the courts, the written, parchment treaty handed to the aboriginal peoples by the Crown constituted the entirety of the agreement.

The fact that the judiciary did not account for Aboriginal understandings of the treaties was only part of the problem with early treaty jurisprudence. In the late 19th and early 20th centuries, treaties were regarded as simple promises existing at the sufferance of the Crown. As Lord Watson commented in *Attorney-General of Ontario v. Attorney-General of Canada: Re Indian Claims*, [1897] A.C. 199 at 213 (P.C.):

> Their Lordships have had no difficulty in coming to the conclusion that, under the treaties, the Indians obtained no right to their annuities ... beyond a promise and agreement, which was nothing more than a personal obligation by its governor.

Since the courts did not regard treaties as binding documents that vested legally enforceable rights in the Aboriginal peoples, the Crown could readily ignore the terms of treaties, either by failing to perform treaty obligations, or by passing legislation that was inconsistent with its treaty promises.

Some of these issues, and others typical of early treaty jurisprudence in Canada, are illustrated in *R. v. Syliboy*, which is a prime example of early judicial attitudes towards treaties.

R. v. SYLIBOY

[1929] 1 D.L.R. 307, 50 C.C.C. 389 (N.S. Co. Ct.) (references omitted)

Patterson (Acting) Co. Ct. J.: — The defendant, who is the grand chief of the Mick Macks of Nova Scotia was convicted under the Lands and Forests Act, 1926 (N.S.), c. 4, of having in his possession ... fifteen green pelts, fourteen muskrat and one fox. He made no attempt to deny having the pelts, indeed frankly admits having them, but claims that as an Indian he is not bound by the provisions of the Act, but has by Treaty the right to hunt and trap at all times. Every now and then for a number of years one has heard that our Indians were making these claims but, so far as I know, the matter has never been before a Court.

The Treaty relied upon is that of 1752, made between Governor Hopson of the Province of Nova Scotia and His Majesty's Council on behalf of His Majesty, and "Major Jean Baptiste Cope, chief Sachem of the Tribe of Mick Mack Indians Inhabiting the Eastern Coast of the said Province, and Andrew Hadley Martin, Gabriel Martin & Francis Jeremiah, Members and Delegates of the said Tribe:" Article 4 in part says: — "It is agreed that the said Tribe of Indians shall not be hindered from but have free liberty to hunt and fish as usual."

Observe the date 1752. Cape Breton between 1748 and 1763 was not part of Nova Scotia. It was owned and governed by the French, while Nova Scotia was a colony of Great Britain. It will be remembered that defendant is a Cape Breton Indian and that the offence alleged against him was committed in Cape Breton. Assuming for the time that the Treaty is still in force in Nova Scotia proper, can defendant claim protection under it? Unless there is something more than I have stated, clearly not. But, say his counsel, the Mick Mack Tribe throughout Nova Scotia, including Cape Breton, is one and indivisible, and the Treaty was made with the tribe, and a very bright and intelligent young Indian testifies that two of the signatories to it were Cape Breton Indians. The language of the Treaty not only lends no support to this contention, but shows that it is untenable, and I am satisfied that the young Indian is mistaken.

"The following Treaty of Peace," reads the minute of Council, "was Signed, Ratifyed and Exchanged with the Mick Mack Tribe of Indians, Inhabiting the Eastern Parts of this Province:" computed to be ninety in number, — Cope himself claimed authority over only forty. Eight years before there had been three hundred Indians engaged in the attack on Canso, all from "the Eastern Parts of this Province" which shows that Cope and the others who joined with him in the Treaty, really represented only a small portion even of these very Indians they claimed to represent. Notice further, how Cope is described as "chief Sachem of the Tribe of Mick Mack Indians Inhabiting the Eastern Coast of the said Province," (*i.e.*, Nova Scotia proper) and his fellow signatories as "Members and Delegates of the said Tribe." Article 3 seems conclusive on the point. There it is provided: — "That the said Tribe" (*i.e.*, the tribe inhabiting the eastern coast of Nova Scotia) "shall use their utmost endeavours to bring in the other Indians to Renew and Ratify this Peace."

. . . . .

In the face of this evidence there can be no doubt, I think, that the Treaty relied upon was not made with the Mick Mack Tribe as a whole but with a small body of that tribe living in the eastern part of Nova Scotia proper, with headquarters in and about Shubenacadie, and that any benefits under it accrued only to that body and their heirs. The defendant being unable to show any connection, by descent or otherwise, with that body cannot claim any protection from it or any rights under it.

But there is much more than what I might not improperly call internal evidence to show that defendant's contention that the Treaty was a general and not a local one is untenable. Between 1752 and 1763 we find negotiations going on between the Governor and council and various tribes or local bodies of Indians for treaties: — for instance with the Fort Lawrence (Missiquash) Indians in 1753 and again in 1755; with the Cape Sable Indians in 1753; with Indians near Halifax in 1760; with Chibenaccadie Indians (the very Indians of our Treaty) in 1760. Between same dates we find treaties entered into with Lehéve (LaHave) Indians in 1753, 1760 and 1761; with the Chibenaccadie and Muscadoboit (Shubenacadie and Musquodoboit) Indians in 1760; with certain Indian chiefs in 1761; with the Missiquash Indians, and with the Pictouck and Malagonich (Pictou and Merigomishe) Indians in the same year. Why these negotiations — why these treaties if the Treaty of 1752 was general applying to all Nova Scotia?

In none of these treaties, or in the negotiations leading up to them is there any reference to the Treaty of 1752, while there are many to the Treaty of 1725. Indeed the only reference to the Treaty of 1752 that I have been able to find is in that infamous proclamation by Governor Lawrence dated May 14, 1756, wherein he offers a reward of £30 for the capture of any Indian, or £25 for any Indian woman. There it is mentioned as a treaty made with a tribe of Mick Macks.

. . . . .

That the Governor in Council of Nova Scotia knew that these treaties were of a local character is evident. On February 29, 1760, that body resolved "to make peace with each chief who came in, and afterwards to have a general treaty signed at Chignecto."

Counsel for the defendant suggest another way in which the benefits from the Treaty were or should be extended to their client and all other Cape Breton Indians. By Royal Proclamation after the Treaty of Paris [the *Royal Proclamation of 1763*], Cape Breton and St. John's (Prince Edward) Island were annexed to Nova Scotia and three years later the Parliament of Nova Scotia by statute declared that the laws of Nova Scotia extended to the Island of Cape Breton. But the expression, "the Laws of Nova Scotia" had reference only to the general laws of the Province and it would be misusing words to speak of the Treaty of 1752 as a law. At any rate the statute of 1766 (N.S.), c. 1, ceased to have any effect in 1784 when Cape Breton was disjoined from Nova Scotia and created a colony with authority to its Governor to convene the Assembly. Separate Cape Breton and Nova Scotia remained until 1820-21 (N.S.), c. 5. After their union in that year an Act was passed enacting that the administration of justice in the Island of Cape Breton should be conformable to the usage and practice of the Province of Nova Scotia. Nothing is said about general laws or treaties. Presumably no mention of general laws was necessary to make them effective, but surely that cannot be said of treaties.

I have referred to the proclamation after the Treaty of Paris. That is relied upon by the defendant for a reason other than that set out in the preceding paragraph. If that proclamation be examined it will be found that it deals only with those territories or countries, of which Nova Scotia was not one, that had been ceded to Great Britain by France. ... The references in it to the Indians are specifically limited to the Indians of the three first named governments [Quebec, East Florida, and West Florida]. One can understand an Indian in Quebec for example making a claim that he was guaranteed certain rights about hunting by the proclamation, but I confess I cannot understand a Cape Breton Indian making any such claim.

I might stop here. If the Treaty did not extend to Cape Breton and the Indians there could make no claim under it or derive any benefits from it, the prosecution must succeed and the conviction of the defendant be confirmed. I think, however, I should express my opinion on the other questions raised for I am in hopes that there will be an appeal from my decision and that upon so important a matter we may have the judgment of an Appeal Court.

Mr. McLennan for the prosecution, whose brief is a joy to read so complete and compact it is, contends that even if the Treaty relied upon by the defendant was made for the whole Mick Mack Tribe and did extend to Cape Breton and included the Indians there, it was almost at once put an end to by the breaking out of war. The ink was not much more than dry on the Treaty when Indians led by a son of Cope (let us hope not that son to whom the complacent Governor had sent a laced hat as a present) were carrying on in the characteristic Indian way a war against Britain. It was the very Indians who were parties to the Treaty that were responsible for the repeated raids upon Dartmouth, and it is a well-known and established fact that right down until the Treaty of Paris put an end to the war between England and France the Indians were on the side of France and were carrying on war in her behalf. Would that clause in the Treaty guaranteeing them the right to hunt be in consequence put an end to, or would it be merely suspended? ... I am inclined to hold it would only be suspended.

. . . . .

A treaty such as that with which we are dealing if made today is one that would require to be ratified by Parliament before becoming effective, and would be invalid until such ratification. Though there was authority in Cornwallis' commission to summon a parliament for Nova Scotia, we all know that none was summoned for some years after the treaty was signed. It is a fair inference I think that after parliament had been assembled and began to legislate this treaty should have been ratified, or otherwise it would lose its validity. At any rate it was not very long after Parliament assumed its functions that a statute was passed which ignored the Treaty and treated it as non-existent.

In 1794 the first of our many Game Acts was passed, 1794 (N.S.), c. 4. It provided that no person within a certain period each year should kill partridge or black duck but Indians and poor settlers. It might be argued that the exception goes to show that the Indians had a special right by treaty, but if they had such a right why mention it in the statute? It would seem to me that the proper interpretation would be that they having no such right by treaty were given it by statute. However that may be the next statute on the subject makes the point clear.

By s. 1 of R.S.N.S. 1851, c. 92, it was enacted that: —

> No person shall take or kill any partridge ... between the first of March and the first of September in any year; but Indians and poor settlers may kill them for their own use at any season.

Section 3 of that Act provides that: — "The sessions may make orders respecting the setting of snares or traps for catching moose," and by s. 5, "may make orders for regulating the periods ... within which moose may be killed." If the Indians were excepted as to the taking or killing of partridge because they had special right by treaty, why were they not so excepted as to setting snares or killing moose?

Then follows a series of statutes prohibiting everyone, Indians not excepted, from hunting during certain seasons until we come to that under which this prosecution was brought. Where a statute and treaty conflict a British Court must follow the statute ... The result therefore is that even assuming the so called Treaty of 1752 is a treaty; assuming that it was valid as such without ratification by parliament, and that any rights under it could be claimed by the Indians of all Nova Scotia as that Province is now constituted, the prosecution would still succeed, because the statute not the treaty prevails.

At the trial there was no discussion as to whether the so called treaty was really a treaty or not. Counsel for the defendant ... did not touch this point. Apparently they are content to accept the description in the document itself ... but the prosecution raised the question and I must deal with it. Two considerations are involved. First, did the Indians of Nova Scotia have status to enter into a treaty? And second, did Governor Hopson have authority to enter into one with them? Both questions must I think be answered in the negative.

(1) "Treaties are unconstrained Acts of independent powers." But the Indians were never regarded as an independent power. A civilized nation first discovering a country of uncivilized people or savages held such country as its own until such time as by treaty it was transferred to some other civilized nation. The savages' rights of sovereignty even of ownership were never recognized. Nova Scotia had passed to Great Britain not by gift or purchase from or even by conquest of the Indians but by treaty with France, which had acquired it by priority of discovery and ancient possession; and the Indians passed with it.

Indeed the very fact that certain Indians sought from the Governor the privilege or right to hunt in Nova Scotia as usual shows that they did not claim to be an independent nation owning or possessing their lands. If they were, why go to another nation asking this privilege or right and giving promise of good behaviour that they might obtain it? In my judgment the Treaty of 1752 is not a treaty at all and is not to be treated as such; it is at best a mere agreement made by the Governor and council with a handful of Indians giving them in return for good behaviour food, presents, and the right to hunt and fish as usual — an agreement that, as we have seen, was very shortly after broken.

(2) Did Governor Hopson have authority to make a treaty? I think not. "Treaties can be made only by the constituted authorities of nations or by persons specially deputed by them for that purpose." Clearly our treaty was not made with the constituted authorities of Great Britain. But was Governor Hopson specially deputed by them? Cornwallis' commission is the manual not only for himself but for his successors and you will search it in vain for any power to sign treaties.

Having called the agreement a treaty, and having perhaps lulled the Indians into believing it to be a treaty with all the sacredness of a treaty attached to it, it may be the Crown should not now be heard to say it is not a treaty. With that I have nothing to do. That is a matter for representations to the proper authorities — representations which if there is nothing else in the way of the Indians could hardly fail to be successful.

On behalf of the defendant one witness testified that all his life he had fished as he would without regard to the Fisheries Law, and defendant himself swears he has started hunting muskrat for the last thirty-four years on Hallowe'en, October 31. Neither of them had ever been interfered with. The suggestion was that they had not been interfered with because they were within their rights in doing what they did by virtue of the treaty. I say nothing about fishing, but as to the hunting it was not until 1927 that the close season was extended to November 15. Until that year whenever there had been a close season on muskrat it had ended on November 1. If defendant did not start his hunting until October 31, the reason he was not proceeded against before seems obvious.

There is abundant evidence also that the Indians have been for many years receiving food, blankets, etc., from the government through the Indian agent because, says the defendant, of this treaty. I cannot agree. Rather I think they received these goods, and other benefits as well, not because of the treaty but by virtue of the successive statutes in that behalf … The good work so begun and carried on when Nova Scotia was a separate Province was taken over by the federal government at Confederation and one is glad to learn is being so generously continued.

On no ground that has been advanced, and I am sure everything has been said or done that with any chance of success could have been said or done, can defendant in my opinion succeed. Such sympathy as a Judge is permitted to have is with defendant. I would gladly allow the appeal if I could find any sound reason for doing so, but I cannot and must confirm the conviction. The very capable Magistrate who heard the case below has, I am pleased to see, fixed the penalty at the very lowest figure that the Act allows. Even so I venture to express the hope that the authorities will not enforce the conviction.

I have no doubt whatever that defendant honestly believed that the treaty was valid and that he was entitled under it to kill muskrat or have their pelts in his possession at any time, and as I pointed out, a year ago or rather in 1926 it was no offence on November 4 to have green muskrat pelts in one's possession. While everyone is presumed to know the law and to know the exact limits of the close season, it is more than likely — is it not a certainty — that the untutored mind of the defendant was not aware that in 1927 the close season had been lengthened to November 15? Of course, ignorance of the law excuses no one, but surely ignorance of the law under such circumstances can be urged as a plea for most lenient treatment — for in such a case as this waiving both penalty and costs.

Appeal dismissed.

Do you agree with Judge Patterson's characterization of the 1752 "treaty"? What of his statement that, "having perhaps lulled the Indians into believing it to be a treaty ... the Crown should not now be heard to say it is not a treaty"? Are there any merits to this argument? The 1752 treaty considered in *Syliboy* is reproduced in its entirety in *Simon v. R.*, [1985] S.C.J. No. 67, [1985] 2 S.C.R. 387, 62 N.R. 366, 23 C.C.C. (3d) 238, 71 N.S.R. (2d) 15, 171 A.P.R. 15, [1986] 1 C.N.L.R. 153, 24 D.L.R. (4th) 390 (S.C.C.), excerpted *infra*.

The English language and concepts implemented in the treaties were not always understood by the Aboriginal peoples. Where they were understood, they were not always understood by the Aboriginals in the same manner that they were by the Crown's representatives. Attempts at translation by the Crown's representatives were also affected by these problems. The Maritime peace and friendship treaties from the late 17th and 18th centuries, such as the 1752 agreement considered in *Syliboy*, are profound examples of the effects of such a lack of common understanding. Compare the approach to these treaties by historian William Wicken with that of either Lord Watson or Patterson J.

WILLIAM WICKEN, "THE MI' KMAQ AND WUASTUKWIUK TREATIES"

(1994) 44 U.N.B.L.J. 241 at 241-42, 249-53 (references omitted)

Between 1722 and 1786, Native people of the Atlantic region signed a series of treaties with the British Crown. In recent years, the Mi' kmaq and Wuastukwiuk have argued that the treaties supersede provincial statutes governing their hunting, fishing and trading rights. The resulting litigation has focused on two principal questions. Firstly, who signed the treaties, and therefore, who can claim their protection, and secondly, how are the treaties to be interpreted?

The courts are seeking answer to historical questions for which conclusive proof is lacking, but do not have the time and materials required to properly evaluate historical documents and testimony. The difficulties which this poses are suggested by errors in historical interpretation made in recent judgments in the Atlantic region. In *R. v. McCoy*, Justice Turnbull of New Brunswick stated that a treaty had been signed "with the Indians . . . at Annapolis Royal in 1750." While treaties were signed in 1749 and 1752, both at Chebouctou (Halifax), none was concluded in 1750 at Annapolis Royal. Moreover, Justice Turnbull based his decision on a number of questionable historical interpretations.

. . . . .

While a court may not have time to grapple with the sometimes tortuous historical debates surrounding 18th century European-Indian relations, it does need to evaluate the historical documentation which is purported by both the treaty claimants and the Crown to validate their particular claims. This article outlines available 18th century documentation and points out some of the difficulties in using these materials to interpret the treaties.

Only by understanding the context in which documents are created is it possible to evaluate opposing interpretations critically. This requires knowing why the document was created, the context in which it was written and the identity of the author. From this it is possible to make some general comments regarding a document's biases, and therefore to evaluate the reliability of the information which it purports to describe. This assists historians in attempting to overcome their greatest difficulty: reconstructing an historical event using documents written by Europeans who are now dead and whose descendants have no memories of these events. What dialogue occurs must be created artificially by constantly questioning one's own assumptions. In doing so, historians must be sensitive to the particular historical context in which they live and question how this influences their perception of the past.

The Sources

Historians and anthropologists have long recognized the difficulties of reconstructing the histories of Native societies. As Native people did not generally produce written records or, in cases where they did, records have not survived, researchers rely almost exclusively on archaeological data to understand North American people prior to European contact, and on European produced documentation after this contact.

. . . . .

The Treaties

Collectively, these records provide the basis for our understanding of the Mi' kmaq and Wuastukwiuk society during the treaty-making period. As is evident, the records are fragmentary, with long silences between mentions of either people. Consequently, it is difficult to reconstruct the precise contours of either society during the 17th and 18th centuries. We do not know, for instance, such basic information as population sizes before and after contact. Indeed, one of the most important aspects of the records is that they show many, if not all, Mi' kmaq and Wuastukwiuk people lived far removed from the sight and pen of European officials. Because of the fragmentary character of this material, it is necessary to consult records produced after 1760. These sources, principally contained in British and Nova Scotian archival series, provide valuable insights into traditional fishing and hunting sites which, in some cases, had been abandoned temporarily in consequence of an expanding imperial rivalry between England and France in the Atlantic region between 1744 and 1760.

Interpretation is complicated further by the fact that the documentary evidence is not readily available. Because of the particular historical circumstances in which Mi' kmaq and Wuastukwiuk lands were invaded by European people, source materials tend to be scattered in archival series housed in Canada, England, France, Massachusetts, New Brunswick, Nova Scotia and Québec. Piecing together this information is a painstaking and time consuming process. Because of the vast quantity of historical document-ation that must be read and analyzed, there may be a tendency, particularly in courtroom situations, to make general conclusions without first sifting through the available evidence. In the Atlantic region this point is particularly important since little new research on the Mi' kmaq and Wuastukwiuk has been published since the late 1970s, forcing an undue reliance on older academic interpretations.

The treaties signed between the British Crown and Mi' kmaq and Wuastukwiuk people illustrate these interpretative difficulties. There are, with one exception, no records of treaty negotiations. Generally, Europeans were not privy to discussions among sakamows and elders, and thus would not have known of community debates which preceded and followed a treaty signing. For example, the Governor of the Ile Royal, Saint-Ovide, wrote in November 1728 that during the previous year the Mi' kmaq had held great meetings at Antigoniche, but he had been unable to obtain much information regarding what had been said in council. Because of this lack of interaction between the Mi' kmaq and European colonial officials, we do not know what Mi' kmaq and Wuastukwiuk delegates were told by English officials about the treaty. This in turn forces reliance on European documentation and European interpretations to understand the treaty's meaning. Indeed, researchers have tended to accept that the English versions of treaties reflect how the Mi' kmaq and Wuastukwiuk understood them. As research on late 19th century treaties signed between Western Native people and the Canadian government has shown, however, there could be a significant difference between the written English document and how Native negotiators understood it. The 1725/26, 1749, 1752 and 1760/61 treaties are cases in point.

According to these treaties, the Mi' kmaq and Wuastukwiuk recognized the English Crown's "jurisdiction and Dominion Over the Territories of the said Province of Nova Scotia or Acadia." Subsequent articles implicitly made both people subjects of the English Crown. Given the lack of English military influence throughout the region before the Loyalist immigration of the early 1780s, such recognition appears unlikely. Indeed, from soon after the English conquest of Port-Royal (Annapolis Royal) through to the mid-1750s, a number of sakamows expressed that neither English nor other European powers held claim to Mi' kmaq land.

How are we to explain this apparent contradiction? One possible explanation is that during the negotiations, the precise content of the treaty was communicated incorrectly to Mi' kmaq and Wuastukwiuk delegates. This is suggested by representations made both by Loron, the speaker for the Penobscot people, and by French speaking delegates who attended the ratification of the 1725 Boston treaty by Abenaki people at Casco Bay in July 1726. In a letter addressed to the Lieutenant-Governor of Massachusetts, Loron stated that[:]

> Having hear'd the Acts read which you have given me I have found the Articles entirely differing from what we have said in presence of one another, 'tis therefore to disown them that I write this letter unto you.

Loron took exception to several of the treaty's articles. Though all of his objections were not included in the letter written to Dummer, Loron was particularly upset by those articles which purported that he and his people had acknowledged King George to be their King and had "declar'd themselves subjects to the Crown of England." According to Loron's memory of those negotiations,

> when you have ask'd me if I acknowedg'd Him for King I answer'd yes butt att the same time have made you take notice that I did not understand to acknowledge Him for my king butt only that I own'd that He was king his kingdom as the King of France is king in His.

Similarly, French-speakers present at the ratification at Casco Bay wrote that articles read to the Indians of Panaouamské had not included references to the fact that they came to submit themselves to the English King, that they accepted responsibility for beginning hostilities with the English, and that they would agree to live according to English law. Rather, the oral translation of these articles had emphasized that the Panaouamské had "come to salute the English Governor to make peace with him and to renew the ancient friendship which had been between them before."

Mistranslation of treaty articles might have occurred for several reasons. As Algonquian based languages, Micmac and Wuastukwiuk were fundamentally different from both English and French. Consequently, many of the words and ideas contained in the treaties could not be translated easily. In translating the treaties, interpreters, some of whom were likely ill-equipped to deal with the subtle nuances of the language, may have misinterpreted those articles of the 1725 treaty in which the Mi' kmaq and Wuastukwiuk recognized King George as their king and accepted his jurisdiction over their lands.

Translation difficulties were exacerbated by a general English distrust of Native people. To English officials, the Mi' kmaq were barbarous and culturally inferior. Native people were, as one New England minister wrote in 1724, a people "living in a state of Nature" who did not possess the two essential components of every civilized nation, agriculture and a system of government. They were unpredictable, unreliable, and therefore not to be trusted. Exemplifying this attitude are remarks made in August 1725 by Hibbert Newton, a member of Nova Scotia's Executive Council, and Captain John Bradstreet in conversation with the Governor of Ile Royal, Joseph de Saint-Ovide. In a frank exchange of views, Newton and Bradstreet said,

> we valued the Indians so very little and knew how little their word was to be depended on that we took no notice of them, nor never shall, till they come in with a method whereby we may be very well assured by hostages and other good pledges at their good behaviour.

Similarly, in October 1749, the governor of Nova Scotia, Edward Cornwallis wrote to the Board of Trade that treaties with Indians meant nothing, and nothing "but force will prevail."

To understand the treaties, we must first evaluate the sources available to interpret them. The usefulness of these sources is limited, as the documents were written by Europeans, and their depictions of Mi' kmaq and Wuastukwiuk society were sporadic and sometimes incorrect. This was particularly true of English documentation before 1760. We should be sceptical, for instance, of letters written by English colonial officials which purport to describe events occurring in Mi' kmaq society when little official contact occurred between the two societies. More useful are French records, as there were extensive cultural, social, economic and political interactions between Mi' kmaq and French-speaking communities in the 17th and 18th centuries. Indeed, it appears there were discrepancies between the English copy of a treaty and the oral understanding of the Mi' kmaq and Wuastukwiuk negotiators.

This complicates a court's task as it suggests that a literal interpretation of the treaties is not always valid. What we need to do, therefore, is move beyond the treaties' literal meaning and describe the context in which they were signed. In doing so, we may be able to visualize the world not only from the European view point, but also from the perspective of Mi' kmaq and Wuastukwiuk people. This can only be done, however, by first recognizing the limitations of the sources traditionally used to interpret the treaties.

What *Syliboy* and other early judicial pronouncements on treaties did not account for, largely because they did not look beyond the "four corners" of written treaties, was the significant discrepancies between the written treaties and the representations made to the Aboriginal peoples who signed them.

Since the Aboriginal peoples could not read written documents, they were dependent upon the explanation of a treaty's terms provided to them by the Crown. As illustrated below, the explanations and representations made by the Crown's agents to the Aboriginal peoples were not always consistent with the final, written version of the treaties.

The following account of the exchange between Alexander Morris, Lieutenant Governor of Manitoba and the North-West Territories and the Crown's chief negotiator for many of the early post-Confederation numbered treaties, and representatives of the Ojibway Indians during the negotiations for Treaty No. 3 demonstrates the different understandings that the parties had regarding the purpose of the treaty. It also provides some insight into the process of Crown-Native treaty-making. It should be noted that this account is one that has been filtered through the eyes and ears of Governor Morris and his aides.

ALEXANDER MORRIS, THE TREATIES WITH THE INDIANS OF MANITOBA AND THE NORTH-WEST TERRITORIES, INCLUDING THE NEGOTIATIONS ON WHICH THEY WERE BASED, AND OTHER INFORMATION RELATING THERETO

(Toronto: Belfords, Clarke, 1880) at 55-65, 74-75

NORTH-WEST ANGLE,

October 1, 1873

The assembled Chiefs met the Governor this morning, as per agreement, and opened the proceedings of the day by expressing the pleasure they experienced at meeting the Commissioners on the present occasion. Promises had many times been made to them, and, said the speaker, unless they were now fulfilled they would not consider the broader question of the treaty.

Mr. S.J. Dawson, one of the Commissioners, reciprocated the expression of pleasure used by the Chiefs through their spokesman. ... He was, he continued, one of the Commission employed by the Government to treat with them and devise a scheme whereby both white men and Indians would be benefitted. ... He would explain to them the proposals he had to make. He had lived long amongst them and would advise them as a friend to take the opportunity of making arrangements with the Governor.

. . . . .

The Chief in reply said his head men and young men were of one mind, and determined not to enter upon the treaty until the promises made in the past were fulfilled; they were tired of waiting. What the Commissioners called "small matters" were great to them, and were what they wished to have settled.

. . . . .

His Excellency [Governor Morris] then addressed them at some length. ... Many of his listeners had come a long way, and he, too, had come a long way, and he wanted all the questions settled at once, by one treaty. He had a message from the Queen, but if his mouth was kept shut, the responsibility would rest on the Indians, and not with him if he were prevented from delivering it. He had authority to tell them what sum of money he could give them in hand now, and what he could give them every year; but it was for them to open his mouth. He concluded his remarks, which were forcibly delivered, with an emphatic, "I have said."

The Chief reiterated that he and his young men were determined not to go on with the treaty until the first question was disposed of. ... [I]t was the Indians' country, not the white man's. Following this the Governor told the Council that ... [h]e was bound by his Government, and was of the same mind to treat with them on all questions, and not on any one separately.

On seeing His Excellency so firm, and feeling that it would not do to allow any more time to pass without coming to business the Chief asked the Governor to open his mouth and tell what propositions he was prepared to make.

His Excellency then said — "I told you I was to make the treaty on the part of our Great Mother the Queen, and I feel it will be for your good and your children's. ... We are all children of the same Great Spirit, and are subject to the same Queen. I want to settle all matters both of the past and the present, so that the white and red man will always be friends. I will give you lands for farms, and also reserves for your own use. I have authority to make reserves such as I have described, not exceeding in all a square mile for every family of five or thereabouts. It may be a long time before the other lands are wanted, and in the meantime you will be permitted to fish and hunt over them. I will also establish schools whenever any band asks for them, so that your children may have the learning of the white man. I will also give you a sum of money for yourselves and every one of your wives and children for this year. I will give you ten dollars per head of the population, and for every other year five dollars-a-head. But to the chief men, not exceeding two to each band, we will give twenty dollars a-year for ever. I will give to each of you this year a present of goods and provisions to take you home, and I am sure you will be satisfied.

After consultation amongst themselves, the Councillors went to have a talk about the matter and will meet the Governor tomorrow morning, when it is expected the bargain will be concluded. Of course the Indians will make some other demands.

．．．．．

THIRD DAY

Proceedings were opened at eleven o'clock by the Governor announcing that he was ready to hear what the Chiefs had to say. The Fort Francis Chief acted as spokesman, assisted by another Chief, Powhassan.

MA-WE-DO-PE-NAIS — ... We think it a great thing to meet you here. What we have heard yesterday, and as you represented yourself, you said the Queen sent you here, the way we understood you as a representative of the Queen. All this is our property where you have come. We have understood you yesterday that Her Majesty has given you the same power and authority as *she* has, to act in this business; you said the Queen gave you her goodness, her charitableness in your hands. This is what we think, that the Great Spirit has planted us on this ground where we are, as you were where you came from. We think where we are is our property. I will tell you what he said to us when he ... planted us here; the rules that we should follow — us Indians — He has given us rules that we should follow to govern us rightly. ... I want to answer what we heard from you yesterday, in regard to the money that you have promised us yesterday to each individual. ... We ask fifteen dollars for all that you see, and for the children that are to be born in the future. This year only we ask for fifteen dollars; years after ten dollars; our Chiefs fifty dollars per year for every year, and other demands of large amounts in writing, say $125,000 yearly."

ANOTHER CHIEF — "I take my standing point from here. Our councillors have in council come to this conclusion, that they should have twenty dollars each; our warriors, fifteen dollars; our population, fifteen dollars. We have now laid down the conclusion of our councils by our decisions. We tell you our wishes are not divided. We are all of one mind." (Paper put in before the Governor for these demands.)

CHIEF — "I now let you know the opinions of us here. We would not wish that anyone should smile at our affairs, as we think our country is a large matter to us. If you grant us what is written on that paper, then we will talk about the reserves; we have decided in council for the benefit of those that will be born hereafter. If you do so the treaty will be finished, I believe."

GOVERNOR — "I quite agree that this is no matter to smile at. I think that the decision of to-day is one that affects yourselves and your children after, but you must recollect that this is the third time of negotiating. If we do not shake hands and make our Treaty to-day, I do not know when it will be done, as the Queen's Government will think you do not wish to treat with her. You told me that you understood that I represented the Queen's Government to you and that I opened my heart to you, but you must recollect that if *you* are a council there is another great council that governs a great Dominion, and they hold their councils the same as you hold yours. I wish to tell you that I am a servant of the Queen. I cannot do my own will; I must do hers. I can only give you what she tells me to give you. I am sorry to see that your hands were very wide open when you gave me this paper. I thought what I promised you was just, kind and fair between the Qeeen [*sic*] and you. It is now three years we have been trying to settle this matter. If we do not succeed to-day I shall go away feeling sorry for you and for your children that you could not see what was good for you and for them. I am ready to do what I promised you yesterday. My hand is open and you ought to take me by the hand and say, "yes, we accept of your offer." I have not the power to do what you ask of me. I ask you once more to think what you are doing, and of those you have left at home, and also of those that may be born yet, and I ask you not to turn your backs on what is offered to you, and you ought to see by what the Queen is offering you that she loves her red subjects as much as her white. I think you are forgetting one thing, that what I offer you is to be while the water flows and the sun rises. You know that in the United States they only pay the Indian for twenty years, and you come here to-day and ask for even more than they get for twenty years. Is that just? I think you ought to accept my offer, and make a treaty with me as I ask you to do. I only ask you to think for yourselves, and for your families, and for your children and children's children, and I know that if you do that you will shake hands with me to-day."

CHIEF — "I lay before you our opinions. Our hands are poor but our heads are rich, and it is riches that we ask so that we may be able to support our families as long as the sun rises and the water runs."

GOVERNOR — "I am very sorry; you know it takes two to make a bargain; you are agreed on the one side, and I for the Queen's Government on the other. I have to go away and report that I have to go without making terms with you. I doubt if the Commissioners will be sent again to assemble this nation."

. . . . .

CHIEF — "My terms I am going to lay down before you; the decision of our Chiefs; ever since we came to a decision you push it back. The sound of the rustling of the gold is under my feet where I stand; we have a rich country; it is the Great Spirit who gave us this; where we stand upon is the Indians' property and belongs to them. If you grant us our requests you will not go back without making the treaty."

ANOTHER CHIEF — "We understood yesterday that the Queen had given you the power to act upon, that you could do what you pleased, and that the riches of the Queen she had filled your head and body with, and you had only to throw them round about; but it seems it is not so, but that you have only half the power that she has, and that she has only half filled your head."

GOVERNOR — "I do not like to be misunderstood. I did not say yesterday that the Queen had given me all the power; what I told you was that I was sent here to represent the Queen's Government, and to tell you what the Queen was willing to do for you. You can understand very well; for instance, one of your great chiefs asks a brave to deliver a message, he represents you, and that is how I stand with the Queen's Government."

CHIEF — "It is your charitableness that you spoke of yesterday — Her Majesty's charitableness that was given you. It is our chiefs, our young men, our children and great grandchildren, and those that are to be born, that I represent here, and it is for them I ask for terms. The white man has robbed us of our riches, and we don't wish to give them up again without getting something in their place."

. . . . .

GOVERNOR — "I have told you already that I cannot grant your demands; I have not the power to do so. I have made you a liberal offer, and it is for you to accept or refuse it as you please."

CHIEF — "Our chiefs have the same opinion; they will not change their decision."

GOVERNOR — "Then the Council is at an end."

CHIEF (of Lac Seule) — "I understand the matter that he asks; if he puts a question to me as well as to the others, I say so as well as the rest. We are the first that were planted here; we would ask you to assist us with every kind of implement to use for our benefit, to enable us to perform our work; a little of everything and money. We would borrow your cattle; we ask you this for our support; I will find whereon to feed them. The waters out of which you sometimes take food for yourselves, we will lend you in return. If I should try to stop you — it is not in my power to do so; even the Hudson's Bay Company — that is a small power — I cannot gain my point with it. If you give what I ask, the time may come when I will ask you to lend me one of your daughters and one of your sons to live with us; and in return I will lend you one of my daughters and one of my sons for you to teach what is good, and after they have learned, to teach us. If you grant us what I ask, although I do not know you, I will shake hands with you. This is all I have to say."

GOVERNOR — "I have heard and I have learned something. I have learned that you are not all of one mind. I know that your interests are not the same — that some of you live in the north far away from the river; and some live on the river, and that you have got large sums of money for wood that you have cut and sold to the steamboats; but the men in the north have not this advantage. What the Chief has said is reasonable; and should you want goods I mean to ask you what amount you would have in goods, so that you would not have to pay the traders' price for them. I wish you were all of the same mind as the Chief who has just spoken. He wants his children to be taught. He is right. He wants to get cattle to help him to raise grain for his children. It would be a good thing for you all to be of his mind, and then you would not go away without making this treaty with me."

. . . . .

BLACKSTONE (Shebandowan) — "I am going to lay down before you the minds of those who are here. I do not wish to interfere with the decisions of those who are before you, or yet with your decisions. The people at the height of land where the waters came down from Shebandowan to Fort Frances, are those who have appointed me to lay before you our decision. We are going back to hold a Council."

. . . . .

GOVERNOR — "I think the nation will do well to do what the Chief has said. I think he has spoken sincerely, and it is right for them to withdraw and hold a Council among themselves."

. . . . .

The Governor decided that he would make a treaty with those bands that were willing to accept his terms, leaving out the few disaffected ones. A Council was held by the Indians in the evening ... After a very lengthy and exhaustive discussion, it was decided to accept the Governor's terms.

. . . . .

The treaty was finally closed on Friday afternoon, and signed on Saturday; after which a large quantity of provisions, ammunition and other goods were distributed.

. . . . .

The business of the treaty having now been completed, the Chief, Mawedopenais, who, with Powhassan, had with such wonderful tact carried on the negotiations, stepped up to the Governor and said: — "Now you see me stand before you all; what has been done here to-day has been done openly before the Great Spirit, and before the nation, and I hope that I may never hear any one say that this treaty has been done secretly; and now, in closing this Council, I take off my glove, and in giving you my hand, I deliver over my birth-right and lands; and in taking your hand, I hold fast all the promises you have made, and I hope they will last as long as the sun goes round and the water flows, as you have said."

The Governor then took his hand and said:

"I accept your hand and with it the lands, and will keep all my promises, in the firm belief that the treaty now to be signed will bind the red man and the white together as friends for ever."

A copy of the treaty was then prepared and duly signed, after which a large amount of presents, consisting of pork, flour, clothing, blankets, twine, powder and shot, etc., were distributed to the several bands represented on the ground.

———————

Compare this exchange of words between Morris and the representatives of the Aboriginal groups signing Treaty No. 3 with the written text of the treaty, reproduced below.

TREATY NO. 3

Between Her Majesty the Queen and the Saulteaux Tribe of the Ojibeway Indians at the northwest angle on the Lake of the Woods with adhesions

ARTICLES OF A TREATY made and concluded this third day of October, in the year of Our Lord one thousand eight hundred and seventy-three, between Her Most Gracious Majesty the Queen of Great Britain and Ireland, by Her Commissioners, the Honourable Alexander Morris, Lieutenant-Governor of the Province of Manitoba and the North-west Territories; Joseph Alfred Norbert Provencher and Simon James Dawson, of the one part, and the Saulteaux Tribe of the Ojibway Indians, inhabitants of the country within the limits hereinafter defined and described, by their Chiefs chosen and named as hereinafter mentioned, of the other part.

Whereas the Indians inhabiting the said country have, pursuant to an appointment made by the said Commissioners, been convened at a meeting at the north-west angle of the Lake of the Woods to deliberate upon certain matters of interest to Her Most Gracious Majesty, of the one part, and the said Indians of the other.

And whereas the said Indians have been notified and informed by Her Majesty's said Commissioners that it is the desire of Her Majesty to open up for settlement, immigration and such other purpose as to Her Majesty may seem meet, a tract of country bounded and described as hereinafter mentioned, and to obtain the consent thereto of Her Indian subjects inhabiting the said tract, and to make a treaty and arrange with them so that there may be peace and good will between them and Her Majesty and that they may know and be assured of what allowance they are to count upon and receive from Her Majesty's bounty and benevolence.

And whereas the Indians of the said tract, duly convened in council as aforesaid, and being requested by Her Majesty's said Commissioners to name certain Chiefs and Headmen, who should be authorized on their behalf to conduct such negotiations and sign any treaty to be founded thereon, and to become responsible to Her Majesty for their faithful performance by their respective bands of such obligations as shall be assumed by them, the said Indians have thereupon named the following persons for that person, that is to say:—

KEK-TA-PAY-PI-NAIS (Rainy River.)
KITCHI-GAY-KAKE (Rainy River.)
NOTE-NA-QUA-HUNG (North-West Angle.)
NAWE-DO-PE-NESS (Rainy River.)
POW-WA-SANG (North-West Angle.)
CANDA-COM-IGO-WE-NINIE (North-West Angle.)
PAPA-SKO-GIN (Rainy River.)
MAY-NO-WAH-TAW-WAYS-KIONG (North-West Angle.)
KITCH-NE-KA-LE-HAN (Rainy River.)
SAH-KATCH-EWAY (Lake Seul.)
MUPA-DAY-WAH-SIN (Kettle Falls.)

ME-PIES (Rainy Lake, Fort Frances.)
OOS-CON-NA-GEITH (Rainy Lake.)
WAH-SHIS-ROUCE (Eagle Lake.)
KAH-KEE-Y-ASH (Flower Lake.)
GO-BAY (Rainy Lake.)
KA-MO-TI-ASH (White Fish Lake.)
NEE-SHO-TAL (Rainy River.)
KEE-JE-GO-KAY(Rainy River.)
SHA-SHA-GANCE (Shoal Lake.)
SHAH-WIN-NA-BI-NAIS (Shoal Lake.)
AY-ASH-A-WATH (Buffalo Point.)
PAY-AH-BEE-WASH (White Fish Bay.)
KAH-TAY-TAY-PA-E-CUTCH (Lake of the Woods.)

And thereupon, in open council the different bands having presented their Chiefs to the said Commissioners as the Chiefs and Headmen for the purposes aforesaid of the respective bands of Indians inhabiting the said district hereinafter described:

And whereas the said Commissioners then and there received and acknowledged the persons so presented as Chiefs and Headmen for the purpose aforesaid of the respective bands of Indians inhabiting the said district hereinafter described;

And whereas the said Commissioners have proceeded to negotiate a treaty with the said Indians, and the same has been finally agreed upon and concluded, as follows, that is to say:—

The Saulteaux Tribe of the Ojibbeway Indians and all other the Indians inhabiting the district hereinafter described and defined do hereby cede, release, surrender and yield up to the Government of the Dominion of Canada for Her Majesty the Queen and Her successors forever, all their rights, titles and privileges whatsoever, to the lands included within the following limits, that is to say:—

Commencing at a point on the Pigeon River route where the international boundary line between the Territories of Great Britain and the United States intersects the height of land separating the waters running to Lake Superior from those flowing to Lake Winnipeg; thence northerly, westerly and easterly along the height of land aforesaid, following its sinuosities, whatever their course may be, to the point at which the said height of land meets the summit of the watershed from which the streams flow to Lake Nepigon; thence northerly and westerly, or whatever may be its course, along the ridge separating the waters of the Nepigon and the Winnipeg to the height of land dividing the waters of the Albany and the Winnipeg; thence westerly and north-westerly along the height of land dividing the waters flowing to Hudson's Bay by the Albany or other rivers from those running to English River and the Winnipeg to a point on the said height of land bearing north forty-five degrees east from Fort Alexander, at the mouth of the Winnipeg; thence south forty-five degrees west to Fort Alexander, at the mouth of the Winnipeg; thence southerly along the eastern bank of the Winnipeg to the mouth of White

Mouth River, thence southerly by the line described as in that part forming the eastern boundary of the tract surrendered by the Chippewa and Swampy Cree tribes of Indians to Her Majesty on the third of August, one thousand eight hundred and seventy-one, namely, by White Mouth River to White Mouth Lake, and thence on a line having the general bearing of White Mouth River to the forty-ninth parallel of north latitude, thence by the forty-ninth parallel of north latitude to the Lake of the Woods, and from thence by the international boundary line to the place beginning.

The tract comprised within the lines above described, embracing an area of fifty-five thousand square miles, be the same more or less. To have and to hold the same to Her Majesty the Queen, and Her successors forever.

And Her Majesty the Queen hereby agrees and undertakes to lay aside reserves for farming lands, due respect being had to lands at present cultivated by the said Indians, and also to lay aside and reserve for the benefit of the said Indians, to be administered and dealt with for them by Her Majesty's Government of the Dominion of Canada, in such a manner as shall seem best, other reserves of land in the said territory hereby ceded, which said reserves shall be selected and set aside where it shall be deemed most convenient and advantageous for each band or bands of Indians, by the officers of the said Government appointed for that purpose, and such selection shall be so made after conference with the Indians; provided, however, that such reserves, whether for farming or other purposes, shall in no wise exceed in all one square mile for each family of five, or in that proportion for larger or smaller families; and such selections shall be made if possible during the course of next summer, or as soon thereafter as may be found practicable, it being understood, however, that if at the time of any such selection of any reserve, as aforesaid, there are any settlers within the bounds of the lands reserved by any band, Her Majesty reserves the right to deal with such settlers as She shall deem just so as not to diminish the extent of land allotted to Indians; and provided also that the aforesaid reserves of lands, or any interest or right therein or appurtenant thereto, may be sold, leased or otherwise disposed of by the said Government for the use and benefit of the said Indians, with the consent of the Indians entitled thereto first had and obtained.

And with a view to show the satisfaction of Her Majesty with the behaviour and good conduct of Her Indians She hereby, through Her Commissioners, makes them a present of twelve dollars for each man, woman and child belonging to the bands here represented, in extinguishment of all claims heretofore preferred.

And further, Her Majesty agrees to maintain schools for instruction in such reserves hereby made as to Her Government of Her Dominion of Canada may seem advisable whenever the Indians of the reserve shall desire it.

Her Majesty further agrees with Her said Indians that within the boundary of Indian reserves, until otherwise determined by Her Government of the Dominion of Canada, no intoxicating liquor shall be allowed to be introduced or sold, and all laws now in force or hereafter to be enacted to preserve Her Indian subjects inhabiting the reserves or living elsewhere within Her North-west Territories, from the evil influences of the use of intoxicating liquors, shall be strictly enforced.

Her Majesty further agrees with Her said Indians that they, the said Indians, shall have right to pursue their avocations of hunting and fishing through-out the tract surrendered as hereinbefore described, subject to such regulations as may from time to time be made by Her Government of Her Dominion of Canada, and saving and excepting such tracts as may, from time to time, be required or taken up for settlement, mining, lumbering or other purposes by Her said Government of the Dominion of Canada, or by any of the subjects thereof duly authorized therefor by the said Government.

It is further agreed between Her Majesty and Her said Indians that such sections of the reserves above indicated as may at any time be required for Public Works or buildings of what nature soever may be appropriated for that purpose by Her Majesty's Government of the Dominion of Canada, due compensation being made for the value of any improvements thereon.

And further, that Her Majesty's Commissioners shall, as soon as possible after the execution of this treaty, cause to be taken an accurate census of all the Indians inhabiting the tract above described, distributing them in families, and shall in every year ensuring the date hereof at some period in each year to be duly notified to the Indians, and at a place or places to be appointed for that purpose within the territory ceded, pay to each Indian person the sum of five dollars per head yearly.

It is further agreed between Her Majesty and the said Indians that the sum of fifteen hundred dollars per annum shall be yearly and every year expended by Her Majesty in the purchase of ammunition and twine for nets for the use of the said Indians.

It is further agreed between Her Majesty and the said Indians that the following articles shall be supplied to any band of the said Indians who are now actually cultivating the soil or who shall hereafter commence to cultivate the land, that is to say: two hoes for every family actually cultivating, also one spade per family as aforesaid, one plough for every ten families as aforesaid, five harrows for every twenty families as aforesaid, one scythe for every family as aforesaid, and also one axe and one cross-cut saw, one hand-saw, one pit-saw, the necessary files, one grind-stone, one auger for each band, and also for each Chief for the use of his band one chest of ordinary carpenter's tools; also for each band enough of wheat, barley, potatoes and oats to plant the land actually broken up for cultivation by such band; also for each band one yoke of oxen, one full and four cows; all the aforesaid articles to be given once for all for the encouragement of the practice of agriculture among the Indians.

It is further agreed between Her Majesty and the said Indians that each Chief duly recognized as such shall receive an annual salary of twenty-five dollars per annum, and each, subordinate officer, not exceeding three for each band, shall receive fifteen dollars per annum; and each such Chief and subordinate officer as aforesaid shall also receive once in every three years a suitable suit of clothing; and each Chief shall receive, in recognition of the closing of the treaty, a suitable flag and medal.

And the undersigned Chiefs, on their own behalf and on behalf of all other Indians inhabiting the tract within ceded, do hereby solemnly promise and engage to strictly observe this treaty, and also to conduct and behave themselves as good and loyal subjects of Her Majesty the Queen. They promise and engage that they will in all respects obey and abide by the law, that they will maintain peace and good order between each other, and also between themselves and other tribes of Indians, and between themselves and others of Her Majesty's subjects, whether Indians or whites, now inhabiting or hereafter to inhabit any part of the said ceded tract, and that they will not molest the person or property of any inhabitants of such ceded tract, or the property of Her Majesty the Queen, or interfere with or trouble any person passing or travelling through the said tract, or any part thereof; and that they will aid and assist the officers of Her Majesty in bringing to justice and punishment any Indian offending against the stipulations of this treaty, or infringing the laws in force in the country so ceded.

IN WITNESS WHEREOF, Her Majesty's said Commissioners and the said Indian Chiefs have hereunto subscribed and set their hands at the North-West Angle of the Lake of the Woods this day and year herein first above named.

Signed by the Chiefs within named, in presence of the following witnesses, the same having been first read and explained by the Honorable James McKay.

The different understanding of the function of post-Confederation "land surrender" treaties held by the Crown and the Aboriginal peoples was not restricted to the scenario surrounding Treaty No. 3. Indeed, the disparate understanding of treaties by the Crown and the Aboriginal peoples is illustrated by the evidence led in *Paulette v. Registrar of Titles (No. 2) (1973)*, 42 D.L.R. (3d) 8 (N.W.T.S.C.), rev'd on other grounds, [1976] 2 W.W.R. 193 (*sub nom. Paulette v. Register of Titles*), 63 D.L.R. (3d) 1 (N.W.T.C.A.), aff'd on other grounds (*sub nom. Paulette v. R.*), [1976] S.C.J. No. 89, [1977] 2 S.C.R. 628, [1977] 1 W.W.R. 321, 12 N.R. 420, 72 D.L.R. (3d) 161 (S.C.C.), reproduced *infra*, in which the effect of Treaties 8 and 11 as land surrender agreements was contemplated. Like Treaty No. 3, Treaties 8 and 11 have been implicated in a number of disputes between Aboriginal peoples and the Crown (note, for example, *R. v. Sikyea*, [1964] S.C.J. No. 42, [1964] S.C.R. 642, 44 C.R. 266, 49 W.W.R. 306, [1965] 2 C.C.C. 129, 50 D.L.R. (2d) 80 (S.C.C.) and *R. v. Horseman*, [1990] S.C.J. No. 39, [1990] 1 S.C.R. 901, [1990] 4 W.W.R. 97, 73 Alta. L.R. (2d) 193, 55 C.C.C. (3d) 353, 108 N.R. 1, 108 A.R. 1, [1990] 3 C.N.L.R. 95 (S.C.C.) cases, reproduced in Chapter 8). The wording and structure of Treaties 8 and 11 take essentially the same form as Treaty No. 3, which was the blueprint for the numbered treaties that came after it.

Treaty No. 11, which was concluded on June 27, 1921, with an adhesion on July 17 of that same year, between the Crown and the Slave, Dogrib, Loucheux, Hare and other Indians, was virtually identical to Treaty No. 8, save for the territory covered, the deletion of the option for the signatories to hold land in severalty and, in the place of the provision of agricultural implements, etc. the following inclusions:

> FURTHER, His Majesty agrees that, each band shall receive once and for all equipment for hunting, fishing and trapping to the value of fifty dollars for each family of such band, and that there shall be distributed annually among the Indians equipment, such as twine for nets, ammunition and trapping to the value of three dollars per head for each Indian who continues to follow the vocation of hunting, fishing and trapping.

> FURTHER, His Majesty agrees that, in the event of any of the Indians aforesaid being desirous of following agricultural pursuits, such Indians shall receive such assistance as is deemed necessary for that purpose.

The Treaty Commissioner's report for Treaty No. 11, as with the report accompanying Treaty No. 8, revealed additional information about the Aboriginals' concerns about signing the treaty and the effect that it would have upon them. Of these concerns, Commissioner H.A. Conroy wrote:

> I had several meetings with them, and explained the terms of the treaty. They were very apt in asking questions, and here, as in all the other posts where the treaty was signed, the questions asked and the difficulties encountered were much the same. The Indians seemed afraid, for one thing, that their liberty to hunt, trap and fish would be taken away or curtailed, but were assured by me that this would not be the case, and the Government will expect them to support themselves in their own way, and, in fact, that more twine for nets and more ammunition were given under the terms of this treaty than under any of the preceding ones; this went a long way to calm their fears. I also pointed out that any game laws made were to their advantage, and, whether they took treaty or not, they were subject to the laws of the Dominion. They also seemed afraid that they would be liable for military service if the treaty was signed, that they would be confined on the reserves, but, when told that they were exempt from military service, and that the reserves mentioned in the treaty would be of their own choosing, for their own use, and not for the white people, and that they would be free to come and go as they pleased, they were satisfied.

What is the relationship between a Treaty Commissioners' Report and the treaty that it corresponds to? Should the text of a Treaty Commissioners' Report be understood as part of a treaty? If not, what weight should it be given *vis-à-vis* the written treaty, if any?

These Treaty Commissioners' Reports reveal that the written text of Crown-Native treaties does not always accurately reflect the nature of the representations made by the Crown or the entirety of the agreement between the parties. This is illustrated as well by the judicial reception of Aboriginal oral history, an early example of which is seen in the *Paulette* case, excerpted below.

In *Paulette,* which was heard in 1973, Justice Morrow of the Northwest Territories Supreme Court received a significant amount of oral evidence from the Aboriginal peoples involved in the dispute. Justice Morrow's decision is interesting not only for its illustration of Aboriginal understandings of the purpose and effect of the treaties, but for its wholesale incorporation of these sentiments in his written reasons for judgment, something that had been infrequently done previously.

PAULETTE v. REGISTRAR OF TITLES (NO. 2)

[1973] N.W.T.J. No. 22, 42 D.L.R. (3d) 8 at 14 (N.W.T.S.C.); rev'd on other
grounds, [1976] 2 W.W.R. 193 (*sub nom. Paulette v. Register of Titles*), 63
D.L.R. (3d) 1 (N.W.T.C.A.); aff'd on other grounds
(*sub nom. Paulette v. R.*) [1976] S.C.J. No. 89, [1977] 2 S.C.R. 628,
[1977] 1 W.W.R. 321, 12 N.R. 420, 72 D.L.R. (3d) 161 (S.C.C.)

. . . . . .

Morrow J.: — Chief Baptiste Cazon, chief of the Fort Simpson Band for some 20 years explained how the members of the present band at Fort Simpson were all descendants from his great-grandfather and that while his people had no written history, as far back as their memories down through each generation could go, his people had made their homes in the general area of Fort Simpson and that such lands had always been considered to be theirs. According to him, for thousands of years, his people had used the land for hunting and fishing, to obtain food and clothing. They roamed all over the country in pursuit of game. He explained that in his capacity as chief, he considered he had a responsibility to his people to take the place of their and his ancestors who had signed the treaty. There are still quite a few of his people even at this time who earn their living from the land in the time-honoured way.

. . . . .

Alexie Arrowmaker, chief at Fort Rae . . . stated that his people, the Dogribs, had never sold their land to anyone.

. . . . .

The chief of the Loucheux Band at Aklavik, Andrew Stewart, described pretty much the same state of affairs in respect of the Indians of his area as has been set forth above. About 12 years old at the time of the treaty he explained he had never heard any of the old people say they had given up their land to the Government.

Louis Norwegian, 64 years of age, was present at Fort Simpson in 1921 when "old" Norwegian as he describes his grandfather, was leader of the Fort Simpson Band and when the treaty was first "paid". He overheard some of the exchange of words between his grandfather and the Government representatives. According to this witness the Commissioner promised a letter on fishing and trapping. When his grandfather, the recognized leader, went home to eat, an Indian by the name of Antoine was left. He took the treaty and became the chief — the white men made him the chief. This man's evidence was to the effect that his grandfather "did not want to the take the money for no reason at all". The promises made that their hunting and fishing would be left to them as long as the sun shall rise and the rivers shall flow. He heard no mention of reserves but he did hear mention that once they took treaty the Government would receive the land. His memory was that the purpose of the treaty was to help the Indians live in peace with the whites and that the Indians would receive a grubstake each treaty payment. Once Antoine took the money, this witness testified the Commissioner said everybody had to take the treaty after that, Antoine was given a medal, the people took the money, and the people being "kind of scared" felt they had to keep Antoine on as chief after that.

Chief Vital Bonnetrouge, chief of the Fort Providence Band ... added a little more to the attitude of the people at the time the treaty was signed. As he states: "the land was not mentioned at the treaty. The old chief said "if this five dollars would be for my land, I am not taking it." This witness, by his testimony, left one with the same impression that came from the stories told by so many, namely, it was a deal to look after the people and nothing else.

. . . . .

Those Indians who had either taken part in the treaty negotiations or who had been present while the negotiations were under way and heard parts or all of the conversation, seemed to be in general agreement that their leaders were concerned about what they were giving up, if anything, in exchange for the treaty money, *i.e.*, they were suspicious of something for nothing; that up to the time of treaty the concept of chief was unknown to them, only that of leader, but the Government man was the one who introduced them to the concept of chief when he placed the medal over the Indian's head after he had signed for his people; that they understood that by signing the treaty they would get a grubstake, money, and the promised protection of the Government from the expected intrusion of white settlers. It is clear also that the Indians for the most part did not understand English and certainly there is no evidence of any of the signatories to the treaties understanding English. Some signatures purport to be what one would call a signature, some are in syllabic form, but most are by mark in the form of an "X". The similarity of the "X"s is suggestive that perhaps the Government party did not even take care to have each Indian make his own "X". Most witnesses were firm in their recollection that land was not to be surrendered, reserves were not mentioned, and the main concern and chief thrust of the discussions centred around the fear of losing their hunting and fishing rights, the Government officials always reassuring them with variations of the phrase that so long as the sun shall rise in the east and set in the west, and the rivers shall flow, their free right to hunt and fish would not be interfered with.

It seems also that very little if any reference to a map was made at any of the settlements. In several cases, also, it is apparent that fairly large segments of the Indian community were not present on the occasion of the first treaty and that the recognized leaders of the respective bands were not always there either.

. . . . .

An Order in Council of January 26, 1891 (never acted upon apparently according to Father Fumoleau's evidence), contained the following paragraph:

> On a Report dated 7th of January 1891, from the Superintendent General of Indian Affairs stating that the discovery in the District of Athabaska and in the Mackenzie River Country that immense quantities of petroleum exists within certain areas of those regions as well as the belief that other minerals and substances of economic value, such as sulphur on the South Coast of Great Slave Lake and Salt on the Mackenzie and Slave Rivers, are to be found therein, the development of which may add materially to the public weal, and the further consideration that several Railway projects in connection with this portion of the Dominion may be given effect to at no such remote date as might be supposed, appear to render it advisable that a treaty or treaties should be made with the Indians who claim those regions as their hunting grounds, with a view to the extinguishment of the Indian title in such portions of the same as it may be considered in the interest of the public to open up for settlement.

A second Order in Council enacted June 27, 1898, contains pretty much the same language in respect to "aboriginal title" and as to how the inhabitants "should be treated with for the relinquishment of their claim to territorial ownership".

The above language is repeated in the Order in Council of December 6, 1898, which deals with the extension of Treaty 8 into British Columbia. Finally on March 3, 1921, the Order in Council which authorized the negotiation of Treaty 11 contains the paragraph:

> The early development of this territory is anticipated and it is advisable to follow the usual policy and obtain from the Indians cession of their aboriginal title and thereby bring them into closer relation with the Government and establish securely their legal position.

Unless, therefore, the negotiation of Treaty 8 and Treaty 11 legally terminated or extinguished the Indian land rights or aboriginal rights, it would appear that there was a clear constitutional obligation to protect the legal rights of the indigenous people in the area covered by the proposed caveat, and a clear recognition of such rights.

5. *Treaty 8 and Treaty 11 could not legally terminate Indian land rights. The Indian people did not understand or agree to the terms appearing in the written version of the treaties, only the mutually understood promises relating to wild life, annuities, relief and friendship became legally effective commitments.*

. . . . .

In the light of the evidence which was adduced during the present hearing it is perhaps of interest to quote H. A. Conroy, the Treaty 11 Commissioner, where in his report to his Deputy Superintendent General, Department of Indian Affairs, he states:

> They were very apt in asking questions, and here, as in all the other posts where the treaty was signed, the questions asked and the difficulties encountered were much the same. The Indians seemed afraid, for one thing, that their liberty to hunt, trap and fish would be taken away or curtailed, but were assured by me that this would not be the case.

While the important phrase in respect to surrender of the land is in each case camouflaged to some extent by being included in one of the preambles, none the less the clear intention would seem to be to obtain from the Indians "all their rights, titles and privileges whatsoever, to the lands . . .". The actual words are: "the said Indians Do HEREBY CEDE, RELEASE, SURRENDER AND YIELD UP". Read in conjunction with "all their rights, titles and privileges" it is about as complete and all-embracing language as can be imagined. If one was to stop there, of course, the Indians were left nothing.

It seems to me that there are two possible qualifications:

(1) That really all the Government did was confirm its paramount title and by assuring the Indians that "their liberty to hunt, trap and fish" was not to be taken away or curtailed was in effect a form of declaration by the Government of continuing aboriginal rights in the Indians.

. . . . .

I am satisfied here that the Caveators have an arguable case under this heading and have at least the possibility of persuading the Federal Court or whichever other Court may be called upon to rule, that the two treaties are not effective instruments to terminate their aboriginal rights for the above reason. In other words the federal Government sought these treaties to reassure their dominant title only.

(2) That, unlike perhaps the previous treaties, the manner of negotiation, the "ultimatum" effect of the discussions between the parties in the Northwest Territories was such as to make it possible for the Caveators to succeed in persuading a Court exercising the final say on these matters that there was either a failure in the meeting of the minds or that the treaties were mere "peace" treaties and did not effectively terminate Indian title — certainly to the extent it covered what is normally referred to as surface rights — the use of the land for hunting, trapping and fishing.

Under this subheading it is necessary to examine the evidence in somewhat closer detail than has been done heretofore in this judgment.

Throughout the hearings before me there was a common thread in the testimony — that the Indians were repeatedly assured they were not to be deprived of their hunting, fishing and trapping rights. To me, hearing the witnesses at first hand as I did, many of whom were there at the signing, some of them having been directly involved in the treaty making, it is almost unbelievable that the Government party could have ever returned from their efforts with any impression but that they had given an assurance in perpetuity to the Indians in the territories that their traditional use of the lands was not affected.

Ted Trindle, present at the signing of Treaty 11 at Fort Simpson, said:

> Well, they talked about land and the Indians were scared that by taking Treaty they would lose all of their rights but the Indians were told not, but if they were taking treaty they would get protection. They were told it was not to get the land but they would still be free to hunt and roam as usual, no interference.

At Fort Wrigley, Phillip Moses remembers that the Commissioner "said nothing would be changed, everything would be the same as way back, and everything would be the same in the future . . . ".

Pretty much the same assurance came at Fort Resolution. When Chief Snuff appeared to be holding out, according to Johnny Jean-Marie Beaulieu, who was there, he was told by the Treaty party: "we will pay out the Treaty to you here and it has no binding on your land or country at all. It has nothing to do with this land."

Almost each Indian witness affirmed how the Indian representatives only signed after being reassured that as one expressed it "If you don't change anything, we will take treaty."

As if the above was not enough, further examination of the evidence, including the material from the archives put in through Father Fumoleau, certainly leaves an impression of haste, almost an "ultimatum" as Bishop Breynat later reported. The uneasy feeling that the negotiations were not all as above-board as one would have hoped for is enhanced by statements like that of Pierre Michel who reported that at Fort Providence the Commissioner said: ". . . if didn't take money, there going to be some sort of trouble for the Indian people".

The comments of Mr. Harris in his report in 1925 for the Simpson Agency lends some credence to the anxiety. He reports:

> I believe it to be my duty to inform you that I know that certain promises were made these Indians at the first Treaty which in my opinion never should have been made. The Indians at Fort Simpson did not wish to accept the Treaty at first, and I think the wisest course would have been to let them alone till they asked for it themselves, though I do not in any way wish to criticise the action of my superiors in the Department.

Confirmation of haste and perhaps irregularities is easy to find from the suggestion put forth during the hearing that at Fort Simpson when the Indians led by Old Norwegian (their recognized spokesman) refused to sign and left, the Treaty party then appointed Antoine as chief and the treaty was signed. Again there is the testimony of Chief Yendo, who is shown as having signed for Fort Wrigley, but who has no memory of having signed and swears he cannot read or write.

The impracticability of expecting the indigenous peoples with whom the treaties were concerned here to be able to sustain themselves on the area of land each was to receive when reserves came to be allocated and set aside offers one more reason to suspect the *bona fides* of the negotiations. Perhaps the extreme south-western area might permit a bare subsistence living to be grubbed from the soil, but most of the area embraced by the treaties is as already described — rock, lake and tundra — with hunting, trapping and fishing offering the only viable method of maintaining life.

In examining agreements such as treaties where as in the present case one side, the Indians, were in such an inferior bargaining position, it is perhaps well to remember the cautionary words of Mr. Justice Matthews in *Choctaw Nation v. United States* (1886), 119 U.S. 1, where, at p. 28, he said:

> The recognized relation between the parties to this controversy, therefore, is that between a superior and an inferior, whereby the latter is placed under the care and control of the former, and which, while it authorizes the adoption on the part of the United States of such policy as their own public interests may dictate, recognizes, on the other hand, such an interpretation of their acts and promises as justice and reason demand in all cases where power is exerted by the strong over those to whom they owe care and protection. The parties are not on an equal footing, and that inequality is to be made good by the superior justice which looks only to the substance of the right, without regard to technical rules framed under a system of municipal jurisprudence, formulating the rights and obligations of private persons, equally subject to the same laws.

Justice Hall in *Calder et al. v. A.-G. B.C.* (1973), 34 D.L.R. (3d) 145 at p. 210, [1973] S.C.R. 313, [1973] 4 W.W.R. 1, in discussing onus, states:

> It would, accordingly, appear to be beyond question that the onus of proving that the Sovereign intended to extinguish the Indian title lies on the respondent and that intention must be "clear and plain". There is no such proof in the case at bar; no legislation to that effect.

With the above principle in mind I conclude under this heading that there is enough doubt as to whether the full aboriginal title had been extinguished, certainly in the minds of the Indians, to justify the Caveators attempting to protect the Indian position until a final adjudication can be obtained.

It has been shown that the Crown and the Aboriginal peoples did not always enter into treaty relations with common purposes or intentions. This reality was not necessarily recognized by the parties at the time. Combining this fact with the differences in the world views held by the parties — as evidenced, in part, by the disparate understandings of land discussed in Chapter 3 — resulted in the treaties being interpreted differently by the parties. This lack of uniformity in interpreting the purpose and effect of treaties has had significant effects on Canadian treaty jurisprudence.

E. MODERN CANADIAN TREATY JURISPRUDENCE — BEGINNING A NEW PROCESS OF INTERPRETATION

As indicated by the introductory quote to this chapter made by Justice M'Lean in *Worcester v. State of Georgia*, early American Aboriginal rights jurisprudence recognized the need to avoid interpreting treaties in a literal fashion. While this principle had become well-entrenched in American jurisprudence before the end of the 19th century, it did not achieve the same recognition in Canada for almost 150 years.

The traditional approach of interpreting treaties literally truly began to change in Canada in the second half of the 20th century. The case of *R. v. White and Bob*, was an early example of this change in judicial approach to treaty interpretation.

R. v. WHITE and BOB

(1964), 50 D.L.R. (2d) 613, 52 W.W.R. 193 (B.C.C.A.); aff'd (1965), 52 D.L.R. (2d) 481*n* (S.C.C.)

Davey J.A.: — The Crown appeals from the respondents' acquittal by Swencisky, Co. Ct. J., on their appeal to him from their summary conviction by L. Beevor-Potts, Esq., P.M. of having game, namely, the carcasses of six deer, in their possession during the closed season without having a valid and subsisting permit under the *Game Act*, contrary to the provisions of that Act. The *Game Act* is an Act of the Provincial Legislature, R.S.B.C. 1960, c. 160.

The Crown concedes that if the respondents, who are native Indians, had a legal right to hunt for food for themselves and their families over the lands in question, they were lawfully in possession of the carcasses, no permit was required, and they were not guilty of the offence.

Section 18 of the *Game Act* forbids any person to kill deer except in open season, subject to certain specified exceptions within which the respondents do not fall. They contend that an agreement (ex. 8) between their ancestors, members of the Saalequun tribe, and Governor Douglas, dated December 23, 1854, for the sale of the land to the Hudson's Bay Company, gave them the right to hunt for food over the land in question and, alternatively, that as native Indians they possess the aboriginal right to hunt for food over unoccupied land lying within their ancient tribal hunting grounds.

For the purposes of this appeal it must be taken that the respondents are native Indians, members of the Saalequun tribe, and descendants of the members who signed ex. 8; that they killed the deer on unoccupied land comprised in the sale to the Hudson's Bay Co., and forming part of the ancient hunting grounds of the tribe, for the purpose of providing food for themselves and their families.

It is common ground that ex. 8 must be taken to include the following clause appearing in all other transfers of Vancouver Island Indian land, which, for reasons that need not be mentioned, does not appear in this instrument:

> The condition of, or understanding of this sale, is this, that our village sites and enclosed fields, are to be kept for our own use, for the use of our children, and for those who may follow after us, and the lands shall be properly surveyed hereafter; it is understood however, that the land itself with these small exceptions, becomes the entire property of the white people forever, it is also understood that we are at liberty to hunt over the unoccupied lands, and to carry on our fisheries as formerly.

The Crown does not deny that the respondents are entitled to exercise and enjoy whatever rights or privileges there may be under ex. 8 until they have been effectively extinguished. It does contend that ex. 8 conferred no hunting rights, and if it did, that these rights have been extinguished by s. 87 of the *Indian Act*, R.S.C. 1952, c. 149, [now s. 88] first enacted in 1951, which the Crown says extends in effect the general provisions of the *Game Act* to Indians.

Section 87 reads as follows:

> 87. Subject to the terms of any treaty and any other Act of the Parliament of Canada, all laws of general application from time to time in force in any province are applicable to and in respect of Indians in the province, except to the extent that such laws are inconsistent with this Act or any order, rule, regulation or by-law made thereunder, and except to the extent that such laws make provision for any matter for which provision is made by or under this Act.

The Crown submits that ex. 8 does not fall within the prefatory saving clause of s. 87 because:

(1) Exhibit 8 did not create any hunting rights but merely recognized pre-existing privileges; that the alleged hunting rights were mere liberties which formed part of the aboriginal rights of the Indians over the soil, and that they existed when Vancouver Island became British territory, and continued until extinguished or abolished by valid legislation; that the saving clause refers only to rights created by Treaties.

(2) That even if ex. 8 did create or recognize rights that could be the subject of a Treaty within the meaning of the saving clause, the document is not such a Treaty.

The force of the first argument seems to depend upon the assumption that s. 87 should be read as if it were subject only to rights created by a Treaty; that would remove from the saving clause rights already in being and excepted from or confirmed by a Treaty. That argument fails to accord full meaning to the words, "subject to the *terms* of any treaty . . ." In my opinion an exception, reservation, or confirmation is as much a term of a Treaty as a grant, (I observe parenthetically that a reservation may be a grant), and the operative words of the section will not extend general laws in force in any Province to Indians in derogation of rights so excepted, reserved or confirmed.

Counsel for the Crown next submits that ex. 8 is not a Treaty. He contends that a Treaty within s. 87 is:

(1) A document that on its face is so described or one that uses that word in the text, and,
(2) deals with fundamental differences between the parties (quaere, political differences?) and not merely with private rights, such as in this case the sale of land, and,
(3) a formal document in which the terms are set out with some degree of formality, and,
(4) an agreement to which the Crown is a party, or which it has authorized one of the parties to make on its behalf.

Counsel submits that ex. 8 meets none of these requirements.

It is unnecessary to venture any extended definition of the word "Treaty" in this context, but it can be safely said that it does not mean an "executive act establishing relationships between what are recognized as two or more independent states acting in sovereign capacities ...", per Rand, J., in *Francis v. The Queen* . ... It is also clear in my opinion that the word is not used in its widest sense as including agreements between individuals dealing with their private and personal affairs. Its meaning lies between those extremes.

. . . . .

In considering whether ex. 8 is a Treaty within the meaning of s. 87, regard ought to be paid to the history of our country: its original occupation and settlement; the fact that the Hudson's Bay Co. was the proprietor, and to use a feudal term contained in its charters, the Lord of the lands in the Northwest Territories and Vancouver Island; and, the part that company played in the settlement and development of this country. In the Charter granting Vancouver Island to the Hudson's Bay Co., it was charged with the settlement and colonization of that Island. That was clearly part of the Imperial policy to head off American settlement of and claims to the territory. In that sense the Hudson's Bay Co. was an instrument of Imperial policy. It was also the long standing policy of the Imperial government and of the Hudson's Bay Co. that the Crown or the company should buy from the Indians their land for settlement by white colonists. In pursuance of that policy many agreements, some very formal, others informal, were made with various bands and tribes of Indians for the purchase of their lands. These agreements frequently conferred upon the grantors hunting rights over the unoccupied lands so sold. Considering the relationship between the Crown and the Hudson's Bay Co. in the colonization of this country, and the Imperial and corporate policies reflected in those agreements, I cannot regard ex. 8 as a mere agreement for the sale of land made between a private vendor and a private purchaser. In view of the notoriety of these facts, I entertain no doubt that Parliament intended the word "Treaty" in s. 87 to include all such agreements, and to except their provisions from the operative part of the section. That being so, s. 87 does not extend the general provisions of the *Game Act* to the respondents in the exercise of their hunting rights under ex. 8 over the lands in question.

We have been referred to no other Act of Parliament or The Colonial Legislature that would have the effect of abrogating or curtailing the respondents' rights under ex. 8, and the only provincial legislation that might to do so is the *Game Act* itself.

Sections 8 [rep. & sub. 1961, c. 21, s. 3] and 15 [rep. & sub. 1961, c. 21, s. 6] of the *Game Act* specifically exempt Indians from the operation of certain provisions of the Act, and from that I think it clear that the other provisions are intended to be of general application and to include Indians. If these general sections are sufficiently clear to show an intention to abrogate or qualify the contractual rights of hunting notoriously reserved to Indians by agreements such as ex. 8 they would, in my opinion, fail in that purpose because that would be legislation in relation to Indians that falls within Parliament's exclusive legislative authority under s. 91(24) of the *B.N.A. Act*, and also because that would conflict with s. 87 of the *Indian Act* passed under that authority. Legislation that abrogates or abridges the hunting rights reserved to Indians under the treaties and agreements by which they sold their ancient territories to the Crown and to the Hudson's Bay Company for white settlement is, in my respectful opinion, legislation in relation to Indians because it deals with rights peculiar to them. Lord Watson's judgment in *St. Catherine's Milling & Lumber Co. v. The Queen* (1888), 58 L.J.P.C. 54, if any authority is needed, makes that clear. At p. 60 he observed that the plain policy of the *B.N.A. Act* is to vest legislative control over Indian affairs generally in one central authority. On the same page he spoke of Parliament's exclusive power to regulate the Indians' privilege of hunting and fishing. In my opinion, their peculiar rights of hunting and fishing over their ancient hunting grounds arising under agreements by which they collectively sold their ancient lands are Indian affairs over which Parliament has exclusive legislative authority, and only Parliament can derogate from those rights.

In the result, the right of the respondents to hunt over the lands in question reserved to them by ex. 8 are preserved by s. 87, and remain unimpaired by the *Game Act*, and it follows that the respondents were rightfully in possession of the carcasses. It becomes unnecessary to consider other aspects of a far-reaching argument addressed to us by the respondents' counsel.

I would dismiss the appeal.

Norris J.A. [at p. 648]: —

. . . . .

As to whether or not the document Exhibit 8 is a Treaty within Section 87 of the Indian Act:

On this branch of this appeal as has been stated, I agree with the conclusions of my brother Davey and substantially with his reasons. What I have to say following is by way of detail and in extension of those reasons. The question is, in my respectful opinion, to be resolved not by the application of rigid rules of construction without regard to the circumstances existing when the document was completed nor by the tests of modern day draftsmanship. In determining what the intention of Parliament was at the time of the enactment of s. 87 of the *Indian Act*, Parliament is to be taken to have had in mind the common understanding of the parties to the document at the time it was executed. In the section "Treaty" is not a word of art and in my respectful opinion, it embraces all such engagements made by persons in authority as may be brought within the term "the word of the white man" the sanctity of which was, at the time of British exploration and settlement, the most important means of obtaining the good will and co-operation of the native tribes and ensuring that the colonists would be protected from death and destruction. On such assurance the Indians relied. ... The transaction in question here was a transaction between, on the one hand, the strong representative of a proprietary company under the Crown and representing the Crown, who had gained the respect of the Indians by his integrity and the strength of his personality and was thus able to bring about the completion of the agreement, and on the other hand, uneducated savages. The nature of the transaction itself was consistent with the informality of frontier days in this Province and such as the necessities of the occasion and the customs and illiteracy of the Indians demanded. The transaction in itself was a primitive one — a surrender of land in exchange for blankets to be divided between the Indian signatories according to arrangements between them — with a reservation of aboriginal rights, the document being executed by the Indians by the affixing of their marks. The unusual (by the standards of legal draftsmen) nature and form of the document considered in the light of the circumstances on Vancouver Island in 1854 does not detract from it as being a "Treaty".

. . . . .

In determining the question as to whether ex. 8 is a "Treaty" within the meaning of s. 87 of the *Indian Act* ... in light of the history and circumstances it is difficult to conceive of a term which would be more appropriate to describe the engagement entered into.

. . . . .

I have no doubt that in enacting s. 87 of the *Indian Act*, Parliament recognized the fact that Indian Treaties would have been completed in degrees of formality varying with the circumstances of each case — some with Government representatives, some with military commanders and others with frontier representatives of the great trading companies. It was necessary that those on the frontier be given wide powers and a wide discretion. So it was with Douglas.

. . . . .

In my opinion, therefore, the document (ex. 8) is a Treaty within the meaning of s. 87 of the Indian Act. As has already been indicated, the right could only be extinguished by Federal legislation.

The Supreme Court of Canada dismissed an appeal from the British Columbia Court of Appeal, explaining that the majority's conclusion that the document in question was a treaty within the meaning of the term in s. 87 of the *Indian Act*, R.S.C. 1970, c. I-6 was correct.

The articulation and adoption of liberal canons of treaty interpretation in *White and Bob* marked an end to the traditionally restrictive interpretations of treaties that had been characteristic of the majority of previous Canadian judicial pronouncements.

In *R. v. Taylor and Williams*, [1981] O.J. No. 3135, 62 C.C.C. (2d) 227, 34 O.R. (2d) 360 (Ont. C.A.), the Ontario Court of Appeal wrote that "[c]ases on Indian or aboriginal rights can never be determined in a vacuum. It is of importance to consider the history and oral traditions of the tribes concerned, and the surrounding circumstances at the time of the treaty, relied on by both parties, in determining the treaty's effect". Taking this approach, the court expanded upon the liberal interpretive principles evident in *White and Bob* and held:

> In approaching the terms of a treaty quite apart from the other considerations already noted, the honour of the Crown is always involved and no appearance of "sharp dealing" should be sanctioned. Mr. Justice Cartwright emphasized this in his dissenting reasons in *R. v. George* ... where he said:
>
> > We should, I think, endeavour to construe the treaty of 1827 and those Acts of Parliament which bear upon the question before us in such a manner that the honour of the Sovereign may be upheld and Parliament not made subject of the reproach of having taken away by unilateral action and without consideration the rights solemnly assured to the Indians and their posterity by treaty.
>
> Further, if there is any ambiguity in the words or phrases used, not only should the words be interpreted as against the framers or drafters of such treaties, but such language should not be interpreted or construed to the prejudice of the Indians if another construction is reasonably possible: *R. v. White and Bob*. ...
>
> Finally, if there is evidence by conduct or otherwise as to how the parties understood the terms of the treaty, then such understanding and practice is of assistance in giving content to the term or terms. As already stated,

counsel for both parties to the appeal agreed that recourse could be had to the surrounding circumstances and judicial notice could be taken of the facts of history. In my opinion, that notice extends to how, historically, the parties acted under the treaty after its execution.

The subsequent Supreme Court of Canada decision in *R. v. Nowegijick*, [1983] S.C.J. No. 5, [1983] 1 S.C.R. 29, [1983] 2 C.N.L.R. 89, [1983] C.T.C. 20, 46 N.R. 41, 144 D.L.R. (3d) 193 at 198 (S.C.C.), in which Justice Dickson, as he then was, stated that "... treaties and statutes relating to Indians should be liberally construed and doubtful expressions resolved in favour of the Indian", affirmed the entrenchment of these canons of treaty interpretation as a fundamental element of Canadian treaty jurisprudence.

With the constitutional entrenchment of Aboriginal and treaty rights in section 35(1) of the *Constitution Act, 1982*, being Schedule B to the *Canada Act 1982* (U.K.), 1982, c. 11, both forms of rights that were in existence on April 17, 1982 — the date that the Act took effect — enjoyed greater protection than ever before. The effect of section 35(1) is dealt with in detail in Chapter 2.

With their constitutionalization in section 35(1), treaty rights were finally afforded the same solemn recognition at law that they had received during the early stages of treaty relations between Britain and the Aboriginal peoples. Yet, the constitutionalization of treaty rights was not the only change in the legal understanding of treaty rights following the adoption of the canons of Aboriginal treaty interpretation. Other, equally significant effects came about as a result of the Supreme Court of Canada's decision in *Simon v. R.*, below.

In reading the *Simon* case, bear in mind that the treaty being discussed therein is the very same treaty that was in issue in *Syliboy*. Note also Chief Justice Dickson's comments on the *Syliboy* decision in the course of his judgment in *Simon*.

SIMON v. R.

[1985] S.C.J. No. 67, [1985] 2 S.C.R 387, 24 D.L.R. (4th) 390 (S.C.C.)

Dickson C.J.C.: — This case raises the important question of the interplay between the treaty rights of native peoples and provincial legislation. The right to hunt, which remains important to the livelihood and way of life of the Micmac people, has come into conflict with game preservation legislation in effect in the province of Nova Scotia. The main question before this Court is whether, pursuant to a Treaty of 1752 between the British Crown and the Micmac, and to s. 88 of the *Indian Act*, R.S.C. 1970, c. I-6, the appellant, James Matthew Simon, enjoys hunting rights which preclude his prosecution for offences under the *Lands and Forests Acts*, R.S.N.S. 1967, c. 163.

I

Facts

The appellant is a member of the Shubenacadie Indian Brook Band (No. 2) of the Micmac people and a registered Indian under the *Indian Act*. He was charged under s. 150(1) of the *Lands and Forest Act* with possession of a rifle and shot-gun cartridges. The two charges read:

> On the 21st day of September, 1980 at West Indian Road, Hants County, Nova Scotia, [he] did unlawfully commit the offence of illegal possession of shotgun cartridge loaded with shot larger than AAA, contrary to s. 150(1) of the *Lands and Forests Act*;

and that:

> On the 21st day of September, 1980 at West Indian Road, Hants County, Nova Scotia, [he] did unlawfully commit the offence of illegal possession of a rifle during closed season contrary to s. 150(1) of the *Lands and Forests Act*.

Section 150(1) of the *Lands and Forests Act* provides:

> 150(1) Except as provided in this Section, no person shall take, carry or have in his possession any shot gun [shot-gun] cartridges loaded with ball or with shot larger than AAA or any rifle,
>
> (a) in or upon any forest, wood or other resort of moose or deer; or
>
> (b) upon any road passing through or by any such forest, wood or other resort; or
>
> (c) in any tent or camp or other shelter (except his usual and ordinary permanent place of abode) in any forest, wood or other resort.

. . . . .

Although all essential elements of the charges were admitted by Simon, it was argued on his behalf at trial that the right to hunt set out in the Treaty of 1752, in combination with s. 88 of the *Indian Act*, offered him immunity from prosecution under s. 150(1) of the *Lands and Forests Act*.

Section 88 of the *Indian Act* reads as follows:

> 88. *Subject to the terms of any treaty* and any other Act of the Parliament of Canada, all laws of general application from time to time in force in any province are applicable to and in respect of Indians in the province, except to the extent that such laws are inconsistent with this Act or any order, rule, regulation or by-law made thereunder, and except to the extent that such laws make provision for any matter for which provision is made by or under this Act.

(Emphasis added.)

The Treaty of 1752, the relevant part of which states at art. 4 that the Micmacs have "free liberty of hunting and Fishing as usual", provides:

Treaty or
Articles of Peace and Friendship Renewed
between

His Excellency Peregrine Thomas Hopson Esquire Captain General and Governor in Chief in and over His Majesty's Province of Nova Scotia or Acadie Vice Admiral of the same & Colonel of One of His Majesty's Regiments of Foot, and His Majesty's Council on behalf of His Majesty.

AND

Major Jean Baptiste Cope chief Sachem of the Tribe of Mick Mack Indians, Inhabiting the Eastern Coast of the said Province, and Andrew Hadley Martin, Gabriel Martin and Francis Jeremiah members & Delegates of the said Tribe, for themselves and their said Tribe their heirs and the heirs of their heirs forever. Begun made and Concluded in the manner form & Tenor following, viz.

1. It is agreed that the Articles of Submission & Agreements made at Boston in New England by the Delegates of the Penobscot Norridgwolk & St. John's Indians in the Year 1725 Ratifyed and Confirmed by all the Nova Scotia Tribes at Annapolis Royal in the Month of June 1726 and lately Renewed with Governor Cornwallis at Halifax and Ratifyed at St. John's River, now read over Explained & Interpreted shall be and are hereby from this time forward renewed, reiterated and forever Confirmed by them and their Tribe, and the said Indians for themselves and their Tribe and their heirs aforesaid do make and renew the same Solemn Submissions and promises for the strict Observance of all the Articles therein Contained as at any time heretofore hath been done.

2. That all Transactions during the late War shall on both sides be buried in Oblivion with the Hatchet, And that the said Indians shall have all favour, Friendship & Protection shewn them from this His Majesty's Government.

3. That the said Tribe shall use their utmost Endeavours to bring in the other Indians to Renew and Ratify this Peace, and shall discover and make known any attempts or designs of any other Indians or any Enemy whatever against His Majesty's Subjects within this Province so soon as they shall know thereof and shall also hinder and Obstruct the same to the utmost of their power, and on the other hand if any of the Indians refusing to ratify this Peace shall make War upon the Tribe who have now Confirmed the same; they shall upon Application have such aid and Assistance from the Government for their defence as the Case may require.

4. It is agreed that the said Tribe of Indians shall not be hindered from, but have *free liberty of hunting and Fishing as usual* and that if they shall think a Truck house needful at the River Chibenaccadie, or any other place of their resort they shall have the same built and proper Merchandize, lodged therein, to be exchanged for what the Indians shall have to dispose of and that in the mean time the Indians shall have free liberty to bring to Sale to Halifax or any other Settlement within this Province, Skins, feathers, fowl, fish or any other thing they shall have to sell, where they shall have liberty to dispose thereof to the best Advantage.

5. That a Quantity of bread, flour, and such other Provisions, as can be procured, necessary for the Familys and proportionable to the Numbers

of the said Indians, shall be given them half Yearly for the time to come; and the same regard shall be had to the other Tribes that shall hereafter Agree to Renew and Ratify the Peace upon the Terms and Conditions now Stipulated.

6. That to Cherish a good harmony and mutual Correspondence between the said Indians and this Government His Excellency Peregrine Thomas Hopson Esq. Capt. General & Governor in Chief in & over His Majesty's Province of Nova Scotia or Accadie Vice Admiral of the same & Colonel of One of His Majesty's Regiments of Foot hereby promises on the part of His Majesty that the said Indians shall upon the first day of October Yearly, so long as they shall Continue in Friendship, Receive Presents of Blankets, Tobacco, some Powder & Shott, and the said Indians promise once every year, upon the said first of October, to come by themselves or their Delegates and Receive the said Presents and Renew their Friendship and Submissions.

7. That the Indians shall use their best Endeavors to save the Lives & Goods of any People Shipwrecked on this Coast where they resort and shall Conduct the People saved to Halifax with their Goods, and a Reward adequate to the Salvadge shall be given them.

8. That all Disputes whatsoever that may happen to arise between the Indians now at Peace and others His Majesty's Subjects in this Province shall be tryed in His Majesty's Courts of Civil Judicature, where the Indians shall have the same benefits, Advantages & Priviledges as any others of His Majesty's Subjects.

In Faith & Testimony whereof the Great Seal of the Province is hereunto appended, and the Partys to these Presents have hereunto interchangeabley Set their Hands in the Council Chamber at Halifax this 22nd day of Nov. 1752 in the 26th Year of His Majesty's Reign.

[signatures deleted]

(Emphasis added.)

. . . . .

III

The issues

This appeal raises the following issues:
1. Was the Treaty of 1752 validly created by competent parties?
2. Does the treaty contain a right to hunt and what is the nature and scope of this right?
3. Has the treaty been terminated or limited?
4. Is the appellant covered by the treaty?
5. Is the treaty a "treaty" within the meaning of s. 88 of the *Indian Act*?
6. Do the hunting rights contained in the treaty exempt the appellant from prosecution under s. 150(1) of the *Lands and Forests Act*?

In addition, the following constitutional question was framed by Chief Justice Laskin:

> Are the hunting rights referred to in the document entitled 'Treaty of Articles of Peace and Friendship Renewed' and executed November 22, 1752, existing treaty rights recognized and affirmed by s. 35(1) of the *Constitution Act, 1982*?

In his factum, the appellant asks this Court to dispose of the appeal on the sole basis of the effect of the Treaty of 1752 and s. 88 of the *Indian Act*. Therefore, if the treaty does not exempt the appellant from s. 150(1) of the *Lands and Forests Act*, he requests that the appeal be dismissed without prejudice to the Micmac position based on other treaties and aboriginal rights. The respondent agreed with this approach. I will, therefore, restrict my remarks to the Treaty of 1752 and s. 88 of the *Indian Act*. It will be unnecessary to deal with aboriginal rights, the Royal Proclamation of 1763, or other treaty rights.

IV

Was the Treaty of 1752 validly created by competent parties?

The respondent raised the issue of the capacity of the parties for two reasons which are stated at p. 8 of the factum:

> The issue of capacity is raised for the purpose of illustrating that the Treaty of 1752 was of a lesser status than an International Treaty and therefore is more easily terminated. The issue is also raised to give the document an historical legal context as this issue has been raised in previous cases.

The question of whether the Treaty of 1752 constitutes an international-type treaty is only relevant to the respondent's argument regarding the appropriate legal tests for the termination of the treaty. I will address this issue, therefore, in relation to the question of whether the Treaty of 1752 was terminated by hostilities between the British and the Micmac in 1753.

The historical legal context provided by the respondent consists primarily of the 1929 decision of Judge Patterson in *R. v. Syliboy* (1928), 50 C.C.C. 389, [1929] 1 D.L.R. 307 (Co. Ct.) and the academic commentary it generated immediately following its rendering. [Refer to the discussion of *Syliboy, supra.*]

. . . . .

It should be noted that the language used by Patterson J. ... reflects the biases and prejudices of another era in our history. Such language is no longer acceptable in Canadian law and, indeed, is inconsistent with a growing sensitivity to native rights in Canada. With regard to the substance of Judge Patterson's words, leaving aside for the moment the question of whether treaties are international-type documents, his conclusions on capacity are not convincing.

. . . . .

The treaty was entered into for the benefit of both the British Crown and the Micmac people, to maintain peace and order as well as to recognize and confirm the existing hunting and fishing rights of the Micmac. In my opinion, both the Governor and the Micmac entered into the treaty with the intention of creating mutually binding obligations which would be solemnly respected. It also provided a mechanism for dispute resolution. The Micmac Chief and the three other Micmac signatories, as delegates of the Micmac people, would have possessed full capacity to enter into a binding treaty on behalf of the Micmac. Governor Hopson was the delegate and legal representative of His Majesty the King. It is fair to assume that the Micmac would have believed that Governor Hopson, acting on behalf of His Majesty the King, had the necessary authority to enter into a valid treaty with them. I would hold that the Treaty of 1752 was validly created by competent parties.

V

Does the treaty contain a right to hunt and what is the nature and scope of this right?

Article 4 of the Treaty of 1752 states, "it is agreed that the said Tribe of Indians shall not be hindered from, but have free liberty of hunting and Fishing as usual . . .". What is the nature and scope of the "liberty of hunting and Fishing" contained in the treaty?

... In my opinion, the treaty, by providing that the Micmac should not be hindered from but should have free liberty of hunting and fishing as usual, constitutes a positive source of protection against infringements on hunting rights. The fact that the right to hunt already existed at the time the treaty was entered into by virtue of the Micmac's general aboriginal right to hunt does not negate or minimize the significance of the protection of hunting rights expressly included in the treaty.

Such an interpretation accords with the generally accepted view that Indian treaties should be given a fair, large and liberal construction in favour of the Indians.

. . . . .

Having determined that the treaty embodies a right to hunt, it is necessary to consider the respondent's contention that the right to hunt is limited to hunting for purposes and by methods usual in 1752 because of the inclusion of the modifier "as usual" after the right to hunt.

First of all, I do not read the phrase "as usual" as referring to the types of weapons to be used by the Micmac and limiting them to those used in 1752. Any such construction would place upon the ability of the Micmac to hunt an unnecessary and artificial constraint out of keeping with the principle that Indian treaties should be liberally construed. Indeed, the inclusion of the phrase "as usual" appears to reflect a concern that the right to hunt be interpreted in a flexible way that is sensitive to the evolution of changes in normal hunting practices. The phrase thereby ensures that the treaty will be an effective source of protection of hunting rights.

Secondly, the respondent maintained that "as usual" should be interpreted to limit the treaty protection to hunting for noncommercial purposes. It is difficult to see the basis for this argument in the absence of evidence regarding the purpose for which the appellant was hunting. In any event, art. 4 of the treaty appears to contemplate hunting for commercial purposes when it refers to the construction of a truck house as a place of exchange and mentions the liberty of the Micmac to bring game to sale.

. . . . .

It should be clarified at this point that the right to hunt to be effective must embody those activities reasonably incidental to the act of hunting itself, an example of which is travelling with the requisite hunting equipment to the hunting grounds. In this case, the appellant was not charged with hunting in a manner contrary to public safety in violation of the *Lands and Forests Act* but with illegal possession of a rifle and ammunition upon a road passing through or by a forest, wood or resort of moose or deer contrary to s. 150(1) of the same Act. The appellant was simply travelling in his truck along a road with a gun and some ammunition. He maintained that he was going to hunt in the vicinity. In my opinion, it is implicit in the right granted under art. 4 of the Treaty of 1752 that the appellant has the right to possess a gun and ammunition in a safe manner in order to be able to exercise the right to hunt. Accordingly, I conclude that the appellant was exercising his right to hunt under the treaty.

VI

Has the treaty been terminated or limited?

(a) *Termination by hostilities*

In accordance with the finding of the Nova Scotia Court of Appeal, the Crown argued that the Treaty of 1752 was terminated and rendered unenforceable when hostilities broke out between the Micmac and the British in 1753. The appellant maintained that the alleged hostilities were sporadic and minor in nature and did not, therefore, nullify or terminate the treaty. It was further argued by the appellant, relying on L. F. S. Upton, *Micmac and Colonists: Indian — White Relations in the Maritimes 1713-1867* (1979), that the English initiated the hostilities and that, therefore, the Crown should not be permitted to rely on them to support the termination of the treaty. Finally, the appellant submitted that, even if the Court finds that there were sufficient hostilities to affect the treaty, at most it was merely suspended and not terminated.

In considering the impact of subsequent hostilities on the peace Treaty of 1752, the parties looked to international law on treaty termination. While it may be helpful in some instances to analogize the principles of international treaty law to Indian treaties, these principles are not determinative. An Indian treaty is unique; it is an agreement *sui generis* which is neither created nor terminated according to the rules of international law.

. . . . .

It may be that under certain circumstances a treaty could be terminated by the breach of one of its fundamental provisions. It is not necessary to decide this issue in the case at bar since the evidentiary requirements for proving such a termination have not been met. Once it has been established that a valid treaty has been entered into, the party arguing for its termination bears the burden of proving the circumstances and events justifying termination. The inconclusive and conflicting evidence presented by the parties makes it impossible for this Court to say with any certainty what happened on the eastern coast of Nova Scotia 233 years ago. As a result, the Court is unable to resolve this historical question. The Crown has failed to prove that the Treaty of 1752 was terminated by subsequent hostilities.

. . . . .

I conclude from the foregoing that the Treaty of 1752 was not terminated by subsequent hostilities in 1753. The treaty is of as much force and effect today as it was at the time it was concluded.

(b) *Termination by extinguishment*

... The respondent submits that absolute title in the land covered by the treaty lies with the Crown and, therefore, the Crown has the right to extinguish any Indian rights in such lands. The respondent further submits ... that the Crown, through occupancy by the white man under Crown grant or lease, has, in effect, extinguished native rights in Nova Scotia in territory situated outside of reserve lands. As the appellant was stopped on a highway outside the Shubenacadie Reserve, the respondent argues that the Treaty of 1752 affords no defence to the appellant regardless of whether the treaty is itself valid.

In my opinion, it is not necessary to come to a final decision on the respondent's argument. Given the serious and far-reaching consequences of a finding that a treaty right has been extinguished, it seems appropriate to demand strict proof of the fact of extinguishment in each case where the issue arises. As Douglas J. said in *United States v. Sante Fe Pacific Ry. Co.*, *supra*, at p. 354, "extinguishment cannot be lightly implied".

In the present appeal the appellant was charged with the offence of possession of a rifle and ammunition on a road passing through or by a forest, wood or other resort. The agreed statement of facts does not disclose whether or where the appellant had hunted or was intending to hunt. In particular, there is no evidence to sustain the conclusion that the appellant had hunted, or intended to hunt, on the highway which might well raise different considerations.

. . . . .

It seems clear that, at a minimum, the treaty recognizes *some* hunting rights in Nova Scotia on the Shubenacadie Reserve and that any Micmac Indian who enjoys those rights has an incidental right to transport a gun and ammunition to places where he could legally exercise them. In this vein, it is worth noting that both parties agree that the highway on which the appellant was stopped "is adjacent to the Shubenacadie Indian Reserve" and "passes through or by a forest, wood, or other resource frequented by moose or deer".

The respondent tries to meet the apparent right of the appellant to transport a gun and ammunition by asserting that the treaty hunting rights have been extinguished. In order to succeed on this argument it is absolutely essential, it seems to me, that the respondent lead evidence as to where the appellant hunted or intended to hunt and what use has been and is currently made of those lands. It is impossible for this Court to consider the doctrine of extinguishment "in the air"; the respondent must anchor that argument in the bedrock of specific lands. That has not happened in this case. In the absence of evidence as to where the hunting occurred or was intended to occur, and the use of the lands in question, it would be impossible to determine whether the appellant's treaty hunting rights have been extinguished. Moreover, it is unnecessary for this Court to determine whether those rights have been extinguished because, at the very least, these rights extended to the adjacent Shubenacadie reserve. I do not wish to be taken as expressing any view on whether, as a matter of law, treaty rights may be extinguished.

VII

Is the appellant an Indian covered by the treaty?

The respondent argues that the appellant has not shown that he is a direct descendant of a member of the original Micmac Indian Band covered by the Treaty of 1752.

. . . . .

In my view, the appellant has established a sufficient connection with the Indian band, signatories to the Treaty of 1752. As noted earlier, this treaty was signed by Major Jean Baptiste Cope, Chief of the Shubenacadie Micmac tribe, and three other members and delegates of the tribe. The Micmac signatories were described as inhabiting the eastern coast of Nova Scotia. The appellant admitted at trial that he was a registered Indian under the *Indian Act*, and was an "adult member of the Shubenacadie —

Indian Brook Band of Micmac Indians and was a member of the Shubenacadie Band Number 02". The appellant is, therefore, a Shubenacadie — Micmac Indian, living in the same area as the original Micmac Indian tribe, party to the Treaty of 1752.

This evidence alone, in my view, is sufficient to prove the appellant's connection to the tribe originally covered by the treaty. True, this evidence is not conclusive proof that the appellant is a *direct* descendant of the Micmac Indians covered by the Treaty of 1752. It must, however, be sufficient, for otherwise no Micmac Indian would be able to establish descendancy. The Micmacs did not keep written records. Micmac traditions are largely oral in nature. To impose an impossible burden of proof would, in effect, render nugatory any right to hunt that a present-day Shubenacadie Micmac Indian would otherwise be entitled to invoke based on this treaty.

The appellant, Simon, as a member of the Shubenacadie Indian Brook Band of Micmac Indians, residing in Eastern Nova Scotia, the area covered by the Treaty of 1752, can therefore raise the treaty in his defence.

VIII

Is the treaty a "treaty" within the meaning of s. 88 of the Indian Act?

Section 88 of the *Indian Act* stipulates that, "Subject to the terms of any treaty ... all laws of general application from time to time in force in any province are applicable to and in respect of Indians in the province ...".

The majority of the Appellate Division held that it was extremely doubtful whether the Treaty of 1752 was a "treaty" within the meaning of s. 88, primarily because it was merely a general confirmation of aboriginal rights and did not grant or confer "new permanent rights". MacDonald J.A. also concluded that the 1752 document could not be considered a "treaty" under s. 88 because it was made by only a small portion of the Micmac Nation and it did not define any land or area where the rights were to be exercised. The respondent urges these views upon this Court. The respondent further submits that the word "treaty" in s. 88 of the *Indian Act* does not include the Treaty of 1752 even under the extended definition of "treaty" enunciated in *R. v. White and Bob* ... because the treaty did not deal with the ceding of land or delineation of boundaries.

... [T]he fact that the treaty did not *create* new hunting or fishing rights but merely *recognized* pre-existing rights does not render s. 88 inapplicable. On this point, Davey J.A. stated in *R. v. White and Bob, supra,* at p. 616:

> The force of the first argument seems to depend upon the assumption that s. 87 should be read as if it were subject only to rights created by a Treaty; that would remove from the saving clause rights already in being and excepted from or confirmed by a Treaty. That argument fails to accord full meaning to the words, "subject to the terms of any treaty . . ." *In my opinion an exception, reservation, or confirmation is as much a term of a Treaty as a grant,* (I observe parenthetically that a reservation may be a grant), and the operative words of the section will not extend general laws in force in any

Province to Indians in derogation of rights so excepted, reserved or confirmed.

(Emphasis added.)

. . . . .

With respect to the respondent's submission that some form of land cession is necessary before an agreement can be described as a treaty under s. 88, I can see no principled basis for interpreting s. 88 in this manner. I would adopt the useful comment of Norris J.A. of the British Columbia Court of Appeal in *R. v. White and Bob, supra,* affirmed on appeal to this Court. In a concurring judgment, he stated at pp. 648-9:

> The question is, in my respectful opinion, to be resolved not by the application of rigid rules of construction without regard to the circumstances existing when the document was completed nor by the tests of modern day draftsmanship. In determining what the intention of Parliament was at the time of the enactment of s. 87 [now s. 88] of the *Indian Act,* Parliament is to be taken to have had in mind the common understanding of the parties to the document at the time it was executed. In the section "Treaty" is not a word of art and in my respectful opinion, it embraces all such engagements made by persons in authority as may be brought within the term 'the word of the white man' the sanctity of which was, at the time of British exploration and settlement, the most important means of obtaining the goodwill and co-operation of the native tribes and ensuring that the colonists would be protected from death and destruction. On such assurance the Indians relied.

In my view, Parliament intended to include within the operation of s. 88 all agreements concluded by the Crown with the Indians that would otherwise be enforceable treaties, whether land was ceded or not. None of the Maritime treaties of the eighteenth century cedes land. To find that s. 88 applies only to land cession treaties would be to limit severely its scope and run contrary to the principle that Indian treaties and statutes relating to Indians should be liberally construed and uncertainties resolved in favour of the Indians.

Finally, it should be noted that several cases have considered the Treaty of 1752 to be a valid "treaty" within the meaning of s. 88 of the *Indian Act* ... The treaty was an exchange of solemn promises between the Micmacs and the King's representative entered into to achieve and guarantee peace. It is an enforceable obligation between the Indians and the white man and, as such, falls within the meaning of the word "treaty" in s. 88 of the *Indian Act.*

IX

Do the hunting rights contained in the treaty exempt the appellant from prosecution under s. 150(1) of the Lands and Forests Act?

As a result of my conclusion that the appellant was validly exercising his right to hunt under the Treaty of 1752 and the fact he has admitted that his conduct otherwise constitutes an offence under the *Lands and Forests Act,* it must now be determined what the result is when a treaty right comes into conflict with provincial legislation. This question is governed by s. 88 of the *Indian Act,* which, it will be recalled, states that "Subject to the terms of any treaty, all laws of general application . . . in force in the province are applicable to ... Indians".

. . . . .

Under s. 88 of the *Indian Act,* when the terms of a treaty come into conflict with federal legislation, the latter prevails, subject to whatever may be the effect of s. 35 of the *Constitution Act, 1982.* It has been held to be within the exclusive power of Parliament under s. 91(24) of the *Constitution Act, 1867,* to derogate from rights recognized in a treaty agreement made with the Indians.

. . . . .

Here, however, we are dealing with provincial legislation. The effect of s. 88 of the *Indian Act* is to exempt the Indians from provincial legislation which restricts or contravenes the terms of any treaty.

. . . . .

Therefore, the question here is whether s. 150(1) of the *Lands and Forests Act,* a provincial enactment of general application in Nova Scotia, restricts or contravenes the right to hunt in art. 4 of the Treaty of 1752. If so, the treaty right to hunt prevails and the appellant is exempt from the operation of the provincial game legislation at issue.

Section 150(1) states that no person shall take, carry or possess a rifle or shot-gun cartridges loaded with ball or with shot larger than AAA in certain areas of the province except as provided in the section.

. . . . .

In my opinion, s. 150 of the *Lands and Forests Act* of Nova Scotia restricts the appellant's right to hunt under the treaty. The section clearly places seasonal limitations and licensing requirements, for the purposes of wildlife conservation, on the right to possess a rifle and ammunition for the purposes of hunting. The restrictions imposed in this case conflict, therefore, with the appellant's right to possess a firearm and ammunition in order to exercise his free liberty to hunt over the lands covered by the treaty. As noted, it is clear that under s. 88 of the *Indian Act* provincial legislation cannot restrict native treaty rights. If conflict arises, the terms of the treaty prevail. Therefore, by virtue of s. 88 of the *Indian Act,* the clear terms of art. 4 of the treaty must prevail over s. 150(1) of the provincial *Lands and Forests Act.*

. . . .

I conclude that the appellant has a valid treaty right to hunt under the Treaty of 1752 which, by virtue of s. 88 of the *Indian Act,* cannot be restricted by provincial legislation. It follows, therefore, that the appellant's possession of a rifle and ammunition in a safe manner, referable to his treaty right to hunt, cannot be restricted by s. 150(1) of the *Lands and Forests Act.*

I would accordingly quash the convictions and enter verdicts of acquittal on both charges.

X

Constitutional question: s. 35 of the Constitution Act, 1982

... In my view, s. 88 of the *Indian Act* covers the present situation and provides the necessary protection to the appellant Simon. As a result, it is not necessary for the determination of this appeal to consider s. 35(1) of the *Constitution Act, 1982.*

. . . . .

Conclusions

To summarize:

1. The Treaty of 1752 was validly created by competent parties.
2. The treaty contains a right to hunt which covers the activities engaged in by the appellant.
3. The treaty was not terminated by subsequent hostilities in 1753. Nor has it been demonstrated that the right to hunt, protected by the treaty has been extinguished.
4. The appellant is a Micmac Indian covered by the treaty.
5. The Treaty of 1752 is a "treaty" within the meaning of s. 88 of the *Indian Act.*
6. By virtue of s. 88 of the *Indian Act,* the appellant is exempt from prosecution under s. 150(1) of the *Lands and Forests Act.*
7. In light of these conclusions, it is not necessary to answer the constitutional question raised in this appeal.

I would, therefore, allow the appeal, quash the convictions of the appellant and enter verdicts of acquittal on both charges.

Appeal allowed; acquittals entered.

How did the Supreme Court's decision in *Simon* clarify the judicial understanding of treaties and treaty rights? What are the implications of its rejection of a "frozen rights" approach to treaty rights and its finding that activities "reasonably incidental" to the exercise of treaty rights must be embodied within the treaty right itself?

The rejection of frozen rights theory in *Simon* was subsequently affirmed by the Supreme Court of Canada in *R. v. Sparrow*, [1990] S.C.J. No. 49, [1990] 1 S.C.R. 1075, [1990] 4 W.W.R. 410, 46 B.C.L.R. (2d) 1, 56 C.C.C. (3d) 263, 70 D.L.R. (4th) 385, 111 N.R. 241, [1990] 3 C.N.L.R. 160 (S.C.C.), which is reproduced in Chapter 2. However, compare the approach towards frozen rights theory in those cases with that endorsed by the Supreme Court's majority decision in *R. v. Van der Peet*, [1996] S.C.J. No. 77, [1996] 9 W.W.R. 1, 23 B.C.L.R. (3d) 1, 50 C.R. (4th) 1, 137 D.L.R. (4th) 289, 109 C.C.C. (3d) 1, 200 N.R. 1, [1996] 4 C.N.L.R. 177 (S.C.C.), reproduced in Chapter 2. Note also how the majority's decision in *Van der Peet* treats activities that are "reasonably incidental" to the exercise of constitutionally protected rights versus the approach endorsed in *Simon*. Were the *Simon* and *Sparrow* precedents discussed here overturned by *Van der Peet*? If not, how are they affected by the *Van der Peet* decision?

F.   MORE RECENT JUDICIAL CONSIDERATIONS OF TREATIES

Following the *Simon* decision, some confusion arose over the use of the canons of interpretation, initially as a result of the Supreme Court of Canada's decision in *R. v. Horse*, [1988] S.C.J. No. 2, [1988] 1 S.C.R. 187, [1988] 2 W.W.R. 289, 39 C.C.C. (3d) 97, [1988] 2 C.N.L.R. 112, 82 N.R. 206, 65 Sask. R. 176, 47 D.L.R. (4th) 526 (S.C.C.) and, later, because of that Court's decision in *R. v. Howard*, [1994] S.C.J. No. 43, [1994] 2 S.C.R. 299, 18 O.R. (3d) 384, [1994] 3 C.N.L.R. 146, 71 O.A.C. 278, 115 D.L.R. (4th) 312, 166 N.R. 282 (S.C.C.). The *Horse* decision, while outwardly affirming most of the canons of treaty interpretation, held that extrinsic evidence could be used only where there was an ambiguity in the terms of a treaty. In *Howard*, the Court stated that a 1923 treaty ought not be interpreted according to the canons of treaty interpretation because the treaty concerned lands close to urbanized Ontario, the Hiawatha signatories included businessmen and a civil servant, and all were literate.

From these decisions, a number of questions arise. Are these decisions reconcilable with the canons of treaty interpretation? Ought different standards of treaty interpretation exist that would be applied based on the perceived or presumed knowledge of the Aboriginal treaty signatories? Should more recent treaties not receive the benefit of the canons of interpretation because of the Aboriginals' greater understanding of English and the concepts employed in treaties? In answering the latter question, it must first be asked what the bases of the canons of interpretation are: inequality in bargaining power? Lack of Aboriginal understanding of English and legal concepts such as land surrenders? The parties' different understandings of language and concepts? The nature of the relationship between the parties? A combination of these?

The Supreme Court appeared to distance itself from the *Horse* judgment in *R. v. Sioui*, where it stated that "a more flexible approach is necessary as the question of the existence of a treaty within the meaning of s. 88 of the

Indian Act is generally closely bound up with the circumstances existing when the document was prepared." Is it possible to interpret treaties in their historical context without looking beyond the four corners of the treaties? Consider what the Supreme Court had to say on this point in *Sioui*.

R. v. Sioui

[1990] S.C.J. No. 48, 70 D.L.R. (4th) 427, [1990] 1 S.C.R. 1025,
109 N.R. 22, 56 C.C.C. (3d) 225,
[1990] 3 C.N.L.R. 30, 30 Q.A.C. 280 (S.C.C.)

The judgment of the court was delivered by

Lamer J.: —

I *Facts and relevant legislation*

The four respondents were convicted by the Court of Sessions of the Peace of cutting down trees, camping and making fires in places not designated in Jacques-Cartier park contrary to ss. 9 and 37 of the *Regulation respecting the Parc de la Jacques-Cartier* (Order in Council 3108-81 of November 11, 1981, (1981) 113 *O.G.* II 3518), adopted pursuant to the *Parks Act*, R.S.Q., c. P-9. The regulations state that:

9. In the Park, users may not:

1. destroy, mutilate, remove or introduce any kind of plant or part thereof.

. . . . .

However, the collection of edible vegetable products is authorized solely for the purpose of consumption as food on the site, except in the preservation zones where it is forbidden at all times;

. . . . .

37. Camping and fires are permitted only in the places designated and arranged for those purposes.

The *Parks Act*, under which the foregoing regulations were adopted, provides the following penalties for an offence:

11. Every person who infringes this act or the regulations is guilty of an offence and liable on summary proceedings, in addition to the costs, to a fine of not less than $50 nor more than $1,000 in the case of an individual and to a fine of not less than $200 nor more than $5,000 in the case of a corporation.

. . . . .

The respondents are Indians within the meaning of the *Indian Act*, R.S.C., 1985, c. I-5 (formerly R.S.C. 1970, c. I-6), and are members of the

Huron band on the Lorette Indian Reserve. They admit that they committed the acts with which they were charged in Jacques-Cartier park, which is located outside the boundaries of the Lorette Reserve. However, they alleged that they were practising certain ancestral customs and religious rites which are the subject of a treaty between the Hurons and the British, a treaty which brings s. 88 of the *Indian Act* into play and exempts them from compliance with the regulations. Section 88 of the *Indian Act* states that:

> 88. Subject to the terms of any treaty and any other Act of Parliament, all laws of general application from time to time in force in any province are applicable to and in respect of Indians in the province, except to the extent that those laws are inconsistent with this Act or any order, rule, regulation or by-law made thereunder, and except to the extent that those laws make provision for any matter for which provision is made by or under this Act.

The document the respondents rely on in support of their contentions is dated September 5, 1760 and signed by Brigadier General James Murray. It reads as follows:

> THESE are to certify that the CHIEF of the HURON Tribe of Indians, having come to me in the name of His Nation, to submit to His BRITANNICK MAJESTY, and make Peace, has been received under my Protection, with his whole Tribe; and henceforth no English Officer or party is to molest, or interrupt them in returning to their Settlement at LORETTE; and they are received upon the same terms with the Canadians, being allowed the free Exercise of their Religion, their Customs, and Liberty of trading with the English: — recommending it to the Officers commanding the Posts, to treat them kindly.

> Given under my hand at Longueil, this 5th day of September, 1760.

> By the Genl's Command,   JA. MURRAY
> JOHN COSNAN,
> Adjut. Genl.

The Hurons had been in the Quebec area since about 1650, after having had to leave their ancestral lands located in territory which is now in Ontario. In 1760, they were settled at Lorette on land given to them by the Jesuits 18 years earlier and made regular use of the territory of Jacques-Cartier park at that time.

III *Points at issue*

The appellants are asking this court to dispose of the appeal solely on the basis of the document of September 5, 1760 and s. 88 of the *Indian Act*.

. . . . .

To decide the case at bar I will consider first the question of whether Great Britain, General Murray and the Hurons had capacity to sign a treaty, assuming that those parties intended to do so. If they had, I will then consider whether the parties actually did enter into a treaty. Finally, if the document of September 5, 1760 is a treaty, I will analyse its contents to determine the nature of the rights guaranteed therein and establish whether they have territorial application.

IV *Analysis*

A. *Introduction*

Our courts and those of our neighbours to the south have already considered what distinguishes a treaty with the Indians from other agreements affecting them. The task is not an easy one. In *Simon v. The Queen*, [1985] 2 S.C.R. 387, this court adopted the comment of Norris J.A. in *R. v. White and Bob* (1964), 50 D.L.R. (2d) 613 (B.C.C.A.) (affirmed in the Supreme Court (1965), 52 D.L.R. (2d) 481*n*, [1965] S.C.R. vi), that the courts should show flexibility in determining the legal nature of a document recording a transaction with the Indians. In particular, they must take into account the historical context and perception each party might have as to the nature of the undertaking contained in the document under consideration.

. . . . .

As the Chief Justice said in *Simon*, *supra*, treaties and statutes relating to Indians should be liberally construed and uncertainties resolved in favour of the Indians (at p. 410). In our quest for the legal nature of the document of September 5, 1760, therefore, we should adopt a broad and generous interpretation of what constitutes a treaty.

In my opinion, this liberal and generous attitude, heedful of historical fact, should also guide us in examining the preliminary question of the capacity to sign a treaty, as illustrated by *Simon* and *White and Bob*.

Finally, once a valid treaty is found to exist, that treaty must in turn be given a just, broad and liberal construction. This principle, for which there is ample precedent, was recently reaffirmed in *Simon*. The factors underlying this rule were eloquently stated in *Jones v. Meehan*, 175 U.S. 1 (1899), a judgment of the United States Supreme Court, and are I think just as relevant to questions involving the existence of a treaty and the capacity of the parties as they are to the interpretation of a treaty (at pp. 10-11):

> In construing any treaty between the United States and an Indian tribe, it must always . . . be borne in mind that the negotiations for the treaty are conducted, on the part of the United States, an enlightened and powerful nation, by representatives skilled in diplomacy, masters of a written language, understanding the modes and forms of creating the various technical estates known to their law, and assisted by an interpreter employed by themselves; that the treaty is drawn up by them and in their own language; that the Indians, on the other hand, are a weak and dependent people, who have no written language and are wholly unfamiliar with all the forms of legal expression, and whose only knowledge of the terms in which the treaty is framed is that imparted to them by the interpreter employed by the United States; and that the treaty must therefore

be construed, not according to the technical meaning of its words to learned lawyers, but in the sense in which they would naturally be understood by the Indians.

The Indian people are today much better versed in the art of negotiation with public authorities than they were when the United States Supreme Court handed down its decision in *Jones*. As the document in question was signed over a hundred years before that decision, these considerations argue all the more strongly for the courts to adopt a generous and liberal approach.

B. *Question of capacity of parties involved*

Before deciding whether the intention in the document of September 5, 1760 was to enter into a treaty within the meaning of s. 88 of the *Indian Act*, this court must decide preliminary matters regarding the capacity of Great Britain, General Murray and the Huron nation to enter into a treaty. If any one of these parties was without such capacity, the document at issue could not be a valid treaty and it would then be pointless to consider it further.

. . . . .

I will first examine the capacity of Great Britain to enter into a treaty and then consider that of Murray and the Hurons.

1. *Capacity of Great Britain*

At this preliminary stage of the analysis, and for purposes of discussion, it has to be assumed that the document of September 5, 1760 possesses the characteristics of a treaty and that the only issue that arises concerns the capacity of the parties to create obligations of the kind contained in a treaty.

The appellant argued that the British Crown could not validly enter into a treaty with the Hurons as it was not sovereign in Canada in 1760. The appellant based this argument on the rules of international law, as stated by certain 18th and 19th century writers, which required that a state should be sovereign in a territory before it could alienate that territory: see E. de Vattel, *The Law of Nations or Principles of the Law of Nature* (1760), vol. II, book III, para. 197; E. Ortolan, *Des moyens d'acquérir le domaine international ou propriété d'État entre les nations* (1851), para. 167.

Without deciding what the international law on this point was, I note that the writers to whom the appellant referred the court studied the rules governing international relations and did not comment on the rules which at that time governed the conclusion of treaties between European nations and native peoples. In any case, the rules of international law do not preclude the document being characterized as a treaty within the meaning of s. 88 of the *Indian Act*. At the time with which we are concerned relations with Indian tribes fell somewhere between the kind of relations conducted between sovereign states and the relations that such states had with their own citizens. The *Simon, supra,* decision, is clear in this regard: an Indian treaty is an agreement *sui generis* which is neither created nor terminated according to the rules of international law (p. 404).

Of course, if the document is a treaty, it could not have been binding on France if Canada had remained under its sovereignty at the end of the war. It would be fair to assume that the Hurons knew enough about warfare to understand that a treaty concluded with the enemy would be of little use to them if the French regained *de facto* control of New France.

Both *Simon* and *White and Bob* make it clear that the question of capacity must be seen from the point of view of the Indians at that time, and the Court must ask whether it was reasonable for them to have assumed that the other party they were dealing with had the authority to enter into a valid treaty with them. I conclude without any hesitation that the Hurons could reasonably have believed that the British Crown had the power to enter into a treaty with them that would be in effect as long as the British controlled Canada. France had not hesitated to enter into treaties of alliance with the Hurons and no one ever seemed to have questioned France's capacity to conclude such agreements. From the Hurons' point of view, there was no difference between these two European states. They were both foreigners to the Hurons and their presence in Canada had only one purpose, that of controlling the territory by force.

2. *General Murray's capacity*

The appellant disputes Murray's capacity to sign a treaty on behalf of Great Britain on the ground that he was at that time only Governor of the City and District of Quebec and a brigadier general in the British Army. As Governor, he was subject to the authority of His Majesty's Secretary of State for the Southern Department, and as a soldier he was the subordinate of General Amherst, the "Commander in Chief of His Britannic Majesty's Troops and Forces in North America". It is true that Murray's capacity to enter into this treaty is less obvious than that of Great Britain to "treat" with the Indians.

. . . . .

To arrive at the conclusion that a person had the capacity to enter into a treaty with the Indians, he or she must thus have represented the British Crown in very important, authoritative functions. It is then necessary to take the Indians' point of view and to ask whether it was reasonable for them to believe, in light of the circumstances and the position occupied by the party they were dealing with directly, that they had before them a person capable of binding the British Crown by treaty. To determine whether the Hurons' perception of Murray's capacity to sign a treaty on behalf of Great Britain was reasonable, the importance of the part played by the latter in Canada in 1760 has to be established.

Although during the siege of Quebec James Murray was the fourth ranking officer in the British military hierarchy in Canada, after the death of Wolfe and the departure of Townshend and Monckton he became the highest ranking officer in the British Army stationed in Canada. General Amherst was the highest military authority in North America and his authority covered all British soldiers in Canada. Murray received the command of the troops at Quebec from him. A very important fact is that since 1759, Murray had also acted as Military Governor of the Quebec district, which included Lorette. He had used his powers to regulate, *inter alia*, the currency exchange rate and the prices of grain, bread and meat and to create civil courts and appoint judges (*Governor Murray's Journal of the Siege of Quebec* (1939), pp. 10-12, 14, and 16-17).

At the time the document under consideration was signed, General Amherst and his troops were occupied in crossing the rapids upstream of Montreal and it was not until some days later, probably on September 8, 1760, that they reached that city: see in this regard the work of F. X. Garneau, *Histoire du Canada français* (1969), vol. 3, at pp. 269-72. In my view, therefore, the respondents are correct in stating that on September 5, 1760, Murray was the highest ranking British officer with whom the Hurons could have conferred. The circumstances prevailing at the time, in my view, thus support the respondents' proposition that Murray in fact had the necessary capacity to enter into a treaty. Furthermore, if there is still any doubt, I think it is clear in any event that Murray had such authority in New France that it was reasonable for the Hurons to believe that he had the power to enter into a treaty with them.

. . . . .

In short, even apart from my conclusion with respect to Murray's actual authority to sign a treaty, I am of the view that the Hurons could reasonably have assumed that, as a general, Murray was giving them a safe conduct to return to Lorette, and that as Governor of the Quebec district, he was signing a treaty guaranteeing the Hurons the free exercise of their religion, customs and trade with the English. In either case no problems concerning Murray's capacity would invalidate the treaty, if there was one.

For all these reasons, therefore, I conclude that Murray had the necessary powers to enter into a treaty with the Hurons that would be binding on the British.

3. *Capacity of the Hurons*

The appellant argues that the Hurons could not enter into a treaty with the British Crown because this Indian nation had no historical occupation or possession of the territory extending from the St-Maurice to the Saguenay. Without going so far as to suggest that there cannot be treaties other than agreements under which the Indians cede land to the Crown, the appellant argues that a treaty could not confer rights on the Indians unless the latter could claim historical occupation or possession of the lands in question.

The appellant deduces this requirement from the fact that most of the cases involving treaties between the British and the Indians concern territories which had traditionally been occupied or held at the time in question by the Indian nation which signed the treaty. The academic commentary cited by the appellant also deals with the aspect of historical occupation or possession of land found in treaties with Indians.

There is no basis either in precedent or in the ordinary meaning of the word "treaty" for imposing such a restriction on what can constitute a treaty within the meaning of s. 88 of the *Indian Act*. In *Simon* [at p. 410], this court in fact rejected the argument that s. 88 applied only to land cession treaties. In the court's opinion that would limit severely the scope of the word "treaty" and run contrary to the principle that Indians treaties should be liberally construed and uncertainties resolved in favour of the Indians. The argument made here must be rejected in the same way. There is no reason why an agreement concerning something other than a territory, such as an agreement about political or social rights, cannot be a treaty within the meaning of s. 88 of the *Indian Act*. There is also no basis for excluding agreements in which the Crown may have chosen to create, for the benefit of a tribe, rights over territory other than its traditional territory. Accordingly, I consider that a territorial claim is not essential to the existence of a treaty.

I therefore conclude that all the parties involved were competent to enter into a treaty within the meaning of s. 88 of the *Indian Act*. This leads me to consider the next question: Did General Murray and the Hurons in fact enter into such a treaty?

C. *Legal nature of the document of September 5, 1760*

1. *Constituent elements of a treaty*

In *Simon* this court noted that a treaty with the Indians is unique, that it is an agreement *sui generis* which is neither created nor terminated according to the rules of international law. ... The following are two extracts illustrating the reasons relied on by the Chief Justice in concluding that a treaty had been concluded between the Micmacs and the British Crown (at pp. 401 and 410):

> In my opinion, both the Governor and the Micmac entered into the treaty with the intention of creating mutually binding obligations which would be solemnly respected. It also provided a mechanism for dispute resolution.

> . . . . .

> The treaty was an exchange of solemn promises between the Micmacs and the King's representative entered into to achieve and guarantee peace. It is an enforceable obligation between the Indians and the white man and, as such, falls within the meaning of the word "treaty" in s. 88 of the *Indian Act*.

From these extracts it is clear that what characterizes a treaty is the intention to create obligations, the presence of mutually binding obligations and a certain measure of solemnity.

. . . . .

In *White and Bob, supra,* Norris J.A. also discussed the nature of a treaty under the *Indian Act.* As he mentioned ... the word "treaty" is not a term of art. It merely identifies agreements in which the "word of the white man" is given and by which the latter made certain of the Indians' co-operation. ... This [case] brings out the importance of the historical context, including the interpersonal relations of those involved at the time, in trying to determine whether a document falls into the category of a treaty under s. 88 of the *Indian Act.* It also shows that formalities are of secondary importance in deciding on the nature of a document containing an agreement with the Indians.

The decision of the Ontario Court of Appeal in *R. v. Taylor and Williams* (1981), 62 C.C.C. (2d) 227, also provides valuable assistance by listing a series of factors which are relevant to analysis of the historical background. In that case the court had to interpret a treaty, and not determine the legal nature of a document, but the factors mentioned may be just as useful in determining the existence of a treaty as in interpreting it. In particular, they assist in determining the intent of the parties to enter into a treaty. Among these factors are:

1. continuous exercise of a right in the past and at present;
2. the reasons why the Crown made a commitment;
3. the situation prevailing at the time the document was signed;
4. evidence of relations of mutual respect and esteem between the negotiators, and
5. the subsequent conduct of the parties.

2. *Analysis of the document in light of these factors*

(a) *Wording*

. . . . .

Several aspects of the wording of the document are consistent with the appellant's position that it was an act of surrender and a safe conduct rather than a treaty. The following is a brief review of the appellant's five main arguments in this regard. First, the document opens with the words "These are to certify that ...", which would suggest that the document in question is a certificate or an acknowledgement of the Hurons' surrender, made official by Murray in order to inform the British troops. Bisson J.A. gave these introductory words an interpretation more favourable to the Hurons: the Hurons did not know how to write and the choice of words only makes it clear that the document of September 5, 1760 recorded an oral treaty.

Secondly, General Murray used expressions which appear to involve him only personally, which do not suggest that he was acting as a representative of the British Crown. Thus, the following expressions are used:

1. "having come to me",
2. "has been received under my Protection",
3. "By the General's Command".

Although the Hurons had surrendered to His Britannic Majesty, wording the document in this way could tend to show that Murray intended only to give his personal undertaking to protect the Hurons, without thereby binding the British Crown in the long term. Murray, it is argued, had only offered the Hurons military protection and had no intention of entering into a treaty.

Thirdly, the orders given to British soldiers stationed in Canada ("no English Officer or party is to molest, or interrupt them in returning to their Settlement at LORETTE ... recommending it to the Officers commanding the Posts, to treat them kindly ... By the Genl's Command") would more naturally form part of a document such as a safe conduct or pass than of a treaty.

These points bring out the unilateral aspect of the document of September 5th: it could be an administrative document issued by General Murray, recognizing that the Hurons had laid down their arms and giving orders to British soldiers accordingly. Finally, the document was signed only by the General's representative with no indication that it had been assented to by the Hurons' in one way or another. The main purpose of the document is thus, it is argued, to recognize the surrender, and what was more important to the Hurons, allow them to return to Lorette safely without fear of being mistaken for enemies by British soldiers they might meet along the way.

Fourthly, the reference to a specific event, namely the return journey to Lorette, as opposed to a document recognizing rights in perpetuity or without any apparent time-limit, could show that the purpose of this document was not to settle long-term relations between the Hurons and the British. The temporary and specific nature of the document would indicate that the parties did not intend to enter into a treaty.

Fifthly, the document does not possess the formality which is usually to be found in the wording of a treaty. First, it is not the General himself who signed the document, but his adjutant on his behalf. Second, the language used in the document does not have the formalism generally accompanying the signature of a treaty with Indians.

. . . . .

The appellant argues that the Hurons did not formalize the document either by their signature (which would not be absolutely necessary to make it a treaty) or by the use of necklaces or belts of shells which were the traditional method used by the Hurons to formalize agreements at the time. Clearly, this argument has weight only if the document accurately indicates all the events surrounding the signature. Otherwise, extrinsic proof of solemnities could help to show that the parties intended to enter into a formal agreement and that they manifested this intent in one way or another.

While the analysis thus far seems to suggest that the document of September 5th is not a treaty, the presence of a clause guaranteeing the free exercise of religion, customs and trade with the English cannot but raise serious doubts about this proposition. It seems extremely strange to me that a document which is supposedly only a temporary, unilateral and informal safe conduct should contain a clause guaranteeing rights of such importance. As Bisson J.A. noted in the Court of Appeal judgment, there would have been no necessity to mention the free exercise of religion and customs in a document the effects of which were only to last for a few days. Such a guarantee would definitely have been more natural in a treaty where "the word of the white man" is given.

The appellant and the Attorney-General of Canada put forward certain explanations for the presence of such guarantees in the document:

1. the free exercise of religion and customs was part of the protection under which General Murray received the Hurons;
2. the free exercise of religion and customs is mentioned because these benefits had been conferred on Canadians laying down their arms earlier.

As this Court recently noted in *R. v. Horse*, [1988] 1 S.C.R. 187 [at p. 201], extrinsic evidence is not to be used as an aid to interpreting a treaty in the absence of ambiguity or where the result would be to alter its terms by adding words to or subtracting words from the written agreement. This rule also applies in determining the legal nature of a document relating to the Indians. However, a more flexible approach is necessary as the question of the existence of a treaty within the meaning of s. 88 of the *Indian Act* is generally closely bound up with the circumstances existing when the document was prepared ... In any case, the wording alone will not suffice to determine the legal nature of the document before the court. On the one hand, we have before us a document the form of which and some of whose subject-matter suggest that it is not a treaty, and on the other, we find it to contain protection of fundamental rights which supports the opposite conclusion. The ambiguity arising from this document thus means that the court must look at extrinsic evidence to determine its legal nature.

(b) *Extrinsic evidence*

It was suggested that the court examine three types of extrinsic evidence to assist it in determining whether the document of September 5th is a treaty. First, to indicate the parties' intent to enter into a treaty, the court was offered evidence to present a picture of the historical context of the period.

Then, evidence was presented of certain facts closely associated with the signing of the document and relating to the existence of the various constituent elements of a treaty. Finally, still with a view to determining whether the parties intended to enter into a treaty, the court was told of the subsequent conduct of the parties in respect of the document of September 5, 1760.

I should first mention that the admissibility of certain documents submitted by the intervener the National Indian Brotherhood/Assembly of First Nations in support of its arguments was contested. The intervener was relying on documents that were not part of the record in the lower courts. The appellant agreed that certain of these documents, namely Murray's journal, letters and instructions, should be included in the record provided this court considered that their admissibility was justified by the concept of judicial notice. I am of the view that all the documents to which I will refer, whether my attention was drawn to them by the intervener or as a result of my personal research, are documents of a historical nature which I am entitled to rely on pursuant to the concept of judicial knowledge. As Norris J.A. said in *White and Bob* (at p. 629):

> The Court is entitled "to take judicial notice of the facts of history whether past or contemporaneous" as Lord du Parcq said in *Monarch Steamship Co., Ld. v. Karlshamns Oljefabriker (A/B)*, [1949] A.C. 196 at p. 234, [1949] 1 All E.R. 1 at p. 20, and it is entitled to rely on its own historical knowledge and researches, *Read v. Bishop of Lincoln*, [1892] A.C. 644, Lord Halsbury, L.C., at pp. 652-4.

The documents I cite all enable the court, in my view, to identify more accurately the historical context essential to the resolution of this case.

The appellant argues that the historical context at the time the document of September 5th was concluded shows that the parties had no intention to enter into a treaty. The respondents and the intervener, the National Indian Brotherhood/Assembly of First Nations, on the other hand, maintain that the historical background to this document supports the existence of a common intent to sign a treaty.

On September 5, 1760, France and England were engaged in a war begun four years earlier, which ended with the Treaty of Paris, 1763, signed on February 10, 1763. About a year earlier, the battle of the Plains of Abraham had allowed the British to take control of Québec City and the surrounding area. During the year following this victory, British troops had worked to consolidate their military position in Canada and to solve the supply and other practical problems engendered by the very harsh winter of 1759.

In his work *An Historical Journal of the Campaigns in North-America for the Years 1757, 1758, 1759 and 1760* (1769), at p. 382 (day of September 3, 1760), Captain Knox also relates the efforts of General Murray to win the loyalty of the Canadians. General Murray at that time invited French soldiers to surrender and Canadians to lay down their arms. He had made it widely known that he would pardon those who surrendered and allow them to keep their land. He had also promised them that he would make larger grants of land and protect them. He gave those who responded to his appeal and took the oath of allegiance to the British Crown safe conducts to return to their parishes. Steps were also taken to inform the Indians who were allies of the British of these changes of allegiance so as to ensure that they would not be attacked on the way back.

As the advantageous position and strength of the British troops became more and more apparent, several groups did surrender and it appears that this movement accelerated in the days preceding that on which the document at issue was signed.

. . . . .

In fact, the total defeat of France in Canada was very near: the "Act of Capitulation of Montreal", by which the French troops stationed in Canada laid down their arms, was signed on September 8, 1760, and signalled the end of France's *de facto* control in Canada.

. . . . .

From the historical situation I have just briefly outlined, the appellant deduced that the document at issue is only a capitulation and that the legal nature of such a document should not be construed differently depending on whether it relates to the Indians or to the French. The court has before it, he submitted, only a capitulation comparable to a capitulation of French soldiers or Canadians, which cannot be elevated to the category of a treaty within the meaning of s. 88 of the *Indian Act* simply because an Indian tribe was a party to it. In other words, as Murray signed the same kind of document with respect to the Indians, the French or the Canadians his intent could not have been any different. The appellant also maintains that, like the capitulations of the Canadians and the French soldiers, this document was only temporary in nature in that its consequences would cease when the fate of Canada was finally settled at the end of the war.

I consider that, instead, we can conclude from the historical documents that both Great Britain and France felt that the Indian nations had sufficient independence and played a large enough role in North America for it to be good policy to maintain relations with them very close to those maintained between sovereign nations.

The mother countries did everything in their power to secure the alliance of each Indian nation and to encourage nations allied with the enemy to change sides. When these efforts met with success, they were incorporated in treaties of alliance or neutrality. This clearly indicates that the Indian nations were regarded in their relations with the European nations which occupied North America as independent nations. The papers of Sir William Johnson (*The Papers of Sir William Johnson*, 14 volumes), who was in charge of Indian affairs in British North America, demonstrate the recognition by Great Britain that nation-to-nation relations had to be conducted with the North American Indians. As an example, I cite an extract from a speech by Sir Johnson at the Onondaga Conference held in April, 1748, attended by the Five Nations (*The Papers of Sir William Johnson*, vol. I, (1921), p.157.):

Brethren of the five Nations I will begin upon a thing of a long standing, our first *Brothership*. My Reason for it is, I think there are several among you who seem to forget it; It may seem strange to you how I a *Foreigner* should know this, But I tell you I found out some of the old Writings of our Forefathers which was thought to have been lost and in this old valuable Record I find, that our first *Friendship* Commenced at the Arrival of the first great Canoe or Vessel at Albany.

(Emphasis added.)

As the Chief Justice of the United States Supreme Court said in 1832 in *Worcester v. State of Georgia*, 31 U.S. 515 at pp. 548-9 (1832) (6 Pet.), about British policy towards the Indians in the mid-18th century:

Such was the policy of Great Britain towards the Indian nations inhabiting the territory from which she excluded all other Europeans; such her claims, and such her practical exposition of the charters she had granted: *she considered them as nations capable of maintaining the relations of peace and war; of governing themselves, under her protection; and she made treaties with them, the obligation of which she acknowledged.*

(Emphasis added.)

Further, both the French and the English recognized the critical importance of alliances with the Indians, or at least their neutrality, in determining the outcome of the war between them and the security of the North American colonies.

Following the crushing defeats of the English by the French in 1755, the English realized that control of North America could not be acquired without the co-operation of the Indians. Accordingly, from then on they made efforts to ally themselves with as many Indian nations as possible. The French, who had long realized the strategic role of the Indians in the success of any war effort, also did everything they could to secure their alliance or maintain alliances already established: Jack Stagg, *Anglo-Indian Relations in North America to 1763* (1981); "Mr. Nelson's Memorial about the State of the Northern Colonies in America", September 24, 1696, reproduced in O' Callaghan (ed.) *Documents relative to the Colonial History of New York* (1856), vol. VII, at p. 206; "Letter from Sir William Johnson to William Pitt", October 24, 1760, in *The Papers of Sir William Johnson*, vol. III, (1921), at pp. 269 *et seq.*; "Mémoire de Bougainville sur l'artillerie du Canada", January 11, 1759, in *Rapport de l'archiviste de la Province de Québec pour 1923-1924* (1924), at p. 58; *Journal du Marquis de Montcalm durant ses campagnes en Canada de 1756 à 1759* (1895), at p. 428.

England also wished to secure the friendship of the Indian nations by treating them with generosity and respect for fear that the safety and development of the colonies and their inhabitants would be compromised by Indians with feelings of hostility. One of the extracts from Knox's work which I cited above reports that the Canadians and the French soldiers who surrendered asked to be protected from Indians on the way back to their parishes. Another passage from Knox, also cited above, relates that the Canadians were terrified at the idea of seeing Sir William Johnson's

Indians coming among them. This proves that in the minds of the local population the Indians represented a real and disturbing threat. The fact that England was also aware of the danger the colonies and their inhabitants might run if the Indians withdrew their co-operation is echoed in the following documents: "Letter from Sir William Johnson to the Lords of Trade", November 13, 1763, reproduced in O' Callaghan, (ed.), *op. cit.*, at pp. 574, 579 and 580; "Letter from Sir William Johnson to William Pitt", October 24, 1760, in *The Papers of Sir William Johnson*, vol. III, at pp. 270 and 274; [M.] Ratelle, *Contexte historique de la localisation des Attikameks et des Montagnais de 1760 à nos jours* (1987); "Letter from Amherst to Sir William Johnson", August 30, 1760, in *The Papers of Sir William Johnson*, vol. X, (1951), at p. 177; "Instructions from George II to Amherst", September 18, 1758, National Archives of Canada (MG 18 L 4 file 0 20/8); C. Colden, *The History of the Five Indian Nations of Canada* (1747), at p. 180; Stagg, *op. cit.*, at pp. 166-7; and by analogy Murray, *Journal of the Siege of Quebec, ibid.*, entry of December 31, 1759, at pp. 15-6.

This "generous" policy which the British chose to adopt also found expression in other areas. The British Crown recognized that the Indians had certain ownership rights over their land, it sought to establish trade with them which would rise above the level of exploitation and give them a fair return. It also allowed them autonomy in their internal affairs, intervening in this area as little as possible.

Whatever the similarities between a document recording the laying down of arms by French soldiers or Canadians and the document at issue, the analogy does not go so far as to preclude the conclusion that the document was nonetheless a treaty.

Such a document could not be regarded as a treaty so far as the French and the Canadians were concerned because under international law they had no authority to sign such a document: they were governed by a European nation which alone was able to represent them in dealings with other European nations for the signature of treaties affecting them. The colonial powers recognized that the Indians had the capacity to sign treaties directly with the European nations occupying North American territory. The *sui generis* situation in which the Indians were placed had forced the European mother countries to acknowledge that they had sufficient autonomy for the valid creation of solemn agreements which were called "treaties", regardless of the strict meaning given to that word then and now by international law. The question of the competence of the Hurons and of the French or the Canadians is essential to the question of whether a treaty exists. The question of capacity has to be examined from a fundamentally different viewpoint and in accordance with different principles for each of these groups. Thus, I reject the argument that the legal nature of the document at issue must necessarily be interpreted in the same way as the capitulations of the French and the Canadians. The historical context which I have briefly reviewed even supports the proposition that both the British and the Hurons could have intended to enter into a treaty on September 5, 1760.

. . . . .

Let us now turn to the second type of extrinsic evidence proposed by the parties, namely evidence relating to facts which were contemporaneous with or which occurred shortly before or after the signing of the document of September 5, 1760.

The respondents first presented evidence that the document of September 5, 1760 was the outcome of negotiations between Murray and certain Indian nations, including the Hurons, who wished to make peace with the British Crown. Knox's journal, *ibid.*, reports the following events for September 6th (at p. 384):

> Eight Sachems, of different nations, lately in alliance with the enemy, have surrendered, for themselves and their tribes, to General Murray: these fellows, after conferring with his Excellency, *and that all matters had been adjusted to their satisfaction*, stepped out to the beach opposite to Montreal, flourished their knives and hatchets, and set up the war-shout; intimating to the French, that they are now become our allies and their enemies. While these Chieftains *were negotiating a peace*, two of our Mohawks entered the apartment where they were with the General and Colonel Burton.

(Emphasis added.)

. . . . .

The foregoing passage shows that the document of September 5th was not simply an expression of General Murray's wishes, but the result of negotiations between the parties.

. . . . .

Knox goes on to say that the Mohawks wanted to turn on the various Indian groups allied with the French who had just concluded peace with the British. Murray and Burton intervened and the Mohawks merely made threats against them. What is significant for purposes of this case is that these threats reflected the Mohawks' perception as to the nature of the agreement which had just been concluded between the eight Sachems and Murray. The Mohawks said the following (at p. 385):

> Do you remember, when you treacherously killed one of our brothers at such a time? Ye shall one day pay dearly for it, ye cowardly dogs, — *let the treaty be as it will*: — I tell you, we will destroy you and your settlement.

(Emphasis added.)

The view taken by these Indians was apparently shared by Murray himself. The note written by Murray in his journal, on September 5, 1760, indicates that he considered that a peace treaty had been concluded with the Indian nations in question:

> Sepr. 5th. March'd with them myself and on the road, met the Inhabitants who were coming to deliver their arms, and take the oaths, there two nations of Indians, of Hurons and Iroquois, came in & *made their Pace*.

(Emphasis added.) (Knox, *Appendix to an Historical Journal or the Campaigns in North America for the Years 1757, 1758, 1759 and 1760* (1916), at p. 831.)

The accounts given by Knox and Murray himself of the events on the days that are critical for this case are quite consistent with British policy, which favoured alliance or at least neutrality for the greatest number of the Indian nations in the newly conquered territories. By holding negotiations to conclude a peace treaty between the Hurons and the British, Murray was only giving effect to this clear policy of Great Britain.

The intervener, the National Indian Brotherhood/Assembly of First Nations, provided the court with some very interesting evidence in this regard. It submitted the minutes of a conference between Sir William Johnson and the representatives of the Eight Nations, including the Lorette Hurons, held in Montreal on September 16, 1760: *The Papers of Sir William Johnson*, vol. XIII, 1962, at p. 163. Although the appellant objected to the court considering this document, I feel it is a reliable source which allows us to take cognizance of a historical fact. Its being submitted by the intervener does not in any way prevent the court from taking judicial notice of it. Indeed, I can only express my appreciation to the intervener for facilitating my research.

The minutes of this conference refer in several places to the peace recently concluded between the Eight Nations and the English and their allies (at pp. 163-4):

> Br. Wy. [Brother Warrigheyagey, a term of endearment for Sir William Johnson, meaning "he who does much business"]
>
> You desired of us to [see] deliver up your People who [may be] are still among us — [We] *As you have now settled all matters wth. us & we are become firm Friends. . . .*
>
> a Belt
> Br. W.
>
> *As we have now made a firm Peace wth. the English & ye. 6 Nats. we shall endeavour all in our Powr. to keep it inviolably.*
>
> a large Belt."

(Emphasis added.)

These words were spoken by spokesmen for the Eight Nations and clearly show that the Indians and Sir William Johnson considered that relations between these Indian nations and the British would now take the form of an alliance ("firm friends"). This new situation was undoubtedly the outcome of the peace concluded between the parties, a peace desired by the Eight Nations as well as the British ("We have now made a firm Peace with the English").

Finally, it is worth noting that each of the contributions made by spokesmen at this conference was followed by the presentation of a belt to solemnize the content of the undertakings that had just been made or the words which had just been spoken. As we saw earlier, the appellant contends that the document of September 5, 1760 is not a treaty, *inter alia*, because the tokens of solemnity that ordinarily accompanied treaties between the Indians and the British are not present. I think it is reasonable to conclude that the circumstances existing on September 5th readily explain the absence of such solemnities. Murray was not given notice of the meeting, and *a fortiori* its purpose, and it was therefore largely improvised. Murray also had very little time to spend on ceremony: his troops were moving towards Montreal and were on a war footing. He himself was busy organizing the final preparations for a meeting between his army and that of Amherst and Haviland in Montreal, for the purpose of bringing down this last significant French bastion in Canada. Although solemnities are not crucial to the existence of a treaty, I think it is in any case reasonable to regard the presentation of belts at the conference on September 16th as a solemn ratification of the peace agreement concluded a few days earlier.

Lastly, the Court was asked to consider the subsequent conduct of the parties as extrinsic evidence of their intent to enter into a treaty. I do not think this is necessary, since the general historical context of the time and the events closely surrounding the document at issue have persuaded me that the document of September 5, 1760 is a treaty within the meaning of s. 88 of the *Indian Act*. The fact that the document has allegedly not been used in the courts or other institutions of our society does not establish that it is not a treaty. Non-use may very well be explained by observance of the rights contained in the document or mere oversight. Moreover, the subsequent conduct which is most indicative of the parties' intent is undoubtedly that which most closely followed the conclusion of the document. Eleven days after it was concluded, at the conference to which I have just referred, the parties gave a clear indication that they had intended to conclude a treaty.

I am therefore of the view that the document of September 5, 1760 is a treaty within the meaning of s. 88 of the *Indian Act*. At this point, the appellant raises two arguments against its application to the present case. First, he argues that the treaty has been extinguished. In the event that it has not been, he argues that the treaty is not such as to render ss. 9 and 37 of the *Regulation respecting the Parc de la Jacques-Cartier* inoperative. Let us first consider whether on May 29, 1982, the date on which the respondents engaged in the activities which are the subject of the charges, the treaty still had any legal effects.

V *Legal Effects of Treaty of September 5, 1760 on May 29, 1982*

The appellant argues that, assuming the document of September 5th is a treaty, it was extinguished by the following documents or events:

1. the Act of Capitulation of Montreal, signed on September 8, 1760;
2. the Treaty of Paris signed on February 10, 1763;
3. the Royal Proclamation of October 7, 1763;
4. the legislative and administrative history of the Hurons' land, and
5. the effect of time and non-use of the treaty.

Neither the documents nor the legislative and administrative history to which the appellant referred the court contain any express statement that the treaty of September 5, 1760 has been extinguished. Even assuming that a treaty can be extinguished implicitly, a point on which I express no opinion here, the appellant was not able in my view to meet the criterion stated in *Simon* regarding the quality of evidence that would be required in any case to support a conclusion that the treaty had been extinguished. That case clearly established that the onus is on the party arguing that the treaty has terminated to show the circumstances and events indicating it has been extinguished. This burden can only be discharged by strict proof, as the Chief Justice said at pp. 405-6:

> Given the serious and far-reaching consequences of a finding that a treaty right has been extinguished, it seems appropriate to demand strict proof of the fact of extinguishment in each case where the issue arises.

The appellant did not submit any persuasive evidence of extinguishment of the treaty. He argues, first, that the treaty had become obsolete because the "Act of Capitulation of Montreal" replaced all other acts of capitulation, thereby extinguishing them. This argument is based on art. 50 of the "Act of Capitulation", which reads as follows:

> The present capitulation shall be inviolably executed in all its articles, and bona fide, on both sides, notwithstanding any infraction, and any other pretence, with regard to the *preceding capitulations*, and without making use of reprisals.

(Emphasis added.)

As I have concluded that this is a peace treaty and not a capitulation, art. 50 has no application in this case, so far as extinguishment of the treaty of September 5th is concerned. That article was designed to ensure that the signatories would comply with the "Act of Capitulation", in spite of the existence of reasons for retaliation which the parties might have had as the result of breaches of an earlier act of capitulation. Article 50 can only apply to preceding acts signed on behalf of France, such as the "Act of Capitulation of Québec" in late 1759. I see nothing here to support the conclusion that this article was also intended to extinguish a treaty between an Indian nation and the British.

The appellant also cites art. 40 of the "Act of Capitulation of Montreal", which provides that:

> The Savages or Indian allies of his most Christian Majesty, shall be maintained in the Lands they inhabit; if they chuse to remain there; they shall not be molested on any pretence whatsoever, for having carried arms, and served his most Christian Majesty. They shall have, as well as the French, liberty of religion, and shall keep their missionaries.

(Emphasis added.)

France could not have claimed to represent the Hurons at the time the "Act of Capitulation" was made, since the latter had abandoned their alliance with the French some days before. As they were no longer allies of the French, this article does not apply to them.

. . . . .

It would be contrary to the general principles of law for an agreement concluded between the English and the French to extinguish a treaty concluded between the English and the Hurons. It must be remembered that a treaty is a solemn agreement between the Crown and the Indians, an agreement the nature of which is sacred: *Simon, supra*, at p. 410, and *White and Bob, supra*, at p. 649. The very definition of a treaty thus makes it impossible to avoid the conclusion that a treaty cannot be extinguished without the consent of the Indians concerned. Since the Hurons had the capacity to enter into a treaty with the British, therefore, they must be the only ones who could give the necessary consent to its extinguishment.

The same reasoning applies to the appellant's argument that the Treaty of Paris of February 10, 1763 between France and England terminated the treaty of September 5, 1760 between the Hurons and the English. England and France could not validly agree to extinguish a treaty between the Hurons and the English, nor could France claim to represent the Hurons regarding the extinguishment of a treaty the Hurons had themselves concluded with the British Crown.

The appellant then argued that it follows that the Royal Proclamation of October 7, 1763 extinguished the rights arising out of the treaty of September 5, 1760, because it did not confirm them. I cannot accept such a proposition: the silence of the Royal Proclamation regarding the treaty at issue cannot be interpreted as extinguishing it.

. . . . .

The proclamation confers rights on the Indians without necessarily thereby extinguishing any other right conferred on them by the British Crown under a treaty.

Legislative and administrative history also provides no basis for concluding that the treaty was extinguished.

. . . . .

The appellant further argues that by adopting the Act to establish the Laurentides National Park, S.Q. 1895, and by making the territory in question a park, the Quebec legislator clearly expressed his intention to prohibit the carrying on of certain activities in this territory, whether or not such activities are protected by an Indian treaty.

Section 88 of the *Indian Act* is designed specifically to protect the Indians from provincial legislation that might attempt to deprive them of rights protected by a treaty. A legislated change in the use of the territory thus does not extinguish rights otherwise protected by treaty. If the treaty gives the Hurons the right to carry on their customs and religion in the territory of Jacques-Cartier Park, the existence of a provincial statute and subordinate legislation will not ordinarily affect that right.

Finally, the appellant argues that non-user of the treaty over a long period of time may extinguish its effect. He cites no authority for this. I do not think that this argument carries much weight: a solemn agreement cannot lose its validity merely because it has not been invoked to, which in any case is disputed by the respondents, who maintain that it was relied on in a seigneurial claim in 1824. Such a proposition would mean that a treaty could be extinguished merely because it had not been relied on in litigation, which is untenable.

In view of the liberal and generous approach that must be adopted towards Indians' rights and the evidence in the record, I cannot conclude that the treaty of September 5th no longer had any legal effect on May 29, 1982.

The question that arises at this point is as to whether the treaty is capable of rendering ss. 9 and 37 of the regulations inoperative. To answer this it will now be necessary to consider the territorial scope of the rights guaranteed by the treaty, since the appellant recognizes that the activities with which the respondents are charged are customary or religious in nature.

VI *Territorial scope of rights guaranteed by treaty of September 5, 1760*

Although the document of September 5th is a treaty within the meaning of s. 88 of the *Indian Act*, that does not necessarily mean that the respondents are exempt from the application of the *Regulation respecting the Parc de la Jacques-Cartier*. It is still necessary that the treaty protecting activities of the kind with which the respondents are charged cover the territory of Jacques-Cartier Park.

. . . . .

The respondents must therefore show that the treaty guaranteed their right to carry on their customs and religious rites in the territory of Jacques-Cartier Park.

The treaty gives the Hurons the freedom to carry on their customs and their religion. No mention is made in the treaty itself of the territory over which these rights may be exercised. There is also no indication that the territory of what is now Jacques-Cartier Park was contemplated. However, for a freedom to have real value and meaning, it must be possible to exercise it somewhere. That does not mean, despite the importance of the rights concerned, that the Indians can exercise it anywhere. Our analysis will be confined to setting the limits of the promise made in the treaty, since the respondents have at no time based their argument on the existence of aboriginal rights protecting the activities with which they are charged.

The respondents suggest that the treaty gives them the right to carry on their customs and religion in the territory of the park because it is part of the territory frequented by the Hurons in 1760, namely the area between the Saguenay and the St-Maurice. In their submission, customs as they existed at the time of the treaty and as they might reasonably be expected to develop subsequently are what the British Crown undertook to preserve and foster.

The appellant argued in the Court of Appeal that the free exercise of the customs mentioned in the document of September 5, 1760 has to be limited to the Lorette territory, a territory of 40 arpents by 40 arpents. ... In his intervention the Attorney-General of Canada argues that the respondents' claim is essentially a territorial one and that in order to establish their rights, the respondents must show a connection between the rights claimed and their exercise in a given territory.

. . . . .

In my view, the treaty essentially has to be interpreted by determining the intention of the parties on the territorial question at the time it was concluded. It is not sufficient to note that the treaty is silent on this point. We must also undertake the task of interpreting the treaty on the territorial question with the same generous approach toward the Indians that applied in considering earlier questions. Now as then, we must do our utmost to act in the spirit of *Simon*.

The historical context, which has been used to demonstrate the existence of the treaty, may equally assist us in interpreting the extent of the rights contained in it. As MacKinnon J.A. said in *Taylor and Williams, supra*, at p. 232:

> Cases on Indian or aboriginal rights can never be determined in a vacuum. It is of importance to consider the history and oral traditions of the tribes concerned, and the surrounding circumstances at the time of the treaty, relied on by both parties, in determining the treaty's effect.

. . . . .

The interpretation which I think is called for when we give the historical context its full meaning is that Murray and the Hurons contemplated that the rights guaranteed by the treaty could be exercised over the entire territory frequented by the Hurons at the time, so long as the carrying on of the customs and rites is not incompatible with the particular use made by the Crown of this territory.

. . . . .

I conclude that in view of the absence of any express mention of the territorial scope of the treaty, it has to be assumed that the parties to the treaty of September 5th intended to reconcile the Hurons' need to protect the exercise of their customs and the desire of the British conquerors to expand. Protecting the exercise of the customs in all parts of the territory frequented when it is not incompatible with its occupancy is in my opinion the most reasonable way of reconciling the competing interests. This, in my view, is the definition of the common intent of the parties which best reflects the actual intent of the Hurons and of Murray on September 5, 1760. Defining the common intent of the parties on the question of territory in this way makes it possible to give full effect to the spirit of conciliation, while respecting the practical requirements of the British. This gave the English the necessary flexibility to be able to respond in due course to the increasing need to use Canada's resources, in the event that Canada remained under British suzerainty. The Hurons, for their part, were protecting their customs wherever their exercise would not be prejudicial to the use to which the territory concerned would be put. The Hurons could not reasonably expect that the use would forever remain what it was in 1760. Before the treaty was signed, they had carried on their customs in accordance with restrictions already imposed by an occupancy incompatible with such exercise. The Hurons were only asking to be permitted to continue to carry on their customs on the lands frequented to the extent that those customs did not interfere with enjoyment of the lands by their occupier. I readily accept that the Hurons were probably not aware of the legal consequences, and in particular of the right to occupy to the exclusion of others, which the main European legal systems attached to the concept of private ownership. None the less I cannot believe that the Hurons ever believed that the treaty gave them the right to cut down trees in the garden of a house as part of their right to carry on their customs.

Jacques-Cartier Park falls into the category of land occupied by the Crown, since the province has set it aside for a specific use. What is important is not so much that the province has legislated with respect to this territory but that it is using it, is in fact occupying the space. As occupancy has been established, the question is whether the type of occupancy to which the park is subject is incompatible with the exercise of the activities with which the respondents were charged, as these undoubtedly constitute religious customs or rites. Since, in view of the situation in 1760, we must assume some limitation on the exercise of rights protected by the treaty, it is up to the Crown to prove that its occupancy of the territory cannot be accommodated to reasonable exercise of the Hurons' rights.

The Crown presented evidence on such compatibility but that evidence did not persuade me that exercise of the rites and customs at issue here is incompatible with the occupancy.

. . . . .

For the exercise of rites and customs to be incompatible with the occupancy of the park by the Crown, it must not only be contrary to the purpose underlying that occupancy, it must prevent the realization of that purpose. First, we are dealing with Crown lands, lands which are held for the benefit of the community. Exclusive use is not an essential aspect of public ownership. Secondly, I do not think that the activities described seriously compromise the Crown's objectives in occupying the park. Neither the representative nature of the natural region where the park is located nor the exceptional nature of this natural site are threatened by the collecting of a few plants, the setting up of a tent using a few branches picked up in the area or the making of a fire according to the rules dictated by caution to avoid fires. These activities also present no obstacle to cross-country recreation. I therefore conclude that it has not been established that occupancy of the territory of Jacques-Cartier Park is incompatible with the exercise of Huron rites and customs with which the respondents are charged.

VII *Conclusion*

For all these reasons, I would dismiss the appeal with costs.

Although it was decided in 1990, the *Sioui* decision, like *Simon* before it, did not contemplate the effects of the constitutionalization of treaty rights in section 35(1). The first treaty case decided by the Supreme Court of Canada that considered the effects of section 35(1) on treaties was *R. v. Badger*. The *Badger* case focused on the rights of three Treaty No. 8 Indians to hunt on private lands. The treaty provided for the right to hunt over the territories surrendered, save for lands that had been taken up for settlement, mining, lumbering, trading, or other purposes. The key question to be determined was whether the appellants, Messrs. Badger, Kiyawasew, and Ominayak, had rights of access to the private lands they were hunting on when they were charged with different violations of the Alberta *Wildlife Act*, S.A. 1984, c. W-9.1.

Mr. Badger had been charged with shooting a moose outside of hunting season on brush land with willow regrowth and scrub. Although the land he was hunting on was private property, there were no fences or signs posted on the land which indicated that it was private property. There was, however, a farm house (that did not appear to be abandoned) located a quarter of a mile from where Badger had shot the moose. Mr. Kiyawasew was charged with hunting without a licence. He had shot a moose on an unfenced, snow-covered field. He testified that he had passed old, run-down barns and that signs were posted on the land, but he was unable to read them from the road. Evidence indicated that, in the fall, a crop had been harvested from the field. Mr. Ominayak was also charged with hunting without a licence. He had been hunting on uncleared muskeg, with no fences, signs, or buildings in the vicinity of where he shot a moose.

The extract from *Badger* reproduced below deals with the Court's explanation of the principles of treaty interpretation and their effects on the issues raised in *Badger*. The effect of the *Natural Resources Transfer Agreement, 1930*, S.C. 1930, c. 3 on the rights contained in Treaty No. 8, the other significant element of the *Badger* case, is examined in Chapter 8.

R. v. BADGER

[1996] S.C.J. No. 39, [1996] 1 S.C.R. 771, 133 D.L.R. (4th) 324, [1996] 4
W.W.R. 457, 37 Alta. L.R. (3d) 153, 195 N.R. 1, 105 C.C.C. (3d) 289 (S.C.C.)
(references omitted)

Sopinka J. (Lamer C.J.C. concurring): —

. . . . .

[9] … The key interpretive principles which apply to treaties are first,
that any ambiguity in the treaty will be resolved in favour of the Indians
and, second, that treaties should be interpreted in a manner that maintains
the integrity of the Crown, particularly the Crown's fiduciary obligation
towards aboriginal peoples. …

. . . . .

Cory J. (La Forest, L'Heureux-Dubé, Gonthier and **Iacobucci JJ.**
concurring): —

[20] Three questions must be answered on this appeal. First, do Indians
who have status under Treaty No. 8 have the right to hunt for food on
privately owned land which lies within the territory surrendered under
that treaty? Secondly, have the hunting rights set out in Treaty No. 8 been
extinguished or modified as a result of the provisions of para. 12 of the
1930 *Natural Resources Transfer Agreement, 1930 (Constitution Act, 1930*, Sch.
2)? Thirdly, to what extent, if any, do ss. 26(1) and 27(1) of the *Wildlife Act*,
S.A. 1984, c. W-9.1, apply to the appellants?
[Only questions 1 and 2 will be dealt with in this extract. Question 3 is
considered in the excerpt of the case in Chapter 8.]

. . . . .

[31] The relevant part of Treaty No. 8, made June 21, 1899, provides:

> And Her Majesty the Queen HEREBY AGREES with the said Indians that
> they shall have right to pursue their usual vocations of hunting, trapping
> and fishing throughout the tract surrendered as heretofore described,
> subject to such regulations as may from time to time be made by the
> Government of the country, acting under the authority of Her Majesty, and
> saving and excepting such tracts as may be required or taken up from time
> to time for settlement, mining, lumbering, trading or other purposes.

The Existing Right to Hunt for Food

. . . . .

The Hunting Right Provided by Treaty No. 8

[39] … Treaty No. 8, made on June 21, 1899, involved the surrender of vast
tracts of land in what is now northern Alberta, north-eastern British
Columbia, north-western Saskatchewan and part of the Northwest Territories.

In exchange for the land, the Crown made a number of commitments. ... However, it is clear that for the Indians the guarantee that hunting, fishing and trapping rights would continue was the essential element which led to their signing the treaties. The report of the commissioners who negotiated Treaty No. 8 on behalf of the government underscored the importance to the Indians of the right to hunt, fish and trap. The commissioners wrote:

> There was expressed at every point the fear that the making of the treaty would be followed by the curtailment of the hunting and fishing privileges.
>
> . . . . .
>
> We pointed out ... that the *same means of earning a livelihood would continue after the Treaty as existed before it*, and that the Indians would be expected to make use of them. ...
>
> Our chief difficulty was the apprehension that the hunting and fishing privileges were to be curtailed. The provision in the treaty under which ammunition and twine is to be furnished went far in the direction of quieting the fears of the Indians, for they admitted that it would be unreasonable to furnish the means of hunting and fishing if laws were to be enacted which would make hunting and fishing so restricted as to render it impossible to make a livelihood by such pursuits. But over and above the provision, *we had to solemnly assure them that only such laws as to hunting and fishing as were in the interest of the Indians and were found necessary in order to protect the fish and fur-bearing animals would be made, and that they would be as free to hunt and fish after the treaty as they would be if they never entered into it.*

(Emphasis added)

[40] Treaty No. 8 then, guaranteed that the Indians "shall have the right to pursue their usual vocations of hunting, trapping and fishing". The treaty, however, imposed two limitations on the right to hunt. First, there was a geographic limitation. The right to hunt could be exercised "throughout the tract surrendered ... saving and excepting such tracts as may be required or taken up from time to time for settlement, mining, lumbering, trading or other purposes". Second, the right could be limited by government regulations passed for conservation purposes.

. . . . .

Principles of Interpretation

[41] At the outset, it may be helpful to once again set out some of the applicable principles of interpretation. First, it must be remembered that a treaty represents an exchange of solemn promises between the Crown and the various Indian nations. It is an agreement whose nature is sacred. ... Second, the honour of the Crown is always at stake in its dealing with Indian people. Interpretations of treaties and statutory provisions which have an impact upon treaty or aboriginal rights must be approached in a manner which maintains the integrity of the Crown. It is always assumed that the Crown intends to fulfil its promises. No appearance of "sharp

dealing" will be sanctioned. ... Third, any ambiguities or doubtful expressions in the wording of the treaty or document must be resolved in favour of the Indians. A corollary to this principle is that any limitations which restrict the rights of Indians under treaties must be narrowly construed. ... Fourth, the onus of proving that a treaty or aboriginal right has been extinguished lies upon the Crown. There must be "strict proof of the fact of extinguishment" and evidence of a clear and plain intention on the part of the government to extinguish treaty rights. ...

[42] These principles of interpretation must now be applied to this case.

. . . . .

Geographical Limitations on the Right to Hunt for Food

[49] ... In the present appeals, the hunting occurred on lands which had been included in the 1899 surrender but were now privately owned. Therefore, it must be determined whether these privately owned lands were "other lands" to which the Indians had a "right of access" under the treaty.

. . . . .

[51] ... While some treaties contain express provisions with respect to hunting on private land, others, such as Treaty No. 8 do not. Under Treaty No. 8, the right to hunt for food could be exercised "throughout the tract surrendered" to the Crown "saving and excepting such tracts as may be required or taken up from time to time for settlement, mining, lumbering, trading or other purposes". Accordingly, if the privately owned land is not "required or taken up" in the manner described in Treaty No. 8, it will be land to which the Indians had a right of access to hunt for food.

[52] [T]he applicable interpretive principles must be borne in mind. Treaties and statutes relating to Indians should be liberally construed and any uncertainties, ambiguities or doubtful expressions should be resolved in favour of the Indians. In addition, when considering a treaty, a court must take into account the context in which the treaties were negotiated, concluded and committed to writing. The treaties, as written documents, recorded an agreement that had already been reached orally and they did not always record the full extent of the oral agreement. ... The treaties were drafted in English by representatives of the Canadian government who, it should be assumed, were familiar with common law doctrines. Yet, the treaties were not translated in written form into the languages (here Cree and Dene) of the various Indian nations who were signatories. Even if they had been, it is unlikely that the Indians, who had a history of communicating only orally, would have understood them any differently. As a result, it is well settled that the words in the treaty must not be interpreted in their strict technical sense nor subjected to rigid modern rules of construction. Rather, they must be interpreted in the sense that they would naturally have been understood by the Indians at the time of

the signing. This applies, as well, to those words in a treaty which impose a limitation on the right which has been granted. ...

[53] The evidence led at trial indicated that in 1899 the Treaty No. 8 Indians would have understood that land had been "required or taken up" when it was being put to a use which was incompatible with the exercise of the right to hunt. Historian John Foster gave expert evidence in this case. His testimony indicated that, in 1899, Treaty No. 8 Indians would not have understood the concept of private and exclusive property ownership separate from actual land use. They understood land to be required or taken up for settlement when buildings or fences were erected, land was put into crops, or farm or domestic animals were present. Enduring church missions would also be understood to constitute settlement. These physical signs shaped the Indians' understanding of settlement because they were the manifestations of exclusionary land use which the Indians had witnessed as new settlers moved into the west. The Indians' experience with the Hudson's Bay Company was also relevant. Although that company had title to vast tracts of land, the Indians were not excluded from and, in fact, continued hunting on these lands. In the course of their trading, the Hudson's Bay Company and the Northwest Company had set up numerous posts that were subsequently abandoned. The presence of abandoned buildings, then, would not necessarily signify to the Indians that land was taken up in a way which precluded hunting on them. Yet, it is dangerous to pursue this line of thinking too far. The abandonment of land may be temporary. Owners may return to reoccupy the land, to undertake maintenance, to inspect it or simply to enjoy it. How "unoccupied" the land was at the relevant time will have to be explored on a case-by-case basis.

[54] An interpretation of the treaty properly founded upon the Indians' understanding of its terms leads to the conclusion that the geographical limitation on the existing hunting right should be based upon a concept of visible, incompatible land use. This approach is consistent with the oral promises made to the Indians at the time the treaty was signed, with the oral history of the Treaty No. 8 Indians, with earlier case law and with the provisions of the Alberta *Wildlife Act* itself.

[55] The Indian people made their agreements orally and recorded their history orally. Thus, the verbal promises made on behalf of the federal government at the times the treaties were concluded are of great significance in their interpretation. ...

Since the Treaty No. 8 lands were not well suited to agriculture, the government expected little settlement in the area. The commissioners ... indicated that "it is safe to say that so long as the fur-bearing animals remain, the great bulk of the Indians will continue to hunt and to trap". The promise that this livelihood would not be affected was repeated to all the bands who signed the treaty. Although it was expected that some white prospectors might stake claims in the north, this was not expected to have an impact on the Indians' hunting rights. For example, one commissioner ... stated:

We are just making peace between Whites and Indians — for them to treat each other well. And we do not want to change your hunting. If Whites should prospect, stake claims, that will not harm anyone.

[56] Commissioner Laird told the Indians that the promises made to them were to be similar to those made with other Indians who had agreed to a treaty. Accordingly, it is significant that the earlier promises also contemplated a limited interference with Indians' hunting and fishing practices. ... In negotiating Treaty No. 1, the Lieutenant-Governor of Manitoba, A.G. Archibald, made the following statement to the Indians ...:

> When you have made your treaty you will still be free to hunt over much of the land included in the treaty. Much of it is rocky and unfit for cultivation, much of it that is wooded is beyond the places where the white man will require to go, at all events for some time to come. *Till these lands are needed for use you will be free to hunt over them, and make all the use of them which you have made in the past. But when lands are needed to be tilled or occupied, you must not go on them any more. There will still be plenty of land that is neither tilled nor occupied where you can go and roam and hunt as you have always done,* and, if you wish to farm, you will go to your own reserve where you will find a place ready for you to live on and cultivate. [Emphasis added.]

With respect to Treaty 4, Lt. Gov. Morris made the following statement to the Indians ...:

> We have come through the country for many days and we have seen hills and but little wood and in many places little water, and it may be a long time before there are many white men settled upon this land, and you will have the right of hunting and fishing just as you have now *until the land is actually taken up.* [Emphasis added.]

With respect to Treaty 6, Lt. Gov. Morris stated ...:

> You want to be at liberty to hunt as before. I told you we did not want to take that means of living from you, you have it the same as before, on this, *if a man, whether Indian or Half-breed, has a good field of grain, you would not destroy it with your hunt.* [Emphasis added.]

[57] The oral history of the Treaty No. 8 Indians reveals a similar understanding of the treaty promises. Dan McLean, an elder from the Sturgeon Lake Indian Reserve, gave evidence in this trial. He indicated that the understanding of the treaty promise was that Indians were allowed to hunt anytime for food to feed their families. They could hunt on unoccupied Crown land and on abandoned land. If there was no fence on the land, they could hunt, but if there was a fence, they could not hunt there. This testimony is consistent with the oral histories presented by other Treaty No. 8 elders whose stories have been recorded by historians. The Indians understood that land would be taken up for homesteads, farming, prospecting and mining and that they would not be able to hunt in these areas or to shoot at the settlers' farm animals or buildings. No doubt the Indians believed that most of the Treaty No. 8 land would remain unoccupied and so would be available to them for hunting, fishing and trapping. ...

[58] Accordingly, the oral promises made by the Crown's representatives and the Indians' own oral history indicate that it was understood that land would be taken up and occupied in a way which precluded hunting when it was put to a visible use that was incompatible with hunting. Turning to the case law, it is clear that the courts have also accepted this interpretation and have concluded that whether or not land has been taken up or occupied is a question of fact that must be resolved on a case-by-case basis.

[59] Most of the cases which have considered the geographical limitations on the right to hunt have been concerned with situations where the hunting took place on *Crown* land. In those cases, it was held that Crown lands were only "occupied" or "taken up" when they were actually put to an active use which was incompatible with hunting. ...

[60] A second but shorter line of cases has considered whether Indians have a treaty right of access to hunt on privately owned lands. While various factual situations have been considered, the courts have not settled the question as to whether the Treaty No. 8 right to hunt for food extends to privately owned land which is not put to visible use.

. . . . .

[65] The "visible, incompatible use" approach, which focuses upon the use being made of the land is appropriate and correct. Although it requires that the particular land use be considered in each case, this standard is neither unduly vague nor unworkable.

[66] In summary, then, the geographical limitation on the right to hunt for food is derived from the terms of the particular treaty if they have not been modified or altered by the provisions of para. 12 of the NRTA. In this case, the geographical limitation on the right to hunt for food provided by Treaty No. 8 has not been modified by para. 12 of the NRTA. Where lands are privately owned, it must be determined on a case-by-case basis whether they are "other lands" to which Indians had a "right of access" under the treaty. If the lands are occupied, that is, put to visible use which is incompatible with hunting, Indians will not have a right of access. Conversely, if privately owned land is unoccupied and not put to visible use, Indians, pursuant to Treaty No. 8, will have a right of access in order to hunt for food. ...

. . . . .

Permissible Regulatory Limitations on the Right to Hunt for Food

[69] Pursuant to the provisions of s. 88 of the *Indian Act*, R.S.C. 1985, c. I-5, provincial laws of general application will apply to Indians. This is so except where they conflict with aboriginal or treaty rights, in which case the latter must prevail. ... In any event, the regulation of Indian hunting rights would ordinarily come within the jurisdiction of the federal government and not the province. However, the issue does not arise in this case since we are dealing with the right to hunt provided by Treaty 8 as

modified by the NRTA. [The NRTA's effect on treaty rights is discussed in Chapter 8.] Both the treaty and the NRTA specifically provided that the right would be subject to regulation pertaining to conservation.

[70] Treaty No. 8 provided that the right to hunt would be "subject to such regulations as may from time to time be made by the Government of the country". In the west, a wide range of legislation aimed at conserving game had been enacted by the government beginning as early as the 1880s. Acts and regulations pertaining to conservation measures continued to be passed throughout the entire period during which the numbered treaties were concluded. In *Horseman, supra*, [reproduced in Chapter 8] the aim and intent of the regulations was recognized. ...:

> Before the turn of the century the federal game laws of the Unorganized Territories provided for a total ban on hunting certain species (bison and musk oxen) in order to preserve both the species and the supply of game for Indians in the future: see the *Unorganized Territories' Game Preservation Act, 1894*, S.C. 1894, c. 31, ss. 2, 4-8 and 26. ... Moreover, beginning in 1890, provision was made in the federal *Indian Act*, R.S.C. 1886, c. 43, for the Superintendent-General to make the game laws of Manitoba and the Unorganized Territories applicable to Indians.

In light of the existence of these conservation laws prior to signing the treaty, the Indians would have understood that, by the terms of the treaty, the government would be permitted to pass regulations with respect to conservation. ...

[Cory J. went on to consider the licensing provisions in the Alberta *Wildlife Act, supra*, which it deemed to be only partially concerned with conservation matters. It found that these provisions infringed upon the hunting rights granted by Treaty No. 8, as modified by the NRTA. The Court then sought to apply the test for the legislative infringement of Aboriginal rights developed in *R. v. Sparrow, supra* — which is discussed in Chapter 2 — to see whether the infringement of the Treaty No. 8 right to hunt by the *Wildlife Act* licensing requirements was justified. However, since the Crown had led no evidence at trial to justify the application of the regulations to Mr. Ominayak and the question of justification was not addressed by the lower courts, a new trial was ordered. The charges against Mr. Ominayak were then stayed. The appeals of Messrs. Badger and Kiyawasew were dismissed, as it was determined that the lands upon which they were hunting were put to a visible, incompatible use and were therefore not lands to which they had a right of access for hunting under the treaty.]

The *Badger* decision raises a number of questions. Would the Treaty No. 8 signatories have understood (as Justice Cory suggests in *Badger*) that the government could regulate Aboriginal hunting (as long as that regulation was aimed at conservation) even though the signatories had been promised by the treaty commissioners (as indicated in their own report) that "they would be as free to hunt and fish after the treaty as they would be if they never entered into it"? Is Justice Cory's conclusion consistent with your interpretation of this treaty promise? Ought one answer this question only by reference to the Aboriginal understanding at the time the treaty was signed? Can extrinsic evidence properly be used in this situation?

In addition to demonstrating concern over Aboriginal understandings of treaties, the Supreme Court of Canada has also sanctioned expansive understandings of the rights associated with treaty promises, following the precedent established in the *Simon* case. This is evidenced particularly well in *R. v. Sundown*, [1999] S.C.J. No. 13, [1999] 1 S.C.R. 393 (S.C.C.), where the Supreme Court allowed a member of the Joseph Bighead First Nation to cut down trees without a permit and to construct a small log cabin to enable him to engage in his First Nation's traditional expeditionary method of hunting, pursuant to which the members ventured out for up to two weeks of hunting.

Justice Cory, for a unanimous Court, made the following statements about the reasonably incidental nature of the cabin to the First Nation's hunting rights under Treaty No. 6:

[27] Both parties submitted that, in order to determine whether the right to shelter is reasonably incidental to the right to hunt, the test set out in *Simon*, *supra*, must be applied. ...

[28] How should the term "reasonably incidental" be defined and applied? In my view it should be approached in this manner. Would a reasonable person, fully apprised of the relevant manner of hunting or fishing, consider the activity in question reasonably related to the act of hunting or fishing? It may seem old fashioned to apply a reasonable person test but I believe it is both useful and appropriate.

[29] The reasonable person must be dispassionate and fully apprised of the circumstances of the treaty rights holder. That reasonable person must also be aware of the manner in which the First Nation hunted and fished at the time the treaty was signed. That knowledge must, of course, be placed to some extent in today's context. For example, in the past it was reasonably incidental to hunting rights to carry a quiver of arrows. Today it is reasonably incidental to hunting rights to carry the appropriate box of shotgun shells or rifle cartridges. A form of shelter was always necessary to carry out the expeditionary hunting of the Joseph Bighead First Nation. At the time of the treaty, the shelter may have been a carefully built lean-to. That shelter appropriately evolved to a tent and then a small cabin. Thus, the reasonable person, informed of the manner of hunting at the time of the treaty, can consider it in the light of modern hunting methods and can determine whether the activity in question — the shelter — is reasonably incidental to the right to hunt.

. . . . .

[31] It is uncontroverted that the Joseph Bighead First Nation has traditionally hunted in what was described as an expeditionary style. Like the spokes of a wheel the hunters radiate out from the base each day to search for game. The hunt may continue for two weeks. The base provides a

place for dressing the game and smoking the fish. Further, it provides the hunters with shelter for the duration of the hunt. Without shelter, expeditionary hunting, the traditional method used by this First Nation, would be impossible. There is no doubt, in the context of this treaty and of this First Nation, that some form of shelter is in fact a necessary part of expeditionary hunting. Accordingly, shelter is also reasonably incidental to this method of hunting.

. . . . .

[33] A hunting cabin is, in these circumstances, reasonably incidental to this First Nation's right to hunt in their traditional expeditionary style. This method of hunting is not only traditional but appropriate and shelter is an important component of it. Without a shelter, it would be impossible for this First Nation to exercise its traditional method of hunting and their members would be denied their treaty rights to hunt. A reasonable person apprised of the traditional expeditionary method of hunting would conclude that for this First Nation the treaty right to hunt encompasses the right to build shelters as a reasonable incident to that right. The shelter was originally a moss-covered lean-to and then a tent. It has evolved to the small log cabin, which is an appropriate shelter for expeditionary hunting in today's society.

The *Sundown* decision affirmed the principle found earlier in *Simon v. R.*, [1985] S.C.J. No. 67, [1985] 2 S.C.R. 387, 24 D.L.R. (4th) 390 (S.C.C.) that practices incidental to the exercise of treaty rights are to be equally protected in order to give true meaning and effect to those rights. This reaffirms the principle that the rights protected in a treaty extend beyond the literal words on the parchment copy of the treaty.

G. TREATIES, TREATY INTERPRETATIONS, AND THE "HONOUR OF THE CROWN"

Modern treaty jurisprudence, as seen in cases such as *Badger* and *Sundown*, has made reference to the notion of the "honour of the Crown" in the process of interpreting Crown-Native treaties. This idea was reflected once again in *R. v. Marshall*, [1999] 3 S.C.R. 456, 177 D.L.R. (4th) 513 (S.C.C.), which is also the leading Canadian case on the principles of treaty interpretation and one of the most controversial Supreme Court of Canada decisions in recent years.

R. v. MARSHALL ("MARSHALL NO. 1")

[1999] S.C.J. No. 55, [1999] 3 S.C.R. 456,
177 D.L.R. (4th) 513 (S.C.C.) (references omitted)

[Donald Marshall Jr., a Mi'kmaq citizen, was charged with selling 463 pounds of eels for $787.10 without a licence, contrary to federal regulations made pursuant to the *Fisheries Act*. Marshall's defence was that he was entitled to sell the eels by virtue of a treaty right agreed to by the British Crown in 1760. The only issue at trial was whether Marshall had an existing treaty right exempting him from compliance with the federal legislation, thus mandating his acquittal. In 1760-61, aboriginal leaders in the Maritimes asked for truckhouses (*i.e.*, trading posts) "for the furnishing them with necessaries, in Exchange for their Peltry" during negotiations leading up to the treaties. However, the written document recording the treaty contained only the promise by the Mi'kmaq not to "Traffick, Barter or Exchange any Commodities in any manner but with such persons, or the Manager of such Truckhouses as shall be appointed or established by His majesty's Governor". As such, the dispute in this case was over whether this "trade clause", framed in negative terms as a restraint on trade, reflected the grant of the positive right to Mi'kmaq people (like Marshall) to bring the products of their hunting, fishing and gathering to a truckhouse to trade. The trial judge held that there was no positive right to trade embodied in the "trade clause", and thus rejected Marshall's defence that he had a treaty right to catch and sell fish. Marshall appealed, and the Nova Scotia Court of Appeal dismissed his appeal. Marshall then appealed to the Supreme Court of Canada.]

The judgment of **Lamer C.J.C.** and **L'Heureux-Dubé**, **Cory**, **Iacobucci** and **Binnie JJ.** was delivered by **Binnie J.**

[5] … The starting point for the analysis of the alleged treaty right must be an examination of the specific words used in any written memorandum of its terms. In this case, the task is complicated by the fact the British signed a series of agreements with individual Mi'kmaq communities in 1760 and 1761 intending to have them consolidated into a comprehensive Mi'kmaq treaty that was never in fact brought into existence. The trial judge, Embree Prov. Ct. J., found that by the end of 1761 all of the Mi'kmaq villages in Nova Scotia had entered into separate but similar treaties. Some of these documents are missing. Despite some variations among some of the documents, Embree Prov. Ct. J. was satisfied that the written terms applicable to this dispute were contained in a Treaty of Peace and Friendship entered into by Governor Charles Lawrence on March 10, 1760, which … provides as follows:

> Treaty of Peace and Friendship concluded by [His Excellency Charles Lawrence] Esq. Govr and Comr. in Chief in and over his Majesty's Province of Nova Scotia or Accadia with Paul Laurent chief of the LaHave tribe of Indians at Halifax in the Province of N.S. or Acadia:
>
> . . . . .
>
> And I do further promise for myself and my tribe that we will not either directly nor indirectly assist any of the enemies of His most sacred Majesty King George the Second, his heirs or Successors, nor hold any manner of Commerce traffick nor intercourse with them, but on the contrary will as much as may be in our power discover and make known to His Majesty's Governor, any ill designs which may be formed or contrived against His Majesty's subjects. *And I do further engage that we will not traffick, barter or Exchange any Commodities in any manner but with such persons or the managers*

of such Truck houses as shall be appointed or Established by His Majesty's Governor at Lunenbourg or Elsewhere in Nova Scotia or Accadia.

[6] The [emphasized] portion of the document, the so-called "trade clause", is framed in negative terms as a restraint on the ability of the Mi'kmaq to trade with non-government individuals. A "truckhouse" was a type of trading post. The evidence showed that the promised government truckhouses disappeared from Nova Scotia within a few years and by 1780 a replacement regime of government licensed traders had also fallen into disuse while the British Crown was attending to the American Revolution. ...

[7] The appellant's position is that the truckhouse provision not only incorporated the alleged right to trade, but also the right to pursue traditional hunting, fishing and gathering activities in support of that trade. It seems clear that the words of the March 10, 1760 document, standing in isolation, do not support the appellant's argument. The question is whether the underlying negotiations produced a broader agreement between the British and the Mi'kmaq, memorialized only in part by the Treaty of Peace and Friendship, that would protect the appellant's activities that are the subject of the prosecution. ...

. . . . .

Evidentiary Sources

[9] The Court of Appeal took a strict approach to the use of extrinsic evidence when interpreting the Treaties of 1760-61. Roscoe and Bateman JJ.A. stated at p. 194: "While treaties must be interpreted in their historical context, extrinsic evidence cannot be used as an aid to interpretation, in the absence of ambiguity". I think this approach should be rejected for at least three reasons.

[10] Firstly, even in a modern commercial context, extrinsic evidence is available to show that a written document does not include all of the terms of an agreement. Rules of interpretation in contract law are in general more strict than those applicable to treaties, yet Professor Waddams states in *The Law of Contracts* (3rd ed. 1993), at para. 316:

> The parol evidence rule does not purport to exclude evidence designed to show whether or not the agreement has been "reduced to writing", or whether it was, or was not, the intention of the parties that it should be the exclusive record of their agreement. Proof of this question is a pre-condition to the operation of the rule, and all relevant evidence is admissible on it. ...

[11] Secondly, even in the context of a treaty document that purports to contain all of the terms, this Court has made clear in recent cases that extrinsic evidence of the historical and cultural context of a treaty may be received even absent any ambiguity on the face of the treaty. MacKinnon A.C.J.O. laid down the principle in *Taylor and Williams* [*R. v. Taylor and Williams* (1981), 34 O.R. (2d) 360 (Ont. C.A.)] at p. 236:

... if there is evidence by conduct or otherwise as to how the parties understood the terms of the treaty, then such understanding and practice is of assistance in giving content to the term or terms. ...

[12] Thirdly, where a treaty was concluded verbally and afterwards written up by representatives of the Crown, it would be unconscionable for the Crown to ignore the oral terms while relying on the written terms, per Dickson J. (as he then was) in *Guerin v. The Queen*, [1984] 2 S.C.R. 335. ...

[13] The narrow approach applied by the Court of Appeal to the use of extrinsic evidence apparently derives from the comments of Estey J. in *R. v. Horse*, [1988] 1 S.C.R. 187, where, at p. 201, he expressed some reservations about the use of extrinsic materials, such as the transcript of negotiations surrounding the signing of Treaty No. 6, except in the case of ambiguity. ... Lamer J., as he then was, mentioned this aspect of *Horse* in *Sioui* [*R. v. Sioui*, [1990] 1 S.C.R. 1025], ... but advocated a more flexible approach when determining the existence of treaties. Lamer J. stated, at p. 1068, that "[t]he historical context, which has been used to demonstrate the existence of the treaty, may equally assist us in interpreting the extent of the rights contained in it".

[14] Subsequent cases have distanced themselves from a "strict" rule of treaty interpretation, as more recently discussed by Cory J., in *Badger* [*R. v. Badger*, [1996] 1 S.C.R. 771, 133 D.L.R. (4th) 324], at para. 52:

> ... when considering a treaty, a court must take into account the context in which the treaties were negotiated, concluded and committed to writing. The treaties, as written documents, recorded an agreement that had already been reached orally and they did not always record the full extent of the oral agreement... The treaties were drafted in English by representatives of the Canadian government who, it should be assumed, were familiar with common law doctrines. Yet, the treaties were not translated in written form into the languages (here Cree and Dene) of the various Indian nations who were signatories. Even if they had been, it is unlikely that the Indians, who had a history of communicating only orally, would have understood them any differently. *As a result, it is well settled that the words in the treaty must not be interpreted in their strict technical sense nor subjected to rigid modern rules of construction.* [Emphasis added.]

"Generous" rules of interpretation should not be confused with a vague sense of after-the-fact largesse. The special rules are dictated by the special difficulties of ascertaining what in fact was agreed to. The Indian parties did not, for all practical purposes, have the opportunity to create their own written record of the negotiations. Certain assumptions are therefore made about the Crown's approach to treaty making (honourable) which the Court acts upon in its approach to treaty interpretation (flexible) as to the existence of a treaty (*Sioui*, at p. 1049), the completeness of any written record (the use, e.g., of context and implied terms to make honourable sense of the treaty arrangement: *Simon v. The Queen*, [1985] 2 S.C.R. 387, and *R. v. Sundown*, [1999] 1 S.C.R. 393), and the interpretation of treaty terms once found to exist (*Badger*). The bottom line is the Court's obligation is to "choose from among the various possible interpretations of the *common* intention [at the time the treaty was made] the one which best reconciles" the Mi'kmaq interests and those of the British Crown (*Sioui*, per Lamer J., at p. 1069 (emphasis added)). ...

[A discussion of a 1752 Mi'kmaq treaty and the trial judge's factual findings are omitted.]

The 1760 Negotiations

[22] I propose to review briefly the documentary record to emphasize and amplify certain aspects of the trial judge's findings. He accepted in general the evidence of the Crown's only expert witness, Dr. Stephen Patterson, a Professor of History at the University of New Brunswick, who testified at length about what the trial judge referred to (at para. 116) as British encouragement of the Mi'kmaq "hunting, fishing and gathering lifestyle". That evidence puts the trade clause in context, and answers the question whether there was something more to the treaty entitlement than merely the right to bring fish and wildlife to truckhouses.

[23] I take the following points from the matters particularly emphasized by the trial judge at para. 90 following his thorough review of the historical background:

> 1. The 1760-61 treaties were the culmination of more than a decade of intermittent hostilities between the British and the Mi'kmaq. Hostilities with the French were also prevalent in Nova Scotia throughout the 1750's, and the Mi'kmaq were constantly allied with the French against the British.

> 2. The use of firearms for hunting had an important impact on Mi'kmaq society. The Mi'kmaq remained dependant on others for gun powder and the primary sources of that were the French, Acadians and the British.

> 3. The French frequently supplied the Mi'kmaq with food and European trade goods. By the mid-18th century, the Mi'kmaq were accustomed to, and in some cases relied on, receiving various European trade goods [including shot, gun powder, metal tools, clothing cloth, blankets and many other things].

> . . . . .

> 6. The British wanted peace and a safe environment for their current and future settlers. Despite their recent victories, they did not feel completely secure in Nova Scotia.

[24] Shortly after the fall of Louisbourg in June 1758, the British commander sent emissaries to the Mi'kmaq, through the French missionary, Father Maillard (who served as translator at the subsequent negotiations), holding out an offer of the enjoyment of peace, liberty, property, possessions and religion ...

[25] In the harsh winter of 1759-1760, so many Mi'kmaq turned up at Louisbourg seeking sustenance that the British Commander expressed concern that unless their demand for necessaries was met, they would become "very Troublesome" and "entirely putt a Stop to any Settling or fishing all along the Coast" or indeed "the Settlement of Nova Scotia" generally. ... It is apparent that the British saw the Mi'kmaq trade issue in

terms of peace, as the Crown expert Dr. Stephen Patterson testified, "people who trade together do not fight, that was the theory". Peace was bound up with the ability of the Mi'kmaq people to sustain themselves economically. Starvation breeds discontent. The British certainly did not want the Mi'kmaq to become an unnecessary drain on the public purse of the colony of Nova Scotia or of the Imperial purse in London, as the trial judge found. To avoid such a result, it became necessary to protect the traditional Mi'kmaq economy, including hunting, gathering and fishing. ...

[26] The trial judge concluded that in 1760 the British Crown entered into a series of negotiations with communities of first nations spread across what is now Nova Scotia and New Brunswick. These treaties were essentially "adhesions" by different Mi'kmaq communities to identical terms because, as stated, it was contemplated that they would be consolidated in a more comprehensive and all-inclusive document at a later date, which never happened. The trial judge considered that the key negotiations took place not with the Mi'kmaq people directly, but with the St. John River Indians, part of the Maliseet First Nation, and the Passamaquody First Nation, who lived in present-day New Brunswick.

[27] The trial judge found as a fact, at para. 108, that the relevant Mi'kmaq treaty did "make peace upon the *same* conditions" (emphasis added) as the Maliseet and Passamaquody. Meetings took place between the Crown and the Maliseet and the Passamaquody on February 11, 1760, twelve days before these bands signed their treaty with the British and eighteen days prior to the meeting between the Governor and the Mi'kmaq representatives, Paul Laurent of LaHave and Michel Augustine of the Richibucto region, where the terms of the Maliseet and Passamaquody treaties were "communicated" and accepted.

[28] The trial judge found (at para. 101) that on February 29, 1760, at a meeting between the Governor in Council and the Mi'kmaq chiefs, the following exchange occurred:

His Excellency then Ordered the Several Articles of the Treaty made with the Indians of St. John's River and Passamaquody to be *Communicated* to the said Paul Laurent and Michel Augustine who expressed their satisfaction therewith, and *declar'd that all the Tribe of Mickmacks would be glad to make peace upon the same Conditions*. [Emphasis added.]

Governor Lawrence afterwards confirmed, in his May 11, 1760 report to the Board of Trade, that he had treated with the Mi'kmaq Indians on "the same terms".

[29] The genesis of the Mi'kmaq trade clause is therefore found in the Governor's earlier negotiations with the Maliseet and Passamaquody First Nations. In that regard, the appellant places great reliance on a meeting between the Governor and their chiefs on February 11, 1760 for the purpose of reviewing various aspects of the proposed treaty. The following exchange is recorded in contemporaneous minutes of the meeting prepared by the British Governor's Secretary:

His Excellency then demanded of them, Whether they were directed by their Tribes, to propose any other particulars to be Treated upon at this time. To which they replied that their Tribes had not directed them to propose any thing further than that *there might be a Truckhouse established, for the furnishing them with necessaries, in Exchange for their Peltry*, and that it might, at present, be at Fort Frederick.

Upon which His Excellency acquainted them *that in case of their now executing a Treaty* in the manner proposed, and its being ratified at the next General Meeting of their Tribes the next Spring, *a Truckhouse should be established at Fort Frederick, agreable to their desire*, and likewise at other Places if it should be found necessary, for furnishing them with such Commodities as shall be necessary for them, in Exchange for their Peltry & and that great care should be taken, that the Commerce at the said Truckhouses should be managed by Persons on whose Justice and good Treatment, they might always depend; and that it would be expected that the said Tribes should not Trafic or Barter and Exchange any Commodities at any other Place, nor with any other Persons. *Of all which* the Chiefs expressed their entire Approbation. [Emphasis added.]

[30] It is true...that the British made it clear from the outset that the Mi'kmaq were not to have any commerce with "any of His Majesty's Enemies". A Treaty of Peace and Friendship could not be otherwise. ...

[31] At a meeting of the Governor's Council on February 16, 1760 (less than a week later), the Council and the representatives of the Indians proceeded to settle the prices of various articles of merchandise ...

[32] In furtherance of this trade arrangement, the British established six truckhouses following the signing of the treaties in 1760 and 1761 ... The existence of advantageous terms at the truckhouses was part of an imperial peace strategy. ... The British were concerned that matters might again become "troublesome" if the Mi'kmaq were subjected to the "pernicious practices" of "unscrupulous traders". The cost to the public purse of Nova Scotia of supporting Mi'kmaq trade was an investment in peace and the promotion of ongoing colonial settlement. The strategy would be effective only if the Mi'kmaq had access both to trade and to the fish and wildlife resources necessary to provide them with something to trade.

. . . . .

[35] In my view, all of this evidence, reflected in the trial judgment, demonstrates the inadequacy and incompleteness of the written memorial of the treaty terms by selectively isolating the restrictive trade covenant. Indeed, the truckhouse system offered such advantageous terms that it hardly seems likely that Mi'kmaq traders had to be compelled to buy at lower prices and sell at higher prices. At a later date, they objected when truckhouses were abandoned. The trade clause would not have advanced British objectives (peaceful relations with a self-sufficient Mi'kmaq people) or Mi'kmaq objectives (access to the European "necessaries" on which they had come to rely) unless the Mi'kmaq were assured at the same time of continuing access, implicitly or explicitly, to wildlife to trade. ...

[A review of Dr. Patterson's comments a trial is omitted.]

[40] In my view, the Nova Scotia judgments erred in concluding that the only enforceable treaty obligations were those set out in the written document of March 10, 1760, whether construed flexibly (as did the trial judge) or narrowly (as did the Nova Scotia Court of Appeal). The findings of fact made by the trial judge taken as a whole demonstrate that the concept of a disappearing treaty right does justice neither to the honour of the Crown nor to the reasonable expectations of the Mi'kmaq people. It is their common intention in 1760 — not just the terms of the March 10, 1760 document — to which effect must be given.

Ascertaining the Terms of the Treaty

[41] Having concluded that the written text is incomplete, it is necessary to ascertain the treaty terms not only by reference to the fragmentary historical record, as interpreted by the expert historians, but also in light of the stated objectives of the British and Mi'kmaq in 1760 and the political and economic context in which those objectives were reconciled.

[42] ... The appellant asserts the right of Mi'kmaq people to catch fish and wildlife in support of trade as an alternative or supplementary method of obtaining necessaries. The right to fish is not mentioned in the March 10, 1760 document, nor is it expressly noted elsewhere in the records of the negotiation put in evidence. This is not surprising. As Dickson J. mentioned with reference to the west coast in *Jack* [*Jack v. The Queen*, [1980] 1 S.C.R. 294], at p. 311, in colonial times the perception of the fishery resource was one of "limitless proportions".

[43] The law has long recognized that parties make assumptions when they enter into agreements about certain things that give their arrangements efficacy. Courts will imply a contractual term on the basis of presumed intentions of the parties where it is necessary to assure the efficacy of the contract, e.g., where it meets the "officious bystander test": ... Here, if the ubiquitous officious bystander had said, "This talk about truckhouses is all very well, but if the Mi'kmaq are to make these promises, will they have the right to hunt and fish to catch something to trade at the truckhouses?", the answer would have to be, having regard to the honour of the Crown, "of course". If the law is prepared to supply the deficiencies of written contracts prepared by sophisticated parties and their legal advisors in order to produce a sensible result that accords with the intent of both parties, though unexpressed, the law cannot ask less of the honour and dignity of the Crown in its dealings with First Nations. The honour of the Crown was, in fact, specifically invoked by courts in the early 17th century to ensure that a Crown grant was effective to accomplish its intended purpose. ...

[44] An example of the Court's recognition of the necessity of supplying the deficiencies of aboriginal treaties is *Sioui, supra*, where Lamer J. considered a treaty document that stated simply (at p. 1031) that the Huron tribe "are received upon the same terms with the Canadians, being allowed the free Exercise of their Religion, their Customs, and Liberty of trading with the English". Lamer J. found that, in order to give real value

and meaning to these words, it was necessary that a territorial component be supplied, as follows, at p. 1067:

> The treaty gives the Hurons the freedom to carry on their customs and their religion. No mention is made in the treaty itself of the territory over which these rights may be exercised. There is also no indication that the territory of what is now Jacques-Cartier park was contemplated. However, *for a freedom to have real value and meaning*, it must be possible to exercise it somewhere. [Emphasis added.]

Similarly, in *Sundown, supra*, the Court found that the express right to hunt included the implied right to build shelters required to carry out the hunt. See also *Simon, supra*, where the Court recognized an implied right to carry a gun and ammunition on the way to exercise the right to hunt. These cases employed the concept of implied rights to support the meaningful exercise of express rights granted to the first nations in circumstances where no such implication might necessarily have been made absent the sui generis nature of the Crown's relationship to aboriginal people. While I do not believe that in ordinary commercial situations a right to trade implies any right of access to things to trade, I think the honour of the Crown requires nothing less in attempting to make sense of the result of these 1760 negotiations.

Rights of the Other Inhabitants

[45] ... [I]t is ... true that a general right enjoyed by all citizens can nevertheless be made the subject of an enforceable treaty promise. ...

. . . . .

[47] ... The settlers and the military undoubtedly hunted and fished for sport or necessaries as well, and traded goods with each other. The issue here is not so much the content of the rights or liberties as the level of legal protection thrown around them. A treaty could, to take a fanciful example, provide for a right of the Mi'kmaq to promenade down Barrington Street, Halifax, on each anniversary of the treaty. Barrington Street is a common thoroughfare enjoyed by all. There would be nothing "special" about the Mi'kmaq use of a common right of way. The point is that the treaty rights-holder not only has the right or liberty "enjoyed by other British subjects" but may enjoy special treaty protection against interference with its exercise. So it is with the trading arrangement. On June 25, 1761, following the signing of the Treaties of 1760-61 by the last group of Mi'kmaq villages, a ceremony was held at the farm of Lieutenant Governor Jonathan Belcher, the first Chief Justice of Nova Scotia, who was acting in the place of Governor Charles Lawrence, who had recently been drowned on his way to Boston. In reference to the treaties, including the trade clause, Lieutenant Governor Belcher proclaimed:

> The Laws will be like a great Hedge about your Rights and properties, if any break this Hedge to hurt and injure you, the heavy weight of the Laws will fall upon them and punish their Disobedience.

[48] Until enactment of the *Constitution Act, 1982*, the treaty rights of aboriginal peoples could be overridden by competent legislation as easily as could the rights and liberties of other inhabitants. The hedge offered no special protection, as the aboriginal people learned in earlier hunting cases such as *Sikyea v. The Queen*, [1964] S.C.R. 642, and *R. v. George*, [1966] S.C.R. 267. On April 17, 1982, however, this particular type of "hedge" was converted by s. 35(1) into sterner stuff that could only be broken down when justified according to the test laid down in *R. v. Sparrow*, [1990] 1 S.C.R. 1075, at pp. 1112 et seq., as adapted to apply to treaties in *Badger*, *supra*, *per* Cory J., at paras. 75 *et seq*. The fact the content of Mi'kmaq rights under the treaty to hunt and fish and trade was no greater than those enjoyed by other inhabitants does not, unless those rights were extinguished prior to April 17, 1982, detract from the higher protection they presently offer to the Mi'kmaq people.

The Honour of the Crown

[49] This appeal puts to the test the principle, emphasized by this Court on several occasions, that the honour of the Crown is always at stake in its dealings with aboriginal people. ...

[50] This principle that the Crown's honour is at stake when the Crown enters into treaties with first nations dates back at least to this Court's decision in 1895, *Province of Ontario v. Dominion of Canada and Province of Quebec; In re Indian Claims* (1895), 25 S.C.R. 434. In that decision, Gwynne J. (dissenting) stated, at pp. 511-12:

> . . . what is contended for and must not be lost sight of, is that the British sovereigns, ever since the acquisition of Canada, have been pleased to adopt the rule or practice of entering into agreements with the Indian nations or tribes in their province of Canada, for the cession or surrender by them of what such sovereigns have been pleased to designate the Indian title, by instruments similar to these now under consideration to which they have been pleased to give the designation of "treaties" with the Indians in possession of and claiming title to the lands expressed to be surrendered by the instruments, and further that *the terms and conditions expressed in those instruments as to be performed by or on behalf of the Crown, have always been regarded as involving a trust graciously assumed by the Crown to the fulfilment of which with the Indians the faith and honour of the Crown is pledged, and which trust has always been most faithfully fulfilled as a treaty obligation of the Crown.* [Emphasis added.] ...

[A review of authorities is omitted.]

[52] I do not think an interpretation of events that turns a positive Mi'kmaq trade demand into a negative Mi'kmaq covenant is consistent with the honour and integrity of the Crown. Nor is it consistent to conclude that the Lieutenant Governor, seeking in good faith to address the trade demands of the Mi'kmaq, accepted the Mi'kmaq suggestion of a trading facility while denying any treaty protection to Mi'kmaq access to the things that were to be traded, even though these things were identified

and priced in the treaty negotiations. This was not a commercial contract. The trade arrangement must be interpreted in a manner which gives meaning and substance to the promises made by the Crown. In my view, with respect, the interpretation adopted by the courts below left the Mi'kmaq with an empty shell of a treaty promise.

. . . . .

The Limited Scope of the Treaty Right

[57] The Crown expresses the concern that recognition of the existence of a constitutionally entrenched right with, as here, a trading aspect, would open the floodgates to uncontrollable and excessive exploitation of the natural resources. Whereas hunting and fishing for food naturally restricts quantities to the needs and appetites of those entitled to share in the harvest, it is argued that there is no comparable, built-in restriction associated with a trading right, short of the paramount need to conserve the resource. ... The ultimate fear is that the appellant, who in this case fished for eels from a small boat using a fyke net, could lever the treaty right into a factory trawler in Pomquet Harbour gathering the available harvest in preference to all non-aboriginal commercial or recreational fishermen. (This is indeed the position advanced by the intervener the Union of New Brunswick Indians.) This fear (or hope) is based on a misunderstanding of the narrow ambit and extent of the treaty right.

[58] The recorded note of February 11, 1760 was that "there might be a Truckhouse established, for the furnishing them with <u>necessaries</u>" (emphasis added). What is contemplated therefore is not a right to trade generally for economic gain, but rather a right to trade for necessaries. The treaty right is a regulated right and can be contained by regulation within its proper limits.

[59] The concept of "necessaries" is today equivalent to the concept of what Lambert J.A., in *R. v. Van der Peet* (1993), 80 B.C.L.R. (2d) 75, at p. 126, described as a "moderate livelihood". Bare subsistence has thankfully receded over the last couple of centuries as an appropriate standard of life for aboriginals and non-aboriginals alike. A moderate livelihood includes such basics as "food, clothing and housing, supplemented by a few amenities", but not the accumulation of wealth (*Gladstone*, [*R. v. Gladstone*, [1996] 2 S.C.R. 723], at para. 165). It addresses day-to-day needs. This was the common intention in 1760. It is fair that it be given this interpretation today. ...

[61] Catch limits that could reasonably be expected to produce a moderate livelihood for individual Mi'kmaq families at present-day standards can be established by regulation and enforced without violating the treaty right. In that case, the regulations would accommodate the treaty right. Such regulations would not constitute an infringement that would have to be justified under the *Badger* standard.

Application to the Facts of this Case

[62] The appellant is charged with three offences: the selling of eels without a licence, fishing without a licence and fishing during the close season with illegal nets. These acts took place at Pomquet Harbour, Antigonish County. For Marshall to have satisfied the regulations, he was required to secure a licence under either the *Fishery (General) Regulations*, SOR/93-53, the *Maritime Provinces Fishery Regulations*, SOR/93-55, or the *Aboriginal Communal Fishing Licences Regulations*, SOR/93-332.

[63] All of these regulations place the issuance of licences within the absolute discretion of the Minister. ...

[64] Furthermore, there is nothing in these regulations which gives direction to the Minister to explain how she or he should exercise this discretionary authority in a manner which would respect the appellant's treaty rights. ... The test for infringement under s. 35(1) of the *Constitution Act, 1982* was set out in *Sparrow, supra*, at p. 1112:

> To determine whether the fishing rights have been interfered with such as to constitute a *prima facie* infringement of s. 35(1), certain questions must be asked. First, is the limitation unreasonable? Second, does the regulation impose undue hardship? Third, does the regulation deny to the holders of the right their preferred means of exercising that right? The onus of proving a *prima facie* infringement lies on the individual or group challenging the legislation.

Lamer C.J. in *Adams* [*R. v. Adams*, [1996] 3 S.C.R. 101], applied this test to licensing schemes and stated as follows at para. 54:

> In light of the Crown's unique fiduciary obligations towards aboriginal peoples, *Parliament may not simply adopt an unstructured discretionary administrative regime which risks infringing aboriginal rights in a substantial number of applications in the absence of some explicit guidance.* If a statute confers an administrative discretion which may carry significant consequences for the exercise of an aboriginal right, the statute or its delegate regulations must outline specific criteria for the granting or refusal of that discretion which seek to accommodate the existence of aboriginal rights. In the absence of such specific guidance, the statute will fail to provide representatives of the Crown with sufficient directives to fulfil their fiduciary duties, and the statute will be found to represent an infringement of aboriginal rights under the Sparrow test. [Emphasis added.]

Cory J. in *Badger, supra*, at para. 79, found that the test for infringement under s. 35(1) of the *Constitution Act, 1982* was the same for both aboriginal and treaty rights, and thus the words of Lamer C.J. in *Adams*, although in relation to the infringement of aboriginal rights, are equally applicable here. There was nothing at that time which provided the Crown officials with the "sufficient directives" necessary to ensure that the appellant's treaty rights would be respected. To paraphrase *Adams*, at para. 51, under the applicable regulatory regime, the appellant's exercise of his treaty right to fish and trade for sustenance was exercisable only at the absolute discretion of the Minister. Mi'kmaq treaty rights were not accommodated in the Regulations because, presumably, the Crown's position was, and continues to be, that no such treaty rights existed. In the circumstances, the purported regulatory prohibitions against fishing without a licence (*Maritime Provinces Fishery Regulations*, s. 4(1)(a)) and of selling eels without a licence (*Fishery (General) Regulations*, s. 35(2)) do *prima facie* infringe the appellant's treaty rights under the Treaties of 1760-61 and are inoperative against the appellant unless justified under the *Badger* test.

[65] Further, the appellant was charged with fishing during the close season with improper nets, contrary to s. 20 of the *Maritime Provinces Fishery Regulations*. Such a regulation is also a *prima facie* infringement, as noted by Cory J. in *Badger*, *supra*, at para. 90: "This Court has held on numerous occasions that there can be no limitation on the method, timing and extent of Indian hunting under a Treaty", apart, I would add, from a treaty limitation to that effect.

[66] The appellant caught and sold the eels to support himself and his wife. Accordingly, the close season and the imposition of a discretionary licensing system would, if enforced, interfere with the appellant's treaty right to fish for trading purposes, and the ban on sales would, if enforced, infringe his right to trade for sustenance. In the absence of any justification of the regulatory prohibitions, the appellant is entitled to an acquittal.

Disposition

[67] The constitutional question stated by the Chief Justice on February 9, 1998, as follows:

> Are the prohibitions on catching and retaining fish without a licence, on fishing during the close time, and on the unlicensed sale of fish, contained in ss. 4(1)(a) and 20 of the *Maritime Provinces Fishery Regulations* and s. 35(2) of the *Fishery (General) Regulations*, inconsistent with the treaty rights of the appellant contained in the Mi'kmaq Treaties of 1760-61 and therefore of no force or effect or application to him, by virtue of ss. 35(1) and 52 of the *Constitution Act, 1982*?

Should be answered in the affirmative. I would therefore allow the appeal and order an acquittal on all charges.

The reasons of **Gonthier** and **McLachlin JJ.** were delivered by

McLachlin J. (dissenting): —

. . . . .

I conclude that the Treaties of 1760-61 created an exclusive trade and truckhouse regime which implicitly gave rise to a limited Mi'kmaq right to bring goods to British trade outlets so long as this regime was extant. The Treaties of 1760-61 granted neither a freestanding right to truckhouses nor a general underlying right to trade outside of the exclusive trade and truckhouse regime. The system of trade exclusivity and correlative British trading outlets died out in the 1780s and with it, the incidental right to bring goods to trade. There is therefore no existing right to trade in the

Treaties of 1760-61 that exempts the appellant from the federal fisheries legislation. The charges against him stand.

Appeal allowed.

In *Marshall*, McLachlin C.J.C. codified the principles of treaty interpretation set out by the Supreme Court of Canada. This codification, while not a part of the majority's judgment in *Marshall*, has been positively cited in many subsequent treaty cases:

1. Aboriginal treaties constitute a unique type of agreement and attract special principles of interpretation: *R. v. Sundown*, [1999] S.C.J. No. 13, [1999] 1 S.C.R. 393 (S.C.C.), at para. 24; *R. v. Badger*, [1996] S.C.J. No. 39, [1996] S.C.J. No. 39, [1996] 1 S.C.R. 771 (S.C.C.), at para. 78; *R. v. Sioui*, [1990] S.C.J. No. 48, [1990] 1 S.C.R. 1025 at 1043 (S.C.C.); *Simon v. R.*, [1985] S.C.J. No. 67, [1985] 2 S.C.R. 387 at 404 (S.C.C.). See also: J. [Sákéj] Youngblood Henderson, "Interpreting *Sui Generis* Treaties" (1997) 36 Alta. L. Rev. 46; L.I. Rotman, "Defining Parameters: Aboriginal Rights, Treaty Rights, and the *Sparrow* Justificatory Test" (1997) 36 Alta. L. Rev. 149.

2. Treaties should be liberally construed and ambiguities or doubtful expressions should be resolved in favour of the Aboriginal signatories: *Simon, supra*, at 402; *Sioui, supra*, at 1035; *Badger, supra*, at para. 52.

3. The goal of treaty interpretation is to choose from among the various possible interpretations of common intention the one which best reconciles the interests of both parties at the time the treaty was signed: *Sioui, supra*, at 1068-69.

4. In searching for the common intention of the parties, the integrity and honour of the Crown is presumed: *Badger, supra*, at para. 41.

5. In determining the signatories' respective understanding and intentions, the court must be sensitive to the unique cultural and linguistic differences between the parties: *Badger, supra*, at paras. 52-54; *R. v. Horseman*, [1990] S.C.J. No. 39, [1990] 1 S.C.R. 901 at 907 (S.C.C.).

6. The words of the treaty must be given the sense which they would naturally have held for the parties at the time: *Badger, supra*, at paras. 53 *et seq.*; *R. v. Nowegijick*, [1983] S.C.J. No. 5, [1983] 1 S.C.R. 29 at 36 (S.C.C.).

7. A technical or contractual interpretation of treaty wording should be avoided: *Badger, supra*; *Horseman, supra*; *Nowegijick, supra*.

8. While construing the language generously, courts cannot alter the terms of the treaty by exceeding what "is possible on the language" or realistic: *Badger, supra*, at para. 76; *Sioui, supra*, at 1069; *Horseman, supra*, at 908.

9. Treaty rights of Aboriginal peoples must not be interpreted in a static or rigid way. They are not frozen at the date of signature. The interpreting court must update treaty rights to provide for their modern exercise. This involves determining what modern practices are

reasonably incidental to the core treaty right in its modern context: *Sundown, supra,* at para. 32; *Simon, supra,* at 402.

What, precisely, is meant by the "honour of the Crown?" Does *Marshall* define the term? Does the discussion in *Marshall* suggest a different interpretation than what was seen in *Badger* and/or *Sundown*? Perhaps more significantly, is this notion a new one, or is it a modern resurrection of a long-standing ideal? Consider this in light of the *Treaty of Albany* and the Covenant Chain alliance, *supra.* See also the discussion of the "honour of the Crown" regarding the Crown's duty to consult with Aboriginal peoples in the *Haida Nation* and *Taku River* decisions, which are examined in Chapter 5.

In the aftermath of the *Marshall* decision, there were violent clashes between Aboriginal and non-Aboriginal fishers in the Maritimes and significant criticism of the Supreme Court's judgment as an example of the excesses of judicial activism. Perhaps not coincidentally, the Supreme Court of Canada revisited its judgment in *Marshall* two months later in the context of dismissing an intervener's motion for a rehearing and stay of the existing *Marshall* judgment pending that rehearing: see *R. v. Marshall,* [1999] S.C.J. No. 66, [1999] 3 S.C.R. 533, 179 D.L.R. (4th) 193 (S.C.C.) ("*Marshall No. 2*").

Some commentators criticized the Court for its "reinterpretation" of the *Marshall* judgment in *Marshall No. 2* while others characterized the *Marshall No. 2* judgment as a method of responding to critics of the *Marshall* judgment. Consider the following excerpts from *Marshall No. 2* and decide for yourself:

> Those opposing the motion object in different ways that the Coalition's motion rests on a series of misconceptions about what the September 17, 1999 majority judgment decided and what it did not decide. These objections are well founded. The Court did not hold that the Mi'kmaq treaty right cannot be regulated or that the Mi'kmaq are guaranteed an open season in the fisheries. ...

> . . . . .

> The September 17, 1999 majority judgment did not rule that the appellant had established a treaty right "to gather" anything and everything physically capable of being gathered. The issues were much narrower and the ruling was much narrower. ... It is of course open to native communities to assert broader treaty rights in that regard, but if so, the basis for such a claim will have to be established in proceedings where the issue is squarely raised on proper historical evidence, as was done in this case in relation to fish and wildlife. Other resources were simply not addressed by the parties, and therefore not addressed by the Court in its September 17, 1999 majority judgment. ...

> . . . . .

> Other limitations apparent in the September 17, 1999 majority judgment include the local nature of the treaties, the communal nature of a treaty right, and the fact it was only hunting and fishing resources to which access was affirmed, together with traditionally gathered things like wild fruit and

berries. ... [T]he Mi'kmaq treaty right to hunt and trade in game is not now, any more than it was in 1760, a *commercial* hunt that must be satisfied before non-natives have access to the same resources for recreational or commercial purposes. The emphasis in 1999, as it was in 1760, is on assuring the Mi'kmaq equitable access to identified resources for the purpose of earning a moderate living. ...

What is, perhaps, most curious about *Marshall No. 2* is that it unanimously affirmed the majority's judgment in *Marshall*, even though two of the judges participating in the *Marshall No. 2* judgment (McLachlin C.J.C. and Gonthier J.) had dissented in *Marshall*.

The Supreme Court of Canada returned to the treaties of 1760-1761 in 2005 and 2006. At issue was the right to harvest wood for commercial purposes (*R. v. Marshall; R. v. Bernard*) and domestic uses (*R. v. Sappier; R. v. Gray*, [2006] S.C.J. No. 54, [2006] 2 S.C.R. 686 (S.C.C.)). These cases further reveal the scope of the peace and friendship treaties in the Maritimes.

R. v. MARSHALL; R. v. BERNARD
[2005] S.C.J. No. 44, [2005] 2 S.C.R. 220 (S.C.C.)

I. Introduction

[1] Can members of the Mi'kmaq people in Nova Scotia and New Brunswick engage in commercial logging on Crown lands without authorization, contrary to statutory regulation? More precisely, do they have treaty rights or aboriginal title entitling them to do so? ...

. . . . .

[6] I conclude that the trial judges in each case correctly held that the respondents' treaty rights did not extend to commercial logging and correctly rejected the claim for aboriginal title in the relevant areas. I would thus allow the appeals, dismiss the cross-appeal in *Marshall* and restore the convictions.

II. Aboriginal Treaty Right

A. *The Background: Marshall 1 and Marshall 2*

[7] In 1760 and 1761, the British Crown concluded "Peace and Friendship" treaties with the Mi'kmaq peoples of the former colony of Nova Scotia, now the Provinces of Nova Scotia and New Brunswick. The British had succeeded in driving the French from the area. The Mi'kmaq and French had been allies and trading partners for almost 250 years. The British, having defeated the French, wanted peace with the Mi'kmaq. To this end, they entered into negotiations, which resulted in the Peace and Friendship treaties. The existence of a treaty and a right to claim under it are questions of fact to be determined in each case. Although different treaties were made with different groups, for the purposes of this case we

assume that the main terms were the same, similar to those in *R. v. Marshall*, [1999] 3 S.C.R. 456 (*"Marshall 1"*).

[8] A critical aspect of the treaties was the trading clause, whereby the British agreed to set up trading posts, or "truckhouses", and the Mi'kmaq agreed to trade only at those posts, instead of with others, like their former allies, the French. In the crucial clause, the Mi'kmaq Chiefs agreed:

> And I do further engage that we will not traffick, barter or Exchange any Commodities in any manner but with such persons or the managers of such Truck houses as shall be appointed or Established by His Majesty's Governor . . . .

The pact was mutual. The English were desirous of ensuring that the Mi'kmaq could continue to peacefully live in the area. To do this, the Mi'kmaq needed to trade for European goods, as they had been doing for more than two centuries. The English wanted the Mi'kmaq to do this with them, and not with the French. For their part, the Mi'kmaq wanted assurance that the English would provide trading posts where they could barter their goods and obtain necessaries. ...

. . . . .

[12] Relying on their interpretation of *Marshall 1*, the respondents commenced logging activities on Crown lands in Nova Scotia and New Brunswick without authorization. They were arrested and charged. They raised the treaties and *Marshall 1* and 2 in support of the defense that they were entitled to log for commercial purposes without permit. Their arguments were rejected at trial and on summary appeal, but accepted on appeal to their respective provincial courts of appeal. The issue of whether the treaties of 1760-61 grant modern Mi'kmaq a right to log contrary to provincial regulation is now squarely before this Court.

B. *The Scope of the Treaty Right*

[13] *Marshall 1* and 2 held that the treaties of 1760-61 conferred on the Mi'kmaq the right to catch and sell fish for a moderate livelihood, on the ground that this activity was the logical evolution of a trading practice that was within the contemplation of the parties to the treaties. The cases now before us raise issues as to the scope of the right.

[14] The respondents argue that the truckhouse clause, as interpreted in *Marshall 1* and 2, confers a general right to harvest and sell all natural resources which they used to support themselves in 1760. Provided they used a form of the resource either for their own needs or for trade at the time of the treaties, they now have the right to exploit it, unless the government can justify limitations on that exploitation in the broader public interest. The respondents argue that they used forest products for a variety of purposes at the time of the treaties, from housing and heat to sleds and snowshoes, and indeed occasionally traded products made of wood, all to sustain themselves. Logging represents the modern use of the same products, they assert. Therefore the treaties protect it.

[15] This interpretation of the truckhouse clause in the treaties asks what resources were used by the Mi'kmaq to sustain themselves at the time of the treaties, and concludes that these resources continue to be available to the Mi'kmaq for the purpose of gaining a moderate livelihood. It takes *Marshall 2* as confirming that the truckhouse clause conferred a perpetual right to use "the types of resources traditionally 'gathered' in an aboriginal economy" (para. 19). The only question is what was "gathered" or used in 1760. If wood was gathered in any way, for any purpose, in 1760, modern Mi'kmaq have the right to log, subject only to such limits as the government can justify in the greater public good.

[16] The appellant Crown takes a narrower view of the import of the truckhouse clause. It accepts *Marshall 1* and *2*, but argues that the respondents misread them. The appellant asserts that these cases did not decide that the truckhouse clause of the treaties granted a perpetual right to any natural resources used or "gathered" at the time, subject only to justification. On its view, the clause merely granted the Mi'kmaq the right to continue to trade in items traded in 1760-61. Only those trading activities were protected; other activities, not within the contemplation of the British and Mi'kmaq of the day, are not protected. The emphasis is not on what products were used, but on what *trading activities* were in the contemplation of the parties at the time the treaties were made. Ancestral trading activities are not frozen in time; the treaty protects modern activities that can be said to be their logical evolution. But new and different trading activities, like modern commercial logging, are not protected. To grant such protection, the appellant asserts, would be to transform the treaty right into something new and different.

[17] For the reasons that follow, I must reject the respondents' interpretation of the scope of the right conferred by the truckhouse clause and endorse the view of the appellant. The purpose of the truckhouse clause, the wording of the clause, and holdings of this Court in *Marshall 1* and *2*, all lead inexorably to this conclusion.

[18] I turn first to the purpose of the truckhouse clause as revealed by the historical record. The truckhouse clause was a *trade* clause. It was concerned with what could be traded. As discussed in *Marshall 1*, the British wanted the Mi'kmaq to cease trading with the French, whom they had just defeated, and trade only with them. The Mi'kmaq were willing to do this, but sought assurances that the British would provide trading posts, or truckhouses, where they could trade. The Mi'kmaq had been trading with Europeans for 250 years by this time, and relied on trading their products, like furs and fish, in exchange for European wares. The purpose of the truckhouse clause was to give the British the exclusive right to trade with the Mi'kmaq and the Mi'kmaq the assurance that they would be able to trade with the British as they had traded with the French in the past.

[19] Thus, the truckhouse clause was concerned with traditionally traded products. The right to trade in traditional products carried with it an implicit right to harvest those resources: *Marshall 1*, at para. 35. But this right to harvest is the adjunct of the basic right to trade in traditional

products. The right conferred is not the right to harvest, in itself, but the right to trade.

[20] This is supported by the wording of the truckhouse clause. It speaks only of trade. The Mi'kmaq affirmed "that we will not traffick, barter or Exchange any Commodities in any manner but with such persons or the managers of such Truck houses as shall be appointed or Established by His Majesty's Governor". Nothing in these words comports a general right to harvest or gather all natural resources then used.

[21] The historic records and the wording of the truckhouse clause indicate that what was in the contemplation of the British and the Mi'kmaq in 1760 was continued trade in the products the Mi'kmaq had traditionally traded with Europeans. The clause affirmed that this trade would continue, but henceforth exclusively with the British.

[22] This view of the truckhouse clause was confirmed by this Court in *Marshall 1* and *2*. In *Marshall 1* the majority, *per* Binnie J., proceeded on the basis that at the time of the treaties the Mi'kmaq had sustained themselves, in part, by trading fish with the Europeans:

> ... the Mi'kmaq people have sustained themselves in part by harvesting and trading fish (including eels) since Europeans first visited the coasts of what is now Nova Scotia in the 16th century. [para. 2]

> . . .

> What is plain from the pre-Confederation period is that the Indian fishermen were encouraged to engage in their occupation and to do so for both food and barter purposes. [para. 25, quoting Dickson J. in *Jack v. The Queen*, [1980] 1 S.C.R. 294, at p. 311]

[23] Thus, the ruling in *Marshall 1* was based on the proposition that *fishing for trade* in 1760 was a traditional activity of the Mi'kmaq. From this, Binnie J. concluded that the treaty conferred a right to continue to obtain necessaries through the traditional Mi'kmaq activity of trading fish. He concluded that "the surviving substance of the treaty is not the literal promise of a truckhouse, but <u>a treaty right to continue to obtain necessaries through hunting and fishing by trading the products of those traditional activities</u>" (para. 56 (emphasis added)).

[24] This is consistent with the assertion in *Marshall 2* that the fundamental issue is whether trade in a particular commodity "was in the contemplation of [the] parties to the 1760 treaty" (para. 20). It is also consistent with the reference in *Marshall 2* to treaty rights to "the type of things traditionally 'gathered' by the Mi'kmaq in a 1760 aboriginal lifestyle" (para. 20) like "fruits and berries" (para. 19). The respondents argued that the reference to fruits and berries shows that the treaty right extends beyond things traditionally traded, to a right to harvest anything the Mi'kmaq used in 1760. However, the evidence in *Marshall 1* in fact referred to the Indians trading fruits and berries with the Europeans.

[25] Of course, treaty rights are not frozen in time. Modern peoples do traditional things in modern ways. The question is whether the modern trading activity in question represents a logical evolution from the traditional trading activity at the time the treaty was made: *Marshall 2*, at

para. 20. Logical evolution means the same sort of activity, carried on in the modern economy by modern means. This prevents aboriginal rights from being unfairly confined simply by changes in the economy and technology. But the activity must be essentially the same. "While treaty rights are capable of evolution within limits, ... their subject matter ... cannot be wholly transformed" (*Marshall 2*, at para. 19).

[26] In summary, what the treaty protects is not the right to harvest and dispose of particular commodities, but the right to practice a traditional 1760 trading activity in the modern way and modern context. The question is whether the logging here at issue is the logical evolution of a traditional Mi'kmaq trade activity, in the way modern eel fishing was found to be the logical evolution of a traditional trade activity of the Mi'kmaq in *Marshall 1*.

C.   *The Test Applied*

[27] The trial judges in both cases applied this test to the evidence before them, asking whether the respondents' logging activity could be considered the logical evolution of a traditional Mi'kmaq trade activity.

[28] Curran Prov. Ct. J. in the *Marshall* case ((2001), 191 N.S.R. (2d) 323, 2001 NSPC 2) asked whether there was any evidence that the Mi'kmaq had traded in wood products and timber at the time of the 1760-61 treaties. He emphasized the trade-based nature of the right and the need that it relate to traditional Mi'kmaq activities. And he asked himself whether the logging activity at issue before him could be considered to be the logical evolution of a traditional trade-based activity.

[29] Lordon Prov. Ct. J. in *Bernard* ([2000] 3 C.N.L.R. 184) asked essentially the same questions. He inquired whether the evidence showed a traditional Mi'kmaq trade in logs and wood. Emphasizing trade, he rejected the broader interpretation of the treaty that the Mi'kmaq were entitled to exploit all natural resources that they had used historically. To permit this would "alter the terms of the treaty" and "wholly transform" (para. 87) the rights it conferred, in his view.

[30] Each judge applied the right test and asked himself the right questions. The remaining question is whether the evidence supports their conclusions of fact.

D.   *The Factual Findings of the Trial Judges and the Evidence*

[31] In each case, the trial judge concluded that the evidence did not support a treaty right to commercial logging.

[32] In *Marshall*, Curran Prov. Ct. J. found no direct evidence of any trade in forest products at the time the treaties were made, but concluded that trade in forest products was likely "at some point":

> There is no doubt the Mi'kmaq in 1760 and for a long time before gathered and used forest products. They made canoes, baskets, snowshoes and toboggans. They also gathered and used forest products in making their wigwams and other dwellings. <u>There was no direct evidence that any of</u>

those items was traded either before the 1760-61 treaties were made or during the time of the truckhouses. Despite that, both [appellants'] and [respondents'] witnesses said it was likely the Mi'kmaq had traded some forest-based items to the British or other Europeans at some point. [Emphasis added; para. 91.]

After comparing the evidence before him with the evidence of fishing for trade in *Marshall 1*, Curran Prov. Ct. J. concluded that the respondents had not met the legal test:

> Trade in logging is not the modern equivalent or a logical evolution of Mi'kmaq use of forest resources in daily life in 1760 even if those resources sometimes were traded. Commercial logging does not bear the same relation to the traditional limited use of forest products as fishing for eels today bears to fishing for eels or any other species in 1760. . . . Whatever rights the defendants have to trade in forest products are far narrower than the activities which gave rise to these charges. [para. 95]

[33] In *Bernard*, Lordon Prov. Ct. J. made similar findings on similar evidence. He held that on the evidence "there was no traditional trade in logs", while "trade in wood products ... such as baskets, snowshoes, and canoes was secondary to fur trade and was occasional and incidental" (para. 85). He noted that Chief Augustine had reluctantly conceded that it is "unlikely ... that the Mi'kmaq contemplated commercial logging during th[e] treaty process" (para. 85). Nor did the evidence suggest that the British ever contemplated trade in anything but traditionally produced products, like fur or fish.

[34] These findings were firmly grounded in the evidence given by expert and aboriginal witnesses at trial, as well as the documentation and the cultural and historical background. As Curran Prov. Ct. J. observed, "[the Mi'kmaq] had no need to cut stands of trees for themselves. ... Trees were readily available and Europeans could cut their own" (para. 92). The experts agreed that it was probably in the 1780s before the Mi'kmaq became involved in logging and then only in a limited fashion as part of British operations. Logging was not a traditional Mi'kmaq activity. Rather, it was a European activity, in which the Mi'kmaq began to participate only decades after the treaties of 1760-61. If anything, the evidence suggests that logging was inimical to the Mi'kmaq's traditional way of life, interfering with fishing which, as found in *Marshall 1*, was a traditional activity.

[35] I conclude that the evidence supports the trial judges' conclusion that the commercial logging that formed the basis of the charges against the respondents was not the logical evolution of traditional Mi'kmaq trading activity protected by the treaties of 1760-61. The trial judge in each case applied the correct test to findings of fact supported by the evidence. It follows that there is no ground upon which an appellate court can properly interfere with their conclusion on this branch of the case.

[36] In view of this conclusion, it is unnecessary to discuss the scope of "moderate livelihood", and the issues of cultural attributes and community authority. It is also unnecessary to consider what territory different treaties may have covered, the precise terms of the treaties, the specific peoples who

concluded treaties, and the need for different respondents to prove membership of a tribe that concluded an applicable treaty.

---

1. *Bernard and Marshall* raises an interesting point regarding treaty interpretation, which builds on issues raised in *Marshall 1* and *Marshall 2*. The Court held that in order for a treaty right to be protected it must have been within the contemplation of the parties at the time the treaty was negotiated (para. 13). When the treaty was signed, was the Crown right to log for commercial purposes contemplated by the parties? If so, how and when did the Crown establish this claim? If not, does the Crown have the right to harvest logs for commercial purposes if this activity was not in the contemplation of both parties at the time the peace and friendship agreements were signed? If the Crown's right to commercial harvests came from another legal principle, what is that principle? If the Crown's right was not established at the time the treaty was signed and cannot be traced to another legal principle, why does the Crown and not the First Nations get the benefit of money raised from logging the Maritimes? For further commentary see Margaret McCallum, "After Bernard and Marshall" (2005) 55 U.N.B.L.J. 73.

2. What is the role of silence within the treaties? In other words, if a matter was not contemplated by the parties and was not expressed in negotiations, what is the fallback position?

3. The Supreme Court of the United States recognized in the *United States v. Winans* case that treaties are "not a grant of rights to the Indians, but a grant of rights from them — a reservation of those not granted: 198 U.S. 371 (1905). This is known as the reserved rights doctrine: the tribes retain everything within their territory unless they affirmatively give it up: *Menominee Tribe v. United States*, 391 U.S. 404 (1968). Is this legal principle applicable within Canadian treaty jurisprudence? If so, how is it expressed? If not, why not, particularly when the Maritimes treaties are primarily concerned with peace and friendship?

4. In *Bernard and Marshall* the Court wrote: "The purpose of the truckhouse clause was to give the British the exclusive right to trade with the Mi'kmaq and the Mi'kmaq the assurance that they would be able to trade with the British as they had traded with the French in the past. Thus, the truckhouse clause was concerned with traditionally traded products" (paras. 18-19). Treaties have been called *sui generis*. In *Sundown* the Court observed: "Treaties may appear to be no more than contracts. Yet they are far more. They are a solemn exchange of promises made by the Crown and various First Nations" (para. 24). In *Marshall 1* the Court wrote: "Rules of interpretation in contract law are in general more strict than those applicable to treaties" (para. 10). They also wrote regarding the 1761 treaty: "This was not a commercial contract" (para. 52). How, if at all, does the Court in *Bernard and Marshall* use contractual principles? What are the alternatives?

5.   Did Chief Justice McLachlin interpret the truckhouse clause correctly? In "Treaty Rights and a Treaty Table" (2005) 55 U.N.B.L.J. 105 at 109, John McEvoy has written:

> McLachlin effectively reads the truckhouse clause as if it read "we will not traffick ... any Commodities that we have not traditionally traded." ... Such a reading fails to give sufficient weight to the reality that trade between individual Mi'kmaq and colonists followed the basic principles of supply and demand and that these principles would indicate a focus on what resources the Mi'kmaq accessed and therefore had available to trade.

Do you agree with his analysis?

6.   While it is settled law that the Crown bears the onus of proving that a treaty right has been extinguished — see, for example, *R. v. Badger*, [1996] S.C.J. No. 39, [1996] 1 S.C.R. 771 (S.C.C.) at para. 41; *R. v. Sioui*, [1990] S.C.J. No. 48, [1990] 1 S.C.R. 1025 at 1061 (S.C.C.); *Simon v. R.*, [1985] S.C.J. No. 67, [1985] 2 S.C.R. 387 at 406 (S.C.C.) — can a treaty right be deemed to be extinguished absent the Crown's proof of extinguishment? See *R. v. Sappier; R. v. Gray*, [2006] S.C.J. No. 54, [2006] 2 S.C.R. 686 (S.C.C.) at paras. 62-65.

H. TREATIES AND FEDERALISM

Recall that the first modern Canadian case that resulted in the protection of treaty rights was *R. v. White and Bob* (1964), 50 D.L.R. (2d) 613, 52 W.W.R. 193 (B.C.C.A.); aff'd (1965), 52 D.L.R. (2d) 481*n* (S.C.C.). It held that the Douglas treaties on Vancouver Island were treaties within the meaning of the term in section 88 of the *Indian Act* and therefore had paramountcy over provincial resources law. Fourteen treaties were signed between Aboriginal peoples and the Hudson Bay Company as representative of the Crown between April 29, 1850 and December 23, 1854 on Vancouver Island. Nine of these treaties were transacted between Governor Douglas and the Indians living around Fort Victoria, two treaties were signed with the Kwa'kwakwak'w of northern Vancouver Island, two treaties with the Indians north of Victoria on the Saanich peninsula and one treaty with the Indians around Nanaimo. When the treaties were entered into there was no text available for the terms of the treaty. It was unilaterally added later by the Crown. The crosses supposedly marking its acceptance were forged "in the sense that they were purported to be made by the Indians but were in fact made by the clerk of the Hudsons Bay Company": *R. v. Morris*, [2004] B.C.J. No. 400, 25 B.C.L.R. (4th) 45 at 64 (B.C.C.A.). For more detail, see also *R. v. Bartleman*, [1984] B.C.J. No. 1760, 12 D.L.R. (4th) 73, 55 B.C.L.R. 78 at 87-89 (B.C.C.A.).

First Nations on Vancouver Island had firm conceptions of their rights to land and resources at the time of the treaties. Governor James Douglas, who negotiated with the Indians, wrote: "As the native Indian population of Vancouver Island have distinct ideas of property in land, and mutually recognize their several exclusive possessory rights in certain districts, they would not fail to regard the occupation of such portions of the Colony as national wrongs; and the sense of injury might produce a feeling of irritation against the settlers, and perhaps disaffection to the Government that would endanger the peace of the country".[4] First Nations who participated in the Douglas treaties were listed as Teechamitsa (now called Esquimalt Band), Kosampson (Esquimalt), Whyomilth (Esquimalt), Swengwhung (Songhees Band), Chilcowitch (Songhees), Che-ko-nein (Songhees), Ka-ky-aakan (Becher Bay), Chewhaytsum (Becher Bay) and Soke, now called Sooke Band. The Fort Rupert Treaties in the Port Hardy area were listed as involving the Queackar (now called Kwakiutl or Kwawkelth Band) and the Quakiolth (Kwakiutl/Kwawkelth). The Saanich treaties were agreed to by people within what are now the Tsawout, Tsartlip, Pauqhachin and Tseycum Indian Bands. The Nanaimo treaty was listed as being with the Saalequun (now called Nanaimo Band) in the present-day Nanaimo area. Other present-day groups that claim Douglas treaty rights are the "Malahat Band, descendants of the South Saanich, which share hunting and fishing rights with the Tsawout and Tsartlip Bands. It is also said the Nanoose Band has a similar relationship with the Nanaimo Band, as do the Nimkish (Nungis) with the Kwakiutl (Kwawkelth). Members of the Comox and Gwa'sala-Nakwaxda'xw Bands are said also to be descendents of the Queackar and Quakiolth".[5]

In examining the history of the treaties, many have concluded that they did not deal with land. In 1875 William S. Green wrote:

> Governor Douglas made agreements with the various families of Indians ... in consideration of certain blankets and other goods possessed by them. But these presents were, as I understand them, made for the purpose of securing friendly relations between those Indians and the settlement of Victoria, then in its infancy, and certainly not in acknowledgement of any general title of the Indians to the land they occupy.[6]

In 1888, an interpreter at the Douglas Treaties, Joseph McKay, stated "Mr. Douglas made no purchase of the country".[7] Chris Arnett wrote that the Douglas treaties would have led the Indians to conclude that their "substantive sovereignty over ancestral lands and resources" was acknowledged by the British.[8] Dennis Madill's analysis concludes that peace was the essential ingredient in the treaties to prevent southerly invasion and encroachment from settlers.[9] In *Land, Man and the Law: The Disposal of Crown Lands in British Columbia, 1871-1913,* Robert Cail wrote:

> Whatever Douglas' intent was, it is now evident that the Indians never really understood what was happening ... As Douglas suggested, they did not understand the principle of usufruct, and the rival Chieftains thought they were yielding to the white interlopers only the right to use land, not the right to anything called exclusive ownership.[10]

In examining the 1852 Douglas treaty Hamar Foster concluded that the Indians "believed that they were agreeing to peaceful relations, to share the right to harvest certain resources, and to allow a limited number of colonists to occupy the lands they were not themselves occupying".[11]

As you read the following case, ask yourself what historical understanding animates the Supreme Court's analysis of the Douglas treaties. Consider how the Court's background assumptions influence the priority it gives to provincial law.

R. v. MORRIS

[2006] S.C.J. No. 59, [2006] 2 S.C.R. 915 (S.C.C.)

Deschamps and **Abella JJ.** (**Binnie** and **Charron JJ.** concurring): —

[1] This case raises the question whether a provincial government acting within its constitutionally mandated powers can interfere with treaty rights and, if so, to what extent.

[2] In 1852, James Douglas, Governor of the Colony of Vancouver Island, representing the British Crown, enshrined in a treaty the recognition that the Saanich Nation would be "at liberty to hunt over the unoccupied lands; and to carry on our fisheries as formerly". Ivan Morris and Carl Olsen, both members of the Tsartlip Band of the Saanich Nation, were charged, among other charges, under s. 27(1)(d) and (e) of British Columbia's *Wildlife Act*, S.B.C. 1982, c. 57, for doing what the Tsartlip have done, as the trial judge noted, "from time immemorial": hunting for food at night with the aid of illuminating devices.

[3] As a defence to the charges under s. 27, Morris and Olsen raised their right to hunt under the North Saanich Treaty of 1852 ("Treaty"). The Crown concedes that Morris and Olsen have a right to hunt but asserts a ban on hunting at night. Morris and Olsen counter that they were observing safe hunting practices and that provincial regulations cannot affect their treaty right.

[4] In this case, we conclude that the Tsartlip's right to hunt at night with the aid of illuminating devices is protected by treaty. Although the prohibition against dangerous hunting contained in s. 29 of the *Wildlife Act* is a limit that does not infringe the treaty right, the complete prohibition on hunting at night with an illuminating device set out in s. 27 is overbroad because it prohibits both safe and unsafe hunting, and, in the case of aboriginal hunters, infringes their treaty right.

[5] The evidence at trial was that the Tsartlip's historic aboriginal practice of hunting at night with illumination has yet to result in a single known accident caused by those engaging in it. In our view, ss. 27(1)(d) and (e) of the *Wildlife Act*, despite being part of a valid provincial law of general application, prohibit the exercise of a protected treaty right and are inapplicable in this case. We would therefore allow the appeal, set aside the convictions and enter acquittals.

1.   *Background*

[6] Morris and Olsen were arrested on November 28, 1996 on Vancouver Island for breaches of prohibitions contained in the *Wildlife Act*: hunting of wildlife with a firearm during prohibited hours (s. 27(1)(d));

hunting by the use or with the aid of a light or illuminating device (s. 27(1)(e)); hunting without reasonable consideration for the lives, safety or property of other persons (s. 29); and, in the case of Olsen only, discharging a firearm at wildlife from a motor vehicle (s. 28(1)).

[7] The backdrop to the prosecution of Morris and Olsen was a change of administrative policy on the part of the provincial Crown, acting through conservation officers. The evidence is that the Tsartlip had hunted at night for generations until the charges were laid in this case. They had received confirmation from the Minister of Forests, David Zirnhelt, that there would be no prosecutions in connection with the exercise of hunting and fishing rights pursuant to the North Saanich Treaty. On the basis of this assurance, the Tsartlip entered into an arrangement with Doug Turner, Chief Enforcement Officer of the Conservation Officer Service for Vancouver Island, whereby any treaty beneficiary charged in relation to night hunting was instructed to phone Mr. Turner. Once Mr. Turner received confirmation that the hunter in question was a member of the Saanich nation, the hunter would be released. This arrangement, it appears, ended with Mr. Turner's retirement in 1996.

[8] In November of that year, not long after Mr. Turner's retirement, a conservation officer was invited to speak at a "rod and gun" club meeting where members expressed dissatisfaction about Indians engaged in night hunting. A decoy operation was promptly organized to trap night hunters, as a result of which Morris and Olsen were arrested and charged. The Tsartlip were not forewarned of the operation and no discussion took place after the charges were laid.

[9] … The conservation officer acknowledged that safety concerns are inversely proportionate to the remoteness and density of the population.

[10] Morris and Olsen led evidence to the effect that night hunting is part of the Tsartlip tradition and has been carried on in safety for generations. They also introduced evidence that the particular night hunt for which they were charged was not dangerous. Morris and Olsen were caught by provincial conservation officers using a mechanical black-tailed deer decoy. The decoy was set up on unoccupied lands 20 metres off a gravel road. It was, one of the conservation officers testified, a spot chosen for its safety. …

[11] The trial judge found that "night hunting with illumination was one of the various methods employed by the Tsartlip [people] from time immemorial" ([1999] B.C.J. No. 3199 (QL), at para. 19). However, despite the evidence that night hunting by Tsartlip hunters had yet to result in an accident, he nonetheless concluded that Morris and Olsen did not have a treaty right to hunt at night because hunting at night with an illuminating device was "inherently unsafe" (para. 25).

[12] However, despite his conclusion that night hunting was inherently unsafe, the trial judge acquitted the appellants on the count of hunting without reasonable consideration for the lives, safety or property of other persons (s. 29). As well, the trial judge conditionally stayed the charges of hunting with the use or aid of a light or illuminating device contrary to s. 27(1)(e) …

[13] The convictions based on the prohibition of night hunting (s. 27(1)(d)) were upheld by a summary conviction appeal judge ([2002] 4 C.N.L.R. 222, 2002 BCSC 780) and by the majority in the Court of Appeal for British Columbia, with Lambert J.A. dissenting ((2004), 25 B.C.L.R. (4th) 45, 2004 BCCA 121). The only provisions at issue in the appeal before us are s. 27(1)(d) and (e).

2. *Analysis*

[14] The analytical framework in which to consider this case can be divided into two parts. The first step is to determine whether the impugned provisions of the *Wildlife Act* impair a treaty right. ... We acknowledge at the outset that there is no treaty right to hunt dangerously. Thus s. 29 of the *Wildlife Act*, which prohibits hunting or trapping "without reasonable consideration for the lives, safety or property of other persons", is a limit that does not impair the treaty rights of aboriginal hunters and trappers. At issue are the limits imposed by ss. 27(1)(d) and (e). In our view these prohibitions, presented as safety measures in relation to the Tsartlip, are overbroad and infringe the treaty right to hunt.

[15] The second step is to analyse whether the impugned provisions of the *Wildlife Act* are valid and applicable under the constitutional division of powers in ss. 91 and 92 of the *Constitution Act, 1867* and under s. 88 of the *Indian Act*, R.S.C. 1985, c. I-5. In our view, because ss. 27(1)(d) and (e) are inconsistent with the Treaty, they do not apply to Morris and Olsen either directly, of their own force, as provincial law, or as incorporated federal law under s. 88 of the *Indian Act*.

2.1 *Evolution of the Treaty Right*

[16] Between 1850 and 1854, fourteen treaties were concluded with bands living on Vancouver Island. These came to be known as the Douglas Treaties, named after James Douglas, Governor of the Colony of Vancouver Island at the time. The Treaty alone covers approximately 22,000 hectares situated on lands that are partly uninhabited and partly inhabited.

[17] In exchange for the surrender by the Saanich of their lands on Vancouver Island, the federal Crown made a number of commitments to them, including the following guarantee:

> [I]t is ... understood that we [the Saanich Tribe] are at liberty to hunt over the unoccupied lands, and to carry on our fisheries <u>as formerly</u>. [Emphasis added.]

Each of the fourteen treaties contained this commitment in the same formulation.

[18] The language of the Treaty stating "we are at liberty to hunt over the unoccupied lands" exemplifies the lean and often vague vocabulary of historic treaty promises. McLachlin J., dissenting on other grounds, stated

in *R. v. Marshall*, [1999] 3 S.C.R. 456 (*Marshall No. 1*), at para. 78, that "[t]he goal of treaty interpretation is to choose from among the various possible interpretations of common intention the one which best reconciles the interests of both parties at the time the treaty was signed". This means that the promises in the treaty must be placed in their historical, political, and cultural contexts to clarify the common intentions of the parties and the interests they intended to reconcile at the time.

[19] The Douglas Treaties were the reflections of oral agreements reduced to writing by agents of the Crown. ... This historical context reveals an overriding intention that the methods by which the Saanich traditionally hunted be brought within the Treaty's protection.

[20] First, it was in the interest of all parties to preserve traditional hunting and fishing practices among the Tsartlip and other Douglas Treaty bands. ...

[21] The interests of the colonial government in preserving the traditional Tsartlip way of life were a reflection of the economic and demographic realities of the region, including concerns for the safety and security of the small number of settlers. Norris J.A. summarized these imperatives as follows in *White and Bob* (BCCA), at p. 657:

> [I]t was at the time of Douglas particularly important for the maintenance of law and order that Indian rights be respected and interpreted broadly in favour of the Indians, not merely for the due administration of law, but also for the safety of the settlers who constituted a minority of, at the most, 1,000 persons, there being 30,000 Indians on Vancouver Island alone, apart from the warlike tribes to the north, who always constituted a raiding threat and against whom the maintenance of friendship with the local Indians afforded a measure of security.

[22] Second, the historical record discloses that Governor Douglas represented to the Indian peoples with whom he entered into treaties that the treaties would secure for them the right to continue their pre-treaty hunting practices. In a letter to the Colonial Secretary dated May 16, 1850, Douglas stated the following:

> I informed the natives that they would not be disturbed in the possession of their Village sites and enclosed fields, which are of small extent, <u>and that they were at liberty to hunt over the unoccupied lands</u>, and to carry on their fisheries <u>with the same freedom as when they were the sole occupants of the country</u>. [Emphasis added.] (See *White*, at p. 651.)

[23] Douglas wrote a similar confirmation to the Speaker and members of the House of Assembly of British Columbia, advising them that:

> [The Indians] were to be protected in their original right of fishing on the Coasts and in the Bays of the Colony, and of hunting over all unoccupied Crown Lands: and they were also to be secured in the enjoyment of their village sites and cultivated fields. [*R. v Bartleman* (BCCA), at p. 89]

[24] These external acknowledgments by Douglas are significant where, as here, the treaty was concluded orally and subsequently reduced to writing. The oral promises made when the treaty was agreed to are as much a part of the treaty as the written words: see *Marshall No. 1*, at para. 12.

[25] The promises made by Douglas confirm that the parties intended the Treaty to include the full panoply of hunting practices in which the Tsartlip people had engaged before they agreed to relinquish control over their lands on Vancouver Island.

[26] One of those practices was night hunting. The trial judge acknowledged the "considerable body of evidence supporting the fact that night hunting has been an accepted practice of the Tsartlip people from pre-treaty days to the present" (para. 18). His most significant finding about night hunting was that it includes, and always has included, hunting with the aid of illuminating devices:

> [N]ight hunting with illumination was one of the various methods employed by the Tsartlip people from time immemorial. [para. 19]

[27] This finding reflected the evidence of Tom Sampson, a member of the Tsartlip band who had hunted for 56 of his 65 years. He described the various ways illumination was historically used in night hunting, including:

> ... a carbide light, it was what the coal miners used to use, and prior to that we used — in fishing, we used the hollowed out part of our canoe and we used pitch from a tree, the stumps we would cut out and shape and put in front of the canoe as a light for hunting and fishing.

[28] The relevant provision of this Treaty, as previously noted, states that the Tsartlip "are at liberty to hunt over the unoccupied lands and to carry on [their] fisheries as formerly". There is no dispute, at least for the purposes of this case, that the words "as formerly" apply to both the hunting and fishing clauses.

[29] As McLachlin J. stated in *Marshall No. 1*, at para. 78, these words "must be given the sense which they would naturally have held for the parties at the time". She also said that " [t]reaties should be liberally construed and ambiguities or doubtful expressions should be resolved in favour of the aboriginal signatories". Even on a literal construction, the language of the Treaty supports the view that the right to hunt "as formerly" means the right to hunt according to the methods used by the Tsartlip at the time of and before the Treaty. This would obviously include those methods the Tsartlip have used in hunting "from time immemorial".

[30] From 1852 to the present, the tools used by the Tsartlip in hunting at night have evolved. From sticks with pitch to spotlights and from canoes to trucks, the tools and methods employed in night hunting have changed over time. These changes do not diminish the rights conferred by the Treaty. The right of the Tsartlip to hunt at night with illuminating devices has of necessity evolved from its pre-treaty tools to its current implements. As McLachlin C.J. observed in *R. v. Marshall*, [2005] 2 S.C.R. 220, 2005 SCC 43, at para. 25:

> ... treaty rights are not frozen in time. Modern peoples do traditional things in modern ways. The question is whether the modern trading activity in question represents a logical evolution from the traditional trading activity at the time the treaty was made .... Logical evolution means the same sort of activity, carried on in the modern economy by modern means. This prevents

aboriginal rights from being unfairly confined simply by changes in the economy and technology.

[31] This approach has led the Court in other cases to acknowledge, for example, that hunting with a rifle and ammunition is the current form of an evolving right whose origins were hunting with a bow and arrow (*Simon v. The Queen*, [1985] 2 S.C.R. 387), and that a treaty right to erect a log cabin for hunting purposes flows from the former use of mossy lean-to shelters (*R. v. Sundown*, [1999] 1 S.C.R. 393).

[32] The evidence in this case makes clear that the use of guns, spotlights, and motor vehicles reflects the current state of the evolution of the Tsartlip's historic hunting practices. Morris testified at trial that the Tsartlip used to hunt at night with

> what they called torch lamps, and I heard this story told to me by our older hunters, that they used sticks with pitch on the end of them to do the same kind of hunt [but that the Tsartlip] had moved into these new tools of the spotlight and of the gun, where it's made it easier for us to hunt. And then we use our vehicles instead of walking or paddling a canoe.

[33] This evidence reveals that the weapons, means of transportation and illuminating devices used in hunting have become more modern. But changes in method do not change the essential character of the practice, namely, night hunting with illumination. What was preserved by the Treaty and brought within its protection was hunting at night with illuminating devices, not hunting at night with a particular *kind* of weapon and source of illumination. This conclusion is dictated by the common intentions of the parties to the Treaty, as distilled from the context in which the Treaty was entered into. The purpose of the hunting clause was to preserve the traditional Tsartlip way of life, including methods of gathering food. It was, in addition, designed to benefit the settlers, whose interests at the time lay in friendship with the Indian majority on Vancouver Island.

[34] Each of these interests could best be met by simultaneously ensuring both the protection of the settlers and the continuation of the hunting methods traditionally used by the Tsartlip. The common intention which best reconciles the interests of the parties is one that brings a right to hunt as they always had within the ambit of the Treaty. This includes the right to hunt at night with illumination.

[35] We agree, as stated earlier, that it could not have been within the common intention of the parties that the Tsartlip would be granted a right to hunt dangerously, since no treaty confers on its beneficiaries a right to put human lives in danger. This limitation on the treaty right flows from the interest of all British Columbians in personal safety. It is also confirmed by the language of the Treaty itself, which restricts hunting to "unoccupied lands," away from any town or settlement. British Columbia is a very large province, and it cannot plausibly be said that a night hunt with illumination is unsafe everywhere and in all circumstances, even within the treaty area at issue in this case.

[36] This Court stated in *R. v. Marshall*, [1999] 3 S.C.R. 533 (*Marshall No. 2*) at para. 37, that "regulations that do no more than reasonably define the ... treaty right in terms that can be administered by the regulator and understood by the ... community that holds the treaty rights do not impair the exercise of the treaty right". As well, as noted in *R. v. Badger*, [1996] 1 S.C.R. 771, at para. 89, "reasonable regulations aimed at ensuring safety do not infringe aboriginal or treaty rights to hunt for food".

[37] The question, therefore, is how to identify and define internal limits on a treaty right. The consensual nature of treaty rights and their specific origin and structure dictate that a respectful approach be adopted. Individual statutory provisions have to be evaluated to determine whether, based on the available historical evidence, they are consistent with the common intention of the parties to the treaty.

[38] In our view, the best reconciliation of the parties' intentions is one that preserves as much as possible the ancient practices the Tsartlip would have understood as forming part of their "liberty to hunt" under the Treaty, subject only to the limit that they do not have a right to put lives or property at risk. Thus, at the very least, the safety limitation in the Treaty should not be drawn so broadly as to exclude *all* night hunting. It could not have been within the common intention of the parties to completely ban night hunting, which was a long-accepted method of hunting for food.

[39] Nor can it be said that such a blanket exclusion should now be implied as a matter of law. If a night hunt is dangerous in particular circumstances, it can (and should) be prosecuted under s. 29. Here, the appellants were acquitted of dangerous hunting. ... Protected methods of hunting cannot, without more, be wholly prohibited simply because in some circumstances they could be dangerous. All hunting, regardless of the time of day, has the potential to be dangerous.

[40] The blanket prohibition of s. 27(1)(d) and (e) applies, of course, throughout British Columbia, including the vast regions of the interior. Much of the north of the province is uninhabited except by aboriginal people, and there are areas where even they are seen only occasionally. To conclude that night hunting with illumination is dangerous everywhere in the province does not accord with reality and is not, with respect, a sound basis for limiting the treaty right.

2.2 *Constitutional Division of Powers*

[41] Having found that the Tsartlip's treaty rights include the right to hunt at night and with illumination, we must now determine whether the impugned provisions of the *Wildlife Act* are nevertheless applicable from the perspective of the constitutional division of powers in ss. 91 and 92 of the *Constitution Act, 1867*. By virtue of s. 91(24), Parliament has exclusive power to make laws in relation to "Indians, and Lands reserved for the Indians". Provincial laws whose "pith and substance" relates to this head of power are *ultra vires* and invalid (*Kitkatla Band v. British Columbia (Minister of Small Business, Tourism and Culture)*, [2002] 2 S.C.R. 146, 2002 SCC 31, at para. 67). However, provincial laws of general application that

affect Indians only incidentally and are enacted under a provincial head of power will be found to be *intra vires* and valid.

[42] In this case, there is no question that the relevant provisions of the *Wildlife Act* are valid provincial legislation under s. 92(13) of the *Constitution Act, 1867*, which refers to Property and Civil Rights in the Province. However, where a valid provincial law impairs "an integral part of primary federal jurisdiction over Indians or Lands reserved for the Indians" (*Four B Manufacturing Ltd. v. United Garment Workers of America*, [1980] 1 S.C.R. 1031, at p. 1047), it will be inapplicable to the extent of the impairment. Thus, provincial laws of general application are precluded from impairing "Indianness". (See, for example, *Dick v. The Queen*, [1985] 2 S.C.R. 309, at p. 326.)

[43] Treaty rights to hunt lie squarely within federal jurisdiction over "Indians, and Lands reserved for the Indians". As noted by Dickson C.J. in *Simon*, at p. 411:

> It has been held to be within the exclusive power of Parliament under s. 91(24) of the *Constitution Act, 1867* to derogate from rights recognized in a treaty agreement made with the Indians.

This Court has previously found that provincial laws of general application that interfere with treaty rights to hunt are inapplicable to particular Aboriginal peoples. (See, for example, *Simon*, at pp. 410-11; *Sundown*, at para. 47.) Where such laws are inapplicable because they impair "Indianness", however, they may nonetheless be found to be applicable by incorporation under s. 88 of the *Indian Act*.

2.3 *Section 88 of the Indian Act*

[44] Section 88 reflects Parliament's intention to avoid the effects of the immunity imposed by s. 91(24) by incorporating certain provincial laws of general application into federal law. Section 88 reads as follows:

> **88.** <u>Subject to the terms of any treaty</u> and any other Act of Parliament, all laws of general application from time to time in force in any province are applicable to and in respect of Indians in the province, except to the extent that those laws are inconsistent with this Act or any order, rule, regulation or by-law made thereunder, and except to the extent that those laws make provision for any matter for which provision is made by or under this Act.

[45] But as the opening words of this provision demonstrate, Parliament has expressly declined to use s. 88 to incorporate provincial laws where the effect would be to infringe treaty rights. And this Court held in *R. v. Côté*, [1996] 3 S.C.R. 139, at para. 86, that one of the purposes of s. 88 is to accord "federal statutory protection to aboriginal treaty rights". Thus, on its face, s. 88 cannot be used to incorporate into federal law provincial laws that conflict with the terms of any treaty.

[46] The clear language of this treaty exception in s. 88 is qualified by statements in this Court's jurisprudence that the provinces may regulate treaty rights under certain circumstances. In *Marshall No. 2*, at para. 24, for example, this Court held that

> the federal and provincial governments [have the authority] within their respective legislative fields to regulate the exercise of the treaty right <u>subject to the constitutional requirement that restraints on the exercise of the treaty right have to be justified on the basis of conservation or other compelling and substantial public objectives</u> .... [Emphasis added.]

That statement must of course be read in the context of the particular right under consideration in *Marshall No. 1*, namely a commercial right of access to resources harvested (and traded) from the outset by aboriginals in common with non-aboriginal inhabitants. ...

[47] Where, as in this case, non-commercial rights are in issue, a distinction must be drawn between insignificant interference with the exercise of the treaty right and *prima facie* infringement of the right.

[48] Regarding insignificant interference, this Court considered in *Côté* whether a provincial regulation requiring the payment of a small access fee for entry into a controlled harvest zone infringed a treaty right to fish. The fee was not revenue generating, but was intended to pay for the ongoing maintenance of roads and facilities within the controlled zone. Lamer C.J. held that this provincial regulation "impose[d] a modest financial burden on the exercise of th[e] alleged treaty right" (para. 88), thereby representing an insignificant interference with a treaty right, and consequently did not infringe that right.

[49] In contrast in *Badger* this Court considered that a licensing scheme that imposed conditions as to the "hunting method, the kind and numbers of game, the season and the permissible hunting area" (para. 92) infringed the appellants' treaty right to hunt. Cory J., writing for the majority, held that this licensing scheme constituted a *prima facie* infringement of the appellants' treaty right to hunt, since it "denie[d] to holders of treaty rights ... the very means of exercising those rights" and was found to be "in direct conflict with the treaty right" (para. 94).

[50] Insignificant interference with a treaty right will not engage the protection afforded by s. 88 of the *Indian Act*. ... Therefore, provincial laws or regulations that place a modest burden on a person exercising a treaty right or that interfere in an insignificant way with the exercise of that right do not infringe the right.

[51] A *prima facie* infringement, however, will trigger the s. 88 treaty right protection. In determining what constitutes a *prima facie* infringement of a treaty right, it is helpful to consider the Court's jurisprudence on this point. In *R. v. Sparrow*, [1999] 1 S.C.R. 1075, at p. 1112, Lamer C.J. and La Forest J. listed three questions that may assist in this determination:

> First, is the limitation unreasonable? Second, does the regulation impose undue hardship? Third, does the regulation deny to the holders of the right their preferred means of exercising that right?

[52] As Lamer C.J. pointed out in *R. v. Gladstone*, [1996] 2 S.C.R. 723, care should be taken, in considering these questions, not to import an element of justification when attempting to identify an infringement. ...

[53] Essentially, therefore, a *prima facie* infringement requires a "meaningful diminution" of a treaty right. This includes anything but an

insignificant interference with that right. If provincial laws or regulations interfere insignificantly with the exercise of treaty rights, they will not be found to infringe them and can apply *ex proprio vigore* or by incorporation under s. 88.

[54] The protection of treaty rights in s. 88 of the *Indian Act* applies where a conflict between a provincial law of general application and a treaty is such that it amounts to a *prima facie* infringement. Where a provincial law of general application is found to conflict with a treaty in a way that constitutes a *prima facie* infringement, the protection of treaty rights prevails and the provincial law cannot be incorporated under s. 88.

[55] Where a *prima facie* infringement of a treaty right is found, a province cannot rely on s. 88 by using the justification test from *Sparrow* and *Badger* in the context of s. 35(1) of the *Constitution Act, 1982*, as alluded to by Lamer C.J. in *Côté* at para. 87. The purpose of the *Sparrow/Badger* analysis is to determine whether an infringement by a government acting within its constitutionally mandated powers can be justified. This justification analysis does not alter the division of powers, which is dealt with in s. 88. Therefore, while the *Sparrow/Badger* test for infringement may be useful, the framework set out in those cases for determining whether an infringement is justified does not offer any guidance for the question at issue here.

3. *Application to this Case*

[56] There is no treaty right to hunt dangerously. Thus, the prohibition against hunting "without reasonable consideration for the lives, safety or property of other persons" set out in s. 29 of the *Wildlife Act* is a limit that does not infringe the Tsartlip's treaty right to hunt. As stated earlier, the requirement to hunt safely was clearly within the common intention of the parties to the Treaty, as reflected by the language of the Treaty itself, which restricts hunting to "unoccupied lands". Where a treaty beneficiary is proven to have hunted dangerously, the Treaty does not provide a defence to charges brought under s. 29.

[57] However, based on an understanding of the common intention of the parties to the Treaty, the Tsartlip's treaty right includes the right to hunt at night with illumination, with the modern incarnation of their ancestral method, namely the use of firearms.

[58] The legislative prohibition set out in s. 27(1)(d) and (e) of the *Wildlife Act* is absolute, and it applies without exception to the whole province, including the most northern regions where hours of daylight are limited in the winter months and populated areas are few and far between. The Legislature has made no attempt to prohibit only those specific aspects or geographic areas of night hunting that are unsafe by, for example, banning hunting within a specified distance from a highway or from residences. The impugned provisions are overbroad, inconsistent with the common intention of the parties to the treaties, and completely eliminate a chosen method of exercising their treaty right.

[59] We respectfully disagree with our colleagues the Chief Justice and Fish J. that nothing short of a total ban on night hunting can address safety concerns. We believe that it would be possible to identify uninhabited areas where hunting at night would not jeopardize safety. This finding is supported by the evidence in this case that the Tsartlip's practice of night hunting with illuminating devices has never been known to have resulted in an accident, and that the conservation officers, in setting up the location for their mechanical decoy, were easily able to locate an area where night hunting could be practised safely. These facts amply demonstrate how something less than an absolute prohibition on night hunting can address the concern for safety.

[60] We have no difficulty concluding, therefore, that the categorical ban on night hunting and hunting with illumination constitutes a *prima facie* infringement of a treaty right. A categorical prohibition clearly constitutes more than an insignificant interference with a treaty right. Although provincial laws of general application that are inapplicable to aboriginal people can be incorporated into federal law under s. 88 of the *Indian Act*, this cannot happen where the effect would be to infringe treaty rights. Because paras. (d) and (e) of s. 27(1) of the *Wildlife Act* constitute a *prima facie* infringement, they cannot be incorporated under s. 88 of the *Indian Act*.

[61] For these reasons, we would allow the appeal, set aside the convictions and enter acquittals.

McLachlin C.J. and Fish JJ. (Bastarache J. dissenting): —

. . . . .

[82] For the reasons that follow, we conclude that the impugned ban on night hunting with a firearm is valid provincial legislation that applies to the appellants. The relevant provisions of the *Wildlife Act* prohibit unsafe hunting practices, which is in pith and substance a matter within the legislative jurisdiction of the provinces. They do not conflict with federal legislation and the doctrine of paramountcy therefore has no application. Finally, the right to hunt protected by the Douglas Treaty is subject to an internal limit: It does not include the right to hunt in an inherently hazardous manner. Or, put differently, the right to hunt under the treaty must be exercised reasonably and hunting practices that are inherently hazardous are antithetical to the reasonable exercise of the right to hunt. The impugned provision of the *Wildlife Act* regulates this internal limit. Since the regulation of dangerous hunting falls outside the scope of the treaty right to hunt, no treaty right is engaged. As there is no aboriginal right asserted, and as the law does not otherwise go to Indianness, the law applies *ex proprio vigore* and does not need to be incorporated by s. 88 in order to apply to Indians.

. . . . .

[98] What type or degree of conflict is required between a provincial law of general application and a treaty to engage the treaty exception's protection? ...

[99] In our view, a *prima facie* infringement test best characterizes the degree of conflict required to engage the protection of the treaty exception. ... Legislation which engages the internal limits of a treaty right does not affect the treaty right at all, and therefore, *a fortiori*, does not constitute a *prima facie* infringement.

. . . . .

[110] In our view, the parties to the Douglas Treaty must have understood that the right to hunt did not carry with it a right to hunt in an unsafe manner. They must have understood as well that the Crown did not abdicate its interests or its responsibilities in this regard. ...

. . . . .

[112] The ninth principle of treaty interpretation laid down in *Marshall No. 1* further supports this conclusion: "Treaty rights of aboriginal peoples must not be interpreted in a static or rigid way. They are not frozen at the date of signature. The interpreting court must update treaty rights to provide for their modern exercise" (para. 78).

[113] The appellants argue that using the ninth principle to restrict rather than expand the scope of a treaty right would "turn this [principle] on its head".

[114] As will be more fully explained below, since 1852, the dangers of night hunting have been amplified with the development of modern weaponry. In our view, treaty rights are not impervious to changes of this sort. They do not evolve in a social, environmental or technological vacuum. A right to hunt is not transformed into a right to hunt in an unsafe manner by disregarding unforeseen dangers or new risks.

[115] Quite the contrary, the ninth principle simply acknowledges that treaties must be interpreted in a manner that contemplates their exercise in modern society. Just as the methods and means of exercising the right should not be frozen in time, neither should the government's legitimate safety concerns. Adapting the exercise of treaty rights to modern weaponry without adapting the corollary legitimate safety concerns would lead to unacceptable results. One cannot reasonably focus on the former and turn a blind eye to the latter.

. . . . .

[119] ... [T]he fact that the treaty protects the means and methods of hunting does not negate the internal limit on the right: the treaty hunting right does not include the right to hunt in a manner that endangers the safety of the hunter or others. Because dangerous hunting falls outside the scope of the protected treaty right, the province is free to regulate in this area. ...

. . . . .

[122] ... We must still determine how this internal limit may be validly expressed in the regulatory context. Are the courts limited to case-by-case after the fact inquiries into whether a particular hunter on a particular occasion exercised the treaty right to hunt unsafely? Or can the province pass legislation or adopt regulations that define the limits of the right in a way that can be administered and understood by the aboriginal community?

[123] The answer to this question is found in this Court's jurisprudence, which affirms the right of the province to determine and direct in advance the limits of a treaty right in a particular regulatory context, provided it does so reasonably. ...

. . . . .

[126] The question before us is thus whether the province's ban on night hunting constitutes a reasonable exercise of the province's power to regulate the internal safety limit on the appellants' treaty right. ...

. . . . .

[129] The conclusion that a ban on night hunting is a reasonable exercise of the Province's regulatory power in defining the internal limit on the treaty right flows naturally and logically from the defining feature of nighttime — that is, darkness. The evidence at trial was more than sufficient to establish that one's ability to identify objects, estimate distances and observe background and surrounding items is greatly diminished in the dark, posing a real danger to other members of the public.

[130] This added danger to hunting causes the risks associated with hunting at nighttime with a firearm to be unacceptably high. The *Wildlife Act* prohibition is a reasonable response to a real danger.

. . . . .

[132] The impugned legislation thus regulates an area which lies entirely outside the treaty right to hunt. It therefore does not conflict at all with the treaty right. No aboriginal right is asserted, and absent a conflicting treaty or aboriginal right, reasonable provincial safety regulation of dangerous hunting practices cannot be said to intrude upon "core Indianness". It follows that the *Wildlife Act* prohibition on night hunting with a firearm is a valid provincial law applicable to the appellants *ex proprio vigore* and without recourse to s. 88.

. . . . .

[140] For these reasons, we would dismiss the appeal.

———————

The dissenting judges in *Morris* wrote, at paras. 105 and 106:

> In the Court of Appeal, Lambert J.A. defined the appellants' treaty right as the right to hunt for food and ceremonial purposes according to the Indians' preferred means in accordance with their own laws, customs, traditions and practices, and the safety practices which regulate the manner of hunting (para. 49) ... In our respectful view Lambert J.A.'s interpretation disregards the internal safety limitations to which that right is necessarily subject.

Read Justice Lambert's reasons relating to safety under the treaty in the following quote and explain why his interpretation would "disregard internal safety limitations" (in dissent in *R. v. Morris*, [2004] B.C.J. No. 400, 2004 BCCA 121, 237 D.L.R. (4th) 693, [2004] 5 W.W.R. 403, [2004] 2 C.N.L.R. 219, 25 B.C.L.R. (4th) 45 (B.C.C.A.) (at paras. 42-46):

> Before the first incomers arrived, all questions of hunting for food and for ceremony, all fishing practices, and all gathering of berries, roots, and shellfish, were resolved and settled in accordance with the laws, customs, traditions, and practices of the Indian peoples. That did not change as soon as the first incomers arrived on the coast. Nor did it change at any time before 1852 or after. ...
>
> In 1852 there was no game ordinance. The first game ordinance for the Colony of Vancouver Island was made in 1859 and it did not deal with safety practices but with preservation of small game birds. There was no basis for enforcement of the incomers' concepts of safe hunting practices. The only control over safe hunting practices lay in the laws, customs, traditions and practices of the Indians themselves as they applied those laws to their hunting for food and ceremonial purposes after first contact, just as they had done before first contact.
>
> In the circumstances I have described can it be doubted that in 1852 the safe hunting practices to be followed by the Indians as they continued their hunting under the treaty were to be the safe hunting practices set on the basis of their own continuing laws, customs, traditions and practices?
>
> I have used the phrase "laws, customs, traditions and practices". In using the word "laws" I am following the terminology used by Chief Justice McLachlin and Mr. Justice Binnie in *Mitchell v. Canada (M.N.R.)*, [2001] 1 S.C.R. 911. See Chief Justice McLachlin at paras. 9 and 10 where she uses the phrases "pre-existing laws" and "customary laws". I am also using the terminology adopted by Chief Justice Lamer in *Delgamuukw v. British Columbia*, [1997] 3 S.C.R. 1010 at para. 147 where he says that the aboriginal perspective on land "includes but is not limited to their systems of law". For applications of aboriginal laws to common law and statutory issues see *Connolly v. Woolrich* (1867), 11 L.C. Jur. 197; 1 C.N.L.C. 70, and *Casimel v. I.C.B.C.* (1993), 82 B.C.L.R. (2d) 387. And see also J. Borrows: "With or Without You: First Nations Law (in Canada)" (1996) 41 McGill L.J. 629.
>
> In this case there was evidence given by the two appellants and by Thomas Sampson, Simon Smith, Curtis Olsen, Joseph Bartleman, David St. Paul and Saul Terry about the laws, customs, traditions and practices of the Tsartlip people with respect to hunting for food, hunting at night, and safety practices with respect to hunting at night and with respect to hunting generally. Those customs were said to go back to much earlier than the Douglas Treaties of 1852. There was evidence that no one had ever been injured by a member of the Tsartlip people hunting at night, with or without a light. ...

I. INTERPRETING MODERN TREATIES AND LAND CLAIMS AGREEMENTS

Modern treaties and land claims agreements are contained within the protection of treaties and treaty rights in section 35 of the *Constitution Act, 1982*. They are expressly contemplated in section 35(3), which states: "For greater certainty, in subsection (1) 'treaty rights' includes rights that now exist by way of land claims agreements or may be so acquired."

Despite their identical protection in section 35, modern treaties and land claims are not exactly like the historical treaties that preceded them. Rather, they involved far more complex negotiations and were often accompanied by governmental legislation that aided their implementation. While modern treaties and land claims agreements do draw upon the canons of treaty interpretation illustrated above, as the following cases illustrate, the courts are still working through the issue of how those canons apply to more contemporary agreements where the Aboriginal signatories were far more familiar with the English language that the treaties were written in and many of the concepts that might be incorporated in those agreements.

QUEBEC (ATTORNEY GENERAL) v. MOSES

[2010] S.C.J. No. 17, [2010] 1 S.C.R. 557 (S.C.C.)

[For ease of reference, the facts of the case are drawn from the dissenting judgment in the case. The discussion of the facts will be followed by the majority judgment and, in turn, the remainder of the dissenting opinion.]

[57] For the first time since the groundbreaking *James Bay and Northern Québec Agreement* ("Agreement") was signed in 1975, this Court must interpret its provisions. At issue are conflicting views about which, or how many, of three possible environmental assessment processes should apply to a mining project in the James Bay area of Quebec that is covered by this agreement between certain First Nations, the governments of Quebec and Canada and several Crown corporations. The parties disagree about whether the project should be reviewed once, twice or three times, or possibly through a combination of competing processes. We find that there is but one answer from both a legal and a practical standpoint: on the facts of this case, only the provincial process provided for in the Agreement applies. ...

. . . . .

[59] In the reasons that follow, we will explore the background and judicial history of this case. We will discuss important issues concerning the nature and interpretation of the Agreement and of modern treaties between the Crown and the First Nations of Canada more generally, and these issues will inform our final disposition of this appeal.

II. Background

A. *James Bay Agreement*

[60] In 1971, the Quebec government announced plans to build an extensive hydro-electric generation complex on the La Grande River in the James Bay area. The project involved flooding vast expanses of land used by the Cree for hunting and fishing in order to build reservoirs that would feed hydro-electric turbines. The Cree responded by initiating litigation. In November 1973, the Quebec Superior Court granted an interlocutory injunction that stopped all work on the project on the basis that it had been undertaken without any consultation about its environmental and social impact on Aboriginal inhabitants. The Court of Appeal reversed that decision, and leave to appeal to this Court was refused ([1975] 1 S.C.R. 48). While the litigation was under way, the Cree and Inuit communities entered into negotiations with the governments of Quebec and Canada that resulted in the signing of the Agreement in November 1975.

[61] The Agreement territory ... comprises more than 1,082,000 square kilometres extending inland from the shores of James Bay ... The Agreement was intended to settle all Aboriginal claims to the land, establish a comprehensive and forward-looking governance regime, and provide a framework for the exercise and performance of the respective rights and obligations of the two First Nations and the two governments in the course of their ongoing relationship. In many respects, the Agreement grants the First Nations parties a form of self-government.

[62] For this purpose, the Agreement established a far-reaching governance scheme under which important powers are conferred on the Cree and Inuit. It created a framework that would govern many aspects of life in the Territory, including Aboriginal hunting and fishing, resource and hydro-electric development, the administration of justice, school administration, Aboriginal economic and social development, health and social services, local governance and — the aspect that is in issue in this case — preservation of the natural environment.

[63] ... Sections 22 and 23 of the Agreement set out detailed and comprehensive procedures for environmental impact assessments that, when drafted, were ahead of their time. Indeed, they predated analogous environmental legislation that has since been enacted by all the provinces and by the federal government. In a sense, the Agreement foreshadowed the increased knowledge of and heightened concern for environmental issues that have since developed throughout Canada. Another significant feature of the Agreement is the explicit affirmation in s. 22.2.2 of its goal of striking a balance between two overarching objectives: economic development and the protection of traditional Aboriginal uses of the land. The resulting environmental impact assessment procedure, which involves the First Nations and the governments of Quebec and Canada, rests on two key principles: guaranteeing Aboriginal participation and consultation at all stages of the assessment process, and avoiding duplication by providing for a single environmental assessment process based on the

nature of the project involved and on whether it falls within provincial or federal constitutional jurisdiction.

B.   *Vanadium Mine Project*

[64] At issue in this appeal is the future of a vanadium mining project ("Project") located at Lac Doré, near Chibougamau, within the James Bay Territory. Lac Doré Mining Inc. ("Proponent") intended to open and exploit the mine. The Project is to be situated in the Agreement Territory on "Category III" lands, with respect to which the Agreement recognizes Quebec's right to regulate natural resource development subject to the environmental protection provisions of s. 22. Vanadium is an element used in the production of steel alloys. The mine contains reserves of 10 million tons, has an anticipated life of 40 years, corresponds to 12 percent of worldwide vanadium consumption, and is the only mine of its kind in North America.

[65] On May 27, 1999, the Proponent forwarded to the Quebec Minister of Environment a Notice of Project in respect of the Project in accordance with the Agreement's procedures. In June 2003, the Proponent submitted its impact statement to the deputy minister, and the impact statement was then forwarded to the provincial Review Committee.

[66] Meanwhile, federal officials concluded that the Project's impact on fisheries engaged s. 35(2) of the *Fisheries Act*, R.S.C. 1985, c. F-14, and required a comprehensive study pursuant to s. 16(*a*) of the Schedule of the *Comprehensive Study List Regulations*, SOR/94-638, made under the *CEAA*. In April 2004, federal officials informed the Cree that the study would be conducted by a review panel under the *CEAA* and not through the federal assessment procedure provided for in Section 22 of the Agreement.

[67] In response, the Cree commenced an action for declaratory relief in the Quebec Superior Court. The commencement of this litigation effectively interrupted the environmental assessment process originally undertaken pursuant to the Agreement.

III.   Judicial History

A.   *Superior Court, 2006 QCCS 1832, [2007] 1 C.N.L.R. 256*

[68] In the Superior Court, the Cree sought a declaration (i) that the *CEAA* was inapplicable in the Agreement Territory because it was inconsistent with the Agreement, and (ii) that the federal and provincial environmental assessments under the Agreement should be conducted instead in light of the nature and impact of the Project. The Attorney General of Quebec ("AGQ") agreed with the Cree that the *CEAA* was inapplicable but argued that because the nature of the Project related to a matter within provincial jurisdiction, only the provincial assessment under the Agreement was applicable. The Attorney General of Canada ("AGC") took a third position: (i) because of the licence requirement in the *Fisheries Act*, the Project's potential impact on fisheries validly triggered the federal

environmental assessment legislation, and (ii) because the nature of the Project related to a matter within provincial jurisdiction, the provincial environmental assessment procedure in the Agreement was also applicable. ...

[69] The parties' divergent positions gave rise to several issues: (i) whether the environmental assessment procedures under the Agreement are consistent with the procedures required by the *CEAA*; (ii) the effect of any inconsistency between the Agreement and the *CEAA*; and (iii) whether the requirement to proceed with a provincial or federal environmental assessment under the Agreement was triggered solely by the nature of the Project, or by both its nature and its impact.

The judgment of **McLachlin C.J.C.** and **Binnie**, **Fish**, **Rothstein** and **Cromwell JJ**. was delivered by **Binnie J**.: —

I. Introduction

[1] The question raised by this appeal is whether a mining project within the territory covered by the *James Bay and Northern Québec Agreement* ("James Bay Treaty" or "Treaty") that "results in the harmful alteration, disruption or destruction of fish habitat" (*Fisheries Act*, R.S.C. 1985, c. F-14, s. 35(1)) is nevertheless exempted by virtue of the Treaty from any independent scrutiny by the federal Fisheries Minister before issuing the federal fisheries permit. All parties to this appeal agree the mine will require the permit before commencing operations. If the permit is not obtained, or if the permit conditions are not complied with, the mine operator would face civil and criminal consequences.

[2] The Attorney General of Quebec contends that the federal Minister will have no choice but to issue the permit once the mine is approved by a provincially appointed Treaty Administrator or the Quebec Cabinet. He contends that despite the anticipated impact of the mine's tailing ponds and other pollutants on fish and fish habitat, and despite fisheries being a matter within exclusive federal jurisdiction under s. 91(12) of the *Constitution Act, 1867*, the James Bay Treaty should be interpreted to exclude what would elsewhere be a compulsory assessment of the project's impact under the *Canadian Environmental Assessment Act*, S.C. 1992, c. 37 ("*CEAA*"), and/or under federal fisheries policy.

[3] My colleagues LeBel and Deschamps JJ. agree with that position. They rely, in particular, on a term of the Treaty that provides that "a project shall not be submitted to more than one (1) impact assessment and review procedure unless such project falls within the jurisdictions of both Québec and Canada" (s. 22.6.7). They then interpret the Treaty to exclude fisheries' "impacts" from the determination of whether the mine is to be considered "exclusively" federal or provincial. In the result, on this view, the provincially appointed Administrator under the Treaty could base a final decision upon an abbreviated fisheries study that is simply unacceptable to the federal Fisheries Minister. Alternatively, the Quebec Cabinet could for its own reasons override the fisheries concerns

altogether and approve the mining project over the objection of the Administrator it has appointed, or lighten the conditions designed to mitigate the adverse effects of the project on the fisheries. In any such circumstances, on this view, the federal Fisheries Minister would be powerless to withhold the permit. I do not agree that the terms of the Treaty support such an anomalous result.

[4] My colleagues go further and accuse the federal government of "unilaterally reneg[ing] on its own solemn [treaty] promises" (para. 58). This is a very serious allegation and, I believe, highlights the importance of paying attention to the actual terms of the treaty to determine what the parties (including the federal government) agreed to, and whether the federal government has (as alleged) gone back on its word and, as my colleagues see it, violated "the honour of the Crown" (para. 58). With respect, I find no support whatsoever for this harsh condemnation in the body of the Treaty, or in the circumstances that gave rise to this dispute.

[5] My colleagues express concern about the "First Nations' participatory rights" (para. 58), but the Cree First Nation — certainly a profoundly important party to the Treaty — considers that it is the Quebec government position, endorsed by my colleagues, that is not only "legally incorrect" but "makes no practical sense". In a factum filed jointly on behalf of Grand Chief Dr. Ted Moses, Grand Council of the Crees (Eeyou Istchee) and Cree Regional Authority (the "Cree respondents"), they write:

> In essence, the Attorney-General of Québec argues that federal authorities responsible for the implementation and enforcement of the *Fisheries Act*, R.S.C. 1985, c. F-14, are required to rely solely on a provincial review (in which they do not participate) to base their decisions under the *Fisheries Act* in regard to the Vanadium project. In addition to being legally incorrect, this approach makes no practical sense. [para. 6]

… While, as will be seen, I do not entirely accept the procedural element of the Cree argument, I agree with their conclusion that on a proper construction of s. 22.7.5 of the Treaty, "a federal assessment in this case is indeed 'required by Federal law or regulation'" (Cree Factum, at para. 80). Furthermore, as I interpret the Treaty, the participatory rights of the Cree are fully protected (contrary to what is said by my colleagues, at para. 58), as will be discussed.

[6] What all of this means, I believe, is that it is necessary to approach this case on the basis of the terms the parties actually negotiated and agreed to as set out in the text of their agreement rather than on general observations and ideas which, in my respectful view, are unsupported by the text. …

A. *Overview*

[7] In *R. v. Badger*, [1996] 1 S.C.R. 771, Cory J. pointed out that Aboriginal "[t]reaties are analogous to contracts, albeit of a very solemn and special, public nature" (para. 76). At issue in that case was an 1899 treaty. The contract analogy is even more apt in relation to a modern

comprehensive treaty whose terms (unlike in 1899) are not constituted by an exchange of verbal promises reduced to writing in a language many of the Aboriginal signatories did not understand (paras. 52-53). The text of modern comprehensive treaties is meticulously negotiated by well-resourced parties. As my colleagues note, "all parties to the Agreement were represented by counsel, and the result of the negotiations was set out in detail in a 450-page legal document" (para. 118). The importance and complexity of the actual text is one of the features that distinguishes the historic treaties made with Aboriginal people from the modern comprehensive agreement or treaty, of which the James Bay Treaty was the pioneer. We should therefore pay close attention to its terms.

[8] I do not agree with the attribution by the Attorney General of Quebec of "trump" status to the reference in s. 22.6.7 to only "one (1) impact assessment and review procedure". This provision merely regulates the *internal* treaty review processes. It does not refer to requirements *external* to the Treaty. Indeed, s. 22.7.1 specifically preserves the external requirement imposed on the vanadium mine promoter, triggered by final approval of the project under the Treaty, to obtain "the necessary authorization or permits from responsible Government Departments and Services", as follows:

> 22.7.1 If the proposed development is approved in accordance with the provisions of this Section, the proponent shall <u>before proceeding with the work obtai[n] where applicable the necessary authorization or permits</u> from responsible Government Departments and Services. The Cree Regional Authority shall be informed of the decision of the Administrator. [Emphasis added.]

If the argument of the Attorney General of Quebec were correct, s. 22.7.1 would be worded to place the obligation on the responsible Government Department and Services to *issue* automatically the necessary authorization or permit, not to put the obligation on the proponent to *obtain* the necessary authorization or permit.

[9] What, then, is the role and function of s. 22.6.7 relied upon by the Attorney General of Quebec whose approach in this respect is adopted by my colleagues? It provides:

> 22.6.7 The Federal Government, the Provincial Government and the Cree Regional Authority may by mutual agreement combine the two (2) impact review bodies provided for in this Section and in particular paragraphs 22.6.1 and 22.6.4 provided that such combination shall be without prejudice to the rights and guarantees in favour of the Crees established by and in accordance with this Section.

> Notwithstanding the above, a project shall not be submitted to more than one (1) impact assessment and review procedure unless such project falls within the jurisdictions of both Québec and Canada or unless such project is located in part in the Territory and in part elsewhere where an impact review process is required.

My colleagues lay stress on the second paragraph ("shall not be submitted to more than one (1) impact assessment and review procedure"), but clearly the second paragraph must be read with the first paragraph. The two paragraphs read together are an elaboration of the internal treaty processes *leading up to* the decision of the Administrator. The rule against duplication simply provides that only one impact assessment is to be conducted *within* the pre-approval treaty process for the benefit of the Administrator. The recommendations forwarded to the relevant Administrator will come from *either* the provincial Committee *or* the federal Panel but (in the absence of governmental agreement) not both, unless the project itself falls within both jurisdictions.

[10] I agree with my colleagues that there is to be only one "impact review" of the mine project *under* the James Bay Treaty. ... The provincial Administrator (or the Quebec Cabinet) will then make an approval decision. However, the agreement of the parties to avoid duplication *internal* to the Treaty does not eliminate the *post*-approval permit requirement contemplated by the Treaty if imposed *externally* by a law of general application, such as the *CEAA* or the *Fisheries Act*, whose operation is preserved by the Treaty itself in s. 22.7.1.

[11] To this group of provisions the parties added a further stipulation which contemplated the possibility of an external "impact assessment review procedure by the Federal Government" as follows:

> 22.7.5 Nothing in the present Section shall be construed as imposing <u>an impact assessment review procedure by the Federal Government unless required by Federal law or regulation</u>. However, this shall not operate to preclude Federal requirement for an additional Federal impact review process as a condition of Federal funding of any development project. [Emphasis added.]

The parties to the Treaty plainly agreed that the Treaty provisions dealing with the environment do not themselves require an independent impact assessment review by the federal government (i.e. the federal government itself as distinguished from the Treaty review bodies on which the federal government may or may not be represented). However, this provision is expressly made subject to such an external requirement being imposed by "Federal law or regulation" (i.e. not the Treaty). Far from excluding a separate federal obligation external to the Treaty, the Treaty thus contemplates the obligation of compliance with federal law whether in existence at the time of the negotiations (e.g. s. 31 of the *Fisheries Act* as it then was) or impact assessments subsequently imposed by federal law (e.g. the *CEAA*). This is the position of the Cree respondents and I agree with it.

. . . . .

IV. Analysis

[36] There is no doubt that a vanadium mining project, considered in isolation, falls within provincial jurisdiction under s. 92A of the *Constitution Act, 1867* over natural resources. There is also no doubt that ordinarily a mining project anywhere in Canada that puts at risk fish

habitat could not proceed without a permit from the federal Fisheries Minister, which he or she could not issue except after compliance with the *CEAA*. The mining of non-renewable mineral resources aspect falls within provincial jurisdiction, but the fisheries aspect is federal.

[37] Parliament, of course, has bound the federal government to comply with the Treaty provisions in all respects: *James Bay and Northern Quebec Native Claims Settlement Act*, S.C. 1976-77, c. 32, s. 8. The Attorney General of Quebec argues that the Treaty review process leading up to a decision by the Administrator is exhaustive of environmental assessment requirements (unless overturned by order of the Cabinet) but, in my view, the effect of the Treaty provisions is as follows. Under s. 22.2.3 of the Treaty, all federal laws of general application respecting environmental protections apply insofar as they are not inconsistent with the Treaty (a similar regime applies to education (s. 16.0.2)). The *CEAA* is a federal law of general application respecting the environment. The question, then, is whether there is any inconsistency between the *CEAA* and the Treaty. I believe not. As stated, s. 22.7.1 of the Treaty provides that once the proposed development is approved by the Administrator following consultation and receipt of "recommendations", the mine promoter is required *notwithstanding such approval* to obtain "the necessary authorization or permits from responsible Government Departments and Services". Nothing in the Treaty relieves the proponent from compliance with the ordinary procedures governing the issuance of the necessary authorization or permits. If the makers of the Treaty had intended the Administrator's approval (or Cabinet's substituted approval) to be the end of the regulatory requirements, they would have said so, but they did not. They said the contrary.

. . . . .

V.   Conclusion

[53] In my view, the vanadium mine cannot lawfully proceed without a fisheries permit. The proponent is unable to obtain, and the federal Minister is unable to issue, a s. 35(2) fisheries permit without compliance with the *CEAA*. ...

[54] It is only after final approval by the Treaty bodies that it can be said that "the proposed development is approved in accordance with the provisions of this Section", which is the condition precedent to the proponent's obligations under s. 22.7.1 to "obtai[n] where applicable the necessary authorization or permits from responsible Government Departments and Services". There is thus no conflict. The need for a *post*-Treaty approval fisheries permit is made mandatory by the Treaty itself ("shall" obtain). In the case of fisheries, it is federal law, not the Treaty, that governs when such a permit may be granted as well as its terms and conditions.

[55] ... I would dismiss the appeal but vary the order of the Quebec Court of Appeal to provide that if the vanadium mine project is approved

pursuant to the Treaty, the proponent may not proceed with the work without authorization under s. 35(2) of the *Fisheries Act*, and that the issuance of any such authorization is to comply with the *Canadian Environmental Assessment Act* in accordance with its procedures, as well as the Crown's duty to consult with the First Nations in relation to matters that may adversely affect their Treaty rights.

. . . . .

The reasons of **LeBel, Deschamps, Abella** and **Charron JJ.** were delivered by **Lebel** and **Deschamps JJ.** (dissenting): —

[The dissenting judgment's recitation of the facts was moved to the beginning of the case.]

IV.   Analysis

[81] The issue remains the same as in the courts below. Which environmental review process applies to the Project: the provincial or the federal process under the Agreement, both those processes, or the federal process under the *CEAA*? To resolve this issue, we must first discuss the nature, interpretation and effect of the Agreement and situate it in its proper legal and constitutional context.

A.   *The James Bay Agreement*

(1)   Nature

[82] The Agreement is both an intergovernmental agreement and an Aboriginal rights agreement. It is binding upon, and creates rights and obligations for, the federal and provincial governments and the First Nations. It may be viewed as a model for the many modern land treaties that have been signed since the 1982 constitutional amendments, which included the protection of what are now referred to as "modern" treaty rights under s. 35(3) of the *Constitution Act, 1982*. However, the Agreement does not just settle and determine the rights and obligations as between the provincial and federal Crowns, on the one hand, and the Aboriginal peoples living in the Territory, on the other. It also settles and determines the obligations, in relation to the Territory, of the federal and provincial governments as between themselves. ...

. . . . . .

[87] The legal status of the Agreement must be considered with this in mind. There is no question that the Agreement establishes a comprehensive and elaborate regime for the administration of the James Bay Territory. ...

. . . . .

(2)   Principles of Interpretation

[108] ... [T]he negotiation of historical treaties was marked by "significant differences" in the signatories' languages, concepts, cultures and world views. ... Because of these contextual factors, Aboriginal treaties are to be interpreted in light of the contexts in which they were signed, and that interpretation must be both liberal and dynamic ... while any ambiguity is to be resolved in favour of the Aboriginal signatories.

[109] Applying these principles, without adaptation, to the interpretation of modern agreements, as opposed to historical ones, is not uncontroversial.

. . . . .

[113] ... [T]his Court has yet to pronounce on this particular issue ... .

[114] ... [An] accurate formulation of the issue ... is whether the rationale for the approach taken in interpreting historical treaties ... ought to apply automatically or systematically to the interpretation of modern agreements. ...

[115] ... [T]he *circumstances* at the root of the principle that ambiguities in historical treaties must be resolved in favour of the Aboriginal signatories — unequal bargaining skill and vulnerability of the Aboriginal parties in particular — do not necessarily exist in the context of a modern agreement ...

[116] Furthermore ... the honour of the Crown infuses both the making of treaties and, ultimately, the interpretation of treaties by the courts ... Modern agreements ... reflect a mixture of rights, obligations, payments and concessions that have already been carefully balanced ... In negotiations, therefore, the Crown must, and does, actively consider the Aboriginal party's interests. ...

. . . . .

[118] When interpreting a modern treaty, a court should strive for an interpretation that is reasonable, yet consistent with the parties' intentions and the overall context ... of the negotiations. ...

. . . . .

(2)   Application

[131] ... [W]e must interpret the provision of s. 22 that is ... determinative of the assessment process, as would have been the case prior to the enactment of the *CEAA*, or whether the enactment of the *CEAA* changed the nature of the constitutional ordering established by the Agreement. For ease of reference, we will reproduce s. 22.6.7 in its entirety:

22.6.7   The Federal Government, the Provincial Government and the Cree Regional Authority may by mutual agreement combine the two (2) impact review bodies provided for in this Section and in particular paragraphs 22.6.1 and 22.6.4 provided that such combination shall be without prejudice to the rights and guarantees in favour of the Crees established by and in accordance with this Section.

Notwithstanding the above, a project shall not be submitted to more than one (1) impact assessment and review procedure unless such project falls within the jurisdictions of both Québec and Canada or unless such project is located in part in the Territory and in part elsewhere where an impact review process is required. [Emphasis added.]

Section 22.6.7 thus creates two exceptions to the general rule that a development project will be subject to only one environmental assessment process: where the project itself falls within the jurisdictions of both the federal and provincial governments, and where the project is located partly in the Territory and partly in an area outside the Territory where an environmental assessment is required. The question is whether, because the impact of the Project on fish habitat — a matter of federal jurisdiction — brings it "within the jurisdictions of both Québec and Canada", the first exception applies to override the general rule of only one assessment.

[132] Those arguing that the answer to this question is yes also rely on s. 22.7.5, which reads as follows:

22.7.5   Nothing in the present Section shall be construed as imposing an impact assessment review procedure by the Federal Government unless required by Federal law or regulation. However, this shall not operate to preclude Federal requirement for an additional Federal impact review process as a condition of Federal funding of any development project.

There is no suggestion that the Project has received any federal funding to which an environmental assessment could be attached as a condition. If it had received such funding, the federal government would be perfectly entitled to require an additional environmental assessment. Whether an additional federal assessment of the Project is required by s. 22.7.5 therefore depends on the interpretation of that provision's first sentence. But that sentence says nothing more than that s. 22 does not impose any obligations on the federal government other than those ordinarily required by general federal law or regulation. In view of the parties' express intention that the Agreement constitute a comprehensive governance scheme for the entire Territory, that there be no other government assessment process, that there be no parallel process in the Agreement itself, that it provide for only one environmental assessment as the general rule, and that it be paramount over all other laws of general application that are inconsistent with it, s. 22.7.5 cannot be interpreted as triggering a separate federal environmental assessment of the Project under the *CEAA*. To agree that the *CEAA* should prevail over the specific provisions of the Agreement would be to subvert the constitutional ordering established and intended by the parties to the Agreement.

[133] Section 22.7.5 must be understood for what it really is: a transitional provision. ... The effect of s. 22.7.5 is that there was to be no federal assessment process until the implementing statute came into force,

at which time the one provided for in the Agreement would be established. If s. 22.7.5 were read as a permanent provision, it would literally say that the federal assessment process under the Agreement will never be applicable and that only a process provided for in other federal legislation will be. As discussed, the Agreement explicitly provides that it is without force of law until legislation, both federal and provincial, is enacted to enforce it. A mechanism was needed to address the application of the law during the period between the signing of the Agreement and its coming into force. ... Section 22.7.5 was therefore included in order to fill this potential legal vacuum, and it would apply to environmental matters until the coming into force of the authorizing legislation. As a result, during the transitional period, the Agreement would not require the federal government to conduct an evaluation process that was not otherwise required under existing federal law. However, the parties judged it necessary to further specify that the federal government was entitled, as a condition of federal funding for any development project, to require an environmental assessment on a purely administrative basis.

[134] The issue, then, is whether the more general exception in s. 22.6.7 applies in this case. More specifically, it must be determined whether the Project is a project "within the jurisdictions of both Québec and Canada" for the purpose of triggering a separate assessment process. From this perspective, it is clear that s. 22, when read as a whole, provides that it is the constitutional jurisdiction applicable to the *nature* of a project that determines which environmental assessment is to be conducted. The Project falls within exclusive provincial jurisdiction and therefore does not fall within both federal and provincial jurisdiction, which means that the exception to the general rule in s. 22.6.7 does not apply. More fundamentally, nothing in the language of s. 22 supports the conclusion that a project's impact can trigger a second environmental review process where the project itself falls within the jurisdiction of one government and it has effects that fall within that of the other government.

[135] If we were to accept the argument that a project's impact could trigger a separate environmental review process, the consequence would be to turn the exception into the rule. Such a conclusion would directly contradict the clear intention of the parties. ...

[136] The signatories to the Agreement were extremely careful to distinguish between projects within federal jurisdiction and those within provincial jurisdiction. The general rule is that there is to be only one environmental assessment and that which one is to be conducted depends on the jurisdiction within which the project itself falls; and there are only two narrow exceptions to this rule. Moreover, in the limited circumstances in which two assessments are required, the Agreement clearly states that the assessments may be combined only with the mutual consent of the parties (s. 22.6.7). If this Court were to find that jurisdiction for environmental assessment purposes depends on both the nature and the impact of a project, the distinctions the parties were so careful to draw would become meaningless. The parties drew these distinctions for a reason, and the Court ought to give effect to them.

[137] A further, related reason exists for concluding that a project's impact cannot trigger a separate environmental assessment process. The Agreement concerns Aboriginal peoples and their territory as well as the environment. The first of these matters is within the exclusive jurisdiction of the federal government, while the second falls within shared provincial and federal jurisdiction. Therefore, *any* proposed project falling within provincial jurisdiction will necessarily have an effect on a federal head of power. If two environmental assessment processes were required every time a project had an effect on either of these two matters, the exception of more than one process would become the rule. ...

[138] The provisions of s. 22, and the objectives and principles that underlie the Agreement as a whole, lead to the conclusion that the Project is subject to a provincial environmental assessment only. The Agreement, which is of course both a s. 35 treaty and an intergovernmental agreement that was made binding by way of statutory implementation, involves no inappropriate delegation of jurisdiction or legislative authority. A plain reading of the Agreement against the backdrop of the circumstances and context in which it was negotiated, drafted, signed and given statutory authorization indicates that it was intended to establish a comprehensive and exhaustive scheme for the governance and management of the Territory and that it is paramount over all other federal and provincial laws of general application to the extent of any inconsistency. It cannot be altered or modified without the consent of all the signatories.

[139] It is also important to stress that s. 22 explicitly addresses the role and participatory rights of the Cree in the environmental assessment process. They have both a substantive and a procedural role at each and every stage of that process. All the section's provisions in combination ensure the continued participation of the Territory's Aboriginal inhabitants in the management, control and regulation of development in the Territory. Finally, the Agreement must now be unequivocally understood as a constitutional document that protects rights. Its status is thus not simply supra-legislative.

[140] A reading of s. 22 as a whole indicates that it is the nature of the project that triggers the applicable environmental assessment process and that the general rule is that there is to be only one assessment process. The Project falls within provincial jurisdiction, which means that there is no basis for setting up a joint review body. The federal process under the *CEAA*, which does not provide for either substantive or procedural participation by the Cree, is inconsistent with the provisions of the Agreement and cannot apply.

[141] The *CEAA* was enacted after the Agreement had been signed and implemented by statute. It is clear from the Agreement and its authorizing legislation that neither party can unilaterally modify its terms. In light of the constitutional normative hierarchy, the *CEAA* cannot prevail to impose a parallel process in addition to the ones provided for in the Agreement. ... The federal government is therefore prohibited from effectively and unilaterally modifying the procedure established by the Agreement, or

derogating from the rights provided for in the Agreement, by purporting to attach conditions based on external legislation of general application.

[142] The practical effect of this interpretation is that, if the Minister determines that a permit must be issued under the *Fisheries Act*, the Minister must issue one on the basis of the environmental processes established by the Agreement and cannot insist that an additional environmental process be undertaken pursuant to the *CEAA*. The environmental review process under the James Bay Agreement is paramount.

V.   Conclusion

[143] For these reasons, we would allow the appeal ... .

Appeal allowed.

Does the Supreme Court's judgment in *Moses* provide much of a distinction between the interpretation of historic treaties and modern land claims agreements like the *James Bay and Northern Quebec Agreement*? What are the primary distinctions that you have uncovered from the judgment? Are they significant in your opinion? Finally, do they provide sufficient guidance for future interpretations of modern treaties and land claims agreements, as distinguished from historic treaties?

Shortly after *Moses*, the Supreme Court had another opportunity to contemplate how to appropriately interpret a modern land claims agreement in *Beckman v. Little Salmon/Carmacks First Nation*, [2010] S.C.J. No. 53, 2010 SCC 53 (S.C.C.). What distinguishes that case from *Moses* is that, in interpreting the treaty in question, the Supreme Court placed far more emphasis on balancing the interpretation of the treaty with the Crown's duty to consult, a topic that is discussed extensively in Chapter 5. The majority judgment in *Beckman v. Little Salmon/Carmacks First Nation* does provide some useful statements about the nature of modern treaties and land claims agreements that are useful to consider here:

> [8] Historically, treaties were the means by which the Crown sought to reconcile the Aboriginal inhabitants of what is now Canada to the assertion of European sovereignty over the territories traditionally occupied by First Nations. The objective was not only to build alliances with First Nations but to keep the peace and to open up the major part of those territories to colonization and settlement. No treaties were signed with the Yukon First Nations until modern times.

> [9] Unlike their historical counterparts, the modern comprehensive treaty is the product of lengthy negotiations between well-resourced and sophisticated parties. The negotiation costs to Yukon First Nations of their various treaties, financed by the federal government through reimbursable loans, were enormous. The LSCFN share alone exceeded seven million dollars. Under the Yukon treaties, the Yukon First Nations surrendered their Aboriginal rights in almost 484,000 square kilometres, roughly the size of

Spain, in exchange for defined treaty rights in respect of land tenure and a quantum of settlement land (41,595 square kilometres), access to Crown lands, fish and wildlife harvesting, heritage resources, financial compensation, and participation in the management of public resources. To this end, the LSCFN Treaty creates important institutions of self-government and authorities such as the Yukon Environmental and Socio-economic Assessment Board and the Carmacks Renewable Resources Council, whose members are jointly nominated by the First Nation and the territorial government.

[10] The reconciliation of Aboriginal and non-Aboriginal Canadians in a mutually respectful long-term relationship is the grand purpose of s. 35 of the *Constitution Act, 1982*. The modern treaties, including those at issue here, attempt to further the objective of reconciliation not only by addressing grievances over the land claims but by creating the legal basis to foster a positive long-term relationship between Aboriginal and non-Aboriginal communities. Thoughtful administration of the treaty will help manage, even if it fails to eliminate, some of the misunderstandings and grievances that have characterized the past. Still, as the facts of this case show, the treaty will not accomplish its purpose if it is interpreted by territorial officials in an ungenerous manner or as if it were an everyday commercial contract. The treaty is as much about building relationships as it is about the settlement of ancient grievances. The future is more important than the past. A canoeist who hopes to make progress faces forwards, not backwards.

[11] Equally, however, the LSCFN is bound to recognize that the $34 million and other treaty benefits it received in exchange for the surrender has earned the territorial government a measure of flexibility in taking up surrendered lands for other purposes.

[12] The increased detail and sophistication of modern treaties represents a quantum leap beyond the pre-Confederation historical treaties such as the 1760-61 Treaty at issue in *R. v. Marshall*, [1999] 3 S.C.R. 456, and post-Confederation treaties such as Treaty No. 8 (1899) at issue in *R. v. Badger*, [1996] 1 S.C.R. 771, and *Mikisew Cree First Nation v. Canada (Minister of Canadian Heritage)*, 2005 SCC 69, [2005] 3 S.C.R. 388. The historical treaties were typically expressed in lofty terms of high generality and were often ambiguous. The courts were obliged to resort to general principles (such as the honour of the Crown) to fill the gaps and achieve a fair outcome. Modern comprehensive land claim agreements, on the other hand, starting perhaps with the *James Bay and Northern Québec Agreement* (1975), while still to be interpreted and applied in a manner that upholds the honour of the Crown, were nevertheless intended to create some precision around property and governance rights and obligations. Instead of *ad hoc* remedies to smooth the way to reconciliation, the modern treaties are designed to place Aboriginal and non-Aboriginal relations in the mainstream legal system with its advantages of continuity, transparency, and predictability. It is up to the parties, when treaty issues arise, to act diligently to advance their respective interests. Good government requires that decisions be taken in a timely way. ...

The remainder of the Supreme Court's judgment in *Beckman v. Little Salmon/Carmacks First Nation* is reproduced in Chapter 5.

J. CONCLUSION

Treaty jurisprudence in Canada has changed considerably in recent years, especially since the adoption and development of the canons of treaty interpretation. That change is still ongoing, as witnessed by the criticism levied against the interpretive canons in cases such as *Horse* and *Howard* and their subsequent reaffirmation in *Marshall, Sappier and Gray* and *Morris*. Governmental, public and judicial attitudes towards treaties continue to provide significant obstacles to achieving contextually and culturally appropriate understandings of treaties as solemn compacts between the Crown and Aboriginal peoples, as opposed to mere contractual agreements.

Consider the approach to treaties articulated in the following excerpt.

JOHN BORROWS, "GROUND RULES: INDIGENOUS TREATIES AND LEGAL FOUNDATIONS"

(2006) 36 N.Z.U. L. Rev. 188 at 195, 197-98 (references omitted)

Treaties between the Crown and indigenous peoples can be a vital part of Canada's … political and legal geology. They could be said to underlie the countries' political orders because they allowed for settlement and development of large portions of country, while at the same time promising certainty for indigenous peoples possession, governance and livelihood. They are also crucial because they can implement indigenous law by grounding indigenous peoples' deepest obligations to the Creator and others in a framework of reciprocity and mutual exchange. …

Most discussions of this issue have focused on indigenous peoples' rights under the treaties. For example, people have debated the meaning of indigenous rights to education, treasures, and intellectual property. There has also been much focus on Indian rights to fish, hunt, log, mine, and receive assistance through money, goods, or services. While these are important inquiries, they miss a fundamental aspect of the treaty relationship. *Indigenous peoples are not the only beneficiaries under the treaties. Non-indigenous peoples also have treaty rights.* As the Supreme Court of the United States recognised in the *Winans* case: "treaty rights are a grant of rights *from* the Indians, not *to* the Indians".

This approach to treaties implies non-indigenous peoples received rights in Canada … from a grant to the Crown by the Indians (as well as other sources such as Crown prerogative, the common law and imperial legislation). Both groups are recipients of promises and bearers of obligations made in the negotiation process; both have treaty rights and responsibilities. As noted, this mutuality is frequently overlooked because indigenous peoples are most often striving to assert their rights. The Crown has had an easier time because it controls the legislative and judicial processes. However there are a number of potential inheritors of treaty rights beyond indigenous nations … The Canadian … Crown certainly received many benefits from the treaties. Their citizens were able to settle and develop large parts of the country with the prior residents' permission. Non-indigenous people could trace many of their entitlements to the consent granted to the Crown by indigenous peoples in the treaty process.

Yet, the notion that non-indigenous peoples might trace certain rights to land or governance through the treaties is, for many, still an emergent concept. Because people have not been exposed to indigenous treaty perspectives, or have not had the time to learn about them, they are only now considering them in this light.

For example, Professor Noel Lyon, who taught for thirty years at Queen's Law School in Kingston, Ontario, Canada, illustrated this point after listening to First Nations elders in Saskatchewan. He said:

> Over the last couple of days as I've listened to the Elders, I have begun to understand that what I've learned about Aboriginal peoples and their situation in Canada has largely come from written sources, from books, and there are a lot of things that were embedded in my legal education that I haven't overcome. The most important one, I think, is that law school indoctrinated me with the belief that the Crown is all powerful, and I think that's a real problem, because I think legal education has a tendency to regard the Crown almost in the way that the First Nations people regard the Creator — as being the source of all things. And from that flows the proposition that the treaties are seen by the non-Aboriginal community as just another body of laws that define the status and rights of Aboriginal peoples, rather than seeing the treaties as a nation-to-nation partnership, intersocietal law. ... It had never occurred to me until Elder Crowe said this yesterday or the day before, that the right of the "white" people to be on this land is founded in the treaty.

... [A]ll people in Canada ... could benefit from calling the treaties their own. It could add an important dimension to our self-understanding as a country. It could build it on a normative base of peace, friendship, respect, consent and cooperation. In this light, the history of Canada is about more than conquering the wilderness, slowly separating from England, and building (then partially dismantling) the welfare state. The country has a broader normative foundations than guarantees of individual liberties through rights documents. If treaties are considered foundational agreements, they allow all to claim their place in their country, not through force, but through peace and agreement.

The Royal Commission on Aboriginal Peoples recommended that the federal government take steps to demonstrate the Crown's commitment to the treaties. To that end, it proposed that the House of Commons and the Senate, by joint resolution, request that the Queen issue a royal proclamation that would establish "a new era of respect for the treaties". This proclamation would, among other things, reaffirm the principles espoused by the *Royal Proclamation of 1763*, R.S.C. 1985, App. II, No. 1 (refer back to the discussion of this document in Chapter 1), acknowledge the detrimental effects suffered by Aboriginal peoples from past governmental practices, and commit the Crown to redressing past breaches of treaty and other obligations.

Along with this royal proclamation, the Royal Commission advocated the introduction of companion legislation to provide symbolic and legal force to the principles contained in the proclamation. It has recommended that this treaty legislation should achieve the following objectives:

1. It should provide for the implementation of existing treaty rights, including the rights to hunt, fish and trap.
2. It should affirm liberal rules of interpretation of treaties, having regard to the context of treaty negotiations, the spirit and intent of each treaty, and the special relationship between the treaty parties, and acknowledge the admissibility of oral and secondary evidence in the courts to make determinations with respect to treaty rights.
3. It should declare the commitment of Parliament and government of Canada to the implementation and renewal of each treaty on the basis of the spirit and intent of the treaty and the relationship embodied in it.
4. It should commit the government of Canada to treaty processes to clarify, implement and, where the parties agree, amend the terms of treaties so as to give effect to the spirit and intent of each treaty and the relationship embodied in it.
5. It should commit the government of Canada to a process of treaty-making with Aboriginal nations that do not yet have a treaty with the Crown and with treaty nations whose treaty does not purport to address land and resource issues.
6. It should clarify that defining the scope of governance for Aboriginal and treaty nations is a vital part of the treaties.
7. It should authorize establishment of the institutions necessary to fulfil the treaty process in consultation with treaty nations.[12]

The proposed royal proclamation would supplement and form a part of the Canadian Constitution, thus serving a similar function as the *Royal Proclamation of 1763* does through the incorporation of its principles in section 25 of the *Constitution Act, 1982* (as discussed in Chapter 3). Although the Commission's recommendations are geared towards federal legislation, it suggests that provincial and territorial governments also participate in this treaty affirmation and renewal process. It remains to be seen whether the federal government would be willing to consider adopting such proposals. In the meantime, it should be asked whether these proposals are feasible and what effect they would have, if any, on existing judicial interpretations of treaties.

ENDNOTES

1. L.I. Rotman, *Parallel Paths: Fiduciary Doctrine and the Crown-Native Relationship in Canada* (Toronto: University of Toronto Press, 1996) at 38-39.

2. As quoted in R. White, *The Middle Ground: Indians, Empires, and Republics in the Great Lakes Region, 1650-1815* (Cambridge: Cambridge University Press, 1991) at 256.

3. D.N. Sprague, "Canada's Treaties with Aboriginal Peoples" (1996) 23 Man. L.J. 341 at 345-46.

4. See Governor Douglas to the Secretary of State for the Colonies, 25 March 1861, British Columbia, *Paper Connected with the Indian Land Question, 1850-1875* (Victoria: Government Printer, 1875) at 19.

5. See Wilson Duff, "The Fort Victoria Treaties" (1969) 3 B.C. Studies 3-57.

6. Report of the Government of British Columbia on the Subject of Indian Reserves, 1875 at 11.

7. Joseph McKay to J.S. Helmcken, Letter of December 3, 1888.

8. Chris Arnett, *The Terror of the Coast* (Burnaby, B.C.: Talon Books, 1999) at 35.

9. Dennis Madill, *British Columbia Indian Treaties in Historical Perspective* (Ottawa: Treaties and Historical Research Centre, Department of Indian Affairs and Northern Development, 1984).

10 (Vancouver: U.B.C. Press, 1974) at 173.

11. Hamar Foster, "The Saanicton Bay Marina Case: Imperial Law, Colonial History and Competing Theories of Aboriginal Title" (1989) 23 U.B.C. L. Rev. 629 at 632.

12. Royal Commission on Aboriginal Peoples, *Report of the Royal Commission on Aboriginal Peoples, Restructuring the Relationship, Volume II, Part I* (Ottawa: Minister of Supply and Services Canada, 1996) at 67.

CHAPTER 5

CROWN OBLIGATIONS

A. INTRODUCTION

The notion that the Crown has legally binding obligations towards Aboriginal peoples in Canada is indisputable. This statement would appear uncontroversial, particularly in light of the entrenchment of section 35 of the *Constitution Act, 1982* (being Schedule B to the *Canada Act 1982* (U.K.), 1982, c. 11) and its recognition and affirmation of existing Aboriginal and treaty rights. For many years, however, Canadian courts seemed unwilling to recognize the legally binding nature of Crown obligations to Aboriginal peoples. Indeed, prior to the landmark judgment in *Calder v. British Columbia (Attorney General)*, [1973] S.C.J. No. 56, [1973] S.C.R. 313 (S.C.C.) (which is excerpted in Chapter 3), Canadian courts largely described the Crown's duties to Aboriginal peoples as political and therefore not enforceable in courts of law. Thus, in 1887, Justice Taschereau of the Supreme Court of Canada described the Crown's duty towards Aboriginal peoples as a "sacred political obligation, in the execution of which the state must be free from judicial control" (*St. Catherine's Milling and Lumber Co. v. R.* (1887), 13 S.C.R. 577 at 649 (S.C.C.)). A year later, Lord Watson of the Judicial Committee of the Privy Council wrote that "the tenure of the Indians was a personal and usufructuary right, dependent upon the good will of the Sovereign" (*St. Catherine's Milling & Lumber Co. v. R.* (1888), 14 App. Cas. 46 (J.C.P.C.)). In 1897 the Privy Council labelled treaty promises to Indians as "nothing more than a personal obligation" (*Attorney-General of Ontario v. Attorney General of Canada: Re Indian Claims*, [1897] A.C. 199 at 213 (J.C.P.C.). Over 60 years later, Justice Rand found the government only had political obligations to Aboriginal peoples (*St. Ann's Island Shooting and Fishing Club Ltd. v. Canada*, [1950] S.C.J. No. 2, [1950] S.C.R. 211 (S.C.C.)). The judicial hesitancy to impose legal obligations on governments existed despite numerous government promises towards Aboriginal peoples, including executive proclamations, treaties, and the nature of the parties' relationship.

This situation only began to truly change in 1973, after the Supreme Court of Canada recognized that the Nisga'a people had *legally enforceable* rights in the *Calder* case. In *Calder*, it was said that Aboriginal possession could be enforced by the courts and given the force of law if its constituent elements were proven. The Court found the source of these rights originated from "the fact that when the settlers came, the Indians were there, organized in societies and occupying the land as their forefathers had done for centuries". It found the scope of these rights were dependent upon historic use and the intention of the legislature to permit their continuance. These declarations brought Aboriginal rights squarely into Canada's legal structure. Subsequently, and as a direct result of the *Calder* case, the Supreme Court of Canada wrote in 2002 that "recognition of aboriginal rights could not be treated merely as an act of grace and favour on the part of the Crown" (*Wewaykum Indian Band v. Canada*, [2002] S.C.J. No. 79, [2002] 4 S.C.R. 245 at 73 (S.C.C.)).

Despite *Calder*'s broad declarations, the Nisga'a failed to secure recognition of their title because they did not have a *fiat justicia* from the Lieutenant Governor of British Columbia that gave them permission to sue the Crown. The Supreme Court found it lacked jurisdiction to decide the case in the absence of the Crown's express willingness to be sued. The requirement for permission squarely raised the notion that Aboriginal rights were related to Crown obligations. If the Crown did not give its consent it was not obliged to answer the case against it. The Crown had sovereign immunity. The Nisga'a could not secure a declaration of title if the Crown did not obligate itself to be sued. As has been observed, the Crown was hesitant to grant a *fiat* to Indigenous peoples in British Columbia because if the courts found in their favour it could drastically undermine Crown land claims and "jeopardize the very large sums of money already invested" in the province.[1] Despite this hurdle, Aboriginal rights have become an integral part of the legal framework of Canada.

What does the recognition of the Crown's legally enforceable obligations to Aboriginal peoples mean for Aboriginal and non-Aboriginal peoples in Canada? What does it mean for Canadian law? Consider the following suggestions.

LET OBLIGATIONS BE DONE

John Borrows (footnotes omitted)

Crown obligations towards Aboriginal peoples are part of Canada's hidden constitution. Commentators have largely overlooked them yet they lie on the frontier of Canada's constitutional development. This fact should be highlighted and Canada's constitutional vision re-focused.

There is a great need for a different kind of legal analysis related to Aboriginal issues which explicitly focuses on Crown obligations. The reciprocal relationship between Aboriginal rights and Crown obligations remains under-theorized and largely unrecognized. This needs to change because rights exist within relationships. Whenever a right exists, a correlative obligation can be found. As W.N. Hohfeld observed: "[A] duty is the invariable correlative of that legal relation which is most properly called a right or claim" (See Wesley Newcomb Hohfeld, *Fundamental Legal Conceptions*, edited by Walter Wheeler Cook (New Haven and London: Yale University Press, 1919) at 35-64). "A duty or a legal obligation is that which one ought or ought not to do. 'Duty' and 'right' are correlative terms. When a right is invaded, a duty is violated" (*Lake Shore & M. S. R. Co. v. Kurtz*, (1894) 10 Ind. App., 60; 37 N.E., 303, 304, cited in Hohfeld,

Ibid.). This is the case with Aboriginal rights in Canada. Wherever an Aboriginal right exists a correlative governmental obligation can be found.

In 1982 when Aboriginal rights were placed in section 35 of Canada's Constitution, Crown obligations followed. Aboriginal rights are severely constrained unless governments have a legal duty to honour Aboriginal peoples' rights. Governments are interposed between Aboriginal peoples and others when it comes to dealing with Aboriginal rights, and thus governments have the greatest potential to erode those rights if they do not possess firm legal obligations (*Canadian Pacific Ltd. v. Paul*, [1988] 2 S.C.R. 654 at p. 677). Historically, government power lead to the imposition of weakened government obligations in those situations where Aboriginal rights were involved. The enactment of section 35(1) strengthened these obligations; in the words of Justice Binnie: it converted them into "sterner stuff" (*R. v. Marshall*, [1999] 3 S.C.R. 456 at para. 48). In *R. v. Sparrow*, the leading case interpreting section 35(1), the Court wrote that "recognition and affirmation [of Aboriginal rights]...import some restraint on the exercise of sovereign power" at 1109. Governmental obligations flow from the limitations placed on Crown sovereignty under section 35(1).

The reconciliation of rights and obligations required under section 35(1) is best obtained through a large, liberal and generous conception of its constitutional purpose. A broad conceptualization of section 35(1) is consistent with the court's purposive approach to section 35(1): "to reconcile the prior presence of aboriginal peoples in North America with the assertion of Crown sovereignty" (*Delgamuukw v. British Columbia*, [1997] 3 S.C.R. 1010 at 141). Mutual isolation is not the constitutional objective underlying section 35(1) (*Mitchell v. M.N.R.*, [2001] 1 S.C.R. 911 at para. 133). Therefore, section 35(1) must be read in a way that incorporates reciprocity. Aboriginal rights have correlative legal consequences, as Hohfeld's theoretical framework suggests. Section 35(1) could thus be seen as incorporating Crown obligations. If this were the case section 35(1) could be read in the following light:

> The existing *Crown* and treaty *obligations* of the *Crown in right of Canada and the provinces* are hereby recognized and affirmed.

This broader conceptualization of section 35(1) places the Crown more squarely in the analysis. It appropriately shifts the focus from Aboriginal peoples to the Crown in a more significant way in working out the section's scope, content and meaning. More relevant and wider remedies to implement Aboriginal rights can be canvassed when the Crown's obligations become more visible within section 35(1).

Just as the recognition of the justiciability of Aboriginal rights in *Calder* was consistent with Canada's legal traditions, the recognition and affirmation of Crown obligations under section 35(1) does not represent a break with Canada's constitutional order. Constraints on Crown sovereignty are consistent with Canada's democratic traditions. The Crown's subjection to the rule of law is at the centre of the nation's political values. Constraints on Crown sovereignty have often been heralded as great breakthroughs for furthering human rights and liberty. For example, many proclaim the date 1215 as significant because the issuance of Magna Carta gave rights to certain classes of individuals relative to the Crown, which expanded through time. Despite its limitations, Magna Carta is applied and commemorated, and is not seen as threatening but supporting Canada's political order. Constraints on the Crown can be a good thing. Similarly, the Glorious Revolution of 1688 in England, where the Crown's authority was made subject to Parliament, is held in high esteem in our democratic traditions. The English Bill of Rights, which flowed from the Revolution, obligated the Crown to raise and spend money with the consent of elected Parliamentary officials, and not of its own accord (*An Act Declaring the Rights and Liberties of the Subject and Settling the Succession of the Crown*, 1689). Judges, lawyers, politicians and the public often refer to the Glorious Revolution as an important source of political authority and regard it as a cornerstone of liberty. British North Americans enjoyed similar restraints to the exercise of Crown prerogatives when Responsible Government came to non-Aboriginal Canadians in the 1850's in the Canada's and the Atlantic colonies. Furthermore, the American and French revolutions of the late 1700's, which also purported to restrain Crown sovereignty relative to individual rights, are also regarded as essential step in democracy's development. Canada's own *Charter of Rights and Freedoms* is in this tradition.

Constraints on Crown actions under section 35(1) should be seen as flowing from this same tradition. There are sound reasons for ensuring that political authority is subject to proper checks and balances. Recognizing Crown obligations relative to Aboriginal peoples is a part of this process. The Supreme Court has been clear that Crown constraints are a part of section 35(1)'s framework. As they observed in the leading case of *R. v. Sparrow*:

> Section 35 calls for a just settlement for aboriginal peoples. It renounces the old rules of the game under which the Crown established courts of law and denied those courts the authority to question sovereign claims made by the Crown. *R. v. Sparrow*, 70 D.L.R. (4th) 385 at 412.

Crown sovereignty is constrained under section 35(1) by its obligations to Aboriginal peoples. The Court has jurisdiction to question the Crown's actions, without an aggrieved party seeking permission from the Crown as required in the *Calder* case. These constraints on government action could be regarded in the same light as the Magna Carta, the Glorious Revolution, Responsible Government and Bills of Rights. Each development significantly restricted the Crown's scope of authority relative to a significant section of the body politic. Freedom was increased when the Crown was obliged to observe constitutional limitations on its power; section 35(1) falls within this tradition.

. . . . .

The Crown also has many voluntary obligations owed to Aboriginal peoples assumed through agreements in treaties, interim measures, contracts, executive proclamations and legislative provisions. Voluntary obligations are generally easier to encourage, monitor and enforce because their adherents freely and consciously make them. One would expect that the Crown's conscious choice to undertake obligations would make their enforcement easier. However, this has not generally been Aboriginal peoples' experience. This must change for Canada's democratic tradition to grow and become applicable to all the people living in this land.

B. THE HONOUR OF THE CROWN

There is a nascent but perceptible change in the Court's approach to Crown obligations relative to Aboriginal peoples in Canada in the past few decades. In the preceding chapters we have already seen many obligations enforced against the federal and provincial governments through the justification analysis developed by the courts relative to section 35(1). The underlying elements of these obligations are nurtured by a concept that has come to be known as the "honour of the Crown".

The "honour of the Crown" has historically been articulated predominantly in the context of Crown-Aboriginal treaty relations. Reference should be made to the discussion of the *Treaty of Albany, 1664* and the Covenant Chain alliance discussed in Chapter 1. Indeed, recognition of the honour of the Crown in the treaty context may be traced to the early stages of Crown-Aboriginal treaty-making. In a letter to the Lords of Trade in 1756, Sir William Johnson, Superintendent-General of Indian Affairs, indicated the need to maintain the honour of the Crown in its relations with the Aboriginal peoples:

> At this critical and interesting conjecture I am sensible the utmost attention be paid to our Indian Alliance and no measures left untried that may have the least tendancy [sic] to strengthen and increase it. Wherefore I would humbly propose a steady and uniform method of conduct, a religious regard to our engagements with them a more unanimous and vigorous extension of our strength than hitherto, and a tender care to protect them and all their Lands against the insults and encroachments of the Common enemy as the most and only effectual method to attach them firmly to the British Interest, and engage them to act heartily in our favour at this or any other time.[2]

One notable example of the recognition of the honour of the Crown in early Canadian jurisprudence may be seen in Gwynne J.'s dissenting judgment in *Ontario v. Dominion of Canada and Province of Quebec: In re Indian Claims*, [1896] 25 S.C.R. 434 at 511-12 (S.C.C.):

> ... [W]hat is contended for and must not be lost sight of, is that the British sovereigns, ever since the acquisition of Canada, have been pleased to adopt the rule or practice of entering into agreement with the Indian nations or tribes in their province of Canada, for the cession or surrender by them of what such sovereigns have been pleased to designate the Indian title, by

instruments similar to these now under consideration to which they have been pleased to give the designation of "treaties" with the Indians in possession of and claiming title to the lands expressed to be surrendered by the instruments, and further that the terms and conditions expressed in those instruments as to be performed by or on behalf of the Crown, have always been regarded as involving a trust graciously assumed by the Crown to the fulfilment of which with the Indians the faith and honour of the Crown is pledged, and which trust has always been most faithfully fulfilled as a treaty obligation of the Crown.

In that same case, Sedgewick J. added to Justice Gwynne's sentiment when he explained, *ibid.* at 535, that "in all questions between Her Majesty and 'Her faithful Indian allies' there must be on her part, and on the part of those who represent her, not only good faith, but more, there must not only be justice, but generosity."

Some 70 years later, in *R. v. George*, [1966] S.C.J. No. 7, [1966] S.C.R. 267, 55 D.L.R. (2d) 386 at 396-97 (S.C.C.), Cartwright J. re-emphasized the importance of these sentiments when he said:

> We should, I think, endeavour to construe the treaty of 1827 and those Acts of Parliament which bear upon the question before us in such manner that the honour of the Sovereign may be upheld and Parliament not made subject to the reproach of having taken away by unilateral action and without consideration the rights solemnly assured to the Indians and their posterity by treaty.

The judicial entrenchment of the honour of the Crown as a fundamental element of Crown-Aboriginal treaties was made explicit in *R. v. Badger*, [1996] S.C.J. No. 39, [1996] 1 S.C.R. 771, [1996] 2 C.N.L.R. 77 at 92 (S.C.C.), where Cory J. stated that:

> ... the honour of the Crown is always at stake in its dealings with Indian people. Interpretations of treaties and statutory provisions which have an impact upon treaty or aboriginal rights must be approached in a manner which maintains the integrity of the Crown. It is always assumed that the Crown intends to fulfil its promises. No appearance of "sharp dealing" will be sanctioned.

Since *Badger*, the honour of the Crown has remained an important element of Crown-Aboriginal treaty rights jurisprudence. The honour of the Crown is not limited to the Crown's treaty obligations, however. It is also foundational to the understanding of Crown-Aboriginal relations as fiduciary, notwithstanding Justice Binnie's curious statement in *Wewaykum Indian Band v. Canada*, [2002] S.C.J. No. 79, [2002] 4 S.C.R. 245 (S.C.C.) at para. 80 that "[s]omewhat associated with the ethical standards required of a fiduciary in the context of the Crown and Aboriginal peoples is the need to uphold the 'honour of the Crown'". The honour of the Crown, expressed through its fiduciary duty, limits the Crown's discretion to act with respect to Aboriginal interests. This may be seen both in regard to private interests, such as the alienation of Aboriginal reserve lands, or *vis-à-vis* Crown legislative jurisdiction over Aboriginal peoples and their lands. As suggested by Judge David Arnot, the Treaty Commissioner for Saskatchewan, in "Treaties as a Bridge to the Future"...

The Supreme Court of Canada's unanimous rebuke of government privilege in *R. v. Guerin* is the milestone in restoring a system of law based on principles of fundamental justice over the exercise of individual discretion. In defining the "fiduciary duty" of the Crown, the Supreme Court restored the concept of holding ministers to a standard of fairness that demands forethought as to what conduct lends credibility and honour to the Crown, instead of what conduct can be technically justified under the current law.[3]

With the entrenchment of section 35(1) of the *Constitution Act, 1982*, the honour of the Crown was found to have limited the Crown's discretion in exercising its legislative power over Aboriginal peoples. As the Court explained this effect in *R. v. Sparrow*, [1990] S.C.J. No. 49, 70 D.L.R. (4th) 385 at 409 (S.C.C.):

> Federal legislative powers continue, including, of course, the right to legislate with respect to Indians pursuant to s. 91(24) of the *Constitution Act, 1867*. These powers must, however, now be read together with section 35(1). In other words, federal power must be reconciled with federal duty and the best way to achieve that reconciliation is to demand the justification of any governmental regulation that infringes upon or denies aboriginal rights. Such scrutiny is in keeping with the liberal interpretive principles enunciated in *Nowegijick* ... and the concept of holding the Crown to a high standard of honourable dealing with respect to the aboriginal peoples of Canada as suggested by *Guerin* ...

Unlike the long-standing association of the honour of the Crown with treaties and treaty relations, however, the notion that the honour of the Crown created fiduciary duties owed by the Crown to Aboriginal peoples is of far more recent vintage. Even more recent still is that the honour of the Crown has created yet another source of legally binding Crown obligation — the Crown's duty to consult with Aboriginal peoples — as a result of the Supreme Court of Canada's judgments in *Haida Nation v. British Columbia (Minister of Forests)*, [2004] S.C.J. No. 70, [2004] 3 S.C.R. 511 (S.C.C.) and *Taku River Tlingit First Nation v. British Columbia (Project Assessment Director)*, [2004] S.C.J. No. 69, [2004] 3 S.C.R. 550 (S.C.C.). These offshoots from the honour of the Crown will be discussed in turn.

C. FIDUCIARY LAW

In the grand scheme of Canadian Aboriginal rights jurisprudence, fiduciary law is a relatively recent addition. In the brief time that it has been a part of Aboriginal rights law, it has captured the imagination of scholars, judges, and Aboriginal peoples alike. The high profile that fiduciary law enjoys within Canadian Aboriginal rights jurisprudence cloaks the fact that the first Canadian judicial characterization of the relationship between the Crown and Aboriginal peoples as fiduciary occurred in 1984 in the Supreme Court of Canada's landmark decision in *Guerin v. R.*, [1984] S.C.J. No. 45, [1984] 2 S.C.R. 335, [1984] 6 W.W.R. 481, 59 B.C.L.R. 301, [1985] 1 C.N.L.R. 120, 20 E.T.R. 6, 36 R.P.R. 1 (*sub nom. Guerin v. Canada*), 55 N.R. 161, 13 D.L.R. (4th) 321 (S.C.C.).

The casual manner in which fiduciary law is discussed in the context of Crown-Native relations implies a sophisticated understanding of the ramifications of applying fiduciary doctrine to that relationship. This picture painted by many existing judicial and academic commentaries on the subject is misleading. The application of fiduciary law to Crown-Native relations is neither a finished work nor even a nearly completed one. As illustrated in the following excerpt, fiduciary law's connection to Crown-Native relations remains a project in its infancy.

LEONARD I. ROTMAN, PARALLEL PATHS: FIDUCIARY DOCTRINE AND THE CROWN-NATIVE RELATIONSHIP IN CANADA

(Toronto: University of Toronto Press, 1996) at 3-4, 11-18
(references omitted)

In the 1984 landmark case of *Guerin v. R.*, the Supreme Court of Canada unanimously declared that the Crown is bound by fiduciary obligations to the aboriginal peoples of Canada. By determining that the nature of the Crown's obligation to aboriginal peoples is fiduciary, hence, legal rather than merely political or moral, the Supreme Court of Canada blazed a new path in Canadian aboriginal rights jurisprudence. Yet, more than ten years later, the Canadian judiciary remains poised at the perimeter of the Crown's duty, refusing to venture into its core.

The implementation of fiduciary doctrine to simultaneously describe and monitor the Crown-Native relationship has created difficulties both for the judiciary and legal scholars. Unlike many other areas of the law, such as contracts, the fiduciary relation — and its concomitant duties, obligations, rights, and benefits — is not very well understood. As one jurist has commented, "It is striking that a principle so long standing and so widely accepted should be the subject of the uncertainty that now prevails." Ironically, the confusion surrounding fiduciary doctrine has neither hampered the tremendous increase in the use of fiduciary arguments by litigants nor their acceptance by the judiciary in recent years.

. . . . .

The Crown's fiduciary duty to the aboriginal peoples applies to virtually every facet of the Crown-Native relationship. It has its basis in the historical relationship between the parties dating back to the time of contact, which describes the period ensuing immediately after the first meeting of Europeans and indigenous peoples in North America. It may also be noted in the terms of various treaties, compacts, and alliances between the groups. In addition to being judicially sanctioned in the *Guerin* case, the Crown's fiduciary duty to Native peoples has been constitutionally entrenched in Section 35(1) of the *Constitution Act, 1982*.

. . . . .

Unfortunately, in a number of judicial considerations since *Guerin*, Canadian courts have neither questioned the application of fiduciary doctrine to Native law nor have they attempted to explain the nature and extent of its application. Academic commentaries written in this area have been similarly plagued. As with existing judicial commentaries, these scholarly attempts to explain the application of fiduciary principles to the Crown-Native relationship have invariably been more descriptive than analytical. Even with all of these shortcomings, the application of fiduciary principles in Native law has become axiomatic. They are now presumed to exist as self-evident truths without ever having been put through any thorough examination of their applicability or appropriateness to the Crown-Native relationship. Indeed, the ramifications flowing from the existence of this relationship have yet to be fleshed out.

. . . . .

The continued application of fiduciary principles to the Crown-Native relationship based on the *Guerin* precedent may be seen to be inversely related to the perceived need to explain its application to that relationship. The more often *Guerin* is cited, without elaboration, for its proposition that the Crown owes fiduciary obligations to aboriginal peoples, the perceived need to explain the basis of the Crown's duty is reduced. Indeed, since *Guerin* has been used as the springboard for the imposition of fiduciary duties upon the Crown towards aboriginal peoples, judicial and academic analysis of the basis of the Crown's duty and its effects has decreased. However, it is of little benefit to state that a fiduciary relationship exists or that it has been breached without illustrating what the relationship encompasses or the ramifications of such a breach. Indeed, the portrayal of a relationship as fiduciary is only an initial step; the explanation of the resultant obligations arising by virtue of the relationship's existence is much more onerous.

. . . . .

The Crown-Native fiduciary relation has its origins in the interaction between the groups in the immediate, post-contact period. During the formative years, which roughly covers the period from contact until the removal of France as a major colonial power in North America in 1760-1, Crown-Native relations were based on mutual need, respect, and trust. Furthermore, when the fiduciary character of these relations was crystallized, the participants conducted themselves on a nation-to-nation basis. Consequently, the nature of the Crown's fiduciary obligations is founded on the mutually recognized and respected sovereign status of the Crown and the aboriginal peoples. This fact was recognized by the Royal Commission on Aboriginal Peoples, which stated: "When Europeans first came to the shores of North America, the continent was occupied by a large number of sovereign and independent Aboriginal peoples with their own territories, laws, and forms of government. These nations entered into relations with incoming European nations on the basis of equality and mutual respect, an attitude that persisted long into the period of colonization." Whereas there have been many changes in the nature of Crown-Native relations in the more than three hundred years that have passed since they were solemnified in the *Treaty of Albany, 1664*, their initial foundation forms the basis of the fiduciary aspect of their interaction.

Although the *Guerin* case may have been the first overt judicial recognition of the fiduciary nature of that relationship, it did not create a form of relationship that did not exist previously. *Guerin* merely gave a title and method of analysis for the subsequent treatment of the reciprocal rights, duties, and responsibilities existing between the groups. Therefore, in the nation-to-nation relationship between the Crown and aboriginal peoples, the interaction of the parties being governed by fiduciary law is not the product of an acceptance of the legitimacy of colonialism in Canada, but, rather, the rigorous, yet malleable principles of fiduciary law which are contextually appropriate to monitor the special needs of this *sui generis* situation.

The use of fiduciary doctrine is a valuable tool to ensure that the Crown performs the duties it owes to aboriginal peoples. It is rigorous in its demands of the Crown, protecting of the interests of the aboriginal peoples, and, as part of the common law, binding upon the Crown and enforceable in Canadian courts. Just as fiduciary doctrine is a part of the common law, though, it is also a part of the special, *sui generis* Crown-Native relationship.

The specific nature of a relationship and the situation under which it germinated is what renders it fiduciary, not the actors involved or whether it fits neatly into an already-established category of fiducial relations. Fiduciary doctrine, therefore, may be described as being *situation-specific*. Its situation-specificity insists that fiduciary principles be applied to a relationship only where the nature of the relationship warrants it. Even then, fiduciary doctrine is applicable only to the extent that its general characteristics and principles are relevant to the relationship under scrutiny.

The Crown-Native fiduciary relationship, in actuality, is comprised of two distinct types, or genres, of fiduciary relationships. The Crown owes a general, overarching fiduciary duty to aboriginal peoples as a result of the historical relationship between the parties dating back to the time of contact. In addition, the Crown also owes specific fiduciary duties or obligations to particular Native groups stemming from its relationships with those groups or from specific treaties, agreements, or alliances that it entered into. Depending on individual circumstances, it is possible for the Crown to owe both a general and one or more specific fiduciary duties to an aboriginal nation as a result of its intercourse with those people. As the Crown's fiduciary obligation may be recognized in the totality of its relationships with aboriginal peoples or in specific events or circumstances, such as treaties, initiatives, or legislation, an aboriginal nation's claim against the Crown for a breach of fiduciary obligation may be based either on the totality of events giving rise to the Crown's general fiduciary duty or on the obligations arising out of any one particular event or occurrence.

. . . . .

Because of the situation-specific basis on which fiduciary doctrine is premised, the unexplained application of fiduciary law to the Crown-Native relationship may clearly be seen to be detrimental to the understanding of that relationship. What is sorely needed before the Crown-Native fiduciary relationship may be truly understood is an explanation of why the relationship is a fiduciary one, who owes the obligations to the Native peoples, and what the ramifications of applying fiduciary doctrine to the Crown-Native relationship are. Thus far, no such commentary exists. It is not surprising, then, that the Crown-Native relationship is not more fully understood in the absence of any thorough examination of its fiduciary basis and effects.

The comfort exhibited by the juridical use of fiduciary rhetoric to characterize Crown-Native relations — and one of the inevitable questions raised as a result of its indiscriminate application — is illustrated in the Supreme Court of Canada's recent decision in *Ontario (Attorney- General) v. Bear Island Foundation*, [1991] 3 C.N.L.R. 79 (S.C.C.). It is insufficient to state, as the Supreme Court of Canada did in *Bear Island*, that "the Crown ... breached its fiduciary obligations to the Indians" without revealing which personifications of the Crown are bound by those obligations. In a juridical context, the phrase "the Crown" has a multitude of meanings which refer to a variety of personae. It may refer to the historical constitutional notion of the single and indivisible Crown, the British Crown in its various personalities, or, domestically, to the Crown in right of Canada or the Crown in right of a particular province.

. . . . .

Despite the manner in which it presents itself and is often regarded, the law is not acontextual. Laws come into being in response to external stimuli, not as a result of a priori assumptions. Consequently, any legal entrenchment of fiduciary obligations upon the Crown towards aboriginal peoples must also arise in response to particular events, circumstances, or requirements. In and of themselves, the *Royal Proclamation of 1763*, the *Indian Act*, and the *Constitution Act, 1982* each provide one basis for ascertaining the nature of the Crown-Native relationship. However, a different light is shed on the legal entrenchment of the Crown's duty once these various components are placed within the context in which they originated.

Focusing exclusively on the legal effects of the *Royal Proclamation of 1763*, for example, provides only one element of the Crown's duty. Recognizing that the Proclamation affects the Crown's responsibilities to the aboriginal peoples renders another component of the Crown's duty. Examining the process by which the Proclamation was promulgated and the underlying rationale for its institution in law is a third component that provides additional information on which the fiduciary character of the Crown-Native relationship may be determined. The result of placing the concrete recognition of the Crown's fiduciary duty in context, then, is a multitiered view of the effect of any one component of the Crown-Native fiduciary relationship on that relationship.

By examining the entirety of events and documents that comprise various elements of the Crown's fiduciary duty, a much richer understanding of the nature of that duty may be obtained. Unless these events and documents are scrutinized for their effects on the legal entrenchment of the Crown's obligations, only a limited understanding of the Crown's duty may be achieved. To avoid this result, a proper accounting for these happenings must itself be well rounded. This includes a consideration of these events as understood by both the Crown and aboriginal peoples.

Traditionally, aboriginal understandings of the Crown-Native relationship are among the most neglected aspects of any examination of the applicability of fiduciary law to that relationship. One of the inherent flaws which has historically plagued the development of Canadian aboriginal rights jurisprudence has been its inability to account for or pay heed to Native perspectives. From an aboriginal standpoint, the nature of the Crown-Native relationship appears fundamentally different than it does from a strictly common law perspective, which is based on colonialist attitudes and the subjugation of aboriginal rights and claims to those more consistent with the common law's European origins and biases. Through the teachings of aboriginal elders and scholars, aboriginal understandings of the nature of their relationship with the Crown and the effects of various documents, events, alliances, and treaties on that relationship may begin to be more fully understood.

By examining the relationship between the Crown and aboriginal peoples in context, it is possible to address the untreated questions and issues arising from previous treatments of the Crown's fiduciary duty to aboriginal peoples. These range from the fundamental issues of the principles applicable to the Crown-Native fiduciary relationship and who is bound by the fiduciary duty to aboriginal peoples to the more specific issues of how the Crown is to discharge its duty and how it may avoid situations of conflict of interest. Only after these issues have been addressed may the full implications and ramifications of the imposition of fiduciary doctrine upon the relationship between the Crown and Aboriginal peoples in Canada begin to be truly understood.

While the above excerpt was published in 1996, little substantive change in the status of Crown-Aboriginal fiduciary relations has been observed since. For further commentary on post-1996 developments, see Leonard I. Rotman, "Crown-Native Relations as Fiduciary: Reflections Almost Twenty Years After *Guerin*" (2003) 22 Windsor Y.B. Access Just. 363; Rotman, *Fiduciary Law* (Toronto: Thomson/Carswell, 2005), ch. 8, "Crown-Native Fiduciary Relations" at pp. 523-608.

1. The Implications of Fiduciary Law

A fiduciary relationship is comprised of at least two parties, one or more of whom possess equitable obligations to one or more others as a result of the nature of their interaction. The party owing those obligations is described as a fiduciary. The party that is owed fiduciary obligations is known as the beneficiary, or *cestui que trust*. The parties to fiduciary relationships need not be natural persons. They may be corporations, Indian bands, or the Crown itself.

In a fiduciary relationship, the beneficiary reposes trust and confidence in the honesty, integrity, and fidelity of the fiduciary and relies upon the latter's care of that trust. Fiduciary law exists to protect those who trust in the ability of others, whether voluntarily or out of necessity, from having that trust abused. Fiduciary law's primary purpose is to preserve the integrity of important, socially and/or economically valuable or necessary relationships that arise as a result of human interdependency. It also provides protection for beneficiaries who are involved in fiduciary relations from the potential for indecorous activities against their interests by unscrupulous fiduciaries.

The following excerpt provides an overview of the fiduciary concept and a blueprint for understanding its application in the context of Crown-aboriginal relations.

LEONARD I. ROTMAN, FIDUCIARY LAW

(Toronto: Thomson/Carswell, 2005) at 244, 247, 253, 278-79,
280, 283-84, 286, 290, 294-96
(references omitted)

The fiduciary concept ... protect[s] certain, though not all forms of interaction. It accomplishes this by imposing onerous duties upon those parties that possess actual or effective power over the interests of others by virtue of the nature of their association. These fiduciary duties require fiduciaries to act selflessly, with honesty, integrity, fidelity, and in the utmost good faith in the interests of their beneficiaries. The beneficiaries, meanwhile, become vulnerable to the latter's use, misuse, or non-use of power within the confines of their fiduciary interaction. This vulnerability needs not be pre-existing, although it may be. Moreover, it does not necessarily extend beyond the fiduciary nature of the interaction to other, non-fiduciary, aspects of the association between the parties.

... The fiduciary concept plays a significant role in ensuring the continued efficacy of ... interdependency ... by governing the conduct of those parties who hold power over others in relations of high trust and confidence in which the latter become utterly dependent upon and vulnerable to the former.

... [T]he fiduciary nature of an interaction, or part thereof, does not stem from simple dependence and vulnerability — which arise in many forms of interaction — but only where dependence and vulnerability is acute. ...

... [A] fiduciary duty will take hold only where the vulnerable party's interests correspond, in some meaningful way, to the fiduciary nature and scope of the parties' affiliation. Since not all aspects of the interaction between parties must be fiduciary for the fiduciary concept to take hold, a would-be fiduciary is not bound to maintain fidelity to *all* interests belonging to the would-be beneficiary, but only those that are relevant to the fiduciary element(s) of their association. Thus, lawyers have a duty to act in their clients' best interests regarding the subject matter contemplated by a retainer, but not *vis-à-vis* any interest that their clients may possess. ...

... [I]mposing strict duties upon ... fiduciaries ... include[s] duties of utmost good faith, full and complete disclosure, the avoidance of conflicts, and the inability to profit ... The imposition of equally strict standards — which entail that fiduciaries bear the onus of disproving *prima facie* demonstrations of fiduciary obligations and their breach and that fiduciary accountability, once established, may transcend the active duration of fiduciary interactions — are similarly designed to enforce the integrity of the fiduciary office.

Finally, where fiduciary interactions exist, Equity compels fiduciaries to serve those beneficiary interests that are tangibly related to those interactions and eschew any correlative personal or third party interests. ... [F]iduciaries may only act in self-interest or in the interests of parties other than their beneficiaries where the express and informed consent of the beneficiaries is obtained. In matters outside the fiduciary nature of their associations, fiduciaries may do whatever they wish. ...

The most vital attribute of the fiduciary concept is its emphasis upon the specific characteristics of individual circumstances or what may alternatively be described as its situation-specificity or case-specific empiricism. ...

The situation-specific character of the fiduciary concept entails that the law of fiduciaries is not properly implemented without regard for the context within which it is to be applied. ...

In summary, the situation-specific nature of the fiduciary concept recognizes that the practical application of fiduciary principles to various persons and relationships may differ to the same degree that those persons or relationships differ from each other, notwithstanding these principles' generic articulation. Consequently, recognition of the situation-specific nature of the fiduciary concept is a primary consideration and a necessary precursor to its application. ...

Since the situation-specific nature of the fiduciary concept precludes the creation of a taxonomy of fiduciary relations, it follows that the frontiers of fiduciary interaction cannot be authoritatively — or, indeed, accurately — established. ... [T]he fiduciary concept ... does not attempt to establish boundaries or limit the types of relationships that may be found to be fiduciary. The only relevant consideration ... is whether the character of the interaction under scrutiny fits within the ambit of the fiduciary concept and its fundamental purpose. ...

As a result ... the forms of potential relations that may properly be described as fiduciary have been said to be no more limited than the categories of negligence at common law. ...

What is truly meant by the open-endedness of the fiduciary concept, then, is that the range of potential fiduciary relations remains open and is not properly subjected to pre-conceived or artificial limits. ...

... A breach of fiduciary duty will exist only where the impugned conduct specifically relates to the fiduciary elements of an interaction and contravenes the nature of the duties imposed upon fiduciaries. Thus, where a fiduciary obligation exists alongside a contractual relationship, it may be that wrongful conduct on the fiduciary's part is simply a breach of contract and not a breach of fiduciary duty where the conduct complained of does not implicate the fiduciary component of the relationship or where it is not inconsistent with fiduciary precepts. Such a determination is only properly made by considering the quality of the impugned conduct, the nature of the fiduciary relationship in question, and the extent of the duties owed under it. In some circumstances, the wrongful conduct may result in a finding of breach, but that will not automatically be presumed in all situations where fiduciary and other duties co-exist. ...

Fiduciary principles exist as guidelines for application rather than a checklist that must be satisfied. ... The fiduciary concept is premised upon principles rather than rules so that it may retain the flexibility to respond to the myriad situations in which it may be applied, but can still provide sufficient guidelines for its informed application to specific scenarios. ...

The fiduciary concept ... arose in response to the need to protect certain forms of vital human interaction and has developed in response to this fundamental purpose. ... [W]hile the underlying purpose of the fiduciary concept is to protect important relationships of high trust and confidence, the manner in which it goes about this function ... requires the maintenance of a delicate balancing of disparate interests.

The above excerpt provides the parameters of the fiduciary concept, a matter which has been far too often overlooked in fiduciary law jurisprudence. The jurisprudence of Crown-Aboriginal relations is no different in this respect. Far too often, fiduciary principles are held to apply to the interaction between the Crown and Aboriginal peoples in the absence of sufficient particulars to provide an adequate understanding of the legal implications of applying these principles to Crown-Aboriginal interactions. To more fully understand what it means to describe Crown-Aboriginal relations as fiduciary, it is necessary to understand the principles of fiduciary obligation on their own terms before one may properly conceive of how they affect the Crown's discharging of its duties to Aboriginal peoples and the expectations of the Aboriginal peoples as beneficiaries of the Crown's duties.

2. Fiduciary Law versus Trust Law

While the notion that the Crown is a fiduciary to Aboriginal peoples in certain contexts is now regarded as axiomatic following the Supreme Court of Canada's decision in the *Guerin* case, prior to *Guerin* the limited judicial consideration of Crown-Native relations was rooted in trust law. For greater discussion of this pre-*Guerin* jurisprudential history, see Leonard I. Rotman, *Parallel Paths: Fiduciary Doctrine and the Crown-Native Relationship in Canada* (Toronto: University of Toronto Press, 1996) at pp. 73-87. Some fundamental problems associated with basing the Crown obligations in trust law are demonstrated by the following case.

PAWIS v. CANADA

(1979), 102 D.L.R. (3d) 602 at 613-15, [1980] 2 F.C. 18 (F.C.T.D.)

Marceau J.: — The basic suggestion here is that the Lake-Huron Treaty of 1850 created a trust, the subject-matter of which was the "full and free privilege to hunt over the territory now ceded by them and to fish in the waters thereof as they have heretofore been in the habit of doing". It is, however, a suggestion that I am again unable to accept.

There is no doubt that the Crown can take upon itself trust obligations which are enforceable in a Court of Equity: *Tito v. Waddell (No. 2)*, [1977] 3 All E.R. 129. It is equally true that no specific form of words is necessary to create a trust, and that a treaty of that nature ought to be liberally construed. But I fail to see how one can find here the prerequisites for the existence of a proper trust that may be the subject-matter of an action before a Court. As was said by Cannon J., in *M.A. Hanna Co. v. Provincial Bank of Canada*, [1935] 1 D.L.R. 545 at p. 565, [1935] S.C.R. 144 at p. 167:

> To completely constitute a trust, four elements are required: —
> (a) A trustee;
> (b) A beneficiary;
> (c) Property the subject-matter of the trust;
> (d) An obligation enforceable in a Court of Equity on the trustee to administer or deal with the property for the benefit of the beneficiary. There must be an equitable interest based on a conscientious obligation which can be enforced against the legal owner of the property alleged to be the subject-matter of the trust. Otherwise there is no trust.

How can the privilege to hunt and to fish be the "property of a trust"? There is no subject-matter here capable of being "held" or "administered" by a trustee for the benefit of a beneficiary. Unless the lands said to be ceded, were to be considered as being the trust property? That suggestion, however, cannot hold since there never has been any doubt that the title to the lands was already vested in the Crown before 1850, and the Treaty cannot be construed as purporting to recognize in favour of the Indians a right different in nature than that of a licensee.

In *A.-G. Can. v. A.-G. Ont.; A.-G. Que. v. A.-G. Ont.*, [1897] A.C. 199, the Judicial Committee of the Privy Council, in deciding questions that turned upon the construction of the very treaty which forms the subject-matter of this trial, and its sister-treaty, the Lake-Superior Treaty, arrived at the following conclusion [at p. 213]:

> Their Lordships have had no difficulty in coming to the conclusion that, under the treaties, the Indians obtained no right to their annuities, whether original or augmented, beyond a promise and agreement, which was nothing more than a personal obligation by its governor, as representing the old province, that the latter should pay the annuities as and when they became due; that the Indians obtained no right which gave them any interest in the territory which they surrendered, other than that of the province; and that no duty was imposed upon the province, whether in the nature of a trust obligation or otherwise, to apply the revenue derived from the surrendered lands in payment of the annuities.

That case was concerned with the payment of the annuities promised in the treaties but it seems to me that the same reasoning must apply with respect to the other promise contained therein, that is the promise of a licence to fish and hunt.

In my view, it cannot be said that, by entering into the Lake-Huron Treaty, the Crown took upon itself a trust obligation. I mean, of course, a trust obligation in the technical sense. The expression "trust obligations" is sometimes used to refer to "governmental obligations" and in that sense it may perhaps be properly applied to the obligations created by the Treaty. But "trust obligations" of that type are not enforceable as such. The distinction between trust obligations enforceable in the Courts of Chancery and these governmental or trust obligations in the higher sense is referred to by Lord Selborne, LC., in *Kinloch v. Secretary of State for India* (1882), 7 App. Cas. 619 at pp. 625-6:

> Now the words 'in trust for' are quite consistent with, and indeed are the proper manner of expressing, every species of trust — a trust not only as regards those matters which are the proper subjects for an equitable jurisdiction to administer, but as respects higher matters, such as might take place between the Crown and public officers discharging, under the directions of the Crown, duties or functions belonging to the prerogative and to the authority of the Crown. In the lower sense they are matters within the jurisdiction of, and to be administered by, the ordinary Courts of Equity; in the higher sense they are not.

(See also *Tito v. Waddell (No. 2)* referred to above.)

In any event, assuming that true trust obligations were in fact created by the Treaty, the problem would remain as to the content thereof and the nature of the duties imposed on the Crown as trustee. ... The facts do not support the allegation of a breach of trust giving rise to an action for damages.

As seen above, Justice Marceau's chief difficulty in applying trust law to the treaty right to hunt and fish in *Pawis* was trust law's requirement that an express trust must have a legally recognizeable property interest that comprises the subject matter, or *res*, of the trust. The "privilege" to hunt and fish, as Marceau J. described it in *Pawis*, was not recognized as a common law property right, thus he found that no trust could exist. Could this situation have been avoided? See the following excerpt from *Guerin v. R.*, below.

3.   The Triumph of Fiduciary Law over Trust Law

The *Guerin* case, like *Pawis* before it, began as an action against the Crown for breach of trust. At the Supreme Court of Canada, the *Guerin* decision initiated an entirely new way of conceptualizing Crown-Native relations by substituting the fiduciary concept as the basis for the Musqueam Band's claim against the federal Crown.

GUERIN v. R.

[1984] S.C.J. No. 45, 13 D.L.R. (4th) 321 at 326, [1984] 2 S.C.R. 335, [1984] 6
W.W.R. 481, 59 B.C.L.R. 301, [1985] 1 C.N.L.R. 120, 20 E.T.R. 6, 36 R.P.R. 1
(sub nom. Guerin v. Canada), 55 N.R. 161 (S.C.C.)

Dickson J.: — The question is whether the appellants, the chief and councillors of the Musqueam Indian Band, suing on their own behalf and on behalf of all other members of the band, are entitled to recover damages from the federal Crown in respect of the leasing to a golf club of land on the Musqueam Indian Reserve. Collier J., of the Trial Division of the Federal Court, declared that the Crown was in breach of trust .... He assessed damages at $10,000,000. The Federal Court of Appeal allowed a Crown appeal, set aside the judgment of the Trial Division and dismissed the action.

I. GENERAL

Before adverting to the facts, reference should be made to several of the relevant sections of the *Indian Act*, R.S.C. 1952, c. 149 as amended. Section 18(1) provides in part that reserves shall be held by Her Majesty for the use of the respective Indian bands for which they were set apart. Generally, lands in a reserve shall not be sold, alienated, leased or otherwise disposed of until they have been surrendered to Her Majesty by the band for whose use and benefit in common the reserve was set apart (s. 37). A surrender may be absolute or qualified, conditional or unconditional (s. 38(2)). To be valid, a surrender must be made to Her Majesty, assented to by a majority of the electors of the band, and accepted by the Governor in Council (s. 39(1)).

The gist of the present action is a claim that the federal Crown was in breach of its trust obligations in respect of the leasing of approximately 162 acres of reserve land to the Shaughnessy Heights Golf Club of Vancouver. The band alleged that a number of the terms and conditions of the lease were different from those disclosed to them before the surrender vote and that some of the lease terms were not disclosed to them at all. The band also claimed failure on the part of the federal Crown to exercise the requisite degree of care and management as a trustee.

II. THE FACTS

... The following summary of the facts derives directly from the judgment at trial. Musqueam Indian Reserve (No. 2) in 1955 contained 416.53 acres, situated within the charter area of the City of Vancouver. The Indian Affairs Branch recognized that the reserve was a valuable one, "the most potentially valuable 400 acres in Vancouver today". In 1956 the Shaughnessy Heights Golf Club was interested in obtaining land on the Musqueam Reserve. There were others interested in developing the land, although the band was never told of the proposals for development.

On April 4, 1957, the president of the golf club wrote to Mr. Anfield, District Superintendent of the Indian Affairs Branch, setting forth a proposal for the lease of 160 acres of the Indian reserve, the relevant terms of which were as follows:

1. The club was to have the right to construct on the leased area a golf course and country club and such other buildings and facilities as it considered appropriate for its membership.
2. The initial term of the lease was to be for fifteen years commencing May 1, 1957, with the club to have options to extend the term for four successive periods of fifteen years each, giving a maximum term of seventy-five years.
3. The rental for the first fifteen year term was to be $25,000 per annum.
4. The rental agreement for each successive fifteen year period was to be detemined by mutual agreement, between the Department and the club and failing agreement, by arbitration, but the rental for any of the fifteen year renewal periods was in no event to be increased or decreased over that payable for the preceding fifteen year period by more than 15% of the initial rent.
5. At any time during the term of the lease, and for a period of up to six months after termination, the club was to have the right to remove any buildings and other structures it had constructed or placed upon the leased area, and any course improvements and facilities.

On April 7, 1957, a band council meeting was held. Mr. Anfield presided. The trial judge accepted evidence on behalf of the plaintiffs that not all of the terms of the Shaughnessy proposal were put before the band council at the meeting. William Guerin, a councillor, said copies of the proposal were not given to them; he did not recall any mention of the $25,000 per year for rental; he described it as a vague general presentation with reference to 15-year periods. Chief Edward Sparrow said he did not recall the golf club proposal being read out in full. At the meeting the band council passed a resolution which the trial judge presumed to have been drawn up by Mr. Anfield. The relevant part of the resolution reads:

That we do approve the leasing of unrequired lands on our Musqueam I.R. 2 and that in connection with the application of the Shaughnessy Golf Club, we do approve the submission to our Musqueam Band of surrender documents for leasing 160 acres approximately as generally outlined on the McGuigan survey in red pencil.

These events followed the band council meeting.

(a) Mr. Bethune, Superintendent of Reserves and Trusts of the Indian Affairs Branch, in Ottawa, questioned the adequacy of the $25,000 annual rental for the first 15 years.... Mr. Bethune suggested that the opinion of Mr. Alfred Howell be obtained. Mr. Howell, with the Veterans Land Act Administration, had earlier made an appraisal of the reserve lands at the request of the Indian Affairs Branch.

(b) On May 15, 1957, Mr. Anfield wrote Mr. Howell asking for the latter's opinion as to whether the $25,000 per year rental for the first 15 years was "just and equitable". Mr. Howell was not given all the details of the Shaughnessy proposal. He was not told that rent increases would be limited to 15%. Nor was he made aware that the golf club proposed to have the right to remove any buildings or improvements.

(c) In his reply to Mr. Anfield, Mr. Howell expressed the view that a 75-year lease, adjustable over 15 years and made with a financially sound tenant, eliminated any risk factor. On that basis he felt the then government bond rate of 3.75% was the most that could be expected.

At trial Mr. Howell said that if he had known the improvements would not revert to the band, he would have recommended a rate of return of 4-6%. He expressed shock at the 15% clause. He had assumed that at the end of the initial term the rental could be renegotiated on the basis of "highest and best use" without any limitation on rental increase.

(d) On September 27, 1957, a band council meeting was held at the reserve, attended by members of the band council, Mr. Anfield, two other officials of the Department of Indian Affairs and representatives of the golf club. Chief Sparrow stipulated for 5% income on the value of 162 acres, amounting to $44,000 per annum. The golf club people balked. They were asked to step outside while the band council and the Indian Affairs personnel had a private discussion. Mr. Anfield said the demand of $44,000 was unreasonable. Eventually, the band council reluctantly agreed to a figure of $29,000. William Guerin testified the councillors agreed to $29,000 because they understood the first lease period was to be 10 years; subsequent rental negotiations would be every five years; and the band council felt it could negotiate for 5% of the subsequent values.

Mr. Grant, officer in charge of the Vancouver agency of the Department of Indian Affairs, testified that there was "absolutely no question that the vote was for a specific lease to a specific tenant on specific terms" and that the band did not give Mr. Anfield "authority to change things around".

(e) On October 6, 1957, a meeting of members of the band was held at the reserve, the so-called "surrender meeting". The trial judge made these findings: (i) those present assumed or understood the golf club lease would be, aside from the first term, for 10-year periods, not 15 years; (ii) those present assumed or understood there would be no 15% limitation on rental increases; (iii) the meeting was not told that the golf club had proposed that it should have the right to remove any buildings, structures, course improvements and facilities.

The trial judge further found that two matters which subsequently found their way into the lease were not even put before the surrender meeting. They were not in the original golf club proposal. They first appeared in draft leases, after the meeting. The first of these terms was the method of determining future rents; failing mutual agreement, the matter was to be submitted to arbitration; the new rent would be the fair rent as if the land were still in an uncleared and unimproved condition and used as a golf club. The second term gave the golf club, but not the Crown, the right at the end of each 15-year period to terminate the lease on six months' prior notice. These two terms were not subsequently brought before the band council or the band for comment or approval.

The surrender, which was approved by a vote of 41 to 2, gave the land in question to Her Majesty the Queen on the following terms:

> TO HAVE AND TO HOLD the same unto Her said Majesty the Queen, her Heirs and Successors forever in trust to lease the same to such person or persons, and upon such terms as the Government of Canada may deem most conducive to our Welfare and that of our people.
>
> AND upon the further condition that all monies received from the leasing thereof, shall be credited to our revenue trust account at Ottawa.
>
> AND WE, the said Chief and Councillors of the said Musqueam Band of Indians do on behalf of our people and for ourselves, hereby ratify and confirm, and promise to ratify and confirm, whatever the said Government may do, or cause to be lawfully done, in connection with the leasing thereof.

(f) On December 6, 1957, the surrender of the lands was accepted by the federal Crown by Order in Council P.C. 1957-1606, "in order that the lands covered thereby may be leased".

(g) On January 9, 1958, a band council meeting was held. A letter was read regarding the proposed golf club lease. The letter indicated the renewal periods were to be 15 years instead of 10 years. Chief Sparrow pointed out that the band had demanded 10-year periods. William Guerin said the council members were "flabbergasted" to learn about the 15-year terms. The band council then passed a resolution agreeing the first term should be 15 years, but insisting the renewal periods be 10-year terms.

(h) The lease was signed January 22, 1958. It provided, *inter alia*:

1. The term is for 75 years unless sooner terminated.
2. The rent for the first 15 years is $29,000 per annum.
3. For the succeeding 15-year periods, annual rent is to be determined by mutual agreement, or failing such agreement, by arbitration, such rent to be equal to the fair rent for the demised premises as if the same were still in an uncleared and unimproved condition and used as a golf course.
4. The maximum increase in rent for the second 15-year period (January 1, 1973 to January 1, 1988) is limited to 15% of $29,000, that is $4,350 per annum.
5. The golf club can terminate the lease at the end of any 15-year period by giving 6 months' prior notice.
6. The golf club can at any time during the lease and up to 6 months after termination, remove any buildings or other structures, and any course improvements and facilities.

The band was not given a copy of the lease, and did not receive one until 12 years later, in March, 1970.

(i) Mr. Grant testified that the terms of the lease ultimately entered into bore little resemblance to what was discussed at the surrender meeting. The judge agreed. He found that the majority of those who voted on October 6, 1957, would not have assented to a surrender of the 162 acres if they had known all the terms of the lease of January 22, 1958.

. . . . .

IV. FIDUCIARY RELATIONSHIP

The issue of the Crown's liability was dealt with in the courts below on the basis of the existence or non-existence of a trust. In dealing with the different consequences of a "true" trust, as opposed to a "political" trust, Le Dain J. noted that the Crown could be liable only if it were subject to an "equitable obligation enforceable in a court of law". I have some doubt as to the cogency of the terminology of "higher" and "lower" trusts, but I do agree that the existence of an equitable obligation is the *sine qua non* for liability. Such an obligation is not, however, limited to relationships which can be strictly defined as "trusts". As will presently appear, it is my view that the Crown's obligations *vis-à-vis* the Indians cannot be defined as a trust. That does not, however, mean that the Crown owes no enforceable duty to the Indians in the way in which it deals with Indian land.

In my view, the nature of Indian title and the framework of the statutory scheme established for disposing of Indian land places upon the Crown an equitable obligation, enforceable by the courts, to deal with the land for the benefit of the Indians. This obligation does not amount to a trust in the private law sense. It is rather a fiduciary duty. If, however, the Crown breaches this fiduciary duty it will be liable to the Indians in the same way and to the same extent as if such a trust were in effect.

The fiduciary relationship between the Crown and the Indians has its roots in the concept of aboriginal, native or Indian title. The fact that

Indian bands have a certain interest in lands does not, however, in itself give rise to a fiduciary relationship between the Indians and the Crown. The conclusion that the Crown is a fiduciary depends upon the further proposition that the Indian interest in the land is inalienable except upon surrender to the Crown.

An Indian band is prohibited from directly transferring its interest to a third party. Any sale or lease of land can only be carried out after a surrender has taken place, with the Crown then acting on the band's behalf. The Crown first took this responsibility upon itself in the Royal Proclamation of 1763. ... It is still recognized in the surrender provisions of the *Indian Act*. The surrender requirement, and the responsibility it entails, are the source of a distinct fiduciary obligation owed by the Crown to the Indians. In order to explore the character of this obligation, however, it is first necessary to consider the basis of aboriginal title and the nature of the interest in land which it represents.

[This discussion of Aboriginal title is reproduced in Chapter 3.]

. . . . .

(c) *The Crown's fiduciary obligation*

The concept of fiduciary obligation originated long ago in the notion of breach of confidence, one of the original heads of jurisdiction in chancery. In the present appeal its relevance is based on the requirement of a "surrender" before Indian land can be alienated.

The Royal Proclamation of 1763 provided that no private person could purchase from the Indians any lands that the Proclamation had reserved to them, and provided further that all purchases had to be by and in the name of the Crown, in a public assembly of the Indians held by the governor or commander-in-chief of the colony in which the lands in question lay. ... [T]his policy with respect to the sale or transfer of the Indians' interest in land has been continuously maintained by the British Crown, by the governments of the colonies when they became responsible for the administration of Indian affairs, and, after 1867, by the federal government of Canada. Successive federal statutes, predecessors to the present *Indian Act*, have all provided for the general inalienability of Indian reserve land except upon surrender to the Crown, the relevant provisions in the present Act being ss. 37-41.

The purpose of this surrender requirement is clearly to interpose the Crown between the Indians and prospective purchasers or lessees of their land, so as to prevent the Indians from being exploited. ... Through the confirmation in the *Indian Act* of the historic responsibility which the Crown has undertaken, to act on behalf of the Indians so as to protect their interests in transactions with third parties, Parliament has conferred upon the Crown a discretion to decide for itself where the Indians' best interests really lie. This is the effect of s. 18(1) of the Act.

This discretion on the part of the Crown, far from ousting, as the Crown contends, the jurisdiction of the courts to regulate the relationship between the Crown and the Indians, has the effect of transforming the Crown's obligation into a fiduciary one. Professor Ernest Weinrib maintains in his article "The Fiduciary Obligation", 25 U.T.L.J. 1 (1975), at p. 7, that "the hallmark of a fiduciary relation is that the relative legal positions are such that one party is at the mercy of the other's discretion". Earlier, at p. 4, he puts the point in the following way:

> [Where there is a fiduciary obligation] there is a relation in which the principal's interests can be affected by, and are therefore dependent on, the manner in which the fiduciary uses the discretion which has been delegated to him. The fiduciary obligation is the law's blunt tool for the control of this discretion.

I make no comment upon whether this description is broad enough to embrace all fiduciary obligations. I do agree, however, that where by statute, agreement, or perhaps by unilateral undertaking, one party has an obligation to act for the benefit of another, and that obligation carries with it a discretionary power, the party thus empowered becomes a fiduciary. Equity will then supervise the relationship by holding him to the fiduciary's strict standard of conduct.

It is sometimes said that the nature of fiduciary relationships is both established and exhausted by the standard categories of agent, trustee, partner, director, and the like. I do not agree. It is the nature of the relationship, not the specific category of actor involved that gives rise to the fiduciary duty. The categories of fiduciary, like those of negligence, should not be considered closed.

. . . . .

It should be noted that fiduciary duties generally arise only with regard to obligations originating in a private law context. Public law duties, the performance of which requires the exercise of discretion, do not typically give rise to a fiduciary relationship. ... [T]he Crown is not normally viewed as a fiduciary in the exercise of its legislative or administrative function. The mere fact, however, that it is the Crown which is obligated to act on the Indians' behalf does not of itself remove the Crown's obligation from the scope of the fiduciary principle. As was pointed out earlier, the Indians' interest in land is an independent legal interest. It is not a creation of either the legislative or executive branches of government. The Crown's obligation to the Indians with respect to that interest is therefore not a public law duty. While it is not a private law duty in the strict sense either, it is none the less in the nature of a private law duty. Therefore, in this *sui generis* relationship, it is not improper to regard the Crown as a fiduciary.

Section 18(1) of the *Indian Act* confers upon the Crown a broad discretion in dealing with surrendered land. ... When, as here, an Indian band surrenders its interests to the Crown, a fiduciary obligation takes hold to regulate the manner in which the Crown exercises its discretion in dealing with the land on the Indians' behalf.

I agree ... that before surrender the Crown does not hold the land in trust for the Indians. I also agree that the Crown's obligation does not somehow crystallize into a trust, express or implied, at the time of surrender. The law of trusts is a highly developed, specialized branch of the law. An express trust requires a settlor, a beneficiary, a trust corpus, words of settlement, certainty of object and certainty of obligation. Not all of these elements are present here. ... As the *Smith* decision [as discussed in Chapter 3 (Aboriginal Title)] ... makes clear, upon unconditional surrender the Indians' right in the land disappears. No property interest is transferred which could constitute the trust *res*, so that even if the other *indicia* of an express or implied trust could be made out, the basic requirement of a settlement of property has not been met. Accordingly, although the nature of Indian title coupled with the discretion vested in the Crown are sufficient to give rise to a fiduciary obligation, neither an express nor an implied trust arises upon surrender.

Nor does the surrender give rise to a constructive trust. ... Any similarity between a constructive trust and the Crown's fiduciary obligation to the Indians is limited to the fact that both arise by operation of law.

. . . . .

The Crown's fiduciary obligation to the Indians is therefore not a trust. To say as much is not to deny that the obligation is trust-like in character. As would be the case with a trust, the Crown must hold surrendered land for the use and benefit of the surrendering band. The obligation is thus subject to principles very similar to those which govern the law of trusts concerning, for example, the measure of damages for breach. The fiduciary relationship between the Crown and the Indians also bears a certain resemblance to agency, since the obligations can be characterized as a duty to act on behalf of the Indian bands who have surrendered lands, by negotiating for the sale or lease of the land to third parties. But just as the Crown is not a trustee for the Indians, neither is it their agent; not only does the Crown's authority to act on the band's behalf lack a basis in contract, but the band is not a party to the ultimate sale or lease, as it would be if it were the Crown's principal. I repeat, the fiduciary obligation which is owed to the Indians by the Crown is *sui generis*. Given the unique character both of the Indians' interest in land and of their historical relationship with the Crown, the fact that this is so should occasion no surprise.

The discretion which is the hallmark of any fiduciary relationship is capable of being considerably narrowed in a particular case. This is as true of the Crown's discretion *vis-à-vis* the Indians as it is of the discretion of trustees, agents, and other traditional categories of fiduciary. The *Indian Act* makes specific provision for such narrowing in ss. 18(1) and 38(2). A fiduciary obligation will not, of course, be eliminated by the imposition of conditions that have the effect of restricting the fiduciary's discretion. A failure to adhere to the imposed conditions will simply itself be a *prima facie* breach of the obligation. In the present case both the surrender and the Order in Council accepting the surrender referred to the Crown leasing the land on the band's behalf. Prior to the surrender the band had also been given to understand that a lease was to be entered into with the Shaughnessy Heights Golf Club upon certain terms, but this understanding was not incorporated into the surrender document itself. The effect of these so-called oral terms will be considered in the next section.

(d) *Breach of the fiduciary obligation*

The trial judge found that the Crown's agents promised the band to lease the land in question on certain specified terms and then, after the surrender, obtained a lease on different terms. The lease obtained was much less valuable. As already mentioned, the surrender document did not make reference to the "oral" terms. I would not wish to say that those terms had none the less somehow been incorporated as conditions into the surrender. They were not formally assented to by a majority of the electors of the band, nor were they accepted by the Governor in Council, as required by s. 39(1)(*b*) and (*c*).

. . . . .

None the less, the Crown, in my view, was not empowered by the surrender document to ignore the oral terms which the band understood would be embodied in the lease. The oral representations form the backdrop against which the Crown's conduct in discharging its fiduciary obligation must be measured. They inform and confine the field of discretion within which the Crown was free to act. After the Crown's agents had induced the band to surrender its land on the understanding that the land would be leased on certain terms, it would be unconscionable to permit the Crown simply to ignore those terms. When the promised lease proved impossible to obtain, the Crown, instead of proceeding to lease the land on different, unfavourable terms, should have returned to the band to explain what had occurred and seek the band's counsel on how to proceed. The existence of such unconscionability is the key to a conclusion that the Crown breached its fiduciary duty. Equity will not countenance unconscionable behaviour in a fiduciary, whose duty is that of utmost loyalty to his principal.

While the existence of the fiduciary obligation which the Crown owes to the Indians is dependent on the nature of the surrender process, the standard of conduct which the obligation imports is both more general and more exacting than the terms of any particular surrender. In the present case the relevant aspect of the required standard of conduct is defined by a principle analogous to that which underlies the doctrine of promissory or equitable estoppel. The Crown cannot promise the band that it will obtain a lease of the latter's land on certain stated terms, thereby inducing the band to alter its legal position by surrendering the land, and then simply ignore that promise to the band's detriment.

. . . . .

In obtaining without consultation a much less valuable lease than that promised, the Crown breached the fiduciary obligation it owed the band. It must make good the loss suffered in consequence.

[Justice Dickson then considered the application of the relevant statutory limitation legislation and held that it did not bar the band's claim since there had been fraudulent concealment of the band's cause of action. He determined that Indian Affairs' conduct toward the band amounted to equitable fraud, thus suspending the operation of the limitation statute until March 1970, when the band first received a copy of the executed lease.]

VII. MEASURE OF DAMAGES

In my opinion, the quantum of damages is to be determined by analogy with the principles of trust law.... I am content to adopt the quantum of damages awarded by the [trial] judge, rejecting, as he did, any claim for exemplary or punitive damages.

I would therefore allow the appeal.

Although *Guerin* single-handedly changed the characterization of Crown-Native relations from trust or quasi-trust to fiduciary, that does not necessarily entail that a specific Crown-Native relation cannot be described as a trust relationship: see *Cardinal v. R.*, [1991] F.C.J. No. 1022, 44 E.T.R. 297 at 316 (*sub nom. Cardinal v. Canada*), 47 F.T.R. 203, [1992] 4 C.N.L.R. 1 (F.C.T.D.), rev'd in part [1993] F.C.J. No. 1254, 72 F.T.R. 309, 164 N.R. 301 (*sub nom. Enoch Band of Stony Plain Indians v. Canada*), [1994] 3 C.N.L.R. 41 (Fed. C.A.), application for reconsideration refused [1994] F.C.J. No. 109 (Fed. C.A.). As seen in the *Pawis* excerpt, there are some difficulties with the use of trust law to describe Crown-Native relations that may be avoided by using fiduciary law instead.

Since fiduciary law does not require the existence of a legally recognizable property interest, there is no doctrinal difficulty in having hunting, trapping, or fishing rights be the subject of a Crown fiduciary obligation to an Aboriginal group. Fiduciary law is thus capable of applying to a wider range of Aboriginal claims against the Crown than trust law. It may also avoid the difficulty of engaging judicial debate as to whether Aboriginal land rights are beneficial or non-beneficial in nature and therefore capable of constituting the *res* of a trust. Refer back to the discussion of *Smith v. R.*, [1983] S.C.J. No. 39, [1983] 1 S.C.R. 554, 47 N.R. 132, 147 D.L.R. (3d) 237 (S.C.C.) in Chapter 3.

4. The Scope of the Crown's Fiduciary Obligations

The release of the *Guerin* decision sparked a wave of litigation based on alleged breaches of the Crown's fiduciary obligations to Aboriginal peoples. The decision also sparked some controversy over the extent of fiduciary law's application to Crown-Native relations. It was questioned whether the Crown's fiduciary duty was restricted to the surrender of Aboriginal lands for leasing purposes, as in *Guerin*, or if it was of wider scope.

While the *Guerin* case did speak specifically to the existence of Crown fiduciary duties pertaining to the surrender of Aboriginal lands for lease, the limited scope of the decision was the result of the specific facts in issue, not because of the restricted nature of the Crown's fiduciary obligations. Justice Dickson, as he then was, expressly contextualized his examination of the Crown's duty in *Guerin* by stating that the relevance of the Crown's fiduciary duty "in the present appeal ... is based on the requirement of a surrender before Indian land can be alienated." Had he intended to limit the Crown's fiduciary obligations to land surrenders, his judgment would have been express on that point, which it clearly was not. This very point was affirmed in *Wewaykum, supra*, at para. 98:

> In *Guerin*, Dickson J. said the fiduciary "interest gives rise *upon surrender* to a distinctive fiduciary obligation on the part of the Crown" (p. 382). These dicta should not be read too narrowly. Dickson J. spoke of surrender because those were the facts of the *Guerin* case. As this Court recently held, expropriation of an existing reserve equally gives rise to a fiduciary duty: *Osoyoos Indian Band v. Oliver (Town)*, [2001] 3 S.C.R. 746, 2001 SCC 85. See also *Kruger v. The Queen*, [1986] 1 F.C. 3 (C.A.).

As indicated in the above quote from *Wewaykum*, this interpretation of the *Guerin* decision had been initially affirmed in *Kruger, infra*. Meanwhile, in the Supreme Court of Canada's decision in *R. v. Sparrow*, below, the scope of the Crown's fiduciary obligations to Aboriginal peoples was expanded considerably from what had been discussed in *Guerin*.

The *Sparrow* case was concerned more particularly with the scope of Aboriginal rights to fish and the extent to which those rights could be affected by governmental regulations. The case is discussed in Chapter 2. Within the scope of the Supreme Court's consideration of that issue, it made the following important pronouncement on the nature of the Crown's fiduciary obligations towards Aboriginal peoples.

R. v. SPARROW

[1990] S.C.J. No. 49, 70 D.L.R. (4th) 385 at 389, [1990] 1 S.C.R. 1075, [1990] 4 W.W.R. 410, 46 B.C.L.R. (2d) 1, 56 C.C.C. (3d) 263, 111 N.R. 241, [1990] 3 C.N.L.R. 160 (S.C.C.)

The judgment of the court was delivered by

Dickson C.J.C. and **La Forest J.:** — This appeal requires this court to explore for the first time the scope of s. 35(1) of the *Constitution Act, 1982*, and to indicate its strength as a promise to the aboriginal peoples of Canada.

. . . . .

The approach to be taken with respect to interpreting the meaning of s. 35(1) is derived from general principles of constitutional interpretation, principles relating to aboriginal rights, and the purposes behind the constitutional provision itself. Here, we will sketch the framework for an interpretation of "recognized and affirmed" that, in our opinion, gives appropriate weight to the constitutional nature of these words.

. . . . .

In our opinion, *Guerin*, together with *R. v. Taylor and Williams* (1981), 62 C.C.C. (2d) 227, 34 O.R. (2d) 360 (C.A.), ground a general guiding principle for s. 35(1). That is, the government has the responsibility to act in a fiduciary capacity with respect to aboriginal peoples. The relationship between the government and aboriginals is trust-like, rather than adversarial, and contemporary recognition and affirmation of aboriginal rights must be defined in light of this historic relationship.

. . . . .

There is no explicit language in the provision that authorizes this court or any court to assess the legitimacy of any government legislation that restricts aboriginal rights. Yet, we find that the words "recognition and affirmation" incorporate the fiduciary relationship referred to earlier and so import some restraint on the exercise of sovereign power. Rights that are recognized and affirmed are not absolute. Federal legislative powers continue, including, of course, the right to legislate with respect to Indians pursuant to s. 91(24) of the *Constitution Act, 1867*. These powers must, however, now be read together with s. 35(1). In other words, federal power must be reconciled with federal duty and the best way to achieve that reconciliation is to demand the justification of any government regulation that infringes upon or denies aboriginal rights. Such scrutiny is in keeping with ... the concept of holding the Crown to a high standard of honourable dealing with respect to the aboriginal peoples of Canada as suggested by *Guerin v. The Queen, supra*.

. . . . .

The way in which a legislative objective is to be attained must uphold the honour of the Crown and must be in keeping with the unique contemporary relationship, grounded in history and policy, between the Crown and Canada's aboriginal peoples.

. . . . .

[T]he honour of the Crown is at stake in dealings with aboriginal peoples. The special trust relationship and the responsibility of the government *vis-à-vis* aboriginals must be the first consideration in determining whether the legislation or action in question can be justified.

———

After the *Sparrow* decision, it was clear that the Crown's fiduciary obligations to Aboriginal peoples extended beyond the surrender of Aboriginal lands to Crown-Native relations more generally and that those obligations were constitutionally entrenched in section 35(1) of the *Constitution Act, 1982*. It was not until 1995, however, that the Supreme Court of Canada released another judgment that contemplated the fiduciary nature of Crown-Native relations in *Blueberry River Indian Band v. Canada*, [1995] S.C.J. No. 99, [1995] 4 S.C.R. 344 (S.C.C.). Following *Blueberry River*, judgments keying on the Crown's fiduciary duties to Aboriginal peoples appeared in *Osoyoos Indian Band v. Oliver (Town)*, [2001] S.C.J. No. 82, [2001] 3 S.C.R. 746 (S.C.C.) and *Wewaykum Indian Band v. Canada*, [2002] S.C.J. No. 79, 2002 SCC 79 (S.C.C.), both of which are excerpted below. Do these cases expand or constrict the notion of Crown fiduciary duties articulated in *Guerin* and *Sparrow*?

5. The Crown's Fiduciary Obligations and Conflict of Interest

As suggested in *Guerin, supra*, the application of fiduciary doctrine to Crown-Native relations entails that the Crown must act with the utmost good faith, or *uberrima fides*, in the best interests of the Aboriginal peoples. The Crown may not allow self-interest, or the interests of third parties, to interfere with its obligations to the Aboriginal peoples. This is known as the rule against conflict of interest.

The rule against conflict of interest imposes a number of restraints upon the Crown as a fiduciary towards Aboriginal peoples. In addition to foregoing personal benefit, the Crown must provide full disclosure of its actions while acting in its fiduciary capacity. A corollary of these two restraints is that the Crown must account for profits wrongfully made while in its fiduciary capacity. The Crown may also be found to be in conflict of interest in the absence of malevolent actions.

As a general rule, fiduciaries who depart from this standard of utmost good faith may be found in breach of duty and be subjected to harsh sanctions by the courts. In some circumstances, however, the Crown's fiduciary duty to Aboriginal peoples may conflict with its other responsibilities, such as the interest of the public at large. Where such potential conflict of interest situations exist, the Crown cannot ignore one interest in favour of the other. Rather, it must attempt to balance its competing responsibilities. In some situations, this may not be possible. Where such an irreconcilable conflict occurs, the judiciary may be required to balance those competing interests and the Crown's duties thereto. While, doctrinally, a fiduciary may not escape liability for a breach of duty by citing competing interests, this general rule may need to be modified, where appropriate, to account for the context of specific fact situations. However, any such modification must be consistent with the fiduciary concept's underlying principles.

The Crown's ability to avoid liability for breach of its fiduciary obligations by citing competing interests is a rather new issue in Canadian Aboriginal rights jurisprudence, but one that is likely to arise more frequently because of the unique position of the Crown as a fiduciary to Aboriginal peoples. This issue was a key element of the Federal Court of Appeal's decision in *Kruger v. R.*, [1985] F.C.J. No. 167, 17 D.L.R. (4th) 591 at 595, [1986] 1 F.C. 3, 32 L.C.R. 65 (*sub nom. Kruger v. Canada*), 58 N.R. 241, [1985] 3 C.N.L.R. 15 (Fed. C.A.); leave to appeal to S.C.C. refused (1985), 33 L.C.R. 192n, 62 N.R. 102*n*.

Until recently, the *Kruger* judgment was the only Crown-Native fiduciary case which considered, in any substantive way, the issue of competing Crown interests and the need for the Crown to balance them. Subsequent decisions have indicated that the Crown has a duty to balance the interests of its various constituents and beneficiaries and cannot avoid liability for breaching its obligations merely by citing competing interests.

For example, in *Wewaykum Indian Band v. Canada*, [2002] S.C.J. No. 79, [2002] 4 S.C.R. 245 (S.C.C.) (excerpted *infra*), it was held that "as a fiduciary, it was the Crown's duty to be even-handed toward and among the various beneficiaries" (para. 97) and that "the role of honest referee does not exhaust the Crown's fiduciary obligation here. The Crown could not, merely by invoking competing interests, shirk its fiduciary duty" (para. 104). As you read the following case, ask yourself whether the Court has appropriately resolved the potential conflict of interest between Crown interests and Aboriginal rights in the test it devises below.

OSOYOOS INDIAN BAND v. OLIVER (TOWN)

[2001] S.C.J. No. 82, [2001] 3 S.C.R. 746 (S.C.C.) (references omitted)

[This case concerned the ability of an Indian band to tax lands taken from its reserve upon which an irrigation canal was built. The canal bisected the band's reserve, which was located near the town of Oliver in the Okanagan Valley of southern British Columbia. Authorization for the taking of the land was uncertain. No attempt to formalize the province's interest in the canal lands was undertaken until some 32 years after the canal was built, at which time a federal Order in Council enacted under section 35 of the 1952 *Indian Act* provided for the use of the land for "irrigation canal purposes" in exchange for the sum of $7,700 from the province. The land was never formally expropriated. In 1962, the canal lands were registered in the name of the Queen in right of the province. At the time of the litigation, the Town of Oliver operated and maintained the canal, although the basis of its authority to do so was uncertain.

Only those aspects of the judgment relevant to the issue of the Crown's fiduciary duty are reproduced below.]

The judgment of **McLachlin C.J.C.** and **Iacobucci**, **Binnie**, **Arbour** and **LeBel JJ.** was delivered by

Iacobucci J.: —

. . . . .

V. Issues and Submissions of the Parties

[34] 1. Can a taking pursuant to s. 35 of the *Indian Act* extinguish an
Indian band's interest in reserve land such that the land is no
longer "in the reserve" and falls outside the jurisdiction of the
band?

2. Did Order in Council 1957-577 remove the land at issue in this
case from the Osoyoos Indian Reserve Number 1?

[35] ... The appellant ... submits that because Indian interests are at
stake, fiduciary principles constrain the discretion of the Governor in
Council to transfer land under s. 35. Consequently, a minimal impairment
rule should be applied in the interpretation of the Order in Council with
the result that the Governor in Council could not have intended to, and
did not in fact, remove the land at issue from the reserve. ...

[36] ... With respect to the interpretation of the Order in Council, the
respondents submit that the Governor in Council is not under any
fiduciary duty to the Band in the context of a taking of an interest in
reserve land under s. 35. Therefore, a minimal impairment rule should not
be applied in this case. ...

VI. Analysis

. . . . .

[38] The determination of the rights and entitlements at issue in this
case will significantly affect the interests of the parties. Yet, the factual
basis upon which that determination must be made is somewhat
unsatisfactory. I share the view of the Court of Appeal that the evidentiary
record in this case is demonstrably incomplete. Important relevant
evidence that could assist the Court in the interpretation and application of
the Order in Council may be available but does not form part of the record
of this case.

[39] In particular, there is no evidence that explains under what
authority, if any, the canal was initially constructed and operated prior to
the enactment of the Order in Council. There is no evidence to indicate
which interests in land were assessed or what methodology was used to
calculate the value of the compensation received by the Band in 1955. The
documentary evidence is thin: none of the correspondence, Band Council
resolutions, minutes of meetings or other documents and reports that
could offer external evidence of intention relating to the transfer effected
by Order in Council 1957-577 was presented. Apart from the fact that the
canal is "concrete lined", we do not know anything about how it was
constructed. Similarly, apart from the fact that the canal lands cover an
area of 56.09 acres, we do not know anything about its specific dimensions.
There was no evidence that would explain what type of tenure is necessary
to maintain and operate the canal or precisely what type of tenure is
enjoyed by the Town of Oliver. There was no evidence of the activities
carried on on the lands in question; whether it is fenced off or occupied

exclusively by the Town of Oliver, or whether the Band members are permitted to cross the canal at certain points.

[40] In my view, as a general matter the Court should be cautious in taking away interests in land in the absence of a complete evidentiary record. This is especially true when the interest at stake is the aboriginal interest in reserve land. ... In this case, we are faced with the difficult task of determining intention without supporting facts and evidence. Having said all this, as the appeal comes by way of a stated case, we must determine the rights of the parties as best we can using the evidence at hand.

. . . . .

[47] Land may be removed from a reserve with the participation of the Crown, which owes a fiduciary duty to the band, as discussed below. Fiduciaries are held to a high standard of diligence. For this reason, as well as by reason of the foregoing principles, it follows that a clear and plain intention must be present in order to conclude that land has been removed from a reserve. ...

. . . . .

4. *The Content of the Crown's Fiduciary Duty in the Context of Section 35*

[51] The intervener the Attorney General of Canada submits that when Canada's public law duty conflicts with its statutory obligation to hold reserve lands for the use and benefit of the band for which they were set apart, then a fiduciary duty does not arise. The Attorney General argues that the existence of a fiduciary duty to impair minimally the Indian interest in reserve lands is inconsistent with the legislative purpose of s. 35 which is to act in the greater public interest and that the opening phrase of s. 18(1) of the *Indian Act*, "Subject to the provisions of this Act . . .", effectively releases the Crown from its fiduciary duty in respect of s. 35 takings. In addition, the Attorney General contends that a fiduciary obligation to impair minimally the Indian interest in reserve lands is inconsistent with the principles of fiduciary law which impose a duty of utmost loyalty on the fiduciary to act only in the interests of the person to whom the duty is owed. Thus, the Attorney General submits that the holding in *Guerin, supra,* that the surrender of an Indian interest of land gives rise to a fiduciary duty on the part of the Crown to act in the best interests of the Indians does not extend to the context of expropriation, and that the duty of the Crown to the band in the case of an expropriation of reserve land is similar to its duty to any other land holder — to compensate the band appropriately for the loss of the lands.

[52] In my view, the fiduciary duty of the Crown is not restricted to instances of surrender. Section 35 clearly permits the Governor in Council to allow the use of reserve land for public purposes. However, once it has been determined that an expropriation of Indian lands is in the public interest, a fiduciary duty arises on the part of the Crown to expropriate or

grant only the minimum interest required in order to fulfill that public purpose, thus ensuring a minimal impairment of the use and enjoyment of Indian lands by the band. This is consistent with the provisions of s. 35 which give the Governor in Council the absolute discretion to prescribe the terms to which the expropriation or transfer is to be subject. In this way, instead of having the public interest trump the Indian interests, the approach I advocate attempts to reconcile the two interests involved.

[53] This two-step process minimizes any inconsistency between the Crown's public duty to expropriate lands and its fiduciary duty to Indians whose lands are affected by the expropriation. In the first stage, the Crown acts in the public interest in determining that an expropriation involving Indian lands is required in order to fulfill some public purpose. At this stage, no fiduciary duty exists. However, once the general decision to expropriate has been made, the fiduciary obligations of the Crown arise, requiring the Crown to expropriate an interest that will fulfill the public purpose while preserving the Indian interest in the land to the greatest extent practicable.

[54] The duty to impair minimally Indian interests in reserve land not only serves to balance the public interest and the Indian interest, it is also consistent with the policy behind the rule of general inalienability in the *Indian Act* which is to prevent the erosion of the native land base: *Opetchesaht Indian Band v. Canada*, [1997] 2 S.C.R. 119, at para. 52. The contention of the Attorney General that the duty of the Crown to the Band is restricted to appropriate compensation cannot be maintained in light of the special features of reserve land discussed above, in particular, the facts that the aboriginal interest in land has a unique cultural component, and that reserve lands cannot be unilaterally added to or replaced.

[55] As the Crown's fiduciary duty is to protect the use and enjoyment of the Indian interest in expropriated lands to the greatest extent practicable, the duty includes the general obligation, wherever appropriate, to protect a sufficient Indian interest in expropriated land in order to preserve the taxation jurisdiction of the band over the land, thus ensuring a continued ability to earn income from the land. Although in this case the taxation jurisdiction given to bands came after the Order in Council of 1957, the principle is the same, namely that the Crown should not take more than is needed for the public purpose and subject to protecting the use and enjoyment of Indians where appropriate.

[Iacobucci J. then turned his attention to the form of interest in the land necessary to operate the canal.]

[65] ... The evidence before the Court is insufficient to provide a clear answer. The respondents argue that since the canal is a permanent structure, they therefore must have the exclusive right to use and occupy the land. However, while the canal seems to be a permanent structure on the land, this fact should not be overstated. There was no evidence to indicate what kind of structure the canal is. Stripped to its essence, it is a ditch lined with concrete. Furthermore, it may be inferred that the fee simple to the land was not necessary to construct the canal since no transfer of title was made at the time of its construction. As well, since the

canal was already built when the transfer was made, the interest in question is that which is reasonably required to operate and maintain the canal only. Moreover, it is obvious that the fee simple is not necessary to operate and maintain the canal since those activities are currently the responsibility of the Town of Oliver, which appears to have some kind of leasehold interest in the land. A canal is similar in nature to a railway in that both are permanent structures on the land involving operation and maintenance activities, and this Court has found that a grant of a statutory easement can be sufficient for the purposes of building and maintaining a railway (*Canadian Pacific Ltd. v. Paul*, [1988] 2 S.C.R. 654, at p. 671). As noted above, as a general matter the Court should be reluctant to take away interests in land in the absence of conclusive evidence.

. . . . .

[81] I conclude that the Order in Council is ambiguous. There are no clear words of exclusion or limitation that make plain the extent of the interest being transferred. Some phrases in the recitals suggest that a transfer of a fee simple is contemplated ("a portion of Osoyoos Indian Reserve number one"), while others suggest a more restricted interest ("for irrigation canal purposes"). Indeed, the phrase "a portion of Osoyoos Indian Reserve number one" is not necessarily indicative of a fee simple transfer. Given that the law views property as a bundle of rights, that the Order in Council grants "a portion" of the reserve is not inconsistent with the granting of an easement or a right to use the land "for irrigation canal purposes". A right to use the land for a restricted purpose is part of the bundle of rights that make up the property interest in the reserve and so may be referred to as "a portion" of the reserve.

[82] In its traditional sense, a "right of way" is a type of easement, and at common law the acquisition of a right of way does not give the holder a fee simple interest or the right to exclusive possession: E. C. E. Todd, *The Law of Expropriation and Compensation in Canada* (2nd ed. 1992). However, as noted by Newbury J.A. in the Court of Appeal, in modern usage the term right of way does not always correspond to the common law concept and in some circumstances may refer to a right to the exclusive use and occupation of a corridor of land. I acknowledge that the term "rights-of-way" can have two meanings and that the degree of occupation will be governed by the document conceding the grant. However, it is not clear from the context in which it appears in the Order in Council whether the term "rights-of-way" necessarily refers to an easement as it is traditionally known, or some greater interest in a corridor of land.

. . . . .

[84] In finding that the Order in Council removed the land from the reserve, the majority of the Court of Appeal relied in part on the fact that there was no indication that the Province was acquiring anything less than exclusive rights to the land. However, this approach is contrary to the clear and plain intention test for extinguishment. While express language is not

strictly necessary, courts should not take away an aboriginal interest in land by implication unless clearly and plainly supported by context.

. . . . .

[89] To summarize, the Order in Council is ambiguous as to the nature of the interest conveyed. It is consistent with the granting of either a fee simple, or a statutory easement for irrigation canal purposes. In light of such ambiguity, resort must be had to the interpretive principles applicable to questions dealing with Indian interests, and the interpretation which impairs the Indian interests as little as possible is to be preferred. Thus, the Order in Council should be read as granting a statutory easement to the Province.

. . . . .

VII. Conclusion

[90] I conclude that the Order in Council is ambiguous as to the nature of the interest transferred. It does not evince a clear and plain intent to extinguish the Band's interest in the reserve land. An interpretation of the instrument as granting only an easement over or right to use the canal lands is both plausible and consistent with the policies of the *Indian Act* relating to taxation (s. 83(1)(*a*)) and expropriation (s. 35). This interpretation is consistent with the minimal impairment of the Band's interest in reserve land. Accordingly, I find that the Order in Council effected a grant of an easement over the land occupied by the canal and did not take away the whole of the Band's interest in the reserve. Therefore, the canal land is still "in the reserve" for the purposes of s. 83(1)(*a*).

[91] I would allow the appeal, set aside the judgment of the British Columbia Court of Appeal, and substitute therefor an order declaring that the canal land is in the reserve for the purposes of s. 83(1)(*a*). Since the appellant did not seek costs, I refrain from making an order for costs.

The reasons of **L'Heureux-Dubé**, **Gonthier**, **Major** and **Bastarache JJ.** were delivered by

Gonthier J. (dissenting): —

. . . . .

[135] Without detailing the content of the Crown's fiduciary obligation, which will vary with the facts, it is fair to assume that the legislation that would guide a s. 35(1) expropriation might inform the extent of the interest and the tract of land that the government ought to transfer in keeping with its fiduciary obligation. In this respect, I agree with my colleague Iacobucci J.'s views expressed under the heading "The Content of the Crown's Fiduciary Duty in the Context of Section 35", though in this case, I cannot agree that the Crown's fiduciary obligation regarding its adoption of the

Order in Council included a duty to protect an Indian interest in expropriated land sufficient to preserve the Band's taxation jurisdiction. The Band had no taxation jurisdiction to preserve in 1957, when the Order in Council was adopted. (The power to tax real property came into effect with the passage of what became s. 83 of the *Indian Act*, R.S.C. 1985, c. I-5, which allowed a band a limited power to tax contingent on a declaration by the Governor in Council that the "band has reached an advanced stage of development". It was not until the 1988 amendment to s. 83 (S.C. 1988, c. 23, s. 10) that all bands were given the broad jurisdiction to tax as exercized by the Band.)

. . . . .

V. Conclusion

[189] I would answer the first stated question — Are lands, taken pursuant to s. 35 of the *Indian Act*, "land or interests in land" in a reserve of a Band within the meaning of s. 83(1)(a) of the *Indian Act* such that those lands are assessable and taxable pursuant to Band Assessment By-laws and taxable pursuant to Band Taxation By-laws — in the negative, where full ownership is expropriated.

[190] I would answer the second stated question — If s. 35 of the *Indian Act* authorizes the removal of lands from reserve status, does federal Order in Council 1957-577, by which the Lands were transferred, remove the Lands from reserve status so that they are not assessable and taxable by the Osoyoos Indian Band — in the affirmative.

I would dismiss the appeal.

Appeal allowed.

The *Osoyoos* judgment is an illustration of the limitations imposed upon the Crown as a result of its fiduciary obligations to Aboriginal peoples. In *Wewaykum*, below, the issue of the Crown's fiduciary duty was connected to damages/loss of benefits alleged by two Indian bands to have occurred as a result of documentation errors by the Crown *vis-à-vis* two reserves.

WEWAYKUM INDIAN BAND v. CANADA

[2002] S.C.J. No. 79, [2002] 4 S.C.R. 245 (S.C.C.) (references omitted)

Binnie J.: —

[1] Two Indian bands on the east coast of Vancouver Island lay claim to each other's reserve land. The reserves, which have been in the possession of the incumbent band since about the end of the 19th century, are located two miles from each other. The inhabitants of both reserves are members of the Laich-kwil-tach First Nation which, in the mid-1800s, managed to displace the Comox First Nation from this area of British Columbia.

[2] Each band claims that but for various breaches of fiduciary duty on the part of the federal Crown, its people would be in possession of *both* reserves. Members of the other band, on this view, should be in possession of neither.

. . . . .

[4] Although the bands seek formal declarations of trespass and possession and injunctive relief against each other, each acknowledges the hardship that such a result would cause the other, and each band therefore says it would be satisfied with financial compensation from the federal Crown. The Cape Mudge appellants say *their* compensation should be in the range of $12.2 to $14.8 million for Reserve No. 11 and the Campbell River appellants say *their* claim is about $4 million for Reserve No. 12. In short, if the appellant bands' claims are allowed, each band will stay where it is but will receive substantial funds by way of "equitable compensation" plus costs on a solicitor-client scale.

[5] We are therefore required to consider (i) the scope of the fiduciary duty of the Crown in the process of the *creation* of Indian reserve lands; (ii) whether the acts of government officials in this case breached any fiduciary duty; and (iii) what equitable remedies (including equitable compensation) are available to remedy such breaches, if any.

. . . . .

[13] The legal requirements for the creation of a reserve within the meaning of the *Indian Act* were considered by this Court in *Ross River Dena Council Band v. Canada*, 2002 SCC 54 … At para. 68, LeBel J. noted "that the process of reserve creation, like other aspects of its relationship with First Nations, requires that the Crown remain mindful of its fiduciary duties and of their impact on this procedure, and taking into consideration the *sui generis* nature of native land rights". The role of the Crown's fiduciary duty in reserve creation was not argued in that case. It is squarely raised in the appeals now before us.

. . . . .

[19] I think there is no doubt on the evidence that when the federal Crown received the B.C. Order-in-Council 1036 dated July 29, 1938, it intended to set apart each of the contested reserves for the beneficial use and occupation of the present incumbent. The claim of each appellant band to *both* reserves is misconceived.

. . . . .

[64] In 1985, the Campbell River Band initiated action against the Crown and the Cape Mudge Band. It did so, as stated in para. 30 of its factum, because of the perceived impact of the decision of this Court in *Guerin v. The Queen*, [1984] 2 S.C.R. 335, where a precedent was set of financial compensation to an Indian band for breach of fiduciary duty in

the disposition of part of its reserve. The Cape Mudge Band counterclaimed for exclusive entitlement to both reserves and, in 1989, added a claim against the Crown. In October 1989, the actions were consolidated.

. . . . .

[71] The solution to these appeals, in my opinion, does not lie in the law of rectification but in the law governing the fiduciary duty alleged and the equitable remedies sought by the appellant bands, as will now be discussed.

M. *The* Sui Generis *Fiduciary Duty*

[72] If, as we affirm, neither band emerged from the reserve-creation process with both reserves, the issue arises whether this outcome establishes in the case of either appellant band a breach of fiduciary duty on the part of the federal Crown.

[73] Prior to its watershed decision in *Guerin*, *supra*, this Court had generally characterized the relationship between the Crown and Indian peoples as a "political trust" or "trust in the higher sense". ...

[74] The enduring contribution of *Guerin* was to recognize that the concept of political trust did not exhaust the potential legal character of the multitude of relationships between the Crown and aboriginal people. A quasi-proprietary interest (e.g., reserve land) could not be put on the same footing as a government benefits program. The latter will generally give rise to public law remedies only. The former raises considerations "in the nature of a private law duty" (*Guerin*, at p. 385). Put another way, the existence of a public law duty does not exclude the possibility that the Crown undertook, in the discharge of that public law duty, obligations "in the nature of a private law duty" towards aboriginal peoples.

. . . . .

[76] [In *Guerin*], Dickson J. ... pointed out that fiduciary duty was imposed on the Crown *despite* rather than *because* of its government functions ... Wilson J., in a concurring opinion, made similar comments ...

. . . . .

[78] The *Guerin* concept of a *sui generis* fiduciary duty was expanded in *R. v. Sparrow*, [1990] 1 S.C.R 1075, to include protection of the aboriginal people's pre-existing and still existing aboriginal and treaty rights within s. 35 of the *Constitution Act, 1982*. In that regard, it was said at p. 1108:

> The *sui generis* nature of Indian title, and the <u>historic powers and responsibility assumed by the Crown</u> constituted the source of such a fiduciary obligation. In our opinion, *Guerin*, together with *R. v. Taylor and Williams* (1981), 34 O.R. (2d) 360, ground a general guiding principle for s. 35(1). That is, the Government has the responsibility to act in a fiduciary capacity with respect to aboriginal peoples. The relationship between the

Government and aboriginals is trust-like, rather than adversarial, and contemporary recognition and affirmation of aboriginal rights must be defined in light of this historic relationship. [Emphasis added.] ...

[79] The "historic powers and responsibility assumed by the Crown" in relation to Indian rights, although spoken of in *Sparrow*, at p. 1108, as a "general guiding principle in s. 35(1)", is of broader importance. All members of the Court accepted in *Ross River* that potential relief by way of fiduciary remedies is not limited to the s. 35 rights (*Sparrow*) or existing reserves (*Guerin*). The fiduciary duty, where it exists, is called into existence to facilitate supervision of the high degree of discretionary control gradually assumed by the Crown over the lives of aboriginal peoples. As Professor Slattery commented:

The sources of the general fiduciary duty do not lie, then, in a paternalistic concern to protect a "weaker" or "primitive" people, as has sometimes been suggested, but rather in the necessity of persuading native peoples, at a time when they still had considerable military capacities, that their rights would be better protected by reliance on the Crown than by self-help. ...

[80] This *sui generis* relationship had its positive aspects in protecting the interests of aboriginal peoples historically (recall, e.g., the reference in *Royal Proclamation, 1763*, R.S.C. 1985, App. II, No. 1, to the "great Frauds and Abuses [that] have been committed in purchasing Lands of the Indians"), but the degree of economic, social and proprietary control and discretion asserted by the Crown also left aboriginal populations vulnerable to the risks of government misconduct or ineptitude. The importance of such discretionary control as a basic ingredient in a fiduciary relationship was underscored in Professor E. Weinrib's statement, quoted in *Guerin*, *supra*, at p. 384, that: "... the hallmark of a fiduciary relation is that the relative legal positions are such that one party is at the mercy of the other's discretion." ... Somewhat associated with the ethical standards required of a fiduciary in the context of the Crown and Aboriginal peoples is the need to uphold the "honour of the Crown" ...

[81] **But there are limits** [emphasis added]. The appellants seemed at times to invoke the "fiduciary duty" as a source of plenary Crown liability covering all aspects of the Crown-Indian band relationship. This overshoots the mark. The fiduciary duty imposed on the Crown does not exist at large but in relation to specific Indian interests. In this case we are dealing with land, which has generally played a central role in aboriginal economies and cultures. Land was also the subject matter of *Ross River* ("the lands occupied by the Band"), *Blueberry River* and *Guerin* (disposition of existing reserves). Fiduciary protection accorded to Crown dealings with aboriginal interests in land (including reserve creation) has not to date been recognized by this Court in relation to Indian interests other than land outside the framework of s. 35(1) of the *Constitution Act, 1982*.

[82] Since *Guerin*, Canadian courts have experienced a flood of "fiduciary duty" claims by Indian bands across a whole spectrum of possible complaints, for example:

(i)   to structure elections (*Batchewana Indian Band (Non-resident members) v. Batchewana Indian Band*, [1997] 1 F.C. 689 (C.A.), at para. 60; subsequently dealt with in this Court on other grounds);

(ii)   to require the provision of social services (*Southeast Child & Family Services v. Canada (Attorney General)*, [1997] 9 W.W.R. 236 (Man. Q.B.));

(iii)   to rewrite negotiated provisions (*B.C. Native Women's Society v. Canada*, [2000] 1 F.C. 304 (T.D.));

(iv)   to cover moving expenses (*Paul v. Kingsclear Indian Band* (1997), 137 F.T.R. 275); *Mentuck v. Canada*, [1986] 3 F.C. 249 (T.D.); *Deer v. Mohawk Council of Kahnawake*, [1991] 2 F.C. 18 (T.D.));

(v)   to suppress public access to information about band affairs (*Chippewas of the Nawash First Nation v. Canada (Minister of Indian and Northern Affairs)* (1996), 116 F.T.R. 37, aff'd (1999), 251 N.R. 220 (F.C.A.); *Montana Band of Indians v. Canada (Minister of Indian and Northern Affairs)*, [1989] 1 F.C. 143 (T.D.); *Timiskaming Indian Band v. Canada (Minister of Indian and Northern Affairs)* (1997), 132 F.T.R. 106);

(vi)   to require legal aid funding (*Ominayak v. Canada (Minister of Indian Affairs and Northern Development)*, [1987] 3 F.C. 174 (T.D.));

(vii)   to compel registration of individuals under the *Indian Act* (rejected in *Tuplin v. Canada (Indian and Northern Affairs)* (2001), 207 Nfld. & P.E.I.R. 292 (P.E.I.T.D.));

(viii) to invalidate a consent signed by an Indian mother to the adoption of her child (rejected in *G. (A.P.) v. A. (K.H.)* (1994), 120 D.L.R. (4th) 511 (Alta. Q.B.)).

[83] I offer no comment about the correctness of the disposition of these particular cases on the facts, none of which are before us for decision, but I think it desirable for the Court to affirm the principle, already mentioned, that not all obligations existing between the parties to a fiduciary relationship are themselves fiduciary in nature (*Lac Minerals, supra*, at p. 597), and that this principle applies to the relationship between the Crown and aboriginal peoples. It is necessary, then, to focus on the particular obligation or interest that is the subject matter of the particular dispute and whether or not the Crown had assumed discretionary control in relation thereto sufficient to ground a fiduciary obligation.

. . . . .

[85] I do not suggest that the existence of a public law duty necessarily excludes the creation of a fiduciary relationship. The latter, however, depends on identification of a cognizable Indian interest, and the Crown's undertaking of discretionary control in relation thereto in a way that invokes responsibility "in the nature of a private law duty", as discussed below.

N. Application of Fiduciary Principles to Indian Lands

[86] For the reasons which follow, it is my view that the appellant bands' submissions in these appeals with respect to the existence and breach of a fiduciary duty cannot succeed:

1.   The content of the Crown's fiduciary duty towards aboriginal peoples varies with the nature and importance of the interest sought to be protected. It does not provide a general indemnity.
2.   Prior to reserve creation, the Crown exercises a public law function under the *Indian Act* — which is subject to supervision by the courts exercising public law remedies. At that stage a fiduciary relationship may also arise but, in that respect, the Crown's duty is limited to the basic obligations of loyalty, good faith in the discharge of its mandate, providing full disclosure appropriate to the subject matter, and acting with ordinary prudence with a view to the best interest of the aboriginal beneficiaries.
3.   Once a reserve is created the content of the Crown's fiduciary duty expands to include the protection and preservation of the band's quasi-proprietary interest in the reserve from exploitation.
4.   In this case, as the appellant bands have rightly been held to lack any beneficial interest in the other band's reserve, equitable remedies are not available either to dispossess an incumbent band that is entitled to the beneficial interest, or to require the Crown to pay "equitable" compensation for its refusal to bring about such a dispossession.
5.   Enforcement of equitable duties by equitable remedies is subject to the usual equitable defences, including laches and acquiescence.

[87] I propose to discuss each of these propositions in turn.

1.   <u>The content of the Crown's fiduciary duty towards aboriginal peoples varies with the nature and importance of the interest sought to be protected. It does not provide a general indemnity.</u>

[88] In *Ross River, supra,* the Court affirmed that "[a]lthough this is not at stake in the present appeal, it should not be forgotten that the exercise of this particular power [of reserve creation] remains subject to the fiduciary obligations of the Crown as well as to the constitutional rights and obligations which arise under s. 35 of the *Constitution Act, 1982*" (LeBel J., at para. 62). Further, "it must not be forgotten that the actions of the Crown with respect to the lands occupied by the Band will be governed by the fiduciary relationship which exists between the Crown and the Band. It would certainly be in the interests of fairness for the Crown to take into consideration in any future negotiations the fact that the Ross River Band has occupied these lands for almost half a century" (para. 77).

[89] In the present case the reserve-creation process dragged on from about 1878 to 1928, a period of 50 years. From at least 1907 onwards, the

Department treated the reserves as having come into existence, which, in terms of actual occupation, they had. It cannot reasonably be considered that the Crown owed no fiduciary duty during this period to bands which had not only gone into occupation of provisional reserves, but were also entirely dependent on the Crown to see the reserve-creation process through to completion.

[90] The issue, for present purposes, is to define the content of the fiduciary duty "with respect to the lands occupied by the Band" (*Ross River, supra*, at para. 77) at the reserve-creation stage insofar as is necessary for the disposition of these appeals.

. . . . . .

[92] ... As stated, even in the traditional trust context not all obligations existing between the parties to a well-recognized fiduciary relationship are themselves fiduciary in nature: *Lac Minerals, supra, per* Sopinka J., at pp. 597 *et seq.* Moreover, as pointed out by La Forest J. in *McInerney v. MacDonald*, [1992] 2 S.C.R. 138, not all fiduciary relationships and not all fiduciary obligations are the same: "These are shaped by the demands of the situation" (p. 149). ... These observations are of particular importance in a case where the fiduciary is also the government, as the Court in *Guerin* fully recognized (p. 385). (In the case of rival bands asserting overlapping claims to s. 35 aboriginal title over the same land, for example, the Crown is caught truly and unavoidably in the middle, but that is not the case here.)

[93] The starting point in this analysis, therefore, is the Indian bands' interest in specific lands that were subject to the reserve-creation process for their benefit, and in relation to which the Crown constituted itself the exclusive intermediary with the province. The task is to ascertain the content of the fiduciary duty in relation to those specific circumstances.

2. Prior to reserve creation, the Crown exercises a public law function under the *Indian Act* — which is subject to supervision by the courts exercising public law remedies. At that stage its fiduciary duty is limited to the basic obligations of loyalty, good faith in the discharge of its mandate, providing full disclosure appropriate to the subject matter, and acting with a view to the best interest of the beneficiaries.

[94] ... In a substantive sense the imposition of a fiduciary duty attaches to the Crown's intervention the additional obligations of loyalty, good faith, full disclosure appropriate to the matter at hand and acting in what it reasonably and with diligence regards as the best interest of the beneficiary. In *Blueberry River* McLachlin J. (as she then was), at para. 104, said that "[t]he duty on the Crown as fiduciary was 'that of a man of ordinary prudence in managing his own affairs'". See also D. W. M. Waters, *Law of Trusts in Canada* (2nd ed. 1984), at pp. 32-33; *Fales v. Canada Permanent Trust Co.*, [1977] 2 S.C.R. 302, at p. 315. Secondly, and perhaps

more importantly, the imposition of a fiduciary duty opens access to an array of equitable remedies, about which more will be said below.

[95] In this case the intervention of the Crown was positive, in that the federal government sought to create reserves for the appellant bands out of provincial Crown lands to which these particular bands had no aboriginal or treaty right. ... [T]he people of the Laich-kwil-tach First Nation arrived in the Campbell River area at about the same time as the early Europeans (1840-1853). Government intervention from 1871 onwards was designed to protect members of the appellant bands from displacement by the other newcomers.

[96] When exercising ordinary government powers in matters involving disputes between Indians and non-Indians, the Crown was (and is) obliged to have regard to the interest of all affected parties, not just the Indian interest. The Crown can be no ordinary fiduciary; it wears many hats and represents many interests, some of which cannot help but be conflicting: *Samson Indian Nation and Band v. Canada*, [1995] 2 F.C. 762 (C.A.). As the Campbell River Band acknowledged in its factum, "[t]he Crown's position as fiduciary is necessarily unique" (para. 96). In resolving the dispute between Campbell River Band members and the non-Indian settlers named Nunns, for example, the Crown was not solely concerned with the band interest, nor should it have been. The Indians were "vulnerable" to the adverse exercise of the government's discretion, but so too were the settlers, and each looked to the Crown for a fair resolution of their dispute. At that stage, prior to reserve creation, the Court cannot ignore the reality of the conflicting demands confronting the government, asserted both by the competing bands themselves and by non-Indians. ...

[97] Here, as in *Ross River*, the nature and importance of the appellant bands' interest in these lands prior to 1938, and the Crown's intervention as the exclusive intermediary to deal with others (including the province) on their behalf, imposed on the Crown a fiduciary duty to act with respect to the interest of the aboriginal peoples with loyalty, good faith, full disclosure appropriate to the subject matter and with "ordinary" diligence in what it reasonably regarded as the best interest of the beneficiaries. As the dispute evolved into conflicting demands between the appellant bands themselves, the Crown continued to exercise public law duties in its attempt to ascertain "the place they wish to have" (as stated at para. 24), and, as a fiduciary, it was the Crown's duty to be even-handed towards and among the various beneficiaries. An assessment of the Crown's discharge of its fiduciary obligations at the reserve-creation stage must have regard to the context of the times. The trial judge concluded that each of these obligations was fulfilled, and we have been given no persuasive reason to hold otherwise.

3.   Once a reserve is created, the content of the fiduciary duty expands to include the protection and preservation of the band's interest from exploitation.

[98] The content of the fiduciary duty changes somewhat after reserve creation, at which the time the band has acquired a "legal interest" in its reserve, even if the reserve is created on non-s. 35(1) lands. In *Guerin*, Dickson J. said the fiduciary "interest gives rise <u>upon surrender</u> to a distinctive fiduciary obligation on the part of the Crown" (p. 382). These dicta should not be read too narrowly. Dickson J. spoke of surrender because those were the facts of the *Guerin* case. As this Court recently held, expropriation of an existing reserve equally gives rise to a fiduciary duty: *Osoyoos Indian Band v. Oliver (Town)*, [2001] 3 S.C.R. 746, 2001 SCC 85. See also *Kruger v. The Queen*, [1986] 1 F.C. 3 (C.A.).

[99] At the time of reserve *disposition* the content of the fiduciary duty may change (e.g. to include the implementation of the wishes of the band members). In *Blueberry River*, McLachlin J. observed at para. 35:

> It follows that under the *Indian Act*, the Band had the right to decide whether to surrender the reserve, and its decision was to be respected. At the same time, if the Band's decision was foolish or improvident — a decision that constituted exploitation — the Crown could refuse to consent. In short, the Crown's obligation was limited to preventing exploitative bargains. ...

[100] It is in the sense of "exploitative bargain", I think that the approach of Wilson J. in *Guerin* should be understood. Speaking for herself, Ritchie and McIntyre JJ., Wilson J. stated that prior to any disposition the Crown has "a fiduciary obligation to protect and preserve the Bands' interests from invasion or destruction" (p. 350). The "interests" to be protected from invasion or destruction, it should be emphasized, are legal interests, and the threat to their existence, as in *Guerin* itself, is the exploitative bargain (e.g. the lease with the Shaughnessy Heights Golf Club that in *Guerin* was found to be "unconscionable"). This is consistent with *Blueberry River* and *Lewis*. Wilson J.'s comments should be taken to mean that ordinary diligence must be used by the Crown to avoid invasion or destruction of the band's quasi-property interest by an exploitative bargain with third parties or, indeed, exploitation by the Crown itself. (Of course, there will also be cases dealing with the ordinary accountability by the Crown, as fiduciary, for its administrative control over the reserve and band assets.)

[101] The Cape Mudge appellants contend that the Crown breached its fiduciary duty with respect to its two reserves (while attacking the trial judge's rejection of this factual premise) by permitting (or even encouraging) the *1907 Resolution*. In the 1907 Resolution, the Cape Mudge Band ceded its claim over Reserve 11 to the Campbell River Band while retaining common fishing rights. The resolution was recorded in a change to the departmental reserve schedule with the name "We-way-akum band" entered opposite Reserve 11. Unfortunately, a clerical error left the impression that Cape Mudge Band Reserve 12 was also transferred to the Campbell River Band. This occurred through a "ditto mark error" which left unchanged the ditto marks against Reserve 12, directly beneath Reserve 11. The Campbell River Band relies on these errors as evidence of its right to both Reserve 11 and Reserve 12. As a result the Cape Mudge

Band claims that they have been deprived of their legal interest in Reserve No. 11, they say, by an "exploitative bargain". They gave away 350 acres for nothing.

[102] While the reserves were not constituted, as a matter of law, until 1938 [when British Columbia "transferred" Indian reserve lands to Canada], I would be prepared to assume that, for purposes of this argument, the fiduciary duty was in effect in 1907. The Cape Mudge Band argument is nevertheless unconvincing. I do not accept what, with respect, is its shaky factual premise, i.e., that the band "gave away" Reserve No. 11 as opposed to entering a quit claim in favour of a sister band with a superior interest. More importantly, this argument rests on a misconception of the Crown's fiduciary duty. The Cape Mudge forbears, whose conduct is now complained of, were autonomous actors, apparently fully informed, who intended in good faith to resolve a "difference of opinion" with a sister band. They were not dealing with non-Indian third parties (*Guerin*, at p. 382). It is patronizing to suggest, on the basis of the evidentiary record, that they did not know what they were doing, or to reject their evaluation of a fair outcome. Taken in context, and looking at the substance rather than the form of what was intended, the *1907 Resolution* was not in the least exploitative.

[103] While courts applying principles of equity rightly insist on flexibility to deal with the unforeseeable and infinite variety of circumstances and interests that may arise, and which will fall to be decided under equitable rules, it must be said that the bold attempt of the appellant bands to extend their claim to fiduciary relief on the present facts is overly ambitious.

[104] On the other hand, the trial judge and the Federal Court of Appeal adopted, with respect, too restricted a view of the content of the fiduciary duty owed by the Crown to the Indian bands with respect to their existing quasi-proprietary interest in their respective reserves. In their view, the Crown discharged its fiduciary duty with respect to existing reserves by balancing "the interests of both the Cape Mudge Indians and the Campbell River Indians and to resolve their conflict regarding the use and occupation of the [Laich-kwil-tach] reserves ... [without favouring] the interests of one Band over the interest of the other" (para. 493 F.T.R. and para. 121 N.R.). With respect, the role of honest referee does not exhaust the Crown's fiduciary obligation here. The Crown could not, merely by invoking competing interests, shirk its fiduciary duty. The Crown was obliged to preserve and protect each band's legal interest in the reserve which, on a true interpretation of events, had been allocated to it. In my view it did so.

4.   As the appellant bands have been held to lack any beneficial interest in the other band's reserve, equitable remedies are not available either to dispossess an incumbent band that is entitled to the beneficial interest, or to require the Crown to pay compensation for its refusal to bring about such a dispossession.

[105] The various technical arguments arrayed by the bands are, in any event, singularly inappropriate in a case where they seek equitable remedies. As noted, each band has, over the past 65 or more years, reasonably relied on the repeated declarations and disclaimers of its sister band, and on the continuance of the *status quo*, to reside on and improve its reserve.

[106] Reserves Nos. 11 and 12 were formally created when the federal Crown obtained administration and control of the subject lands in 1938. At that time, as outlined above, the appellant bands had manifested on several occasions their acknowledgement that the beneficial interest in Reserve No. 11 resided in the Campbell River Band and the beneficial interest in Reserve No. 12 resided in the Cape Mudge Band.

[At paragraphs 59 and 60 the Court wrote: "On November 23, 1936, a declaration was signed by the chief and principal men of the Wewaikai Band stating: 'We the Chiefs and Principal Men of the Cape Mudge Band, do hereby state under oath that the Reserves shown below are the only reserves belonging to this band and this list is complete' (emphasis added). Among these reserves were Reserve No. 10 (Cape Mudge) and Reserve No. 12 (Quinsam). The Campbell River Reserve No. 11 was not mentioned in their list. A parallel declaration was sworn by members of the Campbell River Band in 1937 indicating that 'We the Chiefs and Principal Men of the Campbell River Band, do hereby state under oath that the reserves shown below are the only reserves belonging to this band and that this list is complete' (emphasis added). The list referred to in their declaration, while it mentions 'Reserve No. 11', makes no claim to Reserve No. 12."]

The equitable remedies sought by the appellant bands necessarily address the disposition of the *beneficial* or equitable interest. The trial judge found as a fact (although not using these precise terms) that the equitable interests are reflected in the *status quo*. A mandatory injunction is not available to dispossess the rightful incumbent. Nor is there any requirement on the Crown to pay *equitable* compensation to a claimant band to substitute for an equitable or beneficial interest that does not belong to it.

[**Binnie J.** proceeded to discuss the application of equitable and statutory limitations to the bands' claims, which is excerpted, *infra*.]

. . . . .

Disposition

[138] I would therefore dismiss the appeals with costs.

————————

What did Justice Binnie mean when he said "Somewhat associated with the ethical standards required of a fiduciary in the context of the Crown and Aboriginal peoples is the need to uphold the honour of the Crown ...?" Is this akin to saying that a corpse is "somewhat dead?"

6.   To Whom Do the Crown's Fiduciary Obligations Belong?

A great deal of uncertainty about the nature and scope of the Crown's fiduciary obligations to Aboriginal peoples remains in spite of the continued application of the fiduciary concept to Crown-Native relations since the *Guerin* decision. None of *Guerin*, *Sparrow*, *Blueberry River*, *Osoyoos* or *Wewaykum* have addressed the fundamental question of which emanation(s) of the Crown owe fiduciary obligations to Aboriginal peoples in Canada.

(a) The Provincial Crowns' Fiduciary Obligations

To this point in Canadian Aboriginal rights jurisprudence, the Supreme Court of Canada has yet to definitively state that provincial Crowns owe fiduciary obligations to Aboriginal peoples (although a number of pronouncements at the provincial court of appeal level have done so). There are also valid constitutional arguments that justify the imposition of fiduciary obligations on provincial Crowns, as indicated in the following excerpts.

LEONARD I. ROTMAN, PARALLEL PATHS: FIDUCIARY DOCTRINE AND THE CROWN-NATIVE RELATIONSHIP IN CANADA

(Toronto: University of Toronto Press, 1996) at 221,
238-39, 251-53 (references omitted)

In the aftermath of the *Guerin* decision, the existence of the Crown's fiduciary duty to the aboriginal peoples is no longer in question. In the majority of post-*Guerin* decisions, judicial attention to the fulfilment of the fiduciary duties owed to aboriginal people has been directed to the Crown. However, these decisions have not addressed the issues of which emanations of the Canadian Crown — the Crown in right of Canada, the Crown in right of a province, or both — possess fiduciary obligations to the aboriginal peoples.

. . . . .

When the *British North America Act, 1867* [now the *Constitution Act, 1867* (U.K.), 30 & 31 Vict., c. 3] created federal and provincial Crowns in Canada, it did not affect the existing constitutional understanding of the Crown or the nature and extent of its pre-Confederation obligations and responsibilities. It merely divided the powers, responsibilities, and benefits of a single and indivisible Canadian Crown among the newly created federal and provincial Crowns. This division included the Crown's pre-existing fiduciary obligations to Native peoples. Therefore, the allocation of powers in the *British North America Act, 1867* did not remove or reduce the Crown's fiduciary obligations to the Native peoples, but simply redistributed them.

The fact that the Canadian Crown remained single and indivisible prevented it from escaping its obligations to Native peoples by donning a provincial — or federal — Crown "hat" at its convenience. The Crown could not escape, moreover, liability for adequately discharging its fiduciary duties by virtue of jurisdictional problems, such as those surrounding the establishment of Indian reserves from Indian lands surrendered by treaty: "Each level of government has an independent constitutional role and responsibility. ... Both are, however, subject to the demands of the honour of the Crown, and this must mean, at a minimum, that the aboriginal people to whom the Crown in all its emanations owes an obligation of protection and development, must not lose the benefit of that obligation because of federal-provincial jurisdictional uncertainty."

Mutual power entails mutual responsibility and it is this mutual responsibility, founded in part on the sharing of legislative and executive powers by the federal and provincial Crowns, that underlies the Crown's fiduciary obligations to aboriginal peoples. If a provincial Crown obtains exclusive proprietary and administrative rights over Indian lands surrendered by treaty, then it must, by necessity or logical implication, also obtain a portion of the fiduciary duties owed to the aboriginal signatories to the treaty. Section 109 of the *British North America Act, 1867* is the conduit by which this transfer is effected. Once this transfer takes place, the province is legally bound to cooperate with the federal Crown in fulfilling the terms of the treaty. Brian Slattery has expressed similar sentiments in "First Nations and the Constitution: A Question of Trust": "Where the benefiting Province has the exclusive constitutional authority to fulfill the Crown's promises, it cannot take the benefit of the surrender without incurring corresponding fiduciary obligations. Thus, if the Federal Crown has undertaken to set aside reserves out of the lands surrendered, this promise binds the Province to which the lands pass, because it alone has the power to carry out the promise."

. . . . .

Because of the absence of provincial participation in the majority of the events giving rise to the Crown's fiduciary duties towards Native peoples, provincial obligations stem primarily from the federal-provincial distribution of legislative and authoritative responsibilities in Canada. Areas of provincial jurisdiction in the *British North America Act, 1867* which have direct effects on aboriginal and treaty rights include section 92(5) (management and sale of public lands and timber), section 92(13) (property and civil rights), section 92A (natural resources), and section 109 (ownership of lands, mines, minerals, and royalties). The distribution of legislative and authoritative responsibility between the federal and provincial Crowns entails provincial acceptance of both benefits and obligations from the actions of the federal Crown after 1867 and from its predecessors, including the British Crown, prior to 1867. Provincial obligations also arise from direct provincial actions towards and interaction with aboriginal peoples.

The sharing of legislative responsibility over aboriginal affairs may be seen, for example, in the ability of provinces to pass legislation affecting aboriginal peoples through section 88 of the *Indian Act*. Even though legislative jurisdiction over "Indians, and Lands reserved for the Indians" is an exclusive federal power under section 91(24) of the *British North America Act, 1867*, section 88 of the *Indian Act* allows for provincial laws of general application to be applied to status Indians by referential incorporation, subject to the terms of Indian treaties, the *Indian Act* itself, or other federal legislation.

. . . . .

Where provinces intrude on the federal Crown's section 91(24) legislative sphere, they cannot do so without affecting the nature and scope of their own obligations to Native peoples. As Brian Slattery explains: "[S]o long as the Provinces have powers and rights enabling them to affect adversely Aboriginal interests protected by the relationship, they hold attendant fiduciary obligations." Provinces thereby acquire some measure of the federal Crown's fiduciary responsibility where they pass legislation referentially under section 88 of the *Indian Act*, play an active role in the formulation of land agreements concerning the establishment of Indian reserves, or actively participate in the negotiation of Indian treaties and agreements.

. . . . .

The line between federal and provincial jurisdictional boundaries is becoming increasingly blurred because of the effects of the *Constitution Act, 1982*. For this reason, it is likely that provinces will continue to encroach even further upon the federal Crown's section 91(24) jurisdiction over "Indians, and Lands reserved for the Indians" without reproach. As Dickson C.J.C. noted in *Mitchell* [*Mitchell v. Sandy Bay Indian Band*, [1990] 2 S.C.R. 85, [1990] 3 C.N.L.R. 46, 3 T.C.T. 5219, 110 N.R. 241, 67 Man. R. (2d) 1 (*sub nom. Mitchell v. Peguis Indian Band*), [1990] 5 W.W.R. 97, 71 D.L.R. (4th) 193] the "fluidity of responsibility across lines of jurisdiction accords well with the fact that the newly entrenched s. 35 of the *Constitution Act, 1982* applies to all levels of government in Canada." However, if there is to be a point beyond which provincial action that is consistent with or in fulfilment of its obligation to aboriginal peoples is deemed to be *ultra vires*, some judicial definition of that line and of provincial fiduciary responsibilities to the aboriginal peoples is necessary. Otherwise, instances that approach or even cross that line will be difficult, if not impossible to regulate.

LEONARD I. ROTMAN, FIDUCIARY LAW

(Toronto: Thomson/Carswell, 2005) at 586-91
(references omitted)

At the time this chapter was written, the Supreme Court of Canada had yet to comment expressly on whether provincial Crowns owe fiduciary duties to Aboriginal peoples. However, in *Sparrow*, the Supreme Court indicates that section 35(1) of the *Constitution Act, 1982* "affords aboriginal peoples constitutional protection against provincial legislative power," thereby indicating that provincial legislative powers — and, hence, the legislative branch of provincial Crowns — are also bound by fiduciary duties to Aboriginal peoples. The Supreme Court subsequently made an even stronger inference of provincial fiduciary duty to Aboriginal peoples in *Ontario (Attorney-General) v. Bear Island Foundation*.

In *Bear Island*, the Supreme Court states that "the Crown ... breached its fiduciary obligations to the Indians" without stating which emanation(s) of the Crown both held and breached this duty. It further explains in its brief judgment that the matter involving the breach of duty "currently form the subject of negotiations between the parties." What is intriguing about these statements is that the only parties involved in the negotiations in question were the Teme-Augama Anishnabai ("TAA") and the province of Ontario. The federal Crown was not involved. While nothing was expressly said about who owes the fiduciary duty in question, the only logical conclusion to be derived from these statements is that the Ontario Crown held a fiduciary duty to the TAA which it breached. Curiously, though, judicial statements made in subsequent litigation involving the same parties and the same claims contradict this conclusion.

The inferences of provincial fiduciary duties in *Sparrow* and *Bear Island* may also be seen in lower courts decisions during the same temporal period. For example, in *Cree Regional Authority v. Robinson*, it was correctly said that the Supreme Court's judgment in *Sparrow* did not distinguish between the federal and provincial Crowns in its discussion of fiduciary duties owed to Aboriginal peoples. Consequently, the Federal Court, Trial Division states that "the provincial authorities are also responsible for protecting the rights of the Native population." Meanwhile, in the trial judgment in *Delgamuukw v. British Columbia*, McEachern C.J.B.C. indicates that the Crown has a fiduciary duty to allow the plaintiffs to use unoccupied or vacant Crown lands for subsistence until such lands were dedicated to other purposes. Insofar as such a duty could only be enforced against the province because of the operation of section 109 of the *Constitution Act, 1982*, he determines that British Columbia is bound by the duty found to exist. Subsequent appeals of *Delgamuukw* did not address this fiduciary issue.

More recently, a number of courts have made inferences of provincial fiduciary duties to Aboriginal peoples. In the Ontario Court of Appeal's decision in *Perry v. Ontario*, the court indicates that "government must act in a fiduciary capacity with respect to Aboriginal people." Although this acknowledgment does not distinguish between federal and provincial levels of government, as with the situation existing in *Bear Island*, only the provincial government was a party to the proceedings and it was not specifically excluded from holding fiduciary office towards Aboriginal peoples. A similar result may be seen in *Westbank First Nation v. British Columbia (Ministry of Forests)*, where the British Columbia Supreme Court, in its list of conclusions, states that "[t]here is a fiduciary duty, including a duty to consult, where there is a possible infringement of an existing Aboriginal right or title or a treaty right." As with *Perry*, the discussion was not limited in its application to the federal Crown, but arose where Aboriginal or treaty rights could be infringed. Since provinces have the ability to infringe upon such rights, as specifically contemplated in *Sparrow*, that necessarily entails that provinces possess this duty.

Two more explicit judicial statements in support of provincial fiduciary obligations may be seen in *Haida Nation v. British Columbia (Minister of Forests)* and *Cree School Board v. Canada (Attorney-General)*. In the trial judgment in *Haida Nation*, Halfyard J. expressly finds that "the authorities do establish, as a matter of law, that the federal Crown stands in a fiduciary relationship with all Aboriginal peoples of Canada, and the provincial Crown stands in a similar relationship to the Aboriginal peoples of British Columbia." In the appeal of the *Haida Nation* case, the British Columbia Court of Appeal states that "[i]n *Halfway River* ... this Court confirmed that the fiduciary duty is owed to the Indian people equally by the provincial Crown as by the federal Crown." As indicated above, however, the Supreme Court of Canada has determined that no fiduciary duty exists in relation to the matters in question in *Haida Nation*. Meanwhile, in the *Cree School Board* case, the Quebec Superior Court twice indicates that Quebec possessed fiduciary obligations towards the Crees. Upon appeal, Rousseau-Houle J.A.'s judgment states that certain sections of the impugned agreement "must be interpreted broadly, liberally, and in compliance with the *governments*' fiduciary obligations toward the Crees." The same conclusion is reached in *Gitanyow First Nation v. Canada and British Columbia*, where Williamson J. puts forward the following conclusions on the effect of the 1867 division of powers:

> In 1867, the powers, duties and responsibilities of the Crown pre-Confederation were enumerated and assigned to either the Crown in Right of Canada or the Crown in Right of the Provinces. But, as can be seen above, the fiduciary obligation of the Crown which characterized its relationship with Aboriginal peoples continued after 1867 as before. As a result, in its dealings with Native peoples within its jurisdictional powers, the Crown in Right of British Columbia must act in light of that duty even as its predecessor, the Crown of colonial times should have done.

In opposition to these views is the Ontario Court of Appeal's judgment in the continuing *Bear Island* saga, where Laskin J.A., for the court, states "I am doubtful whether the provincial Crown owes fiduciary duties to Aboriginal people that, on breach, would allow for the transfer of land. The fiduciary duty of the Crown to Aboriginal people is fundamentally a duty of the federal Crown. This equivocal statement is not accompanied by substantive argument or corroboration, which ought to militate against prescribing any weight to it. However, it should be noted that the positive findings in the trial and appellate judgments in *Haida Nation* and *Cree School Board* also have little or no additional reasoning to support their conclusions. The lack of corroboration for any of these statements suggests either that the courts are uneasy with the issue of provincial duties or that they simply are not sufficiently comfortable with federal Crown fiduciary duties to Aboriginal peoples to begin contemplating holding the provinces similarly responsible. However, something rather different occurred in *Bear Island* which has implications for the authority of Laskin J.A.'s assertion. For the purposes of disposing of the matters in issue, Laskin J.A. assumes, without deciding, that Ontario possessed a fiduciary duty to the appellants regarding the matters in issue. Had he intended to make a firm statement that provincial Crowns do not hold fiduciary duties to Aboriginal peoples, it is illogical for him to have made the assumption he did.

In addition to what may be seen in existing jurisprudence, the RCAP also speaks of the fiduciary obligations owed to Aboriginal peoples in Canada as belonging to both federal and provincial Crowns at various places in its landmark report. In its discussion of treaties, the RCAP indicates that:

[t]he courts have ... enunciated new principles in recent years that Aboriginal parties to treaties can use to their advantage, such as the fiduciary obligations owed by federal and provincial governments to Aboriginal peoples and the fact that any violation of treaty promises would be seen by the courts as calling into question the honour and integrity of the Crown.[4]

More expressly, it states that, "[a]s pointed out by the Supreme Court of Canada in *Guerin* and *Sparrow*, Canada's relationship with Aboriginal peoples is a fiduciary one, trust-like in nature. Both orders of government must act in ways that honour this historical relationship between Canada and Aboriginal peoples." Finally, in its list of suggestions, the RCAP proposes:

... provincial and territorial involvement in all phases of the treaty negotiation process. Land settlements, the redistribution of government responsibilities, and co-management schemes all require provincial involvement. The provinces and territories cannot be indifferent about their obligations to Aboriginal peoples. In our view, they also have a fiduciary responsibility. As the principal beneficiaries of Aboriginal peoples' land losses resulting from disregard of treaties or failure to conclude them, they have a legal and moral obligation to participate in creating a new or renewed treaty relationship. We therefore propose formal consultations and negotiations between Aboriginal peoples' representatives and federal, provincial and territorial governments through the development of a Canada-wide framework agreement.[5]

We should make absolutely clear, however, that the federal government does not need the support of all the provinces to take action on Aboriginal issues. Under section 91(24) of the *Constitution Act, 1867*, Parliament has primary jurisdiction with respect to Aboriginal peoples. The federal government cannot, consistent with its fiduciary obligation, sit on its hands in its own jurisdiction while treaties are broken, Aboriginal autonomy is undermined, and Aboriginal lands are destroyed.[6]

Aside from the implications emanating from the very nature of the Canadian constitutional structure, the above excerpts demonstrate that federal and provincial Crown fiduciary responsibilities to the Aboriginal peoples are shown to have been derived from the Crown's historical relationship with the Aboriginal peoples and the treaties and other alliances that it entered into with them. Consequently, it is apparent that these obligations predate the existence of Canadian federal and provincial Crowns. The question, then, is to whom did they belong previously?

The obvious answer to this question is that those duties had belonged to the British Crown. It was the entity in whose name relationships were forged with the Aboriginal peoples and treaties concluded. The British Crown's historical relationship with the Aboriginal peoples and the many treaties and other alliances that it entered into with them — such as the Covenant Chain alliance discussed in Chapter 1 — carried with them continuing obligations of a fiduciary nature. What remains to be answered is whether those historic obligations survived the devolution of British powers over Canadian affairs culminating in the repatriation of the Canadian Constitution in 1982.

(b) The British Crown's Obligations

While the British Crown's divestment of its responsibilities for Canadian affairs entails that Britain no longer holds constitutional power over Canada, the devolution of powers from Britain to Canada would not have absolved Britain of the entirety of her fiduciary obligations to the Aboriginal peoples of Canada. Under the principle *delegatus non potest delegare* (a delegate must not re-delegate), the British Crown would retain ultimate responsibility for any delegations of fiduciary responsibilities it made, whether by formalized constitutional processes or otherwise. While the British Crown may delegate the entirety of its fiduciary *powers*, it may not divest itself of the totality of its fiduciary *responsibilities*. Although these conclusions are consistent with the dictates of the fiduciary concept, they have not been recognized in existing case law.

In two cases launched by Aboriginal groups in the English courts prior to the repatriation of the Canadian Constitution — *R. v. Secretary of State for Foreign & Commonwealth Affairs*, [1982] 2 All E.R. 118, [1982] Q.B. 892, [1982] 2 W.L.R. 641 (C.A.) and *Manuel v. Attorney General*, [1982] 3 All E.R. 786 (Ch. Div.), aff'd [1982] 3 All E.R. 822, [1983] 1 Ch. 77, [1982] 3 W.L.R. 821 (C.A.) — the English courts held that while Britain once possessed certain obligations towards the Aboriginal peoples of Canada, it no longer held any such responsibility; those duties, such as they were, were deemed to have been transferred to Canada. It should be emphasized, however, that neither of these cases dealt with the issue of the British Crown's fiduciary obligations towards the Aboriginal peoples, nor did they address the principle of *delegatus non potest delegare*.

While the passage of time does not forgive a breach of fiduciary duty, allegations of breaches of fiduciary duty may be defeated by applicable statutory limitation periods or equitable bars, such as laches (these are discussed, *infra*). Practically speaking, any attempt to obtain a remedy from the British Crown for a breach of fiduciary duty at this late date would be seriously impeded by its devolution of responsibility over Canadian affairs to the Canadian federal and provincial Crowns. For more detailed consideration of the British Crown's duty and its ramifications, see Rotman, *Parallel Paths, supra*, ch. 11.

7. Equitable and Statutory Bars to Breach of Fiduciary Duty Claims

As seen in many of the cases discussed herein, often a band's claim against the Crown for breach of its fiduciary obligations arises long after the alleged breach of duty occurred. This creates problems for contemporary breach of fiduciary duty claims, insofar as many bands were unaware of their rights for considerable periods of time and, at one time, were statutorily prevented from commencing legal actions against the federal Crown under the *Indian Act* (see s. 149A of R.S.C. 1906, c. 81, as amended by *An Act to Amend the Indian Act*, S.C. 1926-27, c. 32, s. 6, later *Indian Act*, R.S.C. 1927, c. 98, s. 141, repealed by *Indian Act*, R.S.C. 1951, c. 29). The problems associated with the use of breach of fiduciary duty actions by Aboriginal peoples against the Crown have been addressed in a limited way by the Alberta *Limitations Act*, R.S.A. 2000, c. L-12, s. 13, which exempts certain claims for breach of fiduciary duty brought by Aboriginal peoples against the Crown from the application of the current Act and its ultimate limitation period (although they are still subject to the limits established by its predecessor). Section 13 states:

> 13. An action brought on or after March 1, 1999 by an aboriginal people against the Crown based on a breach of a fiduciary duty alleged to be owed by the Crown to those people is governed by the law on limitation of actions as if the *Limitation of Actions Act*, R.S.A. 1980 c. L-15, had not been repealed and this Act were not in force.

Note that the reference in the Act to "the Crown" does not distinguish between federal and provincial Crowns. In addition, section 2(3) of the Ontario *Limitations Act, 2002*, S.O. 2002, c. 24, Sch. B expressly excludes from its operation both "proceedings based on the existing aboriginal and treaty rights of the aboriginal peoples of Canada which are recognized and affirmed in section 35 of the *Constitution Act, 1982*" and "proceedings based on equitable claims by aboriginal peoples against the Crown".

In the *Wewaykum* case, below, the Supreme Court of Canada addressed some of the concerns associated with the use of equitable and statutory bars to allegations of breach of fiduciary duty brought by Aboriginal peoples against the Crown.

WEWAYKUM INDIAN BAND v. CANADA

[2002] S.C.J. No. 79, [2002] 4 S.C.R. 245 (S.C.C.) (references omitted)

[The facts and issues in *Wewaykum* are detailed in the excerpt of the case found earlier in this chapter. The following discussion concerns only the effect of equitable and statutory bars to breach of fiduciary duty claims brought by Aboriginal peoples against the Crown.]

5.   Enforcement of equitable duties by equitable remedies is subject to the usual equitable defences, including laches and acquiescence.

[107] One of the features of equitable remedies is that they not only operate "on the conscience" of the wrongdoer, but require equitable conduct on the part of the claimant. They are not available as of right. Equitable remedies are always subject to the discretion of the court ...

Equity has developed a number of defences that are available to a defendant facing an equitable claim such as a claim for breach of fiduciary duty. One of them, the doctrine of laches and acquiescence, is particularly applicable here. This equitable doctrine applies even if a claim is not barred by statute. ...

. . . . .

[110] The doctrine of laches is applicable to bar the claims of an Indian band in appropriate circumstances ...

[111] It seems to me both branches of the doctrine of laches and acquiescence apply here, namely: (i) where "the party has, by his conduct done that which might fairly be regarded as equivalent to a waiver", and (ii) such conduct "results in circumstances that make the prosecution of the action unreasonable" (*M. (K.) v. M. (H.)*, *supra*, at pp. 76 and 78). Conduct equivalent to a waiver is found in the declaration, representations and failure to assert "rights" in circumstances that required assertion, as previously set out. Unreasonable prosecution arises because, relying on the *status quo*, each band improved the reserve to which it understood its sister band made no further claim. All of this was done with sufficient knowledge "of the underlying facts relevant to a possible legal claim" (*M. (K.) v. M. (H.)*, *supra*, at p. 79).

[112] I conclude therefore that the claims of the appellant bands were rightly rejected on their merits by the trial judge.

O.   In Any Event, the Claims of the Appellant Bands are Statute Barred

[113] Having rejected the appellants' claims to each other's lands on their merits I need not, strictly speaking, address the limitations issue. However, as this ground was extensively canvassed in the courts below and in argument before this Court, it should be dealt with.

[114] This case originated in the Federal Court. It is therefore subject to the limitation provisions contained in the *Federal Court Act* and, in particular, s. 39(1):

> **39.** (1) Except as expressly provided by any other Act, the laws relating to prescription and the limitation of actions in force in any province between subject and subject apply to any proceedings in the Court in respect of any cause of action arising in that province.

Section 39(1) effectively incorporates by reference the applicable British Columbia limitation legislation, but the relevant provisions apply as federal law not as provincial law ...

1. Constitutionality of the Prescription Period

[115] The appellant bands raise the threshold objection that provincial law cannot "extinguish" the Indian interest, which is a matter of exclusive federal legislative competence, *Canadian Pacific Ltd. v. Paul*, [1988] 2 S.C.R. 654, at p. 673. Section 9 of the B.C. Act provides for extinguishment of the cause of action, but, as stated, it applies as federal law.

[116] Parliament is entitled to adopt, in the exercise of its exclusive legislative power, the legislation of another jurisdictional body, as it may from time to time exist: *Coughlin v. Ontario Highway Transport Board*, [1968] S.C.R. 569; *Ontario (Attorney General) v. Scott*, [1956] S.C.R. 137. This is precisely what Parliament did when it enacted what is now s. 39(1) of the *Federal Court Act*.

. . . . .

4. Alleged Harshness of the Prescription Ban

[121] The Cape Mudge Band argues that the limitation periods otherwise applicable in this case should not be allowed to operate as "instruments of injustice" (factum, at para. 104). However, the policies behind a statute of limitations (or "statute of repose") are well known ... Witnesses are no longer available, historical documents are lost and difficult to contextualize, and expectations of fair practices change. Evolving standards of conduct and new standards of liability eventually make it unfair to judge actions of the past by the standards of today. ...

[122] The need for repose is evident in this case. Each band had settled and legitimate expectations with respect to the reserve it now inhabits. Each band still recognizes the need for repose of its sister band (thus seeking compensation from the Crown rather than dispossession of its sister band). Each band claims repose for itself, thus pleading the limitation period in its own defence against the other band.

[123] This is not to say that historical grievances should be ignored, or that injustice necessarily loses its sting with the passage of the years. Here, however, the bands had independent legal advice at least by the 1930s, and were aware at that time of the material facts, if not all the details, on which the present claims are based. While the feeling may not have been

unanimous, each band membership elected not to disturb its neighbours. The conduct of each band between 1907 and 1936 suggests that not only was the other band's open and notorious occupation of its reserve acknowledged, but such occupation was considered, as between the bands, to be fair and equitable.

[124] The Campbell River Band at para. 30 and again at para. 133 of its factum links initiation of these proceedings to a new awareness precipitated by the release of the *Guerin* decision in 1984 of the possibility of financial compensation against the Crown. Awareness of the availability of a claim in equity for financial compensation against the Crown does not, however, turn what the band regarded as an equitable situation into an inequitable situation.

5. Applicable Limitation Period

[125] The causes of action at issue in the present appeal arose prior to July 1, 1975, the date on which the new B.C. *Limitations Act* came into force. If the appellants' causes of action were already extinguished by July 1, 1975 (*Limitation Act* (1979), s. 14(1)), it is *prima facie* the 1897 version of the B.C. *Statute of Limitations*, R.S.B.C. 1897, c. 123, which was in force in British Columbia between 1897 and 1975, that applies. If not so extinguished, the provisions of the new version of this *Limitations Act* apply.

. . . . .

[131] With respect to the claims against the Crown based on breach of fiduciary duty, the 1897 Act imposed no limitation, and the case therefore falls to be decided under the transitional provisions of the 1975 Act. While the new Act is also silent with respect to an action for breach of fiduciary duty, or an action for declaration as to the title to property by a person that is not in possession of it, s. 3(4) of the B.C. *Limitations Act* provides a general six-year limitation period:

> 3(4) Any other action not specifically provided for in this Act or any other Act shall not be brought after the expiration of 6 years after the date on which the right to do so arose.

Section 14(3) of the 1975 *Limitations Act* therefore applied to bar actions for breach of fiduciary duty at the expiry of the grace period on July 1, 1977: *Bera v. Marr* (1986), 1 B.C.L.R. (2d) 1 (C.A.); *Squamish Indian Band v. Canada* (2001), 207 F.T.R.1 , at paras. 724-30; *Kruger, supra*. The appellants' causes of action in these respects were therefore statute barred when they filed their respective statements of claim.

[132] In any event, the claims asserted in these proceedings are all caught by the "ultimate limitation period" in s. 8 of the 1975 *Limitations Act* which says that "no action to which this Act applies shall be brought after the expiration of 30 years from the date on which the right to do so arose". The applicability of this limitation was affirmed in *Blueberry River*, at para.

107. The 30-year "ultimate" limit is subject to very limited exceptions, none of which apply here.

[133] Finally, it is appropriate to note in support of the limitations policy an observation made by the trial judge, at para. 520:

> ... for much of the century, members of both bands had first hand knowledge of the important events which are the subject of these actions. Unfortunately, within the last 30 years, those band members as well as the Indian Agents, have died and many of their documents have been lost or destroyed.

6. The Assertion of Continuing Breach

[134] The appellants contend that every day they are kept out of possession of the other band's reserve is a fresh breach, and a fresh cause of action. As a result, their respective claims are not yet statute barred (and could never be). ...

[135] Acceptance of such a position would, of course, defeat the legislative purpose of limitation periods. For a fiduciary, in particular, there would be no repose. In my view such a conclusion is not compatible with the intent of the legislation. ... It was open to both bands to commence action no later than 1943 when the Department of Indian Affairs finally amended the relevant Schedule of Reserves. There was no repetition of an allegedly injurious act after that date. The damage (if any) had been done. There is nothing in the circumstances of this case to relieve the appellants of the general obligation imposed on all litigants either to sue in a timely way or to forever hold their peace.

[136] Similarly, the "ultimate limitation" in s. 8(1) runs "from the date on which the right to [initiate proceedings] arose". All of the necessary ingredients of the causes of action pleaded in these proceedings could have been asserted more than 30 years prior to the date on which the actions were eventually commenced. The trial judge found that no new or fresh cause of action had arisen at any time within the 30-year period. None of the legislated exceptions being applicable, the 30-year "ultimate limit" applies by reason of its incorporation by reference into federal law.

[137] This conclusion accords with the result on this point reached in *Semiahmoo Indian Band v. Canada*, [1998] 1 F.C. 3 (C.A.), *per* Isaac C.J., at para. 63; *Costigan v. Ruzicka* (1984), 13 D.L.R. (4th) 368 (Alta. C.A.), at pp. 373-74; *Lower Kootenay Indian Band*, *supra*; *Fairford First Nation v. Canada (Attorney General)*, [1999] 2 F.C. 48 (T.D.), at paras. 295-99.

The application of statutory limitation periods to Aboriginal claims in *Wewaykum* was affirmed in *Canada (Attorney General) v. Lameman*, [2008] S.C.J. No. 14, [2008] 1 S.C.R. 372 (S.C.C.).

The following excerpt amplifies the concepts of laches and acquiescence addressed in *Wewaykum*.

LEONARD I. ROTMAN, PARALLEL PATHS: FIDUCIARY DOCTRINE AND THE CROWN-NATIVE RELATIONSHIP IN CANADA

(Toronto: University of Toronto Press, 1996) at 192-93
(references omitted)

Laches and Acquiescence

The applicability of the doctrine of laches to a breach of fiduciary duty is quite rare. Laches is an equitable doctrine which estops, or prevents, a plaintiff from asserting a right or claim by virtue of the combination of having taken too long to assert that right or claim and the prejudice that would result to the adverse party if the allegation was allowed to proceed after such a delay. It should be noted that mere delay alone is insufficient to ground a defence of laches. The delay must have the effect of demonstrating the plaintiff's acquiescence to the defendant's conduct, thereby implying the waiver of any rights or claims belonging to the plaintiff arising from the defendant's conduct. Acquiescence, in this context, entails the plaintiff's objective knowledge of the existence of and right to bring forth any equitable rights or claims based on certain facts — as opposed to merely having knowledge of the facts, but not knowing that they give rise to any right or claim. The plaintiff, therefore, must know of the existence of the defendant's conduct, the wrongfulness of that conduct, and that the wrongful conduct creates the basis of an equitable action. It should also be noted that acquiescence, on its own, may constitute a defence to a claim of breach of fiduciary duty by virtue of the prospective plaintiff's knowledge of and deemed acquiescence to the wrongful activity.

. . . . .

... [L]aches may only be successfully pleaded by a defendant to an equitable proceeding where there is a demonstration of prejudice to the defendant occasioned by the delay in bringing the proceedings caused by the plaintiff's action or inaction. The time from which the reasonableness of any delay is determined is the time at which the plaintiff first acquires sufficient knowledge of the facts which give rise to a cause of action. The determination of whether there has been unreasonable delay sufficient to constitute the basis of a claim of laches is, like all other equitable doctrines, situation-specific. It must, therefore, be made in light of the facts which give rise to the situation leading up to the allegation of delay.

The equitable doctrine of laches prevents a remedy from being granted where it would be unjust to do so in the circumstances. ... Consequently, where a beneficiary asserts a claim against a fiduciary, the doctrine of laches will generally not apply.

Following *Wewaykum*, there was a perceptible shift regarding claims made by Aboriginal groups regarding alleged breaches of the Crown's fiduciary obligations. Paralleling the increase in claims of breach of fiduciary duty following the *Guerin* and *Sparrow* cases, in which such claims were successfully argued and endorsed by the Supreme Court of Canada, the rejection of the claim made in *Wewaykum* and the Supreme Court's limitation of the applicability of breach of fiduciary duty claims resulted in a noticeable reduction of breach of fiduciary duty claims against the Crown. The case of *Ermineskin Indian Band and Nation v. Canada*, [2009] S.C.J. No. 9, [2009] 1 S.C.R. 222 (S.C.C.), which is excerpted immediately below, is the first post-*Wewaykum* case in which the Supreme Court has entertained questions about the Crown's fiduciary duty. As the excerpt demonstrates, however, there is little substantive discussion of the Crown's fiduciary duty that was characteristic of post-*Guerin* and *Sparrow* and pre-*Wewaykum* jurisprudence.

ERMINESKIN INDIAN BAND AND NATION v. CANADA

[2009] S.C.J. No. 9, [2009] 1 S.C.R. 222 (S.C.C.)

The judgment of the Court was delivered by **Rothstein J.**: —

I. Introduction

. . . . . .

[2] The appellants submit that the Crown's fiduciary obligations required it to invest oil and gas royalties received on behalf of the appellants as a prudent investor would, that is, to invest the royalties in a diversified portfolio. Instead, the Crown retained the royalties in the Consolidated Revenue Fund ("CRF") and credited interest to the appellants in accordance with a formula based on the market yield of long-term government bonds. The appellants say that the refusal or neglect of the Crown to invest their royalties has deprived them of hundreds of millions of dollars since 1972.

. . . . . .

II. Facts

[4] The appellants in the *Ermineskin* appeal ("Ermineskin") are Chief John Ermineskin and the Councillors of the Ermineskin Indian Band and Nation ("Ermineskin Nation"), acting on their own behalf and on behalf of the other members of the Ermineskin Nation. The appellants in the *Samson* appeal ("Samson") are the Samson Indian Band and Nation ("Samson Nation") and Chief Victor Buffalo, acting on his own behalf and on behalf of the other members of the Samson Nation.

[5] The Ermineskin Nation and the Samson Nation are "bands" within the meaning of the *Indian Act*, R.S.C. 1985, c. I-5, s. 2 … [and] are "bands" entitled to the benefit of Treaty No. 6, which was entered into in 1876. …

[6] The respondents in both appeals are Her Majesty the Queen in Right of Canada, the Minister of Indian Affairs and Northern Development and the Minister of Finance. I have used the term "the Crown" to refer to the respondents collectively. Indian and Northern Affairs Canada is the "applied title" of the Department of Indian Affairs and Northern Development ("DIAND"). I have used the legal title DIAND throughout these reasons.

[7] Due to the large number of claims, both the Ermineskin and Samson actions have been divided into phases. The trial leading to the present appeals dealt with the first two phases: the "General and Historical Phase", concerning the historical and background evidence relating to the specific claims in the other phases, and the "Money Management Phase", concerning allegations that the Crown has breached its obligations with respect to money held in trust for the bands. The issues on appeal here relate to the "Money Management Phase".

[8] The money held in trust for the bands is composed mainly of royalties derived from the oil and gas reserves found beneath the surface of the Samson Reserve and Pigeon Lake Reserve in Alberta. The Samson Reserve was established in 1889 pursuant to Treaty No. 6 for the Samson Nation. The Pigeon Lake Reserve was established in 1896 pursuant to Treaty No. 6 for four bands (often referred to as the "Four Bands"), including the Samson Nation and the Ermineskin Nation. The reserve belonging to the Ermineskin Nation exclusively has not produced any royalties.

[9] Under the terms of Treaty No. 6 and the *Indian Act*, it was necessary that the bands' interests in the oil and gas under the reserves be surrendered to the Crown so that the Crown could enter into arrangements with third parties in order to exploit the resources. The Four Bands in respect of the Pigeon Lake Reserve and Samson in respect of the Samson Reserve executed instruments of surrender in 1946 (the "Surrenders"). The Surrenders were accepted by the Crown. The terms of the two surrenders were identical.

[10] The statutory scheme governing the handling of Indian moneys, including the oil and gas royalties at issue in this case, involves the *Indian Act*, the *Financial Administration Act*, R.S.C. 1985, c. F-11 ("FAA"), and the *Indian Oil and Gas Act*, R.S.C. 1985, c. I-7 ("IOGA"). …

[11] Under the *Indian Act*, Indian moneys are characterized as "capital moneys" or "revenue moneys", and accounts for each of the two are kept separately by the Crown. There are separate revenue and capital accounts for each of the Four Bands, including the Samson Nation and Ermineskin Nation.

[12] The royalties are characterized as "capital moneys" and have been deposited in the CRF to the credit of the Receiver General of Canada pursuant to the FAA. Interest has been paid on that money by the Crown pursuant to an Order in Council made under s. 61(2) of the *Indian Act*.

[13] In 1859, the interest rate on Indian moneys was fixed by the Province of Canada at 6 percent. In 1861, an Order in Council lowered the rate on newly received money to 5 percent but continued the rate of 6 percent on money already held by the Crown in Right of the Province and, after Confederation in 1867, the Crown in Right of the Dominion of Canada. Between 1861 and 1969, the rate of interest changed from time to time, ranging from 3 percent to 5 percent, although it does appear that the rate of 6 percent remained for those funds in trust prior to 1861.

[14] In 1969, it was proposed by the Minister of Indian Affairs and Northern Development to tie the rate of interest to the market yield of government bonds having terms to maturity of 10 years or over (the "Indian moneys formula"), as well as to discontinue the guarantee of 6 percent on pre-1861 money. The Crown adopted those proposals. As a result, the interest rate has varied with the changes in the market yield on long-term government bonds.

[15] Discussions took place in the late 1970s and early 1980s between the Crown and leaders of various bands, including those of Samson and Ermineskin. This was in part because of an inversion, a situation that resulted in the market yield on short-term debt being greater than that on long-term debt. This situation did not last, but a new Order in Council was enacted in 1981.

[16] The new Order in Council provided that interest would be calculated on the quarterly average of the market yields of the Government of Canada bond issues as published each Wednesday by the Bank of Canada, which have terms to maturity of ten years or over. The discussions between the Crown and the bands also led to a Crown policy of crediting interest semi-annually, rather than annually. From April 1980 to the present, interest has been credited semi-annually at the rate determined in accordance with the 1981 Order in Council.

. . . . .

[18] Pursuant to an order of the trial judge dated December 22, 2005, on February 1, 2006, capital moneys belonging to Samson were transferred from the Samson capital account in the CRF to the Kisoniyaminaw Heritage Trust Fund.

[19] The amounts of money involved in this case are very large. The bands presented evidence at trial estimating the additional amounts which they argued might have been earned had their royalties been invested rather than earning interest under the Indian moneys formula. Using approximate numbers, these estimates ranged from $239 million to $1.53 billion for Samson, and from $156 million to $217 million for Ermineskin.

III. Issues

[20] The primary issue in these appeals is whether the Crown was obligated as a fiduciary to invest the oil and gas royalties that it was holding on behalf of the bands. If it is determined that there was no such

obligation, the issue is then whether the Crown breached its fiduciary obligations in the way in which it calculated and paid interest on the royalties.

[21] The bands also argued that the Crown breached its obligations to the bands because it was in a conflict of interest as a fiduciary by "borrowing" the royalties without permission, and that the Crown was unjustly enriched by this "borrowing".

[22] The appellants have also argued that if ss. 61 to 68 of the *Indian Act* do preclude the Crown from investing the royalties, those provisions infringe their right to equality under s. 15 of the *Canadian Charter of Rights and Freedoms*.

[The portion of the judgment relating to section 15 is omitted.]

. . . . .

V. Analysis

A. *The Source of the Crown's Fiduciary Obligations*

[44] There is no doubt that the Crown in this case has fiduciary obligations with respect to the bands' royalties. The Crown conceded as much. What must be determined is the basis and content of those obligations.

[45] There has been much discussion in this case of the "source" of the Crown's fiduciary obligations. The bands submit that the fiduciary relationship between the Crown and the bands arose initially out of Treaty No. 6, but that it also flows from the Surrenders, the IOGA, the common law and the *Indian Act*.

[46] If the fiduciary relationship arose out of Treaty No. 6, arguably the rights of the bands as beneficiaries of the relationship are treaty rights and thus constitutionally protected under s. 35(1) of the *Constitution Act, 1982*. The bands submit that any legislation purporting to restrict the Crown's fiduciary obligations and the bands' corresponding rights as beneficiaries would be inconsistent with their rights under Treaty No. 6, and therefore unconstitutional and of no force and effect according to s. 52 of the *Constitution Act, 1982*.

[47] Specifically, the bands argue that the Crown is obligated to act in accordance with the same duties as a trustee at common law, which include the duty to invest. The bands are essentially saying that they have a constitutional treaty right to have the royalties invested by the Crown. If this is correct, any provisions of the *Indian Act* which preclude the Crown's ability to invest the royalties would be unconstitutional and of no force and effect.

[48] If, on the other hand, the Crown's fiduciary obligations arose from the Surrenders, the IOGA and/or the *Indian Act*, the bands will have rights as beneficiaries of the Crown's obligations, but they will not be

constitutionally protected rights. As such, legislation that precludes investment of Indian royalties by the Crown will be valid legislation.

B. *Treaty No. 6*

[49] The bands say that Treaty No. 6 imposed on the Crown the duties of a common law trustee. In my view, Treaty No. 6 did not express such an intention. For example, the treaty states that the Plain and Wood Cree Tribes of Indians relinquished "all their rights, titles and privileges whatsoever, to the lands [within the specified territory]". The Treaty further states that reserves would be set aside and that the Crown would be entitled to sell or dispose of the reserve lands "for the use and benefit of the said Indians entitled thereto, with their consent". However, the Crown also retained the right to appropriate reserve land for any public purpose with payment of due compensation.

[50] This language does not support an intention to impose on the Crown the duties of a common law trustee. All rights were relinquished to the Crown, and the Crown then agreed to set aside certain lands for use by the Indian signatories. The language and circumstances point to a conditional transfer of the land, rather than the establishment of a common law trust.

[51] In any event, in my opinion, Treaty No. 6 does not assist the bands. Invoking it as the foundation for the Crown's fiduciary duties does not lead to the result that they seek — an obligation on the part of the Crown to invest royalties.

[52] The bands submit that the following words of Treaty No. 6 give rise to the Crown's obligations with respect to their royalties:

> [T]he aforesaid reserves of land or any interest therein may be sold or otherwise disposed of by Her Majesty's Government for the use and benefit of the said Indians entitled thereto, with their consent first had and obtained.

[53] The bands also submit that the "oral terms" of Treaty No. 6 included a promise by Alexander Morris, Lieutenant-Governor of Manitoba and the North-West Territories, that if any part of the reserves was sold, the proceeds of sale would be "put away to increase". According to the narrative of the negotiations leading to Treaty No. 6 prepared by A. G. Jackes, Secretary to the Commission, Lieut.-Gov. Morris had stated:

> They [other bands], when they found they had too much land, asked the Queen to sell it for them; they kept as much as they could want, and the price for which the remainder was sold was <u>put away to increase</u> for them, and many bands now have a yearly income from the land. [Emphasis added.]

[54] It has been held that it is unconscionable for the Crown to ignore oral terms and rely simply on the written words of a treaty. Extrinsic evidence can be used to give the proper effect to the terms of the treaty as they were understood by all signatories (see *R. v. Marshall*, [1999] 3 S.C.R. 456, at para. 12). While the statement made by Lieut.-Gov. Morris was with

respect to the previous sale of reserve land of other Indians, the representatives of the bands hearing the promise would have considered the statement to be a representation that such an arrangement would apply to them as well.

. . . . .

[56] In this case, the promise of Lieut.-Gov. Morris constituted a representation by the Crown that the proceeds of the sale of any part of the reserve would be "put away to increase". In my opinion, it is likely that the Indian signatories to Treaty No. 6 interpreted and understood Lieut.-Gov. Morris' statement as amounting to a guarantee that the proceeds of the sale of any part of a reserve would be kept for them by the Crown and that it would be safe and secure and over time would increase. In effect, the Crown guaranteed that there would be a return of and a return on the bands' capital funds with no associated risk of loss.

[57] However, the promise that the proceeds of sale would be "put away to increase" did not create a trust in the common law sense, whereby the Crown had the same duties as a common law trustee. There is no duty of a trustee at common law to guarantee against risk of loss to the trust corpus or that the corpus would increase. "Traditionally, the standard of care and diligence required of a trustee in administering a trust is that of a man of ordinary prudence in managing his own affairs", *per* Dickson J. (as he then was) in *Fales v. Canada Permanent Trust Co.*, [1977] 2 S.C.R. 302, at p. 315. However, in *Fales*, Dickson J. observed, at p. 319, that "[a] trustee is not expected to be infallible nor is a trustee the guarantor of the safety of estate assets". ...

[58] Investment always involves some measure of risk to capital. If the Crown were to have invested the royalties, then, depending on when the bands required liquidity, the royalties could have incurred a significant decrease in value.

[59] The interpretation of the treaty promise — that the money would be guaranteed and would increase — is consistent with the historical record, the actual practice of the government and with the Indians' understanding at the time of the treaty.

[60] In 1859, the government of the Province of Canada was faced with the question of the "Management of the Indian Trust and Funds". John A. Macdonald, later Prime Minister, signed a written submission to the Executive Council on August 25, 1859 recommending that Indian funds be carried "at the credit of the Trust to the Consolidated Fund, and to charge the annual interest upon that Fund" rather than continuing the former "System of investment which involves a possible loss to the Trust" (Executive Council Recommendation 1859-08-25, R.R., at pp. 657-58). It was recognized that the possibility of any failure in the payment of annual sums required for the Indians "would certainly be attributed to a breach of faith on the part of the Government and could more [*sic*] be explained to the satisfaction of the Tribes" and that "Parliament would probably find it necessary to make good the losses of the Trust" (R.R., at pp. 657-58).

[61] Thereafter, funds belonging to the Indians were never invested by the government. The consistent position of the government of the Province of Canada and later the Dominion of Canada was to hold funds belonging to the Indians in the CRF and to pay interest on those funds ranging from 3 to 6 percent per annum.

[62] Finally, holding funds to the credit of the Indians and crediting annual interest thereon was consistent with what the Indians themselves would have expected.

[63] The bands argue that the promise that the funds would be "put away to increase" represents "an attempt to convey the concept of investment in simple language to persons presumably unfamiliar with the concept" (Ermineskin factum, at para. 102). I do not think that that is a plausible interpretation of the promise that was made or the way in which the bands' representatives at the time would have understood the promise.
...

[64] While ambiguous treaty promises must be interpreted in a manner most favourable to the Aboriginal signatories (see *R. v. Badger*, [1996] 1 S.C.R. 771, at para. 9), that does not mean that an interpretation that is favourable but unrealistic is to be selected. The promise here was that the funds would be "put away to increase", and the only way that the government could fulfill that promise and that the Indians would be satisfied that it would be fulfilled would be for the government to carry the funds to the credit of the Indians in the CRF.

[65] That treaty promise, therefore, created two alternatives, neither of which required the Crown to invest the royalties. The first was that the Crown would not invest the royalties. The second was that the Crown would invest the royalties, as permitted by the legislation in force at the time, but would have to assume the risk of decrease and would not only be obligated to make good any lost royalties as forecasted by Macdonald, but would also be obligated to provide a return. However, as explained, nothing requires a common law fiduciary to assume such an obligation.

[66] Under the legislation in force until 1951 (*Indian Act*, R.S.C. 1927, c. 98, s. 92), the Crown could have chosen to invest Indian moneys, but could not be forced to do so. Requiring the Crown to invest and to assume the associated risk would take the fiduciary concept too far. If the Crown was unwilling to assume that risk, it was open to it to hold the moneys in the CRF and provide the bands with a return that satisfied its treaty promise that the funds would increase.

[67] For these reasons, I conclude that if Treaty No. 6, including the promise of Lieut.-Gov. Morris, constituted the basis of the Crown's fiduciary obligation to the bands, the obligation was that the royalties would be kept safe and secure and would increase over time. That could be guaranteed by the Crown holding the royalties and paying a rate of interest to the bands so that the funds would indeed increase. Treaty No. 6 did not obligate investment by the Crown. Rather than the Crown having the obligation to invest the royalties, it had the obligation to guarantee that the funds would be preserved and would increase. Because there is no

treaty right to investment by the Crown, s. 35(1) [of the *Constitution Act, 1982*] is not engaged.

C. *The 1946 Surrenders*

[68] The bands argue that under the 1946 Surrenders, the Crown had the obligation of a common law trustee to invest their royalties. The relevant words of the Surrenders are:

> TO HAVE AND TO HOLD the same unto his said Majesty the King, his Heirs and Successors, forever, <u>in trust</u> to grant in respect of such land the right to prospect for, mine, recover and take away any or all minerals contained therein, to such person or persons, and <u>upon such terms and conditions as the Government of the Dominion of Canada may deem most conducive to our welfare and that of our people.</u> [Emphasis added.]

The Surrenders expressly state that the Crown is to hold the mineral interests in trust and the terms on which it may grant rights to others to exploit those interests must be those that are most conducive to the welfare of the bands.

[69] The Crown had discretion with respect to the terms on which it granted rights to exploit the minerals and with respect to the way in which it dealt with the royalties it received on the bands' behalf. It was obligated to exercise that discretion for the benefit of the bands who rendered themselves vulnerable by having ceded their power over the minerals to the Crown by reason of the Surrenders. The bands were entitled to expect that the Crown would exercise its discretionary power with loyalty and care.

. . . . .

[71] In *Guerin v. The Queen*, [1984] 2 S.C.R. 335, Dickson J. explained the nature of the fiduciary relationship in general terms, at p. 384:

> [W]here by statute, agreement, or perhaps by unilateral undertaking, one party has an obligation to act for the benefit of another, and that obligation carries with it a discretionary power, the party thus empowered becomes a fiduciary. Equity will then supervise the relationship by holding him to the fiduciary's strict standard of conduct.

[72] The bands say that the duties of the Crown were that of a common law trustee, which would include the obligation to invest their moneys. While the common law trust relationship is one that has been developed and explained through years of jurisprudence, legislation and commentary, I see no reason why the duties of a common law trustee cannot be applied to any other fiduciary relationship if the nature of the relationship requires it. As La Forest J. stated in *McInerney v. MacDonald*, [1992] 2 S.C.R. 138, "not all fiduciary relationships and not all fiduciary obligations are the same; these are shaped by the demands of the situation" (p. 149).

[73] If a situation is such that a fiduciary is in a position similar to that of a trustee, even though the situation cannot necessarily be categorized as

a "common law trust", I do not see why the common law duties of a trustee cannot be applied to that fiduciary if that is what the particular situation warrants. In this case, the bands have placed particular emphasis on a trustee's duty to invest their royalties — the trust corpus. In my opinion, if the situation is such that the Crown is in the position of a fiduciary, although not strictly speaking a trustee at common law, and holds funds on behalf of the bands, it is not improper to ascribe to the Crown a duty to invest those funds in the manner of a common law trustee, subject to any legislation limiting its ability to do so.

[74] In my view, therefore, the relationship between the Crown and the bands is a fiduciary relationship that is trust-like in nature. The Crown possesses a discretionary power to act in the best interests of the bands, and the bands are vulnerable to the Crown's exercise of that discretion. The Crown may only grant rights over the minerals upon terms that are most conducive to the welfare of the bands, and will hold the proceeds of the granting of those rights on behalf of the bands.

[75] As I have indicated, legislation may limit the discretion and actions of a fiduciary, whether that fiduciary is the Crown or anyone else.

. . . . .

[79] This Court has held ... that when the Crown is a fiduciary, Parliament may legislate in ways that constrain or eliminate the Crown's fiduciary duties. The Crown's obligation is to act in a way that is consistent with its fiduciary duties as constrained by valid legislation. It is therefore necessary to consider whether legislation limits the Crown's fiduciary duties to the bands with respect to their royalties.

D. *The Statutory Framework*

[80] The statutory framework within which the Crown carries out its obligations is composed of the *Indian Act*, the FAA, and the IOGA. The bands argued that the statutory scheme permits investment by the Crown of the royalties, specifically, under s. 61(1) of the *Indian Act*. In my opinion, it does not.

[81] In order to determine the effect of the legislation on the Crown's obligations, it is necessary to examine the entire legislative scheme, starting with the IOGA. It will then be necessary to look at the FAA and the *Indian Act* and, in particular, how the provisions of those two statutes work together to inform the Crown's duties in the management of the oil and gas royalties.

(1) The *Indian Oil and Gas Act*

[82] Section 4(1) of the IOGA reads:

Notwithstanding any term or condition in any grant, lease, permit, licence or other disposition or any provision in any regulation respecting oil or gas or both oil and gas or the terms and conditions of any agreement respecting royalties in relation to oil or gas or both oil and gas, whether granted, issued, made or entered into before or after December 20, 1974, but subject to subsection (2), all oil and gas obtained from Indian lands after April 22, 1977 is subject to the payment to Her Majesty in right of Canada, in trust for the Indian bands concerned, of the royalties prescribed from time to time by the regulations.

[83] The IOGA was assented to in 1974, 28 years after the Surrenders. The Crown's obligations arise from the Surrenders, not the IOGA. The IOGA only confirms that the royalties in relation to oil and gas on reserves are to be paid to the Crown in trust for the bands. The IOGA does not set out any terms of trust or duties of the Crown and therefore does not limit the Crown's fiduciary duties to the bands. It is not a legislative restriction that would preclude investment by the Crown of the royalties.

[84] The interveners Saddle Lake Indian Band and Stoney Indian Band argued that the IOGA is a complete and comprehensive legislative scheme with respect to oil and gas royalties. According to these interveners, statements made during Parliamentary debates on the enactment of the IOGA confirm that the intent was to ensure that bands receive "the fullest benefits" and "[t]he greatest possible return" on oil and gas forming part of reserves (*House of Commons Debates*, vol. I, 1st Sess., 30th Parl., October 21, 1974, at p. 558). These statements formed the basis of commitments to those bands that the Crown will obtain "the greatest possible benefits from the oil and gas interests" (Saddle Lake and Stoney Indian Bands factum para. 45). These interveners argued that the IOGA contains specific "trust" language and that the honour of the Crown obligates the Crown to fulfill these commitments through private law trust duties.

[85] I am unable to infer from these statements of general intent, the specific intent that the Crown was to act as a common law trustee in respect of oil and gas royalties. ...

[86] In any event, I do not think that the above statements in Parliament were made in the context of the investment of royalties. Rather, they were made with a view to ensuring "that equitable benefits from oil and gas production on Indian lands go to the Indian people" and that "[t]he greatest possible return must flow to the band when the oil is taken from the ground and is lost to them forever" (*House of Commons Debates*, vol. I, 1st Sess., 30th Parl., October 21, 1974, at p. 558). Parliament's focus appears to have been on ensuring that bands were getting the best possible proceeds from their oil and gas reserves, not whether royalties would accrue interest from the government or be invested in a portfolio of securities.

[87] The Saddle Lake and Stoney Indian Bands also argued that because the oil and gas royalties can be either money or "in kind" according to s. 33(5) of the *Indian Oil and Gas Regulations, 1995*, SOR/94-753, passed under the IOGA (and previous versions of s. 33(5) since at least April 1, 1974), and because the FAA and *Indian Act* would have no application to "in kind" royalties, "the discretionary monies provisions of the *Indian Act* and the *FAA* [are] incompatible and thus wholly inappropriate legislation through which the trust duties of Her Majesty in relation to Indian oil and

gas royalties are to be considered" (factum, at para. 28). The Crown must therefore manage the royalties as a common law trustee.

[88] In my opinion, there is nothing preventing cash royalties from being dealt with under the FAA and the *Indian Act*. The fact that the IOGA allows for "in kind" royalties does not render these statutes inapplicable to cash royalties. The FAA and the *Indian Act* apply to cash royalties because those funds fall within the definition of "public money" in the FAA. There is nothing inconsistent between the IOGA and the application of the FAA and *Indian Act* to cash royalties.

(2) The *Financial Administration Act*

[89] The FAA governs the administration and management of government, particularly financial management and government spending. It sets out specific rules on the collection, management and spending of public funds.

[90] Section 2 of the FAA defines "public money" as:

… all money belonging to Canada received or collected by the Receiver General or any other public officer in his official capacity or any person authorized to receive or collect such money, and includes

. . . . .

(*d*) all money that is paid to or received or collected by a public officer under or pursuant to any Act, trust, treaty, undertaking or contract, and is to be disbursed for a purpose specified in or pursuant to that Act, trust, treaty, undertaking or contract;

[91] Because the royalties are money collected by Canada on behalf of the bands pursuant to the IOGA, they are "public money" within this definition and as such must be dealt with in accordance with the provisions of the FAA.

[92] Section 17(1) provides that "[s]ubject to this Part, all public money shall be deposited to the credit of the Receiver General."

[93] According to s. 2, all money on deposit to the credit of the Receiver General forms the CRF. The "Consolidated Revenue Fund" is defined as "the aggregate of all public moneys that are on deposit at the credit of the Receiver General". Pursuant to s. 21(1), the royalties, as public money under the definition in para. (*d*), may only be paid out of the CRF "subject to any statute applicable thereto". Section 21(1) states:

Money referred to in paragraph (*d*) of the definition "public money" in section 2 that is received by or on behalf of Her Majesty for a special purpose and paid into the Consolidated Revenue Fund <u>may be paid out of the Consolidated Revenue Fund for that purpose, subject to any statute applicable thereto</u>.

[94] Samson argued that s. 17(1) only requires that money be paid into the CRF and does not require that money be held in the CRF. According to Samson, investment by the Crown is not prohibited. I cannot agree. Section 21(1) provides that funds may only be paid out of the CRF in accordance

with any statute applicable thereto. It is necessarily implied that the royalties must be held in the CRF and only paid out in accordance with any applicable statute. The applicable statute is the *Indian Act*.

[95] Samson also argued that the former s. 18 of the FAA, enacted in 1951 (but repealed in 1999 (S.C. 1999, c. 26, s. 20)), was authority for investment by the Crown. According to Samson, the introduction of s. 18 (which at the time was s. 17) coincided with the 1951 amendments to the *Indian Act*, and was intended to replace the former investment section of the *Indian Act*. Former ss. 18(1) and 18(2) read:

> (1) In this section, "securities" means securities of or guaranteed by Canada and includes any other securities described in the definition "securities" in section 2.

> (2) The Minister may, when he or she deems it advisable for the sound and efficient management of public money or the public debt, purchase or acquire securities, including securities on their issuance, pay for the securities out of the Consolidated Revenue Fund and hold the securities.

[96] Sections 18(1) and 18(2), however, did not authorize investment in the public securities market. Rather, they provided only for the acquisition of "securities", defined in that section and in s. 2 of the FAA as securities representing part of the public debt of Canada. ... Section 90 prohibits any person, unless authorized by an Act of Parliament, to acquire shares of a corporation that would be held by or on behalf of or in trust for the Crown.

. . . . .

[98] ... The former s. 18(2) of the FAA did not authorize external investment by the Crown. Section 90(1)(*b*) of the FAA prohibits the acquisition of securities by the Crown unless authorized by an Act of Parliament. For this reason, it is necessary to find the power to invest and hold securities by or on behalf of or in trust for the Government of Canada in the *Indian Act*. As a result, I am unable to agree with Samson's submission that former s. 18(2) of the FAA authorized the Crown to invest in the public securities market. It is therefore necessary to turn to the *Indian Act* to determine if the Crown had the authority to invest.

(3) The *Indian Act*

[99] The *Indian Act* contains a number of sections under the heading "Management of Indian Moneys", namely ss. 61 to 69. ...

. . . . .

[111] Nowhere in ss. 61 to 69 of the *Indian Act* are investments of Indian moneys made, held and managed by the Crown contemplated.

(c) *The 1951 Amendments*

[112] Prior to the amendments to the *Indian Act* enacted in 1951, there was express permission granted under the Act to the Governor in Council to invest Indian moneys. The former s. 92 of the *Indian Act*, R.S.C. 1927, c. 98, read:

With the exception of such sum not exceeding fifty per centum of the proceeds of any land, timber or other property, as is agreed at the time of the surrender to be paid to the members of the band interested therein, the Governor in Council may, subject to the provisions of this Part, direct how and in what manner, and by whom, the moneys arising from the disposal of Indian lands, or of property held or to be held in trust for Indians, or timber on Indian lands or reserves, or from any other source for the benefit of Indians, shall be <u>invested</u> from time to time, and how the payments or assistance to which the Indians are entitled shall be made or given.

[113] This provision was repealed in 1951 (*The Indian Act*, S.C. 1951, c. 29, s. 123), and no provision authorizing investment took its place. The Assembly of First Nations argued that the investment power formerly contained in the *Indian Act* was transferred to s. 64(1)(*k*) in 1951 [an expenditure provision] …

. . . . .

[115] … After removing a provision expressly permitting investment, it could not have been the intention of Parliament to then preserve that power through a residual clause in a section providing for the "expenditure" of funds.

. . . . .

[117] A further indication of Parliament's intent can be drawn from the fact that from 1859 to 1951, the Crown had not engaged in investing Indian moneys but rather paid interest at rates from 3 to 6 percent. It is reasonable to infer that in repealing the investment power in the *Indian Act*, the Crown was bringing the legislation into conformity with actual practice.

[118] The bands have argued that the Crown could have used s. 4(2) of the *Indian Act* to render ss. 61 to 68 of the Act inapplicable. If those provisions were proclaimed to be inapplicable, it is argued that there would be no legislative restriction on the power of the Crown to invest. Section 4(2) states:

(2) The Governor in Council may by proclamation declare that this Act or any portion thereof, except sections 5 to 14.3 or sections 37 to 41, shall not apply to

(*a*) any Indians or any group or band of Indians, or

(*b*) any reserve or any surrendered lands or any part thereof,

and may by proclamation revoke any such declaration.

[119] However, the use of s. 4(2) in this manner would have had the effect of removing the application of those sections of the *Indian Act* for all purposes relating to the expenditure of capital and revenue moneys of the bands in question, not just in relation to investment of their royalties. By these money management provisions, Parliament created a complete code for the handling of Indian moneys. The inapplicability of the money management provisions would thus have far-reaching implications. For example, it would eliminate the requirement under the Act that the Crown obtain the consent of the bands for the expenditure of funds from the CRF. That the Crown could have used s. 4(2) in the manner suggested by the bands is unrealistic because of its broad impact.

(4) Section 21(1) of the *Financial Administration Act*

[120] The intervener Lac Seul First Nation argued that the FAA and *Indian Act* do not modify the Crown's duty as a common law trustee. It argued that "investment" is not an "expenditure", that s. 64 of the *Indian Act* does not apply, and that the *Indian Act* is therefore not an "applicable" statute within the meaning of s. 21 of the FAA. As a result, s. 21 operates as general authority to pay moneys out of the CRF to satisfy the Crown's common law duties as trustee, which include investment.

[121] I am unable to accept these submissions. Section 21(1) of the FAA says that money may only be paid out of the CRF "subject to any statute applicable thereto". Parliament could not have intended that the Crown retain a residual unilateral power to pay out band moneys from the CRF without consent of the bands for purposes not referred to in the *Indian Act*. Overriding the bands' consent would be contrary to the scheme of the *Indian Act*, which intended to recognize greater self-determination for Indians, while still protecting their interests. In *McDiarmid Lumber Ltd. v. God's Lake First Nation*, 2006 SCC 58, [2006] 2 S.C.R. 846, McLachlin C.J. referred to the Parliamentary debates on the amendments to the *Indian Act* in 1951. ... [where] then-Minister of Citizenship and Immigration Walter Edward Harris put the issue in general terms as follows:

> The problem is to maintain the balance of administration of the Indian Act in such a way as to give self-determination and self-government as the circumstances may warrant to all Indians in Canada, but that in the meantime we should have the legislative authority to afford any necessary protection and assistance.
>
> (*House of Commons Debates*, vol. II, 4th Sess., 21st Parl., March 16, 1951, at p. 1352)

[122] The relevant applicable statute is the *Indian Act* because it is the statutory scheme governing the control and management of Indian moneys. It provides no authority for any expenditure or payment of Indian moneys other than for the purposes provided for in the Act. The *Indian Act* does not provide for investment.

[123] The wording of the *Indian Act* and the legislative changes made in 1951 indicate that no power existed after that time for the Crown to make, hold and manage investments made with Indian moneys.

E. *The Crown's Fiduciary Obligations to the Bands*

[124] It is next necessary to determine whether the Crown's actions under the authority of the FAA and the *Indian Act*, including the Indian moneys formula, were consistent with its fiduciary obligations to the bands.

[125] A fundamental principle underlying the fiduciary relationship is the requirement that a fiduciary acts "exclusively for the benefit of the other, putting his own interests completely aside" (Waters, Gillen and Smith, at p. 877). This is the duty of loyalty and it requires the trustee to avoid conflicts of interest. A fiduciary is required to avoid situations where its duty to act for the sole benefit of the trust and its beneficiaries conflicts with its own self-interest or its duties to another (see Waters, Gillen and Smith, at p. 877, and *Lac Minerals Ltd. v. International Corona Resources Ltd.*, [1989] 2 S.C.R. 574, at pp. 646-47).

[126] At common law, a trustee is not permitted to borrow from the trust, as this would constitute a conflict of interest. The bands argued that the Crown was in a position of conflict of interest and therefore in breach of its fiduciary duty to them because their royalties were held in the CRF for use by the Crown. The bands have characterized the fact that the royalties are held in the CRF for use by the Crown as a "forced borrowing", and that without their consent it is improper or unlawful.

[127] The Crown is in a unique position as a fiduciary with respect to the royalties and the payment of interest. The Crown is borrowing the bands' money held in the CRF. However, the borrowing is required by the legislation. According to s. 61(2) of the *Indian Act*, "[i]nterest on Indian moneys held in the Consolidated Revenue Fund shall be allowed at a rate to be fixed from time to time by the Governor in Council". As the majority of the Court of Appeal noted, this borrowing is an "inevitable consequence of the combined operation of the *Indian Act* and the *Financial Administration Act*" (para. 120).

[128] A fiduciary that acts in accordance with legislation cannot be said to be breaching its fiduciary duty. The situation which the bands characterize as a conflict of interest is an inherent and inevitable consequence of the statutory scheme.

[129] The Crown's position in the setting of the interest rate paid to the bands is also unique. On the one hand, it has fiduciary duties that are owed to the bands, including the duty of loyalty and the obligation to act in the bands' best interests. On the other hand, the Crown must pay the interest owed to the bands with funds from the public treasury financed by taxpayers. The Crown has responsibilities to all Canadians, and some balancing inevitably must be involved.

[130] As Binnie J. stated in *Wewaykum Indian Band v. Canada*, 2002 SCC 79, [2002] 4 S.C.R. 245, at para. 96, "[t]he Crown can be no ordinary

fiduciary; it wears many hats and represents many interests, some of which cannot help but be conflicting". In the present case, the Crown must consider not only the interests of the bands but also the interests of other Canadians when it sets the interest rate paid to the bands.

[131] The standard of care required of the Crown in administering the funds of the bands is that of "a man of ordinary prudence in managing his own affairs", *per* Dickson J. in *Fales*, at p. 315. However, because the Crown "can be no ordinary fiduciary", its obligation to act as a person of ordinary prudence in managing his or her own affairs is modified by relevant legislation and by the kinds of considerations outlined above.

F. *The Test for Determining the Obligations of the Crown in Providing a Return to the Bands*

[132] Within the Crown's discretion as a fiduciary, it had a number of options for setting the interest rate paid to the bands. The range of options included: (1) a flat rate of interest that might be adjusted from time to time; (2) interest at the rate of return of short-term treasury bills; (3) interest equivalent to the return on a diversified portfolio; (4) interest at a rate tied to the yield on long-term government bonds but adjusted periodically; or (5) interest at the yield on long-term government bonds guaranteed for the term of the bonds, i.e. a laddered bond portfolio.

[A detailed discussion of these options is omitted.]

(6) Conclusion Respecting the Methodology Selected By the Crown

[147] Of the alternatives considered, it is apparent that short-term rates would not have been in the best interests of the bands when it was possible for the Crown to pay interest at a higher rate in view of the Crown's diversified borrowing patterns. A fixed rate of interest would not have been sufficiently flexible to account for changes in prevailing interest rates and inflation. Payment of interest equivalent to what might have been earned in a diversified portfolio would have required subsidization from the public treasury. A fiduciary is not required to supplement the return it is legislatively restricted to providing from its own resources, in this case, the public treasury.

[148] The two alternatives that could have been selected by a prudent person managing his or her own affairs but modified by the constraints applicable to the Crown were the fluctuating rate approach adopted by the Crown and the laddered bond approach. When the Indian moneys formula was adopted in 1969, interest rates were tending upwards. In hindsight, because interest rates have tended downwards since the 1980s, investment in a laddered bond portfolio would have produced higher returns for the bands since that time than the long-term floating rate approach that was adopted. However, compliance by the Crown with its fiduciary obligations to the bands must be viewed prospectively.

[149] Without knowing the direction of interest rates and anticipated inflation, it cannot be said that the adoption of a floating long-term rate was an imprudent choice by the Crown. It was a way of contending with interest rates and inflation risk. I am of the opinion that in selecting the floating rate methodology of the Indian moneys formula, there was no breach of the fiduciary duty owed by the Crown to the bands.

G. *Transfer of Funds to the Bands*

[150] An alternative to the payment of interest by the Crown would have been the transfer of funds to the bands or to independent trustees for the benefit of the bands. The funds could then be invested by the bands or their trustees without control or management by the Crown. The bands assert that they had repeatedly demanded that their moneys be released to them by the Crown or to independent trustees but that the Crown had refused to do so. This position was not specifically argued as a breach of trust or fiduciary duty by the Crown. The bands simply argued that the Crown not only refused to invest the royalties, but also refused to allow the bands to invest them.

[151] Before this Court, the parties have argued that s. 64(1)(k) of the *Indian Act* provides authority for the transfer of capital moneys from the Crown to either the bands themselves or to an independent trust for the bands. When funds are transferred, the transfer constitutes an "expenditure" because the funds are no longer held by the Crown in trust. I accept this position.

[152] However, the Crown cannot simply transfer funds. In accordance with its fiduciary obligations and s. 64(1)(k) of the *Indian Act*, it must be satisfied that any transfer is in the best interests of the bands. Once a transfer is effected, the Crown's fiduciary obligations with regard to the funds in question must cease, as it no longer has control over the funds and is not responsible for their management. It is therefore necessary to consider history of dealings between the bands and the Crown to determine whether the Crown should have transferred some or all of the funds to the bands.

(1) Samson

[153] In February and April 1980, Samson requested transfer of $35 million from its capital funds in the CRF to establish Peace Hills Trust. This money was transferred by the Crown. It appears that when the $35 million was transferred to Samson to establish Peace Hills Trust, DIAND officials believed that the transfer was in the best interests of Samson. However, a report prepared for Samson by management consultants P. S. Ross & Partners in December 1979 had found that "[a] lack of long-range planning, including financial planning, prevails across the organization". The report stated:

> Furthermore, major financial decisions are not made as part of an overall plan to achieve specific results, but on an emotional basis, with

consideration only being given to the possible short-term benefits. No serious consideration is given to the long term effects which these investments may have.

(R.R., at p. 2514)

[154] Samson requested a further transfer of all its remaining royalties in the CRF to Peace Hills Trust in December 1980. During discussions between members of Samson and DIAND officials in early 1981, DIAND expressed the view that additional information regarding the requested transfer would be necessary. Some of this additional information was provided to DIAND, but not all the information that was requested.

. . . . .

[169] Throughout the dealings between Samson and the Crown, the evidence indicates that the Crown was supportive of the band's proposals to transfer money for the establishment of Peace Hills Trust and Samson Band Heritage Trust Fund. However, due to difficulties uncovering information as to the disposition of the $35 million actually transferred, the failure of Samson to provide adequate financial plans and assurances of band support and conflict within the Samson band council, the Crown was unable to assure itself that transferring further funds would be in the best interests of Samson.

[170] Having regard to the evidence, in my opinion, for the Crown to have agreed to further transfers prior to the order of Teitelbaum J. in 2005 would have been imprudent.

(2)   Ermineskin

[171] In 1983, the Crown contacted Ermineskin with invitations to consider the transfer of funds from Ermineskin's capital accounts in the CRF to Ermineskin's control and management. In January 1985, the Four Bands (which included Ermineskin) made a presentation to David Crombie, the then-Minister of Indian and Northern Affairs, stating that a Heritage Trust concept had been developed that would require the release of funds from their capital account (R.R., at pp. 2833-38). A November 1985 letter from Crombie to Ermineskin's Chief Littlechild stated that a transfer proposal had not yet been formally submitted by Ermineskin and that a determination could not be made until the details of the proposal were known (R.R., at pp. 3115-16).

[172] For the first time, in September 1988, Ermineskin formally proposed the creation of the Ermineskin Heritage Trust. Ermineskin submitted a band council resolution, draft trust deed, tax ruling and long-range planning memorandum to DIAND. DIAND was supportive of this proposal, although it remained concerned about its responsibilities and authority to approve such a transfer under the *Indian Act*.

[173] A number of discussions took place between the Crown and Ermineskin. Eventually, a plan was developed for legislation specific to

Ermineskin which would satisfy the Crown's concerns about legal authority for the transfer. Ermineskin was sent the drafting instructions for the legislation and offered comments, most of which were accepted by the Crown.

[174] According to the record, in order to effect a transfer of capital funds from the CRF to the Ermineskin Heritage Trust, the Crown asked for a full release of any obligations with respect to the transferred funds. However, at an Ermineskin band council meeting in early 1990, it was decided not to proceed with the Ermineskin Heritage Trust because Ermineskin was unwilling to release the Crown from any future responsibility for the management of the transferred funds (R.R., at pp. 3582-85).

[175] In January 1991, Ermineskin submitted a "Proposal of Ermineskin Indian Band Regarding Management of Indian Moneys", which stated that Ermineskin wished to conduct its own analysis of available money management options (R.R., at p. 3683). The record does not indicate that any further steps were taken.

[176] In November 1990, the Crown had created the Indian Moneys Committee to address the need for Indian participation in and support of legislative reform apparently thought necessary to enable Indian control of capital moneys. Ermineskin actively participated in the Committee. The Committee recommended optional legislation which would allow bands to opt out of the provisions of the *Indian Act* and manage their own moneys. The majority of the recommendations of the Committee were accepted by the Crown, and drafting began.

[177] In May 1992, Ermineskin commenced its action against the Crown. Work continued on the proposed legislation, however, and a final draft of the proposed *First Nations Moneys Management Act* was prepared in 1993. In January 1994, a letter from Ermineskin's counsel to the Crown demanded that the Crown invest Ermineskin's royalties itself. However, a letter from the co-chairs of the Indian Moneys Committee to Ronald Irwin, the then-Minister of Indian Affairs and Northern Development, a month later stated that Ermineskin supported the text of the proposed legislation (R.R., at pp. 4047-48).

[178] The record indicates that at a meeting between DIAND and the Committee in August 1994, representatives of only two bands attended and that the Crown was not willing to proceed with the legislation without widespread support of the bands.

[179] In 1996, Ermineskin again demanded that the Crown invest its capital moneys (Blake, Cassels & Graydon letter, February 15, 1996, [R.R., at p. 4072]). The Crown's response stated that while it would not invest the funds itself, it would be willing to resurrect the Ermineskin Heritage Trust Proposal. Ermineskin continued to reiterate its demand that the Crown invest its moneys, but it appears that no further developments occurred. Ermineskin never revived the Ermineskin Heritage Trust Proposal, and the proposed money management legislation was never enacted.

[180] It appears that the major points of contention were Ermineskin's demands that the Crown invest its royalties and its refusal to release the

Crown of ongoing responsibility in the event of a transfer of the funds for investment by the band itself. Ermineskin stated in its factum that "Ermineskin members have been reluctant to terminate the trust relationship with the Crown" (para. 62). However, the Crown could not agree to ongoing responsibility without having control over the management of the funds.

[181] As I have explained earlier, the Crown was restricted by legislation from investing Ermineskin's royalties and could not accede to the band's demands to do so. In the event of a transfer, the Crown's fiduciary obligations with regard to the funds had to come to an end. The Crown could not be expected to remain responsible for funds over which it no longer had control. In the absence of a release from the band to the Crown, the Crown could not be expected to transfer funds from the CRF to Ermineskin.

[Discussion of whether the Crown was unjustly enriched by making use of the bands' royalties and paying the rate of interest that it did is omitted. The Supreme Court of Canada found no unjust enrichment to have occurred. Arguments regarding the constitutional validity of ss. 61 to 68 of the *Indian Act* as being contrary to s. 15(1) of the Charter are also omitted. No violation of s. 15(1) was found.]

VI. Conclusion

[203] I would dismiss the appeals with costs.

Appeal dismissed.

The *Ermineskin* case was a very specific and limited example of Crown fiduciary duty argued to have existed. Thus, there may not have been much of a need to engage in broader considerations of the Crown's fiduciary obligations in that case. In the subsequent decision in *Lax Kw'alaams Indian Band v. Canada (Attorney General)*, [2011] S.C.J. No. 56, [2011] 3 S.C.R. 535 (S.C.C.), which is excerpted in Chapter 2, the band argued that a fiduciary duty existed to grant it a modern commercial fishery based on its historical fishing practices. In denying the band the right to a modern commercial fishery, the Supreme Court of Canada's unanimous judgment said little about the Crown's fiduciary duty, whether to Aboriginal peoples generally or to the *Lax Kw'alaams* band specifically.

D. THE DUTY TO CONSULT

The creation of an independent Crown duty to consult with and, in appropriate circumstances, to accommodate Aboriginal peoples is a recent development in Canadian jurisprudence. *Haida Nation v. British Columbia (Minister of Forests)* is the leading case articulating principles related to the

Crown's duty to consult with Aboriginal peoples. As you read this case in the following pages, ask yourself whether it represents a logical extension or radical departure from the developed law relating to the Crown's other obligations to Aboriginal peoples in Canada.

HAIDA NATION v. BRITISH COLUMBIA (MINISTER OF FORESTS)

[2004] S.C.J. No. 70, [2004] 3 S.C.R. 511 (S.C.C.)

The judgment of the Court was delivered by **THE CHIEF JUSTICE:** —

I. Introduction

[1] To the west of the mainland of British Columbia lie the Queen Charlotte Islands, the traditional homeland of the Haida people. Haida Gwaii, as the inhabitants call it, consists of two large islands and a number of smaller islands. For more than 100 years, the Haida people have claimed title to all the lands of the Haida Gwaii and the waters surrounding it. That title is still in the claims process and has not yet been legally recognized.

[2] The islands of Haida Gwaii are heavily forested. Spruce, hemlock and cedar abound. The most important of these is the cedar which, since time immemorial, has played a central role in the economy and culture of the Haida people. It is from cedar that they made their ocean-going canoes, their clothing, their utensils and the totem poles that guarded their lodges. The cedar forest remains central to their life and their conception of themselves.

[3] The forests of Haida Gwaii have been logged since before the First World War. Portions of the island have been logged off. Other portions bear second-growth forest. In some areas, old-growth forests can still be found.

[4] The Province of British Columbia continues to issue licences to cut trees on Haida Gwaii to forestry companies. The modern name for these licenses are Tree Farm Licences, or T.F.L.'s. Such a licence is at the heart of this litigation. A large forestry firm, MacMillan Bloedel Limited acquired T.F.L. 39 in 1961, permitting it to harvest trees in an area designated as Block 6. In 1981, 1995 and 2000, the Minister replaced T.F.L. 39 pursuant to procedures set out in the *Forest Act*, R.S.B.C. 1996, c. 157. In 1999, the Minister approved a transfer of T.F.L. 39 to Weyerhaeuser Company Limited ("Weyerhaeuser"). The Haida people challenged these replacements and the transfer, which were made without their consent and, since at least 1994, over their objections. Nevertheless, T.F.L. 39 continued.

[5] In January of 2000, the Haida people launched a lawsuit objecting to the three replacement decisions and the transfer of T.F.L. 39 to Weyerhaeuser and asking that they be set aside. They argued legal encumbrance, equitable encumbrance and breach of fiduciary duty, all grounded in their assertion of Aboriginal title.

[6] This brings us to the issue before this Court. The government holds legal title to the land. Exercising that legal title, it has granted Weyerhaeuser the right to harvest the forests in Block 6 of the land. But the Haida people also claim title to the land — title which they are in the process of trying to prove — and object to the harvesting of the forests on Block 6 as proposed in T.F.L. 39. In this situation, what duty if any does the government owe the Haida people? More concretely, is the government required to <u>consult</u> with them about decisions to harvest the forests and to <u>accommodate</u> their concerns about what if any forest in Block 6 should be harvested before they have proven their title to land and their Aboriginal rights?

[7] The stakes are huge. The Haida argue that absent consultation and accommodation, they will win their title but find themselves deprived of forests that are vital to their economy and their culture. Forests take generations to mature, they point out, and old-growth forests can never be replaced. The Haida's claim to title to Haida Gwaii is strong, as found by the chambers judge. But it is also complex and will take many years to prove. In the meantime, the Haida argue, their heritage will be irretrievably despoiled.

[8] The government, in turn, argues that it has the right and responsibility to manage the forest resource for the good of all British Columbians, and that until the Haida people formally prove their claim, they have no legal right to be consulted or have their needs and interests accommodated.

. . . . .

II. Analysis

. . . .

B. *The Source of a Duty to Consult and Accommodate*

[16] The government's duty to consult with Aboriginal peoples and accommodate their interests is grounded in the honour of the Crown. The honour of the Crown is always at stake in its dealings with Aboriginal peoples: see for example *R. v. Badger*, [1996] 1 S.C.R. 771, at para. 41; *R. v. Marshall*, [1999] 3 S.C.R. 456. It is not a mere incantation, but rather a core precept that finds its application in concrete practices.

[17] The historical roots of the principle of the honour of the Crown suggest that it must be <u>understood generously</u> in order to reflect the underlying realities from which it stems. In all its dealings with Aboriginal peoples, from the assertion of sovereignty to the resolution of claims and the implementation of treaties, the Crown must act honourably. Nothing less is required if we are to achieve "the reconciliation of the pre-existence of aboriginal societies with the sovereignty of the Crown": *Delgamuukw*, *supra*, at para. 186, quoting *Van der Peet*, *supra*, at para. 31.

[18] The honour of the Crown gives rise to different duties in different circumstances. Where the Crown has assumed discretionary control over

specific Aboriginal interests, the honour of the Crown gives rise to a fiduciary duty: *Wewaykum Indian Band v. Canada*, [2002] 4 S.C.R. 245, 2002 SCC 79, at para. 79. The content of the fiduciary duty may vary to take into account the Crown's other, broader obligations. However, the duty's fulfilment requires that the Crown act with reference to the Aboriginal group's best interest in exercising discretionary control over the specific Aboriginal interest at stake. As explained in *Wewaykum*, at para. 81, the term "fiduciary duty" does not connote a universal trust relationship encompassing all aspects of the relationship between the Crown and Aboriginal peoples:

> ... "fiduciary duty" as a source of plenary Crown liability covering all aspects of the Crown-Indian band relationship ... overshoots the mark. The fiduciary duty imposed on the Crown does not exist at large but in relation to specific Indian interests.

[handwritten margin note: why not?]

Here, Aboriginal rights and title have been asserted but have not been defined or proven. The Aboriginal interest in question is insufficiently specific for the honour of the Crown to mandate that the Crown act in the Aboriginal group's best interest, as a fiduciary, in exercising discretionary control over the subject of the right or title.

[19] The honour of the Crown also infuses the processes of treaty making and treaty interpretation. In making and applying treaties, the Crown must act with honour and integrity, avoiding even the appearance of "sharp dealing" (*Badger*, at para. 41). Thus in *Marshall, supra*, at para. 4, the majority of this Court supported its interpretation of a treaty by stating that "nothing less would uphold the honour and integrity of the Crown in its dealings with the Mi'kmaq people to secure their peace and friendship ...".

[20] Where treaties remain to be concluded, the honour of the Crown requires negotiations leading to a just settlement of Aboriginal claims: *R. v. Sparrow*, [1990] 1 S.C.R. 1075, at pp. 1105-6. Treaties serve to reconcile pre-existing Aboriginal sovereignty with assumed Crown sovereignty, and to define Aboriginal rights guaranteed by s. 35 of the *Constitution Act, 1982*. Section 35 represents a promise of rights recognition, and "[i]t is always assumed that the Crown intends to fulfil its promises" (*Badger, supra*, at para. 41). This promise is realized and sovereignty claims reconciled through the process of honourable negotiation. It is a corollary of s. 35 that the Crown act honourably in defining the rights it guarantees and in reconciling them with other rights and interests. This, in turn, implies a duty to consult and, if appropriate, accommodate.

[handwritten margin note: colonial language]

[handwritten margin note: make an ass]

[21] This duty to consult is recognized and discussed in the jurisprudence. In *Sparrow, supra*, at p. 1119, this Court affirmed a duty to consult with west-coast Salish asserting an unresolved right to fish. Dickson C.J. and La Forest J. wrote that one of the factors in determining whether limits on the right were justified is "whether the aboriginal group in question has been consulted with respect to the conservation measures being implemented".

[22] The Court affirmed the duty to consult regarding resources to which Aboriginal peoples make claim a few years later in *R. v. Nikal*, [1996] 1 S.C.R. 1013, where Cory J. wrote: "So long as every reasonable effort is made to inform and to consult, such efforts would suffice to meet the justification requirement" (para. 110).

[23] In the companion case of *R. v. Gladstone*, [1996] 2 S.C.R. 723, Lamer C.J. referred to the need for "consultation and compensation", and to consider "how the government has accommodated different aboriginal rights in a particular fishery ..., how important the fishery is to the economic and material well-being of the band in question, and the criteria taken into account by the government in, for example, allocating commercial licences amongst different users" (para. 64).

[24] The Court's seminal decision in *Delgamuukw, supra,* at para. 168, in the context of a claim for title to land and resources, confirmed and expanded on the duty to consult, suggesting the content of the duty varied with the circumstances: from a minimum "duty to discuss important decisions" where the "breach is less serious or relatively minor"; through the "significantly deeper than mere consultation" that is required in "most cases"; to "full consent of [the] aboriginal nation" on very serious issues. These words apply as much to unresolved claims as to intrusions on settled claims.

[25] Put simply, Canada's Aboriginal peoples were here when Europeans came, and were never conquered. Many bands reconciled their claims with the sovereignty of the Crown through negotiated treaties. Others, notably in British Columbia, have yet to do so. The potential rights embedded in these claims are protected by s. 35 of the *Constitution Act, 1982*. The honour of the Crown requires that these rights be determined, recognized and respected. This, in turn, requires the Crown, acting honourably, to participate in processes of negotiation. While this process continues, the honour of the Crown may require it to consult and, where indicated, accommodate Aboriginal interests.

C. *When the Duty to Consult and Accommodate Arises*

[26] Honourable negotiation implies a duty to consult with Aboriginal claimants and conclude an honourable agreement reflecting the claimants' inherent rights. But proving rights may take time, sometimes a very long time. In the meantime, how are the interests under discussion to be treated? Underlying this question is the need to reconcile prior Aboriginal occupation of the land with the reality of Crown sovereignty. Is the Crown, under the aegis of its asserted sovereignty, entitled to use the resources at issue as it chooses, pending proof and resolution of the Aboriginal claim? Or must it adjust its conduct to reflect the as yet unresolved rights claimed by the Aboriginal claimants?

[27] The answer, once again, lies in the honour of the Crown. The Crown, acting honourably, cannot cavalierly run roughshod over Aboriginal interests where claims affecting these interests are being seriously pursued in the process of treaty negotiation and proof. It must

respect these potential, but yet unproven, interests. The Crown is not rendered impotent. It may continue to manage the resource in question pending claims resolution. But, depending on the circumstances, discussed more fully below, the honour of the Crown may require it to consult with and reasonably accommodate Aboriginal interests pending resolution of the claim. To unilaterally exploit a claimed resource during the process of proving and resolving the Aboriginal claim to that resource, may be to deprive the Aboriginal claimants of some or all of the benefit of the resource. That is not honourable.

[28] The government argues that it is under no duty to consult and accommodate prior to final determination of the scope and content of the right. ...

. . . . .

[31] The government's arguments do not withstand scrutiny. ...

[32] The jurisprudence of this Court supports the view that the duty to consult and accommodate is part of a process of fair dealing and reconciliation that begins with the assertion of sovereignty and continues beyond formal claims resolution. Reconciliation is not a final legal remedy in the usual sense. Rather, it is a process flowing from rights guaranteed by s. 35(1) of the *Constitution Act, 1982*. This process of reconciliation flows from the Crown's duty of honourable dealing toward Aboriginal peoples, which arises in turn from the Crown's assertion of sovereignty over an Aboriginal people and *de facto* control of land and resources that were formerly in the control of that people. ...

[33] To limit reconciliation to the post-proof sphere risks treating reconciliation as a distant legalistic goal, devoid of the "meaningful content" mandated by the "solemn commitment" made by the Crown in recognizing and affirming Aboriginal rights and title: *Sparrow, supra*, at p. 1108. It also risks unfortunate consequences. When the distant goal of proof is finally reached, the Aboriginal peoples may find their land and resources changed and denuded. This is not reconciliation. Nor is it honourable. [*handwritten margin note:* how is this different than what were seeing?]

[34] The existence of a legal duty to consult prior to proof of claims is necessary to understand the language of cases like *Sparrow, Nikal*, and *Gladstone, supra*, where confirmation of the right and justification of an alleged infringement were litigated at the same time. For example, the reference in *Sparrow* to Crown behaviour in determining if any infringements were justified, is to behaviour **before** determination of the right. This negates the contention that a proven right is the trigger for a legal duty to consult and if appropriate accommodate even in the context of justification. [*handwritten margin note:* DTC just postpones this & justifies it!]

[35] But, when precisely does a duty to consult arise? The foundation of the duty in the Crown's honour and the goal of reconciliation suggest that the duty arises when the Crown has knowledge, real or constructive, of the potential existence of the Aboriginal right or title and contemplates conduct that might adversely affect it. ... [*handwritten margin note:* DTC should arise w simple fact of colonization]

. . . . .

[38] I conclude that consultation and accommodation before final claims resolution, while challenging, is not impossible, and indeed is an essential corollary to the honourable process of reconciliation that s. 35 demands. It preserves the Aboriginal interest pending claims resolution and fosters a relationship between the parties that makes possible negotiations, the preferred process for achieving ultimate reconciliation ... Precisely what is required of the government may vary with the strength of the claim and the circumstances. But at a minimum, it must be consistent with the honour of the Crown.

that are a force because no duty to agree! not equal table

D. *The Scope and Content of the Duty to Consult and Accommodate*

[39] The content of the duty to consult and accommodate varies with the circumstances. ... In general terms ... it may be asserted that the scope of the duty is proportionate to a preliminary assessment of the strength of the case supporting the existence of the right or title, and to the seriousness of the potentially adverse effect upon the right or title claimed.

. . . . .

[41] ... While it is not useful to classify situations into watertight compartments, different situations requiring different responses can be identified. In all cases, the honour of the Crown requires that the Crown act with good faith to provide meaningful consultation appropriate to the circumstances. In discharging this duty, regard may be had to the procedural safeguards of natural justice mandated by administrative law.

but isn't the decision really always already made when FN has no veto power

[42] At all stages, good faith on both sides is required. The common thread on the Crown's part must be "the intention of substantially addressing [Aboriginal] concerns" as they are raised (*Delgamuukw, supra*, at para. 168), through a meaningful process of consultation. Sharp dealing is not permitted. However, there is no duty to agree; rather, the commitment is to a meaningful process of consultation. As for Aboriginal claimants, they must not frustrate the Crown's reasonable good faith attempts, nor should they take unreasonable positions to thwart government from making decisions or acting in cases where, despite meaningful consultation, agreement is not reached. ... Mere hard bargaining, however, will not offend an Aboriginal people's right to be consulted.

well listen & smile then do what we had always planned to

[43] Against this background, I turn to the kind of duties that may arise in different situations. In this respect, the concept of a spectrum may be helpful, not to suggest watertight legal compartments but rather to indicate what the honour of the Crown may require in particular circumstances. At one end of the spectrum lie cases where the claim to title is weak, the Aboriginal right limited, or the potential for infringement minor. In such cases, the only duty on the Crown may be to give notice, disclose information, and discuss any issues raised in response to the notice. ...

[Handwritten: Why MAY! why not must · discretion takes any power out of this]

[44] At the other end of the spectrum lie cases where a strong *prima facie* case for the claim is established, the right and potential infringement is of high significance to the Aboriginal peoples, and the risk of non-compensable damage is high. In such cases deep consultation, aimed at finding a satisfactory interim solution, may be required. While precise requirements will vary with the circumstances, the consultation required at this stage may entail the opportunity to make submissions for consideration, formal participation in the decision-making process, and provision of written reasons to show that Aboriginal concerns were considered and to reveal the impact they had on the decision. This list is neither exhaustive, nor mandatory for every case. The government may wish to adopt dispute resolution procedures like mediation or administrative regimes with impartial decision-makers in complex or difficult cases.

[45] Between these two extremes of the spectrum just described, will lie other situations. Every case must be approached individually. Each must also be approached flexibly, since the level of consultation required may change as the process goes on and new information comes to light. The controlling question in all situations is what is required to maintain the honour of the Crown and to effect reconciliation between the Crown and the Aboriginal peoples with respect to the interests at stake. Pending settlement, the Crown is bound by its honour to balance societal and Aboriginal interests in making decisions that may affect Aboriginal claims. The Crown may be required to make decisions in the face of disagreement as to the adequacy of its response to Aboriginal concerns. Balance and compromise will then be necessary. *[Handwritten: FN always the ones compromising]*

[Handwritten margin: not > in general]

[Handwritten margin: Knot poem]

[46] Meaningful consultation may oblige the Crown to make changes to its proposed action based on information obtained through consultations. The New Zealand Ministry of Justice's *Guide for Consultation with Māori* (1997) provides insight (at pp. 21 and 31):

> Consultation is not just a process of exchanging information. It also entails testing and being prepared to amend policy proposals in the light of information received, and providing feedback. Consultation therefore becomes a process which should ensure both parties are better informed ...
>
> ... genuine consultation means a process that involves ...
> – gathering information to test policy proposals
> – putting forward proposals that are not yet finalised
> – seeking Māori opinion on those proposals
> – informing Māori of all relevant information upon which those proposals are based
> – not promoting but listening with an open mind to what Māori have to say
> – being prepared to alter the original proposal
> – providing feedback both during the consultation process and after the decision-process.

[47] When the consultation process suggests amendment of Crown policy, we arrive at the stage of accommodation. Thus the effect of good faith consultation may be to reveal a duty to accommodate. Where a strong *prima facie* case exists for the claim, and the consequences of the

government's proposed decision may adversely affect it in a significant way, addressing the Aboriginal concerns may require taking steps to avoid irreparable harm or to minimize the effects of infringement, pending final resolution of the underlying claim. Accommodation is achieved through consultation ...

[48] This process does not give Aboriginal groups a veto over what can be done with land pending final proof of the claim. The Aboriginal "consent" spoken of in *Delgamuukw* is appropriate only in cases of established rights, and then by no means in every case. Rather, what is required is a process of balancing interests, of give and take.

[49] This flows from the meaning of "accommodate". The terms "accommodate" and "accommodation" have been defined as to "adapt, harmonize, reconcile" ... "an adjustment or adaptation to suit a special or different purpose ... a convenient arrangement; a settlement or compromise": *Concise Oxford Dictionary of Current English* (9th ed. 1995), at p. 9. ...

[50] The Court's decisions confirm this vision of accommodation. The Court in *Sparrow* raised the concept of accommodation, stressing the need to balance competing societal interests with Aboriginal and treaty rights. In *R. v. Sioui*, [1990] 1 S.C.R. 1025, at p. 1072, the Court stated that the Crown bears the burden of proving that its occupancy of lands "cannot be accommodated to reasonable exercise of the Hurons' rights". And in *R. v. Côté*, [1996] 3 S.C.R. 139, at para. 81, the Court spoke of whether restrictions on Aboriginal rights "can be accommodated with the Crown's special fiduciary relationship with First Nations". ...

[51] It is open to governments to set up regulatory schemes to address the procedural requirements appropriate to different problems at different stages, thereby strengthening the reconciliation process and reducing recourse to the courts. As noted in *R. v. Adams*, [1996] 3 S.C.R. 101, at para. 54, the government "may not simply adopt an unstructured discretionary administrative regime which risks infringing aboriginal rights in a substantial number of applications in the absence of some explicit guidance". ...

E. *Do Third Parties Owe a Duty to Consult and Accommodate?*

[52] The Court of Appeal found that Weyerhaeuser, the forestry contractor holding T.F.L. 39, owed the Haida people a duty to consult and accommodate. With respect, I cannot agree. ...

[53] ... The Crown alone remains legally responsible for the consequences of its actions and interactions with third parties that affect Aboriginal interests. The Crown may delegate procedural aspects of consultation to industry proponents seeking a particular development; this is not infrequently done in environmental assessments. ...However, the ultimate legal responsibility for consultation and accommodation rests with the Crown. The honour of the Crown cannot be delegated.

[54] It is also suggested (*per* Lambert J.A.) that third parties might have a duty to consult and accommodate on the basis of the trust law doctrine

of "knowing receipt". ... [W]hile the Crown's fiduciary obligations and its duty to consult and accommodate share roots in the principle that the Crown's honour is engaged in its relationship with Aboriginal peoples, the duty to consult is distinct from the fiduciary duty that is owed in relation to particular cognizable Aboriginal interests. ...

. . . . .

[56] The fact that third parties are under no duty to consult or accommodate Aboriginal concerns does not mean that they can never be liable to Aboriginal peoples. If they act negligently in circumstances where they owe Aboriginal peoples a duty of care, or if they breach contracts with Aboriginal peoples or deal with them dishonestly, they may be held legally liable. But they cannot be held liable for failing to discharge the Crown's duty to consult and accommodate.

harm
require

F. *The Province's Duty*

[57] The Province of British Columbia argues that any duty to consult or accommodate rests solely with the federal government. I cannot accept this argument.

. . . . .

[59] ... [T]he Provinces took their interest in land subject to "any Interest other than that of the Province in the same" (s. 109). The duty to consult and accommodate here at issue is grounded in the assertion of Crown sovereignty which pre-dated the Union. It follows that the Province took the lands subject to this duty. It cannot therefore claim that s. 35 deprives it of powers it would otherwise have enjoyed. As stated in *St. Catherine's Milling and Lumber Co. v. The Queen* (1888), 14 App. Cas. 46 (P.C.), lands in the Province are "available to [the Province] as a source of revenue whenever the estate of the Crown is disencumbered of the Indian title" (p. 59). ...

. . . . .

H. *Application to the Facts*

(1) Existence of the Duty

[64] The question is whether the Province had knowledge, real or constructive, of the potential existence of Aboriginal right or title and contemplated conduct that might adversely affect them. On the evidence before the Court in this matter, the answer must unequivocally be "yes".

[65] The Haida have claimed title to all of Haida Gwaii for at least 100 years. ... The Province has had available to it evidence of the importance of red cedar to the Haida culture since before 1846 (the assertion of British sovereignty).

[66] The Province raises concerns over the breadth of the Haida's claims, observing that "[i]n a separate action the Haida claim aboriginal title to all of the Queen Charlotte Islands, the surrounding waters, and the air space. ... The Haida claim includes the right to the exclusive use, occupation and benefit of the land, inland waters, seabed, archipelagic waters and air space" (Crown's factum, at para. 35). However, consideration of the duty to consult and accommodate prior to proof of a right does not amount to a prior determination of the case on its merits. ...

[67] The chambers judge ascertained that the Province knew that the potential Aboriginal right and title applied to Block 6, and could be affected by the decision to replace T.F.L. 39. On this basis, the honour of the Crown mandated consultation prior to making a decision that might adversely affect the claimed Aboriginal title and rights.

(2) Scope of the Duty

[68] As discussed above, the scope of the consultation required will be proportionate to a preliminary assessment of the strength of the case supporting the existence of the right or title, and to the seriousness of the potentially adverse effect upon the right or title claimed.

(i) *Strength of the Case*

[69] On the basis of evidence described as "voluminous", the chambers judge found, at para. 25, a number of conclusions to be "inescapable" regarding the Haida's claims. He found that the Haida had inhabited Haida Gwaii continuously since at least 1774, that they had never been conquered, never surrendered their rights by treaty, and that their rights had not been extinguished by federal legislation. Their culture has utilized red cedar from old-growth forests on both coastal and inland areas of what is now Block 6 of T.F.L. 39 since at least 1846.

[70] The chambers judge's thorough assessment of the evidence distinguishes between the various Haida claims relevant to Block 6. On the basis of a thorough survey of the evidence, he found, at para. 47:

(1) a "reasonable probability" that the Haida may establish title to "at least some parts" of the coastal and inland areas of Haida Gwaii, including coastal areas of Block 6. There appears to be a "reasonable possibility" that these areas will include inland areas of Block 6;

(2) a "substantial probability" that the Haida will be able to establish an aboriginal right to harvest old-growth red cedar trees from both coastal and inland areas of Block 6. ...

[71] The chambers judge's findings grounded the Court of Appeal's conclusion that the Haida claims to title and Aboriginal rights were "supported by a good *prima facie* case" (para. 49). The strength of the case goes to the extent of the duty that the Province was required to fulfill. In this case the evidence clearly supports a conclusion that, pending a final

resolution, there was a *prima facie* case in support of Aboriginal title, and a strong *prima facie* case for the Aboriginal right to harvest red cedar.

(ii) *Seriousness of the Potential Impact*

[72] The evidence before the chambers judge indicated that red cedar has long been integral to Haida culture. The chambers judge considered that there was a "reasonable probability" that the Haida would be able to establish infringement of an Aboriginal right to harvest red cedar "by proof that old-growth cedar has been and will continue to be logged on Block 6, and that it is of limited supply" (para. 48). ...

[73] Tree Farm Licences are exclusive, long-term licences. T.F.L. 39 grants exclusive rights to Weyerhaeuser to harvest timber within an area constituting almost one quarter of the total land of Haida Gwaii. The chambers judge observed that "it [is] apparent that large areas of Block 6 have been logged off" (para. 59). This points to the potential impact on Aboriginal rights of the decision to replace T.F.L. 39.

. . . . .

[76] I conclude that the Province has a duty to consult and perhaps accommodate on T.F.L. decisions. The T.F.L. decision reflects the strategic planning for utilization of the resource ... If consultation is to be meaningful, it must take place at the stage of granting or renewing Tree Farm Licences.

[77] The last issue is whether the Crown's duty went beyond consultation on T.F.L. decisions, to accommodation. We cannot know, on the facts here, whether consultation would have led to a need for accommodation. However, the strength of the case for both the Haida title and the Haida right to harvest red cedar, coupled with the serious impact of incremental strategic decisions on those interests, suggest that the honour of the Crown may well require significant accommodation to preserve the Haida interest pending resolution of their claims.

(3) Did the Crown Fulfill its Duty?

[78] The Province did not consult with the Haida on the replacement of T.F.L. 39.

[79] It follows, therefore, that the Province failed to meet its duty to engage in something significantly deeper than mere consultation. It failed to engage in any meaningful consultation at all.

III. Conclusion

[80] The Crown's appeal is dismissed and Weyerhaeuser's appeal is allowed. ...

The *Haida Nation* case represents a significant consolidation and application of the principles which underlie Crown obligations to Aboriginal peoples.

In the *Haida Nation* case the Supreme Court found that the duty to consult and accommodate did not extend to third parties, like corporations and private entities. Tanis Fiss of the Canadian Taxpayers Federation indicated the organization's support for this holding in the following terms:

> The Canadian Taxpayers Federation is very pleased the Supreme Court of Canada's requirement for governments to consult does not extend to private companies. If the SCC had included companies, they would have had to hire lawyers and consultants to work with Indian band councils. This would have created costly delays and higher costs that would ultimately have been passed on to consumers and taxpayers.[7]

Does this statement assume that it is economically disadvantageous to recognize obligations to Aboriginal peoples? If there are negative economic implications in recognizing obligations to Aboriginal peoples why does the Court permit them in relation to the Crown? Would it be possible to identify positive economic impacts in the recognition of third party obligations to Aboriginal peoples? In pondering this question consider the following statements made by Dr. Dean Jacobs, Chief of Walpole Island in Bkejwanong territory.

1. Consultation and accommodation create a positive relationship between the corporation and the Aboriginal leadership and membership of a community.
2. Consultation and accommodation avoid litigation. … Litigation is costly and time-consuming, and is a path which most corporations (and First Nations) want to avoid.
3. Consultation and accommodation avoid delay and manage project risk. Most corporations recognize the real and substantive interest that their companies have in the outcome of the consultation process. They want to ensure that adequate consultation and accommodation has happened so that there is a minimized risk of licenses, permits or approvals being set aside. …
4. Consultation and accommodation reflect the reality that industry, not government, is often in the best position to address First Nations' concerns. Industry has the ability to involve First Nations in a project, modify the project's design, implementation or operations to address First Nations' concerns, and the ability to provide the economic benefits to the First Nations to offset some of the impacts of a development.
5. Consultation and accommodation allow the benefit of incorporating and enhancing traditional ecological knowledge in:
   a. baseline environmental studies (e.g., directing the location of the studies so that it properly targets valuable habitat)
   b. environmental monitoring protocols (e.g., by adding parameters that should be monitored for, and identifying appropriate locations where the monitoring should take place)
   c. development of mitigation measures (e.g., including fundamental planning-level mitigation measures like adapting the routing of pipelines, roads and other corridor-type developments to avoid valued habitat)

6. Consultation and accommodation create a partnership approach to resolving environmental problems during a project's construction and operation. Corporations may see having to work with Aboriginal representatives on a joint environmental committee as a cost and administrative burden, but the benefits of a second set of eyes to look at a problem (with eyes who know the territory better than anyone from outside) and come up with ways to solve it, is not to be underestimated.

7. Consultation and accommodation increase the chances that qualified employees from the First Nation membership will work on the project. It is trite to say that not only does a job benefit the employee; it also benefits the employer. Training of potential Aboriginal employees may be a necessary element of achieving this objective, because many Aboriginal people across Canada are at a substantial disadvantage when it comes to obtaining higher education and training. Employers may be called on to contribute some of those training costs, but the long-run benefit of having employees who reside close to a development and have a personal interest in seeing it operate well and with limited environmental impacts must be considered alongside the costs.

8. Consultation and accommodation help to establish clear mechanisms for informing the Aboriginal community affected by a development about developments and impacts in the area affected by the development. This, in turn, reduces the potential degree of community-level frustration with a project. …

9. Consultation and accommodation enhance the opportunities for Aboriginal businesses to supply goods and services to a proponent's project, which can substantially improve community relations, as well as meeting the corporation's needs for those goods and services.

10. Consultation and accommodation provide clear avenues for First Nations to communicate to corporations what their plans for community developments are, so that the corporations and First Nations can work together to make those community developments successful. To give an example, if a First Nation were considering building a facility which required specialized equipment, or wished to build a certain type of building, the corporation and the First Nation might together be able to work out an arrangement for the purchase of a corporation's surplus equipment or infrastructure to the benefit of both.[8]

On the same day that the *Haida Nation* case was released, the Supreme Court issued a companion judgment: *Taku River Tlingit First Nation v. British Columbia*, [2004] S.C.J. No. 69, [2004] 3 S.C.R. 550 (S.C.C.). In the *Taku River* case the Court found that the standard for consultation and accommodation identified in the *Haida Nation* was met.

In the *Taku River* case the Taku River Tlingit First Nation ("TRTFN") argued that a provincial environmental assessment process failed to satisfy British Columbia's duty to consult under section 35(1) of the *Constitution Act, 1982*. The TRTFN alleged that efforts to reopen an old mine in its traditional territory would adversely affect its Aboriginal rights and title, which had not yet been proved to exist by a court. While the First Nation participated in the province's environmental assessment process, related to a mining company's application to redevelop the mine, the First Nation was dissatisfied with the process and result. As a result, the TRTFN argued that the environmental assessment process was insufficient to discharge the Crown's duty. The Supreme Court agreed with the First Nation that the province of British Columbia was required to consult with the TRTFN in the mine's redevelopment. However, the Supreme Court disagreed with the First Nation's claim that the province's three-and-a-half-year environmental assessment was insufficient to uphold the province's duty to consult under section 35(1).

In finding that the Crown owed the TRTFN a duty, the Supreme Court applied the principles articulated in the *Haida* case and found (at para. 32) that

> the TRTFN's claim is relatively strong, supported by a *prima facie* case, as attested to by its acceptance into the treaty negotiation process. The proposed road is to occupy only a small portion of the territory over which the TRTFN asserts title; however, the potential for negative derivative impacts on the TRTFN's claims is high. On the spectrum of consultation required by the honour of the Crown, the TRTFN was entitled to more than the minimum receipt of notice, disclosure of information, and ensuing discussion.

In holding that the province satisfied its duty to consult in this case, the Supreme Court wrote:

> [33] The process of granting project approval to Redfern took three and a half years, and was conducted largely under the *Environmental Assessment Act*. ... The Act requires that Aboriginal peoples whose traditional territory includes the site of a reviewable project be invited to participate on a project committee.
>
> . . . . .
>
> [41] The Act permitted the Committee to set its own procedure, which in this case involved the formation of working groups and subcommittees, the commissioning of studies, and the preparation of a written recommendations report. The TRTFN was at the heart of decisions to set up a steering group to deal with Aboriginal issues and a subcommittee on the road access proposal. The information and analysis required of Redfern were clearly shaped by TRTFN's concerns. By the time that the assessment was concluded, more than one extension of statutory time limits had been granted, and in the opinion of the project assessment director, "the positions of all of the Project Committee members, including the TRTFN had crystallized" (Affidavit of Norman Ringstad, at para. 82 (quoted at para. 57 of the Court of Appeal's judgment)). The concerns of the TRTFN were well understood as reflected in the Recommendations Report and Project Report, and had been meaningfully discussed. The Province had thoroughly fulfilled its duty to consult.
>
> [42] As discussed in *Haida*, the process of consultation may lead to a duty to accommodate Aboriginal concerns by adapting decisions or policies in response. ...
>
> . . . . .
>
> [44] ... Within the terms of the process provided for project approval certification under the Act, TRTFN concerns were adequately accommodated. In addition to the discussion in the minority report, the majority report thoroughly identified the TRTFN's concerns and

recommended mitigation strategies, which were adopted into the terms and conditions of certification. These mitigation strategies included further directions to Redfern to develop baseline information, and recommendations regarding future management and closure of the road.

[45] Project approval certification is simply one stage in the process by which a development moves forward. ...

[46] The Project Committee concluded that some outstanding TRTFN concerns could be more effectively considered at the permit stage or at the broader stage of treaty negotiations or land use strategy planning. The majority report and terms and conditions of the Certificate make it clear that the subsequent permitting process will require further information and analysis of Redfern, and that consultation and negotiation with the TRTFN may continue to yield accommodation in response. For example, more detailed baseline information will be required of Redfern at the permit stage, which may lead to adjustments in the road's course. Further socio-economic studies will be undertaken. It was recommended that a joint management authority be established. It was also recommended that the TRTFN's concerns be further addressed through negotiation with the Province and through the use of the Province's regulatory powers. The Project Committee, and by extension the Ministers, therefore clearly addressed the issue of what accommodation of the TRTFN's concerns was warranted at this stage of the project, and what other venues would also be appropriate for the TRTFN's continued input. It is expected that, throughout the permitting, approval and licensing process, as well as in the development of a land use strategy, the Crown will continue to fulfill its honourable duty to consult and, if indicated, accommodate the TRTFN.

Following the *Haida Nation* and *Taku River* cases, there was considerable confusion about the scope and content of the Crown's duty to consult emanating therefrom. The Supreme Court of Canada revisited the issue shortly thereafter in *Mikisew Cree First Nation v. Canada (Minister of Canadian Heritage)*, [2005] S.C.J. No. 71, [2005] 3 S.C.R. 388, 2005 SCC 69 (S.C.C.), which is excerpted below. Consider how, or to what extent, the notion of the honour of the Crown is expanded in *Mikisew Cree* beyond what was said in either *Haida Nation* or *Taku River*. How does the application of the Crown's duty to consult in *Mikisew Cree* affect traditional understandings of the Crown's treaty obligations to Aboriginal peoples?

MIKISEW CREE FIRST NATION v. CANADA (MINISTER OF CANADIAN HERITAGE)

[2005] S.C.J. No. 71, [2005] 3 S.C.R. 388, 2005 SCC 69 (S.C.C.)

[In 2000, without consulting the Mikisew Cree, the federal government approved the construction of a 118-kilometre-long winter road to run through the Mikisew Cree's remote northern reserve to provide direct winter access between some isolated northern communities and the Alberta highway system to the south. The winter road route was modified, after protests from the Mikisew Cree, to run along the boundary of the reserve, but the road still crossed the traplines of some 14 Mikisew Cree families and affected the hunting grounds of many other band members. Again, the band was not consulted about the modification. The Mikisew

Cree contended that the road would hamper their hunting and trapping rights and have injurious effects on their traditional lifestyle that was central to their culture. The band applied to the Federal Court to set aside the Minister's approval, alleging that the Crown's failure to consult them on the road construction constituted a breach of the Crown's fiduciary duty.]

The judgment of the Court was delivered by **Binnie J.**: —

[1] The fundamental objective of the modern law of aboriginal and treaty rights is the reconciliation of aboriginal peoples and non-aboriginal peoples and their respective claims, interests and ambitions. The management of these relationships takes place in the shadow of a long history of grievances and misunderstanding. The multitude of smaller grievances created by the indifference of some government officials to aboriginal people's concerns, and the lack of respect inherent in that indifference has been as destructive of the process of reconciliation as some of the larger and more explosive controversies. And so it is in this case.

[2] Treaty 8 is one of the most important of the post-Confederation treaties. Made in 1899, the First Nations who lived in the area surrendered to the Crown 840,000 square kilometres of what is now northern Alberta, northeastern British Columbia, northwestern Saskatchewan and the southern portion of the Northwest Territories. Some idea of the size of this surrender is given by the fact that it dwarfs France (543,998 square kilometres), exceeds the size of Manitoba (650,087 square kilometres), Saskatchewan (651,900 square kilometres) and Alberta (661,185 square kilometres) and approaches the size of British Columbia (948,596 square kilometres). In exchange for this surrender, the First Nations were promised reserves and some other benefits including, most importantly to them, the following rights of hunting, trapping, and fishing:

> And Her Majesty the Queen HEREBY AGREES with the said Indians that they shall have right to pursue their usual vocations of hunting, trapping and fishing <u>throughout the tract surrendered</u> as before described, <u>subject to such regulations</u> as may from time to time be made by the Government of the country, acting under the authority of Her Majesty, <u>and saving and excepting such tracts as may be required or taken up</u> from time to time for settlement, mining, lumbering, trading or other purposes. [Emphasis added.]

(Report of Commissioners for Treaty No. 8 (1899), at p. 12)

[3] … The fact the proposed winter road directly affects only about 14 Mikisew trappers and perhaps 100 hunters may not seem very dramatic (unless you happen to be one of the trappers or hunters in question) but, in the context of a remote northern community of relatively few families, it is significant. Beyond that, however, the principle of consultation in advance of interference with existing treaty rights is a matter of broad general importance to the relations between aboriginal and non-aboriginal

peoples. It goes to the heart of the relationship and concerns not only the Mikisew but other First Nations and non-aboriginal governments as well. ...

[4] In this case, the relationship was not properly managed. Adequate consultation in advance of the Minister's approval did not take place. The government's approach did not advance the process of reconciliation but undermined it. The duty of consultation which flows from the honour of the Crown, and its obligation to respect the existing treaty rights of aboriginal peoples (now entrenched in s. 35 of the *Constitution Act, 1982*), was breached. The Mikisew appeal should be allowed, the Minister's approval quashed, and the matter returned to the Minister for further consultation and consideration. ...

. . . . .

[9] According to the trial judge, most of the communications relied on by the Minister to demonstrate appropriate consultation were instances of the Mikisew's being provided with standard information about the proposed road in the same form and substance as the communications being distributed to the general public of interested stakeholders. ... The Minister says that the first formal response from the Mikisew did not come until October 10, 2000, some two months after the deadline she had imposed for "public" comment. Chief Poitras stated that the Mikisew did not formally participate in the open houses, because " ... an open house is not a forum for us to be consulted adequately".

[10] Apparently, Parks Canada left the proponent Thebacha Road Society out of the information loop as well. At the end of January 2001, it advised Chief Poitras that it had just been informed that the Mikisew did not support the road. Up to that point, Thebacha had been led to believe that the Mikisew had no objection to the road's going through the reserve. Chief Poitras wrote a further letter to the Minister on January 29, 2001 and received a standard-form response letter from the Minister's office stating that the correspondence "will be given every consideration".

[11] Eventually, after several more miscommunications, Parks Canada wrote Chief Poitras on April 30, 2001, stating in part: "I apologize to you and your people for the way in which the consultation process unfolded concerning the proposed winter road and any resulting negative public perception of the [Mikisew Cree First Nation]". At that point, in fact, the decision to approve the road with a modified alignment had already been taken.

. . . . .

[13] The Minister now says the Mikisew ought not to be heard to complain about the process of consultation because they declined to participate in the public process that took place. Consultation is a two-way street, she says. It was up to the Mikisew to take advantage of what was on offer. They failed to do so. In the Minister's view, she did her duty.

. . . . .

[15] The Mikisew objection goes beyond the direct impact of closure of the area covered by the winter road to hunting and trapping. The surrounding area would be, the trial judge found, injuriously affected. Maintaining a traditional lifestyle, which the Mikisew say is central to their culture, depends on keeping the land around the Peace Point reserve in its natural condition and this, they contend, is essential to allow them to pass their culture and skills on to the next generation of Mikisew. The detrimental impact of the road on hunting and trapping, they argue, may simply prove to be one more incentive for their young people to abandon a traditional lifestyle and turn to other modes of living in the south.

[16] The Mikisew applied to the Federal Court to set aside the Minister's approval based on their view of the Crown's fiduciary duty, claiming that the Minister owes "a fiduciary and constitutional duty to adequately consult with Mikisew Cree First Nation with regard to the construction of the road" (trial judge, at para. 26).

[17] An interlocutory injunction against construction of the winter road was issued by the Federal Court, Trial Division on August 27, 2001.

. . . . .

IV. Analysis

[24] The post-Confederation numbered treaties were designed to open up the Canadian west and northwest to settlement and development. Treaty 8 itself recites that "the said Indians have been notified and informed by Her Majesty's said Commission that it is Her desire to open for settlement, immigration, trade, travel, mining, lumbering and such other purposes as to Her Majesty may seem meet". This stated purpose is reflected in a corresponding limitation on the Treaty 8 hunting, fishing and trapping rights to exclude such "tracts as may be required or taken up from time to time for settlement, mining, lumbering, trading or other purposes". The "other purposes" would be at least as broad as the purposes listed in the recital, mentioned above, including "travel".

[25] There was thus from the outset an uneasy tension between the First Nations' essential demand that they continue to be as free to live off the land after the treaty as before and the Crown's expectation of increasing numbers of non-aboriginal people moving into the surrendered territory. It was seen from the beginning as an ongoing relationship that would be difficult to manage, as the Commissioners acknowledged at an early Treaty 8 negotiation at Lesser Slave Lake in June 1899:

> The white man is bound to come in and open up the country, and we come before him to explain the relations that must exist between you, and thus prevent any trouble. (C. Mair, *Through the Mackenzie Basin: A Narrative of the Athabasca and Peace River Treaty Expedition of 1899*, at p. 61)

As Cory J. explained in *Badger*, at para. 57, "[t]he Indians understood that land would be taken up for homesteads, farming, prospecting and mining and that they would not be able to hunt in these areas or to shoot at the settlers' farm animals or buildings".

[26] The hunting, fishing and trapping rights were not solely for the benefit of First Nations people. It was in the Crown's interest to keep the aboriginal people living off the land, as the Commissioners themselves acknowledged in their Report on Treaty 8 dated September 22, 1899:

> We pointed out that the Government could not undertake to maintain Indians in idleness; that the same means of earning a livelihood would continue after the treaty as existed before it, and that the Indians would be expected to make use of them. [p. 5]

[27] Thus none of the parties in 1899 expected that Treaty 8 constituted a finished land use blueprint. Treaty 8 signalled the advancing dawn of a period of transition. The key, as the Commissioners pointed out, was to "explain the relations" that would govern future interaction "and thus prevent any trouble" (Mair, at p. 61).

A. *Interpretation of the Treaty*

[28] The interpretation of the treaty "must be realistic and reflect the intention[s] of both parties, not just that of the [First Nation]" (*Sioui*, at p. 1069). ...

[29] The Minister is therefore correct to insist that the clause governing hunting, fishing and trapping cannot be isolated from the treaty as a whole, but must be read in the context of its underlying purpose, as intended by both the Crown and the First Nations peoples. Within that framework, as Cory J. pointed out in *Badger*,

> the words in the treaty must not be interpreted in their strict technical sense nor subjected to rigid modern rules of construction. Rather, they must be interpreted in the sense that they would naturally have been understood by the Indians at the time of the signing. [para. 52]

[30] In the case of Treaty 8, it was contemplated by all parties that "from time to time" portions of the surrendered land would be "taken up" and transferred from the inventory of lands over which the First Nations had treaty rights to hunt, fish and trap, and placed in the inventory of lands where they did not. Treaty 8 lands lie to the north of Canada and are largely unsuitable for agriculture. The Commissioners who negotiated Treaty 8 could therefore express confidence to the First Nations that, as previously mentioned, "the same means of earning a livelihood would continue after the treaty as existed before it" (p. 5).

[31] ... [N]ot every subsequent "taking up" by the Crown constituted an infringement of Treaty 8 that must be justified according to the test set out in *Sparrow*. In *Sparrow*, it will be remembered, the federal government's fisheries regulations infringed the aboriginal fishing right, and had to be strictly justified. This is not the same situation as we have here, where the aboriginal rights have been surrendered and extinguished, and the Treaty 8 rights are expressly limited to lands not "required or taken up <u>from time to time</u> for settlement, mining, lumbering, trading or other purposes" (emphasis added). The language of the treaty could not be clearer in

foreshadowing change. Nevertheless the Crown was and is expected to manage the change honourably.

. . . . .

B. *The Process of Treaty Implementation*

[33] Both the historical context and the inevitable tensions underlying implementation of Treaty 8 demand a *process* by which lands may be transferred from the one category (where the First Nations retain rights to hunt, fish and trap) to the other category (where they do not). The content of the process is dictated by the duty of the Crown to act honourably. Although *Haida Nation* was not a treaty case, McLachlin C.J. pointed out, at paras. 19 and 35:

> The honour of the Crown also infuses the processes of treaty making and treaty interpretation. In making and applying treaties, the Crown must act with honour and integrity, avoiding even the appearance of "sharp dealing" (*Badger*, at para. 41). Thus in *Marshall*, *supra*, at para. 4, the majority of this Court supported its interpretation of a treaty by stating that "nothing less would uphold the honour and integrity of the Crown in its dealings with the Mi'kmaq people to secure their peace and friendship". ...

> But, when precisely does a duty to consult arise? The foundation of the duty in the Crown's honour and the goal of reconciliation suggest that the duty arises when the Crown has knowledge, real or constructive, of the potential existence of the Aboriginal right or title and contemplates conduct that might adversely affect it.

[34] In the case of a treaty the Crown, as a party, will always have notice of its contents. The question in each case will therefore be to determine the degree to which conduct contemplated by the Crown would adversely affect those rights so as to trigger the duty to consult. *Haida Nation* and *Taku River* set a low threshold. The flexibility lies not in the trigger ("might adversely affect it") but in the variable content of the duty once triggered. At the low end, "the only duty on the Crown may be to give notice, disclose information, and discuss any issues raised in response to the notice" (*Haida Nation*, at para. 43). The Mikisew say that even the low end content was not satisfied in this case.

C. *The Mikisew Legal Submission*

[35] The appellant, the Mikisew, essentially reminded the Court of what was said in *Haida Nation* and *Taku River*. This case, the Mikisew say, is stronger. In those cases, unlike here, the aboriginal interest to the lands was asserted but not yet proven. In this case, the aboriginal interests are protected by Treaty 8. They are established legal facts. As in *Haida Nation*, the trial judge found the aboriginal interest was threatened by the proposed development. If a duty to consult was found to exist in *Haida Nation* and *Taku River*, then, *a fortiori*, the Mikisew argue, it must arise here and the majority judgment of the Federal Court of Appeal was quite

wrong to characterise consultation between governments and aboriginal peoples as nothing more than a "good practice" (para. 24).

D. *The Minister's Response*

[36] The respondent Minister seeks to distinguish *Haida Nation* and *Taku River*. Her counsel advances three broad propositions in support of the Minister's approval of the proposed winter road.

1. In "taking up" the 23 square kilometres for the winter road, the Crown was doing no more than Treaty 8 entitled it to do. The Crown as well as First Nations have rights under Treaty 8. The exercise by the Crown of *its* Treaty right to "take up" land is not an infringement of the Treaty but the performance of it.

2. The Crown went through extensive consultations with First Nations in 1899 at the time Treaty 8 was negotiated. Whatever duty of accommodation was owed to First Nations was discharged at that time. The terms of the Treaty do not contemplate further consultations whenever a "taking up" occurs.

3. In the event further consultation was required, the process followed by the Minister through Parks Canada in this case was sufficient.

[37] For the reasons that follow, I believe that each of these propositions must be rejected.

. . . . .

(b) *The Content of Treaty 8*

[42] ... [I]n *Badger* ... Cory J. pointed out that "even by the terms of Treaty No. 8, the Indians' right to hunt for food was circumscribed by both geographical limitations and by specific forms of government regulation" (para. 37). The members of the First Nations, he continued, "would have understood that land had been 'required or taken up' when it was being put to a [visible] use which was incompatible with the exercise of the right to hunt" (para. 53). ...

[43] While *Badger* noted the "geographic limitation" to hunting, fishing and trapping rights, it did not (as it did not need to) discuss the process by which "from time to time" land would be "taken up" and thereby excluded from the exercise of those rights. ...

[44] ... At this stage the winter road is no more than a contemplated change of use. The proposed use would, if carried into execution, reduce the territory over which the Mikisew would be entitled to exercise their Treaty 8 rights. Apart from everything else, there would be no hunting at all within the 200-metre road corridor. More broadly, as found by the trial judge, the road would injuriously affect the exercise of these rights in the surrounding bush. ... [I]t is apparent that the proposed road will adversely affect the existing Mikisew hunting and trapping rights, and therefore that the "trigger" to the duty to consult identified in *Haida Nation* is satisfied.

[45] The Minister ... assert[s] that the test ought to be "whether, after the taking up, it still remains reasonably practicable, <u>within the Province as a whole</u>, for the Indians to hunt, fish and trap for food [to] the extent that they choose to do so" (emphasis added). This cannot be correct. It suggests that a prohibition on hunting at Peace Point would be acceptable so long as decent hunting was still available in the Treaty 8 area north of Jasper, about 800 kilometres distant across the province, equivalent to a commute between Toronto and Quebec City (809 kilometres) or Edmonton and Regina (785 kilometres). One might as plausibly invite the truffle diggers of southern France to try their luck in the Austrian Alps, about the same distance as the journey across Alberta deemed by the Minister to be an acceptable fulfilment of the promises of Treaty 8.

[46] The Attorney General of Alberta tries a slightly different argument, ... adding a *de minimus* element to the treaty-wide approach:

> In this case the amount of land to be taken up to construct the winter road is 23 square kilometres out of 44,807 square kilometres of Wood Buffalo National Park and out of 840,000 square kilometres encompassed by Treaty No. 8. As Rothstein J.A. found, this is not a case where a meaningful right to hunt no longer remains.

[47] The arguments of the federal and Alberta Crowns simply ignore the significance and practicalities of a First Nation's traditional territory. ... More significantly for aboriginal people, as for non-aboriginal people, location is important. Twenty-three square kilometres alone is serious if it includes the claimants' hunting ground or trapline. While the Mikisew may have rights under Treaty 8 to hunt, fish and trap throughout the Treaty 8 area, it makes no sense from a practical point of view to tell the Mikisew hunters and trappers that, while their own hunting territory and traplines would now be compromised, they are entitled to invade the traditional territories of other First Nations distant from their home turf (a suggestion that would have been all the more impractical in 1899). ... *Badger* recorded that a large element of the Treaty 8 negotiations were the assurances of *continuity* in traditional patterns of economic activity. Continuity respects traditional patterns of activity and occupation. The Crown promised that the Indians' rights to hunt, fish and trap would continue "after the treaty as existed before it" (p. 5). This promise is not honoured by dispatching the Mikisew to territories far from their traditional hunting grounds and traplines.

[48] ... The "meaningful right to hunt" is not ascertained on a treaty-wide basis (all 840,000 square kilometres of it) but in relation to the territories over which a First Nation traditionally hunted, fished and trapped, and continues to do so today. If the time comes that in the case of a particular Treaty 8 First Nation "no meaningful right to hunt" remains over *its* traditional territories, the significance of the oral promise that "the same means of earning a livelihood would continue after the treaty as existed before it" would clearly be in question, and a potential action for treaty infringement, including the demand for a *Sparrow* justification, would be a legitimate First Nation response.

(c) Unilateral Crown Action

[49] There is in the Minister's argument a strong advocacy of unilateral Crown action (a sort of "this is surrendered land and we can do with it what we like" approach) which not only ignores the mutual promises of the treaty, both written and oral, but also is the antithesis of reconciliation and mutual respect. ...

[50] The Attorney General of Alberta denies that a duty of consultation can be an implied term of Treaty 8. He argues:

> Given that a consultation obligation would mean that the Crown would be required to engage in meaningful consultations with any and all affected Indians, being nomadic individuals scattered across a vast expanse of land, every time it wished to utilize an individual plot of land or change the use of the plot, such a requirement would not be within the range of possibilities of the common intention of the parties.

The parties *did* in fact contemplate a difficult period of transition and sought to soften its impact as much as possible, and any administrative inconvenience incidental to managing the process was rejected as a defence in *Haida Nation* and *Taku River*. There is no need to repeat here what was said in those cases about the overarching objective of reconciliation rather than confrontation.

[handwritten margin notes: silence the detractors; confrontation almost more honest]

(d) Honour of the Crown

[51] The duty to consult is grounded in the honour of the Crown, and it is not necessary for present purposes to invoke fiduciary duties. The honour of the Crown is itself a fundamental concept governing treaty interpretation and application that was referred to by Gwynne J. of this Court *as a treaty obligation* as far back as 1895, four years before Treaty 8 was concluded: *Province of Ontario v. Dominion of Canada* (1895), 25 S.C.R. 434, at pp. 511-12 *per* Gwynne J. (dissenting). While he was in the minority in his view that the treaty obligation to pay Indian annuities imposed a trust on provincial lands, nothing was said by the majority in that case to doubt that the honour of the Crown was pledged to the fulfilment of its obligations to the Indians. This had been the Crown's policy as far back as the *Royal Proclamation* of 1763, and is manifest in the promises recorded in the report of the Commissioners. The honour of the Crown exists as a source of obligation independently of treaties as well, of course. In *Sparrow, Delgamuukw v. British Columbia* [1997] 3 S.C.R. 1010, *Haida Nation* and *Taku River*, the "honour of the Crown" was invoked as a central principle in resolving aboriginal claims to consultation despite the absence of any treaty.

[52] It is not as though the Treaty 8 First Nations did not pay dearly for their entitlement to honourable conduct on the part of the Crown; surrender of the aboriginal interest in an area larger than France is a hefty purchase price.

(2)   Did the Extensive Consultations with First Nations Undertaken in
      1899 at the Time Treaty 8 Was Negotiated Discharge the Crown's
      Duty of Consultation and Accommodation?

[53] The Crown's second broad answer to the Mikisew claim is that
whatever had to be done was done in 1899. ...

[54] This is not correct. Consultation that excludes from the outset any
form of accommodation would be meaningless. The contemplated process
is not simply one of giving the Mikisew an opportunity to blow off steam
before the Minister proceeds to do what she intended to do all along.
Treaty making is an important stage in the long process of reconciliation,
but it is only a stage. What occurred at Fort Chipewyan in 1899 was not the
complete discharge of the duty arising from the honour of the Crown, but
a rededication of it.

[55] The Crown has a treaty right to "take up" surrendered lands for
regional transportation purposes, but the Crown is nevertheless under an
obligation to inform itself of the impact its project will have on the exercise
by the Mikisew of their hunting and trapping rights, and to communicate
its findings to the Mikisew. The Crown must then attempt to deal with the
Mikisew "in good faith, and with the intention of substantially
addressing" Mikisew concerns (*Delgamuukw*, at para. 168). This does not
mean that whenever a government proposes to do anything in the Treaty 8
surrendered lands it must consult with all signatory First Nations, no
matter how remote or unsubstantial the impact. The duty to consult is, as
stated in *Haida Nation*, triggered at a low threshold, but adverse impact is a
matter of degree, as is the extent of the Crown's duty. Here the impacts
were clear, established and demonstrably adverse to the continued
exercise of the Mikisew hunting and trapping rights over the lands in
question.

[56] In summary, the 1899 negotiations were the first step in a long
journey that is unlikely to end any time soon. Viewed in light of the facts
of this case, we should qualify *Badger*'s identification of two inherent
limitations on Indian hunting, fishing and trapping rights under Treaty 8
(geographical limits and specific forms of government regulation) by a
third, namely the Crown's right to take up lands under the treaty, which
itself is subject to its duty to consult and, if appropriate, accommodate
First Nations' interests before reducing the area over which their members
may continue to pursue their hunting, trapping and fishing rights. Such a
third qualification (not at issue in *Badger*) is fully justified by the history of
the negotiations leading to Treaty 8, as well as by the honour of the Crown
as previously discussed.

[57] As stated at the outset, the honour of the Crown infuses every
treaty and the performance of every treaty obligation. Treaty 8 therefore
gives rise to Mikisew procedural rights (e.g. consultation) as well as
substantive rights (e.g. hunting, fishing and trapping rights). Were the
Crown to have barrelled ahead with implementation of the winter road
without adequate consultation, it would have been in violation of its
procedural obligations, quite apart from whether or not the Mikisew could

have established that the winter road breached the Crown's *substantive* treaty obligations as well.

. . . . .

(3) <u>Was the Process Followed by the Minister Through Parks Canada in this Case Sufficient?</u>

[59] Where, as here, the Court is dealing with a *proposed* "taking up" it is not correct (even if it is concluded that the proposed measure *if implemented* would infringe the treaty hunting and trapping rights) to move directly to a *Sparrow* analysis. The Court must first consider the *process* by which the "taking up" is planned to go ahead, and whether that process is compatible with the honour of the Crown. If not, the First Nation may be entitled to succeed in setting aside the Minister's order on the process ground whether or not the facts of the case would otherwise support a finding of infringement of the hunting, fishing and trapping rights.

[60] I should state at the outset that the winter road proposed by the Minister was a permissible purpose for "taking up" lands under Treaty 8. ...

[61] The question is whether the Minister and her staff pursued the permitted purpose of regional transportation needs in accordance with the Crown's duty to consult. The answer turns on the particulars of that duty shaped by the circumstances here. In *Delgamuukw*, the Court considered the duty to consult and accommodate in the context of an infringement of aboriginal title (at para. 168):

> In occasional cases, when the breach is less serious or relatively minor, it will be no more than a duty to discuss important decisions that will be taken with respect to lands held pursuant to aboriginal title. Of course, even in these rare cases when the minimum acceptable standard is consultation, this consultation must be in good faith, and <u>with the intention of substantially addressing the concerns of the aboriginal peoples whose lands are at issue</u>. In most cases, it will be significantly deeper than mere consultation. Some cases may even require the full consent of an aboriginal nation, particularly when provinces enact hunting and fishing regulations in relation to aboriginal lands. [Emphasis added.]

[62] In *Haida Nation*, the Court pursued the kinds of duties that may arise in pre-proof claim situations, and McLachlin C.J. used the concept of a spectrum to frame her analysis (at paras. 43-45):

> At one end of the spectrum lie cases where the claim to title is weak, the Aboriginal right limited, or the potential for infringement minor. <u>In such cases, the only duty on the Crown may be to give notice, disclose information, and discuss any issues raised in response to the notice</u>. ...
>
> At the other end of the spectrum lie cases where a strong *prima facie* case for the claim is established, the right and potential infringement is of high significance to the Aboriginal peoples, and the risk of non-compensable damage is high. <u>In such cases deep consultation, aimed at finding a satisfactory interim solution, may be required.</u> While precise requirements will vary with the circumstances, the consultation required at this stage may

entail the opportunity to make submissions for consideration, formal participation in the decision-making process, and provision of written reasons to show that Aboriginal concerns were considered and to reveal the impact they had on the decision. This list is neither exhaustive, nor mandatory for every case. . .

Between these two extremes of the spectrum just described, will lie other situations. Every case must be approached individually. Each must also be approached flexibly, since the level of consultation required may change as the process goes on and new information comes to light. The controlling question in all situations is what is required to maintain the honour of the Crown and to effect reconciliation between the Crown and the Aboriginal peoples with respect to the interests at stake. . . . [Emphasis added.]

[63] The determination of the content of the duty to consult will, as *Haida* suggests, be governed by the context. One variable will be the specificity of the promises made. Where, for example, a treaty calls for certain supplies, or Crown payment of treaty monies, or a modern land claims settlement imposes specific obligations on aboriginal peoples with respect to identified resources, the role of consultation may be quite limited. If the respective obligations are clear the parties should get on with performance. Another contextual factor will be the seriousness of the impact on the aboriginal people of the Crown's proposed course of action. The more serious the impact the more important will be the role of consultation. Another factor in a non-treaty case, as *Haida* points out, will be the strength of the aboriginal claim. The history of dealings between the Crown and a particular First Nation may also be significant. Here, the most important contextual factor is that Treaty 8 provides a framework within which to manage the continuing changes in land use already foreseen in 1899 and expected, even now, to continue well into the future. In that context, consultation is key to achievement of the overall objective of the modern law of treaty and aboriginal rights, namely reconciliation.

[64] The duty here has both informational and response components. In this case, given that the Crown is proposing to build a fairly minor winter road on *surrendered* lands where the Mikisew hunting, fishing and trapping rights are expressly subject to the "taking up" limitation, I believe the Crown's duty lies at the lower end of the spectrum. The Crown was required to provide notice to the Mikisew and to engage directly with them (and not, as seems to have been the case here, as an afterthought to a general public consultation with Park users). This engagement ought to have included the provision of information about the project addressing what the Crown knew to be Mikisew interests and what the Crown anticipated might be the potential adverse impact on those interests. The Crown was required to solicit and to listen carefully to the Mikisew concerns, and to attempt to minimize adverse impacts on the Mikisew hunting, fishing and trapping rights. The Crown did not discharge this obligation when it unilaterally declared the road realignment would be shifted from the reserve itself to a track along its boundary. I agree on this point with what Finch J.A. (now C.J.B.C.) said in *Halfway River First Nation* at paras. 159-60.

The fact that adequate notice of an intended decision may have been given does not mean that the requirement for adequate consultation has also been met.

The Crown's duty to consult imposes on it a positive obligation to reasonably ensure that aboriginal peoples are provided with all necessary information in a timely way so that they have an opportunity to express their interests and concerns, *and to ensure that their representations are seriously considered and, wherever possible, demonstrably integrated into the proposed plan of action.* [Emphasis added.]

[65] It is true, as the Minister argues, that there is some reciprocal onus on the Mikisew to carry their end of the consultation, to make their concerns known, to respond to the government's attempt to meet their concerns and suggestions, and to try to reach some mutually satisfactory solution. In this case, however, consultation never reached that stage. It never got off the ground.

[66] Had the consultation process gone ahead, it would not have given the Mikisew a veto over the alignment of the road. As emphasized in *Haida Nation*, consultation will not always lead to accommodation, and accommodation may or may not result in an agreement. ...

[67] The trial judge's findings of fact make it clear that the Crown failed to demonstrate an "'intention of substantially addressing [Aboriginal] concerns' ... through a meaningful process of consultation" (*Haida Nation*, at para. 42). On the contrary, the trial judge held that

[i]n the present case, at the very least, this [duty to consult] would have entailed a response to Mikisew's October 10, 2000 letter, and a meeting with them to ensure that their concerns were addressed early in the planning stages of the project. At the meetings that were finally held between Parks Canada and Mikisew, a decision had essentially been made, therefore, the meeting could not have been conducted with the genuine intention of allowing Mikisew's concerns to be integrated with the proposal. [para. 154]

The trial judge also wrote:

... it is not consistent with the honour of the Crown, in its capacity as fiduciary, for it to fail to consult with a First Nation prior to making a decision that infringes on constitutionally protected treaty rights. [para. 157]

[68] I agree, as did Sharlow J.A., dissenting in the Federal Court of Appeal. She declared that the mitigation measures were adopted through a process that was "fundamentally flawed" (para. 153).

[69] In the result I would allow the appeal, quash the Minister's approval order, and remit the winter road project to the Minister to be dealt with in accordance with these reasons.

Appeal allowed with costs.

The *Mikisew Cree* case continued the process of articulating the Crown's duty to consult with Aboriginal peoples in the *Haida Nation* and *Taku River* cases, but with two major differences: *Mikisew Cree* contemplates rights already demonstrated to exist rather than those only alleged to exist and the rights it considers are treaty rights rather than Aboriginal rights. One important elaboration upon the Crown's duty to consult found in *Mikisew Cree* is Justice Binnie's indication that adequate notice does not equal adequate consultation. Thus, he determines that it was incumbent upon the Crown to actively consult with the Mikisew Cree rather than merely advising them of what it had already decided to do. He further finds that consultation is a two-way street, thereby entailing that First Nations owed a duty of consultation by the Crown must communicate adequately with the Crown and make their concerns known, respond to Crown attempts to meet their suggestions and concerns, and endeavour to arrive at a mutually satisfactory solution.

A key element of the *Mikisew Cree* judgment is its finding that treaties include both *substantive* rights protected by section 35(1) of the *Constitution Act, 1982*, such as hunting, fishing and trapping rights, and *procedural protection* for First Nations. The latter is the basis for the court's finding in the *Mikisew Cree* case the Crown could not simply "take up" land as per its apparent right under Treaty No. 8 without first consulting with the Mikisew Cree and accommodating their interests. The articulation of such proecedural rights in *Mikisew Cree* is entirely consistent with the nature of the negotiations leading up to the conclusion of Crown-Aboriginal treaties, as well as the general historic relationship between the parties in which the honour of the Crown plays a major role.

A failure of the *Mikisew Cree* case is the Supreme Court's inability, or unwillingness, to clarify the distinction between the duty to consult and the Crown's fiduciary duty created by *Haida Nation* and *Taku River*. So, while Justice Binnie indicates that, for the purposes of the *Mikisew Cree* decision, it is not necessary to invoke fiduciary duties, but only the duty to consult, he offers no suggestions as to why this is so, nor what is truly different about these duties.

After reading the *Haida Nation*, *Taku River* and *Mikisew Cree* cases, a number of fundamental questions about the Crown's duty to consult remain. For one, how does the Crown's duty to consult relate to the duty to consult established in *Sparrow*? Is the *Haida Nation* duty to consult an extrapolation from the *Sparrow* duty, which was created as a part of the Crown's fiduciary duty? Alternatively, is it a different basis of obligation? If it is the latter, how is it substantiated as an implication of the honour of the Crown when the duty to consult in *Sparrow* also stems from the honour of the Crown? This is not made sufficiently clear in the jurisprudence. Perhaps as simple a solution as a clarification in terminology would provide some answers.

The more recent case of *Rio Tinto Alcan Inc. v. Carrier Sekani Tribal Council*, [2010] S.C.J. No. 43, [2010] 2 S.C.R. 650 (S.C.C.) took into account the Supreme Court of Canada's formulation and analysis of the Crown's duty to consult from *Haida Nation*, *Taku River* and *Mikisew Cree*. In reading the following excerpt from *Rio Tinto*, consider whether its formulation of the Crown's duty to consult is much different from what had existed in these previous cases.

RIO TINTO ALCAN INC. v. CARRIER SEKANI TRIBAL COUNCIL
[2010] S.C.J. No. 43, [2010] 2 S.C.R. 650 (S.C.C.)

The judgment of the Court was delivered by

McLachlin C.J.C.: —

[1] In the 1950s, the government of British Columbia authorized the building of the Kenney Dam in Northwest British Columbia for the production of hydro power for the smelting of aluminum. The dam and reservoir altered the water flows to the Nechako River, which the Carrier Sekani Tribal Council ("CSTC") First Nations have since time immemorial used for fishing and sustenance. This was done without consulting with the CSTC First Nations. Now, the government of British Columbia seeks approval of a contract for the sale of excess power from the dam to British Columbia Hydro and Power Authority ("BC Hydro"), a Crown corporation. The question is whether the British Columbia Utilities Commission ("the Commission") is required to consider the issue of consultation with the CSTC First Nations in determining whether the sale is in the public interest.

[2] ... This case raises the issues of what triggers a duty to consult, and the place of government tribunals in consultation and the review of consultation. ...

I. Background

A. *The Facts*

[3] In the 1950s, Alcan (now Rio Tinto Alcan) dammed the Nechako River in northwestern British Columbia for the purposes of power development in connection with aluminum production. The project was one of huge magnitude. It diverted water from the Nechako River into the Nechako Reservoir, where a powerhouse was installed for the production of electricity. After passing through the turbines of the powerhouse, the water flowed to the Kemano River and on to the Pacific Ocean to the west. The dam affected the amount and timing of water flows into the Nechako River to the east, impacting fisheries on lands now claimed by the CSTC First Nations. Alcan effected these water diversions under Final Water Licence No. 102324 which gives Alcan use of the water on a permanent basis.

[4] Alcan, the Province of British Columbia, and Canada entered into a Settlement Agreement in 1987 on the release of waters in order to protect fish stocks. Canada was involved because fisheries, whether seacoast-based or inland, fall within federal jurisdiction under s. 91(12) of the *Constitution Act, 1867*. The 1987 agreement directs the release of additional flows in July and August to protect migrating salmon. In addition, a protocol has been entered into between the Haisla Nation and Alcan which regulates water flows to protect eulachon spawning grounds.

[5] The electricity generated by the project has been used over the years primarily for aluminum smelting. Since 1961, however, Alcan has sold its excess power to BC Hydro, a Crown Corporation, for use in the local area and later for transmission to neighbouring communities. The Energy Purchase Agreement ("EPA") entered into in 2007, which is the subject of this appeal is the latest in a series of power sales from Alcan to BC Hydro. It commits Alcan to supplying and BC Hydro to purchasing excess electricity from the Kemano site until 2034. The 2007 EPA establishes a Joint Operating Committee to advise the parties on the administration of the EPA and the operation of the reservoir.

[6] The CSTC First Nations claim the Nechako Valley as their ancestral homeland, and the right to fish in the Nechako River. As was the practice at the time, they were not consulted about the diversion of the river effected by the 1950s dam project. They assert, however, that the 2007 EPA for the power generated by the project should be subject to consultation. This, they say, is their constitutional right under s. 35 of the *Constitution Act, 1982*, as defined in *Haida Nation*.

B. *The Commission Proceedings*

[7] The 2007 EPA was subject to review before the Commission. … The Commission had the power to declare a contract for the sale of electricity unenforceable if it found that it was not in the public interest having regard to the quantity of energy to be supplied, the availability of supplies, the price and availability of any other form of energy, the price of the energy supplied to a public utility company, and "any other factor that the commission considers relevant to the public interest".

[8] The Commission began its work by holding two procedural conferences to determine, among other things, the "scope" of its hearing. "Scoping" is the process by which the Commission determines what "information it considers necessary to determine whether the contract is in the public interest" pursuant to s. 71(1)(b) of the *Utilities Commission Act*. The question of the role of First Nations in the proceedings arose at this stage. The CSTC was not party to the proceedings but the Haisla Nation was. The Haisla people submitted that the Province and BC Hydro "had failed to act on their legal obligation" to them, but "refrained from asking the Commission to assess the adequacy [of consultation] and accommodation afforded … on the 2007 EPA" … . The Commission's Scoping Order therefore addressed the consultation issue as follows:

> Evidence relevant to First Nations consultation may be relevant for the same purpose that the Commission often considers evidence of consultation with other stakeholders. Generally, insufficient evidence of consultation, including with First Nations is not determinative of matters before the Commission.

[9] On October 29, 2007, the CSTC requested late intervener status on the issue of consultation on the basis that the Commission's decision might negatively impact Aboriginal rights and title which were the subject of its

ongoing land claims. At the opening of the oral hearing on November 19, 2007, the CSTC applied for reconsideration of the Scoping Order and, in written submissions of November 20, 2007, it asked the Commission to include in the hearing's scope the issues of whether the duty to consult had been met, whether the proposed power sale under the 2007 EPA could constitute an infringement of Aboriginal rights and title in and of itself, and the related issue of the environmental impact of the 2007 EPA on the rights of the CSTC First Nations.

[10] The Commission established a two-stage process to consider the CSTC's application for reconsideration of the Scoping Order: an initial screening phase to determine whether there was a reasonable evidentiary basis for reconsideration, and a second phase to receive arguments on whether the rescoping application should be granted. ... The Commission confined the proceedings to the question of whether the 2007 EPA would adversely affect potential CSTC First Nations' interests by causing changes in water flows into the Nechako River or changes in water levels of the Nechako Reservoir.

[11] On November 29, 2007, the Commission issued a preliminary decision on the Phase I process called "Impacts on Water Flows". It concluded that the "responsibility for operation of the Nechako Reservoir remains with Alcan under the 2007 EPA", and that the EPA would not affect water levels in the Nechako River ... .

[12] As to fisheries, the Commission stated that "the priority of releases from the Nechako Reservoir [under the 1987 Settlement Agreement] is first to fish flows and second to power service". While the timing of water releases from the Nechako Reservoir for power generation purposes may change as a result of the 2007 EPA, that change "will have no impact on the releases into the Nechako river system". ...

[13] The Commission then embarked on Phase II of the rescoping hearing and invited the parties to make written submissions on the reconsideration application — specifically, on whether it would be a jurisdictional error not to revise the Scoping Order to encompass consultation issues on these facts. The parties did so.

[14] On December 17, 2007, the Commission dismissed the CSTC's application for reconsideration of the scoping order on grounds that the 2007 EPA would not introduce new adverse effects to the interests of the First Nations ... . For the purposes of the motion, the Commission assumed the historic infringement of Aboriginal rights, Aboriginal title, and a failure by the government to consult. ...

[15] The Commission went on to conclude that the 2007 EPA was in the public interest and should be accepted. It stated:

> In the circumstances of this review, evidence regarding consultation with respect to the historical, continuing infringement can reasonably be expected to be of no assistance for the same reasons there is no jurisdictional error, that is, the limited scope of the section 71 review, and there are no new physical impacts.

[16] In essence, the Commission took the view that the 2007 EPA would have no physical impact on the existing water levels in the Nechako River and hence it would not change the current management of its fishery. The Commission further found that its decision would not involve any transfer or change in the project's licences or operations. Consequently, the Commission concluded that its decision would have no adverse impact on the pending claims or rights of the CSTC First Nations such that there was no need to rescope the hearing to permit further argument on the duty to consult.

C. *The Judgment of the Court of Appeal, 2009 BCCA 67, 89 B.C.L.R. (4th) 298*
    (Donald, Huddart and Bauman JJ.A.)

[17] The CSTC appealed the Reconsideration Decision and the approval of the 2007 EPA to the British Columbia Court of Appeal. The Court, *per* Donald J.A., reversed the Commission's orders and remitted the case back to the Commission for "evidence and argument on whether a duty to consult and, if necessary, accommodate the [CSTC First Nations] exists and, if so, whether the duty has been met in respect of the filing of the 2007 EPA" (para. 69).

[18] The Court of Appeal found that the Commission had jurisdiction to consider the issue of consultation. The Commission had the power to decide questions of law, and hence constitutional issues relating to the duty to consult.

. . . . .

[20] The Court of Appeal held that the honour of the Crown obliged the Commission to decide the consultation issue, and that "the tribunal with the power to approve the plan must accept the responsibility to assess the adequacy of consultation" (para. 53). ... In finding that the Commission should have considered the consultation issue, the Court of Appeal appears to have taken a broader view than did the Commission as to when a duty to consult may arise.

[21] The Court of Appeal suggested that a failure to consider consultation risked the approval of a contract in breach of the Crown's constitutional duty. Donald J.A. asked, "How can a contract formed by a Crown agent in breach of a constitutional duty be in the public interest? The existence of such a duty and the allegation of the breach must form part and parcel of the public interest inquiry" (para. 42).

[22] Alcan and BC Hydro appeal to this Court. They argue that the Court of Appeal took too wide a view of the Crown's duty to consult and of the role of tribunals in deciding consultation issues. In view of the Commission's task under its constituent statute and the evidence before it, Alcan and BC Hydro submit that the Commission correctly concluded that it had no duty to consider the consultation issue raised by the CSTC, since, however much participation was accorded, there was no possibility of finding a duty to consult with respect to the 2007 EPA.

[23] The CSTC argues that the Court of Appeal correctly held that the Commission erred in refusing to rescope its proceeding to allow submissions on the consultation issue. It does not pursue earlier procedural arguments in this Court.

II. The Legislative Framework

. . . . .

B. *Legislation on the Commission's Remedial Powers*

[25] … [T]he Commission may issue an order approving the proposed contract under s. 71(2.4) of the *Utilities Commission Act* if it is found to be in the public interest. If it is not found to be in the public interest, the Commission can issue an order declaring the contract unenforceable, either wholly or in part, or "make any other order it considers advisable in the circumstances": s. 71(2), (3).

. . . . .

III. The Issues

[30] The main issues that must be resolved are: (1) whether the Commission had jurisdiction to consider consultation; and (2) if so, whether the Commission's refusal to rescope the inquiry to consider consultation should be set aside. In order to resolve these issues, it is necessary to consider when a duty to consult arises and the role of tribunals in relation to the duty to consult. These reasons will therefore consider:

1. When a duty to consult arises;
2. The role of tribunals in consultation;
3. The Commission's jurisdiction to consider consultation;
4. The Commission's Reconsideration Decision;
5. The Commission's conclusion that approval of the 2007 EPA was in the public interest.

IV. Analysis

A. *When Does the Duty to Consult Arise?*

[31] The Court in *Haida Nation* answered this question as follows: the duty to consult arises "<u>when the Crown has knowledge, real or constructive, of the potential existence of the Aboriginal right or title and contemplates conduct that might adversely affect it</u>" (para. 35). This test can be broken down into three elements: (1) the Crown's knowledge, actual or constructive, of a potential Aboriginal claim or right; (2) contemplated Crown conduct; and (3) the potential that the contemplated

conduct may adversely affect an Aboriginal claim or right. I will discuss each of these elements in greater detail. First, some general comments on the source and nature of the duty to consult are in order.

[32] The duty to consult is grounded in the honour of the Crown. It is a corollary of the Crown's obligation to achieve the just settlement of Aboriginal claims through the treaty process. While the treaty claims process is ongoing, there is an implied duty to consult with the Aboriginal claimants on matters that may adversely affect their treaty and Aboriginal rights, and to accommodate those interests in the spirit of reconciliation ...

[33] The duty to consult described in *Haida Nation* derives from the need to protect Aboriginal interests while land and resource claims are ongoing or when the proposed action may impinge on an Aboriginal right. Absent this duty, Aboriginal groups seeking to protect their interests pending a final settlement would need to commence litigation and seek interlocutory injunctions to halt the threatening activity. These remedies have proven time-consuming, expensive, and are often ineffective. Moreover, with a few exceptions, many Aboriginal groups have limited success in obtaining injunctions to halt development or activities on the land in order to protect contested Aboriginal or treaty rights.

[34] Grounded in the honour of the Crown, the duty has both a legal and a constitutional character ... The duty seeks to provide protection to Aboriginal and treaty rights while furthering the goals of reconciliation between Aboriginal peoples and the Crown. Rather than pitting Aboriginal peoples against the Crown in the litigation process, the duty recognizes that both must work together to reconcile their interests. It also accommodates the reality that often Aboriginal peoples are involved in exploiting the resource. Shutting down development by court injunction may serve the interest of no one. The honour of the Crown is therefore best reflected by a requirement for consultation with a view to reconciliation.

[35] *Haida Nation* sets the framework for dialogue prior to the final resolution of claims by requiring the Crown to take contested or established Aboriginal rights into account *before* making a decision that may have an adverse impact on them ... . The duty is *prospective*, fastening on rights yet to be proven.

[36] The nature of the duty varies with the situation. The richness of the required consultation increases with the strength of the *prima facie* Aboriginal claim and the seriousness of the impact on the underlying Aboriginal or treaty right ... .

[37] The remedy for a breach of the duty to consult also varies with the situation. The Crown's failure to consult can lead to a number of remedies ranging from injunctive relief against the threatening activity altogether, to damages, to an order to carry out the consultation prior to proceeding further with the proposed government conduct ... .

[38] The duty to consult embodies what Brian Slattery has described as a "generative" constitutional order which sees "section 35 as serving a dynamic and not simply static function" ... . This dynamicism was articulated in *Haida Nation* as follows, at para. 32:

... the duty to consult and accommodate is part of a process of fair dealing and reconciliation that begins with the assertion of sovereignty and continues beyond formal claims resolution. Reconciliation is not a final legal remedy in the usual sense. Rather, it is a process flowing from rights guaranteed by s. 35(1) of the *Constitution Act, 1982*.

As the post-*Haida Nation* case law confirms, consultation is "[c]oncerned with an ethic of ongoing relationships" and seeks to further an ongoing process of reconciliation by articulating a preference for remedies "that promote ongoing negotiations" ... .

[39] Against this background, I now turn to the three elements that give rise to a duty to consult.

(1)   Knowledge by the Crown of a Potential Claim or Right

[40] To trigger the duty to consult, the Crown must have real or constructive knowledge of a claim to the resource or land to which it attaches ... . Actual knowledge arises when a claim has been filed in court or advanced in the context of negotiations, or when a treaty right may be impacted ... . Constructive knowledge arises when lands are known or reasonably suspected to have been traditionally occupied by an Aboriginal community or an impact on rights may reasonably be anticipated. While the existence of a potential claim is essential, proof that the claim will succeed is not. What is required is a credible claim. Tenuous claims, for which a strong *prima facie* case is absent, may attract a mere duty of notice. ...

[41] The claim or right must be one which actually exists and stands to be affected by the proposed government action. This flows from the fact that the purpose of consultation is to protect unproven or established rights from irreversible harm as the settlement negotiations proceed ... .

(2)   Crown Conduct or Decision

[42] Second, for a duty to consult to arise, there must be Crown conduct or a Crown decision that engages a potential Aboriginal right. What is required is conduct that may adversely impact on the claim or right in question.

[43] This raises the question of what government action engages the duty to consult. It has been held that such action is not confined to government exercise of statutory powers ... . This accords with the generous, purposive approach that must be brought to the duty to consult.

[44] Further, government action is not confined to decisions or conduct which have an immediate impact on lands and resources. A potential for adverse impact suffices. ...

(3) <u>Adverse Effect of the Proposed Crown Conduct on an Aboriginal Claim or Right</u>

[45] The third element of a duty to consult is the possibility that the Crown conduct may affect the Aboriginal claim or right. The claimant must show a causal relationship between the proposed government conduct or decision and a potential for adverse impacts on pending Aboriginal claims or rights. Past wrongs, including previous breaches of the duty to consult, do not suffice.

[46] Again, a generous, purposive approach to this element is in order …

[47] Adverse impacts extend to any effect that may prejudice a pending Aboriginal claim or right. Often the adverse effects are physical in nature. However, as discussed in connection with what constitutes Crown conduct, high-level management decisions or structural changes to the resource's management may also adversely affect Aboriginal claims or rights even if these decisions have no "immediate impact on the lands and resources" … . This is because such structural changes to the resources management may set the stage for further decisions that will have a *direct* adverse impact on land and resources … .

[48] An underlying or continuing breach, while remediable in other ways, is not an adverse impact for the purposes of determining whether a particular government decision gives rise to a duty to consult. The duty to consult is designed to prevent damage to Aboriginal claims and rights while claim negotiations are underway … . The duty arises when the Crown has *knowledge*, real or constructive, of the potential or actual existence of the Aboriginal right or title "and <u>contemplates conduct that might adversely affect it</u>" … .

[49] The question is whether there is a claim or right that potentially may be adversely impacted by the *current* government conduct or decision in question. Prior and continuing breaches, including prior failures to consult, will only trigger a duty to consult if the present decision has the potential of causing a novel adverse impact on a present claim or existing right. This is not to say that there is no remedy for past and continuing breaches, including previous failures to consult. As noted in *Haida Nation*, a breach of the duty to consult may be remedied in various ways, including the awarding of damages. To trigger a fresh duty of consultation — the matter which is here at issue — a contemplated Crown action must put current claims and rights in jeopardy.

[50] Nor does the definition of what constitutes an adverse effect extend to adverse impacts on the negotiating position of an Aboriginal group. The duty to consult, grounded in the need to protect Aboriginal rights and to preserve the future use of the resources claimed by Aboriginal peoples while balancing countervailing Crown interests, no doubt <u>may have the ulterior effect</u> of delaying ongoing development. The duty may thus serve not only as a tool to settle interim resource issues but also, and incidentally, as a tool to achieve longer term compensatory goals. Thus conceived, the duty to consult may be seen as a necessary element in the

overall scheme of satisfying the Crown's constitutional duties to Canada's First Nations. However, cut off from its roots in the need to preserve Aboriginal interests, its purpose would be reduced to giving one side in the negotiation process an advantage over the other.

(4) An Alternative Theory of Consultation

[51] ... [T]he duty to consult ... requires demonstration of a causal connection between the proposed Crown conduct and a potential adverse impact on an Aboriginal claim or right.

[52] The respondent's submissions are based on a broader view of the duty to consult. It argues that even if the 2007 EPA will have no impact on the Nechako River water levels, the Nechako fisheries or the management of the contested resource, the duty to consult may be triggered because the 2007 EPA is part of a larger hydro-electric project which continues to impact its rights. The effect of this proposition is that if the Crown proposes an action, however limited, that relates to a project that impacts Aboriginal claims or rights, a fresh duty to consult arises. The current government action or decision, however inconsequential, becomes the hook that secures and reels in the constitutional duty to consult on the entire resource.

this makes sense though

[53] I cannot accept this view of the duty to consult. *Haida Nation* ... confines the duty to consult to adverse impacts flowing from the specific Crown proposal at issue — not to larger adverse impacts of the project of which it is a part. The subject of the consultation is the impact on the claimed rights of the *current* decision under consideration.

[54] ... An order compelling consultation is only appropriate where the proposed Crown conduct, immediate or prospective, may adversely impact on established or claimed rights. Absent this, other remedies may be more appropriate.

B. *The Role of Tribunals in Consultation*

[55] The duty on a tribunal to consider consultation and the scope of that inquiry depends on the mandate conferred by the legislation that creates the tribunal. ... It follows that the role of particular tribunals in relation to consultation depends on the duties and powers the legislature has conferred on it.

. . . . .

[60] ... In order for a tribunal to have the power to enter into interim resource consultations with a First Nation, pending the final settlement of claims, the tribunal must be expressly or impliedly authorized to do so. The power to engage in consultation itself, as distinct from the jurisdiction to determine whether a duty to consult exists, cannot be inferred from the mere power to consider questions of law. Consultation itself is not a question of law; it is a distinct and often complex constitutional process

and, in certain circumstances, a right involving facts, law, policy, and compromise. The tribunal seeking to engage in consultation itself must therefore possess remedial powers necessary to do what it is asked to do in connection with the consultation. The remedial powers of a tribunal will depend on that tribunal's enabling statute, and will require discerning the legislative intent … .

[61] A tribunal that has the power to consider the adequacy of consultation, but does not itself have the power to enter into consultations, should provide whatever relief it considers appropriate in the circumstances, in accordance with the remedial powers expressly or impliedly conferred upon it by statute. The goal is to protect Aboriginal rights and interests and to promote the reconciliation of interests called for in *Haida Nation*.

[62] The fact that administrative tribunals are confined to the powers conferred on them by the legislature, and must confine their analysis and orders to the ambit of the questions before them on a particular application, admittedly raises the concern that governments may effectively avoid their duty to consult by limiting a tribunal's statutory mandate. The fear is that if a tribunal is denied the power to consider consultation issues, or if the power to rule on consultation is split between tribunals so as to prevent any one from effectively dealing with consultation arising from particular government actions, the government might effectively be able to avoid its duty to consult.

[63] … [T]he duty to consult with Aboriginal groups, triggered when government decisions have the potential to adversely affect Aboriginal interests, is a constitutional duty invoking the honour of the Crown. It must be met. If the tribunal structure set up by the legislature is incapable of dealing with a decision's potential adverse impacts on Aboriginal interests, then the Aboriginal peoples affected must seek appropriate remedies in the courts … .

[64] Before leaving the role of tribunals in relation to consultation, it may be useful to review the standard of review that courts should apply in addressing the decisions of tribunals. The starting point is *Haida Nation*, at para. 61:

> The existence or extent of the duty to consult or accommodate is a legal question in the sense that it defines a legal duty. However, it is typically premised on an assessment of the facts. It follows that a degree of deference to the findings of fact of the initial adjudicator may be appropriate … Absent error on legal issues, the tribunal may be in a better position to evaluate the issue than the reviewing court, and some degree of deference may be required. In such a case, the standard of review is likely to be reasonableness. To the extent that the issue is one of pure law, and can be isolated from the issues of fact, the standard is correctness. However, where the two are inextricably entwined, the standard will likely be reasonableness
>
> …

[65] It is therefore clear that some deference is appropriate on matters of mixed fact and law, invoking the standard of reasonableness. This, of course, does not displace the need to take express legislative intention into

account in determining the appropriate standard of review on particular issues ... . It follows that it is necessary in this case to consider the provisions of the *Administrative Tribunals Act* and the *Utilities Commission Act* in determining the appropriate standard of review, as will be discussed more fully below.

C. *The Commission's Jurisdiction to Consider Consultation*

[66] Having considered the law governing when a duty to consult arises and the role of tribunals in relation to the duty to consult, I return to the questions at issue on appeal.

[67] The first question is whether consideration of the duty to consult was within the mandate of the Commission. This being an issue of jurisdiction, the standard of review at common law is correctness. The relevant statutes, discussed earlier, do not displace that standard. ... [T]he Commission did not err in concluding that it had the power to consider the issue of consultation.

[68] ... [I]ssues of consultation between the Crown and Aboriginal groups arise from s. 35 of the *Constitution Act, 1982*. They therefore have a constitutional dimension. The question is whether the Commission possessed the power to consider such an issue. ... We must therefore ask whether the *Utilities Commission Act* conferred on the Commission the power to consider the issue of consultation, grounded as it is in the constitution.

[69] It is common ground that the *Utilities Commission Act* empowers the Commission to decide questions of law in the course of determining whether the 2007 EPA is in the public interest. The power to decide questions of law implies a power to decide constitutional issues that are properly before it, absent a clear demonstration that the legislature intended to exclude such jurisdiction from the tribunal's power ... .

[70] Beyond its general power to consider questions of law, the factors the Commission is required to consider under s. 71 of the *Utilities Commission Act*, while focused mainly on economic issues, are broad enough to include the issue of Crown consultation with Aboriginal groups. At the time, s. 71(2)(e) required the Commission to consider "any other factor that the Commission considers relevant to the public interest". The constitutional dimension of the duty to consult gives rise to a special public interest, surpassing the dominantly economic focus of the consultation under the *Utilities Commission Act*. As Donald J.A. asked, "How can a contract formed by a Crown agent in breach of a constitutional duty be in the public interest?"

[71] This conclusion is not altered by the *Administrative Tribunals Act*, which provides that a tribunal does not have jurisdiction over constitutional matters. ...

[72] The application to the Commission by the CSTC for a rescoping order to address consultation issues ... is not a challenge to the constitutional validity or applicability of a law, nor a claim for a constitutional remedy under s. 24 of the *Charter* or s. 52 of the *Constitution*

Act, 1982. In broad terms, consultation under s. 35 of the *Constitution Act, 1982* is a constitutional question ... . However, the provisions of the *Administrative Tribunals Act* and the *Constitutional Question Act* do not indicate a clear intention on the part of the legislature to exclude from the Commission's jurisdiction the duty to consider whether the Crown has discharged its duty to consult with holders of relevant Aboriginal interests. It follows that ... the Commission has the constitutional jurisdiction to consider the adequacy of Crown consultation in relation to matters properly before it.

[73] For these reasons, I conclude that the Commission had the power to consider whether adequate consultation with concerned Aboriginal peoples had taken place.

[74] While the *Utilities Commission Act* conferred on the Commission the power to consider whether adequate consultation had taken place, its language did not extend to empowering the Commission to engage in consultations in order to discharge the Crown's constitutional obligation to consult. ... The Commission's power to consider questions of law and matters relevant to the public interest does not empower it to itself engage in consultation with Aboriginal groups.

[75] ... [T]he duty to consult with Aboriginal groups, triggered when government decisions have the potential to adversely affect Aboriginal interests, is a constitutional duty invoking the honour of the Crown. It must be met. If the tribunal structure set up by the Legislature is incapable of dealing with a decision's potential adverse impacts on Aboriginal interests, then the Aboriginal peoples affected must seek appropriate remedies in the courts ... .

D.   *The Commission's Reconsideration Decision*

[76] The Commission correctly accepted that it had the power to consider the adequacy of consultation with Aboriginal groups. The reason it decided it would not consider this issue was not for want of power, but because it concluded that the consultation issue could not arise, given its finding that the 2007 EPA would not adversely affect any Aboriginal interest.

. . . . .

[79] ... If, in applying the test set out in *Haida Nation*, it is arguable that a duty to consult could arise, the Commission would have been wrong to dismiss the rescoping order.

[80] The first element of the duty to consult — Crown knowledge of a potential Aboriginal claim or right — need not detain us. The CSTC First Nations' claims were well-known to the Crown; indeed, it was lodged in the Province's formal claims resolution process.

[81] Nor need the second element — proposed Crown conduct or decision — detain us. BC Hydro's proposal to enter into an agreement to purchase electricity from Alcan is clearly proposed Crown conduct. BC

Hydro is a Crown corporation. It acts in place of the Crown. No one seriously argues that the 2007 EPA does not represent a proposed action of the Province of British Columbia.

[82] The third element — adverse impact on an Aboriginal claim or right caused by the Crown conduct — presents greater difficulty. The Commission, referring to *Haida Nation*, took the view that to meet the adverse impact requirement, "more than just an underlying infringement" was required. In other words, it must be shown that the 2007 EPA could "adversely affect" a current Aboriginal interest. The Court of Appeal rejected, or must be taken to have rejected, the Commission's view of the matter.

[83] In my view, the Commission was correct in concluding that an underlying infringement in and of itself would not constitute an adverse impact giving rise to a duty to consult. ... Consultation centres on how the resource is to be developed in a way that prevents irreversible harm to existing Aboriginal interests. Both parties must meet in good faith, in a balanced manner that reflects the honour of the Crown, to discuss development with a view to accommodation of the conflicting interests. Such a conversation is impossible where the resource has long since been altered and the present government conduct or decision does not have any further impact on the resource. The issue then is not consultation about the further development of the resource, but negotiation about compensation for its alteration without having properly consulted in the past. The Commission applied the correct legal test.

[84] It was argued that the Crown breached the rights of the CSTC when it allowed the Kenney Dam and electricity production powerhouse with their attendant impacts on the Nechako River to be built in the 1950s and that this breach is ongoing and shows no sign of ceasing in the foreseeable future. But the issue before the Commission was whether a fresh duty to consult could arise *with respect to the Crown decision before the Commission*. ... The issue of ongoing and continuing breach was not before the Commission, given its limited mandate, and is therefore not before this Court.

[85] What then is the potential impact of the 2007 EPA on the claims of the CSTC First Nations? The Commission held there could be none. The question is whether this conclusion was reasonable based on the evidence before the Commission on the rescoping inquiry.

. . . . .

[88] ... The 2007 EPA calls for the creation of a Joint Operating Committee, with representatives of Alcan and BC Hydro (s. 4.13). The duties of the committee are to provide advice to the parties regarding the administration of the 2007 EPA and to perform other functions that may be specified or that the parties may direct (s. 4.14). The 2007 EPA also provides that the parties will jointly develop, maintain, and update a reservoir operating model based on Alcan's existing operating model and "using input data acceptable to both Parties, acting reasonably" (s. 4.17).

[89] The question is whether these clauses amount to an authorization of organizational changes that have the potential to adversely impact on Aboriginal interests. Clearly the Commission did not think so. But our task is to examine that conclusion and ask whether this view of the Commission was reasonable, bearing in mind the generous approach that should be taken to the duty to consult, grounded in the honour of the Crown.

[90] … In cases where adverse impact giving rise to a duty to consult has been found as a consequence of organizational or power-structure changes, it has generally been on the basis that the operational decision at stake may affect the Crown's future ability to deal honourably with Aboriginal interests. Thus, in *Haida Nation*, the Crown proposed to enter into a long-term timber sale contract with Weyerhaeuser. By entering into the contract, the Crown would have reduced its power to control logging of trees, some of them old growth forest, and hence its ability to exercise decision making over the forest consistent with the honour of the Crown. The resource would have been harvested without the consultation discharge that the honour of the Crown required. The Haida people would have been robbed of their constitutional entitlement. A more telling adverse impact on Aboriginal interests is difficult to conceive.

[91] By contrast, in this case, the Crown remains present on the Joint Operating Committee and as a participant in the reservoir operating model. Charged with the duty to act in accordance with the honour of Crown, BC Hydro's representatives would be required to take into account and consult as necessary with affected Aboriginal groups insofar as any decisions taken in the future have the potential to adversely affect them. The CSTC First Nations' right to Crown consultation on any decisions that would adversely affect their claims or rights would be maintained. I add that the honour of the Crown would require BC Hydro to give the CSTC First Nations notice of any decisions under the 2007 EPA that have the potential to adversely affect their claims or rights.

[92] This ongoing right to consultation on future changes capable of adversely impacting Aboriginal rights does not undermine the validity of the Commission's decision on the narrow issue before it: whether approval of the 2007 EPA could have an adverse impact on claims or rights of the CSTC First Nations. The Commission correctly answered that question in the negative. The uncontradicted evidence established that Alcan would continue to produce electricity at the same rates *regardless of whether the 2007 EPA is approved or not*, and that Alcan will sell its power elsewhere if BC Hydro does not buy it, as is their entitlement under Final Water Licence No. 102324 and the 1987 Agreement on waterflows. Moreover, although the Commission did not advert to it, BC Hydro, as a participant on the Joint Operating Committee and the resevoir management team, must in the future consult with the CSTC First Nations on any decisions that may adversely impact their claims or rights. On this evidence, it was not unreasonable for the Commission to conclude that the 2007 EPA will not adversely affect the claims and rights currently under negotiation of the CSTC First Nations.

[93] I conclude that the Commission took a correct view of the law on the duty to consult and hence on the question before it on the application for reconsideration. It correctly identified the main issue before it as whether the 2007 EPA had the potential to adversely affect the claims and rights of the CSTC First Nations. It then examined the evidence on this question. It looked at the organizational implications of the 2007 EPA and at the physical changes it might bring about. It concluded that these did not have the potential to adversely impact the claims or rights of the CSTC First Nations. It has not been established that the Commission acted unreasonably in arriving at these conclusions.

E.   *The Commission's Decision that Approval of the 2007 EPA was in the Public Interest*

[94] The attack on the Commission's decision to approve the 2007 EPA was confined to the Commission's failure to consider the issue of adequate consultation over the affected interests of the CSTC First Nations. The conclusion that the Commission did not err in rejecting the application to consider this matter removes this objection. It follows that the argument that the Commission acted unreasonably in approving the 2007 EPA fails.

V.   Disposition

[95] I would allow the appeal and confirm the decision of the British Columbia Utilities Commission approving the 2007 EPA. Each party will bear their costs.

Appeal allowed.

Does the Supreme Court's judgment in *Rio Tinto* provide any further detail about the scope or content of the Crown's duty to consult, as established in *Haida Nation* and *Taku River*? In some ways, the *Rio Tinto* judgment may be regarded as a wasted opportunity, in that the Supreme Court of Canada failed to infuse the notion of the duty to consult with greater substance or content when it had the opportunity to enhance current understandings of the Crown's duty. What further clarifications would you have wished to see in regard to the duty to consult that were not made in *Rio Tinto* that would have assisted your understanding of the duty to consult? Was it realistic to have expected the Supreme Court to have added this content to its judgment in *Rio Tinto*? Why/why not?

After its judgment in *Rio Tinto*, the Supreme Court revisited the issue of the duty to consult, this time in the context of modern treaties and land claims agreements, in *Beckman v. Little Salmon/Carmacks First Nation*, [2010] S.C.J. No. 53, [2010] 3 S.C.R. 103 (S.C.C.), a portion of which was excerpted in Chapter 4. Does the association of the duty to consult with these modern agreements alter what the Court has said about the duty to consult in its earlier jurisprudence? How does the Court go about reconciling the canons of treaty interpretation with the duty to consult?

BECKMAN v. LITTLE SALMON/CARMACKS FIRST NATION

[2010] S.C.J. No. 53, [2010] 3 S.C.R. 103 (S.C.C.)

The judgment of **McLachlin C.J.C.** and **Binnie**, **Fish**, **Abella**, **Charron**, **Rothstein** and **Cromwell JJ.** was delivered by **Binnie J.**: —

[1] This appeal raises important questions about the interpretation and implementation of modern comprehensive land claims treaties between the Crown and First Nations and other levels of government.

[2] The treaty at issue here is the Little Salmon/Carmacks First Nation Final Agreement (the "LSCFN Treaty"), which was finalized in 1996 and ratified by members of the First Nation in 1997. The LSCFN Treaty is one of eleven that arose out of and implement an umbrella agreement signed in 1993 after twenty years of negotiations between representatives of all of the Yukon First Nations and the federal and territorial governments. It was a monumental achievement. These treaties fall within the protection of s. 35 of the *Constitution Act, 1982*, which gives constitutional protection to existing Aboriginal and treaty rights.

[3] The present dispute relates to an application for judicial review of a decision by the Yukon territorial government dated October 18, 2004, to approve the grant of 65 hectares of surrendered land to a Yukon resident named Larry Paulsen. The plot borders on the settlement lands of the Little Salmon/Carmacks First Nation, and forms part of its traditional territory, to which its members have a treaty right of access for hunting and fishing for subsistence. In the result, Mr. Paulsen still awaits the outcome of the grant application he submitted on November 5, 2001.

[4] The First Nation disclaims any allegation that the Paulsen grant would violate the LSCFN Treaty, which itself contemplates that surrendered land may be taken up from time to time for other purposes, including agriculture. Nevertheless, until such taking up occurs, the members of the LSCFN have an ongoing treaty interest in surrendered Crown lands (of which the 65 hectares form a small part), to which they have a treaty right of access for hunting and fishing for subsistence. The LSCFN contends that the territorial government proceeded without proper consultation and without proper regard to relevant First Nation's concerns. They say the decision of October 18, 2004, to approve the Paulsen grant should be quashed.

[5] The territorial government responds that no consultation was required. The LSCFN Treaty, it says, is a complete code. The treaty refers to consultation in over 60 different places but a land grant application is not one of them. Where not specifically included, the duty to consult, the government says, is excluded.

[6] The important context of this appeal, therefore, is an application for judicial review of a decision that was required to be made by the territorial government having regard to relevant constitutional as well as administrative law constraints. The Yukon Court of Appeal held, as had the trial judge, that the LSCFN Treaty did not exclude the duty of consultation, although in this case the content of that duty was at the lower end of the spectrum (2007 YKSC 28; 2008 YKCA 13). The Court of Appeal went on to hold, disagreeing in this respect with the trial judge, that on the facts the government's duty of consultation had been fulfilled.

[7] I agree that the duty of consultation was not excluded by the LSCFN Treaty, although its terms were relevant to the exercise of the territorial government discretion, as were other principles of administrative and Aboriginal law, as will be discussed. On the facts of the Paulsen application, however, I agree with the conclusion of the Court of Appeal that the First Nation did not make out its case. The First Nation received ample notice of the Paulsen application, an adequate information package, and the means to make known its concerns to the decision maker. The LSCFN's objections were made in writing and they were dealt with at a meeting at which the First Nation was entitled to be present (but failed to show up). Both the First Nation's objections and the response of those who attended the meeting were before the appellant when, in the exercise of his delegated authority, he approved the Paulsen application. In light of the consultation provisions contained in the treaty, neither the honour of the Crown nor the duty to consult were breached. Nor was there any breach of procedural fairness. Nor can it be said that the appellant acted unreasonably in making the decision that he did. I would dismiss the appeal and cross-appeal.

I. Overview

[Discussion of the nature of modern treaties and land claims agreements is reproduced in Chapter 4 and is omitted here.]

[13] There was in this case, as mentioned, an express treaty right of members of the First Nation to hunt and fish for subsistence on their traditional lands, now surrendered and classified as Crown lands. While the LSCFN Treaty did not prevent the government from making land grants out of the Crown's land holdings, and indeed it contemplated such an eventuality, it was obvious that such grants might adversely affect the traditional economic activities of the LSCFN, and the territorial government was required to consult with the LSCFN to determine the nature and extent of such adverse effects.

[14] The delegated statutory decision maker was the appellant David Beckman, the Director of the Agriculture Branch of the territorial Department of Energy, Mines and Resources. He was authorized, subject to the treaty provisions, to issue land grants to non-settlement lands under the *Lands Act*, R.S.Y. 2002, c. 132, and the *Territorial Lands (Yukon) Act*, S.Y. 2003, c. 17. The First Nation argues that in exercising his discretion to

approve the grant the Director was required to have regard to First Nation's concerns and to engage in consultation. This is true. The First Nation goes too far, however, in seeking to impose on the territorial government not only the procedural protection of consultation but also a substantive right of accommodation. The First Nation protests that its concerns were not taken seriously — if they had been, it contends, the Paulsen application would have been denied. This overstates the scope of the duty to consult in this case. The First Nation does not have a veto over the approval process. No such substantive right is found in the treaty or in the general law, constitutional or otherwise. The Paulsen application had been pending almost three years before it was eventually approved. It was a relatively minor parcel of 65 hectares whose agricultural use, according to the advice received by the Director (and which he was entitled to accept), would not have any significant adverse effect on First Nation's interests.

[15] Unlike *Mikisew Cree* where some accommodation was possible through a rerouting of the proposed winter road, in this case the stark decision before the appellant Director was to grant or refuse the modified Paulsen application. He had before him the relevant information. Face-to-face consultation between the First Nation and the Director (as decision maker) was not required. In my view, the decision was reasonable having regard to the terms of the treaty, and in reaching it the Director did not breach the requirements of the duty to consult, natural justice, or procedural fairness. There was no *constitutional* impediment to approval of the Paulsen application and from an *administrative* law perspective the outcome fell within a range of reasonable outcomes.

II.   Facts

[16] On November 5, 2001, Larry Paulsen submitted his application for an agricultural land grant of 65 hectares. He planned to grow hay, put up some buildings and raise livestock. The procedure governing such grant applications was set out in a pre-treaty territorial government policy, *Agriculture for the 90s: A Yukon Policy* (1991) (the "1991 Agriculture Policy").

[17] The Paulsen application (eventually in the form of a "Farm Development Plan") was pre-screened by the Agriculture Branch and the Lands Branch as well as the Land Claims and Implementation Secretariat (all staffed by territorial civil servants) for completeness and compliance with current government policies.

[18] The Paulsen application was then sent to the Agriculture Land Application Review Committee ("ALARC") for a more in-depth technical review by various Yukon government officials. ALARC … predates and is completely independent from the treaty. …

[19] On February 24, 2004, ALARC recommended that the Paulsen application for the parcel, as reconfigured, proceed to the next level of review, namely, the Land Application Review Committee ("LARC"),

which includes First Nation's representatives. LARC also ... existed entirely independently of the treaties.

[20] Reference should also be made at this point to the Fish and Wildlife Management Board — a treaty body composed of persons nominated by the First Nation and Yukon government — which in August 2004 (i.e. while the Paulsen application was pending) adopted a Fish and Wildlife Management Plan ("FWMP") that identified a need to protect wildlife and habitat in the area of the Yukon River, which includes the Paulsen lands. It proposed that an area in the order of some 10,000 hectares be designated as a Habitat Protection Area under the *Wildlife Act*, R.S.Y. 2002, c. 229. The FWMP also recognized the need to preserve the First Nation's ability to transfer its culture and traditions to its youth through opportunities to participate in traditional activities. The FWMP did not, however, call for a freeze on approval of agricultural land grants in the area pending action on the FWMP proposals.

[21] Trapline #143 was registered to Johnny Sam, a member of the LSCFN. His trapline is in a category administered by the Yukon government, not the First Nation. It helps him to earn a livelihood as well as to provide a training ground for his grandchildren and other First Nation youth in the ways of trapping and living off the land. The trapline covers an area of approximately 21,435 hectares. As noted by the Court of Appeal, the 65 hectares applied for by Mr. Paulsen is approximately one-third of one percent of the trapline. A portion of the trapline had already been damaged by forest fire, which, in the LSCFN view, added to the significance of the loss of a further 65 hectares. ...

[22] The LARC meeting to discuss the Paulsen application was scheduled for August 13, 2004. The First Nation received notice and was invited to provide comments prior to the meeting and to participate in the discussion as a member of LARC.

[23] On July 27, 2004, the First Nation submitted a letter of opposition to the Paulsen application. The letter identified concerns about impacts on Trapline #143, nearby timber harvesting, the loss of animals to hunt in the area, and adjacent cultural and heritage sites. No reference was made in the First Nation's letter to Johnny Sam's concerns about cultural transfer or to the FWMP. The letter simply states that "[t]he combination of agricultural and timber harvesting impacts on this already-damaged trapline would certainly be a significant deterrent to the ability of the trapper to continue his traditional pursuits" (A.R., vol. II, at p. 22).

[24] Nobody from the LSCFN attended the August 13, 2004 meeting. Susan Davis, its usual representative, was unable to attend for undisclosed reasons. The meeting went on as planned.

[25] The members of LARC who were present (mainly territorial government officials) considered the Paulsen application and recommended approval in principle. The minutes of the August 13 meeting show that LARC *did* consider the concerns voiced by the LSCFN in its July 27, 2004 letter. Those present at the meeting concluded that the impact of the loss of 65 hectares on Trapline #143 would be minimal as the Paulsen application covered a very small portion of the trapline's overall

area and noted that Johnny Sam could apply under Chapter 16 of the LSCFN Treaty for compensation for any diminution in its value. LARC recommended an archaeological survey to address potential heritage and cultural sites. (An archaeological assessment was later conducted and reported on September 2, 2004, that it was unable to identify any sites that would be impacted adversely by the grant.)

[26] On September 8, 2004, the First Nation representatives met with Agriculture Branch staff who were conducting an agricultural policy review. The meeting did not focus specifically on the Paulsen application. Nevertheless, the First Nation made the general point that its concerns were not being taken seriously. Agriculture Branch officials replied that they consult on such matters through LARC but they were not required by the Final Agreement to consult on such issues. Meetings and discussions with the First Nation had been conducted, they said, only as a courtesy.

[27] On October 18, 2004, the Director approved the Paulsen application and sent a letter to Larry Paulsen, informing him of that fact. He did not notify the LSCFN of his decision, as he ought to have done.

[28] Apparently unaware that the Paulsen application had been approved, the First Nation continued to express its opposition by way of a series of letters from Chief Eddie Skookum to the Yukon government. Johnny Sam also wrote letters expressing his opposition. It seems the government officials failed to disclose that the Director's decision to approve the grant had already been made. This had the unfortunate effect of undermining appropriate communication between the parties.

[29] In the summer of 2005, Susan Davis, representing the First Nation, made enquiries of the Agriculture Branch and obtained confirmation that the Paulsen application had already been approved. She was sent a copy of the October 18, 2004 approval letter.

[30] In response, by letter dated August 24, 2005, the First Nation launched an administrative appeal of the Paulsen grant to the Assistant Deputy Minister.

[31] On December 12, 2005, the request to review the decision was rejected on the basis that the First Nation had no right of appeal because it was a member of LARC, and not just an intervener under the LARC Terms of Reference. The Terms of Reference specify that only applicants or interveners may initiate an appeal. The Terms of Reference had no legislative or treaty basis whatsoever, but the Yukon government nevertheless treated them as binding both on the government and on the First Nation.

[32] Frustrated by the territorial government's approach, which it believed broadly misconceived and undermined relations between the territorial government and the LSCFN, the First Nation initiated the present application for judicial review.

III.   Analysis

[33] The decision to entrench in s. 35 of the *Constitution Act, 1982* the recognition and affirmation of existing Aboriginal and treaty rights,

signalled a commitment by Canada's political leaders to protect and preserve constitutional space for Aboriginal peoples to be Aboriginal. At the same time, Aboriginal people do not, by reason of their Aboriginal heritage, cease to be citizens who fully participate with other Canadians in their collective governance. This duality is particularly striking in the Yukon, where about 25 percent of the population identify themselves as Aboriginal. ...

[34] Underlying the present appeal is not only the need to respect the rights and reasonable expectations of Johnny Sam and other members of his community, but the rights and expectations of other Yukon residents, including both Aboriginal people *and* Larry Paulsen, to good government. The Yukon treaties are intended, in part, to replace expensive and time-consuming *ad hoc* procedures with mutually agreed upon legal mechanisms that are efficient but fair.

[35] I believe the existence of Larry Paulsen's stake in this situation is of considerable importance. ... Mr. Paulsen made his application as an ordinary citizen who was entitled to a government decision reached with procedural fairness within a reasonable time. On the other hand, the entitlement of the trapper Johnny Sam was a derivative benefit based on the collective interest of the First Nation of which he was a member. I agree with the Court of Appeal that he was not, as an individual, a necessary party to the consultation.

A. *The LSCFN Treaty Reflects a Balance of Interests*

[36] Under the treaty, the LSCFN surrendered all undefined Aboriginal rights, title, and interests in its traditional territory in return for which it received:

- title to 2,589 square kilometres of "settlement land" (cc. 9 and 15);
- financial compensation of $34,179,210 (c. 19);
- potential for royalty sharing (c. 23);
- economic development measures (c. 22);
- rights of access to Crown land (except that disposed of by agreement for sale, surface licence, or lease) (c. 6);
- special management areas (c. 10);
- protection of access to settlement land (s. 6.2.7);
- rights to harvest fish and wildlife (c. 16);
- rights to harvest forest resources (c. 17);
- rights to representation and involvement in land use planning (c. 11) and resource management (cc. 14, 16–18).

These are substantial benefits ... . With the substantive benefits, however, came not only rights but duties and obligations. It is obvious that the long-term interdependent relationship thus created will require work and good will on both sides for its success.

[37] The reason for the government's tight-lipped reaction to the unfolding Paulsen situation, as explained to us at the hearing by its

counsel, was the fear that if the duty of consultation applies "these parties will be in court like parties are in areas where there are no treaties, and there will be litigation over whether the consultation applies; what is the appropriate level of the consultation? Is accommodation required? It is all under court supervision" (tr., at p. 18). ...

[38] The denial by the Yukon territorial government of any duty to consult except as specifically listed in the LSCFN Treaty complicated the *Paulsen* situation because at the time the Director dealt with the application the treaty implementation provision contemplated in Chapter 12 had itself not yet been implemented. I do not believe the Yukon Treaty was intended to be a "complete code". Be that as it may, the duty to consult is derived from the honour of the Crown which applies independently of the expressed or implied intention of the parties (see below, at para. 61). In any event, the procedural gap created by the failure to implement Chapter 12 had to be addressed, and the First Nation, in my view, was quite correct in calling in aid the duty of consultation in putting together an appropriate procedural framework.

[39] Nevertheless, consultation *was* made available and *did* take place through the LARC process under the 1991 Agriculture Policy, and the ultimate question is whether what happened in this case (even though it was mischaracterized by the territorial government as a courtesy rather than as the fulfilment of a legal obligation) was sufficient. In *Taku River Tlingit First Nation v. British Columbia (Project Assessment Director)*, 2004 SCC 74, [2004] 3 S.C.R. 550, the Court held that participation in a forum created for other purposes may nevertheless satisfy the duty to consult if *in substance* an appropriate level of consultation is provided.

B.   *The Relationship Between Section 35 and the Duty to Consult*

[40] The First Nation relies in particular on the following statements in *Haida Nation v. British Columbia (Minister of Forests)*, 2004 SCC 73, [2004] 3 S.C.R. 511, at para. 20:

> It is a corollary of s. 35 that the Crown act honourably in defining the rights it guarantees and in reconciling them with other rights and interests. This, in turn, implies a duty to consult and, if appropriate, accommodate.

Further, at para. 32:

> The jurisprudence of this Court supports the view that the duty to consult and accommodate is part of a process of fair dealing and reconciliation that begins with the assertion of sovereignty and <u>continues beyond formal claims resolution</u>. Reconciliation is not a final legal remedy in the usual sense. Rather, it is a process flowing from rights guaranteed by s. 35(1) of the *Constitution Act, 1982*. [Emphasis added.]

[41] Reference should also be made to *R. v. Kapp*, 2008 SCC 41, [2008] 2 S.C.R. 483, at para. 6, where the Court said:

> The decision to enhance aboriginal participation in the commercial fishery may also be seen as a response to the directive of this Court in *Sparrow*, at p. 1119, that the government consult with aboriginal groups in the

implementation of fishery regulation in order to honour its fiduciary duty to aboriginal communities. Subsequent decisions have affirmed the duty to consult and accommodate aboriginal communities with respect to resource development and conservation; <u>it is a constitutional duty, the fulfilment of which is consistent with the honour of the Crown</u>: see e.g. *Delgamuukw v. British Columbia*, [1997] 3 S.C.R. 1010. [Emphasis added.]

[42] The obligation of honourable dealing was recognized from the outset by the Crown itself in the *Royal Proclamation* of 1763 (reproduced in R.S.C. 1985, App. II, No. 1), in which the British Crown pledged its honour to the protection of Aboriginal peoples from exploitation by non-Aboriginal peoples. The honour of the Crown has since become an important anchor in this area of the law … . The honour of the Crown has thus been confirmed in its status as a constitutional principle.

[43] However, this is not to say that every policy and procedure of the law adopted to uphold the honour of the Crown is itself to be treated as if inscribed in s. 35. As the Chief Justice noted in *Haida Nation*, "[t]he honour of the Crown gives rise to different duties in different circumstances" (para. 18). This appeal considers its application in the modern treaty context … .

[44] The respondents' submission, if I may put it broadly, is that because the *duty* to consult is "constitutional", therefore there must be a reciprocal constitutional *right* of the First Nation to be consulted, and constitutional rights of Aboriginal peoples are not subject to abrogation or derogation except as can be justified under the high test set out in *Sparrow*. On this view, more or less every case dealing with consultation in the interpretation and implementation of treaties becomes a constitutional case. The trouble with this argument is that the content of the duty to consult varies with the circumstances. In relation to what *Haida Nation* called a "spectrum" of consultation (para. 43), it cannot be said that consultation at the lower end of the spectrum instead of at the higher end must be justified under the *Sparrow* doctrine. The minimal content of the consultation imposed in *Mikisew Cree* (para. 64), for example, did not have to be "justified" as a limitation on what would otherwise be a right to "deep" consultation. The circumstances in *Mikisew Cree* never gave rise to anything more than minimal consultation. <u>The concept of the duty to consult is a valuable adjunct to the honour of the Crown, but it plays a supporting role, and should not be viewed independently from its purpose.</u>

[45] The LSCFN invited us to draw a bright line between the duty to consult (which it labelled constitutional) and administrative law principles such as procedural fairness (which it labelled unsuitable). At the hearing, counsel for the LSCFN was dismissive of resort in this context to administrative law principles:

[A]dministrative law principles are not designed to address the very unique circumstance of the Crown-Aboriginal history, the Crown-Aboriginal relationship. Administrative law principles, for all their tremendous value, are not tools toward reconciliation of Aboriginal people and other

Canadians. They are not instruments to reflect the honour of the Crown principles. [tr., at p. 62]

However, as Lamer C.J. observed in *R. v. Van der Peet*, [1996] 2 S.C.R. 507, "aboriginal rights exist within the general legal system of Canada" (para. 49). Administrative decision makers regularly have to confine their decisions within constitutional limits ... . In this case, the constitutional limits include the honour of the Crown and its supporting doctrine of the duty to consult.

[46] The link between constitutional doctrine and administrative law remedies was already noted in *Haida Nation*, at the outset of our Court's duty to consult jurisprudence:

In all cases, the honour of the Crown requires that the Crown act with good faith to provide meaningful consultation appropriate to the circumstances. In discharging this duty, regard may be had to the procedural safeguards of natural justice <u>mandated by administrative law</u>. [Emphasis added; para. 41.]

The relevant "procedural safeguards" mandated by administrative law include not only natural justice but the broader notion of procedural fairness. And the content of meaningful consultation "appropriate to the circumstances" will be shaped, and in some cases determined, by the terms of the modern land claims agreement. Indeed, the parties themselves may decide therein to exclude consultation altogether in defined situations and the decision to do so would be upheld by the courts where this outcome would be consistent with the maintenance of the honour of the Crown.

[47] The parties in this case proceeded by way of an ordinary application for judicial review. Such a procedure was perfectly capable of taking into account the constitutional dimension of the rights asserted by the First Nation. There is no need to invent a new "constitutional remedy". Administrative law is flexible enough to give full weight to the constitutional interests of the First Nation. Moreover, the impact of an administrative decision on the interest of an Aboriginal community, whether or not that interest is entrenched in a s. 35 right, would be relevant as a matter of procedural fairness, just as the impact of a decision on any other community or individual (including Larry Paulsen) may be relevant.

C.   *Standard of Review*

[48] In exercising his discretion under the Yukon *Lands Act* and the *Territorial Lands (Yukon) Act*, the Director was required to respect legal and constitutional limits. In establishing those limits no deference is owed to the Director. The standard of review in that respect, including the adequacy of the consultation, is correctness. A decision maker who proceeds on the basis of inadequate consultation errs in law. Within the limits established by the law and the Constitution, however, the Director's decision should be reviewed on a standard of reasonableness ... . In other words, if there was adequate consultation, did the Director's decision to

approve the Paulsen grant, having regard to all the relevant considerations, fall within the range of reasonable outcomes?

D.   *The Role and Function of the LSCFN Treaty*

[49] The territorial government and the LSCFN have very different views on this point. This difference lies at the heart of their opposing arguments on the appeal.

[50] The territorial government regards the role of the LSCFN Treaty as having nailed down and forever settled the rights and obligations of the First Nation community as Aboriginal people. The treaty recognized and affirmed the Aboriginal rights surrendered in the land claim. From 1997 onwards, the rights of the Aboriginal communities of the LSCFN, in the government's view, were limited to the treaty. To put the government's position simplistically, what the First Nations negotiated as terms of the treaty is what they get. Period.

[51] The LSCFN, on the other hand, considers as applicable to the Yukon what was said by the Court in *Mikisew Cree*, at para. 54:

> Treaty making is an important stage in the long process of reconciliation, but it is only a stage. What occurred at Fort Chipewyan in 1899 was not the complete discharge of the duty arising from the honour of the Crown, but a rededication of it. …

[52] I agree with the territorial government that the LSCFN Treaty is a major advance over what happened in Fort Chipewyan in 1899, both in the modern treaty's scope and comprehensiveness, and in the fairness of the procedure that led up to it. The eight pages of generalities in Treaty No. 8 in 1899 is not the equivalent of the 435 pages of the LSCFN Treaty almost a century later. The LSCFN Treaty provides a solid foundation for reconciliation, and the territorial government is quite correct that the LSCFN Treaty should not simply set the stage for further negotiations from ground zero. Nor is that the First Nation's position. It simply relies on the principle noted in *Haida Nation*, that "[t]he honour of the Crown is <u>always</u> at stake in its dealings with Aboriginal peoples" (para. 16 (emphasis added)). Reconciliation in the Yukon, as elsewhere, is not an accomplished fact. It is a work in progress. The "complete code" position advocated by the territorial government is, with respect, misconceived. …

[53] On this point *Haida Nation* represented a shift in focus from *Sparrow*. Whereas the Court in *Sparrow* had been concerned about sorting out the consequences of infringement, *Haida Nation* attempted to head off such confrontations by imposing on the parties a duty to consult and (if appropriate) accommodate in circumstances where development might have a significant impact on Aboriginal rights when and if established. In *Mikisew Cree*, the duty to consult was applied to the management of an 1899 treaty process to "take up" (as in the present case) ceded Crown lands for "other purposes". The treaty itself was silent on the process. The Court held that on the facts of that case the content of the duty to consult

was at "the lower end of the spectrum" (para. 64), but that nevertheless the Crown was wrong to act unilaterally.

[54] The difference between the LSCFN Treaty and Treaty No. 8 is not simply that the former is a "modern comprehensive treaty" and the latter is more than a century old. Today's modern treaty will become tomorrow's historic treaty. The distinction lies in the relative precision and sophistication of the modern document. Where adequately resourced and professionally represented parties have sought to order their own affairs, and have given shape to the duty to consult by incorporating consultation procedures into a treaty, their efforts should be encouraged and, subject to such constitutional limitations as the honour of the Crown, the Court should strive to respect their handiwork: *Quebec (Attorney General) v. Moses*, 2010 SCC 17, [2010] 1 S.C.R. 557.

[55] However, the territorial government presses this position too far when it asserts that unless consultation is specifically required by the Treaty it is excluded by negative inference. Consultation in some meaningful form is the necessary foundation of a successful relationship with Aboriginal people. ...

[56] The territorial government would have been wrong to act unilaterally. The LSCFN had existing treaty rights in relation to the land Paulsen applied for ... The Crown land was subject to being taken up for other purposes (as in *Mikisew Cree*), including agriculture, but in the meantime the First Nation had a continuing treaty interest in Crown lands to which their members continued to have a treaty right of access (including but not limited to the Paulsen plot). It was no less a treaty interest because it was defeasible.

[57] The decision maker was required to take into account the impact of allowing the Paulsen application on the concerns and interests of members of the First Nation. He could not take these into account unless the First Nation was consulted as to the nature and extent of its concerns. Added to the ordinary administrative law duties, of course, was the added legal burden on the territorial government to uphold the honour of the Crown in its dealings with the First Nation. Nevertheless, given the existence of the treaty surrender and the legislation in place to implement it, and the decision of the parties not to incorporate a more general consultation process in the LSCFN Treaty itself, the content of the duty of consultation (as found by the Court of Appeal) was at the lower end of the spectrum. It was not burdensome. But nor was it a mere courtesy.

E.   *The Source of the Duty to Consult Is External to the LSCFN Treaty*

[58] The LSCFN Treaty dated July 21, 1997, is a comprehensive lawyerly document. The territorial government argues that the document refers to the duty to consult in over 60 different places but points out that none of them is applicable here (although the implementation of Chapter 12, which was left to subsequent legislative action, did not foreclose the possibility of such a requirement).

[59] There was considerable discussion at the bar about whether the duty to consult, if it applies at all, should be considered an implied term of the LSCFN Treaty or a duty externally imposed as a matter of law.

. . . . .

[61] ... The duty to consult is treated in the jurisprudence as a means (in appropriate circumstances) of upholding the honour of the Crown. Consultation can be shaped by agreement of the parties, but the Crown cannot contract out of its duty of honourable dealing with Aboriginal people. As held in *Haida Nation* and affirmed in *Mikisew Cree*, it is a doctrine that applies independently of the expressed or implied intention of the parties.

[62] The argument that the LSCFN Treaty is a "complete code" is untenable. For one thing, as the territorial government acknowledges, nothing in the text of the LSCFN Treaty authorizes the making of land grants on Crown lands to which the First Nation continues to have treaty access for subsistence hunting and fishing. The territorial government points out that authority to alienate Crown land exists in the general law. This is true, but the general law exists outside the treaty. The territorial government cannot select from the general law only those elements that suit its purpose. The treaty sets out rights and obligations of the parties, but the treaty is part of a special relationship: "In all its dealings with Aboriginal peoples, from the assertion of sovereignty to the resolution of claims <u>and the implementation of treaties</u>, the Crown must act honourably" (*Haida Nation*, at para. 17 (emphasis added)). As the text of s. 35(3) makes clear, a modern comprehensive land claims agreement is as much a treaty in the eyes of the Constitution as are the earlier pre- and post-Confederation treaties.

[63] At the time the Paulsen application was pending, the implementation of the LSCFN Treaty was in transition. It contemplates in Chapter 12 the enactment of a "development assessment process" to implement the treaty provisions. This was ultimately carried into effect in the *Yukon Environmental and Socio-economic Assessment Act*, S.C. 2003, c. 7 ("*YESAA*"). The territorial government acknowledges that the *YESAA* would have applied to the Paulsen application. Part 2 of the Act (regarding the assessment process) did not come into force until after the Paulsen application was approved (s. 134). The treaty required the government to introduce the law within two years of the date of the settlement legislation (s. 12.3.4). This was not done. The subsequent legislative delay did not empower the territorial government to proceed without consultation.

[64] The purpose of the *YESAA* is broadly stated to "[give] effect to the Umbrella Final Agreement respecting assessment of environmental and socio-economic effects" by way of a "comprehensive, neutrally conducted assessment process" (s. 5) where "an authorization or the grant of an interest in land" would be required (s. 47(2)(*c*)). The neutral assessor is the Yukon Environmental and Socio-economic Assessment Board, to which (excluding the chair) the Council for Yukon Indians would nominate half

the members and the territorial government the other half. The Minister, after consultation, would appoint the chair.

[65] The territorial government contends that this new arrangement is intended to satisfy the requirement of consultation on land grants in a way that is fair both to First Nations and to the other people of the Yukon. Assuming (without deciding) this to be so, the fact remains that no such arrangement was in place at the relevant time.

[66] In the absence of the agreed arrangement, consultation was necessary in this case to uphold the honour of the Crown. It was therefore imposed as a matter of law.

F. *The LSCFN Treaty Does Not Exclude the Duty to Consult and, if Appropriate, Accommodate*

[67] When a modern treaty has been concluded, the first step is to look at its provisions and try to determine the parties' respective obligations, and whether there is some form of consultation provided for in the treaty itself. If a process of consultation has been established in the treaty, the scope of the duty to consult will be shaped by its provisions.

[68] The territorial government argues that a mutual objective of the parties to the LSCFN Treaty was to achieve certainty, as is set out in the preamble:

> ... the parties to this Agreement wish to achieve certainty with respect to the ownership and use of lands and other resources of the Little Salmon/Carmacks First Nation Traditional Territory; the parties wish to achieve certainty with respect to their relationships to each other ... .

Moreover the treaty contains an "entire agreement" clause. Section 2.2.15 provides that:

> Settlement Agreements shall be the entire agreement between the parties thereto and there shall be no representation, warranty, collateral agreement or condition affecting those Agreements except as expressed in them.

[69] However, as stated, the duty to consult is not a "collateral agreement or condition". The LSCFN Treaty *is* the "entire agreement", but it does not exist in isolation. The duty to consult is imposed as a matter of law, irrespective of the parties' "agreement". It does not "affect" the agreement itself. It is simply part of the essential legal framework within which the treaty is to be interpreted and performed.

[70] The First Nation points out that there is an express exception to the "entire agreement" clause in the case of "existing or future constitutional rights", at s. 2.2.4:

> Subject to 2.5.0, 5.9.0, 5.10.1 and 25.2.0, Settlement Agreements shall not affect the ability of aboriginal people of the Yukon to exercise, or benefit from, any existing or future constitutional rights for aboriginal people that may be applicable to them.

Section 2.2.4 applies, the LSCFN argues, because the duty of consultation is a new constitutional duty and should therefore be considered a "future" constitutional right within the scope of the section.

[71] As discussed, the applicable "existing or future *constitutional* right" is the right of the Aboriginal parties to have the treaty performed in a way that upholds the honour of the Crown. That principle is readily conceded by the territorial government. However, the honour of the Crown may not *always require consultation*. The parties may, in their treaty, negotiate a different mechanism which, nevertheless, in the result, upholds the honour of the Crown. In this case, the duty applies, the content of which will now be discussed.

such as?

G.   *The Content of the Duty to Consult*

[72] The adequacy of the consultation … must be assessed in light of the role and function to be served by consultation on the facts of the case and whether that purpose was, on the facts, satisfied.

[73] The Yukon *Lands Act* and the *Territorial Lands (Yukon) Act* created a discretionary authority to make grants but do not specify the basis on which the discretion is to be exercised. It was clear that the Paulsen application might *potentially* have an adverse impact on the LSCFN Treaty right to have access to the 65 hectares for subsistence "harvesting" of fish and wildlife, and that such impact would include the First Nation's beneficial use of the surrounding Crown lands to which its members have a continuing treaty right of access. There was at least the possibility that the impact would be significant in economic and cultural terms. The Director was then required, as a matter of both compliance with the legal duty to consult based on the honour of the Crown *and* procedural fairness to be informed about the nature and severity of such impacts before he made a decision to determine (amongst other things) whether accommodation was necessary or appropriate. The purpose of consultation was not to reopen the LSCFN Treaty or to renegotiate the availability of the lands for an agricultural grant. Such availability was already established in the Treaty. Consultation was required to help manage the important ongoing relationship between the government and the Aboriginal community in a way that upheld the honour of the Crown.

[74] This "lower end of the spectrum" approach is consistent with the LSCFN Treaty itself which sets out the elements the parties themselves regarded as appropriate regarding consultation (where consultation is required) as follows:

"Consult" or "Consultation" means to provide:

(a) to the party to be consulted, notice of a matter to be decided in sufficient form and detail to allow that party to prepare its views on the matter;

(b) a reasonable period of time in which the party to be consulted may prepare its views on the matter, and an opportunity to present such views to the party obliged to consult; and

(c) full and fair consideration by the party obliged to consult of any views presented.

(LSCFN Treaty, c. 1) ...

[75] In my view, the negotiated definition is a reasonable statement of the content of consultation "at the lower end of the spectrum". The treaty does not apply directly to the land grant approval process, which is not a treaty process, but it is a useful indication of what the parties themselves considered fair, and is consistent with the jurisprudence from *Haida Nation* to *Mikisew Cree*.

H.   *There Was Adequate Consultation in This Case*

[76] The First Nation acknowledges that it received appropriate notice and information. Its letter of objection dated July 27, 2004, set out its concerns about the impact on Trapline #143, a cabin belonging to Roger Rondeau (who was said in the letter to have "no concerns with the application") as well as Johnny Sam's cabin, and "potential areas of heritage and cultural interest" that had not however "been researched or identified". The letter recommended an archaeological survey for this purpose (this was subsequently performed *before* the Paulsen application was considered and approved by the Director). Nothing was said in the First Nation's letter of objection about possible inconsistency with the FWMP, or the need to preserve the 65 hectares for educational purposes.

. . . . .

[78] The First Nation complains that its concerns were not taken seriously. It says, for example, the fact that Johnny Sam is eligible for compensation ignores the cultural and educational importance of Trapline #143. He wants the undiminished trapline, not compensation. However, Larry Paulsen also had an important stake in the outcome. The Director had a discretion to approve or not to approve and he was not obliged to decide this issue in favour of the position of the First Nation. Nor was he obliged as a matter of law to await the outcome of the FWMP. The Director had before him the First Nation's concerns and the response of other members of LARC. He was entitled to conclude that the impact of the Paulsen grant on First Nation's interests was not significant.

[79] It is important to stress that the First Nation does not deny that it had full notice of the Paulsen application, and an opportunity to state its concerns through the LARC process to the ultimate decision maker in whatever scope and detail it considered appropriate. Moreover, unlike the situation in *Mikisew Cree*, the First Nation here was consulted *as a First Nation* through LARC and not as members of the general public. While procedural fairness is a flexible concept and takes into account the Aboriginal dimensions of the decision facing the Director, it is nevertheless a doctrine that applies as a matter of administrative law to regulate relations between the government decision makers and all residents of the

Yukon, Aboriginal as well as non-Aboriginal, Mr. Paulsen as well as the First Nation. On the record, and for the reasons already stated, the requirements of procedural fairness were met, as were the requirements of the duty to consult.

. . . . .

I. *The Duty to Accommodate*

[81] The First Nation's argument is that in this case the legal requirement was not only procedural consultation but substantive accommodation. *Haida Nation* and *Mikisew Cree* affirm that the duty to consult *may* require, in an appropriate case, accommodation. The test is not, as sometimes seemed to be suggested in argument, a duty to accommodate to the point of undue hardship for the non-Aboriginal population. Adequate consultation having occurred, the task of the Court is to review the exercise of the Director's discretion taking into account all of the relevant interests and circumstances, including the First Nation entitlement and the nature and seriousness of the impact on that entitlement of the proposed measure which the First Nation opposes.

[82] The 65-hectare plot had already been reconfigured at government insistence to accommodate various concerns. The First Nation did not suggest any alternative configuration that would be more acceptable ... . However, with respect, nothing in the treaty itself or in the surrounding circumstances gave rise to a requirement of accommodation. The government was "taking up" surrendered Crown land for agricultural purposes as contemplated in the treaty.

[83] The concerns raised by the First Nation were important, but the question before the Director was in some measure a policy decision related to the 1991 Agricultural Policy as well as to whether, on the facts, the impact on the First Nation interests were as serious as claimed. He then had to weigh those concerns against the interest of Larry Paulsen in light of the government's treaty and other legal obligations to Aboriginal people. ... The First Nation points out that the Paulsen proposed building would trigger a "no-shooting zone" that would affect Johnny Sam's use of his cabin (as well as his trapline). However, where development occurs, shooting is necessarily restricted, and the LSCFN Treaty is not an anti-development document.

[84] *Somebody* has to bring consultation to an end and to weigh up the respective interests, having in mind the Yukon public policy favouring agricultural development where the rigorous climate of the Yukon permits. The Director is the person with the delegated authority to make the decision whether to approve a grant of land already surrendered by the First Nation. The purpose of the consultation was to ensure that the Director's decision was properly informed.

[85] The Director did not err in law in concluding that the consultation in this case with the First Nation was adequate.

[86] The advice the Director received from his officials after consultation is that the impact would not be significant. There is no evidence that he failed to give the concerns of the First Nation "full and fair consideration". The material filed by the parties on the judicial review application does not demonstrate any palpable error of fact in his conclusion.

. . . . .

[88] Whether or not a court would have reached a different conclusion on the facts is not relevant. The decision to approve or not to approve the grant was given by the Legislature to the Minister who, in the usual way, delegated the authority to the Director. His disposition was not unreasonable.

IV. Conclusion

[89] I would dismiss the appeal and cross-appeal, with costs.

The reasons of **LeBel** and **Deschamps JJ.** were delivered by **Deschamps J.:** —

. . . . .

[91] In Yukon, the parties sat down to negotiate. An umbrella agreement and 11 specific agreements were reached between certain First Nations, the Yukon government and the Government of Canada. Through these agreements, the First Nations concerned have taken control of their destiny. The agreements, which deal in particular with land and resources, are of course not exhaustive, but they are binding on the parties with respect to the matters they cover. The Crown's exercise of its rights under the treaty is subject to provisions on consultation. To add a further duty to consult to these provisions would be to defeat the very purpose of negotiating a treaty. Such an approach would be a step backward that would undermine both the parties' mutual undertakings and the objective of reconciliation through negotiation. This would jeopardize the negotiation processes currently under way across the country. Although I agree with Binnie J. that the appeal and cross-appeal should be dismissed, my reasons for doing so are very different.

[92] Mr. Paulsen's application constituted a project to which the assessment process provided for in Chapter 12 of the Little Salmon/Carmacks First Nation Final Agreement ("Final Agreement") applied. Although that process had not yet been implemented, Chapter 12, including the transitional legal rules it contains, had been. Under those rules, any existing development assessment process would remain applicable. The requirements of the processes in question included not only consultation with the First Nation concerned, but also its participation in the assessment of the project. Any such participation would involve a more extensive consultation than would be required by the common law duty in that regard.

Therefore, nothing in this case can justify resorting to a duty other than the one provided for in the Final Agreement.

. . . . .

[94] I disagree with Binnie J.'s view that the common law constitutional duty to consult applies in every case, regardless of the terms of the treaty in question. And I also disagree with the appellants' assertion that an external duty to consult can never apply to parties to modern comprehensive land claims agreements and that the Final Agreement constitutes a complete code. In my view, *Mikisew Cree First Nation v. Canada (Minister of Canadian Heritage)*, 2005 SCC 69, [2005] 3 S.C.R. 388, stands for the proposition that the common law constitutional duty to consult Aboriginal peoples applies to the parties to a treaty only if they have said nothing about consultation in respect of the right the Crown seeks to exercise under the treaty. Moreover, it is essential to understand that in this context, the signature of the treaty entails a change in the nature of the consultation. When consultation is provided for in a treaty, it ceases to be a measure to prevent the infringement of one or more rights, as in *Haida Nation*, and becomes a duty that applies to the Crown's exercise of rights granted to it in the treaty by the Aboriginal party. This means that where, as in *Mikisew*, the common law duty to consult applies to treaty rights despite the existence of the treaty — because the parties to the treaty included no provisions in this regard — it represents the minimum obligational content.

. . . . .

[99] In the case at bar, all the parties are, in one way or another, bound by the Final Agreement, which settles the comprehensive land claim of the Little Salmon/Carmacks First Nation. Section 35(3) of the *Constitution Act, 1982* provides that "in subsection (1)" the expression "treaty rights" includes "rights that now exist by way of land claims agreements or may be so acquired." The appellants' position is based on one such agreement.

[100] The respondents, intending to rely on *Mikisew*, invoke only the Crown's common law duty to consult Aboriginal peoples, and not the agreement, which, as can be seen from the transcript of the hearing (at p. 46), they do not allege has been breached; they submit that the purpose of the agreement in the instant case was not to define the parties' constitutional duties.

. . . . .

[103] Thus, the constitutional duty to consult Aboriginal peoples involves three objectives: in the short term, to provide "interim" or "interlocutory" protection for the constitutional rights of those peoples; in the medium term, to favour negotiation of the framework for exercising such rights over having that framework defined by the courts; and, in the

longer term, to assist in reconciling the interests of Aboriginal peoples with those of other stakeholders. ... However, the courts must ensure that this duty is not distorted and invoked in a way that compromises rather than fostering negotiation. That, in my view, would be the outcome if we were to accept the respondents' argument that the treaties, and the Final Agreement in particular, do not purport to define the parties' constitutional duties, including what the Crown party must do to consult the Aboriginal party before exercising its rights under the treaty.

. . . . .

[122] ... Where a treaty provides for a mechanism for consulting the Aboriginal party when the Crown exercises its rights under the treaty ... what the treaty does is to override the common law duty to consult the Aboriginal people; it does not affect the general administrative law principle of procedural fairness, which may give rise to a duty to consult rights holders individually. ...

. . . . .

[204] The appellants seek a declaration that the Crown did not have a duty to consult under the Final Agreement with respect to Mr. Paulsen's application. Their interpretation of the Final Agreement is supported neither by the applicable principles of interpretation nor by either the context or the provisions of the Final Agreement. The cross-appellants argue that the common law duty to consult continued to apply despite the coming into effect of the Final Agreement. As I explained above, it is my view that there is no gap in the Final Agreement as regards the duty to consult. Its provisions on consultation in relation to the management of fish and wildlife were in effect. And the Little Salmon/Carmacks First Nation had in fact submitted comments in the process provided for in that respect. Moreover, the administrative law rights of Johnny Sam are governed neither by the common law duty to consult nor by the Final Agreement. Although the Little Salmon/Carmacks First Nation's argument that it had a right to be consulted with respect to Mr. Paulsen's application is valid, the source of that right is not the common law framework. The fact is that the transfer to Mr. Paulsen constituted an agricultural development project that was subject to Chapter 12 of the Final Agreement and that that chapter's transitional provisions established the applicable framework.

[205] In this case, given that Mr. Paulsen's application would have been subject to a mandatory assessment by the local assessment district office, the fact that recourse was had to the existing process to assess the application supports a conclusion that the actual consultation with the respondents was more extensive than the consultation to which they would have been entitled under the *YESAA*.

[206] For these reasons, I would dismiss the appeal and the cross-appeal, both with costs.

Appeal and cross-appeal dismissed with costs.

After reading *Beckman v. Little Salmon/Carmacks First Nation*, ask yourself whether the Court successfully reconciles the canons of treaty interpretation with the duty to consult. If you had to explain the interaction between the two, do you feel that the decision in *Beckman v. Little Salmon/Carmacks First Nation* has given you sufficient guidance to do so?

In her minority judgment in *Beckman v. Little Salmon/Carmacks First Nation*, agreeing in the result, Deschamps J. made the following statement about the notion of the "honour of the Crown":

> [105] This Court has, over time, substituted the principle of the honour of the Crown for a concept — the fiduciary duty — that, in addition to being limited to certain types of relations that did not always concern the constitutional rights of Aboriginal peoples, had paternalistic overtones … . Before being raised to the status of a constitutional principle, the honour of the Crown was originally referred to as the "sanctity" of the "word of the white man" … . The honour of the Crown thus became a key principle for the interpretation of treaties with Aboriginal peoples … .

Justice Deschamps assumes, without further elaboration, that the idea of the "honour of the Crown" has replaced the Crown's fiduciary obligations owed to Aboriginal peoples. What principles or jurisprudence does she rely upon for this statement? Can one point to any judgment that indicates the truth of this assertion? While there have been markedly fewer opportunities for the Supreme Court to consider the application of the Crown's fiduciary duty since its judgment in *Wewaykum*, which marginalized the concept, the Court has never indicated that the Crown's fiduciary duty has been replaced by the "honour of the Crown". Indeed, as indicated above, the "honour of the Crown" is a fundamental element of the Crown's fiduciary obligations. However, as indicated in this section, the honour of the Crown also gives rise to the lesser Crown duty to consult. What still remains to be considered by the Supreme Court is where the Crown's fiduciary duties and duty to consult respectively lie on the spectrum of Crown obligations to Aboriginal peoples and how or to what extent they interact with each other.

E. CONCLUSION

The issue of Crown obligations to Aboriginal peoples, while not fully developed prior to the emergence of the duty to consult as an independent basis of legal obligation in *Haida Nation* and *Taku River*, has become even more cumbersome as a result of this addition. Under the rubric of the "honour of the Crown" now exist three distinct branches of Crown obligation: treaty obligations, fiduciary duties and the duty to consult. While there would certainly appear to be overlap among these, particularly since they may all be traced to the historical interaction between the Crown and Aboriginal peoples, the Supreme Court of Canada has yet to engage directly in such a discussion. This has created an even more fractured and uncertain jurisprudence in which the new and relatively unarticulated duty to consult shares a common foundation with existing treaty and fiduciary obligations, but has yet to be sufficiently distinguished from them other than being said to be a "lesser" duty than the Crown's fiduciary duty. Subsequent jurisprudence on the duty to consult, including the *Mikisew Cree*, *Rio Tinto* and *Beckman v. Little Salmon/ Carmacks First Nation* cases, has failed to provide much assistance to understanding the nature and content of that aspect of the Crown's duty.

Although a combination of the emergence of the duty to consult cases and the judgment in *Wewaykum* has appeared to relegate the Crown's fiduciary duty to the judicial backburner — a conclusion that has not changed despite the more recent consideration of the Crown's fiduciary duty in *Ermineskin* — the Crown's fiduciary duty has not ceased to be an important element of Crown-Aboriginal relations. Much still needs to be done to more fully understand the implications of the Crown's fiduciary duty and how, or to what extent, it differs from the Crown's duty to consult. Yet, rather than addressing such fundamental questions, the Crown's fiduciary duty has been mothballed in favour of applications of the lesser duty to consult. Thus, the legacy of post-*Guerin* fiduciary case law remains in much the same situation that the Supreme Court of Canada initially left after its decision in *Guerin*, albeit with the added wrinkle of its uncertain relationship with the duty to consult as a result of the *Haida Nation* and *Taku River* judgments.

This chapter has attempted to bring together the various strands of Crown obligations emanating from the honour of the Crown in an attempt to more fully understand them and to provides a basis for assessing their similarities and distinctions. What is needed is a fundamental review of the entirety of the Crown's obligations to Aboriginal peoples to better ensure that the Crown lives up to its duties and may not avoid them simply because of the confusion created by an unsatisfactory jurisprudence. Unfortunately, the confusion created by the *Haida Nation* and *Taku River* judgments and the lingering uncertainty over the effects of *Wewaykum* on the Crown's fiduciary duty do not provide a solid foundation for this task. Further, more recent jurisprudence that has had the opportunity to clear up this confusion, like *Rio Tinto*, *Ermineskin* and, to a lesser extent, *Lax Kw'alaams*, has not taken the initiative to address these matters. Thus, resolution of the interplay between the Crown's fiduciary duty and its duty to consult remains for another day.

ENDNOTES

1. Premier McBride to Prime Minister Laurier, 19 November 1910, BCARS, GR 441, Box 149, cited in Jeannie L. Kanakos, *The Negotiations to Relocate the Songhees Indians, 1843-1911* (M.A. thesis, Simon Fraser University, 1974) at 71 (cited in Hamar Foster, "We Are Not O'Meara's Children: Law, Lawyers and the First Campaign for Aboriginal Title in British Columbia, 1909-1928" at <http://www.law.uvic.ca/calder/foster.pdf> at 16).

2. "Sir William Johnson to the Lords of Trade, Fort Johnson, 8 March 1756", as reproduced in E.B. O'Callaghan, ed., *Documents Relative to the Colonial History of the State of New York*, 11 vols. (Albany: Weed, Parsons, 1853-61) VII at 43.

3.   (2001) 50 U.N.B.L.J. 57 at 66-67.
4.   Ottawa, *Report of the Royal Commission on Aboriginal Peoples* (Ottawa: Ministry of Supply and Services Canada, 1996), Vol. 3, Restructuring the Relationship, Part I, at 30.
5.   *Ibid.*, Vol. 4, Perspectives and Realities, at 549.
6.   *Ibid.*, Vol. 5, Renewal: A Twenty-Year Commitment, at 7.
7.   Tanis Fiss, A Matter of the Duty to Consult, November 18, 2004, Canadian Taxpayers Federation News Release.
8.   Dean Jacobs, "Consulting and Accommodating First Nations in Canada: A Duty that Reaps Benefits", July 25, 2005, online at <http://www.bkejwanong.com>.

CHAPTER 6

INUIT RIGHTS

A. INTRODUCTION

Section 35(2) of the *Constitution Act, 1982*, being Schedule B to the *Canada Act 1982* (U.K.), 1982, c. 11 identifies "Aboriginal Peoples of Canada" as including the "Indian, Inuit, and Métis Peoples of Canada". This definition is indicative of at least two things. Initially, it informs us that the contemplation of Aboriginal and treaty rights in section 35(1) is not restricted to those rights pertaining to "Indians", but to any Aboriginal or treaty rights belonging to the Aboriginal Peoples of Canada. Second, section 35(2) tells us that Inuit (and Métis) peoples, while considered "Aboriginal Peoples of Canada," are recognized by the Canadian Constitution as distinct peoples.

This chapter will examine Inuit distinctiveness through an investigation of who Inuit peoples are and some of the issues that are most pertinent to them. A focus on the Inuit, perhaps more than other Aboriginal groups in Canada, illustrates the importance of negotiation and agreement for the resolution of outstanding issues regarding land, resources and governance. Most Inuit groups have entered into land claims agreements over the past 25 years. This has led to some excellent opportunities to incorporate traditional law and legislative power into contemporary Aboriginal governance. At the same time the Inuit are also experiencing a degree of frustration as significant challenges exist regarding government support for the implementation of their land claim agreements. This chapter will investigate different facets of these varied experiences.

B. INUIT LAW IN CULTURAL CONTEXT

Culture is fluid and people adapt to change within such frameworks. Cultures contain variations and these variations allow people to choose different life-courses. Culture is not static and people knit together the past and present in diverse ways. A leading anthropologist who has worked with Inuit people throughout her life has written, "The notion that meaning inheres in culture and that people receive it passively, as dough receives the cookie cutter, is rapidly being replaced by the idea that culture consists of ingredients, potentials, which people actively select, interpret and use in various ways as opportunities, capabilities and experiences allow."[1] Thus, culture is a human resource that enables people to adapt without undermining their broader world-views and relationships.

Law is also fluid. People adapt to change within legal frameworks. Inuit law is a part of Inuit culture. It allows people to choose different life-courses that knit the past and present together in different ways. Inuit law is a resource that allows for adaptation. The following excerpt explains how "tradition" is usually directed toward how people should live in the present and in the future. As you read, identify the various ways in which tradition might be learned. Ask yourself: how are these learning processes similar and different from those you are familiar with in acquiring knowledge about the common law?

INTERVIEWING INUIT ELDERS: THE ORAL TRADITIONS PROJECT, VOLUME 2: PERSPECTIVES ON TRADITIONAL LAW JARICH OOSTEN, FRÉDÉRIC LAUGRAND AND WIM RASING, EDS.

(Iqaluit: Nunavut Arctic College, 1999) at 1-3

Maligait, piqujait and *tirigusuusiit* refer to what had to be followed, done or not done in Inuit culture. Nowadays, these words are often used as equivalents to modern Western notions of law. Through these terms Western notions of law become more accessible to Inuit. In the *Legal Glossary*, authored by Desmond Brice-Bennet, Michèle Therrien (1997: p. 250) states: "New terminology is interesting because it uses 'old' materials to express today's experiences and concepts." In the process of translation, Western concepts as well as Inuit notions are changed.

The Western concepts acquire new connotations and meanings associated with the old words that are not always sufficiently acknowledged by Westerners. The old concepts become imbued with new meanings attached to Western concepts of law. The use of these translations tends to obscure the fact that *maligait, piqujait* and *tirigusuusiit* on one side, and notions such as law on the other, derive from completely different cultural perspectives. In her instructive appendix to the *Legal Glossary*, Michèle Therrien explains some of the key notions in more detail. She is well aware of the risks involved in translating these terms into modern concepts. Her explanations are illuminating, as she carefully expounds the meaning and significance of these terms. Thus *piqujaq* is translated as "Inuit customary law." This translation is useful in the context of the modern law system, but obviously "customary law" is a Western concept that did not exist in Inuit society before the introduction of the Canadian system of law. The back translation of *piqujaq* is "which is asked to be done (by somebody)" and its implicit meaning is "which is asked by an authorized person to be done". Therrien (1997: p. 253) explains that *piqujaq* "is used as a general concept pertaining to the obligation to respect rules imposed within Inuit society. These rules are orally transmitted and not codified. Only authorized persons have the right to make rules. Rules most often taught by parents concern offering help to the family or the elders, and respect due to animals". In this explanation we come much closer to the meaning of piqujaq than in the translation "customary law" but even here it is difficult to avoid such terms as "rules" and "authorized persons" that suggest a much more formalized structure than actually existed in Inuit society. Elders had much authority and were highly respected, but not in any formal way. The term "rule" suggests a general principle, which is always applied whereas the term piqujaq emphasized the importance of the relation involved: people will comply with what those they respect ask from them. To understand how the principle worked we have to understand the social fabric of Inuit society. With respect to the term *maligaq* we are faced with similar problems.

Nowadays, it is often translated as "Canadian law". But *maligaq* is a relational term. According to the glossary *malik* means "to follow a person, an animal, an idea, an object. To travel with somebody not being the leader e.g. not owning the sled" (Therrien, 1997: p. 255). Therrien (1997: p. 256) explains that *maligaq* means, "which is followed in an inherent manner" and comments, "Using *maligaq* or *maliksaq* instead of *piqujaq* for customary law would mean that the focus is put on the result of a request (the obligation to obey) rather than the request itself (the wish to obey)."

The third term, which we use in the title, is *tirigusuusiit*, a term frequently used by the elders in the interviews. In the anthropological literature *tirigusuusiit* are unfortunately often referred to as taboos or superstitions (cf. Spalding, 1998: p. 161) tirigusungniq superstition; belief in taboos). They refer to the observance of specific rules, usually with respect to game and they played an important part in Inuit society before the introduction of Christianity. The more an animal was used the more *tirigusuusiit* there were. The notion of tirigusuusiit is closely associated to that of *pittailiniq*, refraining from doing what is not allowed. In the wider perspective of Inuit society, a clear distinction between ritual and social rules cannot be maintained. In fact, ritual rules such as the *tirigusuusiit* tend to take precedence over general social principles of correct behaviour. The interviews with the elders made quite clear that *tirigusuusiit* played a central role in the preservation of Inuit society. Although most of the *tirigusuusiit* are no longer observed, the necessity of respecting game is still widely acknowledged by Inuit. The awareness, that the continuity of society depends on the maintenance of correct relationships with animals and the land, is still very strong. ...

[T]*irigusuusiit*, *piqujaq* and *maligaq* are embedded in social and cosmic relationships. From this perspective it can be understood why Susan Enuaraq (1995) ... begins her paper on "Traditional Justice among the Inuit" with an account of the famous creation myth of the woman who did not want to get a husband and then married a dog. For Susan, a discussion of traditional law begins with a discussion of the origin of the cosmic order of the world. This woman became the ancestress of different peoples as well as the mother of sea mammals, illustrating that the relations between human beings on one side, and between human beings and game on the other, cannot be separated from each other. ... In the interviews the elders repeatedly emphasized that transgressions were not so much sanctioned by the community as by spiritual "agencies" such as the weather or the game. Stingy people would catch less game. Sins would evoke bad weather. Again, a distinction between social and ritual rules hardly applies to Inuit culture. A murderer would have a short life. In case of transgressions, the elders would try to make the culprit see the foolishness of his behaviour.

... The *maligait* of the Inuit are not on paper. They are inside people's heads and they will not disappear or be torn to pieces. Even if a person dies the *maligait* will not disappear. It is part of a person. It's what makes a person strong. But not only were these laws unwritten, they were of a different nature. ...

1. *Sedna: A Law Story*

The following account of the story of a woman who married a dog and a raven, referenced by Susan Enuaraq above, was recounted by Franz Boas.[2] Sedna's powers are considerable and she is thought to be a judge among some Inuit people:

> ... [T]here lived on a solitary shore an Inu[k] with his daughter Sedna. His wife had been dead for some time and the two led a quiet life. Sedna grew up to be a handsome girl and the youths came from all around to sue for her hand, but none of them could touch her proud heart.
>
> Finally, at the breaking up of the ice in the spring a fulmar [raven] flew from over the ice and wooed Sedna with enticing song. "Come to me," it said; "come into the land of the birds, where there is never hunger, where my tent is made of the most beautiful skins. You shall rest on soft bearskins. My fellows, the fulmars, shall bring you all your heart may desire; their feathers shall clothe you; your lamp shall always be filled with oil, your pot with meat." Sedna could not long resist such wooing and they went together over the vast sea. When at last they reached the country of the fulmar, after a long and hard journey, Sedna discovered that her spouse had shamefully deceived her. Her new home was not built of beautiful pelts, but was covered with wretched fishskins, full of holes, that gave free entrance to wind and snow. Instead of soft reindeer skins her bed was made of hard walrus hides and she had to live on miserable fish, which the birds brought her. Too soon she discovered that she had thrown away her opportunities when in her foolish pride she had rejected the Inuit youth. In her woe she sang: "Aja. O father, if you knew how wretched I am you would come to me and we would hurry away in your boat over the waters. The birds look unkindly upon me the stranger; cold winds roar about my bed; they give me but miserable food. O come and take me back home. Aja."
>
> When a year had passed and the sea was again stirred by warmer winds, the father left his country to visit Sedna. His daughter greeted him joyfully and besought him to take her back home. The father hearing of the outrages wrought upon his daughter determined upon revenge. He killed the fulmar, took Sedna into his boat, and they quickly left the country which had brought so much sorrow to Sedna. When the other fulmars came home and found their companion dead and his wife gone, they all flew away in search of the fugitives. They were very sad over the death of their poor murdered comrade and continue to mourn and cry until this day.
>
> Having flown a short distance they discerned the boat and stirred up a heavy storm. The sea rose in immense waves that threatened the pair with destruction. In this mortal peril the father determined to offer Sedna to the birds and flung her overboard. She clung to the edge of the boat with a death grip. The cruel father then took a knife and cut off the first joints of her fingers. Falling into the sea they were transformed into whales, the nails turning into whalebone. Sedna holding on to the boat more tightly, the second finger joints fell under the sharp knife and swam away as seals; when the father cut off the stumps of the fingers they became ground seals. Meantime the storm subsided, for the fulmars thought Sedna was drowned. The father then allowed her to come into the boat again. But from that time she cherished a deadly hatred against him and swore bitter revenge. After they got ashore, she called her dogs and let them gnaw off the feet and hands of her father while he was asleep. Upon this he cursed himself, his daughter, and the dogs which had maimed him; where upon the earth

opened and swallowed the hut, the father, the daughter, and the dogs. They have since lived in the land of Adlivun, of which Sedna is the mistress.[3]

The Nunavut Court of Justice has an etched glass carving, which is representative of Sedna, embossed in the doors one passes through to enter the courtroom. The artwork is described in a pamphlet introducing the Nunavut Court Building in Iqaluit as follows:

THE GIFTS OF SEDNA

Inuit dance and sing through the swirling strands of Sedna's tangled hair in promise to better their relations with each other and all creatures with love and respect (atoning for their wrongdoing to each other and the earth) so that the sea animals once again offer themselves as food in response to Sedna's compassion towards the people's prayers.[4]

How might the story of Sedna function as law (*maligaq*) among the Inuit? Consider this question as you read the materials in this chapter. One Inuit Elder gave the following interpretation of Sedna's role in Inuit life:

When the people in the camp were unhappy or abusive towards wildlife, the wildlife used to move away from the camp. When the wildlife felt they were not welcome, they felt useless to the camp. The animals would flee to Sedna's shed where they were so numerous they seemed like maggots. It was because they had gone there that the hunters couldn't catch them anymore.[5]

The Inuit have lived in harsh northern climes for thousands of years. They live in parts of Alaska, Greenland, Siberia and Canada. In Canada, they occupy western and central portions of the Arctic, the Keewatin region of the barren lands, Baffin Island and the high Arctic, the coastal areas of Hudson Bay and parts of northern Quebec and Labrador. There are approximately 130,000 Inuit living in the circumpolar north.

According to the 2006 Aboriginal Peoples Survey, approximately 51,000 Inuit live in Canada:

The region with the largest Inuit population was Nunavut, home to 24,635 Inuit who accounted for about one-half of the total Inuit population in Canada. Nunavik was home to 9,565 Inuit, or 19% of the total Inuit population. The Inuvialuit Region had a population of 3,115 Inuit, accounting for 6% of all Inuit nationally. Nunatsiavut in northern Labrador had a population of 2,160 Inuit or 4% of the total Inuit population. Inuit made up the majority of the population in all four regions.[6]

The distinct origins of the Inuit are briefly described below by the Royal Commission on Aboriginal Peoples.

REPORT OF THE ROYAL COMMISSION ON ABORIGINAL PEOPLES: LOOKING FORWARD, LOOKING BACK, VOL. 1

(Ottawa: Ministry of Supply and Services, 1996) at 78-79, 82, 85
(references omitted)

Inuit of the Canadian Arctic are a distinct people, different from other Aboriginal peoples in Canada by virtue of their origins and physical make-up, their language and their technology. For most of their history Inuit, like other Aboriginal peoples, have passed on knowledge to succeeding generations orally. The record of their culture is therefore told in their stories and legends and written in the archaeological remains of the places they have been. ...

The archaeological record of the Arctic and oral accounts of Inuit support each other in affirming that Inuit inhabiting what is now Alaska, Canada and Greenland — who speak variations of the common language, Inuktitut — descend from a people who migrated from what is now Alaska to Canada and Greenland. These were the Thule people, whose arrival in Canada archaeologists date at approximately 1000 AD. However, the Thule did not arrive in an empty land, for there were already people living in these northern regions. These earlier people, called Dorset by archaeologists and Tunit by Inuit, were the descendants of an earlier migration, around 2500 BC, that also originated in Alaska or Siberia.

... The distinguishing characteristic of historical Inuit culture is their way of life, which has enabled them to live year-round on the tundra, north of the tree line, in conditions demanding great resourcefulness, inner strength and quiet patience. Inuit oral tradition links these qualities with the requirements of survival in a harsh environment. Thus, Inuit used snow, animal skins, bone and stone, the elements indigenous to their environment, to fashion "a technology more complex than that of any other pre-industrial culture, which allowed not only an economically efficient but also a comfortable way of life throughout arctic North America." ...

Inuit of different regions clearly share many characteristics rooted in their common ancestry. Variations in culture apparently derive from adaptations to local conditions, whether created by changing climate or intercultural contact. Inuit oral history has received little attention in reconstructing the story of the Inuit past, with the result that written reports are erratic in coverage and rely heavily on archaeological finds and on European or southern Canadian perspectives more generally.

A publication of the Canadian Museum of Civilization suggests that distinct Inuit culture groups can be identified with nine regions: Labrador, Arctic Quebec, Southern Baffin Island, Northern Baffin Island and Foxe Basin, Southampton Island, Western Hudson Bay and the Barren Grounds, Central Arctic Coast, Mackenzie Delta, and the High Arctic. ... The culture of each of these groups has been shaped by the land and its particular historical experience. ...

C. INUIT AS "INDIANS" UNDER SECTION 91(24) OF THE *CONSTITUTION ACT, 1867*

As with other Aboriginal peoples the Inuit have historically been defined by others without their participation. One key question of concern to governments was whether they were considered to be "Indians" for the purpose of section 91(24) of the *Constitution Act, 1867* (U.K.), 30 & 31 Vict., c. 3 and thereby under federal jurisdictional powers. The federal government never enacted legislation to bring the Inuit under its legislative control. Furthermore, in 1924, the federal government decided that it did not want to extend the *Indian Act* to them either. At the same time the provinces also demonstrated an aversion to assuming legislative responsibility for the Inuit. For example, during the Great Depression, the Quebec government found it exceedingly difficult to provide assistance to the Inuit. In fact, there was no provincial presence in the area where the Inuit lived until the 1960s.[7] Therefore, Quebec argued that the federal government had the constitutional responsibility for the Inuit. After a series of administrative compromises through the 1920s and 1930s, the issue was judicially resolved in the case below.

As you read the "Eskimos" reference, identify the reasons why Eskimos were considered to be Indians by the Supreme Court of Canada.

REFERENCE RE TERM "INDIANS"

[1939] S.C.J. No. 5, [1939] 2 D.L.R. 417 (*sub nom. Re Eskimos*),
[1939] S.C.R. 104 (S.C.C.) (references omitted)

REFERENCE to Supreme Court of Canada on the question: "Does the term 'Indians' as used in head 24 of the *B.N.A. Act, 1867*, include Eskimo inhabitants of the Province of Quebec?"

The judgment of **Duff C.J.C., Davis** and **Hudson JJ. (Crocket J.** concurring) was delivered by

Duff C.J.C.: — The reference with which we are concerned arises out of a controversy between the Dominion and the Province of Quebec touching the question whether the Eskimo inhabitants of that Province are "Indians" within the contemplation of head no. 24 of s. 91 of the *B.N.A. Act* which is in these words, "Indians and Lands Reserved for Indians;" and under the reference we are to pronounce upon that question.

Among the inhabitants of the three provinces, Nova Scotia, New Brunswick and Canada that, by the immediate operation of the *B.N.A. Act,* became subject to the constitutional enactments of that statute there were few, if any, Eskimo. But the *B.N.A. Act* contemplated the eventual admission into the Union of other parts of British North America as is explicitly declared in the preamble and for which provision is made by s. 146 thereof.

The Eskimo population of Quebec, with which we are now concerned, inhabits (in the northern part of the Province) a territory that in 1867 formed part of Rupert's Land; and the question we have to determine is whether these Eskimo, whose ancestors were aborigines of Rupert's Land in 1867 and at the time of its annexation to Canada, are Indians in the sense mentioned.

In 1867 the Eskimo population of what is now Canada, then between four and five thousand in number, occupied, as at the present time, the northern littoral of the continent from Alaska to, and including part of, the Labrador coast, within the territories under the control of the Hudson's Bay Co., that is to say, in Rupert's Land and the North-Western Territory which, under the authority given by s. 146 of the *B.N.A. Act* were acquired by Canada in 1871. In addition to these Eskimo in Rupert's Land and the North-Western Territory, there were some hundreds of them on that part of the coast of Labrador (east of Hudson Strait) which formed part of, and was subject to the Government of Newfoundland.

The *B.N.A. Act* is a statute dealing with British North America and, in determining the meaning of the words "Indians" in the statute, we have to consider the meaning of that term as applied to the inhabitants of British North America. In 1867 more than half of the Indian population of British North America were within the boundaries of Rupert's Land and the North-Western Territory; and of the Eskimo population nearly 90% were within those boundaries. It is, therefore, important to consult the reliable sources of information as to the use of the term "Indian" in relation to the Eskimo in those territories. Fortunately, there is evidence of the most authoritative character furnished by the Hudson's Bay Co. itself.

It will be recalled that the Hudson's Bay Co., besides being a trading company, possessed considerable powers of government and administration. Some years before the passing of the *B.N.A. Act*, complaints having been made as to the manner in which these responsibilities had been discharged, a committee of the House of Commons in 1856 and 1857 investigated the affairs of the company. Among the matters which naturally engaged the attention of the Committee was the Company's relations with and conduct towards the aborigines; and for the information of the Committee a census was prepared and produced before it by the officers of the company showing the Indian populations under its rule throughout the whole of the North American continent. This census was accompanied by a map showing the "locations" of the various tribes and was included in the Report of the Committee; and was made an appendix to the Committee's Report which was printed and published by the order of the House of Commons. It is indisputable that in the census and in the map the "Esquimaux" fall under the general designation "Indians" and that, indeed, in these documents, "Indians" is used as synonymous with "aborigines."

. . . . .

Seven years later, the scheme of Confederation, propounded in the Quebec Resolutions of October 10th, 1864, included a declaration that provision should be made "for the admission into the Union on equitable terms of Newfoundland, the North-West Territory, British Columbia, and Vancouver." This declaration was renewed in the Resolutions of the London Conference in December, 1866, and in the *B.N.A. Act* specific provision was made, as we have seen, in s. 146 for the acquisition of Rupert's Land as well as the North-west Territory and, in 1868, a statute of the Imperial Parliament conferred upon the Queen the necessary powers as respects Rupert's Land.

The *B.N.A. Act* came into force on July 1, 1867, and, in December of that year, a joint address to Her Majesty was voted by the Senate and House of Commons of Canada praying that authority might be granted to the Parliament of Canada to legislate for the future welfare and good government of these regions and expressing the willingness of Parliament to assume the duties and obligations of government and legislation as regards those territories. In the Resolution of the Senate expressing the willingness of that body to concur in the joint address is this paragraph:

> Resolved that upon the transference of the Territories in question to the Canadian Government, it will be the duty of the Government to make adequate provisions for the protection of the Indian Tribes, whose interest and well being are involved in the transfer.

By Order in Council of June 23, 1870, it was ordered that from and after July 15, 1870, the North-West Territory and Rupert's Land should be admitted into, and become part of, the Dominion of Canada and that, from that date, the Parliament of Canada should have full power and authority to legislate for the future welfare and good government of the territory. As regards Rupert's Land, such authority had already been conferred upon the Parliament of Canada by s. 5 of the *Rupert's Land Act* of 1868.

The vast territories which by these transactions became part of the Dominion of Canada and were brought under the jurisdiction of the Parliament of Canada were inhabited largely, indeed almost entirely, by aborigines. It appears to me to be a consideration of great weight in determining the meaning of the word "Indians" in the *B.N.A. Act* that, as we have seen, the Eskimo were recognized as an Indian tribe by the officials of the Hudson's Bay Co. which, in 1867, as already observed, exercised powers of government and administration over this great tract; and that, moreover, this employment of the term "Indians" is evidenced in a most unequivocal way by documents prepared by those officials and produced before the Select Committee of the House of Commons which were included in the Report of that Committee. ... It is quite clear from the material before us that this Report was the principal source of information as regards the aborigines in those territories until some years after Confederation.

I turn now to the Eskimo inhabiting the coast of Labrador beyond the confines of the Hudson's Bay territories and within the boundaries and under the Government of Newfoundland. As regards these, the evidence appears to be conclusive that, for a period beginning about 1760 and extending down to a time subsequent to the passing of the *B.N.A. Act*, they were by governors, commanders-in-chief of the navy and other naval officers, ecclesiastics, missionaries and traders who came into contact with them, known and classified as Indians.

First, of the official documents. In 1762, General Murray, then Governor of Quebec, who afterwards became first Governor of Canada, in an official report of the state of the Government of Quebec, deals under the sixth heading with "Indian nations residing within the government." He introduces the discussion with this sentence:

> In order to discuss this point more clearly I shall first take notice of the Savages on the North shore of the River St. Lawrence from the Ocean upwards, and then of such as inhabit the South side of the same River, as far as the present limits of the Government extend on either side of it.

In the first and second paragraphs he deals with the "Savages" on the North Shore and he says: "The first to be met with on this side are the Esquimaux." In the second paragraph he deals with the Montagnais who inhabited a "vast tract" of country from Labrador to the Saguenay.

It is clear that here the Eskimo are classified under the generic term Indian. They are called "Savages," it is true, but so are the Montagnais and so also the Hurons settled at Jeune Lorette. It is useful to note that he speaks in the first paragraph of the Esquimaux as "the wildest and most untamable of any" and mentions that they are "emphatically styled by the other Nations, Savages."

Then there are two reports to His Majesty by the Lords of Trade. The first, dated June 8, 1763, discusses the trade carried on by the French on the coast of Labrador. It is said that they carried on "an extensive trade with the Esquimaux Indians in Oyl, Furs, & ca. [*sic*] (in which they allowed Your Majesty's Subjects no Share)."

In the second, dated April 16, 1765, in dealing with complaints on the part of the Court of France respecting the French fishery on the coast of Newfoundland and in the Gulf of St. Lawrence, their observations on these complaints are based upon information furnished by Commodore Palliser who had been entrusted with the superintendency of the Newfoundland fishery and the Government of the island. In this report, this sentence occurs:

> The sixth and last head of complaint contained in the French Ambassador's letter is, that a captain of a certain French vessel was forbid by your Majesty's Governor from having commerce with the Eskimaux Indians;

and upon that it is observed that the Governor "is to be commended for having forbid the subjects of France to trade or treat with these Indians." "These Indians" are spoken of as "inhabitants ... who are under the protection of and dependent upon your Majesty."

Then there is a series of proclamations by successive Governors and Commanders-in-Chief in Newfoundland, the first of which was that of Sir Hugh Palliser of July 1, 1764. The Proclamation recites, "... Advantages would arise to His Majesty's Trading Subjects if a Friendly Intercourse could be Established with the Esquimeaux Indians, Inhabiting the Coast of Labradore ..." and that the Government "has taken measures for bringing about a friendly communication between the said Indians and His Majesty's subjects." All His Majesty's subjects are strictly enjoined "to treat them in the most civil and friendly manner."

The next is a Proclamation by the same Governor dated April 8, 1765, which recites the desirability of "friendly intercourse with the Indians on the Coast of Labrador" and that "attempts hitherto made for that purpose have proved ineffectual, especially with the Esquimaux in the Northern Ports without the Straits of Belle Isle" and strictly enjoins and requires "all His Majesty's subjects who meet with any of the said Indians to treat them in a most civil and friendly manner."

On April 10, 1772, Governor Shuldham in a Proclamation of that date requires "all His Majesty's subjects coming upon the coast of Labrador to act towards the Esquimaux Indians in a manner agreeable to the Proclamation issued at St. John's the 8th day of July 1769 respecting the savages inhabiting the coast of Labrador." In this Proclamation it should be noted that "Esquimaux savages" and "Esquimaux Indians" are used as convertible expressions.

In 1774, the boundaries of Quebec were extended, and the north eastern coast of Labrador and the Eskimo population therein came under the jurisdiction of the Governor of Quebec and remained so until 1809. Nevertheless, the Governor and Commander-in-Chief of Newfoundland, who at the date was Admiral Edwards, acting under the authority of that Order in Council of March 9, 1774, took measures to protect the missionaries of the Unitas Fratrum and their settlements on the coast of Labrador from molestation or disturbance and, on May 14, 1779, Admiral Edwards issued a Proclamation requiring "all His Majesty's subjects coming upon the Coast of Labrador to act towards the Esquimaux Indians justly, humanely and agreeably to these laws, by which His Majesty's subjects are bound." Here again it is to be observed that the words "savages" and "Indians" are used as equivalents.

A further Proclamation by Admiral Edwards on January 30, 1781, employs the same phrases, the Eskimo being described as "Esquimaux savages" and as "Esquimaux Indians."

On May 15, 1774, Governor Campbell, as Governor and Commander-in-Chief, issued a Proclamation in terms identical with that of 1781.

On December 3, 1821, a Proclamation was issued by Governor Hamilton as Governor and Commander-in-Chief of Newfoundland (now again including the Labrador coast) relating to a "fourth settlement" by the Moravian missionaries requiring all His Majesty's subjects "to act towards the missionaries and the Esquimaux Indians justly and humanely."

. . . . .

Evidence as to subsequent official usage is adduced in a letter of 1824 from the Advocate General of Canada to the Assistant Civil Secretary on some matter of a criminal prosecution in which "Esquimaux Indians" are concerned; and in a report of 1869 by Judge Pinsent of the Court of Labrador to the Governor of Newfoundland in which this sentence occurs: "In this number about 300 Indians and half-breeds of the Esquimaux and Mountaineer races are included."

Reports from missionaries and clergymen are significant. I refer particularly to two. There is a communication in 1821 by the Unitas Fratrum sent to Admiral Hamilton, Governor and Commander-in-Chief of Newfoundland and Labrador, on a visit by H.M.S. "Clinker" to their settlements. In this the Eskimo are mentioned as "Esquimaux Indians" and "Esquimaux Tribes".

. . . . .

In 1849, a report from the Bishop of Newfoundland was printed and published in London for the Society for the Propagation of the Gospel by the Bishop of London ... Extracts from this report, which describes a visit to Labrador ... exemplify in a remarkable way the use of the term Indian, as designating the Eskimo inhabitants of Labrador as well as other classes of Indians there ...

Having regard to the well established usage of designating the Esquimaux of Labrador as Indians or Esquimaux Indians, evidenced by the Proclamations of the Governors of Newfoundland, and other official and unofficial documents, one finds little difficulty in appreciating the significance of the phraseology of the correspondence, in 1879, between Sir John A. Macdonald and Sir Hector Langevin on the subject of the Eskimo on the north shore of the St. Lawrence. The phrase "Esquimaux Indians" is employed in this correspondence as it had been employed for a hundred years in official and other documents to designate the Labrador Esquimaux.

. . . . .

Newfoundland, including the territory inhabited by these Labrador Eskimo was, as already pointed out, one of the British North American colonies the union of which with Canada was contemplated by the *B.N.A. Act*. Thus it appears that, through all the territories of British North America in which there were Eskimo, the term "Indian" was employed by well established usage as including these as well as the other aborigines; and I repeat the *B.N.A. Act*, in so far as it deals with the subject of Indians, must, in my opinion, be taken to contemplate the Indians of British North America as a whole.

. . . . .

Nor do I think that the fact that British policy in relation to the Indians, as evidenced in the Instructions to Sir Guy Carleton and the Royal Proclamation of 1763, did not contemplate the Eskimo (along with many other tribes and nations of British North American aborigines) as within the scope of that policy is either conclusive or very useful in determining the question before us.

. . . . .

Nor can I agree that the context (in head no. 24) has the effect of restricting the term "Indians". If "Indians" standing alone in its application to British North America denotes the aborigines, then the fact that there were aborigines for whom lands had not been reserved seems to afford no good reason for limiting the scope of the term "Indians" itself.

For these reasons I think the question referred to us should be answered in the affirmative.

_____

Although the *Reference re Term "Indians"* case determined that Inuit people were "Indians" for the purposes of section 91(24) of the *Constitution Act, 1867*, the Inuit had far different experiences with Canadian governmental bodies than did Aboriginal peoples residing to the south.

The Inuit were also specifically excluded from the scope of the federal *Indian Act*. Section 4(1) of the current *Indian Act*, R.S.C. 1985, c. I-5 is illustrative of this fact:

> 4(1) A reference in this Act to an Indian does not include any person of the race of aborigines commonly referred to as Inuit.

As a result of their exclusion from the *Indian Act*, the Inuit did not experience many of the benefits and burdens imposed or supported by the *Indian Act*, including the reserve system. However, the Inuit faced other challenges. The following pages briefly discuss recent legal developments surrounding Inuit High Arctic Relocation, Naming Inuit People as Numbers and the RCMP Sled Dog Slaughter.

1. *Inuit High Arctic Relocations*

Because of their geographic locations, the Inuit did not have significant interaction with Canadian governmental authorities until the 1930s. When contact did occur it did not always bring positive results. A series of devastating diseases came with increasing contact. Furthermore, the Government of Canada dispersed many of the Inuit of Baffin Island around the Arctic in this period in an attempt to avoid Indian reserve-like "dependency" in the north. The government wanted the Inuit to hunt and fish in various locations to sustain themselves and avoid government support. These relocations created dire hardship because those relocated did not possess a detailed understanding of their new surroundings. They found it hard to make a living in territories that were not traditional to their families. Unfortunately, the government did not learn from the harms its stereotyping caused the Inuit. Thus, in the 1950s, another round of relocations occurred as a number of Inuit from northern Quebec were also forcibly taken from their homelands to remote locations around the high Arctic. This was also done to further government objectives during the

Cold War. In particular, Canada wanted a human presence in different regions of the north to support its sovereign claims in the area when the D.E.W. (Distant Early Warning) Line was constructed by the United States military to warn of potential Soviet attacks in this era. As the Royal Commission on Aboriginal Peoples wrote about the Inuit and other Aboriginal relocations:

> Governments saw relocation as providing an apparent solution for a number of specific problems. ... [G]overnment administrators saw Aboriginal people as unsophisticated, poor, outside modern society and generally incapable of making the right choices. Confronted with the enormous task of adapting to "modern" society, they faced numerous problems that government believed could be solved only with government assistance. If they appeared to be starving, they could be moved to where game was more plentiful. If they were sick, they could be placed in new communities where health services and amenities such as sewers, water and electricity were available. If they were thought to be "indolent", the new communities would provide education and training facilities, which would lead to integration into the wage economy. If they were in the way of expanding agricultural frontiers or happened to occupy land needed for urban settlements, they could be moved "for their own protection". And if their traditional lands contained natural resources — minerals to be exploited, forests to be cut, rivers to be dammed — they could be relocated "in the national interest".
>
> Justifying its actions by this attitude of paternalism, Canada used its power in an arbitrary manner. Decisions were made with little or no consultation. Communities were relocated on short notice. People's entire lives were disrupted if governments believed it was in their interests to do so. Few Canadians would tolerate the degree of interference in their lives that Aboriginal people have had to endure. In many cases, relocation separated Aboriginal people from their homelands and destroyed their ability to be economically self-sufficient. This loss of economic livelihood contributed to a decline in living standards, social and health problems, and a breakdown of political leadership.

Inuit relocations around the Arctic left a legacy of distrust and suspicion of government actions. The following excerpt recounts the challenges faced by Inuit people as a result of relocation.

EXILES IN THE HIGH ARCTIC
Zebedee Nungak*

Nunavut Department of Education, High Arctic Relocation:
Grade 10 English Language Arts [Draft]
(Iqaluit: Nunavut Department of Education, 2002)

In the 1950s, the Canadian government moved seventeen Inuit families from their homes in Northern Quebec to an area of the High Arctic more than 1,000 miles away. Separated from their families and friends, these people were left without food and shelter to eke out a livelihood as best they could in an inhospitable environment. Those who survived the ordeal recount a horrifying tale of isolation and privation. ...

In 1952, the memorandum lines between the federal government and the RCMP sizzled with brilliant ideas about relocating some Eskimos to the Queen Elizabeth Islands. The strategic importance of the High Arctic was just beginning to dawn on Canada's government in the aftermath of the Second World War. Questions were more than ... about just who had sovereignty over these vast stretches of unoccupied tundra and sea ice. That year, H.A. Larson, navigator of the Northwest Passage and the RCMP officer commanding "G" Division, wrote to the RCMP Commissioner.

> The advantage of placing our Detachment directly across from Greenland would be that we would have full control and supervision of Greenland Eskimos and others travelling back and forth, and over hunting activities they may engage in ... I have also in mind a plan to relieve the over-population of some areas and a brief outline is as follows: Could we not transfer by Department of Transport vessel, to Craig Harbour, Cape Sabine and Dundas Harbour, several needy families to these places where colonization by them appears to be suitable and feasible?

The federal government was the sole authority and administrator of Inuit affairs. What, then, could be simpler than removing a group of Inuit from Port Harrison in Arctic Quebec, and plunking them down in the High Arctic?

"We never volunteered to go, or said to anybody, 'Send us away from here.' We did not have the freedom to refuse being sent away," Markoosie Patsauq told the Aboriginal Affairs Committee of the House of Commons in March this year. The occasion was a special hearing on the High Arctic relocation. "My father just eventually agreed to this because in those days police were feared, their authority unquestioned," Patsauq said. At the same hearing, Samwilly Elijasialuk said:

> At the time we were moved, my adoptive father was given only good and positive expectations, being told only good things, such as being promised that he could return the following year, and being told of the availability of caribou ... He was also told of abundant musk-oxen ... This turned out to be an enticement, a lure — and a false one at that. It was stated by government to attract people to move away. These turned out to be all big lies.

The methods of RCMP recruitment of Eskimo families included the subtle and gentle intimidation of poorer families, laced with glowing descriptions of plentiful wildlife in the new land. And everyone would be together there. For good measure, the RCMP promised the prospective immigrants return passage after two years if they did not like conditions in the new location. ...

It was not until many years later that the heartrending stories of the exiles began to be heard, particularly of the anguish following the realization that families would be divided and sent to several different destinations. In 1986, at a meeting held in Iqaluit to discuss the relocation, Edith Patsauq said:

> We started on the trip believing that we were all going to one place, but further on the trip, as we were nearing Pond Inlet, we were informed that we would be divided three different places. It was shocking to hear that, and

so as we were starting to be separated, there was a lot of crying. It was a big shock that is even difficult to put into words. Even the dogs were crying. ...

At the time, no one realized that years and decades would pass before they would see family members and friends again. Andrew Iqaluk told the Commons committee: "I recall seeing the departure of my ancestral land, my relatives, my sisters, my older brothers. It seemed I was leaving for a place only thirty miles distant. We did not have the sense of occasion [to realize] that it would be a long-term parting." ...

From the first step onto these new lands, the Port Harrison people, especially, were traumatized by the barrenness of the landscape and the onslaught of the early winter. They were immediately perplexed about where they would get their water. Their canvas tents were woefully inadequate shelter against the brutal High Arctic cold.

In the plush surroundings of the House of Commons, the exiles have told the Aboriginal Affairs Committee a consistent tale:

> The landing to our new land was no good. It was already winter; the snow had already come to stay. There was no wood for fire. We had to pitch up our tents. There was no vegetation. There did not seem to be an Qallunaat (non-Eskimos) around ... We were fearful and apprehensive about what was ahead of us, but there was no choice except to carry on.

Sarah Amagoalik

I vividly remember when we landed ... and how cold we were. Some had to be warmed by dogs.

Allie Salluviniq

When we finally landed there, it was as if we had landed on the moon, it was so bare and desolate. There was no food and there was no shelter.

Martha Flaherty

When we landed there, we were put to work unloading drums and coal for the police. We were told that we would not be paid for this work.

Samwillie Elijasialuk

The dismal and bleak first impressions of the "promised land" by the exiles were compounded by the lack of amenities of settlement in Resolute Bay and Craig Harbour. There was no trading post, a *raison d'être* of all settlements in those days. The RCMP was to be the only support for the exiles for many years.

A couple of years later, an RCMP officer on duty at Resolute Bay was quoted in an article in *National Geographic* (April 1955):

> Resolute supports a handful of Eskimos, for whom Constable F. Ross Gibson of the RCMP has special responsibility. He also functions as the game warden, customs officer and immigration registrar, as well as being guardian of the law. "I can't imagine who might immigrate here," Ross said, "though, as a matter of fact, our Eskimos are immigrants. At least, they are

not native here. We brought three families from Quebec and one from Baffin Island, hoping they'd kill enough polar bear and seal to keep going. That way, men would be available to load aircraft and do other chores. But some of those involved knew of the life and death risks involved in this social experiment.

On August 10, 1953, as the first group of exiles steamed toward their destination in the High Arctic, a meeting of bureaucrats was taking place in Room 301 of the Langevin Block in Ottawa. An extract from the minutes reads:

> S/L O'Neil (RCAF) stated that he was afraid that there was not sufficient wildlife in the Resolute area to provide for the proposed Eskimo population.
> ...

Not apparent to the RCMP, however, was the burden felt by the Eskimo elders. The isolation of that small population was made total by the number of factors: the lack of any support from settlement life from anybody except the RCMP; the absence of any means of communication with relatives back home; the three months of High Arctic winter darkness; the lack of transportation other than the annual ship.

At the outset, the elders noted the radical change in food sources and diet in the High Arctic. They longed for the fish, migratory birds, small game and berries of the tundra. In the new land, they now lived on seals and other marine mammals to the point of monotony. In their "happy Eskimo" reports, the RCMP dared not mention that women and children picked through RCMP garbage to supplement their diet. They dared not report that the exiled Eskimos scrounged at the dump for wood scraps to build tiny shacks; that hunters were despondent about restrictions on hunting musk-oxen and caribou; that people were hungry because of scarcities of basic store foods, such as tea and flour, and that people were depressed about the prospect of never seeing their relatives ever again.

More scandalous and insidious are charges by the Inuit exiles of outrageous misbehaviour by RCMP personnel — including testimonies of sexual abuse of Inuit women by certain constables. Most of the alleged incidents involved sexual coercion of women as a condition for being allowed to trade for the meagre food stores over which the officers presided. These allegations have been denied by former members of the force, although they have been considered serious enough for the RCMP to conduct their own internal investigation of them.

On another aspect of RCMP officer's conduct, John Amagoalik, president of Inuit Tapirisat of Canada and himself a former exile, testified to the Commons committee:

> I also remember when members of our relatives were in the hospital for years. We used to try and write letters to them and, to our horror, we found that our letters were thrown in the dump, because we spent a lot of time in the dump ... I also remember my father used to send a little bit of cash to my brother, who was in the hospital for five years. And the RCMP used to come to our house asking if we had any letters. And my father said, "Yes we have a letter. Here it is." And the RCMP would ask, "Did you enclose any money?" And, of course, my father said, "Yes, I enclosed two dollars." And

the RCMP would write on the outside of the letter "two dollars." We found those letters in the dump, too, opened and the money gone. ...

* Zebedee Nungak has served as one of the primary spokesmen for Inuit in the First Ministers conferences on Aboriginal Rights. He is the first vice president of Makivik Corporation, the Inuit development organization of Nunavik (Arctic Quebec). He lives in Kangirsuk (Payne Bay) on the Ungava coast.

As a result of this relocation, a negotiated settlement was developed, which caused the government of Canada to place $10 million in a High Arctic Relocation Trust Fund in the hopes of reconciling Inuit relocatees with the Government of Canada; for a copy of the agreement see <http://www.nunatsiaqonline.ca/pub/docs/EXHIBITP3_1996_Exiles_Agre ement.pdf>. At the time this money was placed in trust (in 1996) the government of Canada refused to apologize for the relocations.

Finally, in August 2010, an apology was issued to the Inuit in the following terms:

APOLOGY FOR THE INUIT HIGH ARCTIC RELOCATION

<http://www.tunngavik.com/wp-content/uploads/2011/02/2011-
naniiliqpita-winter.pdf>

Speaking Notes for The Honourable John Duncan, P.C., M.P.,
Minister of Indian Affairs and Northern Development and Federal
Interlocutor for Métis and Non-Status Indians at the Apology
for the Inuit High Arctic Relocation
August 18, 2010

... Over half a century has gone by since the relocation of Inuit from this community to the High Arctic. I am here on behalf of the Prime Minister, the Government of Canada, and all Canadians to offer an apology for these events.

Today's ceremony is an important step towards healing and reconciliation. Please accept the apology I am about to offer on behalf of all Canadians. I hope that it will form the basis of a strengthened relationship with the Government of Canada.

On behalf of the Government of Canada and all Canadians, we would like to offer a full and sincere apology to Inuit for the relocation of families from Inukjuak and Pond Inlet to Grise Fiord and Resolute Bay during the 1950s.

We would like to express our deepest sorrow for the extreme hardship and suffering caused by the relocation. The families were separated from their home communities and extended families by more than a thousand kilometres. They were not provided with adequate shelter and supplies. They were not properly informed of how far away and how different from Inukjuak their new homes would be, and they were not aware that they would be separated into two communities once they arrived in the High Arctic. Moreover, the Government failed to act on its promise to return anyone that did not wish to stay in the High Arctic to their old homes.

The Government of Canada deeply regrets the mistakes and broken promises of this dark chapter of our history and apologizes for the High Arctic relocation having taken place. We would like to pay tribute to the relocatees for their perseverance and courage. Despite the suffering and hardship, the relocatees and their descendants were successful in building vibrant communities in Grise Fiord and Resolute Bay. The Government of Canada recognizes that these communities have contributed to a strong Canadian presence in the High Arctic.

The relocation of Inuit families to the High Arctic is a tragic chapter in Canada's history that we should not forget, but that we must acknowledge, learn from and teach our children. Acknowledging our shared history allows us to move forward in partnership and in a spirit of reconciliation. The Government of Canada and Inuit have accomplished many great things together, and all Canadians have benefitted from the contributions of Inuit to our culture and history. We must continue to strengthen our connections and deepen our understanding and respect. We must jointly build a stronger, healthier and more vibrant Inuit Nunangat and, in turn, build a stronger, healthier and more vibrant Canada.

The Government of Canada hopes that this apology will help heal the wounds caused by events that began nearly 60 years ago and turn the page on this sad chapter in Canada's history. May it strengthen the foundation upon which the Government of Canada and Inuit can build and help keep the True North Strong and Free.

2. *Numbers as Inuit Names*

There were other Arctic relocations during this period. For further context, see Elisapee Karetak, *Kikkik E1-472*, a documentary produced by the Inuit Broadcasting Corporation:

> During the 1950s famine in the Canadian Arctic, Kikkik, an Inuk woman, killed a man in self-defense and then found herself having to leave two of her five children on the tundra. She was tried for murder and criminal negligence, and subsequently acquitted. Her daughter, Elisapee Karetak, who lives in Arviat, Nunavut, has spent many years tracing the events of her family's story. Elisapee's brothers and sisters as well as many members of the Inuit community who lived through the ordeal recount their memories.[8]

Note the name of the woman who is the subject of the film, *Kikkik E1-472*.

> [I]n the 1940s, the Inuit were given disc numbers, recorded on a special leather ID tag, like a dog tag. They were required to keep the tag with them always. ... The numbers were assigned with a letter prefix that indicated location (E = east), community, and then the order in which the census-taker saw the individual. ... [T]he renaming was abetted by the churches and

missionaries, who viewed the traditional names and their calls to power as related to shamanism and paganism.

They encouraged people to take Christian names. So a young woman who was known to her relatives as "Lutaaq, Pilitaq, Palluq, or Inusiq" and had been baptised as "Annie" was under this system to become Annie E7-121. People adopted the number-names, their family members' numbers, etc., and learned all the region codes (like knowing a telephone area code).

Until Inuit began studying in the south, many didn't know that numbers were not normal parts of Christian and English naming systems. Then in 1969, the government started Project Surname, headed by Abe Okpik, to replace number-names with patrilineal "family surnames". But contemporary Inuit carvers and graphic artists still use their disk number as their signature on their works of art to draw attention to this darker chapter of their past.[9]

3. RCMP Sled Dog Slaughter

Inuit people experienced other colonial abuses, such as residential school, land loss and traditional economic dislocation. At least three reports have chronicled the losses faced by the Inuit through the RCMP slaughter of hundreds of Inuit peoples' sled dogs between 1950 and 1975. In 2006, the RCMP conducted its own investigation into the slaughter and found no evidence of a conspiracy to shoot the dogs, concluding that they were shot for humanitarian, safety and health reasons. In 2010, a report was released by Judge James Igloliorte, head of the Qikiqtani Truth Commission. He concluded that Inuit dogs could be hazardous to the public but that the government response to these problems (mass killing of dogs) was disastrous for the Inuit.[10] A retired Quebec Superior Court Judge, Jean-Jacques Croteau, in a separate report dealing with Nunavik in Quebec, recommended that the governments of Quebec and Canada should apologize and pay compensation to the Inuit of Nunavik for the killing of sled dogs in that province.[11] While the Canadian government has not yet acted on this issue, the Quebec government has apologized and paid compensation.

D. INUIT LAND CLAIMS AND SELF-GOVERNMENT AGREEMENTS

The negotiation of land claims and self-government agreements with the federal government has been a part of Inuit reality for more than two decades, beginning with the *James Bay and Northern Quebec Agreement* (JBNQA) in 1975. The JBNQA was followed in 1984 by the *Inuvialuit Final Agreement*, 1984, approved and given effect by the *Western Arctic (Inuvialuit) Claims Settlement Act*, S.C. 1984, c. 24 [as am. S.C. 1988, c. 16], and, most recently, the *Nunavut Land Claims Agreement* (1993), approved and given effect by the *Nunavut Land Claims Agreement Act*, S.C. 1993, c. 29; and *Nunavut Act*, S.C. 1993, c. 28. The most recent agreement is with the Labrador Inuit of Nunatsiavut in the *Labrador Inuit Land Claims Agreement Act*, S.C. 2005, c. 27.

INUIT LAND CLAIMS — A CHRONOLOGY

<http://www.itk.ca/5000-year-heritage/land-claims.php>

Nunavik — The James Bay and Northern Quebec Agreement — 1975

Responding to encroaching hydroelectric projects on traditional Inuit land, the Inuit of Nunavik, or northern Quebec, formed the Northern Quebec Inuit Association (NQIA). The NQIA, in partnership with the James Bay Cree, responded to these pressures by taking the provincial government and Hydro-Quebec to court to force a stop to development on Inuit land. In 1973, in a dramatic series of events, a judgment came down from the courts in favour of the Inuit and Cree forcing the government and the corporation to halt activity in the area and to negotiate with them. Several days later however, the injunction was overturned, allowing development to continue and placing immense pressure on both Inuit and Cree to negotiate as the bulldozers were kept idling. Thus began the process that culminated in the settlement of the first Inuit comprehensive land claims agreement in 1975.

The JBNQA is the final agreement between the Inuit of Nunavik, the provincial and federal governments, the Grand Council of the Cree and several corporate entities. In all, the agreement's 31 sections define Inuit special rights to land ownership and use, harvesting rights, environmental protection, the creation of a number of regional public institutions including a regional government and school and hospital boards, and provided for the creation of Makivik Corporation. Inuit also received $90 million in compensation to be paid in installments over 20 years, with the final installment paid in 1996. In return, Inuit were required to surrender their aboriginal claims in Quebec.

Inuvialuit — The Final Agreement — 1984

Again under pressure from impending economic development initiatives, the Inuvialuit began a process to settle their land claims during the 1970s. In 1984, the Inuvialuit settled the first comprehensive land claim settlement in the Northwest Territories with the Government of Canada. The Final Agreement stipulates that the Inuvialuit continue to have surface ownership rights to 90,650 square kilometers of land as well as certain subsurface rights to another 12,950 square kilometers of land. The agreement also details a number of other rights afforded to the Inuvialuit including special harvesting rights, environmental protection, Inuvialuit participation in a number of co-management regimes, support for economic development initiatives, and the establishment of a social development fund. Financial compensation in the amount of $45 million was to be paid to the Inuvialuit in annual installments to be completed in 1997.

Nunavut — Nunavut Land Claims Agreement — 1993

By far the largest land claim agreement in Canadian history was the Nunavut Land Claims Agreement signed in 1993. The claim was originally presented to the federal government in 1976 by the Inuit Tapirisat of Canada. Little progress was made during the initial stages of negotiations and in 1982, the Tungavik Federation of Nunavut (TFN) assumed the negotiating role on behalf of the Inuit of Nunavut. In 1990, TFN, the Government of the Northwest Territories and the Government of Canada, ratified and signed an agreement-in-principle (AIP) in 1990. An AIP contains the basic elements of a final agreement but is not legally binding on any of the signatory parties. After Inuit ratified the AIP, a Final Agreement was achieved and on May 25, 1993, the Nunavut Land Claims Agreement was signed in Iqaluit.

The agreement contains 41 articles and has been considered to be one of the most innovative agreements reached to date between governments and aboriginal peoples. In providing title to the Inuit of Nunavut to some 352,240 square kilometers of land in the eastern half of the former Northwest Territories, the agreement provides clear rules of ownership, rights and obligations towards the land, water and resources of Nunavut. Inuit also received $1.14 billion payable over a 14-year period ending in 2007. A $13 million Training Trust Fund was established to ensure Inuit had access to sufficient training dollars to enable them to meet their responsibilities under the claim. As well, Inuit became full participants in a number of co-management bodies that are responsible for the careful management of the territories resources.

Nunavut Territory — 1999

The Final Agreement also included an undertaking by Canada to recommend legislation to Parliament to establish a Nunavut territory. A plebiscite to confirm the boundary between the NWT and the new territory was held in May 1992. A political accord was developed outlining the types of powers, financing and scheduling involved in establishing the new territory. The accord was signed in 1992 thus ensuring the creation of Nunavut. On April 1, 1999, Nunavut became Canada's newest, (and at one-fifth the size of the country) largest territory.

The creation of Nunavut provides Inuit with a form of self-government, as they comprise approximately 85% of the territory's population. While the territory has a public government that represents all Inuit and non-Inuit alike, the large majority of Inuit provides a means to pursue their aspirations to self-determination via a public government structure.

The Government of Nunavut incorporates Inuit values and beliefs into a modern system of government. For example, the working language is Inuktitut although English and French are also used. Each department has an Inuit Employment Plan to increase the number of Inuit within the public service to levels that reflect their proportion of the population. As well, a number of departments are involved in preserving and promoting, Inuit culture and values from the school curriculum to the emphasis placed upon sustainable economic development.

Nunatsiavut — Labrador Inuit Land Claim Agreement — 2005

The Inuit of Nunatsiavut (Labrador), along with the governments of Canada and Newfoundland & Labrador, signed the Labrador Inuit Land Claim Agreement on January 22, 2005, in Nain. The signing was the culmination of decades of work by Labrador Inuit, and the agreement is the fourth and final such agreement for the Inuit of Canada, following claims signed in Nunavik (Northern Quebec), the Inuvialuit region of the NWT, and Nunavut.

Labrador Inuit filed their comprehensive land claim in 1977. It was not until 1990 that Canada, Newfoundland, and the Labrador Inuit Association (LIA) signed a Framework Agreement laying out the details of the claims negotiation process. It took another nine years of intermittent negotiations for an agreement in principle (AIP) to be signed. The Labrador AIP was ratified by the LIA membership on June 25, 2001.

Among the highlights of the AIP are that Inuit will own and govern 15,800 square kilometers, or about six per cent of Labrador. The LIA and the provincial government will also co-manage a larger settlement area of 72,520 square kilometers. Labrador Inuit will also receive 3% of the mining tax earned by the massive Voisey's Bay nickel mining project. In exchange for extinguishing their aboriginal title to the land, Inuit will receive $140 million, as well as an additional $115 million to implement the final agreement.

E. INUIT TRADITIONAL LAW AND THE CREATION OF AN INUIT-FOCUSED JURISPRUDENCE

With the signing of these many land claims agreements Inuit law has come to assume an even greater place in the lives of people in the north. Inuit traditional law has proven to be an enduring source of authority from which to seek guidance in preventing and overcoming conflict. Among the most important legal terms in Inuit law are *maligait*, *piqujait* and *tirigusuusiit*.[12] *Maligait* refers to things that have to be followed. It is a relational term focusing on the result of a request (the obligation to obey). *Piqujait* deals with things that have to be done. The obligation which is the focus of *piqujait* is the wish of an authorized person about something that is to be done. *Tirigusuusiit* refers to things that have to be avoided. If a person transgresses *tirigusuusiit* they will face consequences from their actions, and thus they should avoid such transgressions.

While the Inuit note that their legal traditions are of ancient origin, they believe that they have potential application to present circumstances.

Nunavut Inuk Elder Aupilaarjuk stated: "Today, the problem is to retain from the old traditions what is valuable to the present. When I think about this, I wonder how we can solve the problem. I would like to look at the Inuit *maligait* that we had in the past and compare them with the laws we have today, so we could develop better laws for the future."[13] When Aupilaarjuk was asked which *tirigusuusiit* could be applied today, he said:

> What we are following today is wrong and people are killing themselves. Inuit weren't like that before. We have to look at where we came from and where we are today. Back then we truly believed in *tirigusuusiit*. You need to think about this when you are preparing for your future.

The Inuit are preparing for the future by thinking about what their law counsels them to avoid (*tirigusuusiit*). An example of *tirigusuusiit* relates to the natural environment and its relationship to human settlement. Joan Atuat of Qairnirmiut noted: "We used to have to keep our garbage area in one small place away from children and tents. My grandmother was very strict about people throwing garbage in the lakes. She would not have anything to do with dirty fish ... She was so strict about cleanliness that she didn't even want small pieces lying around the tent.[14] There are also *tirigusuusiit* related to visiting other peoples land, clothing, and hunting and other life activities. One can imagine the impact the application of this law might hold for such concepts as economic development, land use planning and global warming.

When considering *tirigusuusiit*, *Inuit Qaujimajatuqangit* becomes a particularly important concept in Inuit law. *Inuit Qaujimajatuqangit* "includes unwritten traditional knowledge, as well as family and political structures, learning and social development schemes, and even the understanding of local weather patterns".[15] It has also been described as a living technology for rationalizing thought and action, organizing tasks, resources, family and society into a coherent whole. [16] Concepts applied under *Inuit Qaujimajatuqangit* can include: *Pijitsirniq* (serving), *Aajiiqatigiinniq* (decision-making), *Pilimmatsaniq* (passing knowledge and skills through observation, doing and practice); *Piliriqatigiinniq* (working together for a common cause); *Avatittinnik Kamattiarnik* (environmental stewardship); *Qanuqtuurniq* (creatively resourceful problem-solving); *Tunnganarniq* (openness, acceptance and inclusivity); *Ippigusuttiarniq* (caring for others); *Angiqatigiinniq* (proceeding forward with clear understanding); *Ikajuqatigiinniq* (assistance and cooperation without barriers); *Qaujimautittiarniq* (information sharing); *Uppiriqattautiniq* (fair treatment); *Tukisiumaqatigiinniq* (conscious understanding of others is the basis of mutual relationships); *Ilainnasiunnginniq* (sensitivity to difference); *Ilajjuttigiinniq* (encouragement of others); *Aaqqiumatitsiniq* (keeping order in place); *Iqqaqtuijjiqattariaqannginniq* (restraint on personal judgment); *Piviqaqtittiniq* (opportunity for participation and contribution); *Silatuniq* (wisdom to know how to apply your knowledge); and *Ajuqsatittinginniq piviqarialinnik* (support for growth, development and success).[17]

Nunavut has been a living laboratory for the development and application of Inuit law. *Inuit Qaujimajatuqangit*, along with the *Nunavut*

Land Claims Agreement (NLCA), plays an important part in Nunavut's legislative principles. In 2008, the Nunavut Legislative Assembly passed four Acts that develop Inuit law in a democratic setting: the *Midwifery Profession Act*, S.Nu. 2008, c. 18, the *Education Act*, S.Nu. 2008, c. 15, the *Official Languages Act*, R.S.N.W.T. (Nu.) 1988, c. O-1 and the *Inuit Language Protection Act*, S.Nu. 2008, c. 17. Each of these four Acts expresses Inuit aspirations in a way that combines historic and contemporary legal perspectives. These Acts build upon innovative expressions of Inuit tradition in explicit ways. For example, section 27.1 of *the Inuit Language Protection Act* references the applicability of *Inuit Qaujimajatuqangit* in the following terms:

> 27.1(1) The following general principles and concepts related to *Inuit Qaujimajatuqangit* apply in respect of the exercise of the powers and performance of the duties of the Languages Commissioner under sections 28 to 35 and section 37:
>
> (a) Inuuqatigiitsiarniq (respecting others, relationships and caring for people);
> (b) *Tunnganarniq* (fostering good spirit by being open, welcoming and inclusive);
> (c) *Pijitsirniq* (serving and providing for family or community, or both);
> (d) *Aajiiqatigiinniq* (decision making through discussion and consensus);
> (e) *Piliriqatigiinniq* or *Ikajuqtigiinniq* (working together for a common cause);
> (f) *Qanuqtuurniq* (being innovative and resourceful).

Other older Acts also use *Inuit Qaujimajatuqangit* as a guiding legal idea. For example, the Nunavut *Wildlife Act*, S.Nu., 2003, c. 26 states:

> (1) The purpose of this Act is to establish a comprehensive regime for the management of wildlife and habitat in Nunavut, including the conservation, protection and recovery of species at risk, in a manner that implements provisions of the *Nunavut Land Claims Agreement* respecting wildlife, habitat and the rights of Inuit in relation to wildlife and habitat.
>
> (2) To fulfill its purpose, this Act is intended to uphold the following values:
>
> (a) wildlife and habitat should be managed comprehensively since humans, animals and plants in Nunavut are all inter-connected;
> (b) to be comprehensive, the management of wildlife and habitat should include research, analysis, education, harvesting, regulation, conservation, protection, restoration and revitalization;
> (c) Inuit are traditional and current users of wildlife and their rights under the *Nunavut Land Claims Agreement* in relation to wildlife and habitat, which flow from that use, should be given full force and effect;
> (d) the management of wildlife and habitat and the exercise of Inuit harvesting rights should be governed by and subject to the conservation principles;
> (e) the precautionary principle should govern decision making under this Act;

(f)   the guiding principles and concepts of *Inuit Qaujimajatuqangit* are important to the management of wildlife and habitat and should be described and made an integral part of this Act;

(g)   certain provisions of the *Nunavut Land Claims Agreement* respecting wildlife, habitat and the rights of Inuit in relation to wildlife and habitat should be included in this Act to provide Nunavummiut with greater certainty and understanding;

(h)   all wildlife and habitat should be recognized as intrinsically valuable and worth more than just the benefits derived from harvesting and commercial activities;

(i)   the biological diversity of Nunavut should be maintained and wildlife resources should be used in a sustainable manner;

(j)   the management of wildlife and habitat should provide optimum protection to the renewable resource economy; ...

Another example of the application of *Inuit Qaujimajatuqangit* is found in Nunavut's *Family Abuse Intervention Act*, S.Nu. 2006, c. 18:

Preamble –

Recognizing that the values and cultures of Nunavummiut and the guiding principles and concepts of Inuit Qaujimajatuqangit reflect the right of every individual in Nunavut to a full and productive life, free from harm and fear of harm;

Recognizing that family abuse continues to be a serious problem in Nunavut;

Stressing the importance of *inuuqatigiitsiarniq*, which means respecting others, relationships and caring for people, and *tunnganarniq*, which means fostering good spirit by being open, welcoming and inclusive;

Affirming the commitment of the Government of Nunavut to *pijitsirniq*, which means serving and providing for families and communities;

Incorporating and encouraging *qanuqtuurniq*, which means being innovative and resourceful.

In addition, the definitions section contains a definition of *"Inuit Qaujimajatuqangit"* as "means traditional Inuit values, knowledge, behaviour, perceptions and expectations" (section 1), and section 4 contains the following statement of principles:

4. This Act shall be interpreted and administered in accordance with the following principles:

(a)   the paramount objective of this Act is to promote the safety of Nunavummiut;

(b)   all Nunavummiut are entitled to protection from family abuse and the threat of family abuse;

(c)   all Nunavummiut have a responsibility to control their conduct and refrain from engaging in family abuse;

(d)   all Nunavummiut have a responsibility to control their conduct and refrain from damaging the well-being of the family;

(e)   all Nunavummiut are entitled to be treated with respect;

(e.1) the views of elders deserve careful consideration and respect;

(f)   every family's well-being should be supported and promoted;

(g) measures taken for the protection of applicants should, as far as practicable, promote the integrity of the family and the community, while giving priority to the wishes of the applicants;

(h) communities should be encouraged to provide services, wherever possible, to support applicants and respondents and to facilitate the reunification of the family;

(i) members of the extended family should be given the opportunity to be heard and their opinions should be considered when decisions affecting their interests are being made;

(j) there should be no unreasonable delay in making or carrying out an order.

As you read the excerpts below concerning Inuit law, and Canadian constitutional and administrative law, note the significance of their supportive interaction to developing rights and obligations relative to land, animals and people in the north.

Furthermore, in reading this material, remember the Sedna story recounted at the beginning of this chapter for further context.

MARIANO AUPILAARJUK, MARIE TULIMAAQ, EMILE IMARUITTUQ, LUCASSIE NUTARAALUK, AKISU JOAMIE, INTERVIEWING INUIT ELDERS: THE ORAL TRADITIONS PROJECT, VOLUME 2: PERSPECTIVES ON TRADITIONAL LAW, JARICH OOSTEN, FRÉDÉRIC LAUGRAND AND WIM RASING, EDS.

(Iqaluit: Nunavut Arctic College, 1999) at 33, 35-38

Respect for wildlife is a marked feature of Inuit culture, in the past as well as in the present. In many respects it is at the core of the *tiriguusiit, maligait* and *piqujait*. Although it is no longer assumed that game has an *inua*, or spirit, animals are thought to be aware of what is done to them. If game is not respected it will retaliate against the hunter or even the whole community. In the past, that could mean starvation. Today, the emphasis is on management of the wildlife. Respect for wildlife plays an important roll as new and old traditions clash. *Qallunaat* [non-Inuit] are often insufficiently aware of the impact respect for wildlife has on the interactions between Inuit and *qallunaat*. Imaruittuq relates, "When we started dealing with land claims we had to talk a lot about wildlife. This created a lot of fear amongst the elders. They used to tell us not to quarrel about wildlife because this was a very dangerous thing to do. We explained to them that we had to quarrel about the wildlife because we were negotiating with the *qallunaat* and this was a *qallunaat* process. We explained that we were legitimately negotiating over the wildlife. This is a *piqujaq* that we must adhere to. We should not quarrel about wildlife or it will take revenge on us." Respect for wildlife implies that people do not kill for fun. Aupilaarjuk explains. "A long time ago Inuit would prepare for the future. Because we did not want to experience hardship we were told not to kill wildlife just for the sake of killing them."

Aupilaarjuk: Inuit are told not to abuse wildlife. Some wildlife are taken great distances and set in human environments that are too hot for them. In their natural habitat they travel great distances, and they are not confined. When we Inuit hear about incidents where animals, such as walrus, are taken into captivity, we think that this is painful for them because they have feelings also. We have always been told not to abuse wildlife because we believe this causes hardship to the animals. We were told not to make fun of wildlife so we and our children would have a good life. We were constantly told this. We were told to be fearful of something bad happening to us if we abused wildlife. We were told to take good care of our wildlife and our land. Caribou and beluga are abundant. Sometimes when they were too numerous we didn't know how to kill large numbers of them. But now in the winter we use snow machines and we shoot them and they freeze. Some people just take the hindquarters. Some caribou only have the tongues taken and the rest is left behind. This is not a good thing to see. This is something we elders don't like at all. This is not something we Inuit have just started thinking. A long time ago Inuit would prepare for the future. Because we did not want to experience hardship we were told not to kill wildlife just for the sake of killing them. …

What do you think about narwhal and polar bear tags being required?

Imaruittuq: I've never thought of this. I see it as a deterrent. There are now a lot of people up here, both Inuit and *qallunaat,* and if we didn't have this licencing maybe we would just be killing wildlife indiscriminately and that is contrary to Inuit *maligait.* …

Were there natural fluctuations in the polar bear and caribou populations?

Aupilaarjuk: The wildlife up here cannot be treated like domestic animals. They were given to us for our use. At times caribou are very hard to come by and then all of a sudden there is an abundance of them. They are like plants, sometimes they are here and sometimes they are gone. If we are good managers, they are not going to disappear. If we don't manage them, there will be hardship. We have to constantly take care of each other and it is the same for wildlife. This is a strong *maligaq* for Inuit. If we followed this we would be in a much better situation. If educated people included Inuit knowledge when making decisions, the management of wildlife would be much better, even long after we elders are dead.

You were saying that you had to respect wildlife and treat them properly. Let's say I was trying to tire out a polar bear with my snowmobile, what would happen to me?

Imaruittuq: You are not allowed to abuse animals or toy with them. Not too long ago, there was a hunter who tried to tire out a caribou with his snowmobile, to a point where the caribou was having a hard time breathing. Later in life he developed breathing problems.

So it's fine to hunt wildlife as long as you don't mistreat them?

Imaruittuq: If you legitimately hunt wildlife and don't cause them to suffer, if you respect them, then it is fine. There will be suffering on occasion but you have to try and minimize this out of respect for the animal. We should not even make nasty comments about wildlife. We shouldn't quarrel about them amongst ourselves. Wildlife has been placed on this Earth for us to use, but we must treat them with respect. When we started dealing with land claims we had to talk a lot about wildlife. This created a lot of fear amongst the elders. They used to tell us not to quarrel about wildlife because this was a very dangerous thing to do. We explained to them that we had to quarrel about the wildlife because we were negotiating with the *qallunaat* and this was a *qallunaat* process. We explained that we were legitimately negotiating over the wildlife. This is a *piqujaq* that we must adhere to. We should not quarrel about wildlife or it will take revenge on us. ...

What would happen if you over-harvested wildlife?

Imaruittuq: There is no *piqujaq* about over-harvesting wildlife. We are told not to mistreat or abuse wildlife or it can become depleted. For example, there were two lakes that were known to be good for ice fishing. There was a man who grumbled and said bad things about wildlife. Because of what he said, one lake was rapidly depleted of fish and today it is a very bad fishing place even though it is a large lake which should have fish. The fish are coming back to the other lake because they have finished getting even with him. If we are happy and gracious towards wildlife, they will be in great abundance. If we are not thankful and do not appreciate them, they will disappear. ...

––––––––––

In response to the force of Inuit law and the strength of northern land claims agreements, there is an emerging body of Inuit jurisprudence that sheds further light on the unique nature of Inuit rights. The *Kadlak* case, excerpted below, is one such example. *Kadlak* is also illustrative of the clashes between new Inuit administrative regimes and the exercise of traditional rights by Inuit people.

KADLAK v. NUNAVUT (MINISTER OF SUSTAINABLE DEVELOPMENT)

[2001] Nu. J. No. 1, [2001] 1 C.N.L.R. 147, 6 W.W.R. 276 (Nu. C.J.)
(references omitted)

Kilpatrick J.: —

[1] Noah Kadlak lives on Southampton Island in the vastness of Canada's eastern arctic. He is an experienced Inuk hunter, and a beneficiary under the Nunavut Land Claims Agreement. He lives his life

close to the land. In this unforgiving landscape, Noah carries on the proud hunting traditions of his people; traditions that have ensured the survival of the Inuit from time immemorial.

[2] Mr. Kadlak wishes to hunt a polar bear using the traditional methods and technology of his ancestors. The taking of a bear with spear or harpoon is a risky business. There is little room for mistake. The strength, agility and cunning of the bear make it an extremely dangerous and formidable adversary. This form of hunt requires exceptional skill and courage. It is perhaps the ultimate test of the Inuit hunter.

[3] Noah Kadlak has been denied the opportunity to participate in this traditional hunt. The Minister of Sustainable Development for the Government of Nunavut has determined that this form of hunting presents an unwarranted risk to public safety and has refused to grant Mr. Kadlak any exemption from the provisions of section 42(1) of the *Wildlife Act* R.S.N.W.T. 1988, c. W-4. Mr. Kadlak now brings this application to review the Minister's decision. He asks the Court to find that the Minister's exercise of discretion in this case was unreasonable and contrary to law.

Procedural History:

[4] In November 1997, Noah Kadlak applied to the Nunavut Wildlife Management Board (NWMB) for permission to hunt a bear using a spear or harpoon. This application was necessary because section 42(1) of the *Wildlife Act*, R.S.N.W.T. 1988, c. W-4, permits hunting of bears only with certain prescribed weapons. A spear or harpoon is not an approved weapon for this purpose. Article 5.6.48 of the Nunavut Land Claim Agreement gives the NWMB the power to modify or remove this type of restriction in the Nunavut Settlement Area (defined as a non-quota limitation by Article 5.1.1).

[5] In response to Noah Kadlak's application, the NWMB granted Mr. Kadlak permission to carry out the traditional hunt, but made this subject to a number of conditions. These conditions included the following:

a. That the person be at least 19 years of age and be an experienced polar bear hunter;
b. That the person sign a comprehensive Release and Indemnity Agreement;
c. That the person be accompanied by at least one other experienced hunter with a firearm that complies with section 42 of the *Wildlife Act*;
d. That the person first obtain the written endorsement of their HTO and the NWMB.

[6] In accordance with the procedure provided for in the Nunavut Land Claims Agreement, the NWMB forwarded its decision granting permission for the traditional hunt to the Minister of Resources, Wildlife and Economic Development of the NWT by letter dated June 3rd 1998.

[7] On July 17th 1998, The NWT Minister advised the NWMB that he was exercising his jurisdiction under Article 5.3.11 of the Nunavut Land

Claims Agreement to disallow the Board's decision. This decision was made on the basis that the proposed hunt presented an unwarranted risk to public safety within the meaning of Article 5.3.3 of the Nunavut Land Claims Agreement.

[8] The NWMB then reconsidered its original decision as required by Article 5.3.12. The Board reaffirmed the original decision granting the applicant permission to conduct a traditional hunt. This was communicated to the Minister by letter dated September 16th 1998.

[9] The Minister of Sustainable Development for the new Nunavut Territory responded on October 25th, 1999. He confirmed that he was disallowing the Board's decision to grant permission for a traditional bear hunt on the grounds of public safety. It is this decision by the Minister of Sustainable Development that is now under review in this Court.

The Social and Legal Context of The Nunavut Land Claims Agreement:

[10] Before the coming of organized government, the Inuit lived in scattered camps in the remote regions of what is now the new Territory of Nunavut. They survived in this harsh environment through nomadic hunting activities. The Inuit have developed a close symbiotic relationship to the land, and all the creatures of the air, sea and land upon which they have traditionally depended as a people for their survival. The traditions of the hunt are an important focus of Inuit culture. Even today, Inuit language, art, diet and clothing celebrate the hunt and the animals of the hunt. The preservation of Inuit culture remains closely linked to this traditional way of life. The Inuit right to hunt is understandably the central focus of the Nunavut Land Claims Agreement. This is key to their social and cultural identity as a people.

[11] The Inuit right to harvest wildlife is set out in Article 5.6.1 of the Nunavut Land Claims Agreement. This Article provides that:

> … an Inuk shall have the right to harvest up to the full level of his or her economic, social and cultural needs, subject to this Article.

Article 5.1.42 further provides that:

> An Inuk may employ any type, method, or technology to harvest pursuant to the terms of this Article that does not … conflict with the laws of general application regarding humane killing of wildlife, public safety and firearms control.

[12] The provisions of this Agreement were intended by the signatories to be understood and applied in a larger social/legal context that recognized Inuit traditional harvesting practices. As an aid to interpretation, Article 5.1.3 thus proclaims that the Agreement seeks to achieve as one of its objectives:

> … the creation of a system of harvesting rights that reflects the traditional and current levels, patterns and character of Inuit harvesting.

Under the heading "Principles", Article 5.1.2 acknowledges that:

> a. Inuit are traditional and current users of wildlife;

b. The rights of Inuit to harvest wildlife flow from their traditional and current use.

[13] The Inuit right of harvest proclaimed in the Nunavut Land Claims Agreement is constitutionally protected by virtue of the incorporation of this Agreement into section 35 of Canada's *Constitution Act* 1982. In keeping with common law principles of constitutional law and statutory interpretation, the provisions of the Nunavut Land Claims Agreement are to be afforded a large, liberal and purposive interpretation so as to best attain the objectives of this legislation.

The Appropriate Standard of Judicial Review:

[14] The "pragmatic and functional approach" to judicial review of administrative decisions is well entrenched in Canadian jurisprudence. This approach recognizes a continuum of judicial review with certain types of administrative decisions being entitled to more deference from the reviewing Court than others. At the highest end of this continuum, is the standard of correctness. A decision reviewed on this standard will be overturned if it does not fully and strictly comply with the law. At the lowest end, is a standard of patent unreasonableness, where the decision under review can only be overturned if it cannot be rationally supported from the standpoint of a reasonable person. A review conducted on this standard will thus accord significant deference to the administrative body that made the original decision.

[15] It is argued on behalf of the Nunavut Government that the Court should review the Minister's decision in this case on the basis of the lowest possible standard of judicial review; that of patent unreasonableness. It is argued that the fact that the Minister's decision was made in the context of an aboriginal land claims agreement is not helpful in determining the appropriate standard of review.

[16] I disagree with both these submissions. The decision made by the Minister in this case restricts or limits a constitutionally protected right of harvest that I have found to be the central focus of the Nunavut Land Claims Agreement. The decision under review does not involve a delicate balancing of polycentric rights as in the Turbot case recently before the Federal Court (see *NTI v. Minister of Fisheries and Oceans* (1997), 149 D.L.R. (4th) 519). It involves an individual's right of harvest. I find that the individual's right to determine the method of harvest has been directly impacted by the impugned decision. There is a "prima facie infringement of an aboriginal right" within the meaning of the *Sparrow* judgment of the Supreme Court of Canada, [1990] 3 C.N.L.R. 160, 70 D.L.R. (4th) 385.

[17] I find that the highest level of judicial review, the standard of correctness, is demanded by the facts of this case. Any lesser standard of review would not be adequate to effectively protect the right proclaimed under the Nunavut Land Claims Agreement; a right that is both recognized and affirmed by section 35 of the *Constitution Act*. Any lesser standard of review would potentially undermine and erode the very objective that the Nunavut Land Claims Agreement seeks to protect.

[18] In this case, there is no privative clause to limit Court reviews of Ministerial decisions made under Part 6 that limit or restrict the Inuit right of harvesting. The decision under review does not involve difficult technical issues, or issues involving special expertise or competence. It does involve the application of broad public policy considerations to the proposed exercise by the applicant of his right of harvest. It does involve consideration of the legal meaning to attach to the phrase "public safety" as this is found in Article 5.3.3 of the Nunavut Land Claims Agreement. I find that there is nothing about the issues behind this decision that cannot be closely examined by a reviewing Court on a standard of correctness.

[19] The Supreme Court of Canada in the *Pushpanathan* case (160 D.L.R. (4th) 193) identified a number of factors that should be considered in determining the standard of review. The list of factors identified by Justice Bastarache was not intended to be complete or comprehensive. This case did not involve the review of a decision that impacted directly upon a constitutionally protected right. Nor was the Supreme Court called upon to consider the application of section 35 of the *Constitution Act* to the decision then under review. Yet the majority found that the decision of the Immigration and Refugee Board was subject to review on a standard of correctness. In *Pushpanathan*, the Supreme Court of Canada asked the reviewing Court to look to the overall purpose of the legislation in question, and to examine the nature of the issue behind the decision under review.

[20] I infer that a primary objective of the Nunavut Land Claim Agreement is to protect Inuit harvesting rights from unwarranted state interference through the incorporation of these rights into section 35 of the *Constitution Act*. It is entirely appropriate to ask the Court to intervene when government decisions adversely impact, or infringe upon those rights protected by the Constitution of this country. By conferring constitutional status and priority upon the Inuit right to harvest wildlife, Parliament and this Territory have sanctioned challenges to social and economic policy objectives embodied in legislation to the extent that this right is, has been, or will be affected. This Court finds that it is well equipped to monitor and maintain the delicate balance between the public interest represented by government and the private interests defined and protected by the Constitution, on the other. Curial deference has very little place in a review involving constitutional issues of this kind.

[21] Counsel for the Government points to the absence of a right of appeal from the Minister's decision as being a significant indicator of legislative intention to minimize curial review. I disagree. An individual right that is both "recognized and affirmed" by its incorporation into the *Constitution Act* would be meaningless without a means of enforcement or redress. I find that no right of appeal is necessary to justify a standard of correctness on this review for the reasons that I have identified.

The Standard of Correctness:

[22] Section 35(1) of the *Constitution Act* does not promise that the rights under the Nunavut Land Claim Agreement will be immune from all forms of government regulation. It does require the Territorial and Federal Crown to justify any decision that impacts adversely upon the promises made and rights conferred in the Land Claims Settlement. A decision by government that affects the exercise of a substantive aboriginal right will only be upheld if it meets the test for justifying an interference with a right recognized and affirmed under section 35(1). This test, and the analysis that precedes it, has been outlined by the Supreme Court of Canada in the case of *R. v. Sparrow*, [1990] 3 C.N.L.R. 160; (1990) 70 D.L.R. (4th) 385. The Territorial Crown thus has the burden in this case of justifying a decision that clearly restricts the right of harvest, and the right to determine the means of harvest, conferred upon Inuit by the Nunavut Land Claim Agreement.

[23] It is common ground that the only lawful justification for the Minister's decision to deny the traditional hunt in this case must be found in the provision related to "public safety". Unfortunately, the Nunavut Land Claim Agreement does not define this phrase as it appears in Article 5.3.3.

[24] Counsel for the Government argues that the phrase "public safety" should be given a broad and expansive definition. This would allow the regulation of risks assumed by individual hunters as members of the public. Such an interpretation would permit the Minister to effectively regulate a dangerous and risky harvesting activity. It is argued that in the case now before the Court, compelling public policy justified Ministerial intervention. It is argued that a prohibition of this activity is necessary to ensure that public health care and public welfare systems are not burdened by having to support individuals and their dependants who are injured or killed in the course of pursuing these risky hunting activities. It is suggested that the same public policy considerations that ultimately resulted in seat belt legislation being upheld as constitutionally valid are analogous to the case at bar.

[25] The applicant, on the other hand, argues that a very restricted or narrow meaning should attach to the phrase "public safety". It is argued that the Ministerial power to restrict Inuit harvesting should only be allowed to the extent that the hunting activity presents an identifiable risk to the community or public at large. Such a power would thus allow for the imposition of "proximity restrictions" to a harvesting activity in the vicinity of known human population. It would not extend to the risks incurred by individual hunters while pursuing their harvesting activities.

[26] It is argued that to allow the Minister to restrict hunting activities on the basis of risks assumed by individual hunters would "open the door" to significant regulation of the harvesting activities of Inuit. Many Inuit hunting activities contain an element of personal risk. Whaling with a harpoon, walrus hunting on the flow edge, polar bear hunting with a bow and arrow, or crossbow, for example, all pose significant risks, even to the

experienced hunter. It is thus argued that the adoption of the "expansive" definition advocated by government could have a significant adverse affect upon the Inuit harvesting rights recognized under section 35(1) of the *Constitution Act*.

[27] The second stage of the "Sparrow" analysis outlined by the Supreme Court of Canada requires that this Court examine the legislative objective behind the impugned decision. I am satisfied that the decision to restrict the Inuit harvesting right in this case was made pursuant to a "valid" legislative objective within the meaning of the *Sparrow* case. I further find that the decision to prohibit Noah Kadlak from pursuing the bear with a spear falls lawfully within this valid legislative objective of "public safety."

[28] In making this finding, the Court accepts that the broader definition of public safety advanced by the government is correct in law. If this Court adopted the narrow definition advanced by the applicant, then many of the restrictions initially imposed by the NWMB upon Noah Kadlak would also be rendered "invalid". These restrictions appear to have been imposed in an effort to address the risk to the individual hunter pursuing the traditional bear hunt. The provisions of Article 5.3.3 of the Nunavut Land Claim Agreement equally bind the Minister and the NWMB. If the Minister cannot validly restrict hunting activities on the basis of risks assumed by individual hunters, then the NWMB had no basis in law to do so.

[29] While the Court is thus prepared to accord the phrase "public safety" with a broad and expansive definition that would include the assumption of risks by individual hunters, the 2nd stage of the Sparrow type analysis requires that the Minister strictly comply with a "principle" of minimal interference when making his or her decision. Was the Minister's decision to effectively prohibit the traditional hunt the minimum infringement or restriction of the harvesting right possible in order to achieve the desired objective of public safety as I have defined it? Are there reasonable conditions, short of outright prohibition, that could substantially address the Minister's concerns? The principle of minimal interference is to be applied liberally, in accordance with constitutional principles of interpretation, to ensure that the rights recognized and affirmed by section 35 of the *Constitution Act* are not unduly restricted or denied through overzealous government regulation. This Court finds that the concerns raised by the applicant in argument are best addressed in this second stage of analysis.

[30] The "principle" of minimal interference is well entrenched in constitutional litigation in this country. It is a principle adverted to by the majority of the Supreme Court of Canada at p. 187 of the *Sparrow* judgment. I find that it is also a "principle" that has been expressly built into the criteria circumscribing the Minister's decision under Article 5.3.3 of the Nunavut Land Claim Agreement. This Article provides as follows:

Decisions of the NWMB or the Minister made in relation to part 6 shall restrict or limit Inuit harvesting only to the extent necessary:

a. To effect a valid conservation purpose;

b. To give effect to the allocation system outlined in this Article, to other provisions of this Article and to Article 40; or

c. To provide for public health or public safety.

[31] Before any decision is made to prohibit a particular form of harvesting activity, traditional or otherwise, the NWMB or the Minister must first consider whether other reasonable conditions could effectively address the legitimate public safety or public health concerns arising from the activity. It is clear that the NWMB did this when first authorizing the traditional hunt subject to conditions. There is no evidence before me that the Minister has done so.

[32] The outright prohibition of a traditional Inuit harvesting activity is a drastic step. It is a step of last resort. This is so particularly given the principles and objectives of the Nunavut Land Claim Agreement that appear to recognize and accept the validity of traditional harvesting activities, and their continued importance to contemporary Inuit society. For the reasons given earlier, Government must be prepared to have the justification for such a decision closely scrutinized by the Courts. I am not satisfied on the evidence before me that the Minister's decision to disallow the NWMB decision in this case satisfied this principle of minimal interference. I am not satisfied in the circumstances of this case, and on the evidence now before me, that reasonable conditions could not have been crafted to address the Minister's concerns. In the result, the decision of the Minister disallowing the NWMB authorization for a traditional hunt is quashed. It has not met the necessary standard of correctness. The Crown has failed to discharge the burden of justifying the decision under review. This matter is accordingly remitted back to the Minister for his further consideration.

The *Kadlak* case demonstrates that it is not only non-Aboriginal governmental bodies that Aboriginal peoples exercising traditional rights may come into conflict with. Here, the Nunavut government was faced with the difficult task of balancing traditional practices with the rights of others (both Aboriginal and non-Aboriginal) and the exercise of its governmental responsibilities. As with other cases involving the exercise of Aboriginal rights, *Kadlak* demonstrates that such rights are not absolute, regardless of where they may be practised or whether they are used within the jurisdiction of Aboriginal or non-Aboriginal governmental regimes.

While the *Kadlak* case demonstrates that Aboriginal-controlled governments like Nunavut can find themselves in conflict with Aboriginal organizations, there are also times when these two organizations can work effectively together. The following case was brought by Nunavut Tunngavik Incorporated (NTI) with the support of the Nunavut government. NTI's mission is to foster Inuit economic, social and cultural well-being through the implementation of the *Nunavut Land Claims Agreement*. It is also responsible for the management of all Inuit-owned lands in Nunavut and acts as the advocate of Inuit interests in Nunavut. As you read the following case, ask yourself whether the Aboriginal organization would have been as successful if the government had argued that the public interest was less Aboriginal-focused (contrast with *Saskatchewan First Nations and Indian Bands v. Canada (Attorney General)*, [2004] F.C.J. No. 123, [2004] 2 C.N.L.R. 312 (Fed. C.A.)).

NUNAVUT TUNNGAVIK INC. v. CANADA (ATTORNEY GENERAL)

[2003] Nu.J. No. 2, [2004] 1 W.W.R. 122 (Nu. C.J.)

[1] **Kilpatrick J.:** — On December 5th 1995, the Federal government enacted the *Firearms Act*, [S.C.] 1995, c. 39. This legislation has introduced a universal licensing and registration scheme for the possession, use, and purchase of all firearms and ammunition. The Plaintiff Nunavut Tunngavik Incorporated [NTI] resists implementation of this universal licensing and registration system in Nunavut for Inuit enrolled as beneficiaries under the *Nunavut Land Claims Agreement* [NLCA].

[2] It is argued by the Plaintiff that the scheme envisaged by the *Firearms Act* unlawfully infringes upon rights guaranteed to Inuit under the NLCA. Pending trial, the Plaintiff requests an interim order staying application of s. 112 of the *Firearms Act*, and sections 91 and 92 of the *Criminal Code*, R.S.C. 1985, c. C-46 (as amended) as these apply to Inuit beneficiaries. The Plaintiff is supported in this request by the Government of Nunavut, which has been granted intervener status in this action.

[3] The Federal Government opposes this application for an interim stay. It asks the Court to grant an immediate summary judgment against the Plaintiff on the basis that the matter in dispute involves an issue of pure law. It is argued that the Plaintiff's application does not give rise to a genuine issue for trial; there being no apparent conflict between the impugned legislation and the Land Claims Agreement as relied upon by the Plaintiff.

I. The Social Context:

[4] From time immemorial, Inuit survival in a harsh and unforgiving arctic environment has depended upon nomadic hunting activities. It is this activity that today defines the Inuit's social and cultural identity as a people. In the 21st century, Inuit language, art, traditional clothing, and diet continue to reflect the profound relationship of a people to the land, and to all the creatures of air, sea and land that have given life and meaning to Inuit for centuries. The protection of an individual's right of harvest, in the Inuit perspective, remains fundamental to the preservation of Inuit culture.

[5] Change has come swiftly to the Eastern Arctic. Within a short span of approximately 75 years, the Inuit have moved from scattered hunting camps to organized settlements. They now struggle as a people to adjust to sophisticated space age technologies, and a complicated and growing

government infrastructure. Adrift upon this sea of change, the Inuit today insist that their hunting practices and traditions be respected by all levels of government as a means of ensuring their survival as a people, and as a culture. If a right of harvest is a birthright of all Inuit, it is now a birthright that is constitutionally protected by the *Nunavut Land Claims Agreement* through s. 35 of the *Constitution Act, 1982*.

II. The Legal Issues in the Larger Litigation:

[6] Two sections of the NLCA are at issue in this litigation. The individual beneficiary's right of harvest is protected by section 5.7.26 which reads:

> Subject to the terms of this Article, an Inuk with proper identification may harvest up to his or her adjusted basic needs level without any form of license or permit and without imposition of any form of tax or fee.

Section 5.7.42 then provides under the heading "Methods of Harvesting" that:

> An Inuk or assignee pursuant to Sub-section 5.7.34 (a) may employ any type, method or technology to harvest pursuant to the terms of this Article that does not ...
>
> (b) conflict with laws of general application regarding humane killing of wildlife, public safety and firearms control.

[7] The Plaintiff argues that section 5.7.26 should be afforded a broad, liberal and "purposive" interpretation. It is said that the freedoms proclaimed by section 5.7.26 must necessarily apply to all matters that are reasonably incidental to the exercise of the beneficiary's right of harvest. In order to be effective, the right of harvest set out in this section must also include access to the hunting technologies upon which the right of harvest depends. A licensing and fee requirement that limits, or otherwise impairs, Inuit access to the possession and use of a primary hunting technology thus becomes a *prima facie* violation of this section. Absent a broad definition, it is argued that the constitutionally-protected right would become illusory; a mere privilege defined by the limits of a license.

[8] In reply, the Federal Government argues that section 5.7.26 was only intended to provide limited protection from government licensing, taxes or fees for the harvesting activity itself. Section 5.7.26 is by the express terms of the NLCA subject to the provisions of section 5.7.42. Hence, the Inuit right to use any "type, method or technology to harvest" conferred by the Agreement is said to be a limited one; a right that cannot by the terms of the Agreement "conflict with laws of general application regarding ... public safety and firearms control". By choosing to legislate on important public safety and firearms control objectives, Parliament has made the right of Inuit to choose a firearm related harvesting technology subject to licensing, fee and registration requirements that are universal in their application. The Defendant argues that there is thus no real conflict or inconsistency between the *Firearms Act* and the treaty right, because

section 5.7.42 of the NLCA expressly adopts firearm control laws of general application as a limit on Inuit choice of a hunting technology.

[9] The Plaintiff takes issue with this interpretation. It argues that s. 5.7.42 was intended to act as a shield to guard against government interference with a right of harvest. The language used in s. 5.7.42 should be construed as purposive or remedial. Hence only those "types, methods of harvesting, or technologies" that are restricted or prohibited by laws of general application could limit an otherwise unrestricted right of Inuit to employ any technology to harvest. The Plaintiff thus says that the government can limit Inuit access to firearms by laws of general application creating categories of "restricted" or "prohibited" weapons, but not otherwise. It is said that to give effect to the Defendant's broad interpretation of this section would transform the limiting value of this provision into a sword; a sword that could be effectively wielded by government to emasculate, and even extinguish the right sought to be protected by the Agreement. This, it is argued, was not in the contemplation of the Inuit signatories when the agreement was signed.

III. The Summary Judgment Application:

[10] In this application, the moving party has the burden of demonstrating that there is no genuine issue for trial. …

[11] The NLCA cannot be interpreted in a factual vacuum. In order to assign meaning to the provisions now in dispute, the Court must not only divine the parties intention from the actual words used in the Agreement (its internal context), but also must analyze the factual context in which the treaty right was negotiated and ultimately agreed upon. This is particularly important in the context of interpreting treaty provisions that have constitutional force and effect.

[12] The Federal Government argues on this motion that an express term of the NLCA precludes consideration of any evidence as to the treaty's external "context" or factual background. The term relied upon by the Crown is section 2.9.2, which provides as follows:

> The Agreement shall be the entire agreement and there is no representation, warranty, collateral agreement or condition affecting the agreement except as expressed in it.

While this clause was intended to exclude the notion of collateral agreements or representations existing outside the treaty itself, it does not purport to discard settled jurisprudence emphasizing the importance of "context" in treaty interpretation. The Supreme Court of Canada has repeatedly emphasized the importance of context and a case-by-case approach to consideration of agreements entered into under s. 35(1) of the *Constitution Act* (1982). This is because treaty rights are both fact driven and specific to the circumstances under which they are negotiated and signed.

[13] Where the signatories of the NLCA wished to exclude settled common law principles of treaty interpretation, they did so expressly.

Hence, section 2.9.3 excludes the notion of any presumption operating to necessarily resolve ambiguities in favor of the aboriginal signatory. The fact that they did not do so in relation to contextual evidence is telling.

[14] The Crown relies upon the case of *Eastmain Band v. Canada (Federal Administrator)* [1992 CanLII 2415], [1993] 3 C.N.L.R. 55 (F.C.A.) as authority for the proposition that principles of treaty interpretation, laid down by the Supreme Court of Canada in previous decisions made in relation to "historic" treaties, do not necessarily apply with equal force to "contemporary" land claim agreements. Thus it is argued that "context" is less important when interpreting a modern land claim agreement.

[15] The only principle of treaty interpretation at issue in *Eastmain* was the "presumption" that ambiguities be construed in favor of the aboriginal signatory; a principle already expressly excluded by the NLCA. This case does not purport to say that evidence of a treaty's context should not be considered by a Court, or given less weight when interpreting its provisions.

[16] I conclude that contextual evidence is not only admissible, but essential if the treaty provisions now in dispute between the parties are to be afforded a large, liberal and "remedial" interpretation as required by section 2.9.4 of the Agreement and the federal *Interpretation Act*, R.S.C. 1985, c. I-21.

[17] It is apparent from the arguments advanced by the parties on this motion that there continues to be a number of unresolved issues of fact relevant to the context in which this treaty was negotiated. These conflicting positions cannot be resolved on affidavit evidence in the absence of cross-examination before a trier of fact.

[18] Even if this Court has erred in its characterization of the issues in dispute on this application, I find that I still have a residual discretion in law to remit this matter for a trial on the merits, and would do so in this case.

[19] The NLCA was intended to preserve and protect important rights and freedoms of its Inuit beneficiaries. The importance of the interests that are alleged to have been adversely affected, require every Court faced with an alleged treaty violation to review the matter with particular care. As emphasized by counsel for the intervener Government of Nunavut, this litigation raises issues of profound legal and social significance to the general public of this Territory, its elected government, and to Inuit beneficiaries under the NLCA. The issues in dispute also potentially impact upon important public safety initiatives underlying the federal *Firearms Act* and its implementation in Nunavut. These issues are sufficiently complex and too important to be appropriately addressed in a summary application of this kind.

[20] In conclusion, this Court is satisfied that there is a genuine issue for trial … that is properly left to the trial Court to resolve following a full hearing on the evidence. The Federal Government's motion for summary judgment is therefore dismissed, with costs to follow the event.

IV. The Application for an Interlocutory Stay:

[21] The Plaintiff in this application has the burden of demonstrating the following, that:

1. There is a serious constitutional question to be determined;
2. Compliance by Inuit beneficiaries with the compulsory licensing and registration provisions of the Firearms Act will cause irreparable harm;
3. The balance of convenience, taking into account the public interest, favors retention of the status quo until this Court has disposed of the legal issues.

A. Serious Question to Be Tried

[22] A preliminary assessment of the merits of the Plaintiff's case has been made in the course of addressing the Defendant's motion for summary judgment. For all of the reasons set out in the preceding ruling, I am satisfied that the Plaintiff's claim is not frivolous or vexatious, and that it does indeed raise a serious question to be tried. ...

B. Irreparable Harm

[24] At this stage the only issue to be decided is whether a refusal to grant relief would so adversely affect the Plaintiff's interests that the resulting harm could not be effectively remedied after trial.

. . . . .

[27] The Plaintiff's affidavit material suggests that many Inuit have experienced difficulty in complying with the licensing and registration regime of the *Firearms Act*. A significant percentage of Inuit have either very limited command of Canada's two official languages, or are unilingual Inuktitut speakers. The documentation necessary for compliance under the *Firearms Act* is in English or French only. None of this documentation is available in syllabics. It cannot be assumed that all Inuit have sufficient literacy to be able to understand written licensing and registration requirements. Many Inuit elders, in particular, have little or no formal education. The assistance available to Inuit in the settlements to assist with compliance on an ongoing basis is limited.

. . . . .

[30] For the purposes of this motion, it is neither necessary nor helpful to determine where the source of this present difficulty lies. In the circumstances of this case, and on the limited type of evidence before me, I cannot conclude that the "harm" anticipated by the Plaintiff can be avoided by all Inuit simply choosing to comply. For a significant number of Inuit, compliance remains difficult due to circumstances related to literacy and language.

[31] The Plaintiff's affidavit material suggests that country food obtained through harvesting is culturally preferred by Inuit and is, in many respects, more nutritionally valuable than the food available commercially in the remote communities of Nunavut. The Plaintiff argues that the resulting inability of a significant number of Inuit to carry out a "core defining activity" would have significant adverse social and cultural repercussions on Inuit society. Those beneficiaries who risk non compliance with the Act in order to carry out their harvesting activities would face potential prosecution, and the significant consequences provided by law for doing so.

[32] The Crown challenges much of the factual underpinnings used by the Plaintiff to bolster its case on "irreparable harm." The Crown points to a number of anthropological and sociological case studies contained in its affidavit material to suggest that actual participation rates of Inuit in harvesting activity, and Inuit dependence upon harvesting as a food source has declined over time. While the precise participation rate of Inuit and overall level of present dependence on hunting is not clear on the evidence, this Court is satisfied that significant numbers of Inuit beneficiaries continue to exercise their harvesting rights, and remain dependant in part or in whole upon the fruits of these harvesting activities.

[33] The Crown also argues that those Inuit unable to access firearms can always use commercially available foods as an alternative to that ordinarily obtained through Inuit harvesting practices. The Crown thus points to evidence of a growing wage economy in Nunavut. Implicit to this argument, is the assumption that Inuit throughout Nunavut have ready access to a commercially available food source on a consistent basis.

[34] This Court frequently travels to the smaller settlements scattered throughout this Territory. It is uniquely situated to observe local conditions and lifestyle, and to understand and experience the difficulties associated with life in the settlements.

[35] Due to arctic ice conditions, the provision of bulk supplies through sealift is only available to Nunavut's communities during a small window of time every summer. Many of Nunavut's communities receive only one supply ship a year. None of Nunavut's communities are accessible by road or rail. For much of the year, Nunavut's settlements depend upon the airlift of essential commodities and supplies.

[36] It cannot be assumed that fresh produce will always be available to those living in the smaller settlements outside Iqaluit. Nor can it be assumed that daily air service is available to all communities within Nunavut. Supplies brought in by air are subject to the uncertainties of weather. Severe weather conditions are commonplace in Canada's arctic. Scheduled air transport to the settlements is thus frequently preempted, by fog in the spring and arctic summer, or blizzard during the many months of winter. Consistent delivery of basic foodstuffs by air to the smaller settlements is for this reason difficult to achieve. There continues to be real limits to modern air technology in Canada's arctic.

[37] Refrigerated air transport of perishable food items is particularly problematic given the small aircraft utilized for scheduled air service to

the smaller settlements. The lack of pressurized or heated storage compartments on these small aircraft can place severe limits on the type and quantity of foods that can be transported appropriately by air. These same factors can similarly impact upon the quality of produce that "survives" shipment to the smaller communities.

[38] It should not be assumed that the small cooperative stores prevalent in many of Nunavut's smaller settlements are necessarily equipped or of sufficient size to supply basic food staples on a regular basis to everyone in their community. Most Inuit outside of Iqaluit do not have the luxury of going down to a modern, bountifully stocked "supermarket" to pick up daily groceries and fresh produce.

[39] The cost to consumers of supplies airlifted from the south, even with Canada Post's subsidized Food mail program is significant. The cost of food staples in the extremely remote Inuit communities of the high Arctic is therefore many times what it would cost in the south. Given the high rate of unemployment and limited wage economy in the smaller settlements of Nunavut, many of the basic food staples available in the south may be effectively out of the financial reach of many Inuit, particularly if required to depend entirely upon commercially obtained sources of food on an on-going basis.

[40] If, on the failure of this motion, an impairment of Inuit harvesting causes a sudden loss of access to country food by a significant number of Inuit, it can not be assumed that the resulting "hole" in Inuit food supply can be readily filled by recourse to commercially available supplies of basic food staples and fresh produce on a consistent basis. Such an assumption may be warranted in the south. In view of the unique conditions prevailing in Nunavut, however, this will not be assumed by this Court. Evidence is required on this point. This evidence is not before me.

[41] While the precise extent of Inuit participation and dependence on hunting may be a matter for debate, the importance of harvesting to contemporary Inuit society is not. In a solemn exchange inked as recently as 1993, the Inuit agreed through the NLCA to relinquish claims to aboriginal title on lands they occupied in exchange for certain "defined rights and benefits". The *Nunavut Land Claims Agreement Act*, [S.C.] 1993, c. 29 through its preamble thus recognizes as fundamental objectives not only the provision of wildlife harvesting rights for Inuit beneficiaries, but also the encouragement of self-reliance and promotion of "the cultural and social well-being of Inuit". A harvesting right was clearly viewed as important by Inuit society as recently as 1993 when this agreement was signed. I conclude that this right remains as important now to Inuit as it did when the Treaty was first entered into.

[42] If, as claimed by the Plaintiff, the effect of the *Firearms Act*'s mandatory licensing and registration scheme is to impair a core or defining social value, and so diminish Inuit culture, the loss to Inuit would be incalculable. To the Inuit hunters adversely affected by this legislation, the loss or impairment of a traditional lifestyle upon the land would mark the end of living, and the beginning of survival. To the extent that the core values of a hunting culture are damaged or weakened, the elders and

hunters revered by contemporary Inuit society for their traditional knowledge and on the land skills would see their skills devalued and their place in Inuit society diminished. These groups would be at risk of becoming mere anecdotes; anachronisms of a by-gone time and a lifestyle that is passing.

[43] I conclude that in this case the quantification of damage sustained to Inuit beneficiaries caused by the alleged interference or impairment of their treaty rights would be extremely difficult to calculate. ...

. . . . .

[46] This Court, in conclusion, is satisfied that the Plaintiff has established "irreparable" harm within the narrow meaning of the test enunciated by the Supreme Court of Canada in the case of *R.J.R. Macdonald*.

C. The Balance of Convenience

[47] The important public policy considerations that underlie the creation of a scheme of universal licensing and registration of firearms apply with equal force in Nunavut as in southern Canada. In enacting the *Firearms Act*, Parliament has undertaken an important public safety initiative; an initiative that seeks to reduce the potential misuse of firearms. Violent criminal acts involving firearms, including death by suicide, occur in Nunavut as they do in the rest of Canada. Inuit beneficiaries certainly have as great an interest in promoting firearms safety as Canada's population at large.

[48] The order sought would ... not only be limited in temporal terms, but would only affect beneficiaries, who are a distinct and finite group as determined by their status as beneficiaries under the NLCA. The relief requested by the applicant would not affect the responsibility of non-beneficiaries in Nunavut to fully comply with the Act. Nor would it affect the overall implementation of the *Firearms Act* in Nunavut save for those limited sections of the *Criminal Code* and *Firearms Act* caught by this application. Full compliance would still be required for Inuit seeking to purchase new firearms. The proposed order would not exempt Inuit in circumstances where firearms are to be used for non-harvesting purposes. As the relief sought by the Plaintiff in this case amounts to a limited exemption, as opposed to a general suspension of the *Firearms Act*, I conclude that the potential damage to the public interest caused by the proposed order is much reduced.

. . . . .

[50] The relief requested would temporarily limit the ability of the Firearms Center to screen all persons presently possessing ordinary firearms in Nunavut for public safety concerns. However such an order, if granted, would not preclude prohibition applications being made by the authorities under s. 111 of the *Criminal Code* where warranted "in the

interests of safety." Given the very small size of settlements in Nunavut, local police detachments are in a good position to monitor circumstances that impact on public safety and so trigger applications of this kind. The anonymity associated with life in the urban south is simply not present in the smaller settlements of Nunavut. The onus in seeking such a prohibition order would be upon either the local police or firearm authorities. This is not unreasonable, particularly given the impact that such an order may have on a beneficiary's treaty right of harvest.

[51] While there is clearly a significant public interest attached to enforcement of public safety legislation of this kind, the Federal Government on the facts of this case cannot be said to have a "monopoly" on public interest considerations. This broad category includes not only the concerns of society generally, but also the particular interests of a large identifiable group within Nunavut.

[52] There is a significant public interest in Nunavut in ensuring that the constitutional rights of Inuit are respected at all stages of the adjudicative process. This is so particularly where questions of treaty interpretation engage "the honor of the Crown". The public government of the Nunavut Territory, a government charged with responsibility for "the administration of justice", thus joins with the Plaintiff in its request for an interlocutory stay pending trial. In doing so, the Territorial Government argues that a greater public interest is served on the facts of this case by not enforcing the universal licensing and registration on Inuit pending a determination of the merits of the Plaintiff's claim.

[53] I conclude on the basis of the limited evidence before me that the alleged infringement of a treaty right may cause collateral damage to important Inuit interests. It may interfere with Inuit harvesting, whether this is done full time as a livelihood or part time as a means of supplementing diet. It may impact upon the quality of Inuit lifestyle in isolated settlements. It may disrupt Inuit food supply in remote communities. It may cause long term damage to a defining or core social value of Inuit society. The potential for damage is both significant and immediate. This, in the Court's view, tips the balance of convenience in the Plaintiff's favor.

[54] For these reasons, the Court grants an interim stay as requested by the Plaintiff, NTI and the Intervener, Government of Nunavut. Costs will follow this event in an amount to be taxed. Counsel will draft an order and circulate it for approval as to form prior to submitting it for the Court's endorsement.

At paragraph 11, Justice Kilpatrick commented on the importance of understanding legal history as follows:

> The NLCA [*Nunavut Land Claims Agreement*] cannot be interpreted in a factual vacuum. In order to assign meaning to the provisions now in dispute, the Court must not only divine the parties intention from the actual words used in the Agreement (its internal context), but also must analyze

the factual context in which the treaty right was negotiated and ultimately agreed upon. This is particularly important in the context of interpreting treaty provisions that have constitutional force and effect.

What role does legal history and context play in Justice Kilpatrick's decision?

The Inuit of Nunavut have experienced further challenges in the implementation of their land claims agreement. In 2005, lawyer and former judge Thomas Berger was appointed as Conciliator of the *Nunavut Land Claim Agreement* (NLCA) Implementation contract. The main issues Mr. Berger examined related to a disagreement about ongoing funding levels for the institutions of public government created under the NLCA. In particular, he dealt with issues related to the scope of implementation, dispute resolution mechanisms, and implementation of Article 23, which deals with increasing Inuit participation in government employment in Nunavut.

In his report, Mr. Berger found the following issues related to education and language deserved further attention.

THOMAS BERGER, CONCILIATOR'S FINAL REPORT: NUNAVUT LAND CLAIMS AGREEMENT IMPLEMENTATION PLANNING CONTRACT NEGOTIATIONS FOR THE SECOND PLANNING PERIOD

Letter to Minister Prentice, March 1, 2006 at (references omitted) <http://www.ainc-inac.gc.ca/pr/agr/nu/lca/lca1_e.html>

... Since 2002, the Government of Canada, the Government of Nunavut and NTI have been engaged in negotiations to renew the Implementation Contract signed in 1993 (at the same time as the Agreement) to cover the second implementation period, 2003 to 2013.

But Canada, Nunavut and the NTI had been unable to agree on the terms of continuing implementation. ...

In my Final Report, which accompanies this letter, I have had to deal with a subject of even greater import, a subject with profound implications: Article 23 of the Nunavut Land Claims Agreement. Article 23 lies at the heart of the promise of Nunavut.

Article 23 has, as its stated objective, "to increase Inuit participation in government employment in the Nunavut Settlement Area to a representative level." Moreover, this objective applies to "all occupational groupings and grade levels" within government. It is an objective which is shared by the Government of Canada and the Government Nunavut.

On its face, Article 23 speaks only to employment in the public service. But I have found that it is impossible to consider Article 23 in isolation. Any examination of the objective — representative levels of Inuit employment — inevitably leads to a consideration of a range of issues implicated in the future of Nunavut, especially in the fields of employment and education.

The population of Nunavut is now approaching 30,000, of whom 85% are Inuit. Under Article 23 the Inuit ought to have 85% of the positions in the public service. The fact is, however, that only 45% of the employees of the Government of Nunavut are Inuit. This figure was more or less achieved early on, as Inuit took up mainly lower level (e.g. administrative support) positions in government, and has not been improved upon for the simple reason that only a few Inuit are qualified for the executive, management and professional positions that make up the middle and upper echelons of the public service. The result is that, although most of the elected members of the Government of Nunavut are Inuit, the great majority of the higher level positions in the public service are held by non-Inuit; in fact, these latter constitute a large part of the 15% of residents of Nunavut who are not Inuit.

The problem is not on the demand side of the equation. The Government of Nunavut has strived mightily to provide opportunities for virtually all qualified Inuit. The problem is that the supply of qualified Inuit is exhausted. Only 25% of Inuit children graduate from high school, and by no means all of these graduates go on to post-secondary education. The types of jobs where the need for increased Inuit participation is most acute — such as the executive, management and professional categories — have inescapable educational requirements.

The language spoken by the Inuit is Inuktitut. Indeed, for 75 per cent of the Inuit, Inuktitut is still their first language spoken in the home, and fully 15% of Inuit (mostly living in the smaller communities) have no other language. Given the demographics of the new territory Inuktitut ought, generally speaking, to be the language of the governmental workplace in Nunavut and the language of the delivery of government services. But it is not. The principal language of government in Nunavut is English. So the people of the new territory speak a language which is an impediment to obtaining employment in their own public service. ...

Article 23 therefore raises the question: What has to be done to qualify the Inuit for employment in all occupational groupings and grade levels in their own government? There must of course be near-term initiatives to increase the number of Inuit in the public service. ... There will have to be major changes in the education system in order to vastly increase the number of Inuit high school graduates; in my view a new approach is required, a comprehensive program of bilingual education. ...

The Government of Nunavut in 1999 inherited from the old Northwest Territories a school curriculum which, while ostensibly bilingual, emphasized English at the expense of Inuktitut. The system is not working.

Today in Nunavut, Inuktitut is the language of instruction from kindergarten through Grades 3/4. In Grades 4/5 Inuktitut is abandoned as a language of instruction, and Inuit children are introduced to English as the sole language of instruction. Many of them can converse in English. But they can't write in English, nor are their English skills sufficiently advanced to facilitate instruction in English. In Grade 4, they are starting over, and they find themselves behind. Their comprehension is imperfect; it slips and as it does they fall further behind. By the time they reach Grade 8, Grade 9 and Grade 10, they are failing (not all of them, to be sure, but most of them). This is damaging to their confidence, to their faith in themselves. For them, there has been not only an institutional rejection of their language and culture, but also a demonstration of their personal incapacity. The Inuit children have to catch up, but they are trying to hit a moving target since, as they advance into the higher grades, the curriculum becomes more dependent on reading and books, more dependent on a capacity in English that they simply do not have.

In Nunavut this reinforces the colonial message of inferiority. ...

In my judgement the failure of the school system has occurred most of all because the education system is not one that was set up for a people speaking Inuktitut. It is a bilingual system in name only, one that produces young adults who, by and large, cannot function properly in either English (because they never catch up with the English curriculum) or Inuktitut (because they learn only an immature version of their first language before switching to English). ...

The only solution is to provide a bilingual system that works.

The Government of Nunavut with the support of NTI proposes, and the experts agree, that we must undertake nothing less than a new program of bilingual education starting in the pre-school years, and from kindergarten through Grade 12. Inuktitut would still be the principal language of instruction from kindergarten to Grade 3, but it would not be effectively abandoned in Grade 4. Both Inuktitut and English would be languages of instruction right through Grade 12. ...

Why, it may be asked, hasn't the Government of Nunavut gone ahead with such a program? Well, it is a government that was organized only a few years ago. But the main reason is that the Government of Nunavut is not in a position to undertake such a program because *it cannot afford it.*

Such a program and the specific near-term initiatives that I am recommending go well beyond Nunavut's ordinary budget requirements for education and development of human resources. The Government of Nunavut must play its part, but the lion's share of the costs must be borne by the Government of Canada. ...

Nunavut is a unique jurisdiction in Canada, a territory whose population speaks a language which is not predominantly English or French. No other province or territory has a majority of Aboriginal people speaking a single language.

In the late 1960s, the Royal Commission on Bilingualism and Biculturalism (the B & B Commission) warned us that French-speaking Canadians had to be given an opportunity to occupy their fair share of places in the public service of Canada and that their language and their communities should be given an opportunity to flourish throughout Canada.

The B & B Commission found that Francophones did not occupy in the higher echelons of the federal government the places their numbers warranted; that educational opportunities for the francophone minorities in the English-speaking provinces were not commensurate with those provided for the English-speaking minority in Quebec, and that French-speaking Canadians could neither find employment in nor be adequately served in their own language by the federal government.

The resemblance to the situation in Nunavut today is striking. ...

Just as there had to be measures to enable Francophones to take their rightful place in the public service of Canada, and to promote and sustain the use of French, so also in Nunavut today there must be measures to enable the Inuit to take their rightful place in the public service of Nunavut and to promote and sustain the use of Inuktitut. ...

On March 29, 2007, Louis Tapardjuk, the Nunavut Minister of Culture, Language, Elders and Youth issued a press release stating that he planned to introduce a new *Official Languages Act* and an *Inuit Language Protection Act*. Under the proposed *Official Languages Act*, English, French and the Inuit languages of Inuktitut and Inuinnaqtun would be the territory's official languages. The *Inuit Language Protection Act* would give Inuit languages more priority in the workplace, schools and public life.

While there is much to celebrate because of Nunavut's challenge to colonialism, some Inuit people continue to feel that colonialism is omnipresent in their relationship with the federal government. One case that illustrates this feeling is *Canada (Attorney General) v. Nunavut Tunngavik Inc.*: see *Canada (Attorney General) v. Nunavut Tunngavik Inc.*, [2007] Nu.J. No. 32 (Nu. C.J.) and *Canada (Attorney General) v. Nunavut Tunngavik Inc.*, [2008] Nu.J. No. 13 (Nu. C.J.), affd [2009] Nu.J. No. 14 (Nu. C.A.). This case involves allegations that the *Nunavut Land Claims Agreement* (NLCA) has been breached.

Following in line with the tone of Tom Berger's report, the issues in the case were described in the following manner in *Canada (Attorney General) v. Nunavut Tunngavik Inc.*, [2009] Nu.J. No. 14 at paras. 12-14 (Nu. C.A.):

> [12] Numerous breaches are alleged, including inadequate provision of funding for the various boards, organizations and commissions recognized or created under the Agreement, and the failure to implement various monitoring plans, initiatives, analyses, and policies as contemplated by the Agreement. It is also pleaded that the Agreement has created fiduciary obligations in Canada, apart from its contractual obligations, and that Canada is in breach of those obligations. The pleaded fiduciary obligations include an obligation to provide adequate funding to implement the Agreement, and a corresponding duty to negotiate for the necessary funding in good faith.

[13] The Statement of Claim pleads that after its creation the Government of Nunavut was given approximately $2 million per year by Canada for the purposes of implementing the Agreement, but that this sum was "grossly inadequate". It is pleaded that attempts to negotiate a new funding arrangement after the expiry of the Implementation Agreement were unsuccessful, and that Canada has unilaterally determined the level of funding since then. The Statement of Claim seeks numerous declarations that Canada is in breach of the Agreement, an order for specific performance, continuing supervision by the Court of Canada's performance of the Agreement, and $1 billion in damages.

[14] The Statement of Defence includes a general denial of the claims. It is specifically pleaded that proper and adequate funding was provided during the initial implementation period, and that funding has since been increased. It is pleaded that the plaintiff is in breach of the Agreement by refusing to participate in certain decision-making mechanisms provided for in the Agreement. In some specific instances it is pleaded that funding was provided to the Government of Nunavut for use in implementing the provisions of the Agreement, and that this funding was "in addition to the funding provided by the Crown to the GN [Government of Nunavut] under the Territorial Formula Financing arrangement, which provides for financing of many governmental functions that fulfill, in whole or in part, some obligations of the GN under the Agreement".

While the legal validity of these allegations and defences has not been resolved by the courts, the *Canada (Attorney General) v. Nunavut Tunngavik Inc.* litigation indicates that at least some Inuit people feel that colonialism is a continuing feature of their relationship with the federal government. The Nunavut Court of Justice recently ordered Canada to pay $15 million for failure to properly implement the Nunavut Agreement (see *Nunavut Tunngavik Inc. v. Canada (Attorney General)*, 2012 NUCJ 11 (Nu. C.J.)).

Obviously, the future health of the Inuit government will depend on its success in preserving and enhancing Inuit language, traditional law, and economic development through sustainable resource and land use throughout the territory.

F.   CONCLUSION

The geographic location of Inuit communities has meant that the Inuit have only recently been exposed to issues that have confronted other Aboriginal peoples in Canada for quite some time. The relative isolation of the Inuit has allowed Inuit communities to maintain greater connections to their traditional lifestyles and activities than many Aboriginal communities farther south and not be confronted with the same degree of interference from non-Aboriginal authorities as the latter. Not surprisingly, then, the Inuit's recent forays into modern land claims and self-government agreements are, for the most part, their first positive experiences in formal dealings with the federal government on matters concerning their rights.

As seen in the discussion of Inuit land claims and self-government agreements, the Inuit people have been able to negotiate the protection of some of their rights *vis-à-vis* the federal government. That progress has been hampered, though, by government refusals to negotiate agreements that would recognize non-delegated, inherent, or nation-based forms of self-government, as discussed in Chapter 1.

While the Inuit share certain commonalities with other Aboriginal peoples in Canada and may draw upon the situations and precedents involving those other peoples, one must be mindful of the unique situation, rights, and practices of the Inuit. Indeed, as illustrated by the *Kadlak* and *NTI* cases, the uniqueness of Inuit traditional law, rights and practices, as well as the *sui generis* requirements of their geographic locations, have already been factored into Inuit rights jurisprudence.

ENDNOTES

1. Jean Briggs, *Inuit Morality Play: The Emotional Education of a Three-Year-Old* (St. John's: Iser, 1988) at 2.
2. "Central Eskimo" (1888) 6 Bureau of American Ethnology, Annual Report at 175-77.
3. Jarich Oosten, Frédéric Laugrand & William Rasing, eds., *Interviewing Inuit Elders, Volume 2: Perspectives on Traditional Law* (Iqaluit: Nunavut Arctic College, 1999) at 190.
4. See <http://www.numberten.com/news/Nunavut%20Justice%20Centre.pdf>.
5. Jarich Oosten, Frédéric Laugrand & William Rasing, eds., *Interviewing Inuit Elders, Volume 2: Perspectives on Traditional Law* (Iqaluit: Nunavut Arctic College, 1999) at 190.
6. Heather Tait, *Aboriginal Peoples Survey, 2006: Inuit Health and Social Conditions* (Ottawa: Social and Aboriginal Statistics Division, 2009) at 8.
7. See Constance Backhouse, *Colour-Coded: A Legal History of Racism in Canada, 1900-1950* (Toronto: Osgoode Society, 1999).
8. See <http://www.telefilm.gc.ca/en/catalogues/production/kikkik-e1-472>.
9. See <http://en.wikipedia.org/wiki/Inuit_languages>.
10. See Qikiqtani Truth Commission, *Final Report: Achieving Saimaqatigiingniq* (Qikiqtani Inuit Association, October 2010) at <http://www.qtcommission. com/documents/main/QTC_Final_Report_Oct_FINAL.pdf>.
11. See *Final Report of the Honorable Jean-Jacques Croteau, Retired Judge of the Superior Court, Regarding the Allegations Concerning the Slaughter of Inuit Sled Dogs in Nunavik (1950 – 1970)*, March 3, 2010 at <http://homepage.mac.com/puggiq/ officialreports/Final%20Report.pdf >.
12. Mariano Aupilaarjuk, Marie Tulimaaq, Emile Imaruittuq, Lucassie Nutaraaluk, Akisu Joamie, *Interviewing Inuit Elders, Volume 2: Perspectives on Traditional Law*, Jarich Oosten, Frédéric Laugrand and Wim Rasing, eds. (Iqaluit: Nunavut Arctic College, 1999) at 1.
13. *Ibid.*, at 13.
14. John Bennett and Susan Rowley, eds., *Uqalurait: An Oral History of Nunavut* (Montreal: McGill-Queen's Press, 2004) at 110.
15. Law Commission of Canada, *Final Report: Transforming Relationships Through Participatory Justice* (Ottawa, 2003) at chapter 2.
16. Jaypetee Arnakak, "Commentary: What is Inuit Qaujimajatuqangit?", *Nunatsiaq News*, August 25, 2000.
17. For further information see *Review of the Nunavut Community Justice Program: Final Report* (Department of Justice, 2004), appendix 1.

CHAPTER 7

MÉTIS RIGHTS

A. INTRODUCTION

Métis peoples, like the Inuit whose rights are discussed in Chapter 6, fall under the definition of "aboriginal peoples of Canada" in section 35(2) of the *Constitution Act, 1982*, being Schedule B to the *Canada Act 1982* (U.K.), 1982, c. 11. Although for the purposes of section 35(2) Métis peoples are grouped with the Inuit and status Indians (see Chapter 9 for a discussion of the distinction between status and non-status Indians), this chapter will illustrate that the Métis possess distinct practices and cultures that are derived from their unique backgrounds. Indeed, as will be discussed further in the process of determining who Métis persons are, the unique histories of various Métis groups provide for a rich and diverse collectivity within the definition of "Métis".

This chapter will begin by examining the issue of Métis identity, a long-standing matter of debate because of the absence of federal definition, and the historical, cultural and political diversity of Métis communities. It will next address Métis Aboriginal title or land rights, including the process and implications of bringing the Red River Métis into Confederation through the *Manitoba Act, 1870*. The chapter will next consider the issue of Métis Aboriginal rights as separate and distinct rights from the rights belonging to Indian and Inuit peoples. In the process of this examination, we will consider the Supreme Court of Canada's test for the determination of rights-bearing Métis communities.

B. MÉTIS IDENTITY

Because of the Métis' unique origins, a great deal of controversy has surrounded the definition of "Métis" and the nature and extent of their rights. The following excerpt from the Royal Commission on Aboriginal Peoples illustrates the complexity of the Métis constitutional identity.

REPORT OF THE ROYAL COMMISSION ON ABORIGINAL PEOPLES: PERSPECTIVES AND REALITIES, VOL. 4

(Ottawa: Ministry of Supply and Services, 1996)
"Métis Perspectives," at 199-203 (references omitted)

In 1982, the Constitution of Canada was amended to state that Canada's Aboriginal peoples include the Métis. Métis people did not need to be told that: they have always known who they are. They have always known, too, that Canada would be a different place today if they had not played a major role in its development. Modern Canada is the product of a historical partnership between Aboriginal and non-Aboriginal people, and Métis people were integral to that partnership.

Intermarriage between First Nations and Inuit women and European fur traders and fishermen produced children, but the birth of new Aboriginal cultures took longer. At first, the children of mixed unions were brought up in the traditions of their mothers or (less often) their fathers. Gradually, however, distinct Métis cultures emerged, combining European and First Nations or Inuit heritages in unique ways. Economics played a major role in this process. The special qualities and skills of the Métis population made them indispensable members of Aboriginal/non-Aboriginal economic partnerships, and that association contributed to the shaping of their cultures. Using their knowledge of European and Aboriginal languages, their family connections and their wilderness skills, they helped to extend non-Aboriginal contacts deep into the North American interior. As interpreters, diplomats, guides, couriers, freighters, traders and suppliers, the early Métis people contributed massively to European penetration of North America.

The French referred to the fur trade Métis as *coureurs de bois* (forest runners) and *bois brulés* (burnt-wood people) in recognition of their wilderness occupations and their dark complexions. The Labrador Métis (whose culture had early roots) were originally called "livyers" or "settlers", those who remained in the fishing settlements year-round rather than returning periodically to Europe or Newfoundland. The Cree people expressed the Métis character in the term *Otepayemsuak*, meaning the "independent ones". ...

1.2 Métis Identity

... Being Métis ... can mean different things in different contexts: one context may speak to an individual's inner sense of personal identity; another may refer to membership in a particular Métis community; a third may signal entitlement to Métis rights as recognized by section 35 of the *Constitution Act, 1982*. Throughout the following discussion of Métis identity, the meaning of the term is governed largely by the context in which it is used. ...

It is primarily culture that sets the Métis apart from other Aboriginal peoples. Many Canadians have mixed Aboriginal/non-Aboriginal ancestry, but that does not make them Métis or even Aboriginal. ... What distinguishes Métis people from everyone else is that they associate themselves with a culture that is distinctly Métis.

Historically, Métis cultures grew out of ways of life dictated by the resource industry roles of the early Métis. For those who served the fur trade, the birth of the unique Métis language, Michif, was a consequence of using both French and Indian languages. The need to travel inspired mobile art forms: song, dance, fiddle music, decorative clothing. The periodic return to fixed trading bases, the seasonal nature of the buffalo hunt and discriminatory attitudes all shaped settlement patterns. For Métis people of the east, seasonal hunting and gathering expeditions combined with influences that stemmed from a fishing economy. In all cases, the cultures developed organically, their characteristics determined by the social and economic circumstances that germinated and nourished them. ...

Individual identity is a matter of personal choice. ... For acceptance of that identification, however, it is necessary to win the approval of the people or nation with which one identifies. It would be inappropriate for anyone outside that nation to intervene. Therefore, when a government wishes to know a nation's membership for the purpose of engaging in nation-to-nation negotiations, it can legitimately consider only two criteria: self-identification and acceptance by the nation.

This does not mean that other governments can never legitimately concern themselves with who is or is not Métis. Suppose that the government of Canada agreed through negotiation to provide a benefit to Métis residents of a particular area. In the absence of an agreed definition of Métis, it would be necessary for the government to decide who did and did not qualify for the benefit. Or if, pending the negotiated settlement of a Métis issue, it were agreed that a government should administer a program related to the issue, the program's beneficiaries would necessarily have to be identified. It might also be appropriate for a government to identify the membership of an Aboriginal nation in order to assess the ramifications of a decision recognizing its status as a nation. Beyond such purposes, the composition of an Aboriginal nation should be the business of no one other than that nation and its members.

A Métis view on the Métis identity debate which looks at its contemporary social, political, and legal contexts is offered in the following excerpt.

LARRY CHARTRAND, "METIS IDENTITY AND CITIZENSHIP"
(2001) 12 W.R.L.S.I. 5 at 6-10, 19-23, 25-26, 37-41, 47-52
(references omitted)

II. BACKGROUND

Before entering into a discussion of Metis identity and citizenship, it is useful to place such a discussion within the contemporary Metis political and social context. ...

There are a number of organizations that presently claim to represent Metis people in Canada. Indeed, there are serious divisions among self-identifying Metis people about which political organizations are justified in identifying themselves as true Metis organizations. The issue of "Metis identity" is controversial and has generated considerable debate and conflict between various "Metis" organizations.

However, at the outset, it is important to keep in mind an important distinction between those entities that are capable of exercising rights of self-determination, including the right to determine citizenship, and those entities that are incorporated under various federal and provincial statutes as non-profit organizations representing Metis people according to the by-laws of the corporation. ...

A. Metis Political Representation in Canada

Metis peoples are purported to be represented by two national organizations: the Metis National Council and the Congress of Aboriginal Peoples. Each national organization has a number of provincial affiliates that comprise the membership of the national body. There also exists a Metis Settlements General Council that represents the Metis who are situated on the eight land settlements in northern Alberta. This Metis settlement regime is unique to Alberta. In addition, there are some independent regional organizations that purport to represent a particular Metis constituency. ...

B. Social, Cultural and Economic Circumstances

[In 2006, the estimated number of Métis was 404,000. This population almost doubled between 1996 and 2006.] ... In general, the Metis are similar to First Nations people with respect to their social conditions, unemployment and lack of educational attainment. In other words, the Metis have not weathered the storm of social disruption and oppression caused by colonialism any better than Indians or the Inuit. Indeed, in terms of cultural survival, there is every indication that the Metis were particularly hard hit by the pressures of Canadian policies of assimilation. ...

Although Metis continued to practice their culture, the social circumstances of the time no doubt dramatically affected their ability to do so at a level that would ensure maximum freedom and opportunity to pass on their culture to subsequent generations. Another factor relevant to the western Metis that may, in part, have caused such a disparity of culture and language maintenance is the "scrip" program for the Metis living in western Canada. Unlike Indian communities that acquired collective ownership of various tracts of land under the Indian reserve system, the Metis were forced to acquire individual plots of land, often at some distance from their home communities. Although there are problems with the paternalistic nature of the reserve system, at a minimum they at least allow Indian communities to continue practising their culture and maintain a sense of community identity and belonging. Unfortunately, the individualized and alienating scrip system denied the Metis this important condition of cultural continuity. ...

Except for the Metis Settlements in Alberta, the Metis, as communities, are a landless people. Without land, Metis communities have little to no control over their destiny. The important local decision-making is left in the hands of non-aboriginal authorities. Furthermore, without land the

Metis have no financial security or control over resources to protect their traditional avocations for the present or for their children's future. Currently, Metis must often gather as a group to promote collective activities and events either in the basements of churches or community halls when they can afford to rent them.

Furthermore, Metis social and political institutions are often poorly funded. As a result, efforts to provide Metis specific services, such as child care, education and economic development are difficult to establish. Of particular concern is the lack of being able to plan for the long term because of the short-term nature of most funding programs. Agencies, such as Metis Child and Family Services in Edmonton are often put in difficult positions financially, because government funding programs are either temporary, pilot project oriented and administratively complicated due to varying funding criteria and requirements from different funding programs. These problems, in addition to delays and cutbacks, makes it extremely difficult to plan for future expansion and to meet new challenges and needs of the Metis community as they arise.

Much of the problem in developing Metis specific programs is due to the jurisdictional vacuum in which the Metis find themselves. Because of historical circumstances, the federal government denies that they are responsible for the Metis. Likewise, the provinces are not generally prepared to provide Metis-specific funding or services because they run the risk that, if they do so, they might be perceived as accepting jurisdictional responsibility over the Metis which they argue is a federal government responsibility.

Another social concern of the Metis has to do with the public's understanding of the Metis and their history, culture and legal status in Canadian society. This failure to understand who the Metis are often exacerbates problems associated with program service and delivery. Furthermore, government's lack of understanding often causes inequitable responses to Aboriginal issues. For example, an agreement between the Province of Saskatchewan and the Federation of Saskatchewan Indians [FSIN] over the control of Casino revenues in the province excluded the Metis. The FSIN has representation on the Board of the Casino Corporation and are guaranteed 25 per cent of the profits through the First Nations Fund set up under the legislation. Yet the Metis Nation of Saskatchewan was left out of the picture almost entirely, but for a minor reference to the fact that like other charities, they may be eligible for some funding upon application. There is no representation on the Board, no special Metis Nation fund and no guarantee of funds. This is a form of discrimination against the Metis people.

This inequity is well illustrated in the child welfare area. There are several provinces that have legislation requiring child welfare authorities to contact the Indian Band office to which a child belongs if the child is going to become a ward of the state. Similar protections for the Metis do not exist.

Hunting and fishing rights have also been difficult for the Metis to establish and receive equity with First Nations' rights to hunt. ...

Thus, even though the Metis have faced and continue to face racism and discrimination because they are Aboriginal, they also face discrimination because they are not Indians. They are doubly discriminated. They do not get the same level of recognition, as do Indians, in the acquisition of resources and culturally sensitive programs. ...

... The social circumstances facing Metis communities are often exacerbated by Metis exclusion from relevant federal government policies, programs and services that have benefited Indian and Inuit. Provinces, with the exception of Alberta, have denied any jurisdictional responsibility regarding the Metis and have consistently maintained that the Metis are the responsibility of the federal government. Thus, over much of the last 100 years, the Metis have been unable to communicate with the Crown on a nation to nation level — their existence as an Aboriginal people denied. And with that denial, a refusal by both levels of government to recognise the inherent rights of the Metis that exist independent of state or government action. In many cases, the Metis have, out of necessity, only been able to access financial support for their organisations like any other charitable organisation in the province. ...

Under s. 35(2) of the Constitution, the Metis are listed as one of the Aboriginal peoples of Canada; however, the provision does not specifically define who the Metis are. ...

The lack of a definition for the Métis under section 35(1) of the *Constitution Act, 1982* or 91(24) of the *Constitution Act, 1867* has generated political controversy and protracted litigation. The Supreme Court of Canada resolved some definitional issues about what constitutes a rights-bearing Métis community in *R. v. Powley*, [2003] S.C.J. No. 43, [2003] 2 S.C.R. 207 (S.C.C.) (in section D below). The question about whether the Métis are "Indians" under treaties and various constitutional instruments has also been a constant theme. This issue was addressed by the Royal Commission on Aboriginal Peoples in the following excerpt.

REPORT OF THE ROYAL COMMISSION ON ABORIGINAL PEOPLES: PERSPECTIVES AND REALITIES, VOL. 4

(Ottawa: Ministry of Supply and Services, 1996)
at 278-81, 285, 288, 290-92 (references omitted)

Historically, Métis people were closely linked to other Aboriginal peoples. Although the first progeny of Aboriginal mothers and European fathers were genetically both Aboriginal and European, for the most part they followed an Aboriginal lifestyle. Predominant kinship ties also tended to be with the Aboriginal community. In unions between Aboriginal women and Scottish employees of the Hudson's Bay Company, the husbands had a common tendency to treat their "country families" as temporary, to be left behind when they retired to Scotland. The French-Indian families tended to greater permanence, and their lifestyle, at least initially, was closer to Aboriginal patterns than to European ones.

Subsequently, distinctive Métis social patterns of predominantly Aboriginal character evolved in some areas, although not all persons of mixed Aboriginal and European ancestry chose to follow them. ... [There is] evidence of acceptance that Métis persons could avail themselves of Indian status if they chose to do so...in documents relating to early western treaties, such as the report of W.M. Simpson concerning Treaty 1:

> During the payment of the several bands, it was found that in some, and most notably in the Indian settlement and Broken Head River Band, a number of those residing among the Indians, and calling themselves Indians, are in reality half-breeds, and entitled to share in the land grant under the provisions of the Manitoba Act. I was most particular, therefore, in causing it to be explained, generally and to individuals, that any person now electing to be classed with Indians, and receiving the Indian pay and gratuity, would, I believed, thereby forfeit his or her right to another grant as a half-breed; and in all cases where it was known that a man was a half-breed, the matter, as it affected himself and his children, was explained to him, and the choice given him to characterize himself. A very few only decided upon taking their grants as half-breeds. The explanation of this apparent sacrifice is found in the fact that the mass of these persons have lived all their lives on the Indian reserves (so called), and would rather receive such benefits as may accrue to them under the Indian treaty, than wait the realization of any value in their half-breed grant.

Evidence is also found in the transcript of negotiations leading to Treaty 3:

> CHIEF — I should not feel happy if I was not to mess with some of my children that are around me — those children that we call the Half-breed, those that have been born of our women of Indian blood. We wish that they should be counted with us, and have their share of what you have promised. We wish you to accept our demands. It is the Half-breeds that are actually living amongst us — those that are married to our women.

> GOVERNOR — I am sent here to treat with the Indians. In Red River, where I came from, and where there is a great body of Half-breeds, they must be either white or Indian. If Indians, they get treaty money; if the Half-breeds call themselves white, they get land. All I can do is to refer the matter to the Government at Ottawa, and to recommend what you wish to be granted.

The significance of these observations to the present discussion is threefold:

- They indicate that Métis people were recognized, even at that relatively late date, as being entitled to assert Indian status (and thus entitled to Aboriginal rights).
- They show that the operative method of classifying persons for that purpose at the time was self-identification, regulated, presumably, by community confirmation.
- They confirm that Métis rights had not yet been brought under the treaties.

Until recently, the strongest legal evidence that Métis people were entitled to lay claim to Aboriginal rights, even after a distinctive Métis nation had evolved, was section 31 of the *Manitoba Act, 1870*, a statute of the Parliament of Canada that was subsequently accorded constitutional status by the *Constitution Act, 1871*. ...

In the present context [s. 31's] importance lies in the fact that it includes an acknowledgement by both Canadian and British parliaments that the people of the Métis Nation were entitled to share Indian title to the land and, it seems clear by implication, all other elements of Aboriginal rights. Further acknowledgement of the existence of Métis Aboriginal rights is found in subsequent legislation, such as the federal *Dominion Lands Act, 1879*, which referred in section 125(e) to Indian title and its extinguishment by grants to Métis people living outside Manitoba on 15 July 1870. ...

As to the relationship of Métis to First Nation and Inuit Aboriginal rights, there appear to be two fundamentally different views. The first traces Métis rights to the ancient rights of the peoples from whom Métis peoples derive their Aboriginal ancestry. From that point of view, these rights are older than Métis peoples themselves. The other view is that Métis Aboriginal rights were not derived from those of the ancestral Aboriginal nations but sprang into existence when the Métis themselves were born as a distinct people.

The first approach is more consistent with the meaning of the word "Aboriginal": from the beginning. It is also supported by some of the historical evidence referred to above, such as the linkage of Métis to Indian title in the *Manitoba Act, 1870*; the *Dominion Lands Act*; and the revelation in the documents concerning the early western treaties that Métis people who chose to do so were permitted (and presumably considered entitled) to associate themselves with and exercise the rights of Indian peoples.

The other point of view — that an entirely distinct Aboriginal people came into being as a result of contact between the Indigenous population and Europeans and subsequent socio-economic developments — also finds strong support in history. It is unquestionable, for example, that a unique way of life was forged by Métis people of the North American plains and by the mixed-ancestry communities of Labrador. Morris's book recognized the fact for the prairie Métis and suggested that those Métis who chose to live the distinctive life associated with that culture should not be brought under the treaties. This second approach would not do violence to the dictionary meaning of Aboriginal either, since the word could be read to mean "from the beginning of significant European settlement".

In light of this brief historical introduction by RCAP, consider the Supreme Court's treatment of the question of whether Métis are "Indians" under section 13 of the *Natural Resources Transfer Agreement* ("NRTA") in the following case:

R. v. BLAIS
[2003] S.C.J. No. 44, [2003] 2 S.C.R. 236 (S.C.C.)

The Court: —

I. Introduction

[1] This case raises the issue of whether the Métis are "Indians" under the hunting rights provisions of the Manitoba *Natural Resources Transfer Agreement* ("*NRTA*"), incorporated as Schedule (1) to the *Constitution Act, 1930*. We conclude that they are not.

[2] On February 10, 1994, Ernest Blais and two other men went hunting for deer in the District of Piney, in the Province of Manitoba. At that time, deer hunting was prohibited in that area by the terms of the wildlife regulations passed pursuant to *The Wildlife Act* of Manitoba, R.S.M. 1987, c. W130, s. 26, as amended by S.M. 1989-90, c. 27, s. 13. Mr. Blais was charged with unlawfully hunting deer out of season.

[3] The requisite elements of the offence were conceded at trial. However, the appellant asserted ... a constitutional right to hunt for food on unoccupied Crown lands by virtue of para. 13 of the *NRTA*.

. . . . .

[6] Because we agree that para. 13 of the *NRTA* cannot be read to include the Métis, we would dismiss this appeal. We make no findings with respect to the existence of a Métis right to hunt for food in Manitoba under s. 35 of the *Constitution Act, 1982*, since the appellant chose not to pursue this defence.

II. Analysis

[7] Mr. Blais is a "Métis", a member of a distinctive community descended from unions between Europeans and Indians or Inuit. ...The question is whether, as a Métis, he is entitled to benefit from this hunting provision for "Indians".

[8] Paragraph 13 of the *NRTA* reads:

> In order to secure to the Indians of the Province the continuance of the supply of game and fish for their support and subsistence, Canada agrees that the laws respecting game in force in the Province from time to time shall apply to the Indians within the boundaries thereof, provided, however, that the said Indians shall have the right, which the Province hereby assures to them, of hunting, trapping and fishing game and fish for food at all seasons of the year on all unoccupied Crown lands and on any other lands to which the said Indians may have a right of access.

This provision consists of a stipulation and an exception. The stipulation is that "the laws respecting game in force in the Province from time to time shall apply to the *Indians*" (emphasis added). The exception is the continuing right of the Indians to hunt, trap and fish for food on unoccupied Crown lands "provided, however, that the *said Indians* shall have the right, which the Province hereby assures to them, of hunting, trapping and fishing game and fish for food at all seasons of the year on all unoccupied Crown lands and on any other lands to which the said Indians may have a right of access" (emphasis added).

[9] The issue, as stated, is whether the exception addressed to "Indians" applies to the Métis. ... Members of Métis communities in the prairie provinces collectively refer to themselves as the "Métis Nation", and trace their roots to the western fur trade: *Report of the Royal Commission on Aboriginal Peoples: Perspectives and Realities* (1996), vol. 4, at p. 203 ("*RCAP Report*"). ...

A. *An Overview of the NRTA*

[10] Before embarking on our analysis of the meaning of "Indians" in para. 13, it may be useful to set out the history of the *NRTA* in general and para. 13 in particular. The three *NRTA*s arose as part of an effort to put the provinces of Alberta, Manitoba and Saskatchewan on an equal footing with the other Canadian provinces by giving them jurisdiction over and ownership of their natural resources. ...[T]he Agreements were largely concerned with the transfer of contractual and related liabilities from Canada to the provinces. ...

[11] In the midst of these transfer provisions, three out of 25 paragraphs in the Manitoba *NRTA* come under the separate heading "Indian Reserves". Paragraph 13 is one of them. These paragraphs are identical to paras. 10-12 of the Alberta and Saskatchewan *NRTA*s. The three provisions indicate that, notwithstanding the transfer of control over land to Manitoba, responsibility for administering Indian reserves will remain with the federal Crown (para. 11); that the rules set out in the March 24, 1924 agreement between Canada and Ontario will apply to these Indian reserves and to any others subsequently created in the Province (para. 12); and that provincial hunting and fishing laws will apply to Indians <u>except</u> that these laws shall not prevent Indians from hunting and fishing for food on unoccupied Crown lands (para. 13).

[12] ... By enacting para. 13, the federal government specified that hunting and fishing by Indians could be the subject of provincial regulation, while seeking to ensure that its pre-existing obligations towards the Indians with respect to hunting rights would be fulfilled.

[13] Paragraph 13 both affirmed and limited the Province's regulatory power: *Frank v. The Queen*, [1978] 1 S.C.R. 95, at p. 100; *Moosehunter v. The Queen*, [1981] 1 S.C.R. 282, at p. 285; *R. v. Horseman*, [1990] 1 S.C.R. 901, at pp. 931-32; *R. v. Badger*, [1996] 1 S.C.R. 771, at para. 45. It affirmed the Province's power to regulate hunting for conservation purposes (see *Badger, supra*, at para. 71) but it carved out a protected space for hunting by Indians on unoccupied Crown lands and on lands to which the Indians have a right of access. ...

B. *The Regulatory Context*

[14] The Province of Manitoba has used its regulatory power to enact laws designed to protect its wildlife population: *The Wildlife Act*. ...

[15] Seasonal restrictions and licensing requirements for deer hunting under the Manitoba *Wildlife Act* currently do not apply to members of Indian bands. Mr. Blais was arrested and charged with unlawfully hunting deer out of season because he is not a member of an Indian band, but a member of the Manitoba Métis community. ...

C. *Guiding Principles and Application*

[16] Against this background, we turn to the issue before us: whether "Indians" in para. 13 of the *NRTA* include the Métis. ...

[17] The *NRTA* is a constitutional document. It must therefore be read generously within these contextual and historical confines. A court interpreting a constitutionally guaranteed right must apply an interpretation that will fulfill the broad purpose of the guarantee and thus secure "for individuals the full benefit of the [constitutional] protection": *R. v. Big M Drug Mart Ltd.*, [1985] 1 S.C.R. 295, at p. 344. "At the same time it is important not to overshoot the actual purpose of the right or freedom in question, but to recall that the [constitutional provision] was not enacted in a vacuum, and must therefore ... be placed in its proper linguistic, philosophic and historical contexts": *Big M Drug Mart, supra*, at p. 344. This is essentially the approach the Court used in 1939 when the Court examined the historical record to determine whether the term "Indians" in s. 91(24) of the *British North America Act, 1867* includes the Inuit (*Reference as to whether "Indians" in s. 91(24) of the B.N.A. Act includes Eskimo inhabitants of the Province of Quebec*, [1939] S.C.R. 104).

[18] Applied to this case, this means that we must fulfill — but not "overshoot" — the purpose of para. 13 of the *NRTA*. We must approach the task of determining whether Métis are included in "Indians" under para. 13 by looking at the historical context, the ordinary meaning of the language used, and the philosophy or objectives lying behind it.

(1) Historical Context

[19] The *NRTA* was not a grant of title, but an administrative transfer of the responsibilities that the Crown acknowledged at the time towards "the Indians within the boundaries" of the Province — a transfer with constitutional force. In ascertaining which group or groups the parties to the *NRTA* intended to designate by the term "Indians", we must look at the prevailing understandings of Crown obligations and the administrative regimes that applied to the different Aboriginal groups in Manitoba. The record suggests that the Métis were treated as a different group from "Indians" for purposes of delineating rights and protections.

[20] The courts below found, and the record confirms, that the Manitoba Métis were not considered wards of the Crown. ...

[21] The difference between Indians and Métis appears to have been widely recognized and understood by the mid-19th century. In 1870, Manitoba had a settled population of 12,228 inhabitants, almost 10,000 of whom were either English Métis or French Métis. Government actors and

the Métis themselves viewed the Indians as a separate group with different historical entitlements; in fact, many if not most of the members of the Manitoba government at the time of its entry into Confederation were themselves Métis.

[22] The *Manitoba Act, 1870* used the term "half-breed" to refer to the Métis, and set aside land specifically for their use: *Manitoba Act, 1870*, S.C. 1870, c. 3, s. 31 (reprinted in R.S.C. 1985, App. II, No. 8). While s. 31 states that this land is being set aside "towards the extinguishment of the Indian Title to the lands in the Province", this was expressly recognized at the time as being an inaccurate description. Sir John A. Macdonald explained in 1885:

> Whether they [the Métis] had any right to those lands or not was not so much the question as it was a question of policy to make an arrangement with the inhabitants of that Province... 1,400,000 acres would be quite sufficient for the purpose of compensating these men for what was called the extinguishment of the Indian title. That phrase was an incorrect one, the half-breeds did not allow themselves to be Indians.

(*House of Commons Debates*, July 6, 1885, at p. 3113, cited in T. E. Flanagan, "The History of Metis Aboriginal Rights: Politics, Principle, and Policy" (1990), 5 *C.J.L.S.* 71, at p. 74)

[23] Other evidence in the record corroborates this view. For example, at trial, the expert witness Dr. G. Ens attached to his report a book written by Lieutenant-Governor A. Morris entitled *The Treaties of Canada with the Indians of Manitoba and the North-West Territories*, published in 1880. The book includes an account of negotiations between the Governor and an Indian Chief who expresses the concern that his mixed-blood offspring might not benefit from the proposed treaty. The Governor explains, at p. 69: "I am sent here to treat with the Indians. In Red River, where I came from, and where there is a great body of Half-breeds, they must be either white or Indian. If Indians, they get treaty money; if the Half-breeds call themselves white, they get land". This statement supports the view that Indians and Métis were widely understood as distinct groups for the purpose of determining their entitlements *vis-à-vis* the colonial administration.

[24] It could be argued that the ability of individual Métis to identify themselves with Indian bands and to claim treaty rights on this basis weighs against a view of the two groups as entirely distinct. However, the very fact that a Métis person could "choose" either an Indian or a white identity supports the view that a Métis person was not considered Indian in the absence of an individual act of voluntary association.

. . . . .

[26] Placing para. 13 in its proper historical context does not involve negating the rights of the Métis. Paragraph 13 is not the only source of the Crown's or the Province's obligations towards Aboriginal peoples. Other constitutional and statutory provisions are better suited, and were actually intended, to fulfill this more wide-ranging purpose. The sole issue before

us is whether the term "Indians" in the *NRTA* includes the Métis. The historical context of the *NRTA* suggests that it does not.

(2) Language

[27] The common usage of the term "Indian" in 1930 also argues against a view of this term as encompassing the Métis. Both the terms "Indian" and "half-breed" were used in the mid-19th century. Swail Prov. Ct. J. cites a North American census prepared by the Hudson's Bay Company in 1856-57 (pp. 146-47). The census records 147,000 "Indians", and breaks this down into various groups, including "The Plain Tribes", "The Esquimaux", "Indians settled in Canada", and so forth. A separate line indicates the number of "Whites and half-breeds in Hudson's Bay Territory", which is estimated at 11,000, for a total of 158,000 "souls". This document illustrates that the "Whites and half-breeds" were viewed as an identifiable group, separate and distinct from the Indians.

[28] The Red River Métis distinguished themselves from the Indians. For example, the successive Lists of Rights prepared by Métis leaders at the time of the creation of the Province of Manitoba excluded "the Indians" from voting. This provision could not plausibly have been intended to disenfranchise the Métis, who were the authors of the Lists and the majority of the population. The Third and Fourth Lists of Rights emphasized the importance of concluding treaties "between Canada and the different Indian tribes of the Province", with the "cooperation of the Local Legislature" (Morton, *supra*, at pp. 246 and 249). The Local Legislature was, at that time, a Métis-dominated body, underscoring the Métis' own view of themselves and the Indians as fundamentally distinct.

[29] There might not have been absolute consistency in the use of the terms "Indian" and "half-breed", and there appears to have been some mobility between the two groups. However, as evidenced by the historical documents statement cited above, the prevailing trend was to identify two distinct groups and to differentiate between their respective entitlements. ...

[30] This interpretation is supported by the location of para. 13 in the *NRTA* itself. Quite apart from formal rules of statutory construction, common sense dictates that the content of a provision will in some way be related to its heading. Paragraph 13 falls under the heading "Indian Reserves". Indian reserves were set aside for the use and benefit of Status Indians, not for the Métis. ...

. . . . .

(3) The NRTA's Objectives

[32] The purpose of para. 13 of the *NRTA* is to ensure respect for the Crown's obligations to "Indians" with respect to hunting rights. It was enacted to protect the hunting rights of the beneficiaries of Indian treaties and the *Indian Act* in the context of the transfer of Crown land to the provinces. It took away the right to hunt commercially while protecting the right to hunt for food and expanding the territory upon which this

could take place: see ... *Horseman, supra,* at pp. 931-32; and *Badger, supra,* at para. 45. ...

[33] The protection accorded by para. 13 was based on the special relationship between Indians and the Crown. Underlying this was the view that Indians required special protection and assistance. Rightly or wrongly, this view did not extend to the Métis. The Métis were considered more independent and less in need of Crown protection than their Indian neighbours, ...

[34] This perceived difference between the Crown's obligations to Indians and its relationship with the Métis was reflected in separate arrangements for the distribution of land. Different legal and political regimes governed the conclusion of Indian treaties and the allocation of Métis scrip. Indian treaties were concluded on a collective basis and entailed collective rights, whereas scrip entitled recipients to individual grants of land. While the history of scrip speculation and devaluation is a sorry chapter in our nation's history, this does not change the fact that scrip was based on fundamentally different assumptions about the nature and origins of the government's relationship with scrip recipients than the assumptions underlying treaties with Indians.

[35] The historical context of the *NRTA,* the language of the section, and the purpose that led to its inclusion in the *Constitution Act, 1930* support the lower courts' conclusion that para. 13 does not encompass the Métis. ...

D. *Appellant's Counter-Arguments*

(1) Continuity of Language

[36] The appellant asks us to impose a "continuity of language" requirement on the Constitution as a whole in order to support his argument that the term "Indians" in the *NRTA* includes the Métis. We do not find this approach persuasive. To the contrary, imposing a continuity requirement would lead us to conclude that "Indians" and "Métis" are different, since they are separately enumerated in s. 35(2) of the *Constitution Act, 1982.* We emphasize that we leave open for another day the question of whether the term "Indians" in s. 91(24) of the *Constitution Act, 1867* includes the Métis — an issue not before us in this appeal.

(2) The Ambiguity Principle

[37] In the absence of compelling evidence that the term "Indians" in para. 13 includes the Métis, the appellant invokes the principle that ambiguities should be resolved in favour of Aboriginal peoples: see *Nowegijick v. The Queen,* [1983] 1 S.C.R. 29, at p. 36; *R. v. Sutherland,* [1980] 2 S.C.R. 451, at p. 464; see also *Mitchell v. Peguis Indian Band,* [1990] 2 S.C.R. 85, *per* La Forest J., at pp. 142-43 (suggesting refinements to this principle). This principle is triggered when there are doubts about the most fitting interpretation of the provision in question. ...

[38] The ambiguity principle does not assist the appellant in this case. The historical documentation is sufficient to support the view that the term "Indians" in para. 13 of the *NRTA* was not meant to encompass the Métis. ...

(3) The "Living Tree" Principle

[39] We decline the appellant's invitation to expand the historical purpose of para. 13 on the basis of the "living tree" doctrine enunciated by Lord Sankey L.C. with reference to the 1867 *British North America Act*: *Edwards v. Attorney-General for Canada*, [1930] A.C. 124 (P.C.), at p. 136. ...

[40] This Court has consistently endorsed the living tree principle as a fundamental tenet of constitutional interpretation. Constitutional provisions are intended to provide "a continuing framework for the legitimate exercise of governmental power": *Hunter v. Southam Inc.*, [1984] 2 S.C.R. 145, *per* Dickson J. (as he then was), at p. 155. But at the same time, this Court is not free to invent new obligations foreign to the original purpose of the provision at issue. The analysis must be anchored in the historical context of the provision. ... Similarly, Binnie J. emphasized the need for attentiveness to context when he noted in *R. v. Marshall*, [1999] 3 S.C.R. 456, at para. 14, that "'[g]enerous' rules of interpretation should not be confused with a vague sense of after-the-fact largesse." Again the statement, made with respect to the interpretation of a treaty, applies here.

. . . . .

III. Conclusion

[42] We find no reason to disturb the lower courts' findings that neither the Crown nor the Métis understood the term "Indians" to encompass the Métis in the decades leading up to and including the enactment of the *NRTA*. Paragraph 13 does not provide a defence to the charge against the appellant for unlawfully hunting deer out of season. We do not preclude the possibility that future Métis defendants could argue for site-specific hunting rights in various areas of Manitoba under s. 35 of the *Constitution Act, 1982*, subject to the evidentiary requirements set forth in *Powley, supra*. However, they cannot claim immunity from prosecution under the Manitoba wildlife regulations by virtue of para. 13 of the *NRTA*. ...

As indicated in the above excerpts, historically, Métis people were often seen to fit neither entirely within Indian societies nor within non-Aboriginal society, notwithstanding the fact that Métis people trace their ancestry to both groups. The unique position of the Métis people sometimes worked in their favour, but, at other times, was a hindrance to their relations with other groups.

The following decision of the Supreme Court of Canada examines whether the exclusion of status Indians from Métis settlements in Alberta is contrary to section 2(d), section 7 or section 15 of the *Canadian Charter of*

Rights and Freedoms and hinges upon the distinction between Métis and Indian people.

ALBERTA (ABORIGINAL AFFAIRS AND NORTHERN DEVELOPMENT) V. CUNNINGHAM

[2011] S.C.J. No. 37, [2011] 2 S.C.R. 670 (S.C.C.)

The judgment of the Court was delivered by

McLachlin C.J.C.: —

I. Overview

[1] Section 35 of the *Constitution Act, 1982* recognizes three groups of Aboriginal peoples — Indians, Métis and Inuit. The claimants are members of the Métis settlement of Peavine, Alberta; they are also status Indians. The *Metis Settlements Act*, R.S.A. 2000, c. M-14 ("*MSA*"), does not permit status Indians to become formal members of any Métis settlement, including Peavine. The claimants now apply for a declaration that this denial of membership violates the *Canadian Charter of Rights and Freedoms* guarantees of equality, freedom of association and liberty, and is unconstitutional.

. . . . .

II. The History and Framework of the Program

[5] The Métis were originally the descendants of eighteenth-century unions between European men — explorers, fur traders and pioneers — and Indian women, mainly on the Canadian plains, which now form part of Manitoba, Saskatchewan and Alberta. Within a few generations the descendants of these unions developed a culture distinct from their European and Indian forebears. In early times, the Métis were mostly nomadic. Later, they established permanent settlements centered on hunting, trading and agriculture. The descendants of Francophone families developed their own Métis language derived from French. The descendants of Anglophone families spoke English. In modern times the two groups are known collectively as Métis.

[6] Following *The Royal Proclamation* of 1763, R.S.C. 1985, App. II, No. 1, which organized the territories recently acquired by Great Britain and reserved certain lands for Indians, the Crown adopted a practice of making treaties with Indian bands. Thus most Indians on the prairies are Treaty Indians. In exchange for surrendering their traditional lands to the Crown, they were granted reservations and other benefits, such as the right to hunt and trap on Crown land. Today, the welfare of Indians is dealt with under the *Indian Act*, R.S.C. 1985, c. I-5, which provides a variety of benefits to status Indians living on and off reserve.

[7] The Crown did not apply to the Métis its policy of treating with the Indians and establishing reservations and other benefits in exchange for lands. In some regions, it adopted a scrip system that accorded allotments of land to individual Métis. However, Métis communities were not given a collective reservation or land base; they did not enjoy the protections of the *Indian Act* or any equivalent. Although widely recognized as a culturally-distinct Aboriginal people living in culturally-distinct communities, the law remained blind to the unique history of the Métis and their unique needs.

[8] Governments slowly awoke to this legal lacuna. In 1934, the Alberta legislature established the Ewing Commission, a "Royal Commission Appointed to Investigate the Conditions of the Half-Breed Population of Alberta". The mandate of the Commission was to inquire into "the problems of health, education, relief and general welfare of the half-breed population" and to make recommendations based on its investigation.

[9] The Ewing Commission *Report* (1936) defined the terms "Metis" or "half-breed" for its own purposes as "a person of mixed blood, white and Indian, who lives the life of the ordinary Indian, and includes a non-treaty Indian" but excluding persons of mixed blood (Indian and white) who had settled down as farmers and who did not need or desire public assistance (at p. 4).

[10] *The Metis Population Betterment Act*, S.A. 1938, 2nd Sess., c. 6, was enacted as a result of the findings and recommendations of the Ewing Commission. The term "Metis" was defined in s. 2(*a*) of the Act as:

> ... a person of mixed white and Indian blood but <u>does not include either an Indian or a non-treaty Indian</u> as defined in *The Indian Act*, being chapter 98 of the Revised Statutes of Canada, 1927.

[11] Renamed, *The Metis Betterment Act*, R.S.A. 1955, c. 202, continued to exclude anyone registered as an Indian under the *Indian Act* from the definition of "Metis" and expanded the exclusion to encompass anyone with the ability to be registered as an Indian under the *Indian Act*: s. 2(*a*).

[12] *The Metis Betterment Act*, while according limited statutory recognition to Métis, did not compel the Province of Alberta to establish a land base for Métis communities; nor did it provide adequate support for preservation of the distinct Métis identity and culture. Like the predecessor legislation, it continued to deny the Métis any form of self-government.

[13] The landscape shifted dramatically in 1982, with the passage of the *Constitution Act, 1982*. In the period leading up to the amendment of the Constitution, Indian, Inuit and Métis groups fought for constitutional recognition of their status and rights. ... For the first time, the Métis were acknowledged as a distinct rights-holding group.

[14] In anticipation of the coming into force of the *Constitution Act, 1982*, the Province of Alberta struck a Joint Métis-Government Committee to review *The Metis Betterment Act* and Regulations. The Committee, comprised of the chair, the late Grant MacEwan, who was chosen by the Métis and government, along with two members from government and

two from the Métis community, prepared a report, dated July 12, 1984, setting out its conclusions and recommendations (*Foundations for the Future of Alberta's Metis Settlement* (the "MacEwan Report")).

[15] The MacEwan Report defined a "Métis" simply as "an individual of aboriginal ancestry who identifies with Métis history and culture" (at p. 12), and recommended legislation to secure a land base and self-government for Métis communities in the province. The Alberta legislature accepted these recommendations in principle by authorizing an amendment to the *Constitution of Alberta Amendment Act, 1990*, R.S.A. 2000, c. C-24.

[16] A period of negotiation between the Métis of Alberta and the government of Alberta followed. The negotiations centered on establishing settlement lands for Métis communities, extending self-government to those communities, and ensuring the protection and enhancement of Métis culture and identity. Importantly for this case, the negotiations extended to provisions that would allow the Métis to maintain their separate identity as Métis, distinct from Indians.

[17] These negotiations culminated on July 1, 1989, with the *Alberta-Metis Settlements Accord*. The following year, pursuant to the Accord, Alberta granted the Métis Settlements General Council fee simple title to the lands of the eight Métis communities and passed a suite of legislation to protect Métis rights, including the *MSA* at issue here.

[18] The constitution of Alberta, which, in the British tradition, is unwritten, was amended to provide constitutional recognition for the changes. The preamble to the *Constitution of Alberta Amendment Act, 1990* offers crucial insight into the objects of the legislation:

> WHEREAS the Metis were present when the Province of Alberta was established and they and the land set aside for their use form a unique part of the history and culture of the Province; and
>
> WHEREAS it is desired that the Metis should continue to have a land base to provide for the preservation and enhancement of Metis culture and identity and to enable the Metis to attain self-governance under the laws of Alberta and, to that end, Her Majesty in right of Alberta is granting title to land to the Metis Settlements General Council; and
>
> WHEREAS Her Majesty in right of Alberta has proposed the land so granted be protected by the Constitution of Canada, but until that happens it is proper that the land be protected by the constitution of the Province;
>
> ...

[19] The Recital to the *MSA*, added in 2004, contains the following expression of purpose:

> **0.1** This Act is enacted
>
> (a) recognizing the desire expressed in the *Constitution of Alberta Amendment Act, 1990* that the Metis should continue to have a land base to provide for the preservation and enhancement of Metis culture and identity and to enable the Metis to attain self-governance under the laws of Alberta,

(b) realizing that the Crown in right of Alberta granted land to the Metis Settlements General Council by letters patent and that the patented land is protected by an amendment to the *Constitution of Alberta* and by the *Metis Settlements Land Protection Act,*

(c) in recognition that this Act, the *Constitution of Alberta Amendment Act, 1990,* the *Metis Settlements Land Protection Act* and the *Metis Settlements Accord Implementation Act* were enacted in fulfilment of Resolution 18 of 1985 passed unanimously by the Legislative Assembly of Alberta, and

(d) acknowledging that the Government of Alberta and the Alberta Federation of Metis Settlement Associations made The Alberta-Metis Settlements Accord on July 1, 1989.

[20] The *MSA* defined "Metis" for its purposes as "a person of aboriginal ancestry who identifies with Metis history and culture" (s. 1(j)). Consistent with the negotiations that preceded it and the desire to preserve Métis culture and identity, the *MSA* limited the scope for status Indians to be recognized as members of settlement communities. Section 75 provides that persons registered as Indians or Inuit may not apply for membership in a Métis settlement, unless certain conditions are met and membership is authorized by a settlement bylaw. Because its provisions are central to this case, I set out s. 75 in relevant part:

75(1) An Indian registered under the *Indian Act* (Canada) or a person who is registered as an Inuk for the purposes of a land claims settlement is not eligible to apply for membership or to be recorded as a settlement member unless subsection (2) or (3.1) applies.

(2) An Indian registered under the *Indian Act* (Canada) or a person who is registered as an Inuk for the purposes of a land claims settlement may be approved as a settlement member if

(a) the person was registered as an Indian or an Inuk when less than 18 years old,

(b) the person lived a substantial part of his or her childhood in the settlement area,

(c) one or both parents of the person are, or at their death were, members of the settlement, and

(d) the person has been approved for membership by a settlement bylaw specifically authorizing the admission of that individual as a member of the settlement.

(3) If a person who is registered as an Indian under the *Indian Act* (Canada) is able to apply to have his or her name removed from registration, subsection (2) ceases to be available as a way to apply for or to become a settlement member.

(3.1) In addition to the circumstances under subsection (2), an Indian registered under the *Indian Act* (Canada) or a person who is registered as an Inuk for the purposes of a land claims settlement may be approved as a settlement member if he or she meets the conditions for membership set out in a General Council Policy.

. . .

[21] Additionally, the *Transitional Membership Regulation*, Alta. Reg. 337/90, permitted those registered on a settlement membership list upon the entry into force of the *MSA* to maintain their membership even if they were already registered or were eligible to register as Indians under the *Indian Act*. Persons registering as Indians after the coming into force of the *MSA* on November 1, 1990, were not covered by these grandfathering provisions.

[22] Section 90 of the *MSA* confirms that voluntary registration under the *Indian Act* precludes membership in a Métis settlement unless a General Council Policy provides otherwise:

90(1) Unless a General Council Policy provides otherwise, a settlement member terminates membership in a settlement if

(a) the person voluntarily becomes registered as an Indian under the *Indian Act* (Canada), or

(b) the person becomes registered as an Inuk for the purpose of a land claims agreement.

(2) On receipt from the settlement council of notice of a termination of membership under subsection (1), and after any verification of the facts that is considered necessary, the Minister must remove the name of the person concerned from the Settlement Members List.

No General Council Policy addressing settlement membership for status Indians has been passed.

[23] A settlement member who loses membership under these provisions loses any interest in the settlement land, but may continue to reside on a Métis settlement unless expelled. Sections 91 and 93 provide:

91(1) When the membership of a settlement member terminates or is terminated, the member

(a) loses any rights gained by his or her former membership to reside on or occupy patented land, but

(b) does not lose any right to reside on patented land acquired by or under this or any other enactment, a General Council Policy or a settlement bylaw.

(2) The termination of settlement membership does not affect any right acquired by the spouse or adult interdependent partner or minor children of the member to continue to reside on patented land.

(3) A settlement council and a person whose membership has been terminated may agree on the compensation to be paid to the former settlement member for improvements made on land held by the member and if they cannot agree either of them may refer the matter to the Appeal Tribunal.

...

93(1) A person who is permitted to reside in a settlement area under section 92 is entitled to continue to reside in the area unless the settlement council, for just cause, orders the person expelled from the settlement area.

(1.1) A settlement council may order a person who is not permitted to reside in the settlement area expelled from the settlement area if the person refuses to leave the settlement area on the request of the settlement council.

(2) No order can be made under subsection (1) or (1.1) unless the person concerned has been given an opportunity to tell the settlement council why he or she should be able to remain in the settlement area.

[24] While the negotiations proceeded with the Alberta Métis to achieve a land base, self-governance and support for Métis culture and identity, an important change was made to broaden the definition of who could register as an Indian under the federal *Indian Act*. In *An Act to Amend the Indian Act*, S.C. 1985, c. 27 (Bill C-31), Parliament reinstated the right to Indian status for many Métis settlement members who had been previously denied status, including the claimants. Prior to this amendment, Indian women who married Métis men lost their Indian status and could not pass it to their descendants. The new act went some way towards correcting this injustice, recognized the descendants of these unions, and gave them the option of registering as status Indians.

[25] The claimants, members of the Métis settlement of Peavine, opted to register as status Indians in order to obtain medical benefits under the *Indian Act*. They did so outside the limited window provided by the *Transitional Membership Regulation*. As a result, the Registrar of the Métis Settlements Land Registry revoked their membership in the settlement of Peavine, under s. 90 of *MSA*. They sued for a declaration that s. 90 and its companion provision, s. 75, are inconsistent with ss. 15, 2(*d*) and 7 of the *Charter* in a manner that cannot be justified under s. 1 and are thus null and void under s. 52 of the *Constitution Act, 1982*.

[26] Underlying this litigation is the suggestion that the manner in which the Cunninghams' registration was revoked was procedurally unfair. The list that the Peavine Council submitted to the Registrar of the Métis Settlements Land Registry for revocation of membership did not include all of the members who had obtained Indian status, but only the members of the Cunningham family. Following related proceedings (*Alberta (Minister of International and Intergovernmental Relations) v. Peavine Metis Settlement*, 2001 ABQB 165, [2001] 3 C.N.L.R 1), the Registrar removed the claimants from the Peavine membership list on May 10, 2001. Though bad faith and improper motivations were alleged against the then Council, no judicial review or other action was commenced on that basis. Accordingly, the matter of how the revocation proceeded is not before this Court.

. . . . .

IV. The Equality Claim Under Section 15 of the *Charter*

. . . . . .

C. *Application*

1. Is the Distinction Based on an Enumerated or Analogous Ground of Discrimination?

[56] Following the analysis set out in *Kapp*, the first question is whether the distinction between Métis and status Indians in the *MSA* constitutes a distinction on an enumerated or analogous ground, thereby attracting s. 15 protection. Absent such a distinction, no claim lies under s. 15.

[57] The ground advanced and applied in the courts below is registration as a status Indian, as distinguished from non-status Indians or Métis. This ground was accepted as analogous without much discussion below.

[58] I refrain from making a determination as to whether registration as a status Indian constitutes an analogous ground of discrimination. The trial judge's conclusion that it did constitute an analogous ground was not challenged by the Crown in Right of Alberta before the Court of Appeal and the parties have not thoroughly canvassed the issue before this Court. Since the case has proceeded on the assumption that an analogous ground was made out, I will assume that it has been, and consider the remaining aspects of s. 15 as they apply in this case.

2. Is the Program a Genuinely Ameliorative Program?

[59] To qualify as a genuinely ameliorative program, the program must be directed at improving the situation of a group that is in need of ameliorative assistance: *Kapp*, at para. 41. There must be a correlation between the program and the disadvantage suffered by the target group: *Kapp*, at para. 49. The goal is to promote the substantive equality of the group: *Kapp*, at para. 16. To ascertain whether these conditions are met, one looks first to the object of the program, and then asks whether it correlates to actual disadvantage suffered by the target group.

[60] I begin with the object of the *MSA* program. The discussion that follows establishes that the object of the program is to enhance Métis identity, culture and self-government through the establishment of a Métis land base. This is a special type of ameliorative program. Unlike many ameliorative programs, the object of the program is not the direct conferral of benefits onto individuals within a particular group, but the strengthening of the identity of Métis as a group — one of three aboriginal groups recognized in the Constitution.

[61] The object of an ameliorative program must be determined as a matter of statutory interpretation, having regard to the words of the enactment, expressions of legislative intent, the legislative history, and the history and social situation of the affected groups. Defining the objective of

the ameliorative program too broadly or too narrowly will skew the analysis.

[62] Applying this approach, I conclude that the object of the *MSA* program is not the broad goal of benefiting all Alberta Métis, as the claimants contend, but the narrower goal of establishing a Métis land base to preserve and enhance Métis identity, culture and self-governance, as distinct from surrounding Indian cultures and from other cultures in the province.

[63] I turn first to the words of the enactment. The preamble to the amendments to the *Constitution of Alberta Amendment Act* emphasizes the desire to preserve the "unique" Métis culture and identity. It refers to the land set aside for Métis use as forming "a unique part of the history and culture of the Province". It states that it is desirable "that the Metis should continue to have a land base to provide for the preservation and enhancement of Metis culture and identity and to enable the Metis to attain self-governance".

[64] The *MSA* echoes these objects in its Recital, which proclaims that "the Metis should continue to have a land base to provide for the preservation and enhancement of Metis culture and identity and to enable the Metis to attain self-governance under the laws of Alberta".

[65] The wording of the *MSA*'s provisions supports the view that the object of the ameliorative program was to benefit Métis, as distinct from Indians, by setting up a land base that would strengthen an independent Métis identity, culture and desire for self-governance. The title of the statute, the *"Metis Settlements Act"*, suggests that the focus is not on benefiting the Métis generally, but on establishing land-based settlements. The enactment sets out detailed provisions for the establishment of a Métis land base and governance of the land base by Métis members.

[66] The history of the struggle that culminated in the *MSA* supports this view of the object of the challenged legislation. The *MSA*, as discussed earlier, is the result of a negotiation process between the Métis of Alberta and the Province and the outcome of an ongoing struggle for self-preservation. The Métis considered themselves as one of three Aboriginal groups in Canada, but this was not recognized until the *Constitution Act, 1982*. Unlike Indians, however, they enjoyed no land base from which to strengthen their identity and culture or govern themselves. Nor did they enjoy the protection of an equivalent to the *Indian Act*. Their aboriginality, in a word, was not legally acknowledged or protected. Viewed in this perspective, the ameliorative program embodied in the *MSA* emerges as an attempt to provide to Alberta's Métis settlements similar protections to those which various Indian bands have enjoyed since early times.

[67] From the beginning, the quest that led to the *MSA* was premised on the view that the Métis, while Aboriginals, were unique — that they were different from Indians. The first step was the Ewing Commission in 1934, which led to the recognition that the Métis were distinct from other Aboriginal groups, notably Indians, in *The Metis Population Betterment Act* of 1938. The *MSA*, which was the result of a review of *The Metis Betterment Act*, which was in turn prompted by the recognition of the Métis as a

distinct Aboriginal group in the *Constitution Act, 1982,* maintains the historic insistence on the need to exclude Indians from membership in Métis settlements. The current membership provision is less exclusionary and arbitrary than the earlier statutes, which absolutely excluded all actual and potential status Indians, but the *MSA* maintains the requirement for a distinct Métis settlement which, subject to limited exceptions, excludes status Indians from living on settlement lands.

[68] The *Constitution Act, 1982,* gave constitutional recognition to the Métis as one of three distinct Aboriginal groups, provoking review of *The Metis Betterment Act* and Regulations. The MacEwan Committee was conceived as a partnership, composed of a jointly-chosen chair and an equal number of Métis and non-Métis Commissioners. The *MSA* was the ultimate result of the Committee's work and the negotiations that followed over the next five years.

[69] In summary, the preamble, wording, legislative history, and social context of the *MSA* combine to support the conclusion that the *MSA* is not a general benefit program, but a unique scheme that seeks to establish a Métis land base to preserve and enhance Métis identity, culture and self-government, as distinct from Indian identity, culture and modes of governance. In seeking this objective, it reflects the constitutional scheme, which endorses Indians, Métis and Inuit as distinct Aboriginal groups with distinct identities, cultures and rights.

[70] Finally, as required by *Kapp*, there is a correlation between the program and the disadvantage suffered by the target group. In this case, the correlation is manifest. The history of the Métis is one of struggle for recognition of their unique identity as the mixed race descendants of Europeans and Indians. Caught between two larger identities and cultures, the Métis have struggled for more than two centuries for recognition of their own unique identity, culture and governance. The constitutional amendments of 1982 and, in their wake, the enactment of the *MSA*, signal that the time has finally come for recognition of the Métis as a unique and distinct people.

[71] I conclude that the *MSA*, while unique, is a genuinely ameliorative program. Provided that the means of implementation chosen by the legislature serves or advances this end, s. 15(2) protects the *MSA* against the charge of discrimination.

3. Does the Distinction Serve or Advance the Object of the Ameliorative Program?

[72] The object of the *MSA* is to benefit the members of a constitutionally identified and protected group by enhancing the identity, culture and self-governance of the group. In order to achieve this object, the legislature has excluded Métis who are also status Indians from membership in the settlement for purposes of establishing a Métis land base. The question is whether this distinction serves or advances its object.

[73] In my view, the line drawn by the *MSA* between Métis and Métis who are also status Indians with respect to membership, serves and

advances the object of the program. It is supported by historic distinctions between Métis and Indian culture; by the fact that, without the distinction, achieving the object of the program would be more difficult; and by the role of the Métis settlement in defining its membership.

[74] Before discussing these matters in more detail, I note that the chambers judge concluded that exclusion of status Indians from membership in the Peavine Métis Settlement furthered the object of enhancing Métis culture, identity and governance. The Court of Appeal, while accepting that the *MSA* was a genuinely ameliorative program, overturned this finding on the basis there was "no evidence" that the exclusion would enhance those goals. In my view, the Court of Appeal erred in demanding positive proof that an impugned distinction will in the future have a particular impact. As *Kapp* makes clear, all the government need show is that it was "rational for the state to conclude that the means chosen to reach its ameliorative goal would contribute to [its ameliorative] purpose": *Kapp*, at para. 49.

(a) *The Program Recognizes the Historic Uniqueness of the Métis*

[75] The object of the *MSA*, as we have seen, is to promote Métis identity, culture and self-governance in recognition of their unique status — aboriginal, yet neither Indian nor Inuit. This object corresponds to historic differences between the Métis and Indians. Since their emergence as a distinct people on the Canadian prairies in the 1700s, the Métis have claimed an identity based on non-Indianness. They have persistently distinguished themselves as a people from the other dominant Aboriginal group in their territory — Indians. The obverse side of the struggle of the Métis to preserve their distinct identity and culture is the fear that overlap and confusion with the larger Indian cultures would put their identity and culture at risk. The right of the Métis to their own non-Indian culture is confirmed by the *Constitution Act, 1982*, s. 35. Line drawing on this basis, far from being irrational, simply reflects the Constitution and serves the legitimate expectations of the Métis.

[76] The distinction in the *MSA* between Métis and status Indians conforms, in general terms, to the different identities and protections enjoyed by each group and recognized in the Constitution. It thus serves to enhance Métis identity and to further the goal of the ameliorative program. The fact that some people may identify as both Métis and Indian does not negate the general correspondence underlying the distinction between the two groups.

(b) *Realizing the Object of the Program*

[77] To accord membership in the *MSA* communities to Métis who are also status Indians would undermine the object of the program of enhancing Métis identity, culture and governance, and would potentially hollow out the goal of the *MSA* of preserving and enhancing a distinct Métis culture, identity and governance.

[78] Extending membership to significant numbers of people with Indian status may undercut the goals of preserving and enhancing the distinctive Métis culture, identity and self-governance into the future. To the extent that status Indians are members of Métis settlements, the distinctive Métis identity, with its historic emphasis on being distinct from Indian identity, would be compromised. And to the extent that status Indians are members of Métis settlements, the goal of self-governance is hampered. For example, Indians who already enjoy the right to hunt off-reserve may have little interest in promoting the right of Métis to hunt outside settlement lands. The same may be ventured for other benefits and privileges. Because the *Indian Act* provides a scheme of benefits to status Indians, ranging from medical care to housing to tax-free status, status Indian members of Métis settlements may have less interest in fighting for similar benefits than Métis without Indian status.

(c) *The Role of the Métis in Defining their Community*

[79] The exclusion of status Indians from membership in the new land-based Métis settlements was the product of a long period of consultation between the government and the Métis. According a measure of respect to this role serves and advances the object of the ameliorative program. It does not insulate the selection of beneficiaries from *Charter* review, to be sure, but it supports the connection between the object of the program and the means chosen to achieve it.

[80] In *R. v. Powley* ... this Court was seized with the task of developing a test for identifying Métis aboriginal rights under s. 35 of the *Constitution Act, 1982,* and identifying the holders of such rights. We recognized that the term "Métis" used in s. 35 "refers to distinctive peoples who, in addition to their mixed ancestry, developed their own customs, way of life, and recognizable group identity separate from their Indian or Inuit and European forebears" (para. 10; see also para. 11). We further held that "[t]he inclusion of the Métis in s. 35 is based on a commitment to recognizing the Métis and enhancing their survival as distinctive communities" (para. 13).

[81] While this case is not about defining entitlement to s. 35 rights, it is about the identification of membership requirements for Métis settlements for the purpose of establishing a Métis land base. The Court's reasons in *Powley* suggest that Métis communities themselves have a significant role to play in this exercise. We wrote, at para. 29:

> As Métis communities continue to organize themselves more formally and to assert their constitutional rights, it is imperative that membership requirements become more standardized so that legitimate rights-holders can be identified.

[82] The self-organization and standardization of the Métis community in Alberta is precisely what the Alberta legislature and the Alberta Métis have together sought to achieve in developing, agreeing upon and enacting the membership requirements found in the *MSA* and challenged

here. The significant role that the Métis must play in defining settlement membership requirements does not mean that this exercise is exempt from *Charter* scrutiny. Nevertheless, it does suggest that the courts must approach the task of reviewing membership requirements with prudence and due regard to the Métis's own conception of the distinct features of their community.

(d) *Conclusion: The Distinction Serves and Advances the Object of the Ameliorative Program*

[83] I conclude that the exclusion from membership in any Métis settlement, including the Peavine Settlement, of Métis who are also status Indians serves and advances the object of the ameliorative program. It corresponds to the historic and social distinction between the Métis and Indians, furthers realization of the object of enhancing Métis identity, culture and governance, and respects the role of the Métis in defining themselves as a people.

[84] It follows that the distinction between Métis and status Indians in the *MSA* does not fall outside the protective reach of s. 15(2). Rather, the distinction is the type of targeted ameliorative program s. 15 was intended to allow legislatures to adopt. Section 15(2) applies, and the exclusion of the claimants from membership in a Métis settlement does not constitute discrimination.

[85] The argument advanced by the claimants in favour of recognition of the multiple identities of many aboriginal individuals does not undermine this conclusion. The claimants argue that people — particularly Aboriginal people — may, for historical reasons, have multiple identities and that the law should respect those identities in all their complexity.

[86] That people, including many Métis, include mixed ethnic and cultural strands in their particular individual identity is clear. However, this does not mean that every program must recognize everyone who holds some claim to a group targeted by an ameliorative program. Mixed identity is a recurrent theme in Canada's ongoing exercise of achieving reconciliation between its Aboriginal peoples and the broader population. It figures, for example, in land claims negotiations between particular Indian groups and the government. Residents of one Indian group frequently also identify themselves with other Indian groups for historical and cultural reasons. Yet lines must be drawn if agreements are to be achieved. The situation of Métis settlements is similar. In order to preserve the unique Métis culture and identity and to assure effective self-governance through a dedicated Métis land base, some line drawing will be required. It follows of necessity that not every person who is a Métis in the broad sense of having Indian-European ancestry and self-identifying with the Métis community, as discussed in *Powley*, may be entitled to the benefit of membership under the *MSA*.

[87] The conclusion of this Court in *Lovelace, per* Iacobucci J., is apposite:

There are important differences among First Nations bands, Métis communities and non-band First Nations, and as stated by L'Heureux-Dube

J. in *Corbiere*, [1999] 2 S.C.R. 203, *supra*, at para. 94, "[t]aking into account, recognizing, and affirming differences between groups in a manner that respects and values their dignity and difference are not only legitimate, but necessary considerations in ensuring that substantive equality is present in Canadian society." [para. 90]

[88] I conclude that the *MSA* is an ameliorative program protected by s. 15(2) of the *Charter*. It follows that the claimants' s. 15 claim must be dismissed.

[The Supreme Court's discussion of freedom of association and liberty under sections 2(d) and 7 of the Charter is omitted].

. . . . .

VII. *Conclusion*

[96] ... I would answer the constitutional questions as follows:

. . . . .

5. Do ss. 75 and/or 90 of the *Metis Settlements Act*, R.S.A. 2000, c. M-14, infringe s. 15 of the *Canadian Charter of Rights and Freedoms*?

   No.

6. If so, is the infringement a reasonable limit prescribed by law as can be demonstrably justified in a free and democratic society under s. 1 of the *Canadian Charter of Rights and Freedoms*?

   It is not necessary to answer this question.

-----

1. The Court concluded at para. 62 that the objective of the *Métis Settlements Act* was "to preserve and enhance Métis identity, culture and self-governance, as distinct from surrounding Indian cultures and from other cultures in the province". Do you agree with the Court's formulation in light of this reasoning? Why were Indians and not non-Indigenous Albertans chosen as the comparator group? Is it possible to consider that the *Métis Settlements Act* was passed to protect Métis peoples' identity, culture and self-government as distinctive from non-Indigenous peoples in the province? Would such a conclusion change the Court's analysis under section 15(2)?

2. The Court concluded at para. 73 that the exclusion of Métis (who are also status Indians) advances the *Métis Settlements Act*'s object and purpose because this distinction "is supported by historic distinctions between Métis and Indian culture; by the fact that, without the distinction, achieving the object of the program would be more difficult; and by the role of the Métis settlement in defining its

membership". In accepting this, the Court found that it was rational for Alberta to conclude that the means chosen to reach its ameliorative goal would contribute to its ameliorative purpose. As such, the Court did not require actual evidence that the exclusion of Indians from Métis settlements would enhance those settlements, as the Alberta Court of Appeal required. What are the advantages and dangers of accepting government rationales in understanding Indigenous rights in Canada?

3. At para. 78, the Court observed: "To the extent that status Indians are members of Métis settlements, the distinctive Métis identity, with its historic emphasis on being distinct from Indian identity, would be compromised." How might people with dual Indigenous citizenship compromise Métis identity? Does the Court assume that Indigenous identity must be singular or distinctive from other groups to be protected under section 15(2)? The Court, at para. 86, writes that "lines must be drawn if agreements are to be achieved". Why must lines be drawn to advance Indigenous issues? Can you identify the assumptions that may underlie this conclusion, since the Court did not seem to be explicit on this point, other than affirming the importance of difference?

4. At paras. 79-82, the Court found that consultation with Métis peoples was a significant factor in accepting the province's exclusion of status Indians from Métis settlements. If First Nations communities excluded Métis people from band membership in negotiated agreements, would the reasoning in this case support such exclusions? Could First Nations communities exclude non-native people from membership under analogous circumstances?

5. Why was the issue of Métis land and governance in Alberta not dealt with under section 35(1) of the *Constitution Act, 1982*?

C. MÉTIS LAND RIGHTS

JOHN BORROWS, "DOMESTICATING DOCTRINES: ABORIGINAL PEOPLES AFTER THE ROYAL COMMISSION"

(2001) 46 McGill L.J. 615 at 655-57 (references omitted)

Metis peoples' presence in the west prior to Confederation was centrally significant to the economic development and expansion of the country. Without their participation the fur trade would have floundered, and political and economic development on the St. Lawrence River and eastern Great Lakes would have been severely delayed or restricted. The Metis Nation was also crucial to ushering western and northern Canada into Confederation and increasing the wealth of the nation by opening up the prairies to agriculture and settlement. These developments could not have occurred without their intercession. The Dominion Parliament's unilateral attempt to survey the old north-west territories around the Red River in 1869 was strongly resisted by the local Metis settlements. The Metis did not feel it was appropriate that they should become a part of the Dominion without their participation and consent. Therefore, after blocking the surveyors from their work, and thereby preventing Canada's expansion into this region, the Metis compelled the government of Sir John A. Macdonald to recognize their interests.

In particular, the Red River Metis formed a Provisional Government that was given authority to negotiate the terms of union with Ottawa and bring the area into Confederation. Representatives of this government traveled to Ottawa as delegates of the Metis people to negotiate conditions for western Canada's entry. They brought with them a locally developed Bill of Rights that expressed their demands. The negotiations were challenging but an agreement was reached and its terms were embodied in the *Manitoba Act* of 1870. The democratic legitimacy of this process was sealed through the Metis Provisional government's acceptance of the agreement before the Dominion and Imperial Parliament's statutory endorsement that made it part of the constitutional law of Canada. The people of the Metis Nation regard the *Manitoba Act* as embodying a treaty that recognizes and affirms their nation to nation relationship with Canada, even though they argue that its provisions concerning land and resources have not been fulfilled.

The Royal Commission [on Aboriginal Peoples] recommended that outstanding Metis land and resource issues be resolved through negotiation on a nation to nation basis. [As of 2012 this has not occurred]. ... This would enable them to resist assimilative pressures and pursue objectives appropriate to their culture that may somewhat differ from Canada's.

First, the Commission noted that Metis people may have a claim to land and resources because their title and rights were not extinguished by the *Manitoba Act, 1870* or the *Dominion Land Act, 1879*. They wrote that since the Acts "contained provisions that might be read as extinguishment measures, their legal efficacy is open to doubt owing to ambiguous wording and the massive irregularities involved in their negotiation and administration". Clem Chartier, a Metis leader, expressed this same conclusion even more strongly when he wrote: "the government allowed gross injustices to be perpetrated against the half-breed people through the implementation of a [land] grant and scrip system, leaving the half-breeds landless ...". The effect of this dispossession led the Commission to its second observation, that Metis people may have a claim to land and resources because of the fiduciary obligation that the Crown owes to Metis people to act in their best interests. If, as they suggested, Metis rights were extinguished due to irregularities in the negotiation and administration of their land and resource rights, the Commission believed that this would constitute a breach of the Dominion's fiduciary duty. Finally, the Commission suggested that Metis people have specific legal rights to lands and resources through particular provisions of these otherwise flawed legislative Acts which purported to protect their interests. For example, the statutory terms negotiated by the Metis Provisional government entitled Metis children to receive 1.4 million acres of land, and these provisions have never been effectively implemented. As a result of these possibilities, the Royal Commission concluded that Metis people have a legal right to lands and resources.

However, the Commission rested their argument for Metis land and resource rights on a broader foundation than mere legal claims. They found that "it is clear to the Commission that the Metis Nation is entitled, both morally and politically, to have access to land bases and land use rights to fulfill its legitimate aspirations as an Aboriginal people". These findings led the Commission to make two significant recommendations for the implementation of Metis land and resource rights. It was recommended that appropriately sized and located territories be given to Metis people in certain provinces to hold for their own purposes, and that these provinces recognize Metis rights to hunt, trap and fish for food.

Since there have been no significant negotiations concerning or recognizing a Métis land base in Manitoba, Métis peoples have long been attempting to secure a recognition of their status before the courts. The issue of Métis land rights in Manitoba first came to the courts as *Dumont v. Canada (Attorney General)*. In 1988, the Manitoba Court of Appeal denied the justiciablity of this case, as the following excerpt illustrates.

DUMONT v. CANADA (ATTORNEY GENERAL)

[1988] M.J. No. 327, 52 D.L.R. (4th) 25, 52 Man. R. (2d) 291, [1988] 5 W.W.R. 193, [1988] 3 C.N.L.R. 39 (Man. C.A.)

Twaddle J.A.: — The plaintiffs challenge the constitutional validity of several pieces of federal legislation enacted between 1871 and 1886. They say the legislation was unconstitutional because it altered provisions of the *Manitoba Act, 1870*, S.C. 1870, c. 3, contrary to the prohibition against such alteration contained in the *Constitution Act, 1871*, 1871 (U.K.), c. 28. The Attorney-General of Canada seeks to abort the challenge on the ground, amongst others, that the validity of the impugned legislation is a matter of academic interest only.

. . . . .

Historical background is helpful to an understanding of the issues which are raised on this appeal.

Rupert's Land was granted to the Hudson's Bay Company by Charles II in 1670. By 1867, the effective authority of the company in Rupert's Land was on the decline. The United Kingdom Parliament was thus able to foresee, and provide for, the eventual union of Rupert's Land with

Canada. Provisions for this union are to be found in the *Constitution Act, 1867* and the *Rupert's Land Act, 1868*, 1868 (U.K.), c. 105. ...

In anticipation of the union of Rupert's Land with Canada, the Parliament of Canada enacted the *Rupert's Land Act, 1869*, S.C. 1869, c. 3, by which it made provision for the future government of the territory. Also in anticipation of the union, the Government of Canada sent survey teams into the territory.

In August, 1869, a number of half-breeds, fearful of the effect the proposed union would have on their use of land, opposed the making of surveys. What followed was, from Canada's viewpoint, rebellion. A number of local inhabitants openly disputed Canada's right to annex the territory, although others were anxious for union. A state of unrest prevailed. The authority of the Company had been weakened by its own inaction. In the absence of an effective ruling power, a provisional government was formed by some of the people.

The Provisional Government (as it styled itself) sent delegates to Ottawa to negotiate the terms on which the territory might be united with Canada. A draft bill resulted from the negotiations. Before its enactment as the *Manitoba Act, 1870* it was approved by what was known as the Assembly of the Provisional Government. This Act, assented to in May, 1870, preceded the effective date on which legislative authority for the government of the territory was vested in the Parliament of Canada by the Order of Her Majesty in Her Imperial Council dated June 23, 1870.

Land rights within the province were provided for in sections 30, 31 and 32 of the *Manitoba Act, 1870* ...

Doubts having been expressed as to the authority of the Parliament of Canada to establish the Province of Manitoba, the United Kingdom Parliament enacted the *Constitution Act, 1871*, which retroactively validated the *Manitoba Act, 1870*. ...

Subsequent legislation enacted by the Parliament of Canada and by the Governor General in Council regulated the allocation of land to half-breed children and the making of claims to land under s. 32 of the *Manitoba Act, 1870*. The plaintiffs allege that the subsequent legislation went beyond mere regulation. They say that it altered or embellished the original statutory provisions. They also say that this alteration or embellishment was contrary to the provisions of s. 6 of the *Constitution Act, 1871*.

I must say that, when I read the impugned legislation, I do not find provisions which can readily be regarded as alterations to the original enactment. Indeed, one of the impugned statutes actually conferred additional rights on individual half-breeds ("Act respecting the appropriation of certain Dominion Lands in Manitoba", S.C. 1874, c. 20). I do not find it necessary, however, to decide this appeal on the basis that the plaintiffs do not have a reasonable cause of action. It is my view that this appeal can be decided on the question of whether the issue which the plaintiffs wish to raise is justiciable.

Before turning to that question, let me make it clear that, for the purpose of this appeal, I assume the truth of all allegations of fact contained in the statement of claim. Those allegations include the allegation that all half-breeds of 1870 were "Métis"; that the Métis of 1870 were a distinct people; and that all their descendants are included within the undefined group of persons constitutionally recognized today as "the Métis people." These allegations which I assume as true also include the allegation that some half-breeds of 1870 did not receive, or were deprived of, constitutionally entrenched rights and the allegation that their loss of those rights was a result of the impugned legislation.

The plaintiffs do not assert any rights of their own. They acknowledge, at least in argument, that the land of which their forebears were deprived cannot be restored to them and that they, the plaintiffs, have no legal right to compensation for the loss. What they seek is a declaration that the impugned legislation was invalid. They seek this declaration not to establish rights arising from that loss, but for a collateral purpose. That purpose is stated in the statement of claim in these terms:

> [I]t would be greatly to the advantage of the Métis, in seeking to achieve a land claims agreement pursuant to s. 35(3) of the *Constitution Act, 1982,* as amended, to obtain a declaration that the federal ... statutes and orders-in-council ... were unconstitutional measures that had the purpose and effect of stripping the Métis of the land base promised to them under Sections 31 and 32 of the *Manitoba Act, 1870.*

The land claims agreement which the Métis seek is being sought extra-judicially. The land claim is rooted in the aboriginal status of the Métis people, a status recognized by s. 35 of the *Constitution Act, 1982*. ...

The fact that the Métis might acquire a community of interest in land under a land claims agreement does not mean that the plaintiffs are claiming that such an interest in the land was given to half-breeds by the *Manitoba Act, 1870.* I can find no allegation in the statement of claim which suggests that the plaintiffs are asserting in this action a community of interest in any land.

Any doubt as to what the plaintiffs are alleging is removed when one reads para. 13 of the statement of claim. It reads in part:

> Approximately 85% of Métis persons entitled to rights under sections 31 and 32 of the Manitoba Act failed to receive or were deprived of such rights by reason of the unconstitutional ... legislation ...

It must follow that some 15% of Métis retained their rights. Such a result is totally inconsistent with a collective grant to a community of persons. Such a grant must stand or fall as an entirety.

It is, in any event, impossible to construe s. 31 of the *Manitoba Act, 1870* as conferring on half-breed children generally a community of interest in the 1,400,000 acres appropriated for the benefit of the families of half-breed residents. The section makes it quite clear that the land was to be divided "among the children of the half-breed heads of families residing in the Province" and "granted to the said children respectively."

The plaintiffs argue that, by reason of the loss of individual land rights, their forebears were unable to assemble the land which should have been theirs into townships. The argument proceeds on the notion that, but for the impugned legislation, individual titles to land within the townships would have been handed down from one generation to the next so that the present generation of Métis people would not only have enjoyed land rights inherited by them as individuals, but would also have enjoyed the social and economic benefits to be derived from belonging to an integrated community. That argument is purely speculative of what might have been. It offers no justification for a finding that the plaintiffs have a community of interest in some unspecified land or that their own rights are at issue. ...

The plaintiffs are not entitled to a declaration merely for the purpose of demonstrating that their forebears were deprived of their rights unconstitutionally. It is a well-established principle that a declaration is not available as a cure for past ills. ...

The rationale for the grant of a declaration in this case can only be its potential utility to the parties in the resolution of the Métis land claim. The granting of a declaration in aid of an extra-judicial claim is illustrated by a number of cases ...

... [T]he declaration sought in this case will not decide an issue essential to the resolution of the extra-judicial claim. The settlement of the Métis claim will not be promoted in any real sense by the making of the declaration sought by the plaintiffs.

For these reasons, I am of the opinion that the appeal should be allowed, the order made in motions court set aside and an order made striking out the plaintiffs' claim against the Attorney-General of Canada. ...

Appeal allowed.

In 1990, the Supreme Court of Canada unanimously overturned Twaddle J.A.'s judgment: see *Dumont v. Canada (Attorney General)*, [1990] S.C.J. No. 17, [1990] 1 S.C.R. 279 (S.C.C.). Justice Wilson explained that the outcome of the case was neither "plain and obvious" nor "beyond doubt", and therefore the action ought to proceed to trial for determination. As well, she stated that the proper interpretation of the *Manitoba Act, 1870*, the *Constitution Act, 1871* and the impugned ancillary legislation would be better determined at trial once a proper factual basis was established.

Since the *Dumont* case, litigation regarding Métis land rights in Manitoba has proceeded through many preliminary phases between 1990 and 2008, as the parties wrangled over procedural issues related to the framing of the case. Jean Teillet, a prominent Métis lawyer, has written about this case in her comprehensive annual *Métis Law in Canada* (see <http://www.pstlaw.ca/resources/MLIC-2011.pdf> at 41):

> The Manitoba Métis Federation and the Native Council of Canada filed what is usually referred to as a "land claim" case in 1981. ... The case does not actually claim any land. Instead, it asks for a series of declarations that Métis were unjustly deprived of land that they had rights to under the *Manitoba Act 1870*. The MMF and seventeen individual Métis seek a declaration that Canada breached the fiduciary obligation it owed to the Métis of Manitoba by the manner in which it implemented ss. 31 and 32 of

the *Manitoba Act*. They claim that the federal Crown had a fiduciary obligation to act in the best interests of the Métis and that this obligation was breached because: (1) land grants were not made promptly and were not grouped according to family; (2) children received land grants before gaining their majority and those lands were not protected from speculators; and (3) Canada stood "idly by" while Manitoba passed various legislation that was unconstitutional which enabled and facilitated the sale of the children's grants. ...

The substance of the case was finally heard before the Manitoba Court of Queen's Bench in 2008: see *Manitoba Metis Federation Inc. v. Canada (Attorney General)*, [2007] M.J. No. 448, [2008] 4 W.W.R. 402, 223 Man. R. (2d) 42 (Man. Q.B.). In reviewing the issues, MacInnes J. found that the case was barred by the relevant limitation period or laches and concluded that the Manitoba Metis Federation did not have standing to bring the case. Furthermore, MacInnes J. found that that the Métis did not hold Aboriginal title and that the Crown had no fiduciary duty toward the Métis under sections 31 and 32 of the *Manitoba Act*. In his conclusion, MacInnes J. wrote:

[1195] ... a lawsuit is decided on legal principles, not political considerations, applied not in a vacuum, but to a set of facts found upon evidence adduced at trial.

[1196] In my opinion, the facts of this case cause me to conclude that as a matter of law the plaintiffs' claim is fundamentally flawed.

[1197] It seeks relief that is in essence of a collective nature, but is underpinned by a factual reality that is individual.

[1198] At the relevant time, the Métis did not live in a communal or collective setting. True, they lived more or less together in parishes, the common connection being religion, language and culture.

[1199] But they held land on an individual basis and were able to and did sell, buy and otherwise deal with their land as did as any other individual, but Indians.

[1200] Sections 31 and 32 of the Act by their language clearly provided for individual grants, and section 32 was not directed at the Métis qua Métis, but to landholders in the area that became Manitoba.

[1201] Given the factual basis for this litigation, I fail to understand how the plaintiffs can now seek collective entitlement to a land base, something they did not enjoy or seek to enjoy at the material time.

[1202] There is nothing in the evidence to suggest that Canada ever discussed or contemplated the creation of a land base for the Métis at the time. Nor is there anything in the language of section 31 or 32 which speaks of or from which one could infer that a land base was intended.

[1203] Indeed, in my view, the evidence is otherwise.

. . . . .

[1205] As I have concluded, the Métis did not hold aboriginal title to the land in question, no fiduciary obligation existed and no fiduciary duty was owed by Canada to the Métis in respect of the land under section 31 or under section 32, which was simply a quieting of titles section, as it states.

[1206] Rather, the duty owed by Canada under these sections was simply a public law duty. And, the language of section 31 and subsections 32(4) and (5) gave Canada a broad discretion in the fulfillment of that duty.

[1207] It is clear that the grants under both sections were not implemented or administered without error or dissatisfaction.

. . . . .

[1209] ... there is no claim of dishonesty, sharp dealing or bad faith attributable to the defendants in the claim as advanced.

[1210] While clearly less than perfect, the evidence does establish that Canada distributed more than 1.4 million acres to the children of the half-breed heads of families as required under section 31, taking care to consult the Métis as to the location of the reserves. As well, following allocation of the entire grant, Canada gave $240 scrip notes to those children who should have received land under the grant.

[1211] In addition, after excluding the heads of half-breed families from sharing in the 1.4 million acre grant, as the Act required, Canada thereafter passed legislation which gave the heads of families, both men and women, an ex gratia grant of $160 scrip.

[1212] As well, Canada did grant patents under subsections 32(1) to (4) of the Act consistent with its interpretation of its obligations thereunder. ...

[1213] The point is, that while clearly less than perfect, the grants were made with little in the way of complaints and no proceedings commenced.

[1214] In my view, this is a case where the court should be guided by the comments of the Supreme Court of Canada in *Blais* when interpreting the Act. At para. 17 of *Blais*, after commenting that a constitutional document (which the Act is) must be read generously, the Court referred to *R. v. Big M Drug Mart Ltd.*, 1985 CanLII 69 (SCC), [1985] 1 S.C.R. 295 at 344, and wrote:

> At the same time it is important not to overshoot the actual purpose of the right or freedom in question, but to recall that the [constitutional provision] was not enacted in a vacuum, and must therefore ... be placed in its proper linguistic, philosophic and historical contexts.

[1215] As well, I am mindful of the words of Binnie J., writing for the majority of the Supreme Court in *R. v. Marshall*, [1999] 3 S.C.R. 456. Although his comments were made in the context of treaty interpretation, not statutory interpretation, as is the case here, it is my view that his words are apposite to the circumstances of this case. He wrote, at para. 14:

> "Generous" rules of interpretation should not be confused with a vague sense of after-the-fact largesse.

[1216] The plaintiffs' action is dismissed.

The Manitoba Court of Appeal upheld MacInnes J.'s findings and dismissed the MMF appeal: see *Manitoba Metis Federation Inc. v. Canada (Attorney General)*, [2010] M.J. No. 219, [2010] 12 W.W.R. 599 (Man. C.A.). The Manitoba Court of Appeal summarized its conclusions at the end of the judgment. It wrote, at para. 737:

> To conclude, I provide the following summary:

> (a) The appellants' claim for a declaration that the Crown breached its fiduciary duty under ss. 31 and 32 of the Act is statute-barred. The request for a declaration of constitutional invalidity of the relevant Orders in Council and statutes of Canada and Manitoba is not subject to a statutory limitation period.

(b) The equitable doctrine of laches does not apply to the claim that Manitoba's statutory enactments were unconstitutional. While it is arguable that the claim that Canada misinterpreted its constitutional obligations under ss. 31 and 32 of the Act is barred by laches, it is not necessary to decide this question because all proceedings commenced by the appellants are moot.

(c) The trial judge's exercise of his judicial discretion not to grant the declaratory relief sought should not be interfered with.

(d) The trial judge did not exercise his discretion on the basis of a wrong principle or commit an error in law in the exercise of his discretion in denying the appellant Manitoba Métis Federation Inc. standing.

(e) A fiduciary relationship arises between the Crown and Aboriginals; the Métis are Aboriginal.

(f) The test for determining whether a fiduciary obligation exists within a Crown-Aboriginal relationship is composed of two parts; a specific or cognizable interest, and an undertaking of discretionary control by the Crown in the nature of a private law duty. A finding of Aboriginal title is not an essential component of a Crown-Aboriginal fiduciary duty or obligation.

(g) The trial judge did not commit palpable and overriding error when he concluded that the appellants failed to prove any breach of duty with respect to any of the five specific complaints made by the appellants. This being so, it is unnecessary to decide whether in the particular circumstances the Crown did in fact owe a fiduciary obligation to the appellants.

(h) With respect to s. 32, the trial judge did not err when he found the obligations associated with s. 32 did not arise in the context of a Crown-Aboriginal relationship. He was correct to conclude there was no fiduciary duty or obligation owed to the settlers.

The case was appealed to the Supreme Court of Canada and leave to appeal was granted: see *Manitoba Métis Federation Inc. v. Canada (Attorney General)*, [2010] S.C.C.A. No. 344 (S.C.C.). The case was argued before the Court on December 13, 2011. The decision had not been released at the time this edition went to press.

The Supreme Court decision will likely be released soon after this edition is published. In reading the Supreme Court's decision, it may be helpful to consider how the issues were viewed from a Métis perspective. The Métis Nation of Alberta was among the many interveners in the MMF and their factum provides a helpful summary of their point of view: see <http://www.metisnation.org/media/188839/mmf%20case%20-%20inter vener%20factum%20-%20mna.pdf>:

1) This is a case about the promise of land *for the benefit* of one of Canada's aboriginal negotiating partners in Confederation — the Manitoba Métis. It is the story of a growing nation encountering a new aboriginal people, in possession, on the land, in the historic Northwest, and making solemn commitments to them in order to secure its desired westward expansion. It is also the story of a young aboriginal people, uniquely born in the historic Northwest asserting their rights and interests in a territory they called home,

and ultimately securing promises for the protection of their distinct identity[1] and lands in a new province and growing nation. Those promises — solemn linguistic (s. 23), religious (s. 22) and land related (ss. 31 and 32) commitments — are embedded within the *Manitoba Act, 1870*, and are a part of Canada's constitution. This appeal is this Court's first opportunity to consider ss. 31 and 32 — the land related commitments to the Manitoba Métis.

2) In 1870, the Métis, who represented 85% of the total population in the Red River Settlement, agreed to put down their arms, participate as citizens of the new province of Manitoba, and extinguish their "Indian title" throughout the 8.2 million acres that made up the new "postage stamp" province of Manitoba *in exchange* for the protection of their <u>existing</u> land base (s. 32) as well as the protection of their <u>future</u> by way of an additional 1.4 million acres for their children (s. 31), which represented approximately 17% of the new province's land. Read purposively, ss. 31 and 32 represented an attempt to protect the 1870 existence of the Manitoba Métis as well as their collective future *through* a land base. That was the underlying purpose of the constitutional commitment.

3) The Appellants argue, with the support of the Métis Nation of Alberta ("MNA"), that the Crown, in its interpretation and implementation of ss. 31 and 32, breached its fiduciary and constitutional duties owing to the Manitoba Métis. The Manitoba Métis never received *the benefit* that was fundamental to the constitutional compact. Instead, because of government action and inaction (i.e., the great delay, random selection, etc.), they became a marginalized and landless aboriginal people in the province they helped to establish.

[1] The MNA notes this unique Métis identity included many aspects that were at odds with Canada's political establishment at the time. The Métis were predominantly French-speaking and had their own language — Michif — that combined French and Indian languages; they were largely Catholic; they had their own land use customs; they were a mobile aboriginal hunting society. This uniqueness necessitated the *Manitoba Act, 1870* to attempt to reconcile diversity within unity. Today, the Métis Nation continues to work to reconcile their uniqueness — as a distinct aboriginal people — within Canada. It is hoped that this case will assist in the furtherance of this goal.

D. MÉTIS ABORIGINAL RIGHTS

In addition to the controversy surrounding Métis land rights, Métis people face difficulties in attempting to establish other Aboriginal rights under section 35(1) of the *Constitution Act, 1982*. There are serious unanswered questions about the scope and extent of Métis Aboriginal rights. For example, Lamer C.J.C. and L'Heureux-Dubé J. both commented on the definition of Métis Aboriginal rights in their judgments in the Supreme Court of Canada's decision in *R. v. Van der Peet*, below.

R. v. VAN DER PEET

[1996] S.C.J. No. 77, [1996] 4 C.N.L.R. 177, [1996] 9 W.W.R. 1, 23 B.C.L.R.
(3d) 1, 50 C.R. (4th) 1, 137 D.L.R. (4th) 289, 109 C.C.C. (3d) 1, 200 N.R. 1
(S.C.C.)

Lamer C.J.C.: —

[66] ... I would note that basing the identification of aboriginal rights in the period prior to contact is not inconsistent with the fact that s. 35(2) of the *Constitution Act, 1982* includes within the definition of "aboriginal peoples of Canada" the Métis people of Canada.

[67] Although s. 35 includes the Métis within its definition of "aboriginal peoples of Canada", and thus seems to link their claims to those of other aboriginal peoples under the general heading of "aboriginal rights", the history of the Métis, and the reasons underlying their inclusion in the protection given by s. 35, are quite distinct from those of other aboriginal peoples in Canada. As such, the manner in which the aboriginal rights of other aboriginal peoples are defined is not necessarily determinative of the manner in which the aboriginal rights of the Métis are defined. At the time when this Court is presented with a Métis claim under s. 35 it will then, with the benefit of the arguments of counsel, a factual context and a specific Métis claim, be able to explore the question of the purposes underlying s. 35's protection of the aboriginal rights of Métis people, and answer the question of the kinds of claims which fall within s. 35(1)'s scope when the claimants are Métis. The fact that, for other aboriginal peoples, the protection granted by s. 35 goes to the practices, customs and traditions of aboriginal peoples prior to contact, is not necessarily relevant to the answer which will be given to that question. It may, or it may not, be the case that the claims of the Métis are determined on the basis of the pre-contact practices, customs and traditions of their aboriginal ancestors; whether that is so must await determination in a case in which the issue arises.

. . . . .

L'Heureux-Dubé J.: —

[169] ... [W]hen examining the wording of the constitutional provisions regarding aboriginal rights, it appears that the protection should not be limited to pre-contact or pre-sovereignty practices, traditions and customs. Section 35(2) of the *Constitution Act, 1982* provides that the "'aboriginal peoples of Canada' includes the Indian, Inuit and *Métis* peoples of Canada" (emphasis added). Obviously, there were no Métis people prior to contact with Europeans as the Métis are the result of intermarriage between natives and Europeans ... Section 35(2) makes it clear that aboriginal rights are indeed guaranteed to Métis people. As a result, according to the text of the Constitution of Canada, it must be possible for aboriginal rights to arise after British sovereignty, so that Métis people can benefit from the constitutional protection of s. 35(1). The case-by-case

application of s. 35(2) of the *Constitution Act, 1982* proposed by the Chief Justice does not address the issue of the interpretation of s. 35(2).

In *Van der Peet*, Métis Aboriginal rights were not a major focus. Thus, the case did not provide the necessary detail as to how Métis claims could be established as Aboriginal rights within section 35(1) of the *Constitution Act, 1982*. Thus, in 2003, when the Supreme Court of Canada considered a case dealing with Métis rights in Ontario, *R. v. Powley*, [2003] S.C.J. No. 43, [2003] 2 S.C.R. 207 (S.C.C.), it became the leading case on the issue. As you read the *Powley* case in the following pages, try to identify how Métis rights relate to Indian and Inuit rights.

R. v. POWLEY

[2003] S.C.J. No. 43, [2003] 2 S.C.R. 207 (S.C.C.)

THE COURT: —

I. Introduction

[1] This case raises the issue of whether members of the Métis community in and around Sault Ste. Marie enjoy a constitutionally protected right to hunt for food under s. 35 of the *Constitution Act, 1982*. ...

[2] On the morning of October 22, 1993, Steve Powley and his son, Roddy, set out hunting. They headed north from their residence in Sault Ste. Marie, and at about 9 a.m., they shot and killed a bull moose near Old Goulais Bay Road.

[3] Moose hunting in Ontario is subject to strict regulation. The Ministry of Natural Resources ("MNR") issues Outdoor Cards and validation stickers authorizing the bearer to harvest calf moose during open season. ... The validation tag requirement and seasonal restrictions are not enforced against Status Indians, and the MNR does not record Status Indians' annual harvest. ...

[4] After shooting the bull moose near Old Goulais Bay Road, Steve and Roddy Powley transported it to their residence in Sault Ste. Marie. Neither of them had a valid Outdoor Card, a valid hunting licence to hunt moose, or a validation tag issued by the MNR. In lieu of these documents, Steve Powley affixed a handwritten tag to the ear of the moose. The tag indicated the date, time, and location of the kill, as required by the hunting regulations. It stated that the animal was to provide meat for the winter. Steve Powley signed the tag, and wrote his Ontario Métis and Aboriginal Association membership number on it.

[5] Later that day, two conservation officers arrived at the Powleys' residence. The Powleys told the officers they had shot the moose. One week later, the Powleys were charged with unlawfully hunting moose and

knowingly possessing game hunted in contravention of the *Game and Fish Act*, R.S.O. 1990, c. G-1. They both entered pleas of not guilty.

. . . . .

[8] The question before us is whether ss. 46 and 47(1) of the *Game and Fish Act*, which prohibit hunting moose without a licence, unconstitutionally infringe the respondents' aboriginal right to hunt for food, as recognized in s. 35(1) of the *Constitution Act, 1982*.

II. Analysis

. . . . .

[10] The term "Métis" in s. 35 does not encompass all individuals with mixed Indian and European heritage; rather, it refers to distinctive peoples who, in addition to their mixed ancestry, developed their own customs, way of life, and recognizable group identity separate from their Indian or Inuit and European forebears. Métis communities evolved and flourished prior to the entrenchment of European control, when the influence of European settlers and political institutions became pre-eminent. ... "What distinguishes Métis people from everyone else is that they associate themselves with a culture that is distinctly Métis" (*RCAP Report*, vol. 4, at p. 202).

[11] The Métis of Canada share the common experience of having forged a new culture and a distinctive group identity from their Indian or Inuit and European roots. This enables us to speak in general terms of "the Métis". However, particularly given the vast territory of what is now Canada, we should not be surprised to find that different groups of Métis exhibit their own distinctive traits and traditions. This diversity among groups of Métis may enable us to speak of Métis "peoples", a possibility left open by the language of s. 35(2), which speaks of the "Indian, Inuit and Métis peoples of Canada".

[12] We would not purport to enumerate the various Métis peoples that may exist. ...

[13] Our evaluation of the respondents' claim takes place against this historical and cultural backdrop. ...

[14] For the reasons elaborated below, we uphold the basic elements of the *Van der Peet* test (*R. v. Van der Peet*, [1996] 2 S.C.R. 507) and apply these to the respondents' claim. However, we modify certain elements of the pre-contact test to reflect the distinctive history and post-contact ethnogenesis of the Métis, and the resulting differences between Indian claims and Métis claims.

. . . . .

[16] The emphasis on prior occupation as the primary justification for the special protection accorded aboriginal rights led the majority in *Van der Peet* to endorse a pre-contact test for identifying which customs, practices

or traditions were integral to a particular aboriginal culture, and therefore entitled to constitutional protection. However, the majority recognized that the pre-contact test might prove inadequate to capture the range of Métis customs, practices or traditions that are entitled to protection, since Métis cultures by definition post-date European contact. For this reason, Lamer C.J. explicitly reserved the question of how to define Métis aboriginal rights for another day. He wrote at para. 67:

> [T]he history of the Métis, and the reasons underlying their inclusion in the protection given by s. 35, are quite distinct from those of other aboriginal peoples in Canada. As such, the manner in which the aboriginal rights of other aboriginal peoples are defined is not necessarily determinative of the manner in which the aboriginal rights of the Métis are defined. ...

[17] As indicated above, the inclusion of the Métis in s. 35 is not traceable to their pre-contact occupation of Canadian territory. The purpose of s. 35 as it relates to the Métis is therefore different from that which relates to the Indians or the Inuit. The constitutionally significant feature of the Métis is their special status as peoples that emerged between first contact and the effective imposition of European control. The inclusion of the Métis in s. 35 represents Canada's commitment to recognize and value the distinctive Métis cultures, which grew up in areas not yet open to colonization, and which the framers of the *Constitution Act, 1982* recognized can only survive if the Métis are protected along with other aboriginal communities.

[18] With this in mind, we proceed to the issue of the correct test to determine the entitlements of the Métis under s. 35 of the *Constitution Act, 1982*. ... Section 35 requires that we recognize and protect those customs and traditions that were historically important features of Métis communities prior to the time of effective European control, and that persist in the present day. This modification is required to account for the unique post-contact emergence of Métis communities, and the post-contact foundation of their aboriginal rights.

(1) Characterization of the Right

[19] The first step is to characterize the right being claimed: *Van der Peet, supra*, at para. 76. Aboriginal hunting rights, including Métis rights, are contextual and site-specific. The respondents shot a bull moose near Old Goulais Bay Road, in the environs of Sault Ste. Marie, within the traditional hunting grounds of that Métis community. They made a point of documenting that the moose was intended to provide meat for the winter. The trial judge determined that they were hunting for food, and there is no reason to overturn this finding. The right being claimed can therefore be characterized as the right to hunt for food in the environs of Sault Ste. Marie.

[20] We agree with the trial judge that the periodic scarcity of moose does not in itself undermine the respondents' claim. The relevant right is not to hunt moose but to hunt for <u>food</u> in the designated territory.

(2) Identification of the Historic Rights-Bearing Community

[21] The trial judge found that a distinctive Métis community emerged in the Upper Great Lakes region in the mid-17th century, and peaked around 1850. We find no reviewable error in the trial judge's findings on this matter, which were confirmed by the Court of Appeal. The record indicates the following: In the mid-17th century, the Jesuits established a mission at Sainte-Marie-du-Sault, in an area characterized by heavy competition among fur traders. In 1750, the French established a fixed trading post on the south bank of the Saint Mary's River. The Sault Ste. Marie post attracted settlement by Métis — the children of unions between European traders and Indian women, and their descendants. ... According to Dr. Ray, by the early 19th century, "[t]he settlement at Sault Ste. Marie was one of the oldest and most important [Métis settlements] in the upper lakes area". ...

. . . . .

[23] In addition to demographic evidence, proof of shared customs, traditions, and a collective identity is required to demonstrate the existence of a Métis community that can support a claim to site-specific aboriginal rights. We recognize that different groups of Métis have often lacked political structures and have experienced shifts in their members' self-identification. However, the existence of an identifiable Métis community must be demonstrated with some degree of continuity and stability in order to support a site-specific aboriginal rights claim. Here, we find no basis for overturning the trial judge's finding of a historic Métis community at Sault Ste. Marie. This finding is supported by the record and must be upheld.

(3) Identification of the Contemporary Rights-Bearing Community

[24] Aboriginal rights are communal rights: They must be grounded in the existence of a historic and present community, and they may only be exercised by virtue of an individual's ancestrally based membership in the present community. The trial judge found that a Métis community has persisted in and around Sault Ste. Marie despite its decrease in visibility after the signing of the Robinson-Huron Treaty in 1850. While we take note of the trial judge's determination that the Sault Ste. Marie Métis community was to a large extent an "invisible entity" ([1999] 1 C.N.L.R. 153, at para. 80) from the mid-19th century to the 1970s, we do not take this to mean that the community ceased to exist or disappeared entirely.

[25] Dr. Lytwyn describes the continued existence of a Métis community in and around Sault Ste. Marie despite the displacement of many of the community's members in the aftermath of the 1850 treaties:

[T]he Métis continued to live in the Sault Ste. Marie region. Some drifted
into the Indian Reserves which had been set apart by the 1850 Treaty. Others
lived in areas outside of the town, or in back concessions. The Métis
continued to live in much the same manner as they had in the past —
fishing, hunting, trapping and harvesting other resources for their
livelihood. ...

[26] The advent of European control over this area thus interfered with,
but did not eliminate, the Sault Ste. Marie Métis community and its
traditional practices, as evidenced by census data from the 1860s through
the 1890s. Dr. Lytwyn concluded from this census data that "[a]lthough
the Métis lost much of their traditional land base at Sault Ste. Marie, they
continued to live in the region and gain their livelihood from the resources
of the land and waters" (Lytwyn Report, at p. 32). He also noted a
tendency for underreporting and lack of information about the Métis
during this period because of their "removal to the peripheries of the
town", and "their own disinclination to be identified as Métis" in the wake
of the Riel rebellions and the turning of Ontario public opinion against
Métis rights through government actions and the media ...

[27] We conclude that the evidence supports the trial judge's finding
that the community's lack of visibility was explained and does not negate
the existence of the contemporary community. There was never a lapse;
the Métis community went underground, so to speak, but it continued.
Moreover, as indicated below, the "continuity" requirement puts the focus
on the continuing practices of members of the community, rather than
more generally on the community itself, as indicated below.

[28] The trial judge's finding of a contemporary Métis community in
and around Sault Ste. Marie is supported by the evidence and must be
upheld.

(4) Verification of the Claimant's Membership in the Relevant Contemporary Community

[29] While determining membership in the Métis community might not
be as simple as verifying membership in, for example, an Indian band, this
does not detract from the status of Métis people as full-fledged rights-
bearers. As Métis communities continue to organize themselves more
formally and to assert their constitutional rights, it is imperative that
membership requirements become more standardized so that legitimate
rights-holders can be identified. In the meantime, courts faced with Métis
claims will have to ascertain Métis identity on a case-by-case basis. The
inquiry must take into account both the value of community self-
definition, and the need for the process of identification to be objectively
verifiable. In addition, the criteria for Métis identity under s. 35 must
reflect the purpose of this constitutional guarantee: to recognize and affirm
the rights of the Métis held by virtue of their direct relationship to this
country's original inhabitants and by virtue of the continuity between their
customs and traditions and those of their Métis predecessors. This is not an
insurmountable task.

[30] We emphasize that we have not been asked, and we do not purport, to set down a comprehensive definition of who is Métis for the purpose of asserting a claim under s. 35. We therefore limit ourselves to indicating the important components of a future definition, while affirming that the creation of appropriate membership tests before disputes arise is an urgent priority. ... In particular, we would look to three broad factors as indicia of Métis identity for the purpose of claiming Métis rights under s. 35: self-identification, ancestral connection, and community acceptance.

[31] First, the claimant must <u>self-identify</u> as a member of a Métis community. This self-identification should not be of recent vintage: While an individual's self-identification need not be static or monolithic, claims that are made belatedly in order to benefit from a s. 35 right will not satisfy the self-identification requirement.

[32] Second, the claimant must present evidence of an <u>ancestral connection</u> to a historic Métis community. This objective requirement ensures that beneficiaries of s. 35 rights have a real link to the historic community whose practices ground the right being claimed. We would not require a minimum "blood quantum", but we would require some proof that the claimant's ancestors belonged to the historic Métis community by birth, adoption, or other means. ... In this case, the Powleys' Métis ancestry is not disputed.

[33] Third, the claimant must demonstrate that he or she is <u>accepted by the modern community</u> whose continuity with the historic community provides the legal foundation for the right being claimed. Membership in a Métis political organization may be relevant to the question of community acceptance, but it is not sufficient in the absence of a contextual understanding of the membership requirements of the organization and its role in the Métis community. The core of community acceptance is past and ongoing participation in a shared culture, in the customs and traditions that constitute a Métis community's identity and distinguish it from other groups. This is what the community membership criterion is all about. Other indicia of community acceptance might include evidence of participation in community activities and testimony from other members about the claimant's connection to the community and its culture. The range of acceptable forms of evidence does not attenuate the need for an objective demonstration of a solid bond of past and present mutual identification and recognition of common belonging between the claimant and other members of the rights-bearing community.

[34] It is important to remember that, no matter how a contemporary community defines membership, only those members with a demonstrable ancestral connection to the historic community can claim a s. 35 right. Verifying membership is crucial, since individuals are only entitled to exercise Métis aboriginal rights by virtue of their ancestral connection to and current membership in a Métis community.

[35] In this case, there is no reason to overturn the trial judge's finding that the Powleys are members of the Métis community that arose and still exists in and around Sault Ste. Marie. We agree with the Court of Appeal

that, in the circumstances of this case, the fact that the Powleys' ancestors lived on an Indian reserve for a period of time does not negate the Powleys' Métis identity. As the Court of Appeal indicated, "E.B. Borron, commissioned in 1891 by the province to report on annuity payments to the Métis, was of the view that Métis who had taken treaty benefits remained Métis and he recommended that they be removed from the treaty annuity lists" ((2001), 53 O.R. (3d) 35, at para. 139, *per* Sharpe J.A.). We emphasize that the individual decision by a Métis person's ancestors to take treaty benefits does not necessarily extinguish that person's claim to Métis rights. It will depend, in part, on whether there was a collective adhesion by the Métis community to the treaty. Based on the record, it was open to the trial judge to conclude that the rights of the Powleys' ancestors did not merge into those of the Indian band.

(5) Identification of the Relevant Time Frame

[36] As indicated above, the pre-contact aspect of the *Van der Peet* test requires adjustment in order to take account of the post-contact ethnogenesis of the Métis and the purpose of s. 35 in protecting the historically important customs and traditions of these distinctive peoples. While the fact of prior occupation grounds aboriginal rights claims for the Inuit and the Indians, the recognition of Métis rights in s. 35 is not reducible to the Métis' Indian ancestry. The unique status of the Métis as an Aboriginal people with post-contact origins requires an adaptation of the pre-contact approach to meet the distinctive historical circumstances surrounding the evolution of Métis communities.

[37] The pre-contact test in *Van der Peet* is based on the constitutional affirmation that aboriginal communities are entitled to continue those practices, customs and traditions that are integral to their distinctive existence or relationship to the land. By analogy, the test for Métis practices should focus on identifying those practices, customs and traditions that are integral to the Métis community's distinctive existence and relationship to the land. This unique history can most appropriately be accommodated by a post-contact but pre-control test that identifies the time when Europeans effectively established political and legal control in a particular area. The focus should be on the period after a particular Métis community arose and before it came under the effective control of European laws and customs. This pre-control test enables us to identify those practices, customs and traditions that predate the imposition of European laws and customs on the Métis.

[38] We reject the appellant's argument that Métis rights must find their origin in the pre-contact practices of the Métis' aboriginal ancestors. This theory in effect would deny to Métis their full status as distinctive rights-bearing peoples whose own integral practices are entitled to constitutional protection under s. 35(1). The right claimed here was a practice of both the Ojibway and the Métis. However, as long as the practice grounding the right is distinctive and integral to the pre-control Métis community, it will satisfy this prong of the test. This result flows from the constitutional

imperative that we recognize and affirm the aboriginal rights of the Métis, who appeared after the time of first contact.

. . . . .

[40] The historical record indicates that the Sault Ste. Marie Métis community thrived largely unaffected by European laws and customs until colonial policy shifted from one of discouraging settlement to one of negotiating treaties and encouraging settlement in the mid-19th century. The trial judge found, and the parties agreed in their pleadings before the lower courts, that "effective control [of the Upper Great Lakes area] passed from the Aboriginal peoples of the area (Ojibway and Metis) to European control" in the period between 1815 and 1850 (para. 90). The record fully supports the finding that the period just prior to 1850 is the appropriate date for finding effective control in this geographic area, which the Crown agreed was the critical date in its pleadings below.

(6) Determination of Whether the Practice is Integral to the Claimants' Distinctive Culture

[41] The practice of subsistence hunting and fishing was a constant in the Métis community, even though the availability of particular species might have waxed and waned. The evidence indicates that subsistence hunting was an important aspect of Métis life and a defining feature of their special relationship to the land ...

[42] Peterson describes the Great Lakes Métis communities as follows at p. 41:

> These people were neither adjunct relative-members of tribal villages nor the standard bearers of European civilization in the wilderness. Increasingly, they stood apart or, more precisely, in between. By the end of the last struggle for empire in 1815, their towns, which were visually, ethnically and culturally distinct from neighbouring Indian villages and "white towns" along the eastern seaboard, stretched from Detroit and Michilimackinac at the east to the Red River at the northwest.
>
> ... [R]esidents [of these trading communities] ... drew upon a local subsistence base rather than on European imports. ... [S]uch towns grew as a result of and were increasingly dominated by the offspring of Canadian trade employees and Indian women who, having reached their majority, were intermarrying among themselves and rearing successive generations of métis. In both instances, these communities did not represent an extension of French, and later British colonial culture, but were rather "adaptation[s] to the Upper Great Lakes environment." [Emphasis added.]

[43] Dr. Ray emphasized in his report that a key feature of Métis communities was that "their members earned a substantial part of their livelihood off of the land" (Ray Report, *supra*, at p. 56 (emphasis deleted)). Dr. Lytwyn concurred: "The Métis of Sault Ste. Marie lived off the resources of the land. They obtained their livelihood from hunting, fishing, gathering and cultivating" (Lytwyn Report, at p. 2). He reported that "[w]hile Métis fishing was prominent in the written accounts, hunting was

also an important part of their livelihood", and that "[a] traditional winter hunting area for the Sault Métis was the Goulais Bay area" (Lytwyn Report, at pp. 4-5). ...

[44] This evidence supports the trial judge's finding that hunting for food was integral to the Métis way of life at Sault Ste. Marie in the period just prior to 1850.

(7) Establishment of Continuity Between the Historic Practice and the Contemporary Right Asserted

[45] Although s. 35 protects "existing" rights, it is more than a mere codification of the common law. Section 35 reflects a new promise: a constitutional commitment to protecting practices that were historically important features of particular aboriginal communities. ... Hunting for food was an important feature of the Sault Ste. Marie Métis community, and the practice has been continuous to the present. Steve and Roddy Powley claim a Métis aboriginal right to hunt for food. The right claimed by the Powleys falls squarely within the bounds of the historical practice grounding the right.

(8) Determination of Whether or Not the Right Was Extinguished

[46] The doctrine of extinguishment applies equally to Métis and to First Nations claims. There is no evidence of extinguishment here, as determined by the trial judge. The Crown's argument for extinguishment is based largely on the Robinson-Huron Treaty of 1850, from which the Métis as a group were explicitly excluded.

(9) If There Is a Right, Determination of Whether There Is an Infringement

[47] Ontario currently does not recognize any Métis right to hunt for food, or any "special access rights to natural resources" for the Métis whatsoever (appellant's record, at p. 1029). This lack of recognition, and the consequent application of the challenged provisions to the Powleys, infringe their aboriginal right to hunt for food as a continuation of the protected historical practices of the Sault Ste. Marie Métis community.

. . . . .

III. Conclusion

[53] Members of the Métis community in and around Sault Ste. Marie have an aboriginal right to hunt for food under s. 35(1). ...

――――――――

1. In para. 10 of the *Powley* decision, the Court wrote that the term "Métis" in section 35(1) refers to distinctive peoples. Professor Catherine Bell has written about the importance of defining Aboriginal rights as the rights of "peoples" in her article "Métis Aboriginal Rights in Section 35(1)" (1997) 36 Alta. L. Rev. 180 at 184, 189-90:

A consideration of both ancestral origins and legal origins takes comprehensive rights analysis beyond rights sourced in racial descent to rights sourced in essential attributes of "peoplehood or nationhood". Adopting this approach, a proper interpretation of rights in s. 35 is one which places equal emphasis on the words "aboriginal" and "peoples" in assessing the origin, scope and content of Aboriginal rights.

Rights arising from peoplehood are uncertain because the word "peoples" is not defined in Canadian constitutional law and minimal domestic judicial opinion has been rendered on this point. However, it is a term which was used frequently in international political discourse at the time s. 35 was negotiated to distinguish colonized indigenous populations from nation states and ethnic minority immigrant populations within those states. The identification as colonized peoples carried with it potential recognition of land rights sourced in original occupation of colonized territories as well as human rights sourced in existence as a people. The main distinction drawn between the human rights of ethnic minority populations and indigenous peoples was the existence of political rights arising from the injustices perpetrated by the project of colonization. The most fundamental of these political rights are the rights to self-determine membership in, and governmental relations with, nation states, or alternatively, the right to secede. Other human rights attributed to self-determining peoples then and now include: the right to economic, cultural and social development; the right to "maintain and strengthen their distinct identities and characteristics"; the right to "maintain and develop their distinctive spiritual and material relationship with the lands" and the right to restitution for unlawful termination of these rights. ...

Understood in this context, s. 35(1) does not address injustices arising from a theoretical shift in legal and political regimes that occurs as a result of the assertion of sovereignty but actual injustices suffered by "peoples" as a corollary of British sovereignty through the historical process of colonization. Although the date of colonization varies across the country depending on the historical circumstances of colonization, British colonial law is constant in determining the effects of this process on the survival of distinct Aboriginal social and political constitutions. ...

If both the concepts of sovereignty and colonization are adopted as key organizational principles for interpreting s. 35, the inclusion of Canada as colonizer is a natural extension of s. 35 analysis. Prior to its emergence as an independent nation state, the Dominion of Canada operated as the colonizing arm of British Imperial government. It assumed the rights and responsibilities of the Imperial colonizer toward Indian and Inuit peoples under s. 91(24) of the *Constitution Act, 1867* and imposed British rule through negotiation, occupation and force.

Can section 35(1) more effectively address the troubling consequences of colonization for Aboriginal peoples, including the Métis? Should the acceptance of Aboriginal groups as "peoples" within section 35(1) hold broader human rights significance in addressing colonialism?

2.   What is the relationship and relevance of the three different time periods established for proof of section 35(1) rights: Aboriginal rights (contact), Aboriginal title (assertion of sovereignty) and Métis hunting rights (prior to the time of effective European control — as seen in para. 17 and 18 of the *Powley* decision)?

3.   At para. 29 of the *Powley* decision, the Supreme Court of Canada wrote that "it is imperative that [Métis] membership requirements become more standardized so that legitimate rights-holders can be identified." What are the implications of this statement for the control of Aboriginal peoples by the Canadian state? What are the potential positive and negative implications of creating Métis "status" under section 35(1), even if Métis people impose such standardized membership on themselves?

4.   The Supreme Court of Canada wrote that Métis self-identity cannot be of recent vintage (para. 31). What consequences might this finding have for Métis children who had been adopted by non-Aboriginal families and only recently discovered their heritage? What consequences might the Court's ruling regarding "vintage" have for the growth of Métis society through future intermarriage and the extension of non-racially based political membership? What assumptions, stereotypes or ideologies underlie the notion that Métis identity must be old in some way?

5.   The *Powley* judgment states that the claimant must present evidence of an "ancestral connection" to have a "real link" with an historic Métis community (para. 32). When non-Aboriginal traders or farmers married an Indian or Métis person between 1750 and 1850 in Sault Ste. Marie (see para. 21) it was likely such people did not have an ancestral connection to Métis communities prior to their marriage. However, after marriage they often became an important part of that community. How does the Court's insistence on ancestry square with these experiences, which were arguably integral to Métis communities before "European control"? Does the Court's fixation on ancestry mean that a non-Aboriginal person could never have a "real link" with a Métis community, such that this connection would create constitutional rights for them? If ancestry is a key to Métis identity, how does a Métis community grow in modern Canada if non-Aboriginal people cannot become part of these communities when they marry-in or otherwise meaningfully participate in the life of these communities?

6.   If a Métis person must be "accepted by the modern community" to prove rights (para. 33), what might occur if such a person was formally removed from the community because he or she chose to dissent from it in some meaningful way. For example, one could imagine a scenario where a Métis person is struck from community rolls because of opposition to the majority's political will. Would this action disentitle a person to claim Métis rights under the *Powley* guidelines? Note that the Ontario Court of Justice has held that a "modern community" to which Métis rights can attach does not

include a political organization such as the Métis Nation of Ontario: see *R. v. Beaudry*, [2006] O.J. No. 790 (Ont. C.J.).

7. Reconcile these two statements from the *Powley* case: (1) "only those members with an ancestral connection to the historic community can claim a section 35 right" (para. 34); (2) "the recognition of Métis rights in section 35 is not reducible to the Métis' Indian ancestry" (para. 37).

8. When the Court writes that the relevant time frame for establishing Métis rights is post-contact but pre-control (para. 37), does that assume that Canada "controls" the Métis in the present?

9. In para. 40 of *Powley*, the Court writes that "effective control [of the Upper Great Lakes area] passed from the Aboriginal peoples of the area (Ojibway and Métis) to European control in the period between 1815 and 1850." Is this statement true? What implications might this hold for claims to self-government under section 35(1)? Is it significant that the Court assumes the Crown gained control over the area only after its assertion of sovereignty in the area (likely 1763)? If this is true, does this mean Canada does not always control territory after the assertion of sovereignty? What implications might this have for Aboriginal peoples who might claim that, despite the Crown's assertion of sovereignty, the Crown does not have "effective control" over Aboriginal territories and peoples?

10. Since *Powley*, Métis rights cases have been brought in many provinces. In Newfoundland, the Newfoundland and Labrador Court of Appeal found that it was not necessary to determine whether a group of people were Métis or Inuit in order to trigger a duty to consult and accommodate them: see *Labrador Métis Nation v. Newfoundland and Labrador (Minister of Transportation and Works)*, [2007] N.J. No. 421, 272 Nfld. & P.E.I.R. 178, 288 D.L.R. (4th) 641 (N.L.C.A.), leave to appeal refused [2008] S.C.C.A. No. 134 (S.C.C.). It was sufficient for the purposes of this case that the group established that they were an Aboriginal people, and thus they did not need to identify their specific ethnicity. In New Brunswick, the courts have not recognized Métis claims because of findings that Aboriginal ancestral connections are too distant (*R. v. Castonguay*, [2003] N.B.J. No. 350, 265 N.B.R. (2d) 105 (N.B.Q.B.); *R. v. Hopper*, [2008] N.B.J. No. 192, 331 N.B.R. (2d) 177 (N.B.C.A.)) and that there was no identifiable contemporary Métis community in the province (*R. v. Daigle*, [2004] N.B.J. No. 73, 271 N.B.R. (2d) 382 (N.B.Q.B.); *Brideau c. R.*, 2008 NBBR 70 (N.B.Q.B.)). Quebec law is still unsettled in relation to the recognition of Métis rights: see *Québec (Procureure générale) c. Corneau*, [2009] J.Q. no 4492 (Que. C.S.); *Québec (Procureure générale) c. Corneau*, [2011] J.Q. no 1624 (Que. C.S.). Manitoba courts have recognized Métis rights in accord with the *Powley* test: see *R. v. Goodon*, [2009] M.J. No. 3, 234 Man. R. (2d) 278 (Man. Prov. Ct.). In Saskatchewan, Métis claims have been recognized in accordance with the *Powley* test in *R. v. Laviolette*, [2005] S.J. No. 454, [2005] 3 C.N.L.R. 202 (Sask. Prov. Ct.). Alberta courts are currently considering the application of the *Powley* case in southern Alberta: see *R. v. Hirsekorn*, [2011] A.J. No. 1217, 53

Alta. L.R. (5th) 91 (Alta. Q.B.), leave to appeal granted [2012] A.J. No. 44 (Alta. C.A.). In northern Alberta, being a Métis Settlement citizen is sufficient to claim hunting rights under the *Powley* test: see *R. v. Lizotte*, [2009] A.J. No. 1203, [2010] 1 C.N.L.R. 326 (Alta. Prov. Ct.). In British Columbia, the case of *R. v. Willison*, [2006] B.C.J. No. 1505, [2006] 4 C.N.L.R. 253 (B.C.S.C.) held that there was insufficient evidence to establish an historic Métis community in the Falkland area of the province. The court in *Willison* also found that the trial judge erred when he "expanded the definition of community found in *Powley* to include a geographically wide, loosely affiliated group of people of mixed ancestry rather than a group with a distinctive, collective identity, living together in the same geographic area and sharing a common way of life" (para. 48). The judge also found there was no continuity and that the ancestral connection of Mr. Willison was tenuous.

11. Some jurisdictions have implemented Harvesting Agreements to accommodate and apply to Métis rights holders. These agreements may run into difficulties in light of the *Powley* decision: see *R. v. Kelley*, [2007] A.J. No. 67 (Alta. Q.B.). For the text of the Alberta Interim Métis Harvesting Agreement, see para. 9 of the *Kelley* case.

12. How might the *Powley* case interact with provincial legislation? Some provinces have enacted legislation directed at Métis people. In Saskatchewan, see the *Métis Act*, S.S. 2001, c. M-14.01. Section 3 creates a process to deal with issues of common concern, including capacity building, land, harvesting and governance. Section 2 of the Act outlines the following purposes:

> 2. The purpose of this Part is to recognize the contributions of the Métis people to the development and prosperity of Canada, including:
>
> (a) the rich and evolving history of the Métis people;
>
> (b) the cultural distinctiveness of the Métis communities and traditional ways of life of the Métis people;
>
> (c) the importance of the languages of the Métis people, including the Michif language, to Canada's culture and heritage;
>
> (d) the distinctive culture and cultural legacy of the Métis people, as symbolized by the Métis flag, the Métis sash, the Red River cart, the fiddle and the Red River jig;
>
> (e) the significance of the Métis farms and the Batoche historic site; service of the Métis veterans during the two World Wars and the Korean War and in many peace-keeping missions around the world;
>
> (f) the honourable and invaluable service of the Métis veterans during the two World Wars and the Korean War and in many peace-keeping missions around the world;
>
> (g) the importance of Métis entrepreneurs to Canada's economy, beginning in the 18th Century with the historic involvement of the Métis in the North West fur trade;

(h) the leadership role of Métis institutions in providing educational, social and health services to Métis people, and the contribution of those institutions to the delivery of those services; and

(i) the important contribution of the Métis Nation - Saskatchewan in representing the needs and aspirations of the Métis people.

The province of Alberta has recently amended and enacted the *Metis Settlements Act*, R.S.A. 2000, c. M-14 to provide further security in regard to a land base for the Métis to preserve their language and culture. We have already encountered the power of this Act in *Alberta (Aboriginal Affairs and Northern Development) v. Cunningham*, [2011] S.C.J. No. 37, [2011] 2 S.C.R. 670 (S.C.C.), excerpted above. As Métis lawyer Jean Teillet indicates:

> The Métis Settlements legislation is delegated authority from the provincial government. It provides a framework within which Métis Settlement institutions can develop laws concerning membership, land, financial accounting, resource development and other issues pursuant to settlement council bylaws, General Council policies and ministerial regulations. There are also several regulations that have been enacted pursuant to the *Métis Settlements Act* including the *Land Interests Conversion Regulation, Metis Settlements Election Regulation, Metis Settlements Land Registry Regulation, Metis Settlements Subdivision Regulation* and the *Transitional Membership Regulation*.
>
> (Jean Teillet at <http://www.metisnation.org/harvesting/PDF/MLS_2006.pdf> at 102)

E. CONCLUSION

Métis rights have only recently received the attention that rights belonging to other Aboriginal peoples of Canada have received. The *Blais, Dumont* and *Powley* decisions on the nature and content of Métis Aboriginal rights have only outlined future issues in this area in the most general of terms. The interaction of Métis, Indian and Inuit rights and their potential to overlap has not yet been addressed, nor has there been any resolution of how the devastating impact of colonialism on the Métis should factor into judicial decisions. Métis issues remain a vibrant and developing areas of the law dealing with Aboriginal rights in Canada.

CHAPTER 8

FEDERALISM/CONSTITUTIONAL ISSUES

A. INTRODUCTION

In contemporary Canadian Aboriginal rights jurisprudence, when one thinks of constitutional issues pertaining to the Aboriginal peoples of Canada, thoughts generally proceed directly to section 35 of the *Constitution Act, 1982*, being Schedule B to the *Canada Act 1982* (U.K.), 1982, c. 11. Section 35, which is discussed in detail in Chapter 2, includes the substantive guarantee of Aboriginal and treaty rights in the Canadian Constitution in subsection (1). The terms of section 35 read as follows:

> 35(1) The existing aboriginal and treaty rights of the aboriginal peoples of Canada are hereby recognized and affirmed.
>
> (2) In this Act, "aboriginal peoples of Canada" includes the Indian, Inuit, and Métis peoples of Canada.
>
> (3) For greater certainty, in subsection (1) "'treaty rights" includes rights that now exist by way of land claims agreements or may be so acquired.
>
> (4) Notwithstanding any other provision of this Act, the aboriginal and treaty rights referred to in subsection (1) are guaranteed equally to male and female persons.

Section 35 exists as Part II of the *Constitution Act, 1982*. Because of its positioning, section 35 is not subject to the limitation clause in section 1 of the *Canadian Charter of Rights and Freedoms*, Part I of the *Constitution Act, 1982*.

Since some sections of the Charter potentially could have affected section 35 rights — in particular, the equality clause in section 15 — section 25 was included within the Charter to insulate section 35 from such an occurrence. Section 25 modifies and explains the substantive rights guaranteed in section 35. Section 25 also constitutionally entrenches the rights contained in the *Royal Proclamation, 1763* (U.K.), R.S.C. 1985, App. II, No. 1:

> 25. The guarantee in this Charter of certain rights and freedoms shall not be construed so as to abrogate or derogate from any aboriginal, treaty, or other rights or freedoms that pertain to the aboriginal peoples of Canada including
>
> (a) any rights or freedoms that have been recognized by the Royal Proclamation of October 7, 1763; and
>
> (b) any rights or freedoms that now exist by way of land claims agreement or may be so acquired.

The importance of the constitutionalization of Aboriginal and treaty rights in section 35 was recognized by the Supreme Court of Canada in the

Quebec Secession Reference: see *Reference re Secession of Quebec*, [1998] S.C.J. No. 61, [1998] 2 S.C.R. 217 at para. 82:

> ... The "promise" of s. 35, as it was termed in *R. v. Sparrow* ... recognized not only the ancient occupation of land by aboriginal peoples, but their contribution to the building of Canada, and the special commitments made to them by successive governments. The protection of these rights, so recently and arduously achieved ... reflects an important underlying constitutional value.

This characterization appropriately posits section 35 as a bridge between the Crown's historic and contemporary relations with the Aboriginal peoples. It also positions section 35 as a blueprint for the future interaction of the parties in a manner that recognizes the importance of their historic relations and the parties' contributions and commitments to each other and the building of Canada.

While sections 25 and 35 of the *Constitution Act, 1982* receive the bulk of attention when focus shifts to constitutional provisions affecting Aboriginal peoples, as seen in previous chapters, they are not the only provisions in the Canadian Constitution that pertain to the Aboriginal peoples of Canada.

Upon the formation of Canada in 1867, there was a legislative division of powers between the federal Parliament and provincial legislatures. This division of powers is seen primarily in sections 91 and 92 of the *British North America Act, 1867* (U.K.), 30 & 31 Vict., c. 3 (now the *Constitution Act, 1867*). Noteworthy in this division of powers was the allocation of exclusive legislative responsibility over "Indians, and Lands reserved for the Indians" to Parliament in section 91(24) of the *Constitution Act, 1867*. Section 91(24) reads:

> 91. It shall be lawful for the Queen, by and with the Advice and Consent of the Senate and House of Commons, to make Laws for the Peace, Order and good Government of Canada, in relation to all Matters not coming with the Classes of Subjects by this Act assigned exclusively to the Legislatures of the Provinces; and for greater Certainty, but not so as to restrict the Generality of the foregoing Terms of this Section, it is hereby declared that (notwithstanding anything in this Act) the exclusive Legislative Authority of the Parliament of Canada extends to all Matters coming within the Classes of Subjects next hereinafter enumerated; that is to say, —
>
> . . . . .
>
> 24. Indians, and Lands reserved for the Indians.

The federal government used its section 91(24) power to enact the federal *Indian Act, 1876*, S.C. 1876, c. 18, which consolidated all post-Confederation federal statutes pertaining to "Indians", as defined under the Act. The federal government also used this power to engage in treaty negotiations with the Aboriginal peoples. Yet, the *Constitution Act, 1867* had a particular effect on lands surrendered under Crown-Native treaties that had not been foreseen by the federal government at the time it negotiated the treaties.

B. THE IMPLICATIONS OF THE DIVISION OF POWERS ON ABORIGINAL PEOPLES

Until the landmark case of *St. Catherine's Milling & Lumber Co. v. R.* (1888), 14 App. Cas. 46 (P.C.) (reproduced in Chapter 3), little attention was paid to the division of powers in relation to Aboriginal issues. However, the *St. Catherine's Milling* decision profoundly altered previous understandings of the effects of land surrendered under treaties through the Privy Council's interpretation of the effects of sections 91(24) and 109 of the *Constitution Act, 1867*. Section 109 reads as follows:

> 109. All Lands, Mines, Minerals, and Royalties belonging to the several Provinces of Canada, Nova Scotia, and New Brunswick at the Union, and all Sums then due or payable for such Lands, Mines, Minerals, or Royalties, shall belong to the several Provinces of Ontario, Quebec, Nova Scotia, and New Brunswick in which the same are situate or arise, subject to any Trusts existing in respect thereof, and to any Interest other than that of the Province in the same.

Some of the primary effects of the Privy Council's interpretation of sections 91(24) and 109 of the *Constitution Act, 1867* in *St. Catherine's Milling* are summarized in the following excerpt, which also illustrates some of the problems emanating from the judicial interpretation of these sections' effects on lands surrendered under treaties.

LEONARD I. ROTMAN, "PROVINCIAL FIDUCIARY OBLIGATIONS TO FIRST NATIONS: THE NEXUS BETWEEN GOVERNMENTAL POWER AND RESPONSIBILITY"

(1994) 32 Osgoode Hall L.J. 735 at 743-45, 754-58, 760-63
(references omitted)

The *St. Catherine's Milling* decision created a lingering and problematic legacy by juxtaposing the federal Crown's acquisition of Aboriginal lands and "extinguishment" of Aboriginal title by way of treaty to the provincial Crown's acquisition of a beneficial interest in the land once it had been disencumbered of the Aboriginal interest.

. . . . .

The *St. Catherine's Milling* decision centred around a dispute between the Province of Ontario and the Dominion of Canada over the ownership of former Indian lands. The lands had been surrendered under Treaty #3, a post-Confederation treaty signed in 1873, by the Saulteaux Indians. The St. Catherine's Milling and Lumber Company had obtained a licence from the Dominion Crown to cut timber on some of the lands that had been surrendered. The Ontario Crown sought to restrain the lumber company from cutting timber on those lands by claiming that it owned a beneficial interest due to section 109 of the *British North America Act, 1867*. The main issue at bar was which body of the Crown possessed the beneficial interest in the surrendered lands.

. . . . .

[T]he Privy Council found that the federal Crown's section 91(24) power to enter into treaties and obtain surrenders of Indian lands did not give it any interest in the land once its Aboriginal title was extinguished. This conclusion was based upon their Lordships' construction of section 109 and their understanding of that section's effects in the earlier case of *Ontario (A.G.) v. Mercer* [(1883), 8 App. Cas. 767 (P.C.)].

... Section 109 effectively vested the Crown's underlying title to the unsurrendered Indian's lands, which were still subject to Aboriginal title, in the province in which the lands were located. Once those lands were relieved of any Aboriginal interest, the full beneficial interest in those lands became vested in the province.

The Privy Council's finding in *St. Catherine's Milling*, that "the Crown has all along had a present proprietary estate in the land, upon which the Indian title was a mere burden," created a difficult situation. It separated the power to enter into treaties and the power to fulfil the terms of those treaties once they had been concluded. The lasting effect of the decision is to rest exclusive power to obtain a surrender of Indian lands and to create reserves in the federal Crown, and, once a surrender is obtained, to rest exclusive proprietary and administrative rights over the surrendered lands in the provincial Crown.

The practical result of this division of powers is that although only the federal Crown may create a reserve, it cannot use provincial Crown lands (such as those obtained from First Nations by surrender under treaty) for that purpose without the cooperation of the province.

. . . . .

In delivering the judgment in *St. Catherine's Milling* on behalf of the Privy Council, Lord Watson was explicit about Ontario's responsibilities to the treaty signatories. He held that the province was entirely responsible for discharging the annuity obligations incurred under the terms of the treaty:

> Seeing that the benefit of the surrender accrues to her, Ontario must, of course, relieve the Crown, and the Dominion, of all obligations involving the payment of money which were undertaken by Her Majesty, and which are said to have been in part fulfilled by the Dominion government.

. . . . .

The issue of provincial responsibility for treaty obligations arose again in *Seybold* [*Ontario Mining Co. v. Seybold*, [1903] A.C. 73 (P.C.)]. One of the issues in *Seybold* concerned the setting aside and establishment of Indian reserves under the provisions of Treaty #3, the same treaty dealt with in *St. Catherine's Milling*. Out of the lands surrendered under the treaty for the benefit of the treaty signatories, the federal Crown had set aside reserve lands in 1879. It later sold the reserve lands, without the consent of the province, after obtaining their surrender from the Indians. The vital question in *Seybold*, for present purposes, was whether the obligation to set aside reserves under the treaty rightfully belonged to the federal Crown, the Ontario Crown, or both.

. . . . .

The Privy Council determined that the federal Crown's actions in setting aside, and later selling, the reserves were *ultra vires*. In delivering the Privy Council's judgment, Lord Davey stated that Ontario had a duty to fulfil the terms of the treaty. That duty, however, did not exist in a strictly legal sense; rather, it only constituted a moral obligation to cooperate with the federal Crown in setting aside reserves under the treaty:

> [T]he Government of the province, taking advantage of the surrender of 1873, came at least under an *honourable engagement* to fulfil the terms on the faith of which the surrender was made, and, therefore, to concur with the Dominion Government in appropriating certain undefined portions of the surrendered lands as Indian reserves. The result, however, is that the choice and location of the lands to be so appropriated could only be effectively made by the joint action of the two Governments. [emphasis added]

. . . . .

As a result, even if the Aboriginal signatories to the treaty successfully concluded a legal action that affirmed their right to receive reserves under the treaty, the judiciary would have been unable to enforce that right. A court could neither compel Canada to unilaterally fulfil the treaty, since Canada does not possess the jurisdiction on its own to set aside reserves out of surrendered lands, nor compel Ontario to cooperate with Canada in the setting aside of the reserves, since Ontario was not legally bound by any such obligation.

. . . . .

[Yet m]utual power entails mutual responsibility and it is this mutual responsibility, founded in part upon the sharing of legislative and executive powers by the federal and provincial Crowns, that underlies the Crown's fiduciary obligations to First Nations. If a provincial Crown obtains exclusive proprietary and administrative rights over Indian land surrendered by treaty, then it must, by necessity or logical implication, also obtain a portion of the fiduciary duties owed to the Aboriginal signatories to the treaty. Section 109 of the *British North America Act, 1867* is the conduit by which this transfer is effectuated. Once this transfer takes place, the province is legally bound to cooperate with the federal Crown in fulfilling the terms of the treaty.

In short, the result of the *St. Catherine's Milling* decision on the interplay between sections 91(24) and 109 of the *Constitution Act, 1867* is that only the federal government may legislate in respect of Aboriginal lands unless and until those lands are disencumbered of Aboriginal title. At that point, the lands then fall within the legislative jurisdiction of the province in which they are situated. As Lamer C.J.C. explained in *Delgamuukw v. British Columbia*, [1997] S.C.J. No. 108, [1997] 3 S.C.R. 1010, at 1117 (S.C.C.):

> Although that provision [s. 109] vests underlying title in provincial Crowns, it qualifies provincial ownership by making it subject to "any Interest other than that of the Province in the same". In *St. Catherine's Milling*, the Privy Council held that aboriginal title was such an interest, and rejected the argument that provincial ownership operated as a limit on federal jurisdiction. The net effect of that decision, therefore, was to separate the ownership of lands held pursuant to aboriginal title from jurisdiction over those lands.

Aside from obligations existing under treaties, the division of powers in the *Constitution Act, 1867* created other uncertainties for the federal and provincial governments regarding the promulgation of laws pertaining to Aboriginal peoples. One such uncertainty was which level of government possessed jurisdiction over Indian reserves. This issue was dealt with by the Supreme Court of Canada in *Cardinal v. Alberta (Attorney General)*, below.

CARDINAL v. ALBERTA (ATTORNEY GENERAL)

[1973] S.C.J. No. 104, 40 D.L.R. (3d) 553, [1974] S.C.R. 695,
[1973] 6 W.W.R. 205, 13 C.C.C. (2d) 1 (S.C.C.)
(references omitted)

The judgment of **Fauteux C.J.C.** and of **Abbott, Martland, Judson, Ritchie** and **Pigeon JJ.** was delivered by

Martland J.: — On December 8, 1970, the appellant, a treaty Indian, at his home on an Indian Reserve, in the Province of Alberta, sold a piece of moose meat to a non-Indian. He was charged with a breach of s. 37 of the *Wildlife Act*, R.S.A. 1970, c. 391, which provides:

> 37. No person shall traffic in any big game or any game bird except as is expressly permitted by this Act or by the regulations.

The trial Judge found that the appellant had trafficked in big game within the meaning of this section. The appellant was acquitted on the ground that the *Wildlife Act* is *ultra vires* of the Alberta Legislature in its application to the appellant as an Indian on an Indian Reserve. A case was stated on this legal issue, which was considered by a Judge of the Supreme Court of Alberta, who held that the decision was correct. An appeal was taken to the Appellate Division of the Supreme Court of Alberta, which allowed the appeal and overruled the judgment of the Court below. The present appeal is brought, with leave, to this Court.

Section 91(24) of the *British North America Act, 1867*, gives to the Parliament of Canada exclusive authority to legislate in respect of:

> 91(24) *Indians*, and Lands reserved for the *Indians*.

An agreement was made between the Government of Canada and the Government of Alberta, dated December 14, 1929, hereinafter referred to as "the Agreement", for the transfer by the former to the latter of the interest of the Crown in all Crown lands, mines and minerals within the Province of Alberta, and the provisions of the *Alberta Act, 1905* (Can.), c. 3, were modified as in the Agreement set out.

Paragraphs 10 to 12 inclusive appear in the Agreement under the heading "Indian Reserves", and it is paras. 10 and 12 which are of importance in considering this appeal. They provide as follows ... :

10. All lands included in Indian Reserves within the Province including those selected and surveyed but not yet confirmed as well as those confirmed, shall continue to be vested in the Crown and administered by the Government of Canada for the purposes of Canada, and the Province will from time to time, upon the request of the Superintendent General of Indian Affairs, set aside, out of the unoccupied Crown lands hereby transferred to its administration, such further areas as the said Superintendent General may, in agreement with the appropriate Minister of the Province, select, as necessary to enable Canada to fulfil its obligations, under the treaties with the Indians of the Province, and such areas shall thereafter be administered by Canada in the same way in all respects as if they had never passed to the Province under the provisions hereof.

12. In order to secure to the Indians of the Province the continuance of the supply of game and fish for their support and subsistence, Canada agrees that the laws respecting game in force in the Province from time to time shall apply to the Indians within the boundaries thereof, provided however, that the said Indians shall have the right, which the Province hereby assures to them, of hunting, trapping and fishing game and fish for food at all seasons of the year on all unoccupied Crown lands and on any other lands to which the said Indians may have a right of access.

This Agreement was approved by the Parliament of Canada and the Legislature of the Province of Alberta and, thereafter, it and also agreements between the Government of Canada and the Provinces of Manitoba, Saskatchewan and British Columbia were confirmed by the *British North America Act, 1930* (U.K.), c. 26. Section 1 of that Act provided:

1. The agreements set out in the Schedule to this Act are hereby confirmed and shall have the force of law notwithstanding anything in the British North America Act, 1867, or any Act amending the same, or any Act of the Parliament of Canada, or in any Order in Council or terms or conditions of union made or approved under any such Act as aforesaid.

Paragraphs 10 and 12 of the Agreement were, therefore, given the force of law, notwithstanding anything in the *British North America Act, 1867*. The question in issue on this appeal is as to whether s. 12 was effective so as to make the provisions of the *Wildlife Act* applicable to the appellant, a treaty Indian, in respect of an act which occurred on an Indian Reserve in the Province of Alberta.

The submission of the appellant is that the Parliament of Canada has exclusive legislative authority to legislate to control the administration of Indian reserves and that provincial laws cannot apply on such a reserve unless referentially introduced through federal legislation. It is contended that the phrase "on all unoccupied Crown lands and on any other lands to which the said Indians may have a right of access" does not include Indian reserve lands and that the only laws to which Indians are subject, while on a reserve, are the laws of Canada. Paragraph 12, it is said, can only have application to Indians in Alberta outside the Indian reserves.

. . . . .

The present appeal thus raises issues as to the application of para. 12 which have not been considered previously.

As indicated earlier, the appellant starts from the proposition that, prior to the making of the Agreement, Indian reserves were enclaves which were withdrawn from the application of provincial legislation, save by way of reference by virtue of federal legislation. On this premise it is contended that para. 12 should not be construed so as to make provincial game legislation applicable within Indian reserves.

I am not prepared to accept this initial premise. Section 91(24) of the *British North America Act, 1867*, gave exclusive legislative authority to the Canadian Parliament in respect of Indians and over lands reserved for the Indians. Section 92 gave to each Province, in such Province, exclusive legislative power over the subjects therein defined. It is well established, as illustrated in *Union Colliery Company of B.C. v. Bryden*, [1899] A.C. 580, that a Province cannot legislate in relation to a subject-matter exclusively assigned to the Federal Parliament by s. 91. But it is also well established that provincial legislation enacted under a heading of s. 92 does not necessarily become invalid because it affects something which is subject to federal legislation. ...

A provincial Legislature could not enact legislation in relation to Indians, or in relation to Indian reserves, but this is far from saying that the effect of s. 91(24) of the *British North America Act, 1867*, was to create enclaves within a Province within the boundaries of which provincial legislation could have no application. In my opinion, the test as to the application of provincial legislation within a reserve is the same as with respect to its application within the Province and that is that it must be within the authority of s. 92 and must not be in relation to a subject-matter assigned exclusively to the Canadian Parliament under s. 91. Two of those subjects are Indians and Indian reserves, but if provincial legislation within the limits of s. 92 is not construed as being legislation in relation to those classes of subjects (or any other subject under s. 91) it is applicable anywhere in the Province, including Indian reserves, even though Indians or Indian reserves might be affected by it. My point is that s. 91(24) enumerates classes of subjects over which the federal Parliament has the exclusive power to legislate, but it does not purport to define areas within a Province within which the power of a Province to enact legislation, otherwise within its powers, is to be excluded.

. . . . .

I now turn to a consideration of the effect of para. 12 of the Agreement.

It has been noted that this section, along with paras. 10 and 11, appears under the heading "Indian Reserves". It begins with the words:

> In order to secure to the Indians of the Province the continuance of the supply of game and fish for their support and subsistence, Canada agrees that the laws respecting game in force in the Province from time to time shall apply to the Indians within the boundaries thereof. ...

The opening words of the paragraph define its purpose. It is to secure to the Indians of the Province a continuing supply of game and fish for their support and subsistence. It is to achieve that purpose that Indians within the boundaries of the Province are to conform to provincial game laws, subject, always, to their right to hunt and fish for food. This being the purpose of the paragraph, it could not have been intended that the controls which would apply to Indians in relation to hunting and fishing for purposes other than for their own food, should apply only to Indians not on reserves.

Furthermore, if the paragraph were to be so restricted in its scope, it would accomplish nothing towards its purpose. ...

In my opinion, the meaning of para. 12 is that Canada, clothed as it was with legislative jurisdiction over "Indians, and Lands reserved for the Indians", in order to achieve the purpose of the section, agreed to the imposition of provincial controls over hunting and fishing, which, previously, the Province might not have had power to impose. By its express wording, it provides that the game laws of the Province shall apply "to the Indians within the boundaries thereof". To me this must contemplate their application to all Indians within the Province, without restriction as to where, within the Province, they might be.

. . . .

The appellant places emphasis on the words in the proviso to para. 12 of the Agreement "on any other lands to which the said Indians may have a right of access". The contention is that para. 10 provided for continuance of the vesting of title in Indian reserves in the federal Crown, as well as for the creation of additional reserves, and that, in these lands, the Indians who reside thereon have an interest considerably greater than a mere "right of access". The use of that phrase, it is submitted, is inconsistent with any reference to reserve lands, and therefore, as the proviso, by the terms used, does not apply to Indian reserves, the section, as a whole, must be taken not to have application to them.

I am unable to agree that the broad terms used in the first portion of para. 12 can be limited, inferentially, in this way. In my view, having made all Indians within the boundaries of the Province, in their own interest, subject to provincial game laws, the proviso, by which the Province assured the defined rights of hunting and fishing for food, was drawn in broad terms. The proviso assures the right to hunt and fish for food on Indian reserves, because there can be no doubt that, whatever additional rights Indian residents on a reserve may have, they certainly have the right of access to it.

. . . . .

For these reasons, I am of the opinion that para. 12 of the Agreement made the provisions of the *Wildlife Act* applicable to all Indians, including those on reserves, and governed their activities throughout the Province, including reserves. By virtue of s. 1 of the *British North America Act, 1930*, it has the force of law, notwithstanding anything contained in the *British North America Act, 1867*, any amendment thereto, or any federal statute.

Having reached this conclusion, it is not necessary, in the circumstances of this case, to determine the meaning and effect of s. 88 (formerly s. 87) of the *Indian Act*, R.S.C. 1970, c. I-6.

I would dismiss the appeal.

[The judgment of **Hall**, **Spence** and **Laskin JJ.** was delivered by]

Laskin J. (dissenting): — This appeal raises, for the first time in this Court, the question whether provincial game laws apply to a treaty Indian on an Indian reserve so as to make him liable to their penalties for engaging on the reserve in activities prohibited by the provincial legislation. ...

The Alberta Natural Resources Agreement is part of the constitutional order under which Canada and its respective Provinces exist, and the question arises whether and to what extent it affects and is affected by the distribution of legislative power under ss. 91 and 92 of the *British North America Act, 1867*, ... I repeat time-tested words from *Union Colliery Co. of B.C. v. Bryden*, [1899] A.C. 580 ... which express what is now a constitutional axiom:

> The abstinence of the Dominion Parliament from legislating to the full limit of its powers, could not have the effect of transferring to any provincial legislature the legislative power which had been assigned to the Dominion by s. 91 of the Act of 1867.

. . . . .

... Apart entirely from the exclusive power vested in the Parliament of Canada to legislate in relation to Indians, its exclusive power in relation also to Indian reserves puts such tracts of land, albeit they are physically in a Province, beyond provincial competence to regulate their use or to control resources thereon. This is ... because regardless of ultimate title, it is only Parliament that may legislate in relation to reserves once they have been recognized or set aside as such. The issue of title to Indian lands, whether the loosely defined lands referred to in the Royal Proclamation of 1763 or the more precisely defined tracts known as Indian reserves, was considered by the Privy Council in *St. Catherine's Milling and Lumber Co. v. The Queen* ... [discussed in Chapter 3 (Aboriginal Title)]. ... [It] was the result of the *St. Catherine's Milling* case that where such lands are within the limits of a Province, it is only when they are surrendered to the Crown that the full proprietary interest of the Province may be asserted, and that they then become subject to its control and disposition ...

. . . . . .

Where land in a Province is, as in the present case, an admitted Indian reserve, its administration and the law applicable thereto, so far at least as Indians thereon are concerned, depend on federal legislation. Indian reserves are enclaves which, so long as they exist as reserves, are withdrawn from provincial regulatory power. If provincial legislation is applicable at all, it is only by referential incorporation through adoption by the Parliament of Canada. This is seen in the *Indian Act*.

. . . . .

The significance of the allocation of exclusive legislative power to Parliament in relation to Indian reserves merits emphasis in terms of the kind of enclave that a reserve is. It is a social economic community unit, with its own political structure as well according to the prescriptions of the *Indian Act*. The underlying title (that is, upon surrender) may well be in the Province, but during its existence as such a reserve, in my opinion, is no more subject to provincial legislation than is federal Crown property; and it is no more subject to provincial regulatory authority than is any other enterprise falling within exclusive federal competence.

. . . . .

The present case concerns the regulation and administration of the resources of land comprised in a reserve, and I can conceive of nothing more integral to that land as such. If the federal power given by s. 91(24) does not preclude the application of such provincial legislation to Indian reserves, the power will have lost the exclusiveness which is ordained by the Constitution.

. . . . .

Since federal power in relation to "lands reserved for the Indians" is independent and exclusive, its content must embrace administrative control and regulatory authority over Indian reserves. Hence, not only provincial game laws but other provincial regulatory legislation can have no application, of its own force, to such reserves, at least where it is sought to subject Indians thereon to such legislation.

. . . . .

I turn now to the Alberta Natural Resources Agreement which deals separately in its paras. 10 and 12 with reserves and with unoccupied Crown lands and other lands to which Indians may have a right of access. ...

. . . . .

... All Indian reserves are to continue to be administered by the Government of Canada for the purposes of Canada; there is here no qualification to admit any provincial purpose. Moreover, any further reserves that may be established from unoccupied Crown land transferred to the Province are to be administered by Canada in the same way in all respects as if they had never passed to the Province. That points clearly to the exclusion of reserves from provincial control.

. . . . .

The *Indian Act*, defines "reserve" in s. 2(1) to mean a tract of land, the legal title to which is vested in Her Majesty, that has been set apart by Her Majesty for the use and benefit of an Indian band. Sections 18 and 36 of the Act are as follows:

> 18. (1) Subject to this Act, reserves are held by Her Majesty for the use and benefit of the respective bands for which they were set apart; and subject to this Act and to the terms of any treaty or surrender, the Governor in Council may determine whether any purpose for which lands in a reserve are used or are to be used is for the use and benefit of the band.
>
> (2) The Minister may authorize the use of lands in a reserve for the purpose of Indian schools, the administration of Indian affairs, Indian burial grounds, Indian health projects or, with the consent of the council of the band, for any other purpose for the general welfare of the band, and may take any lands in a reserve required for such purposes, but where an individual Indian, immediately prior to such taking, was entitled to the possession of such lands, compensation for such use shall be paid to the Indian, in such amount as may be agreed between the Indian and the Minister, or, failing agreement, as may be determined in such manner as the Minister may direct.
>
> 36. Where lands have been set apart for the use and benefit of a band and legal title thereto is not vested in Her Majesty, this Act applies as though the lands were a reserve within the meaning of this Act.

These, and related provisions which deal with possession by Indians of land within a reserve, reinforce my opinion that provincial regulatory legislation cannot, *ex proprio vigore*, apply to a reserve.

This opinion is unaffected by s. 88 of the *Indian Act* which reads:

> 88. Subject to the terms of any treaty and any other Act of the Parliament of Canada, all laws of general application from time to time in force in any province are applicable to and in respect of Indians in the province, except to the extent that such laws are inconsistent with this Act or any order, rule, regulation or by-law made thereunder, and except to the extent that such laws make provision for any matter for which provision is made by or under this Act.

This section deals only with Indians, not with reserves, and is, in any event, a referential incorporation of provincial legislation which takes effect under the section as federal legislation. I do not read s. 88 as creating any exception to the operation of federal legislation by making way for otherwise competent provincial legislation. ...

. . . . .

Accordingly, I would allow the appeal. ...

Appeal dismissed.

Consider the merits of Justice Laskin's arguments in favour of characterizing Indian reserves as federal enclaves beyond the reach of provincial power. Are his statements consistent with the division of powers envisaged by the *Constitution Act, 1867*? Is the Indian interest in reserve lands a unique, or *sui generis*, interest that differs from the interest that Indians may have in non-reserve lands? If it is not, should it be? In answering these questions, regard should be had to the judgment of Dickson J., as he then was, in *Guerin v. R.*, [1984] S.C.J. No. 45, 13 D.L.R. (4th) 321 at 337 (S.C.C.), as excerpted in Chapter 3, in which he stated that the Aboriginal interest in reserve lands and Aboriginal title lands was the same. Note also the commentary upon this characterization in *Osoyoos Indian Band v. Oliver (Town)*, [2001] S.C.J. No. 82, [2001] 3 S.C.R. 746 (S.C.C.) at paras. 161-64, excerpted in Chapter 5, *per* Iacobucci J., who stated that it:

> ... simply emphasizes ... the fact that lands to which aboriginal title attaches are also reserve lands protected by the *Indian Act* [but] does not change the aboriginal interest in the land insofar as the right to protection by the Crown as fiduciary is at issue.
>
> ... [W]here aboriginal title subsisted in lands that are then appropriated to the use of a band as reserve lands, the aboriginal interest in these lands is no different than that found in traditional lands in which there is an unrecognized aboriginal title — at least for the purposes of understanding the existence and the content of a fiduciary obligation.
>
> I agree with Dickson J. on this point ...
>
> In sum, this quotation from *Guerin* does not speak to identity of aboriginal title and an interest in reserve land with respect to the origin and termination of the respective interests. Dickson J. was merely comparing reserve lands subject to aboriginal title with non-reserve lands subject to aboriginal title, in context of understanding the existence of the Crown's fiduciary obligation in both cases.

Note also Iacobucci J.'s comments, *ibid*. at para. 41:

> ... when describing the features of the aboriginal interest in reserve land it is useful to refer to this Court's recent jurisprudence on the nature of aboriginal title. Although the two interests are not identical, they are fundamentally similar ... (references omitted).

While the majority decision in *Cardinal* rejected the enclave theory (notwithstanding the vociferous dissent of Laskin J.), there were other questions concerning federal and provincial legislative competency pertaining to Aboriginal peoples that were not expressly dealt with in *Cardinal*. The most important of these questions was whether the federal government's exclusive jurisdiction over "Indians, and lands reserved for the Indians", entailed that it would have to enact *all* laws pertaining to Aboriginal peoples, even if the subject matter of the legislation infringed upon provincial jurisdiction. In order to avoid this difficult situation, what is now section 88 of the federal *Indian Act*, R.S.C. 1985, c. I-5, was created.

C. SECTION 88 OF THE *INDIAN ACT*

To avoid the difficulty of legislating in respect of Aboriginal peoples while navigating the division of powers established in the *Constitution Act, 1867*, the amended *Indian Act*, R.S.C. 1951, c. 29, included a new section, section 87. Upon the renumbering of the *Indian Act* in 1970, section 87 became section 88.

Aside from its numbering, this section has remained virtually unchanged since its inclusion in the 1951 *Indian Act*. It reads:

> 88. Subject to the terms of any treaty and any other Act of the Parliament, all laws of general application from time to time in force in any province are applicable to and in respect of Indians in the province, except to the extent that those laws are inconsistent with this Act or the *First Nations Fiscal and Statistical Management Act* or with any order, rule, regulation or law of a band made under those Acts, and except to the extent that those provincial laws make provision for any matter for which provision is made by or under those Acts.

While the rules pertaining to the application of section 88 may seem straightforward, the judicial understanding of that section has evolved since the section's first appearance in the *Indian Act*. The application of provincial laws to Aboriginal peoples and the role played by section 88 was the focus of the Supreme Court of Canada's decision in *Dick v. R.,* below.

DICK v. R.

[1985] S.C.J. No. 62, [1985] 2 S.C.R. 309, [1986] 1 W.W.R. 1, 69 B.C.L.R. 184, [1985] 4 C.N.L.R. 55, 22 C.C.C. (3d) 129, 23 D.L.R. (4th) 33, 62 N.R. 1 (S.C.C.) (references omitted)

The judgment of the Court was delivered by

Beetz J.: —

I   The facts

The facts are not in dispute. They are summarized by Lambert J.A., dissenting in the British Columbia Court of Appeal ...:

> Arthur Dick is a member of the Alkali Lake Band of the Shuswap people. He lives on the Alkali Lake Reserve in the Chilcotin District of the County of Cariboo. He is a non-treaty Indian. The Alkali Lake Band is comprised of about 10 families, or approximately 350 people, all told. They subsist in large measure by foraging. They catch fish for food and they kill deer and moose for food and other uses.
>
> The Shuswap word for May is "Pellcwewlemten". It means "time to go fishing". In response to this imperative Arthur Dick and two other band members, with two members of the Canoe Creek Band, set off on May 4, 1980, for Gustafsen Creek, where they intended to catch fish. On the way they passed Holdon Lake. There Arthur Dick killed a deer with a rifle. His

purpose was to provide food for the members of the foraging party and for other band members. The carcass, cut up in pieces, was taken on to Gustafsen Creek where a provincial conservation officer and four R.C.M.P. constables found the five Indians in possession of dip nets, a number of rainbow trout, and the deer meat.

One precision should perhaps be added. The killing of the deer occurred in the traditional hunting grounds of the Alkali Lake Band but outside a reserve. I now return to the recital of the facts by Lambert J.A.:

> The *Wildlife Act*, R.S.B.C. 1979, c. 433, said it was a closed season for hunting for deer. So Arthur Dick was charged under the Act with two counts; first, with killing wildlife, to wit; one deer, at a time not within the open season, contrary to s. 3(1); and, secondly, with possession of wildlife that was dead, to wit: parts of one deer, during a closed season, contrary to s. 8. It was also a closed season for fishing in Gustafsen Creek. All five Indians were charged with respect to the fishing.

. . . . .

Leave to appeal was granted by the Court of Appeal but the appeal was dismissed, Lambert J.A. dissenting.

Appellant further appealed to this Court by leave of this Court.

II   The issues

Appellant and respondent appear to agree in substance as to the issues raised by this appeal, save one. But they express them differently and I find it preferable to rephrase them as follows:

1.   Is the practice of year-round foraging for food so central to the Indian way of life of the Alkali Lake Shuswap that it cannot be restricted by ss. 3(1) and 8(1) of the *Wildlife Act*, R.S.B.C. 1979, c. 433, without impairment of their status and capacity as Indians, and invasion of the federal field under s. 91(24) of the *Constitution Act, 1867*?
2.   If the answer to the first question is in the affirmative and, consequently, the *Wildlife Act* cannot apply *ex proprio vigore* to the appellant, then is this Act a law of general application referentially incorporated into federal law by s. 88 of the *Indian Act*, R.S.C. 1970, c. I-6.

[A third issue, raised only by the respondent, asked whether the appeal raised a question of law alone for the purpose of s. 114 of the *Offence Act*, R.S.B.C. 1979, c. 305. This issue, and the Court's consideration of it, is omitted.]

In addition, a constitutional question was stated by the Chief Justice:

> Are ss. 3(1)(c) and 8(1) of the *Wildlife Act*, R.S.B.C. 1979, c. 433, constitutionally inapplicable in the circumstances of this case on the ground that the restriction imposed by such sections affects the appellant *qua* Indian and therefore may only be enacted by the Parliament of Canada pursuant to s. 91(24) of the *Constitution Act, 1867*?

. . . . .

One issue that does not arise is that of Aboriginal Title or Rights. In its factum, the appellant expressly states that he has "not sought to prove or rely on the Aboriginal Title or Rights in the case at bar". As in the *Kruger* case, the issue will accordingly not be dealt with any more than the related or included question whether the Indians' right to hunt is a personal right or, as has been suggested by some learned authors, is a right in the nature of a *profit à prendre* or some other interest in land covered by the expression "Lands reserved for the Indians", rather than the word "Indians" in s. 91(24) of the *Constitution Act, 1867*. No submission was made on this last point and in this Court, as well apparently as in the courts below, the case has been argued as if the Indians' right to hunt were a personal one.

III   The first issue

Appellant's main submission ... that the *Wildlife Act* strikes at the core of Indianness, that the question stated in the first issue should accordingly be answered in the affirmative and that the *Wildlife Act*, while valid legislation, should be read down so as not to apply to appellant in the circumstances of the case at bar.

. . . . .

The reasons of Lambert J.A., dissenting [in the British Columbia Court of Appeal's decision in *Dick v. R., supra*], are quite elaborate. For the greater part, they expound the similarities and differences between the case at bar and *Kruger* and his understanding of the tests adopted in the latter case to determine whether a law is one of general application ... But he used the same tests to answer the question stated in the first issue, namely whether the application of the *Wildlife Act* to appellant would regulate him *qua* Indian. Here is what he wrote.

> ... it seems to me that the same tests as are applied to determine whether the application of a provincial law to a particular group of Indians in a particular activity is the application of a law of general application, should also be applied to determine whether the application of a provincial law to a particular group of Indians in a particular activity is legislation in relation to Indians in their Indianness.
>
> So, subject to the question of referential incorporation, which I will come to next, it is my opinion that the evidence and argument which I have set out in Part III of these reasons require the conclusion that the *Wildlife Act* should be "read down" in order to preserve its constitutionality. That "reading down" would prevent it from applying to Arthur Dick in his activity in this case.

It is well worth quoting substantial parts of the evidence and argument set out in Part III of the reasons of Lambert J.A., which, as I just said, were also relied upon by him to resolve the first issue. He wrote:

> In *Kruger and Manuel v. The Queen, supra*, the two accused were members of the Penticton Indian Band. They shot four deer for food on unoccupied

Crown land on the traditional hunting grounds of the Penticton Indian Band. It was the closed season under the *Wildlife Act* and Kruger and Manuel did not have a sustenance permit which would have allowed them to shoot a deer during the closed season.

. . . . .

The evidence in this appeal goes much further than the agreed facts in *Kruger and Manuel v. The Queen.* Here there is evidence which indicates that the line demarking laws of general application from other enactments has been crossed. In *Kruger and Manuel v. The Queen* the only relevant evidence was the statement in the agreed facts that the accused had hunted deer during the closed season on land that was the traditional hunting grounds of the Penticton Indian Band. There was no evidence that the statutory restrictions on the right to hunt impaired the status and capacities of Kruger and Manuel as Indians. There was no evidence that the Penticton Indian Band depended on hunting for their supply of meat. There was no evidence that it would be impracticable to hunt sufficient meat during the open season. There was no evidence as to the amount of meat obtained through hunting, the amount of meat needed to feed an Indian family for a year, or the amount of meat allowed to Indians under the prevailing hunting quotas. Finally, there was no evidence to indicate that hunting was central to the way of life of the Penticton Indian Band. There was, in the words of Mr. Justice Dickson, an 'absence of clear evidence' that the provisions in the *Wildlife Act* crossed the line demarking laws of general application from other enactments.

The situation is entirely different in the present appeal where, in my opinion, the evidence indicates that the line has been crossed.

Nine members of the Alkali Lake Band and three members of the Canoe Creek Band gave evidence. They described their lives and the significance of the rituals of food gathering. They told of their dependence on moose and deer for food and for traditional and valued items of daily clothing and ceremonial clothing. Their evidence was placed in its cultural framework by Dr. Michael Asch, an anthropologist.

In 1980, the year in which Arthur Dick shot the deer at Holdon Lake, there were 45 active hunters in the Alkali Lake Band. They took 117 deer and 48 moose in the year. That provided a yield of 65 to 70 pounds of meat for every man, woman and child in the Band. The meat was shared out among band members in accordance with the institutional practices of the Shuswap people.

The times of year for hunting animals and for fishing, the places to hunt, and the techniques of hunting are taught to young male members of the band by their fathers and grandfathers.

Some of the meat is smoked, some is salted, some is frozen, and some is eaten fresh. The preservation of the meat and the preparation of food is largely done by the women of the band. Women also tan and treat the hides and make the traditional clothing. The skills and techniques for preserving food and making clothing are handed down from one generation to the next.

When the meat supply runs out the hunters go out for more. They go when it is needed. That happens every spring when the supply of preserved meat, from animals killed in the fall, comes to an end. The hunters in the Alkali Lake Band do not hunt for trophies; they do not hunt for recreation, nor do they look on hunting as recreation; they do not leave the carcasses of the animals they kill in the woods. If they work for wages it is not as an alternative to hunting but in order to acquire the means to hunt for food.

Ricky Dick, a member of the Alkali Lake Band, and one of the foraging party on May 4, 1980, gave evidence that his own family needs four or five deer each year for food. But the evidence of the conservation officer at 100 Mile House is that the limit for one hunter in one year from Region 5 is one deer. Of course, if you travel from one region to another, as recreational hunters do, then you can shoot deer in other regions to a total kill of three deer in one year. But, for the hunters of the Alkali Lake Band, the *Wildlife Act* and regulations, if they were to apply, would provide a limit of one deer for each hunter in each year within their hunting grounds.

Dr. Asch drew the relationship between the testimony of the Indian witnesses and the institutions and practices of the traditional way of life of the Alkali Lake Band of the Shuswap people.

In my opinion, it is impossible to read the evidence without realizing that killing fish and animals for food and other uses gives shape and meaning to the lives of the members of the Alkali Lake Band. It is at the centre of what they do and what they are.

In my opinion, this case is distinguishable from *Kruger and Manuel v. The Queen* (1977), 34 C.C.C. (2d) 377, 75 D.L.R. (3d) 434, [1978] 1 S.C.R. 104, because here the appellant has led evidence which, in my opinion, establishes that the *Wildlife Act* in its application to hunting for food impairs the status and capacities of the Alkali Lake Band members and crosses the line demarking laws of general application from other enactments.

And, before concluding ... Lambert J.A. wrote:

> Indeed, I would add that if the facts in this case do not place the killing of the deer within the central core of Indianness, if there is one, or within the boundary that outlines the status and capacities of the Alkali Lake Band, then it is difficult to imagine other facts that would do so.

In *Cardinal v. Attorney General of Alberta* ... it had already been held, apart from any evidence, that provincial game laws do not relate to Indians *qua* Indians. In the case at bar, there was considerable evidence capable of supporting the conclusions of Lambert J.A. to the effect that the *Wildlife Act* did impair the Indianness of the Alkali Lake Band, as well as the opposite conclusions of the courts below.

I am prepared to assume, without deciding, that Lambert J.A. was right on this point and that appellant's submission on the first issue is well taken.

I must confess at being strengthened in this assumption by [the following statement of] Lambert J.A.:

> The question of whether provincial legislation affects Indians as Indians, or Indians in their Indianness, to put it another way, is at the root of both arguments that I have considered in this appeal. I think it is worth adding that I have derived some sense of the nature of Indianness from the fact that the Indians in Alberta, Saskatchewan and Manitoba have the right to hunt and fish for food at all seasons of the year (see the Natural Resources Agreements and the *Constitution Act, 1930*, R.S.C. 1970, Appendix No. 25), and the treaty Indians in British Columbia also have that right: see *R. v. White and Bob* (1965), 52 D.L.R. (2d) 481 *n.*, [1965] S.C.R. vi. I think that those

rights are characteristic of Indianness, at least for those Indians, and if for those Indians, why not for the Alkali Lake Band of the Shuswap people?

On the basis of this assumption and subject to the question of referential incorporation which will be dealt with in the next chapter, it follows that the *Wildlife Act* could not apply to the appellant *ex proprio vigore*, and, in order to preserve its constitutionality, it would be necessary to read it down to prevent its applying to appellant in the circumstances of this case.

IV The second issue

. . . . .

The tests which Lambert J.A. applied in reviewing the evidence in his above quoted reasons are perfectly suitable to determine whether the application of the *Wildlife Act* to the appellant would have the effect of regulating him *qua* Indian, with the consequential necessity of a reading down if it did; but, apart from legislative intent and colourability, they have nothing to do with the question whether the *Wildlife Act* is a law of general application. On the contrary, it is precisely because the *Wildlife Act* is a law of general application that it would have to be read down were it not for s. 88 of the *Indian Act*. If the special impact of the *Wildlife Act* on Indians had been the very result contemplated by the Legislature and pursued by it as a matter of policy, the Act could not be read down because it would be in relation to Indians and clearly *ultra vires*.

The *Wildlife Act* does not differ in this respect from a great many provincial labour laws which are couched in general terms and which, taken literally, would apply to federal works and undertakings. So to apply them however would make them regulate such works and undertakings under some essentially federal aspects. They are accordingly read down so as not to apply to federal works and undertakings. .... But it has never been suggested, so far as I know, that, by the same token, those provincial labour laws cease to be laws of general application.

In his reasons for judgment, Lambert J.A. relied on two passages of *Kruger* which he quoted and commented. The first passage is:

> If the law does extend uniformly throughout the jurisdiction the intention and effects of the enactment need to be considered. The law must not be "in relation to" one class of citizens in object and purpose. But the fact that a law may have graver consequence to one person than to another does not, on that account alone, make the law other than one of general application. There are few laws which have a uniform impact. The line is crossed, however, when an enactment, though in relation to another matter, by its effect, impairs the status or capacity of a particular group.

The second passage of *Kruger* quoted by Lambert J.A. is:

> Game conservation laws have as their policy the maintenance of wildlife resources. It might be argued that without some conservation measures the ability of Indians or others to hunt for food would become a moot issue in consequence of the destruction of the resource. The presumption is for the validity of a legislative enactment and in this case the presumption has to

mean that in the absence of evidence to the contrary the measures taken by the British Columbia Legislature were taken to maintain an effective resource in the province for its citizens and not to oppose the interests of conservationists and Indians in such a way as to favour the claims of the former. If, of course, it can be shown in future litigation that the province has acted in such a way as to oppose conservation and Indian claims to the detriment of the latter — to "preserve moose before Indians" in the words of Gordon J.A. in *R. v. Strongquill* (1953), 8 W.W.R. (N.S.) 247 — it might very well be concluded that the effect of the legislation is to cross the line demarking laws of general application from other enactments. It would have to be shown that the policy of such an Act was to impair the status and capacities of Indians. Were that so, s. 88 would not operate to make the Act applicable to Indians. But that has not been done here and in the absence of clear evidence the Court cannot so presume.

Lambert J.A. then emphasized the importance of the effect of the legislation as opposed to its purpose:

> ... evidence about the motives of individual members of the Legislature or even about the more abstract "intention of the legislature" or "legislative purpose of the enactment" is not relevant. What is relevant is evidence about the effect of the legislation. In fact, evidence about its "application".

With all due deference, it seems to me that the correct view is the reverse one and that what Dickson J., as he then was, referred to in *Kruger* when he mentioned laws which had crossed the line of general application were laws which, either overtly or colourably, single out Indians for special treatment and impair their status as Indians. Effect and intent are both relevant. Effect can evidence intent. But in order to determine whether a law is not one of general application, the intent, purpose or policy of the legislation can certainly not be ignored: they form an essential ingredient of a law which discriminates between various classes of persons, as opposed to a law of general application. This in my view is what Dickson J. meant when in the above quoted passage, he wrote:

> It would have to be shown that the policy of such an Act was to impair the status and capacities of Indians.

. . . . .

It has already been held in *Kruger* that on its face, and in form, the *Wildlife Act* is a law of general application. In the previous chapter, I have assumed that its application to appellant would have the effect of regulating the latter *qua* Indian. However, it has not been demonstrated, in my view, that this particular impact has been intended by the provincial legislator. While it is assumed that the *Wildlife Act* impairs the status or capacity of appellant, it has not been established that the legislative policy of the *Wildlife Act* singles out Indians for special treatment or discriminates against them in any way.

I accordingly conclude that the *Wildlife Act* is a law of general application within the meaning of s. 88 of the *Indian Act*.

It remains to decide whether the *Wildlife Act* has been referentially incorporated to federal laws by s. 88 of the *Indian Act*.

In *Kruger*, Dickson J. wrote:

> There is in the legal literature a juridical controversy respecting whether s. 88 referentially incorporates provincial laws of general application or whether such laws apply to Indians *ex proprio vigore*. ...

This controversy has so far remained unresolved in this Court.

I believe that a distinction should be drawn between two categories of provincial laws. There are, on the one hand, provincial laws which can be applied to Indians without touching their Indianness, like traffic legislation; there are on the other hand, provincial laws which cannot apply to Indians without regulating them *qua* Indians.

Laws of the first category, in my opinion, continue to apply to Indians *ex proprio vigore* as they always did before the enactment of s. 88 in 1951 — then numbered s. 87 (1951 (Can.), c. 29) — and quite apart from s. 88.

I have come to the view that it is to the laws of the second category that s. 88 refers. I agree with what Laskin C.J. wrote in *Natural Parents v. Superintendent of Child Welfare*:

> When s. 88 refers to "all laws of general application from time to time in force in any province" it cannot be assumed to have legislated a nullity but, rather, to have in mind provincial legislation which, *per se*, would not apply to Indians under the *Indian Act* unless given force by federal reference.
>
> I am fully aware of the contention that it is enough to give force to the several opening provisions of s. 88, which, respectively, make the "provincial" reference subject to the terms of any treaty and any other federal Act and subject also to inconsistency with the *Indian Act* and orders, rules, regulations or by-laws thereunder. That contention would have it that s. 88 is otherwise declaratory. On this view, however, it is wholly declaratory save perhaps in its reference to "the terms of any treaty", a strange reason, in my view, to explain all the other provisions of s. 88. I think too that the concluding words of s. 88, "except to the extent that such laws make provision for any matter for which provision is made by or under this Act" indicate clearly that Parliament is indeed effecting incorporation by reference.

I also adopt the suggestion expressed by Professor Lysyk, as he then was:

> Provincial laws of general application will extend to Indians whether on or off reserves. It has been suggested that the constitution permits this result without the assistance of s. 87 of the Indian Act, and that the only significant result of that section is, by expressly embracing *all* laws of general application (subject to the exceptions stated in the section), to contemplate extension of particular laws which otherwise might have been held to be so intimately bound up with the essential capacities and rights inherent in Indian status as to have otherwise required a conclusion that the provincial legislation amounted to an inadmissible encroachment upon s. 91(24) of the British North America Act.

The word "all" in s. 88 is telling but, as was noticed by the late Chief Justice, the concluding words of s. 88 are practically decisive: it would not be open to Parliament in my view to make the *Indian Act* paramount over provincial laws simply because the *Indian Act* occupied the field.

Operational conflict would be required to this end. But Parliament could validly provide for any type of paramountcy of the *Indian Act* over other provisions which it alone could enact, referentially or otherwise.

. . . . .

I accordingly conclude that, in view of s. 88 of the *Indian Act*, the *Wildlife Act* applies to appellant even if, as I have assumed, it has the effect of regulating him *qua* Indian.

. . . . .

VI The constitutional question

I would answer the constitutional question as follows:

Sections 3(1) and 8(1) of the *Wildlife Act*, R.S.B.C. 1979, c. 433, being laws of general application in the Province of British Columbia, are applicable to the appellant either by referential incorporation under s. 88 of the *Indian Act*, R.S.C. 1970, c. I-6, or of their own force.

VII Conclusions

I would dismiss the appeal and make no order as to costs.

Appeal dismissed.

While the *Dick* case attempted to clarify the application of section 88, the judgment in that case has become the subject of debate itself. Some of the issues emanating from section 88 and its interpretation in *Dick* are illustrated in the following excerpt.

KERRY WILKINS, "STILL CRAZY AFTER ALL THESE YEARS: SECTION 88 OF THE INDIAN ACT AT FIFTY"

(2000) 38 Alta. L. Rev. 458 at 465-80, 482-83, 485-87, 497-99, 501-03
(references omitted)

. . . . .

Section 88 displays a clear legislative expectation that provincial laws are to apply, for the most part, to Indians. That much, at least, has always been clear from its phrasing. Initially, though, it was much less clear how s. 88 contributes to realization of that expectation. Is it a mere declaration, for greater certainty, that the kinds of laws specified govern Indians in a province, subject to the restrictions and exceptions it sets out, or does it exist to ensure the application to Indians of those laws (subject, again, to the same exceptions and restrictions) by incorporating them by reference into federal legislation?

... The problems with the "declaratory" view of s. 88 ... were that it left a long and complex statutory provision with very little real work to do, and that, so read, its closing words — "except to the extent that such laws make provision for any matter for which provision is made by or under this Act" — would have to be taken to be suggesting, falsely, that federal and provincial powers are concurrent, not exclusive. The fact that both sets of concerns made sense from a constitutional standpoint was a clear early indication that s. 88 was going to pose problems.

It was only in 1985, in *Dick v. R.*, that the court united behind a single approach to s. 88. That approach takes its shape from a distinction "between two categories of provincial laws[:] ... provincial laws which can be applied to Indians without touching their Indianness, like traffic legislation[, and] provincial laws which cannot apply to Indians without regulating them qua Indians." "[I]t is," the court determined, "to the laws of the second category that s. 88 refers"; "[l]aws of the first category," on the other hand, "continue to apply to Indians *ex proprio vigore*, as they always did before the enactment of s. 88 in 1951 ... and quite apart from s. 88."

We need some background in Canadian constitutional law to understand what the court is saying here. "Indians, and Lands reserved for the Indians" are among the classes of subjects that s. 91 of the Constitution Act, 1867 assigns exclusively to the federal order of government and, by so doing, expressly subtracts from the ambit of provincial authority. This does not mean that Indians are altogether beyond the reach of provincial legislation or executive activity. Generally speaking, valid provincial measures — i.e., those whose primary subject matter is something within the proper scope of provincial authority — apply of their own force (*"ex proprio vigore"*) to Indians, just as they would to anyone else, according to their terms. (Such laws are those in the first category that the Supreme Court identified in *Dick*.) It does mean, though, that there is a certain more limited group of matters over which the provinces, acting as such, may exercise no mandatory control, either directly or indirectly. Each head of federal authority listed in s. 91 has a "basic, minimum and unassailable content": a "core" set of matters from which it takes its definition. As the Supreme Court confirmed in *Dick*, the core of exclusive federal power over "Indians, and Lands reserved for the Indians" includes all matters characteristic of, or unique to, Indians as such: matters relating to "Indianness" or to Indians "qua Indians". Provincial measures that purport to make it their business to govern any such "core" matters are wholly invalid; such laws, altogether without legal force, have no application to anyone. But even otherwise valid provincial measures are "read down" as needed to ensure that they cannot have the effect, even inadvertently, of regulating core federal matters. This last group of provincial laws — those valid but inapplicable, as such, to Indians — are the ones in *Dick*'s second category.

What s. 88 does, then, according to the Supreme Court in *Dick*, is incorporate by reference, and apply as federal law, certain kinds of valid provincial measures ... that, for constitutional reasons, could not otherwise apply to Indians. It leaves undisturbed those provincial laws that apply of their own force to Indians or on Indian lands. Since 1985, the court has reaffirmed repeatedly and unanimously its support for this general proposition.

. . . . .

Doctrinally speaking, the impact of *Dick* is that s. 88 is irrelevant ... unless and until a court determines that the provincial law at issue is both constitutionally valid in its own right and, at the same time, constitutionally inapplicable, considered as provincial law, to Indians. ...

The problem is that the measures to which s. 88 pertains govern everyone else within their intendment as provincial law but apply only as federal law to Indians. This means, in the first place, that such measures, when applied to Indians, are subject, as a matter of course, to federal procedures, policies, priorities, and discretion but to provincial priorities and procedures when applied to anyone else. ... A second, related complication arises when we try to determine whose task it is to administer these measures. Provincial officials have full power to apply them to everyone else but none, while acting as such, to apply them to Indians. Any capacity such officials have to apply or enforce these laws in respect of Indians is necessarily delegated federal authority. Federal officials are, at best, in the same position, only with roles reversed. There seem to be only two administrative options available: asking officials from different orders of government to apply the same laws to different individuals, sometimes in the same situations, or asking officials from, say, the provincial order of government to operate in accordance with different priorities and policies (the federal and the provincial) in applying these same laws at the same time to Indians and to others. From a functional standpoint, neither option has much to recommend it.

These concerns themselves would be troubling enough, but it gets worse. One cannot always tell at a glance whether a given provincial measure applies, as such, to Indians or whether its application to them depends on s. 88 because its effect is to regulate them "qua Indians". ... [T]here is no way of knowing, at least in difficult cases, which policies and procedures (the federal or the provincial) are to govern the application of these measures to Indians, or, perhaps, which officials (the federal or the provincial) have the power to carry out that aspect of their administration.

Finally, s. 88, by intervening to extend the application of certain provincial measures to Indians, is giving a reach to those measures that the provincial legislature must, for constitutional reasons, be taken to have intended that they not have. There is, at a minimum, room for doubt, in circumstances such as these, whether the federal order has constitutional authority to require that provinces assume the added financial and administrative burden of applying these hybrid measures beyond the permissible range of their application as provincial legislation. ... If ... the federal government contemplates provincial assistance in the administration of federal law and policy in matters beyond provincial legislative competence, it seems reasonable for the provinces to expect it to pay for that help. Efforts to identify the extra costs of administration that s. 88 brings about are complicated substantially, however, by the uncertainty of speculating before the fact whether a given provincial measure applies to Indians (if at all) as provincial or as federal law.

. . . . .

Section 88 ... gives Indian treaties and treaty rights virtually complete protection against the provincial laws to which it applies: better quality protection, in fact, than such rights receive generally from s. 35(1) of the *Constitution Act, 1982*. ... The protection that s. 88 affords to treaty rights, therefore, seems clearly to be available only against the effects of such laws as s. 88 incorporates: provincial laws "of general application" that cannot apply, as such, to Indians. Such rights derive no protection at all from s. 88 against the effects of provincial laws that apply of their own force. As the Supreme Court told us in *Dick*, s. 88 has nothing to do with those.

. . . . .

This would indeed be a troubling result if s. 88 were the only protection — apart from s. 35(1) of the *Constitution Act, 1982* — that treaty rights had against provincial law. There is, however, strong authority buttressed by persuasive considerations of constitutional policy, to the effect that Indian treaty rights are matters integral, and therefore exclusive, to the federal government's constitutional authority over Indians and Indian lands ... Insofar as provincial laws interfere with the terms of such treaties, therefore, they can have no relevant application except pursuant to s. 88. And s. 88, as we saw, insulates the rights preserved, acknowledged, or confirmed in such treaties from the effects of the provincial laws it incorporates.

... Properly understood, s. 88 gives treaty rights no independent protection from provincial activity; all it does is shelter this island of pre-existing incapacity from the current of referential incorporation as federal law for which it is more generally responsible.

B. "... And Any Other Act of the Parliament of Canada, ..."

This phrase ensures that provisions in federal legislation other than the *Indian Act* take precedence, in case of conflict, over measures that s. 88 incorporates into federal law. ...

. . . . .

... [T]he phrase is important because the situation that s. 88 addresses differs in two important ways from the standard scenario of federal/provincial conflict. First, as we have seen, s. 88 governs only those provincial laws that cannot apply of their own force to Indians. From a division of powers standpoint, no such laws can give rise, on their own, to questions of paramountcy; true paramountcy issues arise only where provincial and federal laws both apply of their own force. Second, the provincial laws to which s. 88 applies become, upon incorporation, federal legislation, at least in respect of their application to Indians. So understood, such measures no longer give way automatically when they clash with other federal laws; the issue is now one of statutory interpretation, not one of paramountcy. For these reasons, it was not only sensible but important for Parliament to prescribe an explicit hierarchy as between the free-standing federal laws and the s. 88 hybrids. Because of this phrase, the free-standing federal laws will displace the hybrids exactly when and as they would have done apart from s. 88.

Unfortunately, s. 88 does not speak with similar clarity about the relationship between incorporated provincial measures and surviving pre-Confederation legislation including, perhaps most importantly, the Royal Proclamation of 1763. We know as a matter of general law that provinces, acting as such, cannot amend or repeal those parts of the Proclamation that deal with Indians' rights and that those provisions prevail over provincial measures, considered as such, that conflict with them. Once a provincial measure acquires the force of federal law pursuant to s. 88, however, it is from a constitutional standpoint of equal rank with the Proclamation and can operate to curtail the Proclamation's reach. Nothing in s. 88's own text precludes that result. Given the number and the explicitness of the other constraints that s. 88 imposes on the reach of the measures it governs, that omission itself may give courts reason not to protect the Proclamation from the impact of such measures.

C. "... All Laws of General application in Force in Any Province ..."

On its face, this phrasing is broad enough to capture federal, as well as provincial, laws of general application; they too, after all, are "in force in any province." ... The reference, however, is not confined exclusively to laws the provinces have enacted since Confederation; it also includes "any [pre-Confederation] laws which were made a part of the law of a province" as long as those laws count as laws of general application.

But what is a "law of general application"? The Supreme Court, in *Kruger & Manuel*, prescribed two criteria, both of which a provincial law must satisfy to qualify as such a law for purposes of s. 88. The first concerns the territorial reach of the relevant measure. To be "provincial in scope," a law must "extend uniformly throughout the territory"; if it does not, "the inquiry is at an end and the question is answered in the negative." ...

The Supreme Court's second criterion is the one that needs closer examination. It requires attention to "the intention and effects of the enactment" as follows:

> The law must not be "in relation to" one class of citizens in object and purpose. But the fact that a law may have graver consequences to one person than to another does not, on that account alone, make the law other than one of general application. There are few laws which have a uniform impact. The line is crossed, however, when an enactment, though in relation to another matter, by its effect, impairs the status or capacity of a particular group. The analogy may be made to a law which in its effect paralyzes the status and capacities of a federal company. ...

This passage implies that a measure or provision will be "in relation to" a particular class or group, and for that reason will not count as a law of general application, if it has the effect of impairing that group's status or capacity. Later on in the judgment, however, the Supreme Court goes on to say that "[i]t would have to be shown that the policy of the [relevant] Act was to impair the status and capacities of Indians." Relying in part on this latter quotation, it subsequently concluded, in *Dick*, that mere demonstration of such an effect was not sufficient to disqualify a provision or statute from being a law of general application. "Effect and intent," the court said there,

> are both relevant. Effect can evidence intent. But in order to determine whether a law is not one of general application, the intent, purpose or policy of the legislation can certainly not be ignored: they form an essential ingredient of a law which discriminates between various classes of persons, as opposed to a law of general application.

The fact, therefore, that a measure impairs some group's capacity or status will deny it the character of general application if and only if it suffices in all the circumstances to sustain an inference that the measure was enacted to have that effect.

... The only provincial laws, then, even eligible for consideration for federal incorporation pursuant to s. 88 are those whose primary business is not to regulate s. 91(24) lands or Indians (or any other matter within exclusive federal authority) but whose provisions, applied full strength, would nonetheless have the effect of doing so. ... For such laws, that requirement serves as one additional eligibility barrier to federal incorporation. ...

D. "... Are Applicable to and in Respect of Indians in the Province ..."

. . . . .

1. Which Indians?

The first of these questions, though important, is fairly easily answered. "Indian" is a term defined within the *Indian Act*, so the only Indians to whom incorporated measures apply are those that satisfy the statutory definition. ... We know, for example, that Inuit cannot be statutory Indians even though they are, indisputably, s. 91(24) Indians. Section 88, therefore, by its own terms, has no impact on the Inuit or on any other s. 91(24) Indians — or others — who do not qualify as statutory Indians. To those in that group, provincial measures either apply of their own force or not at all. It does, on the other hand, apply incorporated provincial measures to all statutory Indians whether or not they are also s. 91(24) Indians.

2. Provincial Laws About Land

The more difficult issue the current phrase poses — especially when read together with the one just preceding it — is what impact, if any, s. 88 has on the application of provincial measures to interests in, and uses of, reserves and other "Lands reserved for the Indians" ("s. 91(24) lands"). On the one hand, s. 88's text provides that "all laws of general application ... are applicable to and in respect of Indians"; nothing it says excludes provincial laws that happen to deal with land uses or interests. On the other hand, those same words say that "all laws of general application ... are applicable to and in respect of Indians in the province"; they say nothing comparably specific to suggest that such laws are also to govern Indian lands. And therein lies the controversy.

. . . . .

... [P]erhaps most important, the land-related provisions in the *Indian Act* and in its subordinate legislation pertain exclusively to the lands that the *Indian Act* has defined as "reserves". For present purposes ... reserves are by no means the only lands that matter. We have known for over a century that "the words actually used [in s. 91(24) of the *Constitution Act, 1867*] are, according to their natural meaning, sufficient to include all lands reserved, upon any terms or conditions, for Indian occupation," not just those lands that qualify under the statute as "reserves". ... In the absence, therefore, of affirmative federal measures concerning them, it is s. 88, as interpreted, that will determine what mainstream legal regime, if any, is going to govern the use, possession, occupation, or disposition of these lands. It will, to take just one example, determine what rights, if any, provincial laws related to matrimonial property disposition can confer on Aboriginal (or other) women residing off reserve on Aboriginal title lands.

. . . . .

In at least some circumstances, therefore, it will matter profoundly whether s. 88 is understood to apply provincial land regimes to Indian lands. We now must return to consider that primary issue. Does s. 88 (subject only to its other exceptions) impose provincial land regulation on s. 91(24) lands or not?

. . . . .

E.   "... Except to the Extent that Such Laws are Inconsistent with this Act or Any Order, Rule, Regulation or By-law Made Thereunder, ..."

Like the earlier phrase "and any other Act of the Parliament of Canada," and for the same reasons, this phrase ensures that the *Indian Act*'s own provisions, and the provisions of any subordinate legislation passed pursuant to it, prevail over any conflicting provincial measures incorporated as federal law under s. 88. ...

F.   "... And Except to the Extent that such Laws Make Provision for Any Matter for Which Provision is Made By or Under This Act."

These are the words that prompted the Supreme Court to conclude, in *Dick*, that s. 88 as a whole cannot just declare the terms on which provincial laws will apply, of their own force, to statutory Indians. It is the Constitution, as interpreted, that prescribes when and why provincial laws must give way in order not to interfere with the operation of federal schemes. It is not open to Parliament to give its own statutes greater protection from provincial interference than the Constitution already gives them. ...

These consequences ... clarify that these words do indeed confer on the *Indian Act*, and on arrangements enacted under it, extra protection from the effects of the relevant provincial laws, beyond what would be available under the usual paramountcy rules. And they confirm that this extra protection is available only against the effects of those provincial laws whose application to Indians depends on incorporation pursuant to s. 88. It has nothing to do with any provincial laws that apply, as such, to Indian lands or to s. 91(24) Indians.

.....

... When federal authorities, or band councils, enact particular schemes within or pursuant to the *Indian Act*, these words instruct the courts to presume that those schemes are meant to operate to the exclusion of any overlapping provincial arrangements that s. 88 incorporates; those challenging the provincial arrangement need not offer evidence of that intention, let alone demonstrate it. Any competent "substantive scheme or arrangement" set out in an *Indian Act* provision, regulation, or bylaw, therefore, routinely displaces, to the extent of any overlap, any incorporated provincial scheme. This means, for example, that permissive band council bylaws, where authorized by and validly enacted under the *Indian Act*, will almost always override, on the reserves to which they pertain, any related prohibitions contained in incorporated provincial measures about the same matter, unless a bylaw specifically indicates otherwise. Similarly, administrative or enforcement arrangements that band councils validly enact to support their own measures will, other things equal, preclude recourse to any alternative mechanisms provided in overlapping incorporated laws. To displace an overlapping measure, all they have to demonstrate is the overlap.

.....

V. Conclusion

Perhaps the greatest irony about s. 88 is that it may well have been intended, at least in part, as what insiders call a "housekeeping amendment". ...

... If dispelling doubt and confusion was indeed its purpose, I doubt that very many today would agree that it had succeeded in fulfilling it. By any relevant standard, its contribution has been almost entirely negative.

... [S]. 88 reflects confusion and encourages difference of view about the extent of the provinces' own authority to regulate what Indians do and what happens on and to Indian lands, and about the extent of federal power to facilitate, and to channel and limit, that authority. As might be expected, it has not fit comfortably within the framework the courts have developed more recently for dealing with these constitutional questions. ...

... Understood within the larger constitutional framework, however, the court's solution [in *Dick*] gives rise to unacknowledged, inconvenient, and profoundly difficult problems concerning the powers, costs and mechanisms of enforcement of the provincial standards that measures that s. 88 incorporates. At the same time, it seems, of necessity, to deprive the words "laws of general application" of any meaningful function within the section as a whole, except to screen out measures whose territorial application is not uniform. ...

. . . . .

It is fair to say that s. 88 is now in serious need of legislative reconsideration. ... [I]t has created substantially more legal problems than it has solved. It is ... "of doubtful constitutional validity" when and as it operates to restrict the exercise of existing Aboriginal rights. ... [I]t rests, from a policy standpoint, on contentious and unarticulated assumptions: about which s. 91(24) Indians and which aspects of their lives stand in need of mainstream regulation and by whom; and about when, where, and why such regulation is appropriate. These assumptions, and the questions that they purport to answer, deserve re-examination and reflection in light of contemporary law and experience. ...

The controversy surrounding section 88 continued in *R. v. Côté*, [1996] S.C.J. No. 93, [1996] 3 S.C.R. 139, 202 N.R. 161, 138 D.L.R. (4th) 385, 110 C.C.C. (3d) 122, [1996] 4 C.N.L.R. 26 (S.C.C.), where Chief Justice Lamer's majority decision contemplated the addition of a *Sparrow*-type justificatory test to section 88. The Chief Justice made the following statements about section 88 at paras. 86-87:

> Originally adopted in 1951, s. 88 has played a pivotal role in our modern federal system by coordinating the interaction of federal and provincial laws in relation to aboriginal peoples. As I understand the intent of the provision, s. 88 presently serves two distinct purposes. First, s. 88 serves an important jurisdictional purpose. Through the operation of the provision, provincial laws which would otherwise not apply to Indians under the federal and provincial division of powers are made applicable as incorporated federal law: *R. v. Dick*, [1985] 2 S.C.R. 309. Second, s. 88 accords federal statutory protection to aboriginal treaty rights. The application of such generally applicable provincial laws through federal incorporation is expressly made "[s]ubject to the terms of any treaty". Section 88 accords a special statutory protection to aboriginal treaty rights from contrary provincial law through the operation of the doctrine of federal paramountcy. ...

> This second purpose, of course, has become of diminished importance as a result of the constitutional entrenchment of treaty rights in 1982. But I note that, on the face of s. 88, treaty rights appear to enjoy a broader protection from contrary provincial law under the *Indian Act* than under the *Constitution Act, 1982*. Once it has been demonstrated that a provincial law

infringes 'the terms of [a] treaty', the treaty would arguably prevail under s. 88 even in the presence of a well-grounded justification. The statutory provision does not *expressly* incorporate a justification requirement analogous to the justification stage included in the *Sparrow* framework. But the precise boundaries of the protection of s. 88 remains a topic for future consideration. I know of no case which has authoritatively discounted the potential existence of an *implicit* justification stage under s. 88. In the near future, Parliament will no doubt feel compelled to re-examine the existence and scope of this statutory protection in light of these uncertainties and in light of the parallel constitutionalization of treaty rights under s. 35(1).[1]

The Chief Justice ultimately found that section 88 was not engaged in the matter before him and he therefore did not need to consider whether section 88 was subject to a *Sparrow*-type justificatory test. Should section 88 be made subject to such a test?

In *R. v. Alphonse*, [1993] B.C.J. No. 1402, 83 C.C.C. (3d) 417, [1993] 5 W.W.R. 401, 80 B.C.L.R. (2d) 17, 4 C.N.L.R. 19 (B.C.C.A.), the majority judgment of the British Columbia Court of Appeal considered this argument, but held that, insofar as section 88 does not, itself, infringe Aboriginal rights, it did not require justification under the *Sparrow* test. Rather, the court held that if the referentially incorporated provincial laws were found to have infringed section 35(1) rights, they, and not section 88, would need to be justified under the *Sparrow* test.

In criticizing this approach, McNeil stated that the *Alphonse* decision:

> … seems to place the burden of justification on the provinces, when in fact they are not responsible for the application of these referentially incorporated laws to Indians. If the British Columbia Court of Appeal's approach in these cases is correct, then Parliament, through the mechanism of s. 88, has succeeded in casting responsibility onto the provinces without their participation or consent, and has also been able to wash its hands of the matter without justifying this abdication of responsibility to the Aboriginal peoples whose rights are affected. This state of affairs cannot be right if the constitutional principles of division of powers and federal responsibility for s. 91(24) "Indians" have any meaning in this context.[2]

See also K. Wilkins, "Of Provinces and Section 35 Rights" (1999) 22 Dal. L.J. 185, where the author states:

> If Canada had chosen … to enact, one by one, its own measures duplicating, for Indians, the effects of selected existing provincial laws, no one would suggest that any s. 35 inquiry should focus exclusively — or at all — on the inapplicable provincial prototypes. In one respect, s. 88 does exactly that, only by different means.

See also *ibid.* at 230: "An inquiry into s. 88's own justifiability … must be independent of any possible inquiry into the merits of any of the provincial laws it incorporates".[3]

Wilkins suggests, in opposition to *Alphonse*, that section 88 ought to require justification; further, he expresses doubt as to whether that is possible, even assuming that its underlying objectives are "compelling and substantial".[4] He further maintains that section 88 neither meets *Sparrow*'s requirements that there be "as little infringement as possible in order to effect the desired result", nor that there be "sensitivity to and respect for the rights of aboriginal peoples".[5] This is so because, as he states, section 88 "makes no allowance whatever for aboriginal rights, either by according them some statutory priority (as it did for treaty rights), or by requiring some prior review of incorporated statutes to ensure some threshold of sensitivity or of proportionality".[6] See also the following comments in the Supreme Court of Canada's majority judgment in *R. v. Morris*, [2006] S.C.J. No. 59, [2006] 2 S.C.R. 915 (S.C.C.) at para. 55:

> Where a *prima facie* infringement of a treaty right is found, a province cannot rely on s. 88 by using the justification test from *Sparrow* and *Badger* in the context of s. 35(1) of the *Constitution Act, 1982*, as alluded to by Lamer C.J. in *Côté* at para. 87. The purpose of the *Sparrow/Badger* analysis is to determine whether an infringement by a government acting within its constitutionally mandated powers can be justified. This justification analysis does not alter the division of powers, which is dealt with in s. 88. Therefore, while the *Sparrow/Badger* test for infringement may be useful, the framework set out in those cases for determining whether an infringement is justified does not offer any guidance for the question at issue here.

In addition to addressing the application of the *Sparrow* test to section 88, the court in *Alphonse* considered the constitutional validity of section 88 in light of the protections existing in section 35(1) of the *Constitution Act, 1982*. It determined that section 88 remained valid in the face of section 35(1). Academic commentary has largely come to the opposite conclusion. As Brian Slattery has suggested:

> ... [T]he Federal Parliament cannot subvert the overall constitutional scheme by enacting legislation for Aboriginal peoples that referentially incorporates a wide range of Provincial statutes that could not otherwise apply to First Nations under the division of powers. Such Federal legislation, it is submitted, would seriously affect the Aboriginal right of self-government under section 35 of the *Constitution Act, 1982* and cannot meet the *Sparrow* standard of justification. So, section 88 of the current *Indian Act*, which referentially makes applicable to Indians 'all laws of general application from time to time in force in any province' is of doubtful constitutional validity.[7]

In response to the above argument, Kent McNeil stated in "Aboriginal Title and Section 88 of the Indian Act" (2000) 34 U.B.C. L. Rev. 159 at para. 12, that:

> ... Slattery's argument appears to relate only to provincial laws that infringe the rights protected by s. 35(1). Are there provincial laws of general application that could be referentially incorporated by s. 88 without infringing those rights? The answer depends upon whether the "core of Indianness at the heart of s. 91(24)" is limited to matters relating to Aboriginal and treaty rights, or is broader than that. While Chief Justice Lamer did not fully define the extent of the core of federal jurisdiction in *Delgamuukw*, earlier case law indicates that it does include exclusive jurisdiction over the status and capacity of Indians, whether or not Aboriginal or treaty rights are involved. The case law therefore suggests that the core of federal jurisdiction under s. 91(24), to which the doctrine of interjurisdictional immunity applies, extends beyond those rights. If so, then

there is some room for s. 88 to operate without infringing Aboriginal or treaty rights. In that case, if Slattery is correct (as I think he is) that federal authorization of provincial infringements of those rights is unconstitutional, then s. 88 would not be invalid, but would have to be read down in order for referential incorporation to exclude provincial laws having that effect.[8]

McNeil summarizes the situation as follows:

> ... [T]he constitutional validity of s. 88 really depends on whether it incorporates any provincial laws that do not infringe Aboriginal rights. If it does, as the pre-*Delgamuukw* jurisprudence suggests, then it is still valid, but should be read down to limit its application to the incorporation of those laws. However, if the only laws incorporated by it are laws that infringe Aboriginal rights, for the reasons outlined above it should be struck down because it violates s. 35(1). This approach would eliminate the discrepancy in the treatment of Aboriginal and treaty rights under s. 88, the historical justification for which disappeared when Aboriginal rights were acknowledged by the Supreme Court. It would also be more consistent, in the words of Lord Watson, with the "plain policy" of Canada's Constitution, whereby, "in order to ensure uniformity of administration ... Indian affairs generally [were placed] under the legislative control of one central authority." As a result, "the government vested with primary constitutional responsibility for securing the welfare of Canada's aboriginal peoples" would no longer be able to use s. 88 to avoid its fiduciary obligation to respect Aboriginal rights.[9]

D. *EX PROPRIO VIGORE*: THE DIRECT APPLICATION OF PROVINCIAL LAW TO INDIANS

The *Dick* case, in the previous section, held that provincial laws of general application apply *ex proprio vigore* (of their own force) to Indians and lands reserved for Indians, notwithstanding section 91(24) of the *Constitution Act, 1867*. Some more recent Supreme Court of Canada considerations of this issue may be seen in *Delgamuukw v. British Columbia*, [1997] S.C.J. No. 108, [1997] 3 S.C.R. 1010 (S.C.C.); *Kitkatla Band v. British Columbia (Minister of Small Business, Tourism and Culture)*, [2002] S.C.J. No. 33, [2002] 2 S.C.R. 146 (S.C.C.); *R. v. Morris*, [2006] S.C.J. No. 59, [2006] 2 S.C.R. 915 (S.C.C.) and *NIL/TU,O Child and Family Services Society v. B.C. Government and Family Services Employees' Union*, [2010] S.C.J. No. 45, [2010] 2 S.C.R. 696 (S.C.C.), all of which are excerpted below.

DELGAMUUKW v. BRITISH COLUMBIA

[1997] S.C.J. No. 108, [1997] 3 S.C.R. 1010 (S.C.C.)

Cory, McLachlin and Major JJ. concur with

Lamer C.J.C.: —

. . . . .

[177] The extent of federal jurisdiction over Indians has not been definitively addressed by this Court. We have not needed to do so because

the *vires* of federal legislation with respect to Indians, under the division of powers, has never been at issue. The cases which have come before the Court under s. 91(24) have implicated the question of jurisdiction over Indians from the other direction — whether provincial laws which on their face apply to Indians intrude on federal jurisdiction and are inapplicable to Indians to the extent of that intrusion. As I explain below, the Court has held that s. 91(24) protects a "core" of Indianness from provincial intrusion, through the doctrine of interjurisdictional immunity.[10]

[178] It follows, at the very least, that this core falls within the scope of federal jurisdiction over Indians. That core, for reasons I will develop, encompasses aboriginal rights, including the rights that are recognized and affirmed by s. 35(1). Laws which purport to extinguish those rights therefore touch the core of Indianness which lies at the heart of s. 91(24), and are beyond the legislative competence of the provinces to enact. The core of Indianness encompasses the whole range of aboriginal rights that are protected by s. 35(1). Those rights include rights in relation to land; that part of the core derives from s. 91(24)'s reference to "Lands reserved for the Indians". But those rights also encompass practices, customs and traditions which are not tied to land as well; that part of the core can be traced to federal jurisdiction over "Indians". Provincial governments are prevented from legislating in relation to both types of aboriginal rights.

(3) *Provincial Laws of General Application*

[179] The vesting of exclusive jurisdiction with the federal government over Indians and Indian lands under s. 91(24), operates to preclude provincial laws in relation to those matters. Thus, provincial laws which single out Indians for special treatment are *ultra vires*, because they are in relation to Indians and therefore invade federal jurisdiction: see *R. v. Sutherland*, [1980] 2 S.C.R. 451. However, it is a well established principle that (*Four B Manufacturing Ltd.*, *supra*, at p. 1048):

> The conferring upon Parliament of exclusive legislative competence to make laws relating to certain classes of persons does not mean that the totality of these persons' rights and duties comes under primary federal competence to the exclusion of provincial laws of general application.

In other words, notwithstanding s. 91(24), provincial laws of general application apply *proprio vigore* to Indians and Indian lands. Thus, this Court has held that provincial labour relations legislation (*Four B*) and motor vehicle laws (*R. v. Francis*, [1988] 1 S.C.R. 1025), which purport to apply to all persons in the province, also apply to Indians living on reserves.

[180] What must be answered, however, is whether the same principle allows provincial laws of general application to extinguish aboriginal rights. I have come to the conclusion that a provincial law of general application could not have this effect, for two reasons. First, a law of general application cannot, by definition, meet the standard which has been set by this Court for the extinguishment of aboriginal rights without

being *ultra vires* the province. That standard was laid down in *Sparrow* ... as one of "clear and plain" intent. In that decision, the Court drew a distinction between laws which extinguished aboriginal rights, and those which merely regulated them. Although the latter types of laws may have been "necessarily inconsistent" with the continued exercise of aboriginal rights, they could not extinguish those rights. While the requirement of clear and plain intent does not, perhaps, require that the Crown "use language which refers expressly to its extinguishment of aboriginal rights" ... the standard is still quite high. My concern is that the only laws with the sufficiently clear and plain intention to extinguish aboriginal rights would be laws in relation to Indians and Indian lands. As a result, a provincial law could never, *proprio vigore*, extinguish aboriginal rights, because the intention to do so would take the law outside provincial jurisdiction.

[181] Second, as I mentioned earlier, s. 91(24) protects a core of federal jurisdiction even from provincial laws of general application, through the operation of the doctrine of interjurisdictional immunity. That core has been described as matters touching on "Indianness" or the "core of Indianness" (*Dick*, *supra*, at pp. 326 and 315; also see *Four B*, *supra* at p. 1047 and *Francis*, *supra*, at pp. 1028-29). The core of Indianness at the heart of s. 91(24) has been defined in both negative and positive terms. Negatively, it has been held to not include labour relations (*Four B*) and the driving of motor vehicles (*Francis*). The only positive formulation of Indianness was offered in *Dick*. Speaking for the Court, Beetz J. assumed, but did not decide, that a provincial hunting law did not apply *proprio vigore* to the members of an Indian band to hunt and because those activities were "at the centre of what they do and who they are" (*supra*, at p. 320). But in *Van der Peet*, I described and defined the aboriginal rights that are recognized and affirmed by s. 35(1) in a similar fashion, as protecting the occupation of land and the activities which are integral to the distinctive aboriginal culture of the group claiming the right. It follows that aboriginal rights are part of the core of Indianness at the heart of s. 91(24). Prior to 1982, as a result, they could not be extinguished by provincial laws of general application.

(4) *Section 88 of the Indian Act*

[182] Provincial laws which would otherwise not apply to Indians *proprio vigore*, however, are allowed to do so by s. 88 of the *Indian Act*, which incorporates by reference provincial laws of general application ... However, it is important to note, in Professor Hogg's words, that s. 88 does not "invigorate" provincial laws which are invalid because they are in relation to Indians and Indian lands (*Constitutional Law of Canada* (3rd ed. 1992), at p. 676 ... (What this means is that s. 88 extends the effect of provincial laws of general application which cannot apply to Indians and Indian lands because they touch on the Indianness at the core of s. 91(24). For example, a provincial law which regulated hunting may very well touch on this core. Although such a law would not apply to aboriginal people *proprio vigore*, it would still apply through s. 88 of the *Indian Act*,

being a law of general application. Such laws are enacted to conserve game and for the safety of all.

[183] The respondent B.C. Crown argues that since such laws are *intra vires* the province, and applicable to aboriginal persons, s. 88 could allow provincial laws to extinguish aboriginal rights. I reject this submission, for the simple reason that s. 88 does not evince the requisite clear and plain intent to extinguish aboriginal rights. ... I see nothing in the language of the provision which even suggests the intention to extinguish aboriginal rights. Indeed, the explicit reference to treaty rights in s. 88 suggests that the provision was clearly not intended to undermine aboriginal rights.

In the *Kitkatla* case, below, the Supreme Court was faced with determining whether British Columbia heritage object legislation that permitted, *inter alia*, the issuing of permits to "damage, alter, cover, or move" Aboriginal cultural objects was *intra vires* the province or, alternatively, whether the legislation could be validated by section 88.

KITKATLA BAND v. BRITISH COLUMBIA (MINISTER OF SMALL BUSINESS, TOURISM AND CULTURE)

[2002] S.C.J. No. 33, [2002] 2 S.C.R. 146 (S.C.C.)

Le Bel J.: —

I. Introduction

[1] This case concerns a constitutional challenge to the application of provincial legislation on the protection of cultural heritage property. The dispute relates to culturally modified trees or CMTs. These trees have often been altered by aboriginal people as part of their traditional use and have cultural, historical and scientific importance for a number of First Nations in British Columbia. ...

II. The Origins of the Case

[2] The dispute arose during the process of administrative review and authorization of logging operations in British Columbia. The respondent, International Forest Products Limited ("Interfor"), had long held a forest licence over land in the central coast of British Columbia which included an area known as the Kumealon. Provincial forestry legislation required Interfor, as the holder of a forest licence, to propose sequential forest development plans. The legislation also granted the public some participatory rights in the creation of these plans. Interfor provided direct notification of its development plans to the appellant Kitkatla Band ("the Band") since early 1994, but these plans never specifically identified the Kumealon area. The appellants claimed aboriginal rights in this area and had been engaged in treaty negotiations with the province. In early 1998,

aware of its obligations under the Act, Interfor hired a firm of archaeologists in order to report on the impact of future logging operations in an area that included the Kumealon. Coincidentally, it appears, the appellants expressed an interest in the Kumealon at roughly the same time. Interfor was alerted to this claim, and, shortly thereafter, the firm it hired contacted the Band in order to ascertain their views. The Band designated two persons for this purpose. Interfor was concerned with the possible presence of native heritage sites and objects including CMTs in the area to be harvested. The archaeologist eventually reported the presence of a significant number of these trees in seven cutblocks Interfor intended to harvest.

[3] Meanwhile, Interfor applied to the respondent, the Minister of Small Business, Tourism and Culture ("the Minister"), for a site alteration permit under s. 12 of the Act, to authorize the cutting and processing of CMTs during logging operations. The Minister forwarded Interfor's application to the Band, along with a cover letter requesting its written submissions on the application. No submissions were received by the deadline. One week later, on March 31, 1998, and without having considered a single archaeological report, the Minister issued a site alteration permit.

[4] At this stage, the Band commenced proceedings to challenge the legality of the permit. They began judicial review proceedings. These proceedings raised administrative law arguments asserting that the Minister had failed to address all relevant issues — and had violated his fiduciary obligations towards the appellants by failing to provide them with proper notification and the opportunity to consult — before issuing the permit. The Band also challenged the Act as being *ultra vires* the province.

. . . . .

V. Constitutional Questions

[30] On January 22, 2001, the Chief Justice stated the following constitutional questions:

(1) Is s. 12(2)(a) in respect of the subject matter of s. 13(2)(c) and (d) of the *Heritage Conservation Act* in pith and substance law in relation to Indians or Lands reserved for the Indians, or alternatively, is the law in relation to property, and, therefore, within the exclusive legislative competence of the Province under s. 92(13) of the *Constitution Act, 1867*?

(2) If the impugned provisions of the *Heritage Conservation Act* are within provincial jurisdiction under s. 92(13) of the *Constitution Act, 1867* do they apply to the subject matter of s. 13(2)(c) and (d) of the *Heritage Conservation Act*?

(3) If the impugned provisions do not apply to the appellants *ex proprio vigore*, do they nonetheless apply by virtue of s. 88 of the *Indian Act*?

VI. The Issues

. . . . .

[41] ... The Court must first consider the pith and substance of the legislation. Three sub-questions must be discussed in this respect. First, do ss. 12(2)(*a*) and 13(2)(*c*) and (*d*) intrude into a federal head of power, and to what extent? Then, if they do intrude, are they nevertheless part of a valid legislative scheme? At the next step of the analysis, it should be considered whether the impugned provisions are sufficiently integrated with the scheme. If the answer is yes, we may turn to consider the doctrine of interjurisdictional immunity and, if need be, s. 88 of the *Indian Act*. Before I move on to these, I will review the heritage conservation scheme adopted by the province of British Columbia and discuss some evidentiary issues relevant to the rights claimed by the appellants.

C. *Heritage Conservation Legislation in British Columbia*

[42] The *Heritage Conservation Act* is designed to grant a broad protection to the cultural heritage of British Columbia in a very comprehensive manner. The history of the province means that its cultural heritage is in the vast majority of cases an aboriginal one, often going back to pre-contact times and prior to the establishment of the first non-native settlements and the creation of the British colonies on Vancouver Island and on the mainland. The Act was adopted to conserve and protect all forms of cultural property, objects and artifacts as well as sites in British Columbia which have heritage value to the province as a whole, to a community or to an aboriginal people, as appears for example in the definition of "heritage object" in the Act: "heritage object, means, whether designated or not, personal property that has heritage value to British Columbia, a community or an aboriginal people".

[43] The Act attempts to address the importance of the cultural heritage of First Nations in various ways. Section 4 provides for agreements with First Nations with respect to the preservation of aboriginal sites and artifacts. Section 8 states a key interpretive principle in the interpretation and implementation of the Act which is designed to protect aboriginal and treaty rights of First Nations:

> For greater certainty, no provision of this Act and no provision in an agreement entered into under section 4 abrogates or derogates from the aboriginal and treaty rights of a first nation or of any aboriginal peoples.

[44] Native concerns must be weighed at most steps of the administrative procedures created for the application of the Act. For example, prior to the designation of lands as a heritage site, notice must be given to the First Nations within whose traditional territory they lie. Section 13 grants broad protection against any alteration of sites or things in use before 1846, which will usually be part of the cultural heritage of First Nations in British Columbia (see s. 13(2)(*d*)).

[45] The Act considers First Nations' culture as part of the heritage of all residents of British Columbia. It must be protected, not only as an essential part of the collective material memory which belongs to the history and identity of First Nations, but also as part of the shared heritage of all British Columbians. The Act grants protection where none existed before. At the same time, heritage conservation schemes such as the Act here must strike a balance between conservation and other societal interests, which may require the destruction of heritage objects or sites after a careful review by the Minister. Time and nature, as well as mishaps and unforeseen events, may destroy or render the conservation of a site or thing an impossibility. Other needs and concerns may arise and require an assessment of the nature and importance of a site or cultural object. Conservation schemes must thus also provide for removal and destruction. This is what is at issue here. Is the power to order the alteration or even destruction of a cultural object beyond provincial powers when it affects native cultural objects?

D. *Evidentiary Problems*

. . . . .

[48] The appellants' claim in this case is concerned with what archaeologists refer to as culturally modified trees (CMTs). From the evidence, large numbers of CMTs are found in British Columbia. Thousands are reported and registered every year in British Columbia in the archaeology branch of the ministry. For ministry purposes, CMTs are trees which bear the marks of past aboriginal intervention occurring as part of traditional aboriginal use. Bark may have been stripped from them. Pieces or chunks of wood may have been removed from the trees to make tools or build canoes. Sap or pitch may have been collected from the trees. It would appear that the identification of CMTs is an involved process. Sometimes, the modifications found on trees result from the work of nature. On the other hand, modifications may have been made by non-native persons. Therefore, in order to identify true CMTs, archaeologists have developed complex "field" guidelines. In certain cases, these guidelines will prove incapable to the task, and it will be necessary to take a sample or even fell a particular tree to determine whether it is a CMT. In this appeal, the CMTs that the archaeologists were able to identify were generally categorized as either "bark-stripped trees" or "aboriginally-logged trees".

[49] In addition, there is one matter that, as of now, lies beyond the ken from any archaeological expert. Even if there is evidence of native intervention, it is next to impossible to tell which aboriginal group modified them (see Braidwood J.A., at para. 30). In this case, in particular, the trees are found in an area covered by the conflicting claims of the Band and another group, the Lax Kw'alaams, which, like the appellants, also belong to the Tsimshian Tribal Council. This second group has agreed with the forestry management plan proposed by Interfor, and approved by the Minister.

[50] The appellants, in support of their claim, assert that the preservation of the CMTs as living trees is required in order to safeguard evidence of their cultural heritage including the work, activities and endeavours of their forebears. Indeed, they argue that the CMTs constitute the only physical record of their heritage. Unfortunately, the evidence supporting these claims is sparse. Aside from an affidavit sworn by the appellant Chief Hill, there is very little evidence as to the extent to which these trees in the Kumealon had been related to or incorporated into the culture of the Band. In this respect, according to other evidence, the firm of archeologists hired by Interfor identified these CMTs and brought their existence to the attention of the appellants. The constitutional questions must be reviewed in the context of this factual record, with its particular weaknesses. I will now turn to the constitutional issues.

E. *The Division of Powers Issue*

[51] The Constitution of Canada does not include an express grant of power with respect to "culture" as such. Most constitutional litigation on cultural issues has arisen in the context of language and education rights. However, provinces are also concerned with broader and more diverse cultural problems and interests. In addition, the federal government affects cultural activity in this country through the exercise of its broad powers over communications and through the establishment of federally funded cultural institutions. Consequently, particular cultural issues must be analyzed in their context, in relation to the relevant sources of legislative power. In this case, the issues raised by the parties concern the use and protection of property in the province. The Act imposes limitations on property rights in the province by reason of their cultural importance. At first blush, this would seem to be a provincial matter falling within the scope of s. 92(13) of the *Constitution Act, 1867*. This view will have to be tested through a proper pith and substance analysis, in order to establish the relationship between the impugned provisions and the federal power on Indian affairs.

F. *The Pith and Substance of the Provisions of the Heritage Conservation Act*

[52] The beginning of any division of powers analysis is a characterization of the impugned law to determine the head of power within which it falls. This process is commonly known as "pith and substance analysis" ... By thus categorizing the impugned provision, one is able to determine whether the enacting legislature possesses the authority under the constitution to do what it did.

[53] A pith and substance analysis looks at both (1) the purpose of the legislation as well as (2) its effect. First, to determine the purpose of the legislation, the Court may look at both intrinsic evidence, such as purpose clauses, or extrinsic evidence, such as Hansard or the minutes of parliamentary committees.

[54] Second, in looking at the effect of the legislation, the Court may consider both its legal effect and its practical effect. In other words, the Court looks to see, first, what effect flows directly from the provisions of the statute itself; then, second, what "side" effects flow from the application of the statute which are not direct effects of the provisions of the statute itself ...

. . . . .

[58] Dickson C.J. set out in *General Motors of Canada Ltd.*, *supra*, at pp. 666-69, a three-part test for determining the pith and substance of an impugned provision. ... In my view, Dickson C.J.'s test could be re-stated in the following form:

1. Do the impugned provisions intrude into a federal head of power, and to what extent?
2. If the impugned provisions intrude into a federal head of power, are they nevertheless part of a valid provincial legislative scheme?
3. If the impugned provisions are part of a valid provincial legislative scheme, are they sufficiently integrated with the scheme?

In the rest of this section, I will consider these questions and apply the test in the context of this appeal.

G. *Purpose of the Provisions Test*

The first stage of the analysis requires a characterization of the impugned provisions in isolation, looking at both their purpose and effect. For convenience, I reproduce here ss. 12(2)(*a*) and 13(2)(*c*) and (*d*):

12...

(2)   The minister may

(*a*)   issue a permit authorizing an action referred to in section 13, ...

13...

(2)   Except as authorized by a permit issued under section 12 or 14, or an order issued under section 14, a person must not do any of the following:

. . . . .

(*c*)   damage, alter, cover or move an aboriginal rock painting or aboriginal rock carving that has historical or archaeological value;

(*d*) damage, excavate, dig in or alter, or remove any heritage object from, a site that contains artifacts, features, materials or other physical evidence of human habitation or use before 1846; ...

[60] Paragraphs (*c*) and (*d*) of s. 13(2) have as their purpose the protection of certain aboriginal heritage objects from damage, alteration, or removal. In other words, the purpose of these paragraphs is heritage

conservation, specifically the heritage of the aboriginal peoples of British Columbia. The protection extends to all aboriginal rock paintings or aboriginal rock carvings that have historical or archaeological value, as well as to heritage objects, including artifacts, features, materials or other physical evidence of human habitation or use before 1846, which in effect consists almost entirely of aboriginal cultural artifacts.

[61] Paragraph (a) of s. 12(2), on the other hand, provides the minister responsible for the operation of the Act as a whole with the discretion to grant a permit authorizing one of the actions prohibited under s. 13(2)(c) and (d). In other words, this paragraph provides a tempering of the absolute protection otherwise provided by s. 13(2)(c) and (d).

[62] The purpose of such a provision seems obvious when one considers the nature of heritage conservation legislation generally and its specific application in the context of British Columbia. No heritage conservation scheme can provide absolute protection to all objects or sites that possess some historical, archaeological, or cultural value to a society. To grant such an absolute protection would be to freeze a society at a particular moment in time. It would make impossible the need to remove, for example, buildings or artifacts of heritage value which, nevertheless, create a public health hazard or otherwise endanger lives. In other cases, the value of preserving an object may be greatly outweighed by the benefit that could accrue from allowing it to be removed or destroyed in order to accomplish a goal deemed by society to be of greater value. It cannot be denied that ss. 12(2)(a) and 13(2)(c) could sometimes affect aboriginal interests. As will be seen below, these provisions form part of a carefully balanced scheme. As recommended by the Court in *Delgamuukw, supra*, it is highly sensitive to native cultural interests. At the same time, it appears to strike an appropriate balance between native and non-native interests. Native interests must be carefully taken into account at every stage of a procedure under the Act. The Act clearly considers them as an essential part of the interests to be preserved and of the cultural heritage of British Columbia as well as of all First Nations.

[63] Consequently, any heritage conservation scheme inevitably includes provisions to make exceptions to the general protection the legislation is intended to provide. Such a permissive provision strikes a balance among competing social goals.

H. *Effect of the Provisions*

[64] Having looked at the purpose of these provisions, I turn now to consider their effects. Sections 12(2)(a) and 13(2)(c) and (d) grant the Minister a discretion to allow the alteration or removal of aboriginal heritage objects. We have no evidence before us with respect to the total number of aboriginal heritage objects which may be covered by this legislation. Nor do we have any evidence as to how often the Minister has exercised the discretion to permit the removal or destruction of aboriginal heritage objects of whatever type. We know only that, in the present case, the permit granted to the respondent Interfor allowed it to cut 40 out of

about 120 standing CMTs within seven identified cutblocks. Thus, the practical effect, in this case anyway, is to permit the destruction of what are alleged to be Kitkatla heritage objects (although there is no specific proof here that the 40 CMTs in question were indeed the products of Kitkatla ancestors) while protecting 80 CMTs from alteration and removal. In addition, all CMTs allowed to be logged must be catalogued and an archival record of them must be retained. In other words, the effect here is the striking of a balance between the need and desire to preserve aboriginal heritage with the need and desire to promote the exploitation of British Columbia's natural resources.

I. *Effect on Federal Powers*

[65] Given this analysis of the purpose and effect of the legislation in order to characterize the impugned provisions, the Court must then determine whether the pith and substance of ss. 12(2)(*a*) and 13(2)(*c*) and (*d*) fall within a provincial head of power or if, rather, they fall within a federal head of power. If the Court characterizes these provisions as a heritage conservation measure that is designed to strike a balance between the need to preserve the past while also allowing the exploitation of natural resources today, then they would fall squarely within the provincial head of power in s. 92(13) of the *Constitution Act, 1867* with respect to property and civil rights in the province.

[66] On the other hand, one cannot escape the fact that the impugned provisions directly affect the existence of aboriginal heritage objects, raising the issue of whether the provisions are in fact with respect to Indians and lands reserved to Indians, a federal head of power under s. 91(24) of the *Constitution Act, 1867*. In considering this question, the Court must assess a number of factors. First, the Court must remember the basic assumption that provincial laws can apply to aboriginal peoples; First Nations are not enclaves of federal power in a sea of provincial jurisdiction … . The mere mention of the word "aboriginal" in a statutory provision does not render it *ultra vires* the province.

[67] Second, it is clear that legislation which singles out aboriginal people for special treatment is *ultra vires* the province … For example, a law which purported to affect the Indian status of adopted children was held to be *ultra vires* the province: see *Natural Parents v. Superintendent of Child Welfare*, [1976] 2 S.C.R. 751. Similarly, laws which purported to define the extent of Indian access to land for the purpose of hunting were *ultra vires* the provinces because they singled out Indians: see *Sutherland, supra; Moosehunter v. The Queen*, [1981] 1 S.C.R. 282. Further, provincial laws must not impair the status or capacity of Indians: see *Kruger v. The Queen*, [1978] 1 S.C.R. 104, at p. 110; *Dick, supra*, at pp. 323-24.

[68] Nevertheless, "singling out" should not be confused with disproportionate effect. Dickson J. (as he then was) said in *Kruger, supra*, at p. 110, that "the fact that a law may have graver consequence to one person than to another does not, on that account alone, make the law other than one of general application".

[69] In the present case, the impugned provisions cannot be said to single out aboriginal peoples, at least from one point of view. The provisions prohibit everyone, not just aboriginal peoples, from the named acts, and require everyone, not just aboriginal peoples, to seek permission of the Minister to commit the prohibited acts. In that respect, the impugned provisions treat everyone the same. The impugned provisions' disproportionate effects can be attributed to the fact that aboriginal peoples have produced by far the largest number of heritage objects in British Columbia. These peoples have been resident in British Columbia for thousands of years; other British Columbians arrived in the last two hundred years.

[70] A more serious objection is raised with respect to the issue of whether permitting the destruction of aboriginal heritage objects impairs the status or capacity of Indians. The appellants' submission seeks to situate these cultural interests, along with aboriginal rights, at the "core of Indianness", *Delgamuukw*, *supra*, at para. 181. However, as pointed out above, little evidence has been offered by the appellants with respect to the relationship between the CMTs and Kitkatla culture in this area. The appellants argue that aboriginal heritage objects constitute a major portion of their identity and culture in a way that non-aboriginal heritage objects do not go to the centre of non-aboriginal identity. Consequently, they argue, aboriginal people are singled out for more severe treatment. I would reject this argument. Because British Columbia's history is dominated by aboriginal culture, fewer non-aboriginal objects and sites receive protection than aboriginal objects and sites. The Act provides a shield, in the guise of the permit process, against the destruction or alteration of heritage property. When one considers the relative protection afforded aboriginal and non-aboriginal heritage objects, the treatment received by both groups is the same, and indeed is more favourable, in one sense to aboriginal peoples.

[71] In any case, it should be remembered that the Act cannot apply to any aboriginal heritage object or site which is the subject of an established aboriginal right or title, by operation of s. 35(1) of the *Constitution Act, 1982* and by operation of s. 8 of the *Heritage Conservation Act* (and, by implication, s. 12(7) of that Act which states that a permit does not grant a right to alter or remove an object without the consent of the party which has title to the object or site on which the object is situated). The Act is tailored, whether by design or by operation of constitutional law, to not affect the established rights of aboriginal peoples, a protection that is not extended to any other group. On the whole, then, I am of the opinion that ss. 12(2)(*a*) and 13(2)(*c*) and (*d*) of the Act are valid provincial law and that they do not single out aboriginal peoples or impair their status or condition as Indians.

[72] It should be noted that the Attorney General of Canada intervened in support of British Columbia in this case. Dickson C.J. in *OPSEU v. Ontario (Attorney General)*, [1987] 2 S.C.R. 2, at pp. 19-20, commented on the significance of such an intervention in constitutional litigation with respect to the distribution of legislative powers.

I think it is important to note, and attach some significance to, not only the similar federal legislation but also the fact that the federal government intervened in this appeal to support the Ontario law. The distribution of powers provisions contained in the Constitution Act, 1867 do not have as their exclusive addressees the federal and provincial governments. They set boundaries that are of interest to, and can be relied upon by, all Canadians. Accordingly, the fact of federal-provincial agreement on a particular boundary between their jurisdictions is not conclusive of the demarcation of that boundary. Nevertheless, in my opinion the Court should be particularly cautious about invalidating a provincial law when the federal government does not contest its validity or, as in this case, actually intervenes to support it and has enacted legislation based on the same constitutional approach adopted by Ontario. [Emphasis deleted.]

[73] That is essentially the situation in this case: the Attorney General of Canada has intervened in support of the view of the British Columbia government with respect to the latter's right to legislate in this area. While this is not determinative of the issue, as Dickson C.J. said, it does invite the Court to exercise caution before it finds that the impugned provisions of the Act are *ultra vires* the province.

J. *Paramountcy and Federal Powers*

[74] The doctrine of paramountcy does not appear applicable in this case, as no valid federal legislation occupies the same field. ...

[75] I ... find that there is no intrusion on a federal head of power. It has not been established that these provisions affect the essential and distinctive core values of Indianness which would engage the federal power over native affairs and First Nations in Canada. They are part of a valid provincial legislative scheme. The legislature has made them a closely integrated part of this scheme. The provisions now protect native interests in situations where, before, land owners and business undertakings might have disregarded them, absent evidence of a constitutional right.

[76] The Act purports to give the provincial government a means of protecting heritage objects while retaining the ability to make exceptions where economic development or other values outweigh the heritage value of the objects. In the British Columbia context, this generally means that the provincial government must balance the need to exploit the province's natural resources, particularly its rich abundance of lumber, in order to maintain a viable economy that can sustain the province's population, with the need to preserve all types of cultural and historical heritage objects and sites within the province. ...

[77] Given this conclusion, it will not be useful to discuss the doctrine of interjurisdictional immunity. It would apply only if the provincial legislation went to the core of the federal power. ... In these circumstances, no discussion of the principle governing the application of s. 88 of the *Indian Act* would be warranted.

VII. Conclusion and Disposition

[78] Heritage properties and sites may certainly, in some cases, turn out to be a key part of the collective identity of people. In some future case, it might very well happen that some component of the cultural heritage of a First Nation would go to the core of its identity in such a way that it would affect the federal power over native affairs and the applicability of provincial legislation. This appeal does not raise such issues, based on the weak evidentiary record and the relevant principles governing the division of powers in Canada. In the circumstances of this case, the overall effect of the provision is to improve the protection of native cultural heritage and, indeed, to safeguard the presence and the memory of the cultural objects involved in this litigation, without jeopardizing the core values defining the identity of the appellants as Indians. For these reasons, I would dismiss the appeal, without costs. The constitutional questions should be answered as follows:

(1) Is s. 12(2)(*a*) in respect of the subject matter of s. 13(2)(*c*) and (*d*) of the *Heritage Conservation Act* in pith and substance law in relation to Indians or Lands reserved for the Indians, or alternatively, is the law in relation to property, and, therefore, within the exclusive legislative competence of the Province under s. 92(13) of the *Constitution Act, 1867*?

Answer: Section 12(2)(*a*) in respect of the subject matter in s. 13(2)(*c*) and (*d*) of the *Heritage Conservation Act* is in pith and substance law within the legislative competence of the Province under s. 92(13) of the *Constitution Act, 1867*.

(2) If the impugned provisions of the *Heritage Conservation Act* are within provincial jurisdiction under s. 92(13) of the *Constitution Act, 1867* do they apply to the subject matter of s. 13(2)(*c*) and (*d*) of the *Heritage Conservation Act*?

Answer: Yes.

(3). If the impugned provisions do not apply to the appellants *ex proprio vigore*, do they nonetheless apply by virtue of s. 88 of the *Indian Act*?

Answer: No need to answer.

Appeal dismissed.

Following the *Kitkatla* case the Supreme Court decided the *Morris* case, below. It provides a useful synopsis of the primary principles of federalism on Aboriginal and treaty rights.

R. v. MORRIS

[2006] S.C.J. No. 59, [2006] 2 S.C.R. 915 (S.C.C.)
(references omitted)

McLachlin C.J.C. and **Fish J.** (dissenting), **Bastarache J.** concurring: —

[83] Section 91(24) of the *Constitution Act, 1867* gives Parliament exclusive legislative authority over "Indians, and Lands reserved for the Indians". Aboriginal and treaty rights fall squarely within Parliament's jurisdiction under s. 91(24).

[84] Although s. 91(24) attributes exclusive jurisdiction over "Indians" and "Lands reserved for the Indians" to Parliament, valid provincial legislation normally applies to aboriginal persons. It is well established that "First Nations are not enclaves of federal power in a sea of provincial jurisdiction" ...

[85] The validity of a provincial enactment is a condition precedent to its application to aboriginal Canadians. A provincial law that does not fall within a provincial head of power is invalid and of no force or effect. Provincial legislation that, in pith and substance, relates to "Indians" or "Lands reserved for the Indians" — or any other matter within exclusive federal jurisdiction — is *ultra vires*. However, provincial legislation that merely has an incidental effect on a federal head of power is *intra vires*: ... Such incidental effects are without relevance for constitutional purposes .... For instance, in the aboriginal context, provincial traffic legislation applies on reserves. ... Valid provincial laws of this type apply *ex proprio vigore* to aboriginal Canadians.

[86] Determination of the pith and substance of an enactment requires an examination of its purpose as well as its legal and practical effects: *Kitkatla*, at paras. 53 and 54. ... LeBel J. set out in *Kitkatla* (at para. 58) the proper approach for determining the pith and substance of provincial legislation:

1. Do the impugned provisions intrude into a federal head of power, and to what extent?

2. If the impugned provisions intrude into a federal head of power, are they nevertheless part of a valid provincial legislative scheme?

3. If the impugned provisions are part of a valid provincial legislative scheme, are they sufficiently integrated with the scheme?

. . . . .

[89] Under the paramountcy doctrine, valid provincial legislation will be rendered inoperative if it enters into an operational conflict with valid federal legislation. Such conflict will exist if simultaneous compliance with

both provincial and federal legislation is impossible or if the provincial legislation displaces or frustrates the federal legislative purpose ... There is some debate as to the order in which the doctrine of paramountcy and the doctrine of interjurisdictional immunity should be considered by a court, particularly where s. 88 of the *Indian Act* is at issue ...

[90] Under the doctrine of interjurisdictional immunity, valid provincial legislation is constitutionally inapplicable to the extent that it intrudes or touches upon core federal legislative competence over a particular matter. Thus, exclusive federal jurisdiction under s. 91(24) protects "core Indianness" from provincial intrusion ... Valid provincial legislation which does not touch on "core Indianness" applies *ex proprio vigore*. If a law does go to "core Indianness" the impugned provincial legislation will not apply unless it is incorporated into federal law by s. 88 of the *Indian Act*.

[91] Indian treaty rights and aboriginal rights have been held to fall within the protected core of federal jurisdiction ... It follows that provincial laws of general application do not apply *ex proprio vigore* to the hunting activities of Indians that are protected by a treaty.

[92] If, however, a provincial law of general application does not affect a treaty right, and does not otherwise touch upon core Indianness, that law applies *ex proprio vigore*, without recourse to s. 88. Legislation that falls outside the internal limits on the treaty right that the parties to the treaty would have understood and intended would not encroach on the treaty right....

[95] Provincial legislation may apply to matters included within "core Indianness" if it is incorporated by s. 88 of the *Indian Act* ...

[96] The Court clarified the effect of s. 88 of the *Indian Act* in *Dick v. The Queen*, [1985] 2 S.C.R. 309. The Court noted that for the purposes of s. 88 there are two categories of provincial laws: (1) laws which can be applied to Indians without touching their Indianness; and (2) laws which cannot apply to Indians without regulating them *qua* Indians (pp. 326-27). The first category of provincial laws applies to Indians without any constitutional difficulty. The second category cannot apply to Indians by reason of the doctrine of interjurisdictional immunity. It is to this second category of provincial legislation that s. 88 of the *Indian Act* is directed. Thus, s. 88 incorporates provincial laws of general application that are otherwise constitutionally inapplicable to Indians — laws that are precluded from applying to Indians by the doctrine of interjurisdictional immunity because they affect core Indianness, a matter under federal jurisdiction.

[97] ... s. 88 does not incorporate all provincial laws that are otherwise inapplicable by reason of the doctrine of interjurisdictional immunity. Section 88 operates, *inter alia*, "[s]ubject to the terms of any treaty". In other words, s. 88 cannot incorporate a provincial law that conflicts with a treaty right.

[98] What type or degree of conflict is required between a provincial law of general application and a treaty to engage the treaty exception's protection? On the authorities, an insignificant burden on a treaty right is

not enough. ... At the other end of the spectrum, a more searching "unjustified infringement" test would be inappropriate ...

[99] In our view, a *prima facie* infringement test best characterizes the degree of conflict required to engage the protection of the treaty exception. Legislation that places no real burden on the treaty right does not constitute a *prima facie* infringement and would not trigger the treaty exception. Legislation which engages the internal limits of a treaty right does not affect the treaty right at all, and therefore, *a fortiori*, does not constitute a *prima facie* infringement.

[100] On this basis, provincial regulatory authority over Indian treaty rights may be summarized as follows:

1. Provincial laws directed at the regulation of treaty rights are *ultra vires*;

2. Valid provincial laws of general application that do not affect or infringe treaty rights apply to Indians either:

   (a) *ex proprio vigore*; or

   (b) through incorporation under s. 88, if they nevertheless touch upon core Indianness in some other manner; Valid provincial laws that fall outside of the scope of the treaty right, by virtue of an internal limit on the treaty right, do not go to "core Indianness," and thus apply *ex proprio vigore*. They do not need to be incorporated by s. 88; and

3. Valid provincial laws of general application that constitute a *prima facie* infringement of treaty rights trigger the treaty exception in s. 88 and are constitutionally inapplicable. Provincial laws that impose only an insignificant burden on a treaty right (see *Côté*) do not trigger that exception and are therefore incorporated by s. 88.

The *Morris* case also contains a very helpful review of federalism principles in relation to provincially constituted administrative tribunals. The question the Court considered was whether, as a result of the division of powers in the *Constitution Act, 1867*, there were limitations on the ability of courts or tribunals to hear and rule upon arguments relating to Aboriginal or treaty rights. In other words, may only those courts falling under federal jurisdiction or tribunals created by validly enacted federal legislation deal with such matters? In *Paul v. British Columbia (Forest Appeals Commission)*, [2003] S.C.J. No. 34, [2003] 2 S.C.R. 585, 2003 SCC 55 (S.C.C.), the Supreme Court of Canada held that provincially-created administrative tribunals may hear and rule upon arguments relating to Aboriginal or treaty rights in the course of carrying out their constitutionally valid mandates. In contemplating whether section 35(1) rights matters are sufficiently distinct from other constitutional matters to warrant excluding them from the jurisdiction of validly created provincial tribunals, Bastarache J., for the Court, in *R. v. Morris*, [2006] S.C.J. No. 59, [2006] 2 S.C.R. 915 (S.C.C.), stated:

[36] ... there is no basis for requiring an express empowerment that an administrative tribunal be able to apply s. 35 of the *Constitution Act, 1982*. There is no persuasive basis for distinguishing the power to determine

s. 35 questions from the power to determine other constitutional questions, such as the division of powers under the *Constitution Act, 1867* or a right under the *Charter*. Section 35 is not, any more than the *Charter*, "some holy grail which only judicial initiates of the superior courts may touch" ... This Court has rejected the theory that Indian reserves are federal "enclaves" from which provincial laws are excluded ... Similarly, aboriginal rights do not constitute an enclave that excludes a provincially created administrative tribunal from ruling, at first instance, on the border between those aboriginal rights and a provincial law of general application. The arguments that s. 35 rights are qualitatively different — that they are more complex, and require greater expertise in relation to the evidence adduced — have little merit. ...

To the extent that aboriginal rights are unwritten, communal or subject to extinguishment, and thus a factual inquiry is required, it is worth noting that administrative tribunals, like courts, have fact-finding functions. Boards are not necessarily in an inferior position to undertake such tasks. Indeed, the more relaxed evidentiary rules of administrative tribunals may in fact be more conducive than a superior court to the airing of an aboriginal rights claim. ...

. . . . .

[38] I conclude, therefore, that there is no principled basis for distinguishing s. 35 rights from other constitutional questions.

Some issues revolving around the application of provincial law to Indians are more contentious than others. This is particularly true when First Nations take contrary positions on whether federal or provincial governments should have jurisdiction over matters they consider vital to their identities: see Maggie Wente, "Case Comment: *NIL/TUO Child and Family Services Society v. B.C. Government and Service Employees' Union* and *Communications, Energy and Paperworkers of Canada v. Native Child and Family Services of Toronto*" (2011) 10 Indigenous L.J. 133. These challenges arise because federalism leaves almost no room for First Nations to frame their distinct legal status in relation to provincial and federal governments. A recent example may be seen in *NIL/TU,O Child and Family Services Society v. B.C. Government and Services Employees' Union*, [2010] S.C.J. No. 45, [2010] 2 S.C.R. 696 (S.C.C.), in which the Supreme Court of Canada attempted to resolve the jurisdictional overlap between labour relations and child welfare.

NIL/TU,O CHILD AND FAMILY SERVICES SOCIETY v. B.C. GOVERNMENT AND SERVICE EMPLOYEES' UNION

[2010] S.C.J. No. 45, [2010] 2 S.C.R. 696 (S.C.C.)

The judgment of **LeBel, Deschamps, Abella, Charron, Rothstein** and **Cromwell JJ.** was delivered by **Abella J.**: —

[1] NIL/TU,O Child and Family Services Society ("NIL/TU,O") provides child welfare services to certain First Nations children and

families in British Columbia. It has a unique institutional structure, combining provincial accountability, federal funding, and a measure of operational independence.

[2] None of the parties dispute that child welfare is a matter within provincial legislative competence under the *Constitution Act, 1867*. NIL/TU,O does not challenge the constitutional validity of the *Child, Family and Community Service Act*, R.S.B.C. 1996, c. 46, as it applies to Aboriginal people. Nor is the issue whether the federal government can enact labour relations legislation dealing with "Indians". It clearly can. The issue in this appeal is whether NIL/TU,O's labour relations nonetheless fall within federal jurisdiction over Indians under s. 91(24) because its services are designed for First Nations children and families.

. . . . .

Background

[5] In 1997, seven First Nations collectively incorporated NIL/TU,O under British Columbia's *Society Act*, R.S.B.C. 1996, c. 433, to establish a child welfare agency that would provide "culturally appropriate" services to their children and families. NIL/TU,O operates out of offices on the Tsawout reserve and provides its services to the members of the "Collective First Nations", currently comprised of the Beecher Bay, Pacheedaht, Pauquachin, Songhees, T'Sou-ke, Tsartlip and Tsawout First Nations.

[6] In 2005, the British Columbia Government and Service Employees' Union applied to the British Columbia Labour Relations Board to be certified as the bargaining agent for all employees of NIL/TU,O, excluding the executive director. NIL/TU,O objected, arguing that its labour relations fell under federal jurisdiction.

[7] The Board dismissed NIL/TU,O's objection. NIL/TU,O was, in the Board's view, an "'Indian' organization" ((2006), 122 C.L.R.B.R. (2d) 174, at para. 47). However, without some connection to the exercise of federal legislative power, that "'Indian' content" did not attract federal jurisdiction over labour relations (para. 47). The Board accordingly certified the Union under the B.C. *Labour Relations Code*, R.S.B.C. 1996, c. 244. A three-member panel of the Board subsequently dismissed NIL/TU,O's request for reconsideration ((2006), 127 C.L.R.B.R. (2d) 137).

[8] On judicial review, Cullen J. of the Supreme Court of British Columbia granted the application on the grounds that NIL/TU,O's labour relations fell under federal jurisdiction and were therefore not within the Board's authority (2007 BCSC 1080, 76 B.C.L.R. (4th) 322). He found that NIL/TU,O's operations and activities had a federal dimension and, even though those operations served provincial ends, they did so by uniquely Aboriginal means. Cullen J. accordingly overturned the Board's certification order.

[9] The Union then sought and obtained certification from the Canada Industrial Relations Board under the *Canada Labour Code*. Despite its federal certification, the Union appealed Cullen J.'s decision to the British

Columbia Court of Appeal where Groberman J.A., writing for a unanimous court, concluded that NIL/TU,O's operations — and therefore its labour relations — fell under provincial jurisdiction (2008 BCCA 333, 81 B.C.L.R. (4th) 318). In his view, nothing in the *Child, Family and Community Service Act*, the design of NIL/TU,O's operations or the nature of NIL/TU,O's services took NIL/TU,O outside provincial jurisdiction. Primary provincial jurisdiction over labour relations was not "ousted" simply because NIL/TU,O's operations "engage[d] the interests of [A]boriginal groups" or because NIL/TU,O provided services in a "culturally sensitive" manner (para. 62).

. . . . .

Analysis

[11] Jurisdiction over labour relations is not delegated to either the provincial or federal governments under s. 91 or s. 92 of the *Constitution Act, 1867*. But since *Toronto Electric Commissioners v. Snider* [1925] A.C. 396 (P.C.), Canadian courts have recognized that labour relations are presumptively a provincial matter, and that the federal government has jurisdiction over labour relations only by way of exception. ...

[14] [Dickson J.] ... set out a "functional test" for determining whether an entity is "federal" for purposes of triggering federal labour relations jurisdiction [in *Construction Montcalm*]. Significantly, the "core" of the telecommunications head of power was not used to determine, as part of the functional analysis, the nature of the subsidiary's operations:

> (5) The question whether an undertaking, service or business is a federal one depends on the nature of its operation.
>
> (6) In order to determine the nature of the operation, <u>one must look at the normal or habitual activities of the business</u> as those of "a going concern", without regard for exceptional or casual factors; otherwise, the Constitution could not be applied with any degree of continuity and regularity. [Emphasis added; p. 132.]

. . . . .

[18] In ... determining whether an entity's labour relations will be federally regulated, thereby displacing the operative presumption of provincial jurisdiction, *Four B* requires that a court first apply the functional test, that is, examine the nature, operations and habitual activities of the entity to see if it is a federal undertaking. If so, its labour relations will be federally regulated. Only if this inquiry is inconclusive should a court proceed to an examination of whether provincial regulation of the entity's *labour relations* would impair the core of the federal head of power at issue.

[19] Notwithstanding this Court's long-standing approach, a different line of authority has uniquely emerged when courts are dealing with s. 91(24) ... This divergent analysis proceeds, contrary to *Four B*, directly to the question of whether the "core" of the head of power is impaired,

without applying the functional test first. Moreover, rather than considering whether the regulation of the entity's *labour relations* would impair the "core" of a federal head of power, these decisions have examined instead whether the nature of the entity's *operations* lay at the "core" and therefore displaced the presumption that labour relations are provincially regulated.

[20] There is no reason why, as a matter of principle, the jurisdiction of an entity's labour relations should be approached differently when s. 91(24) is at issue. The fundamental nature of the inquiry is — and should be — the same as for any other head of power. It is an inquiry with two distinct steps, the first being the functional test. A court should proceed to the second step only when this first test is inconclusive....

. . . . .

[23] ... The delivery of child welfare services in British Columbia is governed by the *Child, Family and Community Service Act*. The Act sets out a detailed child protection regime for the province that is administered by "directors" appointed by the Minister for Child and Family Development (s. 91).

[24] The province of British Columbia (represented by a director appointed under the Act), the federal government (represented by the Minister of Indian Affairs) and NIL/TU,O (representing the Collective First Nations) are parties to a tripartite delegation agreement, first signed in 1999 and later confirmed in 2004 ("2004 Agreement"). Under this agreement, the provincial government, as the keeper of constitutional authority over child welfare, delegated some of its statutory powers and responsibilities over the delivery of child welfare services to the Collective First Nations to NIL/TU,O. This delegation is anticipated by s. 93(1)(g)(iii) of the Act, which permits a provincial director to make agreements for the delivery of statutory child welfare services with legal entities representing Aboriginal communities. The federal government's role in the arrangement is limited to financing NIL/TU,O's provision of certain services to certain children.

[25] The 2004 Agreement established NIL/TU,O's responsibility for delivering services provided for in the Act to the Collective First Nations' children and their families and confirmed the rights of those children to be connected to their culture and to receive "culturally appropriate" services from NIL/TU,O (arts. 2.1(a) and (d)). It provides that the province of British Columbia has legislative authority in respect of child welfare and that the director is responsible for administering the Act (Preamble, art. D). The 2004 Agreement also provides, however, that NIL/TU,O has the right to "care for and protect NIL/TU,O Children and to preserve their connection to their culture and heritage through the delivery of culturally appropriate Services" (Preamble, art. G).

. . . . .

[31] In all cases, a director under the Act can intervene to ensure NIL/TU,O's compliance with the Act (2004 Agreement, art. 4.3). When a director and NIL/TU,O disagree as to a child's safety or placement or as to the provision of services, the director's decision is paramount (2004 Agreement, art. 14.2). The director is also empowered to revoke, unilaterally, NIL/TU,O's delegated authority upon written notice (2004 Agreement, art. 18.5).

[32] The 2004 Agreement requires that, in addition to delivering delegated services in accordance with the Act, NIL/TU,O must comply with the Aboriginal Operational and Practice Standards and Indicators ("AOPSI") (2004 Agreement, arts. 4.2 and 4.5). The AOPSI were developed collaboratively by the Executive Directors of Aboriginal child and family service agencies, the Department of Indian Affairs and Northern Development, British Columbia's Ministry for Children and Families, and the Caring for First Nations Children Society.   They prescribe the "readiness criteria" that must be met before an Aboriginal child and family services agency receives delegated authority under the Act, and set out practice standards that govern the provision of services by Aboriginal agencies, some of which address the unique circumstances of Aboriginal children (see standards 4, 11 and 15).

[33] In addition to its delegated powers, NIL/TU,O's goals include the delivery of services that are not provided for in the Act. These non-statutory services include after-school programs designed to increase children's appreciation of First Nations' culture, a camp where youth learn traditional practices, youth justice initiatives that pair troubled youth with mentors and elders, and school support programs that provide mentors to children who encounter racism and discrimination. The record does not, as the Court of Appeal pointed out, establish the extent to which these activities form part of NIL/TU,O's day-to-day operations.

[34] NIL/TU,O receives both provincial and federal funding. Before the province delegated to NIL/TU,O some of its authority to provide child welfare services to the Collective First Nations, the federal funds now paid to NIL/TU,O were allocated to the province pursuant to a memorandum of understanding between the federal and provincial governments. The memorandum did not, as the Chief Justice and Fish J. suggest, delegate regulatory or legislative power from the federal to provincial government. Rather, it simply confirmed that the province is responsible for administering the Act for the benefit of "Indian" children under nineteen, and affirmed the parties' understanding that the federal government would reimburse the province for the cost of providing certain services to certain "Indian" children (Memorandum of Understanding, arts. 1.1 and 4.1). The province currently pays NIL/TU,O for those services that are ineligible for federal funding (2004 Agreement, art. 15.6).

[35] Indeed, 65 percent of NIL/TU,O's funding now comes directly from the federal government. Pursuant to federal Program Directives 20-1, the federal government pays for the statutory services NIL/TU,O provides to eligible children in accordance with the following principles:

6.1 The [Department of Indian Affairs] is committed to the expansion of First Nations Child and Family Services on reserve to a level comparable to the services provided off reserve in similar circumstances. . .

6.2 The department will support the creation of Indian designed, controlled and managed services.

6.3 The department will support the development of Indian standards for those services, and will work with Indian organizations to encourage their adoption by provinces/ territor[ies].

6.4 The expansion of First Nations Child and Family Services (FNCPS) will be gradual as funds become available and First Nations are prepared to negotiate the establishment of new services or the takeover of existing services.

6.5 <u>Provincial child and family services legislation is applicable on reserves and will form the basis for this expansion. It is the intention of the department to include the provinces in the process and as party to agreements.</u> [Emphasis added.]

[36] What, then, does all this tell us about the nature of NIL/TU,O's operations? Clearly NIL/TU,O is regulated exclusively by the province, and its employees exercise exclusively provincial delegated authority. This complex operational scheme was undoubtedly created for the benefit of the Collective First Nations. The child welfare services that NIL/TU,O offers are provided primarily by Aboriginal employees to Aboriginal clients and are designed to protect, preserve and benefit the distinct cultural, physical and emotional needs of the children and families of the Collective First Nations. NIL/TU,O serves as the child welfare agency for this community.

[37] NIL/TU,O argues that this distinctively Aboriginal component of its service delivery methodology alters the nature of its operations and activities such that it is a federal undertaking, service or business for the purpose of allocating labour relations jurisdiction. In my view, it does not.

[38] Provincial competence over child welfare is exercised in British Columbia through the *Child, Family and Community Service Act*, and NIL/TU,O's operations are wholly regulated by it. NIL/TU,O is a fully integrated part of this provincial regulatory regime, pursuant to authority that is delegated, circumscribed and supervised by provincial officials. As an organization, it is directly subject to the province's oversight, and NIL/TU,O's employees are directly accountable to the provincial directors, who are empowered to intervene when necessary to ensure statutory compliance. Provincial child welfare workers are, in fact, required to step in when one of NIL/TU,O's cases involves child protection issues since NIL/TU,O's employees are not authorized to provide protection services. Moreover, NIL/TU,O's Constitution and the 2004 Agreement recognize the Act as the statutory authority governing the Society's primary task, namely providing statutory child welfare services. When fulfilling this task, NIL/TU,O must always operate with the Act's two paramount considerations in mind — the safety and well-being of children — and must always comply with the Act as a whole. The

province, therefore, retains ultimate decision-making control over NIL/TU,O's operations.

[39] None of this detracts from NIL/TU,O's distinct character as a child welfare organization for Aboriginal communities. But the fact that it serves these communities cannot take away from its essential character as a child welfare agency that is in all respects regulated by the province. Neither the cultural identity of NIL/TU,O's clients and employees, nor its mandate to provide culturally-appropriate services to Aboriginal clients, displaces the operating presumption that labour relations are provincially regulated. ...

[40] And while it is true that NIL/TU,O receives federal funds pursuant to a federal funding directive, an intergovernmental memorandum of understanding and the 2004 Agreement, this does not rise to the level of federal operational involvement necessary to demonstrate that NIL/TU,O is a federal undertaking, service or business. ...

[41] In my view, British Columbia's *Child, Family and Community Service Act*, by expressly recognizing, affirming and giving practical meaning to the unique rights and status of Aboriginal people in the child welfare context, and by expressly respecting Aboriginal culture and heritage, represents a commendable, constitutionally mandated exercise of legislative power. The very fact that the delivery of child welfare services is delegated to First Nations agencies marks, significantly and positively, public recognition of the particular needs of Aboriginal children and families. It seems to me that this is a development to be encouraged in the provincial sphere, not obstucted.

. . . . .

[44] By virtue of the memorandum of understanding and the tripartite agreement, the federal government actively endorsed the province's oversight of the delivery of child welfare services to Aboriginal children in the province, including those services provided by NIL/TU,O to the Collective First Nations. I see this neither as an abdication of regulatory responsibility by the federal government nor an inappropriate usurpation by the provincial one. It is, instead, an example of flexible and co-operative federalism at work and at its best.

[45] The essential nature of NIL/TU,O's operation is to provide child and family services, a matter within the provincial sphere. Neither the presence of federal funding, nor the fact that NIL/TU,O's services are provided in a culturally sensitive manner, in my respectful view, displaces the overridingly provincial nature of this entity. The community for whom NIL/TU,O operates as a child welfare agency does not change *what* it does, namely, deliver child welfare services. The designated beneficiaries may and undoubtedly should affect how those services are delivered, but they do not change the fact that the delivery of child welfare services, a provincial undertaking, is what it essentially does.

[46] And neither the nature of NIL/TU,O's operation nor the jurisprudence calls for an inquiry into the "core of Indianness" in this appeal. The *Northern Telecom/Four B* principles clearly and conclusively confirm that NIL/TU,O is a provincial undertaking. The past eighty-five

years of labour jurisprudence confirms that no further or alternate analysis is required. The presumption in favour of provincial jurisdiction over labour relations, therefore, remains operative in this case

[47] I would therefore dismiss the appeal with costs.

The reasons of **McLachlin C.J.C.** and **Binnie** and **Fish JJ.** were delivered by **McLachlin C.J.C.** and **Fish J.**: —

. . . . .

[50] We agree with Justice Abella that provincial labour law applies to the appellant and that the appeal should be dismissed. However, we arrive at this conclusion by a somewhat different route.

. . . . .

[55] There is no dispute the power over Indians under s. 91(24) has been held to contain a protected core of federal competency that provincial legislation cannot touch. ... As Lamer C.J. wrote for the majority in *Delgamuukw v. British Columbia*, [1997] 3 S.C.R. 1010, at para. 181:

> ... as I mentioned earlier, s. 91(24) protects a core of federal jurisdiction even from provincial laws of general application, through the operation of the doctrine of interjurisdictional immunity. That core has been described as matters touching on "Indianness" or the "core of Indianness" (*Dick, supra*, at pp. 326 and 315; also see *Four B, supra*, at p. 1047 and *Francis, supra*, at pp. 1028-29).

[56] Unlike Abella J., we conclude the central question is whether the operation at issue falls within the protected "core of Indianness" under s. 91(24) of the *Constitution Act, 1867*, and hence under federal jurisdiction. The starting point is the general rule that labour issues fall within provincial jurisdiction. The only question is whether this case falls within the exception to this rule, i.e., whether applying a functional test, the activity falls within the core of a federal power that is protected from provincial legislation. ...

. . . . .

[59] ... Justice Abella concludes that the core of Indianness should be considered only if the functional test is inconclusive. But the essence of the functional test, ... is whether the function falls within the core of a federal power; only this can displace the presumption of provincial jurisdiction in labour matters. The two-stage test proposed by our colleague would mean that labour jurisdiction would be determined in many cases before consideration of the power under s. 91(24) is reached. With respect, deciding labour jurisdiction in a case such as this without scrutiny of the federal power hollows out the functional test as conceived on the authorities. If a court were satisfied that the operation's normal activities *look provincial* on their face, it would not need to go further.

[60] To exclude consideration of s. 91(24) would negate the federal power. Conversely, to deem any Aboriginal aspect sufficient to trigger federal jurisdiction would threaten to swallow the presumption that labour relations fall under provincial jurisdiction. The proper approach is simply to ask, as the cases consistently have, whether the Indian operation at issue, viewed functionally in terms of its normal and habitual activities, falls within the core of s. 91(24) of the *Constitution Act, 1867.*

. . . . .

[70] ... [T]he core, or "basic, minimum and unassailable content" of the federal power over "Indians" in s. 91(24) is defined as matters that go to the status and rights of Indians. Where their status and rights are concerned, Indians are federal "persons", regulated by federal law: see *Canadian Western Bank*, at para. 60.

[71] It follows that a provincial law of general application will extend to Indian undertakings, businesses or enterprises, whether on or off a reserve, *ex proprio vigore* and by virtue of s. 88 of the *Indian Act*, R.S.C. 1985, c. I-5, *except* when the law impairs those functions of the enterprise which are intimately bound up with the status and rights of Indians. The cases illustrate matters that may go to the status and rights of Indians. These include, *inter alia*:

- Indian status: *Natural Parents v. Superintendent of Child Welfare*, [1976] 2 S.C.R. 751, *per* Laskin C.J., writing for himself and three other Justices, at pp. 760-61, and *per* Beetz J., writing for himself and Pigeon J., at p. 787;
- The "relationships within Indian families and reserve communities": *Canadian Western Bank*, at para. 61;
- "[R]ights so closely connected with Indian status that they should be regarded as necessary incidents of status such for instance as registrability, membership in a band, the right to participate in the election of Chiefs and Band Councils, reserve privileges, etc.": *Four B*, at p. 1048;
- The disposition of the matrimonial home on a reserve: *Paul v. Paul*, [1986] 1 S.C.R. 306
- The right to possession of lands on a reserve and, therefore, the division of family property on reserve lands: *Derrickson v. Derrickson*, [1986] 1 S.C.R. 285, at p. 296;
- Sustenance hunting pursuant to Aboriginal and treaty rights, such as the killing of deer for food: *Dick*;
- The right to advance a claim for the existence or extent of Aboriginal rights or title in respect of a contested resource or lands: *Delgamuukw* and *Kitkatla Band v. British Columbia (Minister of Small Business, Tourism and Culture)*, 2002 SCC 31, [2002] 2 S.C.R. 146; and
- The operation of constitutional and federal rules respecting Aboriginal rights: *Paul v. British Columbia*, among others.

. . . . .

[73] The scope of the core of s. 91(24) is admittedly narrow. That, however, is as it should be. A narrow test for when activities fall within the core of Indianness reserved to the federal government is consistent with the dominant tenor of jurisprudence since *Four B*, as well as the restrained approach to interjurisdictional immunity adopted by this Court in recent cases. It recognizes that Indians are members of the broader population and, therefore, in their day-to-day activities, they are subject to provincial laws of general application. ... Only where the activity is so integrally related to what makes Indians and lands reserved for Indians a fundamental federal responsibility does it become an intrinsic part of the exclusive federal jurisdiction, such that provincial legislative power is excluded.

II. The Normal or Habitual Activities of NIL/TU,O

. . . . .

[76] The function of NIL/TU,O is the provision of child welfare services under the umbrella of the province-wide network of agencies providing similar services. The ordinary and habitual activities of NIL/TU,O do not touch on issues of Indian status or rights. The child welfare services therefore cannot be considered federal activities.

[77] This conclusion is not negated by the fact that the federal government has entered into an intergovernmental agreement with the province of British Columbia and NIL/TU,O, which requires the province, in exchange for funding and reimbursement and acting through NIL/TU,O, to extend child welfare services on reserves. The federal government has ceded its responsibility for the provision of child welfare services on reserve to the province and has agreed to partially fund their delivery, provided that they would be subject to provincial law. NIL/TU,O, as the deliverer of those services, is therefore bound by the applicable provincial legislation.

[78] In the absence of NIL/TU,O's services touching on any of the facets of Indianness which might draw it within federal jurisdiction, NIL/TU,O's operations cannot be said to be federal operations. The fact that NIL/TU,O's services are delivered in a way that is culturally sensitive to Aboriginal identity and values does not change the basic functions of the enterprise. In this, we agree with Justice Abella.

[79] It is argued that because the appellant's services are directed at preserving the cultural identity of Indian children and confirming their Aboriginal traditions and values, the operations go to the core of what it is to be Indian, and that *Four B*, where the activity was making leather shoe uppers, is distinguishable on this basis. However, this is to look at the incidental effect of the activity instead of the operational nature of the business itself. *Four B* is clear that one looks not to the purpose or effects of the enterprise, but to the activity it carries out.

[80] The fact that NIL/TU,O employs Indians and works for the welfare of Indian children in a culturally sensitive way that seeks to enhance Aboriginal identity and preserve Aboriginal values does not alter its essential function – the provision of child welfare services. As stated by Justice Abella, the organization is subject to provincial oversight, regulation, funding and governance. The provision of child welfare services constitutes its normal and principal operation. The rule that Indian operations within a province are subject to generally applicable provincial law is not displaced by the doctrine of interjurisdictional immunity because the operations, viewed from a functional perspective, do not fall within the protected core of s. 91(24).

[81] Nor does the fact that NIL/TU,O's services impact on the Aboriginal family relationship make its operations a federal matter. *Natural Parents*, which is relied on for this proposition, dealt with provincial adoption legislation that had the potential to strip Indian children of their Indian status. It finds no application here, as Indian status is not affected by NIL/TU,O's operations.

III. Conclusion

[82] We would affirm the judgment of the British Columbia Court of Appeal and dismiss the appeal.

Appeal dismissed with costs.

A companion case to the *NIL/TU,O Child and Family Services Society* case, *Communications, Energy and Paperworkers Union of Canada v. Native Child and Family Services of Toronto*, [2010] S.C.J. No. 46, [2010] 2 S.C.R. 737 (S.C.C.), was decided on the same grounds, with a similar split between the majority and minority judgments in the case as in *NIL/TU,O Child and Family Services Society*.

At para. 73 of McLachlin C.J.C.'s concurring judgment in *NIL/TU,O Child and Family Services Society*, she wrote:

> The scope of the core of s. 91(24) is admittedly narrow. That, however, is as it should be. A narrow test for when activities fall within the core of Indianness reserved to the federal government is consistent with the dominant tenor of jurisprudence since *Four B*, as well as the restrained approach to interjurisdictional immunity adopted by this Court in recent cases. It recognizes that Indians are members of the broader population and, therefore, in their day-to-day activities, they are subject to provincial laws of general application. ...

How does this statement align with First Nations views that section 91(24) should be construed in a large, liberal and generous manner to foster inherent and distinctive jurisdictional space under section 35(1) of Canada's Constitution?

E. ABROGATING OR DEROGATING FROM ABORIGINAL AND TREATY RIGHTS

As we have seen, provincial laws can apply to Indians and lands reserved to Indians through section 88 of the *Indian Act*, R.S.C. 1985, c. I-5. Furthermore, provincial laws of general application can apply to Indians *ex proprio vigore* if they do not single out Indians. In this section we will see that these are not the only instances in which legislatures can significantly affect Aboriginal peoples.

In 1916, Great Britain (on behalf of Canada) entered into a convention with the United States to protect migratory birds. The *Migratory Birds Convention Act, 1917*, S.C. 1917, c. 18 [now *Migratory Birds Convention Act, 1994*, S.C. 1994, c. 22] implemented the convention into Canadian domestic law. Under the convention, the ability to hunt migratory birds was restricted, with limited exceptions being made for hunting by Aboriginal peoples. When Treaty No. 11 was signed in 1921, the Aboriginal signatories were assured that their rights to hunt would be protected. No mention was made about the effect, if any, of the Migratory Birds Convention on those rights. This issue came to a head in the case of *R. v. Sikyea*, below, when a charge was laid against a Treaty No. 11 Indian who had shot a migratory bird out of season.

R. v. SIKYEA

(1964), 43 D.L.R. (2d) 150, 43 C.R. 83, 46 W.W.R. 65, [1964] 2 C.C.C. 325 (N.W.T.C.A.), affd [1964] S.C.J. No. 42, [1964] S.C.R. 642, 44 C.R. 266, 49 W.W.R. 306, [1965] 2 C.C.C. 129, 50 D.L.R. (2d) 80 (S.C.C.)

The judgment of the Court was delivered by

Johnson J.A.: — The respondent in this case was convicted by a Magistrate at Yellowknife upon a charge of unlawfully killing a migratory bird in an area described in Schedule A, Part XI, of the *Migratory Bird Regulations* P.C. 1958 1070, SOR/58-308, at a time not during an open season for that bird in the area, in violation of s. 5(1)(a) of the *Migratory Bird Regulations*. He was fined $10 and costs.

. . . . . .

The respondent is an Indian and a member of Band Number 84 under Treaty 11. ... [H]e was on his way out to the bush to see if he was able to do his customary work. He had taken his tent, gun and muskrat traps and was planning to trap muskrats. He expected to be away two or three weeks. He had taken no food, expecting to shoot game. He shot this duck for food.

The right of Indians to hunt and fish for food on unoccupied Crown lands has always been recognized in Canada — in the early days as an incident of their "ownership" of the land, and later by the treaties by which the Indians gave up their ownership right in these lands.

. . . . .

It was not until 1921 that the Indian rights in that part of the Northwest Territories that includes Yellowknife were surrendered by Treaty 11. As part of the consideration for surrendering their interest in the lands covered by the treaty, the Indians received the following covenant:

> And his Majesty the King hereby agrees with the said Indians that they shall have the right to pursue their usual vocations of hunting, trapping and fishing throughout the tract surrendered as heretofore described, subject to such regulations as may from time to time be made by the Government of the Country acting under the authority of His Majesty, and saving and excepting such tracts as may be required or taken up from time to time for settlement, mining, lumbering, trading or other purposes.

. . . . .

These Indians, as well as all others, would have been surprised indeed if in the face of such assurances, the clause in their treaty which purported to continue their rights to hunt and fish could be used to restrict their right to shoot game birds to one and a half months each year. ...

. . . . .

Because of the Government's concern with the Indians' right to pursue "their usual vocations of hunting, trapping and fishing", and that its obligations under the treaties should be performed, it is difficult to understand why these treaties were not kept in mind when the Migratory Birds Convention was negotiated and when its terms were implemented by the *Migratory Birds Convention Act*, R.S.C. 1952, c. 179, and the Regulations made under that Act.

That Convention was entered into by Great Britain (on behalf of Canada), with the United States in August, 1916 and ratified by both Governments in December of that year.

. . . . .

[T]he purpose of the Convention was to save migratory birds "from indiscriminate slaughter" and to assure their preservation. This, it seems to me, would have allowed for exceptions or reservations in favour of the Indians, for there can be no doubt that the amount of game birds taken by the Indians for food during the close season would not have resulted in "indiscriminate slaughter" of birds nor would the preservation of those birds have been threatened. We are told that the treaty between the United States and Mexico negotiated in 1936 permits indigent persons in Mexico to take these types of birds for food.

The *Migratory Birds Convention Act*, 1917 (Can.), c. 18, "sanctioned, ratified and confirmed" the Convention.

. . . . .

It is, I think, clear that the rights given to the Indians by their treaties as they apply to migratory birds have been taken away by this Act and its Regulations. How are we to explain this apparent breach of faith on the part of the Government, for I cannot think it can be described in any other terms? This cannot be described as a minor or insignificant curtailment of these treaty rights, for game birds have always been a most plentiful, a most reliable and a readily obtainable food in large areas of Canada. I cannot believe that the Government of Canada realized that in implementing the Convention they were at the same time breaching the treaties that they had made with the Indians. It is much more likely that these obligations under the treaties were overlooked — a case of the left hand having forgotten what the right hand had done. The subsequent history of the Government's dealing with the Indians would seem to bear this out. When the treaty we are concerned with here was signed in 1921, only five years after the enactment of the *Migratory Birds Convention Act*, we find the Commissioners who negotiated the treaty reporting:

> The Indians seemed afraid, for one thing, that their liberty to hunt, trap and fish would be taken away or curtailed, but were assured by me that this would not be the case, and the Government will expect them to support themselves in their own way, and, in fact, that more twine for nets and more ammunition were given under the terms of this treaty than under any of the preceding ones; this went a long way to calm their fears. I also pointed out that any game laws made were to their advantage, and, whether they took treaty or not, they were subject to the laws of the Dominion.

and there is nothing in this report which would indicate that the Indians were told that their right to shoot migratory birds had already been taken away from them. ... It is of some importance that while the Indians in the Northwest Territories continued to shoot ducks at all seasons for food, it is only recently that any attempt has been made to enforce the Act.

I can come to no other conclusion than that the Indians, notwithstanding the rights given to them by their treaties, are prohibited by this Act and its Regulations from shooting migratory birds out of season. Unless one or other of the matters mentioned in the learned trial Judge's reasons for judgment or raised by the respondent's counsel at the hearing of the appeal is a defence to the charge, the appeal must be allowed and the conviction sustained.

. . . . .

In coming to this conclusion, I regret that I cannot share the satisfaction that was expressed by McGillivray, J.A., in *R. v. Wesley*, [1932] 4 D.L.R. at p. 790, 58 C.C.C. at p. 285, 26 A.L.R. at p. 451, when he was writing his judgment dismissing the appeal in that case:

> It is satisfactory to be able to come to this conclusion and not to have to decide that "the Queen's promises" have not been fulfilled. It is satisfactory to think that legislators have not so enacted but that the Indians may still be "convinced of our justice and determined resolution to remove all reasonable cause of discontent."

Appeal allowed.

The *Sikyea* case was appealed to the Supreme Court of Canada, where it was dismissed. In dismissing the appeal, the Court held that Johnson J.A. "dealt with the important issues fully and correctly in their historical and legal settings". The Supreme Court did not address the issue raised by Johnson J.A. as to whether the curtailment of the Treaty No. 11 Indians' hunting rights pursuant to the furtherance of Canada's obligations under the *Migratory Birds Convention* was "a case of the left hand having forgotten what the right hand had done".

As discussed in Chapter 4, and emphasized by Johnson J.A. in *Sikyea*, there was nothing prohibiting the federal government from unilaterally infringing upon treaty rights at that time. Of course, section 35(1) of the *Constitution Act, 1982* would no longer allow such activity. It is open to question, however, whether the Crown's actions documented in *Sikyea* constituted a breach of either its treaty or fiduciary obligations to the Treaty No. 11 Indians, especially in light of Commissioner H.A. Conroy's assurances to them, as documented in the *Sikyea* case (and reproduced in Chapter 4). Could such an argument be made today?

In the cases of *R. v. Horseman*, [1990] S.C.J. No. 39, [1990] 1 S.C.R. 901 (S.C.C.) and *R. v. Badger* [1996] S.C.J. No. 39, 133 D.L.R. (4th) 324 (S.C.C.) excerpted below, similar situations to that in *Sikyea* arose in relation to the Alberta *Natural Resources Transfer Agreement, 1930*, S.C. 1930, c. 3 (hereinafter "NRTA"), which had been expressly referred to by Johnson J.A. in his judgment.

There was not one, but three NRTAs, one for each of Manitoba, Saskatchewan, and Alberta, although their content was the same. The purpose of the NRTAs was to grant those provinces the same administration and control over Crown lands and natural resources existing within their jurisdictional boundaries as that held by other Canadian provinces. The NRTAs were, essentially, re-enactments of section 109 of the *Constitution Act, 1867* applied to Manitoba, Saskatchewan, and Alberta.

In addition, the NRTAs ensured that land would be made available by those provinces to fulfil the federal Crown's outstanding treaty land entitlements (promises of land made to Aboriginal groups in treaties) — and thus avoid the problem discussed in the Rotman excerpt earlier in this chapter — and provided for the application of provincial game laws to the Aboriginal peoples residing in those provinces. These provisions, taken from the Alberta NRTA, read as follows:

> 10. All lands included in Indian reserves within the Province, including those selected and surveyed but not yet confirmed, as well as those confirmed, shall continue to be vested in the Crown and administered by the Government of Canada for the purposes of Canada, and the Province will from time to time, upon the request of the Superintendent General of Indian Affairs, set aside, out of the unoccupied Crown lands hereby transferred to its administration, such further areas as the said Superintendent General may, in agreement with the appropriate Minister of the Province, select as necessary to enable Canada to fulfil its

obligations under the treaties with the Indians of the Province, and such areas shall thereafter be administered by Canada in the same way in all respects as if they had never passed to the Province under the provisions hereof.

. . . . .

12. In order to secure to the Indians of the Province the continuance of the supply of game and fish for their support and subsistence, Canada agrees that the laws respecting game in force in the Province from time to time shall apply to the Indians within the boundaries thereof, provided however, that the said Indians shall have the right, which the Province hereby assures to them, of hunting, trapping and fishing game and fish for food at all seasons of the year on all unoccupied Crown lands and on any other lands to which the said Indians may have a right of access.

In *Horseman*, the Supreme Court of Canada had to consider the effects of the NRTA on the hunting rights guaranteed by Treaty No. 8, signed in 1899.

R. v. HORSEMAN

[1990] S.C.J. No. 39, [1990] 1 S.C.R. 901, [1990] 4 W.W.R. 97, 73 Alta. L.R. (2d) 193, 55 C.C.C. (3d) 353, 108 N.R. 1, [1990] 3 C.N.L.R. 95 (S.C.C.)

The judgment of **Lamer, La Forest, Gonthier,** and **Cory JJ.** was delivered by

Cory J.: — At issue on this appeal is whether the provisions of s. 42 and s. 1(s) of the *Wildlife Act*, R.S.A. 1980, c. W-9, apply to the appellant, whose forebears were members of one of the Indian Bands party to Treaty No. 8 signed in 1899 which guaranteed substantive hunting rights to certain Indian people.

Factual Background

The facts are not in dispute and were agreed upon at trial. Mr. Bert Horseman is an Indian within the meaning of the *Indian Act*, R.S.C. 1970, c. I-6. He is a descendant of the Indian people who were parties to Treaty No. 8.

. . . . .

In the spring of 1983 the appellant went moose hunting in the territory north of his Reserve in order to feed himself and his family. ... He shot a moose, cut it and skinned it. The moose was too large for the appellant to bring back to the Reserve. He therefore hurried home to obtain the assistance of other Band members to haul it out of the bush. When they arrived at the carcass the appellant and his friends were unpleasantly surprised to find that a grizzly bear had appropriated the moose. The arrival of the appellant was even more unpleasant and upsetting for the bear, which by this time clearly believed it had acquired a valid possessory title to the moose. Faced with the conflicting claim, the bear charged the appellant. Bert Horseman displayed cool courage and skill under attack. He shot and killed the bear, skinned it and took the hide.

... Horseman did not have a licence under the *Wildlife Act* to hunt grizzly bears or sell their hides. This omission ordinarily could be readily excused for neither the presence of the bear nor its attack could have been foreseen.

One year later, in the spring of 1984, the appellant found himself in the unfortunate position of being out of work and in need of money to support his family. In these straitened circumstances he decided to sell the grizzly hide. On or about April 19th he applied for and was issued a grizzly bear licence under s. 18 of the *Wildlife Act*. This licence entitled him to hunt and kill one bear and sell the hide to a licensed dealer as provided by the regulations passed pursuant to that Act. The appellant made use of this licence to sell the hide of his adversary of the year before to a licensed dealer for a price of $200. This isolated sale, which was clearly not part of any organized commercial transaction, took place between April 19th and May 22nd.

There can be no doubt of the financial needs of the appellant nor of his good faith. He certainly made efforts to stay within the spirit of the law. Nevertheless, an information was laid against him in July of 1984 charging him with trafficking in wildlife.

. . . . .

The sole defence raised on behalf of Horseman was that the *Wildlife Act* did not apply to him and that he was within his Treaty 8 rights when he sold the bear hide. Nothing is to turn on the killing of the bear in self-defence. Nor is it argued that Horseman was induced into a mistake of the law by the words of an official of the Government. Rather, it is the appellant's position that he can, at any time, on Crown lands or on lands to which Indians have access, kill a grizzly bear for food. Further, it is said that he can sell the hide of any grizzly bear he kills in order to buy food.

. . . . .

Applicable Legislation

Treaty No. 8, 1899:

> And Her Majesty the Queen HEREBY AGREES with the said Indians that they shall have right to pursue their usual vocations of hunting, trapping and fishing throughout the tract surrendered as heretofore described, subject to such regulations as may from time to time be made by the Government of the country, acting under the authority of Her Majesty, and saving and excepting such tracts as may be required or taken up from time to time for settlement, mining, lumbering, trading or other purposes.

Constitution Act, 1930:

1. The agreements set out in the Schedule to this Act are hereby confirmed and shall have the force of law notwithstanding anything in the Constitution Act, 1867, or any Act amending the same, or any Act of the Parliament of Canada, or in any Order in Council or terms or conditions of union made or approved under any such Act as aforesaid.

Natural Resources Transfer Agreement, 1930 (Alberta):

12 In order to secure to the Indians of the Province the continuance of the supply of game and fish for their support and subsistence, Canada agrees that the laws respecting game in force in the Province from time to time shall apply to the Indians within the boundaries thereof, provided, however, that the said Indians shall have the right, which the Province hereby assures to them, of hunting, trapping and fishing game and fish for food at all seasons of the year on all unoccupied Crown lands and on any other lands to which the said Indians may have a right of access.

Wildlife Act, R.S.A. 1980, c. W-9:

42 No person shall traffic in any wildlife except as is expressly permitted by this Act or by the regulations.

1...

(s) "traffic" means any single act of selling, offering for sale, buying, bartering, soliciting or trading;

Treaty and Hunting Rights

An examination of the historical background leading to the negotiations for Treaty No. 8 and the other numbered treaties leads inevitably to the conclusion that the hunting rights reserved by the Treaty included hunting for commercial purposes. ... It can be seen that the Indians ceded title to the Treaty 8 lands on the condition that they could reserve exclusively to themselves "their usual vocations of hunting, trapping and fishing throughout the tracts surrendered".

The economy of the Indian population at the time of the Treaty had clearly evolved to such a degree that hunting and fishing for commercial purposes was an integral part of their way of life. ... The report of the Commissioners who negotiated Treaty No. 8 on behalf of the government of Canada lends further support to this conclusion [see the Treaty No. 8 Commissioners' Report in Chapter 4 (Treaties)].

.....

... [T]he original Treaty right clearly included hunting for purposes of commerce. The next question that must be resolved is whether or not that right was in any way limited or affected by the Transfer Agreement of 1930.

<u>The Effect of the 1930 Transfer Agreement</u>

At the outset two established principles must be borne in mind. First, the onus of proving either express or implicit extinguishment lies upon the Crown. ... Secondly, any ambiguities in the wording of the Treaty or document must be resolved in favour of the Native people.

. . . . .

The appellant argues that the Transfer Agreement of 1930 was not signed by the Indians. Since they were not a party to it, they could not have agreed to any restriction of their hunting and fishing rights and that these rights could not have been lost as a result of the operation of what has been called the "merger and consolidation" theory.

The Crown on the other hand states that it is clear from the wording of para. 12 itself that the hunting rights were limited by the Agreement.

. . . . .

The Crown argues that the rights granted to the Indians by the Treaty of 1899 were "merged and consolidated" in the 1930 Transfer Agreement.

. . . . .

The merger and consolidation theory was first put forward by McNiven J.A. in *R. v. Strongquill* (1953), 8 W.W.R. (N.S.) 247 (Sask. C.A.).

. . . . .

In later decisions Dickson J., as he then was, adopted this approach. It was his view that the Transfer Agreement operated so as to cut down the scope of Indian hunting rights. In *Frank v. The Queen, supra*, at p. 100, he commented:

> It would appear that the overall purpose of the para. 12 of the Natural Resources Transfer Agreement was to effect a merger and consolidation of the treaty rights theretofore enjoyed by the Indians but of equal importance was the desire to re-state and reassure to the treaty Indians the continued enjoyment of the right to hunt and fish for food.

. . . . .

The appellant contends that these authorities should not be followed. The position is three-fold. Firstly, it is argued that when it is looked at in its historical context, the 1930 Transfer Agreement was meant to protect the rights of Indians and not to derogate from those rights. Secondly, and most importantly, it is contended that the traditional hunting rights granted to Indians by Treaty No. 8 could not be reduced or abridged in any way without some form of approval and consent given by the Indians, the parties most affected by the derogation, and without some form of compensation or *quid pro quo* for the reduction in the hunting rights. Thirdly, it is said that on policy grounds the Crown should not undertake to unilaterally change and derogate the Treaty rights granted earlier. To permit such a course of action could only lead to the dishonour of the Crown. It is argued that there rests upon the Crown an obligation to uphold the original Native interests protected by the Treaty. That is to say, the Crown should be looked upon as a trustee of the Native hunting rights.

. . . . .

It is ... clear that the Transfer Agreements were meant to modify the division of powers originally set out in the *Constitution Act, 1867* (formerly the *British North America Act, 1867*). Section 1 of the *Constitution Act, 1930* is unambiguous in this regard: "The agreements ... shall have the force of law notwithstanding anything in the *Constitution Act, 1867* ...".

In addition, there was in fact a *quid pro quo* granted by the Crown for the reduction in the hunting right. Although the Agreement did take away the right to hunt commercially, the nature of the right to hunt for food was substantially enlarged. The geographical areas in which the Indian people could hunt was widely extended. Further, the means employed by them in hunting for their food was placed beyond the reach of provincial governments. For example, they may hunt deer with night lights and with dogs, methods which are or may be prohibited for others. Nor are the Indians subject to seasonal limitations as are all other hunters. ... Indians are [also] not limited with regard to the type of game they may kill. ... It can be seen that the *quid pro quo* was substantial. Both the area of hunting and the way in which the hunting could be conducted was extended and removed from the jurisdiction of provincial governments.

. . . . .

It is thus apparent that although the Transfer Agreement modified the Treaty rights as to hunting, there was a very real *quid pro quo* which extended the Native rights to hunt for food. In addition, although it might well be politically and morally unacceptable in today's climate to take such a step as that set out in the 1930 Agreement without consultation with and concurrence of the Native peoples affected, nonetheless the power of the Federal Government to unilaterally make such a modification is unquestioned and has not been challenged in this case.

. . . . .

[A]t the time the Treaty was made only the Federal Government had jurisdiction over the territory affected and it was the only contemplated "government of the country". The Transfer Agreement of 1930 changed the governmental authority which might regulate aspects of hunting in the interests of conservation. This change of governmental authority did not contradict the spirit of the original Agreement as evidenced by federal and provincial regulations in effect at the time. Even in 1899 conservation was a matter of concern for the governmental authority.

... [T]he hunting rights granted by the 1899 Treaty were not unlimited. Rather they were subject to governmental regulation. The 1930 Agreement widened the hunting territory and the means by which the Indians could hunt for food thus providing a real *quid pro quo* for the reduction in the right to hunt for purposes of commerce granted by the Treaty of 1899. The right of the Federal Government to act unilaterally in that manner is unquestioned. I therefore conclude that the 1930 Transfer Agreement did alter the nature of the hunting rights originally guaranteed by Treaty No. 8.

Section 42 of the Wildlife Act

At the outset it must be recognized that the *Wildlife Act* is a provincial law of general application affecting Indians not *qua* Indians but rather as inhabitants of the Province. It follows that the Act can be applicable to Indians pursuant to the provisions of s. 88 of the *Indian Act* so long as it does not conflict with a treaty right. ... The courts below correctly found that the sale of the bear hide constituted a hunting activity that had ceased to be that of hunting "for food" but rather was an act of commerce. As a result it was no longer a right protected by Treaty No. 8, as amended by the 1930 Transfer Agreement. Thus the application of s. 42 to Indians who are hunting for commercial purposes is not precluded by s. 88 of the *Indian Act*.

The fact that a grizzly bear was killed by the appellant in self-defence must engender admiration and sympathy, but it is unfortunately not relevant to a consideration of whether there has been a breach of s. 42 of the *Wildlife Act*. ... [T]he prohibition against trafficking in bear hides without a licence cannot admit of any exceptions.

Neither, regrettably, can it be relevant to the breach of s. 42 that the appellant in fact obtained a grizzly bear hunting permit after he was in the possession of a bear hide. The granting of a permit does not bring a hunter any guarantee of success but only an opportunity to legitimately slay a bear. The evidence presented at trial indicated that the limitations placed upon obtaining a licence and the limited chance of success in a bear hunt resulted in the success rate of between 2 and 4 per cent of the licence holder. This must be an important factor in the management of the bear population. Wildlife administrators must be able to rely on the success ratio and proceed on the assumption that those applying for a permit have not already shot a bear. The success ratio will determine the number of licences issued in any year. The whole management scheme which is essential to the survival of the grizzly bear would be undermined if a licence were granted to an applicant who had already completed a successful hunt.

As well, s. 42 of the *Wildlife Act* is consistent with the very spirit of Treaty No. 8, which specified that the right to hunt would still be subject to government regulations. The evidence indicates that there remain only 575 grizzly bears on provincial lands. ... Trafficking in bear hides, other than pursuant to the provisions of the *Wildlife Act*, threatens the very existence of the grizzly bear. The bear may snarl defiance and even occasionally launch a desperate attack upon man, but until such time as it masters the operation of firearms, it cannot triumph and must rely on man for protection and indeed for survival. That protection is provided by the *Wildlife Act*, but if it is to succeed it must be strictly enforced.

Section 42 of the *Wildlife Act* is valid legislation enacted by the government with jurisdiction in the field. It reflects a *bona fide* concern for the preservation of a species. It is a law of general application which does not infringe upon the Treaty 8 hunting rights of Indians as limited by the 1930 Transfer Agreement.

Disposition

In the result, I would dismiss the appeal. ...

. . . . .

The *Wildlife Act* applied to the appellant and Horseman is guilty of violating s. 42 of the Act. Nonetheless he did not seek out the bear and shot it only in self-defence. ... He was in financial difficulties when he sold the bear hide in an isolated transaction. ... If it were not for statutory requirement of a minimum fine, in the unique circumstances of the case, I would vary the sentence by waiving the payment of the minimum fine. Nevertheless, in light of the circumstances of the case, and the time that has elapsed, I would order a stay of proceedings.

[A dissenting opinion was written by Wilson J. She was joined by Dickson C.J.C. and L'Heureux-Dubé J.]

Appeal dismissed.

The majority decision in *Horseman* held that the NRTA unilaterally superseded the terms of Treaty No. 8, thereby extinguishing the rights contained in the latter. Is such a finding consistent with the sanctity of Aboriginal treaties? Is it consistent with the notion of treaties as negotiated compacts? Refer back to the discussion of treaties in Chapter 4. Do the Crown's actions in promulgating the NRTA, assuming it has this effect on treaty rights, implicate its fiduciary obligations to the Aboriginal peoples? See the discussion of Crown-Native fiduciary relations in Chapter 5.

The *Horseman* decision was reconsidered in the Supreme Court of Canada's judgment in *R. v. Badger*, below (which is also discussed in Chapter 4, for its consideration of treaty interpretation). Unlike in the *Horseman* decision, the Court in *Badger* considered the application of section 35(1) of the *Constitution Act, 1982* and its protection of existing treaty rights. The following excerpt from the *Badger* case relates to the Court's discussion of the effect of the Alberta NRTA on hunting rights protected by Treaty No. 8.

R. v. BADGER

[1996] S.C.J. No. 39, [1996] 1 S.C.R. 771, 133 D.L.R. (4th) 324, [1996] 4
W.W.R. 457, 37 Alta. L.R. (3d) 153, 195 N.R. 1, 105 C.C.C. (3d) 289 (S.C.C.)

[The facts of the case are set out in the discussion of the case in Chapter 4.]

Sopinka J. (**Lamer C.J.C.** concurring): —

[1] I have had the benefit of reading the reasons for judgment prepared
in this appeal by my colleague, Justice Cory, and I am in agreement with
his disposition of the appeal and with his reasons with the exception of his
exposition of the relationship between Treaty No. 8, the *Natural Resources
Transfer Agreement, 1930* [*Constitution Act, 1930*, Schedule 2] (NRTA), and
s. 35 of the *Constitution Act, 1982*.

[2] In my view, the rights of Indians to hunt for food provided in Treaty
No. 8 were merged in the NRTA which is the sole source of those rights.
While I agree that the impugned provision of the *Wildlife Act*, S.A. 1984,
c. W-9.1, infringes the constitutional right of Indians to hunt for food, I
disagree that this constitutional right is one covered by s. 35(1) of the
Constitution Act, 1982. I agree, however, that the constitutional right to
hunt for food must be balanced against the right of the province to pass
laws for the purpose of conservation and that this balancing may be
carried out on the basis of the principles set out in *R. v. Sparrow*, [1990] 1
S.C.R. 1075.

[3] There is no disagreement that the NRTA:

(a) duplicated the right of Indians to hunt for food which was contained
in Treaty No. 8;
(b) widely extended the geographical area to include the whole of the
province rather than being limited to the tract of land surrendered;
(c) shifted responsibility for passing game laws from the federal
government to the provinces;
(d) eliminated the right to hunt for commercial purposes;
(e) is a constitutional document and the Treaty is not, although the Treaty
receives constitutional protection by virtue of s. 35(1) of the
Constitution Act, 1982.

[4] In these circumstances, I am of the view that it was clearly the
intention of the framers to merge the rights in the treaty in the NRTA. To
characterize the NRTA as modifying the treaty is to treat it as an amending
document to the treaty. This clearly was not the intent of the NRTA. In
enlarging the area in which hunting for food was permitted to extend to
the whole of the province, it could not be suggested that the NRTA
extended the treaty to all of the province. Rather, the right to hunt for food
was extended by the NRTA to the whole of the province, including the
area covered by the treaty. An Indian hunting on land outside the treaty
lands could not claim to be covered by the treaty. If the NRTA merely
modified the treaty, an Indian hunting on treaty lands could claim the

right under the treaty while an Indian hunting in other parts of the province could claim only under the NRTA. This would invite bifurcation of the rights of Indians hunting for food in the province.

[5] Similarly, the provisions which transferred to the province the power to pass gaming laws for the purpose of conservation could not have been intended simply to amend the treaty. As an amendment to the treaty, this provision would have no constitutional force and could not alter the constitutionally entrenched division of powers. It might be suggested that the NRTA both amended the treaty and, as an independent constitutional document, amended the Constitution. If this were the intent, it is difficult to understand why all the terms of the treaty relating to the right to hunt for food were replicated in NRTA. It must have been the intention to merge these rights in the NRTA so that they could be balanced with the power of the provinces to legislate for conservation purposes. In order to achieve a reasonable balance between them, it was important that they both appear in one document having constitutional status.

[6] I can suggest no reason why the framers of the NRTA would have wanted to maintain any aspects of the treaty except as an interpretative tool. They surely did not do so in order to allow these rights to be recognized under s. 35(1) of the *Constitution Act, 1982* which appears to be the sole present justification for preserving the treaty. However, even that justification loses any force when considered in light of the fact that the NRTA is itself a constitutional document and recognition under s. 35(1) is unnecessary for the protection of these important Indian rights.

[7] From the foregoing, I conclude that it was the intention of the framers of para. 12 of the NRTA to effectuate a merger and consolidation of the treaty rights. ...

[8] If this was the intention, and I conclude that it was, then the proper characterization of the relationship between the NRTA and the treaty rights is that the sole source for a claim involving the right to hunt for food is the NRTA. The treaty rights have been subsumed in a document of a higher order. The treaty may be relied on for the purpose of assisting in the interpretation of the NRTA, but it has no other legal significance.

. . . . .

Validity of the provisions of the Wildlife Act

. . . . .

[11] ... [A]t the time the treaties were signed and, even more so, at the time that the NRTA was agreed to by the provinces and the federal government, it would have been clearly understood that the rights of Indians pursuant to either document would be subject to governmental regulation for conservation purposes. The rights protected by the NRTA thus cannot be viewed as being constitutional rights of an absolute nature for which governmental regulation is prohibited.

[12] How, then, is the governmental regulation permitted by the NRTA, and the extent of the protection of the appellants' rights in the face of such

regulation, to be assessed? ... Section 35(1) was intended to provide constitutional protection for aboriginal rights and treaty rights that did not enjoy such protection. It cannot have been intended to be redundant and provide constitutional protection for rights that already enjoyed constitutional protection. Moreover, para. 12 of the NRTA is a constitutional provision and, as such, s. 35(1) has no direct application to it. Infringements of constitutional rights cannot be remedied by the application of a different constitutional provision.

. . . . .

[13] That is not to say, however, that the principles underlying the interpretation of s. 35(1) have no relevance to the determination of whether a particular legislative enactment has an acceptable purpose and whether it constitutes an acceptable limitation on the rights granted by the NRTA. There is no method provided in the NRTA whereby government measures that may impinge upon the rights the same document grants to Indians can be scrutinized. It is clear, however, that the NRTA does require a balancing of rights. The right of the province to legislate with respect to conservation must be balanced against the right granted to the Indians to hunt for food. ... Although the *Sparrow* test was developed in the context of s. 35(1), the basic thrust of the test, to protect aboriginal rights but also to permit governments to legislate for legitimate purposes where the legislation is a justifiable infringement on those protected rights, applies equally well to the regulatory authority granted to the provinces under para. 12 of the NRTA as to federal power to legislate in respect of Indians.

[14] In this way, the *Sparrow* test is applied to the NRTA by analogy, with the result that the Court will have a means by which to ensure that the rights in the NRTA are protected, but that provincial governments are also provided with some flexibility in terms of their ability to affect those rights for the purpose of legislating in relation to conservation. ...

[15] I agree with Cory J. that, in the absence of evidence with respect to justification, there must be a new trial and I would dispose of the appeal as suggested by him.

. . . . .

[17] The right to hunt for food referred to in Treaty No. 8 was merged in the NRTA which is the sole source of the right.

[18] Sections 26(1) and 27(1) of the *Wildlife Act* did not infringe the constitutional rights of Mr. Badger or Mr. Kiyawasew to hunt for food.

[19] Mr. Ominayak was exercising his constitutional right to hunt for food. Section 26(1) of the *Wildlife Act* is a *prima facie* infringement of his right to hunt for food under NRTA and is invalid unless justified.

[The judgment of **La Forest, L'Heureux-Dubé, Gonthier, Cory** and **Iacobucci JJ.** was delivered by]

Cory J.: —

[20] Three questions must be answered on this appeal. First, do Indians who have status under Treaty No. 8 have the right to hunt for food on privately owned land which lies within the territory surrendered under that treaty? Secondly, have the hunting rights set out in Treaty No. 8 been extinguished or modified as a result of the provisions of para. 12 of the *Natural Resources Transfer Agreement, 1930 (Constitution Act, 1930*, Sch. 2)? Thirdly, to what extent, if any, do s. 26(1) and s. 27(1) of the *Wildlife Act*, S.A. 1984, c. W-9.1, apply to the appellants?

. . . . .

Impact of Paragraph 12 of the NRTA

Principles of Interpretation

. . . . .

[Cory J. discussed the principles of treaty interpretation, which are excerpted in Chapter 4.]

Interpreting the NRTA

[43] The issue at this stage is whether the NRTA extinguished and replaced the Treaty No. 8 right to hunt for food. It is my conclusion that it did not. …

. . . . .

[46] This Court most recently considered the effect the NRTA had upon treaty rights in *Horseman, supra*. There, it was held that para. 12 of the NRTA evidenced a clear intention to extinguish the treaty protection of the right to hunt *commercially*. However, it was emphasized that the right to hunt *for food* continued to be protected and had in fact been expanded by the NRTA. … I might add that *Horseman, supra*, is a recent decision which should be accepted as resolving the issues which it considered. The decisions of this Court confirm that para. 12 of the NRTA did, to the extent that its intent is clear, modify and alter the right to hunt for food provided in Treaty No. 8.

[47] Pursuant to s. 1 of the *Constitution Act, 1930*, there can be no doubt that para. 12 of the NRTA is binding law. It is the legal instrument which currently sets out and governs the Indian right to hunt. However, the existence of the NRTA has not deprived Treaty No. 8 of legal significance. Treaties are sacred promises and the Crown's honour requires the Court to assume that the Crown intended to fulfil its promises. Treaty rights can only be amended where it is clear that effect was intended. It is helpful to recall that Dickson J. in *Frank, supra*, observed at p. 100 that, while the NRTA had partially amended the scope of the treaty hunting right, "*of equal importance* was the desire to re-state and reassure to the treaty Indians

the continued enjoyment of the right to hunt and fish for food" (emphasis added). I believe that these words support my conclusion that the Treaty No. 8 right to hunt has *only* been altered or modified by the NRTA *to the extent that* the NRTA evinces a clear intention to effect such a modification. ... Unless there is a direct conflict between the NRTA and a treaty, the NRTA will not have modified the treaty rights. Therefore, the NRTA language which outlines the right to hunt for food must be read in light of the fact that this aspect of the treaty right continues in force and effect.

. . . . .

[72] [T]he solemn promises made in the treaty should be altered or modified as little as possible. The NRTA clearly intended to modify the right to hunt. It did so by eliminating the right to hunt commercially and by preserving and extending the right to hunt for food. The treaty right thus modified pertains to the right to hunt for food which prior to the treaty was an aboriginal right.

. . . . .

[84] Treaty No. 8 represents a solemn promise of the Crown. ... [I]t can only be modified or altered to the extent that the NRTA clearly intended to modify or alter those rights. The federal government, as it was empowered to do, unilaterally enacted the NRTA. It is unlikely that it would proceed in that manner today. The manner in which the NRTA was unilaterally enacted strengthens the conclusion that the right to hunt which it provides should be construed in light of the provisions of Treaty No. 8.

. . . . .

[90] This Court has held on numerous occasions that there can be no limitation on the method, timing and extent of Indian hunting under a treaty. I would add that a treaty as amended by the NRTA should be considered in the same manner.

. . . . .

Justification

[96] In my view justification of provincial regulations enacted pursuant to the NRTA should meet the same test for justification of treaty rights that was set out in *Sparrow, supra*. The reason for this is obvious. The effect of para. 12 of the NRTA is to place the provincial government in exactly the same position which the federal Crown formerly occupied. Thus the provincial government has the same duty not to infringe unjustifiably the hunting right provided by Treaty No. 8 as modified by the NRTA. Paragraph 12 of the NRTA provides that the province may make laws for a conservation purpose, subject to the Indian right to hunt and fish for food. Accordingly, there is a need for a means to assess which conservation laws will if they infringe that right, nevertheless be justifiable. The *Sparrow*

analysis provides a reasonable, flexible and current method of assessing conservation regulations and enactments.

. . . . .

[98] In the present case, the government has not led any evidence with respect to justification. In the absence of such evidence, it is not open to this Court to supply its own justification. Section 26(1) of the *Wildlife Act* constitutes a *prima facie* infringement of the appellant Mr. Ominayak's treaty right to hunt. Yet, the issue of conservation is of such importance that a new trial must be ordered so that the question of justification may be addressed.

Conclusion

. . . . .

[100] ... The hunting rights confirmed by Treaty No. 8 were modified by para. 12 of the NRTA to the extent indicated in these reasons. Paragraph 12 of the NRTA provided for a continuing right to hunt for food on unoccupied land.

[101] Mr. Badger and Mr. Kiyawasew were hunting on occupied land to which they had no right of access under Treaty No. 8 or the NRTA. Accordingly, ss. 26(1) and 27(1) of the *Wildlife Act* do not infringe their constitutional right to hunt for food.

[102] However, Mr. Ominayak was exercising his constitutional right on land which was unoccupied for the purposes of this case. Section 26(1) of the *Wildlife Act* constitutes a *prima facie* infringement of his treaty right to hunt for food. As a result of their conclusions, the issue of justification was not considered by the courts below. Therefore, in his case, a new trial must be ordered so that the issue of justification may be addressed.

Disposition

[103] The appeals of Mr. Badger and Mr. Kiyawasew are dismissed.

[104] The appeal of Mr. Ominayak is allowed and a new trial directed so that the issue of the justification of the infringement created by s. 26(1) of the *Wildlife Act* and any regulations passed pursuant to that section may be addressed.

———————

From Cory J.'s decision in *Badger*, it may be seen that treaty rights are no longer deemed to be extinguished or replaced by the NRTA, as had been held in *Horseman* and previous decisions. Rather, treaty rights will be modified where they come into conflict with the NRTA. Meanwhile, the treaties are to be used to assist in the interpretation of the NRTA. As Cory J. explained at p. 348 [133 D.L.R. (4th)], citing *R. v. Smith*, [1935] 3 D.L.R. 703, at p. 705, [1935] 2 W.W.R. 433, 64 C.C.C. 131 (Sask. C.A.): "'[I]t is proper to consult th[e] treaty in order to glean from it whatever may throw some light on the meaning to be given to the words' in the NRTA." How can a treaty that states that existing treaty hunting rights are to be preserved (albeit subject to future, unspecified regulation) and a corresponding Treaty Commissioners' report that repeatedly highlights the commissioners' assurances to the Aboriginal peoples that "the same means of earning a livelihood would continue after the treaty as existed before it",[11] help to interpret a unilateral constitutional enactment that extinguishes a principal element of the treaty signatories' hunting practices (as demonstrated by Arthur Ray's report, cited by both Cory and Wilson JJ. in *Horseman*)?

Despite Justice Cory's finding that treaty rights will not be extinguished by the NRTA but will only be modified where they come into conflict with the NRTA, the conflict between Treaty No. 8 and the NRTA over the scope of the treaty right to hunt resulted in commercial hunting rights being extinguished. Is the complete extinguishment of the Treaty No. 8 right to commercially hunt, a right that had been found to exist (at least prior to the NRTA) in *Horseman*, consistent with a "modification" of that right? Alternatively, is this result in *Badger* more consistent with the judgment rendered in that case by Justice Sopinka or with Cory J.'s judgment in *Horseman*?

F.   THE CHARTER AND ABORIGINAL PEOPLES

As explained earlier, the Aboriginal and treaty rights in section 35(1) of the *Constitution Act, 1982* exist outside of the Charter and are, therefore, not affected by it. That does not entail, however, that Aboriginal peoples are not affected by the Charter, although the Charter's application to Aboriginal peoples and governments has been a controversial issue. As indicated in *Lovelace v. Ontario*, [2000] S.C.J. No. 36, [2000] 1 S.C.R. 950 (S.C.C.), a case concerning the Ontario government's plan for distributing profits from one of its casinos to certain Aboriginal bands in the province, the Charter may be used by Aboriginal peoples as a means to protect their interests against government action (even though the action in *Lovelace* was ultimately unsuccessful). This ability exists separate and apart from, or in addition to, the ability of Aboriginal peoples to enforce their rights under section 35(1).

LOVELACE v. ONTARIO

[2000] S.C.J. No. 36, [2000] 1 S.C.R. 950 (S.C.C.)

The judgment of the Court was delivered by

Iacobucci J.: —

I. Introduction

[1] In 1993, the Province of Ontario and representatives from Ontario's First Nations entered into a process of negotiations with the goal of

partnering in the development of the province's first reserve-based commercial casino, which was to become Casino Rama. Profits from the casino were to be shared among Ontario's First Nations. ... Casino Rama opened its doors to the public in the summer of 1996. Meanwhile, the province and representatives of the Chiefs of Ontario had begun a process of negotiating the terms for distributing the casino's proceeds ("First Nations Fund") to the First Nations communities. In the spring of 1996, the province informed the appellant aboriginal communities that the First Nations Fund was to be distributed only to Ontario First Nations communities registered as bands under the *Indian Act*, R.S.C., 1985, c. I-5.

. . . . .

[3] In basic terms, this appeal requires a determination of the constitutionality of the exclusion of non-band aboriginal communities from sharing in the proceeds, and from negotiating the distribution terms for the First Nations Fund. Specifically, the question is whether the First Nations Fund's underinclusiveness violates the appellants' equality rights as guaranteed by s. 15 of the *Canadian Charter of Rights and Freedoms*. We must also determine whether the province's decision to exclude the appellants on the basis that they are not bands under the *Indian Act* was *ultra vires* its jurisdiction under the *Constitution Act, 1867*.

. . . . .

[5] This appeal also raises the question of the proper interpretation of s. 15(2) of the *Charter*. ...

[6] With respect to s. 15(1), in my view the exclusion of the non-band aboriginal communities from the First Nations Fund does not violate s. 15 of the *Charter*. I reach this conclusion despite a recognition that, regrettably, the appellant and respondent aboriginal communities have overlapping and largely shared histories of discrimination, poverty, and systemic disadvantage that cry out for improvement.

[7] In my opinion, a contextual analysis reveals an almost precise correspondence between the casino project and the needs and circumstances of the First Nations bands. The casino project was undertaken by the province of Ontario in order to further develop a partnership or a "government-to-government" relationship with Ontario's First Nations band communities. It is a project that is aimed at supporting the journey of these aboriginal groups towards empowerment, dignity, and self-reliance. It is not, however, designed to meet similar needs in the appellant aboriginal communities, but its failure to do so does not amount to discrimination under s. 15.

[8] Finally, I conclude that the province did not act *ultra vires* in partnering the casino initiative with *Indian Act* registered aboriginal communities. The exclusion of non-registered aboriginal communities did not act to define or impair the "Indianness" of the appellants since the province simply exercised its constitutional spending power in making the casino arrangements.

. . . . .

[43] ... [T]o invoke s. 15(2) a court need only be satisfied that the target of the program was a disadvantaged group, and the purpose of the program was to ameliorate these conditions. ...

[44] ... Since s. 15(2) affirms government initiatives directed at redressing disadvantage, these programs should be shielded to the extent that they address a specific disadvantage. In short, in underinclusive situations, one can find discrimination only if a distinction is made resulting in the denial of a benefit to a member of the group targeted by the program. As a result, the key to the s. 15(2) analysis is properly characterizing the object or the purpose of the program in order to determine whether the claimants are within a group targeted by that program's objects.

. . . . . .

[87] The ameliorative purpose of the overall casino project and the related First Nations Fund has clearly been established. In particular, the First Nations Fund will provide bands with resources in order to ameliorate specifically social, health, cultural, education, and economic disadvantages. It is anticipated that the bands will be able to target the allocation of these monies within these specified areas, thereby increasing the fiscal autonomy of the bands. This aspect of the First Nations Fund is consistent with the related ameliorative purpose of supporting the bands in achieving self-government and self-reliance. Without a doubt, this program has been designed to redress historical disadvantage and contribute to enhancing the dignity and recognition of bands in Canadian society. Furthermore, both of the above ameliorative objectives can be met while, at the same time, ensuring that on-reserve commercial casino gaming is undertaken in compliance with the strict regulations applicable to the supervision of gaming activities. The First Nations Fund has, therefore, a purpose that is consistent with s. 15(1) of the *Charter* and the exclusion of the appellants does not undermine this purpose since it is not associated with a misconception as to their actual needs, capacities and circumstances.

. . . . .

[113] I would answer the constitutional questions as follows:

Question 1: Does the exclusion of the appellant aboriginal groups from the First Nations Fund, and from the negotiations on the establishment and operation of the Fund, set up pursuant to s. 15(1) of the *Ontario Casino Corporation Act, 1993*, S.O. 1993, c. 25, on the grounds that they are not aboriginal groups registered as *Indian Act* bands under the *Indian Act*, R.S.C., 1985, c. I-5, violate s. 15 of the *Canadian Charter of Rights and Freedoms*?

Answer: No.

<u>Question 2</u>: If the answer to question No. 1 is yes, is the violation demonstrably justified under s. 1 of the *Canadian Charter of Rights and Freedoms*?

<u>Answer</u>: In view of the answer to Question 1, it is not necessary to answer this question.

<u>Question 3</u>: Is the exclusion of the appellant aboriginal groups from the First Nations Fund of the Casino Rama Project, and from the negotiations on the establishment and operation of the Fund on the grounds that they are not aboriginal groups registered as *Indian Act* bands under the *Indian Act*, R.S.C., 1985, c. I-5, *ultra vires* the power of the province under the *Constitution Act, 1867*?

<u>Answer</u>: No.

Appeal dismissed.

While the Supreme Court of Canada held that Ontario was not bound to include non-registered bands in its casino revenue redistribution, should it have included them? Why do you think that it did not include them? Can you think of reasons for distinguishing among bands on the basis of *Indian Act* registration?

In addition to the *Lovelace* decision, the Supreme Court of Canada considered the application of section 15(1) to Aboriginal peoples in *Corbiere v. Canada (Minister of Indian and Northern Affairs)*, [1999] S.C.J. No. 24, [1999] 2 S.C.R. 203 (S.C.C.). The controversy in that case surrounded section 77(1) of the *Indian Act*, R.S.C. 1985, c. I-5, which held that only those status Indians "ordinarily resident on a reserve" could vote in band council elections, while those who were band members, but resident off-reserve, could not vote in those elections. The Supreme Court of Canada held that a status Indian's place of residence constituted an analogous form of discrimination in the context of determining who was entitled to vote in band council elections. As a result, the phrase "ordinarily resident on a reserve", was declared inconsistent with section 15(1) of the Charter and struck down, although implementation of the change was suspended for 18 months. The *Corbiere* case is excerpted in Chapter 9.

The application of section 15(2) of the Charter was a primary issue of importance in *R. v. Kapp*, which is reproduced below.

R. v. KAPP

[2008] S.C.J. No. 42, [2008] 2 S.C.R. 483 (S.C.C.)

The judgment of **McLachlin C.J.C.** and **Binnie, LeBel, Deschamps, Fish, Abella, Charron** and **Rothstein JJ.** was delivered by

McLachlin C.J.C. and **Abella J.:** —

A. Introduction

[1] The appellants are commercial fishers, mainly non-aboriginal, who assert that their equality rights under s. 15 of the *Canadian Charter of Rights and Freedoms* were violated by a communal fishing licence granting members of three aboriginal bands the exclusive right to fish for salmon in the mouth of the Fraser River for a period of 24 hours on August 19-20, 1998.

[2] The appellants base their claim on s. 15(1). The essence of the claim is that the communal fishing licence discriminated against them on the basis of race. The Crown argues that the general purpose of the program under which the licence was issued was to regulate the fishery, and that it ameliorated the conditions of a disadvantaged group. These contentions, taken together, raise the issue of the interplay between s. 15(1) and s. 15(2) of the *Charter*. Specifically, they require this Court to consider whether s. 15(2) is capable of operating independently of s. 15(1) to protect ameliorative programs from claims of discrimination — a possibility left open in this Court's equality jurisprudence.

. . . . .

B. Factual and Judicial History

[4] Prior to European contact, aboriginal groups living in the region of the mouth of the Fraser River fished the river for food, social and ceremonial purposes. It is no exaggeration to say that their life centered in large part around the river and its abundant fishery. In the last two decades, court decisions have confirmed that pre-contact fishing practices integral to the culture of aboriginal people translate into a modern-day right to fish for food, social and ceremonial purposes: *R. v. Sparrow*, [1990] 1 S.C.R. 1075. The right is a communal right. It inheres in the community, not the individual, and may be exercised by people who are linked to the ancestral aboriginal community.

[5] The aboriginal right has not been recognized by the courts as extending to fishing for the purpose of sale or commercial fishing: *R. v. Van der Peet*, [1996] 2 S.C.R. 507. The participation of Aboriginals in the commercial fishery was thus left to individual initiative or to negotiation between aboriginal peoples and the government. The federal government determined that aboriginal people should be given a stake in the commercial fishery. The bands tended to be disadvantaged economically, compared to non-Aboriginals. Catching fish for their own tables and ceremonies left many needs unmet.

[6] The government's decision to enhance aboriginal involvement in the commercial fishery followed the recommendations of the 1982 Pearse Final Report, which endorsed the negotiation of aboriginal fishery agreements (*Turning the Tide: A New Policy For Canada's Pacific Fisheries*). The Pearse

Report recognized the problematic connection between aboriginal communities' economic disadvantage and the longstanding prohibition against selling fish — a prohibition that disrupted what was once an important economic opportunity for Aboriginals. Policing the prohibition was also problematic; the 1994 Gardner Pinfold Report addressed the serious conservation issue stemming from a fish sales prohibition "honoured more in the breach than the observance" (*An Evaluation of the Pilot Sale Arrangement of Aboriginal Fisheries Strategy (AFS)*, p. 3). The decision to enhance aboriginal participation in the commercial fishery may also be seen as a response to the directive of this Court in *Sparrow*, at p. 1119, that the government consult with aboriginal groups in the implementation of fishery regulation in order to honour its fiduciary duty to aboriginal communities. Subsequent decisions have affirmed the duty to consult and accommodate aboriginal communities with respect to resource development and conservation; it is a constitutional duty, the fulfilment of which is consistent with the honour of the Crown: see e.g. *Delgamuukw v. British Columbia*, [1997] 3 S.C.R. 1010.

[7] The federal government's policies aimed at giving aboriginal people a share of the commercial fishery took different forms, united under the umbrella of the "Aboriginal Fisheries Strategy". Introduced in 1992, the Aboriginal Fisheries Strategy has three stated objectives: ensuring the rights recognized by the *Sparrow* decision are respected; providing aboriginal communities with a larger role in fisheries management and increased economic benefits; and minimizing the disruption of non-aboriginal fisheries (1994 Gardner Pinfold Report). In response to consultations with stakeholders carried out since its inception, the Aboriginal Fisheries Strategy has been reviewed and adjusted periodically in order to achieve these goals. A significant part of the Aboriginal Fisheries Strategy was the introduction of three pilot sales programs, one of which resulted in the issuance of the communal fishing licence at issue in this case. ...

[8] The licence with which we are concerned permitted fishers designated by the bands to fish for sockeye salmon between 7:00 a.m on August 19, 1998 and 7:00 a.m. on August 20, 1998, and to use the fish caught for food, social and ceremonial purposes, and for sale. Some of the fishers designated by the bands to fish under the communal fishing licence were also licensed commercial fishers entitled to fish at other openings for commercial fishers.

[9] The appellants are all commercial fishers who were excluded from the fishery during the 24 hours allocated to the aboriginal fishery under the communal fishing licence. Under the auspices of the B.C. Fisheries Survival Coalition, they participated in a protest fishery during the prohibited period, for the purpose of bringing a constitutional challenge to the communal licence. As anticipated, they were charged with fishing at a prohibited time. In defence of the charges, they filed notice of a constitutional question seeking declarations that the communal fishing licence, the *ACFLR* and related regulations and the Aboriginal Fisheries Strategy were unconstitutional.

. . . . .

C. Analysis

[13] Section 15 of the *Charter* provides:

> **15.** (1) Every individual is equal before and under the law and has the right to the equal protection and equal benefit of the law without discrimination and, in particular, without discrimination based on race, national or ethnic origin, colour, religion, sex, age or mental or physical disability.
>
> (2) Subsection (1) does not preclude any law, program or activity that has as its object the amelioration of conditions of disadvantaged individuals or groups including those that are disadvantaged because of race, national or ethnic origin, colour, religion, sex, age or mental or physical disability.

1. The Purpose of Section 15

[14] Nearly 20 years have passed since the Court handed down its first s. 15 decision in the case of *Andrews v. Law Society of British Columbia*, [1989] 1 S.C.R. 143. *Andrews* set the template for this Court's commitment to substantive equality — a template which subsequent decisions have enriched but never abandoned.

[15] Substantive equality, as contrasted with formal equality, is grounded in the idea that: "The promotion of equality entails the promotion of a society in which all are secure in the knowledge that they are recognized at law as human beings equally deserving of concern, respect and consideration": *Andrews*, at p. 171, *per* McIntyre J., for the majority on the s. 15 issue. [He pointed] out that the concept of equality does not necessarily mean identical treatment and that the formal "like treatment" model of discrimination may in fact produce inequality. ...

. . . . .

While acknowledging that equality is an inherently comparative concept (p. 164), McIntyre J. warned against a sterile similarly situated test focussed on treating "likes" alike. An insistence on substantive equality has remained central to the Court's approach to equality claims.

[16] Sections 15(1) and 15(2) work together to promote the vision of substantive equality that underlies s. 15 as a whole. Section 15(1) is aimed at preventing discriminatory distinctions that impact adversely on members of groups identified by the grounds enumerated in s. 15 and analogous grounds. This is one way of combatting discrimination. However, governments may also wish to combat discrimination by developing programs aimed at helping disadvantaged groups improve their situation. Through s. 15(2), the *Charter* preserves the right of governments to implement such programs, without fear of challenge under s. 15(1). This is made apparent by the existence of s. 15(2). Thus s. 15(1) and s. 15(2) work together to confirm s. 15's purpose of furthering substantive equality.

. . . . .

[25] The central purpose of combatting discrimination, as discussed, underlies both s. 15(1) and s. 15(2). Under s. 15(1), the focus is on *preventing* governments from making distinctions based on the enumerated or analogous grounds that: have the effect of perpetuating group disadvantage and prejudice; or impose disadvantage on the basis of stereotyping. Under s. 15(2), the focus is on *enabling* governments to pro-actively combat existing discrimination through affirmative measures.

[26] Against this background, we turn to a more detailed examination of s. 15(2) and its role in this appeal.

1.   *Section 15(2)*

[27] Under *Andrews*, as previously noted, s. 15 does not mean identical treatment. ...

[28] Rather than requiring identical treatment for everyone, in *Andrews*, McIntyre J. distinguished between difference and discrimination and adopted an approach to equality that acknowledged and accommodated differences. McIntyre J. proposed the following model, at p. 182:

> [I]n assessing whether a complainant's rights have been infringed under s. 15(1), it is not enough to focus only on the alleged ground of discrimination and decide whether or not it is an enumerated or analogous ground. The effect of the impugned distinction or classification on the complainant must be considered. Once it is accepted that not all distinctions and differentiations created by law are discriminatory, then a role must be assigned to s. 15(1) which goes beyond the mere recognition of a legal distinction. A complainant under s. 15(1) must show not only that he or she is not receiving equal treatment before and under the law or that the law has a differential impact on him or her in the protection or benefit accorded by law but, in addition, must show that the legislative impact of the law is discriminatory.

In other words, not every distinction is discriminatory. By their very nature, programs designed to ameliorate the disadvantage of one group will inevitably exclude individuals from other groups. This does not necessarily make them either unconstitutional or "reverse discrimination". *Andrews* requires that discriminatory conduct entail more than *different* treatment. As McIntyre J. declared at p. 167, a law will not "necessarily be bad because it makes distinctions".

[29] In our view, the appellants have established that they were treated differently based on an enumerated ground, race. Because the government argues that the program ameliorated the conditions of a disadvantaged group, we must take a more detailed look at s. 15(2).

[30] The question that arises is whether the program that targeted the aboriginal bands falls under s. 15(2) in the sense that it is a "law, program or activity that has as its object the amelioration of conditions of disadvantaged individuals or groups". As noted, the communal fishing licence authorizing the three bands to fish for sale on August 19-20 was

issued pursuant to an enabling statute and regulations — namely the *ACFLR*. This qualifies as a "law, program or activity" within the meaning of s. 15(2). The more complex issue is whether the program fulfills the remaining criteria of s. 15(2) — that is, whether the program "has as its object the amelioration of conditions of disadvantaged individuals or groups".

. . . . .

[32] The Royal Commission Report on *Equality in Employment*, whose mandate was to determine whether there should be affirmative action in Canada and on which McIntyre J. relied to develop his theories of discrimination and equality, set out the principles underlying s. 15(2), at pp. 13-14:

> In recognition of the journey many have yet to complete before they achieve equality, and in recognition of how the duration of the journey has been and is being unfairly protracted by arbitrary barriers, section 15(2) permits laws, programs, or activities designed to eliminate these restraints. While section 15(1) guarantees to individuals the right to be treated as equals free from discrimination, section 15(2), though itself creating no enforceable remedy, assures that it is neither discriminatory nor a violation of the equality guaranteed by section 15(1) to attempt to improve the condition of disadvantaged individuals or groups, even if this means treating them differently.
>
> Section 15(2) covers the canvas with a broad brush, permitting a group remedy for discrimination. The section encourages a comprehensive or systemic rather than a particularized approach to the elimination of discriminatory barriers.
>
> Section 15(2) does not create the statutory obligation to establish laws, programs, or activities to hasten equality, ameliorate disadvantage, or eliminate discrimination. But it sanctions them, acting with statutory acquiescence.

[33] In essence, s. 15(2) of the *Charter* seeks to protect efforts by the state to develop and adopt remedial schemes designed to assist disadvantaged groups. This interpretation is confirmed by the language in s. 15(2), "does not preclude".

[34] This Court dealt explicitly with the relationship between s. 15(1) and s. 15(2) in *Lovelace v. Ontario*, [2000] 1 S.C.R. 950, 2000 SCC 37. ...

[35] Iacobucci J. in *Lovelace* perceived two possible approaches to the interpretation of s. 15(2). He believed that the Supreme Court could either read s. 15(2) as an interpretive aid to s. 15(1) (the approach adopted in *Lovelace*) or read it as an exception or exemption from the operation of s. 15(1).

[36] He favoured the interpretive aid approach, while acknowledging that the exemption approach had some support....

[37] In our view, there is a third option: if the government can demonstrate that an impugned program meets the criteria of s. 15(2), it may be unnecessary to conduct a s. 15(1) analysis at all. As discussed at the outset of this analysis, s. 15(1) and s. 15(2) should be read as working together to promote substantive equality. The focus of s. 15(1) is on *preventing*

governments from making distinctions based on enumerated or analogous grounds that have the effect of perpetuating disadvantage or prejudice or imposing disadvantage on the basis of stereotyping. The focus of s. 15(2) is on *enabling* governments to pro-actively combat discrimination. Read thus, the two sections are confirmatory of each other. Section 15(2) supports a full expression of equality, rather than derogating from it. ...

[38] But this confirmatory purpose does not preclude an independent role for s. 15(2). Section 15(2) is more than a hortatory admonition. It tells us, in simple clear language, that s. 15(1) cannot be read in a way that finds an ameliorative program aimed at combatting disadvantage to be discriminatory and in breach of s. 15.

[39] Here the appellants claim discrimination on the basis of s. 15(1). The source of that discrimination — the very essence of their complaint — is a program that may be ameliorative. This leaves but one conclusion: if the government establishes that the program falls under s. 15(2), the appellants' claim must fail.

[40] In other words, once the s. 15 claimant has shown a distinction made on an enumerated or analogous ground, it is open to the government to show that the impugned law, program or activity is ameliorative and, thus, constitutional. ... Should the government fail to demonstrate that its program falls under s. 15(2), the program must then receive full scrutiny under s. 15(1) to determine whether its impact is discriminatory.

[41] We would therefore formulate the test under s. 15(2) as follows. A program does not violate the s. 15 equality guarantee if the government can demonstrate that: (1) the program has an ameliorative or remedial purpose; and (2) the program targets a disadvantaged group identified by the enumerated or analogous grounds. In proposing this test, we are mindful that future cases may demand some adjustment to the framework in order to meet the litigants' particular circumstances. However, at this early stage in the development of the law surrounding s. 15(2), the test we have described provides a basic starting point — one that is adequate for determining the issues before us on this appeal, but leaves open the possibility for future refinement.

[42] We build our analysis of s. 15(2) and its operation around three key phrases in the provision. The subsection protects "any law, program or activity that <u>has as its object</u> the <u>amelioration</u> of conditions of <u>disadvantaged</u> individuals or groups". While there is some overlap in the considerations raised by each of these terms, it may be useful to consider each of them individually.

a) <u>"Has as Its Object"</u>

[43] In interpreting this phrase, two issues arise. The first is whether courts should look to the *purpose* or to the *effect* of legislation. The second is whether, in order to qualify for s. 15(2) protection, a program must have an ameliorative purpose as its sole object, or whether having such a goal as one of several objectives is sufficient.

[44] The language of s. 15(2) suggests that legislative goal rather than actual effect is the paramount consideration in determining whether or not a program qualifies for s. 15(2) protection....

. . . . .

[50] The next issue is whether the program's ameliorative purpose needs to be its exclusive objective. Programs frequently serve more than one purpose or attempt to meet more than one goal. Must the ameliorative object be the sole object, or may it be one of several?

[51] We can find little justification for requiring the ameliorative purpose to be the sole object of a program. It seems unlikely that a single purpose will motivate any particular program; any number of goals are likely to be subsumed within a single scheme. To prevent such programs from earning s. 15(2) protection on the grounds that they contain other objectives seems to undermine the goal of s. 15(2).

[52] The importance of the ameliorative purpose within the scheme may help determine the *scope* of s. 15(2) protection, however. Consider that an ameliorative program may coexist with or interact with a larger legislative scheme. If only the program has an ameliorative purpose, does s. 15(2) extend to protect the wider legislative scheme? We offer as a tentative guide that s. 15(2) precludes from s. 15(1) review distinctions made on enumerated or analogous grounds that serve and are necessary to the ameliorative purpose.

b) "Amelioration"

[53] Section 15(2) protects programs that aim to "ameliorate" the condition of disadvantaged groups identified by the enumerated or analogous grounds. ...

[54] ... [L]aws designed to restrict or punish behaviour would not qualify for s. 15(2) protection. Nor, as already discussed, should the focus be on the effect of the law. This said, the fact that a law has no plausible or predictable ameliorative effect may render suspect the state's ameliorative purpose. Governments, as discussed above, are not permitted to protect discriminatory programs on colourable pretexts.

c) "Disadvantaged"

[55] The interpretation of "disadvantaged", explored in *Andrews, Miron v. Trudel*, [1995] 2 S.C.R. 418, and *Law*, and other cases in the context of s. 15(1), requires little further elaboration here. "Disadvantage" under s. 15 connotes vulnerability, prejudice and negative social characterization. Section 15(2)'s purpose is to protect government programs targeting the conditions of a specific and identifiable disadvantaged group, as contrasted with broad societal legislation, such as social assistance programs. Not all members of the group need to be disadvantaged, as long as the group as a whole has experienced discrimination.

2. *Application of Section 15(2) to This Case*

[56] The appellants have argued they were denied a benefit on the basis of race, a ground enumerated in s. 15 of the *Charter*. As discussed above, once the appellants have demonstrated such a distinction, the government may attempt to show the program is protected under s. 15(2). The government conferred the communal fishing licence valid for August 19-20 to particular aboriginal bands. Therefore, we are satisfied that the appellants have demonstrated a distinction imposed on the basis of race, an enumerated ground under s. 15.

[57] We have earlier suggested that a distinction based on the enumerated or analogous grounds in a government program will not constitute discrimination under s. 15 if, under s. 15(2), (1) the program has an ameliorative or remedial purpose; and (2) the program targets a disadvantaged group identified by the enumerated or analogous grounds. The question is whether the program at issue on this appeal meets these conditions.

[58] The first issue is whether the program that excluded Mr. Kapp and other non-band fishers from the fishery had an ameliorative or remedial purpose. The Crown describes numerous objectives for the impugned pilot sales program. These include negotiating solutions to aboriginal fishing rights claims, providing economic opportunities to native bands and supporting their progress towards self-sufficiency. The impugned fishing licence relates to all of these goals. The pilot sales program was part of an attempt — albeit a small part — to negotiate a solution to aboriginal fishing rights claims. The communal fishing licence provided economic opportunities, through sale or trade, to the bands. Through these endeavours, the government was pursuing the goal of promoting band self-sufficiency. In these ways, the government was hoping to redress the social and economic disadvantage of the targeted bands. The means chosen to achieve the purpose (special fishing privileges for aboriginal communities, constituting a benefit) are rationally related to serving that purpose. It follows that the Crown has established a credible ameliorative purpose for the program.

[59] The government's aims correlate to the actual economic and social disadvantage suffered by members of the three aboriginal bands. The disadvantage of aboriginal people is indisputable. In *Corbiere v. Canada (Minister of Indian and Northern Affairs)*, [1999] 2 S.C.R. 203, the Court noted "the legacy of stereotyping and prejudice against Aboriginal peoples" (para. 66). The Court has also acknowledged that "Aboriginal peoples experience high rates of unemployment and poverty, and face serious disadvantages in the areas of education, health and housing" (*Lovelace*, at para. 69). More particularly, the evidence shows in this case that the bands granted the benefit were in fact disadvantaged in terms of income, education and a host of other measures. This disadvantage, rooted in history, continues to this day. The communal fishing licence, by addressing long-term goals of self-sufficiency and, more immediately, by

providing additional sources of income and employment, relates to the social and economic disadvantage suffered by the bands. ...

. . . . .

[61] We conclude that the government program here at issue is protected by s. 15(2) as a program that "has as its object the amelioration of conditions of disadvantaged individuals or groups". It follows that the program does not violate the equality guarantee of s. 15 of the *Charter*.

3. *Section 25 of the Charter*

[62] Having concluded that a breach of s. 15 is not established, it is unnecessary to consider whether s. 25 of the *Charter* would bar the appellants' claim. ...

. . . . .

D. Conclusion

[66] We would dismiss the appeal on the ground that breach of the s. 15 equality guarantee has not been established.

[Bastarache J., dissenting, held that the appeal was properly disposed of under section 25 of the Charter and its contemplation of "other rights or freedoms", which he argued extends the scope of Aboriginal rights beyond what is contained in section 35(1). In his dissenting judgment in *Kapp*, Bastarache J. established a procedure for the application of section 25. As he stated (at para. 111):

> There are three steps in the application of s. 25. The first step requires an evaluation of the claim in order to establish the nature of the substantive *Charter* right and whether the claim is made out, *prima facie*. The second step requires an evaluation of the native right to establish whether it falls under s. 25. The third step requires a determination of the existence of a true conflict between the *Charter* right and the native right.

As for the substantive nature of section 25, Bastarache J. made the following comments in *Kapp*:]

[78] The enactment of the *Charter* undoubtedly heralded a new era for individual rights in Canada. Nevertheless, the document also expressly recognizes rights more aptly described as collective or group rights. The manner in which collective rights can exist with the liberal paradigm otherwise established by the *Charter* remains a source of ongoing tension within the jurisprudence and the literature. This tension comes to a head in the aboriginal context in s. 25.

[79] Most authors believe that s. 25 is an interpretative provision and does not create new rights.

. . . . .

[86] Most authors have considered the use of the word "construed" as significant in s. 25. In my opinion, the word "construe" is very broad. The *Oxford English Dictionary* (2nd ed. 1989) defines the term as meaning "[t]o analyse or trace the grammatical construction of a sentence; to take its words in such an order as to show the meaning of the sentence" (p. 796). The term accordingly permits the understanding that in constructing and interpreting the scope of *Charter* rights, courts must ensure that they do not abrogate or derogate from an aboriginal right or freedom. ...

. . . . .

[89] ... In my opinion ... s. 25 serves the purpose of protecting the rights of aboriginal peoples where the application of the *Charter* protections for individuals would diminish the distinctive, collective and cultural identity of an aboriginal group. ...

. . . . .

[94] Practically all authors agree with the fact that s. 25 operates as a shield ...

. . . . .

2.1.5 Limitations on the Shield

[97] Is this shield absolute? Obviously not. First, it is restricted by s. 28 of the *Charter* which provides for gender equality "[n]otwithstanding anything in this Charter". Second, it is restricted to its object, placing *Charter* rights and freedoms in juxtaposition to aboriginal rights and freedoms. *R. v. Van der Peet*, [1996] 2 S.C.R. 507, at para. 46, provides guidance in that respect. This means in essence that only laws that actually impair native rights will be considered, not those that simply have incidental effects on natives.

. . . . .

[100] Some would like the Court to ignore s. 25 because of the uncertainty in its application, particularly with regard to legislative powers contemplated by the *Indian Act*. I think it is unreasonable to suggest that a law should not be applied by this Court because it is too difficult. After all, s. 25 is the only provision in the *Charter* which makes express reference to aboriginal people, and the *Charter* is now 25 years old. I also think the concerns are overstated. Even under the present justification in a s. 1 analysis, there is much room for government to establish that *Charter* values should not be overstated when dealing with the requirements of substantive equality of native peoples. ...

. . . . .

[101] In this case, what is significant about the scope of s. 25 protection is the meaning of the words "other rights or freedoms". These words are

"all-embracive" ... this indicates that the protection was meant to be very broad. But the rights and freedoms are only those that "<u>pertain to</u> the aboriginal peoples of Canada", those that are particular to them....

[102] ... In s. 25, the general term "other rights or freedoms" follows the enumerated terms "aboriginal" and "treaty" rights. McLachlin C.J. and Abella J. argue that the rule should apply to limit the rights or freedoms protected to those of a constitutional character. I believe that a broader approach is merited, one more consistent with the interpretative principles outlined above.

[103] I believe that the reference to "aboriginal and treaty rights" suggests that the focus of the provision is the uniqueness of those persons or communities mentioned in the Constitution; the rights protected are those that are unique to them because of their special status. As argued by Macklem, s. 25 "protects federal, provincial and Aboriginal initiatives that seek to further interests associated with indigenous difference from *Charter* scrutiny": see p. 225. Accordingly, legislation that distinguishes between aboriginal and non-aboriginal people in order to protect interests associated with aboriginal culture, territory, sovereignty or the treaty process deserves to be shielded from *Charter* scrutiny.

. . . . .

[109] I do not think it is reasonable to invoke s. 25 once a *Charter* violation is established. One reason for this position is that there would be no rationale for invoking s. 25 in the case of a finding of discrimination that could not be justified under s. 1, simply because, in the context of s. 15, as in this case for instance, considerations that serve to justify that an Act is not discriminatory would have to be relitigated under the terms of s. 25. Another reason is that a true interpretative section would serve to define the substantive guarantee. Section 25 is meant to preserve some distinctions, which are inconsistent with weighing equality rights and native rights. What is called for, in essence, is a contextualized interpretation that takes into account the cultural needs and aspirations of natives. ... I do not believe there are distinct *Charter* rights for aboriginal individuals and non-aboriginal individuals, or that it is feasible to take into account the specific cultural experience of Aboriginals in defining rights guaranteed by the *Charter*. The rights are the same for everyone; their application is a matter of justification according to context.

[110] I also think it is contrary to the scheme of the *Charter* to invoke s. 25 as a factor in applying s. 1. Section 1 does not apply to s. 25 as such because s. 25 does not create rights; to incorporate s. 25 is inconceivable in that context. Section 1 already takes into account the aboriginal perspective in the right case. Section 25 is protective and its function must be preserved. Section 25 was not meant to provide for balancing *Charter* rights against aboriginal rights. There should be no reading down of s. 25 while our jurisprudence establishes that aboriginal rights must be given a broad and generous application, and that where there is uncertainty, every effort should be made to give priority to the aboriginal perspective. It

seems to me that the only reason for wanting to consider s. 25 within the framework of s. 15(1) is the fear mentioned earlier that individual rights will possibly be compromised. Another fear that is revealed by some pleadings in this case is that rights falling under s. 25 will be constitutionalized; this fear is totally unfounded. Section 25 does not create or constitutionalize rights.

———————

1. Do you agree with Bastarache J.'s conceptualization of the purpose and content of section 25? Is it consistent with your understanding of the meaning and interpretation given to section 35(1) rights? Does section 25 have the potential to significantly augment the scope of the rights belonging to the Aboriginal peoples of Canada, as Bastarache J. suggests, or do you see a different purpose/intent behind it? These are significant issues that will, undoubtedly, be fleshed out in greater detail in future jurisprudence.

2. Following the *Kapp* decision, the Supreme Court of Canada had another opportunity to consider the application of section 15(2) of the Charter to a matter involving Aboriginal peoples. In *Alberta (Aboriginal Affairs and Northern Development) v. Cunningham*, [2011] S.C.J. No. 37, [2011] 2 S.C.R. 670 (S.C.C.), which is excerpted in Chapter 7, the Supreme Court of Canada had to consider, *inter alia*, whether sections 75 and 90 of the Alberta *Metis Settlements Act*, R.S.A. 2000, c. M-14, which provided that voluntary registration under the federal *Indian Act*, R.S.C. 1985, c. I-5 precluded membership in a Métis settlement, was discriminatory under section 15(1) of the Charter or whether it was part of an ameliorative program under section 15(2). The Supreme Court held that the *Metis Settlements Act* was an ameliorative program and, as such, protected from claims of discrimination under section 15(1), notwithstanding that it conferred a benefit on one group of people (Métis) that was not provided to others (status Indians), and that drew the distinction based on race. As McLachlin C.J.C. stated in the court's unanimous judgment (at paras. 3, 84 and 85):

> ... The purpose and effect of the *MSA* is to enhance Métis identity, culture, and self-governance by creating a land base for Métis. The exclusion of status Indians from membership in the new Métis land base serves and advances this object and hence is protected by s. 15(2).

> . . . . .

> ... [T]he exclusion from membership in any Métis settlement ... of Métis who are also status Indians serves and advances the object of the ameliorative program. It corresponds to the historic and social distinction between the Métis and Indians, furthers realization of the object of enhancing Métis identity, culture and governance, and respects the role of the Métis in defining themselves as a people.

> It follows that the distinction between Métis and status Indians in the *MSA* does not fall outside the protective reach of s. 15(2) ... and the exclusion of the claimants from membership in a Métis settlement does not constitute discrimination.

The court held that the *Metis Settlements Act* served a similar ameliorative purpose to the program established for the benefit of certain Aboriginal peoples in *Lovelace v. Ontario*, [2000] S.C.J. No. 36, [2000] 1 S.C.R. 950 (S.C.C.), excerpted above, and thus was similarly protected by section 15(2).

G. CONCLUSION

When the Supreme ruled, in *Cardinal v. Alberta (Attorney General)*, [1973] S.C.J. No. 104, [1974] S.C.R. 695 (S.C.C.), that Indian reserves are not "enclaves" and therefore were not withdrawn from the application of provincial legislation, the Court dramatically narrowed the scope of inherent Indigenous and federal jurisdiction on Indian reserves. As the cases in this chapter demonstrate, the Court has not revisited this conclusion despite the existence of section 35(1) of the *Constitution Act, 1982*. As a result, Indigenous peoples in Canada have very little formal jurisdictional space within federalism to act in accordance with their own governmental aspirations. This result does not seem consistent with the entrenchment of section 35(1). In considering whether the Court should continue to narrowly frame the scope of section 91(24), recall the Supreme Court's conclusion in *R. v. Sparrow*, [1990] S.C.J. No. 49, 70 D.L.R. (4th) 385 at 406 (S.C.C):

> Professor Lyon in "An Essay on Constitutional Interpretation" (1988), 26 Osgoode Hall L.J. 95, says the following about s. 35(1), at p. 100:
>
> ... the context of 1982 is surely enough to tell us that this is not just a codification of the case law on aboriginal rights that had accumulated by 1982. Section 35 calls for a just settlement for aboriginal peoples. It renounces the old rules of the game under which the Crown established courts of law and denied those courts the authority to question sovereign claims made by the Crown.

The purposive nature of section 35(1), as indicated by the Supreme Court of Canada in *Sparrow* imposes a constitutional responsibility upon government to act in a manner consistent with the furtherance of Aboriginal rights. Combining the purposive nature of section 35(1) with the Crown's fiduciary and treaty obligations to the Aboriginal peoples, within our federal State, requires that the Crown take positive action to give greater shape and content to Aboriginal and treaty rights and to facilitate timely and equitable settlements of Aboriginal and treaty rights disputes. As the Federal Court, Trial Division explained in *Pacific Fishermen's Defence Alliance v. Canada*, [1987] F.C.J. No. 170, [1987] 3 F.C. 272 at 280-81 (F.C.T.D.):

> Subsection 35(1) of the *Constitution Act, 1982* recognizes and affirms the existing aboriginal and treaty rights of the aboriginal peoples of Canada. It is, therefore, the duty of the federal government to negotiate with Indians in an attempt to settle those rights. ... The government's task is to determine, define, recognize and affirm whatever aboriginal rights existed.[12]

The failure to effectively recognize Aboriginal jurisdictional space within Canadian federalism appears to frustrate section 35(1)'s broader purposes.

ENDNOTES

1. *R. v. Coté*, [1996] S.C.J. No. 93, [1996] 4 C.N.L.R. 26 at 60, [1996] 3 S.C.R. 139 (S.C.C.).
2. See K. McNeil, "Aboriginal Title and Section 88 of the Indian Act" (2000) 34 U.B.C. L. Rev. 159 at para. 13.
3. K. Wilkins, "Of Provinces and Section 35 Rights" (1999) 22 Dal. L.J. 185 at 229.
4. *Ibid.* at 232.
5. *Ibid.*
6. *Ibid.* at 233.
7. B. Slattery, "First Nations and the Constitution: A Question of Trust" (1992) 71 Can. Bar Rev. 261 at 285-86.
8. K. McNeil, *supra* note 2, at para. 12. See also *ibid.* at n. 30, modifying McNeil, "Aboriginal Title and the Division of Powers: Rethinking Federal and Provincial Jurisdiction" (1998) 61 Sask. L. Rev. 431 at 440-41:

    How would th[e] honour of the Crown [which is intimately connected with the Crown's fiduciary obligations] be upheld by Parliamentary delegation of authority to the provinces to infringe Aboriginal rights through the mechanism of referential incorporation? Would this not be a dishonourable abdication of the responsibility that was placed primarily on the federal government by s. 91(24) of the Constitution Act, 1867?

9. McNeil, *supra* note 2, at para. 19.
10. The doctrine of interjurisdictional immunity protects the jurisdiction of either the federal or provincial levels of government from otherwise valid laws promulgated by the other level of government. While the doctrine has been applied only to provincial laws that purport to affect matters of federal jurisdiction, there is nothing inherent in the doctrine that necessitates that it cannot work to immunize provincial areas of jurisdiction from the effect of federal laws. A summary of existing jurisprudence indicates that the doctrine applies where an otherwise-valid provincial law impairs, paralyzes, or sterilizes a federal undertaking or it directly affects a vital part of the management or operation of that undertaking. In these situations, the provincial laws are deemed to be invalid in their application to the federal undertaking in question.
11. *Treaty No. 8 Made June 21, 1899 and Adhesions, Reports, etc.* (Ottawa: Queen's Printer, 1966) at 5.
12. Note also the comments by Lamer C.J.C. in *Delgamuukw v. British Columbia*, [1997] S.C.J. No. 108, [1997] 3 S.C.R. 1010 (S.C.C.), at para. 186 where, in relation to his exhortation that negotiation of the Gitksan and Wet'suwet'en claims should also involve other Aboriginal nations with stakes in the territory being claimed, he stated that the "Crown is under a moral, if not a legal, duty to enter into and conduct those negotiations in good faith".

CHAPTER 9

ABORIGINAL WOMEN

A. INTRODUCTION

Aboriginal women have encountered significant discrimination in their dealings with the Canadian state. They have not only been disadvantaged because of their race, but have also been discriminated against because of their gender. This discrimination is often contrary to the traditional values of many communities which were matrilineal or matrilocal in nature, or which enjoyed a greater degree of equality between the sexes than was the case in many non-native societies. The *Indian Act* [now R.S.C. 1985, c. I-5] played a large part in perpetuating discriminatory stereotypes and denying Indian women a significant role within their communities. The destructive influence of the Act is explored in this chapter. A study of these issues is an investigation into how the law implements colonialism and sexism, and reproduces its effects within Indigenous communities. This chapter reveals that the destructive impact of colonialism is most devastatingly effective when its ideologies are replicated within the group it seeks to legislate. This issue is investigated by studying the legal structures which deny many Aboriginal women matrimonial property, community membership and political representation. Also examined in this chapter are the small steps that have been taken to reverse the exclusion Aboriginal women encounter in Canada.

"ABORIGINAL WOMEN"

A.C. Hamilton and C.M. Sinclair, The Justice System and Aboriginal People: Report of the Aboriginal Justice Inquiry of Manitoba, Vol. 1 (Winnipeg: Queen's Printer, 1991) at 475-87 (references omitted)

Introduction

Aboriginal women and their children suffer tremendously as victims in contemporary Canadian society. They are the victims of racism, of sexism and of unconscionable levels of domestic violence. The justice system has done little to protect them from any of these assaults. At the same time, Aboriginal women have an even higher rate of over-representation in the prison system than Aboriginal men. In community after community, Aboriginal women brought these disturbing facts to our attention. We believe the plight of Aboriginal women and their children must be a priority for any changes in the justice system. In addition, we believe that changes must be based on the proposals that Aboriginal women presented to us throughout our Inquiry.

Women in Traditional Aboriginal Society

Women traditionally played a central role within the Aboriginal family, within Aboriginal government and in spiritual ceremonies. Men and women enjoyed considerable personal autonomy and both performed functions vital to the survival of Aboriginal communities. The men were responsible for providing food, shelter and clothing. Women were responsible for the domestic sphere and were viewed as both life-givers and the caretakers of life. As a result, women were responsible for the early socialization of children.

Traditional Aboriginal society experienced very little family breakdown. Husbands and wives were expected to respect and honour one another, and to care for one another with honesty and kindness. In matriarchal societies, such as of the Mohawk, women were honoured for their wisdom and vision. Aboriginal men also respected women for the sacred gifts which they believed the Creator had given to them. In Aboriginal teachings, passed on through the oral histories of the Aboriginal people of this province from generation to generation, Aboriginal men and women were equal in power and each had autonomy within their personal lives.

Women figured centrally in almost all Aboriginal creation legends. In Ojibway and Cree legends, it was a woman who came to earth through a hole in the sky to care for the earth. It was a woman, Nokomis (grandmother), who taught Original Man (Anishinabe, an Ojibway word meaning "human being") about the medicines of the earth and about technology. When a traditional Ojibway person prays, thanks is given and the pipe is raised in each of the four directions, then to Mother Earth as well as to Grandfather, Mishomis, in the sky.

To the Ojibway, the earth is woman, the Mother of the people, and her hair, the sweet-grass, is braided and used in ceremonies. The Dakota and Lakota (Sioux) people of Manitoba and the Dakotas tell how a woman — White Buffalo Calf Woman — brought the pipe to their people. It is through the pipe that prayer is carried by its smoke upwards to the Creator in their most sacred ceremonies.

The strength that Aboriginal peoples gain today from their traditional teachings and their cultures comes from centuries of oral tradition and Aboriginal teachings, which emphasized the equality of man and woman and the balanced roles of both in the continuation of life. Such teachings hold promise for the future of the Aboriginal community as a whole. We have been told that more and more young Aboriginal people are turning to the beliefs and values of Aboriginal traditions to find answers for the problems which they are facing in this day and age.

Aboriginal author Paula Gunn Allen points out:

> Since the coming of the Anglo-Europeans beginning in the fifteenth century the fragile web of identity that long held tribal people secure has gradually been weakened and torn. But the oral tradition has prevented the complete destruction of the web, the ultimate disruption of tribal ways. The oral tradition is vital: it heals itself and the tribal web by adapting to the flow of the present while never relinquishing its connection to the past.

This revival is necessitated, in large measure, by the assault that Aboriginal culture has experienced during the last century.

The Attack on Aboriginal Culture

Women were never considered inferior in Aboriginal society until Europeans arrived. Women had few rights in European society at the time of first contact with Aboriginal people. Men were considered their social, legal and political masters. Any rights which women had were those derived through their husbands. The law of England, for example, held that women did not have the right to vote, to own property or to enter into contracts. This attitude was ultimately reflected in the *Indian Act*, which blatantly discriminated against women.

This attitude toward women continued until relatively recently in Canada. Women had to fight battles in this century to win the right to vote and to be recognized as legal persons, and it was only within the past few decades that the final legal restrictions upon their right to contract and own property were lifted. ...

Economic factors served as the initial catalyst for change within Aboriginal societies. Aboriginal people were first directed away from hunting into the economic order of the fur trade society. Gradually, more and more of them became removed from the land and went into settlements with a welfare economy. These changes to Aboriginal lifestyle distorted the traditional Aboriginal male and female roles.

> [W]ith the loss of Indian male roles and as a result of being reduced to a state of powerlessness and vulnerability which their own culture deemed highly inappropriate, Indian men came to experience severe role strain.

Cultural changes resulting from the economic factors at play had their greatest impact on the role of Aboriginal women.

Cultural Changes — The Impact upon Aboriginal Women

For Aboriginal women, European economic and cultural expansion was especially destructive. Their value as equal partners in tribal society was undermined completely.

It is only in the past decade that writers have acknowledged the very important role Aboriginal women played in the first centuries of contact with Europeans and their descendants. Yet, while [women's] role within Aboriginal society remained relatively stable for some time after contact, all that changed completely with the advent of the residential school system.

The victimization of Aboriginal women accelerated with the introduction after Confederation of residential schools for Aboriginal children. Children were removed from their families and homes at a young age, some to return eight to 10 years later, some never to return. The ability to speak Aboriginal languages and the motivation to do so were severely undermined. Aboriginal students were taught to devalue everything Aboriginal and value anything Euro-Canadian.

Many Aboriginal grandparents and parents today are products of the residential school system. The development of parenting skills, normally a significant aspect of their training as children within Aboriginal families, was denied to them by the fact that they were removed from their families and communities, and by the lack of attention paid to the issue by residential schools. Parenting skills neither were observed nor taught in those institutions. Aboriginal children traditionally learned their parenting skills from their parents through example and daily direction. That learning process was denied to several generations of Aboriginal parents. In addition to the physical and sexual abuse that Canadians are now hearing took place in residential schools, emotional abuse was the most prevalent and the most severe.

Not only did residential schools not support the development of traditional parental roles among the children, but they taught the children that they were "pagan" — an inferior state of being — and should never use their language or honour their religious beliefs. These messages were imparted to Aboriginal children in a sometimes brutal manner. Several presenters also pointed out that residential schools not only removed children from their families, but they also prevented any closeness, even contact, from occurring between siblings and relatives at the same school.

The damage done by residential schools is evident today as Aboriginal people, long deprived of parenting skills, struggle with family responsibilities and attempt to recapture cultural practices and beliefs so long denied. Grand Chief Dave Courchene Sr. put the experience succinctly:

> Residential schools taught self-hate. That is child abuse. ... Too many of our people got the message and passed it on. It is their younger generations that appear before you (in court).

We believe the breakdown of Aboriginal cultural values and the abuse suffered by Aboriginal children in the schools contributed to family breakdown. This began a cycle of abuse in Aboriginal communities, with women and children being the primary victims. The Canadian government also undermined equality between Aboriginal men and women with the legalization of sexist and racist discrimination in successive pieces of legislation. In 1869 it introduced the concept of enfranchisement, whereby Indian people would lose their status as use in essay

Indians and be treated the same as other Canadians. For Aboriginal women, this process of enfranchisement had particularly devastating consequences, because the role assigned to Canadian women was one of inferiority and subjugation to the male.

Upon becoming enfranchised, Aboriginal people lost their status under the *Indian Act.* An Indian woman lost her status automatically upon marrying a man who was not a status Indian. This was not true for Indian men, whose non-Indian wives gained status as Indians upon marriage. Under subsequent *Indian Acts*, Indian agents could enfranchise an Indian if he were deemed "progressive." In cases where a man became enfranchised, his wife and children automatically lost their status, as well.

While Bill C-31 (1985) [*An Act to Amend the Indian Act*, S.C. 1985, c. 27] addressed many of these problems, it created new ones in terms of the differential treatment of male and female children of Aboriginal people. Under the new Act, anomalies can develop where the children of a status Indian woman can pass on status to their children only if they marry registered Indians, whereas the grandchildren of a status male will have full status, despite the fact that one of their parents does not have status.

Aboriginal women traditionally played a prominent role in the consensual decision-making process of their communities. The *Indian Act* created the chief and council system of local government. The local Indian agent chaired the meetings of the chief and council, and had the power to remove the chief and council from office. Aboriginal women were denied any vote in the new system imposed by the Indian Affairs administration. As a result, they were stripped of any formal involvement in the political process.

The segregation of Aboriginal women, both from wider society and from their traditional role as equal and strong members of tribal society, continues to the present day. This is due partly to the fact that the effects of past discrimination have resulted in the poor socio-economic situation applicable to most Aboriginal women, but it is also attributable to the demeaning image of Aboriginal women that has developed over the years. North American society has adopted a destructive and stereotypical view of Aboriginal women.

The Changing Image of Aboriginal Women

The demeaning image of Aboriginal women is rampant in North American culture. School textbooks have portrayed Aboriginal woman as ill-treated at the hands of Aboriginal men, almost a "beast of burden." These images are more than symbolic — they have helped to facilitate the physical and sexual abuse of Aboriginal women in contemporary society. Emma LaRocque, a Métis woman and professor of Native Studies at the University of Manitoba, wrote to the Inquiry about such demeaning images.

The portrayal of the squaw is one of the most degraded, most despised and most dehumanized anywhere in the world. The "squaw" is the female counterpart to the Indian male "savage" and as such she has no human face; she is lustful, immoral, unfeeling and dirty. Such grotesque dehumanization has rendered all Native women and girls vulnerable to gross physical, psychological and sexual violence. ... I believe that there is a direct relationship between these horrible racist/sexist stereotypes and violence against Native women and girls. I believe, for example, that Helen Betty Osborne was murdered in 1972 by four young men from The Pas, because these youths grew up with twisted notions of "Indian girls" as "squaws" ... Osborne's attempts to fight off these men's sexual advances challenged their racist expectations that an "Indian squaw" should show subservience ... [causing] the whites ... to go into a rage and proceed to brutalize the victim. ...

Our Inquiry was told by the Canadian Coalition for Equality and by the Manitoba Women's Directorate that the media today continue to employ stereotypical images of women. Both presentations compared lurid newspaper coverage of the Helen Betty Osborne murder in The Pas to the more straightforward and sympathetic coverage of the killing of a young non-Aboriginal woman in Winnipeg.

We consider societal attitudes to be an issue that this Inquiry must address. There is a perception among women's groups, both Aboriginal and non-Aboriginal, that abuse of Aboriginal women is more acceptable to the courts than abuse of non-Aboriginal women. While we do not subscribe to the view that there is differential treatment, we are disturbed enough by the perception to suggest that it needs to be addressed. At the heart of the problem is the belief that, fundamentally, justice authorities do not understand, and do not wish to understand, the unique issues facing Aboriginal women.

In order to address the underlying problems that give rise to this perception, the public generally, and those within the justice system specifically, need to be educated about those issues by Aboriginal women. Elsewhere in this report we have recommended that cross-cultural training be provided to a variety of individuals involved in the justice system. We would like to make it clear that Aboriginal women must play a central role in the development and delivery of those programs.

Unfortunately, Aboriginal men, over the centuries, have adopted the same attitude toward women as the European. As a result, the cultural and social degradation of Aboriginal women has been devastating.

According to the Manitoba Women's Directorate, the average annual income for Manitoba's Aboriginal women is less than 75% of that for other women. The labour force participation rate for Aboriginal women is 40%, while 72% of Aboriginal women do not have a high school diploma.

The status of Aboriginal women in the city of Winnipeg is particularly disturbing. Forty-three per cent of Aboriginal families are headed by single women, compared to 10% of non-Aboriginal families.

In her presentation on behalf of the Women's Directorate, Janet Fontaine said:

> Poverty is an unmistakable factor in the lives of Manitoba Native women and children. Poverty has been shown to be positively correlated with conflict with the law, low levels of education, decreased opportunity for employment, and a low level of health.

The Abuse of Women and Children

The presentations of Aboriginal women were blunt and direct. Violence and abuse in Aboriginal communities has reached epidemic proportions.

This violence takes a number of forms. Sometimes it involves physical assaults between adult males. More often — and more disturbingly — it involves the victimization of the least powerful members of the community: women and children.

The Manitoba Women's Directorate submitted to our Inquiry a document entitled "Native Perspective on Rape." According to one of the women interviewed for the study:

- Rape is a common and widespread experience.
- Rape extends back many generations.
- People treat rape as a personal, private pain and do not talk about it unless there is an unavoidable crisis.
- The individual who is raped comes to view violence as [the norm].

The victimization of Aboriginal women has not only been manifested in their abuse, but also in the manner in which Aboriginal female victims are treated. Women victims often suffer unsympathetic treatment from those who should be there to help them. We heard one example of such treatment from the Aboriginal mother of a 16-year-old rape victim. She told of how the police came to her home after her daughter had reported being raped and had undergone hospital examination and police questioning. The police told the mother that her daughter was lying and should be charged with public mischief. According to the mother, the officer added, "Didn't you want it when you were 16?" ...

Spousal Abuse

One study presented to our Inquiry stated that while one in 10 women in Canada is abused by her partner, for Aboriginal women the figure is closer to one in three. The most recent study of Aboriginal women by Aboriginal women, a survey conducted by the Ontario Native Women's Association in 1989, found that 80% of Aboriginal women had personally experienced family violence. Fifty-three per cent of Aboriginal women who responded to a survey conducted for us by the Indigenous Women's Collective indicated they had been physically abused. Seventy-four per cent of those women indicated they did not seek help.

The Thompson Crisis Centre stated that, generally, women are abused at least 20 times before seeking help. A March 1991 study by the Manitoba Association of Women and the Law found that the statistics of a 1980 federal study, Wife Battering in Canada: A Vicious Circle, still held: "women endure anywhere from 11 to 39 episodes of abuse before seeking help, and then they seek help more often from a shelter than from police. The Manitoba government Family Disputes Services branch says that abuse occurs at least 35 times before any outside assistance is sought. ..."

According to the 1991 report of the Manitoba Association of Women and the Law, some improvements have been made since 1983. Nevertheless, over 30% of domestic assault charges are stayed at some stage before trial. The percentage of those sentenced has increased from 48% in 1983 to 64% in 1986. However, only 7% of those sentenced in 1987 were sentenced to a term in jail. While we agree that certain cases need to be prosecuted to the full extent of the law, it does not appear that that avenue has been very effective to date.

Aboriginal women surveyed by the Indigenous Women's Collective indicated that the police response received by others discouraged them from going to the police for help. They complained of the lack of understanding of the problem by officers, and their lack of sensitivity. They believe the police do not understand the situation of the abused woman and the needs of children.

More than one woman who spoke to us told of complaining to the police, only to become the one removed from the home. This happened in spite of the fact that young children were left in the care of an intoxicated father. Others told of situations where police attended in the home, saw the situation was calm when they were there and told the woman everything would be all right. When the police left, the violence became worse than before. With such lack of support from police authorities, it is not surprising that women suffer in silence.

From this information, it is clear that women in abusive situations, particularly in isolated communities in northern Manitoba, do not feel confident in turning to the justice system. We were told that many abused Aboriginal women did not feel safe enough even to bring their personal stories before the inquiry.

Testimony presented to us by the Manitoba Action Committee on the Status of Women in Thompson made it clear why this was the case:

> A man who beat his sister with a length of wood and who had a record of previous convictions for violent acts, was sentenced to seven months. A man who severely beat his common law wife, smashing her face against a fence, kicking her in the face, and slamming her face against the wall, before dragging her into a house, was sentenced to five months in jail, to be followed by probation after his release.

Both these offenders were going to return to their home communities after serving their sentences. Offenders are returned to their community without notice to the victim — and without treatment — and, as a result, their victims were at risk upon their release. Reporting the crime to police authorities provides a temporary respite at best if the causes of abuse are not dealt with. ...

Women's groups expressed concern about the whole criminal justice system, from police to Crown attorneys, judges and correctional institutions. Crisis shelter workers affirmed the experience Aboriginal women have in dealing with the justice system:

> ... indifference/arrogance of lawyers; long police response time; insensitive response of police to spousal abuse; humiliating questioning; failure of police to protect victims; failure of police to take spousal abuse as a serious crime; difficulties obtaining peace bonds; lack of supports to witnesses and treatment of witnesses as criminals; difficulties obtaining protection or getting away from abusive partners in small communities.

In northern, isolated reserve communities, the abused woman is placed in a more difficult situation when the question of calling the police arises. If she calls the police, it may take a day or longer for them to arrive. If they arrive while a party is going on, they may refuse to remove the offender or may simply drive him down the road, from where he can return again, only angrier. There is a lack of housing for families in isolated communities and no "safe house" available for women and children trying to escape an abusive man. They may be forced to spend the night in the bush, or be forced to leave the reserve entirely.

Professor LaRocque points out that women move to urban centres to escape family or community problems. Men, on the other hand, cite employment as the reason for moving. In the new setting Aboriginal women experience personal, systemic, subtle and overt racial discrimination. What they are forced to run to is often as bad as what they had to run from. Why they feel they have to leave is a matter worthy of comment. Most chiefs and council members are male and often exhibit bias in favour of the male partner in a domestic abuse situation. This can effectively chase the woman from her home and community.

The unwillingness of chiefs and councils to address the plight of women and children suffering abuse at the hands of husbands and fathers is quite alarming. We are concerned enough about it to state that we believe that the failure of Aboriginal government leaders to deal at all with the problem of domestic abuse is unconscionable. We believe that there is a heavy responsibility on Aboriginal leaders to recognize the significance of the problem within their own communities. They must begin to recognize, as well, how much their silence and failure to act actually contribute to the problem.

Aboriginal leaders must speak out against abuse within their communities to their own community members, and they must take steps within their own spheres of community influence to assist the true victims. Women and children who report abuse should never feel they have to leave their communities in order to feel safe. Aboriginal communities and their leaders must do what is possible to make the home communities of abused women and children havens from abuse. The problem of abuse is dealt with presently by women either staying on the reserves and putting up with the abuse, or leaving their communities to live elsewhere, just to escape from it. It is clear, however, that most would prefer to stay in their home communities if they could be protected. ...

Rates of violence against Aboriginal women remain as high as when the Manitoba Justice Inquiry was released. In May 2011, Statistics Canada reported:

- In 2009, close to 67,000 Aboriginal women aged 15 or older living in the Canadian provinces reported being the victim of violence in the previous 12 months. Overall, the rate of self-reported violent victimization among Aboriginal women was almost three times higher than the rate of violent victimization reported by non-Aboriginal women.
- Close to two-thirds (63 per cent) of Aboriginal female victims were aged 15 to 34. This age group accounted for just under half (47 per cent) of the female Aboriginal population (aged 15 or older) living in the 10 provinces.[1]

While Aboriginal leaders bear significant responsibility for the violence experienced by Aboriginal women (as suggested in the above excerpt from the Manitoba Justice Inquiry), Amnesty International has also pointed out that the Canadian government should be much more accountable for the tragic circumstances borne by many Aboriginal women. The following excerpt develops this point:

NO MORE STOLEN SISTERS:
THE NEED FOR A COMPREHENSIVE RESPONSE TO DISCRIMINATION AND VIOLENCE AGAINST INDIGENOUS WOMEN IN CANADA

London: Amnesty International Publications International, 2009
<http://www.amnesty.ca/amnestynews/upload/AMR200122009.pdf>
(footnotes omitted)

Indigenous women in Canada face much higher rates of violence than other women. In a 2004 Canadian government survey, Indigenous women reported rates of violence, including domestic violence and sexual assault, 3.5 times higher than non-Indigenous women. Studies suggest that assaults against Indigenous women are not only more frequent, they are also often particularly brutal. According to another government survey, young First Nations women are five times more likely than other women to die as a result of violence.

Such figures almost certainly underestimate the scale and severity of the violence faced by Indigenous women. A 2007 joint committee of government, Indigenous Peoples, police and community groups in Saskatchewan Province reported that 60 per cent of the long-term cases of missing women in the province are Indigenous, although Indigenous women make up only 6 per cent of the population. The fate of these women remains unknown. Significantly, this is the only jurisdiction in Canada where such information has been compiled and made public. In fact, police in Canada often do not even record whether or not the victims of crime are Indigenous.

In the absence of accurate national statistics, Indigenous women have themselves taken the lead in attempting to expose the scale of violence they face. The Native Women's Association of Canada has used the testimony of family members and media reports to create an ongoing list of missing and murdered Indigenous women. As of July 2009, the list included more than 520 women who have gone missing or been murdered in the last three decades. Given the relatively small Indigenous population and the overall low rate of violent crime in Canada, these numbers are truly appalling. However, the Native Women's Association believes that the real number of missing and murdered Indigenous women is even higher than they have been able to record. ...

. . . . .

... [W]idespread and entrenched racism, poverty and marginalization are critical factors exposing Indigenous women to a heightened risk of violence while denying them adequate protection by police and government services.

Deep inequalities in living conditions and access to government services have pushed many Indigenous women into situations, ranging from overcrowded housing to prostitution, where there is a greatly heightened risk of violence. The same inequalities have also denied many Indigenous women access to the services and support, such as emergency shelters, needed to escape violence.

At the same time it appears that some men seek out Indigenous women as targets for extreme acts of violence. These acts of violence against Indigenous women may be motivated by racism, or may be carried out in the expectation that society's indifference to the welfare and safety of Indigenous women will allow the perpetrators to escape justice. Impunity for such violence contributes to a climate where such acts are seen as normal and acceptable rather than criminal, and where women do not seek justice because they know they will not get it. There are additional concerns around police treatment of Indigenous and non-Indigenous women in the sex trade. The threat of arrest could make many women reluctant to report attacks to the police or co-operate with police investigations. As a result, the perpetrators may be encouraged by the belief that they are likely to get away with their crimes.

Justice David Wright, speaking of the 1992 murders of Eva Taysup, Shelley Napope, and Calinda Waterhen in Saskatchewan, said the man responsible for the killings saw the victims as vulnerable for four reasons: "one, they were young; second, they were women; third, they were native; and fourth, they were prostitutes. They were persons separated from the community and their families. The accused treated them with contempt, brutality; he terrorized them and ultimately he killed them. He seemed determined to destroy every vestige of their humanity.

. . . . .

... [T]he ... *Stolen Sisters* report highlights the continuing marginalization and inequality experienced by Indigenous women in five key areas:

1) the role of racism and misogyny in perpetuating violence against Indigenous women;
2) the sharp disparities in the fulfilment of Indigenous women's economic, social, political and cultural rights;
3) the continued disruption of Indigenous societies caused by the historic and ongoing mass removal of children from Indigenous families and communities;
4) the disproportionately high number of Indigenous women in Canadian prisons, many of whom are themselves the victims of violence and abuse; and
5) inadequate police response to violence against Indigenous women as illustrated by the handling of missing persons cases. ...

. . . . .

RECOMMENDATIONS TO THE GOVERNMENT OF CANADA

1. As a matter of urgent priority, the federal government should work with Indigenous women and representative organizations and provincial and territorial officials to develop and implement a comprehensive, co-ordinated national plan of action in keeping with the scale and seriousness of the violence and discrimination experienced by Indigenous women. Such a plan of action should include:

    - The collection and routine publication of gender disaggregated data on health and social and economic conditions for Inuit,

Métis and First Nations women and men, including rates of violence against Indigenous women;

- The promotion of standardized protocols for police handling of missing persons cases including tools for fair and effective assessment of the risk to the missing individual;
- Improved co-ordination of police investigations into long-term missing persons cases and unsolved murders involving Indigenous women and other women at risk;
- Adequate, sustained, long-term funding to ensure the provision of culturally relevant services to meet the needs of Indigenous women and girls at risk of violence or in contact with the police and justice system, including emergency shelters, court workers, victim services and specific programmes to assist women who have been trafficked within Canada;

2. Review all social programmes to ensure that funding for programmes for Indigenous women, children and families is equitable to those available to non-Indigenous people in Canada and is sufficient to ensure effective protection and full enjoyment of their rights. Particular priority should be given to eliminating discrimination in funding for Indigenous child welfare;

3. Restoration of funding to fulfill the commitment set out in the Kelowna Accord (First Ministers and National Aboriginal Leaders: Strengthening Relationships and Closing the Gap) to end inequalities in health, housing, education, and other services for Indigenous peoples;

4. Immediate implementation of recommendations of the Canadian Human Rights Commission and the UN Human Rights Committee concerning the treatment of women prisoners, including the creation of a new security risk assessment system;

5. Publicly commit to fully implement the standards contained in the UN Declaration on the Rights of Indigenous Peoples and to engage Indigenous Peoples in discussions about their implementation.

Governments have only recently taken steps to address the numbers of murdered and missing Aboriginal women in Canada. The Canadian government set aside $10 million to:

- create a National Police Support Centre for Missing Persons to help police forces across Canada by providing coordination and specialized support in missing persons investigations;
- develop a national "tip" website for missing persons;
- enhance the Canadian Police Information Centre database to capture additional missing persons data;
- amend the Criminal Code to streamline the warrants application process where wiretaps are required in missing person cases; and

- develop a comprehensive list of best practices to help communities, law enforcement and justice partners in future work.

British Columbia is conducting a Missing Women Commission of Inquiry, under the direction of The Honourable Wally Oppal, Q.C., Commissioner: see online <http://www.missingwomeninquiry.ca/>. Manitoba has created an Integrated Task Force for Murdered and Missing Women as a joint effort between the government of Manitoba, the RCMP and the Winnipeg Police Services. The government of Saskatchewan also devoted $2 million to a task force dealing with missing persons cases in the province.

The following excerpt rounds out the perspectives offered in this section concerning the socio-economic circumstances of Aboriginal women in Canada.

ABORIGINAL WOMEN: CANADIAN ASSOCIATION OF ELIZABETH FRY SOCIETIES

<http://elizabethfry.ca/wwdcms/uploads/Aboriginal%20Women.pdf>
(footnotes omitted)

- In 2006, the 1 172 785 Aboriginal people in Canada represented 3.8% of the country's total population.
- In 2006, 600 695 Aboriginal women and girls in Canada made up 3% of the total population of women and girls in Canada.
- The population of Aboriginal women is growing much more rapidly than the rest of the population of women and girls in Canada. In the period of 2001 to 2006, the number of Aboriginal women and girls rose by 20.3% in comparison to a 5.6% growth rate in the non-Aboriginal population of women and girls.
- In 2004-2005, Aboriginal women made up 30% of the women in federal prisons. In provincial jails and detention centres in Saskatchewan, women compose 87% of the female prison population, 83% in Manitoba, 54% in Alberta, and 29% in British Columbia. ...

. . . . .

- The gap between employment rates between Aboriginal and non-Aboriginal women was particularly large in the 15-24 age group, in which 35% of Aboriginal women versus 57% of non-Aboriginal women were employed.
- Unemployment rates among Aboriginal women and girls participating in the labour force are twice those of their non-Aboriginal counterparts. In 2001, 17% of Aboriginal women in the labour force were unemployed, compared with a rate of 7% for non-Aboriginal women.
- The incomes of Aboriginal women in Canada tend to be relatively low. In 2000 the median income of an Aboriginal woman was

$12,300 about $5 000 less than that of non-Indigenous women who had an average income of $17,300 that year.

- On average, Aboriginal women in Canadian urban centers are unable to earn enough money to meet their own needs, much less support a family. In the 2001 census, the average annual income of Aboriginal women reserve was $5,500 less than that of non-Indigenous women and substantially less than the amount Statistics Canada estimated people living in a large Canadian city would have needed to provide food, shelter and clothing for themselves.

. . . . .

- The number of Aboriginal women (including Inuit, Métis, and First Nations women) living in poverty was 36% in 2005.

The following figures are taken from Shelly Milligan and Evelyne Bougie, First Nations Women and Postsecondary Education in Canada: Snapshots from the Census.[2]

- According to the 2006 Census, 44 per cent of First Nations women aged 25 to 64 had completed some form of postsecondary education. Of these graduates, 21 per cent had obtained a college diploma. An additional 9 per cent had a university degree, 9 per cent had a trades certificate, and 5 per cent had a university certificate or diploma below the bachelor's level.
- First Nations women were more likely to have college and university credentials than their male counterparts in both 2001 and 2006. In 2006, 21 per cent of First Nations women and 14 per cent of First Nations men had college credentials, while 9 per cent of First Nations women and 5 per cent of First Nations men had university degrees.
- In 2006, the proportion of First Nations women with a postsecondary education was highest among those aged 35 to 39 (48 per cent), whereas for women in the overall Canadian population, this proportion was highest for adults aged 30 to 34 (72 per cent).
- Also, there were proportionately more First Nations women with a postsecondary education among the older age groups (35 to 39 to 50 to 54-year-olds) than among the younger age groups (25 to 29 and 30 to 34-year-olds). This pattern was not found among women in the overall Canadian population, where younger adults were more highly educated than their older counterparts. These data suggest that more First Nations women may defer their postsecondary studies until later in life compared to women in the total Canadian population.

B. MATRIMONIAL PROPERTY

One of the many forms of discrimination and abuse that Indian women face as a result of the *Indian Act* is an inability to effectively access and control property upon marital breakdown. Under the *Indian Act*, title to individual property is often held as a certificate of possession issued by the band council. On many Canadian reserves a strong trend has developed of issuing these certificates in the man's name in a marriage relationship, despite the matrilineal traditions that existed in some communities. Such a practice represents the extension of the patriarchal assumptions underlying the *Indian Act* that unequally distributed Indian status, political power, and property to men:

> There is no equal division of property upon marriage breakdown recognized under the *Indian Act*. This has to be rectified. While we recognize that amending the *Indian Act* is not a high priority for either the federal government or the Aboriginal leadership of Canada we do believe that this matter warrants immediate attention. The Act's failure to deal fairly and equitably with Aboriginal women is not only quite probably unconstitutional, but also appears to encourage administrative discrimination in the provision of housing and other services to Aboriginal women by the Department of Indian Affairs and local governments.[3]

The issue of the division of property upon marital breakdown on a reserve was dealt with in the following case.

DERRICKSON v. DERRICKSON

[1986] S.C.J. No. 16, [1986] 1 S.C.R. 285, 26 D.L.R. (4th) 175 (S.C.C.)

The judgment of the Court was delivered by

Chouinard J.: — The constitutional question stated in this appeal is as follows:

> Whether the provisions of Part 3 of the *Family Relations Act*, R.S.B.C. 1979, c. 121, dealing with the division of family assets, are constitutionally applicable to lands in a reserve held by an Indian, in view of the *Indian Act*, R.S.C. 1970, c. I-6?

The factual background is summarized by Hinkson J.A., who wrote the unanimous judgment of the Court of Appeal of British Columbia, [1984] 2 W.W.R. 754 at p. 755:

> The appellant wife and the respondent husband are members of the Westbank Indian Band. Each of them holds certificates of possession issued to them pursuant to the provisions of the *Indian Act*, R.S.C. 1970, c. I-6.
> The wife brought a petition for divorce and for other relief including a division of family assets pursuant to the provisions of the *Family Relations Act*, R.S.B.C. 1979, c. 121.

At trial, the trial judge raised with counsel the question of whether the provisions of the *Family Relations Act* applied to lands alloted to the spouses by the Westbank Indian Band and for which they held certificates or possession issued pursuant to s. 20 of the *Indian Act*.

The wife sought a declaration pursuant to Pt. 3 of the *Family Relations Act* that she was entitled to an undivided one-half interest in the properties for which her husband held certificates of possession. The husband resisted that claim for relief on the basis that if the lands in question were family assets as defined in the *Family Relations Act*, then that Act had no application to the lands because they were Indian lands.
...

The Interveners

Before this court, the Attorney General of British Columbia and the Attorney General of Ontario intervened in support of the appellant, the Attorney General of Canada in support of the respondent.

The Issues

In the case at bar it is common ground that the *Family Relations Act* is valid provincial legislation of general application. Beyond that the arguments developed in this Court were many and varied, and not always congruent even when supporting the same conclusions.

With respect, however, this appeal can in my view be resolved by consideration of the three following issues:

1. Are the provisions of the *Family Relations Act* applicable of their own force to lands reserved for the Indians?
2. Is the *Family Relations Act* referentially incorporated in the *Indian Act* by the application of s. 88 of the latter Act?
   This issue in turn breaks down into two:

   (a) Does s. 88 of the *Indian Act* apply to lands reserved for the Indians?
   (b) In the affirmative, do the provisions of the *Family Relations Act* fall within one of the exceptions in s. 88?

3. Can an order for compensation be made in accordance with s. 52(2)(c) of the *Family Relations Act* with respect to lands on a reserve in lieu of an order directing division of property?

1. Are the Provisions of the Family Relations Act Applicable of Their Own Force to Lands Reserved for the Indians?

Section 91(24) of the *Constitution Act, 1867* confers exclusive legislative authority on the Parliament of Canada in "all Matters" coming within the subject "Indians, and lands reserved for the Indians".

Title to reserve lands is vested in the Crown, federal or provincial. So long as they remain such, reserve lands are administered by the federal government and Parliament has exclusive legislative authority over them. The *Indian Act*, enacted under that authority, provides in s. 18(1):

> **18**(1) Subject to this Act, reserves are held by Her Majesty for the use and benefit of the respective bands for which they were set apart; and subject to this Act and to the terms of any treaty or surrender, the Governor in Council may determine whether any purpose for which lands in a reserve are used or are to be used is for the use and benefit of the band.

The purpose of the above subsection is to ensure that lands reserved for Indians are and remain used for the use and benefit of the band.

Under s. 20 ... possession of lands in a reserve is allotted to individual members of the band by the band council with the approval of the Minister of Indian Affairs and Northern Development who issues a certificate of possession.

By virtue of s. 24 cited above, a member of the band may transfer his right to possession only to the band or to another member of the band but no such transfer is effective until it is approved by the Minister.

I turn now to the provisions of the *Family Relations Act*.

Section 43 declares that each spouse is entitled to an undivided half-interest in each family asset upon the occurrence of certain events, in this case an order for dissolution of marriage.

Section 45 defines as a family asset property used for a family purpose.

Sections 48 and 49 deal with the effect of marriage and separation agreements upon family assets and provide for the filing, in the land title office, of a notice setting out the provisions of the marriage or separation agreement relating to the land in question.

Section 50 provides for the enforceability of a spouse's interest in matrimonial property.

Section 51 deals with judicial reapportionment of matrimonial property where the division under s. 43 or a marriage agreement would be unfair.

Section 52, already reproduced, governs the determination of the ownership, possession or division of matrimonial property.

Section 53 allows the court to make interim orders in respect of matrimonial property.

The appellant argues that the pith and substance of the *Family Relations Act* is the division of matrimonial property, not the use of Indian lands. She further argues that it in no way encroaches on the exclusive federal jurisdiction as to the use of Indian lands. She is supported in these views by the Attorney-General of British Columbia and the Attorney-General of Ontario.

With respect I do not accept the latter proposition where Indian lands are involved.

The various orders that can be made under s. 52(2) deal, inter alia, with ownership, right of possession, transfer of title, partition or sale of property, severance of joint tenancy. ...

The right to possession of lands on an Indian reserve is manifestly of the very essence of the federal exclusive legislative power under s. 91(24) of the *Constitution Act, 1867*. It follows that provincial legislation cannot apply to the right of possession of Indian reserve lands.

When otherwise valid provincial legislation, given the generality of its terms, extends beyond the matter over which the legislature has jurisdiction and over a matter of federal exclusive jurisdiction, it must, in order to preserve its constitutionality, be read down and given the limited meaning which will confine it within the limits of the provincial jurisdiction.

It follows that the provisions of the *Family Relations Act* dealing with the right of ownership and possession of immovable property, while valid in respect of other immovable property, cannot apply to lands on an Indian reserve.

2. Is the Family Relations Act Referentially Incorporated in the Indian Act by the Application of s. 88 of the Latter Act?

With respect to Indians, valid provincial legislation of general application which would normally have to be read down in order to preserve its constitutionality, may be made applicable to Indians by referential incorporation in the *Indian Act* through the operation of s. 88 of the Act, subject to the exceptions stated in the section.

Section 88 of the *Indian Act* reads:

> 88. Subject to the terms of any treaty and any other Act of the Parliament of Canada, all laws of general application from time to time in force in any province are applicable to and in respect of Indians in the province, except to the extent that such laws are inconsistent with this Act or any order, rule, regulation or by-law made thereunder, and except to the extent that such laws make provision for any matter for which provision is made by or under this Act.

It is now settled that the provincial laws of general application to which s. 88 refers are those laws which could not apply to Indians without regulating them *qua* Indians. It is also settled that those laws that are made applicable to Indians by the operation of s. 88 are not applicable to them *ex proprio vigore* but are so made applicable by referential incorporation in the *Indian Act*: see *Dick v. The Queen*, [1985] 2 S.C.R. 309. ...

It is far from settled, however, that s. 88 contemplates referential incorporation with respect to lands reserved for the Indians.

It follows that the provisions of the *Family Relations Act* at issue will be found not to be referentially incorporated in the *Indian Act* if s. 88 does not apply to lands reserved for the Indians.

If it were found that s. 88 does apply to Indian lands, the provisions of the *Family Relations Act* would still not be referentially incorporated if they fall within one of the exceptions provided for in that section. Hence the two following questions.

(a) Does s. 88 of the Indian Act Apply to Lands Reserved for the Indians?

... The submission that s. 88 does not apply to lands reserved for Indians is quite simple. It is to the effect that not one but two subject-matters are the object of s. 91(24) of the *Constitution Act, 1867*, namely: "Indians" and "Lands reserved for the Indians". Since only Indians are mentioned in s. 88, that section would not apply to lands reserved for the Indians. ...

Be that as it may, it is not essential for the resolution of this case to determine the issue if we find, as I think we must, that even assuming that s. 88 applies to lands reserved for the Indians, the impugned provisions of the *Family Relations Act* are not referentially incorporated in the *Indian Act* since they are excluded by the application of the federal paramountcy set out in the section.

(b) Do the Provisions of the Family Relations Act Fall Within One of the Exceptions in s. 88?

In P.W. Hogg, *Constitutional Law of Canada* (2nd ed. 1985), it is stated at pp. 561-62:

> The Importance of s. 88 lies in its definition of the laws that *do not* apply to Indians. The section is explicitly "subject to the terms of any treaty", which means that any conflict between a treaty made with the Indians and a provincial law of general application has to be resolved in favour of the treaty provision, thus reversing the normal rule for such conflicts.
>
> The section is also subject to "any other act of the Parliament of Canada", so that any conflict between a federal statute and a provincial law has to be resolved in favour of the federal statute. A provincial law is also inapplicable where it is "inconsistent with this Act or any order, rule, regulation or by-law made thereunder". These two parts of the section seem to be intended to make clear that the paramountcy doctrine applies to provincial laws, notwithstanding their adoption by a federal statute. However, the closing language of the section goes on to provide that the provincial laws are applicable "except to the extent that such laws make provision for any matter for which provision is made by or under this Act". This language in its context seems to contemplate that a provincial law which makes provision for any matter for which provision is made by (or under) the *Indian Act* must yield to the provisions of the *Indian Act*. The doctrine of paramountcy, on the other hand, at least as it has been interpreted recently, applies only where there is an express contradiction between a federal and a provincial law. It does not apply where the federal and provincial laws, while not in direct conflict, are merely occupying the same field, or in other words making provision for the same matters. It seems probable therefore that the closing words of s. 88 go further than the paramountcy doctrine and will render inapplicable to Indians some provincial laws which would have been applicable under the general law.

... With respect, in my view, the impugned provisions of the *Family Relations Act* do conflict with the *Indian Act*.

Section 18 of the *Indian Act* provides that reserves are held by Her Majesty for the use and benefit of the bands.

Section 20 provides that the possession by an individual Indian can only come through allotment by the council together with the approval of the Minister. ...

Provisions such as are made in s. 52 of the *Family Relations Act* for orders dealing with ownership, right of possession, transfer of title, partition or sale of property, severance of joint tenancy are, in my view, in "actual conflict" with the above provisions of the *Indian Act*.

Were the provisions of both Acts to be applied at once as was sought in this case, the husband by virtue of his Certificate of Possession issued by the Minister following an allotment by the band council would be entitled to the sole possession of the land while the wife by virtue of an order of the court would be entitled to a half interest in the Certificate of Possession and the rights flowing therefrom.

In my respectful view, to make the order conditional on the approval of the Minister would not change the situation. ...

In the result, even assuming that s. 88 of the *Indian Act* applies to lands reserved for the Indians, the provisions of the *Family Relations Act* would, in my opinion, fall within that exception of s. 88 and would not be applicable to lands reserved for the Indians.

In reaching this conclusion I am not unmindful of the ensuing consequences for the spouses, arising out of the laws in question, according as real property is located on a reserve or not. In this respect I borrow the following sentence, albeit in a different context, from P. W. Hogg, *op. cit.*, at p. 554:

> Whether such laws are wise or unwise is of course a much-controverted question, but it is not relevant to their constitutional validity.

3. Can an Order for Compensation be Made in Accordance With s. 52(2)(c) of the Family Relations Act with Respect to Lands on a Reserve in Lieu of an Order Directing Division of Property?

Section 52(2)(c) of the *Family Relations Act* provides that the court may "order a spouse to pay compensation to the other spouse where property has been disposed of, or for the purpose of adjusting the division". ...

In this respect the trial judge held:

> As there can be no division of the reserve lands under Section 43 then there can be no determination of what "would be unfair". I, therefore, cannot make a substitution of compensation under Section 52(2)(c) for an "unfair division" under Sections 43 or 51.

Reversing on this point the Court of Appeal wrote, at p. 761:

> If the court is unable to award the wife an interest in the Indian reserve lands then the court may make an order for compensation for the purpose of adjusting the division of family assets between the spouses.

The Court of Appeal accordingly ordered that the matter be remitted to the trial judge in order that he may complete the disposition of the family assets involved in this proceeding by awarding compensation for the purpose of adjusting the division of family assets between the spouses.

With this I agree. If the court may make an order for compensation because division is not possible where property has been disposed of, surely it must be empowered to make such an order "for the purpose of adjusting the division", where property exists but cannot be divided because no division can be made of reserve lands.

The rule under s. 43 is that each spouse is entitled to an undivided half interest in all family assets, not immovable property only. Where having regard to the factors listed in s. 51 the division would be unfair, the court may fix different shares. With this we are not concerned here. Section 52(2)(c) provides for a compensation order "for the purpose of adjusting the division". All family assets having been taken into account, where an equal division is not possible because some assets, in this case lands on a reserve, cannot be divided, I fail to see why a compensation order could not be had.

Compensation in lieu of a division of property is not a matter for which provision is made under the *Indian Act* and in my view there is no inconsistency or "actual conflicts" between such a provision for compensation between spouses and the *Indian Act*.

I would answer the constitutional question as follows:

Question: Whether the provisions of Part 3 of the *Family Relations Act*, R.S.B.C. 1979, c. 121, dealing with the division of family assets, are constitutionally applicable to lands in a reserve held by an Indian, in view of the *Indian Act*, R.S.C. 1970, c. I-6?

Answer: No.

I would dismiss the appeal. No order as to costs was made by the Supreme Court nor by the Court of Appeal. I would likewise make no order as to costs.

Appeal dismissed.

MARY-ELLEN TURPEL, "HOME/LAND"

(1991) 10 Can. J. Fam. L. 17 at 30 (references omitted)

The decisions in *Derrickson* and *Paul*, particularly at the Supreme Court of Canada level, project an image of a perfunctory division of powers conflict resolved by application of the constitutional doctrine of exclusivity of federal jurisdiction over Indians and lands reserved for the Indians. This style of reasoning masks the political complexity of the conflict(s) which were at the basis of *Derrickson* and *Paul*. The complexity stems from what can be called the "aboriginal dimension" of the legal dispute. This refers to the fact that the disputes that have arisen in these cases stem directly from the legacy of a colonial regime that continues to be imposed on aboriginal people by decontextualizing these conflicts and ignoring the impact of the law on aboriginal peoples' lives. To do otherwise would demand critical reflection on the inadequacy and oppressive nature of the colonial regime established by the *Constitution Act, 1867* and the *Indian Act.*

The chosen legal issue in *Derrickson* and *Paul* is which branch of the state should control which aspects of aboriginal life, not the very matter of state control itself. The state control of aboriginal life is the central political issue in these cases. Framing the issue in constitutional division of powers doctrine is an effective strategy for depoliticizing the cases and silencing any questioning of the overwhelming state control of (jurisdiction over) aboriginal peoples. The court, as an emanation of the colonial political regime for aboriginal peoples, is blinded to its role and to the political nature of the law it applies in this context.

Insensitivity to Aboriginal Conceptions of Property

The consequence of the *Derrickson* and *Paul* decisions is that an aboriginal woman who resides in a home on a reserve with her spouse cannot make an application under provincial family legislation for occupation or possession of the home upon marriage breakdown or in the event of physical and emotional abuse from her spouse. There is no federal family legislation to govern these conflicts. ...

Even if an aboriginal woman holds a certificate of possession jointly with her spouse under the *Indian Act*, she will have no recourse under provincial family law (the only family law) for access to her home. Moreover, the situation on Indian reserves is such that the certificates of possession are invariably issued to male band members so an appeal to the Department of Indian Affairs or the band council would be equally futile in most, if not all, cases. The practice of issuing certificates to men is a carry-over from the late nineteenth century practice of issuing location tickets to males, an extension of Anglo-European patriarchal notions of land holding and succession. It was this same philosophy that infused the gender discrimination provisions in relation to Indian status.

The *Indian Act* requirement of ministerial approval for any transfer of reserve land likely forecloses the possibility of successfully pursuing a remedy for the situation at common law ... Essentially, an aboriginal woman has no legally recognizable interest in her matrimonial home, unless she solely holds the certificate of possession. Even if this is the case, gaining an interim order for exclusive possession will be impossible as there is no legislation which will apply in this context. While this is an obvious injustice, there is another layer here which makes the injustice particularly cruel and oppressive: that is the cultural significance of property from an aboriginal perspective.

For aboriginal women, it is not the commodity character of property which is vital to her survival. ... The significance of matrimonial property must be understood in the context of what the reserve represents: it is a home of a distinct cultural and linguistic people. It is a community of extended families, tightly connected by history, language and culture. It is often the place where children can be educated in their language and culturally appropriate pedagogies. ... The economic value of the land is secondary to its value as shelter within a larger homeland — the homeland of her people, her family.

The second aspect of matrimonial property theory that infuses this area, the notion of equality of the spouses, is, similarly, not entirely applicable in the aboriginal matrimonial context. In most aboriginal communities, the belief is that women, children and elders come before men and the responsibility of the men is to live life as a good helper toward women, children and elders. Traditional tribal control of property did not lead to the victimization of aboriginal women. As one Mohawk lawyer suggests of property customs in the Iroquois Confederacy:

> The Iroquois woman's rights to the family property was based on political influence via the control over the economic wealth of the family ... she had real property rights even superior to those of her husband ... The property situation of the modern day Iroquois woman is vastly different from her historical sister prior to European contact. Traditionally she had the control of the family assets and family life. There has been a complete demotion. If she is not the legal owner of the family asset situated on an Indian reserve, then upon marriage dissolution she has no possibility of real property rights ... She is truly the forgotten victim in a matrimonial dissolution. Her situation is equivalent to that under the "separate as to property regime" which was remedied by provincial matrimonial legislation in the common law provinces. She has recourse only under common law trust doctrines and provincial compensation schemes. She no longer has her traditional real property rights over family assets.

The decisions in *Derrickson* and *Paul* sanction a situation which is completely opposite to that of the customs of many tribes. There are no obligations on aboriginal men now recognized at law to provide shelter for women, children or elders. Indeed, customary law has no place in matrimonial property disputes as Canadian law will not recognize it — it is the federal or provincial government which exercises jurisdiction over Indians upon marriage breakdown. The impact of this oppression of aboriginal custom on communities cannot be underestimated. When men no longer have to fulfill their responsibilities to women, children and elders, the social control network of the community disintegrates and respect for social responsibilities is lost.

Disregard For the Violence Aboriginal Women Endure

The cultural and spiritual conceptions of property held by aboriginal peoples find no recognition in the cases on matrimonial property. The social reality for aboriginal peoples also does not enter into the discourse of division of powers which has been seized upon by all levels of courts in these cases. The appellants had to structure their arguments into claims based upon alien property notions and legal doctrines foreign to the customs of their communities. Could a claim have been made on the basis of customary law (that is, the aboriginal) practice of the community? Undoubtedly, this was the farthest thing in the minds of lawyers advising the appellants in *Derrickson* and *Paul*, or the court in examining the legitimacy of their claims under Canadian (*i.e.* federal or provincial) law. Moreover, it would be difficult, if not impossible, according to Canadian constitutional law.

The Canadian legal system is revealed, once again, as a thoroughly colonial regime. It is too busy trying to categorize jurisdictional matters between federal and provincial governments to step back and realize the oppressive and presumptuous nature of its exercise. To expect it to do so is to expect too much given that this branch of the state is an emanation and expression of a colonial state. In fact, the role of the judicial branch of the state is going to be, in such a regime, to justify the colonial mentality using legal doctrine. It is little wonder that the legal system enjoys a low level of respect from aboriginal peoples who see this exercise. The actors within the system and, even most academic commentators, often fail to see the violence this situation foists on aboriginal peoples. Aboriginal peoples have nowhere to turn to voice their grievances — taking them to court means accepting an alien system. Doing nothing has only meant continued oppression and an implosion of violence and social upheaval in communities. The violence of silence is difficult to endure, and it is violence. ...

The complete silencing of aboriginal women's experiences and indeed of the aboriginal dimension of *Derrickson* and *Paul*, exposes the deleterious colonial character of Canadian constitutional law. The reasoning employed in the two decisions demonstrates the role played by the Canadian legal system in camouflaging the social and political aspects of aboriginal peoples' conflicts. Courts have been unable to grasp the impact of aboriginal treatment by a colonial legal system because this would require its dismantling and a critical examination of the function of the courts and law in perpetuating the oppression. Dismantling it would require recognizing aboriginal peoples' presence as political communities in Canada with distinct cultural linguistic and social systems. It would require ending bureaucratic regulation of Indian life through the *Indian Act*. No court has been honest or reflective enough to acknowledge the colonial character of the regulation of aboriginal life in Canada. Meanwhile aboriginal peoples have had to endure the violence of a colonial regime which silences aboriginal reality and displays disregard for aboriginal peoples' suffering.

———————————

would you strike down the const as unconst. if you were a judge?!

First Nations Matrimonial Property legislation has been introduced in Parliament three times since 2008. Each time it has failed to pass. On September 28, 2011, Bill S-2, *An Act respecting family homes situated on First Nation reserves and matrimonial interests or rights in or to structures and lands situated on those reserves* (short title: *Family Homes on Reserves and Matrimonial Interests or Rights Act*) was introduced in the Senate. The bill was next referred to the Standing Senate Committee on Human Rights on November 1, 2011, and the committee reported the bill back to the Senate with two amendments. The amended bill was passed by the Senate on December 1, 2011, and the bill subsequently received first reading in the House of Commons on December 8, 2011. The bill remained the same as of June 29, 2012.

> The bill was first introduced as Bill C-47 during the 2nd Session of the 39th Parliament. Bill C-47 died on the *Order Paper* when Parliament was dissolved on 7 September 2008. It was reintroduced as Bill C-8 during the 2nd Session of the 40th Parliament, but it died on the *Order Paper* once again when Parliament was prorogued on 30 December 2009. It was introduced a third time as Bill S-4 during the 3rd Session of the 40th Parliament, and was considered by the Standing Senate Committee on Human Rights in May and June 2010. Bill S-4 was passed by the Senate on 6 July 2010, and was introduced in the House of Commons on 22 September 2010 by then Minister of Indian Affairs and Northern Development, the Honourable John Duncan. Bill S-4, however, died on the *Order Paper* when Parliament was dissolved on 26 March 2011.[4]

The proposed legislation (Bill S-2) is to be "stand-alone legislation, which would require consequential amendments to other acts".[5] This legislation was divided into two parts: Part 1 would recognize First Nations' jurisdiction over matrimonial property, and Part 2 would establish interim federal rules that would apply until a First Nation has exercised its jurisdiction and adopted its own laws.[6]

The proposed Act's preamble reads as follows:

> Whereas it is necessary to address certain family law matters on First Nation reserves since provincial and territorial laws that address those matters are not applicable there and since the *Indian Act* does not address those matters;
>
> Whereas measures are required to provide spouses or common-law partners with rights and remedies during a conjugal relationship, when that relationship breaks down or on the death of a spouse or common-law partner in respect of
>
> the use, occupation and possession of family homes on reserves, including exclusive occupation of those homes in cases of family violence, and
>
> the division of the value of any interests or rights that they hold in or to structures and lands on those reserves;
>
> Whereas it is important that, when spouses or common-law partners exercise those rights and seek those remedies, the decision-maker

take into account the best interests of the children, including the interest of any child who is a First Nation member to maintain a connection with that First Nation, and

be informed by the First Nation with respect to the cultural, social and legal context in the circumstances;

Whereas the Government of Canada has recognized the inherent right of self-government as an aboriginal right and is of the view that implementation of that right is best achieved through negotiations;

Whereas this Act is not intended to define the nature and scope of any right of self-government or to prejudge the outcome of any self-government negotiation;

And whereas the Parliament of Canada wishes to advance the exercise, in a manner consistent with the *Constitution Act, 1982*, of First Nations law-making power over family homes on reserves and matrimonial interests or rights in or to structures and lands on reserves...

If enacted, the heart of the Act would protect married spouses from having matrimonial homes sold without their knowledge or consent, protect married spouses from having the matrimonial home sold without their knowledge or consent, authorize courts to grant applications for compensation orders relating the value of the matrimonial home and authorize courts to develop remedies to reflect First Nations diversity and legal traditions.

Like reaction to its predecessors, reaction to Bill S-2 has been primarily negative. Individuals and organizations who have commented on the new bill have emphasized that for the most part, key issues that had been raised with respect to previous incarnations of the bill (*e.g.*, inadequate consultation, a failure to recognize First Nations' inherent jurisdiction over the issue and the need to improve access to justice) have not been addressed.

Some witnesses who appeared before the Standing Senate Committee on Human Rights in November 2011 acknowledged that removing the verification officer provisions, changing the voting threshold and adding a one-year transitional period between when First Nations are authorized to enact laws and when the provisional federal rules apply were positive differences between Bill S-2 and its predecessors.

When Bill S-2's predecessor, Bill S-4, was considered by the Standing Senate Committee on Human Rights in May and June 2010, witnesses highlighted the following issues:

- shortcomings in the consultation process prior to the drafting of the bill;
- the requirement to recognize First Nations' inherent right to self-government and their jurisdiction over matrimonial interests;
- difficulties accessing the legal system;
- access to alternative dispute resolution mechanisms;

- the need for a comprehensive solution to address underlying issues (family violence, chronic housing shortages, poverty, the lack of shelters and temporary accommodations); and
- a commitment to take non-legislative action (*e.g.*, creation of a legal aid fund).[7]

As noted above, First Nations under the *First Nations Land Management Act* would not be subject to the *Family Homes on Reserves and Matrimonial Interests or Rights Act*. The *First Nations Land Management Act*, which came into force in 1999, contains provisions to deal with matrimonial property. Under the *First Nations Land Management Act*, "every two years, a limited number of First Nations communities have the opportunity to take responsibility for the management of their reserve land. In doing so, each First Nation must write a land code, including rules and procedures on matrimonial real property, in consultation with its members".

Furthermore, some First Nations have undertaken their own initiatives to address matrimonial real property ("MRP") issues in their communities. Some of these initiatives include:

First Nations Laws and Policies

The Aundeck Omni Kaning First Nation Matrimonial Real Property Law

The Aundeck Omni Kaning First Nation undertook a community-developed process to create their own matrimonial real property law and policy for their community. It was part of a larger process to address historical inequities caused by the *Indian Act*. The resulting matrimonial real property law was approved by a large percentage of the community in a referendum. …

The Little Pine First Nation Housing Act

The Little Pine First Nation has developed matrimonial real property law as part of a law relating to housing and land.

The Mistawasis First Nation Housing Policy

The Mistawasis First Nation has developed a housing policy that addresses matrimonial real property. The policy says that in cases of conflict or separation of a common-law union or marriage the spouse deemed by the Housing Authority to be in the greatest need for the unit will be given the title of ownership of a Band and/or Canada Mortgage and Housing Corporation (CMHC) unit.

The Squamish Nation Housing Policy

The Squamish First Nation Housing Policy sets out four categories within their housing list: single, single parent, married/common-law, and pensioner. The Squamish First Nation Council determines how many housing units will be allocated each year within each category.

(<http://www.afn.ca/cmslib/general/MRP-Newsletter.pdf>)

First Nations can also negotiate self-government agreements that contain provisions to address matrimonial property issues. For example, the Westbank First Nation, the community from which the

Derrickson case emanated, has enacted a strong and fair matrimonial property law: see *Westbank First Nation Family Property Law* 2006-02 at <http://wfn.ca/pdf/feb202006_2_.pdf>. The preamble reads:

> Whereas Westbank has jurisdiction over Westbank Lands, Resources and Interests in Westbank lands pursuant to the Westbank Self-Government Agreement effective April 1, 2005;
>
> And whereas Westbank wishes to enact and respect the following rules and procedures applicable on the breakdown of a marriage with respect to the use, occupancy and possession of Westbank lands and the division of Westbank lands;
>
> And whereas Westbank intends to provide rights and remedies without discrimination on the basis of sex to spouses who have or claimed an interest in Westbank lands upon the breakdown of their marriage. ...

Section 9(1) of the *Westbank First Nation Family Property Law* states: "Subject to this law, both spouses have an equal right to possession of the matrimonial home." Section 9 (2) states: "When only one spouse holds an interest in Westbank Lands that is a matrimonial home, the other spouse's right of possession is (a) personal against the spouse who holds the interest." The law also contains provisions for domestic contracts, disposition of matrimonial property, mediation and access to appropriate courts for enforcement.

C. DENIAL OF STATUS UNDER THE INDIAN ACT

The *Indian Act*'s discriminatory provisions extend far beyond the denial of property to women in cases of marital breakdown. Another example of the inequality built into the Act is found in its provisions relating to Indian status. For many years, Indian women who married non-Indian men automatically lost their status under the *Indian Act*. If an Indian man married a non-Indian women, no such disability was incurred. The disparate impact of these provisions reflected the patrilineal assumptions that underlie the Act. Once a woman lost her status she could no longer reside on the reserve, secure treaty promises and policy initiatives designed to assist Indians, or participate in the political and social life of the community. The effect of these provisions was to fracture extended families and exile women from their homes and culture. This legislation sent women from the reserves and undermined their influence and position within their communities. In the last few decades this negative change in gender relations created a drive to reconstruct Indian communities and restore the dignity and respect Indian women once enjoyed. The effort to reinstate this dignity was undertaken by some very courageous women who worked hard against the discrimination they faced. Reform of the provisions of the *Indian Act* that concerned the discriminatory effects of Indian status is explored below through a review of the Act's history, and the efforts of Aboriginal women who brought important cases in the domestic and international realm to challenge its provisions.

REPORT OF THE ROYAL COMMISSION ON ABORIGINAL PEOPLES: PERSPECTIVES AND REALITIES, VOL. 4

(Ottawa: Ministry of Supply and Services, 1996) at 24-33
(references omitted)

Policy Development and its impact on First Nations Women

The First 100 Years: 1850 – 1950

> Historically the Indian Act has thoroughly brainwashed us. Since 1869
> Indian women already were legislated as to who she should be. Six times
> the Indian Act changed on Indian women. But each time she lost a little
> bit of her rights as an Indian.

Nellie Carlson
Indian Rights for Indian Women
Edmonton, Alberta, 11 June 1992

The earliest laws dealing directly and explicitly with Indian people
date from the middle of the nineteenth century and were enacted as
part of the reserve policy of imperial and colonial governments to
protect reserve lands from encroachment by non-Indian settlers. Once
protected lands had been set aside for exclusive Indian use and
occupation, it became necessary to define who was Indian.

The first statutory definition of "Indian" is found in *An Act for the
better protection of the Lands and Property of the Indians in Lower Canada*,
passed in 1850. The definition is quite inclusive. It includes all those of
Indian blood and their descendants, non-Indians who have married
Indians living on the designated lands, and even persons adopted in
infancy by Indians. Within one year, this definition became more
restrictive as a result of amending legislation that denied non-Indian
men who married Indian women the right to acquire Indian status, but
Indian status could still be gained by non-Indian women who married
Indian men.

The descendants of all intermarriages who actually resided on a
reserve would nonetheless still be considered Indians irrespective of the
status of one of the spouses, since they would fall within that part of the
definition of Indian that referred to Indian blood. However, it is
obvious that the same rule did not apply to men and women in mixed
marriages as it had under the earlier legislation. For the first time,
Indian status began to be associated with the male line of descent.

The concept of enfranchisement was introduced in 1857 through *An
Act to encourage the gradual Civilization of the Indian Tribes in the Province,
and to amend the Laws respecting Indians*. The act applied to both Upper
and Lower Canada, and its operating premise was that by removing the
legal distinctions between Indians and non-Indians through
enfranchisement and by facilitating the acquisition of individual
property by Indians, it would be possible in time to absorb Indians fully
into colonial society. An enfranchised Indian was, in effect, actually

renouncing Indian status and the right to live on protected reserve land in order to join non-Aboriginal colonial society. The modern department of Indian affairs describes the nature and effect of the *Gradual Civilization Act* as follows:

> [The Act] ... contained property and monetary inducements to encourage Indians to leave tribal societies and seek enfranchisement. An enfranchised person could receive land and a sum of money equal to the principal of the annuities and other yearly revenues received by the band. The intent of this legislation was that enfranchised Indians would continue to reside in the Native community but would have the same rights as non-Indian citizens.

The Act applied only to adult male Indians. Under s. 3 of the act, to be enfranchised an Indian had to be male, over age 21, able to read and write either English or French, reasonably well educated, free of debt, and of good moral character as determined by a commission of examiners. The right to exercise the franchise depended upon meeting the requirements in federal and provincial legislation in terms of property ownership. Thus, there was no automatic right to vote. Indians were given a three-year qualifying period to acquire these attributes.

Women were not to be enfranchised independently. Yet if an Indian man was enfranchised, his wife and children were automatically enfranchised along with him, regardless of their wishes; willingly or not, they lost their Indian status. From a woman's perspective, this act perpetuated the notion of a wife and children as the husband's property, his chattels. Unlike her husband, the enfranchised woman did not receive a share of reserve lands, because by this time, in keeping with prevailing Victorian notions, maleness and the right to possess and live on reserve lands were becoming fixtures of Indian policy.

If an enfranchised man died, for example, his children of lineal descent were given precedence to inherit the estate and to live on his land. His wife would inherit the estate and land allotted to him if and only if there were no children of lineal descent. She would then have the right to use it only until her re-marriage or death, at which point it would revert to Crown ownership.

In the pre-Confederation period, concepts were introduced that were foreign to Aboriginal communities and that, wittingly or unwittingly, undermined Aboriginal cultural values. In many cases, the legislation displaced the natural, community-based and self-identification approach to determining membership — which included descent, marriage, residency, adoption and simple voluntary association with a particular group — and thus disrupted complex and interrelated social, economic and kinship structures. Patrilineal descent of the type embodied in the *Gradual Civilization Act*, for example, was the least common principle of descent in Aboriginal societies, but through these laws, it became predominant. From this perspective, the *Gradual Civilization Act* was an exercise in government control in deciding who was and was not an Indian.

At Confederation, the secretary of state became the superintendent general of Indian affairs and, in 1868, acquired control over Indian lands and funds through federal legislation. The definition of "Indian" was finalized on a patrilineal model, excluding non-Indian men who married Indian women but including non-Indian women who married Indian men.

The first important piece of post-Confederation legislation, the *Gradual Enfranchisement Act*, was passed in 1869. This Act went further than previous legislation in its "civilizing" and assimilative purposes and in marginalizing Indian women: for the first time, Indian women were accorded fewer legal rights than Indian men in their home communities. The prevailing Victorian social and political norms were now extended to include reserve communities. For example, Indian women were denied the right to vote in band elections; voting was now restricted to adult men, as it was in Canadian society generally. As well, a new provision was added to the provisions carried over from the *Gradual Civilization Act*. Now a woman who married an Indian man from another band lost membership in her home community, as did her children, and she became a member of her husband's band.

In the eyes of Aboriginal women, the most damaging aspects of this legislation were the new provisions that penalized women who married non-Indian men. Under the earlier *Gradual Civilization Act*, there had been no penalty for such a marriage beyond the fact that the non-Indian husband did not gain Indian status upon marriage. Under this new legislation, by contrast, the Indian wife was legally stripped of her recognized Indian identity, and she and the children of the marriage lost the rights that flowed from Indian status. They were no longer entitled to treaty payments, for example, unless the band council agreed to continue them. No similarly disadvantageous provisions applied to Indian men who married non-Indian women. Aside from the inherent unfairness of this policy, there were other potentially damaging consequences for women. A woman could be compelled to leave the reserve — her home community — since her non-Indian husband could be summarily ejected by the superintendent general.

From the perspective of the twentieth century, one may well wonder how such a policy could make its way into federal legislation. The official explanation at the time focused on concerns about control over reserve lands and the need to prevent non-Indian men from gaining access to them. Thus, in 1869 the secretary of state wrote to the Mohawks of Kahnawake regarding the marrying out provisions of the new legislation, stressing that the goal was "preventing men not of Indian Blood having by marrying Indian women either through their Wives or Children any pretext for Settling on Indian lands". The *Gradual Enfranchisement Act* permitted reserves to be subdivided into lots; the superintendent general could then issue "location tickets" allocating specific lots to individual Indian men or women. In the earlier *Gradual Civilization Act*, the fear had been that non-Indian men might gain control over Indian lands; hence the need to exclude them from Indian status and reserve residency rights. In the *Gradual Enfranchisement Act*, that same rationale was extended to justify the exclusion of women from their own communities. Moreover, given the social values of the day, it also seems to have been assumed that Indian women who married non-Indians would be protected by them and would acquire property rights under Canadian law through their non-Indian spouse, thus rendering unnecessary the protection that came from Indian status and the property rights they might have as members of an Indian community on protected reserve lands.

In the relatively short period between the 1850 Lower Canada legislation and the 1863 *Gradual Enfranchisement Act*, it seems apparent that Indian women were singled out for discriminatory treatment under a policy that made their identity as Indian people increasingly dependent on the identity of their husbands. They were subject to rules that applied only to them as women and that can be summarized as follows: they could not vote in band elections; if they married an Indian man from another band, they lost membership in their home communities; if they married out by wedding a non-Indian man, they lost Indian status, membership in their home communities, and the right to transmit Indian status to the children of that marriage; if they married an Indian man who became enfranchised, they lost status, membership, treaty payments and related rights and the right to inherit the enfranchised husband's lands when he died. Despite strong objections, these discriminatory provisions were carried forward into the first *Indian Act* in 1876.

1876: The first Indian Act

In its 100 sections, the 1876 *Indian Act* consolidated and expanded previous Indian legislation, carrying forward the provisions that put Indian women at a disadvantage compared to Indian men. Commenting on these provisions, historian J.R. Miller highlights the irony of the official justification that these measures were necessary to protect Indian lands and social structures:

> The *Indian Act's* tracing of Indian descent and identity through the father was the unthinking application of European patrilineal assumptions by a patriarchal society; but it accorded ill with those Indian societies, such as the Iroquoian, in which identity and authority flowed through the female side of the family. All these attempts at cultural remodelling also illustrate how the first step on the path of protection seemed always to lead to the depths of coercion.

As we will see, a large share of the effects of this coercion was borne by Indian women.

The *Indian Act* went through a number of changes as amendments were introduced and adopted over the years, usually in response to unanticipated administrative problems or to strengthen the assimilative thrust of federal Indian policy. Although most of the provisions that discriminated against women were simply carried forward from earlier legislation, additional measures of the same nature were also adopted. Thus, in 1884, an amendment permitted the wife of an Indian man who held reserve land by location ticket to receive one-third of her husband's estate, if he died without a will. But the amendment stated that the widow might receive it only if she were living with him at the time of death and was "of good moral character" as determined by federal authorities. This amendment applied standards to women that were not applied to men, standards that were, moreover, ambiguous and that could be interpreted arbitrarily by officials outside Indian communities.

Amendments in 1920 increased the power of the superintendent general at the expense of the band council. Until this time, councils had the authority to decide whether an Indian woman who married out would continue to receive treaty annuity payments and band money distributions, or whether she would get a lump sum settlement. Many bands allowed these women to continue receiving payments and distributions so they could retain some link to the home community. The 1920 amendments removed this power from the band and lodged it in the hands of the superintendent general of Indian affairs. The official rationale for this provision was set out in a letter from Deputy Superintendent General Duncan Campbell Scott:

> When an Indian woman marries outside the band, whether a non-treaty Indian or a white man, it is in the interest of the Department, and in her interest as well, to sever her connection wholly with the reserve and the Indian mode of life, and the purpose of this section was to enable us to commute her financial interests. The words "with the consent of the band" have in many cases been effectual in preventing this severance ... The amendment makes in the same direction as the proposed Enfranchisement Clauses, that is it takes away the power from unprogressive bands of preventing their members from advancing to full citizenship.

Importantly, in that same set of amendments were new enfranchisement provisions that allowed the governor in council, on the recommendation of the superintendent general, forcibly to enfranchise any Indian, male or female, if found to be "fit for enfranchisement", along with his or her children.

The 1951 amendments to the Indian Act

The *Indian Act* was completely revised in 1951. A number of provisions were introduced that would affect Indian women. The provisions dealing with status, membership and enfranchisement were significantly modified in a way that further disadvantaged women and their children. The status provisions became vastly more elaborate and spelled out in great detail who was and was not entitled to be registered as an Indian for federal government purposes.

The mention of Indian blood, a feature of the definition of "Indian" since 1876, was replaced by the notion of registration, with a strong emphasis on the male line of descent. The new rules dealt with acquisition and loss of Indian status, referring to persons who were "entitled to be registered" as "Indian". Only they would be recognized as Indian by federal authorities. The result was that many people of Indian ancestry and culture who had been involuntarily enfranchised, who had been deleted from treaty or band lists accidentally. ...

Before these new provisions were introduced in 1951, women who had lost their Indian status through marrying out had often been able to retain their links to their communities. Some Indian agencies would issue an informal identity card known as a "red ticket" identifying such women as entitled to share in band treaty moneys and, in many cases, to continue to live on the reserve. Because they were no longer legally Indians but remained members of the reserve community by virtue of band practice and their red tickets, the precise status in law of such women was unclear to Indian affairs officials and the general Canadian public. With forced enfranchisement upon marrying out, there could no longer be doubt in anyone's mind that they were not Indian and, moreover, not part of any Indian community.

Nonetheless, Indian women who had married out before the 1951 changes were permitted to keep their red ticket status if they did not accept a lump sum settlement in exchange for their treaty payments. However, an amendment to the *Indian Act* in 1956 stopped this practice. After 1956, "red ticket" women were paid a lump sum of 10 times the average annual amount of all payments paid over the preceding 10 years. These women were put in the same unfavourable position as Indian women who married out after the 1951 revision. The children of mixed marriages were not mentioned in the 1951 legislation. Despite the lack of legal authority for it, enfranchisement was forced on them too, under subsection 108(2). To correct this injustice, in 1956 Indian status was restored to these children. But the 1956 *Indian Act* amendments also allowed the governor in council "by order [to] declare that all or any of her children are enfranchised as of the date of the marriage or any such other date as the order may specify". While there do not appear to be any common or consistent criteria regarding how the discretion of the governor in council was to be exercised, the usual practice was that off-reserve children were enfranchised but children living on-reserve were allowed to keep their status.

None of these provisions applied to Indian men. They could not be enfranchised against their will after 1951 except through a stringent judicial inquiry procedure as prescribed in the revised *Indian Act*. This difference in treatment created a huge imbalance between the number of enfranchised men and the number of involuntarily enfranchised women. Between 1955 and 1975 (when forced enfranchisement of women stopped), 1,576 men became enfranchised (along with 1,090 wives and children), while 8,537 women (as well as 1,974 of their children) were forcibly enfranchised and lost their status. From 1965 to 1975, only five per cent of enfranchisements were voluntary; 95 per cent were involuntary, and the great majority of these involved women.

Post-1951 to pre-1985: Growing awareness, growing tension

Between 1951 and 1985, equality and civil rights movements were a prominent feature of the socio-political landscape in North America. Aboriginal voices were being raised, and there was growing awareness of the concerns of Aboriginal people, including the concerns of Indian women. The governments of the day were making some effort to consult Aboriginal people about issues affecting them, but there was little change in the *Indian Act* until the early 1980s.

The status provisions of the *Indian Act* and the exclusion of women who married out were of great concern to the Aboriginal women's groups that sprang up during this period. In 1970, the Royal Commission on the Status of Women tabled its final report. The commission was particularly concerned that the "special kind of discrimination under the terms of the *Indian Act* ... the loss of Indian status, or enfranchisement, implies that rights and privileges given to a member of a band ... will be denied to that person ... Enfranchisement or deletion of the name of an Indian from the Indian Registry is much more frequent for women than for men". The commission recommended that the Act be amended to allow an Indian woman upon marriage to a non-Indian to "(a) retain her Indian status and (b) transmit her Indian status to her children". Two important court cases challenged this inequality head on. Jeannette Corbiere Lavell, an Ojibwa woman and member of the Wikwemikong band on Manitoulin Island in Ontario, had married a non-Indian in 1970. She was living in Toronto when she brought the action in 1971, charging that subsection 12(1)(b) violated the equality clause in the 1960 *Canadian Bill of Rights* on the grounds of discrimination by reason of sex. ... Yvonne Bedard, from the Six Nations Reserve in southern Ontario, lost her status when she married out in 1964. ... Her case was argued on the same grounds as the *Lavell* case. ...

Significantly, both Lavell and Bedard pursued their cases without any support — moral or otherwise — from their communities, band councils, or Indian political organizations. On the contrary, they were actively opposed, not only by the government of Canada but also by their own communities.

CANADA (ATTORNEY GENERAL) v. LAVELL

[1973] S.C.J. No. 128, [1974] S.C.R. 1349, 38 D.L.R. (3d) 481 (S.C.C.)

The judgment of **Fauteux C.J.C.**, and **Martland, Judson** and **Ritchie JJ.** was delivered by

Ritchie J.: — I have had the advantage of reading the reasons for judgment prepared for delivery by my brother Laskin.

These appeals, which were heard together, are from two judgments holding that the provisions of s. 12(1)(*b*) of the *Indian Act*, R.S.C. 1970,

c. I-6, are rendered inoperative by s. 1(*b*) of the *Canadian Bill of Rights*, 1960 (Can.), c. 44, as denying equality before the law to the two respondents.

Both respondents were registered Indians and "Band" members within the meaning of s. 11(*b*) of the *Indian Act* when they elected to marry non-Indians and thereby relinquished their status as Indians in conformity with the said s. 12(1)(*b*) which reads as follows:

> **12.** (1) The following persons are not entitled to be registered, namely,
>
> (*b*) a woman who married a person who is not an Indian, unless that woman is subsequently the wife or widow of a person described in section 11.

It is contended on behalf of both respondents that s. 12(1)(*b*) of the Act should be held to be inoperative as discriminating between Indian men and women and as being in conflict with the provisions of the *Canadian Bill of Rights* and particularly s. 1 thereof which provides:

> **1.** It is hereby recognized and declared that in Canada there have existed and shall continue to exist without discrimination by reason of race, national origin, colour, religion or sex, the following human rights and fundamental freedoms, namely, ...
>
> (*b*) the right of the individual to equality before the law and the protection of the law; ...

I think it desirable at the outset to outline the facts concerning the two respondents separately.

1. *Mrs. Lavell* — This woman was a member of the Wikwemikong Band of Indians who married a non-Indian and whose name was deleted from the Indian Register by the Registrar in charge thereof pursuant to the provisions of section 12(1)(*b*) of the Act. An appeal was taken from the Registrar's decision and was heard before His Honour Judge Grossberg, acting as *persona designata* under the *Indian Act* before whom evidence was taken which disclosed that at the time of the hearing and for some nine years before her marriage Mrs. Lavell had not lived on any Reserve except for sporadic visits to her family, and the learned judge declined to accept the suggestion that she could not visit her family on the Reserve whenever she wished. Mrs. Lavell did not claim to have been deprived of any property rights on the Reserve except those incidental to the right as a Band member.

Judge Grossberg having found that in his opinion section 12(1)(*b*) of the *Indian Act* was not rendered inoperative by the *Bill of Rights*, an appeal was taken from his judgment to the Federal Court of Appeal where a judgment was rendered by Mr. Justice Thurlow who concluded his opinion by saying of section 12(1)(*b*) of the *Indian Act*:

> These provisions are thus laws which abrogate, abridge and infringe the right of an individual Indian woman to equality with other Indians before the law. Though this is not a situation in which an act is made punishable at law on account of race or sex, it is one in which under the provisions here in question the consequences of the marriage of an

Indian woman to a person who is not an Indian are worse for her than for other Indians who marry non-Indians and than for other Indians of her band who marry persons who are not Indians. *In my opinion this offends the right of such an Indian woman as an individual to equality before the law* and the *Canadian Bill of Rights* therefore applied to render the provisions in question inoperative.

(The italics are my own.)

It is from this judgment that the Crown now appeals.

2. *Mrs. Bédard* — In this case the respondent sought an injunction restraining the members of the Six Nations Council from expelling her and her two infant children from the home she occupied on the Six Nations Indian Reserve in the County of Brant, and an order setting aside a resolution passed by the Council ordering her to dispose of such property. By agreement an additional claim was added for a declaratory judgment concerning the respective rights of the parties.

Mrs. Bédard was born on the Six Nations Indian Reserve of Indian parents and she married a non-Indian in May, 1964, by whom she had two children and with whom she resided off the Reserve until June 23, 1970 when, having separated from her husband, she returned to the Reserve to live in a house on a property to which her mother had held a Certificate of Possession under s. 20 of the *Indian Act* and which had been bequeathed to her under her mother's will which had been approved by the Council of the Six Nations and on behalf of the Minister of Indian Affairs as required by the *Indian Act*, (section 45(3)) on August 7, 1969.

When Mrs. Bédard returned to the Reserve with her children in 1970 to occupy her mother's house, the Council passed a series of resolutions giving her permission to reside on the Reserve for a period of six months during which she was to dispose of the property, and extending this permission for a further eight months, after which any further requests for her continued residence would be denied. In accordance with these resolutions this respondent conveyed her interest in the property in question to her brother who was a registered member of the Six Nations Band, and to whom a Certificate of Possession of the property was granted on March 15, 1971 by the Minister. Her brother, however, permitted Mrs. Bédard and her infant children to continue occupying the premises without rent, but the Band Council passed a further resolution on September 15, 1971 by which it was resolved that the Brant District Supervisor should be requested to serve a notice to quit the Reserve upon this respondent. It should be noted that the writ instituting this action was issued on September 14, 1971, more than a year after the brother had obtained his Certificate of Possession and that no notice to quit has been served on Mrs. Bédard pursuant to the resolution which was passed after the writ was issued.

Mrs. Bédard's case was heard by Mr. Justice Osler in the Supreme Court of Ontario where it was contended that the Council's request to the District Supervisor and any action taken by the Supervisor pursuant to such request, and the removal of her name from the Band list simply because of her marriage to a non-Indian, are actions that discriminate against her by reason of her race and sex and deny her "equality before the law". Mr. Justice Osler, basing his decision on the judgment of the Federal Court of Appeal in the *Lavell* case, concluded that:

> Section 12(1)(b) of the Act is ... inoperative and all acts of the Council Band and of the District Supervisor purporting to be based on the provisions of that section can be of no effect.

Leave to appeal from this judgment was granted by order of this Court on January 25, 1972.

The contention which formed the basis of the argument submitted by both respondents was that they had been denied equality before the law *by reason of sex*, and I propose to deal with the matter on this basis. ...

In my opinion the exclusive legislative authority vested in Parliament under s. 91(24) could not have been effectively exercised without enacting laws establishing the qualifications required to entitle persons to status as Indians and to the use and benefit of Crown "lands reserved for Indians". The legislation enacted to this end was, in my view, necessary for the implementation of the authority so vested in Parliament under the constitution.

To suggest that the provisions of the *Bill of Rights* have the effect of making the whole *Indian Act* inoperative as discriminatory is to assert that the Bill has rendered Parliament powerless to exercise the authority entrusted to it under the constitution of enacting legislation which treats Indians living on Reserves differently from other Canadians in relation to their property and civil rights. The proposition that such a wide effect is to be given to the *Bill of Rights* was expressly reserved by the majority of this Court in the case of *The Queen v. Drybones* [[1969] S.C.J. No. 83, [1970] S.C.R. 282 (S.C.C.)], at 298, to which reference will hereafter be made, and I do not think that it can be sustained.

What is at issue here is whether the *Bill of Rights* is to be construed as rendering inoperative one of the conditions imposed by Parliament for the use and occupation of Crown lands reserved for Indians. These conditions were imposed as a necessary part of the structure created by Parliament for the internal administration of the life of Indians on Reserves and their entitlement to the use and benefit of Crown lands situate thereon, they were thus imposed, in discharge of Parliament's constitutional function under s. 91(24) and in my view can only be changed by plain statutory language expressly enacted for the purpose. It does not appear to me that Parliament can be taken to have made or intended to make such a change by the use of broad general language directed at the statutory proclamation of the fundamental rights and freedoms enjoyed by all Canadians, and I am therefore of opinion that the *Bill of Rights* had no such effect....

The contention that the *Bill of Rights* is to be construed as overriding all of the special legislation imposed by Parliament under the *Indian Act* is, in my view, fully answered by Pigeon J. in his dissenting opinion in the *Drybones* [[1969] S.C.J. No. 83, [1970] S.C.R. 282 (S.C.C.)] case where he said, at p. 304:

> If one of the effects of the *Canadian Bill of Rights* is to render inoperative all legal provisions whereby Indians as such are not dealt with in the same way as the general public, the conclusion is inescapable that Parliament, by the enactment of the *Bill*, has not only fundamentally altered the status of the Indians in that indirect fashion but has also made any future use of federal legislative authority over them subject to the requirement of expressly declaring every time 'that the law shall operate notwithstanding the *Canadian Bill of Rights*'. I find it very difficult to believe that Parliament so intended when enacting the *Bill*. If a virtual suppression of federal legislation over Indians as such was meant, one would have expected this important change to be made explicitly not surreptitiously so to speak.

That it is membership in the Band which entitles an Indian to the use and benefit of lands on the Reserve is made plain by the provisions of ss. 2 and 18 of the *Indian Act*; Section 2(1)(*a*) reads as follows:

> 2.(1) In this Act 'band' means a body of Indians
>
> (*a*) for whose use and benefit in common, lands the legal title to which is vested in Her Majesty, have been set apart before, on or after the 4th day of September 1951,
>
> . . . . .

Section 18 reads as follows:

> **18.** (1) Subject to this Act, reserves are held by Her Majesty for the use and benefit of the respective bands for which they were set apart; and subject to this Act and to the terms of any treaty or surrender, the Governor in Council may determine whether any purpose for which lands in a reserve are used or are to be used is for the use and benefit of the band... .

The opening words of s. 2 of the *Bill of Rights* are, in my view, determinative of the test to be applied in deciding whether the section here
impugned is to be declared inoperative. The words to which I refer are:

> **2.** Every law of Canada shall, unless it is expressly declared by an act of the Parliament of Canada that it shall operate notwithstanding *the Canadian Bill of Rights*, be so construed and applied as not to abrogate, abridge or infringe or authorize the abrogation, abridgement [or] infringement of the freedoms herein recognized and declared ...

In the course of the reasons for judgment rendered on behalf of the majority of this Court in *The Queen v. Drybones*, *supra*, this language was interpreted in the following passage at p. 294:

> It seems to me that a more realistic meaning must be given to the words in question and they afford, in my view, the clearest indication that s. 2 is intended to mean and does mean that if a law of Canada cannot be "sensibly construed and applied" so that it does not abrogate, abridge or infringe one of the rights and freedoms, recognized and

declared by the Bill, then such law is inoperative "unless it is expressly declared by an Act of the Parliament of Canada that it shall operate notwithstanding the *Canadian Bill of Rights*".

Accordingly, in my opinion, the question to be determined in these appeals is confined to deciding whether the Parliament of Canada in defining the prerequisites of Indian status so as not to include women of Indian birth who have chosen to marry non-Indians, enacted a law which cannot be sensibly construed and applied without abrogating, abridging or infringing the rights of such women to equality before the law.

In my view the meaning to be given to the language employed in the *Bill of Rights* is the meaning which it bore in Canada at the time when the Bill was enacted, and it follows that the phrase "equality before the law" is to be construed in light of the law existing in Canada at that time.

In considering the meaning to be attached to "equality before the law" as those words occur in section 1(*b*) of the Bill, I think it important to point out that in my opinion this phrase is not effective to invoke the egalitarian concept exemplified by the 14th Amendment of the U.S. Constitution as interpreted by the courts of that country. (See *Smythe v. The Queen* [[1971] S.C.J. No. 62, [1971] S.C.R. 680 (S.C.C.)] per Fauteux C.J. at pp. 683 and 686). I think rather that, having regard to the language employed in the second paragraph of the preamble to the *Bill of Rights*, the phrase "equality before the law" as used in s. 1 is to be read in its context as a part of "the rule of law" to which overriding authority is accorded by the terms of that paragraph.

In this connection I refer to *Stephens Commentaries on the Laws of England*, 21st Ed. 1950, where it is said in Vol. III at p. 337:

> Now the great constitutional lawyer Dicey writing in 1885 was so deeply impressed by the absence of arbitrary governments present and past, that he coined the phrase "the rule of law" to express the regime under which Englishmen lived; and he tried to give precision to it in the following words which have exercised a profound influence on all subsequent thought and conduct.
>
> "That the 'rule of law' which forms a fundamental principle of the constitution has three meanings or may be regarded from three different points of view ...."

The second meaning proposed by Dicey is the one with which we are here concerned and it was stated in the following terms:

> It means again equality before the law or the equal subjection of all classes to the ordinary law of the land administered by the ordinary courts; the "rule of law" in this sense excludes the idea of any exemption of officials or others from the duty of obedience to the law which governs other citizens or from the jurisdiction of the ordinary courts.

"Equality before the law" in this sense is frequently invoked to demonstrate that the same law applies to the highest official of government as to any other ordinary citizen, and in this regard

Professor F.R. Scott, in delivering the Plaunt Memorial Lectures on Civil Liberties and Canadian Federalism in 1959, speaking of the case of *Roncarelli v. Duplessis* [[1959] S.C.J. No. 1, [1959] S.C.R. 121 (S.C.C.)], had occasion to say:

> It is always a triumph for the law to show that it is applied equally to all without fear or favour. This is what we mean when we say that all are equal before the law.

The relevance of these quotations to the present circumstances is that "equality before the law" as recognized by Dicey as a segment of the rule of law, carries the meaning of equal subjection of all classes to the ordinary law of the land *as administered by the ordinary courts*, and in my opinion the phrase "equally before the law" as employed in section 1(*b*) of the *Bill of Rights* is to be treated as meaning equality in the administration or application of the law by the law enforcement authorities and the ordinary courts of the land. This construction is, in my view, supported by the provisions of subsections (*a*) to (*g*) of s. 2 of the Bill which clearly indicate to me that it was equality in the administration and enforcement of the law with which Parliament was concerned when it guaranteed the continued existence of "equality before the law".

Turning to the *Indian Act* itself, it should first be observed that by far the greater part of that Act is concerned with the internal regulation of the lives of Indians on Reserves and that the exceptional provisions dealing with the conduct of Indians off Reserves and their contacts with other Canadian citizens fall into an entirely different category.

It was, of course necessary for Parliament, in the exercise of section 91(24) authority, to first define what Indian meant, and in this regard s. (1) of the Act provides that:

> "Indian" means a person who pursuant to this Act is registered as an Indian or is entitled to be registered as an Indian.

It is therefore clear that registration is a necessary prerequisite to Indian status...

The *Drybones* case can, in my opinion, have no application to the present appeals as it was in no way concerned with the internal regulation of the lives of Indians on Reserves or their right to the use and benefit of Crown lands thereon, but rather deals exclusively with the effect of the *Bill of Rights* on a section of the *Indian Act* creating a crime with attendant penalties for the conduct by Indians off a Reserve in an area where non-Indians, who were also governed by federal law, were not subject to any such restriction.

The fundamental distinction between the present case and that of *Drybones*, however, appears to me to be that the impugned section in the latter case could not be enforced without denying equality of treatment in the administration and enforcement of the law before the ordinary courts of the land to a racial group, whereas no such inequality of treatment between Indian men and women flows as a necessary result of the application of s. 12(1)(*b*) of the *Indian Act*.

To summarize the above, I am of opinion:

1. That the *Bill of Rights* is not effective to render inoperative legislation, such as s. 12(1)(*b*) of the *Indian Act*, passed by the Parliament of Canada in discharge of its constitutional function under s. 91(24) of the *B.N.A. Act*, to specify how and by whom Crown lands reserved for Indians are to be used;

2. that the *Bill of Rights* does not require federal legislation to be declared inoperative unless it offends against one of the rights specifically guaranteed by section 1, but where legislation is found to be discriminatory, this affords an added reason for rendering it ineffective;

3. that equality before the law under the *Bill of Rights* means equality of treatment in the enforcement and application of the laws of Canada before the law enforcement authorities and the ordinary courts of the land, and no such inequality is necessarily entailed in the construction and application of s. 12(1)(*b*).

I would allow the appeal of the *Attorney General of Canada against J.V. Corbiere Lavell*, reverse the judgment of the Federal Court of Appeal and restore the decision of Judge B.W. Grossberg. In accordance with the terms of the order of the Federal Court of Appeal granting leave to appeal to this Court, the appellant will pay to the respondent her solicitor and client costs of the appeal and the application for leave. There should be no further order as to costs.

On the appeal of *Richard Isaac and others v. Yvonne Bédard*, a question was raised in this Court as to the jurisdiction of the trial court. In view of the conclusion reached on the merits, no decision is now necessary on that question. The appeal to this Court should be allowed, the judgment at trial should be reversed and the action dismissed. Under the circumstances, there should be no order as to costs in that case in any court.

Abbott J. (dissenting): — ... I would dismiss both appeals with costs.

The judgment of **Hall**, **Spence** and **Laskin JJ.** (dissenting) was delivered by

Laskin J. (dissenting) — ... In my opinion, unless we are to depart from what was said in *Drybones*, both appeals now before us must be dismissed. I have no disposition to reject what was decided in *Drybones*; and on the central issue of prohibited discrimination as catalogued in s. 1 of the *Canadian Bill of Rights*, it is, in my opinion, impossible to distinguish *Drybones* from the two cases in appeal. If, as in *Drybones*, discrimination by reason of race makes certain statutory provisions

inoperative, the same result must follow as to statutory provisions which exhibit discrimination by reason of sex. ...

The *Drybones* case decided two things. It decided first-hand this decision was a necessary basis for the second point in it — that the *Canadian Bill of Rights* was more than a mere interpretation statute whose terms would yield to a contrary intention; it had paramount force when a federal enactment conflicted with its terms, and it was the incompatible federal enactment which had to give way. ... The second thing decided by *Drybones* was that the accused in that case, an Indian under the *Indian Act*, was denied equality before the law, under s. 1(*b*) of the *Canadian Bill of Rights*, when it was made a punishable offence for him, on account of his race, to do something which his fellow Canadians were free to do without being liable to punishment for an offence. ...

It would be unsupportable in principle to view the *Drybones* case as turning on the fact that the challenged s. 94 of the *Indian Act* created an offence visited by punishment. The gist of the judgment lay in the legal disability imposed upon a person by reason of his race when other persons were under no similar restraint. If for the words "on account of race" there are substituted the words "on account of sex" the result must surely be the same where a federal enactment imposes disabilities or prescribes disqualifications for members of the female sex which are not imposed upon members of the male sex in the same circumstances.

It is said, however, that although this may be so as between males and females in general, it does not follow where the distinction on the basis of sex is limited as here to members of the Indian race. This, it is said further, does not offend the guarantee of "equality before the law" upon which the *Drybones* case proceeded. I wish to deal with these two points in turn and to review, in connection with the first point, the legal consequences for an Indian woman under the *Indian Act* when she marries a non-Indian.

It appears to me that the contention that a differentiation on the basis of sex is not offensive to the *Canadian Bill of Rights* where that differentiation operates only among Indians under the *Indian Act* is one that compounds racial inequality even beyond the point that the *Drybones* case found unacceptable. ...

Section 12(1)(*b*) effects a statutory excommunication of Indian women from this society but not of Indian men. Indeed, as was pointed out by counsel for the Native Council of Canada, the effect of ss. 11 and 12(1)(*b*) is to excommunicate the children of a union of an Indian woman with a non-Indian. There is also the invidious distinction, invidious at least in the light of the *Canadian Bill of Rights*, that the *Indian Act* creates between brothers and sisters who are Indians and who respectively marry non-Indians. The statutory banishment directed by s. 12(1)(*b*) is not qualified by the provision in s. 109(2) for a governmental order declaring an Indian woman who has married a non-Indian to be enfranchised. Such an order is not automatic and no such order was made in relation to Mrs. Bédard; but when made the woman affected is, by s. 110, deemed not to be an Indian within the *Indian Act* or any other statute or law. It is, if anything, an additional legal instrument of separation of an Indian woman from her native society and from her kin, a separation to which no Indian man who marries a non-Indian is exposed. ...

In my opinion, the appellants' contentions gain no additional force because the *Indian Act*, including the challenged s. 12(1)(*b*) thereof, is a fruit of the exercise of Parliament's exclusive legislative power in relation to "Indians, and Lands reserved for the Indians" under s. 91(24) of the *British North America Act*. Discriminatory treatment on the basis of race or colour or sex does not inhere in that grant of legislative power. The fact that its exercise may be attended by forms of discrimination prohibited by the *Canadian Bill of Rights* is no more a justification for a breach of the *Canadian Bill of Rights* than there would be in the case of the exercise of any other head of federal legislative power involving provisions offensive to the *Canadian Bill of Rights*. The majority opinion in the *Drybones* case dispels any attempt to rely on the grant of legislative power as a ground for escaping from the force of the *Canadian Bill of Rights*. The latter does not differentiate among the various heads of legislative power; it embraces all exercises under whatever head or heads they arise. Section 3 which directs the Minister of Justice to scrutinize every Bill to ascertain whether any of its provisions are inconsistent with ss. 1 and 2 is simply an affirmation of this fact which is evident enough from ss. 1 and 2.

Pigeon J.: — I agree in the result with Ritchie J.

---

1. What justifies the government being involved with the internal affairs of Indians according to the majority in this case?
2. Justice Ritchie wrote that: "no inequality of treatment between Indian men and Indian women flows as a necessary result of the application of s. 12(1)(*b*) of the *Indian Act*". Do you agree? How did Justice Ritchie arrive at this conclusion?
3. Do you think the *Lavell and Bédard* case would be decided differently under the Charter?
4. Justice Ritchie characterizes the case as follows: "what is at issue here is rendering inoperative conditions imposed by parliament". Do you agree?

The case of *Lavell and Bédard* illustrates the difficulties Aboriginal women encountered in challenging the *Indian Act* before the Canadian courts. The Supreme Court's deference to federal legislative power and its adherence to select notions of formal equality stood as significant barriers to remedying the inequality of Aboriginal women within their communities. Having exhausted their avenues of appeal within Canada, Aboriginal women continued their efforts to reform the *Indian*

Act before the international community. The following case and commentary from Sandra Lovelace demonstrates the importance of international legal instruments and domestic advocacy in fighting discrimination in Canada.

LOVELACE v. CANADA

36 U.N. GOAR Supp. (No. 40) Annex XVIII; U.N. Doc. A/36/40 (1981)

Views of the Human Rights Committee under Article 5(4) of the Optional Protocol of the International Covenant on Civil and Political Rights concerning Communication No. R.6/24

Submitted by: Sandra Lovelace
Date of communication: 29 December 1977

The Human Rights Committee established under article 28 of the *International Covenant on Civil and Political Rights*

Meeting on 30 July 1981; — having concluded its consideration of communication No. R.6/24 submitted to the Committee by Sandra Lovelace under the Optional Protocol to the *International Covenant on Civil and Political Rights*; — having taken into account the written information made available to it by the authors of the communication and by the state party concerned; adopts the following:

VIEWS UNDER ARTICLE (4) Of THE OPTIONAL PROTOCOL

1. The author of the communication dated 29 December 1977 and supplemented by letters of 17 April 1978, 28 November 1979 and 20 June 1980, is a 32 year old woman, living in Canada. She was born and registered as "Maliseet Indian" but has lost her rights and status as an Indian in accordance with section 12(1)(b) of the *Indian Act*, after having married a non-Indian on 23 May 1970. Pointing out that an Indian man who marries a non-Indian woman does not lose his Indian status, she claims that the Act is discriminatory on the grounds of sex and contrary to articles 2(1), 3, 23(1) and (4), 26 and 27 of the Covenant. As to the admissibility of the communication she contends that she was not required to exhaust local remedies since the Supreme Court of Canada, in *The Attorney General of Canada v. Jeanette Lavell, Richard Isaac et al. v. Yvonne Bedard* (1974) S.C.R. 1349, held that section 12(1)(b) was fully operative, irrespective of its inconsistency with the *Canadian Bill of Rights* on account of discrimination based on sex. ...
5. In its submission under article 4(2) of the Optional protocol concerning the merits of the case, dated 4 April 1980, the state party recognized that "many of the provisions of the ... *Indian Act*, including section 12(l)(b), require serious reconsideration and reform". The government further referred to an earlier public declaration to the effect that it intended to put a reform bill before the Canadian

Parliament. It none the less stressed the necessity of the *Indian Act* as an instrument designed to protect the Indian minority in accordance with article 27 of the Covenant. A definition of the Indian was inevitable in view of the special privileges granted to the Indian communities, in particular their right to occupy reserve lands. Traditionally, patrilineal family relationships were taken into account for determining legal claims. Since, additionally, in the farming societies of the nineteenth century, reserve land was felt to be more threatened by non-Indian men than by non-Indian women, legal enactments as from 1869 provided that an Indian woman who married a non-Indian man would lose her status as an Indian. These reasons were still valid. A change in the law could only be sought in consultation with the Indians themselves who, however, were divided on the issue of equal rights. The Indian community should not be endangered by legislative changes. Therefore, although the government was in principle committed to amending section 12(1)(b) of the *Indian Act*, no quick and immediate legislative action could be expected.

6. The author of the communication, in her submission of 20 June 1980, disputes the contention that legal relationships within Indian families were traditionally patrilineal in nature. ...

9.2 It emerges from statistics provided by the state party that from 1965 to 1978, on an average, 510 Indian women married non-Indian men each year. Marriages between Indian women and Indian men of the same band during that period were 390 on the average each year; between Indian women and Indian men of a different band 422 on the average each year; and between Indian men and non-Indian women 448 on the average each year. ...

9.6 As to Mrs. Lovelace's place of abode prior to her marriage, both parties confirm that she was at that time living on the Tobique Reserve with her parents. Sandra Lovelace adds that as a result of her marriage, she was denied the right to live on an Indian reserve. As to her abode since then, the state party observes:

> Since her marriage and following her divorce, Mrs. Lovelace has, from time to time, lived on the reserve in the home of her parents, and the band Council has made no move to prevent her from doing so. However, Mrs. Lovelace wishes to live permanently on the reserve and to obtain a new house. To do so, she has to apply to the Band Council. Housing on reserves is provided with money set aside by Parliament for the benefit of registered Indians. The Council has not agreed to provide Mrs. Lovelace with a new house. It considers that in the provision of such housing priority is to be given to registered Indians. ...

9.9 On behalf of Sandra Lovelace the following is submitted in this connection:

All the consequence of loss of status persist in that they are permanent and continue to deny the complainant of the right she was born with.

A person who ceases to be an Indian under the *Indian Act* suffers from the following consequences:

1. Loss of the right to possess or reside on lands on a reserve (ss. 25 and 28(1)). This includes loss of the right to return to the reserve after leaving, the right to inherit possessory interest in land from parents and others, and the right to be buried on a reserve;

2. An Indian without status cannot receive loans from the Consolidated Revenue Fund for the purposes set out in section 70;

3. An Indian with benefit cannot benefit from instruction in farming ... (see s. 71);

4. An Indian without status cannot benefit from medical treatment and health services under section 73(1)(g);

5. An Indian without status cannot reside on tax exempt lands (See section 87);

6. A person ceasing to be an Indian loses the right to borrow money for housing from the Band Council (Consolidated Regulations of Canada 1978, c. 949);

7. A person ceasing to be an Indian loses the right to cut timber free of dues on an Indian reserve ...

8. A person ceasing to be an Indian loses traditional hunting and fishing rights that may exist;

9. The major loss to a person ceasing to be an Indian is the loss of cultural benefits of living in an Indian community, the emotional ties to home, family, friends and neighbours, and the loss of identity.

10. The Human Rights Committee, in the examination of the communication before it, has to proceed from the basic fact that Sandra Lovelace married a non-Indian on 23 May 1970 and consequently lost her status as a Maliseet Indian under section 12(l)(b) of the *Indian Act.* This provision was — and still is — based on a distinction de jure on the ground of sex. However, neither its application to her marriage as the cause of her loss of Indian status nor its effects could at that time amount to a violation of the Covenant, because this instrument did not come into force for Canada until 19 August 1976. Moreover, the Committee is not competent, as a rule, to examine allegations relating to events having taken place before the entry into force of the Covenant and the Optional protocol. Therefore, as regards Canada, it can only consider alleged violations of human rights occurring on or after 19 August 1976. ...

11. The Committee recognizes, however, that the situation may be different if the alleged violations, although relating to events occurring before 19 August 1976, continue, or have effects which themselves constitute violations, after that date. In examining the situation of Sandra Lovelace in this respect, the Committee must have regard to all relevant provisions of the Covenant. It has considered, in particular, the

extent to which the general provisions in articles 2 and 3 as well as the rights in articles 12(1), 17(1), 23(1), 44, 26 and 27, may be applicable to the facts of her present situation.

12. The Committee first observes that from 19 August 1976 Canada had undertaken under article 2(1) and (2) of the Covenant to respect and ensure to all individuals within its territory and subject to its jurisdiction, the rights recognized in the Covenant without distinction of any kind such as sex, and to adopt the necessary measures to give effect to these rights. Further, under article 3, Canada undertook to ensure the equal right of men and women to the enjoyment of these rights. These undertakings apply also to the position of Sandra Lovelace. The Committee considers, however, that it is not necessary for the purposes of her communication to decide their extent in all aspects. The full scope of the obligation of Canada to remove the effects or inequalities caused by the application of existing laws to past events, in particular as regards such matters as civil or personal status, does not have to be examined in the present case, for the reasons set out below.

13.1 The Committee considers that the essence of the present complaint concerns the continuing effect of the *Indian Act*, in denying Sandra Lovelace legal status as an Indian, in particular because she cannot for this reason claim a legal right to reside where she wishes to, on the Tobique Reserve. This fact persists after the entry into force of the Covenant, and its effects have to be examined, without regard to their original cause. Among the effects referred to on behalf of the author (quoted in paragraph 9.9, above, and listed (1) to (9)), the greater number, ((1) to (8)), relate to the *Indian Act* and other Canadian rules in fields which do not necessarily adversely affect the enjoyment of rights protected by the Covenant. In this respect the significant matter is her last claim, that "the major loss to a person ceasing to be an Indian is the loss of the cultural benefits of living in an Indian community, the emotional ties to home, family, friends and neighbours, and the loss of identity".

13.2 Although a number of provisions of the Covenant have been invoked by Sandra Lovelace, the Committee considers that the one which is most directly applicable to this complaint is article 27, which reads as follows:

> In those states in which ethnic, religious or linguistic minorities exist, persons belonging to such minorities shall not be denied the right, in community with other members of their group, to enjoy their own culture, to profess and practice their own religion, or to use their own language.

It has to be considered whether Sandra Lovelace, because she is denied the legal right to reside on the Tobique Reserve, has by that fact been denied the right guaranteed by article 27 to persons belonging to minorities, to enjoy their own culture and to use their own language in community with other members of their group.

14. The rights under article 27 of the Covenant have to be secured to "persons belonging" to the minority. At present Sandra Lovelace does not qualify as an Indian under Canadian legislation. However, the *Indian Act* deals primarily with a number of privileges which, as stated above, do not as such come within the scope of the Covenant. Protection under *the Indian Act* and protection under article 27 of the Covenant therefore have to be distinguished. Persons who are born and brought up on a reserve, who have kept ties with their community and wish to maintain these ties must normally be considered as belonging to that minority within the meaning of the Covenant. Since Sandra Lovelace is ethnically a Maliseet Indian and has only been absent from her home reserve for a few years during the existence of her marriage, she is, in the opinion of the Committee, entitled to be regarded as "belonging" to this minority and to claim the benefits of article 27 of the Covenant. The question whether these benefits have been denied to her, depends on how far they extend.

15. The right to live on a reserve is not as such guaranteed by article 27 of the Covenant. Moreover, the *Indian Act* does not interfere directly with the functions which are expressly mentioned in that article. However, in the opinion of the Committee the right of Sandra Lovelace to access to her native culture and language "in community with the other members" of her group, has in fact been, and continues to be interfered with, because there is no place outside the Tobique Reserve where such a community exists. ...

16. In this respect, the Committee is of the view that statutory restrictions affecting the right to residence on a reserve of a person belonging to the minority concerned, must have both a reasonable and objective justification and be consistent with the other provisions of the Covenant. Read as a whole, Article 27 must be construed and applied in the light of the other provisions mentioned above, such as articles 12, 17 and 23 insofar as they may be relevant to the particular case, and also the provisions against discrimination, such as articles 2, 3 and 26, as the case may be. It is not necessary, however, to determine in any general manner which restrictions may be justified under the Covenant, in particular as a result of marriage, because the circumstances are special in the present case.

17. The case of Sandra Lovelace should be considered in the light of the fact that her marriage to a non-Indian has broken up, it is natural that in such a situation she wishes to return to the environment in which she was born, particularly as after the dissolution of her marriage her main cultural attachment again was to the Maliseet band. Whatever may be the merits of the *Indian Act* in other respects, it does not seem to the Committee that to deny Sandra Lovelace the right to reside on the reserve is reasonable, or necessary to preserve the identity of the tribe. The Committee therefore concludes that to prevent her recognition as belonging to the band is an unjustifiable denial of her rights under article 27 of the Covenant, read in the context of the other provisions referred to.

18. In view of this finding, the Committee does not consider it necessary to examine whether the same facts also show separate breaches of the other rights invoked. ...

19. Accordingly, the Human Rights Committee, acting under article 5(4) of the Optional protocol to *the International Covenant on Civil and Political Rights,* is of the view that the facts of the present case, which establish that Sandra Lovelace has been denied the legal right to reside on the Tobique Reserve, disclose a breach by Canada of article 27 of the Covenant.

Do you agree with the Committee's decision to treat Sandra Lovelace's case as a violation of Article 27 (minority rights) of the *International Covenant on Civil and Political Rights,* rather than a violation of Articles 2 and 3 (equality rights) of the *Covenant?*

Should Aboriginal peoples more frequently turn to International Law in dealing with Aboriginal rights in Canada? What are the weaknesses and strengths of this system?

As you consider the success of the *Lovelace* case, it is important to remember that cases such as this are not launched in a vacuum. Intense personal and community decisions and much hard work often lie behind each action. As you read the following excerpt ask yourself: How important to the success of a legal action are the people behind the written decisions?

"RETROSPECTIVE", ENOUGH IS ENOUGH: ABORIGINAL WOMEN SPEAK OUT

(Toronto: The Women's Press, 1987) at 243-45

SANDRA LOVELACE SAPPIER AND KAREN PERLEY

SANDRA: We got into a lot of arguments with the chiefs about the reinstatement issue. They said things like, "You've made your bed, now sleep in it"; "My (white) wife is an Indian because the law says she is."

KAREN: They *believed,* the government says you're Indian, so you're Indian. Therefore the government tell us we're not Indian, so we're not Indians.

SANDRA: Then we'd start arguing. Heavy arguments! (laughter) "I was born an Indian," that's what I'd tell them.

KAREN: If they believed that, where is the reason in all of it! Sometimes your own flesh and blood would say, "You're not an Indian any more. That's the law; that's the *Indian Act.*" See how law abiding Native Indian people are! (laughter) So we'd have these chiefs telling us, "It's our *right* to discriminate."

SANDRA: A few chiefs supported us. Davey, of course. But most of them are chauvinist. They'd say, "You're only a woman, so what do you know! Go watch your babies, clean your house." That's the attitude.

KAREN: Maybe the men will start changing now that the law has changed, though I don't think some of them realize yet that it has really changed. The other day a guy from here wanted to register his white bride. The band office said, "No way," and was he mad. See, that's how "aware" they are. The guy kept arguing, still trying to make her an Indian. What nerve!

SANDRA: Another argument our so-called leaders used against us was, giving women their status back would "dilute the Indian culture." How could it! I teach my children my Indian culture; the white women teach their kids their white culture, because the men are out working. It's mostly the mothers that teach the kids. My children are surrounded by my culture, my language, so how can we dilute it! I think Indian women coming back will *improve* it.

When you hear some of those guys, you get really angry. Then you go out there even if it means scraping together your welfare pennies to do it. If they are going to treat my child different from theirs, that makes me angry. Plus, I have two daughters and I don't want them to have to go through the same thing.

All that lobbying we did! The most devastating experience for me was when Joe Clark's government fell in late 1979. That was disgusting because we knew we were so close; Clark had promised the change. We were so sure. Then we had to start from square one with the Liberals all over again, and we already knew what asses the Liberals are. (laughter) They listen to men.

KAREN: There were so many frustrating experiences, I can't think of which was the worst. The Liberals, Indian Affairs. The Union (of New Brunswick Indians) so much against us, telling the media, "If there is reinstatement, there's going to be violence" — well, there hasn't been any violence yet.

SANDRA: Graydon, the Union president, told the media there was going to be violence if the women were reinstated. Who is going to do the violence? The Union? He said people would burn any houses non-status get. I doubt it. I don't think anyone would dare do that here, because the women would stick together.

KAREN: It was so frustrating when those guys talked so nice to our face, then went against us behind our back; also when the Native Women's Association of Canada wouldn't fight for the same things as us, when it should have been their fight too.

One thing I wish didn't happen was all the tension and bad feeling right here at home during the occupations. God, it was awful. You could feel the hate. Honest, it is just this year I started talking to some of those people — and it is an election year! (laughter) I won't be talking to them for long; things start getting dug up again.

SANDRA: The really painful stuff was right here at home. Plus strain on marriages and relationships because we were always gone lobbying.

Especially towards the end, it started happening to all of us — "Gee, you're going *again*!" But we'd all go. (laughter) Because we knew it was important. We had to get it done and reinstatement was so close.

KAREN: I think we came up with some good strategies along the way, like getting white women's groups involved, writing letters and sending petitions to Ottawa. Some of those organizations were really big, like the United Church and NAC. The women's walk to Ottawa because it was women and children — we knew that would get to people. Getting to know the women M.P.s and senators. They did a lot of lobbying for us. Flora MacDonald, Lynn McDonald. Like in 1981 the women in parliament and senate from all the parties held a press conference and issued a joint statement calling for an end to 12(l)(b).

Then there were the strategies here at home. The petitions. Ninety-five percent of band members signed in favour of reinstatement, and we could tell people outside about that. Another good strategy was near election time when we thought, who can we get in here for chief that would support us! That's when we came up with Dave Perley.

SANDRA: At first he wasn't interested, but then individual people talked to him, "Come on, Davey, go for it." He did and after that, it always helped to tell the media, "Our chief supports us. He backs us up and accepts us." I always made sure I mentioned it, because it would make the other chiefs look bad for not supporting their women.

KAREN: Another thing, I think Glenna and Caroline were talking about, and honestly, I was just waiting for it to happen; having all of our sons marry the non-status women just so they could become status again. We were going to plan a mass wedding, like my son would marry Mavis or Pearl, and so on. (laughter) It sure would have gotten a lot of press!

I was kind of looking forward to that. But we didn't have to go that far.

Another effective strategy was Sandra's case to the United Nations. That's what got the media attention. I mean, it's *history*; it will be in history books, "Sandra Lovelace." (laughter) Once when we were at one of those cocktail parties in Ottawa, Sandra said, "I'd better take it easy. Tomorrow it might be in the papers, 'Sandra Lovelace fell on her face'." (laughter) All those trips to Ottawa.

KAREN: With me, I was still kind of nervous when it came to talking with people; I was always afraid I'd say the wrong thing, or I wouldn't understand what they were saying. (laughter) I never had to go through being interviewed for the press. I never said too much. I would tell Caroline, "Why should I go! I never really say anything." She'd say, "Yes, but you're very good at remembering things and writing stuff down."

SANDRA: There have to be people who watch and take notes.

KAREN: That's right. You sit and watch what's going on in the background while the other person is busy talking, and you learn a lot of things.

SANDRA: Even if we went and relaxed over a drink, we'd talk about it all the time; going over what had just happened, deciding what to do the next day. That's how we lived — it was our life.

KAREN: Another time, way back during the walk, somebody — Glenna, I think — called a cab. It was her first time in Ottawa, and she didn't know where anything was. We were on Parliament Hill and she told the cab driver where we wanted to go. A bunch of us women climbed in, and the guy drove around the corner and stopped. (laughter) The place was right there.

SANDRA: We had our disagreements, but we never disagreed on the most important issue. Our goal was reinstatement and we all agreed to that.

KAREN: If a couple of us disagreed over something, we'd just stay away from each other for a while, and by the next meeting everything would be all right. We never let anything break us up or stand in our way.

I think we were the first group of women to ever stand up to a chief and council on a reserve. We are amongst the reserves I know of. Maybe — I hope — some are doing it now. Why us!

SANDRA: Strong women. Stubborn, too.

KAREN: Strong, political-minded people, I think. Like Glenna is a very strong woman. Gookum. They were the two that started it. My mother was politically minded. When election time came around, she got into it — on the reserve and federal elections, too. We were exposed to politics at an early age.

Another thing is that we all lived in the States and travelled a lot. Maybe if you stay on the reserve all your life, you don't see anything. I mean, you live in a small, little world. But when you leave, and then come back, you see the difference.

SANDRA: You start asking, how come things are happening here that aren't happening anywheres else!

KAREN: And the ones who haven't been anywheres else were the hardest ones to try and convince to change.

Another thing with Tobique is that we've kept our language, whereas other reserves around here haven't so much. Maybe some of the matrilineal stuff and the strength of the women has been passed on, too.

SANDRA: A long time ago, before Christianity got in here, I think the men and women lived together equally. There was no discrimination. It was the women who chose their leader traditionally, because they were the ones raising the children; they knew who was strong.

When the men argued that they didn't want reinstatement for fear of the white men coming in and taking over, I think it's really us women they were afraid of. I think that is the main reason the chiefs opposed us so much. They know we are persistent. If we believe in something, we will fight, we'll keep at it until something comes of it. Maybe the men are afraid of the competition. (laughter)

That's why they want self-government without sexual equality. I never wanted self-government before the women got their rights back. The

men have to work with the women to accomplish anything, and the
sooner they learn that, the better everybody will be. I told a guy in
Ottawa, "Listen, if you men would only work with us in unity." See,
they were the ones always talking about "unity", but they didn't even
want me back on the reserve and I was born here. I said, "If we all
worked together we could have a lot of things accomplished. We could
get Indian self-government, but we have to work together and be
equal." He said, "You're right." But do you think they would do it! Not
yet.

D. AMENDMENTS TO THE *INDIAN ACT*: BILL C-31 AND ITS EFFECTS

The *Lovelace* decision caused Canada considerable international
embarrassment and was regarded by many Indian women as a
significant step towards their reinstatement as Indians and their
restoration to their communities. Following the *Lovelace* case and a
series of Constitutional conferences under s. 37 of the *Constitution Act,
1982* (being Schedule B of the *Canada Act 1982* (U.K.), 1982, c. 11), the
federal government acted to amend the *Indian Act* and remove some
of its offending provisions. These amendments, hereinafter referred to
as Bill C-31 *(An Act to amend the Indian Act*, R.S.C. 1985, c. 32 (1st
Supp.))*, remedied some of the discrimination on the basis of sex found
in the Act. The effects of these amendments are recounted in the
following excerpt.

REPORT OF THE ROYAL COMMISSION ON ABORIGINAL PEOPLES: PERSPECTIVES AND REALITIES, VOL. 4

(Ottawa: Ministry of Supply and Services, 1996) at 33-36
(references omitted)

Bill C-31

The 1982 amendment of the constitution, incorporating the *Canadian
Charter of Rights and Freedoms*, included the provision, in section 15, that
"every individual is equal before and under the law and has the right to
the equal protection and benefit of the law without discrimination
based on race, national or ethnic origin, colour, religion, sex, age, or
mental or physical disability". Section 15 of the *Charter* came into effect
on 17 April 1985. The *Charter* accomplished overnight what the
Canadian Bill of Rights and the *Canadian Human Rights Act* had been
unable to do — motivating the government to eliminate provisions of
the *Indian Act* that had been criticized for discriminating against Indian
women. Some influence was also exerted by the case of *Lovelace v.
Canada,* in which Canada's treatment of Indian women under the *Indian*

Act was strongly criticized by the United Nations Human Rights Committee.

Bill C-31 Provisions

This led to the passage of Bill C-31 in 1985. The bill amended various sections of the *Indian Act*, in particular the status and band membership provisions. While Indian status would continue to be determined by the federal government, status was restored to those who lost it under subsection 12(l)(b) and other similarly discriminatory sections of the status and membership provisions. The general rule was that in future Indian status would be granted to those with at least one parent with status. The concept of enfranchisement, voluntary or otherwise, was totally abolished, and those who lost status through enfranchisement had their status restored. First-generation children of restored persons were granted first-time status. Band membership was guaranteed for some classes of persons restored to status or admitted to status for the first time. Not all were guaranteed automatic band membership, however.

Legal status as an Indian and band membership were formally separated in the act, with the former remaining under federal control. A band may now take control of its own membership from the department of Indian affairs by following the procedures set our in Bill C-31. Once a band has taken control of its membership, persons may be added to or deleted from the list of members according to the rules established by the band in a membership code. In short, the department of Indian affairs will no longer maintain the membership list for that particular band and will no longer have a say in how band membership decisions are made. ...

The amendments concerning restoration of Indian status and band control of membership would be a source of conflict when it came time to implement Bill C-31. There was concern that some bands might reject persons who had acquired or re-acquired Indian status through Bill C-31, whether because of sex discrimination or because of concerns that resources needed to accommodate new members might not be forthcoming from the federal government. To forestall this possibility, subsection 10(4) of the 1985 *Indian Act* included a provision that prohibited First Nations from excluding certain classes of persons from their membership lists. ...

The Impact of Bill C-31

The impact of Bill C-31 was enormous and profound. ... By June 1990, 75,761 applications had been made, representing 133,134 persons. The status Indian population grew by 19 per cent in five years because of Bill C-31 alone and, when natural growth was included, by a total of 33 per cent. ... As of 30 June 1995, Bill C-31 had added 95,429 persons to the status Indian population in Canada, more than half of them (57.2 per cent, 54,589) female.

Despite the amendments to the *Indian Act* that reinstated Aboriginal women to Indian status, many still continue to experience discrimination in their communities. The enormous increase in the status Indian population did not result in an equal increase in the population of reserve communities. This is largely because most persons restored to Indian status or with first-time status under Bill C-31 still live off-reserve. Although most Bill C-31 registrants continue to live off-reserve, it is not always by choice, since it has been difficult for some of them to get reserve residency rights even as band members. Some bands experienced significant population increases from Bill C-31 registrants while others had none. The average band increased in size by 19 per cent, although 80 per cent of the bands had fewer than 15 Bill C-31 registrants living on-reserve.

REPORT OF THE ROYAL COMMISSION ON ABORIGINAL PEOPLES: PERSPECTIVES AND REALITIES, VOL. 4

(Ottawa: Ministry of Supply and Services, 1996) at 36-37, 39-42
(references omitted)

Clearly, the full impact of Bill C-31 on reserve communities has yet to be felt. Some band leaders and community members are concerned about the possibility of crowding and disruption and have been resistant to inclusion of new band members in their communities. Services that could be affected by a population increase include housing, health and post-secondary education.

Indian women have their own concerns about Bill C-31. Women make up the majority of people reinstated under the bill, and fully three-quarters of those whose Indian status was restored — as opposed to those who gained status for the first time — are women. Despite its avowed attempt of bringing about sexual equality in the status and membership provisions of the *Indian Act*, Bill C-31 is nonetheless seen by many Aboriginal women as a continuation of the sexist policies of the past. ...

The bill created two main categories of status Indians. Under subsection 6(1), legal status is assigned to all those who had status before 17 April 1985, all persons who are members of new bands created since 17 April 1985 ... and all individuals who lost status through the discriminatory provisions of the *Indian Act*. ... Subsection 6(2) covers people with only one parent who is or was a status Indian under any part of section 6(1). ... The consequences [for future generations of First Nations people for] falling within subsection 6(1) or subsection 6(2) are felt by the woman's children and grandchildren. For these descendants the way their parents and grandparents acquired status will be important determinants of whether they will have Indian status and, if they do, whether and to what extent they will be able to pass it on to their children. ...

An example helps illustrate the inequality that results from these rules. The following is taken from the *Report of the Aboriginal Justice Inquiry of Manitoba* (which recommended that this form of discrimination cease):

John and Joan, a brother and sister were both registered Indians. Joan married a Metis man before 1985 so she lost her Indian status under section 12(1)(b) of the former Act. John married a white woman before 1985 and she automatically became a status Indian. Both John and Joan have had children over the years. Joan now is eligible to regain her status under section 6(1)(c) and her children will qualify under section 6(2). They are treated as having only one eligible parent, their mother, although both parents are aboriginal. John's children gained status at birth as both parents were Indian legally, even though one was an aboriginal person.

Joan's children can pass on status to their offspring only if they also marry registered Indians. If they marry unregistered aboriginal people or non-aboriginal people, then no status will pass to their children. All John's grandchildren will be status Indians, regardless of who his children marry. Thus, entitlement to registration for the second generation has nothing to do with racial or cultural characteristics. The Act has eliminated the discrimination faced by those who lost status, but has passed it on to the next generation.

The establishment of categories for Indian status was a concoction of the federal government, and instead of devising a bill that would truly repair the situation, it created a "paper blood system" that denied thousands of individuals the opportunity to claim or reclaim their heritage. ... The categorization of Indian status under Bill C-31 has implications for the entire aboriginal population in the coming generations. At present rates of marriage outside the 6(1) and 6(2) categories, status Indians will begin to disappear from the Indian register if the rules are not changed. One report of the problem supports this conclusions in the strongest or terms, noting that Bill C-31 "is the gateway to a world in which some Indians are more equal than others" because the 6(1)/ 6(2) distinction "creates two classes of Indian: *full* Indians and *half* Indians." Moreover, the report concludes, "In the long run these rules will lead to the extinction of First Nations".

Sharon McIvor challenged the residual discrimination that persisted after Bill C-31 and the 1985 *Indian Act* amendments were enacted. She argued that section 6 of the *Indian Act* (the second generation cut-off rule) was discriminatory and violated section 15(1) of the Charter because it treated the descendants of Indian women who married non-Indian men differently from the descendants of Indian men who married non-Indian women.

At trial (*McIvor v. Canada (Registrar, Indian and Northern Affairs)*, [2007] B.C.J. No. 1259, [2007] 3 C.N.L.R. 72 at paras. 192 and 193

(B.C.S.C.)), Ross J. of the British Columbia Supreme Court found that Indian status implicated First Nation citizenship issues:

> In my view, status under the *Indian Act* is a concept that is closely akin to the concepts of nationality and citizenship. Status under the *Indian Act*, like citizenship, is governed by statute. The eligibility of a child in both cases is related to the circumstances of his or her parents. In my view, the eligibility of the child to registration as an Indian based upon the circumstances of the parent, is a benefit of the law in which both the parent and the child have a legitimate interest.
>
> It is my view that the defendants' [Canada's] submission is a strained and unnatural construct that ignores the significance of the concept of Indian as an aspect of cultural identity. The defendants' approach would treat status as an Indian as if it were simply a statutory definition pertaining to eligibility for some program or benefit. However, having created and then imposed this identity upon First Nations peoples, with the result that it has become a central aspect of identity, the government cannot now treat it in that way, ignoring the true essence or significance of the concept.

Later in her judgment (at paras. 286 and 287), Ross J. reinforced the connection between Indian status and identity by observing:

> The record in this case clearly supports the conclusion that registration as an Indian reinforces a sense of identity, cultural heritage, and belonging. A key element of this sense of identity, heritage, and belonging is the ability to pass this heritage to one's children. The evidence of the plaintiffs is that the inability to be registered with full s. 6(1)(a) status because of the sex of one's parents or grandparents is insulting and hurtful and implies that one's female ancestors are deficient or less Indian than their male contemporaries. The implication is that one's lineage is inferior. The implication for an Indian woman is that she is inferior, less worthy of recognition.
>
> It is my conclusion that the current registration provisions have been a blow to the dignity of the plaintiffs. Moreover, they would be so to any reasonable person situated in the plaintiffs' position.

Thus, the British Columbia Supreme Court found that the *Indian Act* favoured male ancestry in the passage of Indian status in a manner that was contrary to section 15(1) of the Charter. Near the end of the decision, Ross J. summarized her findings regarding discrimination (at para. 343), as follows:

> I have concluded that s. 6 of the *1985 Act* violates s. 15(1) of the *Charter* in that it discriminates between matrilineal and patrilineal descendants born prior to April 17, 1985, in the conferring of Indian status, and discriminates between descendants born prior to April 17, 1985, of Indian women who married non-Indian men, and the descendants of Indian men who married non-Indian women. I have concluded that these provisions are not saved by s. 1.

Justice Ross then issued the following remedy (see *McIvor v. Canada (Registrar, Indian and Northern Affairs)*, [2007] B.C.J. No. 2569 at para. 9 (B.C.S.C.)):

(a) Section 6 of the *Indian Act*, R.S.C. 1985, C. 1-5 (the *"1985 Act"*) violates ss. 15 and 28 of the *Canadian Charter of Rights and Freedoms* in that it discriminates, on the grounds of sex and marital status, against matrilineal descendants, born prior to April 17, 1985, and Indian women born prior to April 17, 1985, who married non-Indian men, in the entitlement to be registered as Indians, and is not saved by s. 1 of the *Charter*;

(b) Section 6 of the *1985 Act* is of no force and effect in so far, and only in so far, as it provides for the preferential treatment of Indian men over Indian women born prior to April 17, 1985, and the preferential treatment of patrilineal descendants over matrilineal descendants born prior to April 17, 1985, in the right to be registered as an Indian;

(c) Every person who was registered or was entitled to be registered as an Indian under s. 6(1)(a) of the *1985 Act* shall continue to be registered or entitled to be registered under s. 6(1)(a) as the case may be. Section 6(1)(a) of the *1985 Act* shall, however, be interpreted so as to entitle persons to be registered under s. 6(1)(a), who were previously not entitled to be registered under s. 6(1)(a) solely as a result of the preferential treatment accorded to Indian men over Indian women born prior to April 17, 1985, and to patrilineal descendants over matrilineal descendants, born prior to April 17, 1985;

(d) Nothing in this order shall entitle any person to membership in an Indian band, under s. 11 of the *1985 Act*, or under the membership rules enacted by an Indian band which has assumed control of its own membership under s. 10 of the *1985 Act*. ...

Upon review in *McIvor v. Canada (Registrar, Indian and Northern Affairs)*, [2009] B.C.J. No. 669, 306 D.L.R. (4th) 193 (B.C.C.A.), the British Columbia Court of Appeal agreed that section 6 of the *Indian Act* was discriminatory, but held that the trial judge's characterization of the Charter violation was too broad. Therefore, the Court substituted the following remedy (at paras. 152-161 and 165-166):

The trial judge erred, in my view, in defining the extent of the *Charter* violation. She considered it necessary to redress all discrimination that had occurred prior to 1985. Accordingly, she would have granted Indian status to all individuals who could show that somewhere in their ancestry there was a person who had lost Indian status by virtue of being a woman married to a non-Indian.

In my view, the trial judge erred, as well, in the remedy she granted. In view of the length of time that had passed since the coming into force of the 1985 legislation, she considered it necessary to provide an immediate remedy to the plaintiffs and those in a similar situation. She granted a complex order refashioning the legislation, which she would have had take effect immediately. As I will indicate, I do not think that such an order was in keeping with the proper role of a court in making legislative choices.

The *Charter* violation that I find to be made out is a much narrower one than was found by the trial judge. The 1985 legislation violates the *Charter* by according Indian status to children

i) who have only one parent who is Indian (other than by reason of having married an Indian),

ii) where that parent was born prior to April 17, 1985, and

iii) where that parent in turn only had one parent who was Indian (other than by reason of having married an Indian),

if their Indian grandparent is a man, but not if their Indian grandparent is a woman.

The legislation would have been constitutional if it had preserved only the status that such children had before 1985. By according them enhanced status, it created new inequalities, and violated the *Charter*.

There are two obvious ways in which the violation of s. 15 might have been avoided. The 1985 legislation could have given status under an equivalent of s. 6(1) to people in Mr. Grismer's situation. Equally, it could have preserved only the existing rights of those in the comparator group. While these are the obvious ways of avoiding a violation of s. 15, other, more complicated, solutions might also have been found.

The legislation at issue has now been in force for 24 years. People have made decisions and planned their lives on the basis that the law as it was enacted in 1985 governs the question of whether or not they have Indian status. The length of time that the law has remained in force may, unfortunately, make the consequences of amendment more serious than they would have been in the few years after the legislation took effect.

Contextual factors, including the reliance that people have placed on the existing state of the law, may affect the options currently available to the Federal government in remedying the *Charter* violation. It may be that some of the options that were available in 1985 are no longer practical. On the other hand, options that would not have been appropriate in 1985 may be justifiable today, under s. 1 of the *Charter*, in order to avoid draconian effects.

I cannot say which legislative choice would have been made in 1985 had the violation of s. 15 been recognized. I am even less certain of the options that the government might choose today to make the legislation constitutional. For that reason, I am reluctant to read new entitlements into s. 6 of the *Indian Act*. I am even more reluctant to read down the entitlement of the comparator group, especially given that it is not represented before this Court. In *Schachter v. Canada*, [1992] 2 S.C.R. 679, the Supreme Court of Canada discussed situations in which the appropriate remedy is a declaration of invalidity that is temporarily suspended. At 715-716, the Court said:

> A court may strike down legislation or a legislative provision but suspend the effect of that declaration until Parliament or the provincial legislature has had an opportunity to fill the void. This approach ... may ... be appropriate in cases of underinclusiveness as opposed to overbreadth. For example, in this case some of the interveners argued that in cases where a denial of equal benefit of the law is alleged, the legislation in question is not usually problematic in and of itself. It is its underinclusiveness that is problematic so striking down the law immediately would deprive deserving persons of benefits without providing them to the applicant. At the same time, if there is no obligation on the government to provide the benefits in the first place, it may be inappropriate to go ahead and extend them. The logical remedy is to strike down but suspend the declaration of invalidity to allow the government to determine whether to cancel or extend the benefits.

It seems to me that this reasoning is apt in the case at bar. It would not be appropriate for the Court to augment Mr. Grismer's Indian status, or grant such status to his children; there is no obligation on government to grant such status. On the other hand, it would be entirely unfair for this Court to instantaneously deprive persons who have had status since 1985 of that status as a result of a dispute between the government and the plaintiffs. In the end, the decision as to how the inequality should be remedied is one for Parliament.

Sections 6(1)(a) and 6(1)(c) of the *Indian Act* violate the *Charter* to the extent that they grant individuals to whom the Double Mother Rule applied greater rights than they would have had under s. 12(1)(a)(iv) of the former legislation. Accordingly, I would declare ss. 6(1)(a) and 6(1)(c) to be of no force and effect, pursuant to s. 52 of the *Constitution Act, 1982.* I would suspend the declaration for a period of 1 year, to allow Parliament time to amend the legislation to make it constitutional. ...

Conclusion

While I am in agreement with the trial judge that s. 6 of the *Indian Act* infringes the plaintiffs' right to equality under s. 15 of the *Charter* and that the infringement is not justified by s. 1, I reach this conclusion on much narrower grounds than did the trial judge. In particular, I find that the infringement of s. 15 would be saved by s. 1 but for the advantageous treatment that the 1985 legislation accorded those to whom the Double Mother Rule under previous legislation applied.

I would allow the appeal, and substitute for the order of the trial judge an order declaring ss. 6(1)(a) and 6(1)(c) of the *Indian Act* to be of no force and effect. I would suspend the declaration for a period of 1 year.

The Supreme Court denied leave to appeal in *McIvor v. Canada (Registrar, Indian and Northern Affairs)*, [2009] S.C.C.A. No. 234 (S.C.C.), thus upholding the decision of the British Columbia Court of Appeal.

1. In considering the *McIvor* decision at trial and in the Court of Appeal, which remedy do you think best accords with the aspirations of First Nations women as discussed throughout this chapter?

2. In response to the British Columbia Court of Appeal's order, Parliament enacted the *Gender Equity in Indian Registration Act*, S.C. 2010, c. 18 (Bill C-3). This bill amended provisions of the *Indian Act* found to be unconstitutional in *McIvor v. Canada*. Bill C-3 allows eligible grandchildren of women who lost status as a result of marrying non-Indian men to register as status Indians. It is anticipated that approximately 45,000 persons are entitled to registration because of this legislation.

3. Sharon McIvor, the plaintiff in the *McIvor* case, wrote a letter calling for a rejection of Bill C-3's amendments to the *Indian Act*. She wrote:

    Like the 1985 legislation - Bill C-31, Bill C-3 will provide a remedy for some Aboriginal women and their descendants, but continue the discrimination against many more. Bill C-3 will still exclude: 1) grandchildren born prior to September 4, 1951 who are descendants of a status woman who married out; 2) descendants of Indian women who co-parented in common law unions with non-status men; and 3) the illegitimate female children of male Indians. These Aboriginal women and their descendants are only ineligible for registration as Indians because of the entrenched discrimination in the *Indian Act*, which has been fiercely held onto by Canada, despite years of protest and repeated, damning criticisms by United Nations treaty bodies.[8]

4. Jeanette Corbiere Lavell, one of the plaintiffs in the *Lavell and Bedard* case, was also critical Bill C-3's underinclusiveness. NWAC's critique of the amendments flowing from the *McIvor* case are as follows:

> Despite all of the legislative changes and with the new Bill C-3, the federal government has retained control under sections 6 and 7 of the *Indian Act* over the determination of Indian *status* for all First Nations.
>
> The Court of Appeal in *McIvor* missed its opportunity to provide a meaningful remedy to addressing the preference of following the male line. The main complaint of the McIvor case is that the Indian Act since 1876 said that only the Male could pass along Indian status; even if a woman did not marry out, and was full status herself, she could not pass status along to her children. Only if her child was "illegitimate" and nobody came along to demonstrate that the dad was non-Indian could she give her child her status.
>
> The proposed amendments narrowly address the main issue in McIvor by introducing s. 6(1)(a) and a new subsection s. 6(1)(c).1 — INAC claims this will ensure eligible grandchildren of women who lost status will become eligible for registration. Since 1869, the Federal government has unilaterally changed the definition of who is and who is not an Indian — all without the consent of the First Nations people. The *Indian Act* has created the discriminatory provisions and various classifications of who is or is not an Indian — these people who will be re-instated already belong to our communities — they are our aunties, daughters and mothers and grandmothers.[9]

A federally funded exploratory process is underway to address the remaining issues related to the continuing discrimination under the *Indian Act* (see online: <http://www.nwac.ca/media/release/08-04-11>).

While the cause of this discrimination can rightly be found to have originated in and been perpetrated by the *Indian Act*, some women continue to suffer from adverse treatment from some within their communities. What is disturbing about this form of discrimination is that, at times, it seems to be represented and perpetrated by the leadership within certain communities. Furthermore, recent issues of discrimination raise questions about who should participate in a share of the community's resources, be considered as part of the culture, and have a right to define what are acceptable grounds for determining citizenship. The following case, *Sawridge Band v. Canada (T.D.)*, [1995] F.C.J. No. 1013, [1996] 1 F.C. 3, [1995] 4 C.N.L.R. 121 (F.C.T.D.), raises the issue of the continued discrimination that First Nations women still appear to be encountering under the *Indian Act*.

SAWRIDGE BAND v. CANADA (T.D.)

[1995] F.C.J. No. 1013, [1996] 1 F.C. 3, [1995] 4 C.N.L.R. 121 (F.C.T.D.)

Muldoon J.: — This is a constitutional case, in which the plaintiffs sue for a declaration that key provisions of an Act of Parliament are inconsistent with parts of Section 35 of the Constitution of Canada, and in particular, as enacted by the *Constitution Act, 1982*, Schedule B, *Canada Act 1982*, 1982, c. 11 (U.K.). ...

The Legislation

The plaintiffs' grievance is stated to reside in an Act of Parliament: 33-34 Elizabeth II, *An Act to amend the Indian Act*, S.C. 1985, c. 27 (the 1985 amendment). Section 4 of that 1985 amendment is particularly noticed in enacting new Sections 8, 9, 10, 11 and 12 in the *Indian Act*, R.S.C. 1985,
c. I-5. ...

The matters in issue focus primarily on the 1985 amendments' Sections 11 and 12, by contrast with their repealed predecessors...

The Pleadings

Paragraph 13 of the amended statement of claim alleges that the statutes of Parliament prior to the recognition and affirmation of existing Aboriginal and treaty rights on April 17, 1982 (with a few unstated limited exceptions) confirmed Indians' rights to determine their bands' members and did not impose additional members on the bands. The Attorney General's defence, however, denies all that, and avers those allegations are contrary to the explicit provisions of the successive Indian Acts and to the executive decisions made pursuant to that legislation. ...

Paragraph 14 of the statement of claim alleges as follows:

> 14. With the enactment of an Act entitled An Act to Amend the *Indian Act*, S.C. 1985, c.27 (the "1985 Amendment") Parliament attempted unilaterally to require Indian bands to admit certain persons to membership. The 1985 Amendment imposes members on a band without the necessity of consent by the council of the band or the members of the band itself and, indeed, imposes such persons on the band even if the council of the band or the membership objects to the inclusion of such persons in the band. This exercise of power by Parliament was unprecedented in the predecessor legislation.

The defendant avers in answer to the effect that he denies the allegation expressed in the last sentence and asserts that the 1985 amendment speaks for itself and further regarding the plaintiffs' paragraph 14, that section 91 head 24 of the *Constitution Act, 1867* ... accords Parliament exclusive authority to legislate, and it did legislate the criteria and conditions of band membership, as well as the circumstances in which entitlement can be acquired, held, lost, revoked, regained or restored without the consent of bands or band councils.

To the defendant's statements, the plaintiffs replied and joined issue (certified record: tab 4, page 2, paragraphs 2):

2. With respect to paragraphs 5(b), 11, 12 and 14 the Plaintiffs say that their existence as Indians, Tribes and Bands, living in organized societies, long preceded any statute of the Parliament of Canada or treaty and that no such statute or treaty extinguished the right of such societies to determine their own membership. ...

Concerns About 1985 Amendments in Testimony

The foregoing review of the pleadings on how the 1985 amendment operated or was foreseen to operate, was reflected in the testimony of various witnesses. Perhaps the Court ought not to have permitted such speculative testimony, but it was not wholly inappropriate to hear from an elderly Aboriginal witness who was called and permitted to give "oral history", despite the rule against hearsay. Sophie Makinaw testified through the very excellent oral interpretation services of Harold Cardinal whom the Court praises and thanks for his manifestly first-rate, proficient and dedicated services. Mrs. Makinaw's testimony here is taken not for predictive accuracy, but for the purpose of demonstrating the plaintiffs' worst fears about the practical operation of the 1985 amendments. ...

Now, when we look at this situation, it's got to be clear that we're not talking about only the woman who left our reserve [since 1951] returning to our communities. Those women now have their children, and in some cases they have their grandchildren. And in many cases if they return to our reserves, they will want to come back with their husbands; they will want their husbands to return with them.

I want to talk specifically about the white husband in this instance. It is not clear that the white husband is going to be able to accept our ways and live the way we are. It may be that the white man who comes to live on our reserve will want to impose his own values, his ways which he is familiar with on us, on our communities, and I haven't really thought yet, I haven't had time to really try and determine what all the consequences of this possibility might be.

One of the problems that we're even now encountering and that's going to be aggravating if large numbers of people come back to our reserves is the fact that even now our reserves are getting over populated. ...

The question of who should live on our reserve is really a matter that should be decided by us as people who own and live on the land. That is a decision that should not be taken elsewhere or by someone else for us. ...

The decision on who is a member of our band or not, or who is entitled, should be made by us. We already share ... as Cree people we already share a lot of land with, with the white people. All we retained for ourselves is what we have now in our reserves. If the white people want to give more land, more services, then they should take part of the land that was shared with them because they have an abundance of land to provide these things to these people, if that is what they want to do. ...

We ... my difficulty is with non-Cree people or non-Cree persons because whether we're talking about a white person or a Métis, they are not familiar with our culture, they are not familiar with our ways, and when they come and live with us, they are aggressive, they want to control us. They live in a way that's different from us and often they're not honest, and that's what ... that's a difficulty I have. ...

The Constitution's Textual Provisions

One should return to the theme of the plaintiffs' apprehensions about the 1985 amendment which they allege to be unconstitutional and *ultra vires* of Parliament. What makes it unconstitutional and *ultra vires*, the plaintiffs say, is the existence and operation of s. 35 of the *Constitution Act, 1982.* ...

About one year and two months after s. 35, above recited, came into force, it was amended as is reflected in the *Constitution Amendment Proclamation, 1983* which added the following two subsections:

> (3) For greater certainty in subsection (1) "treaty rights" includes rights that now exist by way of land claims agreements or may be so acquired.
> (4) Notwithstanding any other provision of this Act, the aboriginal and treaty rights referred to in subsection (1) are guaranteed equally to male and female persons.

Subsection 35(4) is Conclusive

Given the nature and main substance of the plaintiffs' complaints (earlier above related), as understood and appreciated by the nature and main substance of the interveners' complaints against the state of the law which existed before the 1985 amendment (described in the testimony of Mary Two-Axe Early — TT48), subsection 35(4) appears to be conclusive. Without going into the plaintiffs' case further, it can be clearly seen that the marital custom, the so-called Aboriginal and treaty rights which permit an Indian husband to bring his non-Indian wife into residence on a reserve, but which forbid an Indian wife from so bringing her non-Indian husband are extinguished utterly by subsection 35(4).

The plaintiffs are firmly caught by the provisions of s. 35 of the *Constitution Act* which they themselves invoke. The more firmly the plaintiffs bring themselves into and under subsection 35(1) the more surely subsection 35(4) acts upon their alleged rights pursuant to subsection 35(1) which, therefore are modified so as to be guaranteed equally to the whole collectivity of Indian men and Indian women.

If ever there was or could be a clear extinguishment of any alleged Aboriginal or treaty right to discriminate within the collectivity of Indians and more particularly against Indian women, subsection 35(4) of the *Constitution Act* is that; and it works that extinguishment, very specifically, absolutely, and imperatively. It operates "notwithstanding any other provision of this Act", that is, the *Constitution Act, 1982.*

The hardship and heartache of those women who were in effect expelled from their homes and home reserves, and even expelled from Indian status, and their grievous sense of injustice of becoming non-Indians while at the same time the "white ladies" who married male band members, became Indians, was well illustrated in the testimony of the interveners' witnesses. Subsection 35(4) is aimed at providing their relief.

That constitutional provision exacts equality of rights between male and female persons, no matter what rights or responsibilities may have pertained in earlier times. On this basis alone, the plaintiffs' action is dismissed. It is the supreme law of Canada which speaks, to end the inequality of marital status of Indian women who are subject to it. The impugned legislation could surely be supported by section 15 of the *Canadian Charter of Rights and Freedoms*, too, were it not perhaps for section 25, but subsection 35(4) of the *Constitution Act* along with the other subsections of the whole of section 35 is in effect an "Indian provision" in an otherwise largely anti-racist constitution, and it speaks deliberately and specifically to the diminution of past inequalities between Indian men and women. Thus the 1985 amendment is doubly validated by maybe section 15 and absolutely by subsection 35(4); and there is no doubt that it is within Parliament's legislative jurisdiction in regard to Indians. So, section 35(4) operates and commands whether pleaded or not; it cannot be evaded. ...

The plaintiffs put forth several other arguments in support of their position, and in justice, the Court ought to consider them all, for some are quite cogent. ...

English and British Sovereignty

The King of England, Charles II, acting in right of England (and apparently not in right of Scotland) by executive act incorporated a trading company of considerable corporate jurisdiction: "The Governor and Company of Adventurers of England Trading into Hudson's Bay", hereinafter HBC. That considerable corporate jurisdiction is, for example, described in that statute of the U.K. known as the *Rupert's Land Act*, 1868, 31-32 Vict., c. 105 (U.K.) refers to the HBC's "lands and territories, rights of government, and other rights, privileges, liberties, franchises, powers and authorities". The HBC's incorporation was effected by means of the king's letters patent often referred to as the company's Royal Charter, granted on May 2, 1670. ...

The Court finds that the assertion of English sovereignty, later to become British sovereignty, was first formally expressed in the HBC Charter, May 2, 1670. Any rights which the plaintiffs can successfully establish must have been exerted before that day, and must not have been extinguished before the coming into force of s-s. 35(1) of the *Constitution Act, 1982* and must withstand Subsection 35(4) thereof. It must be left to others at another time to explain how the revisionists who settled upon Subsection 35(2) thought that they could honestly characterize Metis people as Aboriginal people, wielding Aboriginal rights. Nature has special blessings for hybrid people, the offspring of interracial procreation, as was correctly asserted by the plaintiff Wayne Roan in his testimony, TT8, at p. 837. Only some determined revisionist would seek to regard Metis as being exemplars of only one of their inherently dual lines of ancestors. It will be seen, however, that conduct and lifestyle will be noted in terms of "half-breeds living the 'Indian way of Life'," in this dismally racist subject of litigation.

The Plaintiffs' View of Merger or Subsumption of Aboriginal Rights Under and into Treaty Rights

... The diminution of Aboriginal rights is no doubt true, but the plaintiffs pleaded, and the Court accepts, that the Aboriginal rights so diminished must be rights specified in the treaty, of course, and not all Aboriginal rights at large. The treaties, along with the various versions of the *Indian Act* which preceded the treaties here considered, all bore upon and diminished Aboriginal rights and Aboriginal lifestyle. Even the assertion of sovereignty made the Aboriginal peoples subject to laws of general application in regard to crime, property, civil administration and tort which came into force as English and British sovereignty was secured. To the extent that those general laws impinged on or extinguished Aboriginal rights to such extent they were diminished. The Aboriginal peoples are not "foreigners", but from the time of assertion of sovereignty have been subjects of the sovereign. In that regard, section 88 of the *Indian Act* states, almost redundantly, the evident truth of general status consequent upon the subtraction therefrom of the Indians' special status. It confirms the Aboriginal peoples' status as subjects of the Crown both specially and generally in defining the profile of the boundary between the two.

Like others, no matter how much some judges and public servants seek paternally to patronize them, the western Indians are obliged to obey the laws of [the] land, even if such laws were unknown to their distant ancestors, so long as the law of the land does not abrogate surviving Aboriginal rights, as stated in Subsection 35(1) of the *Constitution Act, 1982*. Before Subsection 35(1) came into force, the law of the land as enacted by Parliament could indeed extinguish Aboriginal rights, but to be clear and unambiguous about such extinguishment or abrogation, the law did not need to state that "such Aboriginal rights as conflict with this law, to wit..., are, to such extent, extinguished". A law which had that clear effect even without those clear words was valid, if enacted in conformity with the wide purview of section 91, head 24 of the *Constitution Act, 1867*. So it was said by the Supreme Court of Canada in regard to treaty rights and State obligations thereto in *Sikyea v. The Queen*, [1964] S.C.R. 642; *The Queen v. George*, [1966] S.C.R. and *The Queen v. Moosehunter*, [1981] 1 S.C.R. 282.

The Treaties

In order to discover which Aboriginal rights were and are truly subsumed into and accordingly extinguished by the treaties, it is necessary to analyze the treaties carefully.

Thereafter, if the particular Aboriginal rights which the plaintiffs contend are theirs unto this very day remain untouched by the treaties, it will be necessary to enquire whether that which the plaintiffs assert be truly an Aboriginal right is indeed such as they assert.

In effect the plaintiffs assert two Aboriginal rights. The first has to do with the plaintiffs' principal but narrower grievance, about permitting Indian women who married non-Indians to live either by remaining in or returning to the women's own reserves of residence, inevitably their natal reserves with membership retained in their natal bands. The plaintiffs claim that their present expression of the Aboriginal right which they assert stems from the Aboriginal principle and practice that, upon marriage the woman followed the man to reside in or at his ordinary residence within his tribal group, not hers. From that narrow principle, the plaintiffs assert more globally that from Aboriginal times Indian groups or encampments controlled their own membership and that such an Aboriginal right either survived the treaty making, or is enshrined in the treaties. The plaintiffs triumphantly state that control of membership is an inevitable incident of their ancestors' "organised societies", which the defendant admitted orally by counsel at trial. These are matters for subsequent analysis.

Basis for the Treaties

The racial and religious hatreds of the historical past provide only a sterile and hopeless basis for nurturing those hatreds into the present and the future. That proposition is a stunningly, obviously, eternal verity as was clear, at least until recent days, in Ireland and is still evident in the present murderous stupidities among the South Slavs in Europe and between the Hutus and Tutsi in Africa. North America was surely going to be occupied and dominated by Europeans because of historical and economic processes which were unavoidable. There is no use in mourning that fact of destiny. The only question was whether the dominant Europeans would be the French, the British or the Spanish, and in the nineteenth century it was as between the Canadians and Americans. ...

There is no doubt that, in entering into the treaties they sought the protection of — and perhaps ill-advisedly — the dependence on, the Crown, as represented by Ottawa's Treaty Commissioners. Those commissioners, unlike General Custer and his government, did have the authority and ability to allow the Indians to live in peace, and to protect them from the Americans — 7th Cavalry and whiskey traders alike.

Among the other important factors of those days inducing the Indians to seek the treaties were: disease and famine and the clearly-to-be-seen demise of the huge natural herds of bison, called buffalo, upon which the Plains Indians depended for food, hides, sinew, bones and horns to maintain their unique pre-industrial life style. Quite possibly the introduction by the Spanish of the horse which quickly became widespread, and the introduction by all the Europeans of the rifle and other firearms, must have contributed to the diminution of the herds.

No doubt the introduction of Euro-settlers also contributed greatly to the buffaloes' disappearance. ...

So there was a quid pro quo inherent in Treaties 6, 7 and 8. The Canadian government wanted to open the Prairies to eastern Canadian settlement — expansionism Canadian style, kept non-murderous with the help of the mounted police — and the Indians, in their straitened circumstances of that different world, wanted the protection from the settlers *inter alia* and wanted the dependent status into which they bargained themselves, seemingly "forever". ... The government's payments work another evil, too. They are an eternal charge on the country's taxpayers, even although the dolorous conditions of the last century lie dead in the past along with its glory, if any, which cannot be now restored. ...

Statutes

Apart from social and economic conditions above mentioned as the basis for the treaties were the various statutes which can be regarded as the historical continuum of the *Indian Act*. That Act precedes the treaties which are under consideration in this litigation. ...

The plaintiffs' asserted right to control their own membership of their "bands" (a wholly statutory term) was emphatically extinguished by the *Indian Act, 1876*. Complete control was taken by Parliament in the enactment of that statute and its predecessors. Even if control of hunting and social groups' or encampments' membership had been a real Aboriginal right it was extinguished by most clear and unambiguous legislation before Treaties 6, 7 and 8 ever came into being. ...

Negotiations

... an Aboriginal right of control of membership it was conclusively extinguished at treaty time and as a condition of concluding the treaty. Governor Morris certainly asserted control over membership by the Canadian government and in consonance with the provisions of the *Indian Act 1876* and preceding legislation enacted by the Parliament of Canada. Other sources of the same historic assertion of control are exhibit 1(4), pp. 36 to 39, and of course the plaintiffs' counsel's reading of the passages into the record in trial transcript (TT) 2, pp. 81 and 82. The government's assertion of control over band membership on reserves, and off, was unambiguously stated by statute and by Alexander Morris, the government's treaty commissioner. ...

Clearly, a people who were experiencing the setting-up of false, puppet chiefs and social granulation "into little parties" due to the influence of traders, cannot be believed to be controlling its own membership. A people which sought governmental establishment of its own "chiefships" in order to have the State make its political and social officers have official recognition in order to avoid that people's willy-nilly granulation at the whim and commercial greed of traders, cannot be held to be controlling its own membership. If such control were truly an Aboriginal practice, then the Indians themselves lost it without any push by the government of Canada which truly asserted and exercised such control. Was this conclusion understood then by the Indians as this Court now understands it? It was they who first acknowledged loss (or absence) of control in the first place; and it was they who requested the government to assert control, for and on their behalf, as in the statutes, so in the treaties.

There is an underlying, sometimes articulated premise in the jurisprudence and among certain cynical activists that the "pitiable Indians" were easy dupes for superior Euro-Canadians and needing protections which applied not only to 19th Century Indians, but also to contemporary Indians, born in the mid-20th Century. This Court finds nothing inferior, genetic, social or intellectual *inter alia* about those Indians who entered into the treaties, nor their descendants today. This Court rejects all stated or implied notions of any inferiority of Indians, whatever. That is why the Court leans against the alleged need, over a century later, of special State protection of Indians, which protection often appears to be excessive and degrading to Indians in comparison with all the other "visible" (and not so "visible") peoples who make up the tax-paying and general population of Canada. Certainly the Morris record (pp. 219-28, 270-71) reveals instances of hard-bargaining and excessive demands beyond the Canadian government's Commissioners' power to yield. There is even at least one instance in which the Commissioners exceeded their authority because of the Indians' persuasion acknowledged that they were taking a risk in hoping to have their so yielding subsequently ratified by Ottawa. The Courts, too, often and too much pretend that the Indians did not understand their bargained treaties. ...

Peoples found to be in a more primitive (i.e. hunting) state of development than the others' state (i.e. industrial or post-industrial) are emphatically not inferior peoples. Their state of development might be likened by analogy to "adolescent" compared with the others' (non-Indians') "adult" state of development. But the law and treaties have protected Indians from "spreading their wings" as may non-Indian adolescents who do and always have made "improvident transactions" until a majority learned not to do so, but to conduct themselves prudently. ...

It is surely apparent that it is not eternal dependence with apartheid, but equal self-reliance, (including Canada's so-called "social safety net" for such as it is and will be) which promote the equal human dignity of all Canadians. It is difficult to understand why the Courts in recent years have promoted dependence. The so-called "honour of the Crown" is surely nothing more than a transparent semantic membrane for wrapping together Indian reserve apartheid and perpetual dependence on Canadian taxpayers. This melancholy situation, being authentically historic, does nothing to support the plaintiffs' claim to control their own membership as is already demonstrated herein. It has contributed to the depression and poverty of many Indians over time. ...

Treaty Text

Taken all-in-all with the Act and the negotiations, no treaty right of Indians to control their band and reserve membership can be discerned. They understood that to be so. The disputed matter of hunting trapping and fishing being subject to governmental regulation is shown in the version reported. As in Treaties 6 and 7, Treaty 8 foresees ever diminishing territory for hunting, trapping and fishing because it was agreed that such activities could be pursued there "saving and excepting such tracts as may be required or taken up from time to time for settlement, mining, lumbering, trading or other purposes."

It was quite obvious and well understood by the Indian parties to all three treaties that the Government of Canada was thereafter to control their band and reserve membership, because the government was committed to pay Indians forever as an eternal charge on taxpayers. Clearly the government was committed also to control who was to be paid individually, and who was not entitled to be paid individually. The Indians were neither simpletons nor crazy. They well understood that "money talks" and that "whoever pays the piper, calls the tune". ...

Woman Follows Man

... It is well known that legislation enacted contrary to the Constitution's provisions is, to the extent of any inconsistency, of no force or effect. Remembering the words of Mr. Justice La Forest in *Mitchell v. Peguis* ... it must be observed that a constitutional recognition and affirmation does not constitutionalize ordinary legislation such as the women's-loss-of-membership-on-marriage-out provisions of previous, successive *Indian Acts*. ...

The plaintiffs assert that the marital régime for which they contend is an Aboriginal right; and that Aboriginal rights are collective rights. Surely, however, the notion of "woman follows man", and is unable to confer her status upon her non-Indian husband, represent a collective right only for men. It was and is not a right for women. If one is going to elevate Aboriginal practices into constitutional imperatives, then the Aboriginal practices of no individual identity for women, and no voice in the encampments' affairs should need constitutional recognition and affirmation, too! It is nonsense to try to keep women silent and invisible. ...

In no time at all historical stories, if ever accurate, soon become mortally skewed propaganda, without objective verity. Since the above mentioned pejorative characteristics, and more, are alas common to humanity they must have been verily evinced by everybody's ancestors, as they are by the present day descendants, but no one, including oral historians wants to admit that. Each tribe or ethnicity in the whole human species raises its young to believe that they are "better" than everyone else. Hence, the wars which have blighted human history. So ancestor advocacy or ancestor worship is one of the most counter-productive, racist, hateful and backward-looking of all human characteristics, or religion, or what passes for thought. People are of course free to indulge in it — perhaps it is an aspect of human nature — but it is that aspect which renders oral history highly unreliable. So saying, the Court is most emphatically not mocking or belittling those who assert that, because their ancestors never developed writing, oral history is their only means of keeping their history alive. It would always be best to put the stories into writing at the earliest possible time in order to avoid some of the embellishments which render oral history so unreliable. ...

The Court finds that in Aboriginal times and up to the making of the treaties, all of the plaintiffs' predecessors had no custom of controlling their groups' or chiefs' peoples' membership. Quite the contrary. The chiefs' stature depended on how many individuals or families attached themselves to the respective chiefs. Even those born into a chief's people were free simply to walk out of the chief's encampment and attach themselves to another. No questions asked. One chief's loss was another's gain. If this freedom to join and depart were an Aboriginal custom, it was the diametric opposite of "control" of membership. ...

If the bands with membership codes think that provisions about "blood quantum" will do what they think "repute" should have done for them, they are calling down untold agonies on themselves and their people. In the first place there is human verity in the old adage: "It's a wise child who knows his own father." There was a sad afternoon at trial herein when one of the plaintiffs' counsel insensitively sought to enlist a witness in his effort to prove that the witness was a so-called illegitimate child. As if any human being can be considered illegitimate! The person being conceived, after all, does not know who are doing it. "Blood quantum" is a highly fascist and racist notion, and puts its practitioners on the path of the Nazi Party led by the late, most unlamented Adolf Hitler. It will bring heartache, for example, to the mother of children sired by different fathers, say an Indian and a non-Indian, who may be required to go into exile rather than to exile some of her children from their siblings. The Court heard testimony to the effect that the Sarcee (Tsuu T'ina) are conjuring with the practice of "blood quantum". One hopes that people who characterize themselves as generous, hospitable and living in tune with Mother Earth and all nature, will not set out to turn some unfortunates among their number against their own grandparents. ...

SAWRIDGE BAND v. CANADA

[1997] F.C.J. No. 794, [1997] 3 F.C. 580 (Fed. C.A.)

Isaac C.J.C., Strayer and **Linden JJ.A.:—**

Introduction

On June 3, 1997 this Court, having heard argument on the first ground of appeal that there was a reasonable apprehension of bias on the part of the Trial Judge, was obliged to dispose of that ground before hearing the remainder of the argument. As a result the Court allowed the appeal on that ground, for reasons to follow. These are those reasons. As will be apparent, they do not address the substance of the Judge's decision.

Facts

This appeal involves an action commenced in 1986 for declarations that certain sections of the *Indian Act* are invalid. These sections were added by an amendment in 1985. Briefly put, this legislation, while conferring on Indian bands the right to control their own band lists, obliged bands to include in their membership certain persons who became entitled to Indian status by virtue of the 1985 legislation. Such persons included: women who had become disentitled to Indian status through marriage to non-Indian men and the children of such women; those who had lost status because their mother and paternal grandmother were non-Indian and had gained Indian status through marriage to an Indian; and those who had lost status on the basis that they were illegitimate offspring of an Indian woman and a non-Indian man. Bands assuming control of their band lists would be obliged to accept all these people as members. Such bands would also be allowed, if they chose, to accept certain other categories of persons previously excluded from Indian status. ...

The trial of this action occupied some seventy-five days commencing September 20, 1993 and ending April 25, 1994. Reasons were issued on July 6, 1995 [[1996] 1 F.C. 3]. ... The Trial Judge dismissed the action for the declarations. ...

The plaintiffs appealed this judgment. ... The two appeals A-779-95 and A-807-95 filed in respect of this matter (the former on behalf of the Ermineskin Band and the latter on behalf of the Sawridge Band and the Sarcee Band, now known as the Tsuu T'ina First Nation) were ordered joined for the hearing of the appeal. These reasons apply to both appeals.

As noted earlier, the first ground of appeal raised by the appellants Sawridge and Sarcee bands was that the record disclosed the basis for a reasonable apprehension of bias on the part of the Trial Judge against the appellants. ...

Counsel for all of the appellants then proceeded to present to the Court, from the trial record, comments or conduct during the trial by the Trial Judge, and passages in his reasons, to support their assertion of a reasonable apprehension of bias. ...

The Court was obliged to dispose of this ground of appeal before proceeding. In allowing the appeal on this basis, with reasons to be delivered later, the Court indicated that it had concluded that there was material in the record upon which a reasonable apprehension of bias could be found.

Analysis

It is first important to underline that no actual bias has been alleged on the part of the Trial Judge, nor does this Court find such bias. ...

We do think, however, that a reasonable observer would have formed the impression that the Trial Judge was strongly opposed to a special regime for some or all Aboriginal peoples different from the system of rights and responsibilities applying to other Canadians. If this apprehension were formed, it could have led such an observer to think that the Trial Judge was thereby influenced in his conclusion that no Aboriginal right had existed for the plaintiff bands to control their own membership or if it had, the right had been extinguished prior to the adoption of section 35 of the *Constitution Act, 1982*.

Such an observer might well have reflected on the fact that, ever since the adoption of the *Constitution Act, 1867* [30 & 31 Vict., c. 3 (U.K.) (as am. by *Canada Act 1982*, 1982, c. 11 (U.K.), Schedule to the *Constitution Act, 1982*, Item 1) [R.S.C., 1985, Appendix II, No. 5]], section 91(24) thereof has given Parliament the power and responsibility to make special laws for Indians in distinction from other persons. This power and responsibility, of necessity, has always required some criteria for defining Indians in order to distinguish them from other Canadians as subjects of legislation. He would further recall that other constitutional documents, treaties and court decisions have distinguished between Aboriginal peoples and others, and section 35 of the *Constitution Act, 1982* has now guaranteed existing Aboriginal rights as rights pertaining to Indians, Inuit, and Métis. The existence of special status for Aboriginal peoples is, therefore, enshrined in our Constitution. It was not for the Trial Judge to dispute this aspect of Canada's constitutional law.

Regrettably, there are a number of passages in the trial transcript and in the Judge's reasons which convey a very negative view of Aboriginal rights or special status for all or some Aboriginal peoples. ...

Conclusions

We believe the foregoing would indeed create in the mind of a fair-minded and reasonably well-informed observer the belief that the Trial Judge held certain views during the trial, which were confirmed in his reasons, that Aboriginal rights are "racist" and a form of "apartheid". Having ascribed these pejorative terms to a system which is recognized in the history, the common law, and the Constitution of Canada, he might well be expected to give the narrowest possible interpretation to, or reject, any newly claimed Aboriginal right asserted by the plaintiffs to have existed in 1982. He might also be taken to assume that this alleged right — the right of bands to control their own membership — would be used to promote racism and apartheid and should therefore not be recognized. ...

Nevertheless, for the reasons indicated earlier we found it necessary to set aside the judgment and order a new trial notwithstanding the great cost and inconvenience which this may cause. It is possible that this situation might have been avoided had counsel for the plaintiffs objected in a clear and timely manner to the Trial Judge's interventions, to make him aware of the unfortunate impression he seems to have given that he had some fixed views on the matters in dispute.

Needless to say, this disposition is in no way a finding that the conclusions of the Judge on the facts and the law were incorrect. These matters remain for determination at the new trial if it proceeds.

Disposition

It is for these reasons that the Court held that the record disclosed a basis for finding a reasonable apprehension of bias, the appeal was allowed, and a new trial ordered with costs to the appellants both here and below and no costs to the interveners either here or below.

---

1. If, as Justice Muldoon held, section 35(4) was conclusive of the matter before him, was it proper for him to consider and comment on issues of English and British sovereignty, treaties, statutes and negotiations, as he did in the remainder of his judgment?
2. Was Justice Muldoon right to characterize this case as being a "dismally racist subject of litigation"? As we have seen, rarely do courts talk about race and racism in the context of Aboriginal rights. Why did Justice Muldoon invoke this language in this particular case? Why was the language of racism not taken up by the Court of Appeal? Why has the language of racism not been taken up in the other cases you have read? What is the place, if there is any at all, of the language of racism in the law dealing with Aboriginal peoples?
3. Could Justice Muldoon draw upon any legal authority in making the statement: "North America was surely going to be occupied and dominated by Europeans because of historical and economic processes which were unavoidable"?
4. Justice Muldoon described treaty annuities as being "an eternal charge on the country's taxpayers". What is wrong with the government having to live up to its promises, and make payments in perpetuity for the use of lands used formerly and exclusively by the Indians? What would be your reaction to an Aboriginal person stating: "Non-Aboriginal peoples' use of our land is an eternal charge on our governments"?

5. Aboriginal leader Sharon McIvor has written:

> As with other existing Aboriginal rights, women's civil and political rights are foundational and do not derive from documents or treaties. The right of Aboriginal women to establish and maintain their civic and political role within the context of Aboriginal self-government has always existed. The regulation of women's political rights through successive Indian Acts did not extinguish their fundamental civil and political rights. Even if the suppression of women's rights was so oppressive it led to their banishment from Aboriginal communities, this, in itself, did not lead to the extinguishment of their rights. There is no extinguishment by regulation in the Aboriginal field ... [Aboriginal women's] rights are part of the inherent right to self-government, of customary laws of Aboriginal people.[10]

Is Ms. McIvor's statement congruent with Justice Muldoon's observation?

6. Is the following statement of Justice Muldoon true?: "Surely, however, the notion of 'woman follows man', and is unable to confer her status upon her non-Indian husband, represents a collective right only for men."

The *Sawridge* case was mired in procedural issues after Justice Muldoon's decision was overturned by the Federal Court of Appeal because it demonstrated a reasonable apprehension of bias. The action was dismissed in *Sawridge Band v. Canada*, [2008] F.C.J. No. 389, 319 F.T.R. 217 (F.C.), affd [2009] F.C.J. No. 465, 391 N.R. 375 (F.C.A.), leave to appeal refused [2009] S.C.C.A. No. 248 (S.C.C.).

Note how issues of discrimination on the basis of sex surrounding Bill C-31 seem to have been submerged in the recent treatment of the case.

Recall that following the passage of Bill C-31 many Indian women and their children wanted to return home to their reserves. However, because of inadequate resources and hostile reactions from some quarters many re-instated women remained off-reserve. The Supreme Court of Canada's decision in *Corbiere v. Canada* (reproduced in part below) made residence a ground of discrimination under section 15 of the *Canadian Charter of Rights and Freedoms* (Part I of the *Constitution Act, 1982*, being Schedule B to the *Canada Act 1982* (U.K.), 1982, c. 11). The issue in *Corbiere* was whether section 77(1) of the *Indian Act* was discriminatory because it restricted the right to vote to band members living on reserve. This provision arguably had the effect of disenfranchising those members who lived off the reserve, which included many women. Consider the Court's treatment of this issue in the following reasons for decision.

CORBIERE v. CANADA (MINISTER OF INDIAN AND NORTHERN AFFAIRS)

[1999] S.C.J. No. 24, [1999] 2 S.C.R. 203 (S.C.C.)

McLachlin and **Bastarache JJ.** (**Lamer C.J.C., Cory, Major JJ.**): —

. . . . .

[3] The narrow issue raised in this appeal is whether the exclusion of off-reserve members of an Indian band from the right to vote in band elections pursuant to s. 77(1) of the *Indian Act*, R.S.C., 1985, c. I-5, is inconsistent with s. 15(1) of the *Canadian Charter of Rights and Freedoms*.

. . . . .

[Note from Justice L'Heureux-Dubé's statement of facts:

[30] ... The number of Batchewana Band members has risen dramatically since 1985, and at the same time the percentage of band members living on the reserves has dramatically fallen. In 1985, 71.1 percent of the 543 registered members of the band lived on-reserve. In 1991, only 32.8 percent of the 1,426 registered members lived on the reserves. The parties agree that this trend is continuing. This dramatic increase in the number of off-reserve members occurred largely because of the passage of *An Act to amend the Indian Act*, S.C. 1985, c. 27 ("Bill C-31"), by Parliament. This legislation restored Indian status to most of those who had lost this status because of the operation of certain sections of the *Indian Act*, as well as to the descendants of such people. Prior to this legislation, women with Indian status who married non-Indian men lost their status, and their children did not get status, though men who married non-Indian women, and their children, maintained Indian status. Registered Indians who voluntarily "enfranchised" also lost Indian status. For the Batchewana Band, approximately 85 percent of the growth in band membership consisted of people who were reinstated to Indian status and band membership because of Bill C-31. Similar trends may be seen in many other bands.]

[6] We agree with L'Heureux-Dubé J. that Aboriginality-residence (off-reserve band member status) constitutes a ground of discrimination analogous to the enumerated grounds.

. . . . .

[14] L'Heureux-Dubé J. ultimately concludes that "Aboriginality-residence" as it pertains to whether an Aboriginal band member lives on or off the reserve is an analogous ground. We agree. L'Heureux-Dubé J.'s discussion makes clear that the distinction goes to a personal characteristic essential to a band member's personal identity, which is no less constructively immutable than religion or citizenship. Off-reserve Aboriginal band members can change their status to on-reserve band members only at great cost, if at all.

[15] Two brief comments on this new analogous ground are warranted. First, reserve status should not be confused with residence. The ordinary "residence" decisions faced by the average Canadians should not be confused with the profound decisions Aboriginal band members make to live on or off their reserves, assuming choice is possible. The reality of their situation is unique and complex. ... Second, we note that the analogous ground of off-reserve status or Aboriginality-residence is limited to a subset of the Canadian population, while s. 15 is directed to everyone. In our view, this is no impediment to its inclusion as an analogous ground under s. 15. Its demographic limitation is no different, for example, from pregnancy, which is a distinct, but fundamentally interrelated form of discrimination from gender. "Embedded" analogous grounds may be necessary to permit meaningful consideration of intra-group discrimination.

[16] Having concluded that the distinction made by the impugned law is made on an analogous ground, we come to the final step of the s. 15(1) analysis: whether the distinction at issue in this case in fact constitutes discrimination. In plain words, does the distinction undermine the presumption upon which the guarantee of equality is based — that each individual is deemed to be of equal worth regardless of the group to which he or she belongs?

[17] Applying the applicable *Law* factors to this case — pre-existing disadvantage, correspondence and importance of the affected interest — we conclude that the answer to this question is yes. The impugned distinction perpetuates the historic disadvantage experienced by off-reserve band members by denying them the right to vote and participate in their band's governance. Off-reserve band members have important interests in band governance which the distinction denies. They are co-owners of the band's assets. The reserve, whether they live on or off it, is their and their children's land. The band council represents them as band members to the community at large, in negotiations with the government, and within Aboriginal organizations. Although there are some matters of purely local interest, which do not as directly affect the interests of off-reserve band members, the complete denial to off-reserve members of the right to vote and participate in band governance treats them as less worthy and entitled, not on the merits of their situation, but simply because they live off-reserve. The importance of the interest affected is underlined by the findings of the Royal Commission on Aboriginal Peoples, *Report of the Royal Commission on Aboriginal Peoples* (1996), vol. 1, *Looking Forward, Looking Back*, at pp. 137-91. The Royal Commission writes in vol. 4, *Perspectives and Realities*, at p. 521:

> Throughout the Commission's hearings, Aboriginal people stressed the fundamental importance of retaining and enhancing their cultural identity while living in urban areas. Aboriginal identity lies at the heart of Aboriginal peoples' existence; maintaining that identity is an essential and self-validating pursuit for Aboriginal people in cities.

And at p. 525:

> Cultural identity for urban Aboriginal people is also tied to a land base or ancestral territory. For many, the two concepts are inseparable. ... Identification with an ancestral place is important to urban people because of the associated ritual, ceremony and traditions, as well as the people who remain there, the sense of belonging, the bond to an ancestral community, and the accessibility of family, community and elders.

[18] Taking all this into account, it is clear that the s. 77(1) disenfranchisement is discriminatory. It denies off-reserve band members the right to participate fully in band governance on the arbitrary basis of a personal characteristic. It reaches the cultural identity of off-reserve Aboriginals in a stereotypical way. It presumes that Aboriginals living off-reserve are not interested in maintaining meaningful participation in the band or in preserving their cultural identity, and are therefore less deserving members of the band. The effect is clear, as is the message: off-reserve band members are not as deserving as those band members who live on reserves. This engages the dignity aspect of the s. 15 analysis and results in the denial of substantive equality.

[19] The conclusion that discrimination exists at the third stage of the *Law* test does not depend on the composition of the off-reserve band members group, its relative homogeneity or the particular historical discrimination it may have suffered. It is the present situation of the group relative to that of the comparator group, on-reserve band members, that is relevant. All parties have accepted that the off-reserve group comprises persons who have chosen to live off-reserve freely, persons who have been forced to leave the reserve reluctantly because of economic and social considerations, persons who have at some point been expelled then restored to band membership through Bill C-31 (*An Act to amend the Indian Act*, S.C. 1985, c. 27), and descendants of these people. It is accepted that off-reserve band members are the object of discrimination and constitute an underprivileged group. It is also accepted that many off-reserve band members were expelled from the reserves because of policies and legal provisions which were changed by Bill C-31 and can be said to have suffered double discrimination. But Aboriginals living on reserves are subject to the same discrimination. Some were affected by Bill C-31. Some left the reserve and returned. The relevant social facts in this case are those that relate to off-reserve band members as opposed to on-reserve band members. Even if all band members living off-reserve had voluntarily chosen this way of life and were not subject to discrimination in the broader Canadian society, they would still have the same cause of action. They would still suffer a detriment by being denied full participation in the affairs of the bands to which they would continue to belong while the band councils are able to affect their interests, in particular by making decisions with respect to the surrender of lands, the allocation of land to band members, the raising of funds and making of expenditures for the benefit of all band members. The effect of the legislation is to force band members to choose between living on the reserve and exercising their

political rights, or living off-reserve and renouncing the exercise of their political rights. The political rights in question are related to the race of the individuals affected, and to their cultural identity. As mentioned earlier, the differential treatment resulting from the legislation is discriminatory because it implies that off-reserve band members are lesser members of their bands or persons who have chosen to be assimilated by the mainstream society.

. . . . .

[21] Having found that s. 77(1) is discriminatory, we must address the s. 1 argument of the appellants. ... We are satisfied that the restriction on voting is rationally connected to the aim of the legislation, which is to give a voice in the affairs of the reserve only to the persons most directly affected by the decisions of the band council. It is admitted that although all band members are subject to some decisions of the band council, most decisions would only impact on members living on the reserve. The restriction of s. 15 rights is however not justified under the second branch of the s. 1 test; it has not been demonstrated that s. 77(1) of the *Indian Act* impairs the s. 15 rights minimally. Even if it is accepted that some distinction may be justified in order to protect legitimate interests of band members living on the reserve, it has not been demonstrated that a complete denial of the right of band members living off-reserve to participate in the affairs of the band through the democratic process of elections is necessary. Some parties and interveners have mentioned the possibility of a two-tiered council, of reserved seats for off-reserve members of the band, of double-majority votes on some issues. The appellants argue that there are important difficulties and costs involved in maintaining an electoral list of off-reserve band members and in setting up a system of governance balancing the rights of on-reserve and off-reserve band members. But they present no evidence of efforts deployed or schemes considered and costed, and no argument or authority in support of the conclusion that costs and administrative convenience could justify a complete denial of the constitutional right. Under these circumstances, we must conclude that the violation has not been shown to be demonstrably justified.

[22] With regard to remedy, the Court of Appeal was of the view that it would be preferable to grant the Batchewana Band a permanent constitutional exemption rather than to declare s. 77(1) of the *Indian Act* to be unconstitutional and without effect generally. With respect, we must disagree. The remedy of constitutional exemption has been recognized in a very limited way in this Court, to protect the interests of a party who has succeeded in having a legislative provision declared unconstitutional, where the declaration of invalidity has been suspended. ... We do not think this is a case where a possible expansion of the constitutional exemption remedy should be considered. There is no evidence of special circumstances upon which this possibility might

be raised. The evidence before the Court is that there are off-reserve members of most if not all Indian bands in Canada that are affected by s. 77(1) of the *Indian Act*, and no evidence of other rights that may be relevant in examining the effect of s. 77(1) with regard to any band other than the Batchewana Band. If another band could establish an Aboriginal right to restrict voting, as suggested by the Court of Appeal, that right would simply have precedence over the terms of the *Indian Act*; this is not a reason to restrict the declaration of invalidity to the Batchewana Band.

[23] Where there is inconsistency between the *Charter* and a legislative provision, s. 52 of the *Constitution Act, 1982* provides that the provision shall be rendered void to the extent of the inconsistency. We would declare the words "and is ordinarily resident on the reserve" in s. 77(1) of the *Indian Act* to be inconsistent with s. 15(1) but suspend the implementation of this declaration for 18 months. We would not grant a constitutional exemption to the Batchewana Band during the period of suspension, as would normally be done according to the rule in *Schachter*. The reason for this is that in the particular circumstances of this case, it would appear to be preferable to develop an electoral process that will balance the rights of off-reserve and on-reserve band members. We have not overlooked the possibility that legislative inaction may create new problems. Such claims will fall to be dealt with on their merits should they arise.

[24] We would therefore dismiss the appeal and modify the remedy by striking out the words "and is ordinarily resident on the reserve" in s. 77(1) of the *Indian Act* and suspending the implementation of the declaration of invalidity for 18 months, with costs to the respondents. We would answer the restated constitutional questions as follows:

1. Do the words "and is ordinarily resident on the reserve" contained in s. 77(1) of the *Indian Act*, R.S.C., 1985, c. I-5, contravene s. 15(1) of the *Canadian Charter of Rights and Freedoms*, either generally or with respect only to members of the Batchewana Indian Band?
   Yes, in their general application.
2. If the answer to question 1 is in the affirmative, is s. 77(1) of the *Indian Act* demonstrably justified as a reasonable limit pursuant to s. 1 of the *Canadian Charter of Rights and Freedoms*?
   No.

L'Heureux-Dubé, Gonthier, Iacobucci and **Binnie JJ.** (concurring in the result).

---

1. Did the Supreme Court inappropriately "duck" the issue of sexual inequality that structured the factual background of the *Corbiere* case? Remember, Justice L'Heureux-Dubé's factual recitation noted that 85 per cent of the growth in band membership in these communities consisted of people who were reinstated to Indian status and band membership because of Bill C-31 (a majority of

those reinstated would have been women). Why didn't this issue figure more prominently in the Court's reasons?

2. The *Indian Act* voting regulations were amended to comply with the *Corbiere* case on October 20, 2000. These regulations apply to votes held on or after November 20, 2000. The *Indian Band Election Regulations and the Indian Referendum Regulations* were published in the *Canada Gazette*, Part II in October of 2000. As a result of these amendments, the following deadlines apply to Indian band elections held on or after January 8, 2001:

- voters must register at least 79 days prior to the election date;
- the voters list must be provided to the Electoral Officer 79 days before the election;
- mail-in ballots will be sent to registered off-reserve voters 35 days before election day;
- the nomination meeting for Chief and Council will be held 42 days before election day; and
- a notice of the nomination meeting will be posted on the reserve and mailed to electors residing off reserve at least 30 days before the nomination meeting.

Do you think these provisions help overcome the legacy of sex discrimination under the *Indian Act*?

3. More than 300 First Nations hold elections according to custom election codes, following the traditions of the individual First Nation community. Many of these custom election codes allow off-reserve members to vote in band elections and on certain key decisions involving lands and money. Although the *Corbiere* decision does not specifically address bands holding elections under custom processes, custom bands have been analyzing their procedures in light of the *Corbiere* decision.

E. ABORIGINAL WOMEN'S ORGANIZATIONS

Aboriginal women formed political organizations to cope with the discrimination that they continued to encounter, and worked for social and legislative reform. These organizations have been influential in affecting the debate and changing law and policy concerning Aboriginal women. While these interventions have sometimes been fractious for Aboriginal communities, at the same time they have served to deepen the level of understanding on the issues in question. The development of the contemporary political and legal landscape regarding Aboriginal peoples cannot be fully understood without taking account of these forces. The following commentary and case describe the role of Aboriginal women's organizations in Canada.

REPORT OF THE ROYAL COMMISSION ON ABORIGINAL PEOPLES: PERSPECTIVES AND REALITIES, VOL. 4

(Ottawa: Ministry of Supply and Services, 1996) at 68-71
(references omitted)

THE RISE OF ABORIGINAL WOMEN'S ORGANIZATIONS

During the period 1951-1970, Aboriginal people became more aware of their legal rights and as a result organized to address their concerns. Aboriginal women's organizations came into being and took on a range of issues, including the development of women in leadership roles and the resolution of health and social problems in their communities. This was a far cry from the first organizations started in 1937 by the Indian affairs department with the stated goal of assisting Indian women "to acquire sound and approved practices for greater home efficiency".

First instituted and promoted by the department during the Depression, Indian homemakers' associations formed on reserves across Canada between 1930 and 1960. In the 1960s, most of these groups underwent a transformation from clubs focusing on home economics to clubs involved in public affairs, tackling issues such as housing standards, living conditions, Aboriginal rights and women's rights. The Indian Homemakers' Association of British Columbia was formed in 1965 to amalgamate clubs throughout the province. Incorporated in 1969, it has the distinction of being the country's oldest provincial Aboriginal women's organization in operation today. Other associations, chapters and locals regrouping Aboriginal women were established across Canada, on reserves, in rural communities and in urban centres.

The idea of a national body to represent Aboriginal women emerged at a 1970 international conference of Aboriginal women in Albuquerque, New Mexico, and in March 1971 the first National Native Women's Conference was held in Canada. In August 1974, the Native Women's Association of Canada (NWAC) convened its first annual assembly in Thunder Bay, Ontario. Until the early 1980s, NWAC spoke on behalf of First Nations, Inuit and Métis women.

In 1984, because of major differences in language, culture, and circumstances, Inuit women felt a need to create their own organization — Pauktuutit. Its mandate is to foster a greater awareness of the needs of Inuit women and to encourage their participation in community, regional and national concerns in relation to social, cultural and economic development.

In 1992, the Métis National Council of Women was incorporated as a federation of six independent provincial and territorial Métis women's organizations: British Columbia, Alberta, Northwest Territories, Saskatchewan, Manitoba and Ontario.

Although stated differently, the goals and objectives of each Aboriginal women's organization are similar: improving the quality of life for Aboriginal women and their children by achieving equal participation in the social, economic, cultural and political life not only of their communities but of Canadian society as a whole.

Throughout the 1970s and '80s, the discriminatory provisions in the *Indian Act* were a central focus of concern. Women such as Yvonne Bedard, Jeannette Corbiere-Lavell, Mary Two Axe Early and Sandra Lovelace instituted legal proceedings challenging the loss of Indian status and rights. Aboriginal women wanted to see major changes in their lives and communities, and they were determined to take action locally, regionally, nationally and internationally.

> In 1981, Sandra Lovelace took her case to the United Nations Human Rights Committee. It held that Canada was in contravention of article 27 of the *International Covenant on Civil and Political Rights*. The committee ruled that the cultural rights guaranteed by article 27 of the Covenant were denied because she was forced to be separate from her community. Only after this decision did the Canadian government try to correct the situation, finally enacting Bill C-31 in 1985. ... This could not have happened if it were not for the Aboriginal women speaking out. ...
>
> Kathy Martin, The Pas, Manitoba 20 May 1992

Although the discriminatory provisions of the *Indian Act* were important, a wide range of other concerns captured the attention of Aboriginal women's organizations. They were also placing increased emphasis on their participation in the decision-making processes of other national Aboriginal organizations.

Discussions on the patriation of the constitution had been occurring for a number of years, but it was not until 1981 that representatives of three national Aboriginal groups — the Assembly of First Nations (AFN), the Inuit Committee on National Issues (ICNI, predecessor of Inuit Tapirisat), and the Native Council of Canada (NCC) — became more involved. A first ministers conference, convened in November 1981, produced a political accord on constitutional reform supported by the federal government and nine provinces. This accord had one glaring omission: Aboriginal rights. The Aboriginal Rights Coalition, led by NCC, ICNI, NWAC, the Dene Nation, the Council for Yukon Indians, the Nisga'a Tribal Council and the National Association of Friendship Centres, initiated a series of public protests. With the support of Canadian women concerned about sexual equality and a support network of Canadian church organizations through Project North, they were able to have Aboriginal and treaty rights — albeit qualified as 'existing' Aboriginal and treaty rights — recognized in section 35(1) of the *Constitution Act, 1982*.

During the first ministers conferences held between 1983 and 1987, NWAC continued to be involved in meetings of AFN's constitutional working group and the Native Council of Canada's constitutional process. During the 1983 first ministers conference, NWAC was instrumental in gaining a further amendment to section 35 of the Act: "Notwithstanding any other provision of this Act, the aboriginal and treaty rights referred to in subsection (1) are guaranteed equally to male and female persons."

NWAC was not a formal participant in these conferences, however. It did not have its own seat at the table, nor was it given equitable funding. During the constitutional talks in 1992, NWAC launched a court case to gain equal participation and funding. In March 1992, the Native Women's Association of Canada put forward legal arguments that the Charter rights of Aboriginal women had been infringed by the Government of Canada. The case that discussed the involvement of Aboriginal women in constitutional reform was *Native Women's Assn. of Canada v. Canada*, [1994] S.C.J. No. 93, [1994] 3 S.C.R. 627 (S.C.C.). In this case, NWAC argued that Aboriginal women's rights to free expression and equality under sections 2(b), 28 and 15(1) of the Charter were denied when money for participation in the conferences was not extended to it, but given to other Aboriginal organizations that NWAC alleged were male-dominated. NWAC also argued that the failure to extend funding for its participation violated section 35(4) of the *Constitution Act, 1982*, which extends Aboriginal and treaty rights equally to male and female persons.

In ruling against NWAC's sections 2(b) and 28 claims, the Supreme Court wrote:

> The freedom of expression guaranteed by s. 2(b) of the *Charter* does not guarantee any particular means of expression or place a positive obligation upon the Government to consult anyone. The right to a particular platform or means of expression was clearly rejected by this Court in *Haig*. The respondents had many opportunities to express their views through the four Aboriginal groups as well as directly to the Government ...

> Even assuming that in certain extreme circumstances, the provision of a platform of expression to one group may infringe the expression of another and thereby require the Government to provide an equal opportunity for the expression of that group, there was no evidence in this case to suggest that the funding or consultation of the four Aboriginal groups infringed the respondents' equal right of freedom of expression. The four Aboriginal groups invited to discuss possible constitutional amendments are all *bona fide* national representatives of Aboriginal people in Canada and, based on the facts in this case, there was no requirement under s. 2(b) of the *Charter* to also extend an invitation and funding directly to the respondents.

In ruling against NWAC's section 15(1) equality claims, the Supreme Court similarly concluded that there was no evidence that the federal government discriminated against the group. It wrote (at paras. 73-74 and 78):

> ... The lack of an evidentiary basis for the arguments with respect to ss. 2(b) and 28 is equally applicable to any arguments advanced under s. 15(1) of the *Charter* in this case.

Finally, the Supreme Court also dismissed NWAC's argument that Aboriginal people have an Aboriginal or treaty right to participate in constitutional discussions. As Sopinka J. wrote for the majority (at para 79):

> I also agree with the conclusions of the Court of Appeal with respect to the inapplicability of s. 35 of the *Constitution Act, 1982* to the present case. The right of the Aboriginal people of Canada to participate in constitutional discussions does not derive from any existing Aboriginal or treaty right protected under s. 35. Therefore, s. 35(4) of the *Constitution Act, 1982*, which guarantees Aboriginal and treaty rights referred to in s. 35(1) equally to male and female persons, is of no assistance to the respondents.

Despite NWAC's failure to compel government funding in the above case, NWAC has remained very active in Canadian social, political and legal circles. Recent initiatives include work related to the environment, health, human rights, international affairs, training and employment, violence against Aboriginal women (in particular its important work with the Sisters in Spirit campaign) and empowering and support Aboriginal youth. For further information, see the NWAC website: <http://www.nwac.ca/home>.

F.   CONCLUSION

This rise and struggle of Aboriginal women's organizations have left their mark on the legal and political community. They have raised important questions that both challenge and clarify critical issues in discussions about self-government. It is clear from their message that Aboriginal women will not accept discrimination in their communities. While this chapter has demonstrated the continued discrimination Aboriginal women encounter in society, it has also reviewed the significant steps that have been taken to counter this challenge. This examination has shown that, in the past 25 years, Aboriginal women have not been passive objects of colonial policy but have been active subjects, influencing and creating the contours of law and policy dealing with Aboriginal rights. Many strong and courageous women have made a difference through their efforts. People like Mary-Two Axe Early, Jeanette Corbière, Yvonne Bédard, Sandra Lovelace, and others, have been influential in changing Canada's law concerning Aboriginal people. As a result, many have begun to rectify the injustice perpetrated by the *Indian Act* and have strengthened their identity, have reunited with their communities, and have had their status reinstated. At the same time, other Aboriginal women continue to experience the double discrimination of racism and sexism. Cases like *Derrickson*, *Sawridge* and *Corbiere* illustrate such issues that still require resolution. The imposition of the *Indian Act* has been destructive. The role of Aboriginal women in nation building and their expressions of justice cannot be ignored. These visions must guide the development of law in Canada for Aboriginal Nations to become healthy, vibrant and strong.

ENDNOTES

1. See Shannon Brennan, "Violent victimization of Aboriginal women in the Canadian provinces, 2009" Juristat (Ottawa: Statistics Canada), May 17, 2011 at 5, online: <http://www.statcan.gc.ca/pub/85-002-x/2011001/article/11439-eng.pdf>.

2. Statistics Canada, October 28, 2009, online: <http://www.statcan.gc.ca/pub/81-004-x/2009004/article/11017-eng.htm>:

3. A.C. Hamilton and C.M. Sinclair, *The Justice System and Aboriginal People: Report of the Aboriginal Justice Inquiry of Manitoba*, Vol. 1 (Winnipeg: Queen's Printer, 1991) at 487.

4. Publication No. 41-1-S2-E, Legislative Summary of Bill S-2: Family Homes on Reserves and Matrimonial Interests or Rights Act, Marlisa Tiedemann, Social Affairs Division, Parliamentary Information and Research Service, Library of Parliament, October 17, 2011 *Revised 24 January 2012*, see online: <http://www.parl.gc.ca/Content/LOP/LegislativeSummaries/41/1/s2-e.pdf>.

5. *Ibid.*

6. *Ibid.*

7. *Ibid.*

8. Letter of May 18, 2010, online: <http://www.nwac.ca/sites/default/files/imce/SharonMay182010MPletterfinal%20%282%29.pdf>.

9. Address of April 13, 2011, President of the Native Women's Association of Canada to the Standing Committee on Aboriginal Affairs, online: <http://www.nwac.ca/fr/node/575>.

10. "Self-Government and Aboriginal Women", in E. Dua and A. Robertson, eds., *Scratching the Surface: Canadian Anti-Racist Feminist Thought* (Toronto: Women's Press, 1999) at 167.

CHAPTER 10

CHILD WELFARE

A.   INTRODUCTION

Children hold a special place in all communities around the world, and Aboriginal communities are no exception. There is a teaching in many Aboriginal communities that stresses today's decisions have to include the needs of the seventh generation of their children. This orientation demonstrates the importance attached to the intergenerational transmission of love, material resources, and cultural values. For many centuries, Aboriginal peoples lived by laws and customs that respected these teachings and promoted such values. Unfortunately, there has been a severe disruption of these laws that has had a devastating effect on child rearing practices. Aboriginal people have encountered numerous difficulties with Canada's treatment of their children. Residential schools, child welfare agencies, institutions of criminal justice, and the courts have all played a damaging role in this calamity. The reasons for this tragedy are numerous, and Canadian law has been among one of its causes. This chapter examines the law relative to Aboriginal child welfare and explores the relationship between government policies of assimilation and the faltering of Aboriginal child-family relationships. It also considers contemporary issues of reform and raises some of the challenges Aboriginal people face in asserting greater responsibility for their children.

REPORT OF THE ROYAL COMMISSION ON ABORIGINAL PEOPLES: GATHERING STRENGTH, VOL. 3

(Ottawa: Ministry of Supply and Services, 1996) at 23 (references omitted)

Today we are in a time of healing for our children, our families, our communities and Mother Earth.

Judy Gingell Teslin, Yukon 27 May 1992

We believe our children are our future, the leadership of tomorrow. If you believe in that, then you have to believe also that you must equip your future with the best possible tools to lead your community and lead your nation into the twenty-first century.

Grand Chief Joe Miskokomon Union of Ontario Indians Toronto, Ontario, 26 June 1992

The Special Place of Children in Aboriginal Cultures

Children hold a special place in Aboriginal cultures. According to tradition, they are gifts from the spirit world and have to be treated very gently lest they become disillusioned with this world and return to a more congenial place. They must be protected from harm because there are spirits that would wish to entice them back to that other realm. They bring a purity of vision to the world that can teach their elders. They carry within them the gifts that manifest themselves as they become teachers, mothers, hunters, counsellors, artisans and visionaries. They renew the strength of the family, clan and village and make the elders young again with their joyful presence.

Failure to care for these gifts bestowed on the family, and to protect children from the betrayal of others, is perhaps the greatest shame that can befall an Aboriginal family. It is a shame that countless Aboriginal families have experienced, some of them repeatedly over generations. Here we examine the genesis of that shame, the efforts to erase it, and the role of [law and] public policy in restoring the trust of children, parents and grandparents in their future.

B. HISTORICAL TREATMENT

"CHILD WELFARE"

In A.C. Hamilton and C.M. Sinclair, *The Justice System and Aboriginal People: Report of the Aboriginal Justice Inquiry in Manitoba*, Vol. 1 (Winnipeg: Queen's Printer, 1991) at 509-15 (references omitted)

... The intrusion by child welfare authorities in the past has been paternalistic and colonial in nature, condescending and demeaning in fact, and often insensitive and brutal to Aboriginal people. Aboriginal children have been taken from their families, communities and societies, first by the residential school system and later by the child welfare system. Both systems have left Aboriginal people and their societies severely damaged. If Aboriginal people are correct, and we believe they are, part of the reason for the high numbers of Aboriginal people in correctional facilities is the fact that Aboriginal people still do not fully control their own lives and destinies, or the lives of their own children. Aboriginal people must have more control over the ways in which their children are raised, taught and protected.

Failing this, we are convinced we will see more, not fewer, Aboriginal people in our correctional facilities in the future. We will see more young Aboriginal people falling into a pattern that is becoming all too familiar. It takes them from institution to institution, from foster home to young offender facility and, finally, on to adult jails. As Oscar Lathlin, the then chief of The Pas Band, asked our Inquiry, "Is the current system conditioning our young for lives in institutions and not in society?"

The implications of these patterns are most obvious to people in Aboriginal communities. People there worry because they know their young people make up a significant proportion of their populations today. The numbers of young people in these communities are increasing at a rate far higher than that of the general population. Aboriginal people worry about the future survival of their languages, cultures and societies if yet another generation is swept into institutions and away from their communities.

It is for these and many other reasons that we have made a careful examination of the child welfare system. We felt it necessary because:

- We feel many of the problems Aboriginal people face with the criminal justice system today have roots in the history of government-Aboriginal relations. No analysis of the justice system can be complete without understanding the devastating effect these relations, guided by government policies, have had on Aboriginal Families. For many Aboriginal societies, existing child welfare practices have ranked as a major destructive force to their Families, communities and cultures.

- Some people have suggested that the child welfare and criminal justice systems are distinct and should function completely independently of each other. We do not agree. We believe many of the reasons why the numbers of Aboriginal people are so disproportionately high in the child welfare system are the same as the reasons why they are so over-represented in the criminal justice system. "Clients" of one system frequently become "clients" of the other system. It would be impossible to present a complete picture of the criminal justice system, and the youth justice system, without also analyzing the field of child and family services.

- The reforms we advocate, particularly in the youth justice area, involve the breaking down of artificial barriers between the criminal justice and child welfare systems. These systems, we believe, must work much more closely together. The needs and problems of Aboriginal families and communities are intertwined, and we feel we cannot separate them completely or relegate them to one system or the other.

- The available evidence indicates that the apprehension of Aboriginal children by the child welfare system tends to set a pattern of multiple foster home placements. The evidence also indicates this pattern often leads the children into young offender institutions and, ultimately, to "graduate" to the adult correctional system. Aboriginal families, communities and their leaders are rightly concerned about these patterns, and about their effects on the future of their children's lives and of their communities.

- There has been some remarkable progress in the child welfare system as Aboriginal people have assumed more control over the lives and well being of their children in their communities. The criminal justice system must move in a similar direction if it hopes to achieve similar success.

- The numbers of Aboriginal children will continue to increase at a rate exceeding that of the general population. Therefore, there is every indication that child and family services will play an increasingly important role in Aboriginal communities in the future.
- Finally, we believe it is essential to review the child welfare system in urban centres, particularly in Winnipeg, where there continue to be significant problems for Aboriginal persons requiring services. We will identify some of these problems and offer suggestions to make this system more effective.

Child Welfare and Education: An Historical Overview of Government-Aboriginal Relations

For some time, governments have undertaken to serve neglected children by taking them into their care or by helping the families of these children through what we now call child welfare services. Services may include family counselling, substance abuse counselling, assistance to an unmarried parent, or taking the child away from a disrupted home or family and placing the child in a foster home, a group home or with a new family, through adoption. In Canada, each province is responsible for developing and maintaining its own child welfare system. Each province gets financial help from the federal government under the Canada Assistance Plan, which pays approximately half the costs of these programs.

At first glance, this system appears to be one most people would support and encourage. It is certainly a far cry from the way Western or European societies have treated children in the past. Historically, the phrase "a man's home is his castle" meant just that. Society took a very dim view of interfering with the manner in which the head of a household treated his children. In ancient Rome, a father had "complete authority over his children, including the legal authority to sell them into slavery or even put them to death." Over time, a father's power over his children was tempered to a limited right of "reasonable chastisement," although this continued to mean a father could beat his children and even sell them into apprenticeship. Eventually, there were laws that forbade parents from killing or maiming their children or failing to provide them with the necessities of life. Nevertheless, children were still subject to abuse and forced labour in mines and factories.

Society's attitudes toward children began to change when social reformers became increasingly concerned at the plight of the working poor and, in particular, with the way children were treated. In the latter part of the 1800s, they pressured governments to pass laws to make the lives of children better. Private children's aid societies formed with the intent of caring for abused, abandoned or neglected children. Governments passed child labour laws and provided for public school systems. For the first time, governments adopted a policy allowing for the intervention by child care workers to protect the life of a child in extreme situations. These laws and policies make up the foundation of the modern child welfare system.

Most of these developments, however, passed by unnoticed in Aboriginal communities and reserves. The history of child welfare in these communities developed separately and much differently from the way it did in the rest of society.

Special Treatment for Aboriginal Children: The Residential School System

Since the time of earliest contact, Aboriginal people and European settlers have seen things from vastly divergent points of view, because their attitudes and philosophies differed. The interaction of the two groups has been characterized as one of "cooperation and conflict but, more importantly, by misconceptions and contradictions." One of the first, and perhaps the most enduring, of these misconceptions was that:

> Europeans assumed the superiority of their culture over that of any Aboriginal peoples. Out of that misconception grew the European conviction that in order for the Indians to survive, they would have to be assimilated into the European social order. ...

This was an impossible task as long as Aboriginal people continued to live in vibrant, self-sufficient communities often far removed from the missionaries' influence. However, this did not prevent the missionaries from forming opinions about the ways Aboriginal people raised and taught their children, or from laying the foundation for future misconceptions of Aboriginal child-rearing methods.

> In view of the current ideal about child-rearing, it is interesting to reflect that no aspect of behavior shocked the French more than their refusal to use physical punishment to discipline their children. On general principles, the Huron considered it wrong to coerce or humiliate an individual publicly. To their own way of thinking, a child was an individual with his or her own needs and rights rather than something amorphous that must be molded into shape. The Huron feared a child who was unduly humiliated, like an adult, might he driven to commit suicide.

Aboriginal parents taught their children

> ... to assume adult roles in an atmosphere of warmth and affection. Learning emphasized such values as respect for all living things, sharing, self-reliance, individual responsibility and proper conduct. Children also had to learn how to utilize the environment most effectively for economic survival. Integral to all aspects of the education of the young was the spiritual, and events in the life cycle from birth to death were marked with ceremonies stressing the individual's link to the spiritual and sacred. Cultural continuity was thus ensured.

The early missionaries also condemned Aboriginal child-rearing methods as being negligent, irresponsible and "uncivilized." This stereotype was to endure even after Aboriginal people had lost much of their independence and "in the point of view of the European, the Indian became irrelevant." From then on, the relationship between Aboriginal people and Europeans became even more one-sided and paternalistic. Aboriginal people were reduced to being "wards of the state". All relevant decision-making power on financial, social or political matters, and even education, came to rest in the hands of the federal government. Eventually, the cause of "civilizing" Aboriginal people to European cultures and values evolved into the government policy of "assimilation," and education became "the primary vehicle in the civilization and advancement of the Indian race."

The federal government had little previous experience in "civilizing" Aboriginal people so it turned to the United States for an example. It sent Nicholas F. Davin to study the Americans' "aggressive civilization policy," based on sending Indian children to large, racially segregated, industrial schools. Davin was convinced the Americans were correct in their approach and the only way to "civilize" Aboriginal people was to remove them from the disruptive influences of the parents and the community. His final comment in the report to Ottawa was representative of attitudes of the time that "... if anything is to be done with the Indian, we must catch him very young." The federal government delegated the job of "civilizing" and "educating" Aboriginal people in Canada to religious organizations and churches. It encouraged the opening of large, industrial residential schools far from reserves and, later, of boarding schools for younger children nearer to their homes. There, every aspect of European life, from dress and behaviour to religion and language, was impressed upon the Aboriginal children. The belief was that Indians were a vanishing race and their only hope of surviving was to assimilate. Their uncivilized and pagan ways would be replaced by good Christian values.

The residential school system was a conscious, deliberate and often brutal attempt to force Aboriginal people to assimilate into mainstream society, mostly by forcing the children away from their languages, cultures and societies. In 1920, during debates in the House of Commons on planned changes to the *Indian Act*, Duncan Campbell Scott, the Deputy Superintendent of Indian Affairs, left no doubt about the federal government's aims:

> Our object is to continue until there is not a single Indian in Canada that has not been absorbed into the body politic and there is no Indian question, and no Indian department, that is the whole object of this Bill.

The experience of residential schools is one shared by many Aboriginal people all across Canada. That experience was marked by emotional, physical and sexual abuse, social and spiritual deprivation, and substandard education. "Even as assimilation was stated as the goal of education for Native people," one researcher wrote, "the assimilation was to take place under conditions which would cause no threat to the surrounding business and farming community." Few Aboriginal people achieved more than a grade five level of education.

The main goal of residential schools and the assimilation policy, however, was not further education, but, rather, to remove Aboriginal children from the influences of their parents and communities, and to rid them of their languages and cultures. The methods, as one former residential school student explained, often were brutally effective:

The elimination of language has always been a primary stage in a process of cultural genocide. This was the primary function of the residential school. My father, who attended Alberni Indian Residential School for four year[s] in the twenties, was physically tortured by his teachers for speaking Tseshaht: they pushed sewing needles through his tongue, a routine punishment for language offenders ... The needle torture, suffered by my father affected all my family (I have six brothers and six sisters). My Dad's attitude became "why teach my children Indian if they are going to be punished for speaking it"? So he would not allow my mother to speak Indian to us in his presence. I never learned how to speak my own language. I am now, therefore, truly a 'dumb Indian'.

After the Second World War, the federal government began to reconsider its assimilation policy. It wanted a more effective means of accomplishing the ultimate aims of the policy. This coincided with yet another revamping of the *Indian Act* and another set of hearings at the House of Commons. This also allowed another famous Canadian, noted anthropologist Diamond Jenness, to unveil his "Plan for Liquidating Canada's Indian Problems Within 25 Years." Jenness proposed abolishing Indian reserves, scrapping the treaties and integrating Indian students into the public school system. For the time being, the federal government shelved most of Jenness' proposals. It did, however, heed his suggestion to change the *Indian Act* to allow Indian children to be enrolled in public schools. This event signaled "the beginning of the end for many residential schools."

The effects upon Aboriginal societies of the federal government's residential school system, and its policy of assimilation, have been astounding. Residential schools denigrated Aboriginal cultures, customs and religions, and disrupted the traditional practices of Aboriginal child-rearing and education. They tore apart families and extended families, leaving the children straddling two worlds, the European one and that of their own Aboriginal societies, but belonging to neither. These policies have caused a wound to fester in Aboriginal communities that has left them diminished to this day. In testimony to our Inquiry, Janet Ross said:

I'd like to begin at the boarding school. The boarding school is where the alienation began. Children were placed there, plucked out of their homes. The bonds between parents and children were fragmented severely — some lost forever. Some searched for the love between parent and child endlessly, searching for it in other ways, never to be restored. The boarding schools taught us violence. Violence was emphasized through physical, corporal punishment, strappings, beatings, bruising and control. We learned to understand that this was power and control.

I remember being very confused when someone told me that my natural mother had died. Hence growing up for me not knowing whether my mother was really mine always created some more confusion. I searched for that love in [foster] parents, but that bond had been broken; you felt that it just wasn't there. The boarding schools were extremely influential towards our low self image and low self-esteem, because we were continuously put down by the use of text books portraying negative images of Indian people.

The loss of successive generations of children to residential schools, the destruction of Aboriginal economic bases, the decimation of their populations through diseases and the increasing dependence on government welfare have led to social chaos. This manifests itself in Aboriginal communities through staggering poverty rates, high unemployment rates, high suicide rates, lower education levels, high rates of alcoholism and high rates of crime. In individuals, the legacy of the residential schools has been lowered self-esteem, confusion of self-identity and cultural identity, and a distrust of, and antagonism toward, authority.

The residential school experience also resulted in a breakdown in traditional Aboriginal methods of teaching child-rearing and parenting. Entire families once took part in the raising of children. Young parents, like young parents everywhere, learned how to raise their children from their own parents, by example. Traditionally, they also drew upon the examples and advice of their extended families, their grand-parents uncles, aunts and siblings. The residential schools made this impossible. Without that example, many Aboriginal parents today feel that they have never learned how to raise their own children.

Aboriginal communities have not yet recovered from the damage caused by the residential schools. It is only in recent times that children are again being taught close to home. For the first time in over 100 years, many families are experiencing a generation of children who live with parents until their teens. The readjustment to this new situation has been difficult for both the parents and their children. The current generation of parents does not even have its own experiences as children growing up in a unified family upon which to draw.

The damage done by these schools is still evident today, as Aboriginal people struggle to recapture their cultural practices and beliefs. The return of self-identity and self-esteem is a slow process. Perhaps, if left alone, this social confusion might have corrected itself to some extent, once children returned to their communities. But, as we will see, there was another dramatic intrusion into their lives after the Second World War.

In 2008, Prime Minister Stephen Harper apologized for the Government of Canada's involvement in residential schools, as follows:

GOVERNMENT OF CANADA, RESIDENTIAL SCHOOL APOLOGY

<http://www.pm.gc.ca/eng/media.asp?id=2149>

The treatment of children in Indian Residential Schools is a sad chapter in our history.

For more than a century, Indian Residential Schools separated over 150,000 Aboriginal children from their families and communities. In the 1870's, the federal government, partly in order to meet its obligation to educate Aboriginal children, began to play a role in the development and administration of these schools. Two primary objectives of the Residential Schools system were to remove and isolate children from the influence of their homes, families, traditions and cultures, and to assimilate them into the dominant culture. These objectives were based on the assumption Aboriginal cultures and spiritual beliefs were inferior and unequal. Indeed, some sought, as it was infamously said, "to kill the Indian in the child". Today, we recognize that this policy of assimilation was wrong, has caused great harm, and has no place in our country.

One hundred and thirty-two federally-supported schools were located in every province and territory, except Newfoundland, New Brunswick and Prince Edward Island. Most schools were operated as "joint ventures" with Anglican, Catholic, Presbyterian or United Churches. The Government of Canada built an educational system in which very young children were often forcibly removed from their homes, often taken far from their communities. Many were inadequately fed, clothed and housed. All were deprived of the care and nurturing of their parents, grandparents and communities. First Nations, Inuit and Métis languages and cultural practices were prohibited in these schools. Tragically, some of these children died while attending residential schools and others never returned home.

The government now recognizes that the consequences of the Indian Residential Schools policy were profoundly negative and that this policy has had a lasting and damaging impact on Aboriginal culture, heritage and language. While some former students have spoken positively about their experiences at residential schools, these stories are far overshadowed by tragic accounts of the emotional, physical and sexual abuse and neglect of helpless children, and their separation from powerless families and communities.

The legacy of Indian Residential Schools has contributed to social problems that continue to exist in many communities today.

It has taken extraordinary courage for the thousands of survivors that have come forward to speak publicly about the abuse they suffered. It is a testament to their resilience as individuals and to the strength of their cultures. Regrettably, many former students are not with us today and died never having received a full apology from the Government of Canada.

The government recognizes that the absence of an apology has been an impediment to healing and reconciliation. Therefore, on behalf of the Government of Canada and all Canadians, I stand before you, in this Chamber so central to our life as a country, to apologize to Aboriginal peoples for Canada's role in the Indian Residential Schools system.

To the approximately 80,000 living former students, and all family members and communities, the Government of Canada now recognizes that it was wrong to forcibly remove children from their homes and we apologize for having done this. We now recognize that it was wrong to separate children from rich and vibrant cultures and traditions that it created a void in many lives and communities, and we apologize for having done this. We now recognize that, in separating children from their families, we undermined the ability of many to adequately parent their own children and sowed the seeds for generations to follow, and we apologize for having done this. We now recognize that, far too often, these institutions gave rise to abuse or neglect and were inadequately controlled, and we apologize for failing to protect you. Not only did you suffer these abuses as children, but as you became parents, you were powerless to protect your own children from suffering the same experience, and for this we are sorry.

The burden of this experience has been on your shoulders for far too long. The burden is properly ours as a Government, and as a country. There is no place in Canada for the attitudes that inspired the Indian Residential Schools system to ever prevail again. You have been working on recovering from this experience for a long time and in a very real sense, we are now joining you on this journey. The Government of Canada sincerely apologizes and asks the forgiveness of the Aboriginal peoples of this country for failing them so profoundly.

> Nous le regrettons
> We are sorry
> Nimitataynan
> Niminchinowesamin
> Mamiattugut

In moving towards healing, reconciliation and resolution of the sad legacy of Indian Residential Schools, implementation of the Indian Residential Schools Settlement Agreement began on September 19, 2007. Years of work by survivors, communities, and Aboriginal organizations culminated in an agreement that gives us a new beginning and an opportunity to move forward together in partnership.

A cornerstone of the Settlement Agreement is the Indian Residential Schools Truth and Reconciliation Commission. This Commission presents a unique opportunity to educate all Canadians on the Indian Residential Schools system. It will be a positive step in forging a new relationship between Aboriginal peoples and other Canadians, a relationship based on the knowledge of our shared history, a respect for each other and a desire to move forward together with a renewed understanding that strong families, strong communities and vibrant cultures and traditions will contribute to a stronger Canada for all of us.

The Government of Canada's Apology was only one part of wider process to deal with the after-effects of residential school. In the 1990s, Aboriginal peoples were successful in suing churches and the federal government for abuse suffered in residential school; see, *inter alia*, *M. (F.S.) v. Clarke*, [1999] B.C.J. No. 1973 (B.C.S.C.), *Blackwater v. Plint*, [2005] S.C.J. No. 59, [2005] 3 S.C.R. 3 (S.C.C.), *A. (T.W.N.) v. Clark*, [2003] B.C.J. No. 2747, 2003 BCCA 670 (B.C.C.A.). However, the courts' adversarial process was a significant burden on residential school survivors, who often felt re-victimized by the trial process. At the same time, the churches bore a heavy financial burden when they were found liable for abuse. Thus, a negotiation process was developed to settle outstanding residential school issues under one umbrella.

On May 8, 2006, the Residential School Settlement Agreement was signed: see <http://www.residentialschoolsettlement.ca/IRS%20Settlement%20Agreement-%20ENGLISH.pdf>. The government of Canada finalized the amount of compensation available through this process in 2007, and pegged it at $1.9 billion. The money is available for survivors of residential school through a common experience payment and a special fund for those who experienced sexual and physical abuse. As part of the Settlement Agreement, the government also funded a $20 million Commemoration initiative, for events, projects and memorials related to residential school. The Aboriginal Healing Foundation was also given an additional $125 million as part of this Settlement.

Finally, the settlement promised an Indian Residential Schools Truth and Reconciliation Commission ("IRSTRC") to examine the tragic legacy of the residential schools. The commission was established on June 1, 2008. The IRSTRC's goals are being implemented through community gatherings, research, witness statements, media outreach and other events. The Commission's goal are expressed as follows:

The goals of the Commission shall be to:

(a) Acknowledge Residential School experiences, impacts and consequences;

(b) Provide a holistic, culturally appropriate and safe setting for former students, their families and communities as they come forward to the Commission;

(c) Witness, support, promote and facilitate truth and reconciliation events at both the national and community levels;

(d) Promote awareness and public education of Canadians about the IRS system and its impacts;

(e) Identify sources and create as complete an historical record as possible of the IRS system and legacy. The record shall be preserved and made accessible to the public for future study and use;

(f) Produce and submit to the Parties of the Agreement a report including recommendations to the Government of Canada concerning the IRS system and experience including: the history, purpose, operation and supervision of the IRS system, the effect and consequences of IRS (including systemic harms, intergenerational consequences and the impact on human dignity) and the ongoing legacy of the residential schools;

(g) Support commemoration of former Indian Residential School students and their families in accordance with the Comme-moration Policy Directive.[1]

The Commission is chaired by the Honourable Justice Murray Sinclair (who co-authored the Manitoba Justice Inquiry Report excerpted in this chapter) and commissioners Marie Wilson and Chief Wilton Littlechild.

With an enhanced understanding of residential schools' relationship to contemporary Aboriginal child welfare issues, we return to the Manitoba Justice Inquiry's discussion of the historical background to Aboriginal child welfare law.

"CHILD WELFARE"

In A.C. Hamilton and C.M. Sinclair, *The Justice System and Aboriginal People: Report of the Aboriginal Justice Inquiry in Manitoba*, Vol. 1 (Winnipeg: Queen's Printer, 1991) at 515-20 (references omitted)

The Child Welfare System

The intrusion by state-run child welfare programs into the lives of Aboriginal children and families did not come about until quite recently, despite the devastating effects which colonization had wreaked on their communities and societies for more than a century. The modern child welfare system, for the most part, is a post-Second World War phenomenon.

. . . . .

However, the end of the Second World War brought about a number of new developments. There was a tremendous proliferation of government-operated and funded social services. These services, once concentrated in urban centres, were increasingly extended to more rural and northern communities, including Aboriginal communities.

This was mirrored by a corresponding proliferation in the new field of professional social work. This profession was anxious to carve a niche for itself. More importantly, the profession provided a means by which the standards of the dominant society could be used to judge traditional Aboriginal family and child care practices. At the same time, Aboriginal peoples became much more visible because of increased mobility and, in particular because of their massive migration to urban centres in search of jobs, an education or a better life. This increased the contacts between Aboriginal people and the dominant society, and led to heightened awareness of the dire social and economic conditions in Aboriginal communities.

One of the first alarms about living conditions on reserves was sounded in 1947 by the Canadian Welfare Council and the Canadian Association of Social Workers. These groups presented a brief to a joint parliamentary committee examining possible changes to the federal *Indian Act*. The brief described living conditions as inadequate and the services delivered to Aboriginal communities as incompatible with similar services provided to non-Aboriginal communities.

In considering Indian adoptions and the role of the Indian agent, the brief stated that "the practice of adopting Indian children is loosely conceived and executed and is usually devoid of the careful legal and social protection afforded to white children." As "wards" of the federal government, "Indian children who are neglected lack the protection afforded under social legislation available to white children in the community." The council's submission also condemned the practice of sending Aboriginal children to residential schools.

In the minds of many experts of the day, the solution to these problems was obvious. They felt existing provincial child welfare programs should be extended to include federal Indian reserves, since the child welfare services provided by the Department of Indian Affairs were very limited or nonexistent. However, there were several problems with this apparently obvious solution.

The federal government had exclusive constitutional authority over "Indians and lands reserved for Indians" under s. 91(24) of the *British North America Act of 1867*. The *Indian Act* reinforced this exclusive federal jurisdiction. To complicate matters, at that time the federal government had no cost-sharing agreement with the provinces for social services, including child welfare programs, and it was reluctant to carry the costs of such programs itself.

Provincial governments, which were under pressure to extend their jurisdiction in certain areas such as education, policing and social services, including child welfare, were reluctant to extend their responsibilities without federal funding. In the end, neither level of government was prepared to provide child welfare to Indians living on- or off-reserve. This jurisdictional wrangling left Indians caught in a legal no-man's land, with devastating results for their children.

In 1951 the federal government amended s. 88 of the *Indian Act* to allow "all laws of general application ... in force in any province" to apply as well to Indians both on- and off-reserve. This included child welfare programs. Unfortunately, while the federal government changed the law, it did not provide any additional money to help pay for these new provincial responsibilities. The result was a patchwork of provincial child welfare services to reserves: some agencies in some provinces extended some services to some reserves, some extended none, and some acted to apprehend children only when they considered them to be in a "life or death" situation.

During the 1960s, public and political attention was once again focused on the living conditions endured by Aboriginal people on reserves and, specifically, on the welfare of Aboriginal children. In 1966 the federal Department of Indian Affairs and Northern Development completed an ambitious survey detailing all aspects of life for Canada's Aboriginal peoples living on reserves. It was called the Hawthorn Report, after its editor. In respect to child welfare services, the report found that "the situation varies from unsatisfactory to appalling."

In the same year, the federal government, attempting once again to expand existing child welfare services to Aboriginal communities, signed an agreement with the provinces to share the costs of extending social services under the Canada Assistance Plan. No Aboriginal people or organizations were consulted about these changes, and there was no commitment to preserve Aboriginal culture or to provide for local Aboriginal control over child welfare services. These services were to be delivered by non-Aboriginal agencies employing non-Aboriginal social workers.

Aboriginal Peoples and the Child Welfare System in Manitoba

The history of Aboriginal child welfare in Manitoba closely parallels the situation across the country. During the late 1970s and 1980s, however, the Manitoba government made a number of changes to its child welfare system in order to provide Aboriginal communities with better and more humane services through greater local control.

Like other provinces, Manitoba had passed various laws over the years, dealing with child welfare matters. In 1887, for example, Manitoba passed the *Apprentices and Minors Act* (S.M. 1877, c. 40), and established a superintendent of neglected and dependent children. The next year, the *Act Respecting Infants* (S.M. 1878, c. 39) was passed. In 1895 the *Humane Societies Act* was amended to provide for the establishment of societies which served children, as well as animals. In 1898 *An Act for the Better Protection of Neglected and Dependent Children* (S.M. 1898, c. 6) was passed, in which provision for the formal establishment of a Children's Aid Society was made. In the same year, the Children's Aid Society of Winnipeg was established. In 1922 Manitoba introduced the *Child Welfare Act* (S.M. 1922, c. 2). Following the introduction of this legislation, the first foster homes were established and, in the 1950s, the first group homes.

The child welfare system had only a limited impact on Aboriginal people before the 1950s and the accompanying government-sponsored boom in social service programs. However, as we have seen, this changed as two things occurred coincidentally. First, there was a massive migration by Aboriginal people into southern and urban areas. Second, there was an expansion into the North of better communication and transportation, and industrial development. With this expansion came southern bureaucracy. Aboriginal and non-Aboriginal people were no longer separated by vast distances or artificial barriers, such as reserve boundaries. To its astonishment and dismay, the latter group quickly learned of the appalling inequities which affected all aspects of the lives of Aboriginal people. Unfortunately, its responses only worsened the situation.

The "Sixties Scoop"

Before the mid-1960s, there was no organized way to provide child welfare services to Aboriginal peoples in Manitoba living on reserves. Then, in 1966 the federal government and the government of Manitoba entered into an agreement that provided for the existing Children's Aid Societies of Central, Eastern and Western Manitoba to deliver child welfare services to 14 bands in southern Manitoba. Three-quarters of the bands in Manitoba were not covered by this arrangement. As in the past the northern bands continued to receive some services from the Department of Indian Affairs, but provincial child welfare authorities would intervene only in emergency or "life and death" situations.

This expansion of child welfare services to Aboriginal communities, which took place across Canada at this time, left a profound and negative impact on these communities. As the Canadian Council on Social Development documented:

> In 1955, there were 3,433 children in the care of B.C.'s child welfare branch. Of that number it was estimated that 29 children, or less than 1 percent of the total, were of Indian ancestry. By 1964, however, 1,446 children in care in B.C. were of Indian extraction. That number represented 34.2 percent of all children in core. Within ten years, in other words, the representation of Native children in B.C.'s child welfare system had jumped from almost nil to a third. It was a pattern being repeated in other parts of Canada as well.

In most provinces, these child welfare services were never provided in any kind of meaningful or culturally appropriate way. Instead of the counselling of families, or consultation with the community about alternatives to apprehending the child, the apprehension of Aboriginal children became the standard operating procedure with child welfare authorities in most provinces.

> In Manitoba, the child welfare system "protected" many Aboriginal children by taking them away from their families and placing them for adoption with non-Aboriginal families. This came to be known as the "Sixties Scoop," but it continued into the 1980s. Although the flaws in this approach would only become evident to most of society later, Aboriginal people immediately condemned the practice. ...

The child welfare system was doing essentially the same thing with Aboriginal children that the residential schools had done. It removed Aboriginal children from their families, communities and cultures, and placed them in mainstream society. Child welfare workers removed Aboriginal children from their families and communities because they felt the best homes for the children were not Aboriginal homes. The ideal home would instill the values and lifestyles with which the child welfare workers themselves were familiar: white, middle-class homes in white, middle-class neighbourhoods. Aboriginal communities and Aboriginal parents and families were deemed to be "unfit". As a result, between 1971 and 1981 alone over 3,400 Aboriginal children were shipped away to adoptive parents in other societies, and sometimes in other countries.

> Gradually, as education ceased to function as the institutional agent of colonization, the child welfare system took its place. It could continue to remove Native children from their parents, devalue Native custom and traditions in the process, but still act "in the best interests of the child." Those who hold to this view argue that the Sixties Scoop was not coincidental; it was a consequence of fewer Indian children being sent to residential school and of the child welfare system emerging or the new method of colonization.

As part of its comprehensive survey of Aboriginal child welfare policies and procedures, in 1983 the Canadian Council on Social Development compiled a statistical overview of Aboriginal children in the care of child welfare authorities across Canada. The director of the project, Patrick Johnston, found that Aboriginal children were highly over-represented in the child welfare system. They represented 40-50 per cent of children in care in the province of Alberta, 60-70 per cent of children in care in Saskatchewan and some 50-60 per cent of children in care in Manitoba. Johnston estimated that, across Canada Aboriginal children were 4.5 times more likely than non-Aboriginal children to be in the care of child welfare authorities. Similar findings have been reported by other experts.

What began in the 1960s, with very few exceptions, carried on through the 1970s and 1980s. Patrick Johnston, in examining the history of Aboriginal children's involvement with the child welfare system, wrote:

> In retrospect, the wholesale apprehension of Native children during the Sixties Scoop appears to have been a terrible mistake. While some individual children may have benefited, many did not. Nor did their families. And Native culture suffered one more of many severe blows. Unfortunately, the damage is still being done. While attitudes may have changed to some extent since the Sixties, Native children continue to be represented in the child welfare system at a much greater rate than non-native children.

C. CONTEMPORARY REALITIES

1. Over-representation in Care: Statistics and Causes

In February 2007 the Assembly of First Nations estimated that there were approximately 27,000 First Nation children in care in First Nations and provincial agencies, on and off reserve. They made the point that this number is three times the number of children that were in residential schools at the height of their operation: First Nations Child and Family Services, Questions and Answers, at <http://64.26.129.156/article.asp?id =3372>.

An Aboriginal child is 9.5 times more likely than a non-Aboriginal child to be in government-supervised care. In British Columbia, Aboriginal children comprise over 50 per cent of the children in care, though Aboriginal children only make up 9 per cent of the general population.[2] In Manitoba, over 13 per cent of Aboriginal children are not living with their parents but are in government care. In fact, Aboriginal children comprise about 20 per cent of the child population, but represent over 70 per cent of the children in care in Manitoba.[3] In Saskatchewan approximately 25 per cent of children in the province are Aboriginal, yet they also represent over 67 per cent of the children in care.[4]

Recently, data has been collected to provide a picture as to the immediate reasons Aboriginal children are apprehended and taken into care (beyond the broader context of colonialism as noted in the Manitoba Justice Inquiry, Royal Commission on Aboriginal Peoples, *etc.*). This information is found in *Wen'de: We Are Coming to the Light of Day*:

[N]eglect continues to be the primary reason why Aboriginal children are reported to child welfare authorities. Amongst the various forms of neglect, physical neglect and failure to supervise were the most frequently reported. Physical neglect relates to the caregivers failure to provide adequately for the child's needs such as nutrition, clothing, hygienic living conditions. CIS [Canadian Incidence Study of Reported Child Abuse and Neglect] requires that the social worker suspect or believe that the parent is at least partially responsible for the situation. CIS-03 data suggests that First Nations children on and off reserve have higher rates of child functioning concerns than their non Aboriginal peers. First Nations children on reserve were more likely to be reported as having depression/anxiety, negative peer involvement, misuse substances, irregular school attendance, and to experience a learning disability than their First Nations peers resident off reserve, other Aboriginal children and non Aboriginal children. On the positive front, First Nations children on reserve were less likely to experience ADD, ADHD, inappropriate sexual behaviour, to have a positive toxicology at birth or young offender involvement than their peers off reserve.

In terms of caregiver functioning, it is clear that First Nations caregivers are facing more pressures than their non Aboriginal counterparts. Although First Nations caregivers on reserve are less likely to be single parents than their non Aboriginal peers, they are more likely to rely on benefits for income and to live in public housing, in unsafe housing, and overcrowded conditions. Alcohol abuse continues to be a key factor affecting 44% of First Nations caregivers on reserve versus 58% for First Nations off reserve, 43% for other Aboriginal caregivers and 11% for non Aboriginal caregivers. First Nations caregivers were more likely to experience drug and solvent abuse (44%) versus 10% for non Aboriginal caregivers. However, the rates for drug and solvent abuse amongst First Nations caregivers resident off reserve were higher at 58% than amongst other Aboriginal caregivers (43%).

In terms of social worker response, cases involving Aboriginal families were two and one half times more likely to be substantiated (49 per thousand) than non Aboriginal families (19.8 per thousand.) In terms of investigative outcomes, cases involving First Nations children were more likely to remain open for services (68%) versus their non Aboriginal peers (41%). Court applications were also more likely for First Nations children on reserve occurring in 10% of cases versus 6% of cases involving non Aboriginal children. Rates for court applications were slightly higher at 13% for both First Nations off reserve and other Aboriginal peoples. When it came to placement First Nations children on reserve were two and a half times more likely to be placed in child welfare care than non Aboriginal children. Specifically, First Nations children on reserve experienced placement rates of 15% as compared to 6% for non Aboriginal children. First Nations children off reserve were placed in child welfare placements in 16% of cases.

CIS-03 compared where Aboriginal children on and off reserve were being placed once admitted to child welfare care. Overall, children on reserve were three times more likely to be placed in either informal kinship care, kinship care or with a family foster home than their non Aboriginal counterparts.

Conclusions

... The profiles of Aboriginal families differ dramatically from the profile of non-Aboriginal families. Aboriginal cases predominantly involve situations of neglect where poverty, inadequate housing and parent substance abuse are a toxic combination of risk factors. Surprisingly, fewer differences were noted at the level of the children themselves. The most systematic pattern to emerge from this first analysis highlights the differences between Aboriginal and non-Aboriginal children. ... [I]t is apparent that one should expect the cost of providing services to Aboriginal children to be significantly higher given that these cases involve a significantly higher rate of intervention at every point of contact.[5]

This finding (that parental neglect accounts for the majority of Aboriginal child apprehensions) is confirmed by a recent Saskatchewan Report, entitled Saskatchewan Child Welfare Review Panel Report, *For the Good of our Children and Youth: A New Vision, A New Direction*:

In our opinion, statistics on the numbers of children and youth entering the provincial child welfare system and the reasons for their involvement support the need for fundamental change. Furthermore, as most involvements in child welfare now relate to neglect as opposed to other forms of maltreatment, a new approach to child welfare seems not only appropriate, but inevitable.

. . . . .

In fact, neglect accounts for nearly six of every 10 new substantiated cases in the province (56 per cent), while physical abuse accounts for less than one-fifth (15 per cent). ...

Given that neglect is the main reason families become involved in child protection and that it drives caseloads of children and youth living out-of-home in this province, it is not surprising that large numbers of parents who come to the attention of child protection are struggling with substance abuse or mental health issues, housing problems, inadequate income, or some combination of these. As recent statistics on substantiated maltreatment in the province clearly indicate, many children and youth are coming into the system because their safety and well-being is compromised by these problems and conditions. Saskatchewan data on parent and household characteristics of those who become involved for substantiated maltreatment from the same recent national study show that:

- 85 per cent of families were living in rental or public housing, 69 per cent had moved frequently, and in 31 per cent of cases there were safety hazards noted in the home;
- 67 per cent of families had no one with a fulltime job in the home, 55 per cent of caregivers had limited social supports, and 51 per cent of families were on social assistance;
- 49 per cent of caregivers had problems with alcohol abuse and 31 per cent had problems with drug/solvent abuse;
- 46 per cent of caregivers had been victims of domestic violence; and
- 27 per cent of caregivers had mental health issues.

If we examine the challenge of increasing numbers of children and youth coming into the system through this lens, it makes sense for us to consider what child welfare in Saskatchewan might look like if the system focused more on getting families the supports they need without requiring them to have an open child protection case. To us, these statistics add more weight to the call for a new way of delivering child protection in Saskatchewan.[6]

D. BEST INTERESTS OF THE CHILD

As noted in the readings thus far, Aboriginal children have been removed from their communities because of parental challenges and different non-native ideologies and programs throughout the years. Federal "civilization" initiatives, residential schools, and provincial child welfare programs have all contributed to this tragedy. As noted, despite the disappearance of residential schools, Aboriginal children continue to be over-represented in government-supervised care. The following extracts examine some further reasons why Aboriginal children continue to be represented in the child welfare system at a much greater rate than non-native children. The role of the "best interests of the child" test is explored in this regard.

1. Best Interests of the Child and Judicial Interpretation

In the 1990s Professor Marlee Kline wrote about a trend she observed in the jurisprudence, in relation to Aboriginal peoples and the "best interests of the child" test. Professor Kline observed:

> ... Child welfare law can [now] be understood as a new modality of colonialist regulation of First Nations, though one less explicit and apparently more "innocent" of colonialist intentions than the aggressive mechanisms of the past. Canadian child welfare law directs judges to make decisions that are "in the best interests of the child". Unlike earlier colonialist mechanisms that openly segregated Indians and treated them as inferiors, the apprehension of First Nations children from their communities and its negative effects are facilitated and legitimated by a legal system that is based upon ideals of universality and neutrality, and which purports to protect individual children and act in their best interests. In other words, there are ideological dimensions of child welfare law which make decisions arrived at within the system appear natural, necessary, and legitimate, rather than coercive and destructive.[7]

As you read the following case, ask yourself about the relationship, if any, between colonialism and the "best interests of the child" test identified by Professor Kline.

RACINE v. WOODS

[1983] S.C.J. No. 70, [1983] 2 S.C.R. 173, 1 D.L.R. (4th) 193 (S.C.C.)

The judgment of the Court was delivered by

Wilson J.: — This appeal emphasizes once more, this time in an interracial context, that the law no longer treats children as the property of those who gave them birth but focuses on what is in their best interests.

Leticia Grace Woods ("Leticia") was born at Portage la Prairie, Manitoba, on September 4, 1976 to Linda Woods, an Indian, who was at the time the wife of Lloyd Woods. Lloyd Woods was not the father of the child and divorce proceedings were underway when Leticia was born. There are two children of the Woods marriage, Jason aged nine and Lydia aged eight. Mrs.

Woods on her own admission had a serious alcohol problem and was unable to care for Leticia. First her brother and then her sister took the infant. The older children, Jason and Lydia, stayed with their father.

On October 20, 1976, when she was six weeks old, Leticia was apprehended by the Children's Aid Society of Central Manitoba pursuant to the protection sections of *The Child Welfare Act*, C.C.S.M., c. C80 ("the Act") and placed in a foster home. In February 1977 Judge Kimmelman, with her mother's consent, made her a ward of the Society for a one-year period which was subsequently extended for a further six months. On February 11, 1977 Leticia was placed in the foster home of Sandra Ransom (later Racine) and her husband Lorne Ransom. The Ransoms separated in the summer of 1977 and in September of that year Sandra started to cohabit with Allan Racine whom she subsequently married. Leticia remained in their home with the sanction of the Children's Aid Society until the wardship order expired in March 1978. Arrangements were then made by the Society to return her to her mother who was living in Brandon with her other two children. The Racines co-operated fully in this transfer which took place on May 4, 1978.

Mrs. Woods had made no effort to contact Leticia during the period of the wardship but had suggested to the Society early in 1978 that her sister might adopt her. The sister apparently had reservations about this and nothing came of it. The Racines by this time had, of course, developed an attachment to the child and were concerned as to whether she was being properly cared for. They therefore took up Mrs. Woods' invitation to pay her a visit. In fact they paid two visits to see Leticia and on the second visit in May 1978, with Mrs. Woods' consent, took Leticia home with them. The evidence as to Mrs. Woods' intention in relinquishing custody of Leticia to the Racines is conflicting. She says they were to have Leticia "just for a while" until she came for her in a couple of weeks' time. The Racines believed that she had surrendered the child to them on a permanent basis. She had confided to them that she was having difficulties with Lloyd Woods with whom she was periodically cohabiting and she appeared to be aware herself that she was in a state of emotional instability. Consistent with the Racines' understanding that they were now to have Leticia on a permanent basis they got in touch with the Children's Aid Society about the possibility of adopting her. Mrs. Woods by this time had returned to the Reserve with Lloyd Woods. The Society advised the Racines that it no longer had responsibility for the child and that if they wished to adopt her they should retain legal counsel. They followed this advice and on October 5, 1978 filed a Notice of Receiving a Child for Private Adoption under s. 102(1) of the Act.

The Racines heard nothing from Mrs. Woods until October 1978 when she arrived at their home announcing that she had left Lloyd Woods because he was abusing her, that she was on her way to Regina and wanted her sister to have Leticia. The Racines refused to give her up. They heard no further word from Mrs. Woods until January 1982 when she launched an application for *habeas corpus*. On February 24, 1982 the Racines applied for an order of *de facto* adoption.

It is apparent from the evidence that Mrs. Woods from January 1978 on was attempting with varying degrees of success to rehabilitate herself. She wanted to rid herself of her alcohol problem, to free herself of her association with Lloyd Woods, and to engage in a program of self-improvement. However, none of this was easy and periods of achievement when she underwent treatment for alcoholism and attended classes to upgrade her education would be followed by periods of backsliding. It took her five years and the support of friends, relatives and her extended family on the Reserve to accomplish her objective. By the time she did, Leticia was five or six years old and an established part of the Racine family. They had brought her up as if she were their own. The evidence discloses that they are a very fine couple, active and respected in their community, and excellent parents. They have two other children, Melissa aged four and two year old Jamie.

Leticia is apparently a well-adjusted child of average intelligence, attractive and healthy, does well in school, attends Sunday School and was baptized in the church the Racine family attends. She knows that Sandra Racine is not her natural mother, that Mrs. Woods is her natural mother, and that she is a native Indian. She knows that Allan Racine is not her natural father and that he is a Métis. This has all been explained to her by the Racines who have encouraged her to be proud of her Indian culture and heritage. None of this seems to have presented any problem for her thus far. She is now seven years old and the expert witnesses agree that the Racines are her "psychological parents".

An unfortunate incident occurred on February 3, 1982. When the court proceedings brought by Mrs. Woods in January 1982 were adjourned for the preparation of home study reports, she decided to take things into her own hands and with the assistance of friends attempted to abduct Leticia first from her school and then from the Racine home. Fortunately, the child was not in the home at the time. The R.C.M.P. had to be called. The Racines obtained an *ex parte* order granting them interim custody and enjoining Mrs. Woods from further attempts at abduction. Mrs. Woods moved to vary the order and was granted supervised access. On her first exercise of access she arranged for a reporter and a photographer from the Winnipeg Free Press to be present. The story was given considerable prominence in the newspaper with a photograph of Mrs. Woods and Leticia. The child was upset by the notoriety.

The Racines' application for adoption and Mrs. Woods' application for custody were heard by Judge Krindle in a trial lasting eight days. The application for custody was dismissed and the adoption order granted. Mrs. Woods appealed to the Manitoba Court of Appeal which overturned the adoption order, made Leticia a ward of the Court of Appeal, granted custody to the Racines and left it open to Mrs. Woods to apply subsequently for access or custody. The Court of Appeal subsequently on a motion for directions referred Mrs. Woods' application for access to Huband J.A., on being advised that an application was being made for leave to appeal to the Supreme Court of Canada, held the application for access in abeyance. This Court gave the Racines leave to appeal on May 17,

1983 and ordered a stay of proceedings. Leticia continued to reside with the Racines and Mrs. Woods has had no access since Judge Krindle's order of adoption on May 12, 1982. Mrs. Woods cross-appealed in this Court on the ground that the Manitoba Court of Appeal erred in not restoring legal custody to her when they set aside the order of adoption in favour of the Racines.

The Racines' application for adoption was made under s. 103 of the Act, *i.e.* a *de facto* adoption based on the fact that Leticia had been cared for and maintained by them for a period of three consecutive years. Section 103(2) states that in the case of such an adoption the consent of the parents or guardian is not required. Judge Krindle found that the Racines had cared for and maintained Leticia for the required three-year period and indeed had rescued her as an infant from an intolerable situation, given her an excellent home, been devoted parents, were fully sensitive to the special problems of raising a native Indian child in a predominantly white environment and were coping with those problems in a mature and responsible fashion. She concluded that the Racines were well able to cope with any identity crisis Leticia might face as a teenager. Moreover, as a Métis Allan Racine was no stranger to the hurt racial prejudice could inflict on a sensitive soul and, in the view of the learned trial judge, was a model for Leticia of how to survive as a member of a much maligned minority. As to Mrs. Woods, Judge Krindle expressed respect and admiration for her courage and determination and the degree of success she had achieved in rehabilitating herself. At the same time, however, she expressed some concern as to whether she was going to be able to maintain her progress. She saw danger signals in "the venom of her anti-white feelings" and wondered what effect "her visible hatred for all things white" would have on her child. She also wondered whether Mrs. Woods' concern was for the child as a person or as a political issue. The media incident, in Judge Krindle's view, manifested an incredible indifference to the effect such an incident might have on her child. It made Leticia, a very private little girl, into a "cause celebre" in her school and community. Judge Krindle concluded that it was in the child's best interests that she remain with the Racines.

In addition to finding that it was in Leticia's best interests to remain with the Racines, Judge Krindle also made a finding that Mrs. Woods had abandoned Leticia between October 1978 and January 1982. She made this finding because of her concern as to whether s. 103(2) had the effect of dispensing with parental rights in the case of a *de facto* adoption. If it did have that effect, then the sole issue was the best interests of the child. However, if it did not, then under the common law a natural mother could lose custody of her child to a stranger in blood only by abandoning it or so misconducting herself that in the opinion of the court it would be improper to leave the child with her: see *Re Baby Duffell: Martin v. Duffell*, [1950] S.C.R. 737; *Hepton v. Maat*, [1957] S.C.R. 606; *Re Agar: McNeilly v. Agar*, [1958] S.C.R. 52.

Having made her findings as to abandonment and the child's best interests, Judge Krindle made the adoption order in favour of the Racines and dismissed Mrs. Woods' application for custody.

As already mentioned, the Court of Appeal overturned the adoption order. Each of the panel of three judges gave separate reasons. Mr. Justice Hall would have affirmed the adoption order but, because his two colleagues were for overturning it, he yielded to the majority and then went on to align himself with the alternate course advanced by O'Sullivan J.A. rather than that advanced by Matas J.A.

O'Sullivan J.A. decided that the best course to follow was to make Leticia a ward of the Court with custody in the Racines, leaving it open to Mrs. Woods at some future time to apply for access. Matas J.A., on the other hand, did not think making the child a ward of the Court was a workable alternative. He favoured a new trial as to custody (as opposed to adoption) with interim custody in the Racines in the meantime and such access to Mrs. Woods as might be agreed upon or as might be ordered by the Court.

On what grounds then did the Court of Appeal upset the judgment of the learned trial judge? Hall J.A. identified the basis on which in his view it should have been affirmed. He pointed out that the trial judge had the tremendous advantage of seeing and hearing the parties and their witnesses and that she had accepted the evidence of some experts in preference to that of others. She had the benefit also of home study reports and reflected in her reasons the concern expressed in them about the consequences of moving the child from the only permanent home she had ever known and separating her from the *de facto* parents to whom she was now psychologically bonded. He referred to the strong statement made by the trial judge after a review of the whole of the evidence:

> I have absolutely no doubt whatsoever that the circumstances of this case demand the granting of an Order of Adoption of Letitia [sic] to the Racines. ...

He found that the findings and conclusions reached by the trial judge were fully supported by the evidence. He pointed out that the trial judge was well aware of the importance of Leticia's cultural background and heritage and the potential difficulties involved in an interracial adoption. She gave particular attention to the evidence of the expert who suggested that Leticia could face a major identity crisis in her teenage years as a result of being reared in a predominantly white environment. She concluded that the Racines would be well able to deal with such a crisis if it arose.

Matas and O'Sullivan JJ.A. had certain concerns in common about the judgment of the learned trial judge. On the issue of abandonment they expressed the view that, when Mrs. Woods attempted to get her child back in 1978, the Racines refused to give her up. How can the Racines rely on abandonment by Mrs. Woods when they at that time had no legal right to keep the child? As Matas J.A. put it:

The actions of the Racines, well motivated though they were, put roadblocks in the path of what Mrs. Woods might have been able to accomplish if she had been dealing with expected reactions of foster parents. In effect, Mr. and Mrs. Racine considered themselves as the equivalent of a court or a child caring agency, in deciding what they thought was best for the child at that time.

In my view, Mr. and Mrs. Racine cannot now rely on a claim that Mrs. Woods abandoned her child when they deliberately refused to return the child to Mrs. Woods in 1978 and embarked on a three-year waiting period to simplify the legal procedures to be followed in adopting Leticia. And it is impossible for us to say now what may have been the result if an application for adoption had been made properly in 1978. At least the court would not have been faced with the argument of the particularly long lapse of time. It is not enough for the Racines to say they have lived at the same address continuously and that Mrs. Woods should have known where to reach them. The custody claimed by the Racines cannot, in my opinion, be a foundation for an application under s. 103 of the Act.

O'Sullivan J.A. said:

> ... it is difficult to know what more Linda Woods could do to recover her child who was being held without legal right except to seek help from child caring agencies, legal aid lawyers and the police. The fact they were unable to help her does not show that she had abandoned her parental rights but that she was unable to assert them effectively.

The trial judge, of course, relied upon the period of four years from 1978 to 1982 for her finding of abandonment and the evidence seems to support her finding that Mrs. Woods:

> ... may have continued to feel for Letitia [sic] from time to time, but the fact is that for four years there was no contact between herself and Letitia [sic], not even an attempt on her part to see how the child was, to let the child know that her mother cared, to see if the child needed help. The only thing that could even be considered, I suppose, a "half-baked" stab at breaking the abandonment was the one time that Miss Woods got into a car with George Beaulieu, looked for the Racine residence, and then because George Beaulieu ran out of money and was low on gas, turned back and went back to Long Plains. That was one day in a period that extended from October of 1978 to January of 1982. During this period of time, from the point of view of the child, she may as well not even have had a natural mother.

It is apparent that Matas and O'Sullivan JJ.A. put an entirely different interpretation on the evidence from that put upon it by the learned trial judge and I agree with the appellants that it is not the function of an appellate court to reinterpret the evidence. In *Stein v. The Ship "Kathy K"*, [1976] 2 S.C.R. 802, this Court (*per* Ritchie J. at p. 807) put its stamp of approval on the following observation of Lord Sumner in *S.S. Hontestroom (Owners) v. S.S. Sagaporack (Owners)*, [1927] A.C. 37, at p. 47.

> ... not to have seen the witnesses puts appellate judges in a permanent position of disadvantage as against the trial judge, and unless it can be shown that he has failed to use or has palpably misused his advantage, the higher Court ought not to take the responsibility of reversing conclusions so arrived at, merely on the result of their own comparisons and criticisms of

the witness and of their own view of the probabilities of the case. The course of the trial and the whole substance of the judgment must be looked at, and the matter does not depend on the question whether a witness has been cross-examined to credit or has been pronounced by the judge in terms to be unworthy of it. If his estimate of the man forms any substantial part of his reasons for his judgment the trial judge's conclusion of fact should, as I understand the decisions, be let alone.

Accordingly, even if a finding of abandonment was a prerequisite for an adoption order under s. 103, I am of the view that the evidence was there to support Judge Krindle's finding.

Nor do I accept the submission of counsel that the trial judge was precluded from finding abandonment by Mrs. Woods on the basis of some kind of estoppel operating against the Racines. The Racines' refusal to return the child to Mrs. Woods in October 1978 when she suddenly appeared at their home at a late hour in the evening and intimated that she had left Lloyd Woods, was moving to Regina and wanted to pass Leticia on to her sister was in my view a perfectly responsible act on the part of the Racines. I do not think they were, as Matas J.A. suggests, setting themselves up as a court to decide the ultimate fate of the child. They had had the care of Leticia since she was an infant except for a brief period in May 1978 following the expiry of the wardship order and had become very attached to her. I believe their conduct was prompted by concern for the child. No doubt they were of the view that if Mrs. Woods' intention in taking Leticia from them was to pass her on to her sister rather than to look after her herself, she might well be better off with them — at least until a proper authority had looked into the kind of home she would have with the sister. It must be recalled that the Racines thought that Mrs. Woods had given Leticia permanently into their care in May and were planning to adopt her. They had heard nothing from her from May until her sudden appearance in October and, indeed, heard nothing further from her until the writ of *habeas corpus* in January 1982. With all due respect to the majority of the Court of Appeal, I think it is quite inappropriate to characterize the conduct of the Racines as some kind of illegal assertion of title! We are dealing with a child who had been brought up in their home after being apprehended by the Children's Aid Society. It was for the Court to decide whether the Racines' conduct in refusing to give up Leticia in October 1978 was reasonable in the circumstances and whether it really prevented Mrs. Woods from pursuing her legal right to custody. The trial judge obviously concluded that it did not. She could have proceeded immediately with her *habeas corpus* application and not waited three years to do so. Matas J.A., in holding the Racines estopped from alleging abandonment by their refusal to give up the child in October 1978, states:

> In my view, Mr. and Mrs. Racine cannot now rely on a claim that Mrs. Woods abandoned her child when they deliberately refused to return the child to Mrs. Woods in 1978 and embarked on a three-year waiting period to simplify the legal procedures to be followed in adopting Leticia. And it is impossible for us to say now what may have been the result if an application

for adoption had been made properly in 1978. At least the court would not have been faced with the argument of the particularly long lapse of time.

With respect, I see nothing "improper" about the Racines proceeding by way of *de facto* adoption. The statute contemplates it. Moreover, in my view the crucial question is not what a court would have done with an adoption application made in 1978 but what it would have done with a *habeas corpus* application. Mrs. Woods might have succeeded on such an application in 1978 had she proceeded with it. Her failure to do so permitted her child to develop a dependency on the Racines as her psychological parents. It seems to me that Mrs. Woods had a responsibility when her rights were challenged to pursue them in the court if necessary and not to wait until her child was bonded to the Racines with all the problems for the child that the disruption of that bond was likely to create.

I frankly cannot see this as a situation for the application of the doctrine of estoppel. I believe there was evidence before the learned trial judge on which she could make her finding of abandonment between October 1978 and January 1982 although I feel impelled to say that I myself would probably not have made that finding. I believe that the significance of a person's conduct must be assessed in the context of that person's circumstances. Acts performed by one may constitute abandonment when the same acts performed by another may not. I think I would have been disposed to take a more charitable view of Mrs. Woods' failure to contact her child given her circumstances than that taken by the learned trial judge.

Be that as it may, I do not think a finding of abandonment was necessary to the trial judge's decision. I think the statute is clear and that s. 103(2) dispenses with parental consent in the case of a *de facto* adoption. This does not mean, of course, that the child's tie with its natural parent is irrelevant in the making of an order under the section. It is obviously very relevant in a determination as to what is in the child's best interests. But it is the parental tie as a meaningful and positive force in the life of the child and not in the life of the parent that the court has to be concerned about. As has been emphasized many times in custody cases, a child is not a chattel in which its parents have a proprietary interest; it is a human being to whom they owe serious obligations. In giving the court power to dispense with the consent of the parent on a *de facto* adoption the legislature has recognized an aspect of the human condition that our own self interest sometimes clouds our perception of what is best for those for whom we are responsible. It takes a very high degree of selflessness and maturity — for most of us probably an unattainable degree — for a parent to acknowledge that it might be better for his or her child to be brought up by someone else. The legislature in its wisdom has protected the child against this human frailty in a case where others have stepped into the breach and provided a happy and secure home for the child for a minimum period of three consecutive years. In effect, these persons have assumed the obligations of the natural parents and taken their place. The natural parents' consent in these circumstances is no longer required.

Counsel for the respondent submits, however, that the word custody as used in s. 103 of the Act should be interpreted to mean legal custody and that Linda Woods never relinquished legal custody of the child and the Racines never obtained it. By legal custody I understood counsel to mean custody pursuant to a court order or some other lawful authority. Because they do not have this counsel submits that the Racines cannot meet the requirements of the section. I find no merit in this submission. Section 103 clearly provides for an application for adoption by a person having *de facto* custody of a child for the prescribed period of time. This is not to say that the means by which the *de facto* custody was obtained is irrelevant under the section. If it were obtained illegally, such as by kidnapping for example, this would certainly be a factor to be considered by the court in determining whether or not it was in the child's best interests to make the order. No such situation obtains here and I cannot read into the section something which is simply not there.

I turn now to the crucial issue on the appeal. Did the learned trial judge err in holding that Leticia's best interests lay with the Racines? The majority of the Court of Appeal thought she did. They appear to share a concern about the finality of an adoption order in terms of cutting Leticia off both from her natural mother and from her Indian heritage and culture. Matas J.A. said:

> As part of his submission, counsel for Mrs. Woods argued that a transracial adoption results in the loss of contact by the child with his heritage and culture and that this would not be in the best interests of the child. I would reject this argument if counsel meant that no transracial adoption order should ever be granted by the courts in this province. The legislation is not restrictive. In an appropriate case, the court may grant a transracial order of adoption. However, I agree that a child's culture and heritage should be considered by the court as one of the factors to be weighed as part of the circumstances envisaged by s. 89 of the Act. Depending on the circumstances, it is a factor which could have greater or lesser influence in the court's final decision. In the case at bar, the evidence supports the view that the factor is an important one.

Hall J.A. did not underestimate the importance of the fact that the child was an Indian. However, he adopted the conclusion the trial judge drew from the expert evidence before her as to the Racines' sensitivity to the interracial aspect and their appreciation of the need to encourage and develop in Leticia a sense of her own worth and dignity and the worth and dignity of her people. The trial judge found that they had amply displayed their ability to guide Leticia through any identity crisis she might face in her teenage years. Hall J.A. also accepted the trial judge's finding based on the psychiatric evidence that to risk the removal of Leticia from the Racines' home at this stage could cause her permanent psychological damage. This was the only home she had ever known and she was securely bonded to the Racines. Hall J.A. concluded that, important a factor as her Indian heritage and culture might be, the duration and strength of her attachment to the Racines was more important.

The majority of the Court of Appeal obviously saw in their alternate courses a means of keeping the door open for access to the natural mother. If the child were a ward of the Court the Court could grant her access while maintaining custody in the Racines if this seemed appropriate. Similarly, if a new trial were ordered as to custody, access rights could be claimed in those proceedings. The majority were loath to close the door on access by the finality of an adoption order. With respect, I think this overlooks something — something adverted to by Mr. Justice Hall when he said:

> In my opinion, it is quite unlikely that a solution to the problem will be found in either of the ways proposed by my colleagues. Rather, my forecast is lengthy, bitter and costly litigation which in itself would not serve the best interests of Leticia. A difficult choice has to be made. Either the order of adoption should stand or she should be returned to Mrs. Woods. The record is as complete as it is ever likely to be.

I agree with Mr. Justice Hall that this child should not be allowed to become a battleground — in the courts or in the media — and I believe that there is a very real risk of this if the Court refuses to "bite the bullet". In my view, when the test to be met is the best interests of the child, the significance of cultural background and heritage as opposed to bonding abates over time. The closer the bond that develops with the prospective adoptive parents the less important the racial element becomes. As the witness, Dr. McCrae, expressed it:

> I think this whole business of racial and Indian and whatever you want to call it all has to do with a parameter of time and if we had gone back to day one and Letitia [sic] Woods is now being relinquished by her mother in terms of priorities at that time, we would have said — supported a hundred times over "let's place the child with its cultural background." That would be a very — would have been very reasonable. But if that is not done and time goes by, that priority drops down. The priority is no longer there, the priority of ethnic and cultural background. That drops and now must go way down because now it's the mother-child relationship. It doesn't matter if Sandra Racine was Indian and the child was white and Linda Woods was white. This same argument would hold. It has nothing to do with race, absolutely nothing to do with culture, it has nothing to do with ethnic background. It's two women and a little girl, and one of them doesn't know her. It's as simple as that; all the rest of it is extra and of no consequence, except to the people involved, of course.

I think the learned trial judge recognized that reality, considered all the factors which were relevant to the determination of what was in the child's best interests including the fact that she was of Indian parentage, and weighed them in the balance. I cannot find that she erred in carrying out this rather difficult process.

Much was made in this case of the interracial aspect of the adoption. I believe that interracial adoption, like interracial marriage, is now an accepted phenomenon in our pluralist society. The implications of it may have been overly dramatized by the respondent in this case. The real issue is the cutting of the child's legal tie with her natural mother. This is always a serious step and clearly one which ought not to be taken lightly. However, adoption — given that the adoptive home is the right one and the trial judge has so found in this case — gives the child secure status as the child of two loving parents. While the Court can feel great compassion for the respondent, and respect for her determined efforts to overcome her adversities, it has an obligation to ensure that any order it makes will promote the best interests of her child. This and this alone is our task.

I would allow the appeal and reinstate the Order of Adoption made by the trial judge. I would dismiss the cross-appeal. I would make no order as to costs.

Appeal allowed and cross-appeal dismissed.

---

1. Justice Wilson's formulation of the best interests of the child in relation to cultural background has endured. As she said near the end of her judgment: "In my view, when the test to be met is the best interests of the child, the significance of cultural background and heritage as opposed to bonding abates over time. The closer the bond that develops with the prospective adoptive parents the less important the racial element becomes." For a recent application of this principle see *M.-C. (C.) v. Winnipeg (Child and Family Services)*, [2006] M.J. No. 32, [2006] 2 C.N.L.R. 14 at 17 (Man. Q.B.); *In the Matter of K. (M.-K.)*, [2004] J.Q. no 5039, [2004] 2 C.N.L.R. 68 at 72 (Que. C.A.); *Catholic Children's Aid Society of Toronto v. C. (B.)*, [2004] O.J. No. 1748, [2004] 3 C.N.L.R. 51 (Ont. C.J.).

2. Professor Jim Anglin has written about the problem of creating "paramount" tests in child welfare cases. He observed:

    One of the central issues identified in this paper has been "the move to paramountcy," in terms of the "rights of the child," the "best interests of the child" and the "safety and well-being of the child" constructs. The problem with the notion of paramountcy is that it almost invariably encourages a pendulum swing that goes too far. It tends to become a type of formula which then is implemented in un-thinking and reductionistic ways. Kline (1995) has argued quite convincingly that making the rights of the child paramount over the rights of the family or parents has the force in law of abstracting children unduly from their family contexts, first conceptually and then in fact.

    A severe interpretation of the "best interests of the child" has led the court to frame parents who wish to maintain their family unit in the face of serious difficulties as "selfish" and having "vested interests" (Kline, 1995, p. 407) implying that they are concerned only with their own benefit. Similarly, by asserting that "the safety and well-being of the child" are the paramount interests in child welfare, and that any child protection worker "who considers that a child is in need of protection should apprehend and remove the child ... and should not try to 'second guess' what a judge will do once the case comes to court" ...

    Thus, the move to paramountcy of the "safety and well-being of the child," while reducing or eliminating one form of risk, has in fact increased other important risks, namely that children will be removed from their families unnecessarily, that their trust in and attachments to their parents will be damaged or even severed, and that children will become entangled in the child protection net and experience greater emotional, psychological, spiritual and perhaps even physical and sexual harm than they would have had they remained at home. Indeed, while many former children-in-care have been protected from harm and healed within the child welfare system, some have had the experience that being removed from their home placed them in equally or more damaging circumstances than those that were occurring, or were likely to occur, in their families.[8]

3.   The late Professor Patricia Monture has written about the distrust the court has created among First Nations peoples because of the way it frames heritage, as abating over time:

> First Nations distrust the child welfare system because it has effectively assisted in robbing us of our children and our future. This distrust is further complicated by the adversarial process itself, which is antithetical to the First Nations consensus method of conflict resolution. Judicial decisions on child welfare reinforce the status quo by applying standards and tests which are not culturally relevant. This is a form of racism.
>
> These racist standards and tests of child welfare law were developed by judges. The most important tests is the "best interests of the child". Madame Justice Wilson wrote for the Supreme Court of Canada: "the law no longer treats children as property of those who gave them birth but focuses on what is in their best interests". ...
>
> There is evidence that the importance of heritage does not abate over time. The assertion that the importance of heritage abates over time really reflects a belief in the value and possibility of the assimilation of racial minorities — particularly in a racist environment. This belief is not grounded in First Nations tradition and culture, but is a reflection of government policies and "white" values. It is a belief that conceptualizes and prioritizes the rights of individuals over collective rights. And it is a test that effectively forces the assimilation and destruction of First Nations peoples. This is racism. ...
>
> Judges seem to "regret" removing First Nations Children from their communities. They express "compassion and sympathy for the mother". Judges feel compelled to indicate that in previous cases that "it was in the best interest of the native child to be raised with his or her own native people". But these comments do not reach the real harm that is being done by forced assimilation. Instead, they are patronizing and are sure flags of racism.[9]

2.   Best Interests of the Child and Bi-cultural Descent

H. (D.) v. M. (H.)
[1999] S.C.J. No. 22, [1999] 1 S.C.R. 761 (S.C.C.)

Decision of the Court (**Lamer C.J.C.** and **L'Heureux-Dubé, Gonthier, Cory, McLachlin, Iacobucci, Major, Bastarache** and **Binnie JJ.**):

. . . . .

[2] The facts of this case are as follows. Ishmael was born March 8, 1995 and is four years old. The putative father is an African-American who lives in the United States, where the adoptive grandparents, the respondents, also live. The mother, Melissa, is an aboriginal Canadian. At birth, she was a member of the Swan Lake First Nation of Manitoba. She and her sister passed through a long list of foster homes in their infancy and were given up for adoption by the applicant and were adopted by the respondents when they were four and six years old respectively. After Melissa became pregnant with Ishmael, she resided with the respondents for some time both before and after his birth. Shortly following the birth, Melissa being unable or unwilling to look after Ishmael, the respondents took over his care. Ishmael was subsequently taken by his mother to British Columbia where, eventually, he came into the care of the British Columbia Ministry of Children and Families. In early 1995 Melissa made contact with her birth parents who were residing separately in Vancouver. In the spring of 1995, D.H. and N.H. paid for Melissa to visit Vancouver to meet her birth parents. Melissa went to Vancouver without Ishmael, made contact with her birth parents, and remained in Vancouver for about two and a half months. During this time, D.H. and N.H. cared for Ishmael. After returning to Connecticut Melissa told the H.'s that she wanted to take Ishmael for a visit to see her sister Melanie in Hartford, Connecticut. On 6 November 1995 Melissa left with Ishmael on the pretense that she was going to visit her sister. Melissa did not go to Melanie's but instead she travelled with the infant by bus to Vancouver and moved into the home of the appellant, H.M. [The respondents found out in late November or early December of 1995 that Melissa and Ishmael were in Vancouver and they asked the Connecticut Department of Children and Families to liaise with the British Columbia Ministry of Children and Families. Ishmael was taken into care in British Columbia for a couple of months but … interim custody was awarded to H.M. The H.'s have travelled to Vancouver on a number of occasions over the past two years to visit Ishmael. The evidence appears to indicate that Ishmael has interacted well with the H.'s during their visits.]

[3] The trial judge found that both the applicant and the respondents were sincere and loving grandparents and each were capable of offering a good home to Ishmael. In his reasons, he gave considerable emphasis to the aboriginal heritage of Ishmael's mother's side. He said that "aboriginal heritage and the ability of his biological grandfather to preserve and

enhance it are important considerations" (para. 46), and that the claims of the applicant to custody were soundly based on "ties of blood, his obvious love and affection for Ishmael, his aboriginal heritage, [and] his demonstrated ability to provide a home and care for his family" (para. 49). At the same time, the trial judge extensively reviewed the other circumstances of the parties, including the stability of the respective homes, and concluded that "[t]he submission that Ishmael's aboriginal heritage is virtually a determining factor here, oversimplifies a very complex case" (para. 47). The trial judge did not agree that an order granting custody of Ishmael to the respondents would uproot him from his culture. Ishmael is African-American on his putative father's side, aboriginal Canadian on his mother's side, and has lived a significant part of his life with his adoptive grandparents, who are neither. As the trial judge said, "[t]his is not a case of taking an aboriginal child and placing him with a non-aboriginal family in complete disregard for his culture and heritage. The fact is that Melissa is the [adopted] daughter of [the respondents] and Ishmael is their grandson" (para. 46).

[4] The trial judgment was reversed by the Court of Appeal, which put emphasis on the apparent stability at the time of the appeal of the relationship between the applicant and J.S., and the fact Ishmael appeared "well integrated into the family unit of [the applicant], J.S., and their daughter, Sharleen. ... J.S. is proving to be a resource of stability to [the applicant] and the family and is able, together with [the applicant], to provide a good home milieu for Ishmael. ... As well, Ishmael has in his present home a young sibling, the child Sharleen, to whom he relates well" (pp. 551 and 554-55). We were advised at the hearing of the appeal that the applicant no longer lives with J.S. and Sharleen, but has returned to live in Manitoba.

[5] Both the trial judge and the Court of Appeal referred to the *Child, Family and Community Service Act*, R.S.B.C. 1996, c. 46, which provides a statutory direction to public authorities in British Columbia to have careful regard to the cultural identity of aboriginal children. In particular, s. 4(2) provides that: "If the child is an aboriginal child, the importance of preserving the child's cultural identity must be considered in determining the child's best interests." The Court of Appeal noted that "[a]s a strict matter of law, the *Child, Family and Community Service Act* is not applicable to the proceedings" (p. 555). That court nevertheless concluded that the trial judge had "underemphasized ties of blood and culture" (p. 554). This Court, on appeal, disagreed. We concluded that in fact the trial judge had given careful attention to the aboriginal ancestry of Ishmael, together with all the other factors relevant to Ishmael's best interest, and that there was no error in his decision, which was reached after five days of evidence and two weeks of reflection, that justified its reversal by the Court of Appeal. The importance of the findings of the trial judge in custody cases cannot be forgotten. They should not be lightly set aside by appellate courts.

PINE TREE LEGAL ASSISTANCE, WABANAKI LEGAL NEWS,
Summer 1999

In February of 1999, the Supreme Court of Canada handed down a decision in a child custody case involving the young son of an aboriginal Canadian mother. The mother is a member of the Swan Lakes First Nation of Manitoba. For several years before the decision, the child had been living with his biological, aboriginal grandfather. The decision gave custody of the child to the mother's non-native, adoptive parents who live in Connecticut. The decision has deeply angered many in the Canadian aboriginal community.

According to Vice Chief Dennis White Bird, the Manitoba representative to the Assembly of First Nations in Canada, during the 1960's until the early 80's, the Canadian Government engaged in "exporting" First Nation children to the United States and Europe. Vice Chief White Bird called this policy "genocidal" and said that it resulted in "decimating our population." The Assembly of Manitoba Chiefs views this case as part of that policy. Vice Chief White Bird explained that the Assembly had been following the progress of this case for an extended period of time and has given its "moral support" to the biological grandfather as well as to the child. ...

ADOPTIVE FAMILY WINS CUSTODY OF NATIVE BOY: SUPREME COURT WILL NOT DELIVER WRITTEN REASONS FOR RULING

Janice Tibetts, *National Post*, Thursday, February 18, 1999
(with permission of Southam News)

OTTAWA — The Supreme Court of Canada ordered yesterday that an aboriginal boy be taken from his poor blood family and returned to his white adoptive family in the United States.

The snap ruling from the bench overturned an earlier decision from the B.C. Court of Appeal that had found three-year-old [IH] was better off being raised by [HM], his biological grandfather, in native culture rather than grow up with adoptive grandparents on a sprawling farm in Connecticut.

The court's nine judges, immediately after hearing both sides in the dispute, instead sided with an earlier ruling from the B.C. Supreme Court, which had awarded custody to the adoptive grandparents, [N] and [DH], saying they offered a superior parenting and family environment compared with Mr. [M], a welfare recipient for the past decade who lives with his common-law wife, [JS], and their young daughter.

[DH] is a newspaper journalist who earns about $52,000 (US) and [NH] works part-time for a computer software company.

[I]'s mother, [MH], had given up custody of the child but intervened in the court case on Mr. [M]'s side.

Ms. [H], an Ojibway originally from Swan Lake, Man., was adopted by the [H]s when she was four years old and said in documents filed with the court that she didn't want her child to grow up like she did, with a feeling that she never belonged. ...

The decision means [I], who has lived with Mr. [M] for the past two years, will return to Connecticut, where he lived for the first eight months of his life.

Mr. [M] recently moved from Vancouver to his original Ojibway reserve north of Winnipeg with [I].

The [H]s had argued that a decision to side with the natural family would have been "excessive multiculturalism rooted in a regrettable form of political correctness." The Supreme Court, in choosing the [H]s, rejected the B.C. Court of Appeal's contention that the courts should abide by recent legislative trends to keep native children in native families. The B.C. Supreme Court also took into account other cultural considerations when it awarded custody to the [H]s. [I] is an American citizen and he has an absentee father who is black. The [H]s have promised to teach [I] about his aboriginal heritage along with his Afro-American heritage.

Both *H. (D.) v. M. (H.)*, [1999] S.C.J. No. 22, [1999] 1 S.C.R. 761 (S.C.C.) and the following case *S. (K.J.) v. T. (M.)*, [2001] N.S.J. No. 188, [2001] 4 C.N.L.R. 96 (N.S. Fam. Ct.) demonstrate the complexities of litigating child welfare cases in a multi-racialized context. Judges must weigh the importance of the child's racialized, cultural or community background against numerous other important factors. As Professor Annie Bunting has observed:

> Judicial decisions on the best interests of Aboriginal children or children of mixed cultural heritage are judgments about the value of culture, race and community in the lives of children and their families. ... Some commentators have asked whether the interests of Aboriginal communities ought to be given greater consideration in these decisions. The best interests of the individual Aboriginal child are often inseparable from the best interests of the wider community. To date such collectivist assumptions have not taken hold in child-placement decisions. For Aboriginal children in out-of-culture placements, other factors associated with best interests have tended to outweigh considerations of cultural background.[10]

As you think about *H. (D.) v. D. (H.)*, ask yourself the following questions:

1. How do judges take race, culture and community into account, and do they undertake this task without reproducing discriminatory stereotypes?
2. Who should define the meaning and importance of a child's cultural identity?
3. Should children in different communities have different weight placed on their cultural heritage?

4. Is it possible for judges to be more explicit about their own assumptions in multi-racialized child placement cases?

To what extent do the legal system and the judiciary play a role in the construction of Aboriginal culture through child placement decisions like *H. (D.) v. M. (H.)*, [1999] S.C.J. No. 22, [1999] 1 S.C.R. 761 (S.C.C.)?

The complex issue of cross-cultural custody disputes involving Aboriginal and non-Aboriginal parents was most prominently profiled in the case of *L. (D.T.) v. L. (Police Service)*, [1999] Q.J. No. 5364 (Que. S.C.). The Quebec Court of Appeal outlined the facts of the case as follows (*L. (D.T.) v. L. (Police Service)*, [2001] Q.J. No. 1444 (Que. C.A.) at paras. 3-8, 11-18, 21-23 and 26):

> [3] Appellant and Respondent were married on June 19, 1988, in the City of La., in the State of Nevada. They moved to California.
>
> [4] Of their union were born twin girls, at S., California, on [...], 1988, namely M.E.L. and V.N.L.
>
> [5] The children were resident at Oceanside, California, until 1993, and from that time, until 1995, in Vista, California.
>
> [6] In 1995, serious matrimonial difficulties arose between the parties.
>
> [7] On March 20, 1995, Respondent commenced divorce proceedings with his affidavit alleging that the Appellant had "a long and serious history of mental instability".
>
> [8] Appellant was served with the proceedings in the morning of March 20 with a notice to be present the same day at 1.30 p.m. She did not appear and the case proceeded *ex parte*.
>
> . . . . .
>
> [11] On September 13, 1995, both parties, with their attorneys, attended a hearing of the Superior Court of California (Judge Etta Oeltman Gillivan). The Court adopted and ordered compliance with the Family Court Services Report for custody and visitation rights.
>
> [12] In this order, the legal custody of the children was granted to the Appellant and the Respondent. ...
>
> [13] As she explains in her brief, the Appellant in desperate financial circumstances and isolated from her family, her people, culture and native homeland in Quebec, left California without the permission of the Respondent and arrived with the children on the L. First Nation Reserve on October 23, 1995.
>
> [14] On November 29, 1995, the Superior Court of California awarded the sole legal and physical custody of the children to the Respondent and ordered the Appellant to return them to the State of California forthwith to the custody of the Respondent. A judgment of divorce was granted *ex parte* on March 1st, 1996.
>
> [15] In June of 1996, Respondent initiated proceedings before the Superior Court in Quebec under the terms of the *Convention on the Civil Aspects of International Child Abduction* (the Hague Convention) as well as the Quebec relevant legislation for the forced return of the two girls to California.
>
> [16] On June 14, 1996, Respondent decided to take matters in his own hands and entered the L. Reserve in disguise, armed with pepper spray and handcuffs and attacked Appellant and her mother. A violent confrontation ended with the Respondent breaking the Appellant's finger and hitting her,

at least ten times in the face and head and dragging the girl's elderly grandmother back towards the house while she was attempting to get help.

[17] He was arrested and pleaded guilty, on June 27, 1996 to six different counts of criminal offences: a) Assault on the Appellant, b) Carrying a weapon, c) Causing bodily harm to the Appellant, d) Assault on her mother, e) Possession of a prohibited weapon, f) Dangerous driving.

[18] On each count, he received a suspended sentence for a period of one year.

. . . . .

[21] [On July 4, 1996] ... [T]he judge ordered the immediate return of the children to their domicile and residence with their father in Vista, California, ordered the Appellant to remit the children no later than July 9, at 11.00 a.m. and ordered the Director of the L. Aboriginal Police Department and any other police force to assist in the execution of this order.

[22] On the same day, the L. Mi'gmaq First Nation Government passed a resolution entitled Order-In-Council whose conclusions read as follows:

Therefore BE IT Resolved

- that the L. Mi'gmaq First Nation Government take the necessary measures to assist A.M.I. and her children;

- that such measures include if necessary intervening in the present legal proceedings or any related proceedings to assert the rights of Mi'gmaq to live in their community with their People and to assert the rights and jurisdiction of the L. Mi'gmaq First Nation and the L. Mi'gmaq First Nation Government under Mi'gmaq Law, Canadian domestic law and international law.

- that Saqamaw Brenda Gideon Miller or failing her Chief Councillor Allison Metallic be and they are hereby authorised to do all things necessary or useful to give effect to this resolution.

[23] The Appellant did not voluntarily turn the children over to the Respondent and the L. police alleging the terms of the "Order-in-Council" did not execute the Court's Order.

. . . . .

[26] The twin girls lived with the Appellant on the Reserve from October 23, 1995 to August 23, 1999, almost four years.

When the decision at the trial level was rendered by Judge Frank Barakett of the Quebec Superior Court, he wrote the following comments at paras. 14-18:

[14] ... Unable to cope with the stress of it all, overcome with her admitted emotional and financial insecurity, her only perceived solution was to abduct the twins (6 ½ years old, born and raised in California) and go to her psychological hideout in Canada, the L. (Mi'gmag) Indian reserve of some 2,000 inhabitants. These blonde freckled twins would be held there, out of reach of the law and their father from October 1995 until March 1999 during which time they lived with their mother, grandmother and their parents and children and were literally indoctrinated into Indian culture, to the exclusion of what they had previously known. It is not contested that from October 1996 until present that they "integrated".

[15] They grew up to believe judges were bad, (until we met) and that their father was a bad guy with a beard, (until they met him pursuant to the undersigned's intervention on March 25th 1999).

[16] Since October 1995, and up to March 1999, the actions of the mother amount to alienation of the father, limiting him to one period of visitation in the presence of armed native guards in March of 1997 and discouraging any telephone or other type of communication. He became a total stranger after 3 ½ years, despite the fact that the mother, before Justice Goodwin, gave her word that she would return them if he so ordered, (July 4th 1996).

[17] She unwittingly taught the children to live as outlaws, which is not what is taught to other children on the reserve.

[18] Perhaps unwittingly and out of a totally misplaced expression of motherly love, they were brainwashed away from the real world into a child like myth of pow-wows and rituals quite different from other children on the reserve who had regular contact with the outside world.

In the Quebec Court of Appeal the Court made the following comments regarding Judge Barakett's treatment of the issues:

[49] We wish first to discuss the bias and prejudice argument. Even though some of the words used by the judge in first instance were inappropriate, we are not convinced in reading all the transcript and the proceedings that his conduct demonstrated on his part a serious apprehension of bias. I rather think that he was in good faith and sincerely motivated by the desire to give to the children an opportunity to vary their experiences of life. Nevertheless, if the argument raised by the Appellant were well founded, the remedy would be to order a new trial. I cannot imagine that the addition of another hearing to the existing saga would be beneficial to the parties and the children. Therefore, this argument is not retained. ...

Eventually, the comments of Judge Barakett resulted in a complaint to the Canadian Judicial Council. The Native Women's Association of Canada wrote:

Leaders representing major national and regional First Nations Organizations in Canada submitted ten formal complaints to the Canadian Judicial Council in regard to the conduct of Judge Frank Barakett of the Quebec Superior Court (Family Division), in the case of *Lavoie v. Isaac-Lavoie*. ...The Lavoie case involved Ms. Audrey Isaac, a citizen of the Listuguj Mi'kmaq First Nation and her two children. She was seeking custody of her twin daughters, after fleeing back to her community in Listuguj from California. Her relationship with her non-native husband severely deteriorated and she found herself in desperate circumstances.

Fourteen months after the complaint was made, a Panel of the Canadian Judicial Council reviewed Justice Barakett's conduct to determine whether an investigation by an Inquiry Committee was warranted to remove him from the bench. Native Women's Association of Canada, *Violations of Human Rights* at 8-10 (December, 2002) (references omitted)

The investigation of Judge Barakett's conduct was dealt with by the Canadian Judicial Council and concluded as follows:

July 24, 2002 …

Dear Mr. Justice Barakett:

Re: CJC File 00-073

I am writing as Chairperson of the Panel of the Canadian Judicial Council appointed to review your conduct related to the October 12, 2000 complaint jointly signed as follows:

- Michèle Audette, Présidente, Femmes Autochtones du Québec;
- Matthew Coon Come, National Chief, Assembly of First Nations;
- Chief Allison Metallic, Listuguj Mi'gmaq First Nation Government;
- Darliea Dorey, President, Native Women's Association of Canada;
- Ghislain Picard, Chef régional, Secrétariat de L'Assemblée des Premières Nations Du Québec et du Labrador.

The other members of the Panel, appointed by Chief Justice Richard Scott of Manitoba, as Chairperson of the Judicial Conduct Committee of the Council, are Associate Chief Justice Jeffrey Oliphant of the Court of Queen's Bench of Manitoba and Madam Justice Louise Charron of the Court of Appeal for Ontario.

The complaint arises out of custody proceedings following Ms. Audrey Isaac's removal of her two young children from the State of California to a reserve in Quebec in violation of a court order from that State. On July 4, 1996, Mr. Justice Ross Goodwin of your Court ordered the return of the children to the United States. The proceedings before you over two years later were to enforce this judgment for the return of the children. Your decision was to the effect that the Goodwin judgment was executory and you ordered the return of the children to the custodial father. Your decision was upheld by a Panel of the Quebec Court of Appeal on April 5, 2001, which concluded that, in light of the California orders related to these children, the Quebec courts lacked jurisdiction to deal with the merits of the custody issue. The Court did observe that "… some of the words used by the judge in the first instance were inappropriate". … The task of the Panel is to decide whether to recommend to the Council that an Inquiry Committee be established pursuant to subsection 63(3) of the *Judges Act* to undertake a formal investigation. The function of such an Inquiry Committee would be to determine whether a recommendation for your removal from office might be warranted on one or more of the grounds specified in subsection 65(2) of the Act as a result of your conduct. In support of their general allegations in the previous paragraph, the complainants list ten more specific complaints. We have considered these individually and then addressed their cumulative effect.

(1) The first of these complaints relates to your characterization of the husband as being "a solid citizen" who had no problems with the law. The allegation is that you blatantly disregarded the criminal assault and related convictions that arose out of his attempts to take back the children in this case. The Panel understands these comments to be in the context of historical background outside of the facts of this case but to be considered in assessing and weighing the facts of this case. The manner in which you assessed and weighed those facts is a legal matter falling within your judicial discretion. The Panel sees no evidence of judicial misconduct in the comments referred to in this first complaint.

(2) The second complaint refers to your characterization of that criminal conduct itself. The conduct was that of the father who went from California to the mother's reserve in Quebec in an unsuccessful attempt to take back the two children. In the course of doing so, he assaulted both the mother and the 68-year-old grandmother of the children. A reading of the transcript suggests that you did not consider the husband's conduct to be unusual. The implication is that since the mother had "kidnapped" the children from California, it was not surprising that the husband would attempt to "kidnap" them back. ... [T]o suggest that such conduct is "not surprising" implies that it is to be expected or is "normal" even if you do not expressly justify it. To suggest that even you, as a judge, might engage in similar conduct in such circumstances is unacceptable. It trivializes serious misconduct on the part of the husband and, in doing so, reflects adversely on the judiciary. ...

(4) The fourth complaint is based on the following statement in your written judgment:

"Perhaps unwittingly and out of a totally misplaced expression of motherly love, they were brainwashed away from the real world into a child like myth of pow-wows and rituals quite different from other children on the reserve who had regular contact with the outside world." (p. 7)

The Panel understands your view that being confined to the reserve may have limited the children's experiences in some ways. However, these comments can only be interpreted as being derogatory to Aboriginal culture. The Panel is very concerned that you would characterize the raising of these children on a reserve as being "brainwashed away from the real world" or that Aboriginal pow-wows and other rituals were a "child like myth". Such observations imply an inherent inferiority in the Aboriginal community and are incompatible with the equality rights guaranteed in the Canadian Charter of Rights and Freedoms which the judiciary must uphold.

(5) The fifth complaint relates to your description of the children as "blond and freckled twins" and your references to blood quantum in attempting to calculate the amount of "Indian blood" in the children. The Panel views these references as a misguided attempt on your part to determine whether these children were "really" Aboriginal. As the Report of the Royal Commission on Aboriginal Peoples has pointed out, and the complainants have quoted:

"... under section 35 of the Constitution Act, 1982, an Aboriginal nation has the right to determine which individuals belong to the nation as members and citizens ... Modern Aboriginal nations, like other nations in the world today, represent a mixture of genetic heritages. Their identity lies in their collective life, their history, ancestry, culture, values, traditions and ties to the land, rather than in their race as such."

Your gratuitous exploration of the children's "Indian blood" was a further reflection of insensitivity towards Aboriginal culture.

(6) The sixth complaint is related to the fourth but emphasizes your references to the children being "brainwashed" and "indoctrinated into Indian culture". The Panel interprets these comments as being critical of the mother's successful efforts to have her children learn about and experience Mi'gmaq culture. We agree with the complainants that every parent has the right to introduce her own cultural and spiritual beliefs to her own children.

Your characterization of these parenting efforts as brainwashing and indoctrinating again imply that Aboriginal culture is inferior and not worthy of equal respect with other cultures and spiritual beliefs.

(7) The seventh complaint has two aspects. The first involves your findings in relation to the custody of the children. This is a legal issue subject to your judicial discretion rather than a conduct issue. However, the second aspect involves gratuitous comments on your part which are of serious concern to the Panel. In response to the mother's comment that she wanted her daughters to be happy, you stated:

"That is easy. Just put them on heroin, they'll be happy all the time."

In response to the mother's explanation of pow-wows and shawl dancing, you stated:

If they had been in Austria with you, if you had run away to Austria, they would be in a beer garden twirling batons with their parents applauding and they would be in their culture, they'd be in Bavaria somewhere.

The latter statement trivializes the mother's commitment to introducing her children to Aboriginal culture. However, both statements suggest a stereotype of Aboriginal peoples related to alcohol and drug abuse which should not be encouraged in any way by a judge. ...

The Panel's findings in relation to these complaints indicate that many of your comments both in the course of the proceedings and in your written judgment were improper for a judge. Some are not only insensitive but also insulting to Aboriginal culture in Canada. ... We were concerned that your comments may reflect an underlying bias against Aboriginal culture which may preclude you from treating all litigants with the equality required by the Charter in future. ...

As mentioned above, the role of this Panel is to decide whether to recommend that an Inquiry Committee be established under the Judges Act. The Inquiry Committee would consider whether a recommendation for your removal from the office of judge may be warranted. The following test for removal was established by the 1990 Marshall Inquiry Committee:

> Is the conduct alleged so manifestly and profoundly destructive of the concept of the impartiality, integrity and independence of the judicial role, that public confidence would be sufficiently undermined to render the judge incapable of executing the judicial office?

... The Panel has noted that you have made a full and unqualified acknowledgment of the impropriety of your comments and have apologized in the attached letter [below]. ... In this case, there is no evidence of malice or improper motive on your part. Your unfortunate comments appear to stem from ignorance of Aboriginal culture rather than contempt for it. In other words, the public could be expected to have confidence that you have learned from this experience and will approach issues related to Aboriginal culture with greater understanding and respect in future. ...

In all of these circumstances, the Panel has decided that no investigation by an Inquiry Committee is warranted as the conduct complained about, while improper, is not serious enough to warrant removal. This file is accordingly closed. ...

Judge Barakett responded to the complaints as follows:

July 3, 2002

Ms. Jeannie Thomas
Canadian Judicial Council ...

In my letter to you of June 10, 2002, I stated that I am truly sorry and sincerely apologize for some of the comments made by me during the trial and in my written judgment in this matter. I also stated that I am willing to offer the complainants a public apology for those comments.

I am writing this letter in order to make that public apology.

I now realize that some of the comments made by me are disparaging to Ms. Isaac and Aboriginal people in general. I sincerely apologize to them for those comments and for the hurt they caused.

Although I reiterate that I have not and do not feel any prejudice against Ms. Isaac or Aboriginal people, I acknowledge that the words used by me are unacceptable.

Would you please transmit the present letter to the Panel considering this matter and indicate to its members my consent to the letter being made public.

Very truly yours,
Frank Barakett, J.S.C.

The Native Women's Association of Canada wrote the following in response to the entire proceedings:

The decision of the Canadian Judicial Council has not convinced Aboriginal people, women, especially, that they should have confidence in the judicial system. There is no confidence that this judge will decide with impartiality any future cases concerning Aboriginal people or women. There are still many valid and significant reasons why many Aboriginal people believe that the system is too often unjust and unfair and that the system "protects its own". As noted by a report of the Quebec Native Women's Association to the CJC, "Many of our people feel that, in relation to Aboriginal peoples, judges within the CJC — as in the courts — are too often incapable of upholding the principles of judicial independence and impartiality. When it comes to disciplining judges, the CJC will too often 'protect their own'. It has also been emphasized that the members of your Council include no Aboriginal people. For many, this helps to explain — but does not excuse — what they perceive as a profound insensitivity within the CJC to the discrimination and other unfair treatment that our people experience."

Do you think the issue of bias was appropriately dealt with by the Canadian Judicial Council in this case?

E. SELF-GOVERNMENT INITIATIVES

Since Aboriginal peoples continue to run into significant challenges with courts and provincially run child welfare agencies, many communities are seeking to make the delivery of these services more culturally appropriate. Others, having less faith in existing systems, seek to take control of Aboriginal child welfare away from the provinces to vest it in the community or Nation. Reform of the child welfare system relative to Aboriginal peoples continues to occupy a prominent place in discussions of self-government and community autonomy. The following case of *S. (E.G.) v. Spallumcheen Band Council*, [1998] B.C.J. No. 2778, [1999] 2 C.N.L.R. 318 (B.C.S.C.), and extracts from the Royal Commission on Aboriginal Peoples and the Manitoba Justice Inquiry illustrate how Aboriginal peoples are taking a larger role in Aboriginal child welfare.

S. (E.G.) v. SPALLUMCHEEN BAND COUNCIL

[1998] B.C.J. No. 2778, [1999] 2 C.N.L.R. 318 (B.C.S.C.)

[1] **Williamson J.:** — [FC] was born on October 27, 1996. Her mother, a member of the Spallumcheen Indian Band (the "Band"), found she was unable to care for the child. She asked the plaintiffs, Mr. and Mrs. [S], to act, in effect, as foster parents. The plaintiffs agreed to do so. However, concerned about this private arrangement, they asked the Provincial Ministry of Children and Families (the "Ministry") to become involved. As a result, the Ministry entered into a voluntary care agreement pursuant to which the [S]s would act as foster parents to [F]. The child's mother had visitation rights.

[2] In 1980 the Band passed a by-law, as it was then empowered to do by s. 81 of the *Indian Act*, R.S.C. 1970, c. I-6 (the "Act") in which it took responsibility for the welfare of children of the Band. This by-law was been approved by the Minister. It has the power of a regulation passed pursuant to the Act and is law.

[3] Thus, the welfare of children of the Spallumcheen Indian Band, unlike that of other children in British Columbia, is the responsibility of the Band rather than of the Ministry.

[4] The Ministry and the Band have a working relationship governed by protocols which have been amended from time to time since the by-law was first approved in 1980.

[5] Over the years the Band has developed a program which emphasizes cultural identity. The affidavits filed disclose the Band also has in place programs and personnel to deal with the physical and psychological health matters that may arise with individual children. The program currently employs three full-time staff, and has other professionals available for consultation. At the time of this application, 25 children were in the care of the Band. In [FC]'s case, several employees of the Provincial Ministry have been involved working with the Band staff.

[6] Although both of [F]'s biological parents are native persons, she was not registered as a member of the Band until February of 1998. When registration occurred, the responsibility for the welfare of [F] passed from the Ministry to the Band.

[7] Initially, the Band was content to leave the child with the plaintiffs and, therefore, entered into a foster parenting agreement with them. The Band decided, however, that it would be in the best interests of the child

and consistent with the provisions of the governing by-law to work towards reuniting the child with her mother.

[8] On March 17, 1998, it was decided that the Band would maintain responsibility for [F], that she would continue to live with the plaintiffs, but that there would be increasing visits by the child's mother geared towards the eventual return of the child to her mother and the reunification of the family.

[9] At that stage, the mother's visits with the child were supervised.

[10] The affidavit material filed discloses that while the plaintiffs provided excellent care for [F] during the entire period that she was in their care, the plaintiffs' relationship with the Band began to break down over the spring.

[11] On June 16, 1998, the Band Council decided that while [F] would remain the responsibility of the Council for a further six months, she would be moved from her foster placement with the plaintiffs to the home of [F]'s maternal aunt and her family, [SW]. Ms. [W] is a member of the Band.

[12] Since [F] was moved to the [W]'s house on June 16, 1998, the plaintiffs have not had access to [F]. In this application, they seek an order for interim access and an order for a custody and access report, pursuant to s. 15 of the *Family Relations Act*, R.S.B.C. 1996, c. 128.

[13] They rely upon the inherent *parens patriae* jurisdiction of the court.

[14] I am not persuaded that this is a case in which that jurisdiction should be asserted.

[15] It is not disputed that pursuant to the by-law passed by the Band in 1980, it is the Band which has the responsibility for welfare of Spallumcheen children.

[16] The affidavit material discloses that the impetus for the passing of this by-law was the conclusion on the part of the Band that the best interests of its children were not being served by a child welfare regime geared to the general population. The Band had concluded that as a result of the loss of children to the residential school system and through apprehensions by Provincial authorities which resulted in Spallumcheen children being placed in non-native foster homes, the survival of the Spallumcheen First Nation was in jeopardy. The preamble to the by-law expressed that view in the following words:

> ... the removal of our children by non-band agencies and the treatment of the children while under the authority of non-band agencies has too often hurt our children emotionally and serves to fracture the strength of our community, thereby contributing to social breakdown and disorder within our reserve.

[17] The by-law went on to say that it was the Band that would have exclusive jurisdiction over any child custody proceeding involving a Spallumcheen child, notwithstanding the residence of that child.

[18] It also specified that where a child was to be placed with a family other than its own, a preference for such placement would be given in the following order:

1) a parent;
2) a member of the extended family living on the reserve;
3) a member of the extended family living on another reserve, although not a reserve to the Indian Band;
4) a member of the extended family living off the reserve;
5) an Indian living on a reserve;
6) an Indian living off a reserve; and
7) only as a last resort shall the child be placed in the home of a non-Indian living off the reserve.

[19] It is the contention of the Band that in placing [F] with her maternal aunt, they were carrying out the objectives of the by-law.

[20] They note that according to the terms of that by-law, it would be preferable to place [F] with a member of her extended family living off the reserve, such as her aunt, rather than with the plaintiffs who would be the preferred placement only as a last resort. Further, the Band says the decision was consistent with other enunciated goals in the by-law including the rebuilding, wherever possible, of the family of the child, and the paramountcy of the best interests of the child.

[21] While they concede the removal of [F] from the plaintiffs in June of this year was too abrupt, the Band says the fault for that cannot be laid at their feet. It is their submission that the relationship between the plaintiffs and the Band had deteriorated and that continued involvement of the plaintiffs would manifest an antagonism which would be apparent to [F] and could not be in her best interests. They observe that since the change in placement, the plaintiffs have been interviewed by the press and that the sensational and inaccurate reporting of this incident has been hurtful and damaging to the Band.

[22] Much of that press coverage was appended to affidavits. I agree that it discloses an apparent lack of verisimilitude and could be interpreted as reinforcing negative stereotypes of native peoples. Certainly there are blatant errors.

[23] For the purposes of this application, however, I am not prepared to accept that the inaccurate reporting in this case is the fault of the plaintiffs rather than the result of the apparent need of some journalists for material conducive to sensational headlines.

[24] The issue to be determined before me is, should this court exercise its inherent jurisdiction of *parens patriae* in the circumstances of this case? Courts once had wide powers pursuant to this inherent jurisdiction. However, in the last century, legislatures in the common law world have increasingly occupied the field. We are now at the stage where there are only limited circumstances where there should be resort to this jurisdiction. These include emergency situations where a child appears in need of some form of protection, in a judicial review of the exercise of a statutory power, or where there is found to be a gap in the legislation being considered. It is the latter which is relied upon by the plaintiffs in this case.

[25] The plaintiffs submit that the by-law, which gives the Band responsibility and power over the welfare of its children, is not as

extensive a code as the statutory framework which applies to non-Spallumcheen children in this Province. Thus, they argue, in a circumstance such as this where the best interests of the child arguably require that she continue to have a relationship with those foster parents who cared for her for most of her life to date, the court should intervene.

[26] While it may be that the by-law is not as extensive as the legislative scheme otherwise in effect, I am satisfied that it provides a clear statutory scheme whereby the Band, consistent with enunciated goals and priorities set out in the by-law, is to exercise its responsibility for the care of children within its care.

[27] I am cognizant of the observations of Associate Chief Judge Stansfield in his reasons given September 30, 1998 when he determined this application could be ruled upon only by a court of inherent jurisdiction. At paragraph 59, he wrote:

> But what of the best interests of a child who has been raised by, and presumably is bonded with, persons who are not within the classes enumerated by the By-Law? One can only presume that it is potentially contrary to the best interest of such a child, and thus could cause a grave injustice, to deny to such caregivers a fair process through which they can offer themselves in the continuing care of the subject child.

[28] The learned judge went on two paragraphs later to say there are "glaring deficiencies" in the by-law, and he suggested that these could and should be addressed through an amendment.

[29] It may be that the fact the legislative framework does not provide foster parents with status to apply for custody or access is a deficiency. But in this respect, the legislative scheme is no different from that applying to foster parents of non-Spallumcheen children in British Columbia.

[30] Foster parents who enter into an agreement with the Ministry to care for a child agree that they will relinquish that child at the request of the Superintendent. *The Family and Child Service Act*, S.B.C. 1980, c. 11, provided in s. 21, that:

> Nothing in this Act limits the inherent jurisdiction of the Crown, through the Supreme Court, over infants, as parens patriae, and the Supreme Court may rescind a permanent order where it is satisfied that to do so is conducive to a child's best interest and welfare.

[31] This legislation was reviewed by the Court of Appeal in *P. (E.) v. B.C. (Supt. of Fam. & Child Service)* (1988), 23 B.C.L.R. (2d) 329. In considering the *parens patriae* jurisdiction of the court, Anderson J.A. noted at p. 340 that as the responsibility for determining the best interests of children who are wards of the Ministry has been given to the Superintendent, the:

> onus is heavy on counsel for the foster parents to persuade us that the reference to the "parens patriae" jurisdiction of the Supreme Court was intended to enable the Supreme Court to "override or disregard the conclusions" of the Superintendent.

In that same case, the court concluded that foster parents have no status to make an application for access under s. 21 of the Act. Nothing in the current legislation renders that comment any less persuasive. See: the *Child, Family and Community Service Act*, R.S.B.C. 1996, c. 46, s. 99.

[32] In my view, foster parents who owe their status to an agreement with the Band Council pursuant to its by-law are in the same circumstance as other foster parents. They have no status to make an application for custody or access. If that be a gap, it is also a gap in the Provincial legislative scheme. And just as with that legislation, it is not a lacuna of such significance that the inherent *parens patriae* jurisdiction of the court should be invoked.

[33] Mrs. [S] deposes that she does not believe it is in the "best interests of the child that the Band be left as the sole decision maker regarding appropriate arrangements for [F]." She would have the court substitute its view of the child's best interests for that of the Band. To do so would be to usurp the very power which the legislation confers upon the Band.

[34] I agree with Judge Stansfield that if former foster parents' lack of a right to apply for access and other rights be a deficiency, the appropriate remedy is legislative action.

[35] The petitioners do not say the child is in need of protection. Rather, they seek access and assessment. I am satisfied, upon a review of the material, that in this case the Band is exercising powers which it has pursuant to the by-law and that there is nothing which would warrant the intrusion upon that jurisdiction sought by the petitioners in this application.

[36] The application is dismissed.

---

1. The following exchange took place in the B.C. legislature concerning the *S. (E.G.)* case (Debates of the Legislative Assembly (Hansard), Wednesday, July 29, 1998 Afternoon, Volume 12, Number 11, Page 10678):

> **V. Anderson:** To the Minister for Children and Families. Last week the official opposition pointed out to the Ministry for Children and Families that on June 22 the Spallumcheen band abruptly removed 20-month-old Baby F. from her foster home without any transition planning. Baby F. has fetal alcohol effect and cannot tolerate sudden and drastic changes. This child has already been separated from her biological mother, and she has now had another primary bond with a foster parent severed. As the Child and Family Review Board found last year in the Murphy case, destroying a developmentally challenged baby's bond with a caregiver is a violation of that child's rights. Why has the Ministry for Children and Families refused to even investigate whether or not this baby's rights have been violated?
>
> **Hon. L. Boone:** The member probably knows — he should know — that the Spallumcheen band was given the right to deal with aboriginal children many years ago. ... In this case here, I certainly understand the concerns of the foster parent. I know that there's great attachment that

comes with foster parents to the children. However, this case actually went before a judge. The judge accepted and approved the plan of care. So this is not something that is being done offhand; it is something that has been approved by the judge. We believe that it's in the best interests of the child.

The Speaker: First supplementary, member for Vancouver-Langara.

V. Anderson: That was the same thing that was said, in essence, in the Murphy case, which was proved to be false afterwards. All children in British Columbia deserve to have their rights protected under provincial law, and this is no exception. Now this government is debating whether or not they even have jurisdiction to protect this little girl. Will the minister acknowledge her responsibility to protect the rights of Baby F. under our provincial legislation and act immediately to ensure that the best interests of this child are put first, as we have committed ourselves to under the convention on the rights of the child?

Hon. L. Boone: It has gone before the courts. I believe that the courts have the final say as to whether the best interests of the child are at stake there. They approved the case plan for that child, so I believe that the best interests of the child are being taken care of.

2. Members of the Spallumcheen Band had most of their children taken away from them before the by-law at issue in the *S. (E.G.)* case was passed in 1980. In fact, of the total Spallumcheen population of approximately 500 people, 80 children were in government care. One particularly poignant event was described as follows:

> A social worker chartered a bus and apprehended 38 children in the 1970's. Spallumcheen became a quiet, dispirited town of adults and Elders, with at times fewer than 14 children left on the reserve. Drinking and despair intensified rather than dissipated and it was generally known that once children were taken, they were never returned.[11]

3. Aboriginal peoples have raised arguments that their responsibilities to raise their children are integral to their distinctive culture and thus protected as Aboriginal rights under section 35(1) of the *Constitution Act, 1982*. Thus far, these arguments have not found much success before the courts because the proper evidentiary base has not been established. In *Algonquins of Pikwakanagan First Nation v. Children's Aid Society of Toronto*, [2004] O.J. No. 1740, [2004] 3 C.N.L.R. 1 (Ont. S.C.J.) the Ontario Superior Court wrote at paras. 39-41:

> The applicant says that, in the circumstances of this case, subsection 64(9) [of the *Child and Family Services Act*] violates the traditional rights guaranteed by section 35 of the *Constitution Act, 1982*. The applicant describes these "traditional rights" as "the child rearing practices and traditions of this band in particular, and first nations in general".
>
> First, I have no evidence of any particular, or even general child-rearing practices of the band, or of first nations in general. Mr. B. appends to his affidavit various reports or studies that support the proposition that native children raised in non-native homes have difficulty integrating into native society as adults and that many suffer from behavioural and psychological problems. These reports and studies are not evidence and, even if they were, say nothing about the traditional

rights the band seeks to protect. They also cannot determine if these difficulties are caused by the native children being adopted by non-natives, or have other, or additional causes.

It is no doubt true that some native children experience the difficulties Mr. B. describes. However, that is not the point. Mr. B.'s affidavit makes a broad statement that, to every extent possible, he and his partner "continue our native traditions, and teach the culture to our children ... and within our home we live a traditional Anishinabe/Wendate relationship." Nowhere are any of these traditions or practices described. The band's motion submits that native child rearing practices are unique customs that have Charter protection. However, there is no evidence before me upon which to conclude that the native child rearing practices are unique in any way. I have no evidence at all of what they are. It is therefore is impossible to find there are any traditional rights that have been guaranteed, and thus infringed. As the court said in *A.P.G. v. K.H.A* "I have heard no evidence as to the contents of any treaty ... nor ... any evidence as to the existence of an inherent aboriginal right of this child to be raised as an Indian ... it is generally impossible to mount a Charter challenge in an evidentiary vacuum.

In *Re T. (R.)*, [2004] S.J. No. 771, [2005] 1 C.N.L.R. 289 (Sask. Q.B.), at paras. 58-61, the Aboriginal litigants met a similar response, as follows:

In this case, the NASC Agency/band argue that aboriginal "notions of community and kinship" are an integral part of aboriginal society. First Nations families and communities share responsibility for the upbringing, training, education and well-being of their children. They submit that the aboriginal right of self-government includes the legal right and moral obligation to speak for persons who are under a legal disability, such as children. As this "right" has never been extinguished, *The Child and Family Services Act* cannot impair it by placing aboriginal children for adoption without the band's consent.

The provincial Attorney General and counsel for the children argue there is no evidence before this Court to establish the aboriginal right claimed.

The only evidence called by the NASC Agency/band was that of Dr. Katz who testified that "kinship" is an aboriginal "value" and that "community" plays an important role in the raising of aboriginal children. There was no evidence of what happens to aboriginal children when no "kinship" or "community" resources are available to care for them. His evidence falls far short of establishing the right asserted by the NASC Agency/band. Moreover, the "right" asserted appears to be of a general nature and not a defining feature of the culture in question. Even if such a right did exist, there is no evidence that its existence was "pre-contact". ...

Because this Court is unable to find the existence of the aboriginal right asserted by the Agency/band, s. 25 of the *Charter* does not apply. As pointed out by Veit J. in *Steinhauer v. R.*, [1985] 3 C.N.L.R. 187 (Alta. Q.B.), s. 25 of the *Charter* does not add to aboriginal rights, it merely "shields" existing aboriginal rights.

Since an Aboriginal or treaty right to child care and protection has not been established under section 35(1), Aboriginal peoples continue to work with provincial governments to secure better laws for children. The following extracts and notes outline the range of legislative and negotiated reforms that have recently developed to facilitate a fuller measure of Aboriginal control in child welfare matters.

REPORT OF THE ROYAL COMMISSION ON ABORIGINAL PEOPLES: GATHERING STRENGTH, VOL. 3

(Ottawa: Ministry of Supply and Services, 1996) at 29-33
(references omitted)

Child Welfare Reform

Some things have changed as a result of efforts begun in the 1980s. Since 1981, when the first agreement was signed authorizing a First Nation agency to deliver child welfare services, responsibility for delivering child welfare services has been delegated progressively to agencies administered by First Nations and some Métis communities. Emphasis is being placed on supporting increased Aboriginal control of the development, design and delivery of child and family services. In 1990-91, DIAND funded 36 Aboriginal child and family agencies covering 212 bands. Also in 1990-91, a total of $1.5 million was allocated to First Nations, over a period of two years, for the development of Aboriginal child and family service standards.

Most Aboriginal child care agencies have adopted placement protocols specifying the following placement priorities: first, with the extended family; second, with Aboriginal members of the community with the same cultural and linguistic identification; and third, other alternative Aboriginal caregivers. As a last resort, placement is considered with non-Aboriginal caregivers. Some work has been done to develop culturally appropriate standards for selecting Aboriginal foster caregivers; however, as discussed later, it has been hampered by funding constraints and limited policy support for developmental work in new Aboriginal agencies.

The following summary illustrates the developments in child welfare in Aboriginal communities:

- Agencies established under the tripartite agreement with the Four Nations Confederacy of Manitoba, signed in 1982.
- Agencies authorized to administer child welfare, particularly in northern and northwestern Ontario under the 1984 *Child and Family Services Act*.
- Child welfare prevention services sponsored jointly by bands and the provincial government in southern Ontario.
- Agreements signed with single bands such as the Blackfoot at Gleichen, Alberta, and the Métis and Cree community of Sandy Bay, Saskatchewan, to provide services under provincial mandates.
- Regional Aboriginal services developed, including Mi'kmaq Family and Children's Service of Nova Scotia and Nuu-chah-nulth Community and Human Services in British Columbia.
- Child welfare and other human services, in regions where land claims agreements have been concluded, delivered through boards under

Aboriginal control, such as Kativik Regional Social Services and Cree Regional Health and Social Services Board in Quebec.

- Social services in the Northwest Territories decentralized to increase community control.

Aboriginal child and family services have been established in metropolitan centres such as Toronto and Winnipeg. They report significant success in recruiting Aboriginal foster homes. For example, Native Child and Family Services of Toronto reported that 62 per cent of the agency's placements in 1993-4 were customary care arrangements, signifying voluntary involvement of parents and placement in Aboriginal homes.

Alberta has the distinction of sponsoring the only Métis-specific child welfare agency yet established. Métis Child and Family Services of Edmonton provides foster care placements and emphasizes traditional values as a component of the assessment process in home studies to screen potential caregivers. According to information provided to Brad McKenzie, who conducted a research study for the Commission,

> An orientation training program and ongoing support meetings for foster parents are provided. As a private agency [Métis Child and Family Services] did not qualify for a 1994 increase of 5 per cent paid to foster parents providing service within the provincial system. Barriers to the recruitment and retention of Aboriginal foster care identified by this agency respondent included limited funding, an inadequate training program for foster parents, limitations in the number of potential families who are able to foster, and a failure on the part of the social service bureaucracy to involve foster parents as meaningful partners in meeting the needs of children in their care.

In the study McKenzie notes that such agencies, administered by Aboriginal people, have achieved considerable success in expanding the number of Aboriginal foster home providers, even though provincial agencies in diverse locations acknowledge difficulties in locating a sufficient number of homes.

Several provinces have moved to make their legislation more sensitive to Aboriginal identity in making plans for children. For example, Alberta specifies that an Aboriginal child must be informed of his or her status and that the chief and council of an Aboriginal child's community must be consulted before permanent wardship hearings. Newfoundland's legislation specifies that "the child's cultural and religious heritage" must be considered in determining a child's best interests." In the Northwest Territories, the objective of the 1994 *Aboriginal Custom Adoption Recognition Act* is "without changing aboriginal customary law, to set out a simple procedure by which a custom adoption may be respected and recognized". The adoptive parent or parents simply provide identification papers along with a written statement from the interested parties that an adoption took place in accordance with Aboriginal custom. Once the custom adoption commissioner is satisfied that the information provided is complete and in order, a certificate of adoption is issued and the adoption is registered in appropriate vital statistics files. Records of the adoption are not sealed. The

Yukon provides that the child's "own cultural background" and "lifestyle in his home community" be considered in adoption cases. Quebec's *Youth Protection Act* stipulates that "Every person having responsibilities towards a child under this Act, and every person called upon to make decisions with respect to a child under this Act shall, in their interventions, take into account the necessity ... of opting for measures in respect of the child and the child's parents ... which take into consideration ... the characteristics of Native communities".

Ontario has the most extensive provisions in relation to Aboriginal child welfare in its *Child and Family Services Act* (1984). The Act seeks to include both status Indian people and others of Aboriginal ancestry by using the term "Native". Special provisions for all children's aid societies serving Aboriginal communities recognize "Indian" and "Native" status as a "best interests" category over and above the obligation to consider cultural background. The Act devotes an entire section to Aboriginal child and family service agencies. It also recognizes customary care and permits these agencies to seek exemptions from the application of any part of the law.

Alberta and Manitoba have created a child advocate office to provide impartial investigations into complaints concerning services rendered to children. About 20 years ago Quebec created a youth protection commission with a similar mandate. This commission was recently merged with Quebec's human rights commission to become the province's human rights and youth rights commission. Its mission is "to ensure ... that the interests of children are protected, and that their rights recognized by the Quebec youth protection act are respected."

In many jurisdictions, exceptions are permitted to culturally inappropriate requirements that might screen out Aboriginal people applying to foster or adopt Aboriginal children. Such exceptions may be explicit, as in Ontario's *Child and Family Services Act*; or implicit, as in the practice of agencies that encourage Aboriginal families to provide care for Aboriginal children.

Expenditures to improve the coverage and quality of Aboriginal-specific child welfare services have been increased substantially for services to registered Indians ordinarily resident on-reserve and Indian child-in-care costs charged back to the federal department of Indian affairs. In 1992-93 the department allocated $ 153.8 million to child and family services, representing 78 per cent of the welfare services budget, which also includes services to enable adults with functional limitations to maintain their independence. The welfare services budget increased from $38.7 million in 1981-82 to $204.8 million in 1992-93 — an annual increase of 16 per cent. Expenditures per child in care increased at an average annual rate of 17 per cent in the same period, rising from $6,754 in 1981-82 to $28,260 in 1991-92.

Despite these welcome reforms, and modest successes in placing children in Aboriginal foster homes, which have stemmed the flow of Aboriginal children out of their communities and nations, it is evident that services to care for neglected and abused children are insufficient to repair the ills plaguing Aboriginal families.

In 1992-93, about 4 per cent of First Nations children living on-reserve were in agency care outside their own homes, a reduction from the highs of between 6 and 6.5 per cent in the 1970s. During the same period, however, child welfare agencies serving the general population made an effort to keep children in their own homes, a move that reduced the general child-in-care rate to 0.63 per cent. The percentage of First Nations children in care is six times that of children from the general population in the care of public agencies. This disparity has increased since the 1970s, when First Nations children were placed in care at five-and-a-half times the rate of children in the general population. As with most statistics on social services, only data on First Nations services provided directly or funded by the federal government are available. The extent of service to Métis people cannot be discerned from existing sources.

A November 1994 publication of Alberta's Commissioner of Services for Children states that "While only nine per cent of all children in Alberta are Aboriginal, nearly 50 per cent of the children in care are Aboriginal". The terminology used would seem to imply that Métis and non-status Aboriginal children are included in the figures, despite the prevailing scarcity of data on the Métis population.

In a more localized study prepared for this Commission in 1994, an Aboriginal child and family service agency in southern Manitoba reported an on reserve child population (0-18 years) of 2,238 and an in-care figure of 257 at 31 March 1994, which translates to an in-care rate of 11.5 per cent. Child welfare agencies are set up to protect the interests of children at risk of neglect or abuse. The continued high rates of children in care outside their homes indicate a crisis in Aboriginal family life.

SONIA HARRIS-SHORT, "THE ROAD BACK FROM HELL? SELF-GOVERNMENT AND THE DECOLONISATION OF ABORIGINAL CHILD WELFARE IN CANADA"

(2003, unpublished)[12]

There have been further developments towards Aboriginal control in child welfare matters since the Royal Commission reported in 1996. For example, British Columbia's *Child, Family and Community Service Act* [R.S.B.C. 1996] c. 46 states: "the cultural identity of aboriginal children should be preserved" and "kinship ties and a child's attachment to the extended family should be preserved if possible" (s. 2 (*e*) & (*f*)). It also stipulates that a child in care has the right "to receive guidance and encouragement to maintain their cultural heritage" (s. 70 (1)(*j*)). These general principles are reflected in several of the Act's more specific provisions. For example, the importance of an aboriginal child's cultural identity is given explicit recognition when determining the child's best interests (s. 4(2)) and the legislation provides that the director's interim plan for a child in care must include details of the steps to be taken to preserve the child's aboriginal identity (s. 35(1)(*b*)).

British Columbia's legislation also strongly recognizes the importance of keeping aboriginal children within their family and community. Therefore the Act contains provisions for voluntary care agreements between the Director and a person who has 'a cultural or traditional responsibility towards a child' (s. 8 (1)(*a*)). The Director can even provide some financial support for a placement arranged under this type of agreement (s. 8 (2)). The Act also contemplates a family conferencing model to enable the family to develop a plan of care that can take into account the role of the child's family, his/her culture and community. To this end, it includes a provision that the child can be placed with a relative or some other person with the director's consent (ss. 20-21).

The BC *Child, Family and Community Service Act* also provides for priority in aboriginal placements. The Act states:

71(3) If the child is an aboriginal child, the director must give priority to placing the child as follows:
  (*a*) with the child's extended family or within the child's aboriginal cultural community;
  (*b*) with another aboriginal family, if the child cannot be safely placed under paragraph (*a*);
  (*c*) in accordance with subsection (2), if the child cannot be safely placed under paragraph (*a*) or (*b*) of this subsection.

Greater community involvement in the design and delivery of aboriginal child protection services is also contemplated in the BC Act. For example, when an aboriginal child is removed from their family, or deemed to be in need of supervised care, a prescribed aboriginal organization or, in the case of a Nisga'a child the Nisga'a Lisms Government, must be given notice of the first presentation hearing (ss. 33.1(4), 34(3), 36(2.1)). Thereafter, the child's band (if the child is registered or entitled to be registered as a member of an Indian band), the Nisga'a Lisms Government (if the child is a Nisga'a child), or an aboriginal community identified by the child or the child's parents (if the child is aboriginal but not a Nisga'a child and not registered or entitled to be registered as a band member) is entitled to be served with notice of the proceedings and, if in attendance at the commencement of the proceedings, will be entitled to full party status (ss. 39(1), 49(3)). As regards service design and delivery, the guiding principles enshrined in the legislation state that:

- aboriginal people should be involved in the planning and delivery of services to aboriginal families and their children (3 (*b*));
- services should be planned and provided in ways that are sensitive to the needs and the cultural, racial and religious heritage of those receiving the services (3 (*c*));
- the community should be involved, wherever possible and appropriate, in the planning and delivery of services, including preventive and support services to families and children (3 (*e*)).

Pursuant to these principles of community participation, the legislative framework allows for a director to enter into an agreement with an Indian band, the Nisga'a Nation, a Nisga'a Village, or a legal entity representing an aboriginal community, to provide services under the Act (s. 93 (1)(g)(iii)). The director may also delegate any or all of his powers, duties and functions to a person or class of person (s. 92(1)). This has facilitated the development in British Columbia of aboriginal controlled child welfare agencies offering a range of child protection and family support services to aboriginal communities. To further this goal the BC government is also establishing five aboriginal regional authorities that will be responsible for the organization and delivery of all child welfare services to any aboriginal person living within the territorial region for which each new authority is responsible. ... [While these are still being set up, it is intended that Regional Aboriginal Authorities will take responsibility for and direct supports and services for Aboriginal children and families.]

Other jurisdictions have also created an enlarged role for Aboriginal peoples in child welfare, see: See *Child and Family Services Act*, 1990, C.11 ss. 1(2)4, 1(2)5, 13(3), 34(2)(*d*), 34(10)(*f*), 35(1)(*e*), 36(4)(*c*), 37(3)3, 37(4), 39(1)4, 47(2)(*c*), 54(3)(*f*), 57(5), 58(2)(*b*), 58(4), 61(2)(*d*), 64(4)(*d*), 64(6)(*e*), 69(1)(*e*), 80(4)(*f*), Part X, 223 (Ontario); *Youth Protection Act*, 2002, P-34.1, ss. 2.4(5)(*c*), 37.5 (Quebec); *Child and Family Services Act*, C-7.2 1989-90, ss. 4(*c*), 23, 37(4)(*c*), 37(10), 37(11), 53, 61 (Saskatchewan); *Child Welfare Act*, 2000, C-12, ss. 2(*f*)(i), 2(*h*)(i), 2(*h*)(iii), 2(*l*) 107, 121, 122 and *Child and Family Services Authorities Act*, C-11 2000, Preamble (Alberta); *Children and Family Services Act* c. 5, 1990, Preamble, ss. 2(*g*), 7(2), 6(1), 9(*i*), 20(*d*), 36(3), 39(8)(*c*), 42(3), 44(3)(*c*), 47(5), 88(1)(*e*) (Nova Scotia); *Children's Act* c. 22, ss. 107, 109, 131(*k*) (Yukon); *Family Services Act* c. F-2.2 1980 ss 1(*g*), 3(1), 45(1)(*a*), 45(3)(*a*) (New Brunswick); *Child, Youth and Family Services Act*, c-12.1 1998, ss. 7(*f*), 7(*g*), 9(*c*), 75(2)(*e*) (Newfoundland); *Child and Family Services Act*, S.N.W.T. 1997, c. 13, Preamble, ss. 2(*f*), 2(*i*), 2(*l*), 3, 7(*l*), 7(*m*), 7(*n*), 15, 25 (*b*.1), 25 (*c*), 54 (3), 56, 57, 58, 58.1, 58.2, 59, 91(*i*) (North West Territories); *Consolidated Child and Family Services Act (Nunavut)* S.N.W.T. 1997, c. 13, Preamble, ss. 2(*f*), 2(*i*), 2(*l*), 3, 7(*l*), 7(*m*), 7(*n*), 15, 25 (*b*.1), 25 (*c*), 54 (3), 56, 57, 58, 58.1, 58.2, 59, 91(i) (Nunavut).

In British Columbia the appointment of Judge Mary-Ellen Turpel, a Cree woman, as the Child and Youth Representative in the province has brought heightened attention to Aboriginal children's issues in the province. Her powers are described in section 6 of the *Representative for Children and Youth Act*, S.B.C. 2006, c. 29, as amended in the *Child and Youth Statutes (Representation Improvement) Amendment Act, 2007*, S.B.C. 2007, c. 5. The Representative for Children and Youth is an independent office of the legislature and does not report through a provincial ministry.

6. The representative is responsible for performing the following functions in accordance with this Act:

(a) support, assist, inform and advise children and their families respecting designated services, which activities include, without limitation,

    (i) providing information and advice to children and their families about how to effectively access designated services and how to become effective self-advocates with respect to those services,

    (ii) advocating on behalf of a child receiving or eligible to receive a designated service, and

    (iii) supporting, promoting in communities and commenting publicly on advocacy services for children and their families with respect to designated services;

(b) monitor, review, audit and conduct research on the provision of a designated service by a public body or director for the purpose of making recommendations to improve the effectiveness and responsiveness of that service, and comment publicly on any of these functions;

(c) review, investigate and report on the critical injuries and deaths of children as set out in Part 4;

(d) perform any other prescribed functions.

Judge Turpel was appointed pursuant to a recommendation of the Hughes Commission Report. In April 2006, the Honourable Ted Hughes released an independent review of B.C.'s child protection system that called for sweeping changes (see <http://www.childyouthreview.ca/down/Chapter_3_Keeping_Aboriginal_Children_Safe_and_Well.pdf> at 60).

Manitoba has recently enacted some innovative legislation to respond to the crisis in that province in Aboriginal child welfare. The following paragraphs by Pamela Gough provide an overview of these developments:

The 2003 *Child and Family Services Authorities Act* fundamentally restructured the provincial child welfare system, establishing four child welfare Authorities, three of which are Aboriginal and one general. These Authorities play a key role in coordinating child welfare services province-wide and are the governing bodies overseeing services. The *Child and Family Services Authorities Act* shifted the power to create and mandate child welfare agencies from the province to the four Authorities.

The four Authorities supervise the operations of the child and family service agencies under their jurisdiction on a province-wide basis, dispersing funds and ensuring culturally appropriate standards and practices, consistent with provincial legislation. Families can choose the Authority that they prefer through coordinated province-wide intake services. There is one central intake service for Winnipeg, which coordinates intakes on behalf of all four Authorities. Elsewhere in the province, existing child welfare agencies have been designated as intake agencies for specific geographic regions, on behalf of all four Authorities. The Northern Authority administers the delivery of child and family services at six child and family service agencies, generally located in the northern half of the province. The Southern Authority oversees eight child and family service agencies in the southern half of the province. The Métis Child and Family Services Authority administers one agency, the Métis Child, Family and Community Services Agency, which covers the entire province and is based in Winnipeg. The General Authority administers the delivery of child and family services throughout the province to families not covered by the other three Authorities. It has six regional offices (run by the provincial government) and also oversees three private family service agencies, which are incorporated non-profit organizations. The Northern and Southern Authorities are also responsible for providing services to out-of province First Nations people living in Manitoba.

Child and family service agencies are community based organizations that provide services to families for the prevention of circumstances requiring the placement of children in protective care or treatment programs. They also investigate allegations of child mistreatment and provide ongoing protection, residential care, adoption services, extended care and maintenance. In addition, child and family service agencies are responsible for licensing, managing and supporting foster homes, which are operated according to province-wide regulations and standards.[13]

"CHILD WELFARE"

In A.C. Hamilton and C.M. Sinclair, *The Justice System and Aboriginal People: Report of the Aboriginal Justice Inquiry in Manitoba*, Vol. 1 (Winnipeg: Queen's Printer, 1991) at 520 (references omitted)

We believe that the Aboriginal child care agencies have been an outstanding success and that they warrant further support and encouragement. They are dealing with Aboriginal families with sensitivity, commitment and ability. At the same time, it must be recognized that their programs and activities sometimes will become the subject of controversy and criticism. Every time an Aboriginal agency stumbles, some critics inevitably will cry out for its dismantling and a return to the old way. But, as we and other inquiries have concluded, the old way was neither the only way, nor the best way. The need for ongoing support and a commitment to Aboriginal child welfare agencies must be recognized and reaffirmed.

Aboriginal people have enjoyed little influence or control over many of the issues which affect them, often adversely. Manitoba's experience in the field of child welfare, however, suggests that when a consensus develops that something must be done, then positive changes can take place. The reform of the child welfare system is an example of that. It is proof that Aboriginal people are ready, willing and able to exercise greater control over aspects of their lives which some erroneously believe can only be dealt with by non-Aboriginal professionals.

We must now do more to support and extend the reforms that have taken place. Positive steps have been taken, but not all Aboriginal people have benefited. Existing agencies must be strengthened and those Aboriginal people not served by Aboriginal agencies must now be afforded this opportunity. Aboriginal peoples must continue to gain more responsibility for the child and family programs and services that affect them. By expanding the range and number of mandated Aboriginal agencies as we have recommended, all Aboriginal Manitobans will have the opportunity to receive culturally appropriate child and family services.

We believe that the rapid and positive development of reserve-based agencies augers well for the future success of Aboriginally administered programs.

In 1999, the Government of Manitoba announced a commitment to address the Aboriginal Justice Inquiry's recommendations. Additionally, the government established the Aboriginal Justice Implementation Commission to advise the government on methods of implementing recommendations of the *Report of the Aboriginal Justice Inquiry* (1991). The Commission prioritized issues of family and child welfare and recommended that:

> The Government of Manitoba seek to enter into agreement with the Assembly of Manitoba Chiefs and the Manitoba Metis Federation to develop a plan that would result in First Nations and Metis communities developing and delivering Aboriginal child welfare services.

Through negotiations with First Nations and Métis representatives, the Province of Manitoba signed three separate three-year agreements (Memoranda of Understanding) with the Manitoba Métis Federation (MMF) (February 22, 2000) representing the Métis; the Assembly of Manitoba Chiefs (AMC) (April 27, 2000) representing southern First Nations; and Manitoba Keewatinowi Okimakanak (MKO) (July 20, 2000) representing northern First Nations. All four parties subsequently signed the Child and Family Services Protocol. The overall purpose of these agreements was to establish a joint initiative under a common process to expand off-reserve jurisdiction for First Nations, establish a province-wide Métis mandate and restructure the existing child care system through legislative and other changes.

The parties have stated that the development of the regional authorities is the key feature of their approach to Aboriginal child welfare services. The authorities do not deliver services directly, but play an integral role in the coordination of services province-wide and are the governing bodies overseeing these services. The responsibilities of the authorities include:

- Delegating the mandate for service delivery to their respective service delivery agencies;
- Developing policies and procedures;
- Assessing needs, setting priorities, planning, funding and service management;
- Ensuring that children and families have access to quality services;
- Ensuring that policies and standards are followed;
- Monitoring and assessing service delivery;
- Working with other authorities, community partners, private bodies and government to coordinate service delivery;
- Promoting collaboration and cooperation among communities, service affiliates and authorities.

On June 10, 2002, legislation to create the new authorities and structure was introduced in The Manitoba Legislative Assembly. The *Child and Family Services Authorities Act*, S.M. 2002, c. 35 (proclaimed in force November 23, 2003) is viewed as an important first step toward a restructured child and family services system in Manitoba.

F.   CHALLENGES OF ABORIGINAL CONTROL

Despite the introduction of provincial legislation that is more sensitive and supportive of Aboriginal issues, many challenges remain.

1.   Jurisdictional and Funding Isues

WEN'DE: WE ARE COMING TO THE LIGHT OF DAY

First Nations Child and Family Caring Society of Canada:
Ottawa, 2005 at 38-40 (references omitted)

First Nations child and family service agencies have long reported that jurisdictional disputes between government departments and levels of government (provincial/federal) have resulted in children unnecessarily being denied services or experiencing delays in service. Moreover, agencies indicated that resolving these disputes was taking an inordinate amount of staff time.

... Survey responses from the 12 agencies indicated that they experienced a staggering 393 jurisdictional disputes this past year requiring an average of 54.25 person hours to resolve each incident or 21,320 person hours each year. If this is typical then agencies across the country are dedicating over 200,000 person hours per year resolving these disputes — and this does not include the time of government officials. If one assumes an average salary of 45K per annum — then jurisdictional disputes cost agencies, and by extension INAC [Indian and Northern Affairs Canada] close to five million dollars per year. The most frequent types of disputes were between federal government departments (36%), between two provincial departments (27%) and between federal and provincial governments (14%). Examples of the most problematic disputes were with regard to children with complex medical and educational needs, reimbursement of maintenance, and the lack of recognition of First Nations jurisdiction. ... Although tripartite tables have been established in some regions with INAC, the province and First Nations child and family service agencies, the efficacy and authority of these tables to resolve jurisdictional disputes is unclear and inconsistent. Moreover, as some jurisdictional disputes involve federal, provincial or tribal authorities outside of these core participants, it is critical that mechanisms for engaging these groups are integrated into a dispute resolution process. Additionally, dispute resolution mechanisms must be reflective of cultural values and processes of the participating First Nation child and family service agency.

Overall, First Nations child and family service agencies report that current funding levels are inadequate in the following areas: prevention services (including least disruptive measures), human resources, capital costs, standards/ evaluation, culturally appropriate services, records management and information technology. Human resources funding was identified as a critical need to support current operations and the anticipated expansion of prevention services in the new formula. Two thirds of agencies in the sample feel there are inadequate funds to pay staff equitable salary and benefits packages. Jurisdictional disputes are a key problem and need to be resolved in order to ensure that Status Indian children on reserve do not face discriminatory allocation of services. In addition, there is likely to be substantial savings in human resources costs should a meaningful dispute resolution mechanism be put in place instead of the current case by case approach that too often places the needs of the child second while governments scramble to see who will pay for the service. [The] principle where the needs of the child come first in the resolution of all jurisdictional disputes is very strongly recommended.

There is a trend toward FNCFSA [First Nations Child and Family Services Agencies] developing their own legislation to ensure culturally based services. This suggests that the new generation funding formula should allow for both tribal based and provincially delegated child welfare legislation. In the meantime, delegation and funding agreement negotiations need to be standardized to create efficiencies in negotiations whilst still allowing for adaptation to reflect community specific needs. First Nations child and family service agencies indicated that there should be a move away from the "take it or leave it" negotiation approach by some provinces and in some situations, by INAC. FNCFSA provide significant gifts in kind to both the provincial and federal governments in terms of consultation services. Although both governments appear to value this input neither is prepared to pay for it — meaning that this service is an additional drain on agencies. Although some agencies were receiving additional funding from other sources, there is clearly a need to clarify the application of the stacking provision in INAC funding agreements with agencies in order to ensure that they can benefit from voluntary sector funding sources and other types of government funding to enhance the range of services provided outside of INAC funding.

The Assembly of First Nations, *Leadership Action Plan on First Nations Child Welfare* (2006) critically commented on the federal government's role in providing inadequate and inequitable assistance to Aboriginal children and families:

> Presently, the Indian and Northern Affairs Canada Child and Family Services Program (CFS) provides 22% less funding per child to First Nations agencies than is received by provincial agencies. The current CFS federal budget is capped at a 2% annual growth rate, even though maintenance costs alone increase by 11% per year.

Amnesty International has recommended in its report to the United Nations Human Rights Committee that "*the Canadian government must act immediately to end the disparity in funding for Indigenous child welfare services and ensure that the best interests of Indigenous children are protected by effective preventative and early intervention programs.*"

This fiscal imbalance has contributed to the over-representation of First Nations children in the child welfare system, and to weakening the ability of First Nations government to take charge of prevention and intervention measures. While INAC provides almost unlimited funding to place First Nations children in outside foster care, virtually no funding exists to support children and families in their communities.[14]

Canada's Auditor General has also critically commented on the lack of resources for First Nations child welfare in Canada. In the *2011 June Status Report of the Auditor General of Canada*, the Auditor General reported:

4.46 First Nations children are among the most vulnerable members of society. In 2008, we noted that over five percent of all children residing on reserves were in care; this was close to eight times the proportion of children residing off reserves. ...

4.47 In 2008, we audited INAC's program for child and family services on reserves. We found that INAC had not defined key policy requirements related to culturally appropriate child and family services and comparability of services with those provided by provinces. Moreover, the Department had no assurance that its First Nations Child and Family Services Program funded child welfare services that were culturally appropriate or reasonably comparable with those normally provided off reserves in similar circumstances. We also found that there was no link between the financial obligations of the program and the way resources were allocated to it. Because the program's expenditures were growing faster than the Department's overall budget, INAC had been reallocating funding from other programs. In our 2008 audit, we also noted that INAC had joined with the Government of Alberta and First Nations in that province to introduce a new child and family services program emphasizing prevention. This was a departure from the existing model, which focused on intervention with families and children at risk.

4.48 In this follow-up audit, we assessed the progress made by INAC to implement two of our recommendations from our 2008 audit on the Department's Child and Family Services Program. We also examined actions taken in relation to the government's commitment in response to a recommendation made by the House of Commons Standing Committee on Public Accounts.

4.49 **Comparability of services**. In our 2008 audit, we recommended that INAC define what is meant by its policy requirement that services be reasonably comparable, define its expectations for culturally appropriate services, and implement these into its program. INAC agreed with the recommendation and committed to a clearer definition, in tripartite agreements, of comparability of services with those provided by provinces. We found that INAC has not defined what is meant by comparability. Until it does so, it is unclear what is the service standard for which the Department is providing funding and what level of services First Nations communities can eventually expect to receive. We also found that the Department had not conducted a review of all social services available in the provinces to see whether they are the same as what is available to children on reserves.

4.50 In our 2008 audit, we noted that INAC had entered into a new funding arrangement in Alberta, enabling First Nations child and family service agencies in that province to deliver services that comply with provincial legislation. However, we noted that the funding model under the new Alberta tripartite agreement did not address all of the funding disparities we had identified. Since that audit, INAC has expanded its Enhanced Prevention Focused Approach and has negotiated new tripartite framework agreements with five other provinces: Manitoba, Nova Scotia, Prince Edward Island, Quebec, and Saskatchewan. The new approach includes greater emphasis on prevention services and is intended to increase comparability with services offered in provinces. INAC officials expect that the approach will reduce the number of children in care, but it is too early to observe results.

4.51 The new tripartite agreements enable the provision of additional services beyond those offered in INAC's initial program. However, without having defined what is meant by comparability, the Department has been unable to demonstrate that its new Enhanced Prevention Focused Approach provides services to children and families living on reserves that are reasonably comparable to provincial services.

4.52 We also found that the Department has not developed a formal definition of what it means by "culturally appropriate services." In response to this recommendation, however, INAC has developed a guiding principle on what culturally appropriate services would entail. This principle has been embedded in the tripartite agreements with the provinces under the new approach. It is also reflected in the business plans of First Nations child and family service agencies. According to INAC, a guiding principle instead of a definition allows service providers to more readily adapt their programs to the culture in each community.

4.53 **Cost determination**. In 2008, we noted that the Department was regularly using funding budgeted for other programs to meet its obligations for its First Nations Child and Family Services Program. We also noted that the Department required a 74 percent increase in its operating and prevention services budget for Alberta to meet the requirements of the new tripartite agreement. We recommended that INAC determine the full costs of meeting the policy requirements of the program. The Department agreed to regularly update its estimate of the cost of delivering the program with the new approach on a province-by-province basis and to periodically review the program budget.

4.54 In this audit, we found that the Department had identified the costs it would have to pay for services in each province before moving to the new Enhanced Prevention Focused Approach. For its operations and prevention services, INAC determined that it would require an incremental increase of between 50 percent and 100 percent in its funding for each of the provinces in which it has established tripartite agreements to date. With all cost components taken into consideration, on average, the agreements led to an increase of over 40 percent in the cost of INAC's Child and Family Services Program in the participating provinces.

4.55 Rather than using funds budgeted for other programs, INAC has obtained increased funding to run its Child and Family Services Program.

The program's budget has increased by 32 percent from $417 million in the 2005–06 fiscal year to $550 million in 2009–10. This rise partly reflects the increased funding levels needed to implement the new framework agreements. The Department also regularly conducts budget reviews and has taken steps to minimize the financial impact of its Child and Family Services Program on other INAC programs.

4.56 **Cost comparisons.** The House of Commons Standing Committee on Public Accounts asked the Department for a comprehensive comparison of its funding to First Nations child and family welfare service agencies with provincial funding to similar agencies. The government committed to providing the Committee with a comparison of its funding for salaries and caseloads for the provinces that have made the transition to the new Enhanced Prevention Focused Approach.

4.57 In preparation for framework negotiations with the provinces, INAC compared some elements central to the operations of child and family services programs with those of the provinces, such as social workers' salaries and benefits. With this information, INAC provided to the Public Accounts Committee a comparison of some of its costs with those of the provinces that have established an agreement under the new approach. We note, however, that the Department has not provided information about social workers' caseloads to the Committee because this is not public information. Moreover, certain services provided by provinces are outside INAC's mandate — for example, services related to health issues and youth justice. The Department therefore does not provide these services.[15]

In light of these and other discouraging findings and statistics, the First Nations Child and Family Caring Society launched a human rights complaint alleging that the federal government is racially discriminating against First Nations children by providing fewer child welfare benefits on reserve. The Canadian Human Rights Tribunal dismissed the claim. After dealing with a host of procedural issues, the Tribunal largely accepted the Crown's argument (see [2011] C.H.R.D. No. 4 at para. 102 (C.H.R.T.)):

> ... that s. 5(b) of the *Act* requires that in order to find adverse differentiation a comparator is required. It further argues that there must be a difference in the provision of services to two different individuals or service recipients. The section does not allow a comparison between two different service providers serving two different "publics". Further, the section does not allow comparisons between the federal government and the provinces. The Crown supports the precepts of the importance of human rights legislation but disagrees that the complaint falls within the statutory mandate of the *Act*. While, the Crown acknowledges that it has a fiduciary obligation towards First Nations peoples, it submits that such a duty and other international commitments do not expand the statutory reach of s. 5(b) of the *CHRA*.

The First Nations Child and Family Caring Society appealed this decision to the Federal Court of Canada and judicial review was allowed ([2012] F.C.J. No. 425 (F.C.)). The grounds of appeal are as follows (see Federal Court File No. T-630-11, April 13, 2011 at <http://iportal.usask.ca/docs/blog/NOTICE%20OF%20APPLICATION%20JR%20Tribunal.pdf>):

The Tribunal unfairly and incorrectly dismissed the Complaint on the sole basis that the discriminatory funding provided by the federal government for child welfare services for on-reserve children could not legally be compared to funding provided to off-reserve children, since off-reserve funding is provided by provincial or territorial governments. The Tribunal incorrectly read into the *Canadian Human Rights Act* a requirement that there be a "comparator group" receiving the same services from the same provider (the federal government) before a finding of discrimination could be made. The Tribunal thereby effectively precluded First Nations people — who receive more services from the federal government than other Canadians because of their *sui generis* constitutional status — from raising human rights complaints in respect of such services regardless of the discriminatory way in which they may be provided.

The Factum of the Canadian Human Rights Commission, which is a separate organization from the Canadian Human Rights Tribunal, challenged the Tribunal decision. One of the important grounds of appeal is as follows (Doc. T-578-11, Memorandum of Fact and Law of the Canadian Human Rights Commission, October 3, 2011):

115. The Tribunal's interpretation amounts to a *prima facie* infringement of section 15 of the *Charter* since only Aboriginal peoples would now be deprived of the ability of filing complaints against the Federal Government. They would be the only ones so deprived by virtue of membership in an ethnic group.

116. When Parliament legislates, it is presumed to have legislated in a manner that is consistent with the law, as well as in a manner consistent with the *Constitution*, including section 15 of the *Charter* and section 2(e) of the *Canadian Bill of Rights*. Where a provision in a statute is capable of more than one meaning, the meaning that is consistent with the *Constitution* is to be attributed to the provision.

117. Where there are multiple possible interpretations of a statute, an interpretation that is constitutional and that does not infringe the *Charter* is the one that must be given to the provision.

118. The Supreme Court of Canada in *Withler* and the Federal Court of Appeal in *Morris* have clearly indicated that there is no rigid requirement for a comparator group as this could deny substantive equality under both statutory human rights law and the *Charter*. The Tribunal's narrow interpretation is inconsistent with those decisions and deprives hundreds of thousands of vulnerable individuals of their rights under the *CHRA* by virtue of membership is a unique ethnic group.

119. The Tribunal ignored the special status of Indians as a unique group falling under Federal jurisdiction under section 91 of the *Constitution Act, 1867*. It ignored the complex evidentiary issues that needed to be developed further at a hearing and, lastly, it failed to give due regard to Parliament's intent in repealing section 67 of the *CHRA*. The decision effectively immunizes federal funding issues from human rights review and provides a greater denial of human rights protection than that which existed prior to Parliament's repeal of section 67. The decision ought to be overturned.

2. Administrative Corruption and Deficiencies

Despite jurisdictional and financial challenges, it should be stressed that many Aboriginal controlled agencies have begun to stem the tide of a century-long trend which devastated the lives of countless individuals and left communities without hope for their future. However, though there have been significant developments with Aboriginal control of child welfare throughout Canada, many challenges remain to be addressed. The well-documented successes of Aboriginally controlled child welfare agencies does not mean they are without problems. As with other child welfare agencies in Canada, violence and abuse can just as easily find their way into Aboriginal institutions and cause great harm to children in care. For example, Manitoba Associate Chief Justice B.D. Giesbrecht reported many of the issues which some communities encounter when he investigated the death of Lester Desjarlais under the *Fatal Inquiries Act* in 1992.

In 1988 Lester Desjarlais took his life, by hanging, while under the supervision of the Dakota Ojibway Child and Family Services (DOCFS), an Aboriginally controlled child welfare agency. The Giesbrecht report made it clear that Aboriginally run child welfare services can at times present as many problems as provincially controlled agencies. He chronicled a sad tale of Lester's neglect at the hands of the DOCFS, which failed to intervene and take action on behalf of Lester when it had knowledge of the severely abusive circumstances he was in. Lester often became a pawn in the larger political struggles occurring within the agency, where people were working at contradictory and cross-purposes. The judge noted that it often seemed as if more attention was being paid to internal political struggles than was being given to the boy's needs. DOCFS failed to explain any special needs or concerns of children being placed in care when the foster placements were made. It did not take sufficient measures to protect Lester from known sex abusers. DOCFS mismanaged and suspiciously lost crucial files related to Lester's care. The agency was subject to political control and interference by the Dakota Ojibway Tribal Council and Band Councils, which led to extreme deference by many members of DOCFS to the disadvantage of children in their care. This enabled band councillors to "interfere" with agency matters and protect people from agency investigation on their reserves. Judge Giesbrecht wrote that "the chiefs and councillors insisted on injecting politics into the system at all levels, and meddling in the daily operation of the agency". He further noted that "The male Indian leaders are not only by and large uninterested in the horrific social problems that are paralyzing their communities, but they are, in too many cases, part of the problem themselves". The judge also observed that the Director of the agency was "virtually absent" and lines of responsibility and accountability for decisions were "completely mangled". These, and many other problems, illustrate the challenges Aboriginal child welfare agencies can encounter when assuming control of this function. While it bears repeating that there are numerous successes in Aboriginally controlled child welfare, the issues raised by the Giesbrecht report should not be ignored. It is absolutely crucial that the issues identified in Lester Desjarlais' death, and the *Jane Doe* case reproduced below, are also the subject of child welfare law reform. Consider the problems in this regard as you read the following case, and the recommendations of the Royal Commission on Aboriginal Peoples that immediately follow it.

JANE DOE (PUBLIC TRUSTEE OF) v. AWASIS AGENCY OF NORTHERN MANITOBA

[1990] M.J. No. 402, [1990] 4 C.N.L.R. 10, 72 D.L.R. (4th) 738 (Man. C.A.)

Krindle J.: — This is an application by The Public Trustee to approve an infant settlement in an action in this court under the above style of cause.

. . . . .

This action arises out of the very tragic events which occurred to a youngster who has been permitted to be named in these proceedings under the pseudonym of "Jane Doe". The child was born on July 30, 1972, in Northern Manitoba. Her natural parents were members of an Indian Band and residents of an isolated reserve in Northern Manitoba. In the fall of 1973 the child was placed in the foster home of a couple living in a Northern mining community, in order that she receive medical treatment not available to her in her remote reserve. The child lived as a member of the foster parents' family for 13 years, moving with them from Northern Manitoba to Southern Manitoba, and ultimately to two locations in Alberta, where the foster parents have resided since 1983. The foster parents adopted the child in Alberta, but the adoption order was later set aside at the instance of the defendant Awasis because the natural parents had not been served. In July of 1986, some 13 years after she had been placed with the foster family, the child was removed (against her will) from the foster family by the defendant Awasis and returned to the care and custody of her natural parents on the isolated reserve in Northern Manitoba. She remained there for approximately six months, at which time she was admitted to hospital in the North, immediately transferred by the hospital to a Winnipeg hospital, and made a ward of this court in order to prevent the defendants, or any of them, from returning her to the Northern Reserve.

During the 13 years that the child lived with her foster family, her contact with her natural family was minimal. By the time she was returned to the reserve by the defendant, Awasis, she was unable to speak the local Dene language. Many of the reserve residents, including her natural parents, could not speak any English. In addition to the purely linguistic barriers between herself and her natural family, they were not well acquainted with one another and communication was extremely difficult. As well, the plaintiff mourned the loss of her foster family, who were the only people whom she knew as family. Life on the reserve was foreign to her. She was in no way accepted into the community and led the life of an outcast. On numerous occasions during the six months that the complainant was on the reserve, she was forcibly confined, sexually assaulted and raped by a number of the male residents of the reserve. She contracted venereal disease as a result of the sexual assaults and rapes. She wrote of her plight to her former foster parents, who contacted the defendants and attempted to seek assistance for her. The defendants did not come to the aid of the child. Ultimately, she was removed from the reserve by a fly-in doctor who had a regular circuit into the area, and to whom she made known her plight. Her former foster parents returned to Manitoba from Alberta to help her. The child was hospitalized in Winnipeg, and the court ordered that the child be returned to her foster parents to live in Alberta, as opposed to the custody of the defendant, Awasis, who wished to return the child to the reserve.

When the child was placed in hospital in Winnipeg she was depressed, suffering from an adjustment disorder, and suffering from a form of venereal disease. Subsequent to her return to Alberta she was referred to counseling in order to assist in resolving the various issues, and particularly to help in dealing with the repeated rapes. She has twice attempted suicide, and was hospitalized on two separate occasions in the year 1989 as a result of those gestures. She is residing in Alberta with her "family" and is undergoing counseling and therapy. The court records disclose that the rape allegations resulted in criminal charges having been laid against several individuals on the reserve. Convictions resulted. The child was required to go through numerous preliminary inquiries and trials in those cases. All of this, while necessary from the perspective of public protection, has exacted an additional toll on the plaintiff herself, who was required repeatedly to relive the incidents in court.

While the name of the child has never been publicized, this entire history of tragic events and the role of public agencies in it, was certainly a matter of media attention and broad public knowledge and concern.

The parties requesting this consent judgment asked that I order that the docket be sealed. I am not disposed to do so. In my opinion, the only thing that might justify removing the whole or any part of this proceeding from public scrutiny is the need to protect the identity of the victim. The child has been tragically and seriously victimized by this whole process. Anything that the courts can do to protect her from further humiliation should be done in her interest. I would not want, in any way, to see her publicly identified through these proceedings. That can be accomplished by referring to her as Jane Doe, and by removing from the docket and sealing or expunging only those documents or portions of documents which might tend to identify her. But having said that, where high profile cases are involved, particularly cases which involve public agencies whose duty it is to protect children, it is important that the public have access to those records, or so much of those records as can be made publicly available without disclosing the identity of the child. Accordingly, the sealing order which was sought is refused.

I order to be removed from the docket and sealed, or to be expunged, only those documents or portions thereof which might tend to identify the child. The rest of the pocket will remain open to the public and the pseudonym "Jane Doe" will continue to be used on these public documents.

Insofar as the proposed settlement is concerned, I approve it, albeit reluctantly. In my opinion the $75,000.00 figure for general damages is low. I recognize, however, the fact that damages in this case do not come within a predictable "range" because of the highly atypical nature of this case.

I recognize that the liability of certain of the defendants was arguable. Most important, however, I note what was said by the child herself and her worker, about the damage the child would likely sustain if she had to go through another trial. The criminal cases are now behind her. She seems to be making progress. She, her foster parents and everyone who is involved with her, stress the need to put the terrible experiences behind her so that she can get on with trying to rebuild her life. Part of putting it behind her involves ending the litigation which causes her to relive those horrors in the most brutal and insensitive of ways. Under those circumstances, I approve the proposed settlement.

I note that in addition to the general damage award, the Government of Canada is providing a fund pursuant to which specialized treatment will continue to be available to the child to help her recovery. I agree with the proposal to have the monies held for her benefit by the Public Trustee for the next few years. The costs charged by the Public Trustee, all of which are being borne by the defendants, are reasonable and are approved.

REPORT OF THE ROYAL COMMISSION ON ABORIGINAL PEOPLES: GATHERING STRENGTH, VOL. 3

(Ottawa: Ministry of Supply and Services, 1996) at 52-53
(references omitted)

Conclusion and Recommendations

Aboriginal institutions in the field of family and children's services are the way of the future. ...

> Our recommendations here focus on affirming and implementing the authority of Aboriginal nations and their communities to act in the field of family and child welfare, and on resolving the tensions between federal, provincial, territorial and Aboriginal authority that interfere with protecting the best interests of Aboriginal children.

While we consider that protecting children's interests can be achieved best in the context of revitalized Aboriginal families, communities and nations, we do not underestimate the difficulties of turning ideals into reality.

In the recent history of Aboriginal child welfare, the best interests of the child have at times been construed as being in conflict with community goals of self-determination. One highly publicized case was the death of

Lester Desjarlais, a child who committed suicide while in the care of an Aboriginal agency in Manitoba.

Associate Chief Judge Dale Giesbrecht concluded from his inquiry into the death that political considerations in the local community had interfered with the agency's discharge of its responsibilities, that policies and lines of responsibility within the agency needed to be clarified and formalized, and that the provincial director of child welfare should take a more active role in monitoring the work of Aboriginal agencies. Concern about issues of political interference, organizational capacity and checks and balances in exercising of community responsibility are not confined to Manitoba.

The tension between individual and group priorities surfaces in another area of child welfare. ... Judgments about guardianship and adoption placements of minor children often entail balancing a child's need for stable parental relationships with the equally compelling need to have community support in developing a mature Aboriginal identity.

Aboriginal and non-Aboriginal agencies and personnel bring different perceptions and approaches to the work of child welfare. Tensions emerge precisely because the well-being of children is such a fundamentally important issue in both Aboriginal and non-Aboriginal societies.

As we reiterate often in this volume, non-Aboriginal institutions will have a continuing role in delivering services to Aboriginal people, even when Aboriginal self-government is fully operative across the country. The best interests of Aboriginal children will be served only by determined and sustained efforts on the part of Aboriginal and non-Aboriginal governments, institutions, and people to recognize and support each other's contributions to the common goal.

RECOMMENDATIONS

The Commission recommends that:

3.2.1 The government of Canada acknowledge a fiduciary responsibility to support Aboriginal nations and their communities in restoring Aboriginal families to a state of health and wholeness.

3.2.2 Aboriginal, provincial, territorial and federal governments promptly acknowledge that child welfare is a core area of self-government in which Aboriginal nations can undertake self-starting initiatives.

3.2.3 Aboriginal, provincial, territorial and federal governments promptly reach agreements on the authority of Aboriginal nations and their communities for child welfare, and its relation to provincial, territorial and federal laws respecting child welfare.

3.2.4 Block funding be provided to child welfare agencies mandated by Aboriginal governments or communities to facilitate a shift in focus from alternative child care to family support.

3.2.5 Until community of interest governments are established in urban and non-reserve areas, voluntary agencies endorsed by substantial numbers of Aboriginal people resident in the areas be authorized under provincial or territorial law to act in the field of child welfare (a) where numbers warrant; and (b) with levels of funding comparable to those of agencies providing comparable services to the general population and sufficient to meet the service needs of Aboriginal people.

G. CUSTOMARY CHILD AND FAMILY RELATIONS

Some Aboriginal communities are attempting to resolve the challenges of child care through their traditional customs and practices. The following commentary and case demonstrate how these customs are a living part of the fabric of contemporary Aboriginal nations. They illustrate the legal foundation on which these rights rest, and contain some important implications for the future exercise of Aboriginal jurisdiction in the area of child welfare.

REPORT OF THE ROYAL COMMISSION ON ABORIGINAL PEOPLES: GATHERING STRENGTH, VOL. 3

(Ottawa: Ministry of Supply and Services, 1996) at 87
(references omitted)

Constitutional scholars have concluded that the affirmation of Aboriginal rights in section 35(1) incorporates into Canadian law the common law principle of continuity. Under this principle the customary laws of Aboriginal peoples were deemed to have survived the Crown's acquisition of their territories, provided that this result was not incompatible with the sovereignty of the Crown.

... Two leading decisions of the United States Supreme Court, *Johnson v. M'Intosh* and *Worcester v. Georgia*, held that Indian tribes in the United States had the status of domestic dependent nations united by special ties to the Crown as ultimate sovereign. In Sioui, Justice Lamer of the Supreme Court of Canada used the words of the chief justice of the United States to describe British policy toward the Indians in the mid-eighteenth century:

[S]he considered them as nations capable of maintaining the relations of peace and war; of governing themselves, under her protection, and she made treaties with them, the obligation of which she acknowledged.

It would appear, therefore, that at least to some extent Aboriginal customary laws survived the advent of the colonizers. Constitutional scholars seem to be in agreement that certain aspects of customary law pertaining to the family have survived. Customary laws on marriage and adoption have been upheld even in the face of legislation that might be taken to have abridged such laws. We referred earlier to the Quebec case, *Connolly v. Woolrich*, which upheld the validity of a marriage contracted under Cree customary law between a non-Aboriginal man and a First Nations woman in the Canadian northwest.

In *Re Katie's Adoption Petition*, Justice Sissons held that adoptions "made according to the laws of the Territories" within the meaning of section 103 of the *Child Welfare Act* included adoptions in accordance with Indian and

Inuit custom."' In *J.T.K. v. Kenora-Patricia Child and Family Services*, the court issued a custody order in favour of relatives of the child's parents over the objections of the Crown. The court found that such an order was in accordance with the tribal tradition of customary adoption among the Ojibway people. ...

With the advent of self-government, Aboriginal nations will be in a position to make their own family law. Indeed, they can proceed with initiatives in this area now, since family law falls within the core of Aboriginal self-governing jurisdiction. While their customary laws in some areas have continuing validity under section 35(1) of the constitution, in other areas they have been preempted by federal or provincial laws. It seems likely, therefore, in view of the fundamental importance of family and family relationships, that Aboriginal people will wish to have their own laws in place as soon as possible. There would seem to be particular urgency in this regard concerning laws and policies affecting children — laws on apprehension, custody and adoption, for example — as well as other areas with an impact on children, including their quality of life and personal security, parental responsibilities with regard to support and maintenance, protection from violence, and property and inheritance. As Aboriginal people have told us, their children are their future.

The *Casimel* case, below, illustrates the court's recognition of the continuity of customary child welfare law within Aboriginal communities. As you read the case, think about the implications of the Royal Commission's finding that child welfare law is a core area of jurisdiction in Aboriginal self-government.

CASIMEL v. INSURANCE CORP. OF BRITISH COLUMBIA
[1993] B.C.J. No. 1834, [1994] 2 C.N.L.R. 22 (B.C.C.A.)

Lambert J.A. (for the Court, allowing the appeal): — The issue in this appeal is whether the plaintiffs, Louise Casimel and Francis Casimel, were dependent parents of Ernest Casimel when he was killed in an automobile accident on 9 November 1988. If they were, they would be entitled to receive "no fault" death benefits under Part VII of the Regulations under the *Insurance (Motor Vehicle) Act*.

The resolution of that issue requires a consideration of the interaction between aboriginal rights arising from aboriginal customary law, on the one hand, and the general statute law of British Columbia, on the other.

I

Louise Casimel is now 79 years old and has been blind for some years. Francis Casimel is 99 years old. They have been married to each other for many years. They are members of the Stellaquo Band of the Carrier People. Until recently they maintained their family home on the Stellaquo

Reserve near Burns Lake. There they raised their family, including their two daughters, Mary Casimel and Charlotte Casimel.

In 1960, Mary Casimel bore a son, Ernest Casimel. Ernest's father was unknown. Mary took no interest in her son and from the beginning he was looked after by Mary's mother and father, Louise and Francis, the present plaintiffs, with the help of Mary's sister, Charlotte. Three or four years later Mary left home to marry. She moved to Vancouver with her husband and lived there for several years. She then returned to live on the Stellaquo Reserve but not with her parents. Charlotte also married and left home. The remaining family unit then consisted of Louise, Francis and Ernest. Ernest was raised by Louise and Francis and he was treated in all respects as their own son. He referred to them as "Mom" and "Dad", and they referred to him as their "son". Charlotte referred to Ernest as her brother and she treated him as her brother. Ernest did not maintain any significant relationship with his biological mother and rarely saw her, even after she returned to the reserve. When he did speak of her he called her "Mary".

As Ernest grew up and Louise and Francis became older, instead of Louise and Francis looking after Ernest, Ernest started looking after them. In due course he became eligible to have a house of his own on the Reserve but he never applied for one. He lived with Louise and Francis and he looked after them. In the words of the trial judge, Mr. Justice Wong: "Ernest washed the clothes, chopped wood for heat and took Louise and Francis shopping since neither of them was able to drive. Ernest did the cooking, washed the dishes and used his money to buy groceries for the whole household. As far as Charlotte can recall, Louise, Francis and Ernest did not have bank accounts and they would simply pool their money together for household expenses. Ernest would cash their cheques and look after the household money. Ernest worked from time to time and when he was not working he received social assistance or unemployment insurance benefits.

Shortly before his death, at age 28, Ernest was elected Chief of the Stellaquo Band. After his death he was succeeded as Chief by Robert Michell who, in an affidavit, said: "The late Ernest Joseph Casimel was raised and cared for by Louise and Francis Casimel and Louise and Francis Casimel were considered by the Stellaquo Band to be his parents."

II

The plaintiffs filed a Statement of Claim seeking "no fault" death benefits under Sections 92, 93 and 94 of Part VII of the Insurance (Motor Vehicle) Regulations as "dependent parents" of Ernest Casimel. The defendant denied that the plaintiffs were "dependent parents". The defendant then brought an application under Rule 18A for the dismissal of the action. The plaintiffs brought a cross-application under Rule 18A for judgment in accordance with their claim. Both 18A applications came on for hearing at the same time before Mr. Justice Wong in Supreme Court Chambers.

Mr. Justice Wong dismissed the action. He decided that the customary adoption under the customs of the Stellaquo Band of the Carrier People gave rise to moral rights and obligations but not to legal rights and obligations, and that for that reason the plaintiffs were not entitled to be treated as parents under the Insurance (Motor Vehicle) Regulations.

Mr. Justice Wong followed the decision of Judge Hutchinson in *Michell v. Dennis and Dennis*, [1984] 2 W.W.R. 449 (B.C.S.C.), where Judge Hutchinson decided that adoption by Indian custom did not give the adopting mother the capacity to sue as a parent under the *Family Compensation Act*.

Mr. Justice Wong's reasons in this case are reported at (1991), 58 B.C.L.R. (2d) 316. Since both the reasons of Mr. Justice Wong and the reasons of Judge Hutchinson *Michell v. Dennis and Dennis* are reported, I do not propose to refer to them at any length. Neither in set of reasons discusses the nature of an Indian customary adoption or the recognition of Indian customary rights by the common law.

I have reached a different conclusion than Mr. Justice Wong and I will set out my reasons for doing so. It is not necessary for me to express any opinion about the decision reached by Judge Hutchinson in *Michell v. Dennis and Dennis*.

III

In the course of his reasons Mr. Justice Wong stated the issue in this way, "At issue is whether the meaning of the words 'dependent parent' in the Regulation includes a dependant customary adoption parent. Mr. Justice Wong also described the plaintiffs as "biological grandparents and customary adoptive parents of [Ernest Casimel]".

I consider therefore that Mr. Justice Wong has found as a fact that a customary adoption in accordance with the customs of the Stellaquo Band of the Carrier People had taken place and that in accordance with those customs Ernest was treated by other band members as the son of Louise and Francis, and Louise and Francis, in turn, were treated by other band members as the parents of Ernest. Both parties to this appeal conceded that such a customary adoption had taken place. In view of Mr. Justice Wong's finding and in view of that concession, I propose to regard Ernest as having been adopted as their son by Louise and Francis in accordance with the customs of the Stellaquo Band of the Carrier People. I also propose to assume that under those customs not only were Francis and Louise regarded as the parents of Ernest, but that Mary was no longer regarded as a parent of Ernest and ceased to have any of the rights or obligations of a parent. That assumption is entirely consistent with the evidence though the precise nature of the customary adoption, which both parties agreed had occurred, was not explored in the evidence. Since the fact of the customary adoption had been agreed, there was no need to explore it.

I consider also that Mr. Justice Wong has found as a fact that Louise and Francis were dependent on Ernest within the meaning of "dependant parent," which is defined in Section 1(1) of the Insurance (Motor Vehicle) Regulations, in this way:

"dependent parent" means a surviving parent of an insured who, at the date of an accident for which a claim is made, resides with the insured and receives most of his financial support from the insured.

Whatever may have been the case in Supreme Court Chambers, the defendant did not admit on this appeal that Louise and Francis were dependant on Ernest. But I consider that Mr. Justice Wong must have found such a dependency or he would not have stated the issue as he did. The defendant brought on an 18A application for dismissal of the claim and the plaintiff brought on an 18A application for judgment. Ernest was described in the evidence as the only member of the family unit who worked. When he was unemployed he received either unemployment insurance or social assistance. At the date of his death he was Chief of the Stellaquo Band. Louise and Francis received the old age pension but that was their only income. In short, there was evidence that Louise and Francis were dependant on Ernest within the terms of the definition and no evidence to rebut the inference of dependency. There is, in my opinion, no basis for interfering with the finding by Mr. Justice Wong that if Louise and Francis were parents of Ernest then they were dependent parents.

IV

The origin and the nature of aboriginal rights were argued very fully in this Court and considered at some length by this Court in *Delgamuukw v. The Queen*, [1993] 5 W.W.R. 97.

All five judges who heard that appeal concluded that aboriginal rights arose from such of the customs, traditions and practices of the aboriginal people in question as formed an integral part of their distinctive culture at the time of the assertion of sovereignty by the incoming power, (which in that case was taken to have occurred in 1846) and which were protected and nurtured by the organized society of that aboriginal people. Those aboriginal rights were then recognized and affirmed by the common law when the common law became applicable following the assertion of sovereignty with the result that those rights became protected as aboriginal rights under the common law. Existing aboriginal rights became constitutionally protected in 1982 as part of the constitutional amendments embodied in the *Constitution Act, 1982*, as Section 35.

When the rights in issue are rights in relation to the social organization of the aboriginal people in question, such as rights arising from marriage, rights of inheritance, and, I would add, rights arising from adoption, Mr. Justice Macfarlane, for himself and Mr. Justice Taggart, said this, at p. 151 (para. 163):

No declaration by this court is required to permit internal self-regulation in accordance with aboriginal traditions, if the people affected are in agreement. But if any conflict between the exercise of such aboriginal traditions and any law of the Province or Canada should arise the question can be litigated. No such specific issue is presented on this appeal.

Mr. Justice Macfarlane, for himself and Mr. Justice Taggart, otherwise confined his consideration of aboriginal rights of social self-regulation to deciding that because of the distribution of legislative powers and judicial powers under the *Constitution Act, 1867* there were no remaining legislative or judicial functions exercisable by aboriginal peoples.

Mr. Justice Wallace confined his consideration of aboriginal rights of social self-regulation in the same way.

Mr. Justice Hutcheon, at p. 394 (para. 1164), said this:

> The traditions of the Gitksan and Wet'suwet'en societies existed long before 1846 and continued thereafter. They included the right to names and titles, the use of masks and symbols in rituals, the use of ceremonial robes and the right to occupy or control places of economic importance. The traditions, in these kinship societies, also included the institution of the clans and of the Houses in which membership descended through the mother and, of course, the Feast system. They regulated marriage and the relations with neighbouring societies.

I note that Mr. Justice Hutcheon referred specifically to marriage customs. I am sure that adoption customs would fall in the same category. Mr. Justice Hutcheon then asked this question: When was the right to practice those traditions lost? At p. 266 (para. 1168) Mr. Justice Hutcheon answered that question by saying that no one could argue that the traditions of the Feast and other traditions such as he was describing of the Gitksan and Wet'suwet'en peoples had been extinguished. At p. 396 (paras. 1172 and 1173), Mr. Justice Hutcheon said this:

> The appellants accept that provincial laws of general application validly apply to aboriginal people subject, of course, to the test arising under s. 88 of the *Indian Act*. It is not necessary at this stage to decide, in a final way, the validity of any specific provincial statute.

What Mr. Justice Hutcheon said at p. 394 (para. 1164) was quoted by Mr. Justice Macfarlane at p. 150 (para. 158) and not disapproved, though Mr. Justice Macfarlane said, at para. 159, "However, what specific system of laws and customs have continued was not made clear."

At p. 363 (para. 1029), I said this:

> I propose to summarize. The Gitksan and Wet'suwet'en peoples had rights of self-government and self-regulation in 1846, at the time of sovereignty. Those rights rested on the customs, traditions and practices of those peoples to the extent that they formed an integral part of their distinctive cultures. The assertion of British Sovereignty only took away such rights as were inconsistent with the concept of British Sovereignty. The introduction of English Law into British Columbia was only an introduction of such laws as were not from local circumstances inapplicable. The existence of a body of Gitksan and Wet'suwet'en customary law would be expected to render much of the newly introduced English Law inapplicable to the Gitksan and Wet'suwet'en peoples, particularly since none of the institutions of English Law were available to them in their territory, so that their local circumstances would tend to have required the continuation of their own laws. The division

of powers brought about when British Columbia entered Confederation in 1871 would not, in my opinion, have made any difference to Gitksan and Wet'suwet'en customary laws. Since 1871, Provincial laws of general application would apply to the Gitksan and Wet'suwet'en people, and Federal laws, particularly the *Indian Act*, would also have applied to them. But to the extent that Gitksan and Wet'suwet'en customary law lay at the core of their Indianness, that law would not be abrogated by Provincial laws of general application nor by Federal laws, unless those Federal laws demonstrated a clear and plain intention of the Sovereign power in Parliament to abrogate the Gitksan or Wet'suwet'en customary laws. Subject to those over-riding considerations, Gitksan and Wet'suwet'en customary laws of self-government and self-regulation have continued to the present day and are now constitutionally protected by s. 35 of the *Constitution Act, 1982*.

I think that the conclusion which should be drawn from the decision of the court in *Delgamuukw v. The Queen* is that none of the five judges decided that aboriginal rights of social self-regulation had been extinguished by any form of blanket extinguishment and that particular rights must be examined in each case to determine the scope and content of the specific right in the aboriginal society, and the relationship between that right with that scope and content and the workings of the general law of British Columbia.

Of course, if the aboriginal right had not been extinguished before 1982, it is now recognized, affirmed and guaranteed by s. 35 of the *Constitution Act, 1982*, not in its regulated form but in its full vigour, subject to the prima facie infringement and justification tests leading to a decision about ultimate justification, all as set out in *R. v. Sparrow*, [1990] 1 S.C.R. 1075.

V

That brings me to the decisive issue in this appeal, namely: the consequences under the general law of the province of a customary adoption brought about in the exercise of aboriginal rights.

I propose in this case to confine my consideration of that question to the narrow point about aboriginal rights which give rise to a particular status in the aboriginal community in question.

Before coming to the Canadian cases, I will refer to this passage from the majority reasons of Mr. Justice Brennan, with which Chief Justice Mason and Mr. Justice McHugh agreed, in the High Court of Australia in *Mabo v. Queensland* (1992), 107 A.L.R. 1:

> The incidents of a particular native title relating to inheritance, *the transmission or acquisition of rights and interests on death or marriage*, the transfer of rights and interests in land and the grouping of persons to possess rights and interests in land are matters to be determined by the laws and customs of the indigenous inhabitants, provided those laws and customs are not so repugnant to natural justice, equity and good conscience that judicial sanctions under the new regime must be withheld: *Idewu Inasa v. Oshodi*, [1934] A.C. 99 (J.C.P.C.).

(my emphasis)

That passage was framed in relation to the holding of native title (or aboriginal title as it is called in Canada), but in my opinion the fact that the acquisition of rights on death and marriage is specifically mentioned is an indication that rights arising from status may properly be determined by the laws and customs of the aboriginal people in question.

I propose now to turn to the Canadian cases. I have been much assisted in a search for the cases and in an understanding of them by an article written by Professor Norman Zlotkin: "Judicial Recognition of Aboriginal Customary Law in Canada: Selected Marriage and Adoption Cases", [1984] 4 C.N.L.R 1.

The leading case, and a most remarkable authority in this field, is the judgment of Mr. Justice Monk of the Superior Court of Quebec in *Connolly v. Woolrich* (1867), 11 L.C. Jur. 197; 17 R.J.R.Q. 75; 1 C.N.L.C. 70. The decision was rendered on 9 July 1867, just 9 days after Confederation. In 1802, William Connolly, at the age of 16, left Montreal as a clerk for the North-west Company and went to live and work at Rivière-aux-rats in the Athabaska District. In 1803 he took to live with him, with her consent and her father's consent, and in accordance with Cree custom, Suzanne Pas-de-nom, a Cree. They lived together from 1802 to 1831 at a number of posts in the North-west country. They had six children or more, of whom the plaintiff was one. By 1831 William Connolly was a chief trader of the Hudson Bay Company and he and Suzanne and a number of their children moved to Montreal.

In 1832 William Connolly went through a form of marriage with Julia Woolrich in accordance with the Quebec civil law and their Catholic faith. William Connolly and Julia Woolrich lived together after that as man and wife and had two children. Suzanne was supported by William and, after his death, by Julia, at a convent at the Red River settlement. The contest in the lawsuit was between one of the children of William Connolly and Suzanne Pas-de-nom, on the one hand, and the heirs of Julia Woolrich on the other.

Mr. Justice Monk decided that William Connolly and Suzanne Pas-de-nom had married in accordance with Cree custom and that for the purposes of Quebec law they were man and wife. Mr. Justice Monk decided further that the status of husband and wife conferred by Cree custom gave rise to community of property between William and Suzanne in accordance with the law of the domicile of origin of William, namely the law of Quebec. As a result the plaintiff was entitled to his proportionate share of half of the property of William Connolly. Mr. Justice Monk's decision was upheld by the Cour du Banc de la Reine, en appel. Chief Justice Duval, Mr. Justice Caron, Mr. Justice Badgley and Mr. Justice McKay agreed with Mr. Justice Monk's reasoning, conclusion, and result. Mr. Justice Loranger dissented. See (1869), 17 R.J.R.Q. 266; 1 R.L.O.S. 253; 1 C.N.L.C 151.

In *R. v. Nan-E-Quis-A-Ka* (1889), 1 Terr. L.R. 211; 2 C.N.L.C. 368 (N.W.T.S.C.), Mr. Justice Wetmore decided that Maggie, a woman married by Inuit custom, was not a compellable witness against her customary law husband. The status conferred by the Inuit customary law marriage was applied to the common law criminal law of evidence and she was not required to testify. A similar conclusion on similar facts was reached by Mr. Justice Gregory in *R. v. Williams* (1921), 30 B.C.R. 303 (B.C.S.C.), though he did not have time to research the point in the middle of an assize. In *Ex parte Côté* (1971), 5 C.C.C. (2d) 49 the Saskatchewan Court of Appeal reached the opposite conclusion on the same question. They considered that the presence of a clergyman was necessary for a simple consensual common law marriage.

In *R. v. Bear's Shin Bone* (1899), 4 Terr. L.R. 173 (N.W.T.S.C.), Mr. Justice Rouleau dealt with a marriage according to the customs of the Blood tribe and concluded that the marriage was valid and could give rise to a conviction for polygamy under the criminal law.

In *Re Noah Estate* (1961), 32 D.L.R. (2d) 185 (N.W.T.S.C.) Mr. Justice Sissons decided that a marriage between two Inuit, celebrated in accordance with Inuit custom in the Northwest Territories, involving simply a trial period and continuing consent of the parties, was a valid marriage and conferred marital status. When the husband had become part of the "white man's society" the Intestate Succession Ordinance of the Northwest Territories applied to confer benefits on his wife as "widow" and his children as "issue".

As Professor Zlotkin says at p. 5, the cases are consistent with the view that before a statute could remove the status confirmed by a marriage according to aboriginal custom the statute would have to be explicit on that point. Or, as the extinguishment cases say, the statute would have to demonstrate a clear and plain intention to extinguish the rights conferred by a marriage in accordance with aboriginal custom.

I propose to move now from the cases involving marriage by aboriginal custom to the cases on adoption by aboriginal custom.

In *Re Katie's Adoption Petition* (1961), 32 D.L.R. (2d) 686 (N.W.T.T.C.) Mr. Justice Sissons decided that an Inuit customary adoption conferred the status of parent and child on the respective parties to the adoption. Mr. Justice Sissons decided that the *Northwest Territories Act*, the Adoption Ordinance and the Child Welfare Ordinance did not end customary adoptions by Inuit custom.

In *Re Beaulieu's Petition* (1969), 3 D.L.R. (3d) 479 (N.W.T.T.C.) Mr. Justice Morrow followed *Re Katie* and decided that a Dogrib Indian customary adoption should be recognized.

In *Re Deborah* (1972), 27 D.L.R. (3d) 225 (N.W.T.S.C.) an Inuit customary adoption was challenged by the natural parents. Mr. Justice Morrow recognized the Inuit customary adoption and the status it conferred and he rejected the challenge of the natural parents. Mr. Justice Morrow's decision was appealed to the Northwest Territories Court of Appeal. Mr. Justice Johnson, for the court, upheld Mr. Justice Morrow's decision. See (1972), 28 D.L.R. (3d) 483 (N.W.T.C.A.). At p. 488, Mr. Justice Johnson set out the legal foundation for the recognition by the common law of adoption by aboriginal custom in this way:

Custom has always been recognized by the common law and while at an earlier date proof of the existence of a custom from time immemorial was required, Tindal C.J. in *Bastard v. Smith* (1838), 2 Mood. & R. 129 at 136, 174 E.R. 238, points out that such evidence is no longer possible or necessary and that the evidence extending "as far back as living memory goes, of a continuous, peaceable, and uninterrupted user of the custom" is all that is now required. Such proof was offered and accepted in this case.

In *Re Wah-Shee* (1975), 57 D.L.R. (3d) 743 and in *Re Tagornak* (1983), 50 A.R. 237 the Supreme Court of the Northwest Territories declared adoption by aboriginal custom to be valid, notwithstanding that in each case one of the adopting parents was caucasian.

I conclude that there is a well-established body of authority in Canada for the proposition that the status conferred by aboriginal customary adoption will be recognized by the courts for the purposes of application of the principles of the common law and the provisions of statute law to the persons whose status is established by the customary adoption. That body of authority is entirely consistent with all of the reasons for judgment of the members of this court in *Delgamuukw v. The Queen* as those reasons discuss the jurisprudential foundation for aboriginal rights in British Columbia.

VI

I turn now to the provincial *Adoption Act* and to the federal *Indian Act* to see whether there is anything in either of those Acts which might be said to qualify, regulate, or in the case of the *Indian Act* extinguish, the status conferred by an aboriginal customary adoption.

Adoption was not known at common law. It is a creation of statute. The first *Adoption Act* in British Columbia was passed in 1920 as S.B.C. 1920 c. 2. There is nothing in that Act or in any amendment to that Act or in the present *Adoption Act*, R.S.B.C. 1979 c. 4, as amended, which could be thought to have qualified or regulated either before or after the constitutional amendment of 1982, the right of aboriginal people to continue their custom of adoption in accordance with the customs, traditions and practices which form an integral part of their distinctive culture.

Indeed, s-s. 11(5) and para. 13.6(1)(b) of the present *Adoption Act* indicate a sensitivity to the protection of aboriginal status in the adoption of Indian children by non-Indian or Indian adoptive parents. That sensitivity is entirely inconsistent with the abrogation of Indian customary adoptions.

Subsection 11(5) reads like this:

11. (5) The status, rights, privileges, disabilities and limitations of an adopted Indian person acquired as an Indian under the *Indian Act* (Canada) or under any other Act or law are not affected by this section.

In my opinion, if aboriginal customary adoptions were not to be recognized and only adoptions under the Adoption Act were to be recognized, then the subsection would have used the words "... an Indian person adopted under this Act ...", rather than the words "... an adopted Indian person ...".

I move on now to the federal *Indian Act*. In that Act "child" is defined in this way in ss. 2(1):

> "child" includes a child born in or out of wedlock, a legally adopted child and *a child adopted in accordance with Indian custom.*

(my emphasis)

That definition was placed in the *Indian Act* in 1985 to replace two former definitions which had been used for two different purposes. At the time of the change, the Honourable David Crombie, Minister of Indian Affairs and Northern Development, said this:

> If an Indian person is capable of transmitting status to his or her natural child, it seems logical to extend that capability to include a child whom the Indian person might adopt, either legally as defined by provincial or territorial law, *or by the custom of his or her people.* The equal treatment of children in an immediate family is important to the preservation and integrity of the family unit. *Band custom adoptions are not uncommon and very frequently involve a relative of the child in question.*

(my emphasis)

See Hansard [Canada, House of Commons, Commons Debates, Vol. IV at pp. 5564-5 (10 June, 1985)].

There is nothing in the *Indian Act* which might be thought to abrogate the status conferred by Indian customary adoptions and, indeed, the definition I have quoted of "child", and the passage I have quoted from Hansard, indicate quite the reverse.

I have discussed both the Provincial *Adoption Act* and the Federal *Indian Act*. Neither of them suggests the qualification, regulation or abrogation of aboriginal customary adoptions. It is therefore not necessary for me to deal with any question relating to the constitutional power to regulate or extinguish aboriginal rights, a subject discussed at some length in *Delgamuukw v. The Queen*.

VII

In my opinion, by the customs of the Stellaquo Band of the Carrier People, Ernest Casimel became the son of Louise Casimel and Francis Casimel, and Louise and Francis Casimel became the parents of Ernest Casimel. Such a customary adoption was an integral part of the distinctive culture of the Stellaquo Band of the Carrier People, (though, of course, other societies may well have shared the same custom or variations of that custom), and as such, gave rise to aboriginal status rights that became recognized, affirmed and protected by the common law and under s. 35 of the *Constitution Act, 1982*.

The status of parent, recognized by the common law and by the constitution of Canada, is sufficient to bring Louise Casimel and Francis

Casimel within the definition of "dependent parent" in Part VII of the Insurance (Motor Vehicle) Regulations and so they are both entitled to the "no fault" death benefits provided under Sections 92, 93, and 94 of those Regulations.

I would allow the appeal and give judgment for the plaintiffs accordingly.

Lambert J.

Hutcheon J.A.: — I agree.

Hinds J.A.: — I agree.

H. CONCLUSION

As this chapter has illustrated, cultural chauvinism has often overshadowed the welfare of Aboriginal children in Canada. While this has largely been evident by the way Aboriginal children have been treated by Canadian governments, unfortunately, it can also exist in Aboriginal communities. Residential schools, the "sixties scoop", and some interpretations of the "best interest of the child" test illustrate the devastating impact that cultural chauvinism can have. However, cases like that of Lester Desjarlais and *Jane Doe (Public Trustee of) v. Awasis Agency of Northern Manitoba* illustrate that cultural chauvinism can also cut the other way. Despite these challenges, there are some hopeful signs that Aboriginal children will be better cared for in the future. The re-emergence of traditions and customs which respect and strengthen the extended family, and implement teachings of sharing, kindness and respect, present some cause for optimism about the future. In any event, no matter what path reform takes to help Aboriginal children, knowledge of the issues identified in this chapter will form the basis upon which the regeneration of Aboriginal peoples is built.

ENDNOTES

1.   See <http://www.trc-cvr.ca>.
2.   Justice Ted Hughes, *BC Children and Youth Review: An Independent Review of BC's Child Protection System*, April 7, 2006 at 48.
3.   Manitoba Aboriginal Affairs Secretariat, *Aboriginal People in Manitoba*, Winnipeg, 2006 at 42.
4.   Saskatchewan Institute of Public Policy, "A Profile of Aboriginal Children in Regina", January 2004 in *Commission on First Nations and Metis Peoples and Justice Reform*, Saskatoon, 2004 at 10-7.
5.   First Nations Child and Family Caring Society of Canada (Ottawa, 2005) at 14-15.
6.   November 2010, online: <http://saskchildwelfarereview.ca/CWR-panel-report.pdf> at 15-17.
7.   "Child Welfare Law, 'Best Interests of the Child' Ideology and First Nations" (1992) 30 Osgoode Hall L.J. 375 at 389.

8. Jim Anglin, "Risk, Well-Being, and Paramountcy in Child Protection: The Need for Transformation" (2002) 31 Child and Youth Care Forum 233 at 248-49.

9. Patricia Monture, "A Vicious Circle: Child Welfare and the First Nations" (1989) 3 C.J.W.L. 1 at 11, 12, 14.

10. Annie Bunting, National Judicial Institute, Aboriginal Law Seminar, Calgary, Alberta, January 23-25, 2003.

11. Suzanne Fournier and Ernie Crey, *Stolen From Our Embrace* (Vancouver: Douglas and McIntyre, 1997. For a description of the by-law's development see: John A. MacDonald, "The Spallumcheen Indian Band By-Law and Its Potential Impact on Child Welfare Policy in British Columbia" (1983) 4 Can. J. Fam. L. 76-95.

12. A revised version was published in *Aboriginal Child Welfare, Self-Government and the Rights of Indigenous Children: Protecting the Vulnerable under International Law* (Farnham, UK: Ashgate, 2012).

13. Pamela Gough, *Manitoba's Child Welfare System* (Toronto: University of Toronto, Faculty of Social Work, 2006 at <http://www.cecw-cepb.ca/DocsEng/ManitobaChildWelfareSystem34E.pdf>) (references omitted).

14. Assembly of First Nations, *Child Welfare Leadership Action Plan on First Nations*, 2006 at 2, online: <http://turtleisland.org/healing/afncf.pdf>.

15. Chapter 4, at pages 23-25, online: <http://www.oag-bvg.gc.ca/internet/docs/parl_oag_201106_04_e.pdf>.

CHAPTER 11

TAXATION

A. INTRODUCTION

Taxation raises fundamental issues of representation, participation and citizenship. As such, the development of the Canadian tax structure has been substantially influenced by constitutional considerations. As earlier chapters have demonstrated, however, Aboriginal peoples have not always received fair treatment within Canada's constitutional structure. This has created considerable tension between Aboriginal peoples and the Crown. Taxation is a significant factor in wealth creation and redistribution, yet materially Aboriginal peoples remain among the poorest group in Canada. This has also generated conflict as Aboriginal people seek to use taxation to produce and retain wealth within their own communities. This chapter explores the history and treatment of Indian taxation in Canada. It provides examples of how the law has interpreted provisions for customs and excise taxes, incomes taxes, sales taxes and corporate income taxes relative to Indians.

B. HISTORY AND CONTEXT

Aboriginal peoples in Canada claim immunities from taxation based on their view that in the face of colonial intrusions they retained sovereignty over their people and territories. The *Chiefs of Ontario Magazine* (1998) Winter edition, outlined this perspective in the following terms:

> The First Nations hold they are comprehensively immune from all forms of Canadian taxation (federal, provincial and municipal). The immunity applies within the traditional territories of First Nations, that is to say, throughout Canada. This immunity, claim First Nations leaders, is not restricted to *Indian Act* reserves.
>
> The immunity flows from the historical relationship between First Nations and the Euro-Canadian settlers.
>
> First Nations exemption from taxation in legislation goes back a long way. In 1850, the Province of Canada enacted a law stating that no taxes would be levied or assessed against an Indian person or anyone married to an Indian person.
>
> It also stated that no taxes or assessments would be levied against either an Indian person or someone married to them if they resided on Indian lands not ceded to the Crown. It went further to say that taxes and assessments would not be levied against them even if they lived on lands that had been ceded to the Crown, but had been set aside for Indian occupancy.

By 1876, this exemption was codified in the *Indian Act*. It remains in the *Indian Act* to this day. ...First Nations leaders negotiated tax exemptions with the Crown as a partial return for the sharing of the land and its enormous potential for the production of wealth through farming, timber, mining and oil exploration. They knew they were sharing something very valuable and, they expected something of value in return. ...

So, by treaty and other means, most First Nations agreed to share some of their lands and resources with the settlers. This generosity has led directly to the immense wealth of the Canadian state and private sector.

In effect, First Nations have paid their "taxes" into eternity. ...

The immunity also flows from the inherent right of self-government held by First Nations. This right is recognized and affirmed by section 35 of the Canadian Constitution Act, 1982. Pursuant to that right, First Nations have complete and exclusive jurisdiction over fiscal issues, including taxation.

First Nations leaders argue that Canadian taxation laws cannot interfere with this inherent jurisdiction.[1]

As we will see in this section, Canadian courts or legislatures have not explicitly accepted the position put forward by First Nations people in regard to taxation. However, it is worth noting that First Nations in Ontario were recently successful in securing an "exemption" to the Harmonized Sales Tax, which came into effect on July 1, 2010. The First Nations secured this benefit after intensive negotiation with the provincial government. First Nations expressed their basis for this action in the following terms:

A. First Nations affirm our rights as Indigenous Peoples to be involved in all decisions regarding our Aboriginal Title, lands and resources.

B. Given our proprietary and inherent rights to our respective territories, lands and resources, First Nations have a right to be involved in the development of policies and decisions that impact our communities, lands and resources.

C. The United Nations Declaration on the Rights of Indigenous Peoples provides in Article 18 that Indigenous peoples have the right to participate in decision-making in matters which would affect their rights, and in Article 19 that States shall consult and cooperate in good faith with the Indigenous peoples concerned through their own representative institutions in order to obtain their free, prior and informed consent before adopting and implementing legislative or administrative measures that may affect them.

D. First Nations' treaty relationship is based on the spirit and intent of our treaties and is reflected in the Treaty of Niagara 1764, the two-row wampum and other treaty agreements First Nations signed with the Crown based on a nation-to-nation relationship.

E. First Nations Aboriginal and Treaty rights are reflected in the Royal Proclamation, 1763 and are also recognized and affirmed in the Canadian Constitution Act, 1982.

F. Canada and Provincial governments continue to exploit First Nation resources without compensation or consideration given to First Nations.

G. Canada signed with Ontario a Memorandum of Agreement to harmonize the 8% Provincial Sales Tax (PST) with the 5% Goods and

Services Tax (GST) into a combined 13% Harmonized Sales Tax (HST).

H.	On November 16, 2009 Ontario tabled legislation on implementing the 13% HST for July 1, 2010.

I.	The proposed 13% HST will be administered by the Canada Revenue Agency and current Point of Sale exemptions Ontario First Nations receive on PST will be eliminated.

J.	The Supreme Court of Canada has clearly stated in Haida that the Crown owes a duty of consultation to a First Nation when the Crown contemplates conduct that might adversely affect rights or title claimed by the First Nation.

K.	The provincial government of British Columbia announced its intentions on September 1, 2009 to adopt the proposed Harmonized Sales Tax ('HST') which combines B.C.'s 7% provincial sales tax (PST) with the 5% federal Goods and Services Tax (GST), and would be applied to the same tax base as GST is currently applied to.

L.	On July 22, 2009 the provincial government of British Columbia signed a Memorandum of Agreement (MOA) with the Government of Canada concerning a Canada-British Columbia Comprehensive Integrated Tax Co-ordination Agreement (CITCA); and according to the MOA, Canada and B.C. will use their best efforts to enter into the CITCA on or before September 30, 2009 and subject to both parties signing and subject to legislative approval, the implementation date for HST will be July 1, 2010.

M.	Canada and both provincial governments failed to meet legal obligations to consult and accommodate and seek First Nation consent on the HST, which will have an immediate negative impact on Ontario First Nation citizens and businesses.

N.	First Nations have never agreed to an imposition of taxation on its citizens and another government cannot unilaterally tax First Nations without derogating Aboriginal and Treaty rights.

O.	First Nations tax immunity is derived from its nation-to-nation relationship with the Crown and Canada administers First Nation exemptions through an oppressive policy called the Indian Act.

P.	First Nations recognize that the Government of Canada imposed the Indian Act on First Nations beginning in 1876, but the Indian Act was never agreed to in any treaty with First Nations.

Q.	First Nations opposed the GST at the time it was implemented and hereby oppose any additional taxes that are administered in the same manner as the GST, including the impending HST.

R.	The administration of the GST fails to recognize First Nations' Aboriginal and Treaty rights beyond the boundaries of First Nation reservations.

S.	First Nations with no land base, but recognized under the Indian Act as First Nations, will not receive any exemptions from the impending HST.

T.	The proposed HST is another example that Canada continues to be an oppressive state against the most marginalized and impoverished people in the country.

U.	Given that exploitative industries such as mining and forestry will benefit through financial savings from the proposed HST, First Nations should also benefit as these developments often occur on First Nations lands.

V.   Many current British Columbia PST exemptions to environmentally sustainable goods and services will not be continued under HST, but instead will be subject to the full 12% HST, and this shift in policy signifies a step away from provincial commitments to environmental preservation and sustainability.

THEREFORE BE IT RESOLVED that the Chiefs-in-Assembly:

1.   Reaffirm our sovereignty as Nations as reflected in our treaty relationships with the Crown.
2.   Declare that First Nations have never relinquished or surrendered their sovereignty or autonomy to the governments of France, Britain, Canada, or provincial governments.
3.   Recognize and affirm that for Treaty peoples our immunity of provincial and Canadian taxes is derived from our rights as Indigenous Peoples, the spirit and intent of our treaties and not from the *Indian Act*.
4.   Recognize and affirm a responsibility to protect the resources and rights of First Nation lands and its citizens.
5.   Hereby oppose a system of taxation on its citizens or governments by other external governments, and also recognize and support other First Nations that oppose the HST.
6.   Invite all First Nations to combine our efforts in protecting Aboriginal and Treaty rights.
7.   Direct the Assembly of First Nations to urge Canada to honour First Nations rights to be consulted and accommodated on any Canadian tax legislation that may impact First Nations Aboriginal and Treaty Rights.
8.   Direct the Assembly of First Nations to declare their support of First Nations Aboriginal and Treaty rights as it pertains to the imposition of taxation.
9.   Direct the Assembly of First Nations to support and participate in any action plans or direct action strategies by First Nations that oppose the HST.
10. Eliminate any future discussions with other provinces regarding harmonization of taxation.[2]

While many First Nations are frustrated by a lack of broader recognition for First Nations tax immunities, Ontario First Nations were relieved to secure the government's agreement to withhold the HST. Other First Nations take encouragement from how Indian taxation issues are treated in the United States Supreme Court, and hope that the Canadian Supreme Court will develop a similar approach. In a case called *Merrion v. Jicarilla Apache Tribe*, 455 U.S. 130 (1982), Justice Thurgood Marshall of the U.S. Supreme Court wrote:

In *Washington v. Confederated Tribes of Colville Indian Reservation*, 447 U.S. 134, 100 S.Ct. 2069, 65 L.Ed.2d 10 (1980) (Colville), we addressed the Indian tribes' authority to impose taxes on non-Indians doing business on the reservation. We held that "[t]he power to tax transactions occurring on trust lands and significantly involving a tribe or its members is a fundamental attribute of sovereignty which the tribes retain unless divested of it by federal law or necessary implication of their dependent status." Id., at 152, 100 S.Ct. at 2080-81. The power to tax is an essential attribute of Indian sovereignty because it is a necessary instrument of self- government and territorial management. This power enables a tribal government to raise revenues for its essential services. The power does not derive solely from the Indian tribe's power to exclude non-Indians from tribal lands. Instead, it derives from the tribe's general authority, as sovereign, to control economic activity within its jurisdiction, and to defray the cost of providing governmental services by requiring contributions from persons or enterprises engaged in economic activities within that jurisdiction.

On the other side of the debate about Aboriginal taxation, special interest groups like the Canadian Taxpayers Federation argue that Aboriginal peoples must not be tax exempt. This view is expressed in Tanis Fiss, "Aboriginal Tax Exemption Must End":

Income — not race or ancestry — is the only valid basis for a tax exemption. Unfortunately, that's not the case in Canada. Aboriginal tax exemptions create an inequality within the tax system. Therefore, the federal government must phase-out the exemption. ...

It is crucial to remember that such tax exemptions are not a constitutional right. Instead, they stem from pieces of legislation. A stroke of the pen, by Parliament can revoke the privilege contained within the Indian Act; similarly a stroke of the pen from provincial legislatures can revoke the provincial tax exemptions for Native Canadians.[3]

As you read the cases in this chapter, try to identify the basis for the differential tax treatment of Indian people within Canadian law. As you consider this issue, ponder the statement made by an Elder before the Commission on First Nations and Metis Peoples and Justice Reform:

f) The Myth of Taxation

"Aboriginal people do not pay taxes," is a belief commonly held. That could not be further from the truth. The right to not pay taxes is land-based. Any Treaty beneficiary living off-reserve and purchasing goods pays the following taxes: property, PST, GST, alcohol, tobacco, income, environment, duty, capital gains, payroll and fuel. Such people pay, in effect, what every other Canadian pays. On-reserve there are exceptions for income, tobacco, fuel, GST and PST. However, given the high unemployment rate on reserves in Saskatchewan, this exemption for income tax is an advantage to very few. Except for Indian Act exemptions on-reserve, First Nations people and corporations do pay taxes. The reason for this exemption is that First Nations land is held "outside" Canada and hence out of Canada's tax jurisdiction. Freedom from taxation and, incidentally, military conscription were also Treaty promises. The taxation promise has been weakened by court interpretation (*Benoit v. Canada*); wrongly, in the opinion of many Aboriginal people.

> Just talking about taxation ... this whole taxation thing came up one day because they're farm people, and one of them said to me, "Well, you're really lucky you don't have to pay taxes." Well, guess what, I probably pay more taxes in that community than anybody else because I have nobody at home with me ... When I talked to them about that they just assumed if you were Aboriginal you paid no taxes, period. They had no understanding, you know, that the people who don't pay taxes are such a small minority. (Elder)[4]

C.   SOVEREIGNTY AND THE CUSTOMS AND EXCISE TAX

As noted, Aboriginal perspectives on Indian taxation usually begin with the idea that they are not merely "exempt" from taxation, but "immune" from its application because of their unique citizenship within Canada. The claim for tax immunity stems from the idea that Indians retain a measure of sovereignty that absolves them from Canadian taxation and obligates them to contribute to their own governments. The United States Supreme Court has taken this approach and recognized a wide range of immunities against state and federal taxation for Indigenous peoples in that country. No Canadian court has pursued the issue of taxation from this perspective or recognized statutory Indian taxation provisions as an immunity from taxation. Despite these rulings, many Aboriginal people continue to claim these immunities, as illustrated in the following cases.

FRANCIS v. CANADA

[1956] S.C.J. No. 38, [1956] S.C.R. 618, 3 D.L.R. (2d) 641 (S.C.C.)

The judgment of **Kerwin C.J.C.**, **Taschereau** and **Fauteux JJ.** was delivered by

The Chief Justice: — This is an appeal against a decision of the Exchequer Court dismissing the Petition of Right of the suppliant (an Indian resident in a reserve in Canada) and the question is whether three articles, a washing machine, a refrigerator and an oil heater, brought by him into Canada from the United States of America are subject to duties of customs and sales tax under the relevant statutes of Canada. None was paid and in fact the articles were not brought into this country at a port of entry; they were subsequently placed under customs detention or seizure and in order to obtain their release, the appellant, under protest, paid the sum demanded by the Crown. The Petition of Right claims the return of this money and a declaration that no duties or taxes were payable by the appellant with respect to the goods. ...

The appellant falls within the definition of "Indian" in s. 2(1)(*g*) of R.S.C. 1951, c. 29 and at all relevant times he resided on the St. Regis Indian Reserve in St. Regis village in the westerly part of the Province of Quebec, which adjoins an Indian reserve in the State of New York in the United States of America, the residents of both reserves belonging to the St. Regis Tribe of Indians. The articles were brought into Canada in the manner already described in order to lay the foundation for the present proceeding as a test case.

The first claim advanced on behalf of the appellant is that these imposts need not be paid because of the following provisions of Article III of the Treaty of Amity, Commerce and Navigation, between His Britannic

Majesty and the United States of America signed on November 19, 1794, and generally known as the *Jay Treaty*: —

> No Duty on Entry shall ever be levied by either Party on Peltries brought by Land, or Inland Navigation into the said Territories respectively, nor shall the Indians passing or re-passing with their own proper Goods and Effects of whatever nature, pay for the same any Impost or Duty whatever. But Goods in Bales or other large Packages unusual among Indians shall not be considered as Goods belonging *bona fide* to Indians.

In view of the conclusion at which I have arrived, it is unnecessary to deal with the question raised by the respondent that the articles imported by the appellant were not his "own proper goods and effects".

The *Jay Treaty* was not a Treaty of Peace and it is clear that in Canada such rights and privileges as are here advanced of subjects of a contracting party to a treaty are enforceable by the Courts only where the treaty has been implemented or sanctioned by legislation. ...

I agree with Mr. Justice Cameron that clause (*b*) of s. 86 of *The Indian Act* does not apply, because customs duties are not taxes upon the personal property of an Indian situated on a Reserve but are imposed upon the importation of goods into Canada. ...

The appeal should be dismissed with costs.

Rand J. (Cartwright J. concurring): — ... The claim is based first on that clause of art. 3 of the Jay Treaty between Great Britain and the United States of 1794 ... and on the 9th article of the *Treaty of Ghent*, 1815, between the same states. ...

... Following [early treaties] large-scale transfers of Indians belonging to the Six Nations and more western tribes took place from the United States to lands north of Lake Erie. ...

In 1794 European settlement of North America was in its early stages. In 1768 a treaty had been made with the Indians that had placed the western boundary of the advance south of the Great Lakes at the Ohio river. The lands to the north and west of those lakes were within the charter granted to the Hudson's Bay Company. The section of the international boundary from the Lake of the Woods to the Rocky Mountains was not fixed until 1818 and that beyond to the Pacific ocean until 1846. Confederation succeeded in 1867 and a few years later drew within its orbit all the territory reaching to the Pacific and the far north. Government in relation to the Indians was thus greatly extended. ...

Indian affairs generally ... have for over a century been the subject of expanding administration throughout what is now the Dominion, superseding the local enactments following the treaty designed to meet an immediate urgency. ... There followed the slow but inevitable march of events ... and today there remain along the border only fragmentary reminders of that past. The strife that had waged over the free and ancient hunting grounds and their fruits, lands which were divided between two powers, but that life in its original mode and scope has long since disappeared.

These considerations seem to justify the conclusion that both the Crown and Parliament of this country have treated the provisional accommodation as having been replaced by an exclusive code of new and special rights and privileges. Appreciating fully the obligation of good faith toward these wards of the state, there can be no doubt that the conditions constituting the raison d'être of the clause were and have been considered such as would in foreseeable time disappear. That a radical change of this nature brings about a cession of such a treaty provision appears to be supported by the authorities available: McNair, *The Law of Treaties*, 378-381. Assuming that art. 9 of the *Treaty of Ghent* extended to the exemption, it was only an "engagement" to restore which, by itself, could do no more than to revive the clause in its original treaty effect, and supplementary action was clearly envisaged. Whether, then, the time of its expiration has been reached or not it is not here necessary to decide; it is sufficient to say that there is no legislation now in force implementing the stipulation. ...

The appeal must therefore be dismissed and with costs if demanded.

Unlike Canada, the United States recognized that the *Jay Treaty* provided authority for some differential treatment for Indians in *Karnuth v. United States* (1929), 23 Am. J. Intl. L. (U.S.S.C.); *U.S. v. Garrow*, 88 F.2d 318 (C.C.P.A. 1937). The issue addressed in *Francis* is still not settled in the minds of many Aboriginal people in Canada. It is difficult for some to accept some of the reasons upon which the judgment rests, that "There followed the slow but inevitable march of events ... and today there remain along the border only fragmentary reminders of [the Aboriginal] past. The strife ... waged over the free and ancient [Aboriginal] hunting grounds and their fruits, [the land] divided between two powers" and the Aboriginal mode of life has long since disappeared. Aboriginal people believe that such justifications amount to an erasure of their continuing presence as contemporary political powers. They are gravely concerned when treaty and other rights are abrogated on the assumption that the development of Canada and the United States inevitably fragmented their rights and way of life such that any justification for the protection of these rights has "long since disappeared".

As a result of dissatisfaction with the Canadian interpretation of the Jay Treaty, Grand Chief Mitchell of the Mohawks of Akwesasne brought the case of *Mitchell v. M.N.R.*, below. In this challenge, however, instead of framing the issue under the Treaty, Chief Mitchell asserted that the Mohawk possessed an existing Aboriginal right to cross the border free of customs and excise taxes.

MITCHELL v. M.N.R.

[2001] S.C.J. No. 33, [2001] 1 S.C.R. 911, 199 D.L.R. (4th) 385 (S.C.C.)

McLachlin C.J.C. (Gonthier, Iacobucci, Arbour and LeBel JJ.): —

Introduction

[1] This case raises the issue of whether the Mohawk Canadians of Akwesasne have the right to bring goods into Canada from the United States for collective use and trade with other First Nations without paying customs duties. Grand Chief Michael Mitchell claims that his people have an aboriginal right that ousts Canadian customs law. The government replies that no such right exists, first because the evidence does not support it and second because such a right would be fundamentally contrary to Canadian sovereignty. At the heart of the case lies the question of the evidence that must be adduced to establish an aboriginal right.

[2] Chief Mitchell is a Mohawk of Akwesasne, a Mohawk community located just west of Montreal, and a descendant of the Mohawk nation, one of the polities comprising the Iroquois Confederacy prior to the arrival of Europeans. On March 22, 1988, Chief Mitchell crossed the international border from the United States into Canada, arriving at the Cornwall customs office. He brought with him some blankets, bibles, motor oil, food, clothing, and a washing machine, all of which had been purchased in the United States. He declared the goods to the Canadian customs agents but asserted that he had aboriginal and treaty rights which exempted him from paying duty on the goods. After some discussion, the customs agents notified Chief Mitchell that he would be charged $142.88 in duty, and they permitted him to continue into Canada. Chief Mitchell, along with other Mohawks of Akwesasne, presented everything but the motor oil to the Mohawk community of Tyendinaga. The gifts were intended to symbolize the renewal of the historic trading relationship between the two communities. The oil was taken to a store in Akwesasne territory for resale to members of that community. In September of 1989, Chief Mitchell was served with a Notice of Ascertained Forfeiture claiming $361.64 for unpaid duty, taxes and penalties.

[3] I conclude that the aboriginal right claimed has not been established. The sparse and tenuous evidence advanced in this case to prove the existence of pre-contact Mohawk trading north of the Canada-United States boundary simply cannot support the claimed right. Even if deference is paid to the trial judge on this finding, any such trade was clearly incidental, and not integral, to the Mohawk culture. As a result, Chief Mitchell must pay duty on the goods he imported to Canada.

. . . . .

A. *What is the Nature of Aboriginal Rights?*

[10] ... European settlement did not terminate the interests of aboriginal peoples arising from their historical occupation and use of the land. To the

contrary, aboriginal interests and customary laws were presumed to survive the assertion of sovereignty, and were absorbed into the common law as rights, unless (1) they were incompatible with the Crown's assertion of sovereignty, (2) they were surrendered voluntarily via the treaty process, or (3) the government extinguished them: see B. Slattery, "Understanding Aboriginal Rights" (1987), 66 Can. Bar Rev. 727. Barring one of these exceptions, the practices, customs and traditions that defined the various aboriginal societies as distinctive cultures continued as part of the law of Canada. ...

[11] The common law status of aboriginal rights rendered them vulnerable to unilateral extinguishment, and thus they were "dependent upon the good will of the Sovereign": see *St. Catherine's Milling and Lumber Co. v. The Queen* (1888), 14 App. Cas. 46 (P.C.), at p. 54. This situation changed in 1982, when Canada's constitution was amended to entrench existing aboriginal and treaty rights. ...

. . . . .

[13] [T]he issue is whether the act which gave rise to the case at bar is an expression of [an Aboriginal] right. Aboriginal rights are not frozen in their pre-contact form: ancestral rights may find modern expression. The question is whether the impugned act represents the modern exercise of an ancestral practice, custom or tradition.

B.   *What is the Aboriginal Right Claimed?*

. . . . .

[16] Chief Mitchell characterizes his claim as the right to enter Canada from the United States with personal and community goods, without paying customs or duties, and the right to trade these goods with other First Nations. On the strength of this claimed right, he crossed the Canada-United States boundary with personal and community goods, the action giving rise to the case at bar. Although the motor oil was the only item transported by Chief Mitchell that was destined for resale, it can only be concluded that Chief Mitchell's actions — and his case — focused in fact on trade. The claimants asserted that "trade and commerce [is] central to their soul". Witness after witness was asked to describe historical Mohawk trading practices. Furthermore, when Chief Mitchell exercised his alleged right, all of the goods brought into Canada were trade-related: they were intended as gifts to seal a trade agreement with Tyendinaga and to signify renewed trading relations, in accordance with customary practice. Therefore the first factor, the action claimed as an exercise of an aboriginal right, suggests that the heart of the claim is the right to bring goods across the Canada-United States border for purposes of trade.

[17] The second factor, the nature of the conflict between the claimed right and the relevant legislation, while more neutral, does not displace this conclusion. The law in conflict with the alleged right is the *Customs Act*. It applies both to personal goods and goods for trade.

[18] The third factor to be considered in characterizing the claim is the relevant traditions and practices of the aboriginal people in question. The ancestral aboriginal practices upon which the claimant relies provide a strong indication of the nature and scope of the right claimed. In this case, the claimants emphasize their ancestral trading practices; indeed these practices and the alleged limitations on them raised by the appellant, lie at the heart of the case. As noted, the claimants assert that historically "trade and commerce [is] central to their soul". One of the claimant's expert witnesses testified that trade "came as easily to the Iroquois as living and breathing". The government, while not denying that the Mohawks traditionally traded, asserts that such trade did not extend north into what is now Canada and that, in any event, the Mohawks traditionally accepted the custom of paying tributes and duties to cross boundaries established by other polities.

[19] I conclude that the *Van der Peet* factors of the impugned action, the governmental action or legislation with which it conflicts, and the ancestral practice relied on, all suggest the claim here is properly characterized as the right to bring goods across the Canada-United States boundary at the St. Lawrence River for purposes of trade.

. . . . .

C. Has the Claimed Aboriginal Right Been Established?

[26] *Van der Peet* set out the test for establishing an aboriginal right protected under s. 35(1). Briefly stated, the claimant is required to prove: (1) the existence of the ancestral practice, custom or tradition advanced as supporting the claimed right; (2) that this practice, custom or tradition was "integral" to his or her pre-contact society in the sense it marked it as distinctive; and (3) reasonable continuity between the pre-contact practice and the contemporary claim. I will consider each of these elements in turn. First, however, it is necessary to consider the evidence upon which claims may be proved, and the approach courts should adopt in interpreting such evidence.

(1) *Evidentiary Concerns — Proving Aboriginal Rights*

[27] Aboriginal right claims give rise to unique and inherent evidentiary difficulties. Claimants are called upon to demonstrate features of their pre-contact society, across a gulf of centuries and without the aid of written records. Recognizing these difficulties, this Court has cautioned that the rights protected under s. 35(1) should not be rendered illusory by imposing an impossible burden of proof on those claiming this protection. ...

(b) *The Interpretation of Evidence in Aboriginal Rights Claims*

[38] [After discussing the admissibility and interpretation of evidence in Aboriginal rights claims Chief Justice McLachlin wrote] ... it must be emphasized that a consciousness of the special nature of aboriginal claims does not negate the operation of general evidentiary principles. While

evidence adduced in support of aboriginal claims must not be undervalued, neither should it be interpreted or weighed in a manner that fundamentally contravenes the principles of evidence law, which, as they relate to the valuing of evidence, are often synonymous with the "general principles of common sense" (Sopinka and Lederman, *supra*, at p. 524). ...

[39] There is a boundary that must not be crossed between a sensitive application and a complete abandonment of the rules of evidence. As Binnie J. observed in the context of treaty rights, "[g]enerous rules of interpretation should not be confused with a vague sense of after-the-fact largesse" (*R. v. Marshall*, [1999] 3 S.C.R. 456, at para. 14). In particular, the *Van der Peet* approach does not operate to amplify the cogency of evidence adduced in support of an aboriginal claim. Evidence advanced in support of aboriginal claims, like the evidence offered in any case, can run the gamut of cogency from the highly compelling to the highly dubious. Claims must still be established on the basis of persuasive evidence demonstrating their validity on the balance of probabilities. Placing "due weight" on the aboriginal perspective, or ensuring its supporting evidence an "equal footing" with more familiar forms of evidence, means precisely what these phrases suggest: equal and due treatment. While the evidence presented by aboriginal claimants should not be undervalued "simply because that evidence does not conform precisely with the evidentiary standards that would be applied in, for example, a private law torts case" (*Van der Peet, supra*, at para. 68), neither should it be artificially strained to carry more weight than it can reasonably support. If this is an obvious proposition, it must nonetheless be stated.

[40] With these principles in mind, I turn now to the consideration of whether the evidence offered in the present case in fact supports an aboriginal right to bring goods across the St. Lawrence River for the purposes of trade.

(2) *Does the Evidence Show an Ancestral Mohawk Practice of Trading North of the St. Lawrence River?*

[41] While the ancestral home of the Mohawks lay in the Mohawk Valley of present-day New York State, the evidence establishes that, before the arrival of Europeans, they travelled north on occasion across the St. Lawrence River. We may assume they travelled with goods to sustain themselves. There was also ample evidence before McKeown J. to support his finding that trade was a central, distinguishing feature of the Iroquois in general and the Mohawks in particular. This evidence indicates the Mohawks were well situated for trade, and engaged in small-scale exchange with other First Nations. A critical question in this case, however, is whether these trading practices and northerly travel coincided prior to the arrival of Europeans; that is, does the evidence establish an ancestral Mohawk practice of transporting goods across the St. Lawrence River for the purposes of trade? Only if this ancestral practice is established does it become necessary to determine whether it is an integral feature of Mohawk culture with continuity to the present day.

[42] With respect, the trial judge's affirmative response to this question finds virtually no support in the evidentiary record. ...

. . . . .

[51] [C]laims must be proven on the basis of cogent evidence establishing their validity on the balance of probabilities. Sparse, doubtful and equivocal evidence cannot serve as the foundation for a successful claim. With respect, this is exactly what has occurred in the present case. The contradiction between McKeown J.'s statement that little direct evidence supports a cross-river trading right and his conclusion that such a right exists suggests the application of a very relaxed standard of proof (or, perhaps more accurately, an unreasonably generous weighing of tenuous evidence). The *Van der Peet* approach, while mandating the equal and due treatment of evidence supporting aboriginal claims, does not bolster or enhance the cogency of this evidence. The relevant evidence in this case — a single knife, treaties that make no reference to pre-existing trade, and the mere fact of Mohawk involvement in the fur trade — can only support the conclusion reached by the trial judge if strained beyond the weight they can reasonably hold. Such a result is not contemplated by *Van der Peet* or s. 35(1). While appellate courts grant considerable deference to findings of fact made by trial judges, I am satisfied that the findings in the present case represent a "palpable and overriding error" warranting the substitution of a different result (*Delgamuukw, supra,* at paras. 78-80). I conclude that the claimant has not established an ancestral practice of transporting goods across the St. Lawrence River for the purposes of trade.

. . . . .

[53] In view of the paucity of evidence of Mohawk trade north of the St. Lawrence River, I need not consider the argument that, even if it were established, any Mohawk trading right should be characterized as inherently subject to border controls, tolls and duties imposed by other peoples, as recognized by ancestral aboriginal custom. ...

. . . . .

[65] I would allow the appeal. Chief Mitchell must pay the duty claimed by the government. I note that the government has undertaken to pay Chief Mitchell's costs.

Binnie J. (Major J. concurring): —

[66] I have read the reasons of the Chief Justice and I concur in the result and with her conclusion that even if Mohawks did occasionally trade goods across the St. Lawrence River with First Nations to the north, this practice was not on the evidence a "defining feature of the Mohawk culture" (para. 54) or "vital to the Mohawk's collective identity" (para. 60) in pre-contact times. There are, however, some additional considerations that have led me to conclude that the appeal must be allowed. ...

[67] It has been almost 30 years since this Court emphatically rejected the argument that the mere assertion of sovereignty by the European powers in North America was necessarily incompatible with the survival and continuation of aboriginal rights: *Calder v. Attorney-General of British Columbia*, [1973] S.C.R. 313. Because not all customs and traditions of aboriginal First Nations are incompatible with Canadian sovereignty, however, does not mean that none of them can be in such conflict. The Chief Justice refrains from addressing the sovereignty issue (para. 64) but she holds, correctly in my view, that "any finding of a *trading* right would also confirm a *mobility* right" (para. 22 (emphasis added)). ...

. . . . .

[69] [H]owever, we are left with [the] court's legitimate concern about the sovereignty implications of the international trading/mobility right claimed by the respondent. ...

[70] Counsel for the respondent does not challenge the reality of Canadian sovereignty, but he seeks for the Mohawk people of the Iroquois Confederacy the maximum degree of legal autonomy to which he believes they are entitled because of their long history at Akwesasne and elsewhere in eastern North America. This asserted autonomy, to be sure, does not presently flow from the ancient Iroquois legal order that is said to have created it, but from the *Constitution Act, 1982*. Section 35(1), adopted by the elected representatives of Canadians, recognizes and affirms existing aboriginal and treaty rights. If the respondent's claimed aboriginal right is to prevail, it does so not because of its own inherent strength, but because the *Constitution Act, 1982* brings about that result.

. . . . .

[73] In terms of traditional aboriginal law, the issue, as I see it, is whether trading/mobility activities asserted by the respondent not as a Canadian citizen but as an heir of the Mohawk regime that existed prior to the arrival of the Europeans, created a legal right to cross international boundaries under succeeding sovereigns. This aspect of the debate, to be clear, is not at the level of fact about the effectiveness of border controls in the 18th century. (Nor is it about the compatibility of internal aboriginal self-government with Canadian sovereignty.) The issue is at the level of law about the alleged incompatibility between European (now Canadian) sovereignty and mobility rights across non-aboriginal borders said by the trial judge to have been acquired by the Mohawks of Akwesasne by reason of their conduct prior to 1609.

. . . . .

5. *The Sovereignty Objection*

[115] ... The *Constitution Act, 1982* ushered in a new chapter but it did not start a new book. Within the framework of s. 35(1) regard is to be had to the common law ("what the law has historically accepted") to enable a court to determine what constitutes an aboriginal right.

. . . . .

[118] Fundamentally, the respondent views his aboriginal rights as a shield against non-aboriginal laws, including what he sees as the imposition of a border that "wasn't meant for [the] Kanienkehaka or the Mohawk Nation or any of the Six Nations". He thus testified at trial:

> Even though my grandfather didn't speak any English he was able to explain to me, as other elders have, that the promises made by the English to the Haudenosaunee that they would continue to recognize our nation as free and independent peoples. At one meeting they would recite it, what exactly were those words and the gist that we had to understand it.
>
> So, when our people in Akwesasne today say this border was not intended for us, they have an understanding in historical terms of the interpretation of those promises. In our language and the way it is passed down, the line of what is now known as the International Border belongs to somebody else. It wasn't meant for Kanienkehaka or the Mohawk Nation or any of the Six Nations. We understand that much.

[119] In this testimony the respondent refers to "promises made by the English to the Haudenosaunee", but his claim to base a trading/mobility right and tax exemptions on an existing treaty right was rejected by the trial judge and has not been appealed to this Court. His contention here is that whether or not the British made a treaty promise to that effect, the Mohawks were in fact free under the Mohawk legal regime "to pass and repass ... across what is now the Canada-United States boundary" with goods for trade and this freedom should now receive s. 35 protection. The claim to trade and mobility across international boundaries as a citizen of Haudenosaunee engages the sovereignty issue.

. . . . .

(7) *The Substance of the Claim Disclosed by the Evidence*

[125] ... [T]he respondent's claim ... is not just about physical movement of people or goods in and about Akwesasne. It is about pushing the envelope of Mohawk autonomy within the Canadian Constitution. It is about the Mohawks' aspiration to live as if the international boundary did not exist. Whatever financial benefit accrues from the ability to move goods across the border without payment of duty is clearly incidental to this larger vision.

. . . . .

[127] In the constitutional framework envisaged by the respondent, the claimed aboriginal right is simply a manifestation of the more fundamental relationship between the aboriginal and non-aboriginal people. In the Mohawk tradition this relationship is memorialized by the "two-row" wampum ... described in the Haudenosaunee presentation to the Parliamentary Special Committee on Indian Self-Government in 1983 as follows:

When the Haudenosaunee first came into contact with the European nations, treaties of peace and friendship were made. Each was symbolized by the Gus-Wen-Tah or Two Row Wampum. There is a bed of white wampum which symbolizes the purity of the agreement. There are two rows of purple, and those two rows have the spirit of your ancestors and mine. There are three beads of wampum separating the two rows and they symbolize peace, friendship and respect.

These two rows will symbolize two paths or two vessels, travelling down the same river together. One, a birch bark canoe, will be for the Indian people, their laws, their customs and their ways. The other, a ship, will be for the white people and their laws, their customs and their ways. We shall each travel the river together, side by side, but in our own boat. Neither of us will try to steer the other's vessel. (Indian Self-Government in Canada: Report of the Special Committee (1983), back cover)

[128] Thus, in the "two-row" wampum there are two parallel paths. In one path travels the aboriginal canoe. In the other path travels the European ship. The two vessels co-exist but they never touch. Each is the sovereign of its own destiny.

[129] The modern embodiment of the "two-row" wampum concept, modified to reflect some of the realities of a modern state, is the idea of a "merged" or "shared" sovereignty. "Merged sovereignty" asserts that First Nations were not wholly subordinated to non-aboriginal sovereignty, but over time became merger partners. The final Report of the Royal Commission on Aboriginal Peoples, vol. 2 (Restructuring the Relationship (1996)), at p. 214, says that "Aboriginal governments give the constitution [of Canada] its deepest and most resilient roots in the Canadian soil." This updated concept of Crown sovereignty is of importance. Whereas historically the Crown may have been portrayed as an entity across the seas with which aboriginal people could scarcely be expected to identify, this was no longer the case in 1982 when the s. 35(1) reconciliation process was established. The Constitution was patriated and all aspects of our sovereignty became firmly located within our borders. If the principle of "merged sovereignty" articulated by the Royal Commission on Aboriginal Peoples is to have any true meaning, it must include at least the idea that aboriginal and non-aboriginal Canadians together form a sovereign entity with a measure of common purpose and united effort. It is this new entity, as inheritor of the historical attributes of sovereignty, with which existing aboriginal and treaty rights must be reconciled.

[130] ... On this view, to return to the nautical metaphor of the "two-row" wampum, "merged" sovereignty is envisaged as a single vessel (or ship of state) composed of the historic elements of wood, iron and canvas. The vessel's components pull together as a harmonious whole, but the wood remains wood, the iron remains iron and the canvas remains canvas. Non-aboriginal leaders, including Sir Wilfrid Laurier, have used similar metaphors. It represents, in a phrase, partnership without assimilation.

. . . . .

[133] In the earlier years of the century the federal government occasionally argued that Parliament's jurisdiction under s. 91(24) of the

Constitution Act, 1867 ("Indians, and Lands reserved for the Indians") was plenary. Indians were said to be federal people whose lives were wholly subject to federal "regulation". This was rejected by the courts, which ruled that while an aboriginal person could be characterized as an Indian for some purposes including language, culture and the exercise of traditional rights, he or she does not cease thereby to be a resident of a province or territory. For other purposes he or she must be recognized and treated as an ordinary member of Canadian society. In a decision handed down soon after the coming into force of the *Constitution Act, 1982*, in *Nowegijick v. The Queen*, a tax case, Dickson J. (as he then was) wrote at p. 36, "Indians are citizens and, in affairs of life not governed by treaties or the *Indian Act*, they are subject to all of the responsibilities ... of other Canadian citizens". ... The constitutional objective is reconciliation not mutual isolation.

[134] The Royal Commission ... recognized the challenge aboriginal self-government poses to the orthodox view that constitutional powers in Canada are wholly and exhaustively distributed between the federal and provincial governments. ...

[135] ... What is significant is that the Royal Commission itself sees aboriginal peoples as full participants with non-aboriginal peoples in a shared Canadian sovereignty. Aboriginal peoples do not stand in opposition to, nor are they subjugated by, Canadian sovereignty. They are part of it.

[136] With this background I return to the point that the respondent does not base his mobility rights in this test case as a Canadian citizen. ...

[137] The respondent's claim thus presents two defining elements. He asserts a trading and mobility right across the international boundary and he attaches this right to his current citizenship not of Canada but of the Haudenosaunee Confederacy with its capital in Onondaga, New York State.

8. *The Legal Basis of the Respondent's Claim*

[138] The respondent initially asserted both a treaty right and an aboriginal right but the conceptual distinction between these two sources of entitlement is important. A treaty right is an affirmative promise by the Crown which will be interpreted generously and enforced in a way that upholds the honour of the Crown. ...

[139] ... A treaty right is itself an expression of Crown sovereignty.

[140] In the case of aboriginal rights, there is no historical event comparable to the treaty-making process in which the Crown negotiated the right or obligation sought to be enforced. The respondent's claim is rooted in practices which he says long preceded the Mohawks' first contact with Europeans in 1609.

. . . . .

[144] Reference has already been made to the fact that one of several sources of the concept of aboriginal rights, now significantly modified by

the more generous principles of constitutional interpretation, is traditional British colonial law. Many of the cases decided by the Judicial Committee of the Privy Council were concerned with rights of property created under a former regime. In *Amodu Tijani v. Southern Nigeria (Secretary)*, [1921] 2 A.C. 399, at p. 407, it was confirmed that "A mere change in sovereignty is not to be *presumed* as meant to disturb rights of private owners" (emphasis added). More recently, Lord Denning, speaking for the Privy Council in *Oyekan v. Adele*, [1957] 2 All E.R. 785, at p. 788, said: "In inquiring ... what rights are recognised, there is one guiding principle. It is this: The courts will *assume* that the British Crown intends that the rights of property of the inhabitants are to be fully respected" (emphasis added). As with the modern law of aboriginal rights, the law of sovereign succession was intended to reconcile the interests of the local inhabitants across the empire to a change in sovereignty.

. . . . .

[148] ... The root of the respondent's argument nevertheless is that the Mohawks of Akwesasne acquired under the legal regimes of 18th century North America, a positive legal right as a group to continue to come and go across any subsequent international border dividing their traditional homelands with whatever goods they wished, just as they had in pre-contact times. In other words, Mohawk autonomy in this respect was continued but not as a mere custom or practice. It emerged in the new European-based constitutional order as a legal trading and mobility right. By s. 35(1) of the *Constitution Act, 1982*, it became a constitutionally protected right. That is the respondent's argument.

9.   *The Limitation of "Sovereign Incompatibility"*

[149] Care must be taken not to carry forward doctrines of British colonial law into the interpretation of s. 35(1) without careful reflection. ...

[150] ... The subject matter of the constitutional provision is "existing" aboriginal and treaty rights and they are said to be "recognized and affirmed" not wholly cut loose from either their legal or historical origins. One of the defining characteristics of sovereign succession and therefore a limitation on the scope of aboriginal rights, as already discussed, was the notion of incompatibility with the new sovereignty. ...

[151] Prior to *Calder*, *supra*, "sovereign incompatibility" was given excessive scope. The assertion of sovereign authority was confused with doctrines of feudal title to deny aboriginal peoples any interest at all in their traditional lands or even in activities related to the use of those lands. To acknowledge that the doctrine of sovereign incompatibility was sometimes given excessive scope in the past is not to deny that it has any scope at all, but it is a doctrine that must be applied with caution.

. . . . .

[154] In my opinion, sovereign incompatibility continues to be an element in the s. 35(1) analysis, albeit a limitation that will be sparingly

applied. For the most part, the protection of practices, traditions and customs that are distinctive to aboriginal cultures in Canada does not raise legitimate sovereignty issues at the definitional stage.

10. *The Alleged Incompatibility Between the Aboriginal Right Disclosed by the Evidence and Canadian Sovereignty*

. . . . .

[158] The question is whether the asserted legal right to the autonomous exercise of international trade and mobility was compatible with the new European (now Canadian) sovereignty and the reciprocal loss (or impairment) of Mohawk sovereignty.

[159] In the resolution of this legal issue, as stated, we are addressing legal incompatibility as opposed to factual incompatibility. The latter emerged more slowly as assertions of sovereignty gave way to colonisation and progressive occupation of land. ...

[160] Control over the mobility of persons and goods into one country is, and always has been, a fundamental attribute of sovereignty. ... In other words, not only does authority over the border exist as an incident of sovereignty, the state is expected to exercise it in the public interest. The duty cannot be abdicated to the vagaries of an earlier regime whose sovereignty has been eclipsed (Cain, *supra*, at pp. 545-46).

[161] The legal situation is further complicated by the fact, previously mentioned, that the respondent attributes his international trading and mobility right not to his status as a Canadian citizen but as a citizen of the Haudenosaunee (Iroquois Confederacy) based at Onondaga, New York. Border conditions in the modern era are vastly different from those in the 18th century. Nevertheless, as stated, borders existed among nations, including First Nations. They were expressions of sovereign autonomy and then, as now, compelled observance.

. . . . .

[163] ... In my view, therefore, the international trading/mobility right claimed by the respondent as a citizen of the Haudenosaunee (Iroquois) Confederacy is incompatible with the historical attributes of Canadian sovereignty.

[164] The question that then arises is whether this conclusion is at odds with the purpose of s. 35(1), i.e. the reconciliation of the interests of aboriginal peoples with Crown sovereignty? In addressing this question it must be remembered that aboriginal people are themselves part of Canadian sovereignty as discussed above. I agree with Borrows, *supra*, at p. 40, that accommodation of aboriginal rights should not be seen as "a zero-sum relationship between minority rights and citizenship; as if every gain in the direction of accommodating diversity comes at the expense of promoting citizenship" (quoting W. Kymlicka and W. Norman, eds., Citizenship in Diverse Societies (2000), at p. 39). On the other hand, the reverse is also true. Affirmation of the sovereign interest of Canadians as a whole, including aboriginal peoples, should not necessarily be seen as a

loss of sufficient "constitutional space for aboriginal peoples to be aboriginal" (Greschner, *supra*, at p. 342). ... In terms of sovereign incompatibility, it is a conclusion that the respondent's claim relates to national interests that all of us have in common rather than to distinctive interests that for some purposes differentiate an aboriginal community. In my view, reconciliation of these interests in this particular case favours an affirmation of our collective sovereignty.

11. *Implications for Internal Aboriginal Self-Government*

[165] In reaching that conclusion, however, I do not wish to be taken as either foreclosing or endorsing any position on the compatibility or incompatibility of internal self-governing institutions of First Nations with Crown sovereignty, either past or present. I point out in this connection that the sovereign incompatibility principle has not prevented the United States (albeit with its very different constitutional framework) from continuing to recognize forms of internal aboriginal self-government which it considers to be expressions of residual aboriginal sovereignty. ...

. . . . .

[169] ... The United States has lived with internal tribal self-government within the framework of external relations determined wholly by the United States government without doctrinal difficulties since *Johnson v. M'Intosh*, 21 U.S. (8 Wheat.) 543 (1823), was decided almost 170 years ago.

. . . . .

[171] The question under consideration here is ... whether the claimed international trading and mobility right could, as a matter of law, have arisen in the first place.

[172] It was, of course, an expression of sovereignty in 1982 to recognize existing aboriginal rights under s. 35(1) of the *Constitution Act, 1982*. However, if the claimed aboriginal right did not survive the transition to non-Mohawk sovereignty, there was nothing in existence in 1982 to which s. 35(1) protection of existing aboriginal rights could attach. It would have been, of course, quite within the sovereign's power to confer specific border privileges by treaty, but the respondent's claim to a treaty right was dismissed.

[173] In my respectful view the claimed aboriginal right never came into existence and it is unnecessary to consider the Crown's argument that whatever aboriginal rights in this respect may have existed were extinguished by border controls enforced by Canada prior to April 17, 1982.

---

1. Is Justice Binnie's concurring decision in *Mitchell* reminiscent of Justice Rand's decision in *Francis*?
2. In *Mitchell*, Justice Binnie wrote: "The *Constitution Act, 1982* ushered in a new chapter but it did not start a new book." Can you reconcile this

statement with the Supreme Court's approach in *R. v. Sparrow*, [1990] S.C.J. No. 49, [1990] 1 S.C.R. 1075 at 1106 (S.C.C.), where the Court wrote: "the context of 1982 is surely enough to tell us that this is not just a codification of the case law on aboriginal rights that had accumulated by 1982. Section 35 calls for a just settlement for aboriginal peoples. It renounces the old rules of the game under which the Crown established courts of law and denied those courts the authority to question sovereign claims made by the Crown."

3. Is it appropriate for Justice Binnie to re-interpret the Two-Row Wampum as he did? See Gordon Christie, "The Court's Exercise of Plenary Power: Rewriting the Two-row Wampum" (2002) 16 S.C.L.R. (2d), at 285-301.

4. If ever accepted as the majority position, does Justice Binnie's theory of sovereign incompatibility herald an expansion or contraction of Aboriginal rights and jurisdiction? Can you develop arguments on both sides of the issue? It may be said that a theory of sovereign incompatibility could severely constrain Aboriginal jurisdiction because — whenever it tried to "push back" Crown interference — an Aboriginal community's every action could be challenged as being incompatible with the Crown's sovereignty. On the other hand, modern theories of federalism have strained to allow coordinate, overlapping spheres between the federal and provincial governments. As a result, each level of government can act in relation to the other's power and not have their actions characterized as being incompatible with the other (*Ross v. Ontario (Registrar of Motor Vehicles)*, [1973] S.C.J. No. 130, [1975] 1 S.C.R. 5 (S.C.C.); *Multiple Access Ltd. v. McCutcheon*, [1982] S.C.J. No. 66, [1982] 2 S.C.R. 161 (S.C.C.)). Could a theory of sovereign incompatibility dealing with Aboriginal peoples take on this approach and actually expand Aboriginal jurisdiction?

D. INCOME TAXATION AND PERSONAL PROPERTY TAX "SITUATE ON RESERVE"

The issue of immunity or exemption from taxation also arises in the field of income tax. The courts have found that Indian property that is not situated on reserve land is subject to taxation. Likewise, they have exempted property that is "situate on reserve" as a result of s. 87 of the *Indian Act* (R.S.C. 1985, c. I-5). The following commentary, and the reproduction of four landmark cases (*R. v. Nowegijick*, [1983] S.C.J. No. 5, [1983] 1 S.C.R. 29, 144 D.L.R. (3d) 193 (S.C.C.); *Mitchell v. Peguis Indian Band*, [1990] S.C.J. No. 63, [1990] 2 S.C.R. 85, [1990] 3 C.N.L.R. 46 (S.C.C.); *Williams v. Canada*, [1992] S.C.J. No. 36, [1992] 1 S.C.R. 877 (S.C.C.); and *McDiarmid Lumber v. God's Lake First Nation*, [2006] S.C.J. No. 58; [2006] 2 S.C.R. 846, 2006 SCC 58 (S.C.C.)) demonstrates the Court's treatment of income tax under ss. 87, 89 and 90 of the *Indian Act*.

In January, 1983, the Supreme Court of Canada rendered its landmark decision on s. 87 of the *Indian Act* in *R. v. Nowegijick*, which is excerpted immediately below.

R. v. NOWEGIJICK

[1983] S.C.J. No. 5, [1983] 1 S.C.R. 29, [1983] 2 C.N.L.R. 89,
144 D.L.R. (3d) 193 (S.C.C.)

The judgment of the Court was delivered by

Dickson J.:— The question is whether the appellant, Gene A. Nowegijick, a registered Indian can claim by virtue of the *Indian Act*, R.S.C. 1970, c. I-6, an exemption from income tax for the 1975 taxation year.

The Facts

The facts are few and not in dispute. Mr. Nowegijick is an Indian within the meaning of the *Indian Act* and a member of the Gull Bay (Ontario) Indian Band. During the 1975 taxation year Mr. Nowegijick was an employee of the Gull Bay Development Corporation, a company without share capital, having its head office and administrative offices on the Gull Bay Reserve. All the directors, members and employees of the Corporation live on the Reserve and are registered Indians.

During 1975 the Corporation in the course of its business conducted a logging operation 10 miles from the Gull Bay Reserve. Mr. Nowegijick was employed as a logger and remunerated on a piece-work basis. He was paid bi-weekly by cheque at the head office of the Corporation on the Reserve.

During 1975, Mr. Nowegijick maintained his permanent dwelling on the Gull Bay Reserve. Each morning he would leave the Reserve to work on the logging operations, and return to the Reserve at the end of the working day.

Mr. Nowegijick earned $11,057.08 in such employment. His assessed taxable income for the 1975 taxation year was $8,698 on which he was assessed tax of $1,965.80. By Notice of Objection he objected to the assessment on the basis that the income in respect of which the assessment was made is the "personal property of an Indian ... situated on a reserve" and thus not subject to taxation by virtue of s. 87 of the *Indian Act*. ...

The Legislation

Mr. Nowegijick, in his claim for exemption from income tax relies upon s. 87 of the *Indian Act*...

Stripped to relevant essentials s. 87 reads:

Notwithstanding any other Act of the Parliament of Canada ... the following property is exempt from taxation, namely:
(*a*) the interest of an Indian or a band in reserve or surrendered lands; and
(*b*) the personal property of an Indian or band situated on a reserve; and no Indian or band is subject to taxation in respect of the ownership, occupation, possession or use of any property mentioned in paragraph (*a*) or (*b*) or is otherwise subject to taxation in respect of any such property ...

The short but difficult question to be determined is whether the tax sought to be imposed under the *Income Tax Act*, 1970-71-72 (Can.), c. 63

upon the income of Mr. Nowegijick can be said to be "in respect of" "any" personal property situated upon a reserve . ...

Construction of section 87 of the Indian Act

Indians are citizens and, in affairs of life not governed by treaties or the *Indian Act*, they are subject to all of the responsibilities, including payment of taxes, of other Canadian citizens.

It is legal lore that, to be valid, exemptions to tax laws should be clearly expressed. It seems to me, however, that treaties and statutes relating to Indians should be liberally construed and doubtful expressions resolved in favour of the Indians. If the statute contains language which can reasonably be construed to confer tax exemption that construction, in my view, is to be favoured over a more technical construction which might be available to deny exemption. In *Jones v. Meehan*, 175 U.S. 1 (1899), it was held that Indian treaties "must ... be construed, not according to the technical meaning of [their] words ... but in the sense in which they would naturally be understood by the Indians".

There is little in the cases to assist in the construction of s. 87 of the *Indian Act.* ...

. . . . .

The prime task of the Court in this case is to construe the words "no Indian ... is ... subject to taxation in respect of any such [personal] property". Is taxable income personal property? The Supreme Court of Illinois in the case of *Bachrach v. Nelson*, 182 N.E. 909 (1932) considered whether "income" is "property" and responded (at p. 914):

> The overwhelming weight of judicial authority holds that it is. The cases of *Eliasberg Bros. Mercantile Co. v. Grimes*, 204 Ala. 492, 86 So. 56, 11 A.L.R. 300, *Tax Commissioner v. Putnam*, 227 Mass. 522, 116 N.E. 904, L.R.A. 1917F, 806, *Stratton's Independence v. Howbert*, 231 U.S. 399, 34 S. Ct. 136, 58 L. Ed. 285, *Doyle v. Mitchell Bros. Co.*, 247 U.S. 179, 38 S. Ct. 467, 62 L. Ed. 1054, *Board of Revenue v. Montgomery Gaslight Co.*, 64 Ala. 269, *Greene v. Knox*, 175 N.Y. 432, 67 N.E. 910, *Hibbard v. State*, 65 Ohio St. 574, 64 N.E. 109, 58 L.R.A. 654, *Ludlow-Saylor Wire Co. v. Wollbrinck*, 275 Mo. 339, 205 S.W. 196, and *State v. Pinder*, 7 Boyce (30 Del.) 416, 108 A. 43, define what is personal property and in substance hold that money or any other thing of value acquired as gain or profit from capital or labour is property, and that, in the aggregate, these acquisitions constitute income, and, in accordance with the axiom that the whole includes all of its parts, income includes property and nothing but property, and therefore is itself property.

I would adopt this language. A tax on income is in reality a tax on property itself. If income can be said to be property I cannot think that taxable income is any less so. Taxable income is by definition, s. 2(2) of the *Income Tax Act*, "his income for the year minus the deductions permitted by Division C". Although the Crown in paragraph 14 of its factum recognizes that "salaries" and "wages" can be classified as "personal property" it submits that the basis of taxation is a person's "taxable" income and that such taxable income is not "personal property" but rather a "concept", that results from a number of operations. This is too fine a distinction for my liking. If wages are personal property it seems to me difficult to say that a person taxed "in respect of" wages is not being taxed in respect of personal property. It is true that certain calculations are needed in order to determine the quantum of tax but I do not think this in any way invalidates the basic proposition. The words "in respect of" are, in my opinion, words of the widest possible scope. They import such meanings as "in relation to", "with reference to" or "in connection with". The phrase "in respect of" is probably the widest of any expression intended to convey some connection between two related subject matters.

Crown counsel submits that the effect of s. 87 of the *Indian Act* is to exempt what can properly be classified as "direct taxation on property" and the judgment of Jackett C.J. in *Minister of National Revenue v. Iroquois of Caughnawaga*, [1977] 2 F.C. 269 is cited. The question in that case was whether the employer's share of unemployment insurance premiums was payable in respect of persons employed by an Indian band at a hospital operated by the band on a reserve. It was argued that the premiums were "taxation" on "property" within s. 87 of the *Indian Act*. Chief Justice Jackett held that even if the imposition by statute on an employer of liability to contribute to the cost of a scheme of unemployment insurance were "taxation" it would not, in the view of the Chief Justice, be taxation on "property" within the ambit of s. 87. The Chief Justice continued (at p. 271):

> From one point of view, all taxation is directly or indirectly taxation on property; from another point of view, all taxation is directly or indirectly taxation on persons. It is my view, however, that when section 87 exempts "personal property of an Indian or band situated on a reserve" from "taxation", its effect is to exempt what can properly be classified as direct taxation on property. The courts have had to develop jurisprudence as to when taxation is taxation on property and when it is taxation on persons for the purposes of section 92(2) of *The British North America Act, 1867*, and there would seem to be no reason why such jurisprudence should not be applied to the interpretation of section 87 of the *Indian Act*. See, for example, with reference to section 92(2), Provincial Treasurer of *Alberta v. Kerr*, [1933] A.C. 710. ...

With respect, I do not agree with Chief Justice Jackett that the effect of s. 87 of the *Indian Act* is only to exempt what can properly be classified as direct taxation on property. Section 87 provides that "the personal property of an Indian ... on a reserve" is exempt from taxation; but it also provides that "no Indian ... is ... subject to taxation in respect of any such property". The earlier words certainly exempt certain property from taxation; but the latter words also exempt certain persons from taxation in respect of such property. As I read it, s. 87 creates an exemption for both persons and property. It does not matter then that the taxation of employment income may be characterized as a tax on persons, as opposed to a tax on property.

We must, I think, in these cases, have regard to substance and the plain and ordinary meaning of the language used, rather than to forensic dialectics. I do not think we should give any refined construction to the section. A person exempt from taxation in respect of any of his personal property would have difficulty in understanding why he should pay tax in respect of his wages. And I do not think it is a sufficient answer to say that the conceptualization of the *Income Tax Act* renders it so.

I conclude by saying that nothing in these reasons should be taken as implying that no Indian shall ever pay tax of any kind. Counsel for the appellant and counsel for the interveners do not take that position. Nor do I. We are concerned here with personal property situated on a reserve and only with property situated on a reserve.

I would allow the appeal, set aside the judgment of the Federal Court of Appeal and reinstate the judgment in the Trial Division of that Court. Pursuant to the arrangement of the parties the appellant is entitled to his costs in all courts to be taxed as between solicitor and client. There should be no costs payable by or to the interveners.

Appeal allowed with costs.

MITCHELL v. PEGUIS INDIAN BAND

[1990] S.C.J. No. 63, [1990] 2 S.C.R. 85, (*sub nom. Mitchell v. Sandy Bay Indian Band*) [1990] 3 C.N.L.R. 46, 67 Man. R. (2d) 81 (S.C.C.)

[This case arose when Manitoba Hydro imposed an invalid tax on the Peguis Indian Band (among other bands) that was related to the sale of electricity on the reserve. The Bands retained a consultant (Mr. Mitchell) to secure a rebate of taxes paid to the Government of Manitoba. The government eventually settled with the Bands. The Bands subsequently refused to pay the consultant because they said the government issued a rebate through processes unrelated to Mr. Mitchell's services. Upon this refusal, the consultant went to court and obtained a prejudgment garnishment order from the Bands' rebate settlement fund, for the amount of his fees for representing the Indians in the negotiations. The Bands applied to have the garnishing order set aside under ss. 89 and 90 of the *Indian Act*. They argued that the tax rebate money was personal property given pursuant to treaty, deemed to be held on a reserve, thus not subject to attachment by a non-Indian under these sections. Both the trial judge and the Court of Appeal agreed with the Bands' argument that the funds could not be garnished under s. 90(1)(*b*) of the *Indian Act*. The Supreme Court of Canada also ruled in the Bands' favour and held that the moneys could not be garnished. Chief Justice Dickson wrote that "the Court of Appeal was correct in the disposition of this case and the trial judge was correct in his reasoning and interpretation of the elements of s. 90(1)(*b*)". He wrote (at para. 46): "'Her Majesty' in s. 90(1)(*b*) of the *Indian Act* refers to both the federal and provincial Crowns. Therefore, the moneys in question are protected from garnishment by virtue of s. 89(1) of the Act." Justice La Forest wrote a concurring judgment which has received the most attention in subsequent cases.]

La Forest J. (Sopinka and Gonthier JJ. concurring): — I have had the advantage of reading the reasons of the Chief Justice. I agree with his proposed disposition of this case, but I do so for quite different reasons. With respect, I am unable to agree with his approach and, in particular, with his adoption of the trial judge's interpretation of s. 90(1)(*b*) of the *Indian Act*, R.S.C. 1970, c. I-6. The Chief Justice has summarized the facts and the judicial history and I need not repeat them. In broad terms, the issue to be determined involves funds in the hands of the Government of Manitoba, which it agreed to pay to the respondent Indians in settlement of a claim for the return of taxes paid by the Indians to Manitoba Hydro in respect of sales of electricity on reserves. The question is whether those funds may be garnisheed by the appellants who are suing the Indians for fees for representing the Indians in negotiating the settlement.

. . . . .

The Historical Record: Sections 87 and 89

As is clear from the comments of the Chief Justice in *Guerin v. The Queen*, [1984] 2 S.C.R. 335, at p. 383, these legislative restraints on the alienability of Indian lands are but the continuation of a policy that has shaped the dealings between the Indians and the European settlers since the time of the *Royal Proclamation of 1763*. The historical record leaves no doubt that native peoples acknowledged the ultimate sovereignty of the British Crown, and agreed to cede their traditional homelands on the understanding that the Crown would thereafter protect them in the possession and use of such lands as were reserved for their use; see the comments of Professor Slattery in his article "Understanding Aboriginal Rights" (1987), 66 Can. Bar Rev. 727, at p. 753. The sections of the *Indian Act* relating to the inalienability of Indian lands seek to give effect to this protection by interposing the Crown between the Indians and the market forces which, if left unchecked, had the potential to erode Indian ownership of these reserve lands. This Court, in its recent decision of *Canadian Pacific Ltd. v. Paul*, [1988] 2 S.C.R. 654, alluded to this point when it noted, at p. 677, that the feature of inalienability was adopted as a protective measure for the Indian population lest it be persuaded into improvident transactions.

I take it to be obvious that the protections afforded against taxation and attachment by ss. 87 and 89 of the *Indian Act* go hand-in-hand with these restraints on the alienability of land. I noted above that the Crown, as part of the consideration for the cession of Indian lands, often committed itself to giving goods and services to the natives concerned. Taking but one example, by terms of the "numbered treaties" concluded between the Indians of the prairie regions and part of the Northwest Territories, the Crown undertook to provide Indians with assistance in such matters as education, medicine and agriculture, and to furnish supplies which Indians could use in the pursuit of their traditional vocations of hunting, fishing, and trapping. The exemptions from taxation and distraint have historically protected the ability of Indians to benefit from this property in two ways. First, they guard against the possibility that one branch of government, through the imposition of taxes, could erode the full measure of the benefits given by that branch of government entrusted with the supervision of Indian affairs. Secondly, the protection against attachment ensures that the enforcement of civil judgments by non-natives will not be allowed to hinder Indians in the untrammelled enjoyment of such advantages as they had retained or might acquire pursuant to the fulfillment by the Crown of its treaty obligations. In effect, these sections shield Indians from the imposition of the civil liabilities that could lead, albeit through an indirect route, to the alienation of the Indian land base through the medium of foreclosure sales and the like; see Brennan J.'s discussion of the purpose served by Indian tax immunities in the American context in *Bryan v. Itasca County*, 426 U.S. 373 (1976), at p. 391.

In summary, the historical record makes it clear that ss. 87 and 89 of the *Indian Act*, the sections to which the deeming provision of s. 90 applies, constitute part of a legislative "package" which bears the impress of an obligation to native peoples which the Crown has recognized at least since the signing of the *Royal Proclamation of 1763*. From that time on, the Crown has always acknowledged that it is honour-bound to shield Indians from any efforts by non-natives to dispossess Indians of the property which they hold qua Indians, i.e., their land base and the chattels on that land base.

It is also important to underscore the corollary to the conclusion I have just drawn. The fact that the modern-day legislation, like its historical counterparts, is so careful to underline that exemptions from taxation and distraint apply only in respect of personal property situated on reserves demonstrates that the purpose of the legislation is not to remedy the economically disadvantaged position of Indians by ensuring that Indians may acquire, hold, and deal with property in the commercial mainstream on different terms than their fellow citizens. An examination of the decisions bearing on these sections confirms that Indians who acquire and deal in property outside lands reserved for their use, deal with it on the same basis as all other Canadians. ...

In summary, I conclude that an interpretation of s. 90(1)(*b*), which sees its purpose as limited to preventing non-natives from hampering Indians from benefitting in full from the personal property promised Indians in treaties and ancillary agreements, is perfectly consistent with the tenor of the obligations that the Crown has always assumed vis-a-vis the protection of native property. ...

Section 90(1)(b) as including the Provincial Crowns

I turn next to the second of the two alternative readings of "Her Majesty" in s. 90(1)(*b*). If this term is meant to include the provincial Crowns, the exemptions and privileges of ss. 87 and 89 will apply to a much wider range of personal property. In effect, it would follow inexorably that the notional situs of s. 90(1)(*b*) will extend these protections to any and all personal property that could enure to Indians through the whole range of agreements that might be concluded between an Indian band and Her Majesty in right of a province.

As I see it, if one is to reject the interpretation advanced above, that s. 90(1)(*b*) refers solely to property which inures to Indians from the federal

Crown through operation of the treaties and ancillary agreements, there is no basis in logic for the further assumption that some, but not all agreements, between Indian bands and Provincial Crown would be contemplated by the provision. Section 90(1)(*b*) does not qualify the term "agreement", and if one interprets "Her Majesty" as including the provincial Crown, it must follow as a matter of due course that s. 90(1)(*b*) takes in all agreements that could be concluded between an Indian band and a provincial Crown.

It follows inexorably that if an Indian band, pursuant to a purely commercial agreement with a provincial Crown, acquires personal property, that property will be exempt from taxation and distraint, regardless of its situs. Moreover, the protections of ss. 87 and 89 would apply in respect of any subsequent dealings by the Indian band respecting that property, even if those dealings were confined to ordinary commercial matters. This would have broad ramifications, and I cannot accept the notion that Parliament, in fulfilling its constitutional responsibility over Indian affairs, intended that the protective envelope of ss. 87 and 89 should apply on such a broad scale.

My conclusion rests on the fact that such a result cannot be reconciled with the scope of the protections that the Crown has traditionally extended to the property of natives. As I stated earlier, a review of the obligations that the Crown has assumed in this area shows that it has done no more than seek to shield the property of Indians that has an immediate and discernible nexus to the occupancy of reserve lands from interference at the hands of non-natives. The legislation has always distinguished between property situated on reserves and property Indians hold outside reserves. There is simply no evidence that the Crown has ever taken the position that it must protect property simply because that property is held by an Indian as opposed to a non-native. Indeed, unless one were to take the view that there exist two laws of contract, one applying to Indians and one to non-Indians, it would be difficult to rationalize a result that saw exemptions against taxation and distraint apply in respect of property simply because the person acquiring it happened to be an Indian. But, as I have intimated above, the interpretation of s. 90(1)(*b*) advanced by the trial judge and affirmed by the Chief Justice must, in logic, lead precisely to this result.

When Indian bands enter the commercial mainstream, it is to be expected that they will have occasion, from time to time, to enter into purely commercial agreements with the provincial Crowns in the same way as with private interests. The provincial Crowns are, after all, important players in the marketplace. If, then, an Indian band enters into a normal business transaction, be it with a provincial Crown, or a private corporation, and acquires personal property, be it in the form of chattels or debt obligations, how is one to characterize the property concerned? To my mind, it makes no sense to compare it with the property that enures to Indians pursuant to treaties and their ancillary agreements. Indians have a plenary entitlement to their treaty property; it is owed to them qua Indians. Personal property acquired by Indians in normal business dealings is clearly different; it is simply property anyone else might have acquired, and I can see no reason why in those circumstances Indians should not be treated in the same way as other people.

There can be no doubt, on a reading of s. 90(1)(*b*), that it would not apply to any personal property that an Indian band might acquire in connection with an ordinary commercial agreement with a private concern. Property of that nature will only be protected once it can be established that it is situated on a reserve. Accordingly, any dealings in the commercial mainstream in property acquired in this manner will fall to be regulated by the laws of general application. Indians will enjoy no exemptions from taxation in respect of this property, and will be free to deal with it in the same manner as any other citizen. In addition, provided the property is not situated on reserve lands, third parties will be free to issue execution on this property. I think it would be truly paradoxical if it were to be otherwise. As the Chief Justice has pointed out in *Nowegijick v. The Queen*, [1983] 1 S.C.R. 29, at p. 36:

> Indians are citizens and, in affairs of life not governed by treaties or the *Indian Act*, they are subject to all of the responsibilities, including payment of taxes, of other Canadian citizens.

But, in my respectful view, the implications flowing from the interpretation the trial judge advanced of s. 90(1)(*b*) go counter to this statement, for as I have pointed out earlier, as a logical consequence of that interpretation, any time Indians acquired personal property in an agreement with a provincial Crown, even one of a purely commercial character, the exemptions and protections of ss. 87 and 89 would apply in respect of that particular asset, regardless of situs. ... As I see it, if Parliament had intended to cast aside these traditional constraints on the Crown's obligations to protect the property of Indians, it would have expressed this in the clearest of terms. I am loathe to conclude that this result can be made to rest on the strength of a supposed ambiguity in s. 90(1)(*b*), which, as I have suggested above, can only arguably be an ambiguity if one turns a blind eye to compelling historical and textual arguments.

To reiterate, I simply cannot reconcile the implications that flow from reading the term "Her Majesty" in s. 90(1)(*b*) as including the provincial Crowns with the scope of the protections that the Crown has accorded Indian property to date. The historical record that so clearly reveals a cogent rationale for protecting the personal property that enures to Indians by operation of treaty obligations regardless of situs, is silent as to any reason why personal property that Indian bands acquire from the provincial Crowns should receive the same extraordinary level of protection.

· · · · ·

I conclude that the statutory notional situs of s. 90(1)(*b*) is meant to extend solely to personal property which enures to Indians through the discharge by "Her Majesty" of her treaty or ancillary obligations. Pursuant to s. 91(24) of the *Constitution Act, 1867*, it is of course "Her Majesty" in right of Canada who bears the sole responsibility for conferring any such property on Indians, and I would, therefore, limit application of the term "Her Majesty" as used in s. 90(1)(b) to the federal Crown.

Nowegijick v. The Queen

While the textual and historical arguments to be made for limiting the meaning of "Her Majesty" in s. 90(1)(b) to the federal Crown appear to me to be irrefutable, I recognize that it is necessary to ask whether the canons of construction generic to the interpretation of statutes relating to Indians change this result. These canons are, of course, those set out by the Chief Justice in *Nowegijick, supra,* at p. 36.

I note at the outset that I do not take issue with the principle that treaties and statutes relating to Indians should be liberally construed and doubtful expressions resolved in favour of the Indians. In the case of treaties, this principle finds its justification in the fact that the Crown enjoyed a superior bargaining position when negotiating treaties with native peoples. From the perspective of the Indians, treaties were drawn up in a foreign language, and incorporated references to legal concepts of a system of law with which Indians were unfamiliar. In the interpretation of these documents it is, therefore, only just that the courts attempt to construe various provisions as the Indians may be taken to have understood them.

But as I view the matter, somewhat different considerations must apply in the case of statutes relating to Indians. Whereas a treaty is the product of bargaining between two contracting parties, statutes relating to Indians are an expression of the will of Parliament. Given this fact, I do not find it particularly helpful to engage in speculation as to how Indians may be taken to understand a given provision. Rather, I think the approach must be to read the Act concerned with a view to elucidating what it was that Parliament wished to effect in enacting the particular section in question. This approach is not a jettisoning of the liberal interpretative method. As already stated, it is clear that in the interpretation of any statutory enactment dealing with Indians, and particularly the *Indian Act*, it is appropriate to interpret in a broad manner provisions that are aimed at maintaining Indian rights, and to interpret narrowly provisions aimed at limiting or abrogating them. Thus if legislation bears on treaty promises, the courts will always strain against adopting an interpretation that has the effect of negating commitments undertaken by the Crown; see *United States v. Powers*, 305 U.S. 527 (1939), at p. 533.

At the same time, I do not accept that this salutary rule that statutory ambiguities must be resolved in favour of the Indians implies automatic acceptance of a given construction simply because it may be expected that the Indians would favour it over any other competing interpretation. It is also necessary to reconcile any given interpretation with the policies the Act seeks to promote.

It is consideration of this factor that leads me to reject the interpretation the trial judge would give to s. 90(1)(b). The provincial Crowns bear no responsibility to provide for the welfare and protection of native peoples, and I am not prepared to accept that Parliament, in enacting s. 90(1)(*b*), intended that the privileges of ss. 87 and 89 exempt Indian bands from taxation and civil process in respect of all personal property that they may acquire pursuant to all agreements with that level of government, regardless of where that property is located. This interpretation is simply too broad. As I have attempted to show, it would take in any agreement relating to purely commercial dealings Indian bands might conclude with the provincial Crowns when competing in the economic mainstream of society. To my mind, such an interpretation takes one beyond the liberal and the generous and subverts the very character of the commitments that the Crown has historically undertaken *vis-à-vis* the protection of native property. ....

In arriving at his conclusion that the trial judge was correct in interpreting "Her Majesty" in s. 90(1)(*b*) as including the provincial Crowns, the Chief Justice sets considerable store on what he takes to be the aboriginal perception of "Her Majesty". With deference, I question his conclusion that it is realistic, in this day and age, to proceed on the assumption that from the aboriginal perspective, any federal-provincial divisions that the Crown has imposed on itself are simply internal to itself, such that the Crown may be considered what one might style an "indivisible entity". But even accepting that assumption, it does not follow that fairness requires one to proceed on the basis that Indians would be justified in concluding that all property they may acquire pursuant to agreements with that "indivisible entity" should be automatically protected, regardless of situs, by the exemptions and privileges conferred by ss. 87 and 89 of the *Indian Act*. I have no doubt that Indians are very much aware that ordinary commercial dealings constitute "affairs of life" that do not fall to be governed by their treaties or the *Indian Act*. Thus I take it that Indians, when engaging in the cut and thrust of business dealings in the commercial mainstream are under no illusions that they can expect to compete from a position of privilege with respect to their fellow Canadians. This distinction, it is fair to say, will be driven home every time Indians do business off their reserve lands. Professor Slattery puts the matter plainly when he notes, *supra*, at p. 776, that the purchases made by Indians in a normal drugstore are governed by laws of general application.

The conclusion I draw is that it is entirely reasonable to expect that Indians, when acquiring personal property pursuant to an agreement with that "indivisible entity" constituted by the Crown, will recognize that the question whether the exemptions of ss. 87 and 89 should apply in respect of that property, regardless of situs, must turn on the nature of the property concerned. If the property in question simply represents property which Indians acquired in the same manner any other Canadian might have done, I am at a loss to see why Indians should expect that the statutory notional situs of s. 90(1)(*b*) should apply in respect of it. In other words, even if the Indians perceive the Crown to be "indivisible", it is unclear to me how it could be that Indians could perceive that s. 90(1)(*b*) is meant to extend the protections of ss. 87 and 89 in an "indivisible" manner to all property acquired by them pursuant to agreements with that entity, regardless of where that property is held. What if the property concerned is property held off the reserve, and was acquired by the Indian band concerned simply with a view to further business dealings in the commercial mainstream?...

Moreover, I would question the conclusion that interpreting "Her Majesty" as including the provincial Crowns in the context of s. 90(1)(*b*) is tantamount to resolving the ambiguity of the meaning of this term in favour of the Indians. Sections 87 and 89, as I have shown above, have been crafted so as to place obstacles in the way of non-natives who would presume to dispossess Indians of personal property that is situated on reserves. But when Indians deal in the general marketplace, the protections conferred by these sections have the potential to become powerful impediments to their engaging successfully in commercial matters. Access to credit is the lifeblood of commerce, and I find it very difficult to accept that Indians would see any advantage, when seeking credit, in being precluded from putting forth in pledge property they may acquire from provincial Crowns. Indians, I would have thought, would much prefer to have free rein to conduct their affairs as all other fellow citizens when dealing in the commercial mainstream.

To elaborate, if Indians are to be unable to pledge or mortgage such personal property as they acquire in agreements with provincial Crowns, businessmen will have a strong incentive to avoid dealings with Indians. This is simply because the fact that Indians will be liable to be distrained in respect of some classes of property, and not in respect of others, will introduce a level of complexity in business dealings with Indians that is not present in other transactions. I think it safe to say that businessmen place a great premium on certainty in their commercial dealings, and that, accordingly, the greatest possible incentive to do business with Indians would be the knowledge that business may be conducted with them on exactly the same basis as with any other person. Any special considerations, extraordinary protections or exemptions that Indians bring with them to the marketplace introduce complications and would seem guaranteed to frighten off potential business partners.

In summary, while I of course endorse the applicability of the canons of interpretation laid down in *Nowegijick*, it is my respectful view that the interpretation proposed in this particular instance takes one beyond the confines of the fair, large and liberal, and can, in fact, be seen to involve the resolution of a supposed ambiguity in a manner most unfavourable to Indian interests. ...

Applicability of the Garnishment Act

It follows from my conclusion that the term "Her Majesty" in s. 90(1)(*b*) is limited to the federal Crown that this section has no application to the agreement that was entered into between the Government of Manitoba and the respondents. This conclusion still leaves to be resolved the question whether it was proper, in the circumstances, to garnish the moneys in question.

… The purpose of s. 87(*b*) of that Act is to protect the personal property of Indians from taxation so as to prevent any impairment by the provincial or federal Crowns with the ability of Indians to possess and enjoy that property. Given the broad social purpose behind this exemption, it would be truly anomalous if, as a result of the imposition of an *ultra vires* tax, the application of provincial law were to impair the ability of Indians to be placed in the same position as they would have been but for the improper tax. In other words, I think it makes no sense to proceed on the basis that Parliament meant to say to Indians, "We will protect you against all taxes in respect of such personal property as is situated on reserves, but if you are taxed improperly that illegal tax is liable to be attached". As I see it, this would be tantamount to allowing provincial law to do, via a circuitous and indirect route, what s. 89 of the *Indian Act* explicitly prohibits it from doing directly, i.e., attach the personal property of Indians situated on a reserve. In my view, this result would be inconsistent with the operation of the *Indian Act*, and I therefore conclude that the garnishment order should not have issued.

Disposition

I would dismiss the appeal with costs throughout.

Lamer, Wilson and **L'Heureux-Dubé JJ.** (concurring), **Dickson C.J.C.** (concurring in the result but differing on the interpretation of "Her Majesty").

In the *Mitchell v. Peguis* case, Justice La Forest was called upon to decide how courts should interpret statutes relating to Indians. Remember, he had to contend with Justice Dickson's point from *Nowegijick* "that treaties and statutes relating to Indians should be liberally construed and doubtful expressions resolved in favour of the Indians". In analyzing this interpretive provision Justice La Forest wrote, "that statutes relating to Indians are an expression of the will of Parliament. Given this fact, I do not find it particularly helpful to engage in speculation as to how Indians may be taken to understand a given provision".

1. Do you agree with Justice La Forest's re-interpretation of *Nowejigick*? What are the implications of this approach?
2. If Justice La Forest does not "find it helpful to engage in speculation as to how Indians may be taken to understand a given provision", how should one deal with his point that "Indians, I would have thought, would much prefer to have free rein to conduct their affairs as all other fellow citizens when dealing in the commercial mainstream". Similarly, if Justice La Forest does not regard it as helpful to speculate

on how Indians understand statutory provisions relating to them, how should one read his point that:

> I have no doubt that Indians are very much aware that ordinary commercial dealings constitute 'affairs of life' that do not fall to be governed by their treaties or the Indian Act. Thus I take it that Indians, when engaging in the cut and thrust of business dealings in the commercial mainstream are under no illusions that they can expect to compete from a position of privilege with respect to their fellow Canadians.

3. What does it mean when an Indian holds land *qua Indian*, in Justice La Forest's judgment? In reflecting on this characterization, Professor Constance MacIntosh wrote, in "From Judging Culture to Taxing 'Indians': Tracing the Legal Discourse of the 'Indian Mode of Life'" (2009) 47 Osgoode Hall L.J. 399 at 424:

> ... Justice La Forest ... interpreted the provisions as operating to "shield Indians from any efforts by non-natives to dispossess Indian of the property which they hold *qua* Indians, *i.e.*, their land base and the chattels on that land base." The awkward phrase "*qua* Indian" is nowhere to be seen in the legislation. So what does it signal, and what difference does adding this phrase make? The following statement, which Justice La Forest adopted as an accurate characterization of how the provision operates, is illuminating: "A tax exemption on the personal property of an Indian will be confined to the place where the holder of such property is *expected* to have it, *namely on the lands which an Indian occupies as an Indian, the reserve.*"

> ... Justice La Forest's interpretation of the provision is provocative. The statutory phrase "of an Indian ... situated on a reserve" has been transformed into "of an Indian *qua* Indian situated on a reserve." This evokes, once again, a conceptual opposition, a splitting of self, that only strikes Aboriginal people, and results in the ebb and flow of their Aboriginality in a judicially determinable manner. The provision's recast scope seems defined less by geography (on a reserve) and whether the owner falls under the statutory definition of "Indian," and more by a manner of occupation ("as an Indian") that is understood ("expected") to map naturally onto that geography. Justice La Forest's comments imply that it is reasonable to expect that Aboriginal people live *qua* "Indians" when they live on reserves, and that the way Aboriginal people live changes — likely becomes less "as an Indian," and more something else — if they live off the reserve.

The next significant case to deal with Indian property situate on reserve is *Williams v. Canada*, [1992] S.C.J. No. 36, [1992] 1 S.C.R. 877 (S.C.C.):

WILLIAMS v. CANADA

[1992] S.C.J. No. 36, [1992] 1 S.C.R. 877 (S.C.C.)

The judgment of the Court was delivered by

Gonthier J.:— At issue in this case is the situs of unemployment insurance benefits received by an Indian for the purpose of the exemption from taxation provided by s. 87 of the *Indian Act*, R.S.C. 1970, c. I-6 (now R.S.C., 1985, c. I-5).

I — Facts and Procedural History

The appellant received a notice of assessment by the Minister of National Revenue which included in his income, for the taxation year 1984, certain unemployment insurance benefits. The appellant contested the assessment. His objection was overruled by the Minister of National Revenue. The appellant appealed to the Federal Court, Trial Division: [1989] 2 F.C. 318, 24 F.T.R. 169, 24 C.C.E.L. 119, 89 D.T.C. 5032, [1989] 1 C.T.C. 117, [1989] 1 C.N.L.R. 184. The appeal proceeded on the basis of an agreed statement of facts.

At all material times, the appellant was a member of the Penticton Indian Band and resided on the Penticton Indian Reserve No. 1. In 1984 he received regular unemployment insurance benefits for which he qualified because of his former employment with a logging company situated on the reserve, and his employment by the Band in a "NEED Project" on the reserve. In both cases, the work was performed on the reserve, the employer was located on the reserve, and the appellant was paid on the reserve. During his employment, contributions to the unemployment insurance scheme were paid both by the appellant and his employers.

All of the regular unemployment insurance benefits were paid by federal government cheques mailed from the Canada Employment and Immigration Commission's regional computer centre in Vancouver. (While the instruments of payment may not technically have been cheques, this is of no consequence in this appeal.)

In addition to regular benefits, the appellant also received "enhanced" unemployment insurance benefits paid in respect of a job creation project administered on the reserve by the Band, pursuant to a written agreement between the Band and the Commission. The appellant was employed pursuant to this project in work which took place on the reserve, during a time in which he would otherwise have received regular benefits. The Band paid the appellant $60 per week during the program. The enhanced benefits constituted the bulk of the appellant's remuneration for his work in this program.

Section 38 of the *Unemployment Insurance Act, 1971*, S.C. 1970-71-72, c. 48, authorized the creation of such programs on a general basis, without any limitation to Indians. The enhanced unemployment insurance benefits were also paid by the Commission's regional computer centre in Vancouver.

The issue at trial was whether the unemployment insurance benefits received by the appellant were exempt from taxation pursuant to s. 87 of the *Indian Act*. With regard to the requirements of that section, the disputed issue was whether the benefits received by the appellant were "situated" on a reserve. ...

III — Framing the Issues

In order to decide the basis upon which a situs is to be assigned to the unemployment insurance benefits in this case, it is necessary to explore the purposes of the exemption from taxation in s. 87 of the *Indian Act*, the nature of the benefits in question, and the manner in which the incidence of taxation falls upon the benefits to be taxed.

A — The Nature and Purpose of the Exemption from Taxation

The question of the purpose of ss. 87, 89 and 90 has been thoroughly addressed by La Forest J. in the case of *Mitchell v. Peguis Indian Band*, [1990] 2 S.C.R. 85. La Forest J. expressed the view that the purpose of these sections was to preserve the entitlements of Indians to their reserve lands and to ensure that the use of their property on their reserve lands was not eroded by the ability of governments to tax, or creditors to seize. The corollary of this conclusion was that the purpose of the sections was not to confer a general economic benefit upon the Indians (at pp. 130-31). ...

La Forest J. also noted that the protection from seizure is a mixed blessing, in that it removes the assets of an Indian on a reserve from the ordinary stream of commercial dealings (at pp. 146-47).

Therefore, under the *Indian Act*, an Indian has a choice with regard to his personal property. The Indian may situate this property on the reserve, in which case it is within the protected area and free from seizure and taxation, or the Indian may situate this property off the reserve, in which case it is outside the protected area, and more fully available for ordinary commercial purposes in society. Whether the Indian wishes to remain within the protected reserve system or integrate more fully into the larger commercial world is a choice left to the Indian.

The purpose of the situs test in s. 87 is to determine whether the Indian holds the property in question as part of the entitlement of an Indian qua Indian on the reserve. Where it is necessary to decide amongst various methods of fixing the location of the relevant property, such a method must be selected having regard to this purpose.

B — Nature of Benefit and the Incidence of Taxation

Section 56 of the *Income Tax Act* is the section which taxes income from unemployment insurance benefits. That section specifies that unemployment insurance benefits which are "received by the taxpayer in the year" are to be included in computing the income of a taxpayer. The parties have approached this question on the basis that what is being taxed is a debt owing from the Crown to the taxpayer on account of unemployment insurance which the taxpayer has qualified for. This is not precisely true, since the liability for taxation arises not when the debt (if that is what it is) arises, but rather when it is paid, and the money is received by the taxpayer. However, it is true that the taxation does not attach to the money in the hands of the taxpayer, but instead to the receipt by the taxpayer of the money. Thus, the incidence of taxation in the case of unemployment insurance benefits is on the taxpayer in respect of the transaction, that is, the receipt of the benefit.

This Court's decision in *Nowegijick v. The Queen*, [1983] 1 S.C.R. 29, stands for the proposition that the receipt of salary income is personal property for the purpose of the exemption from taxation provided by the *Indian Act*. I can see no difference between salary income and income from unemployment insurance benefits in this regard, therefore I hold that the receipt of income from unemployment insurance benefits is also personal property for the purposes of the *Indian Act*.

Nowegijick also stands for the proposition that the inclusion of personal property in the calculation of a taxpayer's income gives rise to a tax in respect of that personal property within the meaning of the *Indian Act*, despite the fact that the tax is on the person rather than on the property directly.

Therefore, most of the requirements of s. 87 of the *Indian Act* have clearly been met in this case. The receipt of unemployment insurance benefits is personal property. That property is owned by an Indian. The Indian is being taxed in respect of that property, since it is being included in his income for the purpose of income taxation. The remaining question is whether the property in question is situated on a reserve.

. . . . .

C — Comments on the "Residence of the Debtor" Test

The factor identified in previous cases as being of primary importance to determine the situs of this kind of property is the residence of the debtor, that is, the person paying the income. This was clearly stated by Thurlow A.C.J. in *The Queen v. National Indian Brotherhood*, [1979] 1 F.C. 103 (T.D.), at p. 109:

> A chose in action such as the right to a salary in fact has no situs. But where for some purpose the law has found it necessary to attribute a situs, in the absence of anything in the contract or elsewhere to indicate the contrary, the situs of a simple contract debt has been held to be the residence or place where the debtor is found. See Cheshire, *Private International Law*, seventh edition, pp. 420 et seq.

This conclusion was cited with approval by this Court in *Nowegijick v. The Queen, supra*, at p. 34:

> The Crown conceded in argument, correctly in my view, that the situs of the salary which Mr. Nowegijick received was sited on the reserve because it was there that the residence or place of the debtor, the Gull Bay Development Corporation, was to be found and it was there that the wages were payable. See Cheshire and North, *Private International Law* (10th ed., 1979) at pp. 536 et seq. and also the judgment of Thurlow A.C.J. in *R. v. National Indian Brotherhood*, [1979] 1 F.C. 103 particularly at pp. 109 et seq.

The only justification given in these cases for locating the situs of a debt at the residence of the debtor is that this is the rule applied in the conflict of laws. The rationale for this rule in the conflict of laws is that it is at the residence of the debtor that the debt may normally be enforced. Cheshire and North, *Private International Law* (11th ed. 1987), quote Atkin L.J. to this effect in *New York Life Insurance Co. v. Public Trustee*, [1924] 2 Ch. 101 (C.A.), at p. 119. ... This may be reasonable for the general purposes of conflicts of laws. However, one must inquire as to its utility for the purposes underlying the exemption from taxation in the *Indian Act*.

. . . . .

In resolving this question, it is readily apparent that to simply adopt general conflicts principles in the present context would be entirely out of keeping with the scheme and purposes of the *Indian Act* and *Income Tax Act*. The purposes of the conflict of laws have little or nothing in common with the purposes underlying the *Indian Act*. It is simply not apparent how the place where a debt may normally be enforced has any relevance to the question whether to tax the receipt of the payment of that debt would amount to the erosion of the entitlements of an Indian qua Indian on a reserve. The test for situs under the *Indian Act* must be constructed according to its purposes, not the purposes of the conflict of laws. Therefore, the position that the residence of the debtor exclusively determines the situs of benefits such as those paid in this case must be closely reexamined in light of the purposes of the *Indian Act*. It may be that the residence of the debtor remains an important factor, or even the exclusive one. However, this conclusion cannot be directly drawn from an analysis of how the conflict of laws deals with such an issue.

IV — The Proper Test

Because the transaction by which a taxpayer receives unemployment insurance benefits is not a physical object, the method by which one might fix its situs is not immediately apparent. In one sense, the difficulty is that the transaction has no situs. However, in another sense, the problem is that it has too many. There is the situs of the debtor, the situs of the creditor, the situs where the payment is made, the situs of the employment which created the qualification for the receipt of income, the situs where the payment will be used, and no doubt others. The task is then to identify which of these locations is the relevant one, or which combination of these factors controls the location of the transaction.

The appellant suggests that in deciding the situs of the receipt of income, a court ought to balance all of the relevant "connecting factors" on a case by case basis. Such an approach would have the advantage of flexibility, but it would have to be applied carefully in order to avoid several potential pitfalls. It is desirable, when construing exemptions from taxation, to develop criteria which are predictable in their application, so that the taxpayers involved may plan their affairs appropriately. This is also important as the same criteria govern an exemption from seizure.

Furthermore, it would be dangerous to balance connecting factors in an abstract manner, divorced from the purpose of the exemption under the *Indian Act*. A connecting factor is only relevant in so much as it identifies the location of the property in question for the purposes of the *Indian Act*. In particular categories of cases, therefore, one connecting factor may have much more weight than another. It would be easy in balancing connecting factors on a case by case basis to lose sight of this.

However, an overly rigid test which identified one or two factors as having controlling force has its own potential pitfalls. Such a test would be open to manipulation and abuse, and in focusing on too few factors could miss the purposes of the exemption in the *Indian Act* as easily as a test which indiscriminately focuses on too many.

The approach which best reflects these concerns is one which analyzes the matter in terms of categories of property and types of taxation. For instance, connecting factors may have different relevance with regard to unemployment insurance benefits than in respect of employment income, or pension benefits. The first step is to identify the various connecting factors which are potentially relevant. These factors should then be analyzed to determine what weight they should be given in identifying the location of the property, in light of three considerations: (1) the purpose of the exemption under the *Indian Act*; (2) the type of property in question; and (3) the nature of the taxation of that property. The question with regard to each connecting factor is therefore what weight should be given that factor in answering the question whether to tax that form of property in that manner would amount to the erosion of the entitlement of the Indian qua Indian on a reserve.

This approach preserves the flexibility of the case by case approach, but within a framework which properly identifies the weight which is to be placed on various connecting factors. Of course, the weight to be given various connecting factors cannot be determined precisely. However, this approach has the advantage that it preserves the ability to deal appropriately with future cases which present considerations not previously apparent.

A — The Test for the Situs of the Unemployment Insurance Benefits

Unemployment insurance benefits are income replacement insurance, paid when a person is out of work under certain qualifying conditions. While one often refers to unemployment insurance "benefits", the scheme is based on employer and employee premiums. These premiums are themselves tax-deductible for both the employer and employee.

There are a number of potentially relevant connecting factors in determining the location of the receipt of unemployment insurance benefits. The following have been suggested: the residence of the debtor, the residence of the person receiving the benefits, the place the benefits are paid, and the location of the employment income which gave rise to the qualification for the benefits. One's attention is naturally first drawn to the traditional test, that of the residence of the debtor. The debtor in this case is the federal Crown, through the Canada Employment and Immigration Commission. The Commission argues that the residence of the debtor in this case is Ottawa, referring to s. 11 of the *Employment and Immigration Department and Commission Act*, S.C. 1976-77, c. 54 (now

R.S.C., 1985, c. E-5, s. 17), which mandates that the head office of the Commission be located in the National Capital Region.

There are, however, conceptual difficulties in establishing the situs of a Crown agency in any particular place within Canada. For most purposes, it is unnecessary to establish the situs of the Crown. The conflict of laws is interested in situs to determine jurisdictional and choice of law questions. With regard to the Crown, no such questions arise, since the Crown is present throughout Canada and may be sued anywhere in Canada. Unemployment insurance benefits are also available anywhere in Canada, to any Canadian who qualifies for them. Therefore, the purposes behind fixing the situs of an ordinary person do not apply to the Crown, and in particular do not apply to the Canada Employment and Immigration Commission in respect of the receipt of unemployment insurance benefits.

This does not necessarily mean that the physical location of the Crown is irrelevant to the purposes underlying the exemption from taxation provided by the *Indian Act*. However, it does suggest that the significance of the Crown being the source of the payments at issue in this case may lie more in the special nature of the public policy behind the payments, rather than the Crown's situs, assuming it can be fixed. Therefore, the residence of the debtor is a connecting factor of limited weight in the context of unemployment insurance benefits. For similar reasons, the place where the benefits are paid is of limited importance in this context.

This leaves two factors to be considered: the residence of the recipient of the benefits, and the location of the employment income which was the basis of the qualification for the benefits. ...

The general scheme of taxation with regard to unemployment insurance premiums and benefits bears further examination in this regard. As noted above, unemployment insurance is premium based. The intent of the scheme is that the premiums received will, overall, largely equal the benefits paid out. This is not to say that the scheme is completely self-financing. However, it is more accurate to characterize an unemployment insurance benefit as something paid for through the premiums of employed persons than to characterize it as a benefit granted by the government out of its general revenues.

. . . . .

Since unemployment insurance benefits are based on premiums arising out of previous employment, not general tax revenue, the connection between the previous employment and the benefits is a strong one. The manner in which unemployment insurance benefits are treated for the purposes of taxation further strengthens this connection, as there is a symmetry of treatment in the taxation of premiums and benefits, since premiums are tax-deductible and benefits are taxed, thereby minimizing the influence of the unemployment insurance scheme on general tax revenues.

The location of the qualifying employment income is therefore an important factor in establishing whether the taxation of subsequent benefits would erode the entitlements of an Indian qua Indian on the reserve. For in the case of an Indian whose qualifying employment income was on the reserve, the symmetry in the tax implications of premiums and benefits breaks down. For such an Indian, the original employment income was tax-exempt. The taxation paid on the subsequent benefits therefore does more than merely offset the tax saved by virtue of the premiums. Instead, it is an erosion of the entitlements created by the Indian's employment on the reserve.

Furthermore, since the duration and extent of the benefits are tied to the terms of employment during a specified period, it is the location of the qualifying employment income during that period that is relevant.

Having regard to the importance of the location of the qualifying employment income as a factor in identifying the location of the unemployment insurance benefits, the remaining factor of the residence of the recipient of the benefits at the time of their receipt is only potentially significant if it points to a location different from that of the qualifying employment.

B — *The Situs of the Appellant's Unemployment Insurance Benefits*

In the present case, the residence of the appellant when he received the benefits was on the reserve.

It has been assumed by the parties that the previous employment of the appellant which gave rise to the qualification for unemployment insurance benefits was also located on the reserve, since the two employers in question were located on the reserve. This question must be reexamined in light of our determination that this conclusion cannot safely be drawn from the principles of the conflicts of laws.

However, this would not be an appropriate case in which to develop a test for the situs of the receipt of employment income. All the potential connecting factors with respect to the qualifying employment of the appellant point to the reserve. The employer was located on the reserve, the work was performed on the reserve, the appellant resided on the reserve, and he was paid on the reserve. A test for the situs of employment income could therefore only be developed in an abstract vacuum in this case, since there is no real controversy of relevant factors pulling in opposite directions. The same would be true of any consideration of the weight, if any, to be given to the residence of the appellant upon receipt of the benefits as this was also on the reserve.

. . . . .

Therefore, for the purposes of the present appeal, we merely note that the employment of the appellant by which he qualified for unemployment insurance benefits was clearly located on the reserve, no matter what the proper test for the situs of employment income is determined to be. Because the qualifying employment was located on the reserve, so too were the benefits subsequently received. The question of the relevance of the residence of the recipient of the benefits at the time of receipt does not arise in this case since it was also on the reserve.

C — The Situs of the Enhanced Unemployment Insurance Benefits

According to s. 38(3) of *the Unemployment Insurance Act, 1971* enhanced benefits are to be considered unemployment insurance benefits for the purpose of the *Income Tax Act*. ...

This is also the manner in which enhanced benefits should be characterized for the purpose of the exemption from taxation in the *Indian Act*, since this only reflects the reality of the situation. The appellant only qualified for participation in the job creation program because he had been receiving regular unemployment insurance benefits, that is, because of his prior employment that had ceased. The benefits which he continued to receive would not have ceased had he quit his employment with the program. The program itself was located on the reserve. Therefore, the conclusion that the unemployment insurance benefits received by the appellant were situated on the reserve applies to both the regular and enhanced benefits.

V — Conclusion

Determining the situs of intangible personal property requires a court to evaluate various connecting factors which tie the property to one location or another. In the context of the exemption from taxation in the *Indian Act*, there are three important considerations: the purpose of the exemption; the character of the property in question; and the incidence of taxation upon that property. Given the purpose of the exemption, the ultimate question is to what extent each factor is relevant in determining whether to tax the particular kind of property in a particular manner would erode the entitlement of an Indian qua Indian to personal property on the reserve.

With regard to the unemployment insurance benefits received by the appellant, a particularly important factor is the location of the employment which gave rise to the qualification for the benefits. In this case, the location of the qualifying employment was on the reserve, therefore the benefits received by the appellant were also located on the reserve. The question of the relevance of the residence of the recipient of the benefits at the time of receipt does not arise in this case.

The appeal is therefore allowed and the cross-appeal dismissed, with costs throughout. The matter is referred back to the Minister of National Revenue to be reassessed on the basis that all of the unemployment benefits in question are exempt from taxation.

After the Supreme Court of Canada's ruling in *Williams*, Revenue Canada (now the Canada Revenue Agency) developed interpretive guidelines to apply the "connecting factors" test for determining whether property was situate on reserve and thus exempt from taxation. These guidelines have been the subject of extensive protests and litigation by Indians. There is concern that they are interpreted too strictly, ignoring Gonthier J.'s caution in *Williams* that "it would be dangerous to balance connecting factors in an abstract manner, divorced from the purpose of the exemption under the *Indian Act*." Gonthier J. further noted (at p. 892):

[a] connecting factor is only relevant in so much as it identifies the location of the property in question for the purposes of the *Indian Act*... In particular categories of cases, therefore, one connecting factor may have much more weight than another. It would be easy in balancing connecting factors on a case by case basis to lose sight of this.

However, an overly rigid test which identified one or two factors as having controlling force has its own potential pitfalls. Such a test would be open to manipulation and abuse, and in focusing on too few factors could miss the purposes of the exemption in the Indian Act as easily as a test which indiscriminately focuses on too many.

This brief excerpt from the *Folster* case illustrates limitations the Court finds in Revenue Canada's guidelines applying the test found in *Williams*.

FOLSTER v. CANADA

[1997] F.C.J. No. 664, [1997] 3 F.C. 269, 148 D.L.R. (4th) 314 (Fed. C.A.)

Isaac C.J. and **Pratte** and **Linden JJ.A.**

The judgment of the Court was delivered by

Linden JJ.A.: — ... Gonthier J. crafted a new test based on the foundation of La Forest J.'s purposive analysis in *Mitchell*. He recognized that, although there are necessarily many factors which may be of assistance in determining the situs of intangible property such as unemployment insurance or employment income, the relevance of these "connecting factors" must be assessed on the basis of their ability to further the purpose of section 87. Further, the weight to be given to each factor may change from case to case. ...

This new test was not designed to extend the tax exemption benefit to all Indians. Nor was it aimed at exempting all Indians living on reserves. Rather, in suggesting reliance on a range of factors which may be relevant to determining the situs of the property, Gonthier J. sought to ensure that any tax exemption would serve the purpose it was meant to achieve, namely, the preservation of property held by Indians qua Indians on reserves so that their traditional way of life would not be jeopardized. ...

... Following the Supreme Court's decision in *Williams*, Revenue Canada issued four guidelines intended to assist in the interpretation of section 87 of the Act according to the connecting factors test. These guidelines are as follows (Indian Act Exemption for employment income, Guidelines, June 1994, Revenue Canada, at 2-8).

When at least 90% of the duties of an employment are performed on a reserve, all of the income of an Indian from that employment will usually be exempt from income tax ... When less than 90% of the duties of an employment are performed on a reserve and the employment income is not exempted by another guideline, the exemption is prorated. The exemption will apply to the portion of the income related to the duties performed on the reserve ...

When: (i) the employer is resident on the reserve; and (ii) the Indian lives on a reserve; all of the income of an Indian from an employment will usually be exempt from income tax ...

When: (i) more than 50% of the duties of an employment are performed on a reserve; and (ii) the employer is resident on a reserve, or the Indian lives on a reserve; all of the income of an Indian from an employment will usually be exempt from income tax ... When: (i) the employer is resident on a reserve; and (ii) the employer is: (a) an Indian band which has a reserve, or a tribal council representing one or more Indian bands which have reserves, or (b) an Indian organization controlled by one or more such bands or tribal councils, if the organization is dedicated exclusively to the social, cultural, educational, or economic development of Indians who for the most part live on reserves; and (iii) the duties of the employment are in connection with the employer's non-commercial activities carried on exclusively for the benefit of Indians who for the most part live on the reserves; all of the income of an Indian from an employment will usually be exempt from income tax.

As is evident, the guidelines understandably are based largely on the residence of the employer and the location where the duties of the employee are performed. While these factors may be useful for the determination of whether employment income falls within section 87, a central premise of *Williams* is that, in the final analysis, the relative weighting of connecting factors must proceed on a case-by-case basis. Consequently, although guidelines may assist in routine cases, it is not possible to establish, in advance, the precise formula by which employment income is to be assessed in all cases.

In *Shilling v. M.N.R.*, [2001] F.C.J. No. 951, 2001 FCA 178 (Fed. C.A.), a status Indian was assessed income tax by the Minister of National Revenue. Ms. Shilling had in the past resided on the Rama reserve and in the present maintained substantial connections with her family and community on the reserve. She had, however, lived and worked in Toronto during the period that she earned the employment income at issue in the case. While her salary was earned off the reserve, it was paid by a person residing on and carrying on business on the reserve (a native employee leasing service). Ms. Shilling's salary payments took the form of transfers of funds from her employer's bank account on the reserve to her bank account on the reserve. The Federal Court, Trial Division determined ([1999] F.C.J. No. 899, [1999] 4 F.C. 178 (F.C.T.D.)) that Ms. Shilling's employment income was tax-exempt as the property of an Indian situated on a reserve. The Crown's appeal to the Federal Court of Appeal was allowed. The Court applied the connecting factors test from *Williams* and held that the employer's head office location was the only factor connecting Ms. Shilling's employment income to a reserve. It held that this was not sufficient to find the *situs* of the employment income to be on the reserve. The fact that Ms. Shilling was employed by a business with its head office and bank account on-reserve was not, in the Court's view, sufficient to make her employment "integral to the life of the reserve". The Court wrote (paras. 65-66):

> Ms. Shilling's employment is to be regarded as in the "commercial mainstream". This conclusion may appear counter-intuitive when applied to a Native person who identifies with her Band and First Nation, and is working with a social agency delivering programmes to assist Native people, in large part through reconnecting them with their culture and traditions.
>
> However, in the context of determining the location of intangible property for the purpose of section 87, "commercial mainstream" is to be contrasted with "integral to the life of a reserve": *Folster, supra*, at paragraph 14. ... The purpose of the tax exemption in paragraph 87(1)(*b*) is not to address the general economically disadvantaged position of Indians in Canada.

Hence, Ms. Shilling's employment income earned while working in Toronto was not situated on a reserve, and was not exempt from taxation under the *Indian Act*. Leave to appeal to the Supreme Court of Canada was denied March 14, 2002, S.C.C. No. 28776.

In *Canada v. Monias*, [2001] F.C.J. No. 1168, 2001 FCA 239 (Fed. C.A.), leave to appeal to S.C.C. denied [2001] S.C.C.A. No. 482, a number of Indians were employed by the Awasis Agency of Northern Manitoba ("Awasis") and assessed taxation. Awasis received its funding from Indian and Northern Affairs Canada pursuant to a series of comprehensive funding arrangements between it and the federal Crown. While the work performed by the taxpayers was mostly for the benefit of people on the reserve, it generally was performed off of the reserve and the taxpayers themselves did not reside on a reserve. The Minister denied the *Indian Act* exemption. The Tax Court allowed the appeals on the basis that the taxpayers' employment was intimately connected with various Indian communities all located on a reserve. The Crown appealed to the Federal Court of Appeal. The Federal Court of Appeal first considered the purpose of the *Indian Act* exemption. Considering the purpose and the facts in the case, the Court concluded the factors connecting the income to a reserve were not sufficient to determine that the income was situated on a reserve. Further, while the taxpayers' work might have helped to maintain and enhance the quality of life on the reserves for members of the bands living there, it did not necessarily connect the acquisition or use of their employment income to the reserves as physical locations. The Federal Court of Appeal wrote (at para. 66):

> That the work from which employment income is earned benefits Indians on reserves, and indeed may be integral to maintaining the reserves as viable social units, is not in itself sufficient to situate the employment income there. It is not the policy of paragraph 87(1)(*b*) to provide a tax subsidy for services provided to and for the benefit of reserves. Rather, it is to protect from erosion by taxation the property of individual Indians that they acquire, hold and use on a reserve, although in the case of an intangible, such as

employment income, it is the *situs* of its *acquisition* that is particularly important.

To summarize *Monias*: the fact that the work from which employment income is earned benefits Indians on reserves (and may even be integral to maintaining the reserves as viable social units) is not in itself sufficient to situate the employment income on the reserve. The taxpayers, therefore, were not entitled to the exemption claimed.

McDIARMID LUMBER LTD. v. GOD'S LAKE FIRST NATION

[2006] S.C.J. No. 58, [2006] 2 S.C.R. 846, 2006 SCC 58 (S.C.C.)

[The Supreme Court of Canada revisited sections 89 and 90 of the *Indian Act* in *McDiarmid Lumber Ltd. v. God's Lake First Nation*. At issue was whether section 89 and 90 "immunities" could extend to band funds deposited in an off-reserve account, when the monies were received pursuant to a Comprehensive Funding Agreement (CFA) between the First Nations and federal government. One of the purposes of the money given to the God's Lake First Nation was on-reserve education. The Court concluded the funds were not protected from seizure by either section 89 or section 90 of the *Indian Act*. In coming to its conclusions regarding section 89, **Chief Justice McLachlin** wrote for the majority (**Bastarache, LeBel, Deschamps, Charron, Rothstein JJ.**)

ISSUE ONE — SECTION 89 (1)]:

[11] Section 89(1) of the *Indian Act* provides that "the real and personal property of an Indian or a band situated on a reserve is not subject to charge, pledge, mortgage, attachment, levy, seizure, distress or execution in favour or at the instance of any person other than an Indian or a band". The question is whether the expression "situated on a reserve" is to be given its plain meaning and subjected to the common law and statutory *situs* rules, or whether it has a more abstract meaning unique to the *Indian Act*.

[12] The band relies on *Williams v. Canada*, [1992] 1 S.C.R. 877…The Court, *per* Gonthier J., found that the *situs* for this purpose was on the reserve, having regard to "a number of potentially relevant connecting factors" relating to the transaction and the parties involved (p. 893). Gonthier J., in *obiter*, suggested that the same approach would apply to seizures.

[13] There is no dispute that under traditional common law approaches and the terms of the *Trust and Loan Companies Act*, the debt at issue here is located off-reserve at the Winnipeg bank branch. The question, therefore, is what approach applies to seizures — the concrete approach of the common law, or the multi-factored notional approach applied to taxation in *Williams*.

[14] The band argues that the *Williams* approach better reflects the broader purpose of this protective provision of the *Indian Act*. That

purpose, it submits, is to protect assets of Indians *qua* Indians where to permit seizure would neglect the realities of the aboriginal community in question or the options available to the parties. ...

[15] Despite its evident appeal, this submission does not withstand scrutiny. Principle, policy and jurisprudence stand against it.

[16] First, *Williams* is distinguishable. It was based on a different section of the *Indian Act* and referred to a different kind of property. At issue was s. 87, which accords an exemption from taxation for "personal property of an Indian or a band situated on a reserve". ...

. . . . .

[19] Second, the cases overwhelmingly support a concrete common law interpretation. In *Union of New Brunswick Indians* (below), writing for the majority of this Court, I confirmed the view of Iacobucci J. in *R. v. Lewis*, [1996] 1 S.C.R. 921, that "on the reserve" is to be given "its ordinary and common sense" meaning throughout the *Indian Act*:

> ... The only qualification the case law admits to the rule that s. 87 catches only property physically located on a reserve is the rule that where property which was on a reserve moves off the reserve temporarily, the court will ask whether its "paramount location" is on the reserve. [paras. 13-14]

The Court of Appeal in the case at bar found this statement to have "foreclosed the existence of a discernible nexus test that would modify the requirement of s. 87 (and of s. 89) that property must be physically located on a reserve" (para. 34). I agree.

[20] Third, this view is supported by the fact that when Parliament wished to depart from the physically situate test for personal property, it did so expressly by statutory language. Thus s. 90 provides that personal property given to Indians by the Crown under treaty obligations or purchased by moneys appropriated by Parliament for the benefit of Indians "shall be deemed always to be situated on a reserve". The existence of a deeming provision of this kind suggests that other provisions addressing location should not be interpreted according to a "notional" test.

[21] I agree with the Court of Appeal that the funds in the Winnipeg bank account were not "situated on a reserve". Accordingly, the exemption granted by s. 89 of the *Indian Act* does not apply.

[ISSUE TWO — SECTION 90(1)]

The Supreme Court in *McDiarmid* next considered whether section 90 would provide an exemption for the funds the First Nations placed in the bank off-reserve. Section 90(1) of the *Indian Act* reads as follows:

> 90. (1) For the purposes of sections 87 and 89, personal property that was
>
> (*a*) purchased by Her Majesty with Indian moneys or moneys appropriated by Parliament for the use and benefit of Indians or bands, or

(b)   given to Indians or to a band under a treaty or agreement between a
      band and Her Majesty,

shall be deemed always to be situated on a reserve.

The Supreme Court wrote:]

[23] The appellant band is a 1909 adherent to Treaty No. 5, concluded at
Norway House in 1875. In exchange for the extinguishment of claims, the
Crown agreed, *inter alia*, to protect traditional activities on the surrendered
land, provide annual grants, and maintain schools. In the case at bar, the
funds in question were provided through a CFA under which funds are to
be delivered to the band's off-reserve bank account on a monthly basis. ...
The parties disagree about both the proper interpretation of the word
"agreement" in s. 90(1) and the proper characterization of the CFA.

[24] The question is one of statutory interpretation. What is the
meaning of "agreement" in s. 90(1)(b)? ...

[25] Precedent, principle and policy all suggest that Parliament's intent
was that the word "agreement" in s. 90(1)(b) should not be accorded a
broad meaning, but should instead be confined to agreements ancillary to
treaties.

5.2.1 Precedent

[26]   This Court has already considered the meaning of "agreement" in
s. 90(1)(b) and concluded that it should be restricted to agreements that
flesh out commitments of the Crown to Indians in the treaty context of the
surrender of their homelands: *Mitchell*, at pp. 124, 131 and 134. The band
would have us overrule *Mitchell*. It is not the practice of this Court to
reverse its previous decisions in the absence of compelling reasons to do
so ...

. . . . .

[28] ... Parliament sought to ensure that the entitlements of Indians
under treaties were not defined in a way that was unduly narrow or
technical. La Forest J. reasoned that "[i]t must be remembered that treaty
promises are often couched in very general terms and that supplementary
agreements are needed to flesh out the details of the commitments
undertaken by the Crown": *Mitchell*, at p. 124. The word "agreement" in
the provision thus served to ensure that agreements that fulfil treaty
obligations are treated as such.

. . . . .

5.2.2 The Principle of Associated Meaning

[30] It is a fundamental principle of statutory interpretation that when
two or more words linked by "and" or "or" serve an analogous
grammatical and logical function within a provision, they should be
interpreted with a view to their common features ...

[31] Applying this principle may result in the scope of the broader term being limited to that of the narrower term ...

. . . . .

[34] ... Where the legislature links two concepts, ambiguity in one of them may be resolved by having regard to the other. As a result, a broad provision may be read more narrowly. ...

[35] In *Mitchell*, this Court applied the principle of associated meaning to clarify the meaning of "agreement" in s. 90(1)(*b*) of the *Indian Act*. La Forest J. echoed the language of Martin J.A. in the earlier case of *Goulis*, at p. 61, stating that "the terms 'treaty' and 'agreement' ... take colour from one another" (p. 124). In my view, the Court did not err in applying this principle.

5.2.3 The Presumption Against Tautology

. . . . .

[37] If "agreement" is interpreted broadly to cover all types of agreements between Indians and the government, the word "treaty" has no role to play. Treaties are special and particularly solemn agreements, but they are agreements nonetheless. This supports the view taken in *Mitchell* that "agreement" in s. 90(1)(*b*) should be read more narrowly as supplementing "treaty".

5.2.4 The Strict Construction of Exceptions and the Protection of Rights

[38] The provincial credit regimes shape an important part of economic life in Canada. They are designed, almost by necessity, to apply universally. The provisions at issue in the case at bar serve to interfere with that scope. They act to carve out certain forms of Indian property from under the applicable credit regime, but leave others in. In short, they establish specific exceptions to the general rule that the provincial credit regime will apply to Indian property.

[39] The wording of the provisions makes clear that Parliament did not seek to exempt Indian property in a broad sense. Instead, specific criteria were set out to describe the features of property that Parliament wanted to exclude from the credit regimes established by the provinces. Given the importance of access to the credit economy, and given Parliament's choice to create only limited exceptions to its application, it is not for the courts to adopt a reading of the statute that distorts that choice. Courts should be hesitant to find exceptions where they are not explicit, particularly when their effect is to materially affect the rights of citizens under statute or common law. The exceptional effect of the provisions at issue here is limited by the precise wording Parliament used and the underlying purpose that the provision serves. It should not be read more broadly than necessary to give meaning to the words and to give effect to Parliament's purpose.

[40] The fact that the effect of the provisions is to suspend the rights of both creditors and debtors provides further support for a narrow interpretation of the exceptions. Provincial credit regimes create important and enforceable rights for the debtors and creditors who are governed by them. They enable debtors to leverage assets and creditors to take measured risks. They are the modern incarnation of the panoply of rules of credit developed at common law. It is against this backdrop that the exceptions created by the *Indian Act* provisions must be understood.

[41] In the absence of express language, it is not the place of courts to read the *Indian Act* exceptions in such a way that would transform them into significant forms of interference with the applicable provincial regime and rights thereunder. Subject to the constraints established by the Constitution, it is for Parliament to make policy choices of that nature. Particularly in the case of a credit regime, courts have a responsibility to ensure a degree of certainty and predictability in the law and to approach the task of statutory interpretation with restraint.

5.2.5 Limiting Access to Credit

[42] A further reason that the word "agreement" in s. 90(1)(*b*) should be read narrowly is that the section limits the ability of aboriginal peoples to access credit. This conclusion was reached by the Royal Commission on Aboriginal Peoples ("RCAP"). In its report, RCAP noted the difficulties that aboriginal peoples have in gaining access to capital, and listed a number of barriers that contribute to this problem: see Canada, *Report of the Royal Commission on Aboriginal* (1996), vol. 2, *Restructuring the Relationship*, at pp. 906-31. Among the barriers listed, the *first* barrier identified was the restrictions imposed by the *Indian Act*. RCAP described these barriers as follows at pp. 906-7: "The *Indian Act* contains certain provisions that make it very difficult for lenders to secure loans using land and other assets located on-reserve as collateral. These provisions serve as a significant deterrent to financing business activity on-reserve." RCAP considered a number of ways to overcome these barriers, including abolishing the restrictions in the *Indian Act*. Although this Court clearly cannot abolish the *Indian Act* restrictions, the concern about limited access to credit resulting from these restrictions is yet another reason that the word "agreement" in s. 90(1)(*b*) should be read narrowly.

. . . . .

5.2.7 The History of Section 90(1)(*b*)

[47] The *Indian Act* seizure exemptions have a long history. The current provision, adopted in 1951 as s. 89 of the *Indian Act*, replaced s. 108 of the *Indian Act*, R.S.C. 1927, c. 98, which in turn was preceded by similar provisions in the 1906, 1886 and 1880 Acts. Section 108 and its predecessors made no reference to property given under a "treaty" or "agreement". Instead they protected from seizure "presents given to

Indians or non-treaty Indians", "annuities or interest on funds" and "moneys appropriated by Parliament, held for any band of Indians", as well as related property purchased with those funds. The 1850 *Act for the protection of the Indians in Upper Canada from imposition, and the property occupied or enjoyed by them from trespass and injury* also protected "annuities and presents" and associated property (S. Prov. C. 1850, 13 & 14 Vict., c. 74).

[48] The scope of these protections was broad. Basically, any monies or gifts from the government to Indians appear to have been covered. By contrast, the words adopted in 1951 and retained to the present are more circumscribed; what is protected is a particular type of money or gifts — personal property which was purchased by the government and personal property "given to Indians or to a band under a treaty or agreement between a band and His Majesty". The change in the language used by Parliament is striking.

[49] Why did Parliament in 1951 abandon the former approach of exempting certain kinds of property, in favour of an approach that based the exemption on whether the property was given under a treaty or agreement? The record reveals no definitive answer. What it does reveal, however, is a change in philosophy after 1951.

[50] The 19th century exemption provisions were born of a fear that Indians and their lands and property were subject to exploitation by others. The aim was thus to provide broad protection for their property. ... This concern with the protection of Indians from those who might take advantage of them and divert funding provided by the Crown is consistent with broad protection against seizure. ...

[51] The paternalism of the 19th century continued to animate many Indian policies and social and political attitudes well into the 20th century. By the 1930s and 1940s, however, other values had also become important. Increasingly, there was a realization that the paternalistic model that had been in place was no longer entirely appropriate. Self-determination and self-government had emerged as an aspiration, if not a reality, and bands were beginning to embark on projects to improve their economic situation.

. . . . .

[53] These changing attitudes were reflected in the work of the Special Joint Committee on the *Indian Act*, struck in 1946 in response to an increasing sense of a need to modernize Indian policy. The participation of Indians in the Second World War and a growing concern for human rights following that conflict had drawn the attention of the public and of Parliament to the conditions faced by Indians: see J. Leslie and R. Maguire, eds., *The Historical Development of the Indian Act* (2nd ed. 1978), at p. 132. The Committee's unprecedented consultative reach in the Indian community revealed the degree to which the needs of Indians varied from region to region and according to socio-economic conditions which were often unique to particular communities. The final report in 1948 made a

series of recommendations "designed to make possible the gradual transition of Indians from wardship to citizenship and to help them to advance themselves": Canada, Special Joint Committee of the Senate and the House of Commons on the Indian Act, *Fourth Report*, June 22, 1948, at p. 187. The recommendations addressed electoral rights, increased funding to communities and the end of Indian-specific alcohol regulation, and revealed a new focus on accession to full citizenship and some form of greater self-government at the band level.

[54] Yet tension between the old ways and the new remained. ...

[55] The adoption of the revised *Indian Act* in 1951, and of the present s. 90(1)(*b*), was born of this tension. Indians were to be encouraged to manage their own affairs and enter into commercial arrangements for their own betterment and economic advantage. This was incompatible with exemption from seizure of virtually all property that could be traced to government gifts and funds. At the same time, it was felt that basic protection from exploitation by others in society was still required. This was consistent with maintaining protection for funds flowing from treaty obligations, as well as for property situated on reserves. ...

[56] The record does not reveal precisely why Parliament chose to define the exemption from seizure in what is now s. 90(1)(*b*) in terms of funds given under a "treaty" or "agreement". It is therefore not possible to say that the history of the provision dictates a particular approach. However, what can be said is that the use of these terms is consistent with the recognition in 1951 that Indians should be encouraged to take steps toward greater self-governance and participation in economic enterprise.

. . . . .

[66] To sum up, the record does not disclose precisely why Parliament chose to replace the pre-1951 categories of protected property with protection based on whether the property had been given pursuant to a "treaty" or "agreement" with the Crown. Nor does it disclose precisely why the word "treaty" was supplemented with "agreement". However, Parliament's documented desire to move away from a purely paternalistic approach and encourage Indian entrepreneurship and self-government is consistent with an intention to confine protection from seizure to benefits flowing from treaties. Exempting property broadly would be inconsistent with self-sufficiency because it would deprive Indian communities of a cornerstone of economic development: credit. Eliminating all protection would neglect the persistent concerns about exploitation. These documented and potentially conflicting policy considerations suggest that Parliament wanted to provide limited protection for treaty entitlements while not interfering with the ability of Indians to achieve great economic independence. This supports the restricted meaning of "agreement" in s. 90(1)(*b*) adopted by this Court in *Mitchell*.

. . . . .

5.2.8 Conclusion on the Meaning of "Agreement"

[69] Textual, historical and policy considerations all support the conclusion of this Court in *Mitchell* that the word "agreement" in s. 90(1)(*b*) of the *Indian Act* should not be construed broadly as extending to any agreement between the government and Indians that confers benefits, or any agreement between the government and Indians that confers "public sector services" benefits. Rather, it should be understood in the sense of an arrangement that fleshes out treaty obligations of the Crown.

[70] I note, for the sake of clarity, that modern land claims agreements (e.g., the Nisga'a Final Agreement (1999)) are protected under the *Mitchell* interpretation of "treaty or agreement". This conclusion flows logically from s. 35(3) of the *Constitution Act, 1982*, which provides that "'treaty rights' includes rights that exist by way of lands claims agreements or may be so acquired". This serves to mitigate, in some small measure, the exclusion of non-treaty Indians from s. 90 protection. Non-treaty Indians that are not currently protected under s. 90 may acquire protection in the future, if their band negotiates a land claims agreement with the federal government.

5.3 Is the CFA at Issue Protected by Section 90(1)(*b*) of the Indian Act?

[71] Is the CFA at issue here an "agreement" that expressly, or by necessary implication, gives effect to the Crown's treaty obligations? This question is complicated for two reasons.

[72] First, the fund created by the CFA is blended and is thus difficult to characterize for the purposes of applying s. 90(1)(*b*). It is a pool of money provided for several different purposes, reflecting the reach of the modern welfare state. It includes funds provided by the federal government in order to enhance the self-sufficiency and living standards of the band in a wide range of areas. If parts of the fund relate to treaty obligations, these have not been segregated by either the Crown or the band.

[73] The solution of the law where blended funds are concerned is usually to require the party claiming protection to segregate or trace the protected portion of the fund from unprotected portions. The same rationale applies to parties claiming protection under the *Indian Act*, but this brings us to the second complication in this case. The record in the case at bar does not permit us to delineate the extent of the Crown's treaty obligations to determine whether, and to what extent, some of the funds may flow directly from those obligations. At the Court of Queen's Bench, Sinclair J. made reference to the Crown's treaty obligation in respect of education, but he failed to engage in an analysis of the relationship, if any, between the treaty obligation and the pool of funds in question. Given his reasoning that s. 90(1)(*b*) provided broad protection, this determination was unnecessary. Under the proper interpretation of the provision set out above, however, it would be determinative of the issues before us.

[74] It is clear that any portion of the CFA funds that flows directly from treaty obligations is entitled to protection under s. 90(1)(*b*). The manner in which the Crown has decided to discharge its obligations under treaties does not alter the degree to which Parliament has decided to protect funds spent for that purpose. To put it another way, there is no magic in the label CFA. The *Indian Act* confers protection on property flowing from treaty obligations, and the onus is on the party claiming the protection to establish that the property it claims to be protected falls within that category. On the findings of the courts below, that burden was not discharged.

[75] Funds given pursuant to treaty obligations will be protected under s. 90(1)(*b*). The nature and extent of those obligations should be determined according to the interpretive principles that this Court has set out in the past, and with due regard to the particular historical context of the relationship between the Crown and the band in each case. The fact that the Crown provides funding for general public services, however, does not alter the fundamental treaty relationship that is the focus of these provisions. The underlying purpose of this statutory protection, as noted by La Forest J. in *Mitchell*, is not to improve socio-economic conditions but instead to protect the treaty property of Indians *qua* Indians. In all cases, the burden will be on the band to demonstrate that disputed funding is protected by virtue of its relationship to treaty obligations.

6. Conclusion

[76] The record before us does not permit us to make a determination about the precise relationship between the funds in question and the treaty obligations of the Crown. As it is the burden of the band to demonstrate this connection, we cannot find that s. 90(1)(*b*) operates in this case to protect the funds. Accordingly, the appeal is dismissed with costs.

---

1. At para. 24 Chief Justice McLachlin writes: "The question is one of statutory interpretation." Are there alternative ways to frame the issue under section 35?
2. How does the *McDiarmid* decision potentially bear on treaty promises? Justice La Forest wrote in *Mitchell v. Peguis* at paras. 118-19:

> I note at the outset that I do not take issue with the principle that treaties and statutes relating to Indians should be liberally construed and doubtful expressions resolved in favour of the Indians. ...

> But as I view the matter, somewhat different considerations must apply in the case of statutes relating to Indians. Whereas a treaty is the product of bargaining between two contracting parties, statutes relating to Indians are an expression of the will of Parliament. Given this fact, I do not find it particularly helpful to engage in speculation as to how Indians may be taken to understand a given provision. Rather, I think the approach must be to read the Act concerned with a view to elucidating what it was that Parliament wished to effect in enacting the particular

section in question. This approach is not a jettisoning of the liberal interpretative method. As already stated, it is clear that in the interpretation of any statutory enactment dealing with Indians, and particularly the *Indian Act*, it is appropriate to interpret in a broad manner provisions that are aimed at maintaining Indian rights, and to interpret narrowly provisions aimed at limiting or abrogating them. Thus if legislation bears on treaty promises, the courts will always strain against adopting an interpretation that has the effect of negating commitments undertaken by the Crown; see *United States v. Powers*, 305 U.S. 527 (1939), at p. 533.

3.   What incentives and disincentives are present in requiring Indians to meet the burden of showing that monies flowing to them by virtue of agreements are connected to treaties?
4.   In para. 38 Chief Justice McLachlin states that provincial credit regimes apply universally, and she appears to say that *Indian Act* provisions that offer exemptions would be specific exceptions to universal provincial law. Why are provincial regimes "universal", and Indian credit regimes the "exception"?
5.   What do you think about Chief Justice McLachlin's historical view of the 1951 amendments to the *Indian Act*?

E.   SALES TAX

Section 87 of the *Indian Act* has also produced litigation concerning the exemption of Indians from provincial sales tax.

UNION OF NEW BRUNSWICK INDIANS v. NEW BRUNSWICK (MINISTER OF FINANCE)

[1998] S.C.J. No. 50, [1998] 1 S.C.R. 1161 (S.C.C.)

The judgment of **Lamer C.J.C.** and **Cory, McLachlin, Iacobucci** and **Major JJ.** was delivered by **McLachlin J.**: —

I.   *Introduction*

[1] This case requires the Court to rule whether Indians living in New Brunswick were required to pay provincial sales tax on goods purchased off the reserve for consumption on the reserve.

. . . . .

IV.   *Analysis*

[6] This appeal requires us to decide whether s. 87 of the *Indian Act* applies to tax levied under the former New Brunswick *Social Services and Education Tax Act*. ...

A. The Application of Section 87 of the Indian Act

[7] Section 87(1) of the *Indian Act* exempts certain property of Indians from taxation. This includes "the personal property of an Indian or a band situated on a reserve": see s. 87(1)(*b*). Section 87(2) describes the types, or modalities, of taxation on the exempted property that are prohibited: taxation "in respect of the ownership, occupation, possession or use of" the property mentioned in s. 87(1).

[8] The purpose of the s. 87 exemption was to "preserve the entitlements of Indians to their reserve lands and to ensure that the use of their property on their reserve lands was not eroded by the ability of governments to tax, or creditors to seize". It "was not to confer a general economic benefit upon the Indians": see *Williams, supra*, at p. 885.

[9] In the past, s. 87(1)(*b*) has been confined to property physically situated on a reserve or property whose "paramount location" is on a reserve. [citations omitted]

[15] These authorities suggest that s. 87 applies only to property physically located on a reserve at the time of taxation or property whose paramount location is on a reserve at the time of taxation. This comports with the purpose of s. 87 to protect the property of Indians on reserves and prevent that property from being eroded: see *Williams, supra*. In determining the applicability of s. 87, one must consider whether the property is located or has its paramount location on a reserve at the time and place that the tax would otherwise attach. In the context of retail sales taxes, this can be called the "point of sale" test.

[16] The remaining question, therefore, is whether the sales tax here at issue is levied on property while it is situated, or has its paramount location on a reserve. The property described in the stated case consists of items for personal use and consumption like clothing and toiletries, purchased by Indians off the reserve for use on the reserve. The *Social Services and Education Tax Act* levies the tax on these items at the time of the off-reserve sale. At the point of sale, the property is not, and has never been located on a reserve. This, without more, suggests that the tax is not levied on goods situated on a reserve or whose paramount location is on a reserve. This would accord with the general view expressed by Richard H. Bartlett, *Indians and Taxation in Canada* (3rd ed. 1992), at p. 92:

> The reasoning employed by the Supreme Court of Canada [in *Francis*] appears applicable to the imposition of sales tax at the point of sale off a reserve. In the vast majority of sales transactions involving Indian purchases in Canada the sales take place off the reserve, and according to *Francis* are not subject to the exemption conferred by section 87.

[17] This, however, does not conclude the matter. The respondents raise a number of arguments in support of their position that s. 87 applies to the tax at issue in this case: (1) that the tax is not a sales tax but a consumption tax collected at the time of purchase but levied in respect of the on-reserve consumption of personal property by Indians; (2) that property purchased for use on-reserve has its paramount location on a reserve; and (3) that s. 87 must be applied to off-reserve purchases by Indians in New

Brunswick in order to fulfill its purpose. I will address each of these arguments in turn. ... [The Court's discussion and rejection of the consumption tax argument omitted: they find the tax is a sales tax.]

C. *The "Paramount Location" Argument*

[33] The respondents submit that tangible personal property which is intended to be consumed primarily on the reserve is "situated on a reserve" for the purposes of s. 87. In doing so, they seek to extend the "paramount location" doctrine to property which has never been on a reserve.

. . . . .

[35] The concept of "paramount location" finds no application to sales taxes on tangible goods. Sales taxes attach at the moment of sale. At this point, the property has but one location — the place of sale. It cannot have its paramount location elsewhere because no pattern of use and safekeeping elsewhere is established. The location of property after the sale and the imposition of tax is irrelevant. This means that goods purchased off-reserve attract tax, while goods purchased on-reserve are exempt, regardless of where the purchaser may intend to use them. To make taxation dependent on place of anticipated use of the article purchased would render the administration of the tax uncertain and unworkable. As Macfarlane J.A. put it in *Danes, supra*, at p. 259:

> An exemption must apply at the moment of purchase. To do so it must be certain. It must not depend upon the consideration of factors such as the extent to which the property may be used on or off the reserve.

[36] In these circumstances, where the location of the property at the time of taxation is readily apparent, there is simply no need to apply the "paramount location" test and I conclude that it does not assist the respondents.

D. *The "Purpose of Section 87" Argument*

[37] The respondents argue that s. 87 is intended to protect Indians from taxation in respect of their use of property on-reserve. Where Indians are obliged to purchase most of their goods off-reserve, as most are in New Brunswick, this protection is eroded. Therefore, they submit that s. 87 should be read as applying to sales tax levied off-reserve on goods purchased by Indians for use on the reserve. This was the view of the majority of the New Brunswick Court of Appeal.

[38] The first difficulty with this argument is that it takes the purpose of s. 87 far beyond that articulated by this Court in *Williams* — to prevent Indian property on Indian reserves from being eroded by taxation or claimed by creditors. No support has been offered for the proposed extension, except that this would economically benefit Indians. But that, this Court has stated, is not the purpose of s. 87: see *Mitchell*; *Williams*. ...

[39] The second difficulty with this argument is that it flies in the face of the wording of s. 87(1)(*b*), which confines the protection from taxation to property situated on a reserve. The respondents attempt to overcome this difficulty by relying on s. 87(2) which provides that "[n]o Indian or band is subject to taxation in respect of the ownership, occupation, possession or use of any property mentioned in paragraph (1)(*a*) or (*b*) or is otherwise subject to taxation in respect of any such property." But this section does not extend the ambit of s. 87(1)(*a*) and (*b*). Section 87(1) states what property is protected from taxation. Section 87(2) states that tax cannot be levied in respect of the ownership, occupation, possession or use of this property. It does not enlarge the class of property subject to the exemption, but merely states the types of tax that are prohibited on a particular type of property. It does not change the rule that for property to be exempt from taxation under s. 87, it must be situated on a reserve. Courts have consistently held that s. 87(1)(*b*) is confined to property physically situated on a reserve or whose paramount location is on a reserve: see *Francis, Mitchell, Williams, Lewis* and *Leighton, supra.*

[40] A third difficulty with this argument is that the history of s. 87 belies the conclusion that Parliament intended it to provide general tax protection for off-reserve property. The tax exemption began in 1850 as a prohibition against taxes on Indians residing on Indian lands. It was amended in 1876 to prevent taxes on Indian property unless it was held outside the reserve. It now prohibits taxation in respect of Indian property that is situated on the reserve: see Bartlett, *supra.* Over the years Parliament has explicitly limited and narrowed the scope of what is now s. 87 to protect from taxation only property that is situated on the reserve.

[41] A fourth difficulty with this argument is that it rests on the assumption that providing a tax exemption to Indians for property purchased off-reserve will benefit Indians uniformly. The argument is that Parliament must have intended the tax to apply to off-reserve purchases because this is required to protect and enhance the position of Indians. Yet it is far from clear that Indians across Canada would benefit from such an interpretation.

[42] Confining s. 87 to property situated on a reserve and excluding off-reserve sales taxes will have varying effects. It is said that in New Brunswick the effects are negative. There are very few retail establishments on New Brunswick reserves where 65-75 percent of status Indians live. Delivery of goods to reserves may partially offset the problem; the trial judge, Savoie J., found that delivery of goods and services to Indians resident on reserves in New Brunswick was available from many of the retail establishments close to reserves. However, delivery may involve additional charges equivalent to a sales tax and, in any event, will not be available in many situations. The reality is that, at present, New Brunswick Indians are unable to live on their reserves without paying a certain amount of provincial sales tax.

[43] At the same time, adopting the "paramount location" test would have adverse consequences for Indians who live off the reserve. They would presumably have to pay tax on purchases made on and off the reserve

because the "paramount location" of the goods would be off-reserve. Indians who lived, and thus consumed their property, off the reserve would always be subject to taxation, while those living on the reserve would be effectively immune. In contrast, the "point of sale" test allows Indians living off-reserve to purchase goods tax-free on reserves regardless of where the goods are ultimately used.

[44] In addition, the "point of sale" test is beneficial to on-reserve Indians in many parts of Canada. First, it provides an incentive for Indians to establish their own retail outlets on reserves and gives a competitive edge to reserve businesses, thereby increasing economic activity and employment. Although the exemption may not yet have been a catalyst in New Brunswick, where until recently off-reserve sales were exempt from tax, it has fostered aboriginal economic development elsewhere. For example, the intervener, the Attorney General of Manitoba, asserted that almost all Manitoba reserves contain some retail businesses. The fact that the exemption is closely tied to the reserve enhances reserve-linked benefits, promotes privatization of reservation economies and encourages an entrepreneurial spirit: see Robert A. Reiter, in *Tax Manual for Canadian Indians* (1990), at p. 1.1.

[45] Second, the "point of sale" approach to the tax exemption permits reserves to impose their own taxes on reserve sales, thus creating a tax base for aboriginal governments: see Peter W. Hogg and Mary Ellen Turpel, "Implementing Aboriginal Self-Government: Constitutional and Jurisdictional Issues" (1995), 74 Can. Bar Rev. 187, at pp. 207 *et seq.* For example, in the *Budget Implementation Act, 1997*, S.C. 1997, c. 26, Parliament granted the Cowichan tribes the authority to impose a direct tax on the on-reserve purchase of tobacco by status Indians. This legislation enabled the Cowichan Tribes to fill the tax void created by s. 87 and raise revenue for the community. If s. 87 is interpreted to provide an exemption for all off-reserve purchases of tobacco destined for use on the reserve, the purpose of this amendment would be frustrated.

[46] These considerations belie the conclusion that s. 87, by its object and purpose, must be read as intending to exempt Indians from all sales taxes, whether on or off a reserve, on property used on reserves. I conclude that the argument that s. 87 must, in keeping with its objects, be read expansively to apply to off-reserve sales cannot succeed.

V. *Conclusion*

[47] I would allow the appeal and set aside the order of the New Brunswick Court of Appeal. I make no comment regarding the validity of the new Harmonized Sales Tax that replaced the tax here at issue.

[48] The following constitutional question was stated:

Question: If as a matter of statutory interpretation, the *Social Services and Education Tax Act*, R.S.N.B. 1973, c. S-10, imposes a tax in respect of tangible personal property purchased at a location off reserve which is destined for use entirely or primarily by an Indian or an Indian band on a reserve, and further, if as a matter of statutory interpretation, s. 87 of the

Indian Act prohibits such taxation, is the *Social Services and Education Tax Act* rendered inoperative to the extent of its inconsistency with s. 87 of the *Indian Act*?

Answer: Section 87 of the *Indian Act* does not prohibit taxation in respect of tangible personal property purchased at a location off reserve which is destined for use entirely or primarily by an Indian or an Indian band on a reserve. As such, the *Social Services and Education Tax Act* is not inconsistent with s. 87 of the *Indian Act* and is not rendered inoperative.

Justice La Forest in *Mitchell v. Peguis Indian Band*, [1990] S.C.J. No. 63, [1990] 2 S.C.R. 85, 71 D.L.R. (4th) 193 (S.C.C.) suggested that "when Indians deal in the general marketplace, the protections conferred by these sections [sections 87-89 of the *Indian Act*] have the potential to become powerful impediments to their engaging successfully in commercial matters" (at p. 146). This characterization, while accurate in one respect, does not capture the potential benefits these sections may hold for economic development more generally. The widely acclaimed *Report of the Royal Commission on Taxation*, 1966 suggested that "the existing tax system and recommendations for its improvement must be predicated on a widely accepted set of goals or objectives that the nation is seeking, and on a knowledge of the potential role that a tax system can play in the achievement of these goals". As a result, this Royal Commission posited four "fundamental objectives" on which it found wide agreement for the Canadian system of taxation:

1.	To maximize the current and future output of goods and services desired by Canadians.
2.	To ensure that this flow of goods and services is distributed equitably among individuals or groups.
3.	To protect the liberties and rights of individuals through the preservation of representative, responsible government and the maintenance of the rule of law.
4.	To maintain and strengthen the Canadian federation.

When Indian exemptions from taxation are judged by these standards (which are the standards for judging the entire tax system), there may be a greater role to consider for Indians aggressively employing their exemptions to secure benefits, even in the commercial mainstream. There is significant potential for these exemptions to: maximize output, ensure equitable flows of resources, protect the rule of law as embodied in Aboriginal rights, and strengthen the Canadian federation. Yet, despite the application of these standards more generally in the Canadian public, there is little sympathy for Indians "marketing their tax exemptions". While federal, provincial and municipal governments are able to manipulate their tax structures to secure economic development, in some sectors there is outrage when Indians attempt to follow the same logic. For example, while many (though not all) praise Alberta's or New Brunswick's use of tax incentives and exemptions to create development in these provinces, there are great cries of unfairness if Indians attempt to use their tax status to follow this same course. If one understands the history and contemporary economic realities of economic development among Aboriginal people, the application of this double standard can be troubling. It may be helpful at this point to inject some economic and empirical considerations relating to Indian taxation.

ANDRE LeDRESSAY, "A BRIEF TAX (ON A ME) OF FIRST NATIONS TAXATION AND ECONOMIC DEVELOPMENT" IN SHARING THE HARVEST: THE ROAD TO SELF RELIANCE, REPORT OF THE NATIONAL ROUND TABLE ON ABORIGINAL ECONOMIC DEVELOPMENT AND RESOURCES

(Ottawa: Ministry of Supply and Services, 1993) 215 at 218-20

87 and Economic Development — The Good, The Bad and The Uncertain

The section 87 taxation exemption employed to its potential can be an effective tool in successful First Nations economic development. It is unfortunately a double-edged sword, clearing a potential path to economic development with one edge, and creating confusion, tension, and red tape with the other. This section briefly reviews the role of the partial exemption in economic development.

The Good

The partial exemption offers several advantages to on-reserve First Nation businesses including the following:

- Exemption from GST, provincial retail sales taxes, and tobacco and fuel taxes means on-reserve First Nation businesses have a significant pricing advantage for their "status" customers. Assuming profit margins are high enough, and competition remains slim or nonexistent, this comparative pricing advantage could in theory be partially passed along to the larger non-status market in some First Nations.
- The income tax exemption for status employees could entail lower labour costs for on-reserve First Nation businesses and a subsequent comparative pricing advantage. This, though, is not a costless advantage, as discussed below.
- On-reserve corporations can distribute the business income to tax-exempt First Nation governments or individuals as a deductible fee, or possibly through dividends, thereby eliminating all its taxable income. This would provide such businesses with a comparative advantage since the opportunity cost (true cost) of doing business is lower.

- If First Nations governments can be considered municipalities and they control over 90 per cent of a corporation, then an exemption can be applied for under 149(l)(*d*) of the *Income Tax Act*. The situs of the income is irrelevant for this exemption (Merry, 1993, p. 17).
- First Nation partnership taxation exemptions will depend on the connecting factors of the business income. When the First Nation partner is tax exempt, this particular business structure may act as an investment incentive since some of the taxable income can be allocated to the tax-exempt partner. This, however, does not apply to joint ventures.
- Band-operated businesses are tax-exempt if the source of income is situated on-reserve or if it uses the *Income Tax Act* municipality provisions alluded to above. It should be cautioned that as an unincorporated entity, the band may unintentionally expose its off-reserve assets to its creditors.

The Bad and The Uncertain

The section 87 exemption, however, is not always advantageous to successful First Nation business and economic development. In fact at least one First Nation business person has suggested that its handicaps almost outweigh its advantages, and may explain its apparent under-use on First Nation land. "Another band of not inconsiderable wealth indicated that on a scale of 1 to 10, the tax exemption didn't even register." (Brown and Strother, 1991, p. 120) Below are listed a few reasons why this may be the case:

- Many non-First Nation businesses believe that First Nation businesses are unfairly advantaged because of the partial taxation exemption. The media often perpetuate the myth that members of First Nations do not pay tax. This may discourage potential First Nation business persons who feel unwilling to wage a political battle just for developing a business.
- The situs provisions in the partial taxation exemption discourage off-reserve business development and expansion to larger markets.
- Use of the income tax exemption for First Nation employees often creates tension when these employees compare their before-tax income with non-First Nation workers doing similar work.
- The bureaucratic requirements of GST and provincial sales tax refunds from tax-exempt sales for on-reserve First Nation businesses (especially gas stations) can seriously affect these businesses' cash flow. Although the customer avoids sales tax at the time of purchase, the retailer may have to wait up to three months to be reimbursed for the tax exemption. For smaller businesses, obtaining these refunds often consumes a disproportionate amount of administrative time.
- There would appear to be a significant communication barrier between the methods for exploiting the section 87 taxation exemption and its effective economic application in First Nation communities. Interpretive difficulties such as the nature of an individual's property and the location of its acquisition complicate section 87. Beyond this

the use of indecipherable legalese, economese, and bureaucratese seldom translates into First Nation community-based economic development action. The uncertainty surrounding the Williams case only exacerbates these problems.

Although it is undoubtedly true that the section 87 partial exemption provides a comparative advantage to First Nation business development, the case study statistical evidence presented in the next section clearly reveals its under-use. ...

Bungee Economics — A Case Study of a First Nations Economy

In order to understand the potential role between taxation and economic development for First Nations, it is crucial to comprehend the workings of a typical First Nations economy. To coin a phrase, most (if not all) First Nation economies are victims of "bungee economics." Money goes in and bounces right back out to the surrounding non-First Nation economy.

. . . . .

Many First Nation leaders object to discussions on taxation because it may ultimately result in the removal of the section 87 tax exemption, and ultimately lead to the direct taxing of First Nation community members. It should be painfully obvious in the indicators above that even if First Nations did tax their own people, there is nothing to tax. ...

The Department of Finance conducted taxation case studies in six First Nation communities in Canada. The study concluded in support of the evidence above; only a small portion of First Nation households would pay tax if the current Canadian taxation system were applied to them. Most First Nation community members would receive tax rebates if they filed a tax return.

Finally, it is important to consider the small number of people who might realistically take advantage of the sales tax exemptions under s. 87 of the *Indian Act*, and the relatively small amount of the "lost" revenue that such exemptions represent for the Department of Finance. See Daniel Wilson, "Checking the Right Wing's Math on First Nations Tax Exemptions":

> The 2006 census identified fewer than 700,000 people who have a North American Indian identity. This number includes about 133,000 who are non-status Indians and slightly more than 565,000 status Indians who might be exempted from paying income tax, if they earned income on-reserve. Bearing in mind that half of Aboriginal people are under 20, more than 40 per cent of status Indians live off-reserve, and Aboriginal people have an unemployment rate more than twice the national average, it is not surprising that the number of people exempted from paying taxes is actually quite small. In fact, the most recent figures tell us that the number of First

Nations citizens living on reserves who had employment or self-employment income was only 103,885.

Unfortunately, Statistics Canada has not made average income numbers for on-reserve employment freely available — which would have allowed for a more precise calculation — but we do know that the median income is $13,637. This allows us to estimate the total employment and self-employment income earned on-reserve as somewhere in the neighbourhood of $1.4 billion.

So what is the total of tax revenues lost to Canada as a result of the exemption?

The federal income tax rate for those earning less than $41,544 is 15 percent. Provincial tax rates vary, but adding them into the calculation puts the tax rate somewhere between 20 and 25 percent across the country. The basic personal deduction is $10,382, which would leave just over $4,000 in taxable income from the median, even with no other deductions. On that amount, one would owe between $800 and $1,000. Multiplying that back out against the 103,885 earners, the exemption amounts to between $84 million and $104 million in foregone revenues.

If all of those earning income on-reserve actually qualify for the exemption, the Receiver General is collecting approximately $100 million less in taxes as a result.

It is possible to quibble with the figures here. I have used the most recent census figures from 2006 with the 2010 tax rates and using the median income level rather than the average leads to a lower total. Nonetheless, even the highest mark-ups on all of this data wouldn't put the lost revenue higher than $120 million.

That number is nothing to sneeze at, of course. But in the context of a 2010 budget of more than $261 billion, it's also not going to make or break the federal government. Nor does it seem disproportional or unfair, when looked at in context. By way of comparison, there are $1.4 billion in annual subsidies for oil and gas companies, equivalent to the total income earned on-reserve, and $120 million in subsidies for ethanol production, equivalent to the highest estimation of revenues lost to the Canadian government through the income tax exemption.

More to the point, the tax exemption in no way compensates for shortfalls in funding to First Nations. The provinces spend more than 20 percent more on children than the federal government does on First Nations children, whether those kids are in school or under child welfare services care. The disadvantage to First Nations children from these two policies alone amounts to far more than the foregone tax revenues, and there are dozens of other examples.

Taxes pay for public services like roads and water, and First Nations communities are notoriously under-serviced. A 2005 study by the Assembly of First Nations found that, per capita federal funding for First Nations citizens is $7,200. That's far lower than the amount that the government spends on the population in general. In Ottawa, for instance, the combined per capita spending by all three levels of government totalled $14,900, more than double the amount being spent on-reserve.

Given the amount of energy certain groups have spent decrying this tax exemption, one might have expected them to conduct an analysis of this nature. The fact that they haven't might suggest that there is another agenda at work in their complaints.[5]

F. INVESTMENT INCOME

Investment income earned by First Nations has often been treated in a manner similar to personal income. The connecting factors test in *Williams v. Canada*, [1992] S.C.J. No. 36, [1992] 1 S.C.R. 877 (S.C.C.) gives a great deal of discretion to judges in determining whether income falls within s. 87's exemption.

In *Recalma v. Canada*, [1998] F.C.J. No 433 (Fed. C.A.), leave to appeal refused [1998] S.C.C.A. No. 250, [1998] 2 C.T.C. 403 (S.C.C.), the Federal Court of Appeal held that a status Indian's investment income in a branch of the Bank of Montreal at the Park Royal Mall on the Squamish Indian Reserve was not exempt from taxation. It reasoned that Recalma's investment income was not situated on a reserve because the funds were not sufficiently connected to the reserve when applying the *Williams* test. The Court held that funds were invested across Canada and the world in "corporations in cities far removed from any reserve" (para. 11). To receive an exemption the Court said such property had to be held Indian *qua* Indian, in a way that was "'intimately connected' to the Reserve, that is an integral part of reserve life" (para. 9). While the capital on the investments was earned through Indian commercial fishing, the Court did not see the investment of such income as being connected to a traditional way of life.

The reasoning in the *Recalma* case was followed in subsequent cases: *Lewin v. Canada*, [2001] T.C.J. No. 242, [2001] 2 C.T.C. 2560 (T.C.C.), upheld [2002] F.C.J. No. 1625, 2002 FCA 461 (Fed. C.A.); *Sero v. Canada*, [2004] 2 C.N.L.R. 333 (Fed. C.A.); and *Large v. Canada*, [2006] T.C.J. No. 398, [2007] 1 C.N.L.R. 178 (T.C.C.). These cases deal with the issue of whether interest paid in respect of an Indian's account at a branch of a financial institution on-reserve is exempt from tax. The cases were also subject to significant criticism; see Donald K. Biberdorf, "Aboriginal Income and the Economic Mainstream" in *Report of Proceedings of the Forty-Ninth Tax Conference*, 1997 Conference Report (Toronto: Canadian Tax Foundation, 1998) at 25:1; Murray Marshall, "Business and Investment Income and Section 87 of the *Indian Act*: *Recalma v. Canada*" (1998) 77 Can. Bar Rev. 528; Bill Maclagan, "Section 87 of the Indian Act: Recent Developments in the Taxation of Investment Income" (2000) 48 Can. Tax J. 1503; Thomas E. McDonnell, "Taxation of an Indian's Investment Income" (2001) 49 Can. Tax J. 954; Martha O'Brien, "Income Tax, Investment Income and the Indian Act: Getting Back on Track" (2002) 50 Can. Tax J. 1570; Constance MacIntosh, "From Judging Culture to Taxing 'Indians': Tracing the Legal Discourse of the 'Indian Mode of Life'" (2009) 47 Osgoode Hall L.J. 399.

In the following case, the Supreme Court appears to accept some of this criticism and reject much of the analysis underlying the *Recalma* case.

BASTIEN ESTATE v. CANADA

[2011] S.C.J. No. 38, 2011 SCC 38 (S.C.C.)

The judgment of **McLachlin C.J.C.** and **Binnie, Fish, Charron** and **Cromwell JJ.** was delivered by **Cromwell J.**: —

. . . . .

[5] The late Rolland Bastien was a status Indian and belonged to the Huron-Wendat Nation. He was born and died on the Wendake Reserve near Quebec City. His wife and children who succeed him are also Huron and live on the reserve. From 1970 until 1997 when he sold the business to his children, Mr. Bastien operated a moccasin manufacturing business on the Wendake Reserve: Les Industries Bastien enr. He invested some of the income from the operation and sale of his business in term deposits with two caisses populaires situated on Indian reserves, the Caisse populaire Desjardins du Village Huron (the "Caisse") situated on the Wendake Reserve and the Caisse populaire Desjardins de Pointe-Bleue situated on the Mashteuiatsh Reserve. Only the income from the investments with the Caisse on the Wendake Reserve is in issue on this appeal. The Caisse has since its founding in 1965 had its head office, its only place of business and its sole fixed asset on the reserve. ...

[6] In 2001, Mr. Bastien held certificates of deposit at the Caisse and these investments paid interest that was deposited in a transaction savings account at the Caisse. Mr. Bastien considered this income to be property exempt from taxation. However, in 2003, the Minister of National Revenue made an assessment in which he added the investment income to Mr. Bastien's income for the 2001 taxation year. The Minister confirmed the assessment and Mr. Bastien's estate appealed unsuccessfully to the Tax Court and the Federal Court of Appeal.

. . . . .

[10] There is only one question before the Court: Was Mr. Bastien's interest income earned on the term deposits with the Caisse populaire Desjardins du Village Huron exempt from income taxation because it was personal property situated on a reserve?

. . . . .

1. *The Statutory Language*

[14] The exemption from taxation (s. 87(1)(*b*)) applies to "the personal property of an Indian or a band situated on a reserve". ...

[15] The phrase "on a reserve" refers throughout the Act to the property being within the boundaries of the reserve. However, different legal tests are used to determine whether various types of property are so situated for the particular purposes. For example, an issue in the *God's Lake* case was whether a bank account in an off-reserve bank was exempt from seizure. The Court looked for guidance to the traditional common law rules and the terms of the *Trust and Loan Companies Act*, S.C. 1991,

c. 45. These made it clear that the account was located at the branch which was off the reserve: para. 13. However, where the question concerns the location of non-physical property generated by a transaction, such as the payment of benefits, for taxation purposes, a more fact-specific analysis is used which weighs factors potentially relevant to identifying the location of the transaction. An important point, however, is that regardless of the type of property or the difficulty of ascribing to it a location, the objective must always be to implement the statutory language, and that requires keeping the focus on whether the property is situated on a reserve.

2. *Determining the Location of Income*

[16] Where, because of its nature or the type of exemption in question, the location of property is not objectively easy to determine, courts must apply the connecting factors approach set out in *Williams v. Canada*, [1992] 1 S.C.R. 877, in order to attribute a location to the property. While this search for location may seem at times to be more the stuff of metaphysics than of law, the attribution of location is what the *Indian Act* provisions require. The difficulty of doing so means that it is not generally possible to apply a simple, standard test to determine the location of intangible property. Gonthier J. recognized this in *Williams*, at p. 891 …

[17] As the location of such property will always be notional, there is a risk that attributing a location to it will be arbitrary. …

[18] To address this challenge, Gonthier J. in *Williams* set out a two-step test. At the first step, the court identifies potentially relevant factors connecting the intangible personal property to a location. "A connecting factor is only relevant", wrote Gonthier J., "in so much as it identifies the location of the property in question for the purposes of the *Indian Act*" (p. 892). Thus, even in this somewhat metaphysical sphere, the focus is clearly on ascribing a physical location to the property in question. Connecting factors mentioned in *Williams* include things such as the residence of the payor and the payee, the place of payment and where the employment giving rise to qualification for the benefit was performed: *Williams*, at p. 893. As Gonthier J. noted, potentially relevant connecting factors have different relevance depending on the categories of property and the types of taxation in issue. So, for example, "connecting factors may have different relevance with regard to unemployment insurance benefits than in respect of employment income, or pension benefits" (p. 892). To take this into account, as well as to ensure that the analysis serves to identify the location of the property for the purposes of the *Indian Act*, at the second step, the court analyses these factors purposively in order to assess what weight should be given to them. This analysis considers the purpose of the exemption under the *Indian Act*; the type of property in question; and the nature of the taxation of that property (p. 892).

[19] *Williams* thus establishes a clearly structured analysis, but one that turns on careful consideration of the particular circumstances of each case assessed against the purpose of the exemption. As Gonthier J. noted at p. 893, the *Williams* approach "preserves the flexibility of the case by case

approach, but within a framework which requires the court to assess the weight which is to be placed on the various connecting factors". The *Williams* approach applies here because we are dealing with the location of a transaction — the payment of interest pursuant to a contract — for the purposes of taxation.

[20] In this case and others, the Tax Court and the Federal Court of Appeal have developed and applied jurisprudence which adapts the *Williams* analysis to the taxation of interest and other investment income. As this is the first case in this Court since *Williams* to address this issue, it is timely to restate and consolidate the analysis that should be undertaken in applying the s. 87 exemption to interest income. I will therefore review the analysis required by *Williams* in more detail, focusing in turn on the purpose of the exemption, the type of property, the nature of the taxation of that property and the potentially relevant connecting factors.

(i) The Purpose of the Exemption

[21] In *Mitchell v. Peguis Indian Band*, [1990] 2 S.C.R. 85, La Forest J. discussed the purpose of both the tax exemption and the immunity from seizure in the *Indian Act*. With respect to the exemption from taxation, he observed that it serves to "guard against the possibility that one branch of government, through the imposition of taxes, could erode the full measure of the benefits given by that branch of government entrusted with the supervision of Indian affairs" (p. 130). ...

. . . . .

[23] The Court returned to the purpose of the exemptions in *Williams*. Gonthier J. confirmed that the purpose of the exemptions "was to preserve the entitlements of Indians to their reserve lands and to ensure that the use of their property on their reserve lands was not eroded by the ability of governments to tax, or creditors to seize" (p. 885). Echoing the limitation described by La Forest J. in *Mitchell*, Gonthier J. added that "the purpose of the sections was not to confer a general economic benefit upon the Indians" (at p. 885) and that "[w]hether the Indian wishes to remain within the protected reserve system or integrate more fully into the larger commercial world is a choice left to the Indian" (p. 887). In light of this, Gonthier J. held that the purpose of the requirement in s. 87 that the property be "situated on a reserve" is to "determine whether the Indian holds the property in question as part of the entitlement of an Indian *qua* Indian on the reserve" (p. 887). In both *Union of New Brunswick Indians* and *God's Lake*, the Court confirmed that the purpose of the exemptions was as set out in *Mitchell* and *Williams*.

[24] It will be useful to make two additional points.

[25] The first is that a purposive approach to the application of the exemption provisions must be rooted in the statutory text and does not give the court "license to ignore the words of the Act ... or otherwise

[circumvent] the intention of the legislature" which that text expresses: *University of British Columbia v. Berg*, [1993] 2 S.C.R. 353, at p. 371. ...

[26] The second and related point concerns the expression "Indian *qua* Indian". In both *Mitchell* and *Williams*, the Court referred to the purpose of the exemption as protecting property which Indians hold *qua* Indians: *Mitchell*, at p. 131; *Williams*, at p. 887. In some of the subsequent jurisprudence, this has been taken as a basis for importing into the s. 87 analysis the question of whether the income in question benefits the traditional Native way of life. For example, in *Canada v. Folster*, [1997] 3 F.C. 269, the Federal Court of Appeal attributed the significance of this factor to La Forest J. in *Mitchell*, observing that he had "characterized the purpose of the tax exemption provision as, in essence, an effort to preserve the traditional way of life in Indian communities by protecting property held by Indians *qua* Indians on a reserve" (para. 14). In *Recalma*, the Federal Court of Appeal identified as a relevant consideration the question of whether the investment income benefits the traditional Native way of life (para. 11). This factor has been relied on in cases in the Tax Court and the Federal Court of Appeal since *Recalma*: see, e.g., *Lewin v. Canada*, 2001 D.T.C. 479, at paras. 36 and 63–64.

[27] The reference to rights of an "Indian *qua* Indian" in *Mitchell*, which was repeated in *Williams*, and the linking of the tax exemption to the traditional way of life have been criticized: C. MacIntosh, "From Judging Culture to Taxing 'Indians': Tracing the Legal Discourse of the 'Indian Mode of Life'" (2009), 47 *Osgoode Hall L.J.* 399, at p. 425. ...The exemption provisions must be read in light of their purpose, but not, as Professor MacIntosh puts it, be "let loose from the moorings of their express language" (p. 425). A purposive interpretation goes too far if it substitutes for the inquiry into the location of the property mandated by the statute an assessment of what does or does not constitute an "Indian" way of life on a reserve. I do not read *Mitchell* or *Williams* as mandating that approach.

[28] In my respectful view, *Recalma* and some of the cases following it have gone too far in this direction. The exemption was rooted in the promises made to Indians that they would not be interfered with in their mode of life: see, e.g., R. H. Bartlett, "The Indian Act of Canada" (1977-1978), 27 *Buff. L. Rev.* 581, at pp. 612-13; *Mitchell*, at pp. 135–36. However, a purposive interpretation of the exemption does not require that the evolution of that way of life should be impeded. Rather, the comments in both *Mitchell* and *Williams* in relation to the protection of property which Indians hold *qua* Indians should be read in relation to the need to establish a connection between the property and the reserve such that it may be said that the property is situated there for the purposes of the *Indian Act*. While the relationship between the property and life on the reserve may in some cases be a factor tending to strengthen or weaken the connection between the property and the reserve, the availability of the exemption does not depend on whether the property is integral to the life of the reserve or to the preservation of the traditional Indian way of life. See M. O'Brien, "Income Tax, Investment Income, and the Indian Act: Getting Back on Track" (2002), 50 *Can. Tax J.* 1570, at pp. 1576 and 1588; B. Maclagan,

"Section 87 of the Indian Act: Recent Developments in the Taxation of Investment Income" (2000), 48 *Can. Tax J.* 1503, at p. 1515; M. Marshall, "Business and Investment Income under Section 87 of the *Indian Act*: *Recalma* v. *Canada*" (1998), 77 *Can. Bar Rev.* 528, at pp. 536-39; T. E. McDonnell, "Taxation of an Indian's Investment Income" (2001), 49 *Can. Tax J.* 954, at pp. 957-58.

[29] Sharlow J.A. in *Sero* acknowledged that this aspect of *Recalma* may be open to criticism, adding that:

> [I]t is not clear to me whether, in determining the *situs* of investment income for purposes of section 87 of the *Indian Act*, it is relevant to consider the extent to which investment income benefits the "traditional Native way of life". This seems to me a difficult test to apply, since it is at least arguable that the "traditional Native way of life" has little or nothing to do with reserves. [para. 25]

[30] I agree with these comments. Section 87 protects the personal property of Indians which is situated on a reserve from taxation. In determining the location of personal property for the purpose of s. 87, there is no requirement that the personal property be integral to the life of the reserve, or that it, in order to be exempted from taxation, must benefit what the court takes to be the traditional Indian way of life.

(ii) The Type of Property

[31] This factor examines the nature of the property in question. The property in issue here is investment income derived from term deposits. As noted, the parties agree that Mr. Bastien's investment income is "personal property" ("*biens meubles*") within the meaning of the s. 87 exemption. However, for the purposes of considering what weight to ascribe to various potentially relevant connecting factors, the nature of the term deposits needs to be considered in more detail.

[32] A term deposit is a basic investment vehicle evidenced by a certificate of deposit. Generally, the investor lends money to a financial institution on condition that he or she can only withdraw the money after the term has ended or forego some or all of the interest if the funds are withdrawn before the end of the term. In return, the financial institution pays a predetermined rate of interest to the investor. Term deposits are similar to savings accounts in that the investor, like the account holder, is a creditor of the financial institution. The investor, as the holder of a certificate of deposit, is not a participant in the equity markets but rather is simply entitled to be paid the agreed-upon rate of interest over the agreed-upon period of time in addition to having the capital returned at the end of that period. ...

[33] The term deposits in issue here were "deposits of money" within the meaning of the Quebec *Deposit Insurance Act*, R.S.Q., c. A-26, and the *Regulation respecting the application of the Deposit Insurance Act*, (1993) 125 G.O.Q. II, 3333, r. 1. However, the Regulation excludes from the definition of "deposit of money" funds used to acquire shares in the capital stock of a savings and credit union or shares of a mutual fund (s. 1). This exclusion

underlines the point that the holder of the certificate is not participating in the equity markets.

[34] To sum up, this investment income is, for the purposes of s. 87 of the *Indian Act*, personal property. ...

. . . . .

(iv) Connecting Factors

[38] *Williams* requires the court to identify the connecting factors for the type of property in question: p. 892. Gonthier J. identified several potentially relevant connecting factors including: "[1] the residence of the debtor, [2] the residence of the person receiving the benefits, [3] the place the benefits are paid, and [4] the location of the employment income which gave rise to the qualification for benefits": p. 893. While it is instructive to review the various connecting factors considered in that case, one must bear in mind that the factors relevant to the receipt of unemployment insurance benefits which were in issue there are not necessarily those relevant to receipt of interest income. The type of property is important in identifying the relevant connecting factors.

. . . . .

[42] These cases [*Williams, Nowegijick, Union of New Brunswick Indians*] underline the point that general legal rules about the location of property are relevant for the purposes of the *Indian Act*. Thus, provisions and jurisprudence relating to the location of income may prove helpful in deciding whether income is located on a reserve: see O'Brien, at pp. 1589-91. While these rules cannot be imported from one context into another without due consideration, they ought to be considered and given appropriate weight in light of the purpose of the exemption, the type of property and the nature of the taxation in issue.

(v) Applying the *Williams* Analysis to Mr. Bastien's Interest Income

[43] In my view, the connecting factors identified in *Williams* are potentially relevant here. When they are considered and weighed in light of the purpose of the exemption, the type of property and the nature of the taxation of that property, all point to the reserve as the location of the interest income in this case.

[44] I turn first to the location of the debtor, a factor traditionally relied on to determine the location of the obligation to pay. Here the debtor is the Caisse whose head office and only place of business as well as its only fixed asset is located on the Wendake Reserve. The income — interest agreed to be paid by the Caisse to Mr. Bastien — arises from a contractual obligation between the taxpayer and the Caisse which was entered into on the reserve. By virtue of the contract, the income was to be paid (and was paid) by the Caisse by depositing it into the taxpayer's account on the reserve: see art. 1566 of the *Civil Code of Québec*. Thus, the location of the

debtor and the place where payment must be made are clearly on the reserve. Unlike the situation facing the Court in *Williams*, where reliance on the location of the debtor involved the complex question of the location of the federal Crown, there is no such complication here. The Caisse's only place of business is on the reserve and its obligation, both under the contract and the *Civil Code*, was to pay on the reserve. [Furthermore] ... the Court in *God's Lake* applied generally applicable legal rules about the location of a bank account for the purposes of the exemption from seizure and while the fact that it applied these rules is not dispositive of the question of the location of the interest income in issue here, it tends to reinforce the conclusion that the interest income is located on the reserve in this case. While the provisions relied on by the Court in *God's Lake* do not apply here because they relate to banks and not to caisses populaires, both the contract between the parties and the provisions of art. 1566 of the *Civil Code* provide that payment of the interest income is to be made on the reserve.

[45] Having regard to the purpose of the exemption, the type of property and the nature of the taxation of that property, the connecting factors of the location of the debtor, the place where the legal obligation to pay must be performed and the location of the term deposits giving rise to the income should in my view be given significant weight in the circumstances of this case. As noted, the property flows from a contractual obligation which, both under the contract and the terms of the *Civil Code* (art. 1566), is to be performed on the reserve. The deposits themselves and the account into which the interest on them is paid are on the reserve. The debtor's only place of business is on the reserve. Thus, the type of property supports the view that the connecting factors of the place of contracting, the place of performance and the residence of the debtor should weigh heavily in attributing a location to the interest income. The nature of the taxation — the income is income from property — reinforces this view. And so does the purpose of the exemption, which is to preserve Indian property on a reserve.

[46] The analysis must also take account of other potentially relevant connecting factors. Here, those factors reinforce rather than detract from the conclusion that the interest income is property situated on the reserve.

[47] Consider the residence of the payee, Mr. Bastien. That of course was on the reserve. As for the source of the capital which was invested to produce the interest income, it too was earned on the reserve. ... In this case, while the interest income was derived from the loan to the Caisse, it was Mr. Bastien's business income, generated on the reserve and not assessed by the Minister, which produced the capital which in turn was invested to produce that income. These other potentially relevant connecting factors do not point to any other location than the reserve and tend to strengthen rather than undermine the connection between the investment income and the reserve.

[48] The Tax Court and the Federal Court of Appeal attached great weight to the fact that the Caisse's income-generating activities were in general commercial markets off the reserve. While that factor may have

weight with respect to other types of investments, it has been given significantly too much weight with respect to the term deposits in issue here. ...

[49] The general legal principles concerning privity of contract reinforce this view. The majority of the Court in *Will-Kare Paving & Contracting Ltd. v. Canada*, 2000 SCC 36, [2000] 1 S.C.R. 915, at para. 31, noted that the *Income Tax Act* does not operate in a vacuum but rather relies implicitly on the general law, especially the law of contract and property. The same, in my view, may be said of the exemption provisions in the *Indian Act*.

[50] I turn therefore to the general law relating to privity of contract. The rule is set out in art. 1440 of the *Civil Code of Québec* which provides:

> 1440. A contract has effect only between the contracting parties; it does not affect third persons, except where provided by law.

[51] Mr. Bastien made a simple loan to the on-reserve Caisse. The Caisse's income-producing actions and contracts after Mr. Bastien invested in term deposits cannot be deemed his own and do not diminish the many and clear connections between his interest income and the reserve. Consequently, the potentially relevant factor of the location of the issuer's income-generating activities is of no importance in this case.

[52] In my respectful view, the *Recalma* line of cases has sometimes wrongly elevated the "commercial mainstream" consideration to one of determinant weight. More precisely, several decisions have looked to whether the debtor's economic activity was in the commercial mainstream even though the investment income payable to the Indian taxpayer was not. This consideration must be applied with care lest it significantly undermine the exemption.

[53] The expression "commercial mainstream" was used in *Mitchell*. In one context, the expression was used to emphasize the distinction between property that is held pursuant to treaty or agreement from property that is not. This distinction is important for the purposes of s. 90 of the *Indian Act*, which deems certain personal property to be on a reserve for the purposes of the tax exemptions. La Forest J.'s reasons in *Mitchell* distinguish between property that is deemed by s. 90 to be on a reserve — that is, property purchased with Indian funds or money appropriated by Parliament for the benefit of Indians, or property given to Indians under a treaty or agreement — from property otherwise acquired and therefore not deemed to be on the reserve. Thus, the expression "commercial mainstream" in this context was not a factor to identify the location of property, but a consideration to help identify property which, although actually located elsewhere, was deemed by s. 90 to be located on a reserve. ...

[54] ... La Forest J. in *Mitchell* also noted that the purpose of the legislation is not to permit Indians to "acquire, hold, and deal with property in the commercial mainstream on different terms than their fellow citizens": p. 131. However, he was clear that, even if an Indian acquired an asset through a purely commercial business agreement with a private concern, the exemption would nonetheless apply if the asset were situated on a reserve. As he emphasized, "[i]t must be remembered that

the protections of ss. 87 and 89 will always apply to property situated on a reserve": p. 139.

[55] The "commercial mainstream" was an important factor in the reasoning of the Federal Court of Appeal in *Folster*. Mrs. Folster challenged the assessment that her employment income was not tax exempt. She lived on a reserve and worked as a nurse in a hospital adjacent to the reserve which was funded by the federal government for the benefit of Indians. Most patients served were Aboriginal and the hospital had once been located on reserve, but had since been relocated. Linden J.A. held:

> Where, therefore, an Aboriginal person chooses to enter Canada's so-called "commercial mainstream", there is no legislative basis for exempting that person from income tax on his or her employment income. Hence, the requirement that the personal property be "situated on a reserve". The *situs* principle provides an internal limit to the scope of the tax exemption provision by tying eligibility for the exemption to Indian property connected with reserve land. Thus, as will be seen, where an Indian person's employment duties are an integral part of a reserve, there is a legitimate basis for application of the tax exemption provision to the income derived from performance of those duties. [Emphasis added; para.14.]

[56] This paragraph is problematic because it might be taken as setting up a false opposition between "commercial mainstream" activities and activities on a reserve. Linden J.A. in *Folster* was alive to this danger when he observed that the use of the term "commercial mainstream" might "... imply, incorrectly, that trade and commerce is somehow foreign to the First Nations" (para. 14, note 27). He was also careful to observe in *Recalma* that the "commercial mainstream" consideration was not a separate test for the determination of the *situs* of investment property, but an "aid" to be taken into consideration in the analysis of the question (para. 9). Notwithstanding this wise counsel, the "commercial mainstream" consideration has sometimes become a determinative test. So, for example, in *Southwind v. Canada* (1998), 156 D.L.R. (4th) 87 (F.C.A.), the court observed that the term "commercial mainstream"

> ... seeks to differentiate those Native business activities that deal with people mainly off the Reserve, not on it. It seeks to isolate those business activities that benefit the individual Native rather than his community as a whole. [para. 14]

[57] Similarly, in *Lewin*, Tardif J. made the following statement which was upheld by the Federal Court of Appeal:

> Thus, the income of the reserve's credit union was derived mainly from off-reserve economic activities, including mortgage loans, personal loans, investments with the Fédération des caisses populaires and purchases of municipal bonds.
>
> If it had been a financial institution created solely for the purposes, concerns and needs of the Indians living on the reserve and if the bulk of its income had primarily been reinvested on the reserve to strengthen, develop and improve the social, cultural and economic well-being of the Indians living there, the situation could have been different. [paras. 35-36]

[58] Then in *Sero*, Sharlow J.A. wrote:

The Royal Bank operates in the "commercial mainstream", to use the phrase from *Mitchell v. Peguis Indian Band*. The source of the interest income earned by Ms. Sero and Mr. Frazer is found in that commercial mainstream, and not on a reserve. I can discern no relevant factual distinction between these cases and *Recalma* and *Lewin*. [para. 22]

[59] The same is true for the decision under appeal. The Tax Court judge concluded:

In the case at bar, it is true that the Reserve was the late Rolland Bastien's place of residence, the source of the capital, the location of the Caisse populaire, the place where the investment income, or a good part of it was used, the location of the investment vehicle, and the place where the investment income was paid. However, these are factors of lesser importance in determining the *situs* of investment income, as for that purpose the emphasis is mainly on the connection between the investment income and the reserve and the extent to which that income can be considered as being derived from an economic mainstream activity. [para. 37]

The Federal Court of Appeal upheld this conclusion: para. 39.

[60] I do not agree that the "commercial mainstream" factor should be given determinative weight in this case. The question is the location of Mr. Bastien's interest income. As I have discussed earlier, the question is not where the financial institution earns the profits to pay its contractual obligation to Mr. Bastien. Yet the focus of the "commercial mainstream" analysis in the courts below led them to concentrate the analysis on the Caisse's income-earning activities rather than on Mr. Bastien's. The exemption from taxation protects an Indian's personal property situated on a reserve. Therefore, where the investment vehicle is, as in this case, a contractual debt obligation, the focus should be on the investment activity of the Indian investor and not on that of the debtor financial institution: see McDonnell, at p. 957; Maclagan, at p. 1522; O'Brien, at pp. 1576 and 1580.

[61] When one focuses, as required by *Williams*, on the connecting factors relevant to the location of Mr. Bastien's interest income arising from his contractual relationship with the Caisse, it is apparent that the other commercial activities of the Caisse should have been given no weight in this case. Mr. Bastien's investment was in the nature of a debt owed to him by the Caisse and did not make him a participant in those wider commercial markets in which the Caisse itself was active.

[62] Of course, in determining the location of income for the purposes of the tax exemption, the court should look to the substance as well as to the form of the transaction giving rise to the income. The question is whether the income is sufficiently strongly connected to the reserve that it may be said to be situated there. Connections that are artificial or abusive should not be given weight in the analysis. For example, if in substance the investment income arises from an Indian's off-reserve investment activities, that will be a significant factor suggesting that less weight should be given to the legal form of the investment vehicle. There is nothing of that nature present in this case. Cases of improper manipulation

by Indian taxpayers to avoid income tax may be addressed as they are in the case of non-Indian taxpayers.

[63] Applying the exemption of interest income in this case is broadly consistent with the purpose of preserving Indian property situated on the reserve. It provides an investment option protected from taxation for Mr. Bastien's property while preserving it against possible seizure.

[64] All potentially relevant factors in this case connect the investment income to the reserve. In the circumstances of this case, the fact that the Caisse produced its revenue in the "commercial mainstream" off the reserve is legally irrelevant to the nature of the income it was obliged to pay to Mr. Bastien. This is true as to both form and substance. Mr. Bastien's investment income should therefore benefit from the s. 87 *Indian Act* exemption.

4. *Conclusion*

[65] I would allow the appeal with costs throughout.

[A dissenting judgment was written by Deschamps J., on behalf of Rothstein J. and herself. At para. 67 she writes: "With all due respect, I find that the analysis proposed by my colleague Cromwell J. gives too much weight to connecting factors that may in some circumstances be artificial, and that it essentially makes a single factor — the debtor's place of residence — determinative." Justice Deschamps would have denied Mr. Bastien an exemption from investment income on the basis that the location of the activity that generated the investment capital was not properly related to the reserve.

In summarizing this point, Deschamps J. wrote (at paras. 102-104 and 107):

> In principle, I cannot agree that significant weight should be given to connecting factors that can be easily manipulated. In my view, that is the effect of the importance attached to the contractual aspects of the investment contract rather than to the property's concrete and discernible connections with the reserve. ...
>
> It can be seen from past experience, as is clear from a number of decisions, that it is easy to set up, on the basis of a purely legal test, a contractual framework that, on its face, meets the requirements for the exemption. The courts have been asked to decide numerous cases concerning employment income in which, in order to gain a financial advantage, employers had designated an establishment on a reserve on the assumption that their employees would be able to benefit from the exemption under the *Indian Act* even though the jobs had no real connection with the reserve (see: *Robinson v. The Queen*, 2010 TCC 649, [2011] 2 C.T.C. 2286; *Horn v. Canada*, 2007 FC 1052, [2008] 1 C.T.C. 140, aff'd 2008 FCA 352, 302 D.L.R. (4th) 472; *Shilling v. M.N.R.*, 2001 FCA 178, [2001] 4 F.C. 364; *Canada v. Monias*, 2001 FCA 239, [2002] 1 F.C. 51; *Southwind v. Canada* (1998), 156 D.L.R. (4th) 87). This type of planning had even extended to other types of businesses (see *Large v. The Queen*, 2006 TCC 509, 2006 D.T.C. 3558). Indeed, what the Aboriginal community seemed to understand from

Nowegijick was that they could, by contract, arrange their affairs to take advantage of the exemption (see Dockstator). Although this approach may seem attractive from a financial perspective, it is hard to see how it can be consistent with the purpose of the exemption. With respect, Cromwell J.'s approach opens the door to setting up contractual frameworks on reserves that have nothing to do with the purpose of the exemption, and it provides an impetus for tax planning aimed solely at benefiting from the exemption (see, on interest income: *Large v. The Queen*). Although such planning is legitimate for contractual purposes, it cannot be endorsed and held to be consistent with the purpose of the exemption provided for in the *Indian Act*.

In my view, it is necessary to continue to emphasize the application of concrete factors. What the *Indian Act* provides for is a right to protect property situated on a reserve, not a right to an exemption that applies to planning measures that notionally situate intangible property on a reserve for the sole purpose of sheltering them from taxation. ...

Moreover, the decision to attach determinative weight to the fact that the payment could be made on the reserve is in my view not only anachronistic, but unrealistic. In this age of electronic transactions, the fact that interest is paid at maturity into an account administered on a reserve seems to me to be a tenuous connection. Indians, like all other citizens, can have access to their funds from almost anywhere. To assume that they go to a Caisse populaire situated on a reserve when they want to have access to their funds, it would be necessary to assume that they do things differently than other citizens. ...]

---

1. In discussing factors connecting Indian income to a reserve, Cromwell J. criticizes lower courts' over-reliance on arguments in the *Mitchell v. Peguis* case involving the commercial mainstream (at paras. 55-61). Recalling the Federal Court's treatment of the connecting factors in the *Folster* case (where fixed percentages were given regarding connections of work to a reserve), do you think reasons underlying the *Bastien* decision will lead to change in the law related to taxation of Indian income?

2. Justice Cromwell's interpretation of s. 87 and investment income would allow Indians to engage in tax planning to take advantage of modern economic realities. On the other hand, Deschamps J. is worried that Indians will set up "contractual frameworks on reserves that have nothing to do with the purpose of the exemption, and it provides an impetus for tax planning aimed solely at benefiting from the exemption" (at para. 103). She further observes, "Although such planning is legitimate for contractual purposes, it cannot be endorsed and held to be consistent with the purpose of the exemption provided for in the *Indian Act*" (at para. 103). Can you identify reasons why it would be inconsistent with the *Indian Act* to set up contractual frameworks that benefit from s. 87 exemptions?

3. The case of *Dubé v. Canada*, [2011] S.C.J. No. 39, 2011 SCC 39 (S.C.C.) was released the same day as the *Bastien* case, and it involved the same issue: "whether Mr. Dubé is exempt from income tax otherwise payable on interest which he earned on term deposits with an on-

reserve caisse populaire, a Quebec savings and credit union" (at para. 1). The factual differences in the *Dubé* case were threefold (at para. 7):

> First, while Mr. Dubé invested in a caisse populaire that was situated on *a* reserve, he did not reside on that reserve and, in fact, the trial judge was not persuaded that his principal residence was on any reserve. Second, the trial judge was unable to conclude that a considerable part of the invested capital had been earned on a reserve. Finally, the trial judge found that Mr. Dubé had not spent his interest income on a reserve.

In finding that Mr. Dubé's investments were exempt under s. 87 of the *Indian Act*, Cromwell J. addressed each of the three above factual differences in turn.

First, in saying that it did not matter that Mr. Dubé invested on a reserve other than his own, Cromwell J. wrote (at paras. 14-15 and 21):

> ... In my view, the first fact — that the Caisse was not on Mr. Dubé's reserve — does not make the income ineligible for the exemption and that fact, as well as the fact that his principal residence was not on a reserve, while potentially relevant, should receive little weight when considered in light of the type of property, the nature of the taxation in issue and the purpose of the exemption. The text of the *Indian Act* and the Court's jurisprudence lead me to this conclusion.
>
> The taxation exemption under s. 87(1)(*b*) of the *Indian Act* refers to an Indian's personal property situated on "a" reserve and not to property on his or her "own" reserve. The Court has consistently held that the meaning of the words "on a reserve" should be approached having regard to their substance and their ordinary, common sense meaning: *Nowegijick v. The Queen*, [1983] 1 S.C.R. 29, at p. 41; *R. v. Lewis*, [1996] 1 S.C.R. 921, at p. 958; *Union of New Brunswick Indians v. New Brunswick (Minister of Finance)*, [1998] 1 S.C.R. 1161, at paras. 13–14; *McDiarmid Lumber Ltd. v. God's Lake First Nation*, 2006 SCC 58, [2006] 2 S.C.R. 846, at para. 19. The ordinary, common sense meaning of "on a reserve" does not require that the property be on any particular reserve.

. . . . .

> As discussed in *Bastien*, the type of property in issue here — income earned on term deposits — strongly connects it to the Mashteuiatsh Reserve. Also, as in *Bastien*, the nature of the taxation of the interest income supports giving considerable weight to the place of contracting, the place of payment and the location of the Caisse. As to the purpose of the exemption, the absence of a financial institution on Mr. Dubé's own reserve tends to weaken the importance of his own place of residence as a possible connecting factor: he would not be able to invest his capital on his own reserve even if he lived there. I conclude that Mr. Dubé's place of residence should be given little weight in the circumstances of this case.

Second, in discussing the next factual difference from Bastien, regarding the ambiguity of where the capital was earned for Mr. Dubé's original investment, Cromwell J. wrote (at para. 30):

> ... [I]n weighing the connecting factors on a case-by-case basis, it is easy to lose sight of the fact that in particular categories of cases, one connecting factor may have much more weight than another: *Williams*, at p. 892. Given the strength of the connecting factors relating to the location

where the contract of investment was entered into, where it was to be performed and the Caisse's place of business, the fact that the bulk of the capital invested was not derived from the tax-exempt activities on a reserve does not in my view appreciably weaken the connection between the income and the Mashteuiatsh Reserve.

Third, in dismissing the significance of where investments were spent as an aspect of the connecting factors test, Cromwell J. wrote (at para. 31):

> During the years under assessment, the appellant lived part time off-reserve and owned real property off-reserve. The trial judge thus inferred that a portion of the interest income may well have been spent off a reserve. The location where the investment income is spent was identified as a potentially relevant factor by the trial judge in *Recalma v. Canada*, [1997] 4 C.N.L.R. 272 (T.C.C.), although one entitled to little weight in determining the location of investment income: pp. 278-79. This factor has also been considered in subsequent investment income cases: see, e.g., *Lewin v. Canada*, 2001 D.T.C. 479, at paras. 43 and 63, aff'd 2002 FCA 461, 2003 D.T.C. 5476. However, in my view, this consideration is not a relevant connecting factor in determining the location of the income earned on the term deposits in issue here. As I see it, the type of property, the nature of the taxation of that property and the purpose of the exemption do not support giving any weight to where the money received as interest income is spent.

Thus, Cromwell J. concluded (at para. 32): "In this case, as in *Bastien*, I am of the view that the relevant factors point to the Mashteuiatsh Reserve as the location of the interest income, and I would hold that it was situated on a reserve and entitled to the s. 87 exemption from taxation."

As in the *Bastien* case, Deschamps and Rothstein JJ. dissented. Justice Deschamps found (at paras. 39 and 40):

> In light of the findings of fact of the Tax Court of Canada judge, it is impossible to identify a sufficient concrete connection with the reserve in this appeal ... It will suffice to mention that Mr. Dubé did not reside on the reserve, that he was unable to explain where large deposits made at the Caisse populaire Desjardins de Pointe-Bleue came from and that the judge was unable to establish a connection between the deposited capital and the transportation company operated by Mr. Dubé. No reason was given for entering into the contract on the reserve that would enable the Court to hold that this fact furthers the purpose of the exemption. Even though the debtor was situated on the reserve and even though this factor does connect the property with the reserve, the other concrete factors outweigh it significantly. While it is true that the contract in this case was signed on the reserve, this factor cannot be considered significant, since the debtor's place of residence was also on the reserve.
>
> To grant the exemption in such circumstances would be tantamount to turning the reserve into a tax haven for Indians engaged in unspecified for-profit activities off the reserve.

G. ABORIGINAL TAXATION POWERS

REPORT OF THE ROYAL COMMISSION ON ABORIGINAL PEOPLES: RESTRUCTURING THE RELATIONSHIP, VOL. 2

(Ottawa: Ministry of Supply and Services, 1996) at 290-93
(references omitted)

We want control of our destiny and a peaceful co-existence with Canadian society. In order for this to happen, First Nations must have an equitable share of lands, resources and jurisdiction, and fiscal capability to fulfill their responsibilities as self-determining peoples.

Chief Clarence T. Jules Kamloops First Nation Ottawa,
Ontario, 5 November 1993

... [A]ttaining a significant measure of fiscal autonomy is a fundamental prerequisite for effective self-government. A people that does not possess the means to finance its own government will be dependent on the priorities of others. This can be mitigated by negotiating long-term arrangements that commit other governments to fiscal transfers. But ultimately, a government that must look to others for most of its financial requirements remains dependent. Hence the importance of own-source revenues and authority for Aboriginal nations to tax their own resources and citizens.

Given the many responsibilities of Aboriginal governments, and assuming that Aboriginal people will want to receive a wide range of high quality services, Aboriginal governments will need to collect significant amounts of revenue. Other governments that support Aboriginal governments through transfers will expect them to do so. Indeed, transfers are likely to depend on the revenue collection effort of the recipient government, as is common in fiscal arrangements between governments in Canada.

There are different ways Aboriginal groups could raise funds and collect revenues through taxation.

1. Inherent Aboriginal Taxation Powers

Canada has not recognized the inherent right of Aboriginal governments to engage in taxation. However, it could be argued that wealth distribution was an activity integral to Aboriginal peoples prior to the arrival of Europeans, and therefore should receive protection under section 35(1) of the *Constitution Act, 1982*. There are many traditions where officially practised wealth redistribution was an important part of Aboriginal societies, such as potlatches, feasts, give-aways, gift-giving, etc.

The United States courts have been willing to recognize inherent or reserved powers of taxation vested in Indian tribes. For example, in *Washington v. Confederated Tribes of the Colville Reservation*, 447 U.S. 134 (U.S.S.C. 1980) the United States Supreme Court wrote: "The power to tax transactions occurring on trust lands and significantly involving a tribe or its members is a fundamental attribute of sovereignty, which the tribes retain unless divested of it by federal law or necessary implication of their dependent status." Similar conclusions are expressed in *Warren Trading Post v. Arizona Tax Commission*, 380 U.S. 685 (U.S.S.C. 1965); *McClanahan v. Arizona State Tax Commission*, 411 U.S. 164 (U.S.S.C. 1973); *White Mountain Apache Tribe v. Bracker*, 448 U.S. 136 (U.S.S.C. 1980); *Merrion v. Jicarilla Apache Tribe*, 455 U.S. 130 (U.S.S.C. 1982). While the plenary power of Congress to extinguish Indian rights to taxation is apparent in the Court's rulings (see especially *Atkinson Trading Company, Inc. v. Shirley*, 532 U.S. 645 (U.S.S.C. 2001), it is significant that the courts have recognized this power, and that the U.S. federal government has encouraged, not extinguished, the Indian taxation power. If Canadian courts and governments were to recognize inherent Indian taxation powers, this could have a positive impact on Aboriginal communities. The existence of inherent powers of taxation in the United States has helped many tribes become self-sufficient: see Stephen Cornell and Joseph P. Kalt, eds., *What Can Tribes Do? Strategies and Institutions in American Indian Economic Development* (Los Angeles: University of California, 1992), 1-61.

2. *Indian Act* Band Taxation

A primary way in which Aboriginal taxation powers have been utilized is under the *Indian Act*. In 1988 Parliament passed Bill C-115 (S.C. 1988, c. 23), known as the Kamloops Amendments, to allow band governments to assume powers of property taxation over non-Aboriginal interests in reserve lands. In particular, the Kamloops Amendments changed section 83 of the *Indian Act*, to read:

> 83(1) ... the council of a band may, subject to the approval of the Minister, make by-laws for any and all of the following purposes, namely,
>
> (a)   subject to subsection (2) and (3), taxation for local purposes of land, or interest in land, in the reserve, including rights to occupy, possess or use land in the reserve;
>
> (a.1)   the licensing of businesses, callings, trades and occupations;
>
> . . . . .
>
> (f)   the raising of money from band members to support band projects;

Thus, according to Parliament, the legislative basis of the Indian Band taxation power stems from section 83 of the *Indian Act*. There is no mention of any reserved or inherent rights of Aboriginal peoples to tax others through band by-laws.

In *Westbank First Nation v. B.C. Hydro and Power Authority*, [1999] S.C.J. No. 38, [1999] 3 S.C.R. 134 (S.C.C.), the Supreme Court of Canada considered the constitutional basis for Indian Band taxation under section 83 of the *Indian Act*. Once again, no reference was made to any reserved or inherent rights that Aboriginal peoples might possess to tax others. As a result, the Court found that the constitutional basis for Indian band taxation powers was section 91(3) of the *Constitution Act, 1867* ("the raising of money by any mode or system of taxation"). In this case the Supreme Court of Canada found that the primary purpose of the taxation by-laws of the Westbank First Nation was in pith and substance taxation. The by-laws were not connected to a regulatory scheme, nor were they a user fee for services directly rendered. Because the by-laws were taxation by-laws, in their pith and substance, the Court found they were enacted pursuant to section 91(3) rather than section 91(24) of the *Constitution Act, 1867*. The Court found that Westbank's tax by-laws could not apply to B.C. Hydro, a provincial Crown agent, since section 125 of the *Constitution Act, 1867* prevents intergovernmental taxation.

In addition to taxation powers under section 83 of the *Indian Act*, First Nations can also implement property taxation under the *First Nations Fiscal and Statistical Management Act*, S.C. 2005, c. 9. The FSMA created four First Nation institutions: First Nations Tax Commission; First Nations Financial Management Board; First Nations Finance Authority; and First Nations Statistical Institute. The FSMA was passed to expand local revenue jurisdiction, provide for financial management certification and expertise, and improve data and statistics quality. The FSMA also provides an alternative to section 83 of the *Indian Act*. The purposes of the FSMA are expressed in the Preamble as follows:

> Whereas the Government of Canada has adopted a policy recognizing the inherent right of self-government as an aboriginal right and providing for the negotiation of self-government;

> Whereas this Act is not intended to define the nature and scope of any right of self-government or to prejudge the outcome of any self-government negotiation;

> Whereas the creation of national aboriginal institutions will assist first nations that choose to exercise real property taxation jurisdiction on reserve lands;

> Whereas economic development through the application of real property tax revenues and other local revenues to support borrowing on capital markets for the development of public infrastructure is available to other governments in Canada;

> Whereas real property taxation regimes on reserves should recognize both the interests of on-reserve taxpayers and the rights of members of first nations communities;

> Whereas accurate, timely and credible statistics are a key element of sound financial planning, management and reporting available to other governments in Canada;

Whereas first nations led an initiative that resulted in 1988 in an amendment to the *Indian Act* so that their jurisdiction over real property taxation on reserve could be exercised and the Indian Taxation Advisory Board was created to assist in the exercise of that jurisdiction;

Whereas, in 1995, the First Nations Finance Authority Inc. was incorporated for the purposes of issuing debentures using real property tax revenues and providing investment opportunities;

Whereas, by 1999, first nations and the Government of Canada recognized the benefits of establishing statutory institutions as part of a comprehensive fiscal and statistical management system;

And whereas first nations have led an initiative culminating in the introduction of this Act ...

To implement the FSMA, section 29 established a First Nations Tax Commission. The mandate of the FNTC is to:

a. ensure the integrity of the system of first nations real property taxation and promote a common approach to first nations real property taxation nationwide, having regard to variations in provincial real property taxation systems;
b. ensure that the real property taxation systems of first nations reconcile the interests of taxpayers with the responsibilities of chiefs and councils to govern the affairs of first nations;
c. prevent, or provide for the timely resolution of, disputes in relation to the application of local revenue laws;
d. assist first nations in the exercise of their jurisdiction over real property taxation on reserve lands and build capacity in first nations to administer their taxation systems;
e. develop training programs for first nation real property tax administrators;
f. assist first nations to achieve sustainable economic development through the generation of stable local revenues;
g. promote a transparent first nations real property taxation regime that provides certainty to taxpayers;
h. promote understanding of the real property taxation systems of first nations;
i. provide advice to the Minister regarding future development of the framework within which local revenue laws are made.

In addition to the above responsibilities, the FNTC also provides advice regarding the approval of section 83 by-laws and it delivers services to First Nations exercising property tax jurisdiction under section 83 of the *Indian Act*. There are over 120 First Nations levying property taxes on reserve. Since 1989 more than $800 million has been raised by First Nations from this revenue source.

When a First Nation enacts a property taxation law or by-law, it occupies the field of taxation jurisdiction over the territory to which the law or by-law applies, which is the land within the reserve boundaries. If provincial or municipal governments have taxed non-Native businesses on a reserve to which FMSA laws or *Indian Act* by-laws apply, the First

Nations law will be paramount, and the provincial or municipal law will be inoperable.

Despite the increasing use of Indian band taxation powers under the *Indian Act* and the *First Nations Fiscal and Statistical Management Act*, this approach has not been without controversy. Non-Aboriginal people and corporations hold most of the land subject to taxation under section 83 by-laws. The types of interests taxed include: commercial land use leases; oil, gas, timber and resources leases; utility leases (hydro, telephone and natural gas lines); rental leases; and agricultural permits and leases. Understandably, entities holding these interests seek to reduce their tax liabilities. As a result, most of the litigation before the Supreme Court of Canada has involved non-Aboriginal people and corporations appealing Indian band taxation decisions. A few examples include:

St. Mary's Indian Band v. Cranbrook (City), [1997] S.C.J. No. 19, [1997] 2 S.C.R. 657 (S.C.C.)

Prior to the Kamloops amendments in 1988, the definition of "reserve" made it doubtful that conditionally surrendered land remained part of the reserve for band taxation purposes. At that time it was therefore unlikely that a band taxation by-law could apply to the non-Indian developments on such land. However, when the *Indian Act* was amended, "conditionally surrendered" lands were renamed "designated" lands. The definition of "reserve" was also changed so that designated lands, for most band by-law purposes, remained within the reserve.

In the *St. Mary's* case the Court was asked to consider the distinction between lands absolutely surrendered (which would not be subject to taxation) and conditionally surrendered or designated lands (which could be subject to taxation). In this case the band surrendered a portion of its reserve for full market value to the federal Crown for use as a municipal airport in 1966. The surrender was subject to the stipulation that it would revert to the band if it ceased to be used for public purposes. The band levied property taxes in 1992 on the ground that the reversionary stipulation to the surrender made the transfer "otherwise than absolut[e]" under the Kamloops amendments, with the result that the surrendered land fell within the "designated lands" category of the reserve. When the city refused to pay, the band sued. The Supreme Court held that the band's reserve lands were absolutely surrendered (and thus not subject to taxation) because at the time of surrender the band intended to part with the land on an absolute basis. The Court said that the mere fact the band included a rider in its surrender (*i.e.* reversion if land ceased to be used as an airport) does not necessarily mean that the surrender was "other than absolute". The Supreme Court held that "absolute" and "conditional" are not mutually exclusive terms — either conceptually or under the scheme of the *Indian Act*. Therefore, the definition of "designated lands" did not capture the airport lands, and these lands were not entitled to be subject to band taxation.

Canadian Pacific Ltd. v. Matsqui Indian Band, [1995] S.C.J. No. 1, [1995] 1 S.C.R. 3 (S.C.C.)

In *Canadian Pacific Ltd. v. Matsqui Indian Band*, [1996] F.C.J. No. 479, 134 D.L.R. (4th) 555 (F.C.T.D.), certain Indian bands tried to tax the railway lines of both the CNR and the CPR. They argued that the railways' interest in the rights of way was less than absolute, because they only held the land so long as it was needed for railway purposes. Thus, they said the railway lands should still be part of the reserves through which they passed and subject to taxation under section 83. It was important to the band's argument that the lands be part of the reserve because band by-laws only have force and effect within the geographical areas of the reserve and apply only to reserve lands. They do not apply to lands held outside the reserve by bands or to absolutely surrendered lands.

The first time the case went to the Supreme Court of Canada, it considered preliminary procedural questions: whether the assessment review board established by the band by-law was the proper forum to consider the jurisdictional question of whether land was in the reserve. The railways argued successfully that the assessment review board was not the proper forum, and established the right to have the assessor's decision reviewed directly by the Federal Court on judicial review. Despite this holding, the Court did write at 24:

> ... it is important that we not lose sight of Parliament's objective in creating the new Indian taxation powers. The regime which came into force in 1988 is intended to facilitate the development of Aboriginal self-government by allowing bands to exercise the inherently governmental power of taxation on their reserves. Though this Court is not faced with the issue of Aboriginal self-government directly, the underlying purpose and functions of the Indian tax assessment scheme provide considerable guidance in applying the principles of administrative law to the statutory provisions at issue here. I will therefore employ a purposive and functional approach where appropriate in this ruling.

Following the Supreme Court of Canada's decision on the procedural questions, there was a series of actions that never did satisfactorily determine the substance of the issue: see *Canadian Pacific Ltd. v. Matsqui Indian Band*, [1996] F.C.J. No. 479, 134 D.L.R. (4th) 555 (F.C.T.D.); affd. [1998] F.C.J. No. 983, 162 D.L.R. (4th) 649 (Fed. C.A.); [1999] 2 C.N.L.R. iv (note) (S.C.C.); [1999] F.C.J. No. 1057, 176 D.L.R. (4th) 35 (Fed. C.A.). The second 1999 Federal Court of Appeal decision contains three sets of reasons. Two judges held that the by-laws' taxation of non-Indian property interests only was not discriminatory. Two judges found the Canadian Pacific rights of way were lands within the reserve, while one judge found that the Canadian Pacific rights of way were held in fee simple absolute and were not lands within the reserve. The Federal Court of Appeal decision was not appealed to the Supreme Court of Canada. Canadian Pacific and the five bands involved in the appeal (the Boothroyd, Cook's Ferry, Matsqui, Seabird Island, and Skuppah Indian Bands) concluded agreements that recognized the bands' property taxation jurisdiction and provided for the passage of a federal regulation under section 83(5) of the *Indian Act*.

Osoyoos Indian Band v. Oliver (Town), [2001] S.C.J. No. 82, [2001] 3 S.C.R. 746 (S.C.C.)

In the *Osoyoos* case the issue was whether expropriated Indian reserve land could still be considered reserve land and thus subject to band taxation. The technical framing of the question was whether lands taken pursuant to section 35 of the *Indian Act* were "land or interests in land" in a reserve of a band within the meaning of section 83(1)(*a*) of the *Indian Act* such that those lands are assessable and taxable pursuant to band assessment by-laws and taxable pursuant to band taxation by-laws?

The Supreme Court of Canada held that section 83(1)(*a*) of the *Indian Act* provides Indian bands with the jurisdiction to impose tax on a very broad range of interests in land, and should be given a broad reading. They held that since the Order in Council that expropriated the lands did not evince a clear and plain intent to extinguish the band's interest in the reserve land, resort must be had to the interpretive principles that impair the Indian interests as little as possible. The Court found that, in light of these interpretive principles, the Order in Council at issue should be read as granting only a statutory easement to the province, and that it be held that the canal land is still "in the reserve" for the purposes of section 83(1)(*a*), and thus subject to taxation.

Musqueam Indian Band v. Glass, [2000] S.C.J. No. 54, [2000] 2 S.C.R. 633 (S.C.C.)

Though not strictly a section 83 taxation case, the *Musqueam* decision may hold important implications for Indian band taxation. The Musqueam dispute arose in 1995 when rent renewal clauses contained in a large number of long-term ground leases of Indian reserve lands first took effect. The Musqueam lands are located adjacent to the City of Vancouver and they form a part of an Indian Reserve that was surrendered for development as a single-family residential development in the early 1960s. Each parcel of land was separately leased on 99-year terms and the rent was fixed in the lease for the first 30 years. The dispute arose because there was no agreement on a condition in the lease that provided that on renewal the annual rent was to be set at 6 per cent of "current land value". Unfortunately, the term "current land value" was not defined precisely enough in the lease. A lengthy and costly dispute followed. This conflict occurred because during the initial 30-year period land values had escalated dramatically. As a result, homeowners would have been faced with significantly higher rents unless the phrase "current land value" was given some constrained meaning.

The phrase was given a restricted meaning by the Supreme Court. This was advantageous to the lease-holding homeowners and less favourable to the Musqueam. The Court resolved the dispute by holding that the annual rent payments should be based upon 6 per cent of the fair market value of fee simple land, less servicing costs, and discounted 50 per cent to adjust for the fact that the land was on an Indian reserve. The decision has been criticized for reducing the fair market value of Indian reserve land. While the case is not, strictly speaking, a section 83 taxation case, it may become relevant for section 83 purposes (if the courts hold that Aboriginal taxation has to be at a lower rate on reserves because of the reserves' lower land values as compared to surrounding provincial lands).

3. Negotiated Aboriginal Taxation Powers

Aboriginal peoples can negotiate for recognition of taxation powers through treaties and agreements. A recent example of Indian taxation provisions relative to self-government is found in the Nisga'a Final Agreement. The Nisga'a are a people in northwestern British Columbia who were the subject of *Calder v. British Columbia (Attorney General)*, [1973] S.C.J. No. 56, [1973] S.C.R. 313, 34 D.L.R. (3d) 145 (S.C.C.) in 1973 before the Supreme Court of Canada. This agreement, the product of 16 years of negotiation, sets out a scheme to assist the Nisga'a in operating their governments, and creating and distributing wealth for their people. It eliminates the taxation provisions of the *Indian Act* and replaces them with an entirely new scheme. The Nisga'a Agreement is a land and self-government agreement that is protected as a treaty under section 35(1) of the *Constitution Act, 1982* (being Schedule B of the *Canada Act 1982* (U.K.), 1982, c. 11).

Under section 1 of chapter 16 (Taxation) of the Nisga'a Final Agreement, the Nisga'a government has the power to make laws with respect to direct taxation of Nisga'a citizens on Nisga'a lands, including property taxation of Nisga'a citizens. That power does not include taxation of non-Nisga'a citizens. As Nisga'a lands are held in fee simple, and are not reserve lands, provincial property taxation laws would normally apply to all interests in those lands. However, under section 13 of chapter 16 (Taxation), certain Nisga'a lands held by the Nisga'a Nation and Nisga'a villages are exempt from real property taxation. These include unimproved lands, lands on which a Nisga'a citizen has a residence, and lands which are improved for public purposes. Provincial taxation laws have been amended to reflect these exemptions: see, for example, section 2.1 of the *Taxation (Rural Area) Act*, R.S.B.C. 1996, c. 448. The Nisga'a treaty provides for possible delegation to the Nisga'a government of provincial taxation powers over non-Nisga'a citizens on Nisga'a lands.[6] Other agreements that contain negotiated taxation powers include: *Sechelt Indian Band Self-Government Act*, S.C. 1986, c. 27; *Sechelt Indian Government District Enabling Act*, R.S.B.C. 1996, c. 416; *Yukon First Nations Self-Government Act*, S.C. 1994, c. 35.

Many people and groups have expressed concern about the fairness and constitutionality of Aboriginal taxation of non-Aboriginal people.[7] Groups like the Canadian Taxpayers Federation, the Fraser Institute, the Saskatchewan Party, the Alliance Party and the B.C. Civil Liberties Association have all written in opposition to Aboriginal taxation of non-Aboriginal people without proper representation. For example, though more supportive than some groups, the B.C. Civil Liberties Association has expressed its position through the following series of principles:

Principle 1

Aboriginal authority to impose property taxes on non-band/First Nations leaseholders under the *Indian Act* raises civil liberties concerns. The use of such authority is an example of a First Nation acting as a government authority, rather than as simply a party in private contract. Aboriginal taxation authority is part of a greater trend to provide First Nations with greater autonomy culminating in self-government treaties.

Principle 2

People who live in aboriginal jurisdictions, but are not band members, have no right to membership in the aboriginal political community.

Principle 3

Residents of aboriginal jurisdictions have a right to participate in decision-making regarding matters that directly affect them.

Principle 4

Canadian citizens who are not members of an Indian band have a right to participate in government decision-making that affects them in aboriginal jurisdictions because they retain some significant degree, though it may be necessarily attenuated in aboriginal jurisdictions, of their sovereign status throughout Canada. The right of citizens to participate meaningfully in decision-making is a fundamental characteristic of Canada's democracy.

Principle 5

To balance the competing principles of aboriginal self-government and non-aboriginal residents' right to participate in decision-making, when the non-Native population is close to, equals or outnumbers the aboriginal population in an aboriginal jurisdiction, then procedures must be weighted to respect aboriginal self-determination.

Principle 6

Non-Aboriginal residents' participation may reflect the process of decision-making used by the aboriginal community. For example, if an aboriginal community uses a consensus-based decision-making process, then non-aboriginal residents might sit at the table and participate as equals in the deliberations. If the aboriginal community uses democratic institutions like voting or appointing representatives, non-aboriginal residents might participate in the same way as First Nations people. A purely advisory body for non-aboriginal residents will only be "meaningful" if the residents agree to forego other types of participation. ...[8]

H. CONCLUSION

The overriding aim of taxation is to provide governments with the funds they require to meet their obligations. As this chapter has demonstrated, however, other important objectives are also recognized and should be considered in the formulation of taxation policy. The 1966 *Royal Commission on Taxation* observed that:

> ... public facilities and services must be made available and public programmes instituted to transfer purchasing power from some individual and groups in the community to others, in order to create an environment which economic activity can expand rapidly and in which the generally accepted social and cultural needs of the people can be met. The government can satisfy these collective needs only if it commands the use of goods and the services of [people].
>
> In addition to obtaining command over goods and services for these purposes, the government must be able to influence the level of private command over goods and services so that it may be able to offset fluctuations in employment and prices, and to ensure that the total output of goods and services expands as rapidly as possible, given the choices of its citizens between present and future consumption, and between work and leisure. To meet this objective the government must be able to increase and reduce private demand over goods and services from time to time so that, together with the public command, all resources are fully utilized.

It is clear that the Canadian government has largely excluded Aboriginal people from its consideration of these wider objectives in taxation. Principles first articulated in outdated Victorian legislation (the *Indian Act*) have been left to develop on a case-by-case basis with little attention to the economic and cultural realities of contemporary Aboriginal communities. Aboriginal peoples have had to be creative in developing arguments that meet their current needs. Yet, since the time the *Indian Act* was first enacted, the Canadian approach to the formulation of taxation policy has undergone a remarkable change. Greater emphasis has been placed on participatory democracy and the development and the more equitable distribution of wealth in Canada. While certain Aboriginal taxation initiatives represent the beginning of a greater attempt to weigh Aboriginal interests in tax policy, much work remains to be done. It is apparent from the legislative history and cases reproduced in this chapter that the purchasing power, social and cultural needs of Aboriginal people have not received the attention needed to enable them to capture a greater share of the wealth that circulates in and around their communities.

ENDNOTES

1. At http://www.chiefs-of-ontario.org/magazine/4-02.html#1.
2. "Imposition of Harmonized Sales Tax", Special Chiefs Assembly, Resolution 32, 2009, December 9, 2009, adopted by consensus, online: <http://www.fns.bc.ca/pdf/2009Dec08_AFN_ResolutionHST.pdf>. It should be noted that British Columbia First Nations did not secure an HST exemption in that province.
3. July 17, 2003 at http://www.taxpayer.com/main/news.php?news_id=454.
4. *Final Report: Legacy of Hope: An Agenda for Change*, Vol. I (Saskatchewan Justice, December 2003) at 7-11.
5. *This Magazine*, June 15, 2011, online: <http://this.org/magazine/2011/06/15/first-nations-tax-exemption/>.

6. For more information see Tom Falconer, "Fiscal Aspects of the Nisga'a Final Agreement" (2000) 48 Can. Tax J. 1829.
7. See Jonathon Kesselman, "Aboriginal Taxation of Non-Aboriginal Residents: Representation, Discrimination and Accountability" (2000) 48 Can. Tax J. 1525; Dominic Belley, "Indian Taxation Powers: Sharing Canadian Prosperity" (2000) 60 R. du B. 185.
8. See: <http://www.bccla.org/positions/political/00nonaboriginal.html>.

CHAPTER 12

ABORIGINAL PEOPLES AND CRIMINAL JUSTICE

The justice system has failed ... Aboriginal people on a massive scale. It has been insensitive and inaccessible, and has arrested and imprisoned Aboriginal people in grossly disproportionate numbers. Aboriginal people who are arrested are more likely than non-Aboriginal people to be denied bail, spend more time in pre-trial detention and spend less time with their lawyers, and if convicted, are more likely to be incarcerated. It is not merely that the justice system has failed Aboriginal people: justice also has been denied to them.

> A.C. Hamilton and C.M. Sinclair,
> *Report of the Aboriginal Justice Inquiry of Manitoba*,
> Vol. 1, The Justice System and Aboriginal People
> (Winnipeg: Queen's Printer, 1991), at 1.

A. INTRODUCTION

The justice system has failed Aboriginal people. These words preface the Aboriginal Justice Inquiry of Manitoba, one of Canada's most comprehensive inquiries into Aboriginal people and the criminal justice system. Unfortunately, its findings are not unique. For over 30 years numerous reports have identified and repeated this same sad fact — "that notwithstanding the hundreds of recommendations from commissions and task forces, the reality for Aboriginal people ... is that the justice system is still failing them". The Royal Commission on Aboriginal Peoples ("RCAP") suggested that this failure has most strongly represented itself through over-representation and systemic discrimination within the system. In some disturbing and astonishing news, the RCAP reports that "these problems are getting worse, not better".

This dismal view of the tragic impact of Canada's criminal law on Aboriginal people has generated a search for positive solutions. Various initiatives have been undertaken in an attempt to heal the horrific scars this law has left on many communities. Change has manifested itself in many ways, from the greater involvement of Aboriginal people in the administration and reform of Canada's current criminal laws, to the creation of more autonomous, Aboriginally controlled systems. Some of these ventures have met with great success, while others have struggled or failed under the weight of a variety of circumstances.

The materials in this chapter illustrate the problems Aboriginal people encounter in the criminal justice system and the opportunities its reform potentially offers them. The search for criminal justice promises to remain a very fluid area of law. Great innovations and upheavals will, no doubt, continue as the disturbing legacy of the failure of Canada's criminal law continues to be felt by Aboriginal peoples.

B. THE FAILURE OF CRIMINAL LAW FOR ABORIGINAL PEOPLES

1. Historical Realities

THE ROYAL COMMISSION ON ABORIGINAL PEOPLES, BRIDGING THE CULTURAL DIVIDE: A REPORT ON ABORIGINAL PEOPLE AND CRIMINAL JUSTICE IN CANADA

(Ottawa: Ministry of Supply and Services, 1996) at xi, 7
(references omitted)

It is rare today to read a newspaper, listen to the radio or watch television without being confronted with issues of crime and punishment, whether in news reports, documentaries or dramatizations. However, the criminal justice system and its effects on the Aboriginal people of Canada reveal themselves in places far removed from the glare of television cameras and reporters' microphones. For Aboriginal people the criminal justice system is not the stuff of drama, real or imagined, but a system in which they, more than any other Canadians, are more likely to become involved, but as victims of crime and as offenders. The over-representation of Aboriginal people in federal, provincial and territorial court systems and prisons casts a long shadow over Canada's claim to be a just society.

Over the last seven years, commissions of inquiry from coast to coast have reviewed the experiences of Aboriginal people with the criminal justice system and have concluded that the system is failing them. Far from addressing the problems they face in their nations, their communities, and their personal lives, it is aggravating them. In large measure these problems are themselves the product of historical processes of dispossession and cultural oppression. ...

We believe that it is essential to frame our discussion of Aboriginal justice issues in the broadest possible context and we have sought to do that. From what we have heard and from what we have read in the reports of the many other justice inquiries, understanding the contemporary realities facing Aboriginal people in the justice system must occur in a historical context of the relationship between Aboriginal and non-Aboriginal people. The sense of oppressiveness, the sense of illegitimacy that has come to characterize Aboriginal peoples' perception and experience of the justice system has deep historical roots.

The trial and execution of Louis Riel for his actions in seeking recognition and respect from Canadian authorities for a Métis homeland have left indelible scars on the collective memory of the Métis people. The perceived injustice of the trial has been compounded by the history of dispossession of Métis people. The trial and execution of eight Cree chiefs who allied themselves with Riel and the Métis, and who were hanged on a single scaffold in the North West Mounted Police courtroom at Battleford,

Saskatchewan, on 27 November 1885, continue to cast a long shadow over the descendants of those who were executed for the "crime" of defending their land.

However, the trials of Louis Riel, of Poundmaker and Big Bear, and of the other Métis and Indian "criminals" were not unique. Many other episodes that have rarely penetrated the history books of Canada remain alive in the oral histories of Aboriginal peoples and provide not simply a backdrop but the bedrock of Aboriginal peoples' experience of "justice" according to Canadian law.

REPORT OF THE CARIBOO-CHILCOTIN JUSTICE INQUIRY (BRITISH COLUMBIA)
Judge Anthony Sarich, Commissioner (1993) at 1

Over the years, the native people of the Cariboo-Chilcotin complained about how they were being treated by the various components of the justice system. Recently, those complaints became louder and more insistent. As a result I was asked by the Honourable Colin Gabelmann, the Attorney General of British Columbia, to check into those complaints. ...

In the Chilcotin ... in every village, the people maintained that the chiefs who were hanged in Quesnel Mouth in 1864 as murderers were, in fact, leaders of a war party defending their land and people. Much has been written but little is known with any certainty of the facts that led to the trials of those chiefs before Judge Matthew B. Begbie. The people of the Chilcotin have long memories. They hold the memory of those chiefs in high esteem and cite the effect of smallpox on their ancestors, the incursions onto their land, and the treatment of their people by the road builders hired by Alfred Penderill Waddington as justification for the war. Many natives consider the trial and subsequent hanging as a political event in a deliberate process of colonization. ...

It became apparent early in the course of the inquiry that the native people of the Cariboo-Chilcotin area were complaining not only about the police and the justice system, but also about all non-native authority structures bearing on their lives. These complaints are long-standing and insistent. They are a product of a conflict of cultural values and beliefs and are driven by the past and present conduct of non-native authority figures. And these complaints go back to the first contact with Europeans.

In every community west of the Fraser River, there was still barely concealed anger and resentment about the trickery that led to the hanging of the Chilcotin Chiefs in 1864 at Quesnel. The village Chiefs spoke with passion about the desecration of their graves, the spread of smallpox that killed so many of their people, and the brutish conduct of Waddington's road builders.

In accusatory tones the Chiefs also spoke about how their land was taken by government agencies, particularly those lands now used by the Canadian army as a weapons proving ground. They railed as well against the many fenced ranches carved from what they considered their traditional lands, and the forced move of a whole village to accommodate a ranching enterprise. ...

It appears that even Judge Begbie was concerned about the fairness of the trial of the Chilcotin Chiefs of Quesnel Mouth in 1864. There was genuine concern that the Chiefs were induced to surrender and give inculpatory statements on a promise of immunity by Magistrate Cox. Many natives still feel that the trial and hangings were more a show piece to impress the natives than an honest search for truth. Whatever the correct version, that episode of history has left a wound in the body of Chilcotin society. It is time for that wound to heal.

REPORT OF THE OSNABURGH/WINDIGO TRIBAL JUSTICE REVIEW COMMITTEE

Attorney General (Ontario) and the Minister Responsible for Native Affairs and the Solicitor General (Ontario), (Toronto: 1990) at 4–6

The arrival of Europeans produced a profound effect on [Aboriginal] societies and their way of life. ... First Nations people have become dispossessed — the Fourth World. ... What Euro-Canadians accept as commonplace for themselves and their children are absent from these communities. ...

While this report addresses the justice system it is but a flash point where the two cultures come in poignant conflict. ... The justice system, in all of its manifestations from police through the courts to corrections, is seen as a foreign one designed to continue the cycle of poverty and powerlessness. It is evident that the frustration of the First Nations communities is internalized; the victims, faced with what they experience as a repressive and racist society, victimize themselves.

The clash of the two cultures has been exacerbated by the attempts of the Euro-Canadian system to address the problems faced by the First Nations people. It lacks legitimacy in their eyes. It is seen as a very repressive system and as an adjunct to ensuring the continuing dominance of Euro-Canadian society. ... Any attempt to reform the justice system must address this central fact; the continuing subjugation of First Nations people.

---

2. Contemporary Realities

(a) Donald Marshall Jr.

On the night of May 28, 1971, Donald Marshall, a 17-year-old native youth in Nova Scotia, was involved in a confrontation that resulted in 11 years in prison for a crime he did not commit. During his trial in November of 1971 Marshall was convicted of murder on the strength of false testimonies obtained through coerced police action. During the trial one of these key witnesses admitted to the Crown that he had lied on the witness stand.

This was not pursued. Ten days after the trial the police received important evidence strongly implicating another as the perpetrator of the crime for which Marshall had been found guilty. The police did not question Marshall again and accepted the denials of the other suspect.

After 11 years of numerous investigations and references, the Nova Scotia Court of Appeal finally heard the truth of Marshall's innocence in the spring of 1982 from the witnesses who had testified at his earlier trial. The Crown also admitted that Marshall should be acquitted. However, in a disturbing turn of events, the Crown asked the court to exonerate the police to preserve the criminal justice system's credibility and the court appeared to oblige. The court accepted arguments that Marshall's supposedly "evasive" statements to the police, and his presumed attempt to "rob" the man with whom he had the confrontation, were the cause of his misfortune. They seemed to imply that Marshall, and not the criminal justice system, was to blame for the tragedy which had befallen him. Five judges of the Court of Appeal declared "any miscarriage of justice is … more apparent that real".

Many were shocked by the court's comments. Public outcry led to a Royal Commission.

EXCERPTS FROM SUMMARY OF FINDINGS OF THE ROYAL COMMISSION ON THE DONALD MARSHALL, JR. PROSECUTION, NOVA SCOTIA JUDGMENTS

[1990] N.S.J. No. 18

The criminal justice system failed Donald Marshall, Jr. at virtually every turn, from his arrest and conviction in 1971, up to — and even beyond — his acquittal by the Supreme Court of Nova Scotia (Appeal Division) in 1983. The tragedy of this failure is compounded by evidence that this miscarriage of justice could have and should have been prevented, or at least corrected quickly, if those involved in the criminal justice system had carried out their duties in a professional and/or competent manner.

These are the inescapable, and inescapably distressing conclusions this Royal Commission has reached after sifting through 16,390 pages of transcript evidence given by 113 witnesses during 93 days of public hearings in Halifax and Sydney in 1987 and 1988; after examining 176 exhibits submitted in evidence during those hearings; after listening to two-and-one-half days of presentations by experts on the criminal justice system's treatment of Blacks and Natives and on the role of the office of the Attorney General in that system; and after examining five volumes of research material prepared for the Royal Commission by leading academics and researchers.

The Royal Commission was not established, however, just to determine whether one individual was the victim of a miscarriage of justice, or even to get to the bottom of how and why that miscarriage occurred. The Nova Scotia Government, which appointed this Royal Commission on October 28, 1986, also asked us to "make recommendations" to help such tragedies from happening in the future. …

We find ...

- that Marshall was not the author of his own misfortune.
- that the miscarriage of justice was real and not simply apparent.
- that the fact that Marshall was a Native was a factor in his wrongful conviction and imprisonment.
- that the fact that Marshall was a Native was one of the reasons [the investigating police officer] identified him as the prime suspect.
- that the Crown prosecutor and the defence counsel in Donald Marshall, Jr.'s 1971 trial failed to discharge their obligations, resulting in Marshall's wrongful conviction.
- that the cumulative effect of incorrect rulings by the trial judge denied Marshall a fair trial.
- in the Appeal Process that counsel for Donald Marshall, Jr. failed to put arguments before the Court of Appeal concerning fundamental errors of law during the trial, and that this failure represented a serious breach of the standard of professional conduct expected and required of defence counsel.
- in the Reference Decision that the Court of Appeal made a serious and fundamental error when it concluded that Donald Marshall, Jr. was to blame for his wrongful conviction.
- that the Court selectively used the evidence before it — as well as information that had not been admitted in evidence — in order to reach its conclusions.
- that the Court took it upon itself to "convict" Marshall of a robbery with which he was never charged.
- that the Court was in error when it stated that Marshall "admittedly" committed perjury.
- that the Court's suggestion that Marshall's "untruthfulness ... contributed in large measure to his conviction" was not supported by any available evidence and was contrary to evidence before the Court.
- that the Court's decision amounted to a defence of the criminal justice system at Marshall's expense, notwithstanding overwhelming evidence to the contrary.
- that the Court's gratuitous comments in the last pages of its decision created serious difficulties for Donald Marshall, Jr., both in terms of his ability to negotiate compensation for his wrongful conviction and also in terms of public acceptance of his acquittal.

An Inquiry before the Canadian Judicial Council was convened (Report to the Canadian Judicial Council of the Inquiry Committee Established Pursuant to Subsection 63(1) of the Judges Act at the Request of the Attorney General of Nova Scotia) at (1991) 40 U.N.B.L.J. 211, to address the following question:

Was it misconduct justifying removal from office for the Court to characterize the conduct of Mr. Marshall as it did having regard to all the circumstances it knew from the record which it had before it? ...

While critical of the judges' treatment of Donald Marshall, the council found that the judges were not guilty of misconduct such as to warrant their removal. It wrote:

> We wish at the outset to state our strong disapproval of some of the language used by the Reference Court in its comments about Mr. Marshall. In reviewing the record before the Reference Court, we cannot help but be struck by the incongruity between the Court's legal conclusion that Mr. Marshall's conviction in 1971 was "unreasonable" and "not now supported by the evidence" and its *obiter* observations that nonetheless "any miscarriage of justice" was "more apparent than real." Surely it cannot be seriously argued that the conviction of an innocent person, let alone one who was at the time an adolescent, who was then unfairly incarcerated for more than ten years, was anything but a blatant miscarriage of justice.
>
> The wrongful conviction and imprisonment of any person constitutes a *real* miscarriage of justice; it cannot be termed "more apparent than real." This is especially so when the conviction is based upon perjured evidence obtained with the complicity of the agencies of the crown. The miscarriage is greater still when crown agencies, subsequent to conviction but while an appeal is pending, receive conclusive or practically conclusive evidence of innocence but do not move promptly, or at all, to have the conviction reviewed. The miscarriage of justice, of course, becomes worse each day the innocent person remains imprisoned. There is no formula that it is possible to suggest that can be applied to redress completely more than ten years of wrongful imprisonment or which will accurately reflect the horror of what happened to Mr. Marshall. We have no difficulty in assuming that any reasonable person, knowing the circumstances adduced in evidence before the Reference Court, would regard some of its language to be at least inappropriate.
>
> .....
>
> Whatever its intention in choosing to refer only to the person it acquitted, there can be no doubt that the impact of the Court's derogatory *obiter* statements created the strong impression that it was not responsive to the injustice of an innocent person spending more than ten years in jail. ...
>
> We would go so far as to suggest that the Court, in seeking to attribute to Marshall exclusive responsibility for the wrongful conviction, and thereby inferentially exculpating the other persons and factors demonstrated in the record to have played a key role in that conviction, so seriously mis-characterized the evidence before it as to commit legal error (*Desgagne v. Fabrique de St. Philippe D'Arvida*, [1984] 1 S.C.R. 19 at 31, *per* Beetz, J.).
>
> We take it as a presumption, however, that judges ought not to be removed from office for legal error. Having found that the five judges in the collegial decision-making capacity were inappropriately harsh in their condemnation of the victim of an injustice they were mandated to correct, we nonetheless accept the submissions of all counsel that their removal from office is not warranted. While their remarks in *obiter* were, in our view, in error, and inappropriate in failing to give recognition to manifest injustice, we do not feel that they are reflective of conduct so destructive that it renders the judges incapable of executing their office impartially and independently with continued public confidence. The three remaining judges collectively had 58 years of judicial experience prior to deciding the Reference and have each served since for seven more years. Moreover, the Court did in fact acquit Mr. Marshall and find his conviction unsustainable.

We do not make our criticisms lightly. We are deeply conscious that criticism can itself undermine public confidence in the judiciary, but on balance conclude in this case that confidence would more severely be impaired by our failure to criticize inappropriate conduct than it would by our failure to acknowledge it.

Conclusion

While we cannot condone or excuse the severity of the Reference Court's condemnation of Donald Marshall, Jr., and in particular its extraordinary observation that any miscarriage of justice was "more apparent than real", we do not find that the comments can lead to the conclusion that the judges cannot execute their office with the impartiality, integrity and independence the public rightly expects from the judiciary. We therefore, do not recommend their removal from office.

---

3. Aboriginal Over-representation

THE ROYAL COMMISSION ON ABORIGINAL PEOPLES, BRIDGING THE CULTURAL DIVIDE: A REPORT ON ABORIGINAL PEOPLE AND CRIMINAL JUSTICE IN CANADA

(Ottawa: Ministry of Supply and Services, 1996) at 28-33
(references omitted)

Injustice Personified — Aboriginal Over-Representation

The justice inquiries that preceded our work documented extensively how this failure has affected the lives of Aboriginal men, women and young people. The clearest evidence appears in the form of the over-representation of Aboriginal people in the criminal justice system. This was first documented in 1967 by the Canadian Corrections Association report, *Indians and the Law,* and in 1974 by the Law Reform Commission of Canada in *The Native Offender and the Law. Reports and inquiries since then have not only confirmed the fact of over representation but, most alarmingly, have demonstrated that the problem is getting worse, not better.*

The over-representation of Aboriginal people in Canadian prisons has been the subject of special attention and appropriately so, because the sentence of imprisonment carries with it the deprivation of liberty and represents Canadian society's severest condemnation. The Canadian Bar Association focused its attention on Aboriginal imprisonment in 1988, arguing that lawyers have a particular responsibility to bring these issues to the forefront of the public and governmental agenda.

As Members of the Bar we see the people that lie behind the statistics. We see them in the courts and prisons of this country and are witnesses to the continuing injustice towards them which we as a society practice in the name, paradoxically, of a criminal justice system.

The Association provided this bleak overview of the measure of this injustice:

Statistics about crime are often not well understood by the public and are subject to variable interpretation by the experts. In the case of the statistics regarding the impact of the criminal justice system on Native people the figures are so stark and appalling that the magnitude of the problem can be neither misunderstood nor interpreted away. Government figures which reflect different definitions of 'Native' and which probably underestimate the number of prisoners who consider themselves Native show that almost 10 per cent of the federal penitentiary population is Native (including about 13 per cent of the federal women's prisoner population) compared to about 2 per cent of the population nationally. In the west and northern parts of Canada where there are relatively high concentrations of Native communities, the over-representation is more dramatic. In the Prairie region, Natives make up about 5 per cent of the total population but 32 per cent of the penitentiary population and in the Pacific region Native prisoners constitute about 12 per cent of the penitentiary population while less than 5 per cent of the region's general population is of Native ancestry. Even more disturbing, the disproportionality is growing. Thus, in 1965 some 22 per cent of the prisoners in Stony Mountain Penitentiary were Native; in 1984 this proportion was 33 per cent. It is realistic to expect that absent radical change, the problem will intensify due to the higher birth rate of Native communities.

Bad as this situation is within the federal system, in a number of the western provincial correctional systems, it is even worse. In B.C. and Alberta, Native people, representing 3-5 per cent of the province's population constitute 16 per cent and 17 per cent of the admissions to prison. In Manitoba and Saskatchewan, Native people, representing 6-7 per cent of the population constitute 46 per cent and 60 per cent of prison admissions.

[A] Saskatchewan study brings home the implications of its findings by indicating that a treaty Indian boy turning 16 in 1976 had a 70 per cent chance of at least one stay in prison by the age of 25 (that age range being the one with the highest risk of imprisonment). The corresponding figure for non-status or Métis was 34 per cent. For a non-Native Saskatchewan boy the figure was 8 per cent. Put another way, this means that in Saskatchewan, prison has become for young Native men, the promise of a just society which high school and college represents for the rest of us. *Placed in a historical context, the prison has become for many young Native people the contemporary equivalent of what the Indian residential school represented for their parents.*

The Association cautioned that "absent radical change, the problem will intensify." The surest evidence that there has been no radical change, and the most damning indictment, is found in the commissions of inquiry appointed since the publication of *Locking Up Natives in Canada*. The Aboriginal Justice Inquiry of Manitoba reported that whereas Aboriginal people accounted for 33 per cent of the population at Stony Mountain Federal Penitentiary in 1984, by 1989 the figure had risen to 46 per cent. In 1983 Aboriginal people accounted for 37 per cent of the population of the provincial Headingly Correctional Institution; by 1989 they accounted for 41 per cent. By 1989 Aboriginal women accounted for 67 per cent of the prison population at the Portage Correctional Institution for Women, and in institutions for young people, the proportion of Aboriginal people was 61 per cent. All together, Aboriginal people made up 56 per cent of the population of correctional institutions (both federal and provincial) in Manitoba in 1989. Aboriginal people account for just under 12 per cent of Manitoba's total population and "thus, Aboriginal people, depending on their age and sex, are present in the jails up to five times more than their presence in the general population."

The figures received by the Task Force on the Criminal Justice System and its Impact on the Indian and Métis People of Alberta also confirmed that Aboriginal over-representation is getting worse in the province of Alberta. Indeed, because Alberta has the second highest rate of imprisonment per person charged in the whole country, over-representation has even harsher effects than elsewhere. Aboriginal men now make up 30 per cent of the male population in provincial jails and Aboriginal women 45 per cent of the female jail population. The most alarming conclusion of the task force is that for Aboriginal young offenders, "over-representation in the criminal justice system is even more dramatic" than it is for adults, and future population projections indicate that the situation will get much worse.

> Projections indicate that by the year 2011, Aboriginal offenders will account for 38.5 per cent of all admissions to federal and provincial correctional centres in Alberta, compared to 29.5 per cent of all such offenders in 1989... In some age categories, for example, the 12-18 years of age group, Aboriginal offenders are projected to account for 40 per cent of the admission of population to correctional facilities by the year 2011.

The fact that in some provinces the coercive intrusion of criminal laws into the lives of Aboriginal people and Aboriginal communities is increasing, not receding, is reflected in the most recent figures from Saskatchewan. John Hylton, a human justice and public policy adviser who has kept a close watch on the situation in Saskatchewan, has broken down total and Aboriginal admissions to provincial correctional centres for the years 1976-77 and compared them to the figures for 1992-93. The breakdown reveals several startling findings:

1. Between 1976-77 and 1992-93, the number of admissions to Saskatchewan correctional centres increased from 4,712 to 6,889, a 46 per cent increase, during a time when the provincial population remained virtually unchanged. The rate of increase was 40.7 per cent for male admissions and 111 per cent for female admissions.
2. During the same period, the number of Aboriginals admitted to Saskatchewan correctional centres increased from 3,082 to 4,757, an increase of 54 per cent. Male Aboriginal admissions increased by 48 per cent, while female Aboriginal admissions increased by 107 per cent.
3. In terms of overall rates of admission, Aboriginals were 65.4 per cent in 1976-77 and 69.1 per cent in 1992-93.

4. Increases in Aboriginal admissions accounted for 77 per cent of the increase in total admissions between 1976-77 and 1992-93.

These data indicate clearly that the problem of disproportionate representation of the Aboriginal people in Saskatchewan's justice system is growing worse, not better. ... Predictions that were prepared in the early 1980's and that were rejected by some as too extreme, have in some instances proven to be conservative, particularly in the case of female Aboriginal admissions.

Aboriginal over-representation in the country's prisons, while presenting the face of injustice in its most repressive form, is only part of the picture. The Aboriginal Justice Inquiry of Manitoba commissioned a great deal of research on the other parts of a system that from beginning to end treats Aboriginal people differently. The Inquiry reported that

> Aboriginal over-representation is the end point of a series of decisions made by those with decision-making power in the justice system. An examination of each of these decisions suggests that the way that decisions are made within the justice system discriminates against Aboriginal people at virtually every point ...

- More than half of the inmates of Manitoba's jails are Aboriginal
- Aboriginal accused are more likely to be denied bail
- Aboriginal people spend more time in pre-trial detention than do non-Aboriginal people
- Aboriginal accused are more likely to be charged with multiple offences than are non-Aboriginal accused
- Lawyers spend less time with their Aboriginal clients than with non-Aboriginal clients
- Aboriginal offenders are more than twice as likely as non-Aboriginal people to be incarcerated

The over-representation of Aboriginal people occurs at virtually every step of the judicial process, from the charging of individuals to their sentencing.

Unfortunately, more recent data continues to show that Aboriginal over representation in the criminal justice system is growing worse, not better.[1]

Province/Territory	Aboriginal People as % of Population	Aboriginal People as % of Provincial Corrections Population	Overrep. Rate
Newfoundland/Labrador	3.7	10	2.7
Prince Edward Island	1.0	3	3.0
Nova Scotia	1.9	7	3.7
New Brunswick	2.4	7	2.9
Quebec	1.1	2	1.8
Ontario	1.7	9	5.3
Manitoba	13.6	69	5.1
Saskatchewan	13.5	77	5.7
Alberta	5.3	38	7.2
British Columbia	4.4	21	4.7
Yukon	22.9	76	3.3
N.W.T.	50.5	90	1.8
Nunavut	85.2	98	1.2

Furthermore, recent research indicates that the number of Aboriginal offenders in federal custody is still increasing, and the parole grant rate for Aboriginal offenders is decreasing.[2] Aboriginal peoples also serve a higher proportion of their sentences before being released.[3]

Research also reveals that Aboriginal peoples are not only over-represented as offenders, but are also over-represented as victims of crime. For example, Savvas Lithopoulos in *International Comparison of Indigenous Policing Models* in a 2007 report for Public Safety Canada observed:

According to the Canadian Centre for Justice Statistics (CCJS, 2006), Aboriginal peoples have the highest rates of actual offences, arrest and incarceration of any group in Canada. In 2004, the on-reserve crime rate was about three times higher than rates in the rest of Canada. Critically, the violent crime rate was even greater at eight times higher than the rest of the country. For specific offences, the on-reserve crime breakdown was as follows:

- The homicide rate was seven times higher than the Canadian average;
- The assault rate was eight times higher than the Canadian average;
- The sexual assault rate was seven times higher than the Canadian average;
- The mischief (vandalism) rate was six times higher than the Canadian average;

- The rate of total property offences was comparable to the Canadian average;
- The rate of disturbing the peace was 12 times higher than the Canadian average;
- The offensive weapons rate was seven times higher than the Canadian average;
- Breaking and entering (burglary) was the single most frequent youth offence type, followed by mischief and theft; and
- Violent crimes tended to be committed by someone known to the victim (56%) such as a relative, friend, or acquaintance, compared with 41% in cases of violence committed against non-Aboriginal people.[4]

PRESENTATION TO THE COMMISSION OF FIRST NATIONS AND MÉTIS PEOPLE AND JUSTICE REFORM (CORRECTIONAL SERVICE OF CANADA, MAY 2003) IN COMMISSION ON FIRST NATIONS AND MÉTIS PEOPLES AND JUSTICE REFORM, FINAL REPORT, VOL. II: SUBMISSIONS TO THE COMMISSION

(Saskatchewan Justice, December 2003) at 3-9 to 3-10 (references omitted)

Some Characteristics of Aboriginal Offenders

As is evident in the Canadian population generally, the population of Aboriginal offenders has unique characteristics that set it apart from the non-Aboriginal population. Although the offender population has characteristics that are common (substance abuse and addictions; lower levels of education; previous criminal history; poor employment history; and dysfunctional family history) the population of Aboriginal offenders stands out as having higher incidences of many of these characteristics:

- 72% of the Aboriginal offender population in the Prairie Region are serving sentences for offences under Schedule 1 of the *Corrections and Conditional Release Act* compared to 55% of the non-Aboriginal offender population. This is significant, as Schedule 1 offences are violent offences and offences against the person. This impacts on risk and need assessment and on the correctional planning process, often resulting in a requirement for more intensive programming to address needs.
- Correctional Services Canada assesses offenders at three levels of risk and need: low, medium and high. 63% of Aboriginal offenders are assessed as both high risk and high need offenders compared to 46% of the non-Aboriginal offender population assessed as high risk/high need.
- Despite the factors described above, Aboriginal offenders tend to be sentenced to shorter periods of incarceration on average than non-Aboriginal offenders. 63.8 % of Aboriginal inmates in the Prairie Region are serving sentences of 5 years or less compared to 60% of non-Aboriginal inmates.

- 20% of Aboriginal offenders in the Prairie Region are sentenced to a sexual offence compared to 15% of non-Aboriginal offenders. Again, this is significant as treatment issues for sex offending behaviour may require greater intensity. Public attitudes toward anyone with a sex offence present special challenges for reintegration.
- Aboriginal offenders have experienced greater dislocation from family. This can be seen in the high numbers of Aboriginal inmates who have been involved in the child welfare system at some point in their lives. Trevethan found that 63% of Aboriginal inmates compared to 36% of non-Aboriginal inmates have been involved with the child welfare system. Also, 50% of Aboriginal inmates reported an unstable adolescence compared to 33.3% of non-Aboriginal inmates.
- Corrado and Cohen found that other indicators of stability, such as family violence, drug/alcohol problems in the same home environment, were evident in young offenders. His research shows that 53.3% of Aboriginal males are victims of physical abuse and 75% of Aboriginal females are victims, while 44.5% of non-Aboriginal males and 55.3% of non-Aboriginal females were victims. 19.3% of Aboriginal males and 57.6 %of Aboriginal females were subject to sexual abuse, where as 17.3% of non-Aboriginal males and 33.8% of non-Aboriginal females have had the same experience. The statistics for the Aboriginal youth offender show a troubling high rate of instability in their families as compared to their non-Aboriginal counterparts.
- 76% of Aboriginal offenders were identified as having some needs in the area of substance abuse. When a link was made to the substance abuse as a contributing factor to their offence, 63% of Aboriginal offenders were found to meet that category. Figures for non-Aboriginal offenders are 60% and 41% respectively.
- Based on tests administered to inmates at intake, only 13.6% of Aboriginal inmates tested at a grade 12 or higher level, compared to 32.6% of non-Aboriginal inmates. 50% of Aboriginal inmates tested at a level of at least grade 9 to grade 11 completion, compared to 51% of non-Aboriginal inmates. This means that 36.4% of Aboriginal inmates did not test beyond the level of grade 8 academic standing whereas 16.4% of non-Aboriginal inmates did not test beyond grade 8.

The foregoing statistical overview of Aboriginal over-representation is deeply troubling and deserves greater public attention and resources for resolution. The Royal Commission on Aboriginal Peoples wrote:

> In a society that places a high value on equality before the law, documenting the appalling figures of over-representation might seem to be enough, without any further analysis, to place resolution of this problem at the very top of the national human rights agenda. However, as compelling as the figures are, we believe that it is equally important to understand what lies

behind these extraordinary figures, which are a primary index of the individual and social devastation that the criminal justice system has come to represent for Aboriginal people. Understanding the root causes is critical to understanding what it will take by way of a national commitment to bring about real change.[5]

What part does racism play, if any, in the context that lies behind the figures in this section?

4. Systemic Racism

Aboriginal people observe that their over representation in the criminal justice system can be explained by reference to systemic racism. The *Report of the Commission on Systemic Racism in the Ontario Criminal Justice System*[6] defined systemic racism as "the social production of racial inequality in decisions about people in the treatment they receive". The Commission noted that systemic racism is produced through the combination of:

- social constructions of races as real, different and unequal (racialization);
- the norms, processes and service delivery of a social system (structure); and
- the actions and decisions of people who work for social systems (personnel).

As the cases and materials in this book have illustrated, Aboriginal people have often been racialized as different and unequal. Albert Memmi, the influential Tunisian Jewish writer of the post World War II African decolonization movement, observed that racism had the following elements:

1. Stressing the real or imaginary differences between the racist and his victim;
2. Assigning values to these differences, to the advantage of the racist and the detriment of the victim;
3. Trying to make them absolutes by generalizing from them and claiming that they are final;
4. Justifying any present or possible aggression or privilege.[7]

Through these processes of selection, sorting, attribution and action, the criminal justice system has sustained and promoted systems which negatively impact Aboriginal people. This has led to legislative and institutional processes that support, transmit and tolerate their unequal and adverse treatment. These patterns are also apparent in the treatment they receive at the hands of the criminal justice system. The operating norms, decision-making processes, service delivery, and actions of the courts' participants have contributed to the high degree of Aboriginal over-representation in the criminal justice system. Consider these ideas in the Court's treatment of racism in the *Williams* case which follows.

R. v. WILLIAMS

[1998] S.C.J. No. 49, [1998] 1 S.C.R. 1128 (S.C.C.)

The judgment of the Court was delivered by

McLachlin J.: —

Introduction

[1] Victor Daniel Williams, an aboriginal, was charged with the robbery of a Victoria pizza parlour in October, 1993. Mr. Williams pleaded not guilty and elected a trial by judge and jury. His defence was that the robbery had been committed by someone else, not him. The issue on this appeal is whether Mr. Williams has the right to question (challenge for cause) potential jurors to determine whether they possess prejudice against aboriginals which might impair their impartiality.

[2] The *Criminal Code*, R.S.C., 1985, c. C-46, s. 638, provides that "... an accused is entitled to any number of challenges on the ground that ... a juror is not indifferent between the Queen and the accused". The section confers discretion on the trial judge to permit challenges for cause. The judge should do so where there is a realistic potential of juror partiality. The evidence in this case established widespread racial prejudice against aboriginals. I conclude that in the circumstances of this case, that prejudice established a realistic potential of partiality and that the trial judge should have exercised his discretion to allow the challenge for cause.

. . . . .

[3] At his first trial, Williams applied to question potential jurors for racial bias under s. 638 of the *Code*. In support of his application, he filed materials alleging widespread racism against aboriginal people in Canadian society and an affidavit which stated, in part, "[I] hope that the 12 people that try me are not Indian haters". ...

. . . . .

Analysis

What is the Rule?

The Prevailing Canadian Approach to Jury Challenges for Lack of Indifference Between the Crown and the Accused

[9] The prosecution and the defence are entitled to challenge potential jurors for cause on the ground that "a juror is not indifferent between the Queen and the accused". Lack of "indifference" may be translated as "partiality", the term used by the Courts below. "Lack of indifference" or "partiality", in turn, refer to the possibility that a juror's knowledge or beliefs may affect the way he or she discharges the jury function in a way that is improper or unfair to the accused. A juror who is partial or "not

indifferent" is a juror who is inclined to a certain party or a certain conclusion. The synonyms for "partial" in *Burton's Legal Thesaurus* (2nd ed. 1992), at p. 370, illustrate the attitudes that may serve to disqualify a juror:

> bigoted, ... discriminatory, favorably disposed, inclined, influenced, ... interested, jaundiced, narrow-minded, one-sided, partisan, predisposed, prejudiced, prepossessed, prone, restricted, ...subjective, swayed, unbalanced, unequal, uneven, unfair, unjust, unjustified, unreasonable.

[10] The predisposed state of mind caught by the term "partial" may arise from a variety of sources. Four classes of potential juror prejudice have been identified — interest, specific, generic and conformity: see Neil Vidmar, "Pretrial prejudice in Canada: a comparative perspective on the criminal jury" (1996), 79 *Jud.* 249, at p. 252. Interest prejudice arises when jurors may have a direct stake in the trial due to their relationship to the defendant, the victim, witnesses or outcome. Specific prejudice involves attitudes and beliefs about the particular case that may render the juror incapable of deciding guilt or innocence with an impartial mind. These attitudes and beliefs may arise from personal knowledge of the case, publicity through mass media, or public discussion and rumour in the community. Generic prejudice, the class of prejudice at issue on this appeal, arises from stereotypical attitudes about the defendant, victims, witnesses or the nature of the crime itself. Bias against a racial or ethnic group or against persons charged with sex abuse are examples of generic prejudice. Finally, conformity prejudice arises when the case is of significant interest to the community causing a juror to perceive that there is strong community feeling about a case coupled with an expectation as to the outcome.

[11] Knowledge or bias may affect the trial in different ways. It may incline a juror to believe that the accused is likely to have committed the crime alleged. It may incline a juror to reject or put less weight on the evidence of the accused. Or it may, in a general way, predispose the juror to the Crown, perceived as representative of the "white" majority against the minority-member accused, inclining the juror, for example, to resolve doubts about aspects of the Crown's case more readily: see Sheri Lynn Johnson, "Black Innocence and the White Jury" (1985), 83 *Mich. L. Rev.* 1611. When these things occur, a juror, however well intentioned, is not indifferent between the Crown and the accused. The juror's own deliberations and the deliberations of other jurors who may be influenced by the juror, risk a verdict that reflects, not the evidence and the law, but juror preconceptions and prejudices. The aim of s. 638 of the *Code* is to prevent effects like these from contaminating the jury's deliberations and hence the trial: see *R. v. Hubbert* (1975), 29 C.C.C. (2d) 279 (Ont. C.A.). The aim, to put it succinctly, is to ensure a fair trial.

[12] The practical problem is how to ascertain when a potential juror may be partial or "not indifferent" between the Crown and the accused. There are two approaches to this problem. The first approach is that prevailing in the United States. On this approach, every jury panel is suspect. Every candidate for jury duty may be challenged and questioned

as to preconceptions and prejudices on any sort of trial. As a result, lengthy trials of jurors before the trial of the accused are routine.

[13] Canada has taken a different approach. In this country, candidates for jury duty are presumed to be indifferent or impartial. Before the Crown or the accused can challenge and question them, they must raise concerns which displace that presumption. Usually this is done by the party seeking the challenge calling evidence substantiating the basis of the concern. Alternatively, where the basis of the concern is "notorious" in the sense of being widely known and accepted, the law of evidence may permit a judge to take judicial notice of it. ...

[14] Judicial discretion, however, must be distinguished from judicial whim. ... To guide judges in the exercise of their discretion, this Court formulated a rule in *Sherratt, supra*: the judge should permit challenges for cause where there is a "realistic potential" of the existence of partiality. *Sherratt* was concerned with the possibility of partiality arising from pre-trial publicity. However, as the courts in this case accepted, it applies to all requests for challenges based on bias, regardless of the origin of the apprehension of partiality.

[15] Applying *Sherratt* to the case at bar, the enquiry becomes whether in this case, the evidence of widespread bias against aboriginal people in the community raises a realistic potential of partiality.

Identifying the Evidentiary Threshold

. . . . .

(1) The Assumption that Prejudice Will be Judicially Cleansed

[20] Underlying the Crown's submissions (as well as the judgments of Esson C.J. and the Court of Appeal) is the assumption that generally jurors will be able to identify and set aside racial prejudice. Only in exceptional cases is there a danger that racial prejudice will affect a juror's impartiality. In contrast, the defence says that jurors may not be able to set aside racial prejudices that fall short of extreme prejudice. Is it correct to assume that jurors who harbour racial prejudices falling short of extreme prejudice will set them aside when asked to serve on a jury? A consideration of the nature of racial prejudice and how it may affect the decision-making process suggests that it is not.

[21] To suggest that all persons who possess racial prejudices will erase those prejudices from the mind when serving as jurors is to underestimate the insidious nature of racial prejudice and the stereotyping that underlies it. As Vidmar, *supra*, points out, racial prejudice interfering with jurors' impartiality is a form of discrimination. It involves making distinctions on the basis of class or category without regard to individual merit. It rests on preconceptions and unchallenged assumptions that unconsciously shape the daily behaviour of individuals. Buried deep in the human psyche, these preconceptions cannot be easily and effectively identified and set aside, even if one wishes to do so. For this reason, it cannot be assumed

that judicial directions to act impartially will always effectively counter racial prejudice ...

[22] Racial prejudice and its effects are as invasive and elusive as they are corrosive. We should not assume that instructions from the judge or other safeguards will eliminate biases that may be deeply ingrained in the subconscious psyches of jurors. Rather, we should acknowledge the destructive potential of subconscious racial prejudice by recognizing that the post-jury selection safeguards may not suffice. Where doubts are raised, the better policy is to err on the side of caution and permit prejudices to be examined. Only then can we know with any certainty whether they exist and whether they can be set aside or not. It is better to risk allowing what are in fact unnecessary challenges, than to risk prohibiting challenges which are necessary ...

. . . . .

(2) Insistence on the Necessity of a Link Between the Racist Attitude and the Potential for Juror Partiality

[26] The Court of Appeal, *per* Macfarlane J.A., stated that the existence of a significant degree of racial bias in the community from which the panel is drawn is, by itself, not sufficient to allow a challenge for cause because bias cannot be equated with partiality. The court held that in order for the appellant to be successful, there must be some evidence of bias against aboriginal persons which is of a particular nature and extent; evidence which only displays a "general bias" against a racial group is insufficient to warrant a challenge for cause. The Crown goes even further, arguing that racial prejudice in the community must be linked to specific aspects of the trial in order to support a challenge for cause. More particularly, it asserts that where, as here, the defence was that another aboriginal committed the crime, race could have no relevance because the jury was obliged to decide between two aboriginals.

[27] I cannot, with respect, accept this contention. In my view, it is unduly restrictive. Evidence of widespread racial prejudice may, depending on the nature of the evidence and the circumstances of the case, lead to the conclusion that there is a realistic potential for partiality. The potential for partiality is irrefutable where the prejudice can be linked to specific aspects of the trial, like a widepread belief that people of the accused's race are more likely to commit the crime charged. But it may be made out in the absence of such links.

[28] Racial prejudice against the accused may be detrimental to an accused in a variety of ways. The link between prejudice and verdict is clearest where there is an "interracial element" to the crime or a perceived link between those of the accused's race and the particular crime. But racial prejudice may play a role in other, less obvious ways. Racist stereotypes may affect how jurors assess the credibility of the accused. Bias can shape the information received during the course of the trial to conform with the bias: see Parks, *supra*, at p. 372. Jurors harbouring racial prejudices may consider those of the accused's race less worthy or perceive

a link between those of the accused's race and crime in general. In this manner, subconscious racism may make it easier to conclude that a black or aboriginal accused engaged in the crime regardless of the race of the complainant: see Kent Roach, "Challenges for Cause and Racial Discrimination" (1995), 37 *Crim. L.Q.* 410, at p. 421.

[29] Again, a prejudiced juror might see the Crown as non-aboriginal or non-black and hence to be favoured over an aboriginal or black accused. The contest at the trial is between the accused and the Crown. Only in a subsidiary sense is it between the accused and another aboriginal. A prejudiced juror might be inclined to favour non-aboriginal Crown witnesses against the aboriginal accused. Or a racially prejudiced juror might simply tend to side with the Crown because, consciously or unconsciously, the juror sees the Crown as a defender of majoritarian interests against the minority he or she fears or disfavours. Such feelings might incline the juror to resolve any doubts against the accused.

[30] Ultimately, it is within the discretion of the trial judge to determine whether widespread racial prejudice in the community, absent specific "links" to the trial, is sufficient to give an "air of reality" to the challenge in the particular circumstances of each case. ...

. . . . .

(3) Confusion Between the Two Phases of the Challenge for Cause Process

[32] Section 638(2) requires two inquiries and entails two different decisions with two different tests. ...

. . . . .

[34] The Crown conflates the two stages of the process. Instead of asking whether there is a potential or possibility of partiality at the stage of determining the right to challenge for cause, it demands proof that widespread racism will result in a partial jury. The assumption is that absent such evidence, no challenge for cause should be permitted. This is not the appropriate question at the preliminary stage of determining the right to challenge for cause. The question at this stage is not whether anyone in the jury pool will in fact be unable to set aside his or her racial prejudices but whether there is a realistic *possibility* that this *could* happen.

(4) Impossibility of Proving That Racism in Society Will Lead to Juror Partiality

[35] To require the accused to present evidence that jurors will in fact be unable to set aside their prejudices as a condition of challenge for cause is to set the accused an impossible task. It is extremely difficult to isolate the jury decision and attribute a particular portion of it to a given racial prejudice observed at the community level. Jury research based on the study of actual trials cannot control all the variables correlated to race. ...

[36] "Concrete" evidence as to whether potential jurors can or cannot set aside their racial prejudices can be obtained only by questioning a juror. If the Canadian system permitted jurors to be questioned after trials

as to how and why they made the decisions they did, there might be a prospect of obtaining empirical information on whether racially prejudiced jurors can set aside their prejudices. But s. 649 of the *Code* forbids this. So, imperfect as it is, the only way we have to test whether racially prejudiced jurors will be able to set aside their prejudices and judge impartially between the Crown and the accused, is by questioning prospective jurors on challenges for cause. In many cases, we can infer from the nature of widespread racial prejudice, that some jurors at least may be influenced by those prejudices in their deliberations. Whether or not this risk will materialize must be left to the triers of impartiality on the challenge for cause. To make it a condition of the right to challenge to cause is to require the defence to prove the impossible and to accept that some jurors may be partial.

(5) Failure to Read s. 638(1)(b) Purposively

[37] The object of s. 638(1)(*b*) must be to prevent persons who may not be able to act impartially from sitting as jurors. This object cannot be achieved if the evidentiary threshold for challenges for cause is set too high.

[38] As discussed above, to ask an accused person to present evidence that some jurors will be unable to set their prejudices aside is to ask the impossible. We may infer in many cases, however, from the nature of racial prejudice, that some prospective jurors, in a community where prejudice against people of the accused's race is widespread, may be both prejudiced and unable to identify completely or free themselves from the effects of those prejudices. It follows that the requirement of concrete evidence that widespread racism will cause partiality would not fulfill the purpose of s. 638(1)(*b*).

[39] Similarly, an evidentiary threshold of extreme prejudice would fail to fulfill the object of s. 638(1)(*b*). Extreme prejudice is not the only sort of prejudice that may render a juror partial. Ordinary "garden-variety" prejudice has the capacity to sway a juror and may be just as difficult to detect and eradicate as hatred. A threshold met only in exceptional cases would catch only the grossest forms of racial prejudice. Less extreme situations may raise a real risk of partiality. Yet there would be no screening of jurors in those situations. The aim of the section — to permit partial jurors to be identified and eliminated — would be only partially achieved. ...

[40] This raises the question of what evidentiary standard is appropriate on applications to challenge for cause based on racial prejudice ...

[41] ... [I]t is not correct to assume that membership in an aboriginal or minority group always implies a realistic potential for partiality. The relevant community for purposes of the rule is the community from which the jury pool is drawn. That community may or may not harbour prejudices against aboriginals. It likely would not, for example, in a community where aboriginals are in a majority position. That said, absent evidence to the contrary, where widespread prejudice against people of

the accused's race is demonstrated at a national or provincial level, it will often be reasonable to infer that such prejudice is replicated at the community level.

. . . . .

(6) Failure to Interpret s. 638(1)(b) in Accordance with the Charter

[44] Parliament's laws should be interpreted in a way that conforms to the constitutional requirements of the *Charter*: see *Slaight Communications Inc. v. Davidson*, [1989] 1 S.C.R. 1038. ...

[45] The s. 11(*d*) of the *Charter* guarantees to all persons charged in Canada the right to be presumed innocent "until proven guilty according to law in a fair and public hearing *by an independent and impartial tribunal*". [Emphasis in original.] A *Charter* right is meaningless, unless the accused is able to enforce it. This means that the accused must be permitted to challenge potential jurors where there is a realistic potential or possibility that some among the jury pool may harbour prejudices that deprive them of their impartiality.

. . . . .

[47] The challenge for cause is an essential safeguard of the accused's s. 11(*d*) *Charter* right to a fair trial and an impartial jury. A representative jury pool and instructions from counsel and the trial judge are other safeguards. But the right to challenge for cause, in cases where it is shown that a realistic potential exists for partiality, remains an essential filament in the web of protections the law has woven to protect the constitutional right to have one's guilt or innocence determined by an impartial jury. If the *Charter* right is undercut by an interpretation of s. 638(1)(*b*) that sets too high a threshold for challenges for cause, it will be jeopardized.

[48] The accused's right to be tried by an impartial jury under s. 11(*d*) of the *Charter* is a fair trial right. But it may also be seen as an anti-discrimination right. The application, intentional or unintentional, of racial stereotypes to the detriment of an accused person ranks among the most destructive forms of discrimination. The result of the discrimination may not be the loss of a benefit or a job or housing in the area of choice, but the loss of the accused's very liberty. The right must fall at the core of the guarantee in s. 15 of the *Charter* that "[e]very individual is equal before and under the law and has the right to the equal protection and equal benefit of the law without discrimination".

. . . . .

[50] Although allowing challenges for cause in the face of widespread racial prejudice in the community will not eliminate the possibility of jury verdicts being affected by racial prejudice, it will have important benefits. Jurors who are honest or transparent about their racist views will be removed. All remaining jurors will be sensitized from the outset of the proceedings regarding the need to confront racial prejudice and will help

ensure that it does not impact on the jury verdict. Finally, allowing such challenges will enhance the appearance of trial fairness in the eyes of the accused and other members of minority groups facing discrimination: see *Parks, supra*.

(7) The Slippery Slope Argument

[51] The Crown concedes that practical concerns cannot negate the right to a fair trial. The Court of Appeal also emphasized this. Yet behind the conservative approach some courts have taken, one detects a fear that to permit challenges for cause on the ground of widespread prejudice in the community would be to render our trial process more complex and more costly, and would represent an invasion of the privacy interests of prospective jurors without a commensurate increase in fairness. Some have openly expressed the fear that if challenges for cause are permitted on grounds of racial prejudice, the Canadian approach will quickly evolve into the approach in the United States of routine and sometimes lengthy challenges for cause of every juror in every case with attendant cost, delay and invasion of juror privacy.

[52] In my view, the rule enunciated by this Court in *Sherratt, supra*, suffices to maintain the right to a fair and impartial trial, without adopting the United States model or a variant on it. *Sherratt* starts from the presumption that members of the jury pool are capable of serving as impartial jurors. This means that there can be no automatic right to challenge for cause. In order to establish such a right, the accused must show that there is a realistic potential that some members of the jury pool may be biased in a way that may impact negatively on the accused. A realistic potential of racial prejudice can often be demonstrated by establishing widespread prejudice in the community against people of the accused's race. As long as this requirement is in place, the Canadian rule will be much more restrictive than the rule in the United States.

. . . . .

[54] In the case at bar, the accused called witnesses and tendered studies to establish widespread prejudice in the community against aboriginal people. It may not be necessary to duplicate this investment in time and resources at the stage of establishing racial prejudice in the community in all subsequent cases. The law of evidence recognizes two ways in which facts can be established in the trial process. The first is by evidence. The second is by judicial notice. ...

. . . . .

Conclusion

[58] Although they acknowledged the existence of widespread bias against aboriginals, both Esson C.J. and the British Columbia Court of Appeal held that the evidence did not demonstrate a reasonable possibility that prospective jurors would be partial. In my view, there was ample

evidence that this widespread prejudice included elements that could have affected the impartiality of jurors. Racism against aboriginals includes stereotypes that relate to credibility, worthiness and criminal propensity. As the Canadian Bar Association stated in *Locking up Natives in Canada: A Report of the Committee of the Canadian Bar Association on Imprisonment and Release* (1988), at p. 5:

> Put at its baldest, there is an equation of being drunk, Indian and in prison. Like many stereotypes, this one has a dark underside. It reflects a view of native people as uncivilized and without a coherent social or moral order. The stereotype prevents us from seeing native people as equals.

There is evidence that this widespread racism has translated into systemic discrimination in the criminal justice system: see Royal Commission on Aboriginal Peoples, *Bridging the Cultural Divide: A Report on Aboriginal People and Criminal Justice in Canada*, at p. 33; Royal Commission on the Donald Marshall Jr., Prosecution, Volume 1: *Findings and Recommendations* (1989), at p. 162; *Report on the Cariboo-Chilcotin Justice Inquiry* (1993), at p. 11. Finally, as Esson C.J. noted, tensions between aboriginals and non-aboriginals have increased in recent years as a result of developments in such areas as land claims and fishing rights. These tensions increase the potential of racist jurors siding with the Crown as the perceived representative of the majority's interests.

[59] In these circumstances, the trial judge should have allowed the accused to challenge prospective jurors for cause. Notwithstanding the accused's defence that another aboriginal person committed the robbery, juror prejudice could have affected the trial in many other ways. Consequently, there was a realistic potential that some of the jurors might not have been indifferent between the Crown and the accused. The potential for prejudice was increased by the failure of the trial judge to instruct the jury to set aside any racial prejudices that they might have against aboriginals. It cannot be said that the accused had the fair trial by an impartial jury to which he was entitled.

[60] I would allow the appeal and direct a new trial.

Appeal allowed.

Is there evidence of widespread bias against Aboriginal peoples in your community? What sources would you look to in answering this question? If you found there was no widespread bias where you live, what would be your response to Justice McLachlin's opinion in *Williams*? If on the other hand you found evidence of widespread bias in your community, would you agree with the Court that such bias could raise the potential for partiality amongst jurors? Should an individual's partiality be questioned because of the community in which he or she lives?

On the other hand, if you agree that widespread bias could lead to partiality, do you agree with the further proposition that such bias can be "judicially cleansed"? Furthermore, if you agree with the Court's opinion that widespread bias against Aboriginal peoples can lead to partiality in jurors and must therefore be judicially cleansed, should there be any issue about the impartiality of judges drawn from communities where there is widespread bias? As you have studied the cases and materials in this book, have you seen any evidence of widespread bias and partiality amongst members of the judiciary? If you do not see bias in the cases, what explains the impartiality of judges? If you do see widespread bias against Aboriginal peoples by judges in the courts, what can be done? Does the *Williams* case hold any answers if this is the case?

Issues of systemic racism come before the courts in other ways. In *Nishnawbe v. Eden*, [2011] O.J. No. 988, 2011 ONCA 187 (Ont. C.A.), the Ontario Court of Appeal found that jury rolls in coroner's inquests were not properly representative of Aboriginal people in the northern Ontario community of Kachechewan. First Nations were excluded from jury rolls in Northern Ontario because the Department of Indian and Northern Affairs did not send band electoral lists to the Provincial Jury Centre, and steps were not taken by court officials to discover from other records who from these reserves might be eligible. As such, the Court found that such juries would not be representative or impartial. As a result, the Court allowed for the summoning of provincial officials to explain how jury rolls were developed and the Court ordered a new inquest to remedy the deficiencies in their development. The Court thus held that the Coroner had jurisdiction to make an order to remedy a juror list drawn from an unrepresentative jury roll.

The Court wrote (at para. 41):

> An inquest into the death of a First Nations person that is adjudicated by a jury chosen from a jury roll that excludes First Nations persons on reserves would not, in my view, be seen as a fair and just inquest or an inquest in which the public would have confidence. It would amount to an abuse of process within s. 50(1) of the [*Coroners Act*, R.S.O. 1990, c. C.37].

Furthermore, the Court observed (at para. 71): "There is no reason to think that the unrepresentativeness of the jury roll in the District of Kenora is unique." This statement, coupled with the facts in the judgment, illustrate how racism can be systemically present in the justice system when Aboriginal peoples' unique circumstances are not accommodated (in this case their political structure outside of provincial municipal rolls, which led to very few Aboriginal peoples being on jury lists). As you consider the above questions related to racism, ask yourself what role, if any, privilege may play in analyzing this issue.

PRESENTATION TO THE COMMISSION OF FIRST NATIONS AND MÉTIS PEOPLE AND JUSTICE REFORM (CORRECTIONAL SERVICE OF CANADA, MAY 2003) IN COMMISSION ON FIRST NATIONS AND MÉTIS PEOPLES AND JUSTICE REFORM, FINAL REPORT, VOL. I: LEGACY OF HOPE: AN AGENDA FOR CHANGE

(Saskatchewan Justice, December 2003) at 7-7 to 7-8 (references omitted)

Race-Based Privilege

One theory is that ignorance is the cause of racism. If people had "the facts" they would change both their beliefs and their behaviour. This is too simple an explanation. In *Racial Healing*, Newkirk and Rutstein state, "We have found that it is actually more difficult for individuals to overcome the emotional attachment to the ignorance than to overcome the ignorance itself. Challenging one's belief system usually provokes resistance because there is a natural desire to protect what makes one feel comfortable and secure." They describe "a gradual process of chipping away" with "patient and unqualified love." While this is surely effective, this gradual process means that while we wait for the changes to occur, the imprisonment rates and other problems remain high.

No one wants to be considered a racist. Many of us think of ourselves as nonracist. To acknowledge our true feelings requires deep reflection. It is troubling to consider the possibility that no one is completely free from racism. ...

Many people resist the idea that they may have biases or may cling to stereotypes. Yet, all may acquire certain biases as part of their "socialization package." Peggy McIntosh wrote an article, *White Privilege: Unpacking the Invisible Knapsack*, which deals with this socialization. A workshop of the same name states:

> It is often easier for white people to look at the disadvantages of racism for people of colour than to recognize the advantages of racism for white people. Focusing only on the negative consequences of disadvantage and marginalization sometimes permits people to feel compassion or pity for others, without having to come to terms with or challenge feelings of one's own superiority. To turn things around, and assess how white people benefit from discrimination on a daily basis, often results in painful reactions, excessive guilt, or denial. In discussions of systemic discrimination that also focus on systemic advantage, some major participants find it especially hard to acknowledge the possibility that their individual achievements may not be based exclusively on their own individual merit, but also depend on the systemically structured advantages available to majority groups. This can create a situation of cognitive dissonance for participants, who have been socialized (as have most of us) to believe that Canadian society is tolerant and fair, and rewards individual excellence and hard work with material and social success.

There are many examples of "white privilege," according to McIntosh: the ease of being able to shop without being followed or harassed; opening the front page of the paper and being able to see people of the white race widely represented; as white parents, being able to protect your children most of the time from people who don't like them; doing well in a challenging situation without being called a credit to the race; never having to speak for all white people; being assured of not being singled out because of racial overtones; being able to choose a bandage, doll or a greeting card that reflects the correct skin colour; taking a job with an affirmative action employer without having coworkers suspect that it was given unfairly because of race.

> We need to help people move towards that and to recognizing that race is a social concept and that it's a way of keeping some people oppressed and others not. And that those who oppose equity programs, those who oppose changes to the system, are ones who want to preserve the status quo and their own group's power and privilege. ...

Facts on 'Privileges'

Racism is increased by lack of accurate information. ... The view seems to be that First Nations people enjoy "unearned privileges" not available to others. ...

a) The Treaties

Treaty and Aboriginal rights form part of the Supreme Law of Canada and are enshrined in the Constitution. According to the *Constitution Act, 1982*, Aboriginal people are defined as the "Indian, Inuit and Metis peoples of Canada." Unfortunately, there is very little public awareness of the Constitution and its implications, including Treaty entitlements.

The post-Confederation Treaty process began in the early 1870s and ran for the next 40 to 50 years, securing for Canada millions of acres of land to fill with mostly white settlers. The current value of this land is hundreds of billions of dollars. This does not include the value of a single drop of oil, a forest that has been harvested, one chunk of potash or any crops that have come from fertile soil. Many Canadians fail to see the value of the earnings on the land gained from First Nations and Metis people for so little as a result of the Treaties. Approximately one per cent of the land in Saskatchewan was given to reserves under Treaties. Settlers received access to farmland, security, and the peace and goodwill of First Nations. Doug Cuthand wrote in the StarPhoenix, December 5, 2003, that the real winner after the numbered Treaty negotiations was Canada:

> It's not often understood, but all Canadian citizens have Treaty rights. When Canada acquired the land for the three Prairie provinces, it received a chunk of land larger than Western Europe. This new land was rich in farm land, minerals and gas and oil. In 2002, the three Prairie provinces had a combined gross domestic product of $223 billion. Now who got the best deal?

> . . . . .

d) Justice

There is a misconception that Aboriginal people receive special consideration in sentencing. The *Gladue* decision [see below], interpreting Section 718.2 of the *Criminal Code*, set a precedent that requires courts to consider social, economic and cultural background factors when sentencing Aboriginal offenders. *Gladue* takes into account the lasting effects of the residential school system and the resulting deterioration of family and culture that has led to so much dysfunction in the Aboriginal community.

C. ABORIGINAL TRADITIONS AND JUSTICE

Some believe that one of the reasons Aboriginal peoples have fared poorly in the criminal justice system is that their guiding norms and values are not appropriately recognized. Canadian institutions have been criticized for failing to recognize and give effect to Aboriginal law and traditions in their operation and decisions. These critics say Aboriginal peoples would not experience the same degree of problems in the criminal justice system if Aboriginal justice traditions had been followed or, at a minimum, given appropriate levels of respect or deference. As you read the materials in the next section, ask yourself whether it is discriminatory to fail to recognize the pre-existing laws and traditions concerning justice in Aboriginal communities. How, for example, would this issue sit with the Doctrine of Continuity discussed in Chapter 2?

All Aboriginal societies relied upon a complex and sophisticated array of mechanisms to maintain order in their societies prior to the arrival of Europeans. For example, after analyzing Ojibwa, Cree and Iroquois methods of justice, Michael Coyle reported that "a number of methods were universally used by Ontario's Indian peoples to prevent anti-social behaviour".[8] These included:

1. Regular teaching of community values by elders and other respected persons in the community;
2. Warning and counselling of particular offenders by leaders or by councils representing the community as a whole;
3. Use of ridicule or ostracism by the community at large to shame offenders and denounce particular wrongs;
4. Public banishment of individuals who persisted in threatening peace in the community;
5. Mediation and negotiations by elders, community members, or clan leaders, aimed at resolving particularly dangerous private disputes and reconciling offenders with the victims of misconduct;
6. Payment of compensation by offenders (or their clans) to their victims or victims' kin even in cases as serious as murder; and
7. In the case of wrongs that posed a grave threat to the community (such as sorcery, murder, and perhaps theft or adultery), physical coercion or execution of the offender, either directly by the community (after

investigation and deliberation by a council) or by the victim of the wrong, who was recognized by the community as having the right to take such action.

The values underlying these mechanisms of social order were of vital significance to the proper functioning of Aboriginal communities. These laws and legal principles varied from nation to nation; one must be careful not to universalize the rules of one group as being consistently applicable to others. However, the study of most First Nations reveals that they each had their own laws, adapted to their unique circumstances. Many of these same laws and systems can still be found in contemporary Aboriginal communities; they are regarded by some as just as significant for the proper functioning of Aboriginal communities today. The existence of these traditions among the Anishinabe (Ojibway) of central Canada can be traced through the following three accounts taken from the 1840s, the 1890s and the 1990s — the report of Mayakaming, the case of *Machekequonabe*, and the *Jacko* case. Consider the possible role of traditional Anishinabek law in contemporary communities in light of the principles these cases reveal.

JARVIS PAPERS COLLECTION # 5 S-125, VOLUME B. 57

Jarvis Papers, Metro Toronto Reference Library,
Collection # S-125, Volume B57
(William Jarvis was the superintendent of Indian Affairs in the 1840s)

Account given by Mayamaking of the murder of an Idiot [*sic*] last winter by a band of Indians near French river during the winter of 1838:

He came among us at the very beginning of last winter having in most severe weather walked six days without either kindling a fire or eating any food.

During the most part of this winter he was quiet enough, but as the sugar season approached got noisy and restless. He went off to a lodge and there remained ten days, frequently eating a whole deer at two meals. After that he went to another lodge when a great change was visible in his person. His form seemed to have dilated and his face was the colour of black. At this lodge he first exhibited the most decided professions of madness and we all considered that he had become a Windigo (giant). He did not sleep but kept on walking round the lodge saying "I shall have a fine feast". Soon this caused plenty of fears in this lodge, both old and young. He then tore open the veins at his wrist with his teeth and drank his blood. The next night was the same, he went out from the lodge and without an axe broke off many saplings about 9 inches in circumference. [He] never slept but worked all that night, and in the morning brought in the poles he had broken off, and at two trips filled a large sugar camp. He continued to drink his blood. The Indians then all became alarmed and we all started off to join our friends. The snow was deep and soft and we sank deeply into it with our snow shoes, but he without shoes or stockings barely left the indent of his toes on the surface. He was stark naked tearing all his clothes given to him off as fast as they were put on. He still continued drinking blood and refused all food eating nothing but ice and snow. We then formed a council to determine how to act as we feared he would eat our children.

It was unanimously agreed that he must die. His most intimate friend undertook to shoot him not wishing any other hand to do it.

After his death we burned the body and all was consumed but the chest which we examined and found to contain an immense lump of ice which completely filled the cavity.

The lad who carried into effect the determination of the council has given himself to the father of him who is no more, to hunt for him, plant and fill all the duties of a son. We also have all made the old man presents and he is now perfectly satisfied.

This deed was not done under the influence of whiskey. There was none there, it was the deliberate act of this tribe in council.

Mayamaking's case illustrates the operation of Anishinabek law outside of the Canadian legal structure. It is an excellent example of protective and restorative justice in traditional Anishinabek communities. Yet it can be difficult to understand these laws without an appreciation of the cultural context from which they grow. Can you identify the legal process followed by the community in coming to its decision? Can you identify the legal principles followed by the Anishinabek in this case? Do you need more information to properly answer these questions? Often, the operation of Aboriginal law has been judged without a fuller appreciation of this background information. Imagine a common law judge from Ontario being called upon to conduct a civil trial in Quebec. What difficulties do you think the judge would encounter?

Mayamaking's case can be analyzed in the following manner. The community dealt with the issue in accordance with their own legal traditions. The community had no other resources for their protection but themselves, their extended family and friends. They used their law to deal with a pressing issue. The onset of their problems with the man was slow and gradual and developed over most of the winter. They tried to help him. His health and mental state seem to have worsened as time went by to the point that he began uttering threats. The group did not take action right away but seemed to wait for two or three weeks, despite the threat to the community and the harm the man was causing himself. When it became clear that he was not getting any better and that his threats were becoming a matter of life and death, they went to council together rather than take action on their own. This is an important Anishinabek legal principle. Their method of making judgments was collective, not individualized. They relied upon one another's viewpoints. They clearly felt that the method of deciding was very important because they travelled through heavy snow to meet together.

When the group finally deliberated, the legal principles that led to the man's death are noteworthy. The matter was not about retribution or anger, but rather defence and compassion (another legal principle related to intent): the man's closest friend was charged with the duty of carrying out the task. The action also has restorative aspects. The father received gifts from the community, and the man who killed the son stepped into his role, also performing restitution. Even the man who lost his son seemed to be satisfied with the council's decision. This example shows how Anishinabek law can be very different from non-Indigenous law. Imagine what our legal systems would be like if judges or lawyers had to take the place of those they have prosecuted or sent to jail.

In analyzing Mayamaking's case it is also important to focus on the process and principles that guided the actions, rather than on the specific outcome. Some might read this case as an example of ad hoc, "uncivilized" Indigenous practices. However, a vast literature shows Anishinabek people following this pattern of dealing over long periods of time, and in different geographic regions where the Anishinabek (also called Ojibway or Chippewa) lived. Furthermore, psychological illness (which the man was probably suffering) would now be handled very differently. The Anishinabek, like other peoples around the world, have developed a more refined understanding of mental disorders. They would most definitely *not* kill the man today. However, the underlying principles in this account remain, even if the process would not lead to the same result today. People could still:

1. Wait, observe and collect information.
2. Meet in council with their friends when it is apparent something is wrong.
3. Help the person who is threatening or causing imminent harm.
4. If the person does not respond to help and becomes an imminent threat to individuals or the community, remove the preson so that he or she does not harm others (though, to re-emphasize, that would not now involve capital punishment).
5. Help those who rely on that person by restoring what might be taken from them by the treatment.
6. Have both the collective and the individual participate in the restoration.

These legal principles provide the important elements of the case, and they show what can be learned from looking at the past. Anishinabek people will likely find many of these approaches familiar in their contemporary lives. As the Supreme Court of Canada wrote in *Rodriguez v. British Columbia*, [1993] S.C.J. No. 94, [1993] 3 S.C.R. 519 (S.C.C.) at para. 143 in determining principles of fundamental justice:

> The way to resolve these problems is not to avoid historical analysis, but to make sure that one is looking not just at the existence of the practice itself ... but the rationale behind that practice and the principles that underlie it.

For Anishinabek people, *windigos* come in different forms today. There are other harmful forms of cannibalistic consumption that destroy lands, people and resources. The principles that underlie the practice in the Mayamaking case are important for dealing with these problems.

Eventually, Canadian courts were called upon to evaluate the operation of Aboriginal law in cases similar to Mayamaking's.

R. v. MACHEKEQUONABE

[1897] O.J. No. 98, 28 O.R. 309 (Ont. Div. Ct.)

Ontario Divisional Court, **Armour C.J.**, **Falconbridge** and **Street** JJ., 8 February 1897

A pagan Indian who, believing in an evil spirit in human shape called a Wendigo, shot and killed another Indian under the impression that he was the Wendigo was held properly convicted of manslaughter.

This was a case reserved under the *Criminal Code* 1892 Statement and amending Act 58 & 59 Vict. ch. 40 (D.) as to whether the prisoner was properly convicted of manslaughter.

The trial took place at Rat Portage on the 3rd of December, 1896, before **Rose**, J., and a jury.

Langford, for the Crown.

Wink, for the prisoner.

It appeared from the evidence that the prisoner was a member of a tribe of pagan Indians who believed in the existence of an evil spirit clothed in human flesh, or in human form called a Wendigo which would eat a human being.

That it was reported that a Wendigo had been seen and it was supposed was in the neighborhood of their camp desiring to do them harm.

That among other precautions to protect themselves, guards and sentries, tho prisoner being one, were placed out in pairs armed with firearms (the prisoner having a rifle); that the prisoner saw what appeared to be a tall human being running in the distance, which he supposed was the Wendigo; that he and another Indian gave chase, and after challenging three times and receiving no answer fired and shot the object, when it was discovered to be his own foster father, who died soon afterward.

The jury found affirmative answers to the following questions:

> Are you satisfied the prisoner did kill the Indian?
>
> Did the prisoner believe the object he shot at to be a Wendigo or spirit?
>
> Did he believe the spirit to be embodied in human flesh?

Was it the prisoner's belief that the Wendigo could be, killed by a bullet shot from a rifle?

Was the prisoner sane apart from the delusion or belief in the existence of a Wendigo?

The learned trial Judge then proceeded with his charged as follows: — "Assuming these facts to be found by you, I think I must direct you as a matter of law that there is no justification here for the killing; and culpable homicide without justification is manslaughter, so that unless you can suggest to yourselves something stated in the evidence to warrant a different conclusion, I think it will be your duty to return a verdict of manslaughter. You may confer among yourselves if you please, and if you take that view, I will reserve a case for consideration by the Court of Appeal as to whether he was properly convicted upon this evidence."

The jury found the prisoner guilty of manslaughter recommending him to mercy, and the learned Judge reserved a case for consideration whether upon the findings of the jury in answer to the questions he had submitted and upon his direction to them and upon the evidence the prisoner was properly found guilty of manslaughter.

The case was argued on February 8th, 1897, before a Divisional Court composed of **Armour, C.J.**, and **Falconbridge**, and **Street, JJ.**

J.K. Kerr, Q.C., for the prisoner. The evidence shews the Indian tribe were pagans, and believed in an evil spirit clothed in human form which they called a Wendigo, and which attacked, killed and ate human beings. The man that was shot was thought to be a Wendigo, a spirit as distinguished from a human being. It is true there was a mistake, but there was no intention even to harm a human being much less to kill. The evidence shews the mistake was not unreasonable. At common law the following of a religious belief would be an excuse. The trial Judge wrongly directed the jury to find the prisoner guilty. There should be a new trial at least. I refer to *Levet's Case*, 1 Hale 474; 1 Bishop on Criminal Law, 7th ed., sec. 305 and note; *Territory v. Fish*, cited in note p.185, is almost a parallel case; *Plummer v. The State*, 4 Texas App. 310; *Regina v. Rose*, 15 Cox C.C. 540; *Regina v. Wagstaffe*, 10 Cox C.C. 530; *State v. Nash*, 88 N. Car. 618; *Regina v. Mawgridge*, Kelyng's C.C. 167 [119].

John Cartwright, Q.C., Deputy Attorney-General was not called on.

The judgement of the Court was delivered by

Armour C.J.: — Upon the case reserved if there was evidence upon which the jury could find the prisoner guilty of manslaughter it is not open to us to reverse that finding, and the question we have to decide is whether there was such evidence.

We think there was, and therefore do not see how we can say that the prisoner was not properly convicted of manslaughter.

Whose standards should have the court applied in determining the reasonableness of Machekequonabe's actions? Should Machekequonabe's belief in Wendigos have been a justifiable defence to manslaughter? Consider what you might do if, in 1897, you were living as an Anishinabe person in a small, isolated community, and you believed a serial murderer, as Wendigo, was attacking you? Do you think your reactions would be influenced by the fact that you had a pre-existing system of custom and conduct that for centuries had enabled you to deal with such issues?

A Canadian court recently examined a defence against a charge of manslaughter in relation to another Anishinabek belief, concerning a Bearwalker. In reading the following decision, ask yourself whether the judge's decision was appropriate in light of all the circumstances?

R. v. JACKO

[1997] O.J. No. 2472, [1998] 1 C.N.L.R. 164 (Ont. Gen. Div.)

Trainor J.: —

. . . . .

[2] Two years have elapsed since this death. ...

[3] This 19 year old Accused, Leon Gavin Jacko, is charged that on the 30 June, 1995, at the First Nation of Sheguiandah, he unlawfully killed Ronald Wilfred Thompson and did thereby commit manslaughter.

[4] The Accused had been charged with murder but the Crown elected to proceed on a manslaughter indictment.

. . . . .

THE EVIDENCE

[6] The Accused and Ronald Thompson (Tab), the victim, were friends. They both resided at the First Nation of Sheguiandah, on Manitoulin Island. The Victim was 45 years old at the time. They were drinking heavily on the 30 June, 1995. The Victim had a lifelong history as a heavy binge drinker. ...

[7] [E]vidence showing extreme levels of alcohol ingested by both men and its impact on them is vividly portrayed in a brief description by Caroline Aguonie. She said that at 4:20 p.m. she drove the two men to Leon's residence. ... The Forensic Centre analysis revealed that at 7:30 p.m. that day the accused had a reading of about 200 milligrams of alcohol in 100 millilitres of his blood. The Victim's reading was in excess of 400 milligrams. The evidence is that as drunk as they were the two were not arguing or fighting and seemed to be getting along fine. Tab was not seen alive after Caroline left at 4:30 p.m., except by Leon. It is clear that their friendly relationship deteriorated dramatically in the next few hours.

[8] At 7:30 p.m. Ronald Roy was at his mother's residence for dinner and cards. ... Roy was outside the home when he heard a loud bellowing noise, like bears fighting, coming from the top of the mountain. He said he had never heard a sound like that coming from a human being. He had in the past heard the sound from bears fighting. He then heard voices cursing and yelling. He thought one of the voices was Tab's.

[9] He said that about 20 minutes later Leon was in the driveway. He was badly cut to the left outer wrist. He was hysterical, screaming words to the effect "I am a warrior — I got the Bearwalker." He repeated this over and over with his arms raised in a V. as in victory salute. He was breathing heavily.

[10] Roy said that Tab was known by some people in the community of Sheguiandah 1st Nation as the Bearwalker, a person who practices witchcraft or black magic.

[11] Winifred Trudeau, Roy's mother, testified that Leon came to the door about 8 p.m. wanting a light for a cigarette. He said he cut his wrist by "killing a f... Bearwalker." He was emotional at times, screaming about "killing the Bearwalker," at other times he cried. He said he "won the victory, the Bearwalker won't bother us anymore." Winifred Trudeau drove Leon to the Chris Aguonie home. On the way he talked about "the militia coming but he had a 25 magnum." When he said this he tapped his right chest. She described Leon as small in stature and frail.

[12] Caroline Aguonie and her sister Brenda Whiteduck decided to investigate the whereabouts of Tab. ... Near the camper they discovered the Victim's body laying on the ground, face down. He was dead.

. . . . .

[15] Several witnesses described Tab. Caroline said she was fond of him even though he had two personalities. She said that when he was drinking he said he used bad medicine. She saw him strangle a cat and cut off its ears to use for bad medicine. She testified that he killed her father's dog and told her he could hurt others. She said he had a reputation as a Bearwalker. She said she was not afraid of him but did not trust him. She was careful to keep her hair out of his reach as she knew if he got a lock of her hair he could bring bad medicine to her. She said that when he was drinking he would go from happy to angry out of the blue and for no reason. She said he had a very dark side. She had seen him become violent on a number of occasions. He had not been violent when she saw the two men together on June 30.

[16] Chris Aguonie was Tab's uncle. Leon is his nephew. He was a life long drinking buddy of the Victim. ... He said Tab and he drank together for 20 years. Tab had taken Leon under his wing and for a week prior to his death they drank together. The witness described Tab as a powerful man when drunk and mad. When drinking it was usual for him to become quite violent. He said that 2 months prior to his death Tab told the witness "I don't know what is wrong but I just feel like killing somebody — something big is coming down."

[17] The witness said Tab told him he had learned bad medicine from an old lady up north. He said he could hurt people and make them suffer. The witness said Tab told him about hurting others. Chris said at times Tab was obsessed with bad medicine. The witness came to fear Tab. He said that when sober Tab was a different person.

. . . . .

[23] Allison Manitawabi ... described the Accused as shy and quiet. She said he was a native traditionalist who enjoyed the outdoors, crafts and beadwork.

[24] Orville Aguonie ... said Leon was physically very weak. He was a person interested in native spirituality and had been so interested since his early teens.

[25] This witness has known Tab for years. Tab was often drunk and when drunk bragged about his spiritual powers as a Bearwalker. He would say he knew a lot of medicine and could hurt people. When sober he was pleasant. When drunk he fought. He had no fear when he was drinking. He talked about his fights when he was intoxicated. The witness had not seen Tab fight for years.

. . . . .

THE DEFENCE EVIDENCE

[49] The defence called Julien Aguonie, the father of the accused. The Accused, the Victim and a majority of the witnesses called in this trial were aboriginal people of the Ojibwe culture and were members of the Sheguiandah 1st Nation. The Accused and his father live in the traditional way of native people and have done so for a number of years prior to June 30th. Julien said Leon came to live with him when he was 12 years old. The witness had stopped drinking when his wife died in 1981. He returned to the traditions of native spiritualism, learning from the elders and studies. During the years he was reunited with Leon he taught him to live in the traditional way. The traditional way is to live in harmony with nature by gathering herbs and creating medicines: gathering food from the land: hunting and fishing and joining in ceremonial traditions such as elders gatherings, pipe ceremonies, sweat lodges and vision quests.

[50] The witness explained that in a pipe ceremony a connection is made with the Creator and with nature. From the directions of the compass, knowledge and wisdom come from the east: a new life from the south: a cleansing from the west and healing and purifying from the north. In a sweat lodge cleansing, healing and guidance take place. The spirits enter through the fire and rocks. In a vision quest the spirit world is contacted and you refocus a troubled life. Food and water is excluded for 4 days. You travel to a secluded place in the forest, after participating in a sweat lodge. Your spirit travels and meets other spirits in the spirit world. You are given directions for your life.

[51] Mr. Aguonie described a positive and negative aspect to the traditional way. The creator makes only good medicine but people, instead of healing others with medicine, cross over and misuse powers by making bad medicine. That is, they use spiritual power to cause harm, get revenge, satisfy greed and use power to harm others. He said Leon was a good student because he is very humble and eager to learn. Leon became a hunter, gathered herbs and made medicine.

[52] The witness explained that a Bearwalker is a belief, known to him since he was a child, when his mother smudged the house to protect it. A Bearwalker is a person who causes harm to others by the use of bad medicine. The Bearwalker can transform himself to animal forms such as a bear. This is known as "shape shifting." The Bearwalker travels as a ball of fire. The Bearwalker strikes fear into people that may result in sickness or death if not treated by good medicine.

[53] This witness testified that he has treated 10 people in the past 4 years. A secret herb is placed in hot coals. The victim of the Bearwalker is covered with a white sheet. The hair of the Bearwalker, symbolizing power, comes through the sheet and is picked up on a Kleenex, wiped across the sheet. The hair tells the healer and victim that the Bearwalker has lost its power and evil influence. The fear and terror is removed.

[54] The Bearwalker, according to tradition and belief, has more than normal physical strength when he is transformed into a bear.

[55] Julien told his son Leon about the Bearwalker. He gave him medicine to protect him, telling him to carry it with him.

. . . . .

[57] This witness has known the Victim all of his life. He testified that Tab's reputation, in the small community of Sheguiandah, is that he is passive when sober but aggressive when drunk. Tab, he said, was drunk a lot of the time. He would brag about his fights and his power as a Bearwalker. He told the witness he could hurt him or his family. He said, "if I can't get the parents because they are too strong I cause them to suffer by getting their children." The witness said he believed Tab had this power. He was not afraid because he had good medicine but he was wary and warned Leon. He told him about Tab's drinking and his evil power. ...

. . . . .

THE ISSUES

[59] The issues in this trial are narrowly focused. It is not contended nor argued that the Victim's death was caused by someone other than this Accused. The sole issue is, whether the death of Ronald Thompson was caused by the unlawful act of Leon Jacko, beyond a reasonable doubt. If the Accused acted in self-defence then he did not commit an unlawful act in killing the Victim. The narrow issue is whether the Accused acted in self defence as that term is defined in s. 34(2) of the *Criminal Code*.

[60] Everyone who is unlawfully assaulted and who causes death or grievous bodily harm in repelling the assault is justified if:

    (a) he causes it under reasonable apprehension of death or grievous bodily harm from the violence with which the assault was originally made or with which the assailant pursues his purposes; and

    (b) he believes, on reasonable grounds that he cannot otherwise preserve himself from death or grievous bodily harm.

[61] The Crown must prove, beyond a reasonable doubt, that one of the essential elements of the section is missing and therefore the Accused is not entitled to rely on the section.

[62] The essential elements are:

1. Has the Crown established that the Accused was not unlawfully assaulted? If the answer is no then,
2. Has the Crown established that the Accused was not under a reasonable apprehension of death or grievous bodily harm from the violence with which the assault was originally made or with which the assailant pursued his purposes? If the answer is no, then,
3. Has the Crown established that the Accused did not believe, on reasonable grounds, that he could not otherwise preserve himself from death or grievous bodily harm? If the answer to any of the questions is yes, beyond a reasonable doubt, then the Accused is not entitled to rely on Section 34(2).

. . . . .

THE LAW

[66] ... The uncontradicted evidence, in my view, is that the Accused was aware of the Victim's propensity for violence and his powers and reputation as a Bearwalker; *R. v. Scopelliti* (1981), 63 C.C.C. (2d) 481, *R. v. Pintar* (1996), 110 C.C.C. (3d) 402, *R. v. Cameron* (1995), 96 C.C.C. (3d) 346.

[68] The reasonableness of the Accused's belief or apprehension must be that of a sober man: *Reilley v. Q.* (1984) 15 C.C.C. (3d) 1.

. . . . .

[70] *R. v. Lavallee*, [1990] 1 S.C.R. 852 was a self-defence case founded on battered wife syndrome. Wilson J. said the question is "whether, given the history, circumstances and perceptions of the appellant, her belief that she could not preserve herself from being killed by [her common-law spouse] that night except by killing him first was reasonable."

CONCLUSION

[71] The only living eyewitness to this case is the Accused. The circumstantial evidence is capable of any number of interpretations and inferences. The difficulty is to draw logical inferences of fact and not conclusions based on speculation.

[72] It has been established beyond a reasonable doubt that this Accused struck at least two blows to the Victim's head with a walrus bone that caused extensive damage to the left side of the skull behind the left ear. Identity is not an issue.

[73] The only direct evidence as to how the altercation unfolded comes from the utterances made by the Accused. His utterances and any reconstruction of the events must be viewed in light of his culture, beliefs and native spirituality.

[74] There is no evidence that would lead me to conclude that the Crown has come close to establishing that his Accused was the instigator of the fight that took place in or beside the camper. It is clear that the Accused was unlawfully assaulted by the Victim. I rely on the utterances and statements to that effect, made by the Accused to a number of witnesses, including the police. In addition, the evidence of the victim's propensity to fight when drunk, coupled with the evidence that the Accused is normally shy and mild mannered, small in stature, not a strong person compared to the Victim and the fact that their is no evidence that the Accused has a violent disposition, even when he is drinking is persuasive.

[75] The fact that the Victim was the aggressor and that he is a powerful man compared to the Accused is significant. It sets the stage in examining the remaining questions in issue.

[76] The difficult issues in this case relate to the reasonableness of the Accused's apprehension of death or grievous bodily harm and the reasonableness of his belief that he could not otherwise preserve himself from death or grievous bodily harm, except by striking out with the walrus bone.

[77] The first of the utterances made by the Accused at the Trudeau home were preceded 20 minutes earlier by a bellowing noise like bears fighting, a sound Ronald Roy had never heard from a human. They were followed by human voices cursing and yelling. One of the voices sounded like Tab's, according to Roy. The utterances made to Roy and other native witnesses, included statements that "I am a warrior." "I got the Bearwalker." "I won the victory." "I cut my wrist by killing a Bearwalker — the bearwalker won't bother us anymore." The native witnesses described the Accused as crying, dazed, looking like a cornered animal, emotional, and screaming as he uttered the words.

[78] Witnesses said his clothes were dirty, his face bloody, he was frail looking, he was talkative, nervous, laughing at times.

[79] His utterances to the aboriginal witnesses must be understood in the context that he was talking to his own people.

[80] Utterances to Constables Goodwin and Rosser were summarized by Constable Goodwin in these words, "his constant theme was Tab went crazy — I had to defend myself — it was an accident." The Accused was now talking to police officers.

[81] His description of himself as a warrior, who killed the Bearwalker, must be understood, not as an act of aggression but as an act of self defence, an act to protect others from an evil spirit.

[82] The Accused referred to Tab's death as an accident. It is clear to me the word accident, repeated many times, is not used in a narrow legal sense but in the sense that he did not mean to kill.

[83] The Accused described the Victim as getting crazy when he drinks wine. The statement reflects his knowledge of the propensity of the Victim

for violence, knowledge gained in part from his father. In other utterances he said words to the effect that Tab went crazy. There is no description in the evidence as to how Tab went crazy and what specific action he took. There is, however, evidence of Tab's strength compared to the accused and his reputation for violence. In addition, the Accused knew of his reputation and power as a Bearwalker, including his ability to transform himself into a bear, adding to his power and strength. That reputation and spiritual belief is not to be looked at or judged by the standards of non-native society. I accept the evidence about native spirituality as being sincerely held beliefs by which I must judge the reasonableness of the Accused's apprehension and belief as to the danger that he was facing when the Victim attacked the Accused.

[84] There is evidence, from which it is not unreasonable to infer, that the Victim attacked the Accused with the jagged end of a wine bottle, after breaking a full bottle to create a dangerous weapon.

[85] ... It is not unreasonable to infer from the physical evidence and the utterances that Tab attacked Leon with the bottle. I do not mean to suggest that the evidence leads solely to this conclusion. However, it is as persuasive as any other reconstruction of the facts. The fact that I cannot say with conviction, based on the evidence, exactly how Tab "went crazy," tends to show that the Crown has not made its case. The obligation on the Crown is to prove, beyond a reasonable doubt, that the Accused did not have a reasonable apprehension of death or grievous bodily harm or that he did not believe on reasonable grounds that he could not otherwise escape.

. . . . .

[91] I do not say that the evidence points solely to the Accused being the unsuspecting victim of a Bearwalker but I do say the evidence in this case is not so clear and convincing that the Crown has satisfied me beyond a reasonable doubt that the Accused did not strike the fatal blow or blows in self defence under s. 34(2) of the *Code*.

[92] I find the Accused not guilty.

_____

Did the judge apply the appropriate standards in judging Tab's actions? Who might be harmed and who might benefit as a result of these standards? Are there dangers that could arise in employing the court's standards?

D. REFORMING THE CRIMINAL JUSTICE SYSTEM

The commentary and cases in this section illustrate the issues and struggles involved in the process of reforming the Canadian criminal justice system from within. By focusing on one type of innovation in this effort, elders' panels and sentencing circles, a greater appreciation of the strengths and weaknesses of this approach can be formulated. The *Moses* and *Gladue* cases are reproduced in the following pages to assist in this evaluation.

THE ROYAL COMMISSION ON ABORIGINAL PEOPLES, BRIDGING THE CULTURAL DIVIDE: A REPORT ON ABORIGINAL PEOPLE AND CRIMINAL JUSTICE IN CANADA

(Ottawa: Ministry of Supply and Services, 1996) at 109, 110, 116
(references omitted)

... Much progress has been made in opening up the sentencing of Aboriginal people to greater Aboriginal input. This advance has come about through the initiative of Aboriginal communities and the support of judges concerned about the problems the justice system causes for Aboriginal people. The development of these initiatives sprang originally from the Yukon and Northwest Territories. ...

Generally speaking these initiatives have come in two forms — elders panels and sentencing circles. In the case of elders panels, elders or clan leaders sit with the judges and provide advice about the appropriate sentence in a case. This advice is given in open court or in private. In a sentencing circle, individuals are invited to sit in a circle with the accused and discuss together what sentence should be imposed. In both cases, the ultimate decision about the sentence rests with the judge.

Regardless of the precise mechanism established, the purpose behind the process is the same — to give the court meaningful input from the people who are most directly affected by his or her conduct. The experience with these programs is that the offender responds more deeply to concerns and suggestions expressed by members of the community than by a judge who is removed in all ways from the offender's world.

The notion of obtaining community input to the sentencing process has spread from the far North to other areas as well. Similar initiatives are in place in Ontario, British Columbia, Quebec, Manitoba and Saskatchewan. ...

Sentencing circles and elders panels should not be seen as an end in themselves. Rather ... they are perhaps best seen as stages in an evolutionary process. The idea of community circles in the Yukon has recently been expanded, so that now they act as an alternative to courts. These initiatives must be allowed to grow and develop on their own. They are helpful not only continuing reform of the existing system, but as useful models in the development of distinct Aboriginal justice systems.

R. v. MOSES

[1992] Y.J. No. 50, 71 C.C.C. (3d) 347 (Y.T. Terr. Ct.)

Stuart Terr. Ct. J.: — The reasons for this sentence will take us on an unusual journey. Unusual, because the process was as influential in moulding the final decision as any substantive factors. Consequently, this judgment examines the process as well as the traditional stuffings of sentences, mitigating and aggravating circumstances.

Many might debate the extent any decision-making process shapes the result, but indisputably process can be as determinative as content. In sentencing, process profoundly influences the result. The process influences, not just what, and how matters are addressed, but who participates and what impact each person has in shaping the final decision. ...

1. Process

(A) Overview

Rising crime rates, especially for violent offences, alarming recidivist rates and escalating costs in monetary and human terms have forced societies the world over to search for alternatives to their malfunctioning justice systems. In the western world much of the energy expended in this search has focused on sentencing. While the underlying problems of crime and the gross inadequacies of the justice system stem from much broader, deeper ills within society, significant immediate improvement within the court process can be achieved by changing the sentencing process.

Currently the search for improving sentencing champions a greater role for victims of crime, reconciliation, restraint in the use of incarceration, and a broadening of sentencing alternatives that calls upon less government expenditure and more community participation. As many studies expose the imprudence of excessive reliance upon punishment as the central objective in sentencing, rehabilitation and reconciliation are properly accorded greater emphasis. All these changes call upon communities to become more actively involved and to assume more responsibility for resolving conflict. To engage meaningful community participation, the sentence decision-making process must be altered to share power with the community, and where appropriate, communities must be empowered to resolve many conflicts now processed through criminal courts.

An important step, towards constructive community involvement must involve significant changes to the sentencing process, before, during and after sentencing.

(B) Before Sentencing

The court circuit flew to Mayo for a special one day circuit to deal with several charges against Philip Moses.

He was found guilty of carrying a weapon, a baseball bat, for the purpose of committing an assault on Constable Alderston. ... Philip picked up a baseball bat to confront Constable Alderston who was standing by his vehicle behind an open car door. Despite several warnings from the Constable to stop, Philip continued to approach in a menacing and angry manner. Philip did not know that behind the vehicle door, the Constable had drawn his revolver. The situation was extremely dangerous. At the last moment, the Constable leapt into his vehicle and sped off. By seeking a less dangerous manner of arresting Philip, the Constable avoided potentially disastrous consequences. Within the hour, the Constable arrested Philip without incident. The prudence, and courage of Constable Alderston averted a violent showdown.

Philip was also found guilty of theft. Philip had stolen clothes from a home within Mayo. Philip pled guilty to a breach of probation.

By evening all trials were completed. A brief adjournment was called to enable counsel and the court to review pre-sentence reports, psychiatric and alcohol assessments that had been before the court in 1989. These documents described an incredulous life history.

Philip, a 26-year-old member of the Na-cho Ny'ak Dun First Nation of Mayo, Yukon, is the third youngest in Tommy Moses and Catherine Germaine's family of four sons and five daughters. Tommy Moses, a respected member of the First Nation, works full-time as a heavy equipment operator and spends all of his spare time pursuing a traditional lifestyle through trapping, hunting and fishing. He suffers from the adverse health ramifications of a survivor from long standing problems of alcohol abuse. Catherine works as a native culture instructor in the Mayo school. A source of strength and stability in the family, she has been sober for eight years. All of Philip's brothers have suffered from substance abuse, and all but one have long criminal records. Philip's sisters survived an early childhood amid extreme alcohol abuse and now raise their own families. Philip has a six year old son, whom he rarely sees and plays no part in parenting.

The litany of desperate, destructive circumstances engulfing Philip's early childhood are sadly typical of families caught in the turmoil of alcohol abuse and poverty. Abuse, and neglect within his home launched Philip from age ten until he was 16 into a series of foster homes, group homes, and ultimately into juvenile centres. Along this painful, destructive road of State imposed care, Philip was physically and sexually abused.

Any hope for a formal education was lost through placements in a series of juvenile facilities. Unable to advance past elementary school, Philip functions at approximately a grade six level. Handicapped by extremely poor reading and writing skills, he encounters severe difficulty with basic literacy and other educational courses.

His limited education frustrates attempts to find gainful employment. With virtually no marketable work skills or work experience, without money or a sober home, without a positive personal support system, and with ready access to others addicted to drugs or alcohol, Philip, once out of jail, quickly drifts into the maelstrom of poverty, substance abuse and crime. He commits crimes while impaired by alcohol or drugs, or to support his addictions.

These circumstances explain the short turnaround time from the street back to jail. With such grim prospects on the street, jail continues to be his primary home. His criminal record of 43 convictions, has imposed jail sentences totalling almost eight years. Jail, as did long stints in juvenile facilities, destroys his self-image, what little there may be, and induces severe depression and suicidal tendencies.

Since 1980, each in depth assessment has described Philip as extremely sensitive, lacking the ability to trust, and suffering from numerous personal problems with significant dysfunctional coping skills. In each assessment, the same theme is repeated: Philip needs "extensive personal counselling, needs to bond with an important helping person who can offer one to one counselling". This has never been provided. Most treatment recommendations have not been carried out. Philip's distrust, anger, lack of discipline, ability to disappear into the street, and poor self-image partially explain why prescribed treatment has not been employed to release Philip from his severe personal problems. ...

... He has extremely poor insight into his behaviour and demonstrates neither the judgment nor perspective to adopt a sensible or realistic course of action.

Against this abjectly dark picture, given his extensive criminal record, and a sentence of months imposed at his last appearance in 1989, common practice marked out a simple task for counsel and judge. How much jail time would be appropriate? Had Mr. Moses now proven by his criminal conduct that a sentence of two years was warranted; a sentence which would send this relatively young aboriginal person out of the Territory to a Federal penitentiary!

The court was being asked once more to remove this violent offender from the community, to again demonstrate the power of society to punish those who break "our" laws.

It was late in the evening, everyone was tired. The police plane waited to return Mr. Moses to jail. The charter plane waited to return the court circuit to Whitehorse. Everyone — including myself — expected the sentencing hearing would be short, directed only to the question of how much time in excess of the last sentence of 15 months would be imposed. Numerous factors which never appear in sentencing decisions but often affect sentencing, pressed the court to "get on with it".

We did not.

Somehow the pernicious cycle plaguing the life of Mr. Moses, has to be broken before he tragically destroys himself or someone else.

Insidiously and predictably, Mr. Moses had for ten years travelled from alcohol abuse, to crime, and then to jail. Each time emerging from jail, angrier, more dysfunctional, and more deeply entrenched in a marginal existence that featured alcohol abuse and crime, which inescapably closed the circuit back to jail. His long history with the criminal justice system had proven two unmistakeable conclusions.

First, the criminal justice system had miserably failed the community of Mayo. Born and raised in Mayo, his family in Mayo, Philip instinctively returned to Mayo after each of the previous seven jail sentences. He would again return after any further jail sentences; each time returning, less capable of controlling either his anger or alcohol abuse; more dangerous to the community and to himself. The criminal justice system had not protected, but had endangered the community.

Secondly, the criminal justice system had failed Mr. Moses. After ten years, after expending in excess of a quarter of a million dollars on Mr.

Moses, the justice system continues to spew back into the community a person whose prospects, hopes and abilities were dramatically worse than when the system first encountered Philip as a wild, undisciplined youth with significant emotional and general life skill handicaps. His childhood had destined him for crime, and the criminal justice system had competently nurtured and assured that destiny.

If the criminal justice system had failed, what could the community do? It was hardly the model case to experiment with community alternatives. What could be lost in trying!

Court was adjourned for three weeks. The probation officer was asked to enquire if the First Nation and Philip's family wished to become involved. The local RCMP Corporal was asked to enlist other community involvement. Crown and defence counsel were asked to consider what else might be done in addition to incarceration to break the vicious cycle that had inextricably captured Philip.

Another special circuit to Mayo was set for on January 9 to sentence Philip and to thereafter hold an open community meeting to discuss how the community, especially the First Nation might constructively participate in the justice system.

Parts of the plan to involve the community were not pursued. However, the crucial parts were implemented. The probation officer met with the Chief and other members of the First Nation. They would assist in searching for a solution. Equally important, the probation officer met with Philip and his family to encourage their participation. A visit to Mayo two days before the sentencing hearing by Crown counsel and the senior Crown, enhanced their knowledge about the community and its concerns. Their time with the local RCMP, the First Nation, the probation officer and others within the community contributed to the collective search for a solution to a difficult case.

The successful use of sentencing remedies primarily depends upon the work invested by counsel, probation officers and the community in exploring and developing proposals for sentencing before a sentencing hearing.

(C) Sentencing Hearing

Spatial dynamics

In any decision-making process, power, control, the overall atmosphere and dynamics are significantly influenced by the physical setting, and especially by the places accorded to participants. Those who wish to create a particular atmosphere, or especially to manipulate a decision-making process to their advantage, have from time immemorial astutely controlled the physical setting of the decision-making forum. Among the great predator groups in the animal kingdom, often the place secured by each member in the site they rest or hunt, significantly influences their ability to control group decisions. In the criminal justice process (arguably one of contemporary society's great predators) the physical arrangement in a courtroom profoundly affects who participates and how they participate. The organization of the courtroom influences the content, scope and importance of information provided to the court. The rules governing the court hearing reinforce the allocation of power and influence fostered by the physical setting.

The combined effect of the rules and the courtroom arrangements entrench the adversarial nature of the process. The judge, defence and Crown counsel, fortified by their prominent places in the courtroom and by the rules, own and control the process and no one in a courtroom can have any doubt about that.

For centuries, the basic organization of the court has not changed. Nothing has been done to encourage meaningful participation by the accused, the victim, or by the community; remarkable, considering how the location of a meeting, the design of the room, furniture arrangements, and the seating of participants are so meticulously considered in most decision making processes to ensure the setting reinforces the objective of the process. If the objective of the sentencing process is now to enhance sentencing options, to afford greater concern to the impact on victims, to shift focus from punishment to rehabilitation, and to meaningfully engage communities in sharing responsibility for sentencing decisions, it may be advantageous for the justice system to examine how court procedures and the physical arrangements within courtrooms militate against these new objectives. It was in this case.

(D) Advantages of Circle

In this case, a change in the physical arrangement of the courtroom produced a major change in the process.

(1) Physical setting

For court, a circle to seat thirty people was arranged as tightly as numbers allowed. When all seats were occupied, additional seating was provided in an outer circle for persons arriving after the "hearing" had commenced.

Defence sat beside the accused and his family. The Crown sat immediately across the circle from defence counsel to the right of the judge. Officials and members from the First Nation, the RCMP officers, the probation officer and others were left to find their own "comfortable" place within the circle.

(2) Dynamics of the circle

By arranging the court in a circle without desks or tables, with all participants facing each other, with equal access and equal exposure to each other, the dynamics of the decision-making process were profoundly changed.

Everyone in turn around the circle introduced themselves. Everyone remained seated when speaking. After opening remarks from the judge, and counsel, the formal process dissolved into an informal, but intense discussion of what might best protect the community and extract Philip from the grip of alcohol and crime.

The tone was tempered by the close proximity of all participants. For the most part, participants referred to each other by name, not by title. While disagreements and arguments were provoked by most topics, posturing, pontification, and the well worn platitudes, commonly characteristic of courtroom speeches by counsel and judges were gratefully absent.

The circle setting dramatically changed the roles of all participants, as well as the focus, tone, content and scope of discussions. The following observations denote the more obvious benefits generated by the circle setting.

(i) Challenges monopoly of professionals

The foreboding courtroom setting discourages meaningful participation beyond lawyers and judges.

The judge presiding on high, robed to emphasize his authoritative dominance, armed with the power to control the process, is rarely challenged. Lawyers, by their deference, and by standing when addressing the judge, reinforce to the community the judge's pivotal importance. All of this combines to encourage the community to believe judges uniquely and exclusively possess the wisdom and resources to develop a just and viable result. They are so grievously wrong.

Counsel, due to the rules, and their prominent place in the court, control the input of information. Their ease with the rules, their facility with the peculiar legal language, exudes a confidence and skill that lay people commonly perceive as a prerequisite to participate.

The community relegated to the back of the room, is separated from counsel and the judge either by an actual bar or by placing their seats at a distinct distance behind counsel tables. The interplay between lawyers and the judge creates the perception of a ritualistic play. The set, as well as the performance, discourages anyone else from participating.

The circle significantly breaks down the dominance that traditional courtrooms accord lawyers and judges. In a circle, the ability to contribute, the importance and credibility of any input is not defined by seating arrangements. The audience is changed. All persons within the circle must be addressed. Equally, anyone in the circle may ask a direct question to anyone. Questions about the community and the accused force discussions into a level of detail usually avoided in the courtroom by sweeping assumptions and broiler plate platitudes. In the courtroom, reliance upon technical legal language imbues the process with the air of resolutely addressing difficult issues. In fact, behind the facade of legalise [*sic*], many crucial considerations are either ignored or superficially considered. The circle denies the comfort of evading difficult issues through the use of obtuse, complex technical language.

(ii) Encourages lay participation

The circle setting drew everyone into the discussion. Unlike the courtroom, where the setting facilitates participation only by counsel and the judge, the circle prompted a natural rhythm of discussion.

The physical proximity of all participants, the ability to see the face of the person speaking, the conversational tone, the absence of incomprehensible rituals, and the intermingling of professionals and lay members of the community during breaks, all a consequence of the circle, broke down many barriers to participation.

The highly defined roles imposed upon professionals by the formal justice process creates barriers to communication. The circle drew out the person buried behind their role, and encouraged a more personal and less professional contribution. The circle, in revealing the person behind the professional facade fostered a greater sense of equality between lay and professional participants in the circle. This sense of equality and the discovery of significant common concerns and objectives is essential to sustain an effective partnership between the community and the justice system.

(iii) Enhances information

The justice system rarely acquires adequate information to competently target the sentencing process on the underlying causes of criminal behaviour. ...

The rituals and specialized language of the sentencing process produce an aura of competence. Rising crime rates (especially rising recidivism) despite staggering increases in expenditures, debunk this illusory aura. Sentencing could be vastly improved by enhancing the quantity and quality of information. ...

Community involvement through the circle generates not only new information, but information not normally available to the court. Through the circle, participants can respond to concerns, fill in gaps, and ensure each new sentencing option is measured against a broader, more detailed base of information. In the circle, the flow of information is alive, flexible and more readily capable of assessing and responding to new ideas. ...

Courtroom procedures and rules often preclude or discourage many sources from contributing crucial information. The circle removes or reduces many of the impediments blocking the flow of essential information into court.

(iv) Creative search for new options

Public censure often focuses on the differences in sentences meted out for the same crime. There should be more, not fewer differences in sentences.

. . . . .

In this case the circle promoted among all participants a desire to find an appropriate sentence that best served all of the above objectives. Their creative search produced a sentence markedly different from customary sentences for such crimes, and radically departed from the pattern of sentences previously imposed upon Philip for similar offences. The circle forged a collective desire for something different, something unlike the sentences imposed in the past ten years, something everyone could support, something they believed would work. Fuelled by the expanded and responsive flow of information, the circle participants worked towards a consensus, towards a unique response to a problem that had plagued the community for ten years and had stolen ten years of productive life from Philip.

I was surprised by the result, but the new information and the option provided by the community rendered the final sentence obvious and compelling. The combination of new information and an array of new sentencing options can dramatically change sentencing dispositions from those based on information normally available and dependant upon the limited range of conventional sentencing remedies.

(v) Promotes a sharing of responsibility

In traditional courtroom settings, all inputs, all representations are directed to the judge. Not surprisingly, all participants, including the community, expect the judge after hearing all submissions to be responsible for rendering a sage and definitive edict. The circle redirected the flow of discussion from a single channel leading to the judge to a flow that followed the natural rhythms of interest around the circle. This in turn redirected expectations over responsibility for developing a workable solution. The circle by engaging everyone in the discussion, engaged everyone in the responsibility for finding an answer. The final sentence, evolved from the input of everyone in the circle. The consensus-based approach fostered not just shared responsibility, but instilled a shared concern to ensure the sentence was successfully implemented. Time will tell how much each participant, especially the offender, will continue to act upon their obligation to the circle and to the decision collectively developed.

This was a first run at a new process. Failures must not daunt further attempts. It may take time for the feelings of shared responsibility inspired by the circle to be translated into concerted and sustained action. There are many well-entrenched bad habits to break. The indolence, apathy and easy but imprudent reliance upon professionals, characteristic of most communities, will not be easily overcome in developing proactive community involvement. Current community leaders now strained beyond normal breaking points cannot be stretched to provide the input necessary to assume meaningful responsibility for community justice. Other community members must be inspired and encouraged to become involved.

However difficult inspiring citizens to become involved may be, the most difficult task will be breaking down the monopoly over conflict resolution tenaciously held by professionals within the justice system. Forging new and meaningful partnerships between professionals and communities will not be easy, we are the professionals after all, we know what to do, we have the power, we know what is best. To many, the existing criminal justice system is sacrosanct. Tampering with its rituals is tantamount to heresy.

The circle provided an important opportunity for both citizens and professionals to put into practice an emerging desire to work together in responding to crime.

(vi) Encouraging the offender's participation

Philip Moses, as is typical of most offenders, had not significantly participated in any of the previous seven sentencing hearings which had instrumentally shaped his life. Most offenders, during formal court proceedings, sit with head bowed, sometimes in fear, more often in anger as incomprehensible discussions ramble on about their life, crimes, and about how communities must be protected from such hardened criminals. ...

In the circle, the police, mother, brother, Chief of the First Nation, the probation officer, and other community members expressed constructive concern about Philip. They repeatedly spoke of the need to "reintegrate" Philip with his family and his First Nation.

This was the first time Philip heard anyone from his community, or from his First Nation offer support. He could no longer believe that the police and the community were solely interested in removing him from their midst.

These comments within the circle drew Philip into the discussion. His eloquence, passion, and pain riveted everyone's attention. His contribution moved the search for an effective sentence past several concerns shared around the circle. No, he did not convince everyone, nor did he ultimately secure what he sought, but his passion and candour significantly contributed to constructing the sentence.

(vii) Involving victims in sentencing

Many offenders perceive only the State as the aggrieved party. They fail to appreciate the very human pain and suffering they cause. Absent an appreciation of the victim's suffering, offenders fail to understand their sentence except as the intrusion of an insensitive, oppressive State bent on punishment. An offender's remorse is more likely be prompted by a desire to seek mercy from the State or by a recognition that they have been "bad". Only when an offender's pain caused by the oppression of the criminal justice system is confronted by the pain that victims experience from crime, can most offenders gain a proper perspective of their behaviour. Without this perspective, the motivation to successfully pursue rehabilitation lacks an important and often essential ingredient.

Much work remains to find an appropriate means of including the victim, or in the very least, including the impact on the victim in the sentencing process. The circle affords an important opportunity to explore the potential of productively incorporating the impact upon victims in sentencing.

(viii) Creates constructive environment

The courtroom, ideally suited to meting out punishment with its potentates on raised podiums, appropriately robed in black, retains its historic function as a degradation ceremony. This atmosphere is counter-productive to developing a constructive rehabilitative plan or to genuinely inspiring offenders (except out of fear) to pursue rehabilitation.

Punishment, if required, can be imposed in a circle as readily as in a courtroom. It is not the trappings surrounding the announcement of punishment, but who imposes, and what is imposed that engages the benefits (if any) of punishment. There is a significantly different sting to a punishment imposed by a community, than to a similar sentence imposed by a circuit court judge.

The circuit court judge is a stranger, in town only for the court circuit. The shame and embarrassment of the few moments of sentencing by the judge quickly dissipates.

Punished by a community, the offender must face his sentencers daily. Punished by a court, the offender confronts the disapproval of a stranger, enforcing strange laws whose punishment carries the authority of the State. Punished by the community, the offender faces the disapproval of his neighbours, friends, and of those within his most immediate environment, whose punishment carries the authority of a consensus within the community.

For purely punitive sanctions, particularly where jail sentences in excess of two years are expected, the circle may be inappropriate. In all other cases where the primary objective is rehabilitation, or reconciliation, the circle in contrast to the courtroom creates a more constructive atmosphere. Whatever sentence is imposed, whether it is purely designed for rehabilitation or punishment or a combination of both, the degrading courtroom ceremony proclaiming the moral inferiority of the offender serves little constructive purpose in achieving contemporary sentencing objectives.

(ix) Greater understanding of justice system limitations

Despite the appalling track record in either stemming the rising tide of crime or in rehabilitating offenders, communities persist in placing excessive reliance upon the justice system. Many conflicts currently channelled into the justice system could be far better processed within the community. For far less money, communities could achieve far better results. Support for families in stress, timely interventions in the budding criminal lives of young offenders, help desperately needed to maintain positive momentum for people faced with crippling pressures that often lead to crime, community involvement in all of these matters could often be more effective than the existing justice system.

For far too long, the expensive, formal, slow, and blunt instruments of the justice system have been employed for too many conflicts within communities. In effect, conflicts are stolen from the community by the justice system. Properly processed, conflict is an essential element in

role of law

building the foundation of community spirit and pride, and most importantly in building the ability to co-operatively develop community based solutions to social problems.

(x) Extending the focus of the criminal justice system

Our criminal justice process has an obdurately narrow focus. Too much attention, too much blame and too much responsibility is placed upon the offender. The court's process, often too engrossed in the administration of the law, is not sufficiently alive to the reality of what happens in the community before and after a sentence is imposed. Within the community, lies many answers to what causes crime, what will prevent crime and what can be done to rehabilitate offenders. The circle, by injecting an awareness of the larger community environment engulfing the offence can immeasurably improve the utility of the sentencing process.

The circle discussions force community members to see beyond the offender, and to explore the causes of crime. This search inevitably leads to assess what characteristics in the community precipitate crime, what should be done to prevent crime, and what could be done to rehabilitate offenders.

(xi) Mobilizing community resources

After several offenders have been processed through the circle, circumstances within the community that directly or indirectly influence criminal behaviour will become patently obvious. For example inadequate recreational activities for teenagers may be a significant part of the reasons they resort to drinking, drug abuse and ultimately to crime to find excitement or the funds to sponsor their expensive substance abuse. Dropping out of school, indolence, unemployment, and strained relationships within the family are only the first ripple of adverse ramifications emanating from early teenage substance abuse. Circle participants, in gaining an appreciation of factors contributing to crime, may exert pressure to realign community expenditures from new roads to new recreational initiatives, and may stimulate local businesses to recognize their best interests are served by developing community based alternatives to prevent crime.

Similarly the circle may discover why, despite heroic efforts to control or cure their substance abuse, anger or other personal problems, some offenders relapse into crime. Circle discussions with repeat offenders may reveal what community based support systems are necessary to reinforce and sustain courageous struggles against substance abuse or other personal difficulties.

Most importantly, the circle stimulates the community to be proactive. Circle discussions generate a collective will to constructively intervene to help individuals or families obviously in trouble. Community support can be more purposefully employed before rather than after crime. ...

(xii) Merging Values; First Nation and western governments

Because aboriginal people use the same language, engage in similar play and work, western society assumes similar underlying values govern and motivate their conduct. Particularly within the justice system, this widely spread erroneous assumption has had a disastrous impact on aboriginal people and their communities.

Much of the systemic discrimination against aboriginal people within the justice system stems from a failure to recognize the fundamental differences between aboriginal and western cultures. Aboriginal culture does not place as high a premium on individual responsibility or approach conflict in the direct confrontational manner championed by our adversarial process. Aboriginal people see value in avoiding confrontation and in refraining from speaking publicly against each other. In dealing with conflict, emphasis is placed on reconciliation, the restoration of harmony and the removal of underlying pressures generating conflict.

After extensive exposure to the justice system, it has been assumed too readily that aboriginal people have adjusted to our adversarial process with its obsession on individual rights and individual responsibility, another tragically wrong assumption. Similarly, we have erroneously assumed by inviting their involvement in our system they will be willing and eager participants. If we generally seek their partnership in resolving crime, a process that fairly accommodates both value systems must emerge.

The circle has the potential to accord greater recognition to aboriginal values, and to create a less confrontational, less adversarial means of processing conflict. Yet the circle retains the primary principles and protections inherent to the justice system. The circle contributes the basis for developing a genuine partnership between aboriginal communities and the justice system by according the flexibility for the respective values to influence the decision making process in sentencing.

(3) Safeguards: protecting individual rights in merging the community and justice in the circle

Courage, patience, and tolerance must accompany all participants in the search for a productive partnership between communities and the justice system. The search need not be foolhardy. Many safeguards can be adapted to protect individual rights while opening the process to community involvement. In this experiment with the circle, the following safeguards were used to cushion any adverse impact on individual rights. Within the justice system, a critical assessment must be made about what is truly inviolable and what has by convention been presumed to be. Many conventions have survived long past the justification for their original creation.

(i) Open court

The courtroom remained the same, only the furniture was rearranged. The door was open, the public retained free access to the room.

The long standing reasons for open court may not be as persuasive in some sentencing hearings where privacy may be essential to precipitate frank exchanges which reveal extremely sensitive family or personal information. Normally such information, vital to competently employing any sentencing option, is rarely available as participants are understandably reluctant to share intimate circumstances of their life in an open public courtroom, especially in small communities where anonymity is impossible.

In most cases there will be no need to limit access. However, where clear advantages flow from a closed session, the long standing reasons for open court must be dusted off and reexamined in light of the advantages derived from acquiring extremely sensitive and personal information from offenders, victims or their families and friends.

(ii) Transcripts

The court reporter remained a part of the circle.

In some cases, there are good reasons to question why a transcript embracing all circle discussions is necessary. Some aspects of the discussion may be best excluded from the transcript, or where the circle is closed to the public, the transcript retained in a confidential manner, available only if required by a court of appeal.

To establish appropriate guidelines in assessing the competing values of an open versus a closed process on a case by case basis, some of the ancient icons of criminal procedures need an airing and reassessment.

The tradition of a circle — "what comes out in a circle, stays in a circle" — runs counter to the justice tradition requiring both an open court and transcripts. A more flexible set of rules for exceptions must be fashioned to establish a balance in merging First Nation, community, and justice system values in the circle.

(iii) Upper limits to sentence

The circle is designed to explore and develop viable sentencing options drawing upon, whenever possible, community based resources. The circle is not designed to extract reasons to increase the severity of punishment. Accordingly at the outset of the circle process, Crown and defence counsel were called upon to make their customary sentencing submissions. Based on these submissions, I indicated the upper limit sentence for the offence.

By stating at the outset an upper limit to the sentence based on conventional sentencing principles and remedies, the offender enters the circle without fearing a harsher jail sentence provoked by candour or anger within the circle. This constitutes an important basis to encourage offenders to participate.

The upper limit also provides a basis for the circle to appreciate what will happen in the absence of community alternatives. The utility of the upper limit sentence can be measured against any new information shared in the circle. Any community based alternative developed by the circle may be substituted for part or all of this sentence.

(iv) Opportunity for offender to speak

The *Criminal Code*, s. 668, ensures the offender has an opportunity to speak in his own words before a sentence is imposed. This opportunity is generally offered after all submissions have been made, and the court has all but formally concluded what the sentence will be. It is generally a perfunctory step in the process, rarely used and generally of little effect.

Defence counsel bears the primary and often exclusive responsibility to represent the offender's interest. How far we have come from the time when lawyers were banned and offenders left to make their own submissions. Somewhere on this journey from exclusive reliance upon the offender to essentially exclusive reliance upon defence counsel, we passed a more fitting balance in the participatory roles of counsel and offender. It may be too cute to suggest courts currently sentence defence counsel not offenders, but the thought does highlight how much sentencing depends upon the work, competence, knowledge, and eloquence of defence counsel. ...

(v) Crown and defence counsel

The traditional and essential functions of Crown and defence counsel are not excluded by the circle.

The Crown at the outset placed before the circle the interests of the State in sentencing the offender. The Crown's participation through questions, and by engaging in the discussions retains the circle's awareness of the larger interests of the State. Aware of community-provided alternatives, having acquired first hand knowledge of a broad spectrum of community concerns and armed with detailed information about the offender, the Crown at the end of the circle discussions can more competently assess how the interests of the State, and the interests of the community are best addressed in sentencing. ...

(vi) Disputed facts

Any disputed fact must be proven in the customary manner. Proof of a disputed fact can be carried out in the circle by the examination of witnesses under oath. Alternatively, during a break in the circle discussions, court can be resumed and all the traditional trappings of the courtroom engaged to resolve a disputed fact.

The circle moves along a different road to consensus than the adversarial character of the formal courtroom hearings. The process in a circle can either resolve disputes in a less adversarial manner, or render the disputed fact irrelevant or unimportant by evolving a sentencing disposition principally relevant upon community based alternatives. However, the formal court process provides a "safe guard" to be called upon by either counsel at any time a matter in the circle necessitates formal proof.

(4) Summary: the circle

These changes to the sentencing process are not the makings of a panacea. They are relatively small steps in a very long journey to move the criminal justice system from its destructive impact on people and communities to doing what it should working closely with communities to prevent crime, protect society, rehabilitate offenders and process conflict in a manner that builds not undermines a sense of community. ...

The circle may not be appropriate for all crimes or all offenders. Experience will explore and test the utility of each new initiative. We must however, continue to search for a less expensive, more purposeful, more humane manner to respond to crime. The current thrust to involve communities in processing and resolving conflict and crime within the community is essential and unavoidable. Costs in monetary and human terms allow no alternative.

Even if funds were unlimited, crime cannot be resolved solely by hiring legions of professionals. This lesson has been repeatedly and expensively learned by many communities who tried to buy their way out of crime. ...

A struggle for a safe community must be led by the community. They, not the justice system must be in the front line of defence against crime. All members of the community must appreciate and accept responsibility to carry their share of the burden in establishing and maintaining a safe community. The safety and overall health of each community is directly related to the extent each citizen participates. This is a fact of family well-being as much as it is of community well-being. The twentieth century is replete with examples of the demise of communities and families that failed to accord the time and take the responsibility to process conflict in a constructive manner. Conflict will always be a part of community life. Creating constructive processes for dealing with conflict is the primary challenge facing society and the criminal justice system.

The current justice system is a very expensive failure, and in many respects undermines the very objectives it champions. There is an increasing recognition within and without the legal community that something more than mere tinkering must be done to create a criminal justice system that is just and offers genuine protection to the community. The existing system notoriously does neither. ...

2. Primary Sentencing Considerations

(A) Criminal Record

Philip began his criminal record as an adult in 1982 with two minor offences. A decade later Philip had amassed a criminal record comprising 43 offences, over eight years of jail sentences, and numerous probation orders. In the past three years his criminal behaviour has significantly intensified (27 offences). The State, despite spending at least a quarter of a million dollars on Philip in the past ten years, has worsened his chances for rehabilitation and lessened public security. ...

(B) Appropriateness of Jail

Jail is an undeniably important part of the numerous options required to competently address the infinite variety of offenders and offences. In Philip's case, as with many others, jail sentences are unfortunately not simply the last resort, but the most expedient means of sweeping out of the community, off the court docket, a difficult problem. Crime will mysteriously disappear, society naively presumes, if criminals are sent away to jail. Sweeping offenders into the hands of prison officials simply moves the problem from one incompetent process to another. The dust bins of society, the jails, are so overwhelmed that prison officials struggle with maintaining security and desperately attempt against impossible overcrowding to provide more than an expensive method of warehousing offenders. An undue reliance upon jail sentences, creates an intolerable task for prison officials. Despite resourceful, imaginative, and dedicated efforts by many prison officials, overall their efforts do little to rectify the problems dumped upon them by the courts.

Judges and prison officials elude responsibility for the abysmal failures of incarceration by shifting blame to the "system". This is partly true. The absence of reasonable alternatives creates a difficult choice. Faced with the prospect of leaving an offender in the community without any programs offering a reasonable prospect of rehabilitation, or sending the offender to jail, where at least any question of control is resolved, begrudgingly, often in frustration, jail is chosen. The tenaciously held belief against overwhelming evidence to the contrary that jail can be rehabilitative provides an illusory solace for the court, and enables communities and courts to avoid confronting reality. The destructive impact on offenders and ultimately future victims, and the squandering of scarce public resources is reason enough to exercise restraint in relying upon punishment and especially upon jail to protect the public.

Public protection is diminished when we throw away the key and return offenders to the street unreformed and unsupervised. Lengthy sentences employed to punish offenders increase the chance the offender will offend again.

Courts call upon ancient incantations to bless the process of sending offenders to jail: "The public must be protected"; "A clear denunciatory sentence must be imposed to send a clear message to others and to reaffirm society's values"; "Only jail can rehabilitate the offender, all else has failed".

For many years experiences in countries the world over have debunked these reverently expressed ancient myths. The legal community, and particularly the courtroom can no longer comfortably hide behind principles and practices universally questioned by other disciplines. The intended purpose of jail sentences must be subject to the scrutiny of what actually takes place in jail and of what objectives jail can realistically achieve. ...

The criminal record, the information shared by Philip in the circle about his experiences in jail, and the singularly constant theme in all professional assessments, provide compelling reasons to conclude that further punishment, particularly incarceration, would continue to lock Philip into a life of crime and self-destruction. For any prospect of rehabilitation, something other than punishment, something other than jail must be used. ...

(C) Jail: Unique Circumstances of Each Offender

. . . . .

In this case, the evidence revealed the particularly harsh and destructive impact of jail on Philip. The prison system expressed as much trouble with Philip as he did with it. Degradation, depression, and suicidal tendencies provoked by jail, bitterly flowed through Philip's story of his life as a "dog" in jail. Previous psychiatric assessments and pre-sentence reports indicated why jail was particularly difficult and potentially destructive for Philip. ...

Anyone reading Philip's personal history would simply not believe someone could be subjected to such abuse and survive. Conversely, most justice professionals who read such personal histories, having been conditioned by reading so many similar stories, tend to discount its significance in affecting the offender's ability to function within society.

The standard measure of what offenders can or ought to do is based upon western middle class values, opportunities and lifestyles, which bear little relevance to evaluating either Philip's past or what he can do in the future. There is simply no appropriate basis within the justice system to properly consider the devastating impact a life like Philip's can have on the ability to function, least of all, avoid criminal behaviour. Failing to take properly into account the cultural or personal life circumstances of offenders may help explain why we repeatedly err, repeatedly increase the prospect that the very thing we so religiously strive to prevent will happen again. Each time we punish Philip with jail, and the more severe the sentence, the sooner once on the street, Philip returns to crime. Perhaps if we knew more about Philip's personal circumstances, then if protecting society and rehabilitating Philip were our primary goals, punishment would not be our primary remedy.

(D) Rehabilitation: A New Direction

The probation officer vividly described why, despite a commonly shared perception that Philip had been given many chances for rehabilitation in the past, that Philip persisted in believing that he had never been given a chance. Most of Philip's chances were incorporated in a probation order that came into play upon the termination of a lengthy jail sentence. Philip's *bona fide* intentions to change his life at the time of sentencing were obliterated by jail. His self image, courage, and will to change were drained by his experience in jail. Upon his release the "good times" of "bad company" and substance abuse easily recaptured a despondent, defeated, and angry Philip whose self image had once again been severely damaged by jail. ...

(E) First Nation Involvement

In First Nation communities, the first challenge in exercising control over their future must be in healing and rehabilitating their members. The impact of incarcerating so many of their members adversely affects the community's ability to. First Nation's have the best knowledge and ability to prevent and resolve the long list of tragedies plaguing their communities.

Philip's First Nation and his family responded to the challenge. Their involvement was the singularly most important reason for focusing the sentence on rehabilitation. Without their involvement, the destructive cycle would be sustained, as the justice system could only turn once again to jail. ...

3. Sentencing Plan

(A) Overview

By the end of the circle discussion, the search for an appropriate sentence had shifted from punishment to rehabilitation. The resources contributed by Philip's family, his First Nation, and his community created a practical, realistic alternative to incarceration. Without this investment, despite the obvious need for rehabilitation, jail once again would have been the only option. ...

The leaders of the community where Philip will live out his life are willing to risk their safety in a rehabilitative program, his family and First Nation are willing to invest in Philip. After many years of counselling Philip, the local probation officer, a long time resident of Mayo, believes Philip deserves an opportunity to try and believes he can succeed. Philip recognizes all of this support and spoke eloquently of his motivation to try to change his life. In the face of all of these compelling grounds for a rehabilitation sentence, neither the offences before the court, nor his criminal record deny taking a risk. What risk could there be. We knew the risks of jail (further offenses)! Neither a trial judge nor an appellate court should hesitate to take a calculated risk when satisfied by so doing there is a reasonable possibility that the offender may change his life.

The doubts properly raised and fairly expressed by Crown counsel were simply not enough to offset the support of the community for Philip and for the plan that had evolved. The Crown and judge who do not live in the community and are not familiar with the community must be cautious in opposing, on the basis of a need to "protect the public", a rehabilitative plan developed by the community.

(B) The Plan

A suspended sentence, coupled with a two-year probation order provides the legal packaging for the sentencing plan that contains three distinct parts.

The first part commences Philip's rehabilitation by immediately calling upon his family to reintegrate him into their family and lifestyle. Foster homes, juvenile facilities and eight years of jail sentences, removed Philip from any positive interaction with his family and directed his life into an urban context. Consequently, he lost contact with the culture and practices of his family. Philip is required to reside with his family on the trapline located 60 miles outside Mayo. His family will ensure a member of the family will stay with Philip.

The plan's second part sends Philip from the trapline to a two month residential program for native alcoholics in southern British Columbia. Other members of his First Nation have benefited from this program. His brother may attend with him and in the very least, his family, First Nation and the probation officer will maintain regular contact. Unfortunately as yet, no such program exists in the Yukon. (A local program, reliant upon local resources, constructively engaging local community and family support systems, would significantly increase the likelihood of success at significantly less cost per patient.)

The plan's third part brings Philip back to Mayo where his family will provide an alcohol free home. The First Nation will develop a support program for Philip to upgrade life and employment skills, and provide continuing counselling for substance abuse. The probation officer will add additional support and counselling services. All efforts will be made within the community to help Philip acquire gainful employment.

At each stage, a court review will be held in the circle to fine-tune the plan and offer whatever further support may be required. The plan depends upon a concerted investment from Philip, his family, his First Nation, his community and from government. Combining all of these resources created for the first time a viable alternative to jail, and incorporates the values and concerns of the First Nation, the justice system, and most importantly, Philip.

4. Conclusion

. . . . .

Tragically, Philip's is not a unique story. There are many other victims of the current justice system and will be many more if we irresponsibly believe simply keeping the current machinery of justice in gear defines the parameters of our "professional" responsibility. Unless the system is changed, the community will be victimized by the very system charged with the responsibility of protecting it. We must find a way to change. We must find communities, First Nations, professionals and lay people willing to work together to explore "truly new ways". We will; we have no choice.

In making the circle work, the Na-cho Ny'ak Dun First Nation took an important first step. Can we follow?

Judgment accordingly.

In 1996 the Parliament of Canada set out the purposes and principles of sentencing in an amendment to the *Criminal Code*. As a result of these amendments, section 718.2(*e*) of the *Code* now reads:

> 718.2 A court that imposes a sentence shall also take into consideration the following principles: . . .
>
> (*e*) all available sanctions other than imprisonment that are reasonable in the circumstances should be considered for all offenders, with particular attention to the circumstances of aboriginal offenders.

Three years later, the Supreme Court of Canada considered this provision in the case of *R. v. Gladue*.

R. v. GLADUE

[1999] S.C.J. No. 19, [1999] 1 S.C.R. 688 (S.C.C.)

The judgment of the Court was delivered by **Cory** and **Iacobucci JJ.**: —

I. *Factual Background*

. . . . .

[2]... The appellant and the victim Reuben Beaver started to live together in 1993, when the appellant was 17 years old. Thereafter they had a daughter, Tanita. In August 1995, they moved to Nanaimo. ... By September 1995, the appellant and Beaver were engaged to be married, and the appellant was five months pregnant with their second child, a boy, whom the appellant subsequently named Reuben Ambrose Beaver in honour of his father.

[3] In the early evening of September 16, 1995, the appellant was celebrating her 19th birthday. She and Reuben Beaver, who was then 20, were drinking beer with some friends and family members in the townhouse complex. The appellant suspected that Beaver was having an affair with her older sister, Tara. During the course of the evening she voiced those suspicions to her friends. The appellant was obviously angry with Beaver. She said, "the next time he fools around on me, I'll kill him". ...

[4] The appellant's sister Tara left the party, followed by Beaver. After he had left, the appellant told her friend, "He's going to get it. He's really going to get it this time." The appellant, on several occasions, tried to find Beaver and her sister. She eventually located them coming down the stairs together in her sister's suite. The appellant suspected that they had been engaged in sexual activity and confronted her sister, saying, "You're going to get it. How could you do this to me?"

[5] The appellant and Beaver returned separately to their townhouse and they started to quarrel. During the argument, the appellant confronted him with his infidelity and he told her that she was fat and ugly and not as good as the others. A neighbour, Mr. Gretchin, who lived next door was awakened by some banging and shouting and a female voice saying "I'm sick and tired of you fooling around with other women." The disturbance was becoming very loud and he decided to ask his neighbours to calm down. He heard the front door of the appellant's residence slam. As he opened his own front door, he saw the appellant come running out of her suite. He also saw Reuben Beaver banging with both hands at Tara Chalifoux's door down the hall saying, "Let me in. Let me in."

[6] Mr. Gretchin saw the appellant run toward Beaver with a large knife in her hand and, as she approached him, she told him that he had better run. Mr. Gretchin heard Beaver shriek in pain and saw him collapse in a pool of blood. The appellant had stabbed Beaver once in the left chest, and the knife had penetrated his heart. As the appellant went by on her return to her apartment, Mr. Gretchin heard her say, "I got you, you fucking bastard." The appellant was described as jumping up and down as if she had tagged someone. Mr. Gretchin said she did not appear to realize what she had done. At the time of the stabbing, the appellant had a blood-alcohol content of between 155 and 165 milligrams of alcohol in 100 millilitres of blood.

[7] On June 3, 1996, the appellant was charged with second degree murder.

. . . . .

[9] There was ... evidence that Beaver had subjected the appellant to some physical abuse in June 1994, while the appellant was pregnant with their daughter Tanita. Beaver was convicted of assault, and was given a 15-day intermittent sentence with one year's probation. ... However, the trial judge found that the facts as presented before him did not warrant a finding that the appellant was a "battered or fearful wife".

. . . . .

[13] The appellant was sentenced to three years' imprisonment and to a ten-year weapons prohibition. Her appeal of the sentence to the British Columbia Court of Appeal was dismissed.

. . . . .

IV. *Issue*

[24] The issue in this appeal is the proper interpretation and application to be given to s. 718.2(*e*) of the *Criminal Code*. The provision reads as follows:

718.2 A court that imposes a sentence shall also take into consideration the following principles: . . .

(e) all available sanctions other than imprisonment that are reasonable in the circumstances should be considered for all offenders, with particular attention to the circumstances of aboriginal offenders.

. . . . .

V. *Analysis*

[27] This is the first occasion on which this Court has had the opportunity to construe and apply the provision.

. . . . .

[33] In our view, s. 718.2(e) is *more* than simply a re-affirmation of existing sentencing principles. The remedial component of the provision consists not only in the fact that it codifies a principle of sentencing, but, far more importantly, in its direction to sentencing judges to undertake the process of sentencing aboriginal offenders differently, in order to endeavour to achieve a truly fit and proper sentence in the particular case. It should be said that the words of s. 718.2(e) do not alter the fundamental duty of the sentencing judge to impose a sentence that is fit for the offence and the offender. For example...it will generally be the case as a practical matter that particularly violent and serious offences will result in imprisonment for aboriginal offenders as often as for non-aboriginal offenders. What s. 718.2(e) does alter is the method of analysis which each sentencing judge must use in determining the nature of a fit sentence for an aboriginal offender. ...

[34] ... In our view, s. 718.2(e) creates a judicial duty to give its remedial purpose real force.

. . . . .

[36] Section 718.2(e) directs a court, in imposing a sentence, to consider all available sanctions other than imprisonment that are reasonable in the circumstances for all offenders, "with particular attention to the circumstances of aboriginal offenders". The broad role of the provision is clear. As a general principle, s. 718.2(e) applies to all offenders, and states that imprisonment should be the penal sanction of last resort. Prison is to be used only where no other sanction or combination of sanctions is appropriate to the offence and the offender.

[37] The next question is the meaning to be attributed to the words "with particular attention to the circumstances of aboriginal offenders". ... [T]he logical meaning to be derived from the special reference to the circumstances of aboriginal offenders, juxtaposed as it is against a general direction to consider "the circumstances" for all offenders, is that sentencing judges should pay particular attention to the circumstances of aboriginal offenders *because those circumstances are unique*, and different from those of non-aboriginal offenders.

. . . . .

[43] Section 718 now sets out the purpose of sentencing in the following terms:

> 718. The fundamental purpose of sentencing is to contribute, along with crime prevention initiatives, to respect for the law and the maintenance of a just, peaceful and safe society by imposing just sanctions that have one or more of the following objectives:
>
>   (*a*)   to denounce unlawful conduct;
>   (*b*)   to deter the offender and other persons from committing offences;
>   (*c*)   to separate offenders from society, where necessary;
>   (*d*)   to assist in rehabilitating offenders;
>   (*e*)   *to provide reparations for harm done to victims or to the community*; and
>   (*f*)   *to promote a sense of responsibility in offenders, and acknowledgment of the harm done to victims and to the community.* [Emphasis added by Court.]

Clearly, s. 718 is, in part, a restatement of the basic sentencing aims, which are listed in paras. (*a*) through (*d*). What are new, though, are paras. (*e*) and (*f*), which along with para. (*d*) focus upon the restorative goals of repairing the harms suffered by individual victims and by the community as a whole, promoting a sense of responsibility and an acknowledgment of the harm caused on the part of the offender, and attempting to rehabilitate or heal the offender. The concept of restorative justice, which underpins paras. (*d*), (*e*), and (*f*)..., involves some form of restitution and reintegration into the community. ...

[44] Just as the context of Part XXIII supports the view that s. 718.2(*e*) has a remedial purpose for all offenders, the scheme of Part XXIII also supports the view that s. 718.2(*e*) has a particular remedial role for aboriginal peoples.

. . . . .

D. The Context of the Enactment of Section 718.2(*e*)

. . . . .

[50] The parties and interveners agree that the purpose of s. 718.2(*e*) is to respond to the problem of overincarceration in Canada, and to respond, in particular, to the more acute problem of the disproportionate incarceration of aboriginal peoples. ...

[51] The fact that the parties and interveners are in general agreement among themselves regarding the purpose of s. 718.2(*e*) is not determinative of the issue as a matter of statutory construction. However, as we have suggested, on the above points of agreement the parties and interveners are correct. A review of the problem of overincarceration in Canada, and of its peculiarly devastating impact upon Canada's aboriginal peoples, provides additional insight into the purpose and proper application of this new provision.

(1) [Discussion on the problem of over-incarceration in Canada is omitted]

(2) The Overrepresentation of Aboriginal Canadians in Penal Institutions

[58] If overreliance upon incarceration is a problem with the general population, it is of much greater concern in the sentencing of aboriginal Canadians. In the mid-1980s, aboriginal people were about 2 percent of the population of Canada, yet they made up 10 percent of the penitentiary population. In Manitoba and Saskatchewan, aboriginal people constituted something between 6 and 7 percent of the population, yet in Manitoba they represented 46 percent of the provincial admissions and in Saskatchewan 60 percent: see M. Jackson, "Locking Up Natives in Canada" (1988-89), 23 *U.B.C. L. Rev.* 215 (article originally prepared as a report of the Canadian Bar Association Committee on Imprisonment and Release in June 1988), at pp. 215-16. The situation has not improved in recent years. By 1997, aboriginal peoples constituted closer to 3 percent of the population of Canada and amounted to 12 percent of all federal inmates: Solicitor General of Canada, Consolidated Report, *Towards a Just, Peaceful and Safe Society: The Corrections and Conditional Release Act — Five Years Later* (1998), at pp. 142-55. The situation continues to be particularly worrisome in Manitoba, where in 1995-96 they made up 55 percent of admissions to provincial correctional facilities, and in Saskatchewan, where they made up 72 percent of admissions. A similar, albeit less drastic situation prevails in Alberta and British Columbia: Canadian Centre for Justice Statistics, *Adult Correctional Services in Canada, 1995-96* (1997), at p. 30.

. . . . .

[61] Not surprisingly, the excessive imprisonment of aboriginal people is only the tip of the iceberg insofar as the estrangement of the aboriginal peoples from the Canadian criminal justice system is concerned. Aboriginal people are overrepresented in virtually all aspects of the system. As this Court recently noted in *R. v. Williams*, [1998] 1 S.C.R. 1128 at para. 58, there is widespread bias against aboriginal people within Canada, and "[t]here is evidence that this widespread racism has translated into systemic discrimination in the criminal justice system".

. . . . .

[64] These findings cry out for recognition of the magnitude and gravity of the problem, and for responses to alleviate it. The figures are stark and reflect what may fairly be termed a crisis in the Canadian criminal justice system. The drastic overrepresentation of aboriginal peoples within both the Canadian prison population and the criminal justice system reveals a sad and pressing social problem. It is reasonable to assume that Parliament, in singling out aboriginal offenders for distinct sentencing treatment in s. 718.2(*e*), intended to attempt to redress this social problem to some degree. The provision may properly be seen as Parliament's direction to members of the judiciary to inquire into the causes of the

problem and to endeavour to remedy it, to the extent that a remedy is possible through the sentencing process.

[65] It is clear that sentencing innovation by itself cannot remove the causes of aboriginal offending and the greater problem of aboriginal alienation from the criminal justice system. The unbalanced ratio of imprisonment for aboriginal offenders flows from a number of sources, including poverty, substance abuse, lack of education, and the lack of employment opportunities for aboriginal people. It arises also from bias against aboriginal people and from an unfortunate institutional approach that is more inclined to refuse bail and to impose more and longer prison terms for aboriginal offenders. There are many aspects of this sad situation which cannot be addressed in these reasons. What can and must be addressed, though, is the limited role that sentencing judges will play in remedying injustice against aboriginal peoples in Canada. Sentencing judges are among those decision-makers who have the power to influence the treatment of aboriginal offenders in the justice system. They determine most directly whether an aboriginal offender will go to jail, or whether other sentencing options may be employed which will play perhaps a stronger role in restoring a sense of balance to the offender, victim, and community, and in preventing future crime.

E. *A Framework of Analysis for the Sentencing Judge*

(1) *What Are the "Circumstances of Aboriginal Offenders"?*

[66] How are sentencing judges to play their remedial role? The words of s. 718.2(*e*) instruct the sentencing judge to pay particular attention to the circumstances of aboriginal offenders, with the implication that those circumstances are significantly different from those of non-aboriginal offenders. The background considerations regarding the distinct situation of aboriginal peoples in Canada encompass a wide range of unique circumstances, including, most particularly:

(A)   The unique systemic or background factors which may have played a part in bringing the particular aboriginal offender before the courts; and

(B)   The types of sentencing procedures and sanctions which may be appropriate in the circumstances for the offender because of his or her particular aboriginal heritage or connection.

(a) *Systemic and Background Factors*

[67] The background factors which figure prominently in the causation of crime by aboriginal offenders are by now well known. Years of dislocation and economic development have translated, for many aboriginal peoples, into low incomes, high unemployment, lack of opportunities and options, lack or irrelevance of education, substance abuse, loneliness, and community fragmentation. ...

[68] ... However, it must be recognized that the circumstances of aboriginal offenders differ from those of the majority because many

aboriginal people are victims of systemic and direct discrimination, many suffer the legacy of dislocation, and many are substantially affected by poor social and economic conditions. Moreover, as has been emphasized repeatedly in studies and commission reports, aboriginal offenders are, as a result of these unique systemic and background factors, more adversely affected by incarceration and less likely to be "rehabilitated" thereby, because the internment milieu is often culturally inappropriate and regrettably discrimination towards them is so often rampant in penal institutions.

[69] In this case, of course, we are dealing with factors that must be considered by a judge sentencing an aboriginal offender. While background and systemic factors will also be of importance for a judge in sentencing a non-aboriginal offender, the judge who is called upon to sentence an aboriginal offender must give attention to the unique background and systemic factors which may have played a part in bringing the particular offender before the courts. In cases where such factors have played a significant role, it is incumbent upon the sentencing judge to consider these factors in evaluating whether imprisonment would actually serve to deter, or to denounce crime in a sense that would be meaningful to the community of which the offender is a member. In many instances, more restorative sentencing principles will gain primary relevance precisely because the prevention of crime as well as individual and social healing cannot occur through other means.

(b) Appropriate Sentencing Procedures and Sanctions

[70] Closely related to the background and systemic factors which have contributed to an excessive aboriginal incarceration rate are the different conceptions of appropriate sentencing procedures and sanctions held by aboriginal people. A significant problem experienced by aboriginal people who come into contact with the criminal justice system is that the traditional sentencing ideals of deterrence, separation, and denunciation are often far removed from the understanding of sentencing held by these offenders and their community. The aims of restorative justice as now expressed in paras. (d), (e), and (f) of s. 718 of the *Criminal Code* apply to all offenders, and not only aboriginal offenders. However, most traditional aboriginal conceptions of sentencing place a primary emphasis upon the ideals of restorative justice. This tradition is extremely important to the analysis under s. 718.2(e).

[71] The concept and principles of a restorative approach will necessarily have to be developed over time in the jurisprudence, as different issues and different conceptions of sentencing are addressed in their appropriate context. In general terms, restorative justice may be described as an approach to remedying crime in which it is understood that all things are interrelated and that crime disrupts the harmony which existed prior to its occurrence, or at least which it is felt should exist. The appropriateness of a particular sanction is largely determined by the needs of the victims, and the community, as well as the offender. The focus is on the human beings closely affected by the crime. ...

[72] The existing overemphasis on incarceration in Canada may be partly due to the perception that a restorative approach is a more lenient approach to crime and that imprisonment constitutes the ultimate punishment. Yet in our view a sentence focussed on restorative justice is not necessarily a "lighter" punishment. Some proponents of restorative justice argue that when it is combined with probationary conditions it may in some circumstances impose a greater burden on the offender than a custodial sentence. …

[73] In describing in general terms some of the basic tenets of traditional aboriginal sentencing approaches, we do not wish to imply that all aboriginal offenders, victims, and communities share an identical understanding of appropriate sentences for particular offences and offenders. Aboriginal communities stretch from coast to coast and from the border with the United States to the far north. Their customs and traditions and their concept of sentencing vary widely. What is important to recognize is that, for many if not most aboriginal offenders, the current concepts of sentencing are inappropriate because they have frequently not responded to the needs, experiences, and perspectives of aboriginal people or aboriginal communities.

[74] … What is important to note is that the different conceptions of sentencing held by many aboriginal people share a common underlying principle: that is, the importance of community-based sanctions. Sentencing judges should not conclude that the absence of alternatives specific to an aboriginal community eliminates their ability to impose a sanction that takes into account principles of restorative justice and the needs of the parties involved. Rather, the point is that one of the unique circumstances of aboriginal offenders is that community-based sanctions coincide with the aboriginal concept of sentencing and the needs of aboriginal people and communities. It is often the case that neither aboriginal offenders nor their communities are well served by incarcerating offenders, particularly for less serious or non-violent offences. Where these sanctions are reasonable in the circumstances, they should be implemented. In all instances, it is appropriate to attempt to craft the sentencing process and the sanctions imposed in accordance with the aboriginal perspective.

(2) The Search for a Fit Sentence

[75] The role of the judge who sentences an aboriginal offender is, as for every offender, to determine a fit sentence taking into account all the circumstances of the offence, the offender, the victims, and the community. Nothing in Part XXIII of the *Criminal Code* alters this fundamental duty as a general matter. However, the effect of s. 718.2(*e*), viewed in the context of Part XXIII as a whole, is to alter the method of analysis which sentencing judges must use in determining a fit sentence for aboriginal offenders. Section 718.2(*e*) requires that sentencing determinations take into account the unique circumstances of aboriginal peoples.

[76] ... [T]he appropriateness of a sentence will depend on the particular circumstances of the offence, the offender, and the community in which the offence took place. Disparity of sentences for similar crimes is a natural consequence of this individualized focus.

. . . . .

[78] In describing the effect of s. 718.2(*e*) in this way, we do not mean to suggest that, as a general practice, aboriginal offenders must always be sentenced in a manner which gives greatest weight to the principles of restorative justice, and less weight to goals such as deterrence, denunciation, and separation. It is unreasonable to assume that aboriginal peoples themselves do not believe in the importance of these latter goals, and even if they do not, that such goals must not predominate in appropriate cases. Clearly there are some serious offences and some offenders for which and for whom separation, denunciation, and deterrence are fundamentally relevant.

[79] Yet, even where an offence is considered serious, the length of the term of imprisonment must be considered. In some circumstances the length of the sentence of an aboriginal offender may be less and in others the same as that of any other offender. Generally, the more violent and serious the offence the more likely it is as a practical reality that the terms of imprisonment for aboriginals and non-aboriginals will be close to each other or the same, even taking into account their different concepts of sentencing.

[80] As with all sentencing decisions, the sentencing of aboriginal offenders must proceed on an individual (or a case-by-case) basis: For this offence, committed by this offender, harming this victim, in this community, what is the appropriate sanction under the *Criminal Code*? What understanding of criminal sanctions is held by the community? What is the nature of the relationship between the offender and his or her community? What combination of systemic or background factors contributed to this particular offender coming before the courts for this particular offence? How has the offender who is being sentenced been affected by, for example, substance abuse in the community, or poverty, or overt racism, or family or community breakdown? Would imprisonment effectively serve to deter or denounce crime in a sense that would be significant to the offender and community, or are crime prevention and other goals better achieved through healing? What sentencing options present themselves in these circumstances?

[81] The analysis for sentencing aboriginal offenders, as for all offenders, must be holistic and designed to achieve a fit sentence in the circumstances. There is no single test that a judge can apply in order to determine the sentence. The sentencing judge is required to take into account all of the surrounding circumstances regarding the offence, the offender, the victims, and the community, including the unique circumstances of the offender as an aboriginal person. Sentencing must proceed with sensitivity to and understanding of the difficulties aboriginal

people have faced with both the criminal justice system and society at large. When evaluating these circumstances in light of the aims and principles of sentencing as set out in Part XXIII of the *Criminal Code* and in the jurisprudence, the judge must strive to arrive at a sentence which is just and appropriate in the circumstances. By means of s. 718.2(*e*), sentencing judges have been provided with a degree of flexibility and discretion to consider in appropriate circumstances alternative sentences to incarceration which are appropriate for the aboriginal offender and community and yet comply with the mandated principles and purpose of sentencing. In this way, effect may be given to the aboriginal emphasis upon healing and restoration of both the victim and the offender.

(3) The Duty of the Sentencing Judge

[82] ... The provision expressly provides that a court that imposes a sentence should consider all available sanctions other than imprisonment that are reasonable in the circumstances, and should pay particular attention to the circumstances of aboriginal offenders. There is no discretion as to whether to consider the unique situation of the aboriginal offender; the only discretion concerns the determination of a just and appropriate sentence.

[83] How then is the consideration of s. 718.2(*e*) to proceed in the daily functioning of the courts? ... In all instances it will be necessary for the judge to take judicial notice of the systemic or background factors and the approach to sentencing which is relevant to aboriginal offenders. However, for each particular offence and offender it may be that some evidence will be required in order to assist the sentencing judge in arriving at a fit sentence. Where a particular offender does not wish such evidence to be adduced, the right to have particular attention paid to his or her circumstances as an aboriginal offender may be waived. Where there is no such waiver, it will be extremely helpful to the sentencing judge for counsel on both sides to adduce relevant evidence. Indeed, it is to be expected that counsel will fulfil their role and assist the sentencing judge in this way.

[84] However, even where counsel do not adduce this evidence, where for example the offender is unrepresented, it is incumbent upon the sentencing judge to attempt to acquire information regarding the circumstances of the offender as an aboriginal person. Whether the offender resides in a rural area, on a reserve or in an urban centre the sentencing judge must be made aware of alternatives to incarceration that exist whether inside or outside the aboriginal community of the particular offender. The alternatives existing in metropolitan areas must, as a matter of course, also be explored. Clearly the presence of an aboriginal offender will require special attention in pre-sentence reports. Beyond the use of the pre-sentence report, the sentencing judge may and should in appropriate circumstances and where practicable request that witnesses be called who may testify as to reasonable alternatives.

[85] Similarly, where a sentencing judge at the trial level has not engaged in the duty imposed by s. 718.2(*e*) as fully as required, it is

incumbent upon a court of appeal in considering an appeal against sentence on this basis to consider any fresh evidence which is relevant and admissible on sentencing. In the same vein, it should be noted that, although s. 718.2(e) does not impose a statutory duty upon the sentencing judge to provide reasons, it will be much easier for a reviewing court to determine whether and how attention was paid to the circumstances of the offender as an aboriginal person if at least brief reasons are given.

. . . . .

VII. Was There an Error Made in This Case?

[94] From the foregoing analysis it can be seen that the sentencing judge, who did not have the benefit of these reasons, fell into error. ...

[95] The majority of the Court of Appeal, in dismissing the appellant's appeal, also does not appear to have considered many of the factors referred to above. ...

[96] In most cases, errors such as those in the courts below would be sufficient to justify sending the matter back for a new sentencing hearing. It is difficult for this Court to determine a fit sentence for the appellant according to the suggested guidelines set out herein on the basis of the very limited evidence before us regarding the appellant's aboriginal background. However, as both the trial judge and all members of the Court of Appeal acknowledged, the offence in question is a most serious one, properly described by Esson J.A. as a "near murder". Moreover, the offence involved domestic violence and a breach of the trust inherent in a spousal relationship. That aggravating factor must be taken into account in the sentencing of the aboriginal appellant as it would be for any offender. For that offence by this offender a sentence of three years' imprisonment was not unreasonable.

[97] More importantly, the appellant was granted day parole on August 13, 1997, after she had served six months in the Burnaby Correctional Centre for Women. She was directed to reside with her father, to take alcohol and substance abuse counselling and to comply with the requirements of the Electronic Monitoring Program. On February 25, 1998, the appellant was granted full parole with the same conditions as the ones applicable to her original release on day parole.

[98] In this case, the results of the sentence with incarceration for six months and the subsequent controlled release were in the interests of both the appellant and society. In these circumstances, we do not consider that it would be in the interests of justice to order a new sentencing hearing in order to canvass the appellant's circumstances as an aboriginal offender.

Appeal dismissed.

The principles discussed in *Gladue* were affirmed in the Supreme Court of Canada's decision in *R. v. Wells*, [2000] S.C.J. No. 11, [2000] 1 S.C.R. 207 (S.C.C.). In that case, Justice Iacobucci stated (at para. 37) that:

[w]hile the objective of restorative justice, by virtue of s. 718.2(*e*), applies to all offenders, the requirement to pay "particular attention to the circumstances of aboriginal offenders" recognizes that most traditional aboriginal conceptions of sentencing hold restorative justice to be the primary objective. In addition, s. 718.2(*e*) has a particular remedial purpose for aboriginal peoples, as it was intended to address the serious problem of overincarceration of aboriginal offenders in Canadian penal institutions. In singling out aboriginal offenders for distinct sentencing treatment in s. 718.2(*e*), it is reasonable to assume that Parliament intended to address this social problem, to the extent that a remedy was possible through sentencing procedures.

Iacobucci J. also took pains to emphasize (at para. 41) that

the guidelines as set out in *Gladue*, and reiterated in the present appeal, are not intended to provide a single test for a sentencing judge to apply in determining a reasonable sentence in the circumstances. Section 718.2(*e*) imposes an affirmative duty on the sentencing judge to take into account the surrounding circumstances of the offender, including the nature of the offence, the victims and the community.

He indicated (at para. 42) that

[a]s held in *Gladue*, at para. 79, to the extent that generalizations may be made, the more violent and serious the offence, the more likely as a practical matter that the appropriate sentence will not differ as between aboriginal and non-aboriginal offenders, given that in these circumstances, the goals of denunciation and deterrence are accorded increasing significance.

And (at para. 50) he explains that

[t]he generalization drawn in *Gladue* to the effect that the more violent and serious the offence, the more likely as a practical matter for similar terms of imprisonment to be imposed on aboriginal and non-aboriginal offenders, was not meant to be a principle of universal application. In each case, the sentencing judge must look to the circumstances of the aboriginal offender. In some cases, it may be that these circumstances include evidence of the community's decision to address criminal activity associated with social problems, such as sexual assault, in a manner that emphasizes the goal of restorative justice, notwithstanding the serious nature of the offences in question.

What is clear from both *Gladue* and *Wells* is that generalizations in the absence of the specific facts of the particular case are inappropriate and that the unique situations of individual offenders are afforded appropriate weight rather than relying solely upon the categorization of their crimes in considering fair and apt sentencing.

Some of the following issues arising from *Gladue* and *Wells* were considered in the following case, *R. v. Ipeelee*. As you read the following questions, try to predict the Supreme Court of Canada's approach to these issues based on the materials you have read thus far.

1. Should Aboriginal peoples be singled out as requiring particular attention in sentencing decisions? One opposition Member of Parliament, discussing the passage of section 718.2(e), stated in Commons debate:

    > Finally, again with respect to the purpose and principles of sentencing, it is deplorable that the bill tries to sneak through the back door the concept of a parallel system of justice for Aboriginals. It is so well hidden that it is almost necessary to read Clause 718.2(e) twice to discover this enormity hidden under nine sneaky words. (*House of Commons Debates*, 20 September, 1994 at 5876 by Ms. Venne)

    Do you agree with the Member's characterization of section 218.2(e)?

2. Should *Gladue* only be applied when an Aboriginal person has strong connections to an Aboriginal community? The Alberta Court of Appeal considered but did not decide this question in *R. v. Wilson*, [2009] A.J. No. 781, 9 Alta. L.R. (5th) 283 at para. 12 (Alta. C.A.), where the Crown argued:

    > [*Gladue* and s. 718.2(e)] should have got little or no weight here. That is because the accused respondent was two years old when he left an aboriginal community, and has lived the rest of his life in general society, largely non-aboriginal, in the City of Fort McMurray ... . The pre-sentence report says that the respondent's "family was not involved much with their cultural background." The Fort McKay Band, from which the parents came, is modern, less traditional, and says that the family are not active members; indeed the Band do not want the respondent with them. ... He grew up in a prosperous, united and happy family in the City of Fort McMurray ... spending but a few isolated months later in two aboriginal communities.

    In *R. v. Brizard*, [2006] O.J. No. 729, 2006 CanLII 5444 (Ont. C.A.), the Ontario Court of Appeal applied *Gladue* to an Aboriginal person who had very little contact with an Aboriginal community. In *R. v. R. (J.)*, [2006] O.J. No. 4777, 2006 CanLII 40236 (Ont. S.C.J.), Ducharme J. of the Ontario Superior Court wrote (at footnote 2):

    > [I]t should be remembered that the ability of any particular offender to prove his or her aboriginal status may be significantly compromised by the fact that past Canadian governments pursued a policy of displacement and assimilation towards Canada's aboriginal peoples. As noted by the Royal Commission on Aboriginal Peoples, for more than 100 years following confederation the Canadian federal government "attempted to promote the eventual break-up of Aboriginal societies and the assimilation of Aboriginal people into mainstream — that is, non-Aboriginal — society." ... This historical reality is a part of the 'the distinct situation of aboriginal peoples in Canada' that *Gladue* instructs sentencing judges to consider.

    In considering this question further, see Brian R. Pfefferle, "Gladue Sentencing: Uneasy Answers to the Hard Problem of Aboriginal Over-Incarceration" (2008) 32 Man. L.J. 113.

3. *Gladue* principles have been applied to a case involving Aboriginal peoples found guilty of contempt of court as a result of blockades and other activities designed to protect Aboriginal and treaty rights. In

Frontenac Ventures Corp. v. Ardoch Algonquin First Nation, [2008] O.J. No. 2651, 295 D.L.R. (4th) 108 at paras. 54-65 (Ont. C.A.), the Ontario Court of Appeal held the "special circumstances of Aboriginal peoples" spoken of in s. 718.2(e) of the *Criminal Code* had to inform sentences arising from Aboriginal and treaty disputes. In this case the Court reduced sentences based on the fact of ongoing land-claims negotiations, the broad nature of Ontario's *Mining Act*, R.S.O. 1990, c. M.14, and the harsher nature of the original sentences compared to others given for participation in blockades held in contempt of a court order. Should *Gladue* be applied this broadly?

4. A *Gladue* (Aboriginal Persons) Court has been set up in Toronto. It convenes Tuesdays and Fridays in Courtroom 126 at the Old City Hall Courts in Toronto. At present, the Court only hears cases from Aboriginal people whose matters are going through the Old City Hall Courts — charges cannot be brought into the *Gladue* Court from other Toronto Courts. The Court accepts guilty pleas, sentences offenders and does bail hearings. Eventually it is anticipated that the Court will also take on trials. Aboriginal Legal Services of Toronto has three staff who assist the court, called *Gladue* Caseworkers. They write reports on the life circumstances of an Aboriginal offender at the request of defence counsel, the Crown Attorney or the judge. These reports also contain recommendations that the court can consider in sentencing in light of the circumstances of the offender. These reports, "*Gladue* Reports" as they are often called, can be done for Aboriginal offenders in any court in Toronto as well as for Aboriginal offenders in the Hamilton and Brantford areas.

5. "In May 2002, the Solicitor General of Canada investigated whether imprisonment reduces crime. A review, by P. Smith, C. Goggin and P. Gendreau, was done of 111 studies involving 442,000 offenders sentenced in a variety of ways. The conclusion was that harsher punishment did not reduce future criminal acts. In fact, harsher punishment actually increased chances that offenders would commit an offence again": Commission on First Nations and Métis Peoples and Justice Reform, Final Report, Vol. I: *Legacy of Hope: An Agenda for Change* (Saskatchewan Justice, December 2003) at 6-33. In light of this finding, why is the *Gladue* approach to using prison as the last resort the subject of so much criticism?

6. Should the circumstances of Aboriginal offenders be taken into account in every case, including those involving serious offences? The Ontario Court of Appeal has written in *R. v. Kakekagamick*, [2006] O.J. No. 3346 at paras. 38 and 39 (Ont. C.A.):

> ... this Court held in *R. v. Jensen* (2005), 74 O.R. (3d) 561 at para. 27, that the law in Ontario requires that the *Gladue* analysis be performed in all cases involving an Aboriginal offender, regardless of the seriousness of the offence. I would note that this is also the law in Alberta: see *R. v. Abraham* (2000), 261 A.R. 192 (C.A.). See also *Gladue*, para. 79.

> The sentencing judge therefore has a statutory duty to consider the unique circumstances of Aboriginal offenders; the only discretion is

with respect to the determination of a just and appropriate sentence (*Gladue*, para. 82). To fulfil their duty, sentencing judges must undertake the sentencing of Aboriginal offenders individually — as with all offenders — but also differently, because the circumstances of Aboriginal people are unique and call for a special approach (*Gladue*, para. 6).

This question was answered in the following case, *R. v. Ipeelee*, [2012] S.C.J. No. 13, 2012 SCC 13 (S.C.C.).

R. v. IPEELEE

[2012] S.C.J. No. 13, 2012 SCC 13 (S.C.C.)

The judgment of **McLachlin C.J.C.** and **Binnie, LeBel, Deschamps, Fish** and **Abella JJ.** was delivered by

LeBel J. : —

I. Introduction

[1] These two appeals raise the issue of the principles governing the sentencing of Aboriginal offenders for breaches of long-term supervision orders ("LTSO"). Both appeals concern Aboriginal offenders with long criminal records. They provide an opportunity to revisit and reaffirm the judgment of this Court in *R. v. Gladue*, [1999] 1 S.C.R. 688. I propose to allow the offender's appeal in *Ipeelee* and to dismiss the Crown's appeal in *Ladue*.

[In this case two Aboriginal men were declared long-term offenders under the *Criminal Code* and they had long-term supervision orders (LTSOs) imposed.

Manasie Ipeelee was a 39-year-old Inuk man who was born and raised in Iqaluit, Nunavut. He was labelled an alcoholic with a history of committing violent offences when intoxicated. His mother was an alcoholic too, and she froze to death when Manasie Ipeelee was five years old. Mr. Ipeelee was raised by his maternal grandmother and grandfather, both of whom were deceased. Mr. Ipeelee began consuming alcohol when he was 11 years old and quickly developed a serious alcohol addiction. He dropped out of school shortly thereafter. His involvement with the criminal justice system began in 1985, when he was only 12 years old. He spent a significant proportion of his life in custody or under some form of community supervision. Mr. Ipeelee was designated a long-term offender and was under an LTSO after one six-year prison term. After his release from prison, he committed an offence while intoxicated which breached a condition of his LTSO. In 2009 the Ontario Court of Justice sentenced Ipeelee to three years' imprisonment, less six months of pre-sentence custody at a 1:1 credit rate. The Ontario Court of Appeal dismissed Mr. Ipeelee's appeal.

Frank Ladue was a 49-year-old member of the Ross River Dena Council Band. He was addicted to drugs and alcohol and had a history of committing sexual assaults when intoxicated. He was sentenced to three years' imprisonment followed by an LTSO after being designated a long-term offender. After his release from prison, he failed a urinalysis test, thereby breaching a condition of his LTSO. The British Columbia Provincial Court sentenced Mr. Ladue to three years' imprisonment, less five months of pre-sentence custody at a 1.5:1 rate. The British Columbia Court of Appeal allowed Mr. Ladue's appeal and reduced the sentence to one year's imprisonment.]

. . . . .

V. Analysis

A. *The Principles of Sentencing*

[34] The central issue in these appeals is how to determine a fit sentence for a breach of an LTSO in the case of an Aboriginal offender. In particular, the Court must address whether, and how, the *Gladue* principles apply to these sentencing decisions. ...

. . . . .

B. *The Offence — Sentencing for Breach of a Long-Term Supervision Order*

. . . . .

[48] Reading the *Criminal Code*, the *CCRA* [*Corrections and Conditional Release Act*, S.C. 1992, c. 20] and the applicable jurisprudence together, we can therefore identify two specific objectives of long-term supervision as a form of conditional release: (1) protecting the public from the risk of re offence, and (2) rehabilitating the offender and reintegrating him or her into the community. The latter objective may properly be described as the ultimate purpose of an LTSO, as indicated by s. 100 of the *CCRA*, though it is inextricably entwined with the former. Unfortunately, provincial and appellate courts have tended to emphasize the protection of the public at the expense of the rehabilitation of offenders. This, in turn, has affected their determinations of what is a fit sentence for breaching a condition of an LTSO.

. . . . .

[50] The ... long-term offender regime is ... two-fold: to protect the public *and* to rehabilitate offenders and reintegrate them into the community. In fact, s. 100 of the *CCRA* singles out rehabilitation and reintegration as the purpose of community supervision including LTSOs. [R]ehabilitation is the key feature of the long-term offender regime that distinguishes it from the dangerous offender regime. To suggest, therefore, that rehabilitation has been determined to be impossible to achieve in the long-term offender context is simply wrong. Given this context, it would be contrary to reason to conclude that rehabilitation is not an appropriate sentencing objective and should therefore play "little or no role" (as stated in *W. (H.P.)*), in the sentencing process.

[51] This is not to say that rehabilitation will always be the foremost consideration when sentencing for breach of an LTSO. The duty of a

sentencing judge is to apply all of the principles mandated by ss. 718.1 and 718.2 of the *Criminal Code* in order to devise a sentence that furthers the overall objectives of sentencing. The foregoing simply demonstrates that there is nothing in the provisions of the *Criminal Code* or the *CCRA* to suggest that any of those principles or objectives will not apply to the breach of an LTSO. As with any sentencing decision, the relative weight to be accorded to each sentencing principle or objective will vary depending on the circumstances of the particular offence. In all instances, the sentence must be proportionate to both the gravity of the offence and the degree of responsibility of the offender.

. . . . .

[55] It is the sentencing judge's duty to determine, within this open range of sentencing options, which sentence will be proportionate to both the gravity of the offence and the degree of responsibility of the offender. The severity of a particular breach of an LTSO will depend, in large part, on the circumstances of the breach, the nature of the condition breached, and the role that condition plays in managing the offender's risk of reoffence in the community. This requires a contextual analysis. As Smith J.A. states in *R. v. Deacon*, 2004 BCCA 78, 193 B.C.A.C. 228, at para. 51, "the gravity of an offence under s. 753.3 must be measured with reference not only to the conduct that gave rise to the offence, but also with regard to what it portends in light of the offender's entire history of criminal conduct". Breach of an LTSO is not subject to a distinct sentencing regime or system. In any given case, the best guides for determining a fit sentence are the well-established principles and objectives of sentencing set out in the *Criminal Code*.

C. *The Offender — Sentencing Aboriginal Offenders*

[56] Section 718.2(*e*) of the *Criminal Code* directs that "all available sanctions other than imprisonment that are reasonable in the circumstances should be considered for all offenders, <u>with particular attention to the circumstances of aboriginal offenders</u>". This provision was introduced into the *Code* as part of the 1996 Bill C-41 amendments to codify the purpose and principles of sentencing. According to the then Minister of Justice, Allan Rock, "the reason we referred specifically there to aboriginal persons is that they are sadly overrepresented in the prison populations of Canada" ...

. . . . .

[58] The overrepresentation of Aboriginal people in the Canadian criminal justice system was the impetus for including the specific reference to Aboriginal people in s. 718.2(*e*). It was not at all clear, however, what exactly the provision required or how it would affect the sentencing of Aboriginal offenders. In 1999, this Court had the opportunity to address these questions in *Gladue*. ...

. . . . .

[60] Courts have, at times, been hesitant to take judicial notice of the systemic and background factors affecting Aboriginal people in Canadian society (see, e.g., *R. v. Laliberte*, 2000 SKCA 27, 189 Sask. R. 190). To be clear, courts must take judicial notice of such matters as the history of colonialism, displacement, and residential schools and how that history continues to translate into lower educational attainment, lower incomes, higher unemployment, higher rates of substance abuse and suicide, and of course higher levels of incarceration for Aboriginal peoples. These matters, on their own, do not necessarily justify a different sentence for Aboriginal offenders. Rather, they provide the necessary *context* for understanding and evaluating the case-specific information presented by counsel. Counsel have a duty to bring that individualized information before the court in every case, unless the offender expressly waives his right to have it considered. In current practice, it appears that case-specific information is often brought before the court by way of a *Gladue* report, which is a form of pre-sentence report tailored to the specific circumstances of Aboriginal offenders. Bringing such information to the attention of the judge in a comprehensive and timely manner is helpful to all parties at a sentencing hearing for an Aboriginal offender, as it is indispensable to a judge in fulfilling his duties under s. 718.2(*e*) of the *Criminal Code*.

[61] It would have been naive to suggest that sentencing Aboriginal persons differently, without addressing the root causes of criminality, would eliminate their overrepresentation in the criminal justice system entirely. In *Gladue*, Cory and Iacobucci JJ. were mindful of this fact, yet retained a degree of optimism ...

[62] This cautious optimism has not been borne out. In fact, statistics indicate that the overrepresentation and alienation of Aboriginal peoples in the criminal justice system has only worsened. In the immediate aftermath of Bill C-41, from 1996 to 2001, Aboriginal admissions to custody increased by 3 percent while non-Aboriginal admissions declined by 22 percent (J. V. Roberts and R. Melchers, "The Incarceration of Aboriginal Offenders: Trends from 1978 to 2001" (2003), 45 *Can. J. Crim. & Crim. Just.* 211, at p. 226). From 2001 to 2006, there was an overall decline in prison admissions of 9 percent. During that same time period, Aboriginal admissions to custody increased by 4 percent (J. Rudin, "Addressing Aboriginal Overrepresentation Post-*Gladue*: A Realistic Assessment of How Social Change Occurs" (2008-2009), 54 *Crim. L.Q.* 447, at p. 452). As a result, the overrepresentation of Aboriginal people in the criminal justice system is worse than ever. Whereas Aboriginal persons made up 12 percent of all federal inmates in 1999 when *Gladue* was decided, they accounted for 17 percent of federal admissions in 2005 (J. Rudin, "Aboriginal Over-representation and *R. v. Gladue*: Where We Were, Where We Are and Where We Might Be Going", in J. Cameron and J. Stribopoulos, eds., *The Charter and Criminal Justice: Twenty-Five Years Later* (2008), 687, at p. 701). As Professor Rudin asks: "If Aboriginal overrepresentation was a crisis in 1999, what term can be applied to the situation today?" ("Addressing Aboriginal Overrepresentation Post-*Gladue*", at p. 452).

[63] Over a decade has passed since this Court issued its judgment in *Gladue*. As the statistics indicate, section 718.2(*e*) of the *Criminal Code* has not had a discernible impact on the overrepresentation of Aboriginal people in the criminal justice system. Granted, the *Gladue* principles were never expected to provide a panacea. There is some indication, however, from both the academic commentary and the jurisprudence, that the failure can be attributed to some extent to a fundamental misunderstanding and misapplication of both s. 718.2(*e*) and this Court's decision in *Gladue*. The following is an attempt to resolve these misunder-standings, clarify certain ambiguities, and provide additional guidance so that courts can properly implement this sentencing provision.

1. Making Sense of Aboriginal Sentencing

[64] Section 718.2(*e*) of the *Criminal Code* and this Court's decision in *Gladue* were not universally well-received. Three interrelated criticisms have been advanced: (1) sentencing is not an appropriate means of addressing overrepresentation; (2) the *Gladue* principles provide what is essentially a race-based discount for Aboriginal offenders; and (3) providing special treatment and lesser sentences to Aboriginal offenders is inherently unfair as it creates unjustified distinctions between offenders who are similarly situated, thus violating the principle of sentence parity. In my view, these criticisms are based on a fundamental misunderstanding of the operation of s. 718.2(*e*) of the *Criminal Code*.

[65] Professors Stenning and Roberts describe the sentencing provision as an "empty promise" to Aboriginal peoples because it is unlikely to have any significant impact on levels of overrepresentation (P. Stenning and J. V. Roberts, "Empty Promises: Parliament, the Supreme Court, and the Sentencing of Aboriginal Offenders" (2001), 64 Sask. L. Rev. 137, at p. 167). As we have seen, the direction to pay particular attention to the circumstances of Aboriginal offenders was included in light of evidence of their overrepresentation in Canada's prisons and jails. This overrepresentation led the Aboriginal Justice Inquiry of Manitoba to ask in its Report: "Why, in a society where justice is supposed to be blind, are the inmates of our prisons selected so overwhelmingly from a single ethnic group? Two answers suggest themselves immediately: either Aboriginal people commit a disproportionate number of crimes, or they are the victims of a discriminatory justice system" (at p. 85); see also RCPA, at p. 33). The available evidence indicates that both phenomena are contributing to the problem (RCAP). Contrary to Professors Stenning and Roberts, addressing these matters does not lie beyond the purview of the sentencing judge.

[66] First, sentencing judges can endeavour to reduce crime rates in Aboriginal communities by imposing sentences that effectively deter criminality and rehabilitate offenders. These are codified objectives of sentencing. To the extent that current sentencing practices do not further these objectives, those practices must change so as to meet the needs of Aboriginal offenders and their communities. As Professors Rudin and Roach ask, "[if an innovative sentence] can serve to actually assist a person

in taking responsibility for his or her actions and lead to a reduction in the probability of subsequent re-offending, why should such a sentence be precluded just because other people who commit the same offence go to jail?" (J. Rudin and K. Roach, "Broken Promises: A Response to Stenning and Roberts' 'Empty Promises'" (2002), 65 Sask. L. Rev. 3, at p. 20).

[67] Second, judges can ensure that systemic factors do not lead inadvertently to discrimination in sentencing. Professor Quigley aptly describes how this occurs:

> Socioeconomic factors such as employment status, level of education, family situation, etc., appear on the surface as neutral criteria. They are considered as such by the legal system. Yet they can conceal an extremely strong bias in the sentencing process. Convicted persons with steady employment and stability in their lives, or at least prospects of the same, are much less likely to be sent to jail for offences that are borderline imprisonment offences. The unemployed, transients, the poorly educated are all better candidates for imprisonment. When the social, political and economic aspects of our society place Aboriginal people disproportionately within the ranks of the latter, our society literally sentences more of them to jail. This is systemic discrimination. (T. Quigley, "Some Issues in Sentencing of Aboriginal Offenders", in R. Gosse, J. Y. Henderson and R. Carter, eds., *Continuing Poundmaker and Riel's Quest: Presentations Made at a Conference on Aboriginal Peoples and Justice* (1994), 269, at pp. 275-76)

Sentencing judges, as front-line workers in the criminal justice system, are in the best position to re-evaluate these criteria to ensure that they are not contributing to ongoing systemic racial discrimination.

[68] Section 718.2(*e*) is therefore properly seen as a "direction to members of the judiciary to inquire into the causes of the problem and to endeavour to remedy it, <u>to the extent that a remedy is possible through the sentencing process</u>" (*Gladue*, at para. 64 (emphasis added)). Applying the provision does not amount to "hijacking the sentencing process in the pursuit of other goals" (Stenning and Roberts, at p. 160). The purpose of sentencing is to promote a just, peaceful and safe society through the imposition of just sanctions that, among other things, deter criminality and rehabilitate offenders, all in accordance with the fundamental principle of proportionality. Just sanctions are those that do not operate in a discriminatory manner. Parliament, in enacting s. 718.2(*e*), evidently concluded that nothing short of a specific direction to pay particular attention to the circumstances of Aboriginal offenders would suffice to ensure that judges undertook their duties properly.

[69] Certainly sentencing will not be the sole — or even the primary — means of addressing Aboriginal overrepresentation in penal institutions. But that does not detract from a judge's fundamental duty to fashion a sentence that is fit and proper in the circumstances of the offence, the offender, and the victim. Nor does it turn s. 718.2(*e*) into an empty promise. The sentencing judge has an admittedly limited, yet important role to play. ...

[70] The sentencing process is therefore an appropriate forum for addressing Aboriginal overrepresentation in Canada's prisons. Despite

being theoretically sound, critics still insist that, in practice, the direction to pay particular attention to the circumstances of Aboriginal offenders invites sentencing judges to impose more lenient sentences simply because an offender is Aboriginal. In short, s. 718.2(*e*) is seen as a race-based discount on sentencing, devoid of any legitimate tie to traditional principles of sentencing. A particularly stark example of this view was expressed by Bloc Québecois M.P. Pierrette Venne at the second reading for Bill C-41 when she asked: "Why should an Aboriginal convicted of murder, rape, assault or of uttering threats not be liable to imprisonment like any other citizen of this country? Can we replace all this with a parallel justice, an ethnic justice, a cultural justice? Where would it stop? Where does this horror come from?" (*House of Commons Debates*, vol. 133, 1st Sess., 35th Parl., September 20, 1994, at p. 5876).

[71] In *Gladue*, this Court rejected Ms. Gladue's argument that s. 718.2(*e*) was an affirmative action provision or, as the Crown described it, an invitation to engage in "reverse discrimination" (para. 86). Cory and Iacobucci JJ. were very clear in stating that "s. 718.2(*e*) should not be taken as requiring an automatic reduction of a sentence, or a remission of a warranted period of incarceration, simply because the offender is aboriginal" (*Gladue*, at para. 88 (emphasis added)). This point was reiterated in *R. v. Wells*, 2000 SCC 10, [2000] 1 S.C.R. 207, at para. 30. There is nothing to suggest that subsequent decisions of provincial and appellate courts have departed from this principle. In fact, it is usually stated explicitly. For example, in *R. v. Vermette*, 2001 MBCA 64, 156 Man. R. (2d) 120, the Manitoba Court of Appeal stated, at para. 39:

> The section does not mandate better treatment for aboriginal offenders than non-aboriginal offenders. It is simply a recognition that the sentence must be individualized and that there are serious social problems with respect to aboriginals that require more creative and innovative solutions. This is not reverse discrimination. It is an acknowledgement that to achieve real equity, sometimes different people must be treated differently.

[72] While the *purpose* of s. 718.2(*e*) may not be to provide "a remission of a warranted period of incarceration", critics argue that the *methodology* set out in *Gladue* will inevitably have this effect. As Professors Stenning and Roberts state: "[T]he practical effect of this alternate methodology is predictable: the sentencing of an Aboriginal offender is less likely to result in a term of custody and, if custody is imposed, it is likely to be shorter in some cases than it would have been had the offender been non-Aboriginal" (p. 162). These criticisms are unwarranted. The methodology set out by this Court in *Gladue* is designed to focus on those unique circumstances of an Aboriginal offender which could reasonably and justifiably impact on the sentence imposed. *Gladue* directs sentencing judges to consider: (1) the unique systemic and background factors which may have played a part in bringing the particular Aboriginal offender before the courts; and (2) the types of sentencing procedures and sanctions which may be appropriate in the circumstances for the offender because of his or her particular Aboriginal heritage or connection. Both sets of

circumstances bear on the ultimate question of what is a fit and proper sentence.

[73] First, systemic and background factors may bear on the culpability of the offender, to the extent that they shed light on his or her level of moral blameworthiness. ... Canadian criminal law is based on the premise that criminal liability only follows from voluntary conduct. Many Aboriginal offenders find themselves in situations of social and economic deprivation with a lack of opportunities and limited options for positive development. While this rarely — if ever — attains a level where one could properly say that their actions were not *voluntary* and therefore not deserving of criminal sanction, the reality is that their constrained circumstances may diminish their moral culpability. As Greckol J. of the Alberta Court of Queen's Bench stated, at para. 60 of *R. v. Skani*, 2002 ABQB 1097, 331 A.R. 50, after describing the background factors that lead to Mr. Skani coming before the court, "[f]ew mortals could withstand such a childhood and youth without becoming seriously troubled." Failing to take these circumstances into account would violate the fundamental principle of sentencing — that the sentence must be proportionate to the gravity of the offence *and the degree of responsibility of the offender*. The existence of such circumstances may also indicate that a sanction that takes account of the underlying causes of the criminal conduct may be more appropriate than one only aimed at punishment *per se*. ...

[74] The second set of circumstances — the types of sanctions which may be appropriate — bears not on the degree of culpability of the offender, but on the effectiveness of the sentence itself. As Cory and Iacobucci JJ. point out, at para. 73 of *Gladue*: "What is important to recognize is that, for many if not most aboriginal offenders, the current concepts of sentencing are inappropriate because they have frequently not responded to the needs, experiences, and perspectives of aboriginal people or aboriginal communities." As the RCAP indicates, at p. 309, the "crushing failure" of the Canadian criminal justice system *vis-à-vis* Aboriginal peoples is due to "the fundamentally different world views of Aboriginal and non-Aboriginal people with respect to such elemental issues as the substantive content of justice and the process of achieving justice." The *Gladue* principles direct sentencing judges to abandon the presumption that all offenders and all communities share the same values when it comes to sentencing and to recognize that, given these fundamentally different world views, different or alternative sanctions may more effectively achieve the objectives of sentencing in a particular community.

[75] Section 718.2(*e*) does not create a race-based discount on sentencing. The provision does not ask courts to remedy the overrepresentation of Aboriginal people in prisons by artificially reducing incarceration rates. Rather, sentencing judges are required to pay particular attention to the circumstances of Aboriginal offenders in order to endeavour to achieve a truly fit and proper sentence in any particular case. This has, and continues to be, the fundamental duty of a sentencing judge. *Gladue* is entirely consistent with the requirement that sentencing

judges engage in an individualized assessment of all of the relevant factors and circumstances, including the status and life experiences, of the person standing before them. *Gladue* affirms this requirement and recognizes that, up to this point, Canadian courts have failed to take into account the unique circumstances of Aboriginal offenders that bear on the sentencing process. Section 718.2(*e*) is intended to remedy this failure by directing judges to craft sentences in a manner that is meaningful to Aboriginal peoples. Neglecting this duty would not be faithful to the core requirement of the sentencing process.

[76] A third criticism, intimately related to the last, is that the Court's direction to utilize a method of analysis when sentencing Aboriginal offenders is inherently unfair as it creates unjustified distinctions between offenders who are otherwise similarly situated. This, in turn, violates the principle of sentence parity. This criticism is premised on the argument that the circumstances of Aboriginal offenders are not, in fact, unique. As Professors Stenning and Roberts put it (at p. 158):

> If the kinds of factors that place many Aboriginal people at a disadvantage *vis-à-vis* the criminal justice system also affect many members of other minority or similarly marginalized non-Aboriginal offender groups, how can it be fair to give such factors more particular attention in sentencing Aboriginal offenders than in sentencing offenders from those other groups who share a similar disadvantage?

[77] This critique ignores the distinct history of Aboriginal peoples in Canada. The overwhelming message emanating from the various reports and commissions on Aboriginal peoples' involvement in the criminal justice system is that current levels of criminality are intimately tied to the legacy of colonialism (see, e.g., RCAP, p. 309). As Professor Carter puts it, "poverty and other incidents of social marginalization may not be unique, but how people get there is. No one's history in this country compares to Aboriginal people's" (M. Carter, "Of Fairness and Faulkner" (2002), 65 Sask. L. Rev. 63, at p. 71). Furthermore, there is nothing in the *Gladue* decision which would indicate that background and systemic factors should not also be taken into account for other, non-Aboriginal offenders. Quite the opposite. Cory and Iacobucci JJ. specifically state, at para. 69, in *Gladue*, that "background and systemic factors will also be of importance for a judge in sentencing a non-aboriginal offender".

[78] The interaction between s. 718.2(*e*) and 718.2(*b*) — the parity principle — merits specific attention. Section 718.2(*b*) states that "a sentence should be similar to sentences imposed on similar offenders for similar offences committed in similar circumstances". Similarity, however, is sometimes an elusory [*sic*] concept. As J.-P. Brodeur describes ("On the Sentencing of Aboriginal Offenders: A Reaction to Stenning and Roberts" (2002), 65 Sask. L. Rev. 45, at p. 49):

> "[H]igh unemployment" has a different meaning in the context of an Aboriginal reservation where there are simply no job opportunities and in an urban context where the White majority exclude Blacks from segments of the labour-market; "substance abuse" is not the same when it refers to young men smoking crack cocaine and to kids committing suicide by

sniffing gasoline; "loneliness" is not experienced in a similar way in bush reservations and urban ghettoes.

[79] In practice, similarity is a matter of degree. No two offenders will come before the courts with the same background and experiences, having committed the same crime in the exact same circumstances. Section 718.2(*b*) simply requires that any disparity between sanctions for different offenders be justified. To the extent that *Gladue* will lead to different sanctions for Aboriginal offenders, those sanctions will be justified based on their unique circumstances — circumstances which are rationally related to the sentencing process. Courts must ensure that a formalistic approach to parity in sentencing does not undermine the remedial purpose of s. 718.2(*e*). As Professor Quigley cautions (at p. 286):

> Uniformity hides inequity, impedes innovation and locks the system into its mindset of jail. It also prevents us from re-evaluating the value of our aims of sentencing and their efficacy. ...

2.   Evaluating Aboriginal Sentencing Post-*Gladue*

[80] An examination of the post-*Gladue* jurisprudence applying s. 718.2(*e*) reveals several issues with the implementation of the provision. These errors have significantly curtailed the scope and potential remedial impact of the provision, thwarting what was originally envisioned by *Gladue*.

[81] First, some cases erroneously suggest that an offender must establish a causal link between background factors and the commission of the current offence before being entitled to have those matters considered by the sentencing judge. The decision of the Alberta Court of Appeal in *R. v. Poucette*, 1999 ABCA 305, 250 A.R. 55, provides one example. In that case, the court concluded, at para. 14:

> It is not clear how Poucette, a 19 year old, may have been affected by the historical policies of assimilation, colonialism, residential schools and religious persecution that were mentioned by the sentencing judge. While it may be argued that all aboriginal persons have been affected by systemic and background factors, *Gladue* requires that their influences be traced to the particular offender. Failure to link the two is an error in principle. (See also *R. v. Gladue*, 1999 ABCA 279, 46 M.V.R. (3d) 183; *R. v. Andres*, 2002 SKCA 98, 223 Sask. R. 121.)

[82] This judgment displays an inadequate understanding of the devastating intergenerational effects of the collective experiences of Aboriginal peoples. It also imposes an evidentiary burden on offenders that was not intended by *Gladue*. As the Ontario Court of Appeal states in *R. v. Collins*, 2011 ONCA 182, 277 O.A.C. 88, at paras. 32-33:

> There is nothing in the governing authorities that places the burden of persuasion on an Aboriginal accused to establish a causal link between the systemic and background factors and commission of the offence. ...

> As expressed in *Gladue*, *Wells* and *Kakekagamick*, s. 718.2(e) requires the sentencing judge to "give attention to the unique background and systemic factors which may have played a part in bringing the particular offender

before the courts": *Gladue* at para. 69. This is a much more modest requirement than the causal link suggested by the trial judge. (See also *R. v. Jack*, 2008 BCCA 437, 261 B.C.A.C. 245.)

[83] As the Ontario Court of Appeal goes on to note in *Collins*, it would be extremely difficult for an Aboriginal offender to ever establish a direct causal link between his circumstances and his offending. The intercomnections are simply too complex. The Aboriginal Justice Inquiry of Manitoba describes the issue, at p. 86:

> Cultural oppression, social inequality, the loss of self-government and systemic discrimination, which are the legacy of the Canadian government's treatment of Aboriginal people, are intertwined and interdependent factors, and in very few cases is it possible to draw a simple and direct correlation between any one of them and the events which lead an individual Aboriginal person to commit a crime or to become incarcerated.

Furthermore, the operation of s. 718.2(*e*) does not logically require such a connection. Systemic and background factors do not operate as an excuse or justification for the criminal conduct. Rather, they provide the necessary context to enable a judge to determine an appropriate sentence. ...

[84] The second and perhaps most significant issue in the post-*Gladue* jurisprudence is the irregular and uncertain application of the *Gladue* principles to sentencing decisions for serious or violent offences. As Professor Roach has indicated, "appellate courts have attended disproportionately to just a few paragraphs in these two Supreme Court judgments — paragraphs that discuss the relevance of *Gladue* in serious cases and compare the sentencing of Aboriginal and non-Aboriginal offenders" (K. Roach, "One Step Forward, Two Steps Back: *Gladue* at Ten and in the Courts of Appeal" (2008-2009), 54 *Crim. L.Q.* 470, at p. 472). The passage in *Gladue* that has received this unwarranted emphasis is the observation that "[g]enerally, the more violent and serious the offence the more likely it is as a practical reality that the terms of imprisonment for Aboriginals and non-Aboriginals will be close to each other or the same, even taking into account their different concepts of sentencing" (*Gladue*, at para. 79; see also *Wells*, at paras. 42-44). Numerous courts have erroneously interpreted this generalization as an indication that the *Gladue* principles do not apply to serious offences (see, e.g., *R. v. Carrière* (2002), 164 C.C.C. (3d) 569 (Ont. C.A.)).

[85] Whatever criticisms may be directed at the decision of this Court for any ambiguity in this respect, the judgment ultimately makes it clear, at para. 82, that sentencing judges have a *duty* to apply s. 718.2(*e*): "There is no discretion as to whether to consider the unique situation of the Aboriginal offender; the only discretion concerns the determination of a just and appropriate sentence." Similarly, in *Wells*, Iacobucci J. reiterated, at para. 50, that "[t]he generalization drawn in *Gladue* to the effect that the more violent and serious the offence, the more likely as a practical matter for similar terms of imprisonment to be imposed on aboriginal and non-aboriginal offenders, was not meant to be a principle of universal

application. In each case, the sentencing judge must look to the circumstances of the aboriginal offender. ...

[86] In addition to being contrary to this Court's direction in *Gladue*, a sentencing judge's failure to apply s. 718.2(*e*) in the context of serious offences raises several questions. First, what offences are to be considered "serious" for this purpose? As Ms. Pelletier points out: "Statutorily speaking, there is no such thing as a 'serious' offence. The *Code* does not make a distinction between serious and non-serious crimes. There is also no legal test for determining what should be considered 'serious'" (R. Pelletier, "The Nullification of Section 718.2(e): Aggravating Aboriginal Over-representation in Canadian Prisons" (2001), 39 Osgoode Hall L.J. 469, at p. 479). Trying to carve out an exception from *Gladue* for serious offences would inevitably lead to inconsistency in the jurisprudence due to "the relative ease with which a sentencing judge could deem any number of offences to be 'serious'" (Pelletier, at p. 479). It would also deprive s. 718.2(*e*) of much of its remedial power, given its focus on reducing overreliance on incarceration. A second question arises: who are courts sentencing if not the offender standing in front of them? If the offender is Aboriginal, then courts must consider all of the circumstances of that offender, including the unique circumstances described in *Gladue*. There is no sense comparing the sentence that a particular Aboriginal offender would receive to the sentence that some hypothetical non-Aboriginal offender would receive, because there is only one offender standing before the court.

[87] The sentencing judge has a statutory duty, imposed by s. 718.2(*e*) of the *Criminal Code*, to consider the unique circumstances of Aboriginal offenders. Failure to apply *Gladue* in any case involving an Aboriginal offender runs afoul of this statutory obligation. As these reasons have explained, such a failure would also result in a sentence that was not fit and was not consistent with the fundamental principle of proportionality. Therefore, application of the *Gladue* principles is required in every case involving an Aboriginal offender, including breach of an LTSO, and a failure to do so constitutes an error justifying appellate intervention.

VI. Application

A. *Manasie Ipeelee*

[88] Megginson J. sentenced Mr. Ipeelee to three years' imprisonment, less credit for pre-sentence custody. The Court of Appeal upheld that sentence. Both courts emphasized the serious nature of the breach, given the documented link between Mr. Ipeelee's use of alcohol and his propensity to engage in violence. As a result, both courts emphasized the objectives of denunciation, deterrence, and protection of the public.

[89] In my view, the courts below made several errors in principle warranting appellate intervention. First, the courts reached the erroneous conclusion that protection of the public is the paramount objective when sentencing for breach of an LTSO and that rehabilitation plays only a small

role. As discussed, while protection of the public is important, the legislative purpose of an LTSO as a form of conditional release set out in s. 100 of the *CCRA* is to rehabilitate offenders and reintegrate them into society. The courts therefore erred in concluding that rehabilitation was not a relevant sentencing objective.

[90] As a result of this error, the courts below gave only attenuated consideration to Mr. Ipeelee's circumstances as an Aboriginal offender. Relying on *Carrière*, the Court of Appeal concluded that this was the kind of offence where the sentence will not differ as between Aboriginal and non-Aboriginal offenders, and relying on *W. (H.P.)*, held that features of Aboriginal sentencing play little or no role when sentencing long-term offenders. Given certain trends in the jurisprudence discussed above, it is easy to see how the court reached this conclusion. Nonetheless, they erred in doing so. These errors justify the Court's intervention.

[91] It is therefore necessary to consider what sentence is warranted in the circumstances. Mr. Ipeelee breached the alcohol abstention condition of his LTSO. His history indicates a strong correlation between alcohol use and violent offending. As a result, abstaining from alcohol is critical to managing his risk in the community. That being said, the conduct constituting the breach was becoming intoxicated, not becoming intoxicated and engaging in violence. The Court must focus on the actual incident giving rise to the breach. A fit sentence should seek to manage the risk of reoffence he continues to pose to the community in a manner that addresses his alcohol abuse, rather than punish him for what might have been. To engage in the latter would certainly run afoul of the principles of fundamental justice.

[92] At the time of the offence, Mr. Ipeelee was eighteen months into his LTSO. He was living in Kingston, where there were few culturally-relevant support systems in place. There is no evidence, other than one isolated instance of refusing urinalysis, that he consumed alcohol on any occasion prior to this breach. Mr. Ipeelee's history indicates that he has been drinking heavily since the age of 11. Relapse is to be expected as he continues to address his addiction.

[93] Taking into account the relevant sentencing principles, the fact that this is Mr. Ipeelee's first breach of his LTSO and that he pleaded guilty to the offence, I would substitute a sentence of one year's imprisonment. Given the circumstances of his previous convictions, abstaining from alcohol is crucial to Mr. Ipeelee's rehabilitation under the long-term offender regime. Consequently, this sentence is designed to denounce Mr. Ipeelee's conduct and deter him from consuming alcohol in the future. In addition, it provides a sufficient period of time without access to alcohol so that Mr. Ipeelee can get back on track with his alcohol treatment. Finally, the sentence is not so harsh as to suggest to Mr. Ipeelee that success under the long-term offender regime is simply not possible.

B. *Frank Ralph Ladue*

[94] Bagnall Prov. Ct. J. sentenced Mr. Ladue to three years' imprisonment, less credit for pre-sentence custody. The majority of the

Court of Appeal intervened and substituted a sentence of one year's imprisonment. Bennett J.A., writing for the majority, held that the sentencing judge made two errors warranting appellate intervention.

[95] First, the majority of the Court of Appeal held that the sentencing judge failed to give sufficient weight to Mr. Ladue's circumstances as an Aboriginal offender. Although she acknowledged Mr. Ladue's Aboriginal status in her reasons for sentence, she failed to give it any "tangible consideration" (para. 64). In my view, the Court of Appeal was right to intervene on this basis. The sentencing judge described Mr. Ladue's history in great detail, but she failed to consider whether and how that history ought to impact on her sentencing decision. As a result, she failed to give effect to Parliament's direction in s. 718.2(*e*) of the *Criminal Code*. ...

[96] Second, the majority of the Court of Appeal held that a sentence of three years' imprisonment was not proportionate to the gravity of the offence and the degree of responsibility of the offender. The Court of Appeal placed particular emphasis on the manner in which Mr. Ladue came to arrive at Belkin House rather than Linkage House. In my view, this emphasis was entirely warranted. Mr. Ladue is addicted to opiates — incidentally, a form of the same drug he first began using while incarcerated in a federal penitentiary. He had arranged to be released to Linkage House where he would have access to culturally-relevant programming and the resources of an Elder. Instead, as a result of errors made by correctional officials, he was released to Belkin House where he was immediately tempted by drugs. The Court of Appeal was therefore justified in reaching the following conclusion:

> I acknowledge that Mr. Ladue's repeated failure to abstain from substances while on release required some time back in prison. However, in my respectful opinion, a sentence of one year would properly reflect the principles and purpose of sentencing. I say this because it is enough time for Mr. Ladue to achieve sobriety, and enough time for the correctional staff to find an appropriate placement for him, preferably Linkage House or another halfway house which emphasizes Aboriginal culture and healing. In addition, a one-year sentence is more reflective of and more proportionate to the nature of his offence and his circumstances. ...

> [T]he circumstances of Mr. Ladue's background played an instrumental part in his offending over his lifetime and his rehabilitation is critical to the protection of the public. [paras. 81-82]

[97] The judgment of the Court of Appeal is well founded. Bennett J.A. cogently analysed this Court's decisions in *Gladue* and *L.M.* and correctly applied those principles to the facts of the specific case. A sentence of one year of imprisonment adequately reflects the principles and objectives of sentencing set out in the *Criminal Code*. As a result, I would dismiss the Crown's appeal and affirm the sentence of one year's imprisonment imposed by the majority of the Court of Appeal.

VII. Conclusion

[98] For the foregoing reasons, I would allow the offender's appeal in *Ipeelee* and substitute a sentence of one year's imprisonment. I would dismiss the Crown's appeal in *Ladue*.

[Rothstein J. (dissenting in part) wrote:]

[99] I have had the opportunity of reading the reasons of my colleague Justice LeBel. While I am in agreement with much of what my colleague has written in the context of general sentencing principles and application of those principles to Aboriginal offenders, I am of the respectful opinion that he does not specifically address the issue of the sentencing of Aboriginal offenders who have been found to be long-term offenders and have been found guilty of breaching a condition of a long-term supervision order ("LTSO").

[100] I believe that LeBel J.'s reasons conflate the purpose and objective of LTSOs with the purpose and objective of sentencing for breaches of such orders. My concern is that the message they send to sentencing judges as to the weight to be given to considerations relevant to the sentencing for breaches in such cases is not consistent with Parliamentary intent. In my opinion, Parliament has said that protection of society is the paramount consideration when it comes to such sentencing. Elevating rehabilitation and reintegration into society to a more significant factor diverts the sentencing judge from adhering to the expressed intention of Parliament.

[101] With respect to sentencing of Aboriginal offenders, I agree that s. 718.2(*e*) of the *Criminal Code*, R.S.C. 1985, c. C-46, pertaining to Aboriginal offenders, is mandatory and must be applied in all cases, including the case of long-term Aboriginal offenders. However, once an Aboriginal individual is found to be a long-term offender, and the offender has breached one or more conditions of his or her LTSO, alternatives to a significant prison term will be limited. The risk the Aboriginal offender poses in the community is substantial and the management of that risk has been compromised. That is the reality facing the judge charged with fixing an appropriate sentence in such circumstances.

E.   ABORIGINAL JUSTICE SYSTEMS

"THE ARGUMENT FOR ABORIGINAL JUSTICE SYSTEMS"

in A.C. Hamilton and C.M. Sinclair, *The Justice System and Aboriginal People: Report of the Aboriginal Justice Inquiry of Manitoba*, Vol. 1
(Winnipeg: Queen's Printer, 1991) at 256-64 (references omitted)

The call for separate, Aboriginally controlled justice systems was made repeatedly in our public hearings throughout Manitoba as one solution to all or most of the problems with the present system. ...

Aboriginal self-government is a reality. It exists. It benefits the Aboriginal person and his or her community, and takes nothing away from Canadian society. In fact, we believe that Aboriginal self-government adds to the overall positive growth and development of Canada.

It is time to apply similar advances to the administration of all aspects of the justice system. Aboriginal governments need to establish systems to deal appropriately with those people causing problems in their own communities and provide a means for other community members to provide them with culturally appropriate ways to achieve the ultimate result of restoring and ensuring peace among individuals, and stability in the community.

To enable this to be done, Aboriginal communities must have the right, as part of self-government to establish their own rules of conduct, to develop means of dealing with disputes (such as courts and peacemakers), appropriate sanctions (such as holding facilities or jails), and the full range of probation, parole, counselling and restorative mechanisms once applied by First Nations. ...

The reality is that approaches taken by a non-Aboriginal justice system in Aboriginal communities will not address the social needs, development, culture or right to self-determination of those communities. A court system is not seen as an institution that belongs to them, and that is able to adapt to their indigenous concepts and mechanisms of justice, will not work in Aboriginal communities. ...

This means that in establishing a system of justice for Aboriginal people, the laws enacted by Aboriginal peoples themselves, or deliberately accepted by them for their purposes, must form the foundation of the system's existence.

In the United States, separate tribal justice systems have been an important part of Aboriginal community development. The Harvard Project on Economic Development found that the existence of a separate justice system was crucial to the creation of social, political and legal stability within a tribe. While the organization of tribal courts was initially suspect because of their heavy reliance on the Bureau of Indian Affairs, in the last 25 years many have grown to become independent bodies capable of addressing the most challenging issues courts can face.

One particularly strong example of this power comes from the decision *In Re Certified Question II: Navajo Nation v. MacDonald*. In *MacDonald*, the Navajo court was asked to consider, among other things, whether their tribal chairman had breached any fiduciary duties by receiving "bribes and kickbacks from contractors doing business with the Navajo Nation" (*In Re Certified Question II: Navajo Nation v. MacDonald* (1989) 16 Indian Law Reporter 6086 (Navajo Supreme Court)). This case was significant for the Navajo courts because it asked them to solve their nation's most pressing problem without resorting to external legal institutions.

In *MacDonald*, the Navajo Court drew upon "Western" principles of law to articulate the fiduciary duty a tribal executive officer owes to tribal members. In finding this duty the Court did that which any other court would have done. It examined general principles of law and applied them to the facts of the case to arrive at an appropriate solution. However, in finding that the chairman owed and violated fiduciary duties to the nation, the Court referred to other legal norms that only it would be qualified to draw upon in facing down this problem. In particular, the Navajo justices drew on Navajo common law to give meaning to the fiduciary duty in the context of principles of normative order within their communities. The Court wrote of a story concerning two "Hero Twins" who slew monsters and overcame other troubles faced by the Navajo at the time of their creation. The Court held that this story embodied the "Navajo traditional concept of fiduciary trust of a leader (*naat'aanii*)". In applying the principles embedded in this story the Court wrote:

> After the epic battles were fought by the Hero Twins, the Navajo people set on the path of becoming a strong nation. It became necessary to elect *naat'aaniis* by consensus of the people. A *naat'aanii* was not a powerful politician nor was he a mighty chief. A *naat'aanii* was chosen based on his ability to help the people survive and whatever authority he had was based upon that ability and the trust placed in him by the people. If *naat'aanii* lost the trust of his people, the people simply ceased to follow him or even listen to his words. ... The Navajo Tribal Council can place a Chairman or Vice Chairman on administrative leave if they have reasonable grounds to believe that the official seriously breached his fiduciary trust to the Navajo people. ...

The Court's explanation of how an ancient story about Hero Twins gave rise to fiduciary duties for a tribal chairman gives a view about the utility of tribal justice systems that suggests that these systems enable Native American tribes to solve pressing legal problems more appropriately by fitting general legal principles to the specific realities of their community.

Another example of the broad powers exercised by Aboriginal Tribal Courts in the United States is illustrated in the following case from an Anishinabek Court of Appeal in Michigan.

PEOPLE OF THE LITTLE RIVER BAND OF OTTAWA INDIANS v. CHAMPAGNE

Little River Band of Ottawa Indians Court of Appeals
No. 06-178-AP
35 (2007) Indian L. Rep. 6004

Before **Edmondson, Fletcher** and **Kraus**, Justices

Fletcher J.: —

I. Introduction

There are many trickster tales told by the Anishinaabek involving the godlike character Nanabozho. One story relevant to the present matter is a story that is sometimes referred to as "The Duck Dinner." See, *e.g.*, John

Borrows, Recovering Canada: The Resurgence of Indigenous Law 47-49 (2002); Charles Kawbawgam, *Nanabozho in a Time of Famine*, in Ojibwa Narratives of Charles and Charlotte Kawbawgam and Jacques LePique, 1893-1895, at 33 (Arthur P. Bourgeios, ed. 1994); Beatrice Blackwood, *Tales of the Chippewa Indians*, 40 Folklore 315, 337-38 (1929). There are many, many versions of this story, but in most versions, Nanabozho is hungry, as usual. After a series of failures in convincing (tricking) the woodpecker and muskrat spirits into being meals, Nanabozho convinces (tricks) several ducks and kills them by decapitating them. He eats his fill, saves the rest for later, and takes a nap. He orders his buttocks to wake him if anyone comes along threatening to steal the rest of his duck dinner. During the night, men approach. Nanabozho's buttocks warn him twice: "Wake up, Nanabozho. Men are coming." Kawbawgam, *supra*, at 35. Nanabozho ignores his buttocks and continues to sleep. When he awakens to find the remainder of his food stolen, he is angry. But he does not blame himself. Instead, he builds up his fire and burns his buttocks as punishment for their failure to warn him. To some extent, the trick has come back to haunt Nanabozho — and in the end, with his short-sightedness, he burns his own body.

The relevance of this timeless story to the present matter is apparent. The trial court, per Judge Brenda Jones Quick, tried and convicted the defendant and appellant, Hon. Ryan L. Champagne, a tribal member, an appellate justice, and a member of this Court, of the crime of attempted fraud. Justice Champagne's primary job during the relevant period in this case was with the Little River Band of Ottawa Indians. Part of his job responsibilities included leaving the tribal place of business in his personal vehicle to visit clients. While on one of these trips, Justice Champagne took a personal detour and was involved in an accident. The Band and later the trial judge concluded that his claim for reimbursement from the Band was fraudulent. Judge Quick found that Justice Champagne "attempted to obtain money by seeking reimbursement from the Tribe for the loss of his vehicle by intentionally making a false assertion that he was on his way to a client's home at the time of the accident." *People v. Champagne*, Opinion and Judgment at 6, No. 06-131-TM (Little River Band Tribal Court, Dec. 1, 2006) (*Champagne III*). Justice Champagne was neither heading toward the tribal offices nor toward a client's home.

Like Nanabozho, Justice Champagne perpetrated a trick upon the Little River Ottawa community — a trick that has come back to haunt him. It would seem to be a small thing involving a relatively small sum of money, but because the Little River Ottawa people have designated this particular "trick" a criminal act, Justice Champagne has burned himself.

Among the many legal arguments made before this Court at oral argument that will be addressed later in this Opinion and Order, Justice Champagne argues that the tribal customs and traditions of the Ottawa people do not recognize the crime of "attempt." Justice Champagne further appears to argue more generally that the Little River Band statute adopting relevant Michigan state criminal is inconsistent with Anishinaabek traditional tribal law and therefore this Court should not apply it to him.

Cf. LaPorte v. Fletcher, No. 04142AP, at 9-10 (Little River Band Tribal Court of Appeals 2006) (Champagne, J.) ("It is the custom of the Little River Band of Ottawa Indians to believe that society must be mended to make whole again."). These are laudable and compelling arguments relating to the seeming contradiction between tribal goals to develop a modern and sophisticated legal system based on Anglo-American legal models while attempting to preserve the cultural distinctiveness of Ottawa culture through the development of tribal law and the preservation of tribal customs and traditions. *See generally* Michael D. Petoskey, *Tribal Courts,* 67 Michigan Bar Journal, May 1988, at 366, 366-69; Frank Pommersheim, Braid of Feathers: American Indian Law and Contemporary Tribal Life 66-67 (1995). As such, we take these arguments seriously. In other factual and legal circumstances, we might be compelled to consider such an argument as dispositive, but this matter does not oblige us to question current tribal law. As Justice Champagne all but admitted at trial and at oral argument, he attempted to procure money that was not owed him by the Little River Band for his own purposes. It is not obvious to this Court that Justice Champagne's failure in his attempt should excuse him from liability. More importantly, Justice Champagne does not and cannot identify an Ottawa custom or tradition that would excuse him for his actions. In fact, it would be a sad day for this community to acknowledge that an action reflecting an intention of an individual to fraudulently procure money from the Band is excused because the word "attempt" does not exist in Anishinaabemowin, as Justice Champagne alleged at oral argument.

As the remainder of this Opinion and Order shows, we have no choice but to AFFIRM the judgment below.

II. Scope of Review

This Court's review of the judgment of the trial judge over matters of fact is extremely limited. Section 5.401(A) of the appellate court rules provides that "[a] finding of fact by a judge shall be sustained unless clearly erroneous." Other than one minor factual question raised at oral argument and discussed below, Justice Champagne has not challenged the findings of fact made by Judge Quick. ... As such, this Court's review is limited to the legal arguments made by Justice Champagne at various times during the litigation. We review the trial court's conclusions of law *de novo* in accordance with Section 5.401(E).

III. Discussion

Justice Champagne offered several legal challenges to the complaint filed against him by the Little River Band. Justice Champagne's challenges derive from his pre-trial motions that, respectively, asserted that the complaint should be dismissed for (1) lack of a criminal statute; (2) lack of probable cause; and (3) lack of jurisdiction. On August 21, 2006, the trial court denied the motions to dismiss and filed an Opinion and Order. *See People v. Champagne,* Opinion and Order, No. 06-131-TM (Little River Band Tribal Court Aug. 21, 2006) (*Champagne I*). Justice Champagne sought review of these motions to dismiss from this Court. We declined to address the merits of the motions at that time. *See Champagne v. People*, Opinion and Order, No. 06-178-AP (Little River Band Tribal Court of Appeals, Oct. 24, 2006) (*Champagne II*). Justice Champagne raised additional legal arguments in his notice of appeal and at oral argument on May 4, 2007.

We address each of these legal arguments in turn.

A. Jurisdiction

As always, we must begin our analysis with jurisdiction, for this Court has no authority without jurisdiction. *See generally* Const. art. VI, § 8. Justice Champagne asserts that the Little River Band does not have territorial jurisdiction over this matter. We disagree.

The Constitution of the Little River Band of Ottawa Indians provides that "[t]he territory of the Little River Band of Ottawa Indians shall encompass all lands which are now or hereinafter owned or reserved for the Tribe ... and all lands which are now or at a later date owned by the Tribe or held in trust for the Tribe or any member of the Tribe by the United States of America." Const. art. I, § 1. The Tribal Council has defined the criminal jurisdiction of this Court to include the territory of the Band and all American Indians. *See* Law and Order – Criminal Offenses – Ordinance §§ 4.02 – 4.03, Ordinance #03-400-03 (last amended July 19, 2006); Criminal Procedures Ordinance § 8.08, Ordinance #03-300-03 (effective Oct. 10, 2003). In other words, this Court has jurisdiction over all crimes committed on both reservation lands and trust lands of the Little River Band. Such lands include the lands upon which the Little River Band's governmental and commercial entities rest.

The Constitution provides that the Band must exercise jurisdiction over the Band's territory, subject to three limitations. Specifically, the Constitution provides that "[t]he Tribe's jurisdiction over its members and territory shall be exercised to the fullest extent consistent with this Constitution, the sovereign powers of the Tribe, and federal law." Const. art. I, § 2. As to the <u>first</u> limitation, the Constitution mandates that this Court take jurisdiction over criminal matters arising within the territory of the Band that involve tribal members. The Constitution provides that this Court must "adjudicate all ... criminal matters arising within the jurisdiction of the Tribe or to which the Tribe or an enrolled member of the Tribe is a party." Const. art. VI, § 8(a)(1). *See also* Tribal Court Ordinance § 4.01, Ordinance #97-300-01 (Aug. 4, 1997). As the trial court correctly concluded, the locus of the crime was the territory of the Little River Band, not the accident location or Justice Champagne's residence. *See People v. Champagne*, Opinion and Order, No. 06-131-TM, at 5-6 (Little River Band Tribal Court Aug. 21, 2006) (*Champagne I*). The act of attempted fraud against the tribal government committed by a tribal member such as Justice Champagne is within this definition of the Band's jurisdiction.

As to the <u>second</u> limitation, the Constitution authorizes the Tribal Council "to govern the conduct of members of the Little River Band and other persons within its jurisdiction" through the enactment of ordinances and resolutions. Const. art. IV, § 7(a)(1). The Little River Band is a sovereign nation capable of exercising the inherent governmental powers that every sovereign retains in accordance with its governing, organic documents. In this instance, the Constitution authorizes the government to exercise criminal jurisdiction over its members. The Tribal Council has adopted a criminal code and authorized a prosecutor to exercise the sovereign powers of the Band to prosecute the criminal code. *See* Tribal Court Ordinance § 8.02, Ordinance #97-300-01 (Aug. 4, 1997). *See also* Law and Order – Criminal Offenses – Ordinance §§ 4.02 – 4.03, Ordinance #03-400.03 (last amended July 19, 2006). As such, the sovereign powers of the Band as defined by the Constitution and the ordinances of the Tribal Council authorize the prosecution of this matter.

As to the <u>third</u> limitation, federal law, nothing in federal law prohibits the prosecution of Justice Champagne for this crime. Congress reaffirmed the federal recognition of the Little River Band in 1994. *See* Pub. L. 103-324; 25 U.S.C. § 1300k-2(a). In that statute, Congress expressly reaffirmed "[a]ll rights and privileges" of the Band. 25 U.S.C. § 1300k-3(a). Federal law has long recognized the rights and authority of federally recognized Indian tribes to exercise criminal jurisdiction over American Indians for crimes committed within Indian Country. *See, e.g.*, 25 U.S.C. § 1301(2) (recognizing tribal authority "to exercise criminal jurisdiction over all Indians"); *United States v. Lara*, 541 U.S. 193 (2004); *United States v. Wheeler*, 435 U.S. 313 (1978); Cohen's Handbook of Federal Indian Law § 9.04 (Nell Jessup Newton et al. eds. 2005). In short, the Band possesses ample authority recognized under federal law to prosecute Justice Champagne.

In his pre-trial motion, Justice Champagne argued that the State of Michigan should have exclusive jurisdiction in this matter. At oral argument, Justice Champagne asserted that the federal government should have exclusive jurisdiction. Justice Champagne is incorrect on both counts. As Judge Quick pointed out:

> Defendant is a member of the Tribe. The allegation against Defendant is that he engaged in criminal conduct against the Tribe. To assume a sovereign other than the Little River Band of Ottawa Indians has jurisdiction over this matter would be tantamount to determining that the Tribe has no power to govern its own affairs. Certainly, the Tribe's right of governance is unquestionable. The Little River Band of Ottawa Indians, through its inherent power to rule itself, does have jurisdiction over this matter.

Champagne I, *supra*, at 6. Regardless of whether either the State of Michigan or the United States has jurisdiction over this matter, this Court is obligated by the Constitution of the Little River Band and by the ordinances of the Tribal Council to assert jurisdiction. ...

C. Lack of a Criminal Statute

The Little River Band's Tribal Council has both adopted an indigenous criminal code and incorporated provisions of the Michigan state criminal law statutes as a means of exercising its constitutional authority "to govern the conduct of members of the Little River Band...." Const. art. IV, § 7(a)(1). The Band charged Justice Champagne with attempted fraud in accordance with the Law and Order – Criminal Offenses – Ordinance

§ 11.02, Ordinance #03-400-03 (last amended July 19, 2006) (criminalizing and defining "fraud") and the Tribal Court Ordinance § 8.02, Ordinance #97-300-01 (Aug. 4, 1997) ("Any matters not covered by the laws or regulations of the Little River Band of Ottawa ... may be decided by the Courts according to the laws of the State of Michigan."). Through the state law incorporation statute, Section 8.02, the Band asserted that Michigan Compiled Laws Section 750.92 also applies to Justice Champagne. Section 750.92 is the State's "attempt" statute and provides, "Any person who shall attempt to commit an offense prohibited by law, and in such attempt shall do any act towards the commission of such offense, but shall fail in the perpetration, or shall be intercepted or prevented in the execution of the same, when no express provision is made by law for the punishment of such attempt, shall be punished...." The Little River Band's criminal law statute has no parallel provision criminalizing "attempt." Justice Champagne, who attempted to defraud the Band but failed, was charged under this collection of statutes.

Justice Champagne forcefully argues that the lack of an indigenous "attempt" statute excuses his actions. His argument rests on the basis that the Little River Band's choice to incorporate elements of Michigan's criminal code is an abrogation of tribal sovereignty and a violation of tribal customs and traditions. This appears to be a facial attack on the validity of Section 8.02. As Judge Quick noted, however, "It does not diminish a sovereign's power to enact, by incorporation, laws as set forth by another jurisdiction, particularly when it is a matter of convenience. ... Certainly, when the Tribal Council enacted specific laws, it could have done away with Ordinance #97-300-01, Section 8.02. This, it did not do. There, the Ordinance is binding on Defendant." *Champagne I, supra*, at 2. Regardless, whether or not the Tribal Council's decision to adopt state law was wise is irrelevant — the statutes apply to Justice Champagne as a member of the Band. We are bound to apply the law of the Little River Band. See Tribal Court Ordinance § 8.01, Ordinance #97-300-01 (Aug. 4, 1997).

At oral argument, Justice Champagne referred this Court to his separate opinion in our 2006 decision in *LaPorte v. Fletcher*, No. 04-142-AP (Little River Band Tribal Court of Appeals 2006) (Champagne, J.). Justice Champagne represented the opinion to mean that the tribal courts should refrain from applying state law, especially where it is inconsistent with tribal customs and traditions. That opinion, the reasoning of which both of the other justices deciding that matter explicitly rejected, has no precedential value to this Court. Moreover, the subject of the separate opinion — whether the losing party to a closely contested civil suit should receive an award of attorney fees — is all but irrelevant to this matter. Finally, the separate opinion — arguing on a general level that tribal law should be used to bring the parties together to make the parties whole — tends to support a view that does not favor Justice Champagne's position in this matter. As noted in the introduction to this opinion, it does no justice to the tribal community to excuse the actions of a presiding appellate justice in attempting (and failing) to defraud the Little River Band. ...

Conclusion

This Court is aware of the gravity of a criminal case involving a sitting appellate justice as a defendant. It is a sad day for the Little River Band Ottawa community and to this Court to be forced to sit in judgment of one of its own, but we are obligated to do so. At oral argument, Justice Champagne raised the possibility that his prosecution was "political." We have no doubt that Justice Champagne's assertion is true, but not in the way he means it. As one of the leaders of the community — *ogemuk* — Justice Champagne was held — and should be held — to a higher standard of conduct. *See generally* Const. art. VI, § 2(a); art. VI, §§ 6(b)(1)-(2). As to Justice Champagne's claim that he was singled out by other leaders of this community, we have no competence or authority to make judgments as to the sound discretion of the tribal prosecutor to initiate a criminal proceeding.

For the above reasons, we AFFIRM the judgment of the trial court.

---

1. In the above case the Court of Appeals held jurisdiction off the reservation. Would the Court's reasons be applicable in Canada? If so, what would be the scope of a Canadian Aboriginal Court's jurisdiction? For discussion of this idea, see John Borrows, *Canada's Indigenous Constitution* (Toronto: University of Toronto Press, 2010) at 155-65.

2. Like the trial judge in this case, some people might argue that a law is not Indigenous if it is influenced by non-Aboriginal laws. What was the Court's response to this point of view? Ponder the following quote in considering your answer to this question:

   > ... we have spent several years in a distracting debate over whether justice reform involves separate justice systems or reforming the mainstream system. This is a false dichotomy and a fruitless distinction because it is not an either/or choice. The impetus for change can better be described as getting away from the colonialism and domination of the Criminal Justice system.[9]

3. How should Aboriginal peoples deal with the fact that there might be disagreement about the nature and scope of their laws? Note that the *Champagne* case successfully overcame this problem by having an appeal process. In this regard, John Borrows suggested, in *Canada's Indigenous Constitution* (Toronto: University of Toronto Press, 2010) at 59-60:

   > Care must be taken not to over-simplify Indigenous societies by presenting each group's laws as completely isolated and self-contained. Law, like culture, is not frozen. Legal traditions are permeable and subject to cross-cutting influences. When making laws, Indigenous peoples often draw upon the best legal ideas from their own culture, and then combine them with others. They compare, contrast, accept and reject legal standards from many sources, including their own. ... [T]his is an

important aspect in making Indigenous law a living system of social order. Some might label the contemporary and comparative nature of Indigenous law as revisionist, and thereby seek to undermine Indigenous governance and law by regarding these developments as inauthentic or potentially even non-Aboriginal. This criticism would be unfortunate and inaccurate. Legal systems are at their healthiest when they are at least somewhat revisionist. Legal traditions must continually be re-interpreted and re-applied in order to remain relevant amidst changing conditions. Law can become unjust and irrelevant if it is not continually reviewed and revised. Indigenous law is no different, and should not be held to unrealistic standards. ...

It should also be remembered that all legal traditions are subject to various interpretations. Disagreement is endemic in human affairs. Indigenous peoples are no different, and their societies are likely to contain divergent interpretations of any law that could be examined. ... The complexity of Indigenous laws demands that we see them in their great variety and allow for the existence of significant internal conflicts. Incongruities and differing interpretations should not be taken as a clear sign that the community does not have law. On the contrary, multiple perspectives of a legal tradition could be a signal that the tradition is vibrant and strong. Internal diversity about how law is created, interpreted and enforced can allow those with opposing viewpoints to maintain a relationship within the tradition. As long as there is a way to temporarily resolve inconsistencies for the finite moments when decisions actually require deference, legal systems can live with a great deal of variation. Canada's other legal traditions admit wide disagreements internally and *vis à vis* each other and are still accorded legitimacy and relevance. The dissenting opinions found in case law judgments and the opposing parties formed in legislatures and Parliament illustrate that complete accord is not needed in a functioning legal system. We should give at least the same degree of deference to dissent within Indigenous legal traditions, and perhaps even more, since these traditions are often less centralized or hierarchical than is the case with the common law or civil law.

4.   How should we deal with the fact that people within Aboriginal justice will not be perfect? Aboriginal justice officials will sometimes fail to live by the community's highest laws, as the *Champagne* case illustrates. In answering this question, consider the following observation from John Borrows, *Canada's Indigenous Constitution* (Toronto: University of Toronto Press, 2010) at 10-11:

Indigenous peoples are as susceptible to petty squabbles and large-scale controversies as other societies in the world. There is no romantic time of pre-contact idyllic existence for Indigenous societies, at least over extended periods. Violence, tension, creation, destruction, harmony and tenuous peace have always been with us in varying degrees. Colonialism has compounded the challenges Indigenous peoples have always faced. ... Therefore, we should not idealize Indigenous laws in our attempts to constructively apply their precepts. Indigenous law remains relevant as long as there is discord and dissension in the world and the desire to address its consequences. Indigenous peoples participate in this discord. They also participate in the search for harmony. Thus, in dealing with disharmony, Indigenous laws may contain some guidance in curtailing our worst excesses. Such laws are especially relevant when Indigenous peoples are involved. Disputes within Indigenous communities and with other societies could potentially be reduced if their laws were more widely applied.

F. CONCLUSION

Aboriginal peoples continue to encounter a criminal justice system in which they do not receive justice. It has failed them on a massive scale. Individualized and systemic racism have adversely impacted these populations and left them with severe disproportional representation in charges laid, court appearances, and rates of incarceration. For most Aboriginal people the system remains vast and inaccessible. It does not promise to heal lives, but continues to grind up the bodies and souls of those who are pulled into its clutches. Anishinabe elder Art Solomon observed this truth when he wrote:

They say that

The wheels of "Justice",

They grind slowly.

Yes we know.

But they grind

And they grind

And they grind

And they grind.

It seems like they grind

Forever ...[10]

This chapter has examined this sentiment and some of the causes for the criminal justice system's spectacular failure for Aboriginal peoples.

This chapter has also attempted to present some of the initiatives being taken to transform and revolutionize criminal justice for Aboriginal peoples in Canada. While Aboriginal legal traditions have been submerged in Canada for many years, their reappearance is providing creativity for both the reform of Canada's criminal law and the development of separate practices. While this process has not been without its setbacks or problems, it holds some promise for individuals and communities. Despite these reforms however, at present, the problem Aboriginal people encounter in the criminal justice system is getting worse, not better.

In the *Report on the Cariboo-Chilcotin Inquiry*, at 28, Judge Sarich wrote:

One constant drum beat that followed the commission from reserve to reserve was the message that native people want to control their own lives and manage their own affairs. That means a process of justice that is comprehensible and culturally acceptable to them. To achieve these ends some of the communities will institute their own justice process and others will experiment with an adaptation of the non-native process.

Aboriginal peoples will continue to search for ways in which they can receive justice. These will not be easy discussions, proposals or actions. The deep dysfunction the system has participated in creating will not immediately disappear. There will be many successes, set-backs and reformulations.

ENDNOTES

1. See Jonathan Rudin, *Aboriginal Peoples and the Criminal Justice System*, prepared for the Ipperwash Inquiry, (2005) at <http://www.ipperwashinquiry.ca/policy_part/research/pdf/Rudin.pdf> at 14, combining census information and data from the Centre for Justice Statistics for 2001, to generate a more current vision of the issue of Aboriginal over-representation.

2. See Public Safety Canada Portfolio Corrections Statistics Committee, *Corrections and Conditional Release Overview, Annual Report 2010* (Public Works and Government Services Canada, December 2010) at 61, 62, 78; online: <http://www.publicsafety.gc.ca/res/cor/rep/_fl/2010-ccrso-eng.pdf>.

3. *Ibid.*, at 83-84.

4. See <http://www.publicsafety.gc.ca/prg/le/ap/_fl/ipm-eng.pdf>.

5. The Royal Commission on Aboriginal People, *Bridging the Cultural Divide: A Report on Aboriginal People and Criminal Justice in Canada* (Ottawa: Ministry of Supply and Services, 1996) at 33.

6. (Toronto: Queen's Printer, December 1995).

7. Albert Memmi, *The Colonizer and the Colonized* (New York: Orion Press, 1965).

8. "Traditional Indian Justice in Ontario: A Role for the Present?" (1986) 24 Osgoode Hall L.J. 605.

9. Mary Ellen Turpel-Lafond, "Reflections on Thinking Concretely About Criminal Justice Reform" in R. Gosse, J.Y. Henderson and R. Carter, eds. *Continuing Poundmaker's and Riel's Quest* (Saskatoon: Purich Publishing, 1994) at 208.

10. *Songs for the People: Teachings on the Natural Way* (Toronto: W.C. Press, 1990) at 126.

INDEX

Note: A page number in boldface type indicates
materials excerpted in the text.